CONSTRUCTION DETAILS

Ramsey/Sleeper

CONSTRUCTION DETAILS

from
ARCHITECTURAL GRAPHIC STANDARDS
Eighth Edition

Edited by
JAMES AMBROSE

THE AMERICAN INSTITUTE OF ARCHITECTS

John Wiley & Sons, Inc.
New York / Chichester / Brisbane / Toronto / Singapore

In recognition of the importance of preserving what has been
written, it is the policy of John Wiley & Sons, Inc., to have books
of enduring value published in the United States printed on
acid-free paper, and we exert our best efforts to that end.

Library of Congress Cataloging in Publication Data:

Ramsey, Charles George, 1884–1963.
    Construction details from Architectural graphic standards, eighth
edition / Ramsey/Sleeper; edited by James Ambrose.
        p.   cm.
    "The American Institute of Architects."
    Abridgement of 8th ed. of Architectural graphic standards designed
to provide a concise reference for production of details for
building construction.
    Includes bibliographical references and index.
    ISBN 0-471-54899-5 (cloth):
    1. Building—Details—Drawings—Handbooks, manuals, etc.
I. Sleeper, Harold Reeve, 1893–1960. II. Ambrose, James E.
III. Ramsey, Charles George, 1884–1963. Architectural graphic
standards. IV. American Institute of Architects. V. Title.
VI. Title: Ramsey/Sleeper construction details from Architectural
graphic standards, eighth edition.
TH2031.R353 1992
721′.022′2—dc20   91-25165
                                                        CIP

Printed in the United States of America

10 9 8 7 6 5 4 3 2

CONTENTS

PUBLISHER'S NOTE

Through eight editions spanning nearly 60 years, *Architectural Graphic Standards* has become *the* benchmark reference for the building design and construction professions. Originally the work of two authors, Charles Ramsey and Harold Sleeper, over the years *Architectural Graphic Standards* has continued to grow through the collaborative efforts of many publishing professionals at both Wiley and, since 1964, the American Institute of Architects.

This new volume on architectural details is a continuation of our effort to provide the user with essential information from *Architectural Graphic Standards*, in the format most suitable for your needs. The success of the special abridgement entitled *Residential and Light Construction* has shown us that *Architectural Graphic Standards* can continue to provide important and up-to-date information for the design community. This new volume provides basic information for the professional who specializes in the creation and production of architectural details.

Again the product of Wiley's long-time collaboration with the AIA, this volume is also the result of the expert editorial guidance of James Ambrose. In his 30 years as an educator, editor, and author, James Ambrose has consistently brought intelligence, insight, and clarity to the communication of complex technical information. His experience as the editor of Harry Parker's series of *Simplified Design Guides,* and as author of his own books on structural design topics, makes Jim an expert in assessing the specific needs of the small-scale construction professional.

Building on the example of excellence set by Ramsey and Sleeper, John Wiley and the AIA will continue to serve the design and construction professions with the best in graphic information and design details. We trust that you will use this book with confidence. We look forward to your suggestions for improvements and modifications in the future.

KENNETH R. GESSER
Publisher
Professional, Reference, and Trade Group
John Wiley & Sons, Inc.

PREFACE

This abridged edition of the 8th edition of *Architectural Graphic Standards* has been developed for the purpose of providing a more concise reference for those persons whose primary interest is in the production of details for building construction. The preparation of precise details for construction is a critical part of the activity of building design, as the drawings that are produced become a major device for transmitting the design to those who execute the construction work.

This book is primarily intended for those persons who have the direct responsibility for the making of the construction drawings, or working drawings as they are sometimes called. In the past, this activity generally took place on drafting boards, with drawings produced on tracing paper by hand drafting. Increasingly today, this work is aided by computers that assist in storage of supportive information, making of individual details, and assemblage of pages and sets of drawings.

The drawing activity and the production processes for development of construction drawings may be managed in many ways, appropriate to the size and complexity of design projects and to the general organization, staff, and available equipment in design offices. Details for construction must relate to many standards, deriving from existing codes, current construction practices, and available building materials and products. In many cases, for the most common elements of construction, details may approach something like a single standard. However, the range of available materials and products, variations in climate, peculiarities of local codes, and personal opinions of designers and builders make this highly problematic.

While the details shown in this book are described as "standards," and the attempt by the many contributors has been to make them so, there is hardly any case where some room for modifications is not possible. If you don't think so, try asking ten randomly selected professional designers for their opinions about any single detail.

The 8th edition of *Architectural Graphic Standards* is an extensive and rich source of reference materials and is well worth the investment for persons with broader scopes of concerns. Duplicating the contents of the 8th edition with a collection of other publications would assuredly cost the buyer several times over the price of the single volume. This book is not a substitute for the 8th edition, but merely allows the reader to more quickly focus on areas of particular interest.

This partial presentation of materials from the Ramsey and Sleeper book follows on other recent publications that have sought to extend the rich resource of this book, which has been in continuous publication since 1932, through eight editions.

In addition to the materials taken from the 8th edition of *Architectural Graphic Standards*, there are lists of references for additional information. Such lists are provided at the ends of the chapters, relating to the topic scope of the chapters. A list of general references—relating to the general topic of the book—is provided in the General References section at the back of the book.

I must acknowledge the contributions of the many individuals and organizations who contributed to the development of the 8th edition. Developers of individual book pages are listed at the bottoms of the pages, and the many organizations providing book materials are listed in the General References section at the back of the book.

I must also acknowledge the contributions of the many generations of people—beginning with George Ramsey and Harold Sleeper—who made inputs to the development and continuation of this work over the almost 60 years of its publication. This includes the many authors, graphic artists, and editors, as well as the many people at the American Institute of Architects and at John Wiley & Sons who worked on the several editions of the book.

For this book I am grateful for the contributions and support of my editor, Everett Smethurst, my publisher, Kenneth R. Gesser, and the many other editors, marketing, and production personnel at John Wiley & Sons, especially Robert J. Fletcher and Joseph Keenan.

I am also grateful for the support and direct assistance of my wife, Peggy, who did most of the work of redeveloping the extensive index—a major component of this book.

JAMES AMBROSE
Westlake Village, California
September, 1991

CONSTRUCTION DETAILS

GENERAL PLANNING AND DESIGN DATA

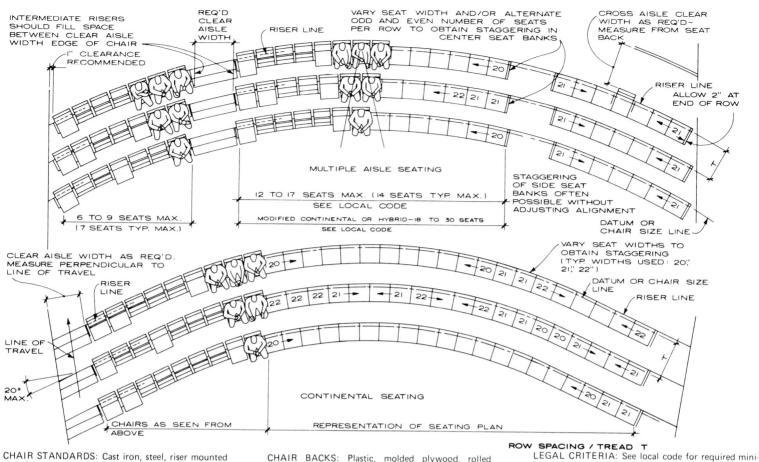

INTERMEDIATE RISERS SHOULD FILL SPACE BETWEEN CLEAR AISLE WIDTH EDGE OF CHAIR

1" CLEARANCE RECOMMENDED

REQ'D CLEAR AISLE WIDTH

RISER LINE

VARY SEAT WIDTH AND/OR ALTERNATE ODD AND EVEN NUMBER OF SEATS PER ROW TO OBTAIN STAGGERING IN CENTER SEAT BANKS

CROSS AISLE CLEAR WIDTH AS REQ'D— MEASURE FROM SEAT BACK

RISER LINE ALLOW 2" AT END OF ROW

MULTIPLE AISLE SEATING

6 TO 9 SEATS MAX. (7 SEATS TYP. MAX.)

12 TO 17 SEATS MAX. (14 SEATS TYP. MAX.) SEE LOCAL CODE

MODIFIED CONTINENTAL OR HYBRID—18 TO 30 SEATS SEE LOCAL CODE

STAGGERING OF SIDE SEAT BANKS OFTEN POSSIBLE WITHOUT ADJUSTING ALIGNMENT

DATUM OR CHAIR SIZE LINE

CLEAR AISLE WIDTH AS REQ'D. MEASURE PERPENDICULAR TO LINE OF TRAVEL

RISER LINE

LINE OF TRAVEL

20° MAX.

VARY SEAT WIDTHS TO OBTAIN STAGGERING (TYP WIDTHS USED: 20", 21", 22")

DATUM OR CHAIR SIZE LINE

RISER LINE

CONTINENTAL SEATING

CHAIRS AS SEEN FROM ABOVE

REPRESENTATION OF SEATING PLAN

CHAIR STANDARDS: Cast iron, steel, riser mounted and floor mounted. Also pedestal mounting using continuous beam support or cantilevered standards. Folding tablet arms usually available.

CHAIR ARMS: Upholstered fabric, wood, plastic, metal.

CHAIR BACKS: Plastic, molded plywood, rolled stamped metal, upholstered front, rear. Higher backs and bottom extension for scuff protection also available.

CHAIR SEATS: Upholstered, plywood, plastic, metal pan, coil or serpentine springs, polyurethane foam.

ROW SPACING / TREAD T

LEGAL CRITERIA: See local code for required minimum spacing. Codes typically stipulate a minimum clear plumbline distance measured between the unoccupied chair and the rear of the back of the chair in front.

32"–33": typical minimum for multiple aisle seating
34"–37": typical minimum for modified continental seating
38"–42": typical minimum for continental seating

COMFORT FOR THE SEATED PERSON:
32": knees will touch chair back; uncomfortable
34": minimum spacing for comfort
36": ideal spacing for maximum comfort
38" and up: audience cohesiveness may suffer

EASE OF PASSAGE IN FRONT OF SEATED PERSONS:
32"–34": seated person must rise to allow passage
36"–38": some seated persons will rise
40" and up: passage in front of seated persons possible

SAFETY: Excessive plumbline distance may entice exiting persons to squeeze ahead and cause jam.

EFFICIENCY: Choice of minimum spacing satisfying criteria above reduces maximum distance to stage.

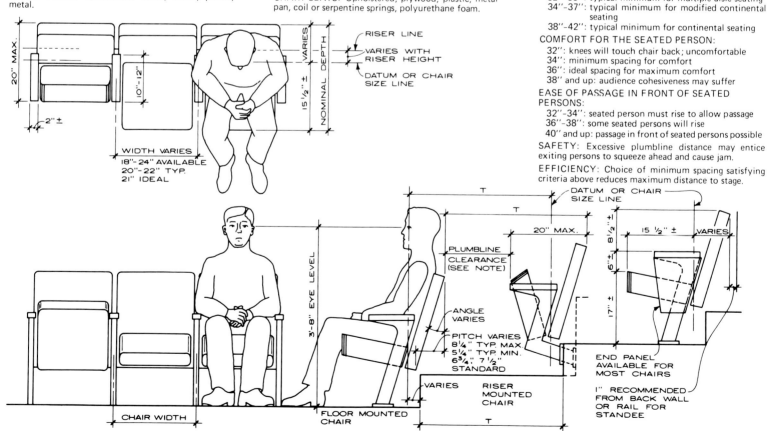

20" MAX.

2"±

10"–12"

WIDTH VARIES
18"–24" AVAILABLE
20"–22" TYP.
21" IDEAL

VARIES

RISER LINE

VARIES WITH RISER HEIGHT

DATUM OR CHAIR SIZE LINE

15 1/2" ± NOMINAL DEPTH

3'-8" EYE LEVEL

CHAIR WIDTH

FLOOR MOUNTED CHAIR

PLUMBLINE CLEARANCE (SEE NOTE)

ANGLE VARIES

PITCH VARIES
8 1/4" TYP. MAX.
5 1/4" TYP. MIN.
6 3/4", 7 1/2" STANDARD

VARIES   RISER MOUNTED CHAIR

T

20" MAX.

8 1/2" ±

6" ±

17" ±

15 1/2" ±   VARIES

END PANEL AVAILABLE FOR MOST CHAIRS

1" RECOMMENDED FROM BACK WALL OR RAIL FOR STANDEE

DATUM OR CHAIR SIZE LINE

Peter H. Frink; Frink and Beuchat: Architects; Philadelphia, Pennsylvania

1   **THEATER DESIGN**

IMPACT NOISE DESIGN CRITERIA

Floors are subject to impact or structure-borne sound transmission—noises such as footfalls, dropped objects, and scraping furniture. Parallel to development of laboratory Sound Transmission Class (STC) ratings for partition constructions is Impact Insulation Class (IIC), a single-number rating system to evaluate the effectiveness of floor construction to prevent impact sound transmission to spaces underneath the floor. The current IIC rating method replaces the previously used Impact Noise Rating (INR) method. To compare the ratings, note that IIC = INR + 51 $\pm$. [The amount of deviation is relatively small (± 2), but should still be noted.] For example, INR = +4 would be equivalent basically to IIC = 55.

IMPACT SOUND PRESSURE LEVELS MEASUREMENT (ASTM E492.77)

$$L_n = L_p - 10 \log (A_0/A_2)$$

where L_n = normal impact sound pressure
L_p = sound pressure level in the receiving room
A_2 = sound absorption of the receiving room
A_0 = reference absorption (108 sabins)

SUMMARY OF METHOD (ASTM E492.77)

A standard tapping machine is used on a test floor specimen, which forms a horizontal separation between two rooms, one directly above the other. The transmitted impact sound is characterized by the one-third octave band spectrum of the average sound pressure level produced by the tapping machine in the receiving room located directly beneath the test floor specimen.

Since the noise levels depend on the absorption of the receiving room, it is desirable to normalize the impact sound pressure levels to a reference absorption for purposes of comparing results obtained in different receiving rooms that differ in absorption.

To achieve adequate acoustical privacy in multifamily dwellings and other structures where both air-borne and structure-borne sound transmission are concerns, controlling impact sound transmission is as important as the control of air-borne sound transmission, or, expressed in its simplest terms: IIc $\geq$ STC for a given construction. Again, as with STC ratings, the higher the IIC number, the greater the sound control.

This method is based on the use of a standard tapping machine, which produces a series of continuous uniform impacts at a uniform rate on a test floor. It generates broadband sound pressure levels in the receiving room below which are sufficiently high to accurately reproduce them. The tapping machine, however, is not designed to simulate any one type of impact, for example, male or female footsteps.

Because it is portable, the tapping machine cannot simulate the weight of a human walker. Therefore, the creak or boom of a limber floor caused by such footsteps cannot be reflected in the single-figure impact rating. The correlation between tapping machine tests in the laboratory and field performance of floors under typical conditions may vary, depending on floor construction and the nature of the impact.

Often the greatest annoyance caused by footfall noise is generated by low-frequency sound energy beyond standardized test frequency range. Sometimes it is near or at the resonant frequency of the building structure.

To summarize, think resiliency. Wherever possible, use carpet with padding on floors of residential buildings. Use resilient, suspended ceilings with cavity insulation. For especially critical situations such as those involving pedestrian bridges or tunnels, use an acoustics consultant.

Other sources of impact noise are slamming of doors or drawers of cabinets. If possible, bureaus should not be placed directly against a wall. Door closers or stops can be added to cushion the impact of the energy so that it is not imparted directly into the structure. Common sense arrangements can help minimize problems in multi-family dwellings. Kitchen cabinets should not be placed on a common wall to a neighbor's bedroom, for example.

Carl J. Rosenberg, AIA; BBN Laboratories, Inc.; Cambridge, Massachusetts

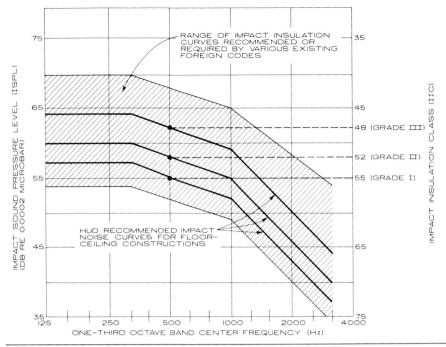

IMPACT NOISE INSULATION CRITERIA

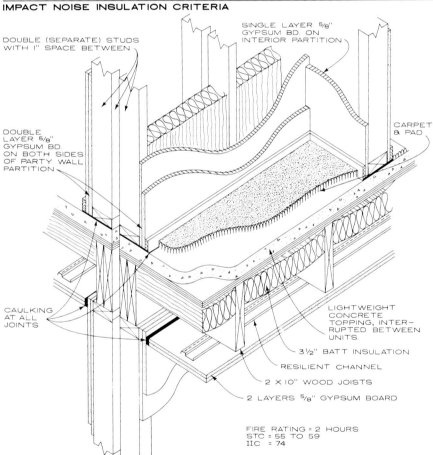

GOOD SOUND ISOLATION CONSTRUCTION

NOTE

Edge attachment and junctions of walls, partitions, floors, and ceilings can cause large differences in TL performance. The transverse waves set up in continuous, stiff, lightweight walls or floors can carry sound a long distance from the source to other parts of the structure with little attenuation. Curtain walls, thin concrete floors on bar joists, and wood framed structures are particularly subject to this weakness.

Properly designed discontinuities such as interrupted floor slab/toppings are helpful in reducing structural flanking.

A resilient (airtight) joint between exterior wall and partition or partition and floor can appreciably improve TL.

Continuous pipes, conduits, or ducts can act as transmission paths from room to room. Care must be taken to isolate such services from the structure.

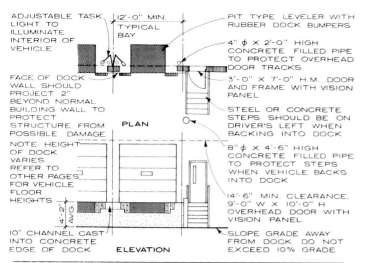

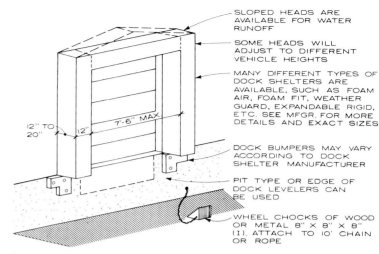

TYPICAL LOADING DOCK BAY

Provides positive weather seal; protects dock from wind, rain, snow, and dirt. Retains constant temperature between dock and vehicle.

CUSHIONED DOCK SHELTER

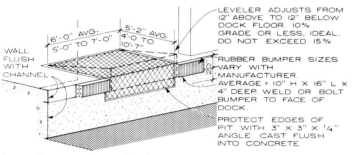

Automatic or manual operation for high volume docks where incoming vehicle heights vary widely; must be installed in a preformed concrete pit. Exact dimensions provided by manufacturer.

PIT TYPE DOCK LEVELER

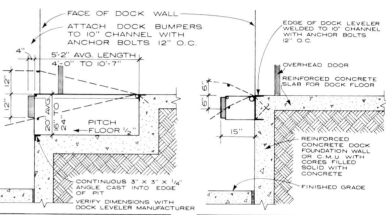

SILL FOR PIT LEVELER

SILL FOR EDGE OF DOCK LEVELER

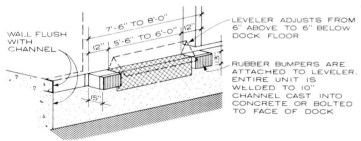

Manual operation for high or medium volume docks where pit type levelers are impractical or leased facilities are being used.

EDGE OF DOCK LEVELER

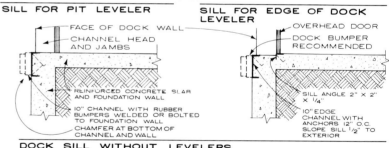

DOCK SILL WITHOUT LEVELERS

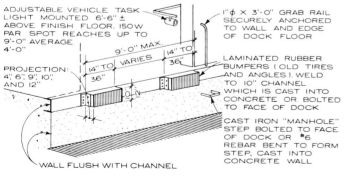

Used for low volume docks where incoming vehicle heights do not vary. Use portable type leveler such as a throw plate.

LOADING DOCK WITHOUT LEVELER

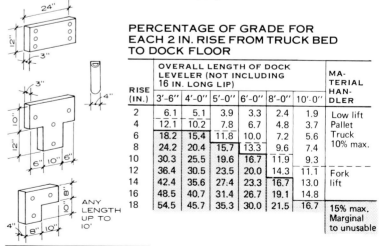

MOLDED HARD RUBBER DOCK BUMPERS

PERCENTAGE OF GRADE FOR EACH 2 IN. RISE FROM TRUCK BED TO DOCK FLOOR

RISE (IN.)	OVERALL LENGTH OF DOCK LEVELER (NOT INCLUDING 16 IN. LONG LIP)						MATERIAL HANDLER
	3'-6''	4'-0''	5'-0''	6'-0''	8'-0''	10'-0''	
2	6.1	5.1	3.9	3.3	2.4	1.9	Low lift Pallet Truck 10% max.
4	12.1	10.2	7.8	6.7	4.8	3.7	
6	18.2	15.4	11.8	10.0	7.2	5.6	
8	24.2	20.4	15.7	13.3	9.6	7.4	
10	30.3	25.5	19.6	16.7	11.9	9.3	
12	36.4	30.5	23.5	20.0	14.3	11.1	Fork lift
14	42.4	35.6	27.4	23.3	16.7	13.0	
16	48.5	40.7	31.4	26.7	19.1	14.8	
18	54.5	45.7	35.3	30.0	21.5	16.7	15% max. Marginal to unusable

Robert H. Lorenz, AIA; Preston Trucking Company, Inc.; Preston, Maryland

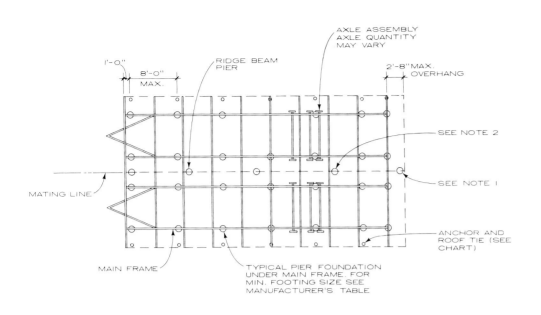

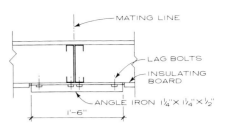

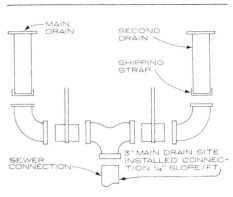

NOTES

1. Required pier capacity at each end of home equals the total distance in feet to the next ridge beam post multiplied by 165 lb/lin. ft.

2. Required pier capacity at interior ridge beam posts equals the distance between each post on each side, in feet, multiplied by 165 lb/lin. ft.

NOTE

Gutters, overflows not hooked up with the drain system shall discharge outside the home perimeter.

EXAMPLES OF FOOTING MAIN FRAME TIE-DOWN

DRAIN SYSTEM HOOKUP

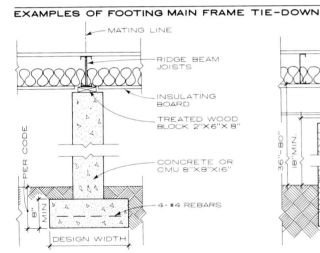

RIDGE BEAM PIER

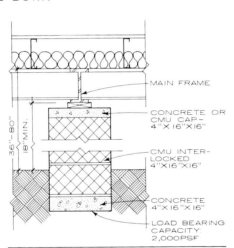

MAIN FRAME PIER

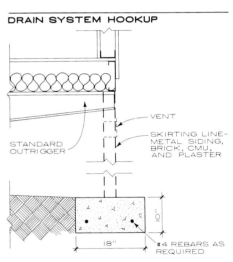

TYPICAL SIDEWALL

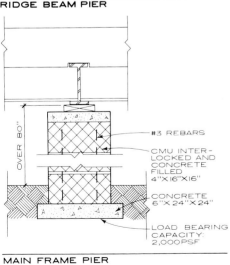

MAIN FRAME PIER

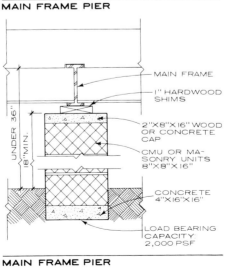

MAIN FRAME PIER

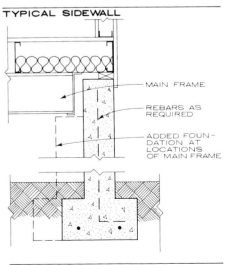

TYPICAL ENDWALL

Walter Hart Associates, AIA; White Plains, New York
Charles W. Graham, AIA; Texas A & M University; College Station, Texas

TRANSPORTATION   1

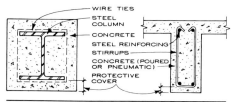

CONCRETE ENCASEMENT

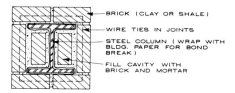

MASONRY ENCLOSURE

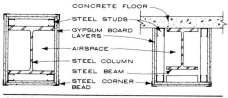

GYPSUM MEMBRANE ENCLOSURE

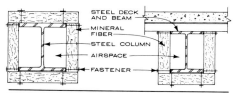

MINERAL FIBER MEMBRANE ENCLOSURE

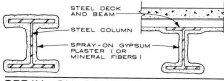

SPRAY-ON CONTOUR

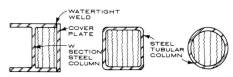

LIQUID FILLED COLUMN

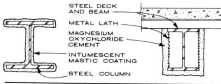

COATINGS

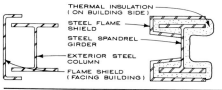

FLAME SHIELDS

UNPROTECTED STEEL

At temperatures greater than 1000°F, mild steel loses about one half of its ultimate room temperature strength. Consequently, fire tests on steel beams and columns are terminated when the steel's surface temperatures reach a predetermined limit or when the applied design loading can no longer be sustained (specific alternate test procedures are given by ASTM Standard Methods E 119). Fire resistance ratings are expressed in terms of duration in hours of fire exposure to standard temperature conditions in a test furnace (e.g., ³/₄ hr, 1 hr, 2 hr, 3 hr). For further information on fire resistance tests and fire protection of steel, see American Iron and Steel Institute's handbook, "Fire-Resistant Steel-Frame Construction."

CONCRETE ENCASEMENT

Achieved fire resistance for steel members encased in concrete depends on thickness of protective concrete cover, concrete mixture, and structural restraint (i.e., method of support and method of confining thermal expansion). Lightweight aggregate concrete has better fire resistance than normal weight concrete because of its higher moisture content and higher thermal resistance to heat flow. Heavier members require less cover for equivalent fire resistance, since they have greater mass. For data on columns encased in concrete, see National Fire Protection Association's "Fire Protection Handbook." Gunite, a mixture of cement, sand, and water, can be spray-applied by air pressure, but requires steel reinforcing. For exterior applications, reinforcing steel with less than 2 in. of concrete cover usually requires corrosion resistant primers.

MASONRY ENCLOSURE

Masonry materials (brick, concrete block, gypsum block, hollow clay tile) can be used to encase steel columns. The cores (or cells), which provide openings for reinforcing, also can be filled with mortar or insulating materials such as vermiculite to increase thermal resistance to heat flow. For data on fire resistance of masonry constructions, see National Concrete Masonry Association's "Fire Safety with Concrete Masonry."

GYPSUM MEMBRANE ENCLOSURE

Gypsum board or troweled plaster (e.g., vermiculite-gypsum, perlite-gypsum) or lath can be used to protect steel at building locations not exposed to moisture. Gypsum retards heat flow to steel by releasing chemically combined water (called "calcination") at temperatures above 180°F. To protect steel columns, gypsum board layers can be attached to steel studs by means of self-tapping screws or installed behind a galvanized or stainless sheet steel cover. For data on fire resistance of gypsum constructions, see Gypsum Association's "Fire Resistance Design Data Manual."

MINERAL FIBER MEMBRANE ENCLOSURE

When exposed to fire, mineral fiber (made from molten rock or slag) retards heat flow to steel because of its low thermal conductivity (it can withstand temperatures above 2000°F without melting). Mineral fiber requires a protective covering when exposed to outdoor conditions or the possibility of damage from accidental impact or abrasion.

SPRAY-ON CONTOUR

Spray-on applied cementitious mixtures (lightweight aggregate plasters with insulating fibers or vermiculite) or mineral fibers mixed with inorganic binders provide thermal barrier to heat from fire. The steel surface must be clean and free of loose paint, rust, oil, and grease before spraying, and a protective primer may be required. In addition, spraying should not be scheduled during cold conditions. Lightweight spray-on contours can be easily damaged during installation of nearby gas and water pipes, air ducts, and the like, and they are subject to flaking during normal use. Pins, studs, and other mechanical fasteners can be used to secure moisture or abrasion resistant protective finish coatings. Applications more than 2 in. thick generally require wire mesh or lath reinforcement.

LIQUID FILLED COLUMNS

During a fire the liquid, circulating by convection from fire floor columns, removes heat. Storage tanks or city water mains can be used to replace water converted to steam (vented by pressure relief valves or rupture discs). Pumps also may be used to avoid stagnant areas within an interconnected water circulation system of columns and piping. To prevent corrosion, use a rust inhibitor such as potassium nitrate. To prevent freezing in cold climates, use an antifreeze such as potassium carbonate. During construction, strict quality control is essential to achieve a watertight system.

COATINGS

Intumescent mastic coatings can be spray-applied like paint. When exposed to fire, the coating absorbs heat above about 300°F by expanding into a thick, lightweight thermal barrier more than about 150 times its initial thickness. This gas filled multicellular layer retards heat flow by releasing cooling gases and blocks off oxygen supply. Coatings should only be applied to steel surfaces that are free of dirt, scale, and oil. A multilayer system, consisting of intumescent mastic layers with glass fiber reinforcing between, is needed to achieve fire resistance ratings greater than 1 hr.

When exposed to heat, magnesium oxychloride cement retards heat flow to steel by releasing water of hydration at temperatures above about 570°F. Corrosion resistant priming may be required to assure proper adhesion of magnesium oxychloride to steel surfaces. In high intensity fires (e.g., flammable liquid or gas fires), magnesium oxychloride does not spall and the magnesium oxide residue acts as an efficient heat reflector.

FLAME SHIELDS

Steel flame shields can deflect heat and flames from burning building away from exterior structural steel members. For example, girder top and bottom flanges avoid direct flame impingement during fire by having flame shield protection with thermal insulation behind girder.

NOTES

1. Check prevailing building code for required fire resistance ratings of building constructions. Begin planning steel fire protection during the early stages of a project so that it can be integrated into building design. Consult early with authority having jurisdiction and insurance underwriting groups such as Industrial Risk Insurers, American Insurance Association, or Factory Mutual System.
2. Refer to fire resistance data based on ASTM E 119 test procedures from Underwriters' Laboratories, Factory Mutual, and other nationally recognized testing laboratories.
3. In general, fire resistance of constructions with cavity airspace (e.g., walls, floor-ceilings) will be greater than similar identical weight constructions without airspace.
4. If possible, locate cavity airspace on side of construction opposite potential fire exposure.
5. For most situations, fire resistance of constructions with thermal insulating materials such as mineral fiber and glass fiber in cavity airspace (e.g., doors, walls) will be greater than identical constructions without cavity insulation. Be careful, however, since adding thermal insulation to suspended floor-ceiling assemblies may lower fire resistance by causing metal suspension grid system to buckle or warp from elevated surface temperatures.
6. When plenum spaces above suspended ceilings are used for mechanical system return airflow, fire resistance of floor-ceiling assemblies will be diminished. Conversely, plenums under positive pressure from supply airflow can achieve greater fire resistances than under neutral pressure conditions (e.g., no air circulation in plenum).
7. For beams and columns, the higher the ratio of weight (e.g., pounds per unit length) to heated perimeter (i.e., surface area exposed to fire) the greater the fire resistance.
8. Beams and columns with membrane enclosure protection will have less surface area exposed to fire than identical members with spray-on applied contour protection. In addition, membrane enclosures (e.g., gypsum board, mineral fiber, magnesium oxychloride, or metal lath) form airspaces on both sides of W and S section webs.

M. David Egan, P.E.; College of Architecture, Clemson University; Clemson, South Carolina

1   FIRE PROTECTION

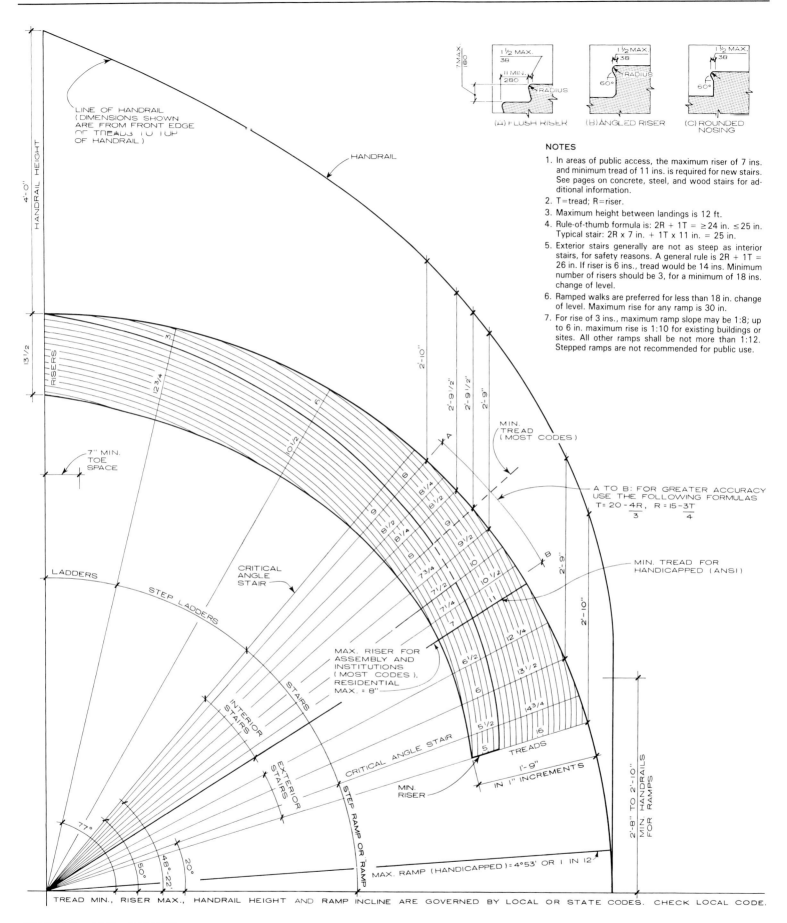

(A) FLUSH RISER   (B) ANGLED RISER   (C) ROUNDED NOSING

LINE OF HANDRAIL (DIMENSIONS SHOWN ARE FROM FRONT EDGE OF TREADS TO TOP OF HANDRAIL)

HANDRAIL

NOTES

1. In areas of public access, the maximum riser of 7 ins. and minimum tread of 11 ins. is required for new stairs. See pages on concrete, steel, and wood stairs for additional information.

2. T = tread; R = riser.

3. Maximum height between landings is 12 ft.

4. Rule-of-thumb formula is: 2R + 1T = ≥ 24 in. ≤ 25 in. Typical stair: 2R x 7 in. + 1T x 11 in. = 25 in.

5. Exterior stairs generally are not as steep as interior stairs, for safety reasons. A general rule is 2R + 1T = 26 in. If riser is 6 ins., tread would be 14 ins. Minimum number of risers should be 3, for a minimum of 18 ins. change of level.

6. Ramped walks are preferred for less than 18 in. change of level. Maximum rise for any ramp is 30 in.

7. For rise of 3 ins., maximum ramp slope may be 1:8; up to 6 in. maximum rise is 1:10 for existing buildings or sites. All other ramps shall be not more than 1:12. Stepped ramps are not recommended for public use.

HANDRAIL HEIGHT 4'-0"

RISERS 13½

7" MIN. TOE SPACE

LADDERS

STEP LADDERS

CRITICAL ANGLE STAIR

INTERIOR STAIRS

STAIRS

EXTERIOR STAIRS

CRITICAL ANGLE STAIR

STEP RAMP OR RAMP

MAX. RISER FOR ASSEMBLY AND INSTITUTIONS (MOST CODES). RESIDENTIAL MAX. = 8"

MIN. RISER

MIN. TREAD (MOST CODES)

A TO B: FOR GREATER ACCURACY USE THE FOLLOWING FORMULAS $T = \frac{20 - 4R}{3}$, $R = \frac{15 - 3T}{4}$

MIN. TREAD FOR HANDICAPPED (ANSI)

TREADS

1'-9" IN 1" INCREMENTS

2'-8" TO 2'-10" MIN. HANDRAILS FOR RAMPS

77°   50°   48°-22'   20°

MAX. RAMP (HANDICAPPED) = 4°53' OR 1 IN 12

TREAD MIN., RISER MAX., HANDRAIL HEIGHT AND RAMP INCLINE ARE GOVERNED BY LOCAL OR STATE CODES. CHECK LOCAL CODE.

TREADS AND RISERS

Paul Vaughan, AIA; Charleston, West Virginia

ANTHROPOMETRIC 1

REFERENCES

GENERAL REFERENCES

American National Standards Institute (ANSI) *ASTM Standards in Building Codes*, American Society for Testing and Materials (ASTM)

BOCA National Building Code, Building Officials and Code Administrators International (BOCA)

Fire Protection Handbook, National Fire Protection Association (NFPA)

Minimum Guidelines and Requirements for Accessible Design, Architectural and Transportation Barriers Compliance Board

Southern Standard Building Code, Southern Building Code Congress (SBCC)

Uniform Building Code, International Conference of Building Officials (ICBO)

DATA SOURCES: ORGANIZATIONS

American Insurance Association, 6

American National Standards Institute (ANSI), 7

American Society for Testing and Materials (ASTM), 6

Factory Mutual System, 6

Federal Housing Administration (FHA), U.S. Department of Housing and Urban Development (HUD), 3

Industrial Risk Insurers, 6

National Building Code, American Insurance Association, 7

DATA SOURCES: PUBLICATIONS

Basic Building Code, Building Officials and Code Administrators International (BOCA), 7

Concepts in Building Fire Safety, M. David Egan, Wiley, 6

Fire Protection Handbook, 15th ed., National Fire Protection Association (NFPA), 1981. Reprinted with permission of the publisher, 6

Fire Resistance Design Data Manual, Gypsum Association, 6

Fire Safety with Concrete Masonry, National Concrete Masonry Association (NCMA), 6

Fire-Resistant Steel-Frame Construction, American Iron and Steel Institute (AISI), 6

Southern Standard Building Code, 1985 ed., Southern Building Code Congress (SBCC), 7

CHAPTER 2

SITEWORK

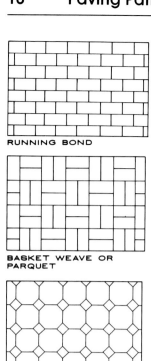

RUNNING BOND

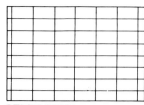

STACK BOND

STACK BOND

BASKET WEAVE OR PARQUET

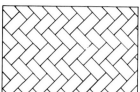

HERRINGBONE

DIAGONAL RUNNING BOND

OCTAGON AND DOT

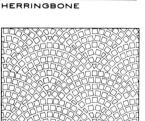

ROMAN COBBLE

HEXAGON

TYPICAL UNIT PAVER TYPES AND NOMINAL SIZES

BRICK PAVERS: 4 in. x 4 in., 4 in. x 8 in., 4 in. x 12 in.; ½ in. to 2¼ in. thick.

PRESSED CONCRETE BRICKS: 4 in. x 8 in., 2½ in. to 3 in. thick.

PRESSED CONCRETE PAVERS: 12 in. x 12 in., 12 in. x 24 in., 18 in. x 18 in., 18 in. x 24 in., 24 in. x 24 in., 24 in. x 30 in., 24 in. x 36 in., 30 in. x 30 in., 36 in. x 36 in.; 1½ in. to 3 in. thick.

ASPHALT PAVERS: 5 in. x 12 in., 6 in. x 6 in., 6 in. x 12 in., 8 in. x 8 in., 8 in. hexagonal, 1¼ in. to 3 in. thick.

NOTES
1. Face brick, marble, and granite sometimes are used for paving.
2. See index for tile paver sizes and shapes.
3. Paving patterns shown often are rotated 45° for diagonal patterns.
4. Maximum 3 percent absorption for brick applications subject to vehicular traffic.
5. For pressed concrete and asphalt pavers subject to vehicular traffic, use 3 in. thickness.
6. Use modular size for brick paver patterns other than running and stack bond set with mortar joints. Use full size when set without mortar joints.

UNIT PAVERS

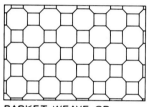

BASKET WEAVE OR PARQUET

DIAGONAL RUNNING BOND

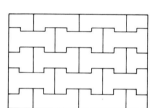

RUNNING BOND

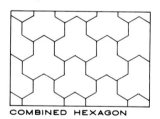

COMBINED HEXAGON

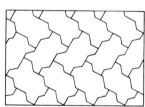

HERRINGBONE

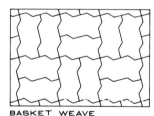

BASKET WEAVE

NOTES
1. Interlocking pavers are available in concrete, hydraulically pressed concrete, asphalt, and brick, and in different weight classifications, compressive strengths, surface textures, finishes, and colors. Consult local suppliers for availability.
2. Subject to manufacturer's recommendations and local code requirements, interlocking concrete pavers may be used in areas subject to heavy vehicle loads at 30 to 40 mph speeds.
3. Continuous curb or other edge restraint is required to anchor pavers in applications subject to vehicular traffic.
4. Concrete interlocking paver sizes are based on metric dimensions. Dimensions indicated are to nearest ⅛ in.
5. Where paver shape permits, herringbone pattern is recommended for paving subject to vehicular traffic.
6. Portions have been adapted, with permission, from ASTM C 939.

INTERLOCKING PAVERS

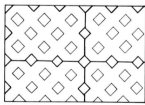

DIAGONAL SQUARES

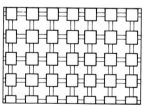

RUNNING SQUARES

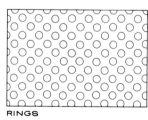

RINGS

NOTES
1. Appearance of grass pavers when voids are filled are shown by stipple to the right of the cut line. Voids may be filled with grass, a variety of ground cover, or gravel.
2. Grass pavers may be used to control erosion.
3. Herringbone pattern is recommended for concrete grass pavers subject to vehicular traffic.
4. Grass rings are available with close ring spacing for pedestrian use or wide ring spacing for vehicular use.

GRASS PAVERS

STACK BOND

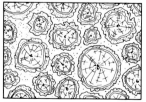

RANDOM

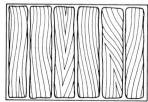

STACK BOND

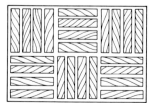

BASKET WEAVE OR PARQUET

WOOD PAVERS

Jeffrey R. Vandevoort; Talbott Wilson Associates, Inc.; Houston, Texas
John R. Hoke, Jr., AIA, Architect; Washington, D.C.

 PAVING AND SURFACING

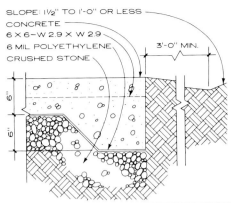

SLOPE: 1½" TO 1'-0" OR LESS
CONCRETE
6 × 6—W 2.9 × W 2.9
6 MIL POLYETHYLENE
CRUSHED STONE
3'-0" MIN.
6"
6"

CONCRETE PAVING WITHOUT CURB

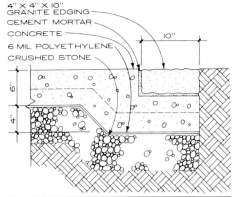

4" × 4" × 10"
GRANITE EDGING
CEMENT MORTAR
CONCRETE
6 MIL POLYETHYLENE
CRUSHED STONE
10"
6"
4"

GRANITE EDGING

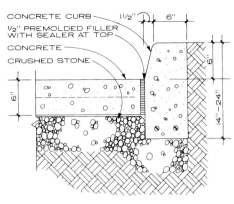

CONCRETE CURB
1½" 6"
½" PREMOLDED FILLER
WITH SEALER AT TOP
CONCRETE
CRUSHED STONE
6"
6"
14"–24"

SEPARATE CONCRETE CURB

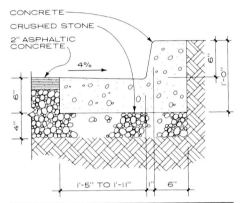

CONCRETE
CRUSHED STONE
2" ASPHALTIC
CONCRETE
4%
6"
1'-0"
6"
4"
1'-5" TO 1'-11" 1" 6"

CONCRETE CURB AND GUTTER

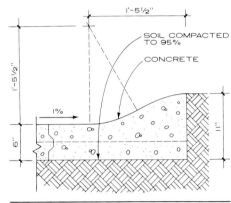

1'-5½"
1'-5½"
SOIL COMPACTED
TO 95%
CONCRETE
1%
6"
11"

MOUNTABLE CONCRETE CURB

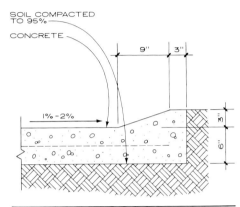

SOIL COMPACTED
TO 95%
CONCRETE
9" 3"
1%–2%
3"
6"

IOWA CONCRETE CURB

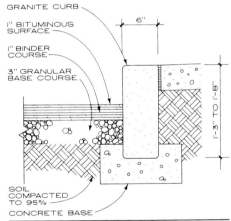

GRANITE CURB
1" BITUMINOUS
SURFACE
1" BINDER
COURSE
3" GRANULAR
BASE COURSE
6"
1'-3" TO 1'-8"
SOIL
COMPACTED
TO 95%
CONCRETE BASE

ASPHALT PAVING WITH STONE CURB

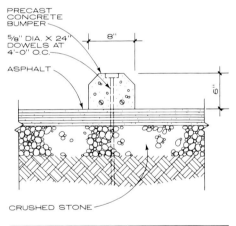

PRECAST
CONCRETE
BUMPER
⅝" DIA. × 24"
DOWELS AT
4'-0" O.C.
ASPHALT
8"
6"
CRUSHED STONE

**ASPHALT PAVING WITH PRECAST
CONCRETE BUMPER**

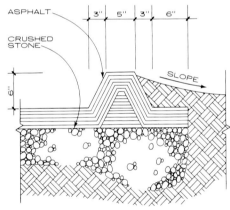

ASPHALT
CRUSHED
STONE
3" 5" 3" 6"
SLOPE
6"

NOT RECOMMENDED AS WHEEL STOP

ASPHALT CURB AND PAVING

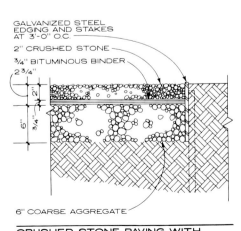

GALVANIZED STEEL
EDGING AND STAKES
AT 3'-0" O.C.
2" CRUSHED STONE
¾" BITUMINOUS BINDER
2¾"
2"
6"
¾"
6" COARSE AGGREGATE

**CRUSHED STONE PAVING WITH
METAL EDGE**

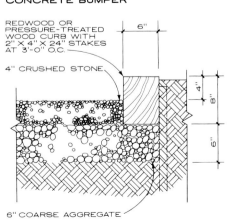

REDWOOD OR
PRESSURE-TREATED
WOOD CURB WITH
2" × 4" × 24" STAKES
AT 3'-0" O.C.
4" CRUSHED STONE
6"
4"
8"
6"
6" COARSE AGGREGATE

**CRUSHED STONE PAVING WITH
TIMBER CURB**

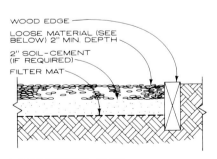

WOOD EDGE
LOOSE MATERIAL (SEE
BELOW) 2" MIN. DEPTH
2" SOIL-CEMENT
(IF REQUIRED)
FILTER MAT

LOOSE MATERIAL SIZES
WOOD CHIPS – 1" NOMINAL
SHREDDED BARK MULCH
¼" STONE CHIPS
¾" PEA GRAVEL

½" DECOMPOSED
GRANITE
¾" CRUSHED
STONE
1"–2" WASHED
STONE

NOTE: ORGANIC MATERIALS WILL DECOMPOSE

**LOOSE MATERIAL PAVING WITH
WOOD EDGE**

Francisco J. Menendez; Washington, D.C.
Richard J. Vitullo; Washington Grove, Maryland

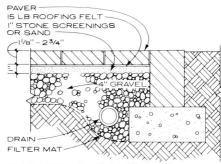

PAVER
15 LB ROOFING FELT
1" STONE SCREENINGS OR SAND
1 1/8" - 2 3/4"
4" GRAVEL
DRAIN
FILTER MAT

PAVER SIZES: 4" X 4", 4" X 8", 4" X 12", 6" X 6", 8" X 8", 12" X 12", 5 3/4", 8", AND 12" HEXAGON
PAVER THICKNESS: 1 1/8"-2 3/4"

BRICK, CLAY TILE, OR ASPHALT BLOCK PAVERS

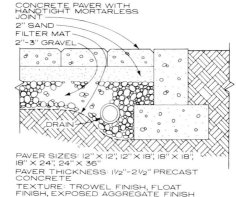

CONCRETE PAVER WITH HANDTIGHT MORTARLESS JOINT
2" SAND
FILTER MAT
2"-3" GRAVEL
DRAIN

PAVER SIZES: 12" X 12", 12" X 18", 18" X 18", 18" X 24", 24" X 36"
PAVER THICKNESS: 1 1/2"-2 1/2" PRECAST CONCRETE
TEXTURE: TROWEL FINISH, FLOAT FINISH, EXPOSED AGGREGATE FINISH

CONCRETE PAVERS AND LONDON WALKS

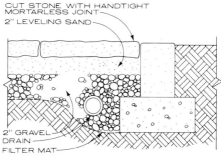

CUT STONE WITH HANDTIGHT MORTARLESS JOINT
2" LEVELING SAND
2" GRAVEL
DRAIN
FILTER MAT

STONE SIZES: 12" X 12", 12" X 18", 18" X 18", 18" X 24", 24" X 36", OR RANDOM SHAPES
STONE THICKNESS: 1"-2" CUT STONE
TEXTURE: HONED, NATURAL CLEFT, OR FLAME TREATED FOR NONSLIP FINISH

CUT STONE PAVERS

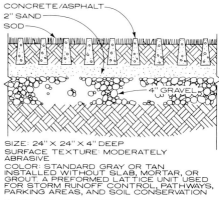

CONCRETE/ASPHALT
2" SAND
SOD
4" GRAVEL

SIZE: 24" X 24" X 4" DEEP
SURFACE TEXTURE: MODERATELY ABRASIVE
COLOR: STANDARD GRAY OR TAN
INSTALLED WITHOUT SLAB, MORTAR, OR GROUT. A PREFORMED LATTICE UNIT USED FOR STORM RUNOFF CONTROL, PATHWAYS, PARKING AREAS, AND SOIL CONSERVATION.

GRID PAVING BLOCKS

UNIT PAVERS ON FLEXIBLE BASE

GENERAL NOTES

1. Drainpipes may be omitted at well-drained areas.
2. Provide positive outflow for drainpipes.
3. Do not use unsatisfactory soil (expanding organic).
4. Satisfactory soil shall be compacted to 95%.

Charles A. Szoradi; Washington, D.C.
Richard J. Vitullo; Washington Grove, Maryland

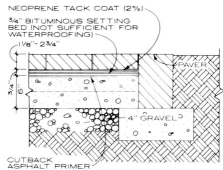

NEOPRENE TACK COAT (2%)
3/4" BITUMINOUS SETTING BED (NOT SUFFICIENT FOR WATERPROOFING)
1 1/8" - 2 3/4"
PAVER
3/4"
6"
4" GRAVEL
CUTBACK ASPHALT PRIMER

WHERE WEATHER PERMITS, LATEX-MODIFIED MORTAR MAY BE USED FOR JOINTS AND SETTING BED

BRICK, CLAY TILE, OR ASPHALT BLOCK PAVERS

CONCRETE PAVER WITH HANDTIGHT MORTARLESS JOINT
3/4" BITUMINOUS SETTING BED (NOT SUFFICIENT FOR WATERPROOFING)
CONCRETE
4" GRAVEL

WHERE WEATHER PERMITS, LATEX-MODIFIED MORTAR MAY BE USED FOR JOINTS AND SETTING BED

CONCRETE PAVERS AND LONDON WALKS

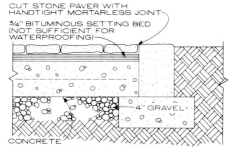

CUT STONE PAVER WITH HANDTIGHT MORTARLESS JOINT
3/4" BITUMINOUS SETTING BED (NOT SUFFICIENT FOR WATERPROOFING)
4" GRAVEL
CONCRETE

SIZES: CAN BE SMALLER THAN FOR FLEXIBLE BASE WHERE WEATHER PERMITS LATEX-MODIFIED MORTAR. MAY BE USED FOR JOINT AND SETTING BEDS. JOINTS MAY BE STAGGERED OR RANDOM
STONE THICKNESS: 1/2" SLATE OR 1"-2" CUT STONE

CUT STONE PAVERS

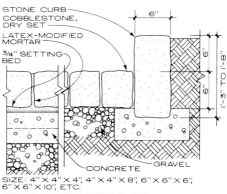

STONE CURB COBBLESTONE, DRY SET
LATEX-MODIFIED MORTAR
3/4" SETTING BED
6"
6"
6"
6"
1'-3" TO 1'-8"
CONCRETE
GRAVEL

SIZE: 4" X 4" X 4", 4" X 4" X 8", 6" X 6" X 6", 6" X 6" X 12", ETC.
STONE: GRANITE, BASALT, ETC.

COBBLESTONE PAVERS

UNIT PAVERS ON RIGID BASE

5. Flexible and suspended bases shown are for light duty only.
6. Edging width: 2, 4, 8, 12 in.; depth: 8, 12, 16, 24 in.

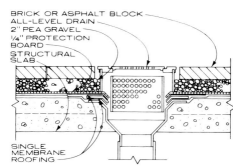

BRICK OR ASPHALT BLOCK
ALL-LEVEL DRAIN
2" PEA GRAVEL
1/4" PROTECTION BOARD
STRUCTURAL SLAB
SINGLE MEMBRANE ROOFING

FOR HEATED SPACES UNDER STRUCTURAL SLAB, USE CLOSED CELL INSULATION UNDER PAVERS

BRICK, CLAY TILE, ASPHALT BLOCK, CONCRETE, OR STONE PAVERS OVER UNINSULATED BASE

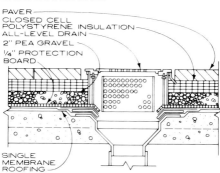

PAVER
CLOSED CELL POLYSTYRENE INSULATION
ALL-LEVEL DRAIN
2" PEA GRAVEL
1/4" PROTECTION BOARD
SINGLE MEMBRANE ROOFING

THIS SYSTEM SUITABLE FOR PEDESTRIAN TRAFFIC ONLY

BRICK, CLAY TILE, ASPHALT BLOCK, CONCRETE, OR STONE PAVERS OVER INSULATED BASE

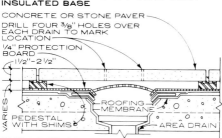

CONCRETE OR STONE PAVER
DRILL FOUR 3/8" HOLES OVER EACH DRAIN TO MARK LOCATION
1/4" PROTECTION BOARD
1 1/2" - 2 1/2"
ROOFING MEMBRANE
PEDESTAL WITH SHIMS
AREA DRAIN
VARIES

FINISH SURFACE: LEVEL, JOINTS ACTING AS DRAINS
DRAINAGE SURFACE: SLOPE TO DRAIN 1/8"-1/4" PER FT
HEIGHT OF PEDESTALS: 1/2"-1 1/2"
PEDESTAL MATERIAL: NEOPRENE, METAL, VINYL, MORTAR
SHIMS: MULTIPLE OF 1/8"

CONCRETE OR CUT STONE PAVER ON PEDESTALS OVER UNINSULATED BASE

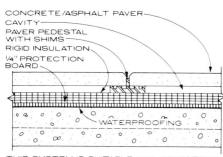

CONCRETE/ASPHALT PAVER
CAVITY
PAVER PEDESTAL WITH SHIMS
RIGID INSULATION
1/4" PROTECTION BOARD
WATERPROOFING

THIS SYSTEM IS SUITABLE FOR PEDESTRIAN TRAFFIC ONLY. RIGID INSULATION SHALL BE SUITABLE TO CARRY PEDESTRIAN LOADS
PEDESTAL MATERIAL: NEOPRENE, METAL, VINYL, MORTAR
SHIMS: SAME AS PEDESTAL MATERIAL

CONCRETE OR STONE PAVERS ON PEDESTALS OVER INSULATED BASE

UNIT PAVERS ON SUSPENDED BASE

7. Footing of edging width: 8, 12, 16, 20 in.; depth: 6, 8 in.
8. If freezing, depth is deeper than bottom of footing; provide gravel at footing.

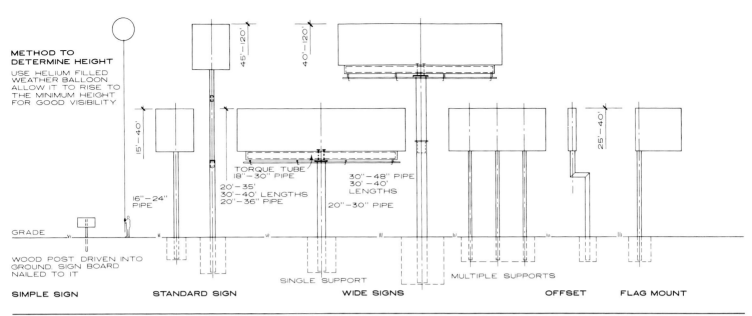

METHOD TO DETERMINE HEIGHT

USE HELIUM FILLED WEATHER BALLOON ALLOW IT TO RISE TO THE MINIMUM HEIGHT FOR GOOD VISIBILITY

WOOD POST DRIVEN INTO GROUND. SIGN BOARD NAILED TO IT

16''—24'' PIPE

TORQUE TUBE 18''—30'' PIPE

20'—35'
30'—40' LENGTHS
20'—36'' PIPE

30''—48'' PIPE
30'—40' LENGTHS

20''—30'' PIPE

GRADE

SIMPLE SIGN   STANDARD SIGN   SINGLE SUPPORT   WIDE SIGNS   MULTIPLE SUPPORTS   OFFSET   FLAG MOUNT

TYPES OF SIGNS

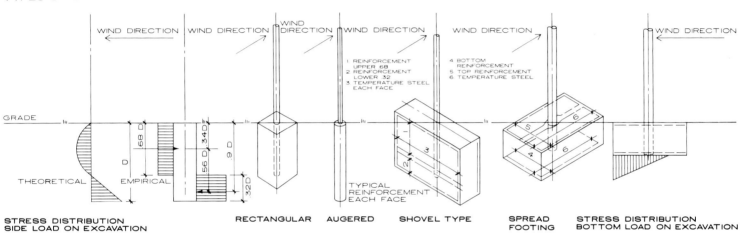

WIND DIRECTION

GRADE

THEORETICAL   EMPIRICAL

1 REINFORCEMENT UPPER 68
2 REINFORCEMENT LOWER 32
3 TEMPERATURE STEEL EACH FACE

4 BOTTOM REINFORCEMENT
5 TOP REINFORCEMENT
6 TEMPERATURE STEEL

TYPICAL REINFORCEMENT EACH FACE

STRESS DISTRIBUTION SIDE LOAD ON EXCAVATION   RECTANGULAR   AUGERED   SHOVEL TYPE   SPREAD FOOTING   STRESS DISTRIBUTION BOTTOM LOAD ON EXCAVATION

FOOTING TYPES

STRUCTURAL DESIGN OF SIGNS

Signs are structurally designed primarily by wind forces and secondarily by gravitational forces. Wind forces are determined by wind speed, height, location, time interval for maximum wind (100 year, 50 year, etc.), gust factor, distribution on the surface, and codes. Although the basic wind load p is computed by the formula $p = 0.00258 \, V$ where V = velocity of the wind in miles per hour, the factors that modify it vary in different regions by the codes that apply. Therefore wind loads are computed differently in different parts of the country. A state code may also be modified by a local ordinance, so a designer has to make sure that code requirements are met. By following the applicable code requirements utilizing wind maps, tables, and directions, the designer is able to determine the wind load per square foot acting on the sign surface in the locality in which the sign is being erected.

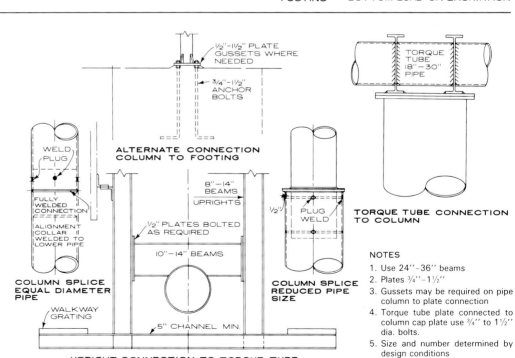

1/2''—11/2'' PLATE GUSSETS WHERE NEEDED

3/4''—11/2'' ANCHOR BOLTS

ALTERNATE CONNECTION COLUMN TO FOOTING

WELD PLUG

FULLY WELDED CONNECTION

ALIGNMENT COLLAR WELDED TO LOWER PIPE

COLUMN SPLICE EQUAL DIAMETER PIPE

WALKWAY GRATING

8''—14'' BEAMS
UPRIGHTS

1/2'' PLATES BOLTED AS REQUIRED

10''—14'' BEAMS

5'' CHANNEL MIN.

UPRIGHT CONNECTION TO TORQUE TUBE

1/2''
PLUG WELD

COLUMN SPLICE REDUCED PIPE SIZE

TORQUE TUBE 18''—30'' PIPE

TORQUE TUBE CONNECTION TO COLUMN

NOTES

1. Use 24''—36'' beams
2. Plates 3/4''—11/2''
3. Gussets may be required on pipe column to plate connection
4. Torque tube plate connected to column cap plate use 3/4'' to 11/2'' dia. bolts.
5. Size and number determined by design conditions

Leon Seligson, AIA; Columbus, Ohio

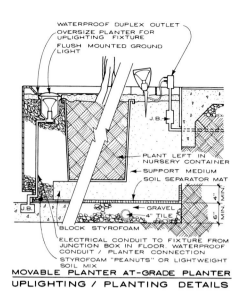

MOVABLE PLANTER AT-GRADE PLANTER UPLIGHTING / PLANTING DETAILS

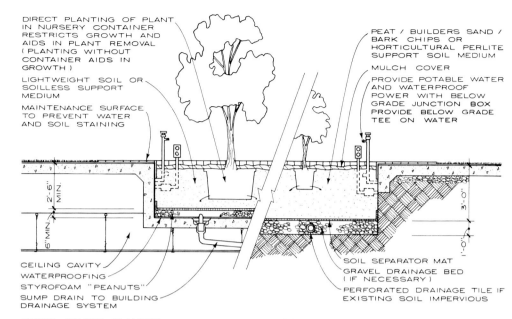

ABOVE-GRADE PLANTER   **AT-GRADE PLANTER**
FLOOR PLANTER DETAILS

UPLIGHTING AND ELECTRICAL NEEDS

1. May be of some benefit to plants, but inefficient for plant photosynthesis because of plant physiological structure. Chlorophyll is usually in upper part of leaf.

2. Uplighting should never be utilized as sole lighting source for plants.

3. Waterproof duplex outlets above soil line with a waterproof junction box below soil line are usually adequate for "atmosphere" uplighting and water fountain pumps.

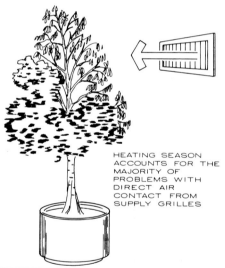

FOLIAGE BURN FROM DIRECT HEAT CONTACT

HVAC EFFECT ON PLANTS

1. Air-conditioning (cooled air) is rarely detrimental to plants, even if it is "directed" at plants. The ventilation here is what counts! Good ventilation is a must with plants; otherwise oxygen and temperatures build up. Heat supply, on the other hand, when "directed" at plants, can truly be disastrous. Plan for supplies directed away from plants, but maintain adequate ventilation.

2. Extended heat or power failures of sufficient duration can damage plant health. The lower limit of temperature as a steady state is 65°F for plant survival. Brief drops to 55°F (less than 1 hr) are the lower limit before damage. Temperatures up to 85°F for only 2 days a week can usually be tolerated.

3. The relative humidity should not be allowed to fall below 30%, as plants prefer a relative humidity of 50-60%.

Richard L. Gaines, AIA; Plantscape House; Apopka, Florida

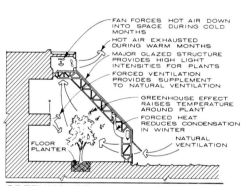

GREENHOUSE EFFECT RAISES NEED FOR ADEQUATE VENTILATION

TEMPERATURE REQUIREMENTS

1. Most plants prefer human comfort range: 70-75°F daytime temperatures and 60-65°F nighttime temperatures.

2. An absolute minimum temperature of 50°F must be observed. Plant damage will result below this figure. Rapid temperature fluctuations of 30-40°F can also be detrimental to plants.

3. "Q-10" phenomenon of respiration: for every 10°C rise in temperature, plants' respiration rate and food consumption doubles.

4. Both photosynthesis and respiration decline and stop with time, as temperatures go beyond 80°F. Beware of the greenhouse effect!

WATER SUPPLY REQUIREMENTS

1. Movable and railing planters are often watered by watering can. Provide convenient access to hot and cold potable water by hose bibbs and/or service sinks (preferably in janitor's closet) during normal working hours, with long (min. 24 in.) faucet-to-sink or floor distances. Provide for maximum of 200 ft travel on all floors.

2. At-grade floor planters are usually watered by hose and extension wand. Provide hose bibbs above soil line (for maximum travel of 50 ft) with capped "tee" stub-outs beneath soil line. If soil temperature is apt to get abnormally low in winter, provide hot and cold water by mixer-faucet type hose bibbs.

3. High concentrations of fluoride and chlorine in water supply can cause damage to plants. Provide water with low concentrations of these elements and with a pH value of 5.0-6.0. Higher or lower pH levels can result in higher plant maintenance costs.

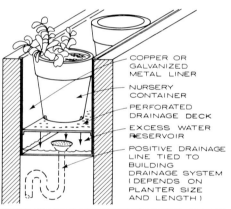

RAILING PLANTER DETAIL

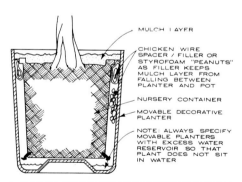

MOVABLE DECORATIVE PLANTER DETAIL

STORAGE REQUIREMENTS

Provide a secured storage space of approximately 30 sq ft for watering equipment and other maintenance materials. It may be desirable to combine water supply and janitor needs in the same storage area.

AIR POLLUTION EFFECTS ON PLANTS

Problems result from inadequate ventilation. Excessive chlorine gas from swimming pool areas can be a damaging problem, as well as excessive fumes from toxic cleaning substances for floor finishes, etc. Ventilation a must here!

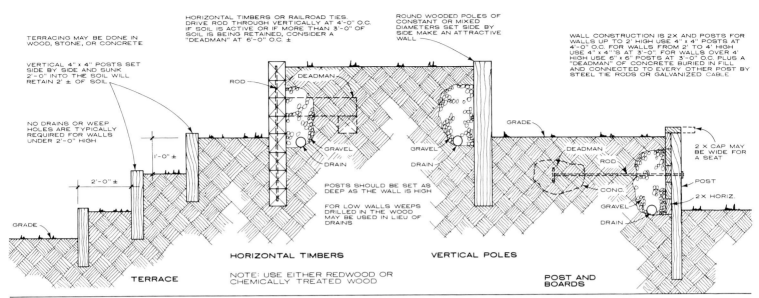

VERTICAL POLES

HORIZONTAL TIMBERS

TERRACE

POST AND BOARDS

NOTE: USE EITHER REDWOOD OR CHEMICALLY TREATED WOOD

WOOD APPLICATIONS

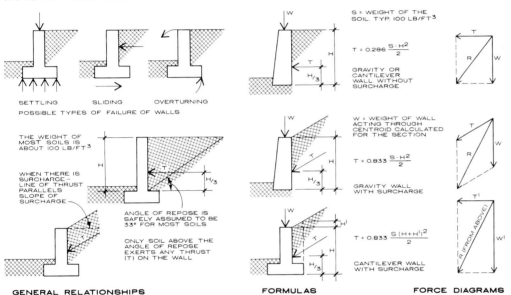

POSSIBLE TYPES OF FAILURE OF WALLS

GENERAL RELATIONSHIPS

FORMULAS

FORCE DIAGRAMS

SLIDING

The thrust on the wall must be resisted. The resisting force is the weight of the wall times the coefficient of soil friction. Use a safety factor of 1.5. Therefore:

$$W(C.F.) \geq 1.5T$$

Average coefficients:

Gravel	0.6
Silt/dry clay	0.5
Sand	0.4
Wet clay	0.3

OVERTURNING

The overturning moment equals $T(H/3)$. This is resisted by the resisting moment. For symmetrical sections, resisting moment equals W times (width of base/2). Use a safety factor of 2.0. Therefore:

$$M_R \geq 2(M_0)$$

SETTLING

Soil bearing value must resist vertical force. For symmetrical sections that force is W (or W') / bearing area. Use a safety factor of 1.5. Therefore:

$$S.B. \geq 1.5(W/A)$$

STRUCTURAL DESIGN CONSIDERATIONS

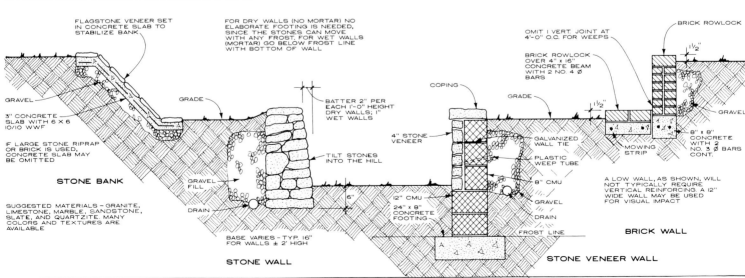

STONE BANK

STONE WALL

BRICK WALL

STONE VENEER WALL

STONE AND MASONRY APPLICATIONS

Charles R. Heuer, AIA; Washington, D.C.

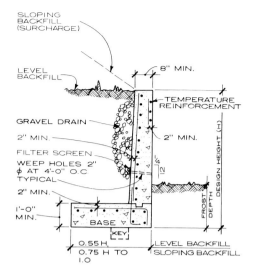

L TYPE RETAINING WALLS

Place base below frost line. Dimensions are approximate.

Soil pressure at toe equals 0.2 times the height in kips per square foot. Dimensions are preliminary.

GRAVITY RETAINING WALL

VERTICAL CONTROL JOINT

VERTICAL EXPANSION JOINT

RETAINING WALL JOINTS

NOTES

Provide control and/or construction joints in concrete retaining walls about every 25 ft and expansion joints about every fourth control and/or construction joint. Coated dowels should be used if average wall height on either side of a joint is different.

Consult with a structural engineer for final design of concrete retaining walls. An engineer's seal may be required for final design approval by local code officials.

Use temperature bars if wall is more than 10 in. thick.

Keys shown dashed may be required to prevent sliding in high walls and those on moist clay.

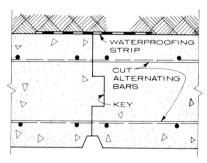

T TYPE RETAINING WALLS

PRELIMINARY DIMENSIONS

	BACKFILL SLOPING φ = 29° 45' (1¾:1)				
	APPROXIMATE CONCRETE DIMENSIONS				
HEIGHT OF WALL H (FT)	WIDTH OF BASE B (FT)	WIDTH OF WALL a (FT)	HEEL b (FT)	TOE c (FT)
3	2'-8''	0'-9''	1'-5''	0'-6''
4	3'-5''	0'-9''	2'-0''	0'-8''
5	4'-6''	0'-10''	2'-6''	1'-2''
6	5'-4''	0'-10''	2'-11''	1'-7''
7	6'-3''	0'-10''	3'-5''	2'-0''
8	7'-0''	1'-0''	3'-8''	2'-4''
9	7'-6''	1'-0''	4'-2''	2'-4''
10	8'-6''	1'-0''	4'-9''	2'-9''
11	11'-0''	1'-1''	7'-2''	2'-9''
12	12'-0''	1'-2''	7'-10''	3'-0''
13	13'-0''	1'-4''	8'-5''	3'-3''
14	14'-0''	1'-5''	9'-1''	3'-6''
15	15'-0''	1'-6''	9'-9''	3'-9''
16	16'-0''	1'-7''	10'-5''	4'-0''
17	17'-0''	1'-8''	11'-1''	4'-3''
18	18'-0''	1'-10''	11'-8''	4'-6''
19	19'-0''	1'-11''	12'-4''	4'-9''
20	20'-0''	2'-0''	13'-0''	5'-0''
21	21'-0''	2'-2''	13'-7''	5'-3''
22	22'-0''	2'-4''	14'-4''	5'-4''

	BACKFILL LEVEL—NO SURCHARGE				
	APPROXIMATE CONCRETE DIMENSIONS				
HEIGHT OF WALL H (FT)	WIDTH OF BASE B (FT)	WIDTH OF WALL a (FT)	HEEL b (FT)	TOE c (FT)
3	2'-1''	0'-8''	1'-0''	0'-5''
4	2'-8''	0'-8''	1'-7''	0'-5''
5	3'-3''	0'-8''	2'-2''	0'-5''
6	3'-9''	0'-8''	2'-5''	0'-8''
7	4'-2''	0'-8''	2'-6''	1'-0''
8	4'-8''	1'-0''	2'-8''	1'-0''
9	5'-2''	1'-0''	3'-2''	1'-0''
10	5'-9''	1'-0''	3'-7''	1'-2''
11	6'-7''	1'-1''	4'-1''	1'-5''
12	7'-3''	1'-2''	4'-7''	1'-6''
13	7'-10''	1'-2''	5'-0''	1'-8''
14	8'-5''	1'-3''	5'-5''	1'-9''
15	9'-0''	1'-4''	5'-9''	1'-11''
16	9'-7''	1'-5''	6'-2''	2'-0''
17	10'-3''	1'-6''	6'-7''	2'-2''
18	10'-10''	1'-6''	7'-1''	2'-3''
19	11'-5''	1'-7''	7'-5''	2'-5''
20	12'-0''	1'-8''	7'-10''	2'-6''
21	12'-7''	1'-9''	8'-2''	2'-8''
22	13'-3''	1'-11''	8'-7''	2'-9''

Kenneth D. Franch, AIA, PE; Phillips Swager Associates, Inc.; Dallas, Texas
Neubaur · Sohn, Engineers; Washington, D.C.

DIMENSIONS AND REINFORCEMENT

WALL	H	B	T	A	"V" BARS	"F" BARS
8"	3' 4"	2' 4"	9"	8"	#3 @ 32"	#3 @ 27"
	4' 0"	2' 9"	9"	10"	#4 @ 32"	#3 @ 27"
	4' 8"	3' 4"	10"	12"	#5 @ 32"	#3 @ 27"
	5' 4"	3' 8"	10"	14"	#4 @ 16"	#4 @ 30"
	6' 0"	4' 2"	12"	16"	#6 @ 24"	#4 @ 25"
12"	5' 4"	3' 8"	10"	14"	#4 @ 24"	#3 @ 25"
	6' 0"	4' 2"	12"	15"	#4 @ 16"	#4 @ 30"
	6' 8"	4' 6"	12"	16"	#6 @ 24"	#4 @ 22"
	7' 4"	4' 10"	12"	18"	#5 @ 16"	#5 @ 26"
	8' 0"	5' 4"	12"	20"	#7 @ 24"	#5 @ 21"
	8' 8"	5' 10"	14"	22"	#6 @ 8"	#6 @ 26"
	9' 4"	6' 2"	14"	24"	#8 @ 8"	#6 @ 21"

NOTE: See General Notes for design parameters.

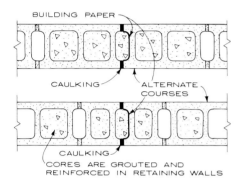

SHEAR - RESISTING CONTROL JOINT

NOTE

Long retaining walls should be broken into panels 20 ft. to 30 ft. long by vertical control joints designed to resist shear and other lateral forces while permitting longitudinal movement.

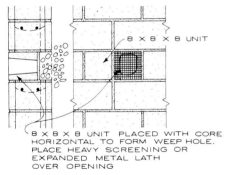

ALTERNATE WEEP HOLE DETAIL

NOTE

Four inch diameter weepholes located at 5 to 10 ft spacing along the base of the wall should be sufficient. Place about 1 cu ft of gravel or crushed stone around the intake of each weephole.

GENERAL NOTES

1. Materials and construction practices for concrete masonry retaining walls should comply with "Building Code Requirements for Concrete Masonry Structures (ACI 531)."

2. Use fine grout where grout space is less than 3 in. in least dimension. Use coarse grout where the least dimension of the grout space is 3 in. or more.

3. Steel reinforcement should be clean, free from harmful rust, and in compliance with applicable ASTM standards for deformed bars and steel wire.

4. Alternate vertical bars may be stopped at wall midheight. Vertical reinforcement usually is secured in

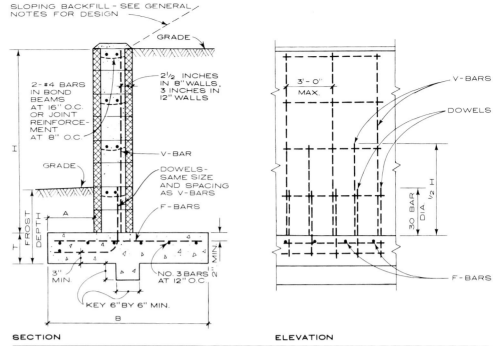

SECTION   **ELEVATION**

TYPICAL CANTILEVER RETAINING WALL

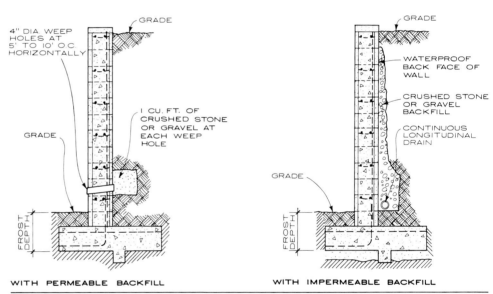

WITH PERMEABLE BACKFILL   **WITH IMPERMEABLE BACKFILL**

DRAINAGE DETAILS FOR VARYING SOIL CONDITIONS

place after the masonry work has been completed and before grouting.

5. Designs herein are based on an assumed soil weight (vertical pressure) of 100 pcf. Horizontal pressure is based on an equivalent fluid weight for the soil of 45 pcf.

6. Walls shown are designed with a safety factor against overturning of not less than 2 and a safety factor against horizontal sliding of not less than 1.5. Computations in the table for wall heights are based on level backfill. One method of providing for additional loads due to sloping backfill or surface loads is to consider them as an additional depth of soil, that is, an extra load of 300 psf can be treated as 3 ft. of extra soil weighing 100 psf.

7. Top of masonry retaining walls should be capped or otherwise protected to prevent entry of water into unfilled hollow cells and spaces. If bond beams are used, steel is placed in the beams as the wall is constructed. Horizontal joint reinforcement may be

placed in each joint (8 in. o.c.) and the bond beams omitted.

8. Allow 24 hours for masonry to set before grouting. Pour grout in 4 ft. layers, 1 hour between each pour. Break long walls into panels of 20 ft. to 30 ft. in length with vertical control joints. Allow 7 days for finished wall to set before backfilling. Prevent water from accumulating behind wall by means of 4 in. diameter weepholes at 5 ft. to 10 ft. spacing (with screen and graded stone) or by a continuous drain with felt-covered open joints combined with waterproofing.

9. Where backfill height exceeds 6 ft., provide a key under the footing base to resist the wall's tendency to slide horizontally.

10. Heavy equipment used in backfilling should not approach closer to the top of the wall than a distance equal to the height of the wall.

11. A structural engineer should be consulted for final design.

Kenneth D. Franch, AIA, PE; Phillips Swager Associates, Inc.; Dallas, Texas
Stephen J. Zipp, AIA; Wilkes and Faulkner Associates; Washington, D.C.

REFERENCES

GENERAL REFERENCES

Building Foundation Design Handbook, 1988, K. Labs, J. Carmody, et al., Underground Space Center, Minneapolis

Concrete Basements for Residential and Light Construction, Portland Cement Association (PCA)

Energy Conserving Site Design, 1984, E. G. McPherson, American Society of Landscape Architects (ASLA)

Graphic Standards for Landscape Architecture, 1986, Richard Austin, Van Nostrand Reinhold

Handbook of Landscape Architectural Construction, American Society of Landscape Architects (ASLA)

Simplified Design of Building Foundations, 1988, James Ambrose, Wiley

Site Design and Construction Detailing, 1988, Theodore D. Walker, PDA Publishers

Site Details, 1989, Gregory W. Jameson and Michael A. Verson, Van Nostrand Reinhold

Time-Saver Standards for Landscape Architecture, 1988, Charles W. Harris and Nicholas T. Dines, McGraw-Hill

Time-Saver Standards for Site Planning, 1984, Joseph DeChiara and Lee E. Koppleman, McGraw-Hill

DATA SOURCES: ORGANIZATIONS

American Society for Testing and Materials (ASTM), 10, 17

Endicott Clay Products Company, 10

Hanover Prest-Paving Company, 10

Hastings Pavement Company, Inc., 10

National Concrete Masonry Association (NCMA), 17

Outdoor Advertising Association of America, Inc. (OAAA), 13

Pavestone Company, 10

Paving Stones of Texas, 10

Pee Dee Ceramics, 10

Ritterings USA, Inc., 10

DATA SOURCES: PUBLICATIONS

Interior Plantscaping: Building Design for Interior Foliage Plants, Richard L. Gaines, AIA; Architectural Record Books, 14

Landscape Architecture, 1982, Linda Jewell, American Society of Landscape Architects Publication Board, 10

CHAPTER 3

CONCRETE

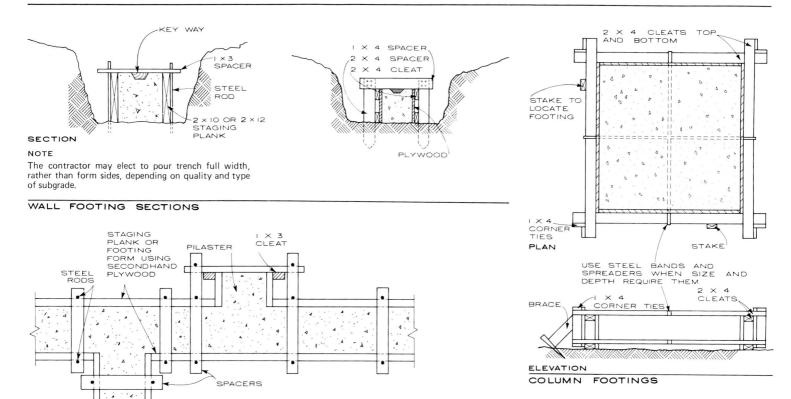

SECTION

NOTE

The contractor may elect to pour trench full width, rather than form sides, depending on quality and type of subgrade.

WALL FOOTING SECTIONS

PLAN

COLUMN FOOTINGS

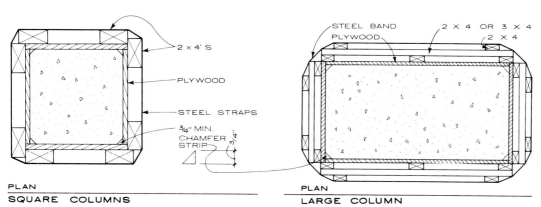

PLAN OF WALL FOOTINGS

PLAN
SQUARE COLUMNS

PLAN
LARGE COLUMN

NOTE

Height of column will change thickness and spaces of steel bands. Consult manufacturers' catalogs. Selection of sheathing (or plywood), type of column clamps (job built or patented metal types), and their spacing will depend on column height, rate of concrete pour (ft/hr), and concrete temperature (°F), as well as on whether the concrete is to be vibrated during pour. Consult design guides for correct selection of materials to ensure safe column forms.

It is recommended that chamfer strips be used at all outside corners to reduce damage to concrete when forms are removed.

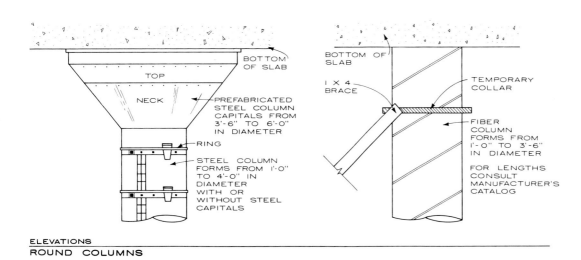

ELEVATIONS
ROUND COLUMNS

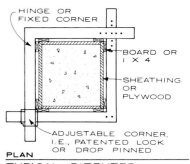

PLAN
TYPICAL PATENTED COLUMN CLAMP

Tucker Concrete Form Co.; Malden, Massachusetts

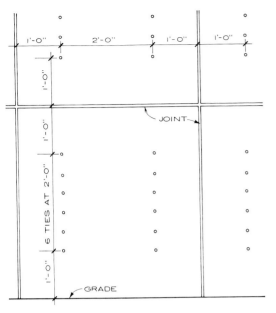

ELEVATION

EXPOSED CONCRETE WITH RUSTICATION STRIP (IF DESIRED)

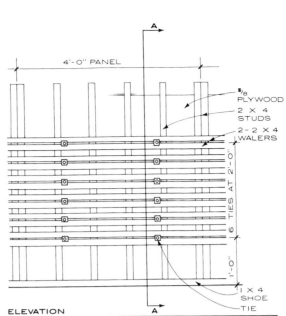

ELEVATION

SAMPLE WALL FORM

Mortar-tight forms are required for architectural exposed concrete. Consult manufacturers' literature on the proper use of metal forms or plywood forms with metal frames.

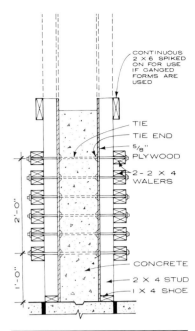

SECTION A-A

The section above will change if there are any variations in the thickness of plywood used, the type and strength of ties, or the size of studs and walers.

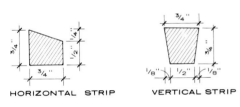

HORIZONTAL STRIP   **VERTICAL STRIP**

RUSTICATION STRIPS

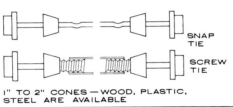

1" TO 2" CONES—WOOD, PLASTIC, STEEL ARE AVAILABLE

TYPICAL TIES

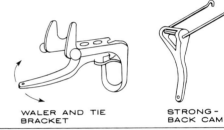

WALER AND TIE BRACKET   **STRONG-BACK CAM**

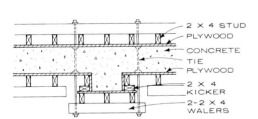

PLAN

SMALL PILASTER

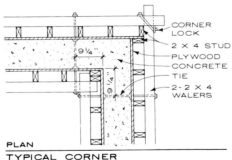

PLAN

TYPICAL CORNER

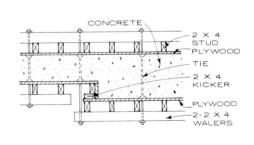

PLAN

TYPICAL WALL WITH OFFSET

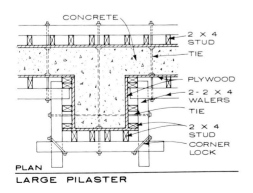

PLAN

LARGE PILASTER

Tucker Concrete Form Co.; Malden, Massachusetts

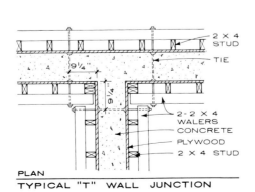

PLAN

TYPICAL "T" WALL JUNCTION

FORM DESIGN NOTES

1. Pressure depends on rate of pour (ft/hr) and concrete temperature (°F). Vibration of concrete is also a factor in form pressure.
2. Provide cleanout doors at bottom of wall forms.
3. Various types of form ties are on the market. Some are not suitable for architectural concrete work, i.e., they cannot be withdrawn from the concrete.
4. Various plastic cones 1½ in. in diameter and ½ in. deep can be used and the holes are left ungrouted to form a type of architectural feature.
5. Consult manufacturers' catalogs for form design and tie strength information.

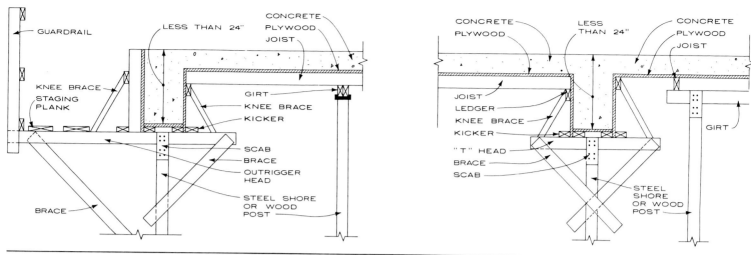

TYPICAL SLAB AND SHALLOW BEAM FORMING

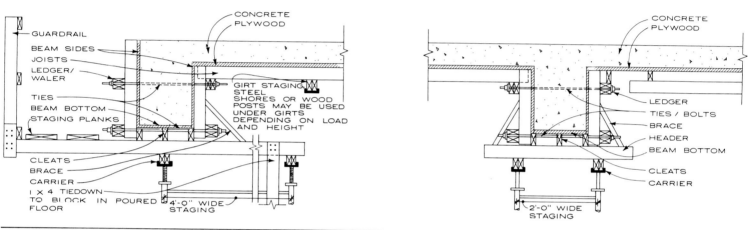

TYPICAL SLAB AND HEAVY BEAM FORMING

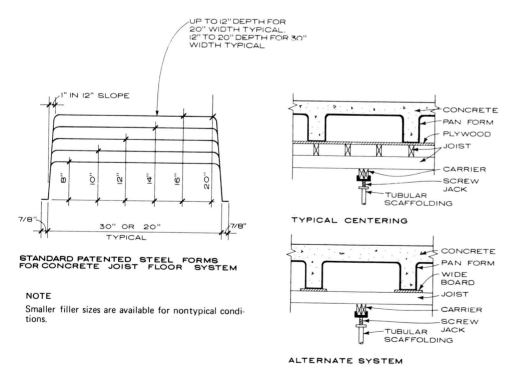

STANDARD PATENTED STEEL FORMS FOR CONCRETE JOIST FLOOR SYSTEM

NOTE

Smaller filler sizes are available for nontypical conditions.

TYPICAL CENTERING

ALTERNATE SYSTEM

NOTES

1. Staging, steel shores, or wood posts may be used under girts depending on loads and height requirements.
2. For flat slabs of flat plate forming, metal "flying forms" are commonly used.
3. Patented steel forms or fillers are also available for nontypical conditions on special order. See manufacturer's catalogs. Fiber forms, too, are on the market in similar sizes. Plywood deck is required for forming.
4. Plywood is usually $^5/_8$" minimum thickness, Exposure 1.

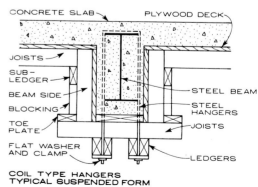

COIL TYPE HANGERS TYPICAL SUSPENDED FORM

Tucker Concrete Form Co.; Malden, Massachusetts

3   **CONCRETE FORMWORK**

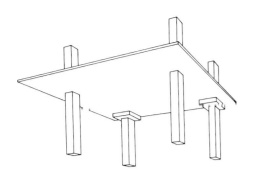

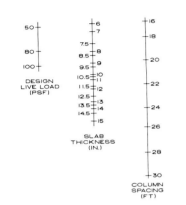

FLAT SLABS TO HAVE DROP
PANELS OR COLUMN CAPITALS.
FOR SUPERIMPOSED LOADS
OVER 100 PSF, USE BOTH DROP
PANELS AND COLUMN CAPITALS

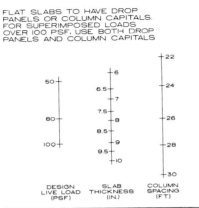

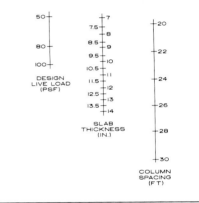

FLAT PLATE

FLAT SLAB WITHOUT BEAMS

FLAT SLAB WITH BEAMS

IF REQUIRED, USE
TAPERED PANS AT GIRDER TO
RESIST SHEAR FORCES

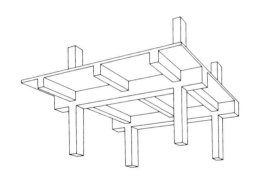

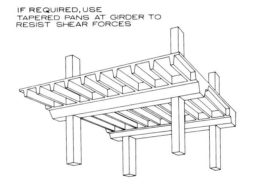

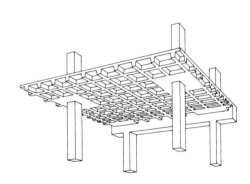

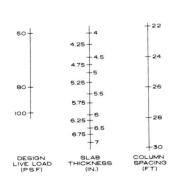

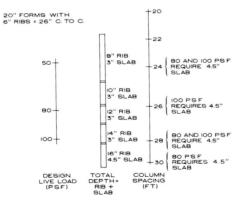

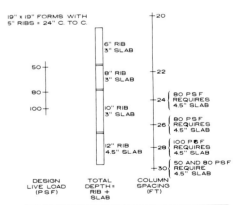

ONE-WAY SLAB WITH BEAMS
(SPAN = ½ THE COLUMN SPACING)

ONE-WAY JOISTS WITH BEAMS
(METAL PAN CONSTRUCTION)

TWO-WAY JOISTS WITHOUT BEAMS
(WAFFLE FLAT PLATE CONSTRUCTION)

GENERAL NOTES

To use bar graphs, lay straight edge across chart and line up with design live load required on left bar and with selected column spacing on right bar. Slab thickness required is indicated where straight edge intersects center bar.

The examples above are all calculated by the ultimate design strength method around the following parameters:

1. Concrete strength of 4000 psi at 28 days.
2. Steel reinforcing strength of 60,000 psi.
3. Steel to concrete ratio of minimum steel.

The information represented on this page is intended to be used as a preliminary design guide only and not to replace complete analysis and calculation of each project condition by a licensed professional engineer.

Killebrew/Rucker/Associates, Inc.; Architects/Planners/Engineers; Wichita Falls, Texas

CAST-IN-PLACE CONCRETE   3

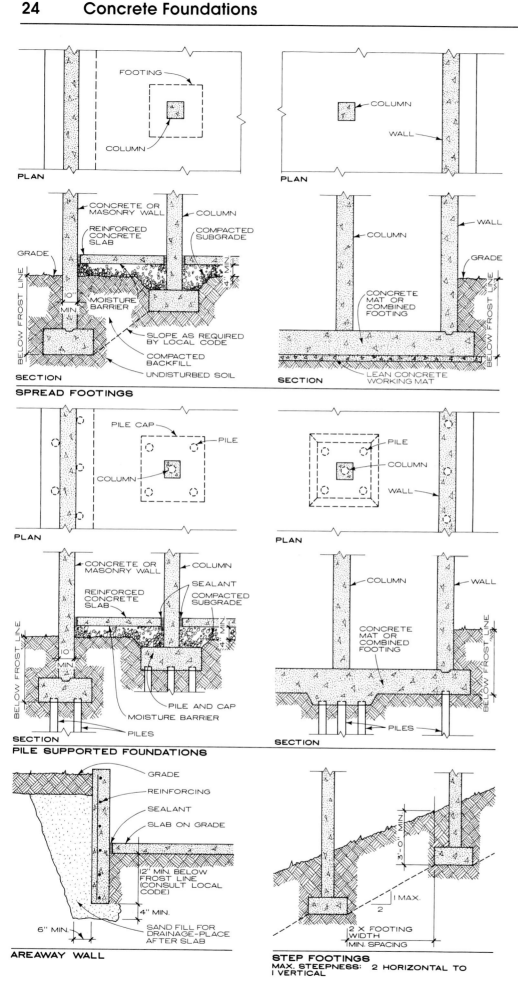

SPREAD FOOTINGS

PILE SUPPORTED FOUNDATIONS

AREAWAY WALL

STEP FOOTINGS
MAX. STEEPNESS: 2 HORIZONTAL TO 1 VERTICAL

STEP FOOTING (FOR CONTINUOUS WALL)
MAX. STEEPNESS: 2 HORIZONTAL TO 1 VERTICAL

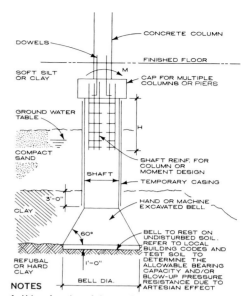

NOTES

1. H is a function of the passive resistance of the soil, generated by the moment applied to the pier cap.
2. Piers may be used under grade beams or concrete walls. For very heavy loads, pier foundations may be more economical than piles.

BELL PIER FOUNDATION

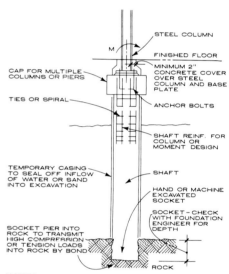

NOTES

1. Pier shaft should be poured in the dry if possible, but tremie pours can be used with appropriate control.
2. Grout bottom of shaft against artesian water or sulphur gas intrusion into the excavation.

SOCKET PIER FOUNDATION

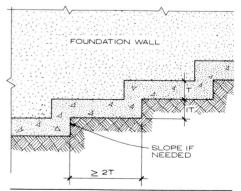

Mueser, Rutledge, Johnston & DeSimone; New York, New York

GENERAL NOTES

Factors to consider in construction of all concrete slabs on grade include assurance of uniform subgrade, quality of concrete, adequacy of structural capacity, type and spacing of joints, finishing, curing, and the application of special surfaces. It is vital to design and construct the subgrade as carefully as the floor slab itself. The subgrade support must be reasonably uniform, and the upper portion of the subgrade should be of uniform material and density. A subbase, a thin layer of granular material placed on the subgrade, should be used in most cases to cushion the slab.

Wear resistance is directly related to concrete strength. A low water-cement ratio improves the surface hardness and finishability as well as internal strength of concrete. Low water-cement ratio, low slump, and well graded aggregates with coarse aggregate size as large as placing and finishing requirements will permit and enhance the quality of concrete.

Exterior concrete subjected to freeze-thaw cycles should have 6 to 8% entrained air. Reinforcement is unnecessary where frequent joint spacing is used. Where less frequent joint spacing is necessary, reinforcement is put in the top one third depth to hold together any shrinkage cracks that form. Control joint spacing of 15 to 25 ft square is recommended. Checkerboard pouring patterns allow for some shrinkage between pours, but the process is more costly and is not recommended for large areas. The total shrinkage process takes up to one year. Strip pouring, allowing for a continuous pour with control joints cut after concrete has set, is a fast economical method, recommended for large areas.

Three types of joints are recommended:

1. ISOLATION JOINTS (also called expansion joints): Allow movement between slab and fixed parts of the building such as columns, walls, and machinery bases.
2. CONTROL JOINTS: Induce cracking at preselected locations.
3. CONSTRUCTION JOINTS: Provide stopping places during floor construction. Construction joints also function as control and isolation joints.

Sawcut control joints should be made as early as is practical after finishing the slab and should be filled in areas with wet conditions, hygienic and dust control requirements, or considerable traffic

by hard wheeled vehicles, such as forklift trucks. A semirigid filler with Shore Hardness "A" of at least 80 should be used.

Concrete floor slabs are monolithically finished by floating and troweling the concrete to a smooth dense finish. Depressions of more than 1/8 in. in 10 ft or variations of more than 1/4 in. from a level plane are undesirable. Special finishes are available to improve appearance. These include sprinkled (shake) finishes and high strength concrete toppings, either monolithic or separate (two-stage floor).

A vaporproof barrier should be placed under all slabs on grade where the passage of water vapor through the floor is undesirable. Permeance of vapor barrier should not exceed 0.20 perms.

Generally the controlling factor in determining the thickness of a floor on ground is the heaviest concentrated load it will carry, usually the wheel load plus impact of an industrial truck. Because of practical considerations, the minimum recommended thickness for an industrial floor is about 5 in. For Class 1, 2, and 3 floors, the minimum thickness should be 4 in.

The floor thickness required for wheel loads on relatively small areas may be obtained from the table for concrete; an allowable flexural tensile stress (psi) can be estimated from the approximate formula $f_t = 4.6\sqrt{f'_c}$ in which f'_c is the 28-day concrete compressive strength. If f_t is not 300 psi, the table can be used by multiplying the actual total load by the ratio of 300 to the stress used and entering the chart with that value.

Assume that a 5000 psi concrete slab is to be designed for an industrial plant floor over which there will be considerable traffic—trucks with loads of 10,000 lb/wheel, each of which has a contact area of about 30 sq in. Assume that operating conditions are such that impact will be equivalent to about 25% of the load. The equivalent static load will then be 12,500 lb. The allowable flexural tensile stress for 5000 psi concrete is

$$4.6\sqrt{5000} = 325 \text{ psi}$$

The allowable loads in the table are based on a stress of 300 psi, so that the design load must be corrected by the factor 300/325. Thus 11,500 lb on an area of 30 sq in. requires a slab about 7 1/2 in. thick.

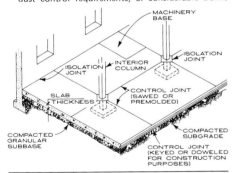

CONTROL JOINTS FOR A SLAB ON GRADE

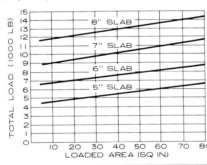

MAXIMUM WHEEL LOADS FOR INDUSTRIAL FLOORS (FLEXURAL TENSILE STRESS = 300 PSI)

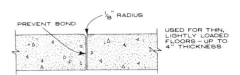

BUTT TYPE CONSTRUCTION JOINT

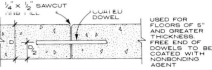

BUTT TYPE CONSTRUCTION JOINT WITH DOWELS

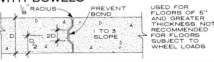

TONGUE AND GROOVE CONSTRUCTION JOINT

SAWED OR PREMOLDED CONTROL JOINT FOR SLABS < 4"

TONGUE AND GROOVE CONTROL JOINT

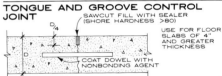

CONTROL JOINT WITH DOWELS

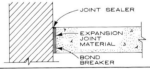

ISOLATION JOINT

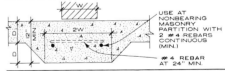

THICKENED SLAB

CLASSIFICATION OF CONCRETE SLABS ON GRADE

CLASS	SLUMP RANGE (IN.)	MINIMUM COMPRESSIVE STRENGTH (PSI)	USUAL TRAFFIC	USE	SPECIAL CONSIDERATION	CONCRETE FINISHING TECHNIQUE
1	2-4	3500	Light foot	Residential or tile covered	Grade for drainage; plane smooth for tile	Medium steel trowel
2	2-4	3500	Foot	Offices, schools, hospitals, residential	Nonslip aggregate, mix in surface Color shake, special	Steel trowel; special finish for nonslip Steel trowel, color exposed aggregate
3	2-4	3500	Light foot and pneumatic wheels	Drives, garage floors, sidewalks for residences	Crown; pitch joints	Float, trowel, and broom
4	1-3	4000	Foot and pneumatic wheels	Light industrial, commercial	Careful curing	Hard steel trowel and brush for nonslip
5	1-3	4500	Foot and wheels—abrasive wear	Single course industrial, integral topping	Careful curing	Special hard aggregate, float and trowel
6	2-4	3500	Foot and steel tire vehicles—severe abrasion	Bonded two-course, heavy industrial	Base: textured surface and bond Top: special aggregate	Base: surface leveled by screeding Top: special power floats
7	1-3	4000	Same as Classes 3, 4, 5, 6	Unbonded topping	Mesh reinforcing; bond breaker on old concrete surface	—

Setter, Leach & Lindstrom, Inc.; Minneapolis, Minnesota

GENERAL CONSIDERATIONS

1. Concrete strength usually 5000 psi at 28 days and at least 3000 psi at time of prestressing. Hardrock aggregate or lightweight concrete used. Low slump controlled mix is required to reduce shrinkage. Shrinkage after prestressing increases prestress losses.

2. Post-tensioning systems can be divided into three categories depending on whether the tendon is wire, strand, or bar. Wire systems use 0.25 in. diameter wires that have a minimum strength of 240,000 psi and are usually cut to length in the shop. Strand systems use tendons composed of seven wires wrapped together that have a minimum strength of 270,000 psi and are cut in the field. Bar systems use bars ranging in diameter from $5/8$ to $1 3/8$ in. in diameter, with a minimum strength of 145,000 psi; they may be smooth or deformed. The system used will determine the type of anchorage used, which in turn will affect the size of blockout required in the edge of slab or beam for the anchorage to be recessed.

3. Tendons are greased and wrapped, or placed in conduits to reduce frictional losses during stressing operations. Length of continuous tendons limited to about 100 ft if stressed from one end. Long tendons require simultaneous stressing from both ends to reduce friction losses. Tendons may be grouted after stressing or left unbonded. Bonded tendons have structural advantages that are more important for beams and primary structural members.

4. Minimum average prestress (net prestress force/area of concrete) = 150 to 250 psi for flat plates, 200 to 500 psi for beams. Exceeding these values very much will cause excessive prestress losses because of creep.

5. Field inspection of post-tensioned concrete is critical to ensure proper size and location of tendons and to monitor the tendon stress. Tendon stress should be checked by measuring elongation of the tendon, and by gauge pressures on the stressing jack.

6. Provisions must be made for the shortening of post-tensioned beams and slabs caused by elastic compression, shrinkage, and creep. Shearwalls, curtain walls, or other stiff elements that adjoin post-tensioned members should be built after the post-tensioning has been done or should be isolated from these members with an expansion joint. Otherwise, additional post-tensioning force will be required to overcome the stiffness of the walls; cracking of the walls may also occur.

7. Fire tests have been conducted on prestressed beam and slab assemblies according to ASTM E119 test procedures; they compare favorably with conventionally reinforced concrete. There is little difference between beams using grouted tendons and those using ungrouted tendons.

8. References for further study:
   a. Post-Tensioning Institute, "Post-Tensioning Manual."
   b. Prestressed Concrete Institute, "Design Handbook for Precast and Prestressed Concrete."
   c. Lin, T.Y., "Design of Prestressed Concrete Structures."
   d. American Concrete Institute, "Building Code Requirements for Reinforced Concrete" (ACI-318-83).

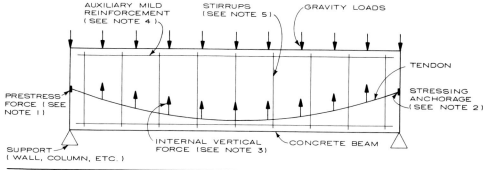

PRESTRESSED OR POST-TENSIONED BEAM

NOTES

1. Prestressing force puts entire beam cross-section into compression, thereby reducing unwanted tension cracks.

2. Permanent tension is introduced into tendon and "locked in" with the stressing anchorage in one of two ways. In prestressed concrete, the tendon is elongated in a stressing bed before the concrete is poured. In post-tensioned concrete, the tendon is elongated after concrete has been poured and allowed to cure by means of hydraulic jacks pushing against the beam itself. The principle in both cases is the same. Post-tensioned beams permit casting at the site for members too large or heavy for transporting from factory to site.

3. Vertical internal force on beam is caused by tendency of tendon to "straighten out" under tension.

It reduces downward beam deflection and allows shallower beams and longer spans than in conventionally reinforced beams.

4. Auxiliary mild reinforcement provides additional strength, controls cracking, and produces more ductile behavior.

5. Stirrups are used to provide additional shear strength in the beam and to support the tendons and longitudinal mild reinforcement. Stirrups should be open at the top to allow the reinforcing to be fabricated and placed before the tendon is placed.

6. Shoring must be left in place until the post-tensioning operation is performed. After stressing, reshoring may be required to prevent overloading during additional construction.

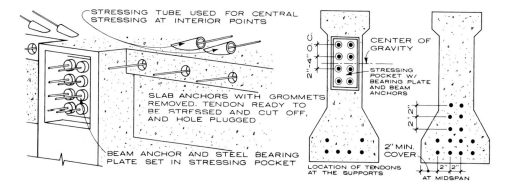

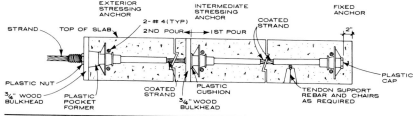

TYPICAL UNBONDED SINGLE STRAND TENDON INSTALLATION

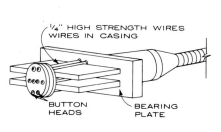

8 WIRE BBRV POST-TENSIONING ANCHOR (GROUTED)

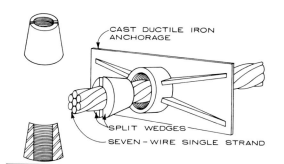

SINGLE STRAND TENDON ANCHORAGE (UNBONDED)

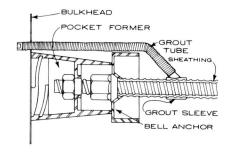

THREAD BAR ANCHORAGE (GROUTED)

Leo A. Daly, Architecture-Engineering-Planning; Omaha, Nebraska

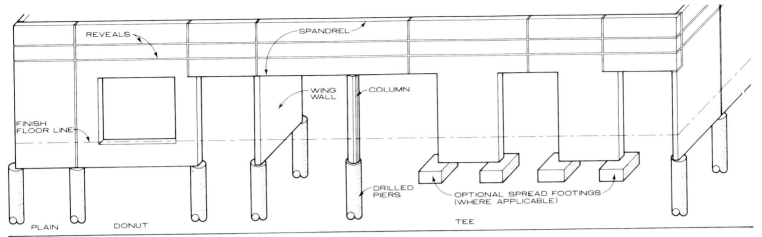

PANEL TYPES

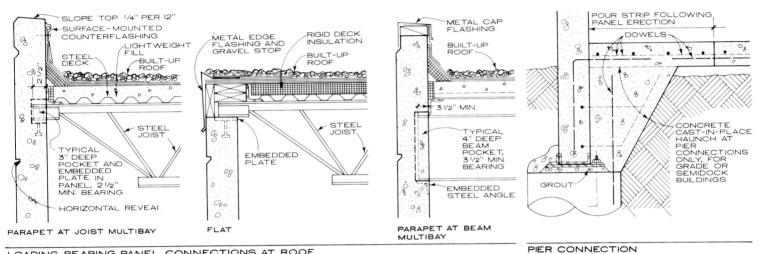

LOADING BEARING PANEL CONNECTIONS AT ROOF

PIER CONNECTION

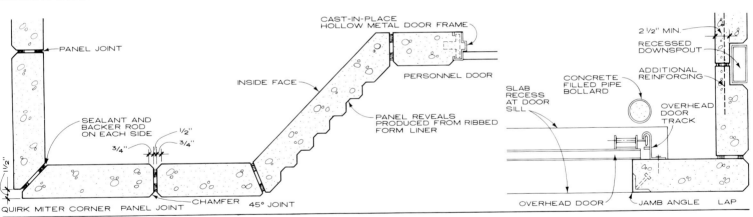

PANEL DETAILS

GENERAL

Tilt-up concrete construction is a fast and economical method of enclosing a building with durable, load-bearing walls. Tilt-up concrete panels are cast horizontally on site utilizing the building's floor slab as a casting bed. Wood formwork is typically used to define the edges, reveals, details, and fenestrations of the panel. Once the concrete has reached sufficient strength, the panels are lifted, or "tilted up" by crane and placed on isolated footings where they are temporarily braced until they are attached to the interior structural framing system.

DESIGN

Panel thickness varies from $5\frac{1}{2}$ in. to $11\frac{1}{4}$ in., depending on height, span, depth of reveals, or surface finish, as well as local codes and construction practices. Full-height panel widths of 15 ft and weights of 30,000–50,000 lb are typical. Spans of 30 ft are common for spandrel panels, as are cantilevers of 10–15 ft. Panels are designed structurally to resist lifting stresses, which frequently exceed in-place loads. Floor slab design must accommodate panel and crane loads.

FINISH

Most of the finishes used for factory precast concrete are possible in tilt-up construction. Panels can be cast either facedown or faceup, depending on desired finish and formwork methods. The facedown method, however, is usually easier to erect. Casting method, finish desired, and available aggregates will affect concrete mix design. Control of the concrete mix design and placement of the concrete in the forms are more difficult than with factory cast units. Discoloration will occur if cracks and joints in the casting bed are not sealed. Commonly used finishes are as follows:

Sandblast (light, medium, or heavy exposure)
Fractured (similar to bushhammer)
Form liner (metal deck, plastic, fiberglass, EPS)
Paint
Brick/tile veneer
Aggregate (cast facedown in sand bed)

Harry Gendel Architects; Houston, Texas
Haynes Whaley Associates, Inc., Structural Engineers; Houston, Texas

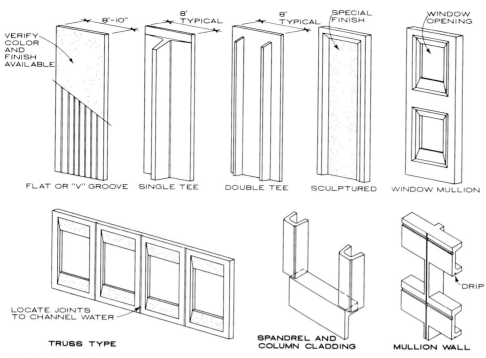

FLAT OR "V" GROOVE   SINGLE TEE   DOUBLE TEE   SCULPTURED   WINDOW MULLION

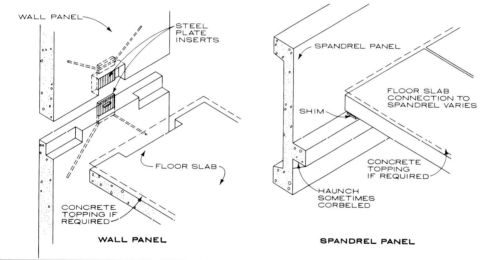

TRUSS TYPE   SPANDREL AND COLUMN CLADDING   MULLION WALL

PANEL VARIATIONS

WALL PANEL   SPANDREL PANEL

BEARING PANEL CONDITIONS

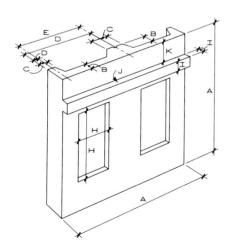

A. Overall height and width measured at face adjacent to mold at time of casting or neutral axis of ribbed member:
   10 ft or under: $\pm\,^1/_8$ in.
   10 ft to 20 ft: $\pm\,^1/_8$ in. to $\pm\,^3/_{16}$ in.
   20 ft to 30 ft: $\pm\,^1/_8$ in. to $\pm\,^1/_4$ in.
   Above 30 ft: $\pm\,^1/_4$ in.

B. Thickness, total or flange: $^1/_4$ in. to $^1/_8$ in.

C. Rib thickness: $\pm\,^1/_8$ in.

D. Rib to edge of flange: $\pm\,^1/_8$ in.

E. Distance between ribs: $\pm\,^1/_8$ in.

F. Angular deviation of plane of side mold: $^1/_{32}$ in. per 3 in. of depth or $^1/_{16}$ in. total, whichever is greater

G. Deviation from square or designated skew (difference in length of the two diagonal measurements): $^1/_8$ in. per 6 ft or $^1/_4$ in. total, whichever is greater

H. Length and width of blockouts and openings with one unit: $\pm\,^1/_4$ in.

I. Depth and width of haunches: $\pm\,^1/_4$ in.

J. Haunch-bearing surface deviation from specified plane: $^1/_8$ in.

K. Difference in relative position of adjacent haunch-bearing surfaces from specified relative position: $^1/_4$ in.

All other tolerances not defined above: $\pm\,^1/_8$ in.

DIMENSIONAL TOLERANCES FOR FLAT AND VERTICAL RIBBED WALL PANELS

Bruce Lambert, AIA; Columbia, South Carolina

WALL PANELS

Carefully distinguish between the more specialized architectural wall panel and the structural wall panel which is a derivative of floor systems. Always work with manufacturers early in the design process. Careful attention must be given to manufacturing and joint tolerances during design. Thoroughly examine joint sealants for adhesion and expected joint movement.

FINISHES

Form liner molds provide a wide variety of smooth and textured finishes. Finishes after casting but prior to hardening include exposed aggregate, broom, trowel, screed, float, or stippled. After hardening finishes include acid etching, sandblasting, honed, polished, or hammered rib.

COLORS

Select a color range, as complete uniformity cannot be guaranteed. White cement offers the best color uniformity; gray cement is subject to color variations even when supplied from one source. Pigments require high-quality manufacturing and curing standards. Fine aggregate color requires control of the mixture graduation; coarse aggregate color should be chosen for durability and appearance.

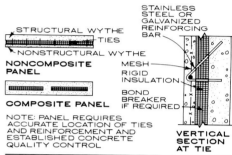

NOTE: PANEL REQUIRES ACCURATE LOCATION OF TIES AND REINFORCEMENT AND ESTABLISHED CONCRETE QUALITY CONTROL

SANDWICH WALL CONSTRUCTION

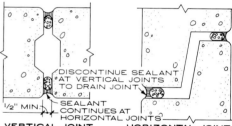

VERTICAL JOINT   HORIZONTAL JOINT

TWO-STAGE SEALANT JOINTS

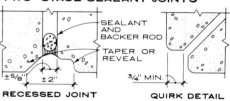

RECESSED JOINT   QUIRK DETAIL

JOINT DETAILS

JOINT TAPER: $^1/_{40}$ IN. PER FT LENGTH (MAX. LENGTH OF TAPERING IN ONE DIRECTION OF 10 FT)

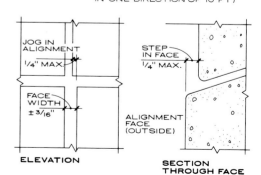

ELEVATION   SECTION THROUGH FACE

JOINT TOLERANCES

PRECAST CONCRETE

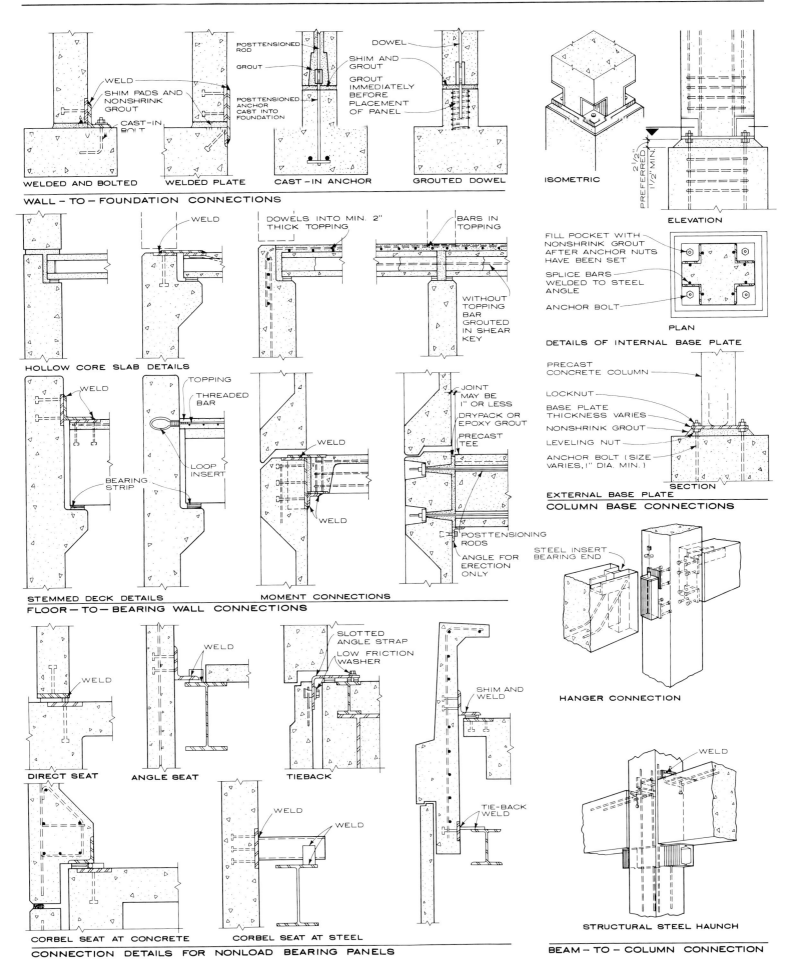

WELDED AND BOLTED   WELDED PLATE   CAST-IN ANCHOR   GROUTED DOWEL

WALL-TO-FOUNDATION CONNECTIONS

WELD
SHIM PADS AND NONSHRINK GROUT
CAST-IN BOLT

POSTTENSIONED ROD
GROUT
POSTTENSIONED ANCHOR CAST INTO FOUNDATION

DOWEL
SHIM AND GROUT
GROUT IMMEDIATELY BEFORE PLACEMENT OF PANEL

ISOMETRIC

PREFERRED 2 1/2"
1 1/2" MIN.

ELEVATION

FILL POCKET WITH NONSHRINK GROUT AFTER ANCHOR NUTS HAVE BEEN SET
SPLICE BARS WELDED TO STEEL ANGLE
ANCHOR BOLT

PLAN

DETAILS OF INTERNAL BASE PLATE

HOLLOW CORE SLAB DETAILS

WELD
DOWELS INTO MIN. 2" THICK TOPPING
BARS IN TOPPING
WITHOUT TOPPING BAR GROUTED IN SHEAR KEY

PRECAST CONCRETE COLUMN
LOCKNUT
BASE PLATE THICKNESS VARIES
NONSHRINK GROUT
LEVELING NUT
ANCHOR BOLT (SIZE VARIES, 1" DIA. MIN.)

EXTERNAL BASE PLATE
SECTION

COLUMN BASE CONNECTIONS

STEMMED DECK DETAILS   MOMENT CONNECTIONS

WELD
TOPPING
THREADED BAR
LOOP INSERT
BEARING STRIP

WELD
WELD

JOINT MAY BE 1" OR LESS
DRYPACK OR EPOXY GROUT
PRECAST TEE
POSTTENSIONING RODS
ANGLE FOR ERECTION ONLY

FLOOR-TO-BEARING WALL CONNECTIONS

STEEL INSERT BEARING END

HANGER CONNECTION

DIRECT SEAT   ANGLE SEAT   TIEBACK

WELD
WELD
SLOTTED ANGLE STRAP
LOW FRICTION WASHER
SHIM AND WELD
TIE-BACK WELD

CORBEL SEAT AT CONCRETE   CORBEL SEAT AT STEEL

WELD
WELD

WELD

STRUCTURAL STEEL HAUNCH

CONNECTION DETAILS FOR NONLOAD BEARING PANELS

BEAM-TO-COLUMN CONNECTION

Bruce Lambert, AIA; Columbia, South Carolina

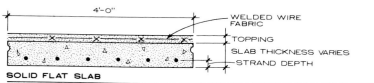

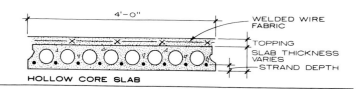

FLAT DECK MEMBERS

TABLE 1 *
SAFE SUPERIMPOSED SERVICE LOADS (PSF) FOR SOLID FLAT SLABS (4 FT WIDTH)

SLAB THICKNESS (IN.)	SLAB DESIGNATION	TOPPING THICKNESS (IN.)	SPAN (FT)														
			11	12	13	14	15	16	17	18	19	20	21	22	23	24	25
4" STRAND DESIGNATION CODE: 58-S	FS4	NONE	212	180	154	127	104	86	70								
	FS4+2	2			274	214	166	127	95								
6" STRAND DESIGNATION CODE: 78-S	FS6	NONE	320	287	257	236	213	196	183	168	155	144	134	126	109	94	81
	FS6+2	2					298	273	252	231	216	199	185	169	140	115	93
8" STRAND DESIGNATION CODE: 68-S	FS8	NONE				318	291	266	245	227	209	196	181	169	155	136	119
	FS8+2	2								304	283	261	245	225	197	167	140

TABLE 2 *
SAFE SUPERIMPOSED SERVICE LOADS (PSF) FOR HOLLOW CORE SLABS (4 FT WIDTH)

SLAB THICKNESS (IN.)	SLAB DESIGNATION	TOPPING THICKNESS (IN.)	SPAN (FT)														
			12	14	16	18	20	22	24	26	28	30	32	34	36	38	40
6" STRAND DESIGNATION CODE: 66-S	4HC6	NONE	257	197	154	113	84	63	47								
	4HC6+2	2		278	215	153	102	65									
8" STRAND DESIGNATION CODE: 58-S	4HC8	NONE					275	221	175	140	112	91	73	59			
	4HC8+2	2						273	215	170	136	108	84	60			
10" STRAND DESIGNATION CODE: 78-S	4HC10	NONE					298	264	237	214	192	160	134	113	95	80	67
	4HC10+2	2							278	250	218	181	150	125	103	85	67
12" STRAND DESIGNATION CODE: 68-S	4HC12	NONE									182	165	150	120	109	92	78
	4HC12+2	2							249	224	200	183	164	137	114	95	78

LOAD TABLES FOR FLAT DECK MEMBERS

* NOTE: 1. NORMAL WEIGHT (150 PCF) CONCRETE SLAB AND TOPPING
2. SLABS f_c = 5000 PSI
3. STRAND DESIGNATION CODE
78-S
└ STRAIGHT
└ DIAMETER OF STRANDS IN 16THS
└ NUMBER OF STRANDS

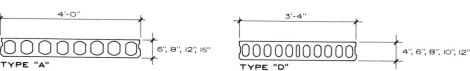

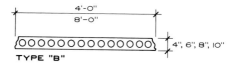

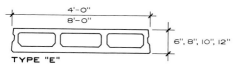

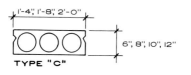

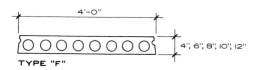

HOLLOW CORE SLAB TYPES
ALL SECTIONS ARE NOT AVAILABLE FROM ALL PRODUCERS
CHECK AVAILABILITY WITH LOCAL MANUFACTURERS

NOTES

1. Normal weight (150 pcf) or lightweight concrete (115 pcf) is used in standard slab construction. Topping concrete is usually normal weight concrete with a cylinder strength of 3000 psi. All units are prestressed with strand release when concrete strength is 3500 psi.

2. Strands are available in various sizes and strengths according to individual manufacturers. Strand placement may vary, which will change load capacity, camber values, and fire resistance. Contact the local supplier for strand placement and allowable loading.

3. Camber will vary substantially depending on slab design, span, and loading. Nonstructural components attached to members may be affected by camber variations. Calculations of topping quantities should recognize camber variations.

4. Safe superimposed service loads include a dead load of 10 psf for untopped concrete and 15 psf for topped concrete. The remainder is live load.

5. Smooth or textured soffits may be available in some types; check with the supplier.

Bruce Lambert, AIA; Columbia, South Carolina

PRECAST CONCRETE

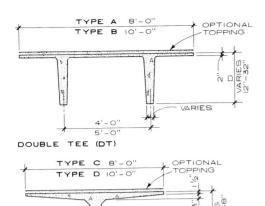

TYPE A 8'-0"
TYPE B 10'-0"
OPTIONAL TOPPING
DOUBLE TEE (DT)

TYPE C 8'-0"
TYPE D 10'-0"
OPTIONAL TOPPING
SINGLE TEE (ST)

STRAND PATTERN DESIGNATION
— NO. OF STRANDS (20)
S = STRAIGHT   D = DEPRESSED
208·D1
— NO. OF DEPRESSION POINTS
— DIAMETER OF STRAND IN 16THS
TOPPING CONCRETE = 3000 PSI, 150 LB./CU. FT. f'_c = 5000 PSI FOR NORMAL OR LIGHTWEIGHT DECK

NOTES
1. Safe loads shown indicate dead load of 10 psf for untopped members and 15 psf for topped members. Remainder is live load.
2. Designers should contact the manufacturers in the geographic area of the proposed structure to determine availability, exact dimensions, and load tables for various sections.
3. Camber should be checked for its effect on non-structural members (i.e., partitions, folding doors, etc.), which should be placed with adequate allowance for error. Calculations of topping quantities should also recognize camber variations.
4. Normal weight concrete is assumed to be 150 lb/cu ft; lightweight concrete is assumed to be 115 lb/cu ft.

STEMMED DECK MEMBERS
SEE CHART FOR APPROXIMATE MAX. SPANS

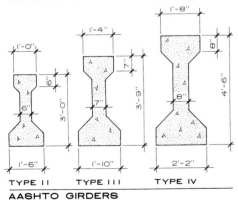

TYPE II   TYPE III   TYPE IV
AASHTO GIRDERS

APPROXIMATE MAXIMUM SPAN FOR STEMMED DECK SECTIONS

DECK TYPE	DEPTH D (IN.)	CONCRETE WEIGHT	DESIGNATION	TOPPING DEPTH (IN.)	STRAND DESIGNATION	MAX. SPAN (FT)	SAFE LOAD (PSF)
A	12	Normal weight	8DT12	0	88·D1	40	40
			8DT12 + 2	2	68·D1	34	39
		Lightweight	8LDT12	0	68·D1	40	35
			8LDT12 + 2	2	68·D1	36	36
A	18	Normal weight	8DT18	0	108·D1	58	34
			8DT18 + 2	2	88·D1	46	48
		Lightweight	8LDT18	0	108·D1	60	37
			8LDT18 + 2	2	88·D1	50	39
A	24	Normal weight	8DT24	0	148·D1	74	38
			8DT24 + 2	2	128·D1	60	56
		Lightweight	8LDT24	0	148·D1	80	35
			8LDT24 + 2	2	108·D1	62	44
A	32	Normal weight	8DT32	0	228·D1	88	56
			8DT32 + 2	2	208·D1	76	76
		Lightweight	8LDT32	0	228·D1	100	41
			8LDT32 + 2	2	208·D1	82	67
B	32	Normal weight	10DT32	0	228·D1	86	49
			10DT32 + 2	2	208·D1	74	62
		Lightweight	10LDT32	0	228·D1	98	35
			10LDT32 + 2	2	208·D1	78	59
C	36	Normal weight	8ST36	0	228·D1	100	44
			8ST36 + 2	2	188·D1	82	61
		Lightweight	8LST36	0	228·D1	110	38
			8LST36 + 2	2	168·D1	86	50
D	48	Normal weight	10ST48	0	248·D1	112	42
		Lightweight	10LST48	0	248·D1	120	41

TABLE OF SAFE SUPERIMPOSED SERVICE LOAD* (PLF) FOR PRECAST BEAM SECTIONS

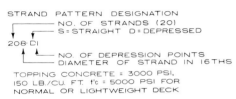

TYPE	DESIGNATION	NO. STRAND	H (IN.)	H1/H2 (IN.)	18	22	26	30	34	38	42	46	50
RECTANGULAR BEAM (B = 12" OR 16")	12RB24	10	24		6726	4413	3083	2248	1684	1288	1000		
	12RB32	13	32			7858	5524	4059	3080	2394	1894	1519	1230
	16RB24	13	24		8847	5803	4052	2954	2220	1705	1330		
	16RB32	18	32			7434	5464	4147	3224	2549	2036	1642	
	16RB40	22	40				8647	6599	5163	4117	3332	2728	
L-SHAPED BEAM	18LB20	9	20	12/8	5068	3303	2288	1650	1218				
	18LB28	12	28	16/12		6578	4600	3360	2531	1949	1524	1200	
	18LB36	16	36	24/12			7903	5807	4405	3422	2706	2168	1755
	18LB44	19	44	28/16				8729	6666	5219	4166	3370	2752
	18LB52	23	52	36/16					9538	7486	5992	4871	4007
	18LB60	27	60	44/16							8116	6630	5481
INVERTED TEE BEAM	24IT20	9	20	12/8	5376	3494	2412	1726	1266				
	24IT28	13	28	16/12		6951	4848	3529	2648	2030			
	24IT36	16	36	24/12			8337	6127	4644	3598	2836	2265	1825
	24IT44	20	44	28/16				9300	7075	5514	4378	3525	2868
	24IT52	24	52	36/16						7916	6326	5132	4213
	24IT60	28	60	44/16							8616	7025	5800

*Safe loads shown indicate 50% dead load and 50% live load; 800 psi top tension has been allowed, therefore additional top reinforcement is required.

TABLE OF SAFE SUPERIMPOSED SERVICE LOAD* (PLF) FOR AASHTO GIRDER

DESIGNATION	NO. OF STRANDS	36	40	44	48	52	56	60
Type II	14	3520	2785	2241	1826			
Type III	22	7231	5757	4667	3837	3192	2679	2266
Type IV	32		9848	7996	6588	5492	4622	3920

Bruce Lambert, AIA; Columbia, South Carolina

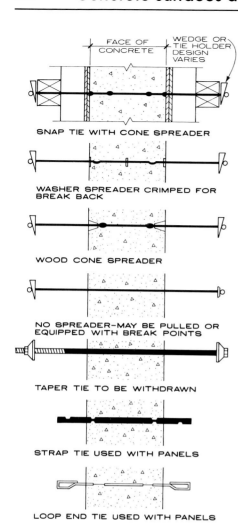

SNAP TIE WITH CONE SPREADER

WASHER SPREADER CRIMPED FOR BREAK BACK

WOOD CONE SPREADER

NO SPREADER—MAY BE PULLED OR EQUIPPED WITH BREAK POINTS

TAPER TIE TO BE WITHDRAWN

STRAP TIE USED WITH PANELS

LOOP END TIE USED WITH PANELS

TYPICAL SINGLE MEMBER TIES

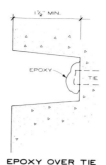

EPOXY OVER TIE

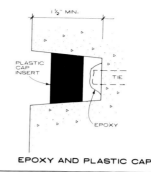

EPOXY AND PLASTIC CAP

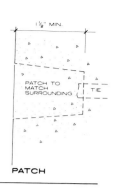

PATCH

TIE HOLE TREATMENT OPTIONS

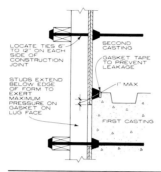

TYPICAL CONSTRUCTION JOINT

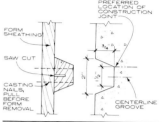

RUSTICATION AT CONSTRUCTION JOINT

CONCRETE SURFACES—GENERAL

The variety of architectural finishes is as extensive as the cost and effort expended to achieve them. There are three basic ways to improve or change the appearance of concrete:

1. Changing materials, that is, using a colored matrix and exposed aggregates.
2. Changing the mold or form by such means as a form liner.
3. By treating or tooling the concrete surface in the final stages of hardening.

The aim is to obtain maximum benefit from one of three features—color, texture, and pattern—all of which are interrelated. Color is the easiest method of changing the appearance of concrete. It should not be used on a plain concrete surface with a series of panels, since color matches are difficult to achieve. The exception is possible when white cement is used, usually as a base for the pigment to help reduce changes of color variation. Since white cement is expensive, many effects are tried with gray cement to avoid an entire plain surface. Colored concrete is most effective when it is used with an exposed aggregate finish.

FORM LINERS

1. Sandblasted Douglas fir or long leaf yellow pine dressed one side away from the concrete surface.
2. Flexible steel strip formwork adapted to curved surfaces (Schwellmer System).
3. Resin coated, striated, or sandblasted plywood.
4. Rubber mats.
5. Thermoplastic sheets with high gloss or texture laid over stone, for example.
6. Formed plastics.
7. Plaster of Paris molds for sculptured work.
8. Clay (sculpturing and staining concrete).
9. Hardboard (screen side).

10. Standard steel forms.
11. Wood boarding and reversed battens.
12. Square-edged lumber dressed one side.
13. Resawn wood boards.

RELEASE AGENTS

1. Oils, petroleum based, used on wood, concrete, and steel forms.
2. Soft soaps.
3. Talcum.
4. Whitewash used on wood with tannin in conjunction with oils.
5. Calcium stearate powder.
6. Silicones used on steel forms.
7. Plastics used on wood forms.
8. Lacquers used on plywood and plaster forms.
9. Resins used on plywood forms.
10. Sodium silicate.
11. Membrane used over any form.
12. Grease used on plaster forms.
13. Epoxy resin plastic used on plywood.

CATEGORIES OF COMMON AGGREGATE

1. QUARTZ: Clear, white, rose.
2. MARBLE: Green, yellow, red, pink, blue, gray, white, black.
3. GRANITE: Pink, gray, black, white.
4. CERAMIC: Full range.
5. VITREOUS/GLASS: Full range.

CRITICAL FACTORS AFFECTING SURFACES

DESIGN DRAWINGS should show form details, including openings, control joints, construction joints, expansion joints, and other important specifics.

1. CEMENT: Types and brands.
2. AGGREGATES: Sources of coarse and fine aggregates.
3. TECHNIQUES: Uniformity in mixing and placing.
4. FORMS: Closure techniques or concealing joints in formwork materials.
5. SLUMP CONTROL: Ensure compliance with design.
6. CURING METHODS: Ensure compliance with design.

TIES

A concrete tie is a tensile unit adapted to hold concrete forms secure against the lateral pressure of unhardened concrete. Two general types of concrete ties exist:

1. Continuous single member where the tensile unit is a single piece and the holding device engages the tensile unit against the exterior of the form. Standard types: working load = 2500 to 5000 lb.
2. Internal disconnecting where the tensile unit has an inner part with threaded connections to removable external members, which have suitable devices of securing them against the outside of the form. Working load = 6000 to 36,000 lb.

GUIDELINES FOR PATCHING

1. Design the patch mix to match the original, with small amount of white cement; may eliminate coarse aggregate or hand place it. Trial and error is the only reliable match method.
2. Saturate area with water and apply bonding agent to base of hole and to water of patch mix.
3. Pack patch mix to density of original.
4. Place exposed aggregate by hand.
5. Bristle brush after setup to match existing material.
6. Moist cure to prevent shrinking.
7. Use form or finish to match original.

CHECKLIST IN PLANNING FOR ARCHITECTURAL CONCRETE PLACING TECHNIQUES:

Pumping vs. bottom drop or other type of bucket.

1. FORMING SYSTEM: Evaluate whether architectural concrete forms can also be used for structural concrete.
2. SHOP DRAWINGS: Determine form quality and steel placement.
3. VIBRATORS: Verify that proper size, frequency, and power are used.
4. RELEASE AGENTS: Consider form material, color impact of agents, and possible use throughout job.
5. CURING COMPOUND: Determine how fast it wears off.
6. SAMPLES: Require approval of forms and finishes. Field mock-up is advised to evaluate appearance of panel and quality of workmanship.

D. Neil Rankins; SHWC, Inc.; Dallas, Texas

③ ARCHITECTURAL CONCRETE

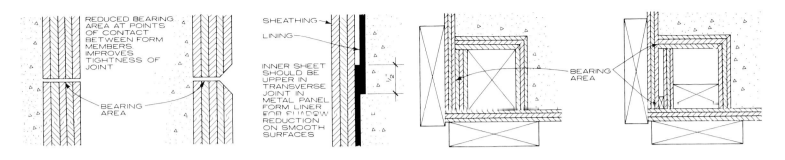

USUAL · RECOMMENDED · LINER JOINT · USUAL · RECOMMENDED

FORM JOINTS

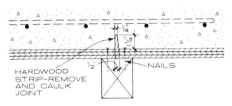

RUBBER FORM INSERT

WOOD FORM INSERT

SHEET METAL FORM INSERT

CONTROL JOINTS

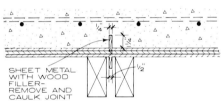

RUSTICATION (PREFERRED)

TAPED (MEDIUM LIGHT BLAST)

EPOXY ON 45° CUT

GASKETED

TONGUE AND GROOVED

SPLINED

IMPERVIOUS LINER (1/4" TO 3/8")

SHIPLAP

PLYWOOD BUTT JOINTS FOR EXPOSED AGGREGATE FINISHES

D. Neil Rankins; SHWC, Inc.; Dallas, Texas

CATEGORIES OF ARCHITECTURAL CONCRETE SURFACES

CATEGORY	FINISH	COLOR	FORMS	CRITICAL DETAILS
1. As cast	Remains as is after form removal— usually board marks or wood grain	Cement first influence, fine aggregate second influence	Plastic best All others • Wire-brushed plywood • Sandblasted plywood • Exposed-grain plywood • Unfinished sheathing lumber • Ammonia sprayed wood • Tongue-and-groove bands spaced	Slump = 2½'' to 3½'' Joinery of forms Proper release agent Point form joints to avoid marks
2. Abrasive blasted surfaces A. Brush blast	Uniform scour cleaning	Cement plus fine aggregate have equal influence	All smooth	Scouring after 7 days Slump = 2½'' to 3½''
B. Light blast	Sandblast to expose fine and some coarse aggregate	Fine aggregate primary coarse aggregate plus cement secondary	All smooth	10% more coarse aggregate Slump = 2½'' to 3½'' Blasting between 7 and 45 days
C. Medium exposed aggregate	Sandblasted to expose coarse aggregate	Coarse aggregate	All smooth	Higher than normal coarse aggregate Slump = 2'' to 3'' Blast before 7 days
D. Heavy exposed aggregate	Sandblasted to expose coarse aggregate 80% viable	Coarse aggregate	All smooth	Special mix coarse aggregate Slump = 0'' to 2'' Blast within 24 hours Use high frequency vibrator
3. Chemical retardation of surface set	Chemicals expose aggregate Aggregate can be adhered to surface	Coarse aggregate and cement	All smooth, glass fiber best	Chemical Grade determines etch depth Stripping scheduled to prevent long drying between stripping and washoff
4. Mechanically fractured surfaces, scaling, bush hammering, jackhammering, tooling	Varied	Cement, fine and coarse Aggregate	Textured	Aggregate particles ⅜'' for scaling and tooling Aggregate particles
5. Combination/fluted	Striated/abrasive blasted/irregular pattern Corrugated/abrasive Vertical rusticated/abrasive blasted Reeded and bush hammered Reeded and hammered Reeded and chiseled	The shallower the surface, the more influence aggregate fines and cement have	Wood or rubber strips, corrugated sheet metal or glass fiber	Depends on type of finish desired Wood fluke kerfed and nailed loosely

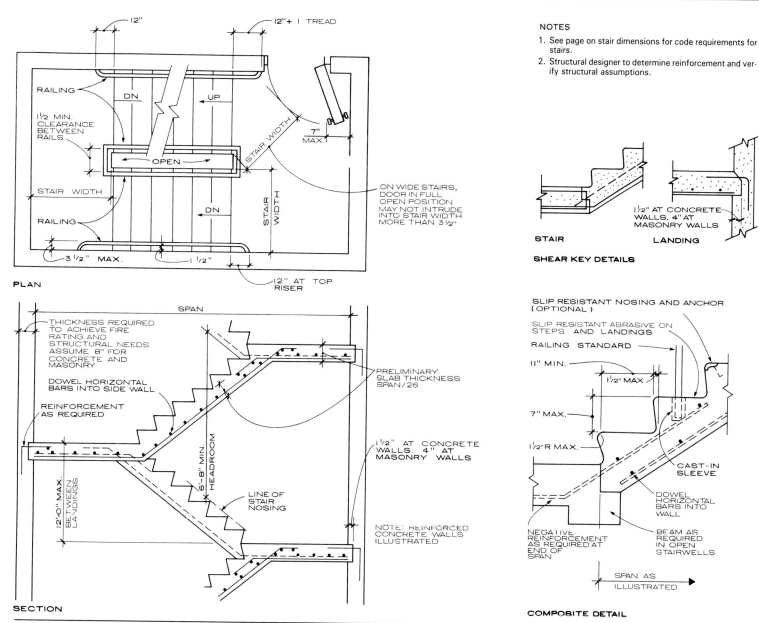

NOTES

1. See page on stair dimensions for code requirements for stairs.
2. Structural designer to determine reinforcement and verify structural assumptions.

PLAN

RAILING

DN   UP

1½ MIN. CLEARANCE BETWEEN RAILS

OPEN

STAIR WIDTH

STAIR WIDTH

DN

RAILING

3½" MAX.   1½"   12" AT TOP RISER

12"   12"+ 1 TREAD

STAIR WIDTH

7" MAX.

ON WIDE STAIRS, DOOR IN FULL OPEN POSITION MAY NOT INTRUDE INTO STAIR WIDTH MORE THAN 3½"

SHEAR KEY DETAILS

STAIR   LANDING

1½" AT CONCRETE WALLS. 4" AT MASONRY WALLS

SECTION

SPAN

THICKNESS REQUIRED TO ACHIEVE FIRE RATING AND STRUCTURAL NEEDS. ASSUME 8" FOR CONCRETE AND MASONRY

DOWEL HORIZONTAL BARS INTO SIDE WALL

REINFORCEMENT AS REQUIRED

12'-0" MAX. BETWEEN LANDINGS

6'-8" MIN. HEADROOM

LINE OF STAIR NOSING

PRELIMINARY SLAB THICKNESS SPAN/26

1½" AT CONCRETE WALLS. 4" AT MASONRY WALLS

NOTE: REINFORCED CONCRETE WALLS ILLUSTRATED

U — TYPE CONCRETE STAIRS

COMPOSITE DETAIL

SLIP RESISTANT NOSING AND ANCHOR (OPTIONAL)

SLIP RESISTANT ABRASIVE ON STEPS AND LANDINGS

RAILING STANDARD

11" MIN.

1½" MAX

7" MAX.

1½"R MAX.

NEGATIVE REINFORCEMENT AS REQUIRED AT END OF SPAN

CAST-IN SLEEVE

DOWEL HORIZONTAL BARS INTO WALL

BEAM AS REQUIRED IN OPEN STAIRWELLS

SPAN AS ILLUSTRATED

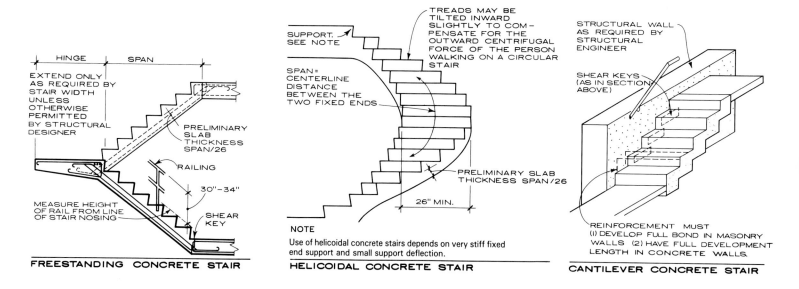

FREESTANDING CONCRETE STAIR

HINGE   SPAN

EXTEND ONLY AS REQUIRED BY STAIR WIDTH UNLESS OTHERWISE PERMITTED BY STRUCTURAL DESIGNER

PRELIMINARY SLAB THICKNESS SPAN/26

RAILING

30"–34"

SHEAR KEY

MEASURE HEIGHT OF RAIL FROM LINE OF STAIR NOSING

HELICOIDAL CONCRETE STAIR

SUPPORT. SEE NOTE

SPAN= CENTERLINE DISTANCE BETWEEN THE TWO FIXED ENDS

TREADS MAY BE TILTED INWARD SLIGHTLY TO COMPENSATE FOR THE OUTWARD CENTRIFUGAL FORCE OF THE PERSON WALKING ON A CIRCULAR STAIR

PRELIMINARY SLAB THICKNESS SPAN/26

26" MIN.

NOTE

Use of helicoidal concrete stairs depends on very stiff fixed end support and small support deflection.

CANTILEVER CONCRETE STAIR

STRUCTURAL WALL AS REQUIRED BY STRUCTURAL ENGINEER

SHEAR KEYS (AS IN SECTION ABOVE)

REINFORCEMENT MUST (1) DEVELOP FULL BOND IN MASONRY WALLS (2) HAVE FULL DEVELOPMENT LENGTH IN CONCRETE WALLS

Krommenhoek/McKeown & Associates; San Diego, California
Karlsberger and Associates, Inc.; Columbus, Ohio

REFERENCES

GENERAL REFERENCES

ACI Detailing Manual, American Concrete Institute (ACI)

Building Code Requirements for Reinforced Concrete, American Concrete Institute (ACI)

CRSI Handbook, Concrete Reinforcing Steel Institute (CRSI)

Design and Typical Details of Connections for Precast and Prestressed Concrete, Precast/Prestressed Concrete Institute (PCI)

PCI Design Handbook: Precast and Prestressed Concrete. Precast/Prestressed Concrete Institute (PCI)

Structural Details for Concrete Construction, 1988, Morton Newman, McGraw-Hill

DATA SOURCES: ORGANIZATIONS

American Concrete Institute (ACI), 26, 32, 33

American National Standards Institute, (ANSI), 34

Concrete Reinforcing Steel Institute (CRSI), 23

Dynamold Corporation, 30

Dyroform Engineering, 30

Flexicore Company, 30

Portland Cement Association (PCA), 25

Precast Concrete Institute, 28–31

Spancrete Industries, Inc., 30

Span-Deck, Inc., 30

DATA SOURCES: PUBLICATIONS

Architectural Precast Concrete, Prestressed Concrete Institute, 28

Basic Building Code, Building Officials and Code Administrators International (BOCA), 34

Design Handbook, 2nd and 3rd editions, Prestressed Concrete Institute, 28–30

Guide Specifications for Precast, Prestressed Concrete for Buildings, Prestressed Concrete Institute, 28

Load Bearing Architectural Wall Panels, Prestressed Concrete Institute, 28

Manual for Quality Control for Plants and Production of Architectural Precast Concrete Products, Prestressed Concrete Institute, 28

Manual for Structural Design, Prestressed Concrete Institute, 28

Manual for Structural Design of Architectural Prescast Concrete, Prestressed Concrete Institute, 29

CHAPTER 4

MASONRY

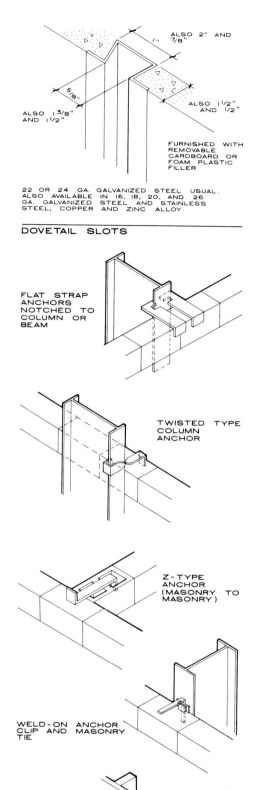

ALSO 2" AND 7/8"

ALSO 1 1/2" AND 1/2"

ALSO 1 3/8" AND 1 1/2"

FURNISHED WITH REMOVABLE CARDBOARD OR FOAM PLASTIC FILLER

22 OR 24 GA. GALVANIZED STEEL USUAL. ALSO AVAILABLE IN 16, 18, 20, AND 26 GA. GALVANIZED STEEL AND STAINLESS STEEL, COPPER AND ZINC ALLOY

DOVETAIL SLOTS

FLAT STRAP ANCHORS NOTCHED TO COLUMN OR BEAM

TWISTED TYPE COLUMN ANCHOR

Z-TYPE ANCHOR (MASONRY TO MASONRY)

WELD-ON ANCHOR CLIP AND MASONRY TIE

VENEER ANCHORS (PLAIN AND CORRUGATED TYPES SHOWN)

MISCELLANEOUS ANCHORS

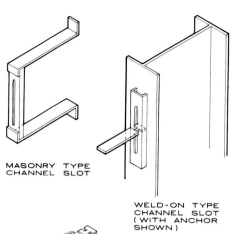

MASONRY TYPE CHANNEL SLOT

WELD-ON TYPE CHANNEL SLOT (WITH ANCHOR SHOWN)

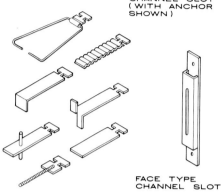

ANCHOR CONFIGURATIONS

FACE TYPE CHANNEL SLOT

CHANNEL SLOTS AND ANCHORS

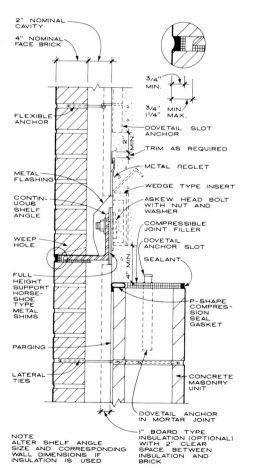

2" NOMINAL CAVITY

4" NOMINAL FACE BRICK

3/4" MIN.

3/4" MIN. 1 1/4" MAX.

FLEXIBLE ANCHOR

DOVETAIL SLOT ANCHOR

TRIM AS REQUIRED

METAL REGLET

WEDGE TYPE INSERT

ASKEW HEAD BOLT WITH NUT AND WASHER

COMPRESSIBLE JOINT FILLER

DOVETAIL ANCHOR SLOT

SEALANT

P-SHAPE COMPRESSION SEAL GASKET

METAL FLASHING

CONTINUOUS SHELF ANGLE

WEEP HOLE

FULL HEIGHT SUPPORT HORSESHOE TYPE METAL SHIMS

PARGING

LATERAL TIES

CONCRETE MASONRY UNIT

DOVETAIL ANCHOR IN MORTAR JOINT

NOTE ALTER SHELF ANGLE SIZE AND CORRESPONDING WALL DIMENSIONS IF INSULATION IS USED

1" BOARD TYPE INSULATION (OPTIONAL) WITH 2" CLEAR SPACE BETWEEN INSULATION AND BRICK

CAVITY WALL SHELF ANGLE SUPPORT

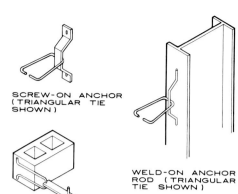

SCREW-ON ANCHOR (TRIANGULAR TIE SHOWN)

WELD-ON ANCHOR ROD (TRIANGULAR TIE SHOWN)

ADJUSTABLE U-BAR ANCHOR (FLAT TYPE PIN SHOWN)

1	Rectangular	Available with or without moisture drip in 3/16 in. or 1/4 in. mill or hot dipped galvanized steel; conforms to ASTM (A-82); space 16 in. vertically and 24 in. horizontally
2	Z	
3	Adjustable Z	
4	Mesh	1/2 in. mesh x 16 ga. hot dipped galvanized
5	Corrugated	mill or hot dipped galvanized steel 7/8 in. wide and 7 in. long; 12 to 28 ga.

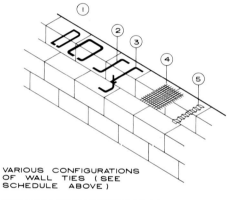

VARIOUS CONFIGURATIONS OF WALL TIES (SEE SCHEDULE ABOVE)

WIRE TIES

Masonry veneer and facing must be anchored to back-up construction. Codes usually require one anchor for 3 sq. ft. of surface area. Inserts usually are spaced 2 ft. on center horizontally, and ties usually are spaced 16 to 18 in. on center vertically. Spandrel beams over 18 in. deep require inserts and anchors for tying masonry facing to the beam. Most anchor systems permit differential movement in one or two directions. An anchoring system that allows movement only in the intended direction should be selected. See ASTM STP 778.

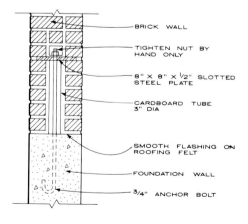

BRICK WALL

TIGHTEN NUT BY HAND ONLY

8" X 8" X 1/2" SLOTTED STEEL PLATE

CARDBOARD TUBE 3" DIA

SMOOTH FLASHING ON ROOFING FELT

FOUNDATION WALL

3/4" ANCHOR BOLT

WALL ANCHORAGE TO FOUNDATION

Narcisa P. Sanchez; Sanchez & Sanchez; Falls Church, Virginia
Metz Train Olson & Youngren, Inc.; Chicago, Illinois

4    **MASONRY ACCESSORIES**

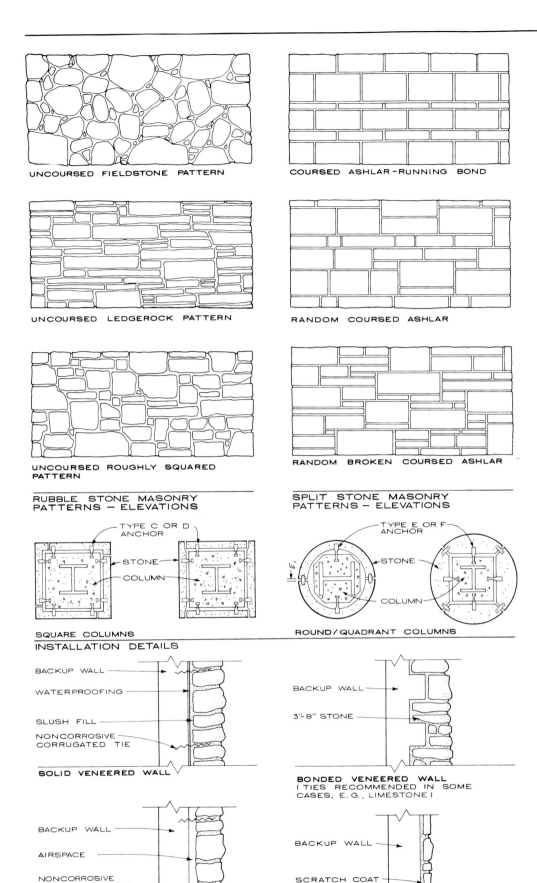

UNCOURSED FIELDSTONE PATTERN

COURSED ASHLAR - RUNNING BOND

ONE - HEIGHT PATTERN (SINGLE RISE)

UNCOURSED LEDGEROCK PATTERN

RANDOM COURSED ASHLAR

TWO - HEIGHT PATTERN (40% - 2¹/₄"; 60% - 5")

UNCOURSED ROUGHLY SQUARED PATTERN

RANDOM BROKEN COURSED ASHLAR

THREE - HEIGHT PATTERN (15% - 2¹/₄"; 40% - 5"; 45% - 7³/₄")

RUBBLE STONE MASONRY PATTERNS — ELEVATIONS

SPLIT STONE MASONRY PATTERNS — ELEVATIONS

SPLIT STONE MASONRY HEIGHT PATTERNS — ELEVATIONS

TYPE C OR D ANCHOR — STONE — COLUMN

SQUARE COLUMNS

TYPE E OR F ANCHOR — STONE — COLUMN

ROUND / QUADRANT COLUMNS

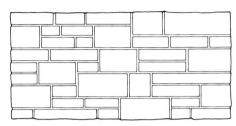
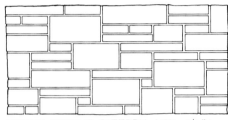
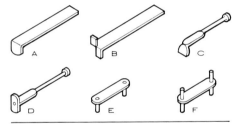

ANCHORS

INSTALLATION DETAILS

BACKUP WALL — WATERPROOFING — SLUSH FILL — NONCORROSIVE CORRUGATED TIE

SOLID VENEERED WALL

BACKUP WALL — 3'-8" STONE

BONDED VENEERED WALL (TIES RECOMMENDED IN SOME CASES, E.G., LIMESTONE)

BACKUP WALL — AIRSPACE — NONCORROSIVE CORRUGATED TIE

CAVITY VENEERED WALL

BACKUP WALL — SCRATCH COAT

THIN VENEERED WALL

TYPICAL WALL SECTIONS

NOTES

1. A course is a horizontal row of stone. Bond pattern is described by the horizontal arrangement of vertical joints. (See also Brickwork.) Structural bond refers to the physical tying together of load bearing and veneer portions of a composite wall. Structural bond can be accomplished with metal ties or with stone units set as headers into the backup.

2. Ashlar masonry is composed of squared-off building stone units of various sizes. Cut Ashlar is dressed to specific design dimensions at the mill. Ashlar is often used in random lengths and heights, with jointing worked out on the job.

3. All ties and anchors must be made of noncorrosive material. Chromium-nickel stainless steel types 302 and 304 and eraydo alloy zinc are the most resistant to corrosion and staining. Hot dipped galvanized is widely used, but is not as resistant, hence is prohibited by some building codes. Copper, brass, and bronze will stain under some conditions. Local building codes often govern the types of metal that may be used for stone anchors.

4. Nonstaining cement mortar should be used on porous and light colored stones. At all corners use extra ties and, when possible, larger stones. Joints are usually ¹/₂ to 1¹/₂ in. for rough work and ³/₈ to ³/₄ in. for Ashlar.

Building Stone Institute; New York, New York
George M. Whiteside, III, AIA, and James D. Lloyd; Kennett Square, Pennsylvania
Alexander Keyes; Darrel Downing Rippeteau, Architect; Washington, D.C.

STONE

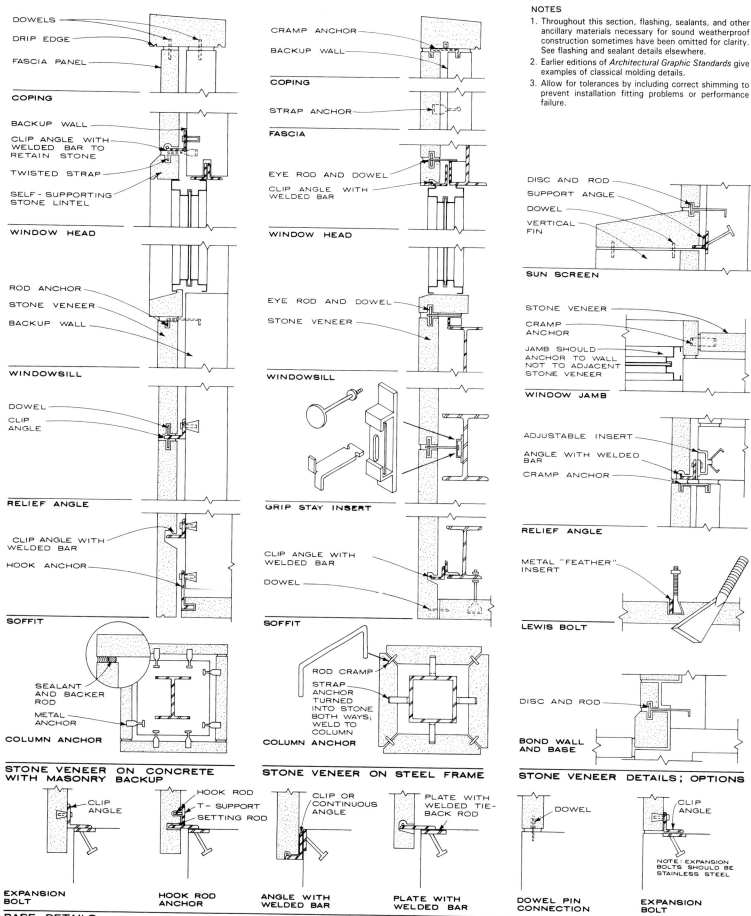

NOTES
1. Throughout this section, flashing, sealants, and other ancillary materials necessary for sound weatherproof construction sometimes have been omitted for clarity. See flashing and sealant details elsewhere.
2. Earlier editions of *Architectural Graphic Standards* give examples of classical molding details.
3. Allow for tolerances by including correct shimming to prevent installation fitting problems or performance failure.

COPING

WINDOW HEAD

WINDOWSILL

RELIEF ANGLE

SOFFIT

COLUMN ANCHOR

STONE VENEER ON CONCRETE WITH MASONRY BACKUP

COPING

FASCIA

WINDOW HEAD

WINDOWSILL

GRIP STAY INSERT

SOFFIT

COLUMN ANCHOR

STONE VENEER ON STEEL FRAME

SUN SCREEN

WINDOW JAMB

RELIEF ANGLE

LEWIS BOLT

BOND WALL AND BASE

STONE VENEER DETAILS; OPTIONS

EXPANSION BOLT

HOOK ROD ANCHOR

ANGLE WITH WELDED BAR

PLATE WITH WELDED BAR

DOWEL PIN CONNECTION

EXPANSION BOLT

NOTE: EXPANSION BOLTS SHOULD BE STAINLESS STEEL

BASE DETAILS

Building Stone Institute; New York, New York
George M. Whiteside, III, AIA, and James D. Lloyd; Kennett Square, Pennsylvania
Alexander Keyes; Darrel Downing Rippeteau, Architect; Washington, D.C.

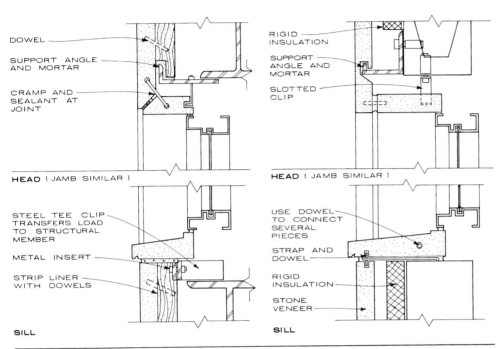

- STAINLESS STEEL DOWEL WITH HOOK ANCHOR
- SEALANT AND FOAM ROD
- SETTING BED
- FLASHING
- STONE VENEER

DOWEL CONNECTION

HORIZONTAL CONNECTION; DOWEL AND CRAMP

ANCHOR BOLT

COPINGS

ANCHOR DIMENSIONS

Standard flat stock anchors are made from strap 1 in. and 1¼ in. wide by ⅛ in., ³⁄₁₆ in., and ¼ in. thick. Lengths vary up to 6 in., 8 in., 10 in. and 12 in. standards. Dovetail anchors are usually 4¼ in. overall with 3½ in. projection from face of concrete. Bends are ¾ in., 1 in., and 1¼ in.

Round stock anchors are made from stock of any diameter; ¼ in. and ⅜ in. are most common for rods; ⅛ in. (#11 gauge) through ³⁄₁₆ in. (#6 gauge) for wire anchors; and ¼ in. and ⅜ in. are most common for dowels. Dowel lengths are usually 2 in. to 6 in.

Refer to page on 3 in. stone veneer for additional anchorage information.

Allow for tolerances by including correct shimming to prevent installation fitting problems or performance failure.

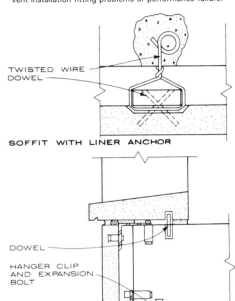

- TWISTED WIRE DOWEL

SOFFIT WITH LINER ANCHOR

- DOWEL
- HANGER CLIP AND EXPANSION BOLT

SOFFIT AND SILL DETAIL

- DOWEL
- SUPPORT ANGLE AND MORTAR
- CRAMP AND SEALANT AT JOINT

HEAD (JAMB SIMILAR)

- RIGID INSULATION
- SUPPORT ANGLE AND MORTAR
- SLOTTED CLIP

HEAD (JAMB SIMILAR)

- STEEL TEE CLIP TRANSFERS LOAD TO STRUCTURAL MEMBER
- METAL INSERT
- STRIP LINER WITH DOWELS

SILL

- USE DOWEL TO CONNECT SEVERAL PIECES
- STRAP AND DOWEL
- RIGID INSULATION
- STONE VENEER

SILL

WINDOW DETAILS

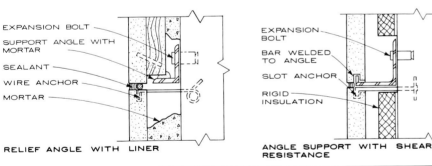

- EXPANSION BOLT
- SUPPORT ANGLE WITH MORTAR
- SEALANT
- WIRE ANCHOR
- MORTAR

RELIEF ANGLE WITH LINER

- EXPANSION BOLT
- BAR WELDED TO ANGLE
- SLOT ANCHOR
- RIGID INSULATION

ANGLE SUPPORT WITH SHEAR RESISTANCE

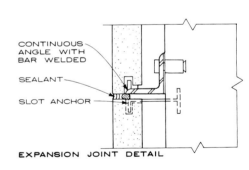

- CONTINUOUS ANGLE WITH BAR WELDED
- SEALANT
- SLOT ANCHOR

EXPANSION JOINT DETAIL

RELIEF ANGLE SUPPORTS

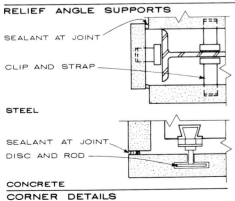

- SEALANT AT JOINT
- CLIP AND STRAP

STEEL

- SEALANT AT JOINT
- DISC AND ROD

CONCRETE

CORNER DETAILS

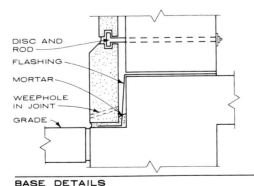

- DISC AND ROD
- FLASHING
- MORTAR
- WEEPHOLE IN JOINT
- GRADE

BASE DETAILS

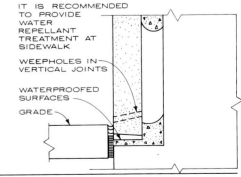

IT IS RECOMMENDED TO PROVIDE WATER REPELLANT TREATMENT AT SIDEWALK

- WEEPHOLES IN VERTICAL JOINTS
- WATERPROOFED SURFACES
- GRADE

Building Stone Institute; New York, New York
George M. Whiteside, III, AIA, and James D. Lloyd; Kennett Square, Pennsylvania
Alexander Keyes; Darrel Downing Rippeteau, Architect; Washington, D.C.

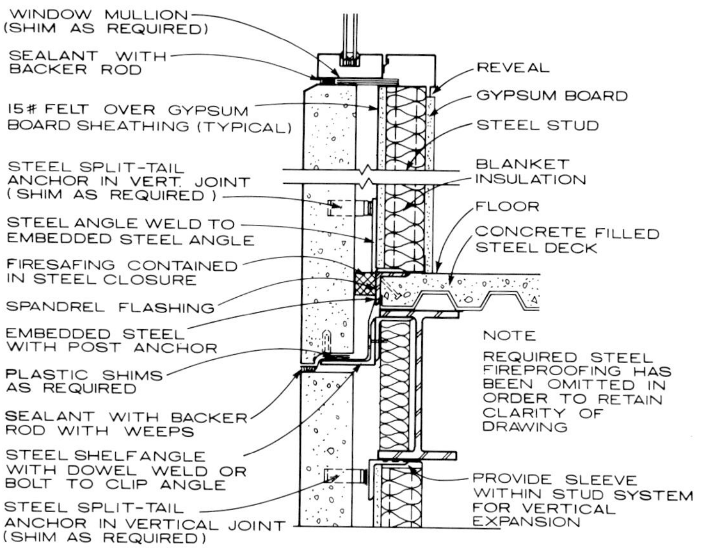

WINDOW MULLION (SHIM AS REQUIRED)
SEALANT WITH BACKER ROD
15# FELT OVER GYPSUM BOARD SHEATHING (TYPICAL)
STEEL SPLIT-TAIL ANCHOR IN VERT. JOINT (SHIM AS REQUIRED)
STEEL ANGLE WELD TO EMBEDDED STEEL ANGLE
FIRESAFING CONTAINED IN STEEL CLOSURE
SPANDREL FLASHING
EMBEDDED STEEL WITH POST ANCHOR
PLASTIC SHIMS AS REQUIRED
SEALANT WITH BACKER ROD WITH WEEPS
STEEL SHELF ANGLE WITH DOWEL WELD OR BOLT TO CLIP ANGLE
STEEL SPLIT-TAIL ANCHOR IN VERTICAL JOINT (SHIM AS REQUIRED)
REVEAL
GYPSUM BOARD
STEEL STUD
BLANKET INSULATION
FLOOR
CONCRETE FILLED STEEL DECK
NOTE
REQUIRED STEEL FIREPROOFING HAS BEEN OMITTED IN ORDER TO RETAIN CLARITY OF DRAWING
PROVIDE SLEEVE WITHIN STUD SYSTEM FOR VERTICAL EXPANSION

SECTION THROUGH HARD STONE PANEL AT WINDOW WALL

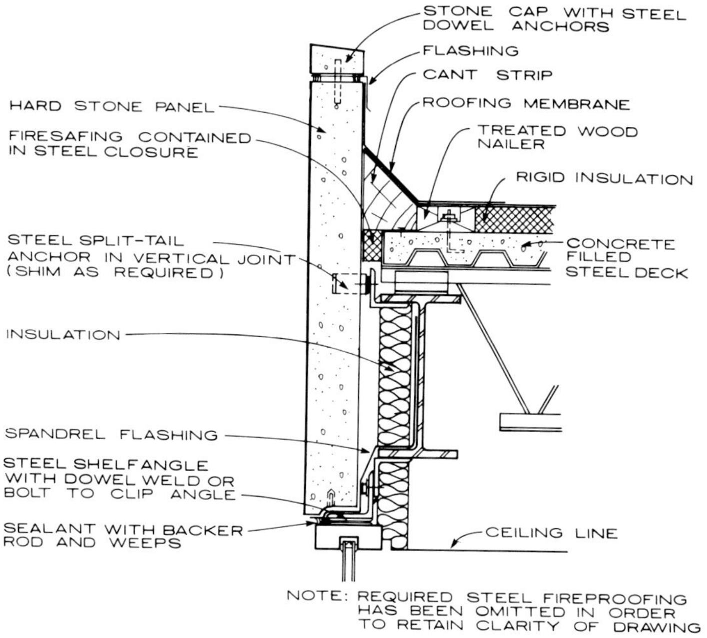

STONE CAP WITH STEEL DOWEL ANCHORS
FLASHING
CANT STRIP
ROOFING MEMBRANE
TREATED WOOD NAILER
RIGID INSULATION
HARD STONE PANEL
FIRESAFING CONTAINED IN STEEL CLOSURE
CONCRETE FILLED STEEL DECK
STEEL SPLIT-TAIL ANCHOR IN VERTICAL JOINT (SHIM AS REQUIRED)
INSULATION
SPANDREL FLASHING
STEEL SHELF ANGLE WITH DOWEL WELD OR BOLT TO CLIP ANGLE
SEALANT WITH BACKER ROD AND WEEPS
CEILING LINE
NOTE: REQUIRED STEEL FIREPROOFING HAS BEEN OMITTED IN ORDER TO RETAIN CLARITY OF DRAWING

SECTION THROUGH ROOF PARAPET AT HARD STONE PANEL

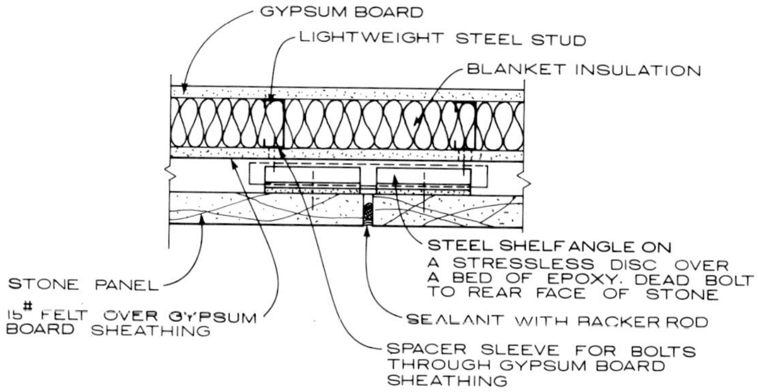

GYPSUM BOARD
LIGHTWEIGHT STEEL STUD
BLANKET INSULATION
STONE PANEL
15# FELT OVER GYPSUM BOARD SHEATHING
STEEL SHELF ANGLE ON A STRESSLESS DISC OVER A BED OF EPOXY. DEAD BOLT TO REAR FACE OF STONE
SEALANT WITH BACKER ROD
SPACER SLEEVE FOR BOLTS THROUGH GYPSUM BOARD SHEATHING

SECTION AT VERTICAL JOINT

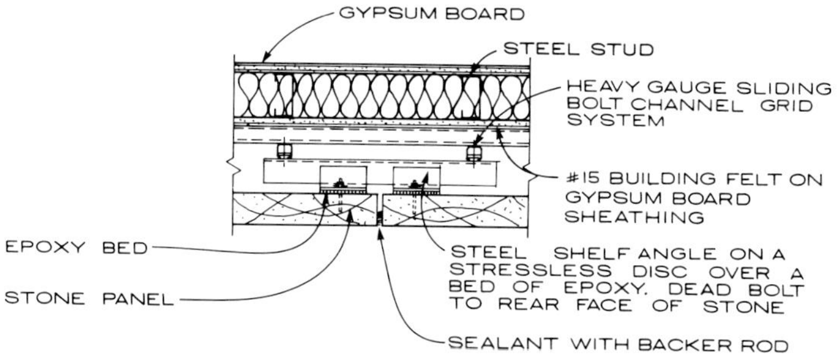

GYPSUM BOARD
STEEL STUD
HEAVY GAUGE SLIDING BOLT CHANNEL GRID SYSTEM
#15 BUILDING FELT ON GYPSUM BOARD SHEATHING
EPOXY BED
STONE PANEL
STEEL SHELF ANGLE ON A STRESSLESS DISC OVER A BED OF EPOXY. DEAD BOLT TO REAR FACE OF STONE
SEALANT WITH BACKER ROD

SECTION AT VERTICAL JOINT

NOTES

Use of the steel stud support system as shown requires an architect or engineer to develop adequate and realistic performance criteria, including thorough consideration of the long-term durability and corrosion resistance of light gauge members, mechanical fasteners, and other system components; provisions for adequate thermal movement; development of adequate system strength and stiffness; recognition of the structural interaction between the stone support system; and consideration of vapor retarders and flashing to control moisture migration. It also is important that adequate provisions be developed to ensure quality workmanship necessary to implement the system and to achieve the expected quality and durability.

The stone thickness depicted is a minimum of 1½ in. Thicker stone materials can use the same type of support system; however, engineering analyses of the system will be necessary to ensure proper performance and compliance with recommended design practices.

Design criteria for stone anchorage must include consideration of the particular stone's average as well as lowest strength values for safety, particularly at anchorage points. The proposed stone should be tested for adequate design properties and values. Stone anchorage size and location depend on establishing the particular stone's strength values, natural faults, and other properties; the stone's thickness and supported area; the expected lateral as well as gravity loading; and the amount of thermal movement to be accommodated.

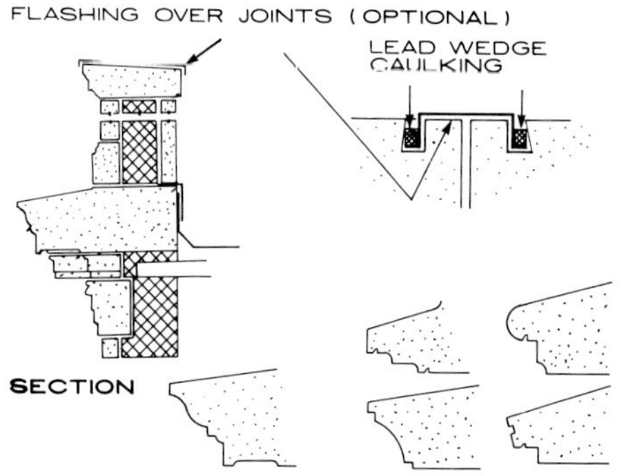

FLASHING OVER JOINTS (OPTIONAL)
LEAD WEDGE CAULKING
SECTION

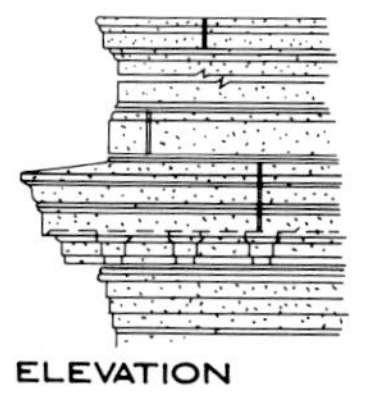

ELEVATION

NOTE

Shown are five possible cornice designs. Indiana limestone can be fabricated easily and economically to almost any profile. See examples.

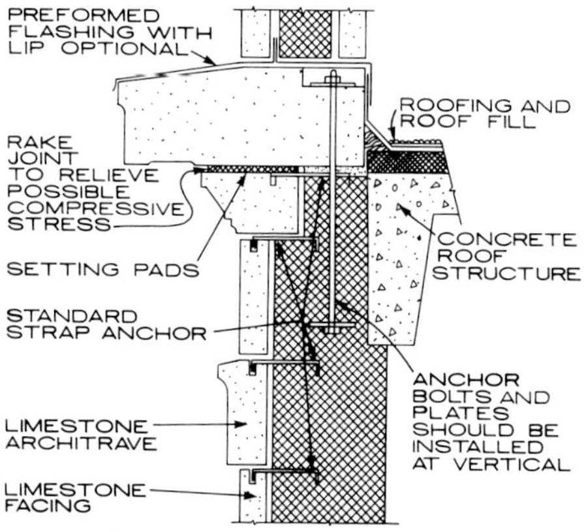

PREFORMED FLASHING WITH LIP OPTIONAL
ROOFING AND ROOF FILL
RAKE JOINT TO RELIEVE POSSIBLE COMPRESSIVE STRESS
SETTING PADS
CONCRETE ROOF STRUCTURE
STANDARD STRAP ANCHOR
ANCHOR BOLTS AND PLATES SHOULD BE INSTALLED AT VERTICAL
LIMESTONE ARCHITRAVE
LIMESTONE FACING

WALL SECTION

Shown here is the most common method of anchoring a cornice, which has a large enough projection to be unbalanced in the wall.

The bed joint immediately below the heavy cornice is open far enough back to remove any compressive stress that would have a tendency to break off stone below.

TRADITIONAL CORNICES

The Spector Group; North Hills, New York

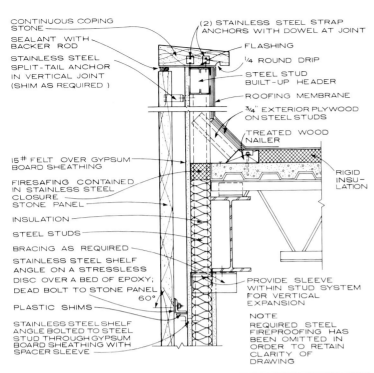

CONTINUOUS COPING STONE
SEALANT WITH BACKER ROD
STAINLESS STEEL SPLIT-TAIL ANCHOR IN VERTICAL JOINT (SHIM AS REQUIRED)
(2) STAINLESS STEEL STRAP ANCHORS WITH DOWEL AT JOINT
FLASHING
¼ ROUND DRIP
STEEL STUD BUILT-UP HEADER
ROOFING MEMBRANE
¾" EXTERIOR PLYWOOD ON STEEL STUDS
TREATED WOOD NAILER
15# FELT OVER GYPSUM BOARD SHEATHING
FIRESAFING CONTAINED IN STAINLESS STEEL CLOSURE
STONE PANEL
INSULATION
STEEL STUDS
BRACING AS REQUIRED
STAINLESS STEEL SHELF ANGLE ON A STRESSLESS DISC OVER A BED OF EPOXY; DEAD BOLT TO STONE PANEL 60°
PLASTIC SHIMS
STAINLESS STEEL SHELF ANGLE BOLTED TO STEEL STUD THROUGH GYPSUM BOARD SHEATHING WITH SPACER SLEEVE
RIGID INSULATION
PROVIDE SLEEVE WITHIN STUD SYSTEM FOR VERTICAL EXPANSION
NOTE REQUIRED STEEL FIREPROOFING HAS BEEN OMITTED IN ORDER TO RETAIN CLARITY OF DRAWING

SECTION AT ROOF PARAPET AND WINDOWLESS WALL

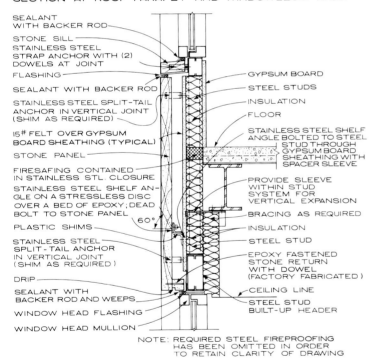

SEALANT WITH BACKER ROD
STONE SILL
STAINLESS STEEL STRAP ANCHOR WITH (2) DOWELS AT JOINT
FLASHING
SEALANT WITH BACKER ROD
STAINLESS STEEL SPLIT-TAIL ANCHOR IN VERTICAL JOINT (SHIM AS REQUIRED)
15# FELT OVER GYPSUM BOARD SHEATHING (TYPICAL)
STONE PANEL
FIRESAFING CONTAINED IN STAINLESS STL. CLOSURE
STAINLESS STEEL SHELF ANGLE ON A STRESSLESS DISC OVER A BED OF EPOXY; DEAD BOLT TO STONE PANEL 60°
PLASTIC SHIMS
STAINLESS STEEL SPLIT-TAIL ANCHOR IN VERTICAL JOINT (SHIM AS REQUIRED)
DRIP
SEALANT WITH BACKER ROD AND WEEPS
WINDOW HEAD FLASHING
WINDOW HEAD MULLION
GYPSUM BOARD
STEEL STUDS
INSULATION
FLOOR
STAINLESS STEEL SHELF ANGLE BOLTED TO STEEL STUD THROUGH GYPSUM BOARD SHEATHING WITH SPACER SLEEVE
PROVIDE SLEEVE WITHIN STUD SYSTEM FOR VERTICAL EXPANSION
BRACING AS REQUIRED
INSULATION
STEEL STUD
EPOXY FASTENED STONE RETURN WITH DOWEL (FACTORY FABRICATED)
CEILING LINE
STEEL STUD BUILT-UP HEADER

NOTE: REQUIRED STEEL FIREPROOFING HAS BEEN OMITTED IN ORDER TO RETAIN CLARITY OF DRAWING

STONE SPANDREL AT WINDOW HEAD AND SILL

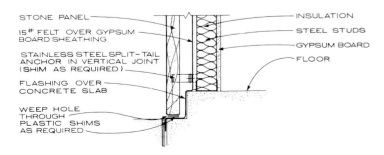

STONE PANEL
15# FELT OVER GYPSUM BOARD SHEATHING
STAINLESS STEEL SPLIT-TAIL ANCHOR IN VERTICAL JOINT (SHIM AS REQUIRED)
FLASHING OVER CONCRETE SLAB
WEEP HOLE THROUGH PLASTIC SHIMS AS REQUIRED
INSULATION
STEEL STUDS
GYPSUM BOARD
FLOOR

STONE SPANDREL AT GRADE

The Spector Group; North Hills, New York

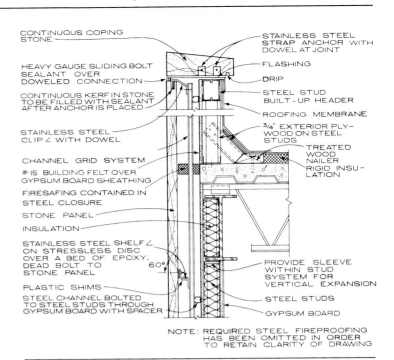

CONTINUOUS COPING STONE
HEAVY GAUGE SLIDING BOLT SEALANT OVER DOWELED CONNECTION
CONTINUOUS KERF IN STONE TO BE FILLED WITH SEALANT AFTER ANCHOR IS PLACED
STAINLESS STEEL CLIP ∠ WITH DOWEL
CHANNEL GRID SYSTEM
#15 BUILDING FELT OVER GYPSUM BOARD SHEATHING
FIRESAFING CONTAINED IN STEEL CLOSURE
STONE PANEL
INSULATION
STAINLESS STEEL SHELF ∠ ON STRESSLESS DISC OVER A BED OF EPOXY, DEAD BOLT TO STONE PANEL 60°
PLASTIC SHIMS
STEEL CHANNEL BOLTED TO STEEL STUDS THROUGH GYPSUM BOARD WITH SPACER
STAINLESS STEEL STRAP ANCHOR WITH DOWEL AT JOINT
FLASHING
DRIP
STEEL STUD BUILT-UP HEADER
ROOFING MEMBRANE
¾" EXTERIOR PLYWOOD ON STEEL STUDS
TREATED WOOD NAILER
RIGID INSULATION
PROVIDE SLEEVE WITHIN STUD SYSTEM FOR VERTICAL EXPANSION
STEEL STUDS
GYPSUM BOARD

NOTE: REQUIRED STEEL FIREPROOFING HAS BEEN OMITTED IN ORDER TO RETAIN CLARITY OF DRAWING

SECTION AT ROOF PARAPET AND WINDOWLESS WALL

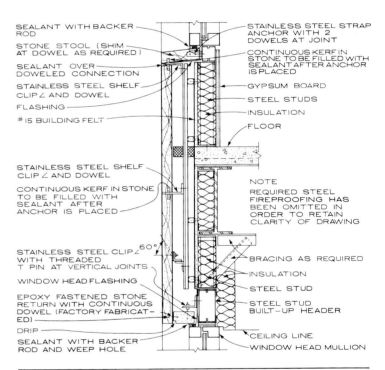

SEALANT WITH BACKER ROD
STONE STOOL (SHIM AT DOWEL AS REQUIRED)
SEALANT OVER DOWELED CONNECTION
STAINLESS STEEL SHELF CLIP ∠ AND DOWEL
FLASHING
#15 BUILDING FELT
STAINLESS STEEL SHELF CLIP ∠ AND DOWEL
CONTINUOUS KERF IN STONE TO BE FILLED WITH SEALANT AFTER ANCHOR IS PLACED
STAINLESS STEEL CLIP ∠ WITH THREADED T PIN AT VERTICAL JOINTS 60°
WINDOW HEAD FLASHING
EPOXY FASTENED STONE RETURN WITH CONTINUOUS DOWEL (FACTORY FABRICATED)
DRIP
SEALANT WITH BACKER ROD AND WEEP HOLE
STAINLESS STEEL STRAP ANCHOR WITH 2 DOWELS AT JOINT
CONTINUOUS KERF IN STONE TO BE FILLED WITH SEALANT AFTER ANCHOR IS PLACED
GYPSUM BOARD
STEEL STUDS
INSULATION
FLOOR
NOTE REQUIRED STEEL FIREPROOFING HAS BEEN OMITTED IN ORDER TO RETAIN CLARITY OF DRAWING
BRACING AS REQUIRED
INSULATION
STEEL STUD
STEEL STUD BUILT-UP HEADER
CEILING LINE
WINDOW HEAD MULLION

STONE SPANDREL AT WINDOW HEAD AND SILL

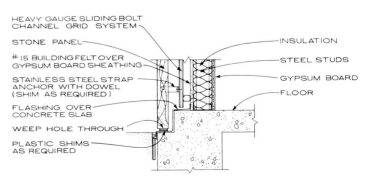

HEAVY GAUGE SLIDING BOLT CHANNEL GRID SYSTEM
STONE PANEL
#15 BUILDING FELT OVER GYPSUM BOARD SHEATHING
STAINLESS STEEL STRAP ANCHOR WITH DOWEL (SHIM AS REQUIRED)
FLASHING OVER CONCRETE SLAB
WEEP HOLE THROUGH
PLASTIC SHIMS AS REQUIRED
INSULATION
STEEL STUDS
GYPSUM BOARD
FLOOR

STONE SPANDREL AT GRADE

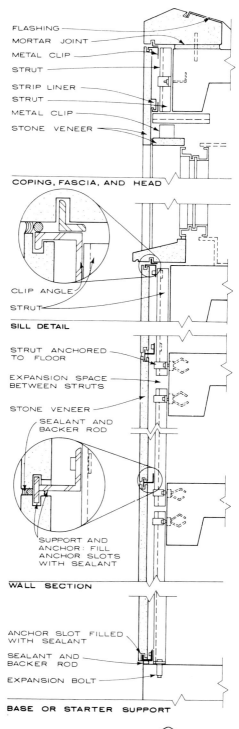

FLASHING
MORTAR JOINT
METAL CLIP
STRUT
STRIP LINER
STRUT
METAL CLIP
STONE VENEER

COPING, FASCIA, AND HEAD

CLIP ANGLE
STRUT

SILL DETAIL

STRUT ANCHORED TO FLOOR
EXPANSION SPACE BETWEEN STRUTS
STONE VENEER
SEALANT AND BACKER ROD
SUPPORT AND ANCHOR: FILL ANCHOR SLOTS WITH SEALANT

WALL SECTION

ANCHOR SLOT FILLED WITH SEALANT
SEALANT AND BACKER ROD
EXPANSION BOLT

BASE OR STARTER SUPPORT

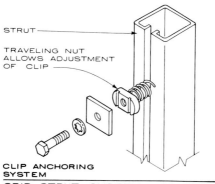

STRUT
TRAVELING NUT ALLOWS ADJUSTMENT OF CLIP

CLIP ANCHORING SYSTEM

GRID STRUT SYSTEM — CONCRETE FRAME

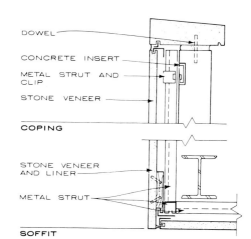

DOWEL
CONCRETE INSERT
METAL STRUT AND CLIP
STONE VENEER

COPING

STONE VENEER AND LINER
METAL STRUT

SOFFIT

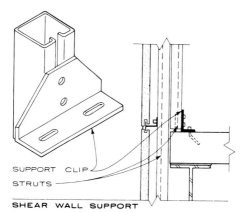

SUPPORT CLIP
STRUTS

SHEAR WALL SUPPORT

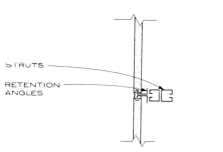

STRUTS
RETENTION ANGLES

SHEAR WALL SIDE RETENTION (PLAN)

GRID STRUT SYSTEM — METAL FRAME

GRID STRUT SPACING RELATIVE TO SLAB HEIGHT—MARBLE

HEIGHT OF SLAB UP TO	GRID STRUT SPACING	
	⁷⁄₈″ THICK	1¼″ THICK
2'-6"	4'-9"	4'-0"
3'-0"	4'-6"	3'-9"
3'-6"	4'-3"	3'-6"
4'-0"	4'-0"	3'-3"
4'-6"	3'-9"	3'-0"
5'-0"*	3'-6"	2'-9"
5'-6"*	3'-3"	2'-6"
6'-0"*	3'-3"	2'-3"

*For slabs over 4'-6" height use intermediate vertical joint anchoring.

NOTE: Engineering design of all supports for this type of construction is essential.

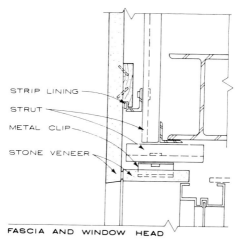

STRIP LINING
STRUT
METAL CLIP
STONE VENEER

FASCIA AND WINDOW HEAD

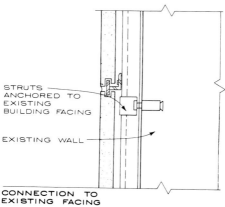

STRUTS ANCHORED TO EXISTING BUILDING FACING
EXISTING WALL

CONNECTION TO EXISTING FACING

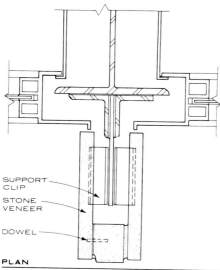

SUPPORT CLIP
STONE VENEER
DOWEL

PLAN
COLUMN RETURN

GRID ANCHOR SPACING AND STRUT SIZE—MARBLE

MAXIMUM SPACING		ANCHOR	STRUT SIZE
⁷⁄₈″ THICK	1¼″ THICK		WIDTH, DEPTH, AND SHAPE
4'-0"	4'-0"		1⁵⁄₈″ x 1⁵⁄₈″
7'-0"	6'-0"		1⁵⁄₈″ x 2⁷⁄₁₆″
10'-0"	9'-0"		1⁵⁄₈″ x 3¼″
15'-0"	13'-0"		1⁵⁄₈″ x 4⁷⁄₈″

NOTES
1. "X" = dimension between strut and outside face of stone.
2. "X" = 1⁵⁄₈″ for ⁷⁄₈″ marble.
3. "X" = 1³⁄₄″ for 1¼″ marble.

Building Stone Institute; New York, New York
George M. Whiteside, III, AIA, and James D. Lloyd; Kennett Square, Pennsylvania
Alexander Keyes; Darrel Downing Rippeteau, Architect; Washington, D.C.

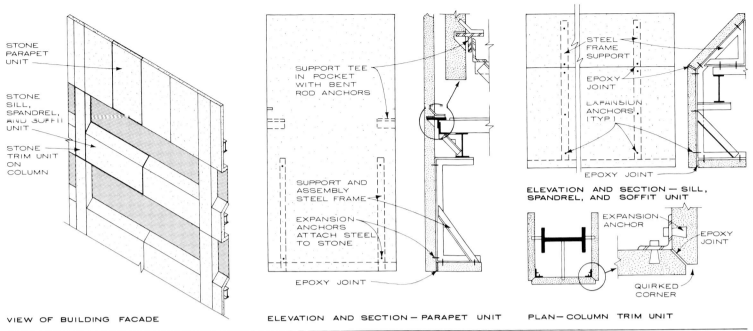

STONE PARAPET UNIT

STONE SILL, SPANDREL, AND SOFFIT UNIT

STONE TRIM UNIT ON COLUMN

VIEW OF BUILDING FACADE

SUPPORT TEE IN POCKET WITH BENT ROD ANCHORS

SUPPORT AND ASSEMBLY STEEL FRAME

EXPANSION ANCHORS ATTACH STEEL TO STONE.

EPOXY JOINT

ELEVATION AND SECTION — PARAPET UNIT

STEEL FRAME SUPPORT

EPOXY JOINT

EXPANSION ANCHORS (TYP)

EPOXY JOINT

ELEVATION AND SECTION — SILL, SPANDREL, AND SOFFIT UNIT

EXPANSION ANCHOR

EPOXY JOINT

QUIRKED CORNER

PLAN — COLUMN TRIM UNIT

PREASSEMBLED STONE UNIT WITH EPOXY ON STEEL FRAME

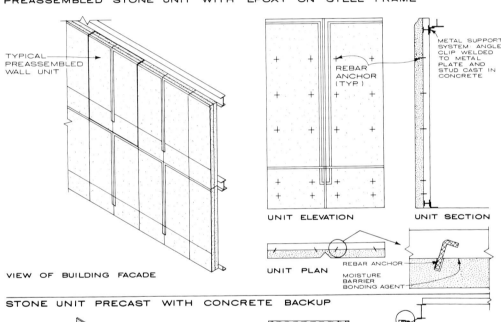

TYPICAL PREASSEMBLED WALL UNIT

VIEW OF BUILDING FACADE

REBAR ANCHOR (TYP)

UNIT ELEVATION

METAL SUPPORT SYSTEM ANGLE CLIP WELDED TO METAL PLATE AND STUD CAST IN CONCRETE

UNIT SECTION

REBAR ANCHOR

UNIT PLAN

MOISTURE BARRIER BONDING AGENT

PREASSEMBLED PANELS

Savings in on-site labor and accurate component stone unit joining are available through preassembled stone panel technology.

Shipping and erection stresses on the stone panels and stone anchorage system to the preassembled units should be evaluated.

Design of sealant joints between preassembled units should include at least the following: thermal movement, fabrication and erection tolerances, irreversible material growth or shrinkage, and sealant movement potential.

STONE ON STEEL FRAME WITH EPOXY JOINTS

Stone units are mounted on a steel frame with expansion bolts and dowel pins (as recommended by manufacturer). Joints in stone are epoxied and held to approximately ⅛ in. when finished for delivery. All stones in the assembly are anchored as a unit to the structure. Preassembled unit installation reduces individual leveling, plumbing, and aligning, and on-site joint sealing is not as extensive as with individual stone panels.

COMPOSITE ASSEMBLIES OF STONE AND CONCRETE

Stone units are bonded to reinforced precast concrete panels with bent stainless steel anchors. A moisture barrier and a bonding agent are installed between the stone and concrete in conditions where concrete alkali salts may stain stone units.

STONE AND STEEL ASSEMBLIES WITH SEALANT JOINTS

Stone units are shimmed and anchored to a steel frame using standard stone connecting hardware. Joints may be sealed on site, along with joints between assemblies.

STONE UNIT PRECAST WITH CONCRETE BACKUP

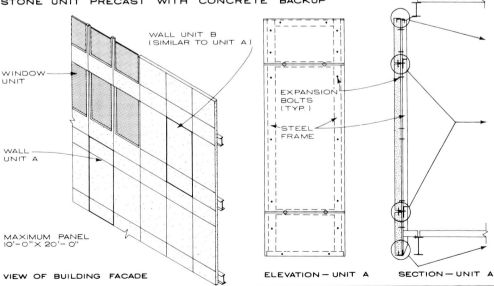

WALL UNIT B (SIMILAR TO UNIT A)

WINDOW UNIT

WALL UNIT A

MAXIMUM PANEL 10'-0" X 20'-0"

VIEW OF BUILDING FACADE

EXPANSION BOLTS (TYP.)

STEEL FRAME

ELEVATION — UNIT A

SECTION — UNIT A

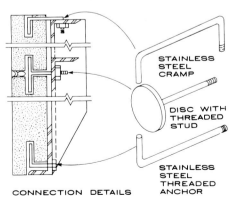

STAINLESS STEEL CRAMP

DISC WITH THREADED STUD

STAINLESS STEEL THREADED ANCHOR

CONNECTION DETAILS

PREASSEMBLED STONE UNIT ON STEEL FRAME
Building Stone Institute; New York, New York
George M. Whiteside, III, AIA, and James D. Lloyd; Kennett Square, Pennsylvania
Alexander Keyes; Darrel Downing Rippeteau, Architect; Washington, D.C.

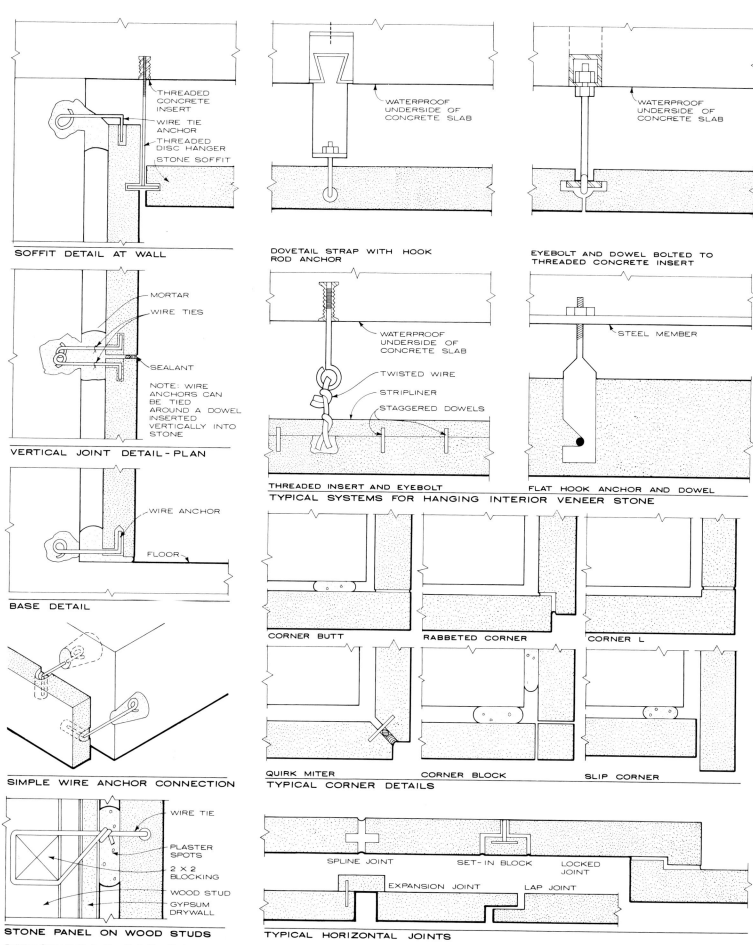

SOFFIT DETAIL AT WALL

THREADED CONCRETE INSERT
WIRE TIE ANCHOR
THREADED DISC HANGER
STONE SOFFIT

VERTICAL JOINT DETAIL-PLAN

MORTAR
WIRE TIES
SEALANT

NOTE: WIRE ANCHORS CAN BE TIED AROUND A DOWEL INSERTED VERTICALLY INTO STONE

BASE DETAIL

WIRE ANCHOR
FLOOR

SIMPLE WIRE ANCHOR CONNECTION

STONE PANEL ON WOOD STUDS

WIRE TIE
PLASTER SPOTS
2 X 2 BLOCKING
WOOD STUD
GYPSUM DRYWALL

DOVETAIL STRAP WITH HOOK ROD ANCHOR

WATERPROOF UNDERSIDE OF CONCRETE SLAB

EYEBOLT AND DOWEL BOLTED TO THREADED CONCRETE INSERT

WATERPROOF UNDERSIDE OF CONCRETE SLAB

THREADED INSERT AND EYEBOLT

WATERPROOF UNDERSIDE OF CONCRETE SLAB
TWISTED WIRE
STRIPLINER
STAGGERED DOWELS

FLAT HOOK ANCHOR AND DOWEL

STEEL MEMBER

TYPICAL SYSTEMS FOR HANGING INTERIOR VENEER STONE

CORNER BUTT   RABBETED CORNER   CORNER L

QUIRK MITER   CORNER BLOCK   SLIP CORNER

TYPICAL CORNER DETAILS

SPLINE JOINT   SET-IN BLOCK   LOCKED JOINT
EXPANSION JOINT   LAP JOINT

TYPICAL HORIZONTAL JOINTS

Building Stone Institute; New York, New York
George M. Whiteside, III, AIA, and James D. Lloyd; Kennett Square, Pennsylvania
Alexander Keyes; Darrel Downing Rippeteau, Architect; Washington, D.C.

 STONE

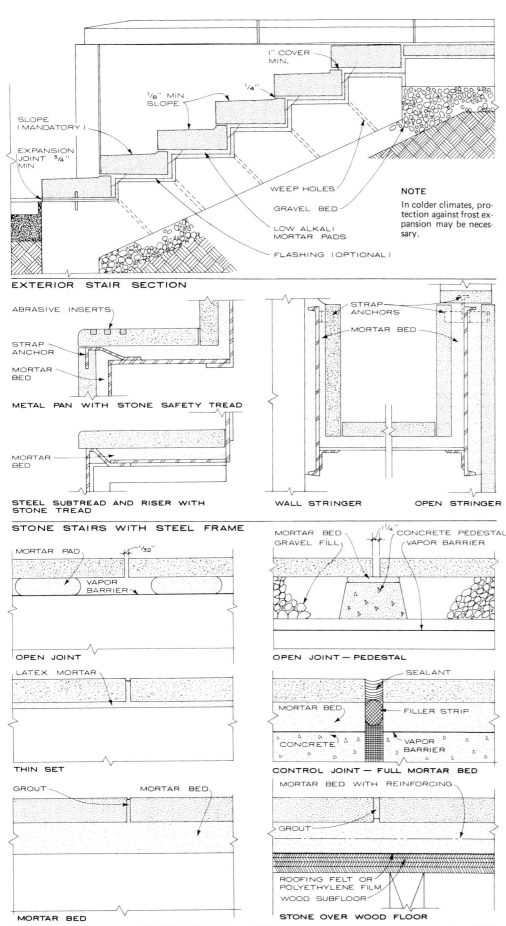

EXTERIOR STAIR SECTION

NOTE

In colder climates, protection against frost expansion may be necessary.

METAL PAN WITH STONE SAFETY TREAD

STEEL SUBTREAD AND RISER WITH STONE TREAD

STONE STAIRS WITH STEEL FRAME

WALL STRINGER   **OPEN STRINGER**

OPEN JOINT

THIN SET

MORTAR BED

STONE FLOORING

OPEN JOINT — PEDESTAL

CONTROL JOINT — FULL MORTAR BED

STONE OVER WOOD FLOOR

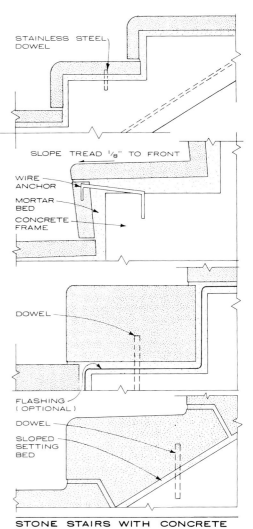

STONE STAIRS WITH CONCRETE FRAME

DESIGN FACTORS FOR STONE STAIRS

Stone used for steps should have an abrasive resistance of 10 (measured on a scale from a minimum of 6 to a maximum of 17). When different varieties of stone are used, their abrasive hardness should be similar to prevent uneven wear.

Dowels and anchoring devices should be noncorrosive.

If a safety tread is not used on stairs, a light bush hammered soft finish or nonslip finish is recommended.

To prevent future staining, dampproof the face of all concrete or concrete block, specify low alkali mortar, and provide adequate drainage (slopes and weepholes).

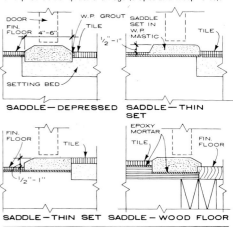

SADDLE — DEPRESSED   **SADDLE — THIN SET**

SADDLE — THIN SET   **SADDLE — WOOD FLOOR**

STONE THRESHOLDS

Building Stone Institute; New York, New York
George M. Whiteside, III, AIA, and James D. Lloyd; Kennett Square, Pennsylvania
Alexander Keyes; Darrel Downing Rippeteau, Architect; Washington, D.C.

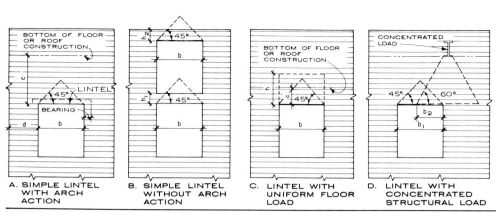

A. SIMPLE LINTEL WITH ARCH ACTION

B. SIMPLE LINTEL WITHOUT ARCH ACTION

C. LINTEL WITH UNIFORM FLOOR LOAD

D. LINTEL WITH CONCENTRATED STRUCTURAL LOAD

NOTES FOR LINTEL CONDITIONS

A. Simple lintel with arch action carries wall load only in triangle above opening:

$$c \geq b \quad \text{and} \quad d \geq b$$

B. Simple lintel without arch action carries less wall load than triangle above opening:

$$h_1 \text{ or } h_2 < 0.6b$$

C. Lintel with uniform floor load carries both wall and floor loads in rectangle above opening:

$$c < b$$

D. Lintel with concentrated load carries wall and portion of concentrated load distributed along length b_2.

LINTEL LOADING CONDITIONS (CONSULT STRUCTURAL HANDBOOK FOR DESIGN FORMULAS)

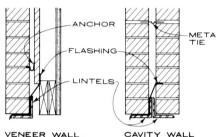

VENEER WALL   CAVITY WALL

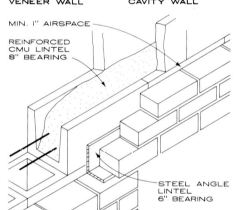

BRICK AND CMU WALL

LOOSE STEEL LINTELS FOR MASONRY WALLS

ALLOWABLE UNIFORM SUPERIMPOSED LOAD (IN LB) PER LINEAR FOOT FOR STEEL ANGLE LINTELS

HORIZONTAL LEG	ANGLE SIZE	WEIGHT PER FT. (LB)	SPAN IN FEET (CENTER TO CENTER OF REQUIRED BEARING)									
			3	4	5	6	7	8	9	10	11	12
$3\frac{1}{2}$	$3 \times 3\frac{1}{2} \times \frac{1}{4}$	5.4	956	517	262	149	91	59				
	$\times \frac{5}{16}$	6.6	1166	637	323	184	113	73				
	$\times \frac{3}{8}$	7.9	1377	756	384	218	134	87	59			
$3\frac{1}{2}$	$3\frac{1}{2} \times 3\frac{1}{2} \times \frac{1}{4}$	5.8	1281	718	406	232	144	94	65			
	$\times \frac{5}{16}$	7.2	1589	891	507	290	179	118	80			
	$\times \frac{3}{8}$	8.5	1947	1091	589	336	208	137	93	66		
$3\frac{1}{2}$	$4 \times 3\frac{1}{2} \times \frac{1}{4}$	6.2	1622	910	580	338	210	139	95	68		
	$\times \frac{5}{16}$	7.7	2110	1184	734	421	262	173	119	85	62	
	$\times \frac{3}{8}$	9.1	2434	1365	855	490	305	201	138	98	71	
	$\times \frac{7}{16}$	10.6	2760	1548	978	561	349	230	158	113	82	60
4	$4 \times 4 \times \frac{7}{16}$	11.3	2920	1638	1018	584	363	239	164	116	85	62
	$\times \frac{1}{2}$	12.8	3246	1820	1141	654	407	268	185	131	95	70
$3\frac{1}{2}$	$5 \times 3\frac{1}{2} \times \frac{1}{4}$	7.0	2600	1460	932	636	398	264	184	132	97	73
	$\times \frac{5}{16}$	8.7	3087	1733	1106	765	486	323	224	161	119	89
	$\times \frac{7}{16}$	12.0	4224	2371	1513	1047	655	435	302	217	160	120
	$\times \frac{1}{2}$	13.6	4875	2736	1746	1177	736	488	339	244	179	134
$3\frac{1}{2}$	$6 \times 3\frac{1}{2} \times \frac{1}{4}$	7.9	3577	2009	1283	888	650	439	306	221	164	124
	$\times \frac{5}{16}$	9.8	4390	2465	1574	1090	798	538	375	271	201	151
	$\times \frac{3}{8}$	11.7	5200	2922	1865	1291	945	636	443	320	237	179
	$\times \frac{1}{2}$	15.3	6828	3834	2448	1695	1228	818	570	412	305	230
4	$6 \times 4 \times \frac{1}{4}$	8.3	3739	2099	1340	928	679	458	319	231	171	129
	$\times \frac{5}{16}$	10.3	4552	2556	1632	1129	827	562	391	283	209	158
	$\times \frac{3}{8}$	12.3	5365	3012	1923	1331	974	665	463	335	248	187
	$\times \frac{7}{16}$	14.3	6178	3469	2214	1533	1122	764	532	384	284	215
	$\times \frac{1}{2}$	16.2	6990	3925	2506	1734	1270	857	597	431	319	241

NOTE: Allowable loads to the left of the heavy line are governed by moment, and to the right by deflection. $F_y = 36,000$ psi. Maximum deflection $\frac{1}{700}$. Consult structural engineer for long spans.

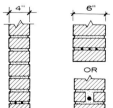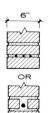

CONCRETE

COMMON U-BLOCK

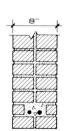

CMU

DOUBLE CORE

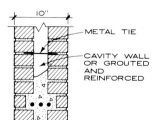

BEARING END DETAIL

PRECAST CONCRETE AND CMU LINTELS

NUMBER AND SIZE OF REBARS REQUIRED

Precast Concrete and Reinforced CMU Lintels (no superimposed loads)

LINTEL TYPE	CLEAR SPAN (MAX)	8" BRICK WALL (80 LB/SQ FT)	8" CMU WALL (50 LB/SQ FT)
Reinforced concrete (7⅝" square section)	4'-0"	4-#3	4-#3
	6'-0"	4-#4	4-#3
	8'-0"	4-#5	4-#4
CMU (7⅝" square section) nominal 8 x 8 x 16 unit	4'-0"	2-#4	2-#3
	6'-0"	2-#5	2-#4
	8'-0"	2-#6	2-#5

NOTE: fc' = 3000 psi concrete and grout
fy = 60,000 psi

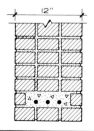

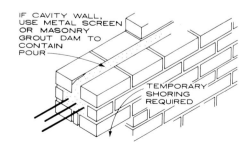

REINFORCED BRICK LINTELS

Christine Beall, AIA, CCS; Austin, Texas
Metz, Train, Olson and Youngren, Inc.; Chicago, Illinois

UNIT MASONRY

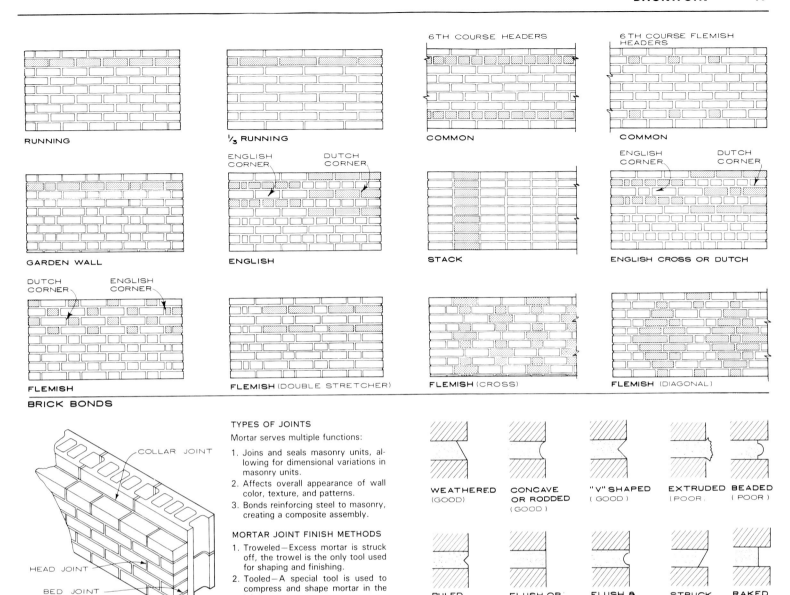

RUNNING

⅓ RUNNING

COMMON
6TH COURSE HEADERS

COMMON
6TH COURSE FLEMISH HEADERS

GARDEN WALL

ENGLISH
ENGLISH CORNER — DUTCH CORNER

STACK

ENGLISH CROSS OR DUTCH
ENGLISH CORNER — DUTCH CORNER

FLEMISH
DUTCH CORNER — ENGLISH CORNER

FLEMISH (DOUBLE STRETCHER)

FLEMISH (CROSS)

FLEMISH (DIAGONAL)

BRICK BONDS

COLLAR JOINT

HEAD JOINT

BED JOINT

TERMS APPLIED TO JOINTS

BRICK JOINTS

TYPES OF JOINTS

Mortar serves multiple functions:

1. Joins and seals masonry units, allowing for dimensional variations in masonry units.
2. Affects overall appearance of wall color, texture, and patterns.
3. Bonds reinforcing steel to masonry, creating a composite assembly.

MORTAR JOINT FINISH METHODS

1. Troweled—Excess mortar is struck off, the trowel is the only tool used for shaping and finishing.
2. Tooled—A special tool is used to compress and shape mortar in the joint.

WEATHERED (GOOD)   CONCAVE OR RODDED (GOOD)   "V" SHAPED (GOOD)   EXTRUDED (POOR)   BEADED (POOR)

RULED (FAIR)   FLUSH OR PLAIN CUT (FAIR)   FLUSH & RODDED (FAIR)   STRUCK (POOR)   RAKED (POOR)

TYPES OF JOINTS (WEATHERABILITY)

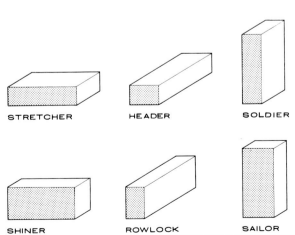

STRETCHER   HEADER   SOLDIER

SHINER   ROWLOCK   SAILOR

TERMS APPLIED TO VARIED BRICK POSITIONS

SIZES OF MODULAR BRICK

UNIT DESIGNATION	NOMINAL DIMENSIONS			MODULAR COURSING
	THICKNESS	HEIGHT	LENGTH	
MODULAR	4″	2⅔″	8″	3C = 8″
ENGINEER	4″	3⅕″	8″	5C = 16″
ECONOMY	4″	4″	8″	1C = 4″
DOUBLE	4″	5⅓″	8″	3C = 16″
ROMAN	4″	2″	12″	2C = 4″
NORMAN	4″	2⅔″	12″	3C = 8″
NORWEGIAN	4″	3⅕″	12″	5C = 16″
UTILITY[1]	4″	4″	12″	1C = 4″
TRIPLE	4″	5⅓″	12″	3C = 16″
SCR BRICK	6″	2⅔″	12″	3C = 8″
6″ NORWEGIAN	6″	3⅕″	12″	5C = 16″
6″ JUMBO	6″	4″	12″	1C = 4″
8″ JUMBO	8″	4″	12″	1C = 4″
8″ SQUARE	4″	8″	8″	1C = 8″
12″ SQUARE	4″	12″	12″	1C = 12″

[1] Also called Norman Economy, General and King Norman.
*For special shapes contact local brick manufacturers.

Brick Institute of America; Reston, Virginia
Raso·Greaves An Architecture Corporation; Waco, Texas

UNIT MASONRY **4**

STANDARD MODULAR
4″ x 2 2/3″ x 8″ NOMINAL

BRICK SIZES:
* For 3/8″ Joint   3 5/8″ x 2 1/4″ x 7 5/8″
** For 1/2″ Joint   3 1/2″ x 2 3/16″ x 7 1/2″

NORMAN
4″ x 2 2/3″ x 12″ NOMINAL

BRICK SIZES:
* For 3/8″ Joint   3 5/8″ x 2 1/4″ x 11 5/8″
** For 1/2″ Joint   3 1/2″ x 2 3/16″ x 11 1/2″

SCR BRICK
6″ x 2 2/3″ x 12″ NOMINAL
    For 1/2″ Joint   5 1/2″ x 2 1/8″ x 11 1/2″

Joint selected determines brick size
3 courses = 2 modules (8″)

NOMINAL HEIGHT OF 2 2/3″ COURSES

Course	Height	Course	Height
31	6′ – 10 2/3″	61	13′ – 6 2/3″
30	6′ – 8″	60	13′ – 4″
29	6′ – 5 1/3″	59	13′ – 1 1/3″
28	6′ – 2 2/3″	58	12′ – 10 2/3″
27	6′ – 0″	57	12′ – 8″
26	5′ – 9 1/3″	56	12′ – 5 1/3″
25	5′ – 6 2/3″	55	12′ – 2 2/3″
24	5′ – 4″	54	12′ – 0″
23	5′ – 1 1/3″	53	11′ – 9 1/3″
22	4′ – 10 2/3″	52	11′ – 6 2/3″
21	4′ – 8″	51	11′ – 4″
20	4′ – 5 1/3″	50	11′ – 1 1/3″
19	4′ – 2 2/3″	49	10′ – 10 2/3″
18	4′ – 0″	48	10′ 8″
17	3′ – 9 1/3″	47	10′ – 5 1/3″
16	3′ – 6 2/3″	46	10′ – 2 2/3″
15	3′ – 4″	45	10′ – 0″
14	3′ – 1 1/3″	44	9′ – 9 1/3″
13	2′ – 10 2/3″	43	9′ – 6 2/3″
12	2′ – 8″	42	9′ – 4″
11	2′ – 5 1/3″	41	9′ – 1 1/3″
10	2′ – 2 1/3″	40	8′ – 10 2/3″
9	2′ – 0″	39	8′ – 8″
8	1′ – 9 1/3″	38	8′ – 5 1/3″
7	1′ – 6 2/3″	37	8′ – 2 2/3″
6	1′ – 4″	36	8′ – 0″
5	1′ – 1 1/3″	35	7′ – 9 1/3″
4	10 2/3″	34	7′ – 6 2/3″
3	8″	33	7′ – 4″
2	5 1/3″	32	7′ – 1 1/3″
1	2 2/3″		

ENGINEER
4″ x 3 1/5″ x 8″ NOMINAL

BRICK SIZES:
* For 3/8″ Joint   3 5/8″ x 2 13/16″ x 7 5/8″
   For 1/2″ Joint   3 1/2″ x 2 11/16″ x 7 1/2″

Joint selected determines brick size.
5 courses = 4 modules (16″).

NOMINAL HEIGHTS OF 3 1/5″ COURSES

Course	Height	Course	Height
29	7′ – 8 4/5″	59	15′ – 8 4/5″
28	7′ – 5 3/5″	58	15′ – 5 3/5″
27	7′ – 2 2/5″	57	15′ – 2 2/5″
26	6′ – 11 1/5″	56	14′ – 11 1/5″
25	6′ – 8″	55	14′ – 8″
24	6′ – 4 4/5″	54	14′ – 4 4/5″
23	6′ – 1 3/5″	53	14′ – 1 3/5″
22	5′ – 10 2/5″	52	13′ – 10 2/5″
21	5′ – 7 1/3″	51	13′ – 7 1/5″
20	5′ – 4″	50	13′ – 4″
19	5′ – 0 4/5″	49	13′ – 0 4/5″
18	4′ – 9 3/5″	48	12′ – 9 3/5″
17	4′ – 6 2/5″	47	12′ – 6 2/5″
16	4′ – 3 1/5″	46	12′ – 3 1/5″
15	4′ – 0″	45	12′ – 0″
14	3′ – 8 4/5″	44	11′ – 8 4/5″
13	3′ – 5 3/5″	43	11′ – 5 3/5″
12	3′ – 2 2/5″	42	11′ – 2 2/5″
11	2′ – 11 1/5″	41	10′ – 11 1/5″
10	2′ – 8″	40	10′ – 8″
9	2′ – 4 4/5″	39	10′ – 4 4/5″
8	2′ – 1 3/5″	38	10′ – 1 3/5″
7	1′ – 10 2/5″	37	9′ – 10 2/5″
6	1′ – 7 1/5″	36	9′ – 7 1/5″
5	1′ – 4″	35	9′ – 4″
4	1′ – 0 4/5″	34	9′ – 0 4/5″
3	9 3/5″	33	8′ – 9 3/5″
2	6 2/5″	32	8′ – 6 2/5″
1	3 1/5″	31	8′ – 3 1/5″
		30	8′ – 0″

ECONOMY
4″ x 4″ x 8″ NOMINAL

BRICK SIZES:
* For 3/8″ Joint   3 5/8″ x 3 5/8″ x 7 5/8″
** For 1/2″ Joint   3 1/2″ x 3 1/2″ x 7 1/2″

UTILITY
4″ x 4″ x 12″ NOMINAL

BRICK SIZES:
   For 3/8″ Joint   3 5/8″ x 3 5/8″ x 11 5/8″
   For 1/2″ Joint   3 1/2″ x 3 1/2″ x 11 1/2″

Joint selected determines brick size
1 course = 1 module (4″)

NOMINAL HEIGHTS OF 4″ COURSES

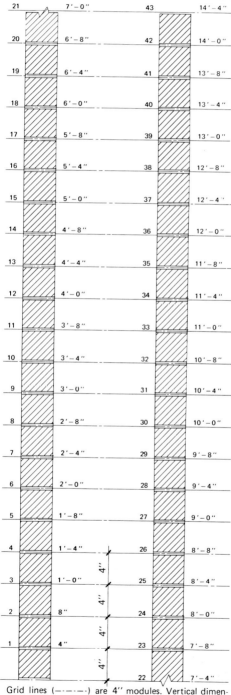

Course	Height	Course	Height
21	7′ – 0″	43	14′ – 4″
20	6′ – 8″	42	14′ – 0″
19	6′ – 4″	41	13′ – 8″
18	6′ – 0″	40	13′ – 4″
17	5′ – 8″	39	13′ – 0″
16	5′ – 4″	38	12′ – 8″
15	5′ – 0″	37	12′ – 4″
14	4′ – 8″	36	12′ – 0″
13	4′ – 4″	35	11′ – 8″
12	4′ – 0″	34	11′ – 4″
11	3′ – 8″	33	11′ – 0″
10	3′ – 4″	32	10′ – 8″
9	3′ – 0″	31	10′ – 4″
8	2′ – 8″	30	10′ – 0″
7	2′ – 4″	29	9′ – 8″
6	2′ – 0″	28	9′ – 4″
5	1′ – 8″	27	9′ – 0″
4	1′ – 4″	26	8′ – 8″
3	1′ – 0″	25	8′ – 4″
2	8″	24	8′ – 0″
1	4″	23	7′ – 8″
		22	7′ – 4″

NOTES

Not all sizes made in all sections of U.S.; check with local manufacturers for sizes available.

Brick Institute of America; Reston, Virginia

*3/8″ Joint used for facing brick.
**1/2″ Joint used for glazed and structural units and building brick.

Grid lines (—·—·—) are 4″ modules. Vertical dimensions are from bottom of mortar joint to bottom of mortar joint.

VERTICAL BRICK COURSES

NUMBER OF BRICKS AND JOINTS	HEIGHT 3/8" JOINTS	HEIGHT 1/2" JOINTS
1 brk. & 1 jt.	2 5/8"	2 3/4"
2 brks. & 2 jts.	5 1/4"	5 1/2"
3 brks. & 3 jts.	7 7/8"	8 1/4"
4 brks. & 4 jts.	10 1/2"	11"
5 brks. & 5 jts.	1'- 1 1/8"	1'- 1 3/4"
6 brks. & 6 jts.	1'- 3 3/4"	1'- 4 1/2"
7 brks. & 7 jts.	1'- 6 3/8"	1'- 7 1/4"
8 brks. & 8 jts.	1'- 9"	1'-10"
9 brks. & 9 jts.	1'-11 5/8"	2'- 0 3/4"
10 brks. & 10 jts.	2'- 2 1/4"	2'- 3 1/2"
11 brks. & 11 jts.	2'- 4 7/8"	2'- 6 1/4"
12 brks. & 12 jts.	2'- 7 1/2"	2'- 9"
13 brks. & 13 jts.	2'-10 1/8"	2'-11 3/4"
14 brks. & 14 jts.	3'- 0 3/4"	3'- 2 1/2"
15 brks. & 15 jts.	3'- 3 5/8"	3'- 5 1/4"
16 brks. & 16 jts.	3'- 6"	3'- 8"
17 brks. & 17 jts.	3'- 8 5/8"	3'-10 3/4"
18 brks. & 18 jts.	3'-11 1/4"	4'- 1 1/2"
19 brks. & 19 jts.	4'- 1 7/8"	4'- 4 1/4"
20 brks. & 20 jts.	4'- 4 1/2"	4'- 7"
21 brks. & 21 jts.	4'- 7 1/8"	4'- 9 3/4"
22 brks. & 22 jts.	4'- 9 3/4"	5'- 0 1/2"
23 brks. & 23 jts.	5'- 0 3/8"	5'- 3 1/4"
24 brks. & 24 jts.	5'- 3"	5'- 6"
25 brks. & 25 jts.	5'- 5 5/8"	5'- 8 3/4"
26 brks. & 26 jts.	5'- 8 1/4"	5'-11 1/2"
27 brks. & 27 jts.	5'-10 7/8"	6'- 2 1/4"
28 brks. & 28 jts.	6'- 1 1/2"	6'- 5"
29 brks. & 29 jts.	6'- 4 1/8"	6'- 7 3/4"
30 brks. & 30 jts.	6'- 6 3/4"	6'-10 1/2"
31 brks. & 31 jts.	6'- 9 3/8"	7'- 1 1/4"
32 brks. & 32 jts.	7'- 0"	7'- 4"
33 brks. & 33 jts.	7'- 2 5/8"	7'- 6 3/4"
34 brks. & 34 jts.	7'- 5 1/4"	7'- 9 1/2"
35 brks. & 35 jts.	7'- 7 7/8"	8'- 0 1/4"
36 brks. & 36 jts.	7'-10 1/2"	8'- 3"
37 brks. & 37 jts.	8'- 1 1/8"	8'- 5 3/4"
38 brks. & 38 jts.	8'- 3 3/4"	8'- 8 1/2"
39 brks. & 39 jts.	8'- 6 3/8"	8'-11 1/4"
40 brks. & 40 jts.	8'- 9"	9'- 2"
41 brks. & 41 jts.	8'-11 5/8"	9'- 4 3/4"
42 brks. & 42 jts.	9'- 2 1/4"	9'- 7 1/2"
43 brks. & 43 jts.	9'- 4 7/8"	9'-10 1/4"
44 brks. & 44 jts.	9'- 7 1/2"	10'- 1"
45 brks. & 45 jts.	9'-10 1/8"	10'- 3 3/4"
46 brks. & 46 jts.	10'- 0 3/4"	10'- 6 1/2"
47 brks. & 47 jts.	10'- 3 3/8"	10'- 9 1/4"
48 brks. & 48 jts.	10'- 6"	11'- 0"
49 brks. & 49 jts.	10'- 8 5/8"	11'- 2 3/4"
50 brks. & 50 jts.	10'-11 1/4"	11'- 5 1/2"
51 brks. & 51 jts.	11'- 1 7/8"	11'- 8 1/4"
52 brks. & 52 jts.	11'- 4 1/2"	11'-11"
53 brks. & 53 jts.	11'- 7 1/8"	12'- 1 3/4"
54 brks. & 54 jts.	11'- 9 3/4"	12'- 4 1/2"
55 brks. & 55 jts.	12'- 0 3/8"	12'- 7 1/4"
56 brks. & 56 jts.	12'- 3"	12'-10"
57 brks. & 57 jts.	12'- 5 5/8"	13'- 0 3/4"
58 brks. & 58 jts.	12'- 8 1/4"	13'- 3 1/2"
59 brks. & 59 jts.	12'-10 7/8"	13'- 6 1/4"
60 brks. & 60 jts.	13'- 1 1/2"	13'- 9"
61 brks. & 61 jts.	13'- 4 1/8"	13'-11 3/4"
62 brks. & 62 jts.	13'- 6 3/4"	14'- 2 1/2"
63 brks. & 63 jts.	13'- 9 3/8"	14'- 5 1/4"
64 brks. & 64 jts.	14'- 0"	14'- 8"
65 brks. & 65 jts.	14'- 2 5/8"	14'-10 3/4"
66 brks. & 66 jts.	14'- 5 1/4"	15'- 1 1/2"
67 brks. & 67 jts.	14'- 7 7/8"	15'- 4 1/4"
68 brks. & 68 jts.	14'-10 1/2"	15'- 7"
69 brks. & 69 jts.	15'- 1 1/8"	15'- 9 3/4"
70 brks. & 70 jts.	15'- 3 3/4"	16'- 0 1/2"
71 brks. & 71 jts.	15'- 6 3/8"	16'- 3 1/4"
72 brks. & 72 jts.	15'- 9"	16'- 6"
73 brks. & 73 jts.	15'-11 5/8"	16'- 8 3/4"
74 brks. & 74 jts.	16'- 2 1/4"	16'-11 1/2"
75 brks. & 75 jts.	16'- 4 7/8"	17'- 2 1/4"
76 brks. & 76 jts.	16'- 7 1/2"	17'- 5"

Brick Institute of America; Reston, Virginia

HORIZONTAL BRICK COURSES

NUMBER OF BRICKS AND JOINTS	LENGTH OF COURSE 3/8" JOINTS	LENGTH OF COURSE 1/2" JOINTS
1 brk. & 0 jt.	0'- 8"	0'- 8"
1 1/2 brks. & 1 jt.	1'- 0 3/8"	1'- 0 1/2"
2 brks. & 1 jt.	1'- 4 3/8"	1'- 4 1/2"
2 1/2 brks. & 2 jts.	1'- 8 3/4"	1'- 9"
3 brks. & 2 jts.	2'- 0 3/4"	2'- 1"
3 1/2 brks. & 3 jts.	2'- 5 1/8"	2'- 5 1/2"
4 brks. & 3 jts.	2'- 9 1/8"	2'- 9 1/2"
4 1/2 brks. & 4 jts.	3'- 1 1/2"	3'- 2"
5 brks. & 4 jts.	3'- 5 1/2"	3'- 6"
5 1/2 brks. & 5 jts.	3'- 9 7/8"	3'-10 1/2"
6 brks. & 5 jts.	4'- 1 7/8"	4'- 2 1/2"
6 1/2 brks. & 6 jts.	4'- 6 1/4"	4'- 7"
7 brks. & 6 jts.	4'-10 1/4"	4'-11"
7 1/2 brks. & 7 jts.	5'- 2 5/8"	5'- 3 1/2"
8 brks. & 7 jts.	5'- 6 5/8"	5'- 7 1/2"
8 1/2 brks. & 8 jts.	5'-11"	6'- 0"
9 brks. & 8 jts.	6'- 3"	6'- 4"
9 1/2 brks. & 9 jts.	6'- 7 3/8"	6'- 8 1/2"
10 brks. & 9 jts.	6'-11 3/8"	7'- 0 1/2"
10 1/2 brks. & 10 jts.	7'- 3 3/4"	7'- 5"
11 brks. & 10 jts.	7'- 7 3/4"	7'- 9"
11 1/2 brks. & 11 jts.	8'- 0 1/8"	8'- 1 1/2"
12 brks. & 11 jts.	8'- 4 1/8"	8'- 5 1/2"
12 1/2 brks. & 12 jts.	8'- 8 1/2"	8'-10"
13 brks. & 12 jts.	9'- 0 1/2"	9'- 2"
13 1/2 brks. & 13 jts.	9'- 4 7/8"	9'- 6 1/2"
14 brks. & 13 jts.	9'- 8 7/8"	9'-10 1/2"
14 1/2 brks. & 14 jts.	10'- 1 1/4"	10'- 3"
15 brks. & 14 jts.	10'- 5 1/4"	10'- 7"
15 1/2 brks. & 15 jts.	10'- 9 5/8"	10'-11 1/2"
16 brks. & 15 jts.	11'- 1 5/8"	11'- 3 1/2"
16 1/2 brks. & 16 jts.	11'- 6"	11'- 8"
17 brks. & 16 jts.	11'-10"	12'- 0"
17 1/2 brks. & 17 jts.	12'- 2 3/8"	12'- 4 1/2"
18 brks. & 17 jts.	12'- 6 3/8"	12'- 8 1/2"
18 1/2 brks. & 18 jts.	12'-10 3/4"	13'- 1"
19 brks. & 18 jts.	13'- 2 3/4"	13'- 5"
19 1/2 brks. & 19 jts.	13'- 7 1/8"	13'- 9 1/2"
20 brks. & 19 jts.	13'-11 1/8"	14'- 1 1/2"
20 1/2 brks. & 20 jts.	14'- 3 1/2"	14'- 6"
21 brks. & 20 jts.	14'- 7 1/2"	14'-10"
21 1/2 brks. & 21 jts.	14'-11 7/8"	15'- 2 1/2"
22 brks. & 21 jts.	15'- 3 7/8"	15'- 6 1/2"
22 1/2 brks. & 22 jts.	15'- 8 1/4"	15'-11"
23 brks. & 22 jts.	16'- 0 1/4"	16'- 3"
23 1/2 brks. & 23 jts.	16'- 4 5/8"	16'- 7 1/2"
24 brks. & 23 jts.	16'- 8 5/8"	16'-11 1/2"
24 1/2 brks. & 24 jts.	17'- 1"	17'- 4"
25 brks. & 24 jts.	17'- 5"	17'- 8"
25 1/2 brks. & 25 jts.	17'- 9 3/8"	18'- 0 1/2"
26 brks. & 25 jts.	18'- 1 3/8"	18'- 4 1/2"
26 1/2 brks. & 26 jts.	18'- 5 3/4"	18'- 9"
27 brks. & 26 jts.	18'- 9 3/4"	19'- 1"
27 1/2 brks. & 27 jts.	19'- 2 1/8"	19'- 5 1/2"
28 brks. & 27 jts.	19'- 6 1/8"	19'- 9 1/2"
28 1/2 brks. & 28 jts.	19'-10 1/2"	20'- 2"
29 brks. & 28 jts.	20'- 2 1/2"	20'- 6"
29 1/2 brks. & 29 jts.	20'- 6 7/8"	20'-10 1/2"
30 brks. & 29 jts.	20'-10 7/8"	21'- 2 1/2"
30 1/2 brks. & 30 jts.	21'- 3 1/4"	21'- 7"
31 brks. & 30 jts.	21'- 7 1/4"	21'-11"
31 1/2 brks. & 31 jts.	21'-11 5/8"	22'- 3 1/2"
32 brks. & 31 jts.	22'- 3 5/8"	22'- 7 1/2"
32 1/2 brks. & 32 jts.	22'- 8"	23'- 0"
33 brks. & 32 jts.	23'- 0"	23'- 4"
33 1/2 brks. & 33 jts.	23'- 4 3/8"	23'- 8 1/2"
34 brks. & 33 jts.	23'- 8 3/8"	24'- 0 1/2"
34 1/2 brks. & 34 jts.	24'- 0 3/4"	24'- 5"
35 brks. & 34 jts.	24'- 4 3/4"	24'- 9"
35 1/2 brks. & 35 jts.	24'- 9 1/8"	25'- 1 1/2"
36 brks. & 35 jts.	25'- 1 1/8"	25'- 5 1/2"
36 1/2 brks. & 36 jts.	25'- 5 1/2"	25'-10"
37 brks. & 36 jts.	25'- 9 1/2"	26'- 2"
37 1/2 brks. & 37 jts.	26'- 1 7/8"	26'- 6 1/2"
38 brks. & 37 jts.	26'- 5 7/8"	26'-10 1/2"
38 1/2 brks. & 38 jts.	26'-10 1/4"	27'- 3"

NUMBER OF BRICKS AND JOINTS	LENGTH OF COURSE 3/8" JOINTS	LENGTH OF COURSE 1/2" JOINTS
39 brks. & 38 jts.	27'- 2 1/4"	27'- 7"
39 1/2 brks. & 39 jts.	27'- 6 5/8"	27'-11 1/2"
40 brks. & 39 jts.	27'-10 5/8"	28'- 3 1/2"
40 1/2 brks. & 40 jts.	28'- 3"	28'- 8"
41 brks. & 40 jts.	28'- 7"	29'- 0"
41 1/2 brks. & 41 jts.	28'-11 3/8"	29'- 4 1/2"
42 brks. & 41 jts.	29'- 3 3/8"	29'- 8 1/2"
42 1/2 brks. & 42 jts.	29'- 7 3/4"	30'- 1"
43 brks. & 42 jts.	29'-11 3/4"	30'- 5"
43 1/2 brks. & 43 jts.	30'- 4 1/8"	30'- 9 1/2"
44 brks. & 43 jts.	30'- 8 1/8"	31'- 1 1/2"
44 1/2 brks. & 44 jts.	31'- 0 1/2"	31'- 6"
45 brks. & 44 jts.	31'- 4 1/2"	31'-10"
45 1/2 brks. & 45 jts.	31'- 8 7/8"	32'- 2 1/2"
46 brks. & 45 jts.	32'- 0 7/8"	32'- 6 1/2"
46 1/2 brks. & 46 jts.	32'- 5 1/4"	32'-11"
47 brks. & 46 jts.	32'- 9 1/4"	33'- 3"
47 1/2 brks. & 47 jts.	33'- 1 5/8"	33'- 7 1/2"
48 brks. & 47 jts.	33'- 5 5/8"	33'-11 1/2"
48 1/2 brks. & 48 jts.	33'-10"	34'- 4"
49 brks. & 48 jts.	34'- 2"	34'- 8"
49 1/2 brks. & 49 jts.	34'- 6 3/8"	35'- 0 1/2"
50 brks. & 49 jts.	34'-10 3/8"	35'- 4 1/2"
50 1/2 brks. & 50 jts.	35'- 2 3/4"	35'- 9"
51 brks. & 50 jts.	35'- 6 3/4"	36'- 1"
51 1/2 brks. & 51 jts.	35'-11 1/8"	36'- 5 1/2"
52 brks. & 51 jts.	36'- 3 1/8"	36'- 9 1/2"
52 1/2 brks. & 52 jts.	36'- 7 1/2"	37'- 2"
53 brks. & 52 jts.	36'-11 1/2"	37'- 6"
53 1/2 brks. & 53 jts.	37'- 3 7/8"	37'-10 1/2"
54 brks. & 53 jts.	37'- 7 7/8"	38'- 2 1/2"
54 1/2 brks. & 54 jts.	38'- 0 1/4"	38'- 7"
55 brks. & 54 jts.	38'- 4 1/4"	38'-11"
55 1/2 brks. & 55 jts.	38'- 8 5/8"	39'- 3 1/2"
56 brks. & 55 jts.	39'- 0 5/8"	39'- 7 1/2"
56 1/2 brks. & 56 jts.	39'- 5"	40'- 0"
57 brks. & 56 jts.	39'- 9"	40'- 4"
57 1/2 brks. & 57 jts.	40'- 1 3/8"	40'- 8 1/2"
58 brks. & 57 jts.	40'- 5 3/8"	41'- 0 1/2"
58 1/2 brks. & 58 jts.	40'- 9 3/4"	41'- 5"
59 brks. & 58 jts.	41'- 6 1/8"	42'- 1 1/2"
59 brks. & 58 jts.	41'- 1 3/4"	41'- 9"
59 1/2 brks. & 59 jts.	41'- 6 1/8"	42'- 1 1/2"
60 brks. & 59 jts.	41'-10 1/8"	42'- 5 1/2"

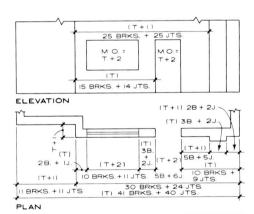

ELEVATION

PLAN

EXAMPLE SHOWING USE OF TABLE

T: Dimensions and number of joints as given in the table, that is, one joint less than the number of bricks.

T + 1: One brick joint added to figure given in the table, that is, the number of bricks is equal to the number of joints.

T + 2: Two brick joints added to figure given in the table, that is, one joint more than the number of bricks.

UNIT MASONRY 4

GENERAL NOTES

1. Fire resistance ratings vary according to the ultimate composition of a masonry wall. Designers should refer to local codes to obtain this information.
2. Straight metal ties should be used in rigidly insulated masonry walls. Metal ties with drips should be used in noninsulated cavity masonry walls.
3. Water and vapor migration into a masonry wall may be controlled by designing a drainage-type wall or a barrier-type wall. Drainage walls are provided with damp course flashing and weep holes 24 in. o.c. just above the flashing. Barrier walls have a mortar-parged or fully grouted joint between wythes. Damp course flashing should also be used with the barrier-type wall. Most water migration occurs at mortar joints. Mortar

selection should be based on the "initial" rate of absorption of the brick selected, as well as on regional weather conditions; mortars containing air-entering agents should be avoided.
4. All anchors, ties, and attachments should be stainless steel or of corrosion-resistant metal or be coated with such metal.
5. Block and brick quality varies throughout the industry. Masonry units should be chosen on the basis of availability, historical product quality of the manufacturer, strength, cost, and appearance. As with most construction assemblies, the final product will only be as good as the design and installation.

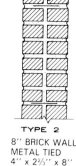

TYPE 1
4'' BRICK WALL
MODULAR BRICK
4'' x 2⅔'' x 8''

TYPE 3
CMU WALL

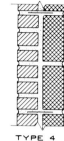

TYPE 2
8'' BRICK WALL
METAL TIED
4'' x 2⅔'' x 8''

TYPE 4
4'' MODULAR BRICK
4'' CMU WALL
METAL TIED

HEIGHT/THICKNESS RATIO OF MASONRY WALLS

BEARING CONDITION	TYPE 1	TYPE 2	TYPE 3
Maximum bearing wall height[1]	$\frac{H}{T} \leq 18$	$\frac{H}{T} \leq 18$	$\frac{H}{T} \leq 18$
Maximum nonbearing wall height[1]	$\frac{H}{T} \leq 20$	$\frac{H}{T} \leq 20$	$\frac{H}{T} \leq 20$
	TYPE 4	TYPE 5	TYPE 6
Maximum bearing wall height[1]	$\frac{H}{T} \leq 18$	$\frac{H}{T} \leq 25$	$\frac{H}{T} \leq 25$
Maximum nonbearing wall height[1]	$\frac{H}{T} \leq 20$	$\frac{H}{T} \leq 48$	$\frac{H}{T} \leq 48$
	TYPE 7	TYPE 8	TYPE 9
Maximum bearing wall height[1]	$\frac{H}{T} \leq 25$	$\frac{H}{T} \leq 18^2$	$\frac{H}{T} \leq 18^2$
Maximum nonbearing wall height[1]	$\frac{H}{T} \leq 48$	$\frac{H}{T} \leq 20^2$	$\frac{H}{T} \leq 20^2$

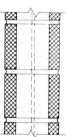

TYPE 5
REINFORCED
CMU WALL

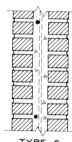

TYPE 6
REINFORCED
BRICK MASONRY
WALL (RBM)

NOTES

1. Maximum unsupported wall heights should be determined by local codes. Formulas given are for planning purposes only and solutions should be verified by a structural engineer. In the formulas,
   H = height of wall (in feet)
   T = thickness of wall (in feet)

2. Resultant thickness is the net wall thickness of masonry units. Up to a 2 in. cavity may be used with this formula as long as the wythes are tied together with cavity wall ties.
3. Empirical formulas are taken from the 1982 Uniform Building Code.

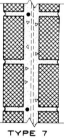

TYPE 7
REINFORCED
CMU WALL

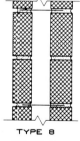

TYPE 8
CAVITY WALL
SPLIT FACE CMU
AND CMU

PROPERTIES OF MASONRY WALL COMPONENTS

MATERIAL	WEIGHT (LB/SQ FT)	QUANTITY (100 SQ FT)[1]	U VALUE[2]	STC
4 in. brick	40	675 units	2.27	39
4 in. CMU	22	113 units	0.71	40
6 in. CMU	32	113 units	0.65	44
8 in. CMU	35	113 units	0.57	45
10 in. CMU	45	113 units	0.50	50
12 in. CMU	55	113 units	0.47	55
2 in. vermiculite (loose)	1.16	116 lb	0.22	—
2 in. perlite (loose)	1.08	108 lb	0.18	—
2 in. polystyrene (rigid)	0.58	100 sq ft	0.09	—
2 in. polyurethane (rigid)	0.25	100 sq ft	0.08	—
2 in. Airspace	—	—	0.40	4
Air film exterior[3]	—	—	4.76	—
Air film interior[4]	—	—	1.39	—

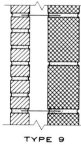

TYPE 9
CAVITY
WALL—BRICK
AND CMU

WALL TYPES

NOTES

1. Waste is not included, as this will vary with the job. A waste factor of 2–5% is often applied for masonry units.
2. U values are tabulated from various sources and represent an average value for the given material. Check with manufacturers for actual U values.
3. U value given is an average of both winter and summer winds.
4. U value given is an average of still air on all surface positions and direction of heat flow.

Charles L. Goodman, AIA; Everett I. Brown Company; Indianapolis, Indiana
Robert Joseph Sangiamo, AIA; New York, New York
Davis, Brody & Associates; New York, New York

International Conference of Building Officials, see data sources

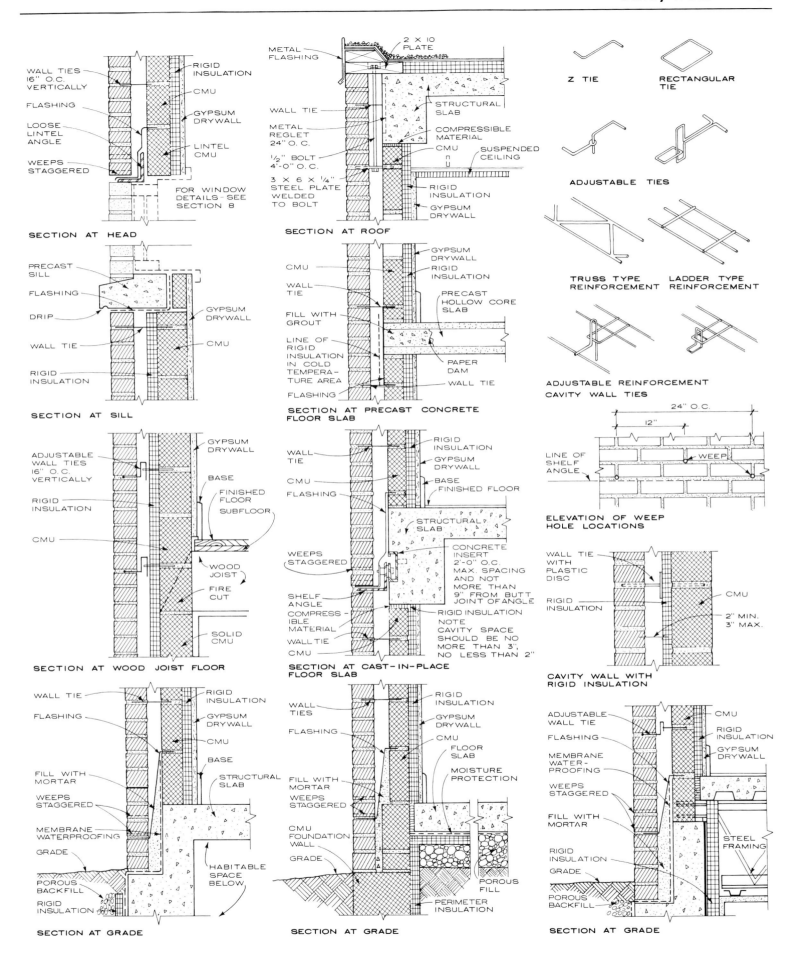

SECTION AT HEAD

SECTION AT ROOF

Z TIE

RECTANGULAR TIE

ADJUSTABLE TIES

TRUSS TYPE REINFORCEMENT

LADDER TYPE REINFORCEMENT

ADJUSTABLE REINFORCEMENT CAVITY WALL TIES

SECTION AT SILL

SECTION AT PRECAST CONCRETE FLOOR SLAB

ELEVATION OF WEEP HOLE LOCATIONS

SECTION AT WOOD JOIST FLOOR

SECTION AT CAST-IN-PLACE FLOOR SLAB

CAVITY WALL WITH RIGID INSULATION

SECTION AT GRADE

SECTION AT GRADE

SECTION AT GRADE

Robert J. Sangiamo, AIA; New York, New York
Davis, Brody & Associates; New York, New York

UNIT MASONRY 4

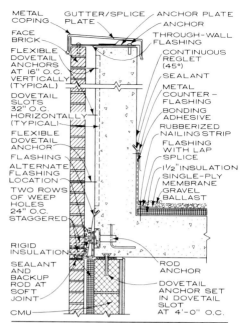

CAVITY WALL AT CONCRETE PARAPET

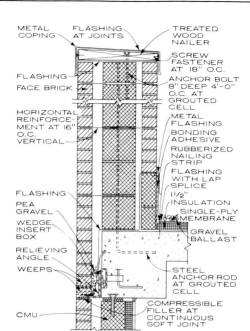

PARAPET WALL WITH DOUBLE CAVITY

PARAPET WALL WITH STEEL REINFORCING

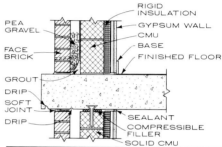

EXPOSED SLAB DETAIL

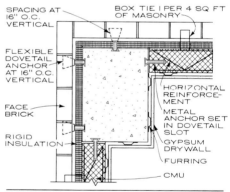

DOVETAIL ANCHORS AT CORNER

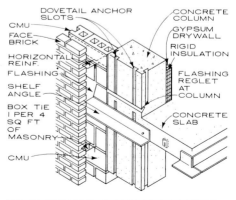

SHELF ANGLE AT CORNER COLUMN

GENERAL NOTES

1. Relieving angles should be designed to limit deflection to $1/700$ of span between wedge inset centerlines.
2. The horizontal reinforcing whose primary purposes are to prevent cracks in the mortar of the CMU wythe of masonry and aid in spanning wind load to supports should also be used to attach the brick masonry ties. The ties are required only to transfer forces due to positive and negative wind pressure on the brick wythe of the CMU wythe.
3. "Z" type masonry ties should not be used with hollow CMU masonry.
4. Type S mortar should be used where the winds are greater than 80 miles per hour.
5. Exterior brick should conform to the requirements of ASTM-216.
6. The exterior wythe of brick masonry should be panelized by the use of horizontal and vertical control joints.
7. Control joint sizes should accommodate the following Brick Institute of America Formula Technical Note 18A:

$$w = [0.0002 + 0.000004 \ (T \ \text{max.} - T \ \text{min.})] \ L$$

where: L = length of wall in inches
   T max. = maximum mean wall temperature in degrees Fahrenheit
   T min. = minimum mean wall temperature in degrees Fahrenheit
   w = total expansion of wall in inches

Actual joint width in masonry is determined by anticipated movement times the limit of compressibility and expandability of the sealant. Typically for polysulfide sealants one multiplies anticipated movement by four, and for urethane sealants by two. Consult manufacturers' recommendations for the actual products proposed for use.

8. When the structural frame of a building is of reinforced concrete, horizontal control joints must also accommodate the dimensional change due to anticipated shrinkage and creep of the concrete columns.
9. Aligning vertical control joints with the window jambs is good practice for economy.
10. The number of vertical control joints required should be doubled at the parapet, and vertical control joints should also be added at 5 to 10 ft from each corner.
11. CMU masonry and brick masonry should not be exposed on the same parapet, as the CMU expands and contracts at different rates than the brick masonry, causing parapet cracking.
12. The spacing and size of the vertical reinforcing in a parapet are a function of parapet height wall and local wind pressure. For high-rise buildings, structural design is required.
13. For lateral support requirements consult local codes.
14. Refer to Brick Institute of America Technical Note 21, Brick Masonry Cavity Walls, for additional information.

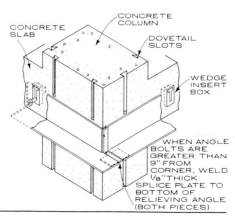

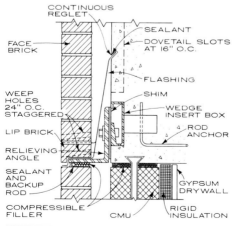

HORIZONTAL CONTROL JOINT

Theodore D. Sherman; Lev Zetlin Associates, Inc.; New York, New York
Robert J. Sangiamo, AIA; New York, New York
Davis, Brody & Associates; New York, New York

GENERAL NOTE : VERMICULITE SHOULD NOT BE USED TO FILL CAVITY WALLS

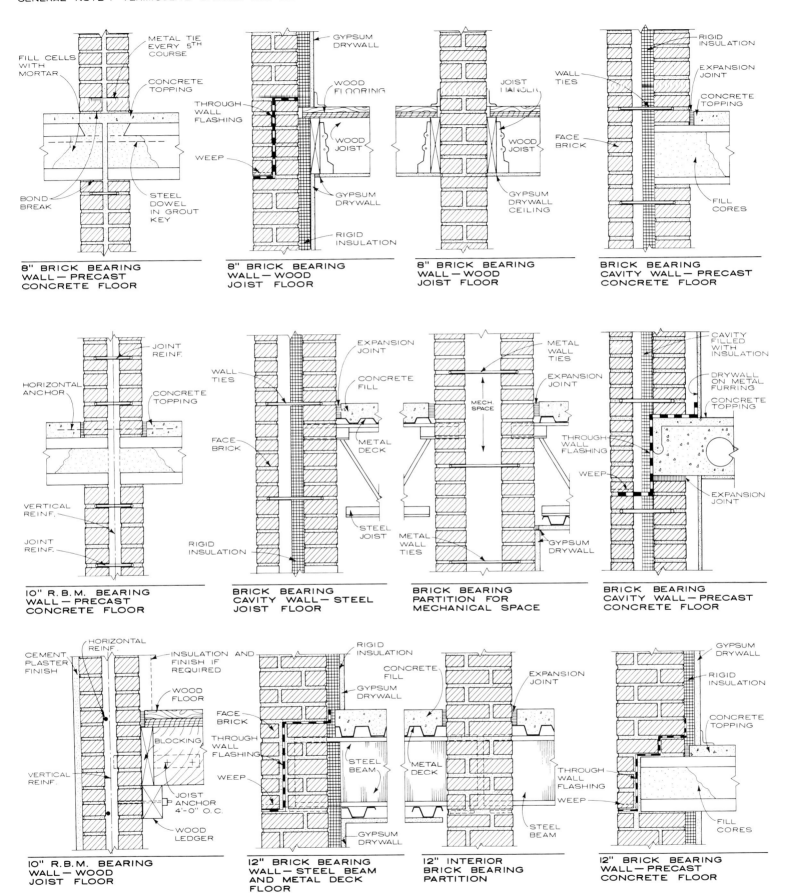

8" BRICK BEARING WALL — PRECAST CONCRETE FLOOR

8" BRICK BEARING WALL — WOOD JOIST FLOOR

8" BRICK BEARING WALL — WOOD JOIST FLOOR

BRICK BEARING CAVITY WALL — PRECAST CONCRETE FLOOR

10" R.B.M. BEARING WALL — PRECAST CONCRETE FLOOR

BRICK BEARING CAVITY WALL — STEEL JOIST FLOOR

BRICK BEARING PARTITION FOR MECHANICAL SPACE

BRICK BEARING CAVITY WALL — PRECAST CONCRETE FLOOR

10" R.B.M. BEARING WALL — WOOD JOIST FLOOR

12" BRICK BEARING WALL — STEEL BEAM AND METAL DECK FLOOR

12" INTERIOR BRICK BEARING PARTITION

12" BRICK BEARING WALL — PRECAST CONCRETE FLOOR

Robert Joseph Sangiamo, AIA; New York, New York
Davis, Brody & Associates; New York, New York

UNIT MASONRY 4

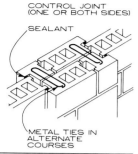

CONTROL JOINT AT PIER

FLUSH WALL AND PLASTER CONTROL JOINTS

CONTROL JOINT BLOCK

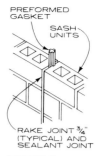

FLUSH WALL CONTROL JOINTS

PRINCIPLES

Masonry materials expand and contract in response to temperature changes. Dimensional changes also occur in masonry because of moisture variations. To compensate for these dimensional changes and thus control cracking in masonry, keep the following in mind:

1. Proper product specifications and construction procedures limit moisture related movements. For example, Type I moisture controlled concrete masonry units are manufactured to minimize moisture related movement.
2. Proper steel reinforcing, including horizontal joint reinforcing, increases the tensile resistance of masonry walls.
3. Properly placed expansion joints and control joints accommodate movement and provide for controlled crack locations.

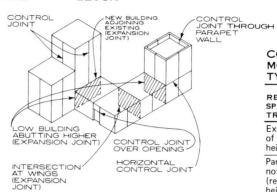

LOCATION OF CONTROL AND EXPANSION JOINTS

CONTROL JOINT SPACING FOR MOISTURE CONTROLLED ASTM C90 TYPE I BLOCK UNITS

RECOMMENDED SPACING OF CONTROL JOINTS	VERTICAL SPACING OF JOINT REINFORCEMENT			
	NONE	24"	16"	8"
Expressed as ratio of panel length to height (L/H)	2	2½	3	4
Panel length (L) not to exceed (regardless of height (H))	40'	45'	50'	60'

EXPANSION JOINTS

The purpose of expansion joints is to relieve tension and compression between separate portions of a masonry wall resulting from temperature and/or moisture induced dimensional movements.

Exterior and interior masonry wythes of cavity walls should be connected with flexible metal ties. Horizontal expansion joints should be located below shelf angles or structural frames supporting masonry walls or panels. Shelf angles should contain sufficient interruptions to accommodate thermal movements. Horizontal expansion joints (soft joints, slip channel, etc.) should also be provided above exterior masonry walls or panels abutting structural frames and at interior non-load-bearing masonry walls abutting the underside of floor or roof structures above.

CONTROL JOINTS

The purpose of control joints is to provide tension relief between individual portions of a masonry wall that may change from their original dimensions. They must provide for lateral stability across the joint and contain a through wall seal.

Control joints should be located in long straight walls, at major changes in wall heights, at changes in wall thickness, above changes in foundations, at columns and pilasters, at one or both sides of wall openings, near wall intersections, and near junctions of walls in L, T, or U shaped buildings. Joints should continue through roof parapets.

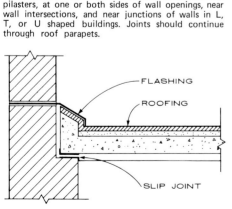

PARAPET AND RIGID ROOF SLAB

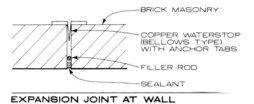

EXPANSION JOINT AT WALL

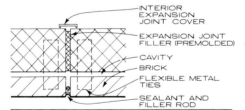

EXPANSION JOINT AT MASONRY CAVITY WALL

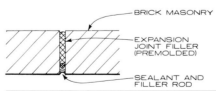

EXPANSION JOINT AT WALL

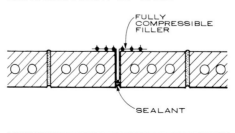

WALL EXPANSION JOINT

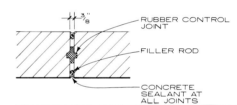

CONTROL JOINT AT STRAIGHT WALL

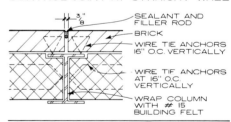

CONTROL JOINT AT STEEL COLUMN

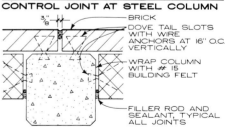

CONTROL JOINT AT CONCRETE COLUMN

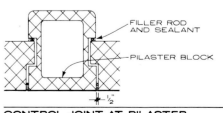

CONTROL JOINT AT PILASTER

Setter, Leach & Lindstrom, Inc.; Minneapolis, Minnesota

UNIT MASONRY

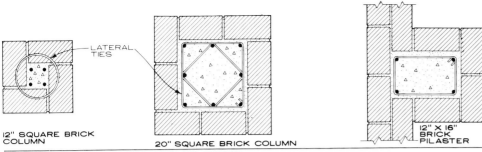

12" SQUARE BRICK COLUMN

20" SQUARE BRICK COLUMN

12" X 16" BRICK PILASTER

REINFORCED COLUMNS AND PILASTER

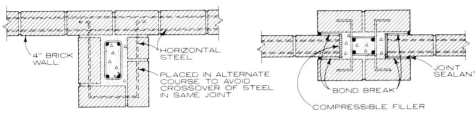

4" BRICK WALL

HORIZONTAL STEEL

PLACED IN ALTERNATE COURSE TO AVOID CROSSOVER OF STEEL IN SAME JOINT

BOND BREAK

COMPRESSIBLE FILLER

JOINT SEALANT

REINFORCED BRICK MASONRY COLUMN

REINFORCED BRICK MASONRY PILASTER

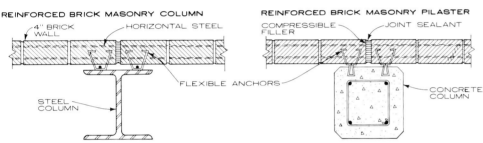

4" BRICK WALL

HORIZONTAL STEEL

COMPRESSIBLE FILLER

JOINT SEALANT

FLEXIBLE ANCHORS

STEEL COLUMN

CONCRETE COLUMN

STEEL COLUMN

REINFORCED CONCRETE COLUMN

BRICK CURTAIN WALL AND PANEL WALL REINFORCEMENT AND ANCHORAGE

TYPICAL RETAINING WALL DESIGN VALUES

H	B	L	D BARS	V BARS	F BARS
2'-0"	1'-9"	1'-10"	#3 @ 40"		#3 @ 40"
2'-6"	1'-9"	2'-4"	#3 @ 40"		#3 @ 40"
3'-0"	2'-0"	2'-10"	#3 @ 40"		#3 @ 40"
3'-6"	2'-0"	3'-4"	#3 @ 40"		#3 @ 40"
4'-0"	2'-4"	1'-4"	#3 @ 27" #4 @ 40"	#3 @ 27" #3 @ 40"	#3 @ 27" #3 @ 40"
4'-6"	2'-8"	1'-6"	#3 @ 19" #4 @ 35"	#3 @ 38" #3 @ 35"	#3 @ 19" #3 @ 35"
5'-0"	3'-0"	1'-8"	#3 @ 14" #4 @ 25" #5 @ 40"	#3 @ 28" #3 @ 25" #4 @ 40"	#3 @ 14" #3 @ 25" #4 @ 40"
5'-6"	3'-3"	1'-10"	#3 @ 11" #4 @ 20" #5 @ 31"	#3 @ 22" #4 @ 40" #4 @ 31"	#3 @ 11" #3 @ 20" #4 @ 31"
6'-0"	3'-6"	2'-0"	#3 @ 8" #4 @ 14" #5 @ 20"	#3 @ 16" #4 @ 28" #5 @ 40"	#3 @ 8" #3 @ 14" #4 @ 20"

NOTE: For convenience, this table was developed to aid the nondesigner in a typical application. However, materials must meet these additional minimum requirements:

1. Brick strength in excess of 6000 psi in compression.
2. Steel design tensile strength, F_s, of 20,000 psi.
3. No surcharge.

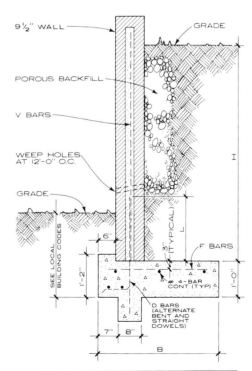

9½" WALL

GRADE

POROUS BACKFILL

V BARS

WEEP HOLES AT 12'-0" O.C.

GRADE

SEE LOCAL BUILDING CODES

6"

3" (TYPICAL)

F BARS

4-BAR CONT (TYP)

D BARS (ALTERNATE BENT AND STRAIGHT DOWELS)

7" 8"

B

LOW BRICK MASONRY RETAINING WALL (LESS THAN 6'-0")

NOTE

Consult a qualified engineer and local code requirements for design of all grouted, reinforced masonry construction.

Christine Beall, AIA, CCS; Austin, Texas
John R. Hoke, Jr., AIA, Architect; Washington, D.C.

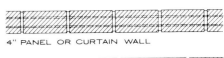
4" PANEL OR CURTAIN WALL

8" GROUTED HOLLOW BRICK WALL

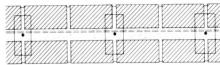
10" DOUBLE-WYTHE GROUTED, REINFORCED BRICK WALL

WALL TYPES

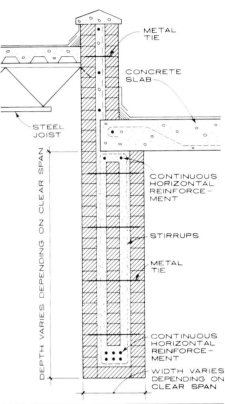

METAL TIE

CONCRETE SLAB

STEEL JOIST

DEPTH VARIES DEPENDING ON CLEAR SPAN

CONTINUOUS HORIZONTAL REINFORCEMENT

STIRRUPS

METAL TIE

CONTINUOUS HORIZONTAL REINFORCEMENT

WIDTH VARIES DEPENDING ON CLEAR SPAN

REINFORCED BRICK BEAM

The design of load-bearing masonry buildings is based on a rational analysis of the magnitude, line of action, and direction of all forces acting on the structure. Dead loads, live loads, lateral loads, and other forces such as those resulting from temperature changes, impact, and unequal settlement are considered. The combination of loads producing the greatest stresses is used to size the members. Reinforced masonry is used where compressive, flexural, and shear stresses are greater than those permitted for unreinforced or partially reinforced masonry. The minimum amount of steel reinforcing required by code is designed for seismic zones 3 and 4 where high winds or earthquake activity subject buildings to severe lateral dynamic loads. Reinforcing steel adds ductility and strength to the wall, which then bears the load with minimum deflection and maximum damping of the earthquake energy. For further technical information:

Masonry Design and Detailing, 2nd edition.
   Christine Beall. New York: McGraw-Hill, 1987.
Recommended Practice for Engineered Brick Masonry.
   Brick Institute of America. McLean, VA, 1969.
Reinforced Masonry Design. R. Schneider and W. Dickey.
   New York: Prentice-Hall, Inc., 1980.
Technical Notes Series. Brick Institute of America.

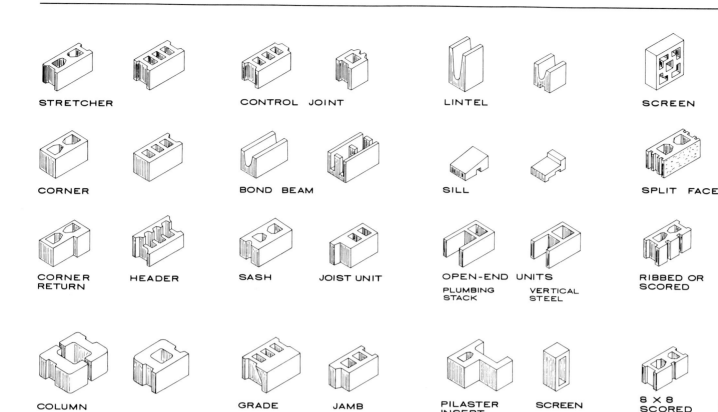

STRETCHER   CONTROL JOINT   LINTEL   SCREEN

CORNER   BOND BEAM   SILL   SPLIT FACE

CORNER RETURN   HEADER   SASH   JOIST UNIT   OPEN-END UNITS (PLUMBING STACK, VERTICAL STEEL)   RIBBED OR SCORED   FLUTED

COLUMN   GRADE   JAMB   PILASTER INSERT   SCREEN   8 X 8 SCORED FACE   SPLIT RIBBED

TYPICAL CONCRETE MASONRY UNIT SHAPES

CONCRETE MASONRY UNIT SPECIFICATIONS AND FIRE RESISTANCE DATA

1. A solid (load bearing) concrete block is a unit whose cross-sectional area in every plane parallel to the bearing surface is not less than 75% of the gross cross-sectional area measured in the same plane. (ASTM C145—75.)

2. A hollow concrete block is a unit whose cross-sectional area in every plane parallel to the bearing surface is less than 75% of the gross cross-sectional area measured in the same plane. (ASTM C90—75.)

3. Actual dimension is 3/8 in. less than nominal shown.

4. All shapes shown are available in all dimensions given in chart except for width (W) which may be otherwise noted.

5. Because the number of shapes and sizes for concrete masonry screen units is virtually unlimited, it is advisable for the designer to check on availability of any specific shape during early planning.

6. Screen units should be of high quality, even though they seldom are employed in load bearing construction. When tested with their hollow cells parallel to the direction of the load, screen units should have a compressive strength exceeding 1000 psi of gross area; a quality of concrete unit comparable to "Specifications for Hollow Load-Bearing Concrete Masonry Units" ASTM C90—75.

7. Building codes are quite specific in the degree of fire protection required in various areas of buildings. Local building regulations will govern the concrete masonry wall section best suited for specific applications. Fire resistance ratings of concrete masonry walls are based on fire tests made at Underwriters' Laboratories, Inc., National Bureau of Standards, Portland Cement Association, and other recognized laboratories. Methods of test are described in ASTM E119 "Standard Method of Fire Tests of Building Construction and Materials."

8. The fire resistance ratings of most concrete masonry walls are determined by heat transmission measured by temperature rise on the cold side. Fire endurance can be calculated as a function of the aggregate type used in the block unit,

and the solid thickness of the wall, or the equivalent solid thickness of the wall when working with hollow units.

9. Equivalent thickness of hollow units is calculated from actual thickness and the percentage of solid materials. Both needed items of information are normally reported by the testing laboratory using standard ASTM procedures, such as ASTM C140 "Methods of Sampling and Testing Concrete Masonry Units." When walls are plastered or otherwise faced with fire resistant materials, the thickness of these materials is included in calculating the equivalent thickness effective for fire resistance. Estimated fire resistance ratings shown in the table are for fully protected construction in which all structural members are of incombustible materials. Where combustible members are framed into walls, equivalent solid thickness protecting each such member should not be less than 93% of the thicknesses shown. Plaster is effective in increasing fire resistance when combustible members are framed into masonry walls, as is filling core spaces with various fire resistant materials.

10. Walls and partitions of 1- to 4-hr ratings are governed by code requirements for actual or equivalent solid thickness computed on the percent of core area in the unit. Increasing the wall thickness or filling the cores with grout increases the rating. Units with more than 25% core area are classified as hollow, and the equivalent solid thickness must first be computed in order to determine the fire rating. Since core size and shape will vary, either manufacturer's data or laboratory test data must be used to establish exact figures. A nominal 8 in. hollow unit reported to be 55% solid would be calculated as follows: equivalent solid thickness = 0.55 x 7.625 in. (actual thickness) = 4.19 in. Lightweight aggregates such as pumice, expanded slag, clay, or shale offer greater resistance to the transfer of heat in a fire because of their increased air content. Units made with these materials require less thickness to achieve the same fire rating as a heavyweight aggregate unit.

NOMINAL DIMENSIONS OF TYPICAL CONCRETE MASONRY UNIT SHAPES

Height (H) =	4", 8"
Length (L) =	8", 12", 16", 24"
Width (W) =	4", 6", 8", 10", 12"

EQUIVALENT THICKNESS FOR FIRE RATING

	1 HR	2 HR	3 HR	4 HR
Expanded slag or pumice	2.1	3.2	4.0	4.7
Expanded clay or shale	2.6	3.8	4.8	5.7
Limestone, cinders, air-cooled slag	2.7	4.0	5.0	5.9
Calcareous gravel	2.8	4.2	5.3	6.2
Siliceous gravel	3.0	4.5	5.7	6.7

R VALUE OF SINGLE WYTHE CMU, EMPTY AND WITH LOOSE-FILL INSULATION*

NOMINAL UNIT THICKNESS (IN.)	CORES	DENSITY OF CONCRETE IN CMU (PCF)				
		60	80	100	120	140
4	insul.	3.36	2.79	2.33	1.92	1.14
	empty	2.07	1.68	1.40	1.17	0.77
6	insul.	5.59	4.59	3.72	2.95	1.59
	empty	2.25	1.83	1.53	1.29	0.86
8	insul.	7.46	6.06	4.85	3.79	1.98
	empty	2.30	2.12	1.75	1.46	0.98
10	insul.	9.35	7.45	5.92	4.59	2.35
	empty	3.00	2.40	1.97	1.63	1.08
12	insul.	10.98	8.70	6.80	5.18	2.59
	empty	3.29	2.62	2.14	1.81	1.16

*Vermiculite or perlite insulation.

Robert J. Sangiamo, AIA, and Davis, Brody & Associates; New York, New York
Christine Beall, AIA, CCS; Austin, Texas

 UNIT MASONRY

NOTES
Concrete masonry unit walls are susceptible to cracking due to the differential or restrained movements of building elements. These stresses may be controlled through reinforcement in the form of bond beams and horizontal joint reinforcing and through separation, as in control joints which accommodate movement of the wall.

In seismic zones, concrete masonry unit walls should be reinforced horizontally and vertically to resist the lateral forces acting nonconcurrently in the direction of each of the main axes of the building.

Reference state and local building codes and The National Concrete Masonry Association for design requirements and recommendations.

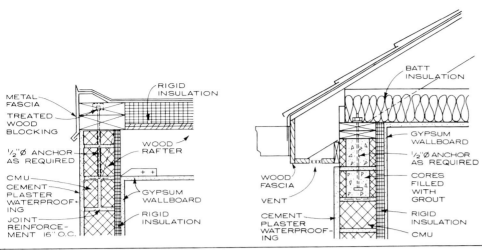

WALL – ROOF ANCHORAGE

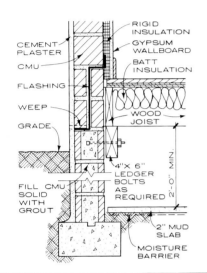

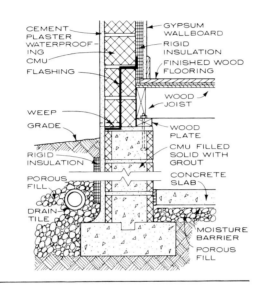

FOUNDATION DETAILS

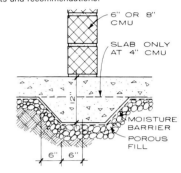

NONBEARING WALL

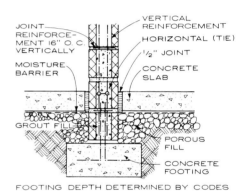

FOOTING DEPTH DETERMINED BY CODES

BEARING WALL

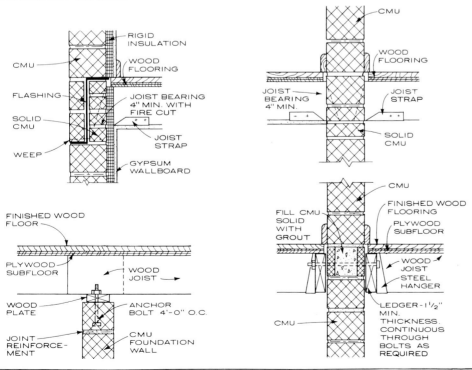

WALL – FLOOR ANCHORAGE DETAILS

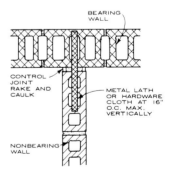

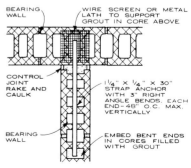

INTERSECTING WALL DETAILS

Robert J. Sangiamo, AIA; New York, New York
Davis, Brody & Associates; New York, New York
Ted B. Richey, AIA; The InterDesign Group; Indianapolis, Indiana

UNIT MASONRY

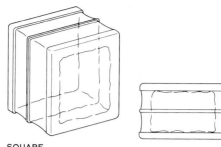

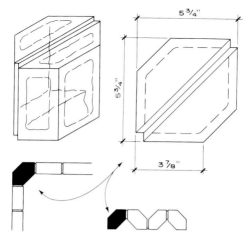

SQUARE

4½ in. x 4½ in.
6 in. x 6 in. (5¾ in. x 5¾ in. actual)
7½ in. x 7½ in.
8 in. x 8 in. (7¾ in. x 7¾ in. actual)
9½ in. x 9½ in.
12 in. x 12 in. (11¾ in. x 11¾ in. actual)

115 mm x 115 mm
190 mm x 190 mm
240 mm x 240 mm
300 mm x 300 mm

Metric sizes are available from foreign manufacturers through distributors in the U.S.

RECTANGULAR

4 in. x 8 in. (3¾ in. x 7¾ in. actual)
6 in. x 8 in. (5¾ in. x 7¾ in. actual)
9½ in. x 4½ in.*

*240 mm x 115 mm

THICKNESSES

Square and rectangular glass block are available in thicknesses ranging from a minimum of 3 in. for solid units to a maximum of 4 in. for hollow units. Metric thicknesses range from 80 mm to 100 mm.

SPECIAL SHAPES (CORNERS)

A limited number of manufacturers have special shapes to execute corner designs. These units also may be placed together for varying patterns and forms.

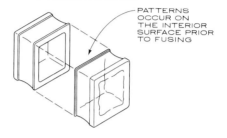

PATTERNS OCCUR ON THE INTERIOR SURFACE PRIOR TO FUSING

The basic glass block unit is made of two halves fused together with a partial vacuum inside. Faces may be clear, figured, or with integral relief forms.

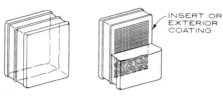

INSERT OR EXTERIOR COATING

Solid glass block units (glass bricks) are impact resistant and allow through vision.

Solar control units have either inserts or exterior coatings to reduce heat gain. Coated units require periodic cleaning to remove alkali and metal ions that can harm the surface coating. Edge drips are required to prevent moisture rundown on surface.

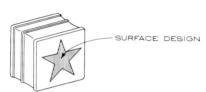

SURFACE DESIGN

Surface decoration may be achieved with fused-on ceramic, etching, or sandblasting. Glass block units may be split or shipped in halves in order to apply some decoration to the inside. Blocks then must be resealed. Resealed blocks will not perform the same under various stresses as factory sealed units. Placement in walls or panels should be limited to areas receiving minimum loading.

STANDARD BLOCK DESIGN

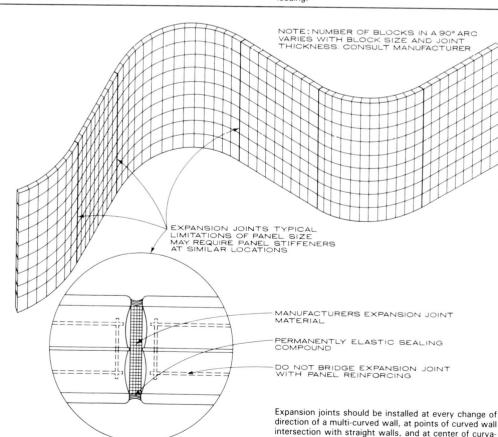

NOTE: NUMBER OF BLOCKS IN A 90° ARC VARIES WITH BLOCK SIZE AND JOINT THICKNESS. CONSULT MANUFACTURER

12" GLASS BLOCK
9½" GLASS BLOCK
8" GLASS BLOCK
7½" GLASS BLOCK
6" GLASS BLOCK
4½" GLASS BLOCK
4" GLASS BLOCK

32" 38½" 48½" 63" 65" 80" 96½"

⅝" OUTSIDE JOINT
⅛" OR ³/₁₆" INSIDE JOINT

EXPANSION JOINTS TYPICAL LIMITATIONS OF PANEL SIZE MAY REQUIRE PANEL STIFFENERS AT SIMILAR LOCATIONS

MANUFACTURERS EXPANSION JOINT MATERIAL

PERMANENTLY ELASTIC SEALING COMPOUND

DO NOT BRIDGE EXPANSION JOINT WITH PANEL REINFORCING

Curved walls may be constructed to the minimum radii (to the inside surface) indicated above. There are no maximum radii.

Table is based on an outside joint thickness of ⅝ in. and an inside joint thickness of ⅛ in. Some manufacturers prefer a minimum inside joint thickness of ³/₁₆ in. Wider joints require a slightly larger radius.

Expansion joints should be installed at every change of direction of a multi-curved wall, at points of curved wall intersection with straight walls, and at center of curvature in excess of 90 degrees.

CURVED WALL DESIGN

Raso·Greaves An Architecture Corporation; Waco, Texas

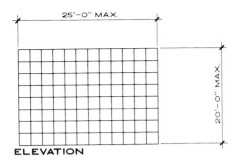

ELEVATION

25'-0" MAX.

20'-0" MAX.

NOTES

Area of exterior unbraced panel should not exceed 144 sq ft. Maximum size may be increased to 250 sq ft with the addition of mortared stiffeners.

Area of interior unbraced panel should not exceed 250 sq ft.

Panels are designed to be mortared at sill, with head and jambs providing for movement and settling. Deflection of lintel at head should be anticipated.

Consult manufacturers for specific design limitations of glass block panels. Thickness of block used also determines maximum panel size.

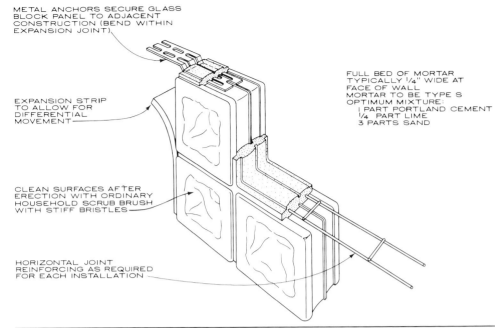

METAL ANCHORS SECURE GLASS BLOCK PANEL TO ADJACENT CONSTRUCTION (BEND WITHIN EXPANSION JOINT)

EXPANSION STRIP TO ALLOW FOR DIFFERENTIAL MOVEMENT

CLEAN SURFACES AFTER ERECTION WITH ORDINARY HOUSEHOLD SCRUB BRUSH WITH STIFF BRISTLES

HORIZONTAL JOINT REINFORCING AS REQUIRED FOR EACH INSTALLATION

FULL BED OF MORTAR TYPICALLY 1/4" WIDE AT FACE OF WALL MORTAR TO BE TYPE S OPTIMUM MIXTURE:
1 PART PORTLAND CEMENT
1/4 PART LIME
3 PARTS SAND

GLASS BLOCK PANEL

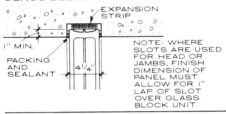

EXPANSION STRIP

1" MIN.

PACKING AND SEALANT

4 1/4"

NOTE: WHERE SLOTS ARE USED FOR HEAD OR JAMBS, FINISH DIMENSION OF PANEL MUST ALLOW FOR 1" LAP OF SLOT OVER GLASS BLOCK UNIT

GLASS BLOCK PANEL COMPONENTS

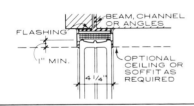

FLASHING

1" MIN.

BEAM, CHANNEL OR ANGLES

4 1/4"

OPTIONAL CEILING OR SOFFIT AS REQUIRED

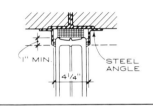

1" MIN.

4 1/4"

STEEL ANGLE

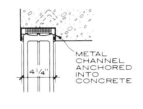

4 1/4"

METAL CHANNEL ANCHORED INTO CONCRETE

HEAD SECTIONS

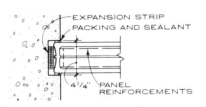

EXPANSION STRIP

PACKING AND SEALANT

4 1/4"

PANEL REINFORCEMENTS

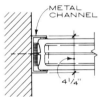

METAL CHANNEL

4 1/4"

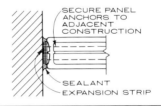

SECURE PANEL ANCHORS TO ADJACENT CONSTRUCTION

SEALANT

EXPANSION STRIP

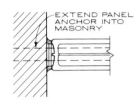

EXTEND PANEL ANCHOR INTO MASONRY

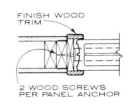

FINISH WOOD TRIM

2 WOOD SCREWS PER PANEL ANCHOR

JAMB SECTIONS

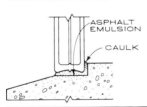

ASPHALT EMULSION

CAULK

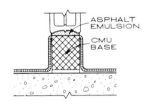

ASPHALT EMULSION

CMU BASE

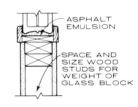

ASPHALT EMULSION

SPACE AND SIZE WOOD STUDS FOR WEIGHT OF GLASS BLOCK

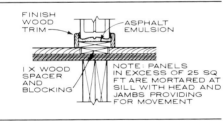

FINISH WOOD TRIM

ASPHALT EMULSION

1 X WOOD SPACER AND BLOCKING

NOTE: PANELS IN EXCESS OF 25 SQ FT ARE MORTARED AT SILL WITH HEAD AND JAMBS PROVIDING FOR MOVEMENT

SILL SECTIONS

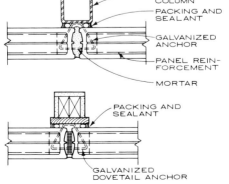

TUBE OR COLUMN

PACKING AND SEALANT

GALVANIZED ANCHOR

PANEL REINFORCEMENT

MORTAR

PACKING AND SEALANT

GALVANIZED DOVETAIL ANCHOR

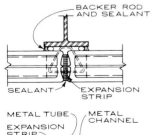

BACKER ROD AND SEALANT

SEALANT

EXPANSION STRIP

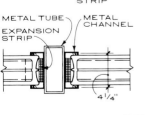

METAL TUBE

METAL CHANNEL

EXPANSION STRIP

4 1/4"

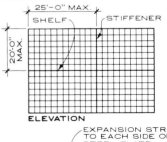

25'-0" MAX.

SHELF

STIFFENER

20'-0" MAX.

ELEVATION

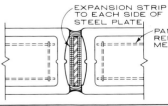

EXPANSION STRIP TO EACH SIDE OF STEEL PLATE

PANEL REINFORCEMENT

NOTE: PANELS WITH AN EXPANSION JOINT STIFFENER INCORPORATING A CONCEALED VERTICAL PLATE SHOULD BE LIMITED TO 10 FT MAX HEIGHT

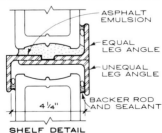

ASPHALT EMULSION

EQUAL LEG ANGLE

UNEQUAL LEG ANGLE

4 1/4"

BACKER ROD AND SEALANT

SHELF DETAIL

STIFFENER SECTIONS

Raso·Greaves An Architecture Corporation; Waco, Texas

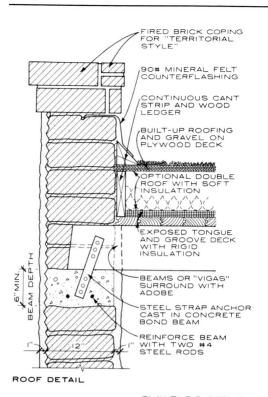

FIRED BRICK COPING FOR "TERRITORIAL STYLE"

90# MINERAL FELT COUNTERFLASHING

CONTINUOUS CANT STRIP AND WOOD LEDGER

BUILT-UP ROOFING AND GRAVEL ON PLYWOOD DECK

OPTIONAL DOUBLE ROOF WITH SOFT INSULATION

EXPOSED TONGUE AND GROOVE DECK WITH RIGID INSULATION

BEAMS OR "VIGAS" SURROUND WITH ADOBE

STEEL STRAP ANCHOR CAST IN CONCRETE BOND BEAM

REINFORCE BEAM WITH TWO #4 STEEL RODS

6" MIN. BEAM DEPTH

1" 12" 1"

ROOF DETAIL

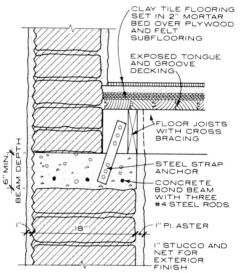

CLAY TILE FLOORING SET IN 2" MORTAR BED OVER PLYWOOD AND FELT SUBFLOORING

EXPOSED TONGUE AND GROOVE DECKING

FLOOR JOISTS WITH CROSS BRACING

STEEL STRAP ANCHOR

CONCRETE BOND BEAM WITH THREE #4 STEEL RODS

1" PLASTER

1" STUCCO AND NET FOR EXTERIOR FINISH

6" MIN. BEAM DEPTH

1" 18" 1"

SECOND FLOOR DETAIL

OPTIONAL WOOD BASE

TILE FLOORING ON REINFORCED CONCRETE SLAB

KEY TOP OF PIER AND WATERPROOF

REINFORCED CONCRETE STEM WALL

" SAND BED WITH VAPOR BARRIER

PERIMETER INSULATION

6" MIN.

18"

FOUNDATION DETAIL

WALL SECTIONS (TERRITORIAL STYLE)

P. G. McHenry, Jr., AIA; Albuquerque, New Mexico

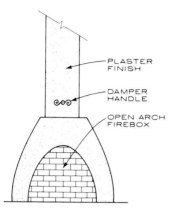

ADOBE WALL WITH RUBBLE FILLED CORNER

FIREBRICK CORNER LINING AND HEARTH

PLAN

PLASTER FINISH

DAMPER HANDLE

OPEN ARCH FIREBOX

ELEVATION

"HORNO" FIREPLACES

TYPICAL SIZES OF ADOBE BRICK

HEIGHT	LENGTH	WIDTH
4''	8''	16''
4''	10''	16''
4''	9''	18''
4''	12''	18''
5''	12''	16''
5''	10''	20''
5''	12''	18''
6''	12''	24''

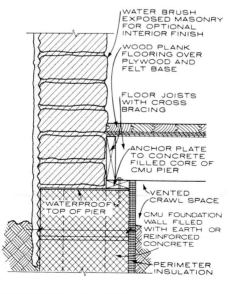

WATER BRUSH EXPOSED MASONRY FOR OPTIONAL INTERIOR FINISH

WOOD PLANK FLOORING OVER PLYWOOD AND FELT BASE

FLOOR JOISTS WITH CROSS BRACING

ANCHOR PLATE TO CONCRETE FILLED CORE OF CMU PIER

VENTED CRAWL SPACE

WATERPROOF TOP OF PIER

CMU FOUNDATION WALL FILLED WITH EARTH OR REINFORCED CONCRETE

PERIMETER INSULATION

FIREPLACES

A traditional feature of most adobe homes is one or more corner "Kiva" or "Horno" fireplaces. The main masonry structure is provided by the adobe wall at a corner. If a corner is not available, sometimes a "Padercita" (little wall) is projected from another wall to provide a corner. The corner is lined with firebrick, and a masonry shell encloses the firebox and fireplace flue. A vitreous flue liner or masonry flue is projected through the roof. The curved back wall and open fire-box reflect heat efficiently into the room, and the curve provides a smoke shelf. A butterfly damper in the flue or throat is controlled by a decorative wrought iron handle.

New seismic requirements in some areas require vertical steel reinforcement in the masonry of fireplaces.

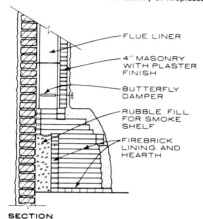

FLUE LINER

4" MASONRY WITH PLASTER FINISH

BUTTERFLY DAMPER

RUBBLE FILL FOR SMOKE SHELF

FIREBRICK LINING AND HEARTH

SECTION

ADOBE WALL CONSTRUCTION

The strength of an adobe wall lies in its mass and homogeneous nature, using the same material, mud, for mortar. The addition of reinforcing bars or anchor bolts may weaken joints. An international use standard for adobe wall thickness-height ratio is approximately 1:10. Uniform sizes for sundried bricks vary widely with different locales. The bricks should be made near the point of use and will vary with tradition and the standards of the manufacturer. Larger sizes of great weight will increase the labor cost. Minimum bonding distance is approximately 4 in.

One story walls should be 12 in. thick in Arizona and 10 in. in New Mexico and should not exceed 12 ft in height. Two story walls should be 18 in. thick at first floor and 12 in. at second and not over 22 ft in height.

Avoidance of flowing water on mud surfaces is the most important detail consideration. Rising damp is of no consequence if the site immediately adjacent is well drained and moisture is not trapped by water-proofing materials. Unstabilized mud brick or plaster (without the addition of waterproofing compounds) bonds well to itself and to wood without the use of normal lathing reinforcement. Rain erosion of un-stabilized mud surfaces will only approximate 1 in. in 20 years in rainfall areas of 10 to 25 in. per year. Monolithic slab/foundations are not desirable with mud adobe because possible concentrations of rain-water on the slab during construction may damage lower courses.

"Effective" U values for insulation are more significant than the ASHRAE "steady-state" values in common use. The "effective" values take into account the thermal mass, storage, insulation gains in various climate zones, wall compass orientation, and color.

"Burned adobe," which is merely a low fired brick, should be dealt with in the manner normal for brick masonry. Its use is not recommended in climate zones where high daily temperature fluctuations can cause severe freeze-thaw cycle damage. Mud bricks can be stabilized (waterproofed) by the addition of cement, asphalt emulsion, or other compounds. These materials often do not bond well with themselves in repeated layers and may accelerate the deterioration at the point of contact with the mud material.

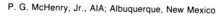

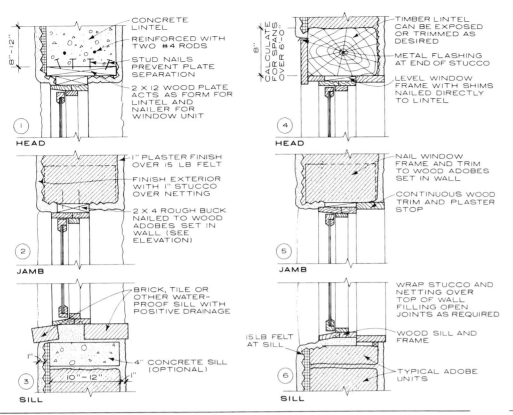

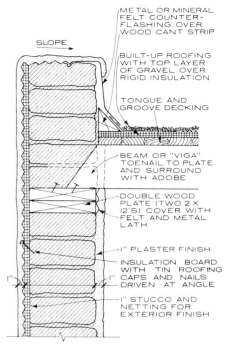

WINDOW DETAILS (SEE ELEVATION FOR ANCHORAGE OF FRAME)

PARAPET WITH WOOD COLLAR

NOTES

Details deal with the use of sundried mud bricks. They may be stabilized with additives or simply made of mud. Proportions for the mud mixture of sand, silt, and clay normally are not critical. Gravel and small stones can also be present if they do not exceed 50% of the volume. Adobe is approved by local building officials in areas where adobe use is traditional or familiar to builders or construction officials. Information concerning local codes should be sought.

Nailing anchors are best provided by the use of wood adobes ("Gringo blocks"), either solid or made of scrap lumber, laid up with the wall in locations where door and window jambs may require attachment. Nails will not hold permanently when nailed into adobe bricks unless additionally secured by plaster or other material. Later attachments can be made by the use of wooden triple wedges driven into a pilot hole. Channels for wiring, pipes, and decorative features may be easily cut in the wall after it is in place.

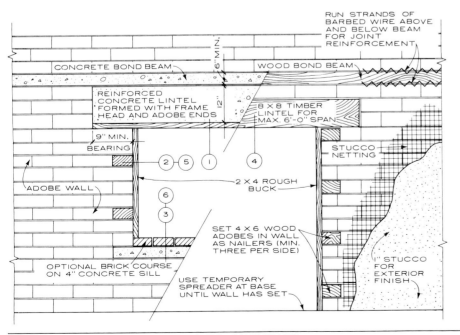

ELEVATION OF TYPICAL FRAMED OPENINGS

P. G. McHenry, Jr., AIA; Albuquerque, New Mexico

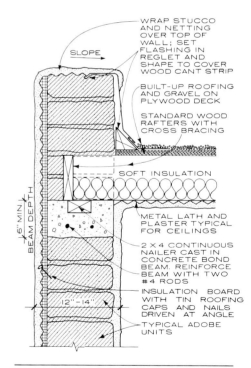

PARAPET WITH CONCRETE COLLAR

GENERAL NOTE

Some building codes may require additional thicknesses and reinforcement of concrete bond beams. The anchorage of pitched roof structures may be done by normal attachment to the bond beams shown.

ADOBE

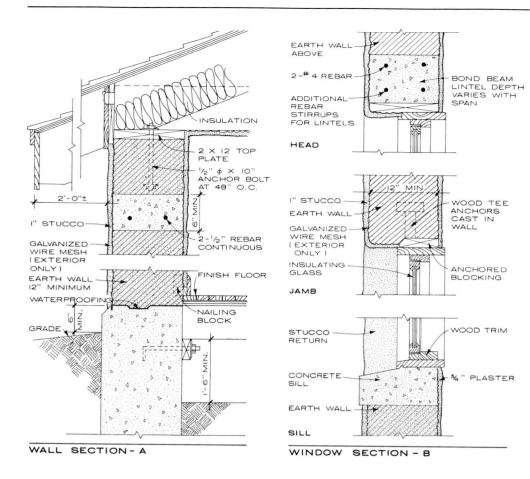

WALL SECTION - A

- INSULATION
- 2 X 12 TOP PLATE
- 1/2" φ X 10" ANCHOR BOLT AT 48" O.C.
- 2'-0"±
- 6" MIN.
- 1" STUCCO
- 2-1/2" REBAR CONTINUOUS
- GALVANIZED WIRE MESH (EXTERIOR ONLY)
- EARTH WALL 12" MINIMUM
- WATERPROOFING
- FINISH FLOOR
- NAILING BLOCK
- 6" MIN.
- GRADE
- 1'-6" MIN.

WINDOW SECTION - B

HEAD
- EARTH WALL ABOVE
- 2-#4 REBAR
- ADDITIONAL REBAR STIRRUPS FOR LINTELS
- BOND BEAM LINTEL DEPTH VARIES WITH SPAN

JAMB
- 12" MIN.
- 1" STUCCO
- EARTH WALL
- GALVANIZED WIRE MESH (EXTERIOR ONLY)
- INSULATING GLASS
- WOOD TEE ANCHORS CAST IN WALL
- ANCHORED BLOCKING

SILL
- STUCCO RETURN
- CONCRETE SILL
- EARTH WALL
- WOOD TRIM
- 3/4" PLASTER

NOTES

1. Rammed earth wall construction is an old technique used effectively in many parts of the world. The basic material is earth, with allowable proportions of clay, silt, and aggregate, commonly found almost everywhere. The soil in most locations has naturally usable proportions that do not require further tempering. The ideal soil mixture will have less than 50% clay and silt, and a maximum aggregate size of 1/4 in. The solid is dampened to a moisture content of approximately 10% by weight, of dry soil. Saltwater should not be used under any circumstances.

2. The walls are constructed by the use of slip forms, (24 to 36 in. high x 8 to 12 ft long) placed level and secure. The forms are filled with damp (not wet) earth in 4 in. lifts. Each lift is rammed with a tamper until full compaction is reached. The tamp should be flat, approximately 6 x 6 in., weighing 18 to 25 lb, tamped by hand or mechanically. Full compaction can be determined by a ringing sound when the tamp compacts the fill. When the form is full and compacted, it is moved to a new location and secured and the process is repeated. The corners should be placed first, with special corner forms. When the full circumference is completed, the next course is started. The form heights (courses) are best coordinated with heights of window and door lintels. Form replacement can begin as soon as compaction is reached, without further drying.

3. Exterior wall thickness should be a minimum of 12 in. for one story, 18 in. to support a second story, and interior walls of not less than 9 in. Wall thickness can be increased as appropriate to the design. Basic rammed earth walls have many of the same characteristics of sundried adobe. The insulation value of the walls is not as great as more efficient insulating materials, but will provide thermal mass for heat storage, sound control, and other benefits.

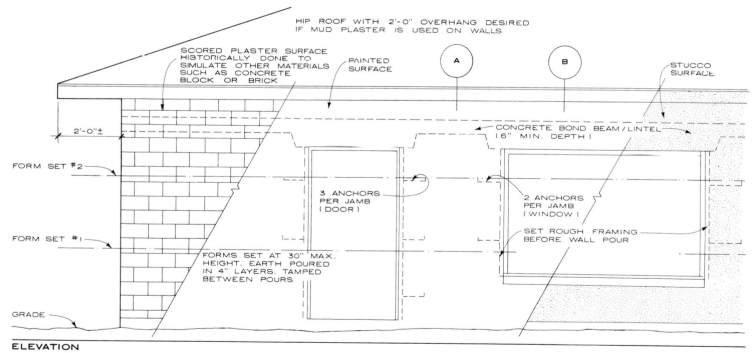

ELEVATION

- HIP ROOF WITH 2'-0" OVERHANG DESIRED IF MUD PLASTER IS USED ON WALLS
- SCORED PLASTER SURFACE HISTORICALLY DONE TO SIMULATE OTHER MATERIALS SUCH AS CONCRETE BLOCK OR BRICK
- PAINTED SURFACE
- A
- B
- STUCCO SURFACE
- 2'-0"±
- CONCRETE BOND BEAM / LINTEL (6" MIN. DEPTH)
- FORM SET #2
- FORM SET #1
- 3 ANCHORS PER JAMB (DOOR)
- 2 ANCHORS PER JAMB (WINDOW)
- SET ROUGH FRAMING BEFORE WALL POUR
- FORMS SET AT 30" MAX. HEIGHT. EARTH POURED IN 4" LAYERS. TAMPED BETWEEN POURS
- GRADE

NOTES

1. Foundations are normally conventional spread footings of sufficient width to support the heavy (3000 # per lin ft) walls. The foundation wall should be of a waterproof material, topped with a vapor barrier to prevent capillary moisture rise. Attachment anchors in the form of wood tees or plugs are placed in the wall as it is erected, in the positions required to secure window and door frames. A continuous steel reinforced concrete beam (6 in. thick) is placed as a continuous lintel beam to support walls above the openings.

2. A top plate of wood is secured by means of anchor bolts cast in the top of the walls. The plate provides load distribution and an attachment point for the roof structure. Interior and exterior walls can be finished by the application of conventional stucco or plaster. Simpler treatment can be achieved by smoothing or texturing the earth wall with a sponge rubber float, wet burlap, or sheepskin, and painting it. Sealing and preparation of the surface before painting is the same as for plaster. If waterproof stucco is not used, roof overhangs should be of sufficient width to protect the walls from rain erosion.

P. G. McHenry, Jr., AIA; Albuquerque, New Mexico

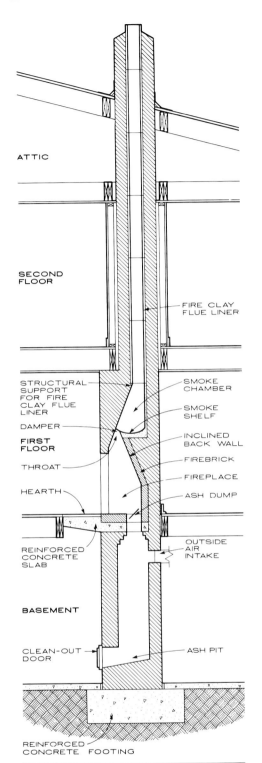

ATTIC

SECOND FLOOR

FIRE CLAY FLUE LINER

STRUCTURAL SUPPORT FOR FIRE CLAY FLUE LINER

DAMPER

FIRST FLOOR

SMOKE CHAMBER

SMOKE SHELF

INCLINED BACK WALL

FIREBRICK

FIREPLACE

ASH DUMP

THROAT

HEARTH

REINFORCED CONCRETE SLAB

OUTSIDE AIR INTAKE

BASEMENT

CLEAN-OUT DOOR

ASH PIT

REINFORCED CONCRETE FOOTING

SECTION

INTRODUCTION

A masonry chimney is usually the heaviest single part of a wood frame structure; therefore, it requires a special foundation. The same is true for masonry buildings where walls are not thick enough to incorporate the chimney or where the chimney is not designed into a masonry wall. Beyond the structural requirements, a fireplace and chimney must be designed so spaces and relationships between spaces sustain combustion and carry smoke away safely. Fireplace design is bound by various building and mechanical codes. The internal diagram of a working fireplace shows the several required parts and their vertical organization. Each part is illustrated further on succeeding pages. Other pages describe more efficient prefabricated fireplace units that incorporate air heating and circulating devices.

Most important in fireplace design is the location of the fireplace and chimney. It is best located at the center of the house to prevent heat loss to the exterior. For best efficiency, a fireplace should not be located opposite an outside door, near an open stairway leading to an upper floor, near a forced-air furnace, or near a return air register. Two factors primarily affect the chimney draft: height of the flue above the fireplace, and the pressure differential between the heated exhaust and cooler outside air.

The even combustion of wood fuel is improved by providing a measured supply of air, independent of room air, to the firebox. This is done by: installing an air duct from the exterior access to the ash dump, letting the ash door serve as a damper; or by providing a separate chase directly to the firebox. When a separate chase to the firebox is coupled with operable doors in the fireplace opening, the user can control the rate of combustion and maintain positive room air pressure; air infiltration and drafts are avoided.

DEFINITIONS

FLUE—Takes smoke from the smoke chamber to the outside. Flue area (in plan) is proportionally related to flue height and area of fireplace opening. A tight, lined flue is an important safety feature. Flue termination must be located according to codes. As an exterior building part, it requires weatherproofing.

SMOKE CHAMBER—Directs smoke into the flue by tapering up and in.

DAMPER—Allows throat size adjustment from fully open to tightly closed.

THROAT—Passes smoke from fireplace up into smoke chamber.

FIREPLACE—Where burning takes place. Size and proportions determine size of other components.

HEARTH—Extends fireplace floor beyond opening to protect room flooring from sparks, heat, and flames.

ASH DUMP—Operable louver in fireplace floor providing efficient ash removal. An air intake may be installed in the ash pit wall to introduce outside air into the fireplace via the ash dump.

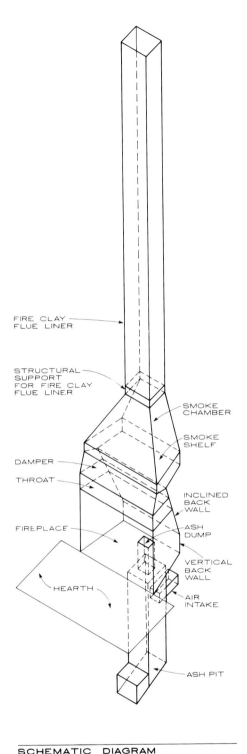

FIRE CLAY FLUE LINER

STRUCTURAL SUPPORT FOR FIRE CLAY FLUE LINER

SMOKE CHAMBER

SMOKE SHELF

DAMPER

THROAT

INCLINED BACK WALL

FIREPLACE

ASH DUMP

VERTICAL BACK WALL

HEARTH

AIR INTAKE

ASH PIT

SCHEMATIC DIAGRAM

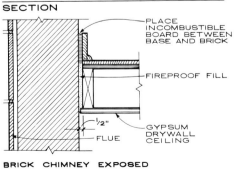

PLACE INCOMBUSTIBLE BOARD BETWEEN BASE AND BRICK

FIREPROOF FILL

GYPSUM DRYWALL CEILING

1/2"

FLUE

BRICK CHIMNEY EXPOSED

FLUE

STUD AND DRY WALL

POROUS NON-METALLIC, INCOMBUSTIBLE FILL

SHEET METAL OR LATH SUPPORT

4" 2"

BRICK CHIMNEY CONCEALED BEHIND A STUD WALL

INSULATION OF WOOD FRAMING MEMBERS AT A CHIMNEY

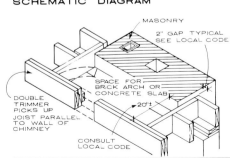

MASONRY

2" GAP TYPICAL SEE LOCAL CODE

SPACE FOR BRICK ARCH OR CONCRETE SLAB

DOUBLE TRIMMER PICKS UP JOIST PARALLEL TO WALL OF CHIMNEY

20'±

CONSULT LOCAL CODE

WOOD FLOOR FRAMING AROUND CHIMNEY AND HEARTH

Darrel Downing Rippeteau, Architect; Washington, D.C.
Timothy B. McDonald; Washington, D.C.

FIREPLACES 4

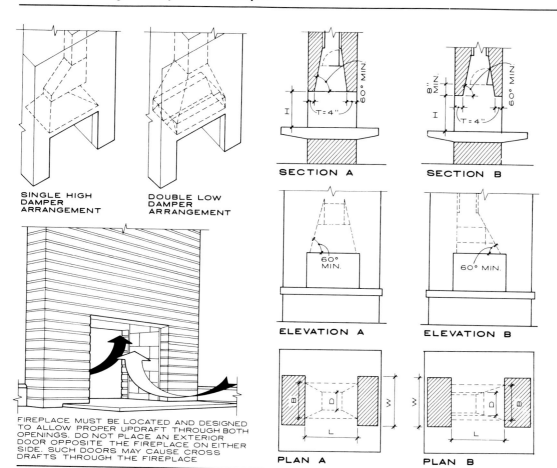

SINGLE HIGH DAMPER ARRANGEMENT

DOUBLE LOW DAMPER ARRANGEMENT

SECTION A

SECTION B

ELEVATION A

ELEVATION B

PLAN A

PLAN B

FIREPLACE MUST BE LOCATED AND DESIGNED TO ALLOW PROPER UPDRAFT THROUGH BOTH OPENINGS. DO NOT PLACE AN EXTERIOR DOOR OPPOSITE THE FIREPLACE ON EITHER SIDE. SUCH DOORS MAY CAUSE CROSS DRAFTS THROUGH THE FIREPLACE

FIREPLACE OPEN FRONT AND BACK

FIREPLACE OPEN FRONT AND BACK

H   Height from top of hearth to bottom of facing.

B   (Depth of burning area) $\frac{5}{8}$ H minus 8 in. but never less than 16 in.

W   (Width of fireplace) B + 2T.

D   (Damper at bottom of flue, see Section A) equal to free area of flue.

D   (Damper closer to fire, see Section B) equal to twice the free area of flue. Set damper a minimum of 8 in. from bottom of smoke chamber. Open damper should extend entire length of smoke chamber.

TYPICAL FIREPLACE DIMENSIONS

L	H	B	FLUE
28	24	16	13 x 13
30	28	16	13 x 18
36	30	17	18 x 18
48	32	19	20 x 24
54	36	22	24 x 24

NOTE: W should not be less than 24".

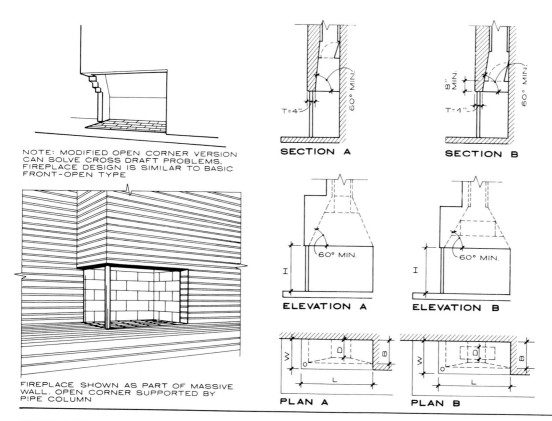

NOTE: MODIFIED OPEN CORNER VERSION CAN SOLVE CROSS DRAFT PROBLEMS. FIREPLACE DESIGN IS SIMILAR TO BASIC FRONT-OPEN TYPE

SECTION A

SECTION B

ELEVATION A

ELEVATION B

PLAN A

PLAN B

FIREPLACE SHOWN AS PART OF MASSIVE WALL. OPEN CORNER SUPPORTED BY PIPE COLUMN

FIREPLACE OPEN FRONT AND SIDE

FIREPLACE OPEN FRONT AND SIDE

H   Height from top of hearth to bottom of facing.

B   (Depth of burning area) $\frac{2}{3}$ H minus 4 in.

W   (Width of fireplace) B + T.

D   (Damper at bottom of flue, see Section A) equal to twice the free area of the flue. Set damper a minimum of 8 in. from bottom of smoke chamber.

TYPICAL FIREPLACE DIMENSIONS

L	H	B	FLUE
28	24	16	12 x 12
30	28	18	13 x 18
36	30	20	13 x 18
48	32	22	18 x 18

Darrel Downing Rippeteau, AIA, Architect; Washington, D.C.

FIREPLACES

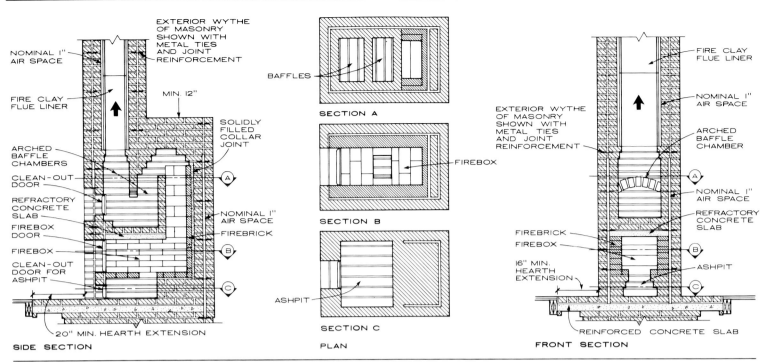

NOMINAL 1" AIR SPACE

FIRE CLAY FLUE LINER

ARCHED BAFFLE CHAMBERS

CLEAN-OUT DOOR

REFRACTORY CONCRETE SLAB

FIREBOX DOOR

FIREBOX

CLEAN-OUT DOOR FOR ASHPIT

20" MIN. HEARTH EXTENSION

SIDE SECTION

EXTERIOR WYTHE OF MASONRY SHOWN WITH METAL TIES AND JOINT REINFORCEMENT

MIN. 12"

SOLIDLY FILLED COLLAR JOINT

NOMINAL 1" AIR SPACE

FIREBRICK

BAFFLES

SECTION A

FIREBOX

SECTION B

ASHPIT

SECTION C

PLAN

FIRE CLAY FLUE LINER

NOMINAL 1" AIR SPACE

ARCHED BAFFLE CHAMBER

EXTERIOR WYTHE OF MASONRY SHOWN WITH METAL TIES AND JOINT REINFORCEMENT

NOMINAL 1" AIR SPACE

REFRACTORY CONCRETE SLAB

FIREBRICK

FIREBOX

16" MIN. HEARTH EXTENSION

ASHPIT

REINFORCED CONCRETE SLAB

FRONT SECTION

RUSSIAN MASONRY STOVE

INTRODUCTION

Brick masonry stoves are adapted from prototypes used in northern and eastern Europe and were used for a number of heating functions, including cooking. Masonry stoves utilize two basic principles to obtain high combustion and heating efficiencies, namely, controlled air intake to the combustion chamber/firebox, and a heat exchange system of baffle chambers through which the combustion gases are circulated.

FINNISH MASONRY STOVES

Finnish or contra-flow stoves are so called because heated air is forced from the top of the smoke chamber down through baffles on the sides of the stove while room air rises by convection along the exterior surface of the masonry. This allows for even heating of the masonry and efficient radiant heating of the room. The baffles converge below the firebox and open out to the flue from the base of the chimney.

RUSSIAN MASONRY STOVES

Russian stoves are typically deep with a small opening to the firebox with a system of either vertically or horizontally aligned baffles above, which replace the smoke chamber. After circulating through the baffle system exhaust gases pass directly into the flue. There is no decided advantage to either baffle alignment, though the horizontal system is easier to construct. Clean-outs are optional on either system, but are recommended to observe creosote build-up.

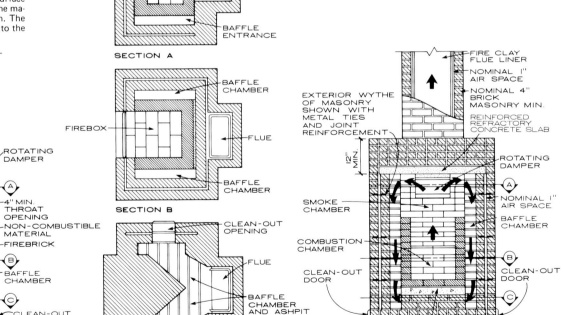

FIRE CLAY FLUE LINER
NOMINAL 1" AIR SPACE
NOMINAL 4" BRICK MASONRY MIN.
REINFORCED REFRACTORY CONCRETE SLAB

12" MIN

NOMINAL 1" AIR SPACE
FIREBRICK
STEEL ANGLE LINTEL
FIREBOX DOOR
FIREBOX
RAISED HEARTH

20" MIN. HEARTH EXTENSION

REINFORCED CONCRETE SLAB

16" MIN. HEARTH EXTENSION

SIDE SECTION

ROTATING DAMPER

4" MIN. THROAT OPENING

NON-COMBUSTIBLE MATERIAL

FIREBRICK

BAFFLE CHAMBER

CLEAN-OUT DOOR

SMOKE CHAMBER
THROAT OPENING

BAFFLE ENTRANCE

ROTATING DAMPER

FLUE

BAFFLE ENTRANCE

SECTION A

BAFFLE CHAMBER

FIREBOX

FLUE

BAFFLE CHAMBER

SECTION B

CLEAN-OUT OPENING

FLUE

BAFFLE CHAMBER AND ASHPIT

CLEAN-OUT OPENING

SECTION C

PLAN

FIRE CLAY FLUE LINER
NOMINAL 1" AIR SPACE
NOMINAL 4" BRICK MASONRY MIN.
REINFORCED REFRACTORY CONCRETE SLAB

EXTERIOR WYTHE OF MASONRY SHOWN WITH METAL TIES AND JOINT REINFORCEMENT

12" MIN

SMOKE CHAMBER

COMBUSTION CHAMBER

CLEAN-OUT DOOR

ROTATING DAMPER

NOMINAL 1" AIR SPACE

BAFFLE CHAMBER

CLEAN-OUT DOOR

16" MIN. HEARTH EXTENSION

REINFORCED CONCRETE SLAB

16" MIN. HEARTH EXTENSION

FRONT SECTION

FINNISH MASONRY STOVE

Timothy B. McDonald; Washington, D.C.

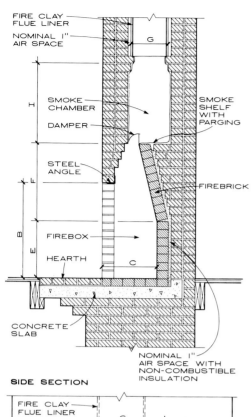

SIDE SECTION

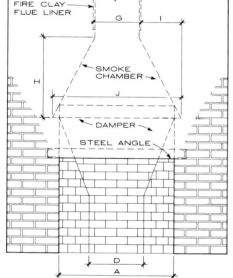

FRONT ELEVATION

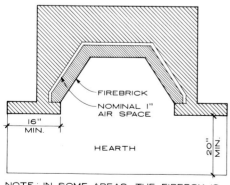

NOTE: IN SOME AREAS, THE FIREBOX IS SET 1" LOWER THAN THE HEARTH

PLAN

RUMFORD FIREPLACE

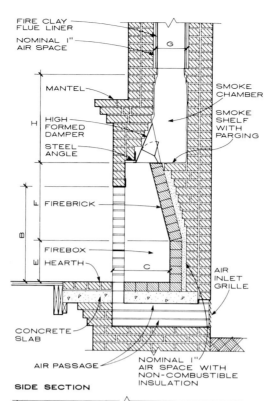

SIDE SECTION

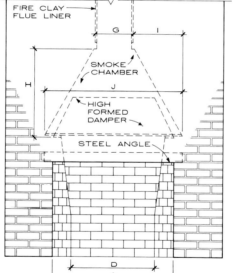

FRONT ELEVATION

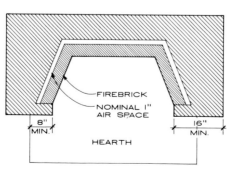

PLAN

SINGLE FACE FIREPLACE

SINGLE FACED FIREPLACES

The design of single faced fireplaces has been well documented, thus a reasonably accurate set of design dimensions of fireplace openings, dampers and flue linings has been developed.

Single faced fireplaces can be efficient radiant heaters. The amount of heat radiated and reflected into the room is directly proportional to the masonry surface area exposed to the fire. The Rumford fireplace is a variation of the single faced fireplace with a shallow firebox, a high throat, and widely splayed sides, all features for optimal direct radiant heating.

In addition, the energy efficiency of new fireplaces can be improved by:
1. Placing the fireplace on the interior of the house, preferably as close to the center as possible.
2. Supplying outside air for combustion and maintenance of positive room pressure.
3. Providing glass screens to prevent unwanted air infiltration.

RECOMMENDED DIMENSIONS FOR WOOD BURNING FIREPLACES (IN.)

TYPICAL FIREPLACES

FIREPLACE OPENINGS			BACKWALL (Inclined)			FLUE LINING (Outside Dim.)	SMOKE CHAMBER	
A	B	C	D	E	F	G	H	I	J
24	24	16	11	14	18	8 x 12	19	10	32
28	24	16	15	14	18	8 x 12	21	12	36
30	29	16	17	14	23	12 x 12	24	13	38
36	29	16	23	14	23	12 x 12	27	16	44
42	32	16	29	14	26	16 x 16	32	17	50
48	32	18	33	14	26	16 x 16	37	20	56
54	37	20	37	16	29	16 x 16	45	26	68
60	37	22	42	16	29	16 x 20	45	26	72
60	40	22	42	16	31	16 x 20	45	26	72
72	40	22	54	16	31	20 x 20	56	32	84

RUMFORD FIREPLACES

A	B	C	D	E	F	G	H	I	J
36	32	19	19	19	25	12 x 16	14	10	27
40	32	19	19	19	25	16 x 16	16	15	29
40	40	19	19	19	30	16 x 16	16	15	29
48	40	19	19	19	32	16 x 20	18	15	35
48	48	20	20	20	40	20 x 20	18	18	37
54	48	20	20	20	40	20 x 20	23	18	45
60	48	20	20	20	40	20 x 24	24	18	45

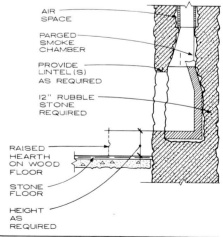

SIDE SECTION

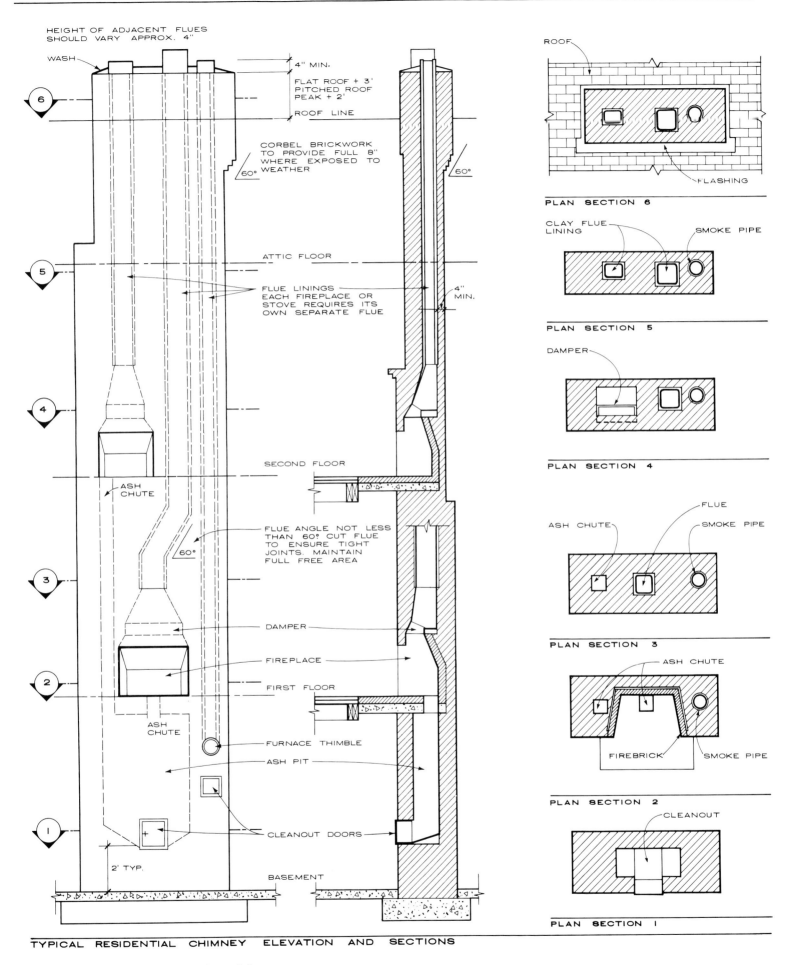

HEIGHT OF ADJACENT FLUES
SHOULD VARY APPROX. 4"

WASH

6

4" MIN.

FLAT ROOF + 3'
PITCHED ROOF
PEAK + 2'

ROOF LINE

CORBEL BRICKWORK
TO PROVIDE FULL 8"
WHERE EXPOSED TO
60° WEATHER

60°

5

ATTIC FLOOR

FLUE LININGS
EACH FIREPLACE OR
STOVE REQUIRES ITS
OWN SEPARATE FLUE

4"
MIN.

4

ASH
CHUTE

SECOND FLOOR

FLUE ANGLE NOT LESS
THAN 60° CUT FLUE
TO ENSURE TIGHT
JOINTS. MAINTAIN
FULL FREE AREA

60°

3

DAMPER

FIREPLACE

2

FIRST FLOOR

ASH
CHUTE

FURNACE THIMBLE

ASH PIT

1

CLEANOUT DOORS

2' TYP.

BASEMENT

TYPICAL RESIDENTIAL CHIMNEY ELEVATION AND SECTIONS

Darrel Downing Rippeteau, Architect; Washington, D.C.

ROOF

FLASHING

PLAN SECTION 6

CLAY FLUE
LINING

SMOKE PIPE

PLAN SECTION 5

DAMPER

PLAN SECTION 4

ASH CHUTE

FLUE

SMOKE PIPE

PLAN SECTION 3

ASH CHUTE

FIREBRICK

SMOKE PIPE

PLAN SECTION 2

CLEANOUT

PLAN SECTION 1

FIREPLACES   4

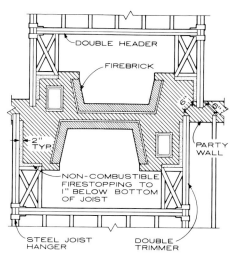

FIREPLACES BACK TO BACK IN
PARTY WALL

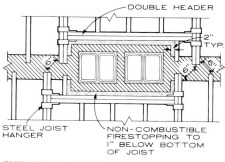

FIREPLACES CONSTRUCTED
INTEGRALLY WITH BRICK
PARTY WALL

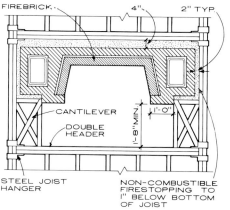

FLOOR FRAMING AT FIREPLACE

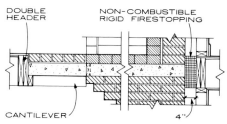

HEARTH FRAMING

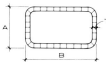

RECTANGULAR FLUE LINING (STANDARD)

AREA (SQ IN.)	A	B	T
51	8½''	8½''	⅝''
79	8½''	13''	¾''
108	8½''	18''	⅞''
125	13''	13''	⅞''
168	13''	18''	⅞''
232	18''	18''	1⅛''
279	20''	20''	1⅜''
338	20''	24''	1½''
420	24''	24''	1½''

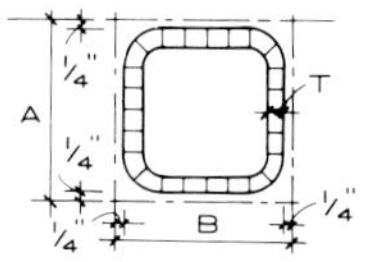

RECTANGULAR FLUE LINING (MODULAR)

AREA (SQ IN.)	A	B	T
57	8''	12''	¾''
74	8''	16''	⅞''
87	12''	12''	⅞''
120	12''	16''	1''
162	16''	16''	1⅛''
208	16''	20''	1¼''
262	20''	20''	1⅜''
320	20''	24''	1½''
385	24''	24''	1⅝''

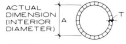

ROUND FLUE LINING

AREA (SQ IN.)	A	T	LENGTH
47	8''	¾''	2'-0''
74.5	10''	⅞''	2'-0''
108	12''	1''	2'-0''
171	15''	1⅛''	2'-0''
240	18''	1¼''	2'-0''
298	20''	1⅜''	2'-0''
433	24''	1⅝''	2'-0''

CLAY FLUE LININGS

NOTES

1. Availability of specific clay flue lining shapes varies according to location. Generally, oval and round flue linings, used in construction with steel reinforcing bars, are available in the western states, while rectangular flue linings are found commonly throughout the eastern states. Check with local manufacturers for available types and sizes.
2. U.L. approved lightweight concrete flues are available in the western states in modular sizes 8 x 8 in. and 16 x 16 in.
3. Nominal flue size for round flues is interior diameter; nominal flue sizes for standard rectangular flues are the exterior dimensions and, for modular flue linings, the outside dimensions plus ½ in.

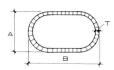

OVAL FLUE LINING

NOMINAL SIZE	AREA (SQ IN.)	A	B
8½'' x 13''	69	8½''	12¾''
8½'' x 17''	87	8½''	16¾''
10'' x 18''	112	10''	17¾''
10'' x 21''	138	10''	21''
13'' x 17''	134	12¾''	16¾''
13'' x 21''	173	12¾''	21''
17'' x 17''	171	16¾''	16¾''
17'' x 21''	223	16¾''	21''
21'' x 21''	269	21''	21''

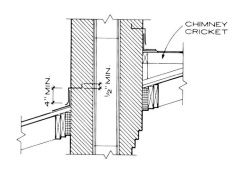

INSULATION OF WOOD FRAMING
MEMBERS AT A CHIMNEY

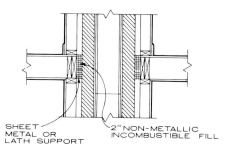

BRICK CHIMNEY CONCEALED
BEHIND STUD WALL

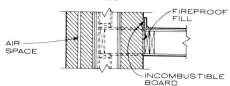

BRICK CHIMNEY EXPOSED

CHIMNEY FRAMING AND INSULATION

4. Areas shown are net minimum inside areas.
5. Wall thicknesses shown are minimum required. Flue dimensions vary ±½ in. about the nominal sizes shown.
6. All flue linings listed are generally available in 2 ft lengths. Verify other lengths with local supplier.
7. Fireplace flue sizes: One-tenth the area of fireplace opening recommended; one-eighth the area of opening recommended if chimney is higher than 20 ft and rectangular flues are used; one-twelfth the area is minimum required; verify with local codes.
8. Flue area should never be less than 70 sq in. for fireplace of 840 sq in. opening or smaller.

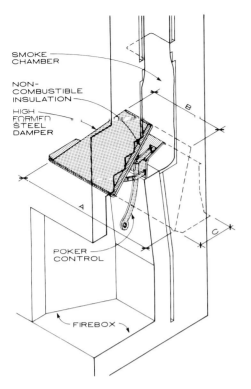

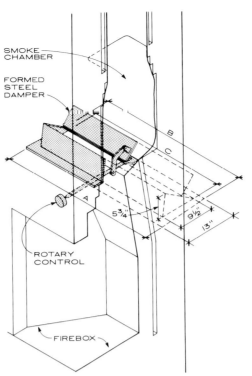

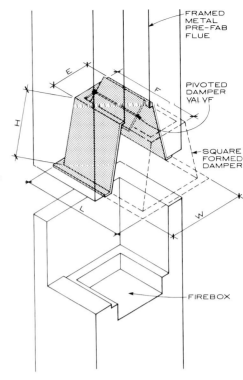

HIGH FORMED DAMPER (IN.)

A	B	C
32	15¼	9¾
36	19¼	9¾
40	23¼	9¾
44	27¼	9¾
48	31¼	9¾

HIGH FORMED DAMPERS provide correct ratio of throat-to-fireplace opening with an optional preformed smoke shelf, which can reduce material and labor requirements. They are useful for both single and multiple opening fireplaces.

FORMED DAMPER (IN.)

WIDTH OF OPENING	DAMPER DIMENSIONS (IN.)		
	A	B	C
24 to 26	28¼	26¾	24
27 to 30	32¼	30¾	28
31 to 34	36¼	34¾	32
35 to 38	40¼	38¾	36
39 to 42	44¼	42¾	40
43 to 46	48¼	46¾	44
47 to 50	52¼	50¾	48

FORMED STEEL DAMPERS are designed to provide the correct ratio of throat-to-fireplace opening, producing maximum draft. These dampers are equipped with poker type control and are easily installed.

SQUARE FORMED DAMPER (IN.)

TOP OUTLET			OVERALL SIZE	
E	F	H	L	W
17	17	17	41	27
17	17	25	45	27
17	23	25	49	27

SQUARE FORMED DAMPERS have high sloping sides that promote even draw on all sides of multiple opening fireplaces. They are properly proportioned for a strong draft and smokefree operation.

FORMED STEEL DAMPERS

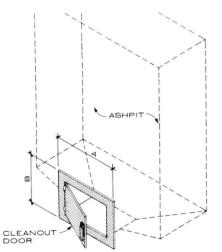

DOOR DIMENSIONS (IN.)

A	B
6	8
8	8, 10
10	10, 12
12	8, 10, 12, 16, 18

CLEANOUT OR ASHPIT DOOR

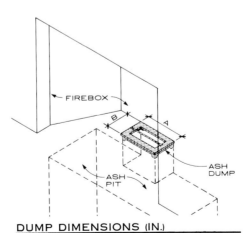

DUMP DIMENSIONS (IN.)

A	3½	4½	7
B	7	9	10

NOTE

Ash dumps and cleanout doors are available in heavy gauge steel or cast iron. See local manufacturers for available types and sizes.

ASH DUMP

NOTES

1. Locate bottom of damper minimum 6 to 8 in. from top of fireplace opening.
2. Mineral wool blanket allows for expansion of metal damper walls.
3. Dampers are available in heavy gauge steel or cast iron. Check with local suppliers for specific forms and sizes.
4. A cord of wood consists of 128 cu. ft or a stack 4 ft. high and 8 ft. wide, with logs 4 ft. long.
5. A face cord of wood consists of 64 cu ft, or a stack 4 ft high and 8 ft wide, with logs 2 ft long.
6. Logs are cut to lengths of 1 ft 4 in., 2 ft 0 in., 2 ft 6 in., and 4 ft. Allow 3 in. minimum clearance between logs and each side of fireplace.

Timothy B. McDonald; Washington, D.C.

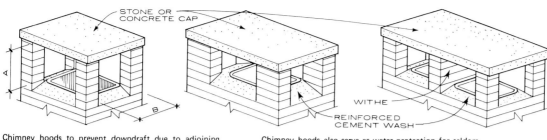

Chimney hoods to prevent downdraft due to adjoining hills, buildings, trees, etc.

A should be $\frac{1}{4}$ greater than B in all hooded chimneys

Chimney hoods also serve as water protection for seldom used flues

Withe between flues is the best method of preventing downdraft

CHIMNEY HOODS

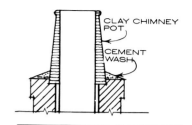

CHIMNEY POT

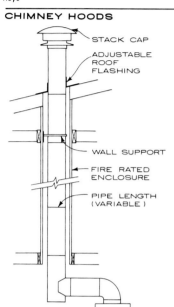

PREFAB METAL FLUE ASSEMBLY

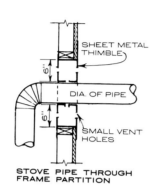

STOVE PIPE THROUGH FRAME PARTITION

Metal chimneys, connections, and flues are designed to be assembled with other pipes and accessory parts of the same model without requiring field construction. Pipes are single, double, or triple metal walls separated by $\frac{1}{2}$ to 1 in. airspace. Sizes range from 3 to 14 in. I.D. round pipe and $4\frac{5}{6}$ in. oval pipe for use in 2 x 6 stud walls. Provide 1 to 2 in. clearance from enclosure walls and roof structure. Verify with manufacturer's listings for approved uses and specifications.

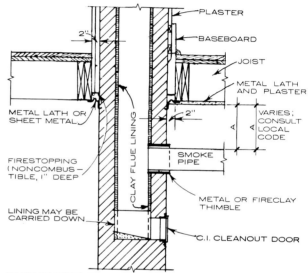

SMOKE PIPE FOR STOVES, H.W. HEATERS AND SMALL RANGES—CONNECTIONS AND CLEARANCES

FLUES, VENTS, AND SMOKE CONNECTIONS—RESIDENTIAL

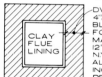

Chimneys for stoves, cooking ranges, warm air, hot water and low pressure steam heating furnaces, low heat industrial appliances, portable type incinerators, fireplaces.

LOW HEAT APPLIANCES

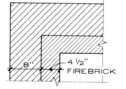

Chimneys for high pressure steam boilers, smokehouses, and other medium heat appliances other than incinerators. Continue firebrick up 25' min. N.Y.C. firebrick up 50' min.

MEDIUM HEAT APPLIANCES

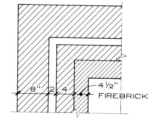

Chimneys for cupolas, brass furnaces, porcelain baking kilns, and other high heat appliances.

HIGH HEAT APPLIANCES

For domestic type incinerators where firebox or charging compartment is not larger than 5 cu ft

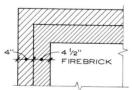

For apartment house type incinerators. Continue firebrick up 10' above roof of combustion chamber for grate area 7 sq ft or less; 40' above for grate area exceeding 7 sq ft.

FOR RESIDENCE BLDGS, INSTITUTIONAL BLDGS CHURCHES, SCHOOLS, & RESTAURANTS.

CHIMNEYS FOR INCINERATORS

CHIMNEY REQUIREMENTS— VARIOUS USE TYPES

Alexander Keyes; Darrel Downing Rippeteau, Architect; Washington, D.C.

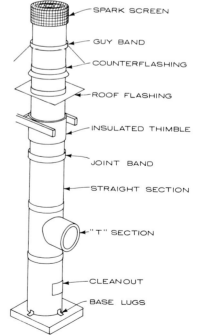

U.L. approved metal chimney systems with refractory linings are available in 10 to 60 in. I.D. in 4 ft lengths.

INDUSTRIAL CHIMNEY SYSTEM

FIREPLACES

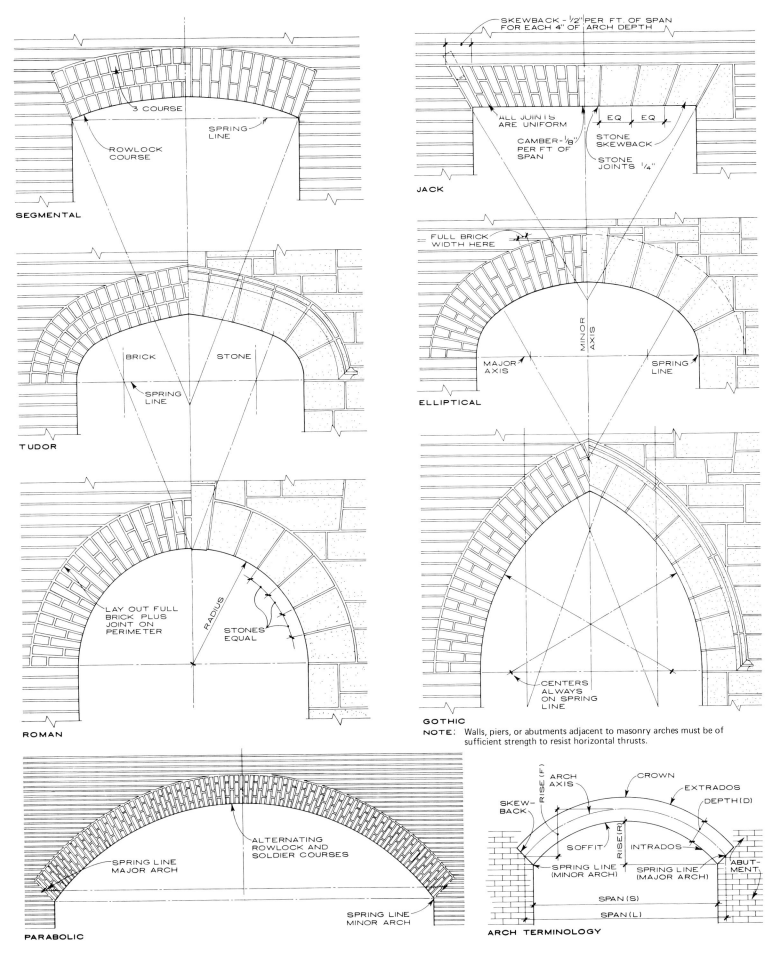

SEGMENTAL

3 COURSE

SPRING LINE

ROWLOCK COURSE

TUDOR

BRICK STONE

SPRING LINE

ROMAN

LAY OUT FULL BRICK PLUS JOINT ON PERIMETER

RADIUS

STONES EQUAL

JACK

SKEWBACK - 1/2" PER FT. OF SPAN FOR EACH 4" OF ARCH DEPTH

ALL JOINTS ARE UNIFORM

CAMBER - 1/8" PER FT OF SPAN

EQ EQ

STONE SKEWBACK

STONE JOINTS 1/4"

ELLIPTICAL

FULL BRICK WIDTH HERE

MINOR AXIS

MAJOR AXIS

SPRING LINE

GOTHIC

CENTERS ALWAYS ON SPRING LINE

NOTE: Walls, piers, or abutments adjacent to masonry arches must be of sufficient strength to resist horizontal thrusts.

PARABOLIC

ALTERNATING ROWLOCK AND SOLDIER COURSES

SPRING LINE MAJOR ARCH

SPRING LINE MINOR ARCH

ARCH TERMINOLOGY

RISE (F)

ARCH AXIS

CROWN

SKEW-BACK

EXTRADOS

DEPTH (D)

RISE (R)

SOFFIT

INTRADOS

SPRING LINE (MINOR ARCH)

SPRING LINE (MAJOR ARCH)

ABUT-MENT

SPAN (S)

SPAN (L)

Brick Institute of America; Reston, Virginia

ARCHES 4

REFERENCES

GENERAL REFERENCES

Architectural and Engineering Concrete Masonry Details for Building Construction, National Concrete Masonry Association (NCMA)

BIA Technical Notes on Brick Construction, Brick Institute of America (BIA)

Building Code Requirements for Masonry Structures, American Concrete Institute (ACI)

Dimensional Stone, Marble Institute of America

Indiana Limestone Institute of America, Inc., Handbook, Indiana Limestone Institute of America, Inc.

Masonry Design and Detailing, 2nd ed., 1987, Christine Beall, Prentice-Hall

Masonry Design Manual, Masonry Institute of America

Structural Details for Masonry Construction, 1988, Morton Newman, McGraw-Hill

DATA SOURCES: ORGANIZATIONS

American Society for Testing and Materials (ASTM), 56–58

Brick Institute of America (BIA), 48–52, 55–57, 73

Building Stone Institute (BSI), 39–41, 46, 47

Castellucci & Sons, Inc., 42, 43

Everett I. Brown Company, 52

Intrepid Enterprises, Inc., 42, 43

National Bureau of Standards (NBS), 58

National Concrete Masonry Association (NCMA), 58, 59

Pittsburgh Corning Corporation, 60, 61

Portland Cement Association (PCA), 58

Solaris, 60, 61

Susquehanna Concrete Products, Inc., 72

Underwriters' Laboratories, Inc. (U.L.), 58, 72

DATA SOURCES: PUBLICATIONS

American Standards Building Code for Masonry, American National Standards Institute (ANSI), 52

Masonry Accessories, National Wire Products Corporation, 38

Masonry Anchors and Ties, Heckman Building Products, 38

Masonry Design and Detailing, Christine Beall, AIA, 48, 57, 59

Shelf Angle Component Considerations in Cavity Wall Construction, C. J. Parise, American Society for Testing and Materials, 38

Uniform Building Code, 1982 ed., 1985 ed., International Conference of Building Officials (ICBO). Reprinted with permission of the publisher, 52

METALS

S SHAPES—DIMENSIONS FOR DETAILING

DESIGNA-TION	DEPTH d (IN.)	FLANGE WIDTH b_f (IN.)	AVERAGE THICKNESS t_f (IN.)	WEB THICKNESS t_w (IN.)
S 24 x 120	24	8	1 1/8	13/16
x 105.9	24	7 7/8	1 1/8	5/8
S 24 x 100	24	7 1/4	7/8	3/4
x 90	24	7 1/8	7/8	5/8
x 79.9	24	7	7/8	1/2
S 20 x 95	20	7 1/4	15/16	13/16
x 85	20	7	15/16	5/8
S 20 x 75	20	6 3/8	13/16	5/8
x 65.4	20	6 1/4	13/16	1/2
S 18 x 70	18	6 1/4	11/16	11/16
x 54.7	18	6	11/16	7/16
S 15 x 50	15	5 5/8	5/8	9/16
x 42.9	15	5 1/2	5/8	7/16
S 12 x 50	12	5 1/2	11/16	11/16
x 40.8	12	5 1/4	11/16	7/16
S 12 x 35	12	5 1/8	9/16	7/16
x 31.8	12	5	9/16	3/8
S 10 x 35	10	5	1/2	5/8
x 25.4	10	4 5/8	1/2	5/16
S 8 x 23	8	4 1/8	7/16	7/16
x 18.4	8	4	7/16	1/4
S 7 x 20	7	3 7/8	3/8	7/16
x 15.3	7	3 5/8	3/8	1/4
S 6 x 17.25	6	3 5/8	3/8	7/16
x 12.5	6	3 5/8	3/8	1/4
S 5 x 14.75	5	3 1/4	5/16	1/2
x 10	5	3	5/16	3/16
S 4 x 9.5	4	2 3/4	5/16	5/16
x 7.7	4	2 5/8	5/16	3/16
S 3 x 7.5	3	2 1/2	1/4	3/8
x 5.7	3	2 3/8	1/4	3/16

HP SHAPES—DIMENSIONS FOR DETAILING

DESIGNA-TION	DEPTH d (IN.)	FLANGE WIDTH b_f (IN.)	AVERAGE THICKNESS t_f (IN.)	WEB THICKNESS t_w (IN.)
HP14 x 117	14 1/4	14 7/8	13/16	13/16
x 102	14	14 3/4	11/16	11/16
x 89	13 7/8	14 3/4	5/8	5/8
x 73	13 5/8	14 5/8	1/2	1/2
HP12 x 74	12 1/8	12 1/4	5/8	5/8
x 53	11 3/4	12	7/16	7/16
HP10 x 57	10	10 1/4	9/16	9/16
x 42	9 3/4	10 1/8	7/16	7/16
HP8 x 36	8	8 1/8	7/16	7/16

AMERICAN STANDARD CHANNELS

DESIGNA-TION	DEPTH d (IN.)	FLANGE WIDTH b_f (IN.)	AVERAGE THICKNESS t_f (IN.)	WEB THICKNESS t_w (IN.)
C 15 x 50	15	3 3/4	5/8	11/16
x 40	15	3 1/2	5/8	1/2
x 33.9	15	3 3/8	5/8	3/8
C 12 x 30	12	3 1/8	1/2	1/2
x 25	12	3	1/2	3/8
x 20.7	12	3	1/2	5/16
C 10 x 30	10	3	7/16	11/16
x 25	10	2 7/8	7/16	1/2
x 20	10	2 3/4	7/16	3/8
x 15.3	10	2 5/8	7/16	1/4
C 9 x 20	9	2 5/8	7/16	7/16
x 15	9	2 1/2	7/16	5/16
x 13.4	9	2 3/8	7/16	1/4
C 8 x 18.75	8	2 1/2	3/8	1/2
x 13.75	8	2 3/8	3/8	5/16
x 11.5	8	2 1/4	3/8	1/4
C 7 x 14.75	7	2 1/4	3/8	7/16
x 12.25	7	2 1/4	3/8	5/16
x 9.8	7	2 1/8	3/8	3/16
C 6 x 13	6	2 1/8	5/16	7/16
x 10.5	6	2	5/16	5/16
x 8.2	6	1 7/8	5/16	3/16
C 5 x 9	5	1 7/8	5/16	5/16
x 6.7	5	1 3/4	5/16	3/16
C 4 x 7.25	4	1 3/4	5/16	5/16
x 5.4	4	1 5/8	5/16	3/16
C 3 x 6	3	1 5/8	1/4	3/8
x 5	3	1 1/2	1/4	1/4
x 4.1	3	1 3/8	1/4	3/16

MISCELLANEOUS CHANNELS—DIMENSIONS FOR DETAILING

DESIG-NATION	DEPTH d (IN.)	FLANGE WIDTH b_f (IN.)	AVERAGE THICKNESS t_f (IN.)	WEB THICKNESS t_w (IN.)
MC 18 x 58	18	4 1/4	11/16	5/8
x 51.9	18	4 1/4	5/8	5/8
x 45.8	18	4	1/2	5/8
x 42.7	18	4	7/16	5/8
MC 13 x 50	13	4 3/8	13/16	5/8
x 40	13	4 1/8	9/16	5/8
x 35	13	4 1/8	7/16	5/8
x 31.8	13	4	3/8	5/8
MC 12 x 50	12	4 1/8	13/16	11/16
x 45	12	4	11/16	11/16
x 40	12	3 7/8	9/16	11/16
x 35	12	3 3/4	7/16	11/16
MC 12 x 37	12	3 5/8	5/8	5/8
x 32.9	12	3 1/2	1/2	5/8
x 30.9	12	3 1/2	7/16	5/8
MC 12 x 10.6	12	1 1/2	3/8	5/16
MC 10 x 41.1	10	4 3/8	13/16	9/16
x 33.6	10	4 1/8	9/16	9/16
x 28.5	10	4	7/16	9/16
MC 10 x 28.3	10	3 1/2	1/2	9/16
x 25.3	10	3 1/2	7/16	9/16
x 24.9	10	3 3/8	3/8	9/16
x 21.9	10	3 1/2	5/16	1/2
MC 10 x 8.4	10	1 1/2	3/16	1/4
MC 10 x 6.5	10	1 1/8	1/8	3/16
MC 9 x 25.4	9	3 1/2	9/16	7/16
9 x 23.9	9	3 1/2	9/16	3/8
MC 8 x 22.8	8	3 1/2	1/2	7/16
x 21.4	8	3 1/2	1/2	3/8
MC 8 x 20	8	3	1/2	3/8
x 18.7	8	3	1/2	3/8
MC 8 x 8.5	8	1 7/8	5/16	3/16
MC 7 x 22.7	7	3 5/8	1/2	1/2
x 19.1	7	3 1/2	1/2	3/8
MC 7 x 17.6	7	3	1/2	3/8
MC 6 x 18	6	3 1/2	1/2	3/8
x 15.3	6	3 1/2	1/2	5/16
MC 6 x 16.3	6	3	1/2	3/8
x 15.1	6	3	1/2	5/16
MC 6 x 12	6	2 1/2	3/8	5/16

ANGLES (EQUAL LEGS)—DIMENSIONS FOR DETAILING

SIZE AND THICKNESS (IN.)

L 8 x 8 x 1 1/8, 1, 7/8, 3/4, 5/8, 9/16, 1/2
L 6 x 6 x 1, 7/8, 3/4, 5/8, 9/16, 1/2, 7/16, 3/8, 5/16
L 5 x 5 x 7/8, 3/4, 5/8, 1/2, 7/16, 3/8, 5/16
L 4 x 4 x 3/4, 5/8, 1/2, 7/16, 3/8, 5/16, 1/4

SIZE AND THICKNESS (IN.)

L 3 1/2 x 3 1/2 x 1/2, 7/16, 3/8, 5/16, 1/4
L 3 x 3 x 1/2, 7/16, 3/8, 5/16, 1/4, 3/16
L 2 1/2 x 2 1/2 x 1/2, 3/8, 5/16, 1/4, 3/16
L 2 x 2 x 3/8, 5/16, 1/4, 3/16, 1/8
L 1 3/4 x 1 3/4 x 1/4, 3/16, 1/8
L 1 1/2 x 1 1/2 x 1/4, 3/16, 5/32, 1/8
L 1 1/4 x 1 1/4 x 1/4, 3/16, 1/8
L 1 x 1 x 1/4, 3/16, 1/8

ANGLES (UNEQUAL LEGS)—DIMENSIONS FOR DETAILING

SIZE AND THICKNESS (IN.)

L 9 x 4 x 1, 7/8, 3/4, 5/8, 9/16, 1/2
L 8 x 6 x 1, 7/8, 3/4, 5/8, 9/16, 1/2, 7/16
L 8 x 4 x 1, 7/8, 3/4, 5/8, 9/16, 1/2, 7/16
L 7 x 4 x 7/8, 3/4, 5/8, 9/16, 1/2, 7/16, 3/8

SIZE AND THICKNESS (IN.)

L 6 x 4 x 7/8, 3/4, 5/8, 9/16, 1/2, 7/16, 3/8, 5/16, 1/4
L 6 x 3 1/2 x 1/2, 3/8, 5/16, 1/4
L 5 x 3 1/2 x 3/4, 5/8, 1/2, 7/16, 3/8, 5/16, 1/4
L 5 x 3 x 1/2, 7/16, 3/8, 5/16, 1/4

SIZE AND THICKNESS (IN.)

L 4 x 3 1/2 x 5/8, 1/2, 7/16, 3/8, 5/16, 1/4
L 4 x 3 x 5/8, 1/2, 7/16, 3/8, 5/16, 1/4
L 3 1/2 x 3 x 1/2, 7/16, 3/8, 5/16, 1/4
L 3 1/2 x 2 1/2 x 1/2, 7/16, 3/8, 5/16, 1/4
L 3 x 2 1/2 x 1/2, 7/16, 3/8, 5/16, 1/4, 3/16

SIZE AND THICKNESS (IN.)

L 3 x 2 x 1/2, 7/16, 3/8, 5/16, 1/4, 3/16
L 2 1/2 x 2 x 3/8, 5/16, 1/4, 3/16
L 2 1/2 x 1 1/2 x 5/16, 1/4, 3/16
L 2 x 1 1/2 x 1/4, 3/16, 1/8
L 2 x 1 1/4 x 1/4, 3/16, 1/8
L 1 3/4 x 1 1/4 x 1/4, 3/16, 1/8

W SHAPES-DIMENSIONS FOR DETAILING

DESIGNATION	DEPTH d (IN.)	FLANGE WIDTH b_f (IN.)	FLANGE THICKNESS t_f (IN.)	WEB THICKNESS t_w (IN.)
W36 x 300	36³/₄	16⁵/₈	1¹¹/₁₆	¹⁵/₁₆
x 280	36¹/₂	16⁵/₈	1⁹/₁₆	⁷/₈
x 260	36¹/₄	16¹/₂	1⁷/₁₆	¹³/₁₆
x 245	36¹/₈	16¹/₂	1³/₈	¹³/₁₆
x 230	35⁷/₈	16¹/₂	1¹/₄	³/₄
W36 x 210	36³/₄	12¹/₈	1³/₈	¹³/₁₆
x 194	36¹/₂	12¹/₈	1¹/₄	³/₄
x 182	36³/₈	12¹/₈	1³/₁₆	³/₄
x 170	36¹/₈	12	1¹/₈	¹¹/₁₆
x 160	36	12	1	⁵/₈
x 150	35⁷/₈	12	¹⁵/₁₆	⁵/₈
x 135	35¹/₂	12	¹³/₁₆	⁵/₈
W33 x 241	34¹/₈	15⁷/₈	1³/₈	¹³/₁₆
x 221	33⁷/₈	15³/₄	1¹/₄	³/₄
x 201	33⁵/₈	15³/₄	1¹/₈	¹¹/₁₆
W33 x 152	33¹/₂	11⁵/₈	1¹/₁₆	⁵/₈
x 141	33¹/₄	11¹/₂	¹⁵/₁₆	⁵/₈
x 130	33¹/₈	11¹/₂	⁷/₈	⁹/₁₆
x 118	32⁷/₈	11¹/₂	³/₄	⁹/₁₆
W30 x 211	31	15¹/₈	1⁵/₁₆	³/₄
x 191	30⁵/₈	15	1³/₁₆	¹¹/₁₆
x 173	30¹/₂	15	1¹/₁₆	⁵/₈
W30 x 132	30¹/₄	10¹/₂	1	⁵/₈
x 124	30¹/₈	10¹/₂	¹⁵/₁₆	⁹/₁₆
x 116	30	10¹/₂	⁷/₈	⁹/₁₆
x 108	29⁷/₈	10¹/₂	³/₄	⁹/₁₆
x 99	29⁵/₈	10¹/₂	¹¹/₁₆	¹/₂
W27 x 178	27³/₄	14¹/₈	1³/₁₆	³/₄
x 161	27⁵/₈	14	1¹/₁₆	¹¹/₁₆
x 146	27³/₈	14	1	⁵/₈
W27 x 114	27¹/₄	10¹/₂	¹⁵/₁₆	⁹/₁₆
x 102	27¹/₈	10	¹³/₁₆	¹/₂
x 94	26⁷/₈	10	³/₄	¹/₂
x 84	26³/₄	10	⁵/₈	⁷/₁₆
W24 x 162	25	13	1¹/₄	¹¹/₁₆
x 146	24³/₄	12⁷/₈	1¹/₁₆	⁵/₈
x 131	24¹/₂	12⁷/₈	¹⁵/₁₆	⁵/₈
x 117	24¹/₄	12³/₄	⁷/₈	⁹/₁₆
x 104	24	12³/₄	³/₄	¹/₂
W24 x 94	24¹/₄	9¹/₈	⁷/₈	¹/₂
x 84	24¹/₈	9	³/₄	¹/₂
x 76	23⁷/₈	9	¹¹/₁₆	⁷/₁₆
x 68	23³/₄	9	⁹/₁₆	⁷/₁₆
W24 x 62	23³/₄	7	⁹/₁₆	⁷/₁₆
x 55	23⁵/₈	7	¹/₂	³/₈
W21 x 147	22	12¹/₂	1¹/₈	³/₄
x 132	21⁷/₈	12¹/₂	1¹/₁₆	⁵/₈
x 122	21⁵/₈	12¹/₂	¹⁵/₁₆	⁵/₈
x 111	21¹/₂	12³/₈	⁷/₈	⁹/₁₆
x 101	21³/₈	12¹/₄	¹³/₁₆	¹/₂
W21 x 93	21⁵/₈	8³/₈	¹⁵/₁₆	⁹/₁₆
x 83	21³/₈	8³/₈	¹³/₁₆	¹/₂
x 73	21¹/₄	8¹/₄	³/₄	⁷/₁₆
x 68	21¹/₈	8¹/₄	¹¹/₁₆	⁷/₁₆
x 62	21	8¹/₄	⁵/₈	¹/₂
W21 x 57	21	6¹/₂	⁵/₈	¹/₂
x 50	20⁷/₈	6¹/₂	⁹/₁₆	³/₈
x 44	20⁵/₈	6¹/₂	⁷/₁₆	³/₈
W18 x 119	19	11¹/₄	1¹/₈	⁵/₈
x 106	18³/₄	11¹/₄	¹⁵/₁₆	⁹/₁₆
x 97	18⁵/₈	11¹/₈	⁷/₈	⁹/₁₆
x 86	18³/₈	11¹/₈	³/₄	¹/₂
x 76	18¹/₄	11	¹¹/₁₆	⁷/₁₆

DESIGNATION	DEPTH d (IN.)	FLANGE WIDTH b_f (IN.)	FLANGE THICKNESS t_f (IN.)	WEB THICKNESS t_w (IN.)
W18 x 71	18¹/₂	7⁵/₈	¹³/₁₆	¹/₂
x 65	18³/₈	7⁵/₈	³/₄	⁷/₁₆
x 60	18¹/₄	7¹/₂	¹¹/₁₆	⁷/₁₆
x 55	18¹/₈	7¹/₂	⁵/₈	³/₈
x 50	18	7¹/₂	⁹/₁₆	³/₈
W18 x 46	18	6	⁵/₈	³/₈
x 40	17⁷/₈	6	¹/₂	⁵/₁₆
x 35	17³/₄	6	⁷/₁₆	⁵/₁₆
W16 x 100	17	10³/₈	1	⁹/₁₆
x 89	16³/₄	10³/₈	⁷/₈	⁹/₁₆
x 77	16¹/₂	10¹/₄	³/₄	⁷/₁₆
x 67	16³/₈	10¹/₄	¹¹/₁₆	³/₈
W16 x 57	16³/₈	7¹/₈	¹¹/₁₆	⁷/₁₆
x 50	16¹/₄	7¹/₈	⁵/₈	³/₈
x 45	16¹/₈	7	⁹/₁₆	³/₈
x 40	16	7	¹/₂	⁵/₁₆
x 36	15⁷/₈	7	⁷/₁₆	⁵/₁₆
W16 x 31	15⁷/₈	5¹/₂	⁷/₁₆	¹/₄
x 26	15³/₄	5¹/₂	³/₈	¹/₄
W14 x 730	22³/₈	17⁷/₈	4¹⁵/₁₆	3¹/₁₆
x 665	21⁵/₈	17⁵/₈	4¹/₂	2¹³/₁₆
x 605	20⁷/₈	17³/₈	4³/₁₆	2⁵/₈
x 550	20¹/₄	17¹/₄	3¹³/₁₆	2³/₈
x 500	19⁵/₈	17	3¹/₂	2³/₁₆
x 455	19	16⁷/₈	3³/₁₆	2
W14 x 426	18⁵/₈	16³/₈	3¹/₁₆	1⁷/₈
x 398	18¹/₄	16⁵/₈	2⁷/₈	1³/₄
x 370	17⁷/₈	16¹/₂	2¹¹/₁₆	1⁵/₈
x 342	17¹/₂	16³/₈	2¹/₂	1⁹/₁₆
x 311	17¹/₈	16¹/₄	2¹/₄	1⁷/₁₆
x 283	16³/₄	16¹/₈	2¹/₁₆	1⁵/₁₆
x 257	16³/₈	16	1⁷/₈	1³/₁₆
x 233	16	15⁷/₈	1³/₄	1¹/₁₆
x 211	15³/₄	15³/₄	1⁹/₁₆	1
x 193	15¹/₂	15³/₄	1⁷/₁₆	⁷/₈
x 176	15¹/₄	15⁵/₈	1⁵/₁₆	¹³/₁₆
x 159	15	15⁵/₈	1³/₁₆	³/₄
x 145	14³/₄	15¹/₂	1¹/₁₆	¹¹/₁₆
W14 x 132	14⁵/₈	14³/₄	1	⁵/₈
x 120	14¹/₂	14⁵/₈	¹⁵/₁₆	⁹/₁₆
x 109	14³/₈	14⁵/₈	⁷/₈	¹/₂
x 99	14¹/₈	14⁵/₈	³/₄	¹/₂
x 90	14	14¹/₂	¹¹/₁₆	¹/₂
W14 x 82	14¹/₄	10¹/₄	⁷/₈	¹/₂
x 74	14¹/₈	10¹/₈	¹³/₁₆	⁷/₁₆
x 68	14	10	³/₄	⁷/₁₆
x 61	13⁷/₈	10	⁵/₈	³/₈
W14 x 53	13⁷/₈	8	¹¹/₁₆	³/₈
x 48	13³/₄	8	⁵/₈	⁵/₁₆
x 43	13⁵/₈	8	¹/₂	⁵/₁₆
W14 x 38	14¹/₈	6³/₄	¹/₂	⁵/₁₆
x 34	14	6³/₄	⁷/₁₆	⁵/₁₆
x 30	13⁷/₈	6³/₄	³/₈	¹/₄
W14 x 26	13⁷/₈	5	⁷/₁₆	¹/₄
x 22	13³/₄	5	⁵/₁₆	¹/₄
W12 x 336	16⁷/₈	13³/₈	2¹⁵/₁₆	1³/₄
x 305	16³/₈	13¹/₄	2¹¹/₁₆	1⁵/₈
x 279	15⁷/₈	13¹/₈	2¹/₂	1¹/₂
x 252	15³/₈	13	2¹/₄	1³/₈
x 230	15	12⁷/₈	2¹/₁₆	1⁵/₁₆
x 210	14³/₄	12³/₄	1⁷/₈	1³/₁₆

DESIGNATION	DEPTH d (IN.)	FLANGE WIDTH b_f (IN.)	FLANGE THICKNESS t_f (IN.)	WEB THICKNESS t_w (IN.)
W12 x 190	14³/₈	12⁵/₈	1³/₄	1¹/₁₆
x 170	14	12⁵/₈	1⁹/₁₆	¹⁵/₁₆
x 152	13³/₄	12¹/₂	1³/₈	⁷/₈
x 136	13³/₈	12³/₈	1¹/₄	¹³/₁₆
x 120	13¹/₈	12³/₈	1¹/₈	¹¹/₁₆
x 106	12⁷/₈	12¹/₄	1	⁵/₈
x 96	12³/₄	12¹/₄	⁷/₈	⁹/₁₆
x 87	12¹/₂	12¹/₄	¹³/₁₆	¹/₂
x 79	12³/₈	12¹/₄	³/₄	¹/₂
x 72	12¹/₄	12	¹¹/₁₆	⁷/₁₆
x 65	12¹/₈	12	⁵/₈	³/₈
W12 x 58	12¹/₄	10	⁵/₈	³/₈
x 53	12	10	⁹/₁₆	³/₈
W12 x 50	12¹/₄	8¹/₈	⁵/₈	³/₈
x 45	12	8	⁹/₁₆	⁵/₁₆
x 40	12	8	¹/₂	⁵/₁₆
W12 x 35	12¹/₂	6¹/₂	¹/₂	⁵/₁₆
x 30	12³/₈	6¹/₂	⁷/₁₆	¹/₄
x 26	12¹/₄	6¹/₂	³/₈	¹/₄
W12 x 22	12¹/₄	4	⁷/₁₆	¹/₄
x 19	12¹/₄	4	³/₈	¹/₄
x 16	12	4	¹/₄	¹/₄
x 14	11⁷/₈	4	¹/₄	³/₁₆
W10 x 112	11³/₈	10³/₈	1¹/₄	³/₄
x 100	11¹/₈	10³/₈	1¹/₈	¹¹/₁₆
x 88	10⁷/₈	10¹/₄	1	⁵/₈
x 77	10⁵/₈	10¹/₄	⁷/₈	¹/₂
x 68	10³/₈	10¹/₈	³/₄	¹/₂
x 60	10¹/₄	10¹/₈	¹¹/₁₆	⁷/₁₆
x 54	10¹/₈	10	⁵/₈	³/₈
x 49	10	10	⁹/₁₆	⁵/₁₆
W10 x 45	10¹/₈	8	⁵/₈	³/₈
x 39	9⁷/₈	8	¹/₂	⁵/₁₆
x 33	9³/₄	8	⁷/₁₆	⁵/₁₆
W10 x 30	10¹/₂	5³/₄	¹/₂	⁵/₁₆
x 26	10³/₈	5³/₄	⁷/₁₆	¹/₄
x 22	10¹/₈	5³/₄	³/₈	¹/₄
W10 x 19	10¹/₄	4	³/₈	¹/₄
x 17	10¹/₈	4	⁵/₁₆	¹/₄
x 15	10	4	¹/₄	¹/₄
x 12	9⁷/₈	4	³/₁₆	¹/₄
W8 x 67	9	8¹/₄	¹⁵/₁₆	⁹/₁₆
x 58	8³/₄	8¹/₄	¹³/₁₆	¹/₂
x 48	8¹/₂	8¹/₈	¹¹/₁₆	³/₈
x 40	8¹/₄	8¹/₈	⁹/₁₆	⁵/₁₆
x 35	8¹/₈	8	¹/₂	⁵/₁₆
x 31	8	8	⁷/₁₆	⁵/₁₆
W8 x 28	8	6¹/₂	⁷/₁₆	⁵/₁₆
x 24	7⁷/₈	6¹/₂	³/₈	¹/₄
W8 x 21	8¹/₄	5¹/₄	³/₈	¹/₄
x 18	8¹/₈	5¹/₄	⁵/₁₆	¹/₄
W8 x 15	8¹/₈	4	¹/₄	¹/₄
x 13	8	4	¹/₄	¹/₄
x 10	7⁷/₈	4	³/₁₆	³/₁₆
W6 x 25	6³/₈	6¹/₈	⁷/₁₆	⁵/₁₆
x 20	6¹/₄	6	³/₈	¹/₄
x 15	6	6	¹/₄	¹/₄
W6 x 16	6¹/₄	4	³/₈	¹/₄
x 12	6	4	¹/₄	¹/₄
x 9	5⁷/₈	4	³/₁₆	³/₁₆
W5 x 19	5¹/₈	5	⁷/₁₆	¹/₄
x 16	5	5	³/₈	¹/₄
W4 x 13	4¹/₈	4	³/₈	¹/₄

M SHAPES-DIMENSIONS FOR DETAILING

DESIGNATION	DEPTH d (IN.)	FLANGE WIDTH b_f (IN.)	FLANGE THICKNESS t_f (IN.)	WEB THICKNESS t_w (IN.)
M 14 x 17.2	14	4	¹/₄	³/₁₆
M 12 x 11.8	12	3¹/₈	¹/₄	³/₁₆
M 10 x 29.1	9⁷/₈	5⁷/₈	³/₈	⁷/₁₆
x 22.9	9⁷/₈	5³/₄	³/₈	¹/₄
M 10 x 9	10	2³/₄	³/₁₆	³/₁₆
M 8 x 37.7	8¹/₈	8	¹/₂	³/₈
x 34.3	8	8	⁷/₁₆	³/₈
x 32.6	8	8	⁷/₁₆	⁵/₁₆
M 8 x 22.5	8	5³/₈	³/₈	³/₈
x 18.5	8	5¹/₄	³/₈	¹/₄
M 8 x 6.5	8	2¹/₄	³/₁₆	¹/₈
M 7 x 5.5	7	2¹/₈	³/₁₆	¹/₈
M 6 x 33.75	6¹/₄	6¹/₈	⁵/₈	¹/₂
x 22.5	6	6	³/₈	³/₈
x 20	6	6	³/₈	¹/₄
M 6 x 4.4	6	1⁷/₈	³/₁₆	¹/₈
M 5 x 18.9	5	5	⁷/₁₆	⁵/₁₆
M 4 x 16.3	4¹/₄	4	¹/₂	⁵/₁₆
x 13.8	4	4	³/₈	⁵/₁₆
x 13	4	4	³/₈	¹/₄

NOTE

The following tables show sizes and shapes usually stocked or readily available. Manufacturers' data should be checked for availability of sizes other than those in these tables. Where necessary, and where extra cost is warranted, other sections may be produced by welding, cutting, or other methods.

STEEL CHANNEL

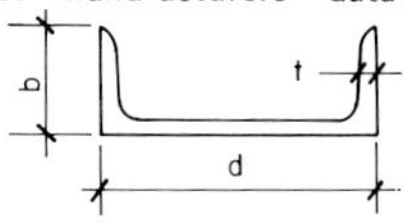

STEEL CHANNELS—BAR SIZE (IN.)

d x b x t	d x b x t	d x b x t
3/4 x 5/16 x 1/8	1 1/4 x 1/2 x 1/8	2 x 9/16 x 3/16
3/4 x 3/8 x 1/8	1 1/2 x 1/2 x 1/8	2 x 5/8 x 1/4
7/8 x 3/8 x 1/8	1 1/2 x 9/16 x 3/16	2 x 1 x 1/8
7/8 x 7/16 x 1/8	1 1/2 x 3/4 x 1/8	2 x 1 x 3/16
1 x 3/8 x 1/8	1 1/2 x 1 1/2 x 3/16	2 1/2 x 5/8 x 3/16
1 x 1/2 x 1/8	1 3/4 x 1/2 x 3/16	
1 1/8 x 9/16 x 3/16	2 x 1/2 x 1/8	

NOTE: For structural channel sizes (d = 3 in. and larger) see Dimensions of Channel Shapes in this chapter.

STEEL TEES

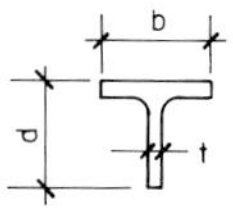

STEEL TEES—BAR SIZE (IN.)

b x d x t	b x d x t	b x d x t
3/4 x 3/4 x 1/8	1 1/2 x 1 1/2 x 3/16	2 x 2 x 5/16
1 x 1 x 1/8	1 1/2 x 1 1/2 x 1/4	2 1/4 x 2 1/4 x 1/4
1 x 1 x 3/16	1 3/4 x 1 3/4 x 3/16	2 1/2 x 2 1/4 x 1/4
1 1/4 x 1 1/4 x 1/8	1 3/4 x 1 3/4 x 1/4	2 1/2 x 2 1/2 x 5/16
1 1/4 x 1 1/4 x 3/16	2 x 1 1/2 x 1/4	2 1/2 x 2 1/2 x 3/8
1 1/4 x 1 1/4 x 1/4	2 x 2 x 1/4	
STRUCTURAL		
3 x 2 1/2 x 5/16	3 x 3 x 3/8	4 x 4 x 1/2
3 x 3 x 5/16	4 x 3 x 3/8	5 x 3 1/8 x 1/2

ALUMINUM ANGLE STRUCTURAL

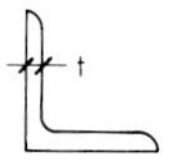

ALUMINUM ANGLES—STRUCTURAL —EQUAL LEGS (IN.)

SIZE x t	SIZE x t	SIZE x t
3/4 x 3/4 x 1/8	2 x 2 x 3/16	3 1/2 x 3 1/2 x 1/4
1 x 1 x 1/8	2 x 2 x 1/4	3 1/2 x 3 1/2 x 3/8
1 x 1 x 3/16	2 x 2 x 5/16	3 1/2 x 3 1/2 x 1/2
1 x 1 x 1/4	2 x 2 x 3/8	4 x 4 x 1/4
1 1/4 x 1 1/4 x 1/8	2 1/2 x 2 1/2 x 1/8	4 x 4 x 5/16
1 1/4 x 1 1/4 x 3/16	2 1/2 x 2 1/2 x 3/16	4 x 4 x 3/8
1 1/4 x 1 1/4 x 1/4	2 1/2 x 2 1/2 x 1/4	4 x 4 x 1/2
1 1/2 x 1 1/2 x 1/8	2 1/2 x 2 1/2 x 5/16	4 x 4 x 3/4
1 1/2 x 1 1/2 x 3/16	2 1/2 x 2 1/2 x 3/8	5 x 5 x 3/8
1 1/2 x 1 1/2 x 1/4	3 x 3 x 3/16	5 x 5 x 1/2
1 3/4 x 1 3/4 x 1/8	3 x 3 x 1/4	6 x 6 x 3/8
1 3/4 x 1 3/4 x 3/16	3 x 3 x 5/16	6 x 6 x 1/2
1 3/4 x 1 3/4 x 1/4	3 x 3 x 3/8	8 x 8 x 1/2
2 x 2 x 1/8	3 x 3 x 1/2	
UNEQUAL LEGS (IN.)		
1 1/2 x 1 1/4 x 1/8	2 1/2 x 2 x 5/16	4 x 3 x 1/2
1 1/2 x 1 1/4 x 3/16	2 1/2 x 2 x 3/8	5 x 3 x 3/8
1 1/2 x 1 1/4 x 1/4	3 x 2 x 3/16	5 x 3 x 1/2
1 3/4 x 1 1/4 x 1/8	3 x 2 x 1/4	5 x 3 1/2 x 5/16
1 3/4 x 1 1/4 x 3/16	3 x 2 x 3/8	5 x 3 1/2 x 3/8
1 3/4 x 1 1/4 x 1/4	3 x 2 1/2 x 1/4	5 x 3 1/2 x 1/2
2 x 1 1/2 x 1/8	3 x 2 1/2 x 3/8	6 x 3 1/2 x 5/16
2 x 1 1/2 x 3/16	3 1/2 x 2 1/2 x 1/4	6 x 3 1/2 x 1/2
2 x 1 1/2 x 1/4	3 1/2 x 2 1/2 x 3/8	6 x 4 x 3/8
2 1/2 x 1 1/2 x 1/4	3 1/2 x 3 x 1/4	6 x 4 x 1/2
2 1/2 x 2 x 3/16	4 x 3 x 1/4	6 x 4 x 5/8
2 1/2 x 2 x 1/4	4 x 3 x 3/8	8 x 6 x 3/4

STEEL ANGLES UNEQUAL LEGS

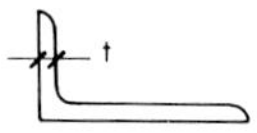

STEEL ANGLES —UNEQUAL LEGS—BAR SIZE (IN.)

SIZE x t	SIZE x t	SIZE x t
1 x 5/8 x 1/8	2 x 1 1/4 x 1/4	2 1/2 x 1 1/2 x 5/16
1 x 3/4 x 1/8	2 x 1 1/2 x 1/8	2 1/2 x 2 x 3/16
1 3/8 x 7/8 x 1/8	2 x 1 1/2 x 3/16	2 1/2 x 2 x 1/4
1 3/8 x 7/8 x 3/16	2 x 1 1/2 x 1/4	2 1/2 x 2 x 5/16
1 1/2 x 1 1/4 x 3/16	2 1/4 x 1 1/2 x 3/16	2 1/2 x 2 x 1/8
1 3/4 x 1 1/4 x 1/8	2 1/2 x 1 1/2 x 3/16	
2 x 1 1/4 x 3/16	2 1/2 x 1 1/2 x 1/4	

NOTE: For structural angle sizes (3 x 2 x 3/16 in. and larger) see Dimensions of Angle Shapes in this chapter.

STEEL ZEES

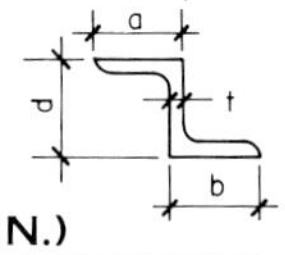

STEEL ZEES—BAR SIZE (IN.)

d x a x b x t	d x a x b x t
1 x 1/2 x 5/8 x 1/8	1 3/8 x 3/4 x 1 3/16 x 1/8
1 3/16 x 5/8 x 3/4 x 1/8	1 3/4 x 1 1/4 x 3/4 x 3/16
STRUCTURAL	
3 x 2 11/16 x 2 11/16 x 1/4	4 1/8 x 3 3/16 x 3 3/16 x 3/8
3 x 2 11/16 x 2 11/16 x 3/8	5 x 3 1/4 x 3 1/4 x 5/16
3 x 2 11/16 x 2 11/16 x 1/2	5 x 3 1/4 x 3 1/4 x 1/2
4 x 3 1/16 x 3 1/16 x 1/4	5 1/16 x 3 5/16 x 3 5/16 x 3/8
4 1/16 x 3 1/8 x 3 1/8 x 5/16	6 x 3 1/2 x 3 1/2 x 3/8

ALUMINUM ANGLE SQUARE CORNERS

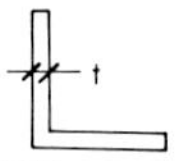

ALUMINUM ANGLES—SQUARE CORNERS—EQUAL LEGS (IN.)

SIZE x t	SIZE x t	SIZE x t
1/2 x 1/2 x 1/16	1 1/8 x 1 1/8 x 3/16	2 x 2 x 3/16
1/2 x 1/2 x 1/8	1 1/4 x 1 1/4 x 1/8	2 x 2 x 1/4
5/8 x 5/8 x 1/8	1 1/4 x 1 1/4 x 3/16	2 1/2 x 2 1/2 x 1/8
3/4 x 3/4 x 1/16	1 1/2 x 1 1/2 x 1/8	3 x 3 x 1/8
3/4 x 3/4 x 1/8	1 1/2 x 1 1/2 x 3/16	3 x 3 x 3/16
1 x 1 x 1/16	1 1/2 x 1 1/2 x 1/4	3 1/2 x 3 1/2 x 1/8
1 x 1 x 1/8	1 3/4 x 1 3/4 x 1/8	4 x 4 x 1/8
1 x 1 x 3/16	2 x 2 x 1/8	
UNEQUAL LEGS (IN.)		
3/4 x 3/8 x 3/32	2 x 3/4 x 1/8	3 1/2 x 2 x 1/8
1 x 1/2 x 1/8	2 x 1 x 1/8	3 1/2 x 2 1/2 x 1/8
1 x 3/4 x 1/8	2 x 1 x 3/16	3 1/2 x 3 x 1/8
1 1/4 x 1/2 x 1/8	2 x 1 1/2 x 1/8	4 x 2 x 1/8
1 1/2 x 1/2 x 1/8	2 1/2 x 1 x 1/8	4 x 3 x 1/8
1 1/2 x 3/4 x 1/8	2 1/2 x 1 1/2 x 1/8	5 x 3 x 1/8
1 1/2 x 1 x 1/8	2 1/2 x 2 x 1/8	5 x 4 x 1/8
1 3/4 x 1 x 1/8	3 x 1 x 1/8	5 1/4 x 2 1/4 x 1/8
1 3/4 x 1 1/2 x 1/8	3 x 2 x 1/8	
2 x 1/2 x 1/8	3 1/2 x 1 1/4 x 1/8	

ALUMINUM ZEES SQUARE CORNERS

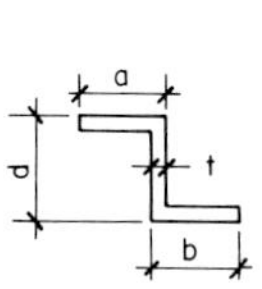

ALUMINUM ZEES— SQUARE CORNERS (IN.)

d x a x b x t	d x a x b x t
1/2 x 1/2 x 1/2 x 3/32	1 x 1 1/8 x 1 1/8 x 1/8
3/4 x 3/4 x 3/4 x 1/8	1 x 5/8 x 7/8 x 1/8
7/8 x 3/4 x 3/4 x 1/8	

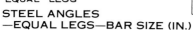

STEEL ANGLES EQUAL LEGS

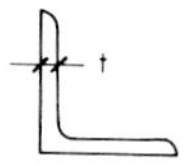

STEEL ANGLES —EQUAL LEGS—BAR SIZE (IN.)

SIZE x t	SIZE x t	SIZE x t
1/2 x 1/2 x 1/8	1 1/4 x 1 1/4 x 3/16	2 x 2 x 3/16
5/8 x 5/8 x 1/8	1 1/4 x 1 1/4 x 1/4	2 x 2 x 1/4
3/4 x 3/4 x 1/8	1 1/2 x 1 1/2 x 1/8	2 x 2 x 5/16
7/8 x 7/8 x 1/8	1 1/2 x 1 1/2 x 3/16	2 x 2 x 3/8
1 x 1 x 1/8	1 1/2 x 1 1/2 x 1/4	2 1/2 x 2 1/2 x 3/16
1 x 1 x 3/16	1 3/4 x 1 3/4 x 1/8	2 1/2 x 2 1/2 x 1/4
1 x 1 x 1/4	1 3/4 x 1 3/4 x 3/16	2 1/2 x 2 1/2 x 5/16
1 1/8 x 1 1/8 x 1/8	1 3/4 x 1 3/4 x 1/4	2 1/2 x 2 1/2 x 3/8
1 1/4 x 1 1/4 x 1/8	2 x 2 x 1/8	2 1/2 x 2 1/2 x 1/2

NOTE: For structural angle sizes (3 x 3 x 3/16 in. and larger) see Dimensions of Angle Shapes in this chapter.

ALUMINUM CHANNEL SQUARE CORNERS

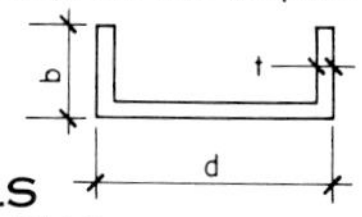

ALUMINUM CHANNELS —SQUARE CORNERS (IN.)

d x b x t	d x b x t	d x b x t
3/8 x 3/8 x 7/64	1 1/4 x 3/4 x 1/8	2 1/2 x 3/4 x 1/8
1/2 x 3/8 x 1/8	1 1/4 x 1 1/4 x 1/8	2 1/2 x 1 1/2 x 1/8
1/2 x 1/2 x 3/32	1 1/2 x 1/2 x 1/8	2 1/2 x 2 1/2 x 1/8
1/2 x 3/4 x 1/8	1 1/2 x 5/8 x 1/8	3 x 1/2 x 1/8
5/8 x 5/8 x 1/8	1 1/2 x 3/4 x 1/8	3 x 1 x 1/8
5/8 x 1 x 1/8	1 1/2 x 1 x 1/8	3 x 2 x 1/8
3/4 x 3/8 x 1/8	1 1/2 x 1 1/2 x 1/8	3 x 3 x 1/8
3/4 x 1/2 x 1/8	1 3/4 x 1/2 x 1/8	4 x 1 1/2 x 1/8
3/4 x 3/4 x 1/8	1 3/4 x 3/4 x 1/8	4 1/2 x 2 x 1/8
1 x 1/2 x 1/8	1 3/4 x 1 x 1/8	5 x 2 x 3/16
1 x 3/4 x 1/8	2 x 1/2 x 1/8	
1 x 1 x 1/8	2 x 1 x 1/8	
1 1/4 x 1/2 x 1/8	2 x 2 x 1/8	
1 1/4 x 5/8 x 1/8	2 1/4 x 7/8 x 1/8	

NOTE: For aluminum channels in American Standard sizes and Aluminum Association Standard sizes, see Dimensions of Channel Shapes in this chapter.

ALUMINUM TEES SQUARE CORNERS

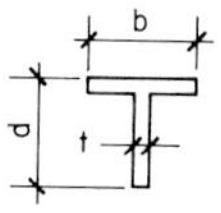

ALUMINUM TEES— SQUARE CORNERS (IN.)

b x d x t	b x d x t	b x d x t
3/4 x 3/4 x 1/8	1 1/8 x 1/2 x 3/8	2 x 3/4 x 1/8
3/4 x 1 1/4 x 1/8	1 1/8 x 1 1/8 x 1/8	2 x 2 x 3/16
1 x 3/4 x 1/8	1 1/4 x 7/8 x 1/8	
1 x 1 x 1/8	1 1/2 x 1 1/2 x 1/8	

ALUMINUM TEES SQUARE CORNERS

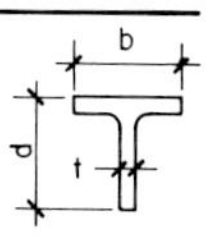

STRUCTURAL (IN.)

1 1/2 x 1 1/2 x 1/4	2 1/4 x 2 1/4 x 1/4	4 x 4 x 3/8
2 x 2 x 1/4	3 x 3 x 3/8	

STAINLESS STEEL ANGLES

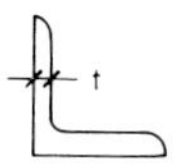

STAINLESS STEEL ANGLES (IN.)

SIZE x t	SIZE x t	SIZE x t
3/4 x 3/4 x 1/8	1 1/2 x 1 1/2 x 3/16	2 1/2 x 2 1/2 x 1/4
1 x 1 x 1/8	1 1/2 x 1 1/2 x 1/4	3 x 3 x 1/4
1 x 1 x 3/16	2 x 2 x 1/8	3 x 3 x 5/16
1 1/4 x 1 1/4 x 1/8	2 x 2 x 3/16	3 x 3 x 3/8
1 1/4 x 1 1/4 x 3/16	2 x 2 x 1/4	
1 1/2 x 1 1/2 x 1/8	2 1/2 x 2 1/2 x 3/16	

Harnish, Morgan, and Causey, Architects; Ontario, California

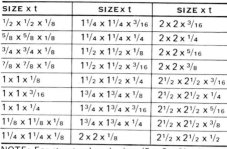

STRUCTURAL TEES CUT FROM W SHAPES—DIMENSIONS FOR DETAILING

DESIGNATION	DEPTH OF SECTION d (IN.)	FLANGE WIDTH b_f (IN.)	FLANGE AVERAGE THICKNESS t_f (IN.)	STEM THICKNESS t_w (IN.)
WT18 x 150	18.370	16.655	1.680	0.945
x 140	18.260	16.595	1.570	0.885
x 130	18.130	16.550	1.440	0.840
x 122.5	18.040	16.510	1.350	0.800
x 115	17.950	16.470	1.260	0.760
WT18 x 105	18.345	12.180	1.360	0.830
x 97	18.245	12.115	1.260	0.765
x 91	18.165	12.075	1.180	0.725
x 85	18.085	12.030	1.100	0.680
x 80	18.005	12.000	1.020	0.650
x 75	17.925	11.975	0.940	0.625
x 67.5	17.775	11.950	0.790	0.600
WT16.5 x 120.5	17.090	15.860	1.400	0.830
x 110.5	16.965	15.805	1.275	0.775
x 100.5	16.840	15.745	1.150	0.715
WT16.5 x 76	16.745	11.565	1.055	0.635
x 70.5	16.650	11.535	0.960	0.605
x 65	16.545	11.510	0.855	0.580
x 59	16.430	11.480	0.740	0.550
WT15 x 105.5	15.470	15.105	1.315	0.775
x 95.5	15.340	15.040	1.185	0.710
x 86.5	15.220	14.985	1.065	0.655
WT15 x 66	15.155	10.545	1.000	0.615
x 62	15.085	10.515	0.930	0.585
x 58	15.005	10.495	0.850	0.565
x 54	14.915	10.475	0.760	0.545
x 49.5	14.825	10.450	0.670	0.520
WT13.5 x 89	13.905	14.085	1.190	0.725
x 80.5	13.795	14.020	1.080	0.660
x 73	13.690	13.965	0.975	0.605
WT13.5 x 57	13.645	10.070	0.930	0.570
x 51	13.545	10.015	0.830	0.515
x 47	13.460	9.990	0.745	0.490
x 42	13.355	9.960	0.640	0.460
WT12 x 81	12.500	12.955	1.220	0.705
x 73	12.370	12.900	1.090	0.650
x 65.5	12.240	12.855	0.960	0.605
x 58.5	12.130	12.800	0.850	0.550
x 52	12.030	12.750	0.750	0.500
WT12 x 47	12.155	9.065	0.875	0.515
x 42	12.050	9.020	0.770	0.470
x 38	11.960	8.990	0.680	0.440
x 34	11.865	8.965	0.585	0.415
WT12 x 31	11.870	7.040	0.590	0.430
x 27.5	11.785	7.005	0.505	0.395
WT10.5 x 73.5	11.030	12.510	1.150	0.720
x 66	10.915	12.440	1.035	0.650
x 61	10.840	12.390	0.960	0.600
x 55.5	10.755	12.340	0.875	0.550
x 50.5	10.680	12.290	0.800	0.500
WT10.5 x 46.5	10.810	8.420	0.930	0.580
x 41.5	10.715	8.355	0.835	0.515
x 36.5	10.620	8.295	0.740	0.455
x 34	10.565	8.270	0.685	0.430
x 31	10.495	8.240	0.615	0.400
WT10.5 x 28.5	10.530	6.555	0.650	0.405
x 25	10.415	6.530	0.535	0.380
x 22	10.330	6.500	0.450	0.350

DESIGNATION	DEPTH OF SECTION d (IN.)	FLANGE WIDTH b_f (IN.)	FLANGE AVERAGE THICKNESS t_f (IN.)	STEM THICKNESS t_w (IN.)
WT9 x 59.5	9.485	11.265	1.060	0.655
x 53	9.365	11.200	0.940	0.590
x 48.5	9.295	11.145	0.870	0.535
x 43	9.195	11.090	0.770	0.480
x 38	9.105	11.035	0.680	0.425
WT9 x 35.5	9.235	7.635	0.810	0.495
x 32.5	9.175	7.590	0.750	0.450
x 30	9.120	7.555	0.695	0.415
x 27.5	9.055	7.530	0.630	0.390
x 25	8.995	7.495	0.570	0.355
WT9 x 23	9.030	6.060	0.605	0.360
x 20	8.950	6.015	0.525	0.315
x 17.5	8.850	6.000	0.425	0.300
WT8 x 50	8.485	10.425	0.985	0.585
x 44.5	8.375	10.365	0.875	0.525
x 38.5	8.260	10.295	0.760	0.455
x 33.5	8.165	10.235	0.665	0.395
WT8 x 28.5	8.215	7.120	0.715	0.430
x 25	8.130	7.070	0.630	0.380
x 22.5	8.065	7.035	0.565	0.345
x 20	8.005	6.995	0.505	0.305
x 18	7.930	6.985	0.430	0.295
WT8 x 15.5	7.940	5.525	0.440	0.275
x 13	7.845	5.500	0.345	0.250
WT7 x 365	11.210	17.890	4.910	3.070
x 332.5	10.820	17.650	4.520	2.830
x 302.5	10.460	17.415	4.160	2.595
x 275	10.120	17.200	3.820	2.380
x 250	9.800	17.010	3.500	2.190
x 227.5	9.510	16.835	3.210	2.015
WT7 x 213	9.335	16.695	3.035	1.875
x 199	9.145	16.590	2.845	1.770
x 185	8.960	16.475	2.660	1.655
x 171	8.770	16.360	2.470	1.540
x 155.5	8.560	16.230	2.260	1.410
x 141.5	8.370	16.110	2.070	1.290
x 128.5	8.190	15.995	1.890	1.175
x 116.5	8.020	15.890	1.720	1.070
x 105.5	7.860	15.800	1.560	0.980
x 96.5	7.740	15.710	1.440	0.890
x 88	7.610	15.650	1.310	0.830
x 79.5	7.490	15.565	1.190	0.745
x 72.5	7.390	15.500	1.090	0.680
WT7 x 66	7.330	14.725	1.030	0.645
x 60	7.240	14.670	0.940	0.590
x 54.5	7.160	14.605	0.860	0.525
x 49.5	7.080	14.565	0.780	0.485
x 45	7.010	14.520	0.710	0.440
WT7 x 41	7.155	10.130	0.855	0.510
x 37	7.085	10.070	0.785	0.450
x 34	7.020	10.035	0.720	0.415
x 30.5	6.945	9.995	0.645	0.375
WT7 x 26.5	6.960	8.060	0.660	0.370
x 24	6.895	8.030	0.595	0.340
x 21.5	6.830	7.995	0.530	0.305
WT7 x 19	7.050	6.770	0.515	0.310
x 17	6.990	6.745	0.455	0.285
x 15	6.920	6.730	0.385	0.270
WT7 x 13	6.955	5.025	0.420	0.255
x 11	6.870	5.000	0.335	0.230

DESIGNATION	DEPTH OF SECTION d (IN.)	FLANGE WIDTH b_f (IN.)	FLANGE AVERAGE THICKNESS t_f (IN.)	STEM THICKNESS t_w (IN.)
WT6 x 95	7.100	12.070	1.735	1.060
x 85	7.015	12.570	1.560	0.960
x 76	6.855	12.480	1.400	0.870
x 68	6.705	12.400	1.250	0.790
x 60	6.560	12.320	1.105	0.710
x 53	6.445	12.220	0.990	0.610
x 48	6.355	12.160	0.900	0.550
x 43.5	6.265	12.125	0.810	0.515
x 39.5	6.190	12.080	0.735	0.470
x 36	6.125	12.040	0.670	0.430
x 32.5	6.060	12.000	0.605	0.390
WT6 x 29	6.095	10.010	0.640	0.360
x 26.5	6.030	9.995	0.575	0.345
WT6 x 25	6.095	8.080	0.640	0.370
x 22.5	6.030	8.045	0.575	0.335
x 20	5.970	8.005	0.515	0.295
WT6 x 17.5	6.250	6.560	0.520	0.300
x 15	6.170	6.520	0.440	0.260
x 13	6.110	6.490	0.380	0.230
WT6 x 11	6.155	4.030	0.425	0.260
x 9.5	6.080	4.005	0.350	0.235
x 8	5.995	3.990	0.265	0.220
x 7	5.955	3.970	0.225	0.200
WT5 x 56	5.680	10.415	1.250	0.755
x 50	5.550	10.340	1.120	0.680
x 44	5.420	10.265	0.990	0.605
x 38.5	5.300	10.190	0.870	0.530
x 34	5.200	10.130	0.770	0.470
x 30	5.110	10.080	0.680	0.420
x 27	5.045	10.030	0.615	0.370
x 24.5	4.990	10.000	0.560	0.340
WT5 x 22.5	5.050	8.020	0.620	0.350
x 19.5	4.960	7.985	0.530	0.315
x 16.5	4.865	7.960	0.435	0.290
WT5 x 15	5.235	5.810	0.510	0.300
x 13	5.165	5.770	0.440	0.260
x 11	5.085	5.750	0.360	0.240
WT5 x 9.5	5.120	4.020	0.395	0.250
x 8.5	5.055	4.010	0.330	0.240
x 7.5	4.995	4.000	0.270	0.230
x 6	4.935	3.960	0.210	0.190
WT4 x 33.5	4.500	8.280	0.935	0.570
x 29	4.375	8.220	0.810	0.510
x 24	4.250	8.110	0.685	0.400
x 20	4.125	8.070	0.560	0.360
x 17.5	4.060	8.020	0.495	0.310
x 15.5	4.000	7.995	0.435	0.285
WT4 x 14	4.030	6.535	0.465	0.285
x 12	3.965	6.495	0.400	0.245
WT4 x 10.5	4.140	5.270	0.400	0.250
x 9	4.070	5.250	0.330	0.230
WT4 x 7.5	4.055	4.015	0.315	0.245
x 6.5	3.995	4.000	0.255	0.230
x 5	3.945	3.940	0.205	0.170
WT3 x 12.5	3.190	6.080	0.455	0.320
x 10	3.100	6.020	0.365	0.260
x 7.5	2.995	5.990	0.260	0.230
WT3 x 8	3.140	4.030	0.405	0.260
x 6	3.015	4.000	0.280	0.230
x 4.5	2.950	3.940	0.215	0.170

STRUCTURAL TEES CUT FROM S SHAPES—DIMENSIONS FOR DETAILING

DESIGNATION	d	b_f	t_f	t_w
ST12 x 60	12.00	8.048	1.102	0.798
x 52.95	12.00	7.875	1.102	0.625
ST12 x 50	12.00	7.247	0.871	0.747
x 45	12.00	7.124	0.871	0.624
x 39.95	12.00	7.001	0.871	0.501
ST10 x 47.5	10.00	7.200	0.916	0.800
x 42.5	10.00	7.053	0.916	0.653
ST10 x 37.5	10.00	6.391	0.789	0.641
x 32.7	10.00	6.250	0.789	0.500
ST9 x 35	9.00	6.251	0.691	0.711
x 27.35	9.00	6.001	0.691	0.461

DESIGNATION	d	b_f	t_f	t_w
ST7.5 x 25	7.50	5.640	0.622	0.550
x 21.45	7.50	5.501	0.622	0.411
ST6 x 25	6.00	5.477	0.659	0.687
x 20.4	6.00	5.252	0.659	0.462
ST6 x 17.5	6.00	5.078	0.544	0.428
x 15.9	6.00	5.000	0.544	0.350
ST5 x 17.5	5.00	4.944	0.491	0.594
x 12.7	5.00	4.661	0.491	0.311
ST4 x 11.5	4.00	4.171	0.425	0.441
x 9.2	4.00	4.001	0.425	0.271

DESIGNATION	d	b_f	t_f	t_w
ST3.5 x 10	3.50	3.860	0.392	0.450
x 7.65	3.50	3.662	0.392	0.252
ST3 x 8.625	3.00	3.565	0.359	0.465
x 6.25	3.00	3.332	0.359	0.232
ST2.5 x 7.375	2.50	3.284	0.326	0.494
x 5	2.50	3.004	0.326	0.214
ST2 x 4.75	2.00	2.796	0.293	0.326
x 3.85	2.00	2.663	0.293	0.193
ST1.5 x 3.75	1.50	2.509	0.260	0.349
x 2.85	1.50	2.330	0.260	0.170

RECTANGULAR TUBING

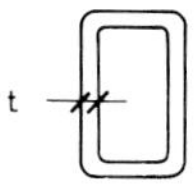

RECTANGULAR TUBING—STEEL

SIZE (IN.)	T - WALL THICKNESS (BW GAUGE OR IN.)				
1½ x ¾	0.073				
1½ x 1	16	14	11		
2 x 1	16	14	11		
2 x 1¼	14				
2 x 1½	11				
2½ x 1	14				
2½ x 1¼	14				
2½ x 1½	14	0.145	7	5	¼''
3 x 1	14				
3 x 1½	16	14	11	7	
3 x 2	14	11	9/64''	3/16''	¼''
4 x 2	14	11	5/32''	3/16''	¼''
4 x 2½	11				
4 x 3	11	5/32''	3/16''	¼''	5/16''
5 x 2	3/16''	¼''			
5 x 2½	11	7			
5 x 3	3/16''	¼''	5/16''	3/8''	½''
6 x 2	3/16''	¼''			
6 x 3	3/16''	¼''	5/16''	3/8''	½''
6 x 4	3/16''	¼''	5/16''	3/8''	½''
7 x 4	¼''	3/8''			
7 x 5	3/16''	¼''	5/16''	3/8''	½''
8 x 2	3/16''				
8 x 3	3/16''	¼''			
8 x 4	3/16''	¼''	5/16''	3/8''	½''
8 x 6	3/16''	¼''	5/16''	3/8''	½''
10 x 2	3/16''				
10 x 4	3/16''	¼''			
10 x 5	¼''				
10 x 6	¼''	5/16''	3/8''	½''	
10 x 8	¼''	3/8''	½''		
12 x 2	3/16''				
12 x 4	¼''	3/8''			
12 x 6	¼''	3/8''	½''		
ALUMINUM					
2 x 3	3/16''				
2 x 4	3/16''				
2 x 6	3/16''				
STAINLESS STEEL					
½ x 1½	0.065				
¾ x 1¼	0.065				
¾ x 1½	0.065				
1 x 1½	0.065				
1 x 2	0.065				
1¼ x 2½	0.065				
1¾ x 3	0.065				
1¾ x 4	0.065				

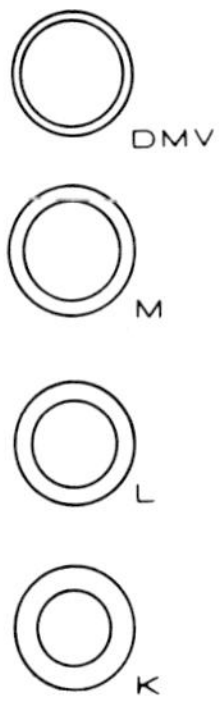

ROUND TUBING—COPPER

SIZE (IN.) NOMINAL INSIDE DIA.	OUTSIDE DIA. (BW GAUGE)	INSIDE DIAMETER (BW GAUGE)			
		TYPE K	TYPE L	TYPE M	TYPE DWV
¼	0.375	0.305	0.315		
½	0.625	0.527	0.545	0.569	
¾	0.875	0.745	0.785	0.811	
1	1.125	0.995	1.025	1.055	
1½	1.625	1.481	1.505	1.527	1.541
2	2.125	1.959	1.985	2.009	2.041
4	4.125	3.857	3.905	3.935	4.009

RECTANGULAR ALUMINUM TUBING

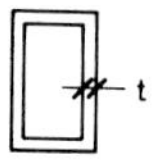

RECTANGULAR ALUMINUM TUBING (IN.)

SIZE x T	SIZE x T	SIZE x T
½ x 1 x ⅛	1½ x 2½ x ⅛	2 x 3 x ⅛
¾ x 1½ x ⅛	1½ x 6 x ⅛	2 x 4 x ⅛
1 x 1½ x ⅛	1¾ x 2¼ x ⅛	2 x 5 x ⅛
1 x 2 x ⅛	1¾ x 3 x ⅛	2 x 6 x ⅛
1 x 3 x ⅛	1¾ x 3½ x ⅛	3 x 5 x ⅛
1¼ x 2½ x ⅛	1¾ x 4 x ⅛	3 x 5 x ⅛
1¼ x 3 x ⅛	1¾ x 4½ x ⅛	
1½ x 2 x ⅛	1¾ x 5 x ⅛	

SQUARE ALUMINUM TUBING

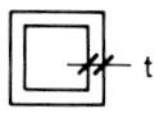

SQUARE ALUMINUM TUBING (IN.)

SIZE x T	SIZE x T	SIZE x T
½ x ½ x 1/16	1¼ x 1¼ x 5/64	2 x 2 x ⅛
⅝ x ⅝ x 1/16	1¼ x 1¼ x ⅛	2½ x 2½ x ⅛
¾ x ¾ x 1/16	1½ x 1½ x 5/64	3 x 3 x ⅛
¾ x ¾ x ⅛	1½ x 1½ x ⅛	4 x 4 x ⅛
1 x 1 x 1/16	1¾ x 1¾ x ⅛	
1 x 1 x ⅛	2 x 2 x 5/64	

NOTE: Rectangular and square aluminum tubing with sharp corners is usually used for miscellaneous architectural metalwork.

NOTE

Round tubing, usually manufactured for mechanical purposes, is used for architectural metalwork to supplement round pipe. Round tubing is measured by the outside diameter and the wall thickness by gauge, fractions, or decimals of an inch. Round tubing is used where a high grade finish is required and exact diameters are necessary.

Round tubing is available in steel, aluminum, copper, stainless steel, and other metals. Individual manufacturers' catalogs should be consulted for availability of materials and sizes.

ROUND PIPE

ROUND PIPE—STEEL

SIZE (IN.) NOMINAL INSIDE DIA.	OUTSIDE DIA. (BW GAUGE)	INSIDE DIAMETER (BW GAUGE)		
		STAN-DARD	EXTRA STRONG	DOUBLE EXTRA STRONG
⅛	0.405	0.269	0.215	
¼	0.540	0.364	0.302	
⅜	0.675	0.493	0.423	
½	0.840	0.622	0.546	0.252
¾	1.050	0.824	0.742	0.434
1	1.315	1.049	0.957	0.599
1¼	1.660	1.380	1.278	0.896
1½	1.900	1.610	1.500	1.100
2	2.375	2.067	1.939	1.503
2½	2.875	2.469	2.323	1.771
3	3.500	3.068	2.900	2.300
3½	4.000	3.548	3.364	2.728
4	4.500	4.026	3.826	3.152
5	5.563	5.047	4.813	4.063
6	6.625	6.065	5.761	4.897
8	8.625	7.981	7.625	6.875
10	10.750	10.020	9.750	8.750
12	12.750	12.000	11.750	10.750

NOTE

Round pipe is made in primarily three weights: Standard, Extra Strong (or Extra Heavy), and Double Extra Strong (or Double Extra Heavy). Outside diameters of the three weights of pipe in each size are always the same, extra thickness always being on the inside and therefore reducing the inside diameter of the heavier pipe. All sizes are specified by what is known as the "nominal inside diameter."

Round pipe is also available in aluminum and stainless steel. Individual manufacturers' catalogs should be consulted for sizes.

SQUARE TUBING

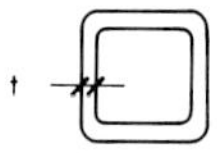

SQUARE TUBING—STEEL

SIZE (IN.)	T - WALL THICKNESS (BW GAUGE OR IN.)										SIZE (IN.)	T
½ x ½	18	16									**ALUMINUM**	
⅝ x ⅝	18	0.060	16								2 x 2	0.120
¾ x ¾	20	18	0.060	16	11						3 x 3	3/16''
⅞ x ⅞	18	16									4 x 4	3/16''
1 x 1	20	18	0.060	16	14	13	0.102	12	11		**STAINLESS STEEL**	
1⅛ x 1⅛	18	16									¾ x ¾	0.049
1¼ x 1¼	18	0.060	16	0.075	0.090	11	3/16''				1 x 1	0.049	0.065
1½ x 1½	18	0.060	16	14	11	0.140	7	3/16''	¼''		1¼ x 1¼	0.065
1¾ x 1¾	16	14	13	11							1½ x 1½	0.065
2 x 2	0.060	18	16	14	11	⅛''	0.145	3/16''	¼''		1¾ x 1¾	0.065
2½ x 2½	16	14	11	0.141	¼''						2 x 2	0.065
3 x 3	16	14	13	11	3/16''	¼''						
3½ x 3½	11	5/32''	5	¼''								
4 x 4	14	11	3/16''	¼''	3/8''	½''						
4½ x 4½	3/16''	¼''										
5 x 5	3/16''	¼''	5/16''	3/8''								
6 x 6	3/16''	¼''	5/16''	3/8''								
7 x 7	3/16''	¼''	5/16''	3/8''								
8 x 8	¼''	5/16''	3/8''	½''								
10 x 10	¼''	5/16''	3/8''	½''								

ROUND TUBING COPPER

Harnish, Morgan, and Causey, Architects; Ontario, California

STRUCTURAL METAL FRAMING

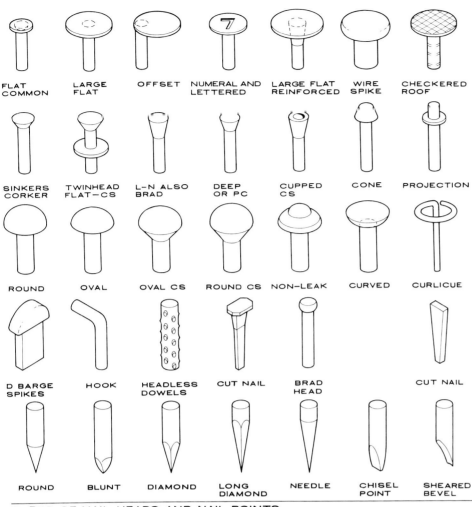

Row 1: FLAT COMMON | LARGE FLAT | OFFSET | NUMERAL AND LETTERED | LARGE FLAT REINFORCED | WIRE SPIKE | CHECKERED ROOF

Row 2: SINKERS CORKER | TWINHEAD FLAT—CS | L-N ALSO BRAD | DEEP OR PC | CUPPED CS | CONE | PROJECTION

Row 3: ROUND | OVAL | OVAL CS | ROUND CS | NON-LEAK | CURVED | CURLICUE

Row 4: D BARGE SPIKES | HOOK | HEADLESS DOWELS | CUT NAIL | BRAD HEAD | | CUT NAIL

Row 5: ROUND | BLUNT | DIAMOND | LONG DIAMOND | NEEDLE | CHISEL POINT | SHEARED BEVEL

TYPES OF NAIL HEADS AND NAIL POINTS

NOTES

1. Nail diameter, length, shape and surface affect holding power (withdrawal resistance and lateral resistance). See NFPA publications.

2. Materials: Zinc, brass, monel, copper, aluminum, iron or steel, stainless steel, copper bearing steel, muntz metal.

3. Coatings: Tin, copper, cement, brass plated, zinc, nickel, chrome, cadmium, etched acid, parkerized.

4. Forms: Smooth, barbed, helical, annular-ring.

5. Colors: Blue, bright, coppered, black (annealed).

6. Gauges shown are for steel wire (Washburn and Moen).

7. Abbreviations (for the following pages of nails only):

B = blunt	F = flat	O = oval
CS = countersunk	L = long	PC = pointing cone
D = diamond	N = narrow	R = round

FASTENER FINISHES AND COATINGS

COATINGS OR FINISH	USED ON:	COMMENTS
Anodizing	Aluminum	Excellent corrosion protection
Chromate: black, clear, colored	Zinc and cadmium plated	Colors usually offer better protection than clear
Cadmiumplate	Most metals	
Copperplate	Most metals	Electroplated, fair protection
Copper, brass, bronze	Most metals	Indoor, decorative finishes
Lacquering	All metals	Some specially designed for humid conditions
Lead-tin	Steel	Applied by hot-dip. Gives good lubrication to tapping screws.
Nickel, bright and dull	Most metals	Indoor; outdoor if at least .0005 in. thick
Phosphate rust preventative	Steel	Rustproofs steel. Oils increase corrosion resistance
Phosphate paint-base preparations	Steel, aluminum zinc plate	Chemical process for painting or lacquering
Colored phosphate coatings	Steel	Superior to regular phosphated or oiled surfaces
Rust preventatives	All metals	Usually applied to phosphate and black oxide finishes
Electroplated zinc or tin; electrogalvanized zinc; hot-dip zinc or tin	All metals	Zinc or Tin
Hot-dip aluminum	Steel	Maximum corrosion protection, withstands high temperatures

Timothy B. McDonald; Washington, D.C.

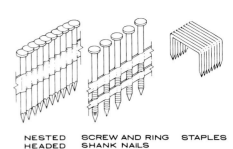

Row: NESTED HEADED NAILS | SCREW AND RING SHANK NAILS | STAPLES

STAPLES AND NAILS FOR PNEUMATIC FASTENERS
ALLOWABLE LOADS FOR DESIGNED STRUCTURES

FAS-TENER	WIRE DIAM-ETER	WIRE GAUGE	PENE-TRA-TION INTO MAIN MEM-BER	ALLOWABLE LOAD (LBS.) (6,7)	
				LAT-ERAL (4,5)	WITH-DRAWAL
T-nail	.097	12½	1⅛	52	29
T-nail	.113	11½	1¼	63	34
T-nail	.131	10¼	1½	78	39
T-nail	.148	9	1⅝	94	44
staple	.0625	16	1	52	36
staple	.072	15	1	64	42
staple	.080	14	1	75	46
staple	.0915	13	1	92	53
staple	.1055	12	1⅛	113	62

NOTES

1. Refer to Industrial Stapling and Nailing Technical Association, HUD-FHA Bulletin No. UM-25d (1973), for complete data.

2. Crown widths range from ³⁄₁₆ in. to 1 in. Leg lengths vary from ⁵⁄₃₂ in. to 3½ in. Gauge should be chosen for shear value needed.

3. Screw shank and ring shank nails have the same allowable loads as common nails.

4. Nested nails are manufactured with a crescent-shaped piece missing in the head.

5. For wood diaphragms resisting wind or seismic loading these values may be increased 30 percent in addition to the 33⅓ percent increase permitted for duration of load.

6. The tabulated allowable lateral values are for fasteners installed in Douglas Fir-Larch or Southern Pine.

7. Allowable values shall be adjusted for duration of load in accordance with standard engineering practices. Where metal side plates are used, lateral strength values may be increased 25 percent.

8. Withdrawal values are for fasteners inserted perpendicular to the grain in pounds per linear inch of penetration into the main member based on a specific gravity of approximately 0.545.

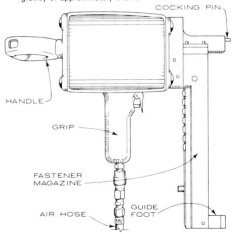

COCKING PIN

HANDLE

GRIP

FASTENER MAGAZINE

AIR HOSE

GUIDE FOOT

PNEUMATIC NAILERS AND STAPLERS

Pneumatic nailers and staplers, connected to compressors or CO_2 bottles, are capable of attaching a variety of fasteners to concrete and steel as well as wood. Consult manufacturer for special features and interchangeability of fasteners.

NAIL TYPE		SIZE		MATERIAL
F D #14 GAUGE	BARBED NAILS	1/4" TO 1½"		CEMENT COATED, BRASS, STEEL
LCSN D #14 GAUGE	CASING NAILS	2d TO 40d 6d TO 10d		BRIGHT, CEMENT COATED CUPPED HEADS AVAILABLE IN ALUMINUM
O ALSO FLAT HEAD CS D #5 TO #10 GAUGE	CEMENT NAILS ALSO CALLED CONCRETE NAILS AND HARDENED NAILS	1/2" TO 3"		SMOOTH, BRIGHT OIL QUENCHED
L N F CUP HEAD AVAILABLE #15 TO #2 GAUGE	COMMON BRAD	2d TO 60d		BRIGHT—MAY BE SECURED WITH CUPPED HEAD, CEMENT COATED—USUALLY MADE IN HEAVY GAUGES
F	CUT COMMON NAILS OR CUT COMMON SPIKE	2d TO 60d 20d TO 100d		STEEL OR IRON PLAIN OR ZINC COATED
L N F GAUGE	COMMON NAILS (SHINGLE NAILS)	2d TO 60d		COPPER—CLAD
F D LIGHT GAUGE .095" HEAVY GAUGE .120"	COMMON BRASS WIRE NAILS	LIGHT GAUGE	1/2" 1" TO 3½"	BRASS, ALUMINUM
		HEAVY GAUGE	3/4"—6"	
F D .109 (ABOUT 12 GAUGE)	COMMON NAILS (SHINGLE NAILS)	5/8" TO 6"		COPPER WIRE, ALUMINUM
F	STANDARD CUT NAILS (NON-FERROUS)	5/8" TO 6"		COPPER, MUNTZ METAL OR ZINC
F 2"LONG D #11½ GAUGE DOUBLE HEADED		1¾," 2," 2¼," 2½," 2¾," 3," 3½," 4," 4½"		BRIGHT, CEMENT COATED, MADE IN SEVERAL DESIGNS
CUPPED HEAD AVAILABLE D MADE IN 5 DIAMETERS	DOWEL PINS	5/8" TO 2"		BARBED – CUPPED HEAD AVAILABLE
O D MADE IN 3 GAUGES	ESCUTCHEON PINS	1/4" TO 2"		BRIGHT STEEL, BRASS PLATED, BRASS, ALSO NICKEL, SILVER, COPPER, ALUMINUM
F 6d–2" D #10 GAUGE FENCE NAILS		5d TO 20d		SMOOTH; BRIGHT, CEMENT COATED (GAUGE HEAVIER THAN COMMON)
L N F D #15 GAUGE	FINISHING NAIL, WIRE	2d TO 20d		SMOOTH; CUPPED HEADS AVAILABLE (SMALLER GAUGE THAN USUAL COMMON BRAD)
	FINISHING NAILS	STANDARD FINE	3d TO 20d 6d TO 10d	CUT IRON AND STEEL
3d–1⅛" #15 & #16 GAUGE	FINE NAILS	2d & 2d EX. FINE 3d & 3d EX. FINE		BRIGHT—SMALLER GAUGE AND HEADS THAN COMMON NAILS
PC B (ALSO WITH D. POINT) #14 GAUGE FLOORING NAILS		3d TO 20d 6d TO 20d		BRIGHT AND CEMENT COATED (DIFFERENT GAUGE) CUPPED HEADS AVAILABLE
L N CS 6d–2" D OR BLUNT D #11 GAUGE FLOORING BRAD		6d TO 20d		SMOOTH; BRIGHT AND CEMENT COATED CUPPED HEADS AVAILABLE

5   METAL FASTENING

NAIL TYPE		SIZE	MATERIAL
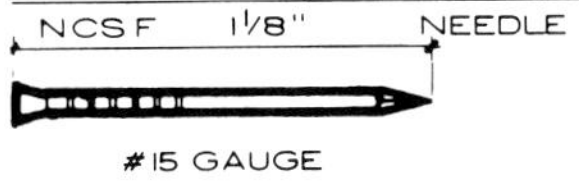 NCSF 1⅛" NEEDLE #15 GAUGE	PARQUET FLOORING NAIL OR BRAD	1", 1⅛", 1¼"	SMOOTH OR BARBED
	FLOORING NAILS	4d TO 10d	IRON OR STEEL (CUT)
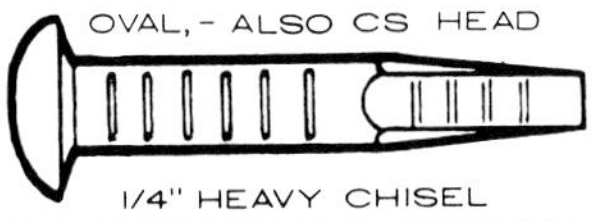 OVAL, - ALSO CS HEAD 1/4" HEAVY CHISEL	HINGE NAILS	HEAVY: 1/4" TO 3/8" DIA. / LIGHT–3/16" TO 1/4" DIA — 1½" TO 4" LONG	SMOOTH, BRIGHT OR ANNEALED
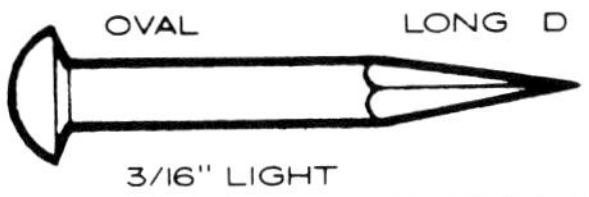 OVAL LONG D 3/16" LIGHT	HINGE NAILS	HEAVY-1/4" DIA. / LIGHT – 3/16" DIA. — 1½" TO 3" ALSO TO 4"	SMOOTH, BRIGHT OR ANNEALED
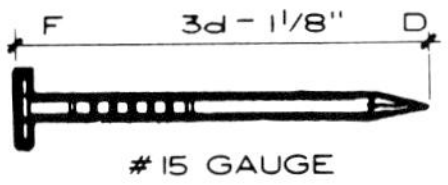 F 3d – 1⅛" D #15 GAUGE	LATH NAILS (WOOD)	2d, 2d LIGHT, 3d, 3d LIGHT, 3d HEAVY 4d.	BRIGHT (NOT RECOMMENDED), BLUED OR CEMENT COATED
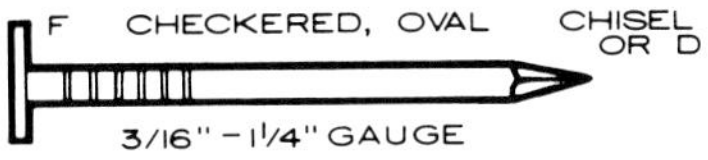 F CHECKERED, OVAL CHISEL OR D 3/16" – 1/4" GAUGE	GUTTER SPIKES	6" TO 10"	STEEL, ZINC COATED
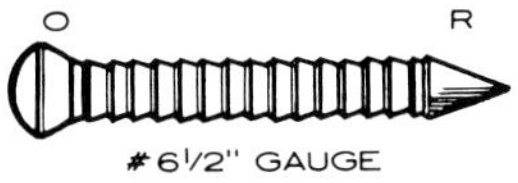 O R #6½" GAUGE	HINGE NAILS	1½" TO 3"	STEEL, ZINC COATED
 HOOK 1⅛" #12 GAUGE	LATH NAILS (METAL)	1⅛"	BRIGHT, BLUED, ZINC COATED, ANNEALED
 #14 & #15 GAUGE	LATH STAPLES	1" TO 1½"	BRIGHT, BLUED, ZINC COATED, ANNEALED
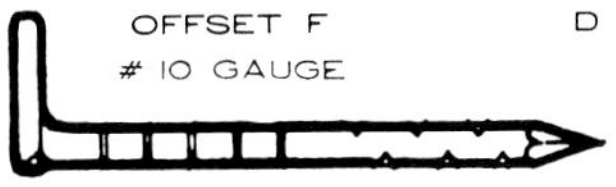 OFFSET F D #10 GAUGE	LATH OFFSET HEAD NAILS FOR SELF FURRING METAL LATH	1¼" TO 1¾"	BRIGHT, ZINC COATED
 F #7 – #9 GAUGE	MASONRY NAILS USED FOR FURRING STRIPS CLEATS, PLATES	½" TO 4"	HIGH CARBON STEEL, HEATED & TEMPERED
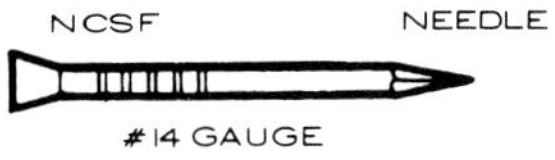 NCSF NEEDLE #14 GAUGE	MOLDING NAILS (BRADS)	⅞" TO 1¼"	SMOOTH, BRIGHT OR CEMENT COATED
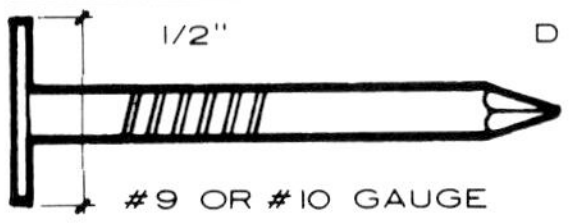 1/2" D #9 OR #10 GAUGE	PLASTER-BOARD NAILS USED ALSO FOR WALL-BOARD ROCK LATH (5/16" HEAD)	1" TO 1¾" 1⅛" TO 1½"	SMOOTH, BRIGHT OR CEMENT COATED, BLUED ALUMINUM
 F D #10 GAUGE	ROOFING NAILS (STANDARD)	3/4" TO 2"	BRIGHT, CEMENT COATED, ZINC COATED BARBED
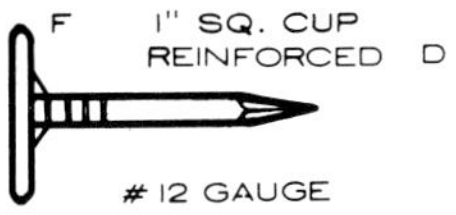 F 1" SQ. CUP REINFORCED D #12 GAUGE	ROOFING NAILS FOR BUILT-UP ROOFING	3/8" TO 2"	STEEL, ZINC COATED
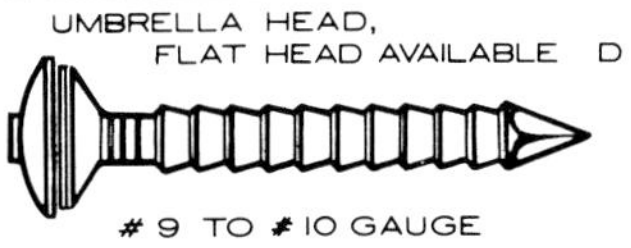 UMBRELLA HEAD, FLAT HEAD AVAILABLE D #9 TO #10 GAUGE	NEOPRENE WASHER ROOFING NAILS	1½" TO 2½"	STEEL, ZINC COATED
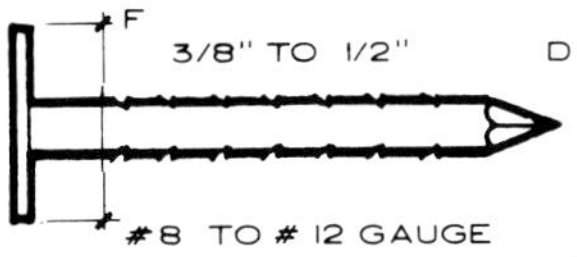 F 3/8" TO 1/2" D #8 TO #12 GAUGE	ROOFING NAILS LARGE HEAD	3/4" TO 1¾" ALSO 2" 3/4" TO 2½"	BARBED, BRIGHT OR ZINC COATED CHECKERED HEAD AVAILABLE ALUMINUM (ETCHED) NEOPRENE WASHER OPTIONAL

NAIL TYPE	SIZE	MATERIAL
F REINFORCED 5/8" DIA. 1¼" NEEDLE OR D # 11 TO # 12 GAUGE ALSO # 10 GAUGE **ROOFING NAILS LARGE HEAD**	3/4" TO 1¼"	BRIGHT OR ZINC COATED
#10 GAUGE **NON-LEAKING ROOFING NAIL**	1¾" TO 2"	ZINC COATED, ALSO WITH LEAD HEADS
CUT SHEATHING NAILS	3/4" TO 3"	COPPER OR MUNTZ METAL
F LARGE HEAD AVAILABLE 1/4" TO 9/32" 5/16" DIA. #12 GAUGE D **SHINGLE NAILS**	3d TO 6d 2d TO 6d	SMOOTH, BRIGHT, ZINC, CEMENT COATED, LIGHT AND HEAVY ALUMINUM
CUT SHINGLE NAILS	2d TO 6d	IRON OR STEEL (CUT) PLAIN OR ZINC COATED
F D # 14 GAUGE **SIDING NAILS**	2d TO 40d 6d TO 10d	SMOOTH, BRIGHT OR CEMENT COATED SMALLER DIAMETER THAN COMMON NAILS ALUMINUM
F D # 11 GAUGE **SIDING NAILS USED FOR FENCES, TANKS, GATES, ETC.**	2½" TO 3"	STEEL ZINC COATED
F 5/16" TO 3/8" SEVERAL GAUGES **SLATING NAILS**	3/8" HEAD | 1"TO 2" SMALL HEADS | 1"TO 2" COPPER WIRE | 7/8"-1½"	ZINC COATED, BRIGHT, CEMENT COATED, COPPER CLAD, COPPER
CUT SLATING NAILS, NON-FERROUS	1¼" TO 2"	COPPER, ZINC OR MUNTZ METAL
OVAL, SQUARE OR ROUND HEAD CHISEL POINT 1/4" TO 5/8" SQ. **BARGE SPIKE, SQUARE**	3" TO 12" ALSO 16"	PLAIN AND ZINC COATED USED FOR HARDWOOD
SQUARE OR DIAMOND HEAD 7/32" TO 1⅛" DIA. CHISEL POINT 1/4" TO 5/8" SQ. **BOAT SPIKE, SQUARE**	3" TO 12"	PLAIN AND ZINC COATED USED FOR HARD WOOD
1" HEAD **ROOF DECK NAILS**	1" AND 1¾"	GALVANIZED - NAILS STEEL TUBE
F OR OCS D OR CHISEL POINT # 6 TO 3/8" GAUGE **ROUND WIRE SPIKES**	10d TO 60d & 7" TO 12" ALSO 16"	SMOOTH, BRIGHT OR ZINC COATED

MACHINE BOLT ANCHORS AND SHIELDS (IN.)

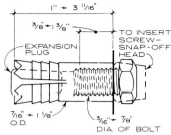

SELF-DRILLING EXPANSION SION ANCHOR
(SNAP-OFF TYPE)

BOLT DIA.	THDS PER INCH	DECIMAL EQUIV. (IN.)	SINGLE EXPANDING ANCHOR (CAULKING)		SINGLE EXPANDING ANCHOR (NONCAULKING)		MULTIPLE EXPANDING ANCHOR (PLAIN STYLE)			MULTIPLE EXPANDING ANCHOR (THREADED STYLE)			DOUBLE ACTING SHIELD	
								L UNITS			L UNITS			
			A	L	A	L	A	2	3	A	2	3	A	L
6	32	.138	5/16	1/2										
8	32	.164	5/16	1/2										
10	24	.190	3/8	5/8										
12	24	.216	1/2	7/8										
1/4	20	.250	1/2	7/8	1/2	1 3/8	1/2"	1 1/8		1/2	1		1/2	1 1/4
5/16	18	.312	5/8	1	5/8	1 5/8							5/8	1 1/2
3/8	16	.375	3/4	1 1/4	5/8	1 5/8	3/4	1 1/2		3/4	1 1/2		3/4	1 3/4
1/2	13	.500	7/8	1 1/2	7/8	2 1/2	1	1 3/4	2 3/8	1	1 3/4	2 1/4	7/8	2 1/4
5/8	11	.625	1 1/8	2	1	2 3/4	1 1/8	*	2 5/8	1 1/8	*	2 1/2	1	2 1/2
3/4	10	.750	1 1/4	2 1/4	1 1/4	2 7/8	1 3/8	*	3	1 3/8	*	3 1/8	1 1/4	3 1/2
7/8	9	.875					1 1/2	*	3 1/2	1 1/2	*	3 5/8	1 5/8	4"
1	8	1.00					1 5/8	*	3 7/8	1 5/8	*	3 3/4	1 3/4	4 1/4

*Use of three units in these diameters is recommended.

NOTE
1. Extension sleeve for deep setting.
2. Expansion shields and anchors shown are representative of many types, some of which may be used in single or multiple units.
3. Many are threaded for use with the head of the screw outside, some with the head inside and some types require setting tools to install.
4. In light construction plastic expansion shields are used frequently.

NOTE
1. Refer to manufacturers for size variations within the limits shown, and for different types of bolts.
2. The anchor is made of case hardened steel and drawn carburizing steel.

HOLLOW WALL ANCHORS

ANCHOR DIA. (IN.)	A	L	A	L
1/8	5/16	1-2 9/16		XS-L
3/16	7/16	2 1/4-3 1/2		
1/4	1/2	2 1/4-3 1/2		

SHIELDS FOR LAG BOLTS AND WOOD SCREWS (IN.)

LAG SCREW DIA. (IN.)	WOOD SCREW SIZES	DECIMAL EQUIV. (IN.)	LAG BOLT EXPANSION SHIELD A	L SHORT	L LONG	LEAD SHIELD FOR LAG BOLT OR WOOD SCREW A	L
	6	.138				1/4	3/4-1 1/2
	8	.164				1/4	3/4-1 1/2
	10	.190				5/16	1-1 1/2
	12	.216				5/16	1-1 1/2
1/4	14	.250	1/2	1	1 1/2	5/16	1-1 1/2
	16	.268				3/8	1 1/2
	18	.294				3/8	1 1/2
5/16	20	.320	1/2	1 1/4	1 3/4	7/16	1 3/4
3/8	24	.372	5/8	1 3/4	2 1/2	7/16	1 3/4
1/2		.500	3/4	2	3		
5/8		.625	7/8	2	3 1/2		
3/4		.750	1	2	3 1/2		

ONE PIECE ANCHORS (IN.)

ANCHOR SIZE AND DRILL SIZE	DECIMAL EQUIV. (IN.)	WEDGE ANCHOR L	MIN. HOLE DEPTH D	STUD ANCHOR L	MIN. HOLE DEPTH D	SLEEVE ANCHOR L	MIN. HOLE DEPTH D	HEAD STYLE
1/4	.250	1 3/4-3 1/4	1 3/8	1 3/4-3 1/4	1 3/8	5/8-2 1/4	1/2-1 1/8	Acorn nut
5/16	.320			1 1/2-2 1/2	1 1/8			Hex nut
3/8	.375	2 1/4-5	1 3/4	2 1/4-6	1 5/8	1 7/8-3	1 1/2	''
1/2	.500	2 3/4-7	2 1/8	2 3/4-5 1/4	1 7/8	2 1/4-4	1 7/8	''
5/8	.625	3 1/2-8 1/2	2 5/8	3 3/8-7	2 3/8	2 1/4-6	2	''
3/4	.750	4 1/4-10	3 1/4	4 1/4-8 1/2	2 7/8	2 1/2-8	2 1/4-5 1/2	''
7/8	.875	6-10	3 3/4					
1	1.00	6-12	4 1/2					
1 1/4	1.25	9-12	5 1/2					

Sleeve anchors available in acorn nut, hex nut, flat head, round head, Phillips round head, and tie wire head styles.

METAL FASTENING 5

MACHINE SCREW AND STOVE BOLT (INS.)

STOVE BOLT DIAM.	MACHINE SCREW DIAM.	ROUND HEAD	FLAT HEAD	FILLISTER HEAD	OVAL HEAD	OVEN HEAD
	2	1/8-7/8		1/8-7/8		
	3	1/8-7/8		1/8-7/8		
	4	1/8-1 1/2	40 N.C.	1/8-1 1/2		
	4	1/8-1 1/2	36 N.C.	1/8-1 1/2		1/8-3/4
1/8	5	1/8-2		1/8-2		3/8-2
	6	1/8-2		1/8-2		1/8-1
5/32	8	3/16-3		3/16-3		3/16-2
3/16	10	3/16-6		3/16-3		1/4-6
	12	1/4-3		1/4-3		
1/4	1/4	5/16-6		5/16-3		3/8-6
5/16	5/16	3/8-6		3/8-3		3/4-6
3/8	3/8	1/2-5		1/2-3		3/4-5
1/2	1/2	1-4				

Length intervals = 1/16 in. increments up to 1/2 in., 1/8 in. increments from 5/8 in. to 1 1/4 in., 1/4 in. increments from 1 1/2 in. to 3 in., 1/2 in. increments from 3 1/2 in. to 6 in.
NOTE: N.C. = Course thread

SCREW AND BOLT LENGTHS (INS.)

DIAMETER (INS.)	CAP SCREWS				BOLTS		
	BUTTON HEAD	FLAT HEAD	HEXAGON HEAD	FILLISTER HEAD	MACHINE BOLT	CARRIAGE BOLT	LAG BOLT
1/4	1/2-2 1/4		1/2-3 1/2	3/4-3	1/2-8	3/4-8	1-6
5/16	1/2-2 3/4		1/2-3 1/2	3/4-3 3/4	1/2-8	3/4-8	1-10
3/8	5/8-3		1/2-4	3/4-3 1/2	3/4-12	3/4-12	1-12
7/16	3/4-3		3/4-4	3/4-3 3/4	3/4-12	1-12	1-12
1/2	3/4-4		3/4-4 1/2	3/4-4	3/4-24	1-20	1-12
9/16	1-4		1-4 1/2	1-4	1-30	1-20	
5/8	1-4		1-5	1 1/4-4 1/2	1-30	1-20	1 1/2-16
3/4	1-4		1 1/4-5	1 1/2-4 1/2	1-30	1-20	1 1/2-16
7/8			2-6	1 3/4-5	1 1/2-30		2-16
1			2-6	2-5	1 1/2-30		2-16

Length intervals = 1/8 in. increments up to 1 in., 1/4 in. increments from 1 1/4 in. to 4 in., 1/2 in. increments from 4 1/2 in. to 6 in.

Length intervals = 1/4 in. increments up to 6 in., 1/2 in. increments from 6 1/2 in. to 12 in., 1 in. increments over 12 in.

Length intervals = 1/2 in. increments up to 8 in., 1 in. increments over 8 in.

ROUND — FLAT — OVAL — PAN — FILLISTER — TRUSS — HEX — WASHER

HEAD TYPES

SQUARE — HEX — LOCK

 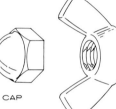

CASTELLATED — CAP — WING

FLAT — LOCK (SPRING) — COUNTERSUNK

TOOTHLOCK (INTERNAL) — (EXTERNAL)

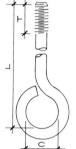

EYE BOLT (CLOSED) — EYE BOLT (OPEN) — J-BOLT

Self-locking nuts have a pin that acts as a rachet, sliding down the thread as the bolt is tightened, to prevent loosening from shock and vibration.

LOCK

NUTS

The bolt's clamping force causes protrusions on the washer to flatten partially, closing the gap between the washer and the bolt head. Measurement of the gap indicates whether the bolt has been tightened adequately.

LOAD INDICATOR

WASHERS

U-BOLT ROUND BEND — U-BOLT SQUARE BEND — HOOK BOLT ROUND BEND

Fiberglass nuts and bolts are noncorrosive and nonconductive. Bolts are available in 3/8 in., 1/2 in., 5/8 in., 3/4 in., and 1 in. standard diameters.

FIBERGLASS NUTS AND BOLTS

High tension, stainless steel helical inserts are held in place by spring-like pressure, and they are used to salvage damaged threads. They also eliminate thread failure due to stress conditions.

HELICAL INSERTS

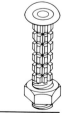

Interference body bolts are driven into reamed or drilled holes to create a joint in full bearing.

INTERFERENCE BODY BOLTS

NOTES
1. Bent bolts are specialty items made to order.
2. D = bolt diameter; C = inside opening width; T = thread length; L = inside length of bolt; A = inside depth.

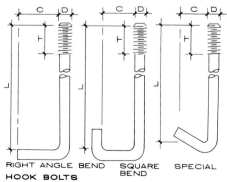

RIGHT ANGLE BEND — SQUARE BEND — SPECIAL

HOOK BOLTS

Timothy B. McDonald; Washington, D.C.

METAL FASTENING

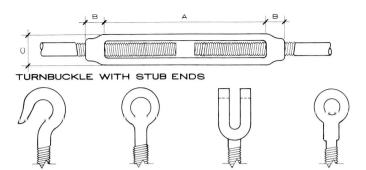

TURNBUCKLE WITH STUB ENDS

HOOK EYE CLEVIS

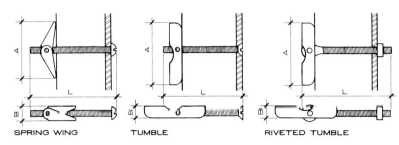

SPRING WING   TUMBLE   RIVETED TUMBLE

TOGGLE BOLTS (IN INCHES)

DIAMETER		1/8	5/32	3/16	1/4	5/16	3/8	1/2
DECIMAL EQUIV.		.138	.164	.190	.250	.313	.375	.500
SPRING WING	A	1.438	1.875	1.875	2.063	2.750	2.875	4.625
	B	.375	.500	.500	.688	.875	1.000	1.250
	L	2-4	2 1/2-4	2-6	2 1/2-6	3-6	3-6	4-6
TUMBLE	A	1.250	2.000	2.000	2.250	2.750	2.750	
	B	.375	.500	.500	.688	.875	.875	
	L	2-4	2 1/2-4	3-6	3-6	3-6	3-6	
RIVETED TUMBLE	A		2.000	2.000	2.250	2.750	2.750	3.375
	B		.375	.375	.500	.625	.688	.875
	L		2 1/2-4	3-6	3-6	3-6	3-6	3-6

TURNBUCKLES (IN INCHES)

DIAMETER	1/4	5/16	3/8	1/2	5/8	3/4	7/8	1
DECI.EQUIV.	.250	.313	.375	.500	.625	.750	.875	1.00
A	4	4 1/2	6"	6"	6"	6"	6"	6"
				9"	9"	9"		
				12"	12"	12"	12"	12"
B	7/16	1/2	9/16	3/4	29/32	1 1/16	1 7/32	1 3/8
C	3/4	7/8	31/32	1 7/32	1 1/2	1 23/32	1 7/8	2 1/32

DIAMETERS OVER 1" AVAILABLE, NOT ALWAYS STOCKED.

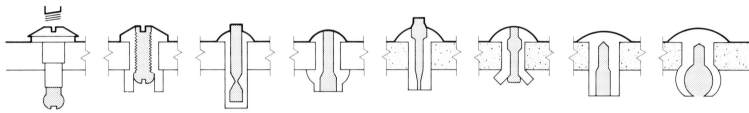

THREADED   PULL MANDREL   DRIVE PIN   CHEMICALLY EXPANDED

BLIND RIVETS FOR USE IN A JOINT THAT IS ACCESSIBLE FROM ONLY ONE SIDE

ROUND   TRUSS   FLAT   COUNTERSUNK   PAN

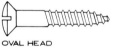
OVAL HEAD

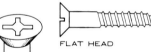
ROUND HEAD

SLOTTED

RIVETS
STANDARD RIVETS AVAILABLE WITH SOLID, TUBULAR AND SPLIT SHANKS OF STEEL, BRASS, COPPER, ALUMINUM, MONEL METAL AND STAINLESS STEEL; IN DIAMETERS OF 1/8" TO 7/16" AND LENGTHS OF 3/16" TO 4 IN.

FLAT HEAD

Self-drilling fasteners: used to attach metal to metal, wood, and concrete. Consult manufacturer for sizes and drilling capabilities.

PHILLIPS

SHEET METAL GIMLET POINT
Sheet metal gimlet point: hardened, self-tapping. Used in 28 gauge to 6 gauge sheet metal; aluminum, plastic, slate, etc. Usual head types.

SELF-DRILLING FASTENERS

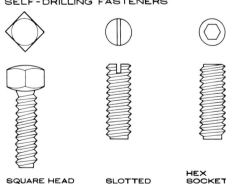

SQUARE HEAD   SLOTTED   HEX SOCKET

Set Screws: headless with socket or slotted top; made in sizes 4 in. to 1/2 in., and in lengths 1/2 in. to 5 in. Square head sizes 1/4 in. to 1 in., and lengths 1/2 in. to 5 in.

SET SCREWS

SHEET METAL BLUNT POINT
Sheet metal blunt point: hardened, self-tapping. Used in 28 to 18 gauge sheet metal. Made in sizes 4 to 14 in usual head types.

FREARSON

THREAD CUTTING- CUTTING SLOT
Thread cutting, cutting slot: hardened. Used in metals up to 1/4 in. thick in sizes 4 in. to 5/16 in. in usual head types.

WOOD SCREWS (IN IN.)

DIA.	DECI. EQUIV.	LENGTH
0	.060	1/4 - 3/8
1	.073	1/4 - 1/2
2	.086	1/4 - 3/4
3	.099	1/4 - 1
4	.112	1/4 - 1 1/2
5	.125	3/8 - 1 1/2
6	.138	3/8 - 2 1/2
7	.151	3/8 - 2 1/2
8	.164	3/8 - 3
9	.177	1/2 - 3
10	.190	1/2 - 3 1/2
11	.203	5/8 - 3 1/2
12	.216	5/8 - 4
14	.242	3/4 - 5
16	.268	1 - 5
18	.294	1 1/4 - 5
20	.320	1 1/2 - 5
24	.372	3 - 5

SHEET METAL & THREADING SCREWS

DRIVE TYPES

Timothy B. McDonald; Washington, D.C.

METAL FASTENING 5

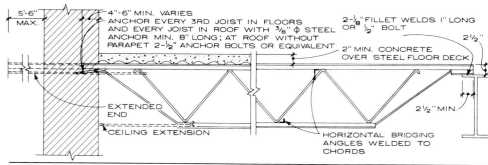

SECTION THROUGH JOIST BEARING

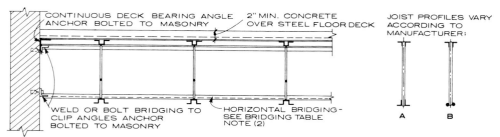

SECTION THROUGH JOISTS

NOTES

The following information applies to both open web and long span steel joists.

JOIST DESIGNATION:

25 LH 10 ← Chord
└─ Type of steel
└─ Longspan (DL-deep longspan)
└─ Nominal depth (in.)

For greater economy, the K-series joist replaced the H-series joist in 1986.

1. ROOF CONSTRUCTION: Joists are usually covered by steel deck topped with either rigid insulation board or lightweight concrete fill and built-up felt and gravel roof. Plywood, poured gypsum, or structural wood fiber deck systems can also be used with built-up roof.

2. CEILINGS: Ceiling supports can be suspended from or mounted directly to bottom chords of joists, although suspended systems are recommended because of dimensional variations in actual joist depths.

3. FLOOR CONSTRUCTION: Joists usually covered by 2 to $2\frac{1}{2}$ in. concrete on steel centering. Concrete thickness may be increased for electrical conduit or electrical/communications raceways. Precast concrete, gypsum planks, or plywood can also be used for the floor system.

4. VIBRATION: Objectionable vibrations can occur in open web joist and $2\frac{1}{2}$ in. concrete slab designs for open floor areas at spans between 24 and 40 ft, especially at 28 ft. When a floor area cannot have partitions, objectionable vibrations can be prevented or reduced by increasing slab thickness, joist spacing, or floor spans. Attention should also be given to support framing beams which can magnify a vibration problem.

5. OPENINGS IN FLOOR OR ROOF SYSTEMS: Small openings between joists are framed with angles of channel supported on the adjoining two joists. Larger openings necessitating interruption of joists are framed with steel angle or channel headers spanning the adjoining two joists. The interrupted joists bear on the headers.

6. ROOF DRAINAGE: Roof drainage should be carefully considered on level or near level roofs especially with parapet walls. Roof insulation can be sloped, joists can be sloped or obtained with sloping top chords in one or both directions, and overflow scuppers should be provided in parapet walls.

PRELIMINARY JOIST SELECTION: The tables below are not to be used for final joist design but are intended as an aid in speeding selection of steel joists for preliminary design and planning. The final design must be a separate and thorough process, involving a complete investigation of the pertinent conditions. This page is not for that purpose. Consult structural engineer.

EXAMPLE: Assume a particular clear span. By assuming a joist spacing and estimating the total load a joist can immediately be selected from the table. Then proceed with preliminary design studies.

NOTES
1. Total safe load = live load + dead load. Dead load includes weight of joist. For dead loads and recommended live loads, see pages on weights of materials. Local codes will govern.
2. Span not to exceed a depth 24 times that of a nominal joist.
3. For more detailed information refer to standard specifications and load tables adopted by the Steel Joist Institute.

NUMBER OF ROWS OF BRIDGING (FT)
DISTANCES ARE CLEAR SPAN DIMENSIONS

CHORD SIZE[1]	1 ROW	2 ROWS	3 ROWS	4 ROWS[2]	5 ROWS[2]
#1	Up to 16	16–24	24–28	—	—
#2	Up to 17	17–25	25–32	—	—
#3	Up to 18	18–28	28–38	38–40	—
#4	Up to 19	19–28	28–38	38–48	—
#5	Up to 19	19–29	29–39	39–50	50–52
#6	Up to 19	19–29	29–39	39–51	51–56
#7	Up to 20	20–33	33–45	45–58	58–60
#8	Up to 20	20–33	33–45	45–58	58–60
#9	Up to 20	20–33	33–46	46–59	59–60
#10	Up to 20	20–37	37–51	51–60	
#11	Up to 20	20–38	38–53	53–60	
#12	Up to 20	20–39	39–53	53–60	

1. Last digit(s) of joist designation shown in load table below.
2. Where four or five rows of bridging are required, a row nearest the midspan of the joist shall be diagonal bridging with bolted connections at chords and intersections.

SELECTED LOAD TABLES: K SERIES—TOTAL SAFE UNIFORMLY DISTRIBUTED LOAD (LB/FT)

JOIST DESIGNATION		8	12	16	20	24	28	32	36	42	48	54	60
K SERIES f_s = 30,000 psi	8K1	550	444	246									
	10K1		550	313	199								
	12K3		550	476	302	208							
	14K4			550	428	295	216						
	16K5			550	550	384	281	214					
	18K6				550	473	346	264	208				
	20K7				550	550	430	328	259				
	22K9					550	550	436	344	252			
	24K9					550	550	478	377	276	211		
	26K10						550	549	486	356	272		
	28K10						550	549	487	384	294	232	
	30K11							549	487	417	362	285	231
	30K12							549	487	417	365	324	262

Note: Number preceding letter is joist depth; 14K4 is 14 in. deep.

Kenneth D. Franch, AIA, PE; Phillips Swager Associates, Inc.; Dallas, Texas
Setter, Leach & Lindstrom, Inc.; Minneapolis, Minnesota

METAL JOISTS

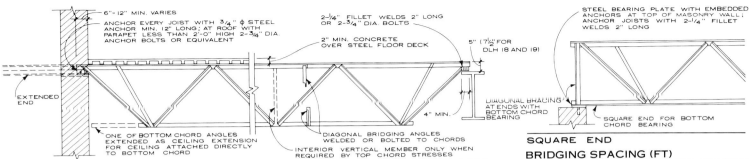

SECTION THROUGH JOIST BEARING

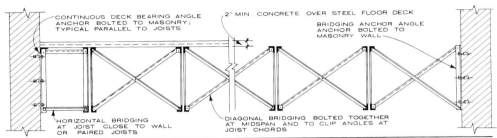

SECTION THROUGH JOISTS

SQUARE END
BRIDGING SPACING (FT)

LH CHORD SIZE†	MAXIMUM SPACING (FT)
02-09	11
10-14	16
15-17	21

DLH CHORD SIZE†	MAXIMUM SPACING (FT)
10	14
11-14	16
15-17	21
18-19	26

†Last two digits of joist designation shown in load tables.

PRELIMINARY JOIST SELECTION

The tables below are not to be used for final joist design but are intended as an aid in speeding selection of steel joists for preliminary design and planning.

The final design must be a separate thorough process, involving a complete investigation of the pertinent conditions. This page is not for that purpose. Consult a structural engineer.

EXAMPLE

Assume a particular clear span. By assuming a joist spacing and estimating the total load a joist can immediately be selected from the table. Then proceed with preliminary design studies.

NOTES

1. Total safe load = live load + dead load. Dead load includes weight of joist. For dead loads and recommended live loads, see pages on weights of materials. Local codes will govern.
2. Span not to exceed 24 times depth of a nominal joist for roofs; 20 times depth for floors.
3. For more detailed information refer to standard specifications and load tables adopted by the Steel Joist Institute.

FIRE RESISTANCE RATINGS

TIME (HR)	FLOOR ASSEMBLIES	TIME (HR)	ROOF ASSEMBLIES
1 or 1½	2″ reinforced concrete, listed ½″ (⅝″ for 1½ hr) acoustical tile ceiling, concealed ceiling grid suspended from joists	1	Built-up roofing on 2″ structural wood fiber units, listed ¾″ acoustical ceiling tiles, concealed ceiling grid suspended from joists
	2″ reinforced concrete, listed ½″ acoustical board ceiling, listed exposed ceiling grid suspended from joists		Built-up roofing and insulation on 26 gauge min. steel deck, listed ⅝″ acoustical ceiling boards, listed exposed ceiling grid suspended from joists
	2″ reinforced concrete, listed ½″ gypsum board ceiling fastened to joists		Built-up roofing over 2″ vermiculite on centering, listed ½″ acoustical ceiling boards, listed exposed ceiling grid suspended from joists
2	2½″ reinforced concrete, listed ⅝″ acoustical tile ceiling, listed concealed ceiling grid suspended from joists		
	2½″ reinforced concrete, listed ½″ acoustical board ceiling, listed exposed ceiling grid suspended from joists	2	Built-up roofing on 2″ listed gypsum building units, listed ⅝″ acoustical ceiling boards, listed exposed ceiling grid suspended from joists
	2″ reinforced concrete, listed ⅝″ gypsum board ceiling fastened to joists		Built-up roofing on 22 gauge min. steel deck, suspended ⅞″ metal lath and plaster ceiling
	2½″ reinforced concrete, listed ½″ gypsum board ceiling fastened to joists		

NOTE: Listed by Underwriters Laboratories or Factory Mutual approved, as appropriate. Ratings are the result of tests made in accordance with ASTM Standard E 119. A more complete list can be obtained from the SJI Technical Digest concerning the design of fire resistive assemblies with steel joists.

SELECTED LOAD TABLES: LH AND DLH SERIES—TOTAL SAFE UNIFORMLY DISTRIBUTED LOAD (LB/FT)

JOIST DESIGNATION		CLEAR SPAN (FT)												
		28	32	36	42	48	54	60	66	72	78	84	90	96
LH Series $f_s = 30,000$ psi	18LH05	581	448	355										
	20LH06	723	560	444										
	24LH07			588	446	343								
	28LH09				639	499	401							
	32LH10					478	389							
	36LH11						451	378	322					
	40LH12							472	402	346				
	44LH13									423	369			
	48LH14											444	390	346
		90	96	102	108	114	120	126	132	138	144			
DLH Series $f_s = 30,000$ psi	52DLH13	433	381	338										
	56DLH14		411	368										
	60DLH15			442	398	361								
	64DLH16				466	421	382							
	68DLH17					460	420							
	72DLH18						505	463	426					

NOTE: Number preceding letter is joist depth; 32LH10 is 32 in. deep.

Setter, Leach & Lindstrom, Inc.; Minneapolis, Minnesota

METAL JOISTS   5

EXAMPLES OF THE MANY TYPES OF DECK AVAILABLE (SEE TABLES)

1. Roof deck.
2. Floor deck (noncomposite).
3. Composite floor deck interacting with concrete.
4. Permanent forms for self-supporting concrete slabs.
5. Cellular deck (composite or noncomposite).
6. Acoustical roof deck.
7. Acoustic cellular deck (composite or non-composite).
8. Electric raceway cellular deck.
9. Prevented roof deck (used with lightweight insulating concrete fill).

All metal floor and roof decks must be secured to all supports, generally by means of "puddle welds" made through the deck to supporting steel. Steel sheet lighter than 22 gauge (0.0295 in. thick) should be secured by use of welding washers (see illustration).

Shear studs welded through floor deck also serve to secure the deck to supporting steel. Power actuated and pneumatically driven fasteners may also be used in certain applications.

Side laps between adjacent sheets of deck must be secured by button-punching standing seams, welding, or screws, in accordance with manufacturer's recommendations.

Decks used as lateral diaphragms must be welded to steel supports around their entire perimeter to ensure development of diaphragm action. More stringent requirements may govern the size and/or spacing of attachments to supports and side lap fasteners or welds.

Roof deck selection must take into consideration construction and maintenance loads as well as the capacity to support uniformly distributed live loads. Consult current Steel Deck Institute recommendations and Factory Mutual requirements.

Floor deck loadings are virtually unlimited in scope, ranging from light residential and institutional loads to heavy duty industrial floors utilizing composite deck with slabs up to 24 in. thick. The designer can select the deck type, depth, and gauge most suitable for the application.

Fire resistance ratings for roof deck assemblies are published by Underwriters Laboratories and Factory Mutual. Ratings of 1 to 2 hr are achieved with spray-on insulation: a 1 hr rating with suspended acoustical ceiling and a 2 hr rating with a metal lath and plaster ceiling.

Floor deck assembly fire resistive ratings are available both with and without spray-applied fireproofing, and with regular weight or lightweight concrete fill. From 1 to 3 hr ratings are possible using only concrete fill—consult Underwriters Laboratory Fire Resistance Index for assembly ratings.

Consult manufacturer's literature and technical representatives for additional information. Consult "Steel Deck Institute Design Manual for Floor Decks and Roof Decks" and "Tentative Recommendations for the Design of Steel Deck Diaphragms" by the Steel Deck Institute.

ADVANTAGES OF METAL ROOF DECKS

1. High strength-to-weight ratio reduces roof dead load.
2. Can be erected in most weather conditions.
3. Variety of depths and rib patterns available.
4. Acoustical treatment is possible.
5. Serve as base for insulation and roofing.
6. Fire ratings can be obtained with standard assemblies.
7. Provide lateral diaphragm.
8. Can be erected quickly.
9. Can be erected economically.

The use of vapor barriers on metal deck roofs is not customary for normal building occupancies. For high relative humidity exposure a vapor barrier may be provided as part of the roofing system, but the user should be aware of the great difficulties encountered in installing a vapor barrier on metal deck. Punctures of the vapor barrier over valleys might reduce or negate entirely the effectiveness of the vapor barrier.

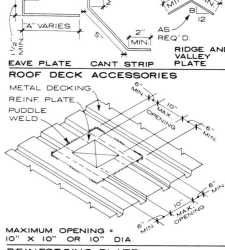

ROOF DECK ACCESSORIES

REINFORCING PLATE

Small openings (up to 6 x 6 in. or 6 in. dia.) may usually be cut in roof or floor deck without reinforcing the deck. Openings up to 10 x 10 in. or 10 in. dia. require reinforcing of the deck by either welding a reinforcing plate to the deck all around the opening, or by providing channel shaped headers and/or supplementary reinforcing parallel to the deck span. Reinforcing plates should be 14 gauge sheets with a minimum projection of 6 in. beyond all sides of the opening, and they should be welded to each cell of the deck.

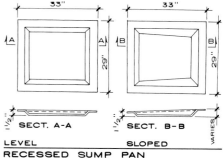

RECESSED SUMP PAN

Preformed recessed sump pans are available from deck manufacturers for use at roof drains.

FRAMED OPENING

Larger openings should be framed with supplementary steel members so that all free edges of deck are supported.

Roof-mounted mechanical equipment should not be placed directly on metal roof deck. Equipment on built-up or prefabricated curbs should be supported directly on main and supplementary structural members and the deck must also be supported along all free edges (see illustration). Heavy items such as cooling towers which must be elevated should be supported by posts extending through pitch pockets directly onto structural members below the deck. Openings through the deck may be handled as previously discussed.

ROOF DECK (ACOUSTICAL ROOF DECKS ARE AVAILABLE IN MANY OF THESE PROFILES - CONSULT MANUFACTURERS)

TYPICAL EXAMPLES	ECONOMICAL SPANS	USUAL WIDTH	MAX. LENGTH AVAILABLE
1½" NARROW RIB	4'- 6'	24"– 36"	36'– 42'
1½" INTERMEDIATE RIB	5'- 7'	24"–36"	40'– 42'
1½" WIDE RIB	6'- 9'	24"– 30"	32'– 42'
3"	8'- 16'	24"	40'
4½"	15'-18'	12"	32'
1½"	7'- 11'	24"	32'
3/16"	10'- 20'	24"	40'
7½" / 6" / 4½" / 3"	12'- 30'	12"	40'– 42'
7½" / 6" / 4½" / 3"	13'- 33'	24"	40'

Walter D. Shapiro, P.E.; Tor, Shapiro & Associates; New York, New York

METAL DECKING

FLOOR DECK – COMPOSITE WITH CONCRETE FILL

TYPICAL EXAMPLES	ECONOMICAL SPANS	USUAL WIDTH	MAX. LENGTH AVAILABLE
1 1/2"	4'–9'	30"	36'
2"	8'–12'	30"	40'–45'
3"	8'–15'	24"	40'
7 1/2" 6" 4 1/2" 3"	8'–24'	12"	40'

FLOOR DECK – COMPOSITE CELLULAR (ACOUSTIC DECK AVAILABLE IN SOME PROFILES; CONSULT MANUFACTURERS)

	ECONOMICAL SPANS	USUAL WIDTH	MAX. LENGTH AVAILABLE
1 1/2" 6"	6'–12'	24"	40'
5/8"	6'–12'	24"	40'
2"	6'–12'	30"	36'–45'
3"	10'–16'	24"	40'
7 1/2" 6" 4 1/2" 3"	8'–24'	24"	40'

CORRUGATED FORMS FOR CONCRETE SLABS – NONCOMPOSITE

	ECONOMICAL SPANS	USUAL WIDTH	MAX. LENGTH AVAILABLE
1/2"	1'–2'	96"	2'–6'
9/16"	1'–6"–3'	30"	40'
15/16"	3'–5'	29"	40'
1" 4"	3'–5'	28"	30'–40'
15/16" 4 1/2"	4'–9'	27"	30'–40'
2" 6"	7'–12'	24"	30'–40'

Walter D. Shapiro, P.E.; Tor, Shapiro & Associates; New York, New York

ADVANTAGES OF METAL FLOOR DECKS:

1. Provide a working platform, eliminating temporary wood planking in highrise use.
2. Composite decks provide positive reinforcement for concrete slabs.
3. Noncomposite and composite decks serve as forms for concrete, eliminate forming and stripping.
4. Fire ratings can be achieved without spray-on fireproofing or rated ceilings.
5. Acoustical treatment is possible.
6. Electric raceways may be built into floor slab.
7. Economical floor assemblies.

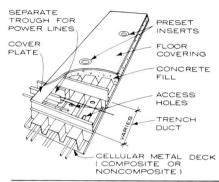

ELECTRICAL TRENCH DUCT

Electric raceways may be built into floor slabs by use of cellular deck or special units that are blended with plain deck. Two-way distribution is achieved by use of trench ducts that sit astride the cellular units at right angles. Use of trench ducts with composite floor deck may reduce or eliminate entirely the effectiveness of composite action at the trench duct. This is also true for composite action between steel floor beams and concrete fill. Trench duct locations must be taken into account in deciding whether composite action is possible.

Openings in composite deck may be blocked out on top of the deck and the deck can be burned out after the concrete has set and become self-supporting. Reinforcing bars can be added alongside openings to replace positive moment deck steel area lost at openings.

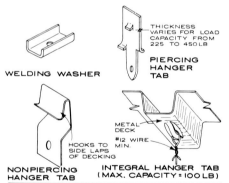

DECKING ATTACHMENTS

A convenient and economical means for supporting lightweight acoustical ceilings is by attaching suspension system to hanger tabs at side laps, piercing tabs driven through deck, or prepunched tabs in roof deck (see illustrations above). These tabs and metal decks must not be used to support plaster ceilings, piping, ductwork, electric equipment, or other heavy loads. Such elements must be supported directly from structural joists, beams, girders, and so on, or from supplementary subframing, and not from metal deck.

ALLOWABLE LOADS FOR SIMPLE SPAN STEEL "C" JOISTS (LB/LINEAR FOOT) MADE OF 40 KSI MATERIAL

SPAN	SECTION (DEPTH/GAUGE)	SINGLE MEMBER TOTAL ALLOWABLE LOAD	ALLOWABLE LIVE LOAD	DOUBLE MEMBER TOTAL ALLOWABLE LOAD	ALLOWABLE LIVE LOAD
8'	6"/18	201	189	402*	378
	6"/16	245	230	490	460
	6"/14	301	283	602	566
	8"/18	295	295	590*	590
	8"/16	359	359	718*	718
	8"/14	442	442	884*	884
	10"/16	506	506	1012*	1012
	10"/14	627	627	1254*	1254
10'	6"/18	129	97	258	194
	6"/16	157	118	314	236
	6"/14	193	144	386	288
	8"/18	188	186	376*	372
	8"/16	230	228	460*	456
	8"/14	283	280	566	560
	10"/16	326	326	652*	652
	10"/14	401	401	802*	802
12'	6"/18	89	56	178	112
	6"/16	109	68	218	136
	6"/14	134	83	268	166
	8"/18	131	108	262*	216
	8"/16	159	131	318	262
	8"/14	196	162	392	324
	10"/16	226	226	452*	452
	10"/14	278	278	556*	556
14'	6"/18	65	35	130	70
	6"/16	80	43	160	86
	6"/14	98	52	196	204
	8"/18	96	68	192	136
	8"/16	117	83	234	166
	8"/14	144	102	288	204
	10"/16	166	150	332*	300
	10"/14	204	184	408	368
16'	6"/18	50	23	100	46
	6"/16	61	28	122	56
	6"/14	75	35	150	70
	8"/18	73	45	146	90
	8"/16	89	55	178	110
	8"/14	110	68	220	136
	10"/16	127	100	254	200
	10"/14	156	123	312	246
18'	8"/18	58	32	116	64
	8"/16	71	39	142	78
	8"/14	87	48	174	96
	10"/16	100	70	200	140
	10"/14	123	86	246	172
20'	8"/18	47	23	94	46
	8"/16	57	28	114	56
	8"/14	70	35	140	70
	10"/16	81	51	162	102
	10"/14	100	63	200	126
22'	8"/18	39	17	78	34
	8"/16	47	21	94	42
	8"/14	58	26	116	52
	10"/16	67	38	134	76
	10"/14	82	47	164	94
24'	10"/16	56	29	112	58
	10"/14	69	36	138	72

NOTES
The tables on this page are not to be used for final design.
They are intended to serve only as aids in the preliminary selection of members.
Consult appropriate manufacturers' literature for final and/or additional information.
*Ends of members require additional reinforcing, such as by end clips.

Ed Hesner; Rasmussen & Hobbs Architects; Tacoma, Washington

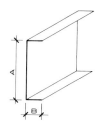
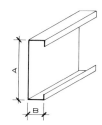
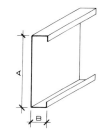

CHANNEL STUDS A	B	"C" STUDS A	B	"C" JOISTS A	B
2½"	1"	2½"	1¼"	5½"	1⅞"
3¼"	1⅜"	3"	1⅜"	6"	1⅝"
3⅝"		3⅝"	1½"	7¼"	1¾"
4"		3¼"	1⅝"	8"	2"
6"		3½"		9¼"	2½"
		4"		10"	
		5½"		12"	
		6"			
		7½"			
		8"			

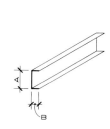
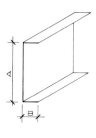
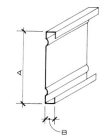

FURRING CHANNEL A	B	"C" JOIST CLOSURE A	B	NESTABLE JOIST A	B
¾"	½"	5½"	1¼"	7¼"	1¾"
1½"	17/32"	6"		7½"	
		7¼"		8"	
		8"		9¼"	
		9¼"		9½"	
		10"		11½"	
		12"		13½"	
				Normally available in all joist sizes	

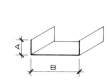
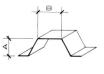
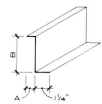

RUNNER CHANNEL A	B	FURRING HAT CHANNEL A	B	"Z" FURRING A	B
¾"	2 11/16"	⅞"	1⅜"	¾"	1"
1"	3 13/16"	1½"	1¼"		1½"
1⅜"	3 7/16"				2"
1¼"	4 3/16"				3"
1½"	6 3/16"				
1¾"	8 3/16"				
3½"					

LIGHT GAUGE FRAMING MEMBERS
MEMBERS AVAILABLE IN 14, 16, 18, 20 & 22 GAUGE MATERIAL

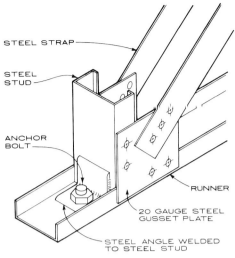

DIAGONAL STEEL STRAPPING

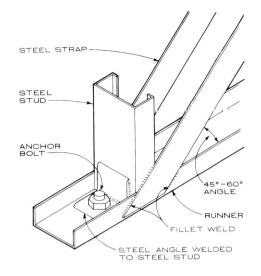

DIAGONAL STEEL STRAPPING

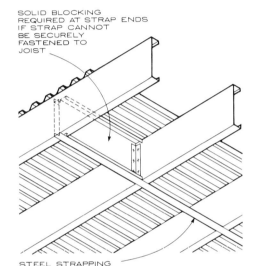

JOIST BRACING

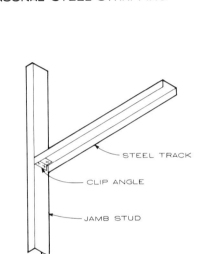

SILL ATTACHMENT

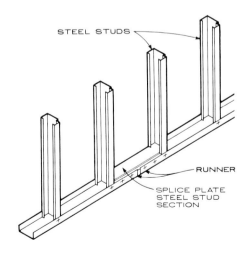

RUNNER SPLICE

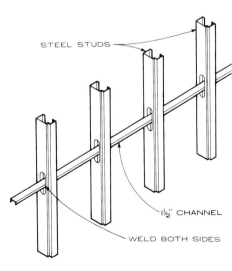

HORIZONTAL BRACING

Timothy B. McDonald; Washington, D.C.

LIMITING HEIGHT TABLES FOR INTERIOR PARTITIONS AND CHASE WALL PARTITIONS

STUD WIDTH	STUD SPACING	ALLOW. DEFL.	PARTITION ONE LAYER	PARTITION TWO LAYERS	FURRING ONE LAYER
LIMITING HEIGHTS 25 GAUGE STEEL STUD ASSEMBLIES					
1 5/8"	16"	1/120	10'9"f	10'9"d	10'3"d
		1/240	9'6"d	10'6"d	8'3"d
	24"	1/120	8'9"f	8'9"f	8'9"f
		1/240	8'3"d	8'9"f	7'3"d
2 1/2"	16"	1/120	14'3"f	14'3"f	14'0"d
		1/240	12'6"d	13'6"d	11'0"d
	24"	1/120	11'6"f	11'6"f	11'6"f
		1/240	10'9"d	11'6"f	9'9"d
3 5/8"	16"	1/120	18'3"f	18'3"f	18'3"f
		1/240	16'0"d	17'0"d	14'6"d
	24"	1/120	15'0"f	15'0"f	15'0"f
		1/240	14'0"d	14'9"d	12'9"d
4"	16"	1/120	19'6"f	19'6"f	19'6"f
		1/240	17'3"d	18'3"d	15'9"d
	24"	1/120	16'0"f	16'0"f	16'0"f
		1/240	15'0"d	15'9"d	13'9"d
6"	16"	1/120	26'0"f	26'0"f	26'0"f
		1/240	23'0"d	24'0"d	21'6"d
	24"	1/120	21'3"f	21'3"f	21'3"f
		1/240	20'3"d	21'0"d	18'9"d
20 GAUGE STEEL STUDS ASSEMBLIES					
2 1/2"	16"	1/120	17'9"d	18'6"d	16'6"d
		1/240	14'0"d	14'9"d	13'0"d
	24"	1/120	15'6"d	16'3"f	14'6"d
		1/240	12'3"d	13'0"d	11'6"d
3 5/8"	16"	1/120	23'0"d	24'0"d	21'9"d
		1/240	18'3"d	19'0"d	17'3"d
	24"	1/120	20'0"d	20'9"f	19'0"d
		1/240	16'0"d	16'6"d	15'0"d
4"	16"	1/120	24'9"d	25'9"d	23'6"d
		1/240	19'6"d	20'3"d	18'9"d
	24"	1/120	21'6"d	22'0"f	20'6"d
		1/240	17'3"d	17'9"d	16'3"d
6"	16"	1/120	33'6"d	34'6"d	32'3"d
		1/240	26'6"d	27'6"d	25'6"d
	24"	1/120	29'3"d	29'6"f	28'0"d
		1/240	23'3"d	24'0"d	22'3"d
LIMITING HEIGHT 25 GAUGE CHASE WALL PARTITIONS					
1 5/8"	16"	1/120	15'3"f	15'3"f	
		1/240	13'3"d	14'6"d	
	24"	1/120	12'6"f	12'6"f	
		1/240	11'6"d	12'6"f	
2 1/2"	16"	1/120	20'3"f	20'3"f	
		1/240	17'6"d	19'0"d	
	24"	1/120	16'6"f	16'6"f	
		1/240	15'6"d	16'6"f	
3 5/8"	16"	1/120	25'9"f	25'9"f	
		1/240	22'9"d	24'3"d	
	24"	1/120	21'0"d	21'0"f	
		1/240	19'9"d	21'0"f	
2 1/2" *	16"	1/120	24'3"d	25'9"d	
		1/240	19'3"d	20'6"d	
	24"	1/120	21'3"d	22'6"f	
		1/240	17'0"d	18'0"d	

NOTE

1. Limiting height for 1/2 in. or 5/8 in. thick panels and 5 psf uniform load perpendicular to partition or furring. Use one-layer heights for unbalanced assemblies. Limiting criteria: d-deflection, f-bending stress. Consult local code authority for limiting criteria.

* 20 Gauge chase wall partitions

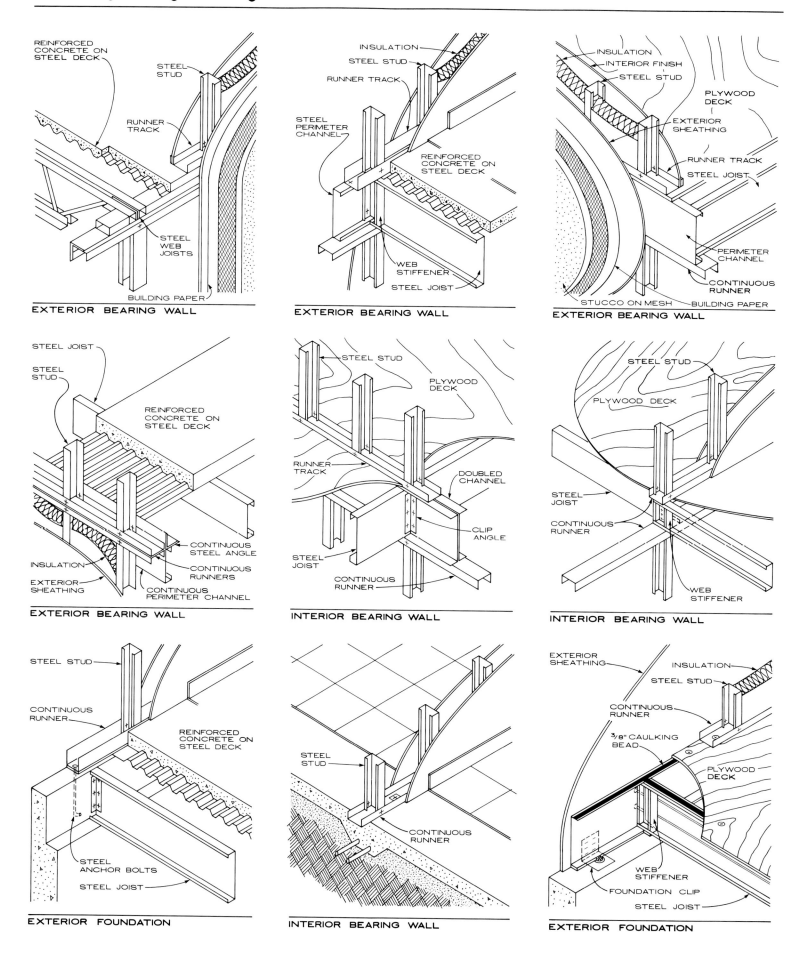

REINFORCED CONCRETE ON STEEL DECK
STEEL STUD
RUNNER TRACK
STEEL WEB JOISTS
BUILDING PAPER

EXTERIOR BEARING WALL

INSULATION
STEEL STUD
RUNNER TRACK
STEEL PERIMETER CHANNEL
REINFORCED CONCRETE ON STEEL DECK
WEB STIFFENER
STEEL JOIST

EXTERIOR BEARING WALL

INSULATION
INTERIOR FINISH
STEEL STUD
PLYWOOD DECK
EXTERIOR SHEATHING
RUNNER TRACK
STEEL JOIST
PERIMETER CHANNEL
CONTINUOUS RUNNER
STUCCO ON MESH
BUILDING PAPER

EXTERIOR BEARING WALL

STEEL JOIST
STEEL STUD
REINFORCED CONCRETE ON STEEL DECK
CONTINUOUS STEEL ANGLE
CONTINUOUS RUNNERS
INSULATION
EXTERIOR SHEATHING
CONTINUOUS PERIMETER CHANNEL

EXTERIOR BEARING WALL

STEEL STUD
PLYWOOD DECK
RUNNER TRACK
DOUBLED CHANNEL
CLIP ANGLE
STEEL JOIST
CONTINUOUS RUNNER

INTERIOR BEARING WALL

STEEL STUD
PLYWOOD DECK
STEEL JOIST
CONTINUOUS RUNNER
WEB STIFFENER

INTERIOR BEARING WALL

STEEL STUD
CONTINUOUS RUNNER
REINFORCED CONCRETE ON STEEL DECK
STEEL ANCHOR BOLTS
STEEL JOIST

EXTERIOR FOUNDATION

STEEL STUD
CONTINUOUS RUNNER

INTERIOR BEARING WALL

EXTERIOR SHEATHING
INSULATION
STEEL STUD
CONTINUOUS RUNNER
3/8" CAULKING BEAD
PLYWOOD DECK
WEB STIFFENER
FOUNDATION CLIP
STEEL JOIST

EXTERIOR FOUNDATION

Timothy B. McDonald; Washington, D.C.

5 **COLD-FORMED METAL FRAMING**

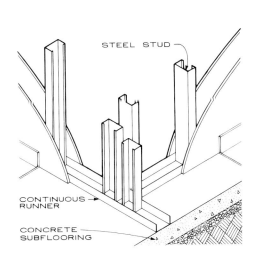

PARTITION INTERSECTION

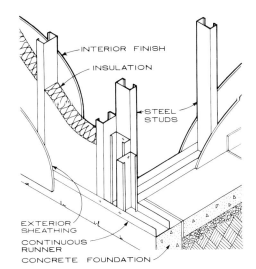

PARTITION / EXTERIOR WALL

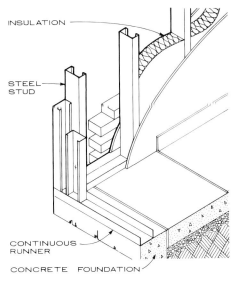

EXTERIOR CORNER

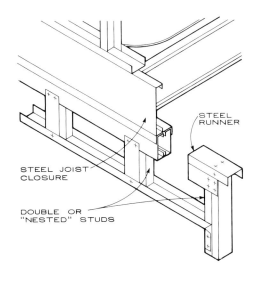

TWO MEMBER LINTEL

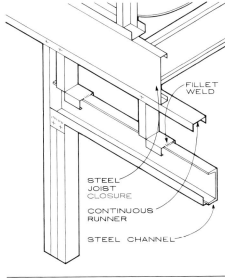

LONG SPAN LINTEL

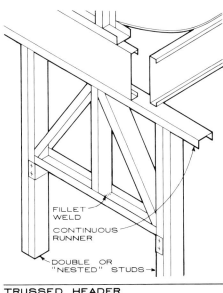

TRUSSED HEADER

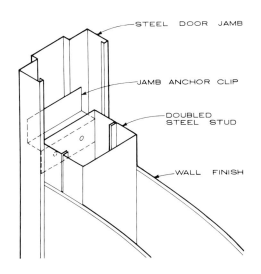

STUD-TO-DOOR BUCK

Timothy B. McDonald; Washington, D.C.

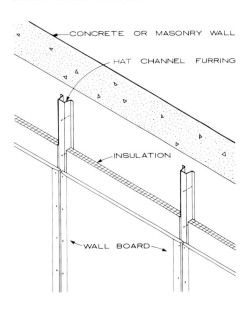

FURRING

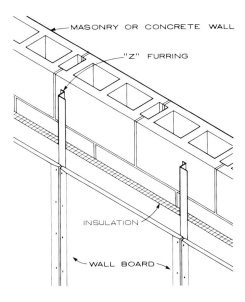

FURRING

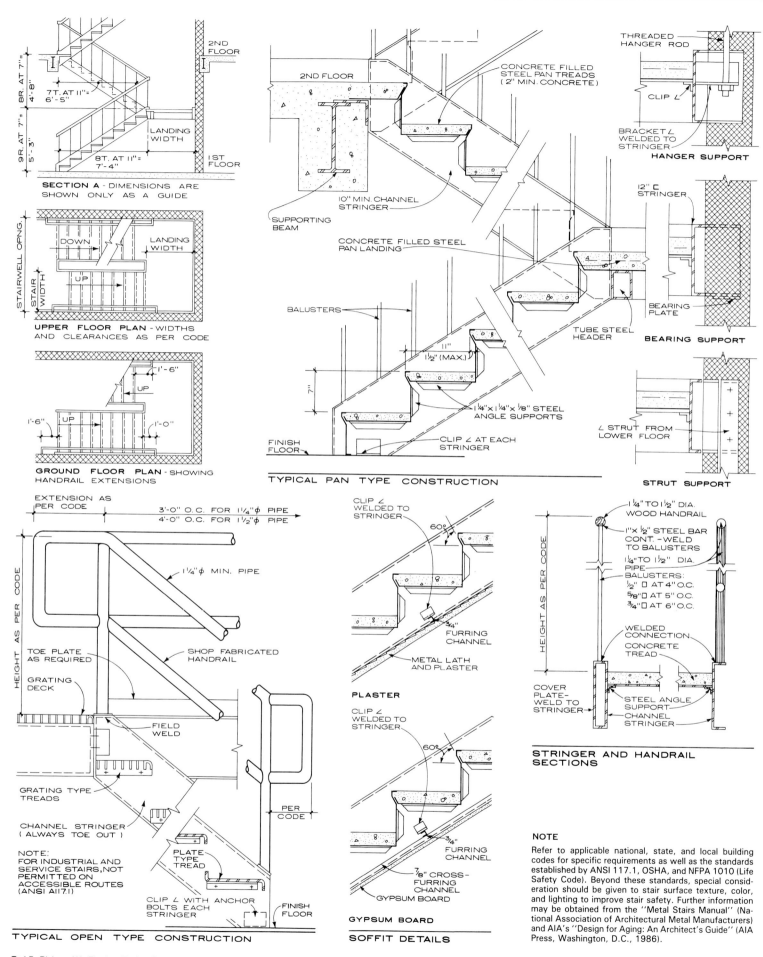

SECTION A - DIMENSIONS ARE SHOWN ONLY AS A GUIDE

8R AT 7" = 4'-8"
7T. AT 11" = 6'-5"
9R. AT 7" = 5'-3"
8T. AT 11" = 7'-4"

2ND FLOOR
1ST FLOOR
LANDING WIDTH

UPPER FLOOR PLAN - WIDTHS AND CLEARANCES AS PER CODE

DOWN
UP
STAIRWELL OPNG.
STAIR WIDTH
LANDING WIDTH

GROUND FLOOR PLAN - SHOWING HANDRAIL EXTENSIONS

1'-6"
UP
1'-6"
UP
1'-0"

2ND FLOOR
SUPPORTING BEAM
10" MIN. CHANNEL STRINGER
CONCRETE FILLED STEEL PAN LANDING
BALUSTERS
11"
1½" (MAX.)
7"
1¼"x1¼"x⅛" STEEL ANGLE SUPPORTS
FINISH FLOOR
CLIP ∠ AT EACH STRINGER

CONCRETE FILLED STEEL PAN TREADS (2" MIN. CONCRETE)
TUBE STEEL HEADER

TYPICAL PAN TYPE CONSTRUCTION

THREADED HANGER ROD
CLIP ∠
BRACKET ∠ WELDED TO STRINGER

HANGER SUPPORT

12" C STRINGER
BEARING PLATE

BEARING SUPPORT

∠ STRUT FROM LOWER FLOOR

STRUT SUPPORT

EXTENSION AS PER CODE
3'-0" O.C. FOR 1¼"φ PIPE
4'-0" O.C. FOR 1½"φ PIPE
1¼"φ MIN. PIPE
SHOP FABRICATED HANDRAIL
TOE PLATE AS REQUIRED
GRATING DECK
HEIGHT AS PER CODE
FIELD WELD
GRATING TYPE TREADS
CHANNEL STRINGER (ALWAYS TOE OUT)
PLATE TYPE TREAD
PER CODE
CLIP ∠ WITH ANCHOR BOLTS EACH STRINGER
FINISH FLOOR

NOTE:
FOR INDUSTRIAL AND SERVICE STAIRS, NOT PERMITTED ON ACCESSIBLE ROUTES (ANSI A117.1)

TYPICAL OPEN TYPE CONSTRUCTION

CLIP ∠ WELDED TO STRINGER
60°
¾" FURRING CHANNEL
METAL LATH AND PLASTER

PLASTER

CLIP ∠ WELDED TO STRINGER
60°
¾" FURRING CHANNEL
⅞" CROSS-FURRING CHANNEL
GYPSUM BOARD

GYPSUM BOARD

SOFFIT DETAILS

1¼" TO 1½" DIA. WOOD HANDRAIL
1"x½" STEEL BAR CONT.-WELD TO BALUSTERS
1¼" TO 1½" DIA. PIPE
BALUSTERS:
½" ◻ AT 4" O.C.
⅝" ◻ AT 5" O.C.
¾" ◻ AT 6" O.C.
HEIGHT AS PER CODE
WELDED CONNECTION
CONCRETE TREAD
COVER PLATE-WELD TO STRINGER
STEEL ANGLE SUPPORT
CHANNEL STRINGER

STRINGER AND HANDRAIL SECTIONS

NOTE

Refer to applicable national, state, and local building codes for specific requirements as well as the standards established by ANSI 117.1, OSHA, and NFPA 1010 (Life Safety Code). Beyond these standards, special consideration should be given to stair surface texture, color, and lighting to improve stair safety. Further information may be obtained from the "Metal Stairs Manual" (National Association of Architectural Metal Manufacturers) and AIA's "Design for Aging: An Architect's Guide" (AIA Press, Washington, D.C., 1986).

Ted B. Richey, AIA; The InterDesign Group; Indianapolis, Indiana
John D. Harvey, AIA; Wheatley Associates; Charlotte, North Carolina

METAL FABRICATIONS

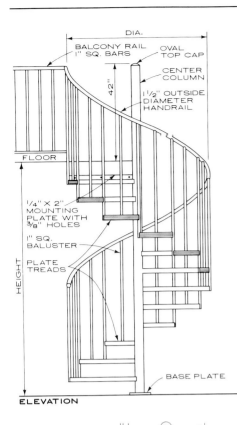

ELEVATION

NOTES

1. Dimensions: Spiral stairs are manufactured in a variety of diameters. Larger diameters increase perceived comfort, ease of use, and safety.

2. Tread and platform materials: The most common materials are steel, aluminum, and wood. Steel and aluminum can be smooth plate, checker plate, pan type, and bar. A variety of hardwoods can be used, although many manufacturers use steel substructures to support the finish wood surface. Plywood usually is used under carpeting.

3. Factory finishes: Standard for exterior and wet area interiors are zinc-chromated rust inhibitor or hot-dipped galvanized. Other coatings are black acrylic enamel and black epoxy.

4. Handrails and balusters: A large variety of materials are available, including steel, aluminum, brass, bronze, wood, glass, and plastic laminate.

5. Platform dimensions usually are 2 in. larger than the stair radius. Various anchorage connections are available to suit the floor structure.

6. Refer to local and national codes for dimension and construction requirements and allowable uses.

SPECIFICATIONS (IN.)

Diameter	40	48	52	60	64	72	76	88	96
Center Column	4	4	4	4	4	4	4	$6\frac{5}{8}$	$6\frac{5}{8}$
Lb per 9 ft	205	220	235	250	265	310	325	435	485
Tread Detail A	4	4	4	4	4	4	4	$6\frac{5}{8}$	$6\frac{5}{8}$
Tread Detail B	18	22	24	28	32	34	36	42	48
27° Tread Detail C	$9\frac{1}{4}$	$11\frac{1}{8}$	$12\frac{1}{8}$	$13\frac{15}{16}$	$14\frac{7}{8}$	$16\frac{3}{4}$	$17\frac{5}{8}$	$20\frac{1}{2}$	$22\frac{5}{16}$
27° Tread Detail D	$7\frac{5}{8}$	8	$8\frac{1}{4}$	$8\frac{3}{8}$	$8\frac{1}{2}$	$8\frac{5}{8}$	$8\frac{3}{4}$	10	$10\frac{1}{2}$
30° Tread Detail C	$10\frac{1}{2}$	$12\frac{9}{16}$	$13\frac{5}{8}$	$15\frac{3}{4}$	$16\frac{3}{4}$	$18\frac{7}{8}$	$19\frac{7}{8}$	23	$25\frac{1}{8}$
30° Tread Detail D	$8\frac{1}{2}$	$8\frac{5}{8}$	$8\frac{3}{4}$	$8\frac{7}{8}$	9	$9\frac{1}{4}$	$9\frac{3}{8}$	$11\frac{3}{8}$	$11\frac{1}{2}$
Landing Size	22	26	28	32	34	38	40	46	52

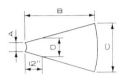

TREAD DETAIL

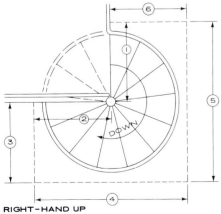

LEFT-HAND UP
12 TREADS/CIRCLE 8" TO 9½" RISERS
MAY BE RIGHT-HAND UP

RIGHT-HAND UP
13 TREADS/CIRCLE 7½" TO 8" RISERS
MAY BE LEFT-HAND UP

Framing dimensions are used when the stair passes through the flooring. The opening is "L" shaped, not square. For maximum head room, taper joist #2 45°. For standard 27° treads and 10 in. or over joist, delete one step to increase head room.

27° RISER TABLE

FINISH FLOOR HEIGHT (IN.)	NUMBER OF STEPS	CIRCLE DEGREE
90 to 96	11	297°
97 to 104	12	324°
105 to 112	13	351°
113 to 120	14	375°
121 to 128	15	405°
129 to 136	16	432°
137 to 144	17	459°
145 to 152	18	486°
153 to 160	19	513°
161 to 168	20	540°

30° RISER TABLE

FINISH FLOOR HEIGHT (IN.)	NUMBER OF STEPS	CIRCLE DEGREE
85 to 95	9	270°
96 to 104	10	300°
105 to 114	11	330°
115 to 123	12	360°
124 to 133	13	390°
134 to 142	14	420°
143 to 152	15	450°
153 to 161	16	480°
162 to 171	17	510°
172 to 180	18	540°

FRAMING DIMENSIONS (IN.)

STAIR DIAMETER	1	2	3	4	5	6
40	20	20	24	44	44	24
48	24	24	28	52	52	28
52	26	26	30	56	56	30
60	30	30	34	64	64	34
64	32	32	36	68	68	36
72	36	36	40	76	76	40
76	38	38	42	80	80	42
88	44	44	48	92	92	48
96	48	48	52	100	100	52

SPIRAL STAIRS

David W. Johnson; Washington, D.C.

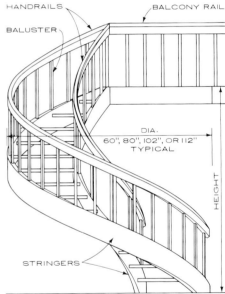

ELEVATION

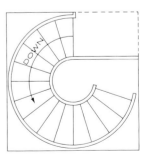

PLAN

Design considerations are similar to those for spiral stairs. Made of fabricated steel tube one-piece stringer with treads bolted or welded to the stringer. Treads also are made of laminated wood. Numerous finishes are available, with wood the most common. Risers can be open or closed, and they can be carpeted.

CIRCULAR STAIRS

METAL FABRICATIONS   5

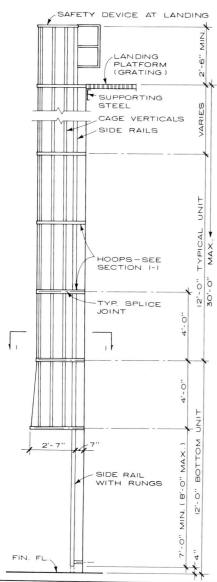

TYPICAL SIDE ELEVATION
(EXTRUDED ALUMINUM LADDER)
MEETS OSHA REQUIREMENTS
AND ANSI SPECIFICATIONS
A 14.3

NOTE

All ladder safety devices such as those that incorporate lifebelts, friction brakes, and sliding attachments shall meet the design requirements of fire escape ladders; by U.S. Department of Labor-Occupational Safety and Health Administration.

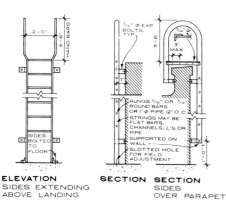

ELEVATION
SIDES EXTENDING
ABOVE LANDING

SECTION
SIDES OVER PARAPET

VERTICAL AND SHIPS LADDERS

Jan M. Sprawka; Symmes, Maini and McKee Associates, Inc.; Cambridge, Massachusetts
Max O. Urbahn Associates, Inc.; New York, New York
NFPA, see data sources

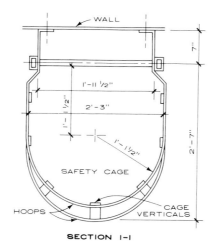

SECTION 1-1

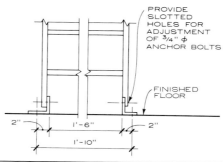

TYPICAL LADDER FOOTING CONNECTIONS

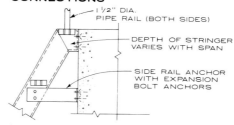

SHIPS LADDER HEAD CONNECTION

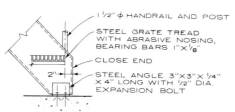

FIRE ESCAPE FOOTING CONNECTION

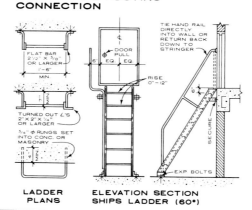

LADDER PLANS

ELEVATION SECTION
SHIPS LADDER (60°)

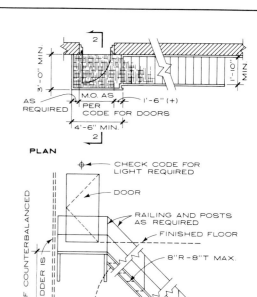

PLAN

ELEVATION

NOTE: WEATHER PROTECTION FROM ICE AND SNOW IS REQUIRED IN SOME AREAS

NOTES

1. Freestanding stairways that are independently supported on steel columns with platforms at exits can be used on new and existing buildings. This type of exterior stair is subject to height limitations, occupancy classifications, and fire separation ratings.

2. Stairways supported on brackets attached to building walls with platforms at exits may be used for existing buildings, but only when outside stairways are not practical. This type of fire escape stair is subject to occupancy provisions: ''Fire escape stairs may be used in existing buildings as permitted in applicable existing occupancy chapters but shall not constitute more than 50 percent of the required exit capacity'' (NFPA 101 National Fire Code 1985, 5-2.8.1.4).

3. Slide fire escapes, used chiefly in institutional buildings, must be designed in accordance with state or local laws and ordinances. Frames for platforms can be angles or channels bolted to brackets; grating can be bolted or welded to the frame. Alternate brackets may be round or square steel, sized by a structural engineer.

4. Ships' ladder railings are ¾ in., 1 in., or larger pipe railing on one or both sides, bolted or welded to strings. Tread may be channels, angles, bent plates, grating, or cast metals, with or without abrasives. Brackets are to be 2½ in. x ⅜ in. or larger, and may be welded, bolted, or clamped to strings, but spaced not over 10 ft. Fastening to wall should be through bolts, bolts set in wall, or by expansion bolts. Rungs, ⅝ in. or ¼ in. diameter bars, usually are set into holes in string and welded together.

5. Galvanic corrosion (electrolysis) potential between common flashing materials and selected construction materials should be considered.

6. Portable ladders, rope fire escapes, and similar emergency escape devices may be useful in buildings that lack adequate standard exits. Their use is not recognized by the Life Safety Code as satisfying requirements for means of egress. Many such devices are unsuited for use by aged or infirm persons or small children. Such devices may give a false sense of security and should not substitute for standard exit facilities.

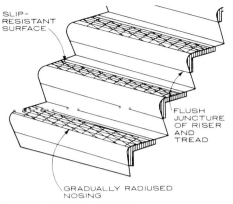

"SAFE" STAIR ELEMENTS

TREAD AND RISER SIZES

Riser and tread dimensions must be uniform for the length of the stair. ANSI specifications recommend a minimum tread dimension of 11 in. nosing to nosing and a riser height of 7 in. maximum. Open risers are not permitted on stairs accessible to the handicapped.

TREAD COVERING

OSHA standards require finishes to be "reasonably slip resistant" with nosings of slip-resistant finish. Treads without nosings are acceptable provided that the tread is serrated or is of a definite slip-resistant design. Uniform color and texture are recommended for clear delineation of edges.

NOSING DESIGN

ANSI specifications recommend nosings without abrupt edges that project no more than 1½ in. beyond the edge of the riser. A safe stair uses a ½ in. radius abrasive nosing firmly anchored to the tread, with no overhangs and a clearly visible edge.

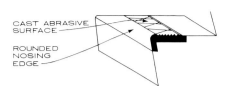

PREFERRED CAST METAL ABRASIVE NOSING

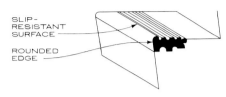

PREFERRED CAST METAL NOSING FOR CONCRETE STAIR

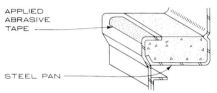

PREFERRED ABRASIVE TAPE NOSING

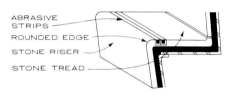

PREFERRED STONE TREAD

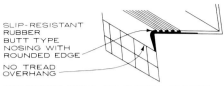

PREFERRED VINYL OR RUBBER NOSING

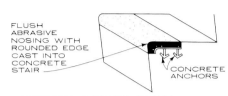

PREFERRED ABRASIVE EPOXY

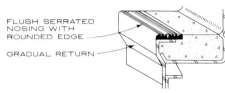

PREFERRED STEEL SUBTREAD

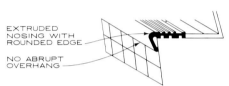

PREFERRED ALUMINUM NOSING

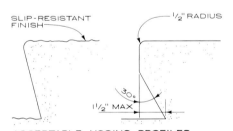

ACCEPTABLE NOSING PROFILES

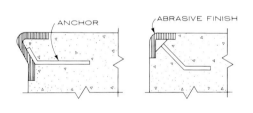

PREFERRED CAST NOSINGS FOR CONCRETE

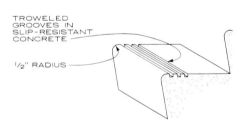

PREFERRED CONCRETE TREAD

DESIGN OF A "SAFE" STAIR, USABLE BY THE PHYSICALLY HANDICAPPED

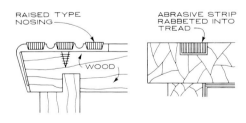

OTHER ALUMINUM NOSINGS WITH ABRASIVE FILLER

NOTE

Cast nosings for concrete stairs are iron, aluminum, or bronze, custom-made to exact size. Nosings and treads come with factory-drilled countersunk holes, with riveted strap anchors, or with wing-type anchors.

NOTE

Abrasive materials are used as treads, nosings, or inlay strips for new work and as surface-mounted replacement treads for old work. A homogeneous epoxy abrasive is cured on an extruded aluminum base for a smoother surface, or it is used as a filler between aluminum ribs.

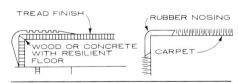

OTHER SLIP-RESISTANT VINYL AND RUBBER NOSINGS

OTHER EXTRUDED ALUMINUM NOSINGS

Olga Barmine; Darrel Downing Rippeteau, Architect; Washington, D.C.
Krommenhoek/McKeown & Associates; San Diego, California

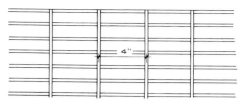

WITH SPACER BARS WELDED 4" O.C.

WITH SPACER BARS WELDED 2" O.C.

RECTANGULAR (WELDED OR PRESSURE LOCKED)

NOTES

Constructed of flat bearing bars of steel or aluminum I-bars, with spacer bars at right angles. Spacer bars may be square, rectangular, or of another shape. Spacer bars are connected to bearing bars by pressing them into prepared slots or by welding. They have open ends or perhaps ends banded with flat bars that are of about the same size as welded bearing bars. Standard bar spacings are $^{15}/_{16}$ and $1^3/_{16}$ in.

NOSING OF ANGLE AND ABRASIVE STRIP AND BAR ENDS

HEAVY FRONT AND BACK BEARING BARS AND BAR END PLATES

FLOOR PLATE NOSING, BAR END PLATES

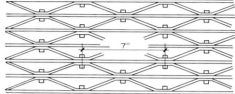

WITH SPACER BARS RIVETED APPROX. 7" O.C. USED FOR AVERAGE INSTALLATION

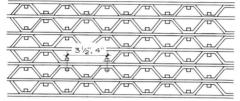

WITH SPACER BARS RIVETED 3½" OR 4" USED FOR HEAVY TRAFFIC AND WHERE WHEELED EQUIPMENT IS USED

NOSING OF CLOSELY SPACED BARS, ANGLE ENDS

CHECKER PLATE NOSING, BAR END PLATES

RETICULATED (RIVETED)

NOTES

Flat bearing bars are made of steel or aluminum, and continuous bent spacer or reticulate bars are riveted to the bearing bars. Usually they have open ends or ends that are banded with flat bars of the same size as bearing bars, welded across the ends. Normal spacing of bars: $^3/_4$, $1^1/_8$, or $2^5/_{16}$ in. Many bar gratings cannot be used in areas of public pedestrian traffic (crutches, canes, pogo sticks, women's shoes, etc.). Close mesh grating ($^1/_4$ in.) is available in steel and aluminum, for use in pedestrian traffic areas.

EXTRUDED ALUMINUM CORRUGATED NOSING, BAR END PLATES

TREADS

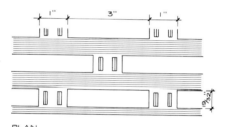

PLAN

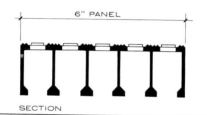

6" PANEL

SECTION

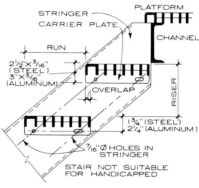

STAIR STRINGER AND TREAD CARRIER

ALUMINUM PLANK

NOTES

Grating is extruded from aluminum alloy in one piece with integral I-beam ribs and can have a natural finish or be anodized. Top of surface may be solid or punched. Standard panel width is 6 in.

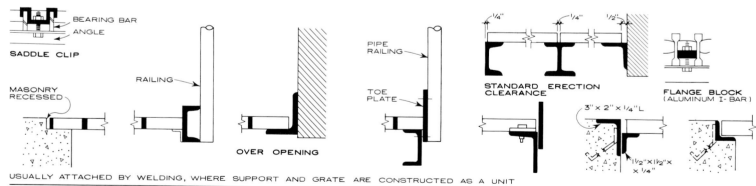

USUALLY ATTACHED BY WELDING, WHERE SUPPORT AND GRATE ARE CONSTRUCTED AS A UNIT

FIXED OR LOOSE GRATINGS

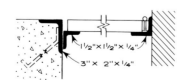

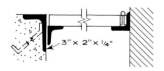

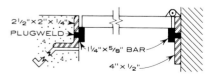

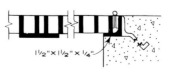

SIZES OF ANGLES SUPPORTING GRATING DEPEND ON DEPTH OF GRATING BARS

HINGED AREA GRATINGS

Vicente Cordero, AIA; Arlington, Virginia

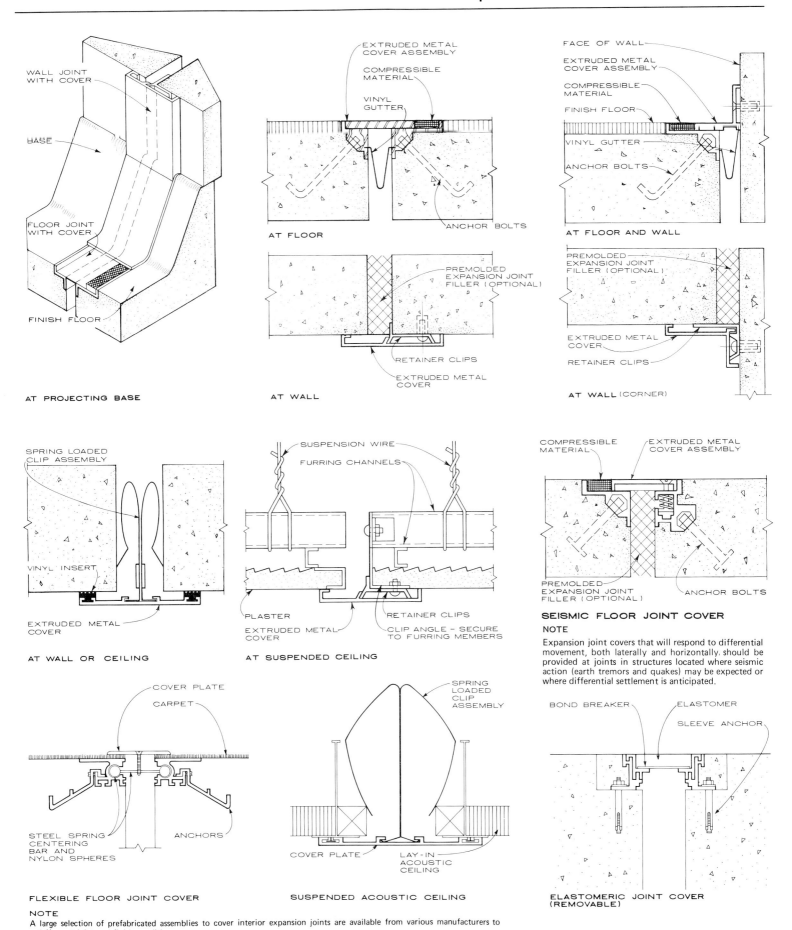

WALL JOINT WITH COVER

BASE

FLOOR JOINT WITH COVER

FINISH FLOOR

AT PROJECTING BASE

EXTRUDED METAL COVER ASSEMBLY

COMPRESSIBLE MATERIAL

VINYL GUTTER

ANCHOR BOLTS

AT FLOOR

FACE OF WALL

EXTRUDED METAL COVER ASSEMBLY

COMPRESSIBLE MATERIAL

FINISH FLOOR

VINYL GUTTER

ANCHOR BOLTS

AT FLOOR AND WALL

PREMOLDED EXPANSION JOINT FILLER (OPTIONAL)

RETAINER CLIPS

EXTRUDED METAL COVER

AT WALL

PREMOLDED EXPANSION JOINT FILLER (OPTIONAL)

EXTRUDED METAL COVER

RETAINER CLIPS

AT WALL (CORNER)

SPRING LOADED CLIP ASSEMBLY

VINYL INSERT

EXTRUDED METAL COVER

AT WALL OR CEILING

SUSPENSION WIRE

FURRING CHANNELS

PLASTER

EXTRUDED METAL COVER

RETAINER CLIPS

CLIP ANGLE – SECURE TO FURRING MEMBERS

AT SUSPENDED CEILING

COMPRESSIBLE MATERIAL

EXTRUDED METAL COVER ASSEMBLY

PREMOLDED EXPANSION JOINT FILLER (OPTIONAL)

ANCHOR BOLTS

SEISMIC FLOOR JOINT COVER

NOTE

Expansion joint covers that will respond to differential movement, both laterally and horizontally, should be provided at joints in structures located where seismic action (earth tremors and quakes) may be expected or where differential settlement is anticipated.

COVER PLATE

CARPET

STEEL SPRING CENTERING BAR AND NYLON SPHERES

ANCHORS

FLEXIBLE FLOOR JOINT COVER

NOTE

A large selection of prefabricated assemblies to cover interior expansion joints are available from various manufacturers to satisfy most joint and finish conditions.

SPRING LOADED CLIP ASSEMBLY

COVER PLATE

LAY-IN ACOUSTIC CEILING

SUSPENDED ACOUSTIC CEILING

BOND BREAKER

ELASTOMER

SLEEVE ANCHOR

ELASTOMERIC JOINT COVER (REMOVABLE)

PREFABRICATED INTERIOR EXPANSION JOINT COVERS

Robert D. Abernathy; J. N. Pease Associates; Charlotte, North Carolina

ORNAMENTAL METAL   5

GENERAL NOTES

Many variations of the typical types shown are available such as slanted, rounded, or tapered tops and ends; grooved, ribbed, fluted and shaped faces; as well as other decorative treatment.

Refer to the following sections for:	a) Standard Metal Shapes	b) Metal Stair Nosings

D.O.F. = DEPTH OF FACE

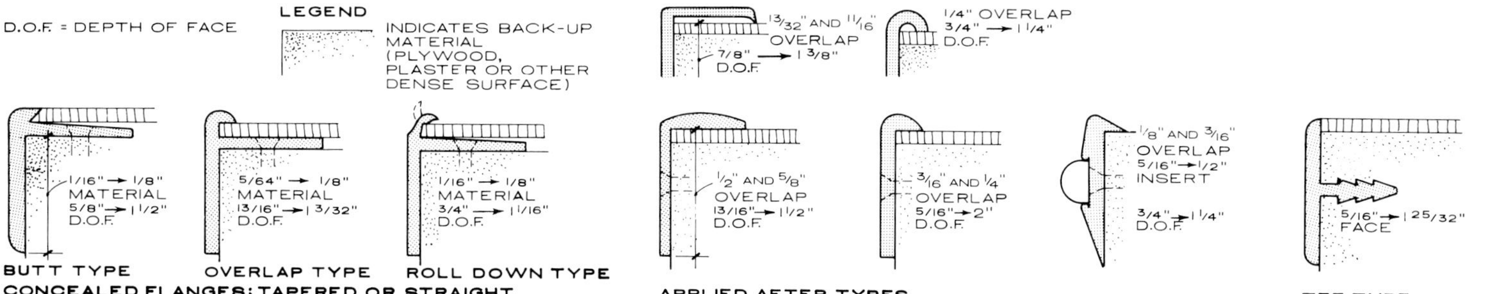

LEGEND

INDICATES BACK-UP MATERIAL (PLYWOOD, PLASTER OR OTHER DENSE SURFACE)

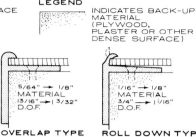

13/32" AND 11/16" OVERLAP
7/8" → 1 3/8" D.O.F.

1/4" OVERLAP
3/4" → 1 1/4" D.O.F.

1/16" → 1/8" MATERIAL
5/8" → 1 1/2" D.O.F.

BUTT TYPE

5/64" → 1/8" MATERIAL
13/16" → 1 3/32" D.O.F.

OVERLAP TYPE

1/16" → 1/8" MATERIAL
3/4" → 1 1/16" D.O.F.

ROLL DOWN TYPE

CONCEALED FLANGES: TAPERED OR STRAIGHT

1/2" AND 5/8" OVERLAP
13/16" → 1 1/2" D.O.F.

3/16" AND 1/4" OVERLAP
5/16" → 2" D.O.F.

APPLIED AFTER TYPES

1/8" AND 3/16" OVERLAP
5/16" → 1/2" INSERT
3/4" → 1 1/4" D.O.F.

5/16" → 1 25/32" FACE

TEE TYPE

NOSINGS

5/64" → 1/8" MATERIAL

1/8" AND 1/4" UNDER FLANGE

1/16" → 3/16" MATERIAL

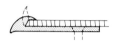

1/16" → 1/8" MATERIAL

**SINK (FLAT RIM) OR DOORWAY: BUTT & ROLL DOWN TYPES
CONCEALED FLANGES: TAPERED OR STRAIGHT**

1/8" AND 3/16" MATERIAL

1/8" AND 3/16" MATERIAL

BUTT TYPES

EDGINGS

3/32" → 5/32" MATERIAL
3/8" → 1 3/16" WIDTHS

**EDGE BINDER
OVERLAP TYPES**

3/4" → 1 9/32" WIDTHS

SEAM BINDER

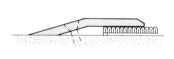

1" → 2 1/2" WIDTHS

**OVERLAP TYPE
CARPET EDGE BINDERS**

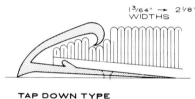

13/64" → 2 1/8" WIDTHS

TAP DOWN TYPE

EDGINGS

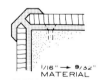

1/16" → 9/32" MATERIAL

**OUTSIDE TYPES
CONCEALED FLANGES: TAPERED**

1/32" → 1/4" MATERIAL

1/16" → 1/8" MATERIAL

INSIDE TYPE

1/16" → 3/8" MATERIAL

21/64" OVERLAP

**OUTSIDE
APPLIED AFTER TYPE**

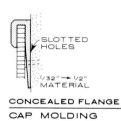

SLOTTED HOLES

1/32" → 1/2" MATERIAL

CONCEALED FLANGE

CAP MOLDING

CORNERS

1/32" → 3/8" MATERIAL

CONCEALED FLANGE - TAPERED

1/16" → 5/32" MATERIAL

APPLIED AFTER

7/16" → 2" FACE

COVE

COVE AND BATHTUB EDGING

HANDLE MOLDINGS FOR 1/4" MATERIAL

SHOW CASE MOLDINGS

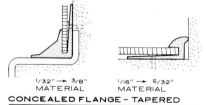

TAG PLACED HERE

1/16" → 1/2" MATERIAL

CONCEALED FLANGE

DIVISION BAR

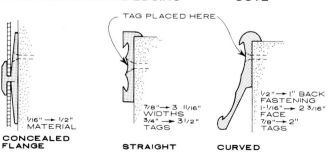

7/8" → 3 11/16" WIDTHS
3/4" → 3 1/2" TAGS

STRAIGHT

1/2" → 1" BACK FASTENING
1 1/16" → 2 3/16" FACE
7/8" → 2" TAGS

CURVED

TAG MOLDINGS

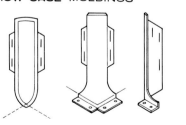

**INSIDE CORNERS
UP TO 5/32" MATERIAL**

OUTSIDE

RIGHT / LEFT END STOPS

COVE BASE

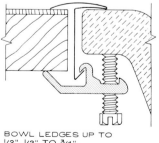

BOWL LEDGES UP TO 1/2", 1/2" TO 3/4", 3/4" TO 1 1/8"

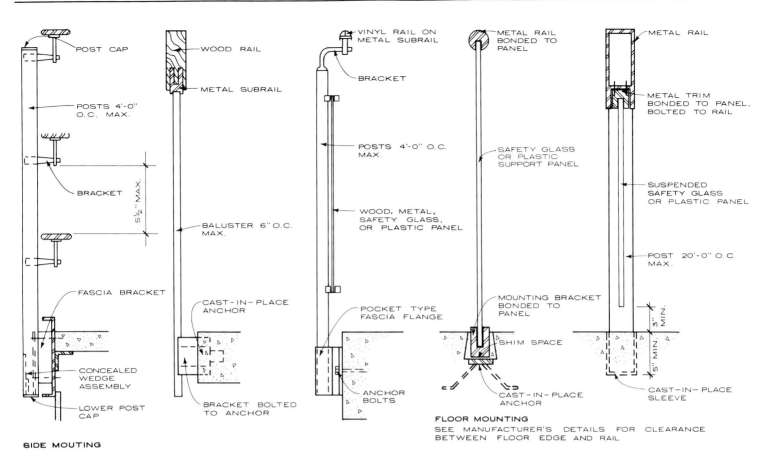

SIDE MOUTING

FLOOR MOUNTING
SEE MANUFACTURER'S DETAILS FOR CLEARANCE
BETWEEN FLOOR EDGE AND RAIL

CONSULT CODE FOR RAILING HEIGHT, POST RAIL, AND BALUSTER SPACING, AND LOADING REQUIREMENTS

TYPICAL POST AND RAIL DETAILS

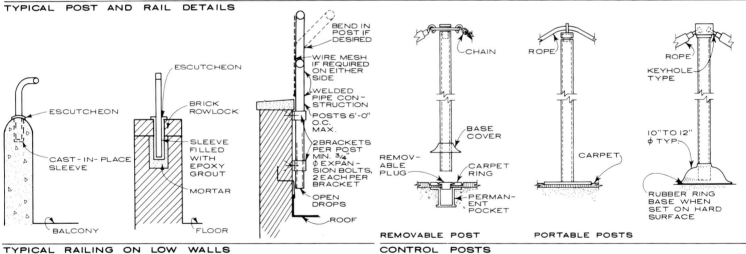

TYPICAL RAILING ON LOW WALLS

CONTROL POSTS

REMOVABLE POST   PORTABLE POSTS

GUIDELINES

Factors to consider for railing design include:

1. Follow all local code requirements, especially as they relate to handicap requirements, ramps, rail diameter, and rail clearances.

2. Verify allowable design stresses of rails, posts, and panels.

3. Verify the structural value of fasteners and anchorage to building structure for both vertical and lateral (horizontal) forces.

4. Requirements for uniform loading may vary from 100 to 200 lb/linear foot.

5. Requirements for concentrated loads, at any point along the rail, may vary from 200 to 300 lb.

6. Horizontal guardrail or rail at ramps is 42 in. above floor surface.

7. Guardrails and rails at stairs should be designed to prevent passage of a 6 in. diameter sphere, at any opening, in areas accessible to the public.

8. Refer to ASTM E-985 for additional information.

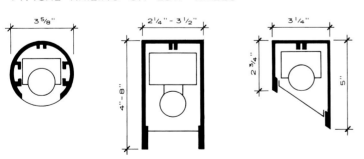

FLUORESCENT FIXTURES AND PLASTIC DIFFUSERS, SMALLER HANDRAILS AVAILABLE WITH INCANDESCENT FIXTURES

LIGHTED HANDRAILS

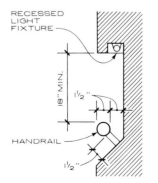

RECESSED HANDRAIL

John McCartney, AIA; Washington, D.C.

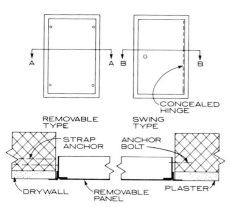

SECTION A-A

NOTES

1. Frames usually are set into building construction; doors are constructed to fit later. Doors may be hinged, set in with clips, or fastened with screws. Hinges may be butt or pivot, separate or continuous, surface or concealed. Assorted stock sizes range from 8 in. x 8 in. to 24 in. x 36 in.
2. Access panels should have a fire rating similar to the wall in which they occur. Access panels of more than 144 sq. ins. require automatic closers.
3. Minimum size for attic and crawl space access often is specified by building code.

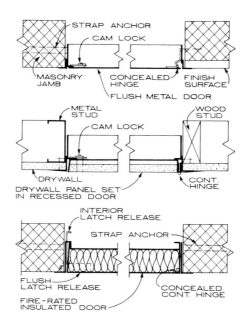

SECTION B-B

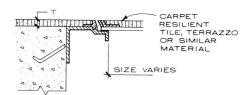

PLASTER

ACOUSTICAL PLASTER

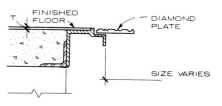

ACOUSTICAL TILE

NOTES

1. Spring-operated, swingdown panels and swingup panels frequently are used for ceiling access.
2. Standard sizes range from 12 in. x 12 in. to 24 in. x 36 in.
3. Other finish ceiling panels are detailed similar to acoustical tiles.

ACCESS DOORS

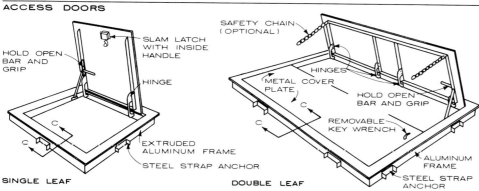

SINGLE LEAF

1. MATERIAL: Steel or aluminum.
2. SIZES: Single leaf—2 ft. x 2 ft., 2 ft. 6 in. x 2 ft. 6 in., 2 ft. 6 in. x 3 ft., 3 ft. x 3 ft. Double leaf—3 ft. 6 in. x 3 ft. 6 in., 4 ft. x 4 ft., 4 ft. x 6 ft., 5 ft. x 5 ft.

DOUBLE LEAF

Thickness "T" varies from 1/8 in. for resilient flooring to 3/16 in. for carpet; some manufacturers offer 3/4 in. for terrazzo and tile floor.

Double-leaf floor hatch is recommended for areas where there is danger a person could fall into the opening. Safety codes require that floor openings be protected. Check local codes for special requirements.

CEILING ACCESS PANELS

FLOOR HATCH — SECTION C-C

FLOOR HATCH — SECTION C-C

FLOOR HATCHES

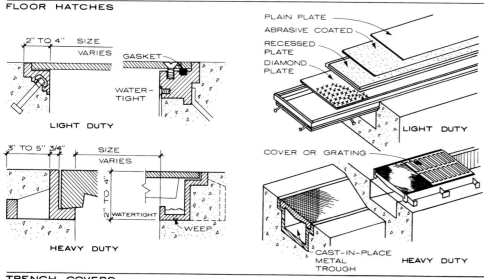

LIGHT DUTY

HEAVY DUTY

TRENCH COVERS

LIGHT-DUTY TRENCH COVERS

1. MATERIAL: Extruded aluminum.
2. SIZE: 2 in. to 36 in. wide. Side frames are available in cut length of 20 ft. stocks that can be spliced to any length. Recessed cover plates are available in 20 ft. stock; other covers are available in 10 ft. and 12 ft. stock.
3. Side frames normally are cast in concrete around trough form.

HEAVY-DUTY TRENCH COVERS

1. MATERIAL: Cast iron or ductile iron.
2. SIZES: Heavy duty cast iron trench covers should be planned carefully to use standard stock length to avoid cutting, or special length casting should be ordered.
3. STOCK COVER SIZE: To 48 in. wide and 24 in. long. Frames are manufactured in standard lengths of 24 in. or 36 in. depending on size and manufacturer. Cast iron troughs are 8 in. deep, 6 in. to 24 in. wide, and 48 in. in stock lengths.
4. Minimum grating size in walkways is specified in ANSI A117.1-1986.

Cohen, Karydas & Associates, Chartered; Washington, D.C.
Harold C. Munger, FAIA; Munger Munger + Associates Architects, Inc.; Toledo, Ohio

ORNAMENTAL METAL

REFERENCES

GENERAL REFERENCES

Architectural Metal Handbook, National Association of Architectural Metal Manufacturers

Design Manual for Composite Decks, Form Decks, and Roof Decks, Steel Deck Institute (SDI)

Fire-Resistant Steel Frame Construction, American Iron and Steel Institute (AISI)

Manual of Steel Construction, Allowable Stress Design, American Institute of Steel Construction (AISC)

Residential Masonry Fireplace and Chimney Handbook, 1989, James E. Amrhein, Masonry Institute of America

Standard Specifications, Load Tables, and Weight Tables for Steel Joists and Joist Girders, Steel Joist Institute (SJI)

Structural Details for Steel Construction, 1988, Morton Newman, McGraw-Hill

Structural Steel in Architecture and Building Technology, 1988, Irvin Engel, Prentice-Hall

DATA SOURCES: ORGANIZATIONS

American Bolt, Nut and Rivet Manufacturers (ABNRM), 85

American Iron and Steel Institute (AISI), 92

American National Standards Institute (ANSI), 96, 99

American Society for Testing and Materials (ASTM), 89

Blumcraft of Pittsburgh, 103

Factory Mutual System, 89, 90

Independent Nail and Packing Company, 82–84

Irving Grating, IKG Industries, Harsco Corporation, 100

Julius Blum and Company, Inc., 103

Occupational Safety and Health Administration (OSHA), U.S. Department of Labor, 96, 98, 99

Rawplug Company, Inc., 85

Red Head, ITT Phillips Drill Division, 85

Simplex Nails, Inc., 82–84

Underwriters' Laboratories, Inc. (U.L.), 89, 90

U.S. Steel Corporation, 92

Youngstown Aluminum Products, 102

DATA SOURCES: PUBLICATIONS

Architectural Metal Handbook, National Association of Architectural Metal Manufacturers, 96, 100

Design Manual for Floor Decks and Roof Decks, Steel Deck Institute (SDI), 90, 91

Life Safety Code, 5-2.8.1.4 NFPA 101, 1985, National Fire Protection Association. Reprinted with permission, 98

Manual of Steel Construction, American Institute of Steel Construction (AISC), 77, 76

Standard Specifications Load Tables and Weight Tables for Steel Joists, Steel Joist Institute (SJI), 88, 89

CHAPTER 6

WOOD

NOMINAL AND MINIMUM DRESSED SIZES OF LUMBER PRODUCTS (IN.)

The thicknesses apply to all widths and all widths to all thicknesses.

LUMBER PRODUCT	THICKNESSES NOMINAL	MIN DRESSED DRY	MIN DRESSED GREEN	FACE WIDTHS NOMINAL	MIN DRESSED DRY	MIN DRESSED GREEN
Boards	1	$3/4$	$25/32$	2	$1\,1/2$	$1\,9/16$
	$1\,1/4$	1	$1\,1/32$	3	$2\,1/2$	$2\,9/16$
	$1\,1/2$	$1\,1/4$	$1\,9/32$	4	$3\,1/2$	$3\,9/16$
				5	$4\,1/2$	$4\,5/8$
				6	$5\,1/2$	$5\,5/8$
				7	$6\,1/2$	$6\,5/8$
				8	$7\,1/4$	$7\,1/2$
				9	$8\,1/4$	$8\,1/2$
				10	$9\,1/4$	$9\,1/2$
				11	$10\,1/4$	$10\,1/2$
				12	$11\,1/4$	$11\,1/2$
				14	$13\,1/4$	$13\,1/2$
				16	$15\,1/4$	$15\,1/2$
Dimension lumber	2	$1\,1/2$	$1\,9/16$	2	$1\,1/2$	$1\,9/16$
	$2\,1/2$	2	$2\,1/16$	3	$2\,1/2$	$2\,9/16$
	3	$2\,1/2$	$2\,9/16$	4	$3\,1/2$	$3\,9/16$
	$3\,1/2$	3	$3\,1/16$	5	$4\,1/2$	$4\,5/8$
				6	$5\,1/2$	$5\,5/8$
				8	$7\,1/4$	$7\,1/2$
				10	$9\,1/4$	$9\,1/2$
				12	$11\,1/4$	$11\,1/2$
				14	$13\,1/4$	$13\,1/2$
				16	$15\,1/4$	$15\,1/2$
	4	$3\,1/2$	$3\,9/16$	2	$1\,1/2$	$1\,9/16$
	$4\,1/2$	4	$4\,1/16$	3	$2\,1/2$	$2\,9/16$
				4	$3\,1/2$	$3\,9/16$
				5	$4\,1/2$	$4\,5/8$
				6	$5\,1/2$	$5\,5/8$
				8	$7\,1/4$	$7\,1/2$
				10	$9\,1/4$	$9\,1/2$
				12	$11\,1/4$	$11\,1/2$
				14		$13\,1/2$
				16		$15\,1/2$
Timbers	5 and thicker		$1/2$ off	5 and wider		$1/2$ off
Shiplap $3/8''$ lap	1	$3/4$	$25/32$	4	$3\,1/8$	$3\,3/16$
				6	$5\,1/8$	$5\,1/4$
				8	$6\,7/8$	$7\,1/8$
				10	$8\,7/8$	$9\,1/8$
				12	$10\,7/8$	$11\,1/8$
				14	$12\,7/8$	$13\,1/8$
				16	$14\,7/8$	$15\,1/8$
Shiplap $1/2''$ lap	1	$3/4$	$25/32$	4	3	$3\,1/16$
				6	5	$5\,1/8$
				8	$6\,3/4$	7
				10	$8\,3/4$	9
				12	$10\,3/4$	11
				14	$12\,3/4$	13
				16	$14\,3/4$	15
Centermatch $1/4''$ tongue	1	$3/4$	$25/32$	4	$3\,1/8$	$3\,3/16$
	$1\,1/4$	1	$1\,1/32$	5	$4\,1/8$	$4\,1/4$
	$1\,1/2$	$1\,1/4$	$1\,9/32$	6	$5\,1/8$	$5\,1/4$
				8	$6\,7/8$	$7\,1/8$
				10	$8\,7/8$	$9\,1/8$
				12	$10\,7/8$	$11\,1/8$
2'' dressed and matched $3/8''$ tongue	2	$1\,1/2$	$1\,9/16$	4	3	$3\,1/16$
				6	5	$5\,1/8$
				8	$6\,3/4$	7
				10	$8\,3/4$	9
				12	$10\,3/4$	11
2'' shiplap $1/2''$ lap	2	$1\,1/2$	$1\,9/16$	4	3	$3\,1/16$
				6	5	$5\,1/8$
				8	$6\,3/4$	7
				10	$8\,3/4$	9
				12	$10\,3/4$	11

NOTE: For dry lumber moisture content is 19% or less and for green lumber moisture content is in excess of 19%.

NOMINAL AND MINIMUM DRESSED DRY SIZES OF LUMBER PRODUCTS (IN.)

The thicknesses apply to all widths and all widths to all thicknesses.

LUMBER PRODUCT	THICKNESSES NOMINAL	MIN DRESSED	FACE WIDTHS NOMINAL	MIN DRESSED
Finish	$3/8$	$5/16$	2	$1\,1/2$
	$1/2$	$7/16$	3	$2\,1/2$
	$5/8$	$9/16$	4	$3\,1/2$
	$3/4$	$5/8$	5	$4\,1/2$
	1	$3/4$	6	$5\,1/2$
	$1\,1/4$	1	7	$6\,1/2$
	$1\,1/2$	$1\,1/4$	8	$7\,1/4$
	$1\,3/4$	$1\,3/8$	9	$8\,1/4$
	2	$1\,1/2$	10	$9\,1/4$
	$2\,1/2$	2	11	$10\,1/4$
	3	$2\,1/2$	12	$11\,1/4$
	$3\,1/2$	3	14	$13\,1/4$
	4	$3\,1/2$	16	$15\,1/4$
Flooring; dimension given is face dimension excluding tongue	$3/8$	$5/16$	2	$1\,1/8$
	$1/2$	$7/16$	3	$2\,1/8$
	$5/8$	$9/16$	4	$3\,1/8$
	1	$3/4$	5	$4\,1/8$
	$1\,1/4$	1	6	$5\,1/8$
	$1\,1/2$	$1\,1/4$		
Ceiling	$3/8$	$5/16$	3	$2\,1/8$
	$1/2$	$7/16$	4	$3\,1/8$
	$5/8$	$9/16$	5	$4\,1/8$
	$3/4$	$11/16$	6	$5\,1/8$
Partition	1	$23/32$	3	$2\,1/8$
			4	$3\,1/8$
			5	$4\,1/8$
			6	$5\,1/8$
Stepping	1	$3/4$	8	$7\,1/4$
	$1\,1/4$	1	10	$9\,1/4$
	$1\,1/2$	$1\,1/4$	12	$11\,1/4$
	2	$1\,1/2$		
Bevel siding	$1/2$	$7/16$ butt, $3/16$ tip	4	$3\,1/2$
	$9/16$	$15/32$ butt, $3/16$ tip	5	$4\,1/2$
	$5/8$	$9/16$ butt, $3/16$ tip	6	$5\,1/2$
	$3/4$	$11/16$ butt, $3/16$ tip	8	$7\,1/4$
	1	$3/4$ butt, $3/16$ tip	10	$9\,1/4$
			12	$11\,1/4$
Bungalow siding	$3/4$	$11/16$ butt, $3/16$ tip	8	$7\,1/4$
			10	$9\,1/4$
			12	$11\,1/4$
Rustic and drop siding shiplapped $3/8''$	$5/8$	$9/16$	4	3
	1	$23/32$	5	4
			6	5
Rustic and drop siding shiplapped $1/2''$	$5/8$	$9/16$	4	$2\,7/8$
	1	$23/32$	5	$3\,7/8$
			6	$4\,7/8$
			8	$6\,5/8$
			10	$8\,5/8$
			12	$10\,5/8$
Rustic and drop siding dressed and matched	$5/8$	$9/16$	4	$3\,1/8$
	1	$23/32$	5	$4\,1/8$
			6	$5\,1/8$
			8	$6\,7/8$
			10	$8\,7/8$

NOTE: Maximum moisture content is 19%.

NOTE

For additional information reference should be made to the National Bureau of Standards, Product Standard PS20-70 American Softwood Lumber Standard. Available through U.S. Government Printing Office.

NOTE

Wood is preserved by pressure treatment with an EPA registered pesticide to protect it from insect attack and decay. Treated wood should be used only where such protection is required. Exposure to preservatives may present certain hazards. Precautions should be taken in handling, using, and disposing of treated wood. Refer to local codes.

DECAY AND INSECT RESISTANT WOOD

WOLMANIZED PRESSURE TREATED WOOD AND OUTDOOR BRAND WOOD

Wolmanized wood has been pressure treated with a water solution of preservative chemicals. Has outstanding durability under any condition of exposure. Use is limited to the treatment of fully air seasoned or kiln dried material. Wolman salts, the preservative used, impart a light green, blue-green, or brownish color to the wood, depending on the species. Wolmanized wood weathers to a silver gray.

1. GENERAL USE: In the ground; in water; in contact with masonry, or when the wood will be exposed to wetting.
2. SPECIFIC USE: Decks, patios, walkways, fences, boat docks, sill plates, soffits, fascia, all weather wood foundations, pole houses, and pole buildings.
3. ADVANTAGES: Provides lasting protection against decay producing fungi and insects. Clean, oil free. Odorless. Can be painted or stained. Preservative chemicals are fiberfixed in the wood to prevent leaching. Harmless to people, plants, and animals.
4. LIMITATIONS: Air seasoning or kiln drying is required after treatment to make Wolmanized lumber paintable and to guard further against shrinkage in service. Moisture content should be 19% or less. Because undercoated steel rusts quickly, nails or bolts should be galvanized.

CELLON PRESSURE TREATED WOOD

The Cellon pressure treatment process utilizes liquefied butane gas as a solvent to carry pentachlorophenol, the preservative, deep into the wood. After treatment, the solvent is evaporated. Particularly suitable for treating hardwoods and all plywoods.

1. GENERAL USE: Ground contact, in contact with masonry, or when the wood will be exposed to wetting.
2. SPECIFIC USE: Glued laminated beams, lighting standards, pole houses and pole buildings, decking.
3. ADVANTAGES: Provides lasting protection against decay producing fungi and insects. Clean and dry to the touch. Can be painted, stained, and glued. Since neither water nor oil is used in the Cellon process, air seasoning and kiln drying are not required after treatment. Retains the wood's original texture and color. Weathers naturally.
4. LIMITATIONS: Will not protect against attack from marine organisms. Certain species such as Douglas fir, southern pine, and ponderosa pine may exude resin from knots and heartwood after treatment. Wood rich in tannin, such as redwood and oak, may develop a blue-black surface stain if the lumber has not been well seasoned prior to treatment; however, the sun's rays will bleach out the stain in several months.

PENTACHLOROPHENOL PRESSURE TREATED WOOD

Pentachlorophenol is the principal preservative in the "oil borne" category. Toxic to insects and fungi.

1. GENERAL USE: In the ground.
2. SPECIFIC USE: Industrial and farm buildings; fence posts.
3. ADVANTAGES: Protects against fungi and insect attack. Seasoned hardwoods and softwoods can be treated without fear of grain raising, checking, or splitting.
4. LIMITATIONS: Penta treated forest products may become blotchy when exposed to the weather; this condition disappears after extended service. Penta-in-oil treated wood would NOT be used as a subflooring, or in contact with materials subject to staining (plaster, wallboard). Not readily paintable; would not be used in direct contact with roofing felt, since it can cause the tar to drip. Not recommended for use in saltwater.

Derek Martin, FAIA; Pittsburgh, Pennsylvania
Domenic F. Valente, AIA; D. F. Valente, Architect & Planner; Medford, Massachusetts

CREOSOTE

Creosote is the oldest commercial wood preservative currently being used. It has demonstrated, through years of actual service, outstanding durability, dependability, and general utility. Creosote contains a multitude of chemical compounds which are toxic to fungi, insects, and most marine organisms. Average life expectancy of a creosoted wood pole in the ground is 35 to 40 years, but some creosoted poles are still standing fast after more than 75 years of rugged service.

1. GENERAL USE: In the ground and in water.
2. SPECIFIC USE: Foundation piles, landscape ties, fence posts, highway guard rails, marine piling, and bulkheads.
3. ADVANTAGES: Creosote is a coal tar product that derives its effectiveness from its persistent high toxicity to wood destroying insects and fungi. Creosote effectively protects wood from the ravages of most marine organisms.
4. LIMITATIONS: Pressure creosoted lumber should NOT be used as a subflooring or in contact with materials subject to staining (plaster, wallboard). It is not readily paintable, and should not be used in direct contact with roofing felt, since it can cause the tar to drip.

CORROSION RESISTANT WOOD

KP RESIN IMPREGNATED WOOD

KP resin impregnated wood has been impregnated with a phenolic resin solution to obtain a high degree of acid resistance and excellent dimensional stability. The treatment is limited to southern pine, hard maple, cativo, and kempas. Natural wood color.

1. GENERAL USE: Where corrosion resistance or dimensional stability is required.
2. SPECIFIC USE: Filter press plates and frames, flumes, stacks, tank covers, tanks, troughs and trays, die models.
3. ADVANTAGES: High degree of acid resistance. Dimensional stability far greater than untreated wood. Can be machined. Gouging the surface does not reduce the protection.
4. LIMITATIONS: Should not be exposed to alkaline solutions, aniline, chlorine gas, strong bleaching solutions, strong oxidizing acids.

ASIDBAR IMPREGNATED WOOD

Asidbar impregnated wood has been impregnated with topped coal tar material that provides the natural structural properties of wood as well as the chemical resistant properties of coal tar composites. Color is coal-tar black. Treatment is for southern pine lumber, and southern pine and Douglas fir plywood.

1. GENERAL USE: Where corrosion resistance is required.
2. SPECIFIC USE: Beams, interior wall cladding, decking, effluent systems, platforms, roof systems, walkways.
3. ADVANTAGES: High degree of acid resistance. Gouging of surface does not reduce the protection.
4. LIMITATIONS: Tends to soften and expand in severe temperatures above 130°F. Not suitable for use with acetate solvents, benzene or benzol, ethers, trichloroethylene, xylene, or xylol.

FIRE RETARDANT TREATED WOOD

NON-COM FIRE RETARDANT TREATED WOOD

Non-Com fire retardant treated wood is used indoors where the relative humidity is normally below 80%. The wood is pressure impregnated with inorganic salts that react chemically at temperatures below the ignition point of untreated wood. This chemical reaction reduces the flammable vapors emitted by wood subjected to fire. A protective char is formed and wood underneath remains structurally sound longer than untreated and surface treated wood.

1. CLASSIFIED: Non-Com fire retardant treated lumber and plywood have an Underwriters' Laboratories designated rating of FRS, which means that the material has a fire hazard classification of 25 or less for flame spread, fuel contributed, and smoke developed, and shows no sign of progressive combustion when the 10 minute fire hazard classification test is continued for an additional 20 minutes.
2. APPROVED: The Factory Mutual Engineering Division, the Factory Insurance Association, all state insurance rating bureaus, and all branches of the Insurance Services Office frequently permit the use of Non-Com fire retardant treated wood as an alternative to materials classified as noncombustible.
3. GENERAL USE: In buildings (interior).
4. SPECIFIC USE: Studs, wall plates, and fire stops with metal lath and plaster or drywall construction of interior nonbearing walls and partitions in fire resistive buildings. Roof systems including deck, purlins, and joists.
5. ADVANTAGES: Reduces flame spread and fuel contributed. Requires no maintenance to retain its fire retardant properties. Can be installed by regular carpenter crews. Low sound transmission makes it an excellent product for remodeling as well as for new construction.
6. LIMITATIONS: If Non-Com is to be painted, sealed, or varnished, it must be kiln dried to a maximum moisture content of 12%. Not recommended for use in the ground or for exposed locations that are subject to weathering or humidity normally above 80%. At jobsite, dry lumber should be stored indoors if possible. Otherwise, it should be stored on raised platforms and covered with suitable weatherproof protective covering such as tarpaulins or polyethylene film. NOTE: NCX fire retardant treated wood is recommended for architectural appearance applications.

NCX FIRE RETARDANT TREATED WOOD

NCX fire retardant treated wood is used outside or where the relative humidity is frequently above 80%. The wood is pressure impregnated with a fire retardant monomeric resin solution. After impregnation, the wood is kiln dried to cure the chemicals in the wood. The cured chemicals in the wood are not affected by direct outdoor weather exposure and high humidity.

1. CLASSIFIED: NCX fire retardant treated lumber and plywood have an Underwriters' Laboratories designated rating of FRS, which means that the material has a fire hazard classification of 25 or less for flame spread, fuel contributed, and smoke developed, and shows no sign of progressive combustion when the 10 minute fire hazard classification test is continued for an additional 20 minutes.
2. APPROVED: The Factory Mutual Engineering Division, the Factory Insurance Association, all state insurance rating bureaus, and all branches of the Insurance Services Office frequently permit the use of NCX as an alternative to materials classified as noncombustible.
3. RECOGNIZED: For certain applications by numerous state and city building codes. Also by BOCA, ICBO, SBCC, Southern Standard, AIA, and American Insurance Association.
4. GENERAL USE: Exterior use and where humidity is frequently above 80%. Also, interior appearance applications.
5. SPECIFIC USE: Balconies and steps. Roof systems. Soffit and fascia. Architectural hardwood molding and paneling. Western red cedar shingles and shakes.
6. ADVANTAGES: Suitable for exposure to the weather or high humidity conditions. Clear architectural finishes can be applied without causing below-film blushes.
7. LIMITATIONS: Although NCX wood has excellent weathering characteristics, it is not recommended for use in the ground or in ground contact. Treatment may darken wood slightly, but basic tone or hue remains almost unchanged. Treated wood may show sticker marks after drying. Underwriters' Laboratories permits milling of some species after drying. Where marks are objectionable, milling is recommended.

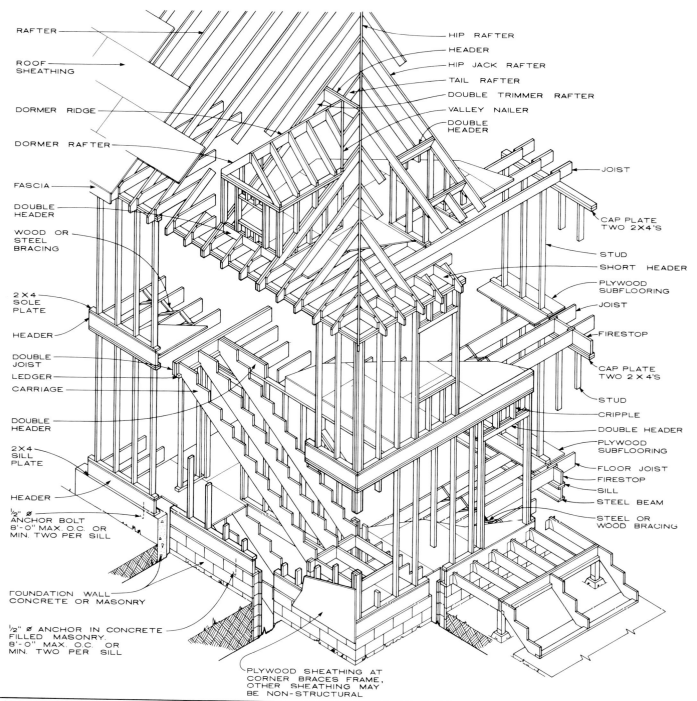

RAFTER
ROOF SHEATHING
DORMER RIDGE
DORMER RAFTER
FASCIA
DOUBLE HEADER
WOOD OR STEEL BRACING
2 × 4 SOLE PLATE
HEADER
DOUBLE JOIST
LEDGER
CARRIAGE
DOUBLE HEADER
2 × 4 SILL PLATE
HEADER
½" Ø ANCHOR BOLT 8'-0" MAX. O.C. OR MIN. TWO PER SILL
FOUNDATION WALL CONCRETE OR MASONRY
½" Ø ANCHOR IN CONCRETE FILLED MASONRY. 8'-0" MAX. O.C. OR MIN. TWO PER SILL

HIP RAFTER
HEADER
HIP JACK RAFTER
TAIL RAFTER
DOUBLE TRIMMER RAFTER
VALLEY NAILER
DOUBLE HEADER
JOIST
CAP PLATE TWO 2 × 4'S
STUD
SHORT HEADER
PLYWOOD SUBFLOORING
JOIST
FIRESTOP
CAP PLATE TWO 2 × 4'S
STUD
CRIPPLE
DOUBLE HEADER
PLYWOOD SUBFLOORING
FLOOR JOIST
FIRESTOP
SILL
STEEL BEAM
STEEL OR WOOD BRACING

PLYWOOD SHEATHING AT CORNER BRACES FRAME, OTHER SHEATHING MAY BE NON-STRUCTURAL

PLATFORM FRAMING

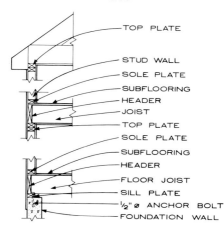

TOP PLATE
STUD WALL
SOLE PLATE
SUBFLOORING
HEADER
JOIST
TOP PLATE
SOLE PLATE
SUBFLOORING
HEADER
FLOOR JOIST
SILL PLATE
½" Ø ANCHOR BOLT
FOUNDATION WALL

Timothy B. McDonald; Washington, D.C.

NOTES
WESTERN OR PLATFORM FRAMING
Before any of the superstructure is erected, the first floor subflooring is put down making a platform on which the walls and partitions can be assembled and tilted into place. The process is repeated for each story of the building. This framing system is used frequently .

FIRESTOPPING
All concealed spaces in framing, with the exception of areas around flues and chimneys, are to be fitted with 2 in. blocking arranged to prevent drafts between spaces.

EXTERIOR WALL FRAMING
One story buildings: 2 x 4's, 16 in. or 24 in. o.c.;
       2 x 6's, 24 in. o.c.
Two and three stories: 2 x 4's, 16 in. o.c.;
       2 x 6's, 24 in. o.c.

BRACING EXTERIOR WALLS
Because floor framing and wall frames do not interlock, adequate sheathing must act as bracing and provide the necessary lateral resistance. Where required for additional stiffness or bracing, 1 x 4's may be let into outer face of studs at 45° angle secured at top, bottom, and to studs.

BRIDGING FOR FLOOR JOISTS
May be omitted when flooring is nailed adequately to joist; however, where nominal depth-to-thickness ratio of joists exceeds 6, bridging would be installed at 8 ft. 0 in. intervals. Building codes may allow omission of bridging under certain conditions.

Steel bridging is available. Some types do not require nails.

ROUGH CARPENTRY

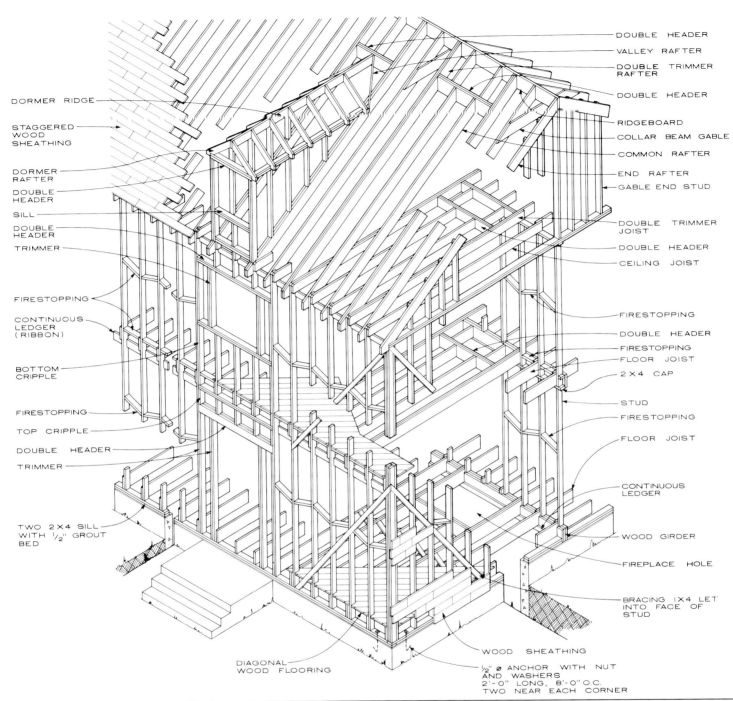

DORMER RIDGE
STAGGERED WOOD SHEATHING
DORMER RAFTER
DOUBLE HEADER
SILL
DOUBLE HEADER
TRIMMER
FIRESTOPPING
CONTINUOUS LEDGER (RIBBON)
BOTTOM CRIPPLE
FIRESTOPPING
TOP CRIPPLE
DOUBLE HEADER
TRIMMER
TWO 2×4 SILL WITH 1/2" GROUT BED
DIAGONAL WOOD FLOORING

DOUBLE HEADER
VALLEY RAFTER
DOUBLE TRIMMER RAFTER
DOUBLE HEADER
RIDGEBOARD
COLLAR BEAM GABLE
COMMON RAFTER
END RAFTER
GABLE END STUD
DOUBLE TRIMMER JOIST
DOUBLE HEADER
CEILING JOIST
FIRESTOPPING
DOUBLE HEADER
FIRESTOPPING
FLOOR JOIST
2×4 CAP
STUD
FIRESTOPPING
FLOOR JOIST
CONTINUOUS LEDGER
WOOD GIRDER
FIREPLACE HOLE
BRACING 1X4 LET INTO FACE OF STUD
WOOD SHEATHING
1/2" Ø ANCHOR WITH NUT AND WASHERS 2'-0" LONG, 8'-0" O.C. TWO NEAR EACH CORNER

BALLOON FRAMING

NOTES

BALLOON FRAMING

Balloon Framing's principal characteristics are that wall studs and joists rest on an anchored sill, with the studs extending in one continuous piece from sill to roof. At the second floor level a ribbon is let into the studs. The floor joists rest on the ribbon and are fastened to the studs: supporting and tying the structure together. This type of framing can be found in older structures and is generally not used today.

FIRESTOPPING

The flue effect created by continuous studs from sill to roof make firestopping mandatory in this type of framing. Firestopping is provided at each floor level and at the mid wall level.

TYPICAL EXTERIOR WALL FRAMING

One story: 2 x 4's 16 in. o.c.
Two story: 2 x 4's 16 in. o.c.

Timothy B. McDonald; Washington, D.C.

BRACING EXTERIOR WALLS

There are no braces in the balloon frame itself; hence, two methods are used to provide lateral rigidity. Previously diagonal sheathing was used. The other method, sometimes used in conjunction with diagonal sheathing, is to let continuous 1 x 4's into the outer face of corner studs at a 45° angle, and fastened top, bottom, and to the studs.

BRIDGING FOR FLOOR JOISTS

May be omitted when flooring is properly nailed to joists. However, where nominal depth-to-thickness ratio of joists exceeds 6 bridging should be installed at 8 ft 0 in. intervals. (F.H.A. also allows omission of bridging under certain conditions—see F.H.A. publication No. 300, revised 1965.)

Steel bridging is available. Some types do not require nails.

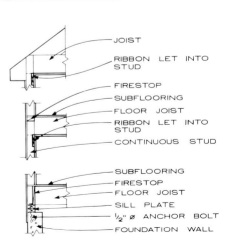

JOIST
RIBBON LET INTO STUD
FIRESTOP
SUBFLOORING
FLOOR JOIST
RIBBON LET INTO STUD
CONTINUOUS STUD
SUBFLOORING
FIRESTOP
FLOOR JOIST
SILL PLATE
1/2" Ø ANCHOR BOLT
FOUNDATION WALL

ROUGH CARPENTRY

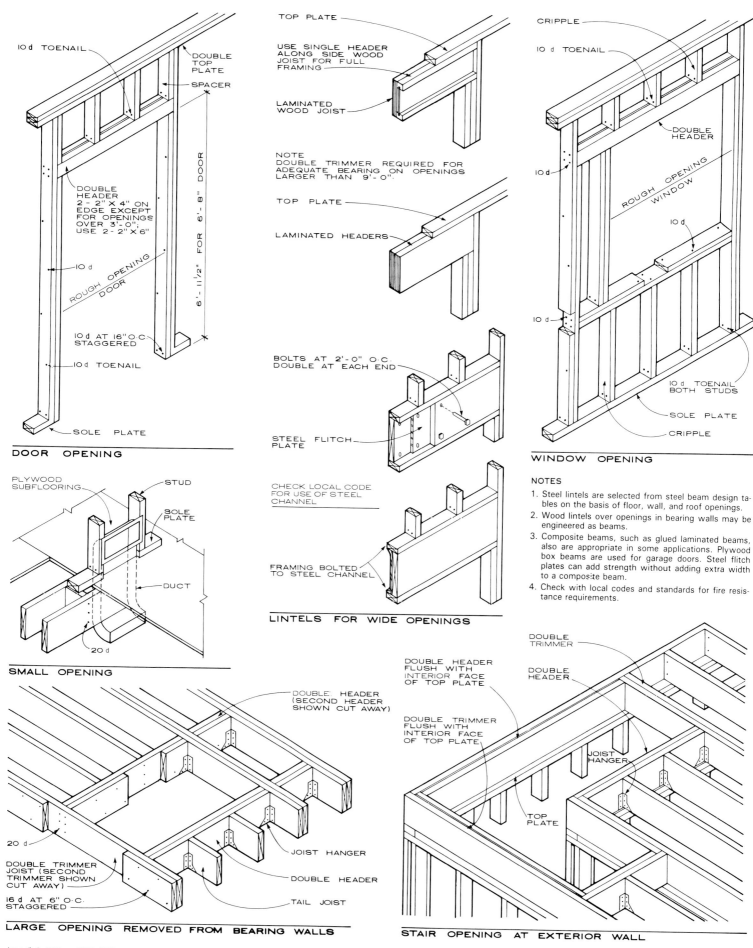

10d TOENAIL

DOUBLE TOP PLATE

SPACER

DOUBLE HEADER 2-2"X4" ON EDGE EXCEPT FOR OPENINGS OVER 3'-0"; USE 2-2"X6"

6'-11½" FOR 6'-8" DOOR

10d

ROUGH OPENING DOOR

10d AT 16"O.C. STAGGERED

10d TOENAIL

SOLE PLATE

DOOR OPENING

TOP PLATE

USE SINGLE HEADER ALONG SIDE WOOD JOIST FOR FULL FRAMING

LAMINATED WOOD JOIST

NOTE
DOUBLE TRIMMER REQUIRED FOR ADEQUATE BEARING ON OPENINGS LARGER THAN 9'-0".

TOP PLATE

LAMINATED HEADERS

BOLTS AT 2'-0" O.C. DOUBLE AT EACH END

STEEL FLITCH PLATE

CHECK LOCAL CODE FOR USE OF STEEL CHANNEL

FRAMING BOLTED TO STEEL CHANNEL

LINTELS FOR WIDE OPENINGS

CRIPPLE

10d TOENAIL

DOUBLE HEADER

10d

ROUGH OPENING WINDOW

10d

10d

10d TOENAIL BOTH STUDS

SOLE PLATE

CRIPPLE

WINDOW OPENING

NOTES

1. Steel lintels are selected from steel beam design tables on the basis of floor, wall, and roof openings.
2. Wood lintels over openings in bearing walls may be engineered as beams.
3. Composite beams, such as glued laminated beams, also are appropriate in some applications. Plywood box beams are used for garage doors. Steel flitch plates can add strength without adding extra width to a composite beam.
4. Check with local codes and standards for fire resistance requirements.

PLYWOOD SUBFLOORING

STUD

SOLE PLATE

DUCT

20d

SMALL OPENING

DOUBLE HEADER (SECOND HEADER SHOWN CUT AWAY)

20d

DOUBLE TRIMMER JOIST (SECOND TRIMMER SHOWN CUT AWAY)

16d AT 6" O.C. STAGGERED

JOIST HANGER

DOUBLE HEADER

TAIL JOIST

LARGE OPENING REMOVED FROM BEARING WALLS

DOUBLE HEADER FLUSH WITH INTERIOR FACE OF TOP PLATE

DOUBLE TRIMMER FLUSH WITH INTERIOR FACE OF TOP PLATE

DOUBLE TRIMMER

DOUBLE HEADER

JOIST HANGER

TOP PLATE

STAIR OPENING AT EXTERIOR WALL

Joseph A. Wilkes, FAIA; Wilkes and Faulkner; Washington, D.C.

ROUGH CARPENTRY

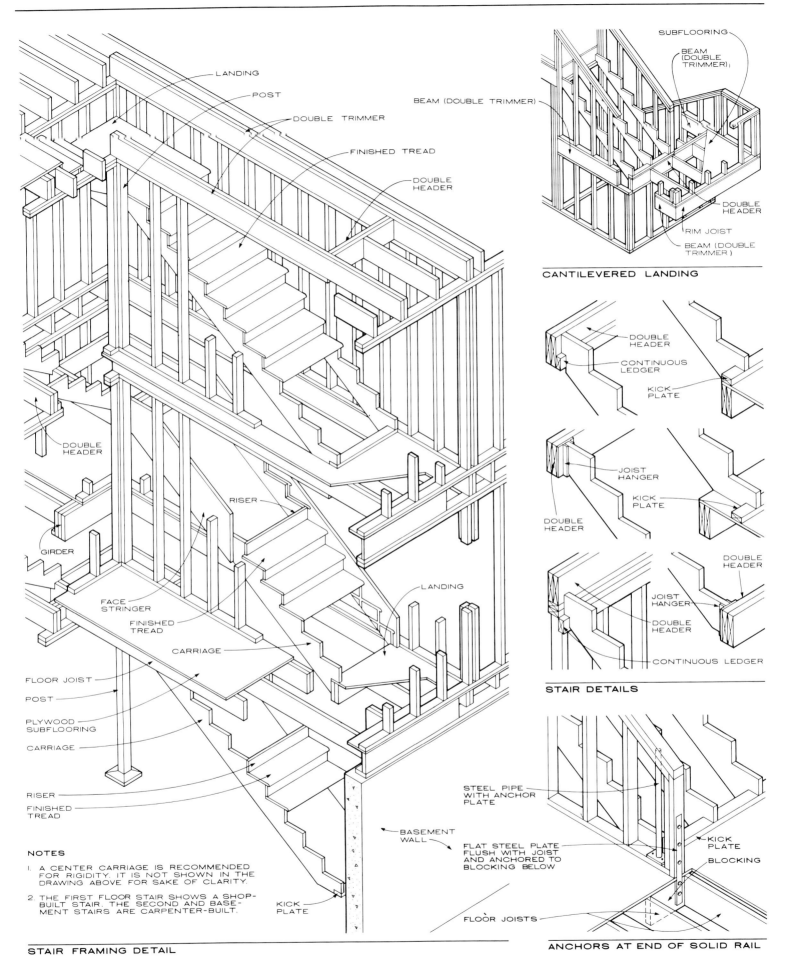

SUBFLOORING

BEAM (DOUBLE TRIMMER)

BEAM (DOUBLE TRIMMER)

DOUBLE HEADER

RIM JOIST

BEAM (DOUBLE TRIMMER)

CANTILEVERED LANDING

DOUBLE HEADER

CONTINUOUS LEDGER

KICK PLATE

JOIST HANGER

KICK PLATE

DOUBLE HEADER

DOUBLE HEADER

JOIST HANGER

DOUBLE HEADER

CONTINUOUS LEDGER

STAIR DETAILS

LANDING

POST

DOUBLE TRIMMER

FINISHED TREAD

DOUBLE HEADER

DOUBLE HEADER

RISER

GIRDER

FACE STRINGER

FINISHED TREAD

CARRIAGE

LANDING

FLOOR JOIST

POST

PLYWOOD SUBFLOORING

CARRIAGE

RISER

FINISHED TREAD

BASEMENT WALL

KICK PLATE

STEEL PIPE WITH ANCHOR PLATE

FLAT STEEL PLATE FLUSH WITH JOIST AND ANCHORED TO BLOCKING BELOW

KICK PLATE

BLOCKING

FLOOR JOISTS

ANCHORS AT END OF SOLID RAIL

NOTES

1. A CENTER CARRIAGE IS RECOMMENDED FOR RIGIDITY. IT IS NOT SHOWN IN THE DRAWING ABOVE FOR SAKE OF CLARITY.

2. THE FIRST FLOOR STAIR SHOWS A SHOP-BUILT STAIR. THE SECOND AND BASE-MENT STAIRS ARE CARPENTER-BUILT.

STAIR FRAMING DETAIL

Timothy B. McDonald; Washington, D.C.

ROUGH CARPENTRY 6

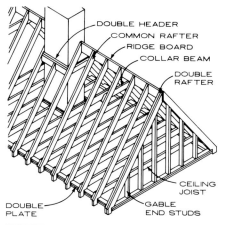

DOUBLE HEADER
COMMON RAFTER
RIDGE BOARD
COLLAR BEAM
DOUBLE RAFTER
CEILING JOIST
DOUBLE PLATE
GABLE END STUDS

GABLE ROOF

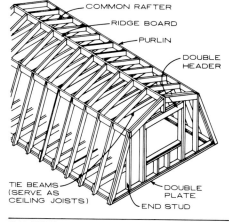

COMMON RAFTER
RIDGE BOARD
PURLIN
DOUBLE HEADER
DOUBLE PLATE
END STUD
TIE BEAMS (SERVE AS CEILING JOISTS)

GAMBREL ROOF

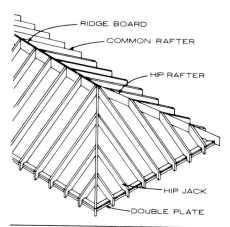

RIDGE BOARD
COMMON RAFTER
HIP RAFTER
HIP JACK
DOUBLE PLATE

HIP ROOF

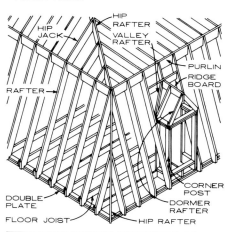

HIP RAFTER
HIP JACK
VALLEY RAFTER
PURLIN
RIDGE BOARD
RAFTER
CORNER POST
DORMER RAFTER
HIP RAFTER
DOUBLE PLATE
FLOOR JOIST

MANSARD ROOF

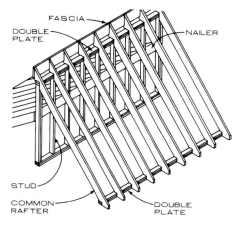

FASCIA
DOUBLE PLATE
NAILER
STUD
COMMON RAFTER
DOUBLE PLATE

SHED ROOF

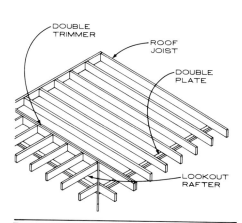

DOUBLE TRIMMER
ROOF JOIST
DOUBLE PLATE
LOOKOUT RAFTER

FLAT ROOF

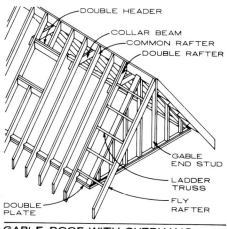

DOUBLE HEADER
COLLAR BEAM
COMMON RAFTER
DOUBLE RAFTER
GABLE END STUD
LADDER TRUSS
DOUBLE PLATE
FLY RAFTER

GABLE ROOF WITH OVERHANG

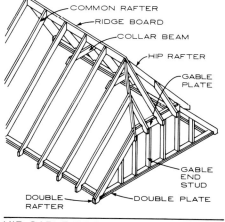

COMMON RAFTER
RIDGE BOARD
COLLAR BEAM
HIP RAFTER
GABLE PLATE
GABLE END STUD
DOUBLE RAFTER
DOUBLE PLATE

HIP GABLE ROOF

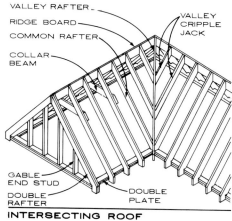

VALLEY RAFTER
RIDGE BOARD
COMMON RAFTER
COLLAR BEAM
VALLEY CRIPPLE JACK
GABLE END STUD
DOUBLE RAFTER
DOUBLE PLATE

INTERSECTING ROOF

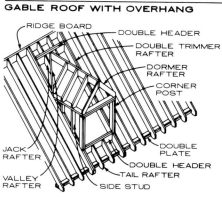

RIDGE BOARD
DOUBLE HEADER
DOUBLE TRIMMER RAFTER
DORMER RAFTER
CORNER POST
JACK RAFTER
DOUBLE PLATE
VALLEY RAFTER
DOUBLE HEADER
TAIL RAFTER
SIDE STUD

DORMER

SHED RAFTER
RIDGE BOARD
DOUBLE HEADER
DOUBLE PLATE
END STUD
DOUBLE TRIMMER RAFTER

SMALL SHED DORMER

CEILING JOIST
WALL STUD
RAFTER
HIP RAFTER
CRIPPLE
DOUBLE HEADER
SOLE PLATE
FLOORING
STUD
HEADER

BAY WINDOW

Timothy B. McDonald; Washington, D.C.

ROUGH CARPENTRY

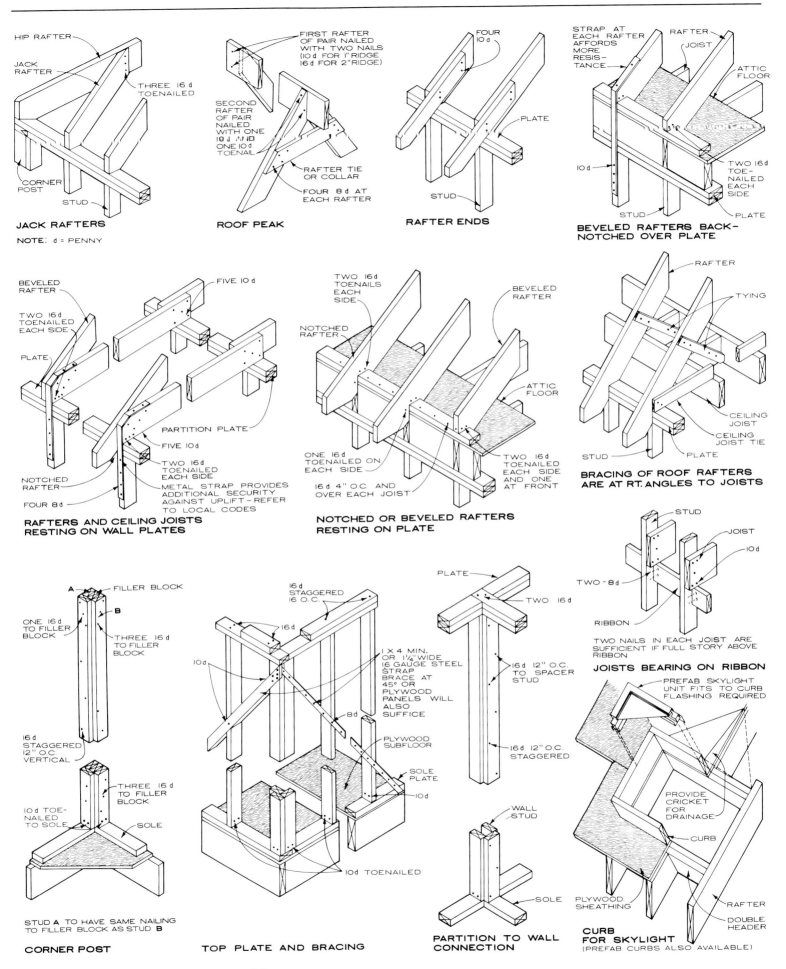

JACK RAFTERS
HIP RAFTER
JACK RAFTER
THREE 16 d TOENAILED
CORNER POST
STUD
NOTE: d = PENNY

ROOF PEAK
FIRST RAFTER OF PAIR NAILED WITH TWO NAILS (10 d FOR 1" RIDGE 16 d FOR 2" RIDGE)
SECOND RAFTER OF PAIR NAILED WITH ONE 10 d AND ONE 10 d TOENAIL
RAFTER TIE OR COLLAR
FOUR 8 d AT EACH RAFTER

RAFTER ENDS
FOUR 10 d
PLATE
STUD

BEVELED RAFTERS BACK-NOTCHED OVER PLATE
STRAP AT EACH RAFTER AFFORDS MORE RESISTANCE
RAFTER
JOIST
ATTIC FLOOR
10 d
TWO 16 d TOENAILED EACH SIDE
STUD
PLATE

RAFTERS AND CEILING JOISTS RESTING ON WALL PLATES
BEVELED RAFTER
TWO 16 d TOENAILED EACH SIDE
PLATE
FIVE 10 d
PARTITION PLATE
FIVE 10 d
TWO 16 d TOENAILED EACH SIDE
NOTCHED RAFTER
FOUR 8 d
METAL STRAP PROVIDES ADDITIONAL SECURITY AGAINST UPLIFT – REFER TO LOCAL CODES

NOTCHED OR BEVELED RAFTERS RESTING ON PLATE
TWO 16 d TOENAILS EACH SIDE
NOTCHED RAFTER
BEVELED RAFTER
ATTIC FLOOR
ONE 16 d TOENAILED ON EACH SIDE
16 d 4" O.C. AND OVER EACH JOIST
TWO 16 d TOENAILED EACH SIDE AND ONE AT FRONT

BRACING OF ROOF RAFTERS ARE AT RT. ANGLES TO JOISTS
RAFTER
TYING
CEILING JOIST
CEILING JOIST TIE
STUD
PLATE

CORNER POST
A
FILLER BLOCK
B
ONE 16 d TO FILLER BLOCK
THREE 16 d TO FILLER BLOCK
16 d STAGGERED 12" O.C. VERTICAL
THREE 16 d TO FILLER BLOCK
10 d TOENAILED TO SOLE
SOLE
STUD A TO HAVE SAME NAILING TO FILLER BLOCK AS STUD B

TOP PLATE AND BRACING
16 d STAGGERED 16 O.C.
16 d
10 d
1 X 4 MIN. OR 1¼" WIDE 16 GAUGE STEEL STRAP BRACE AT 45° OR PLYWOOD PANELS WILL ALSO SUFFICE
8 d
PLYWOOD SUBFLOOR
SOLE PLATE
10 d
10 d TOENAILED

PARTITION TO WALL CONNECTION
PLATE
TWO 16 d
16 d 12" O.C. TO SPACER STUD
16 d 12" O.C. STAGGERED
WALL STUD
SOLE

JOISTS BEARING ON RIBBON
STUD
JOIST
10 d
TWO - 8 d
RIBBON
TWO NAILS IN EACH JOIST ARE SUFFICIENT IF FULL STORY ABOVE RIBBON

CURB FOR SKYLIGHT
(PREFAB CURBS ALSO AVAILABLE)
PREFAB SKYLIGHT UNIT FITS TO CURB FLASHING REQUIRED
PROVIDE CRICKET FOR DRAINAGE
CURB
PLYWOOD SHEATHING
RAFTER
DOUBLE HEADER

Joseph A. Wilkes, FAIA; Wilkes and Faulkner; Washington, D.C.

ROUGH CARPENTRY   6

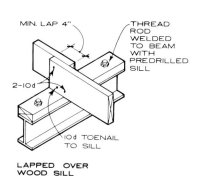

LAPPED OVER
WOOD SILL

ON LOWER FLANGE

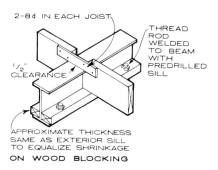

ON WOOD BLOCKING

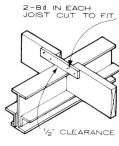

ON STEEL ANGLES

WOOD JOISTS SUPPORTED ON STEEL GIRDERS

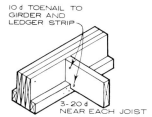

**JOIST NOTCHED OVER
LEDGER STRIP**
NOTCHING OVER BEARING
NOT RECOMMENDED

**JOIST IN JOIST
HANGER IRON**
ALSO CALLED STIRRUP
OR BRIDLE IRON

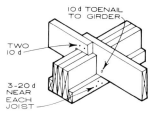

**OVERLAPPING JOISTS
NOTCHED OVER GIRDER**
BEARING ONLY ON LEDGER,
NOT ON TOP OF GIRDER

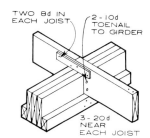

**JOISTS NOTCHED
OVER GIRDER**
BEARING ONLY ON
LEDGER, NOT ON TOP
OF GIRDER

WOOD JOISTS SUPPORTED ON WOOD GIRDERS

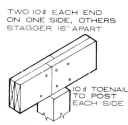

TWO PIECE GIRDER
GIRDER JOINTS ONLY
AT SUPPORTS
STAGGER JOINTS

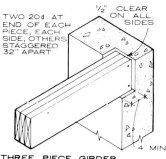

THREE PIECE GIRDER
FOR FOUR PIECE GIRDER: ADD
NAILS

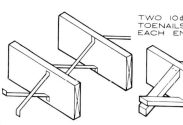

STEEL BRIDGING
SOME HAVE BUILT-IN
TEETH, NEEDS NO
NAILS

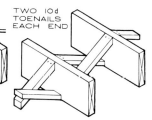

1" X 3" CROSS BRIDGING
LOWER ENDS NOT NAILED,
UNTIL SUBFLOORING
IS LAYED

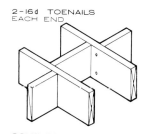

SOLID BRIDGING
USED UNDER PARTITIONS
FOR HEAVY LOADING
STAGGER BOARDS FOR
EASE OF NAILING

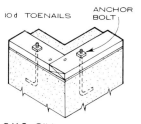

2 X 6 SILL

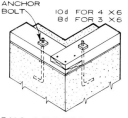

3 X 6, 4 X 6 SILL
HALVED AT CORNERS

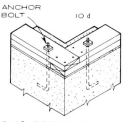

4 X 6 DOUBLE SILL
NAILS STAGGERED ALONG
SILL 24" ON CENTER

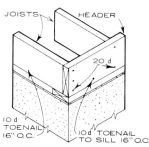

PLATFORM FRAMING
TOENAIL TO SILL NOT
REQUIRED IF DIAGONAL
SHEATHING USED

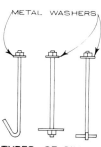

**TYPES OF SILL
ANCHOR BOLTS**

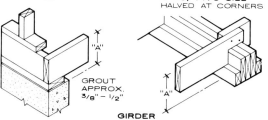

SHRINKAGE
SELECT JOIST-GIRDER DETAIL THAT HAS
APPROXIMATE SAME SHRINKAGE "A" AS THE
SILL DETAIL USED

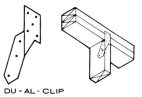

DU-AL-CLIP
METAL FRAMING DEVICES

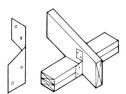

TY-DOWN ANCHOR

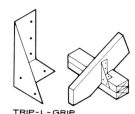

TRIP-L-GRIP
16-18 GAUGE ZINC COATED STEEL

Joseph A. Wilkes, FAIA; Wilkes and Faulkner; Washington, D.C.

  ROUGH CARPENTRY

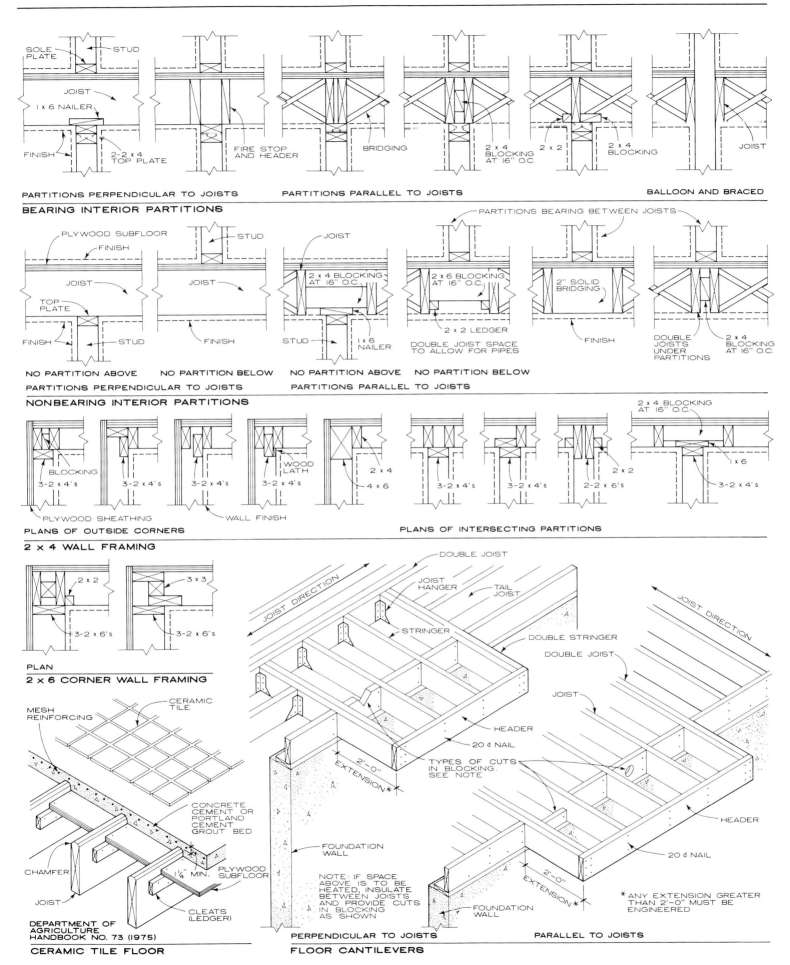

SOLE PLATE
STUD
JOIST
1 x 6 NAILER
FINISH
2-2 x 4 TOP PLATE
FIRE STOP AND HEADER
BRIDGING
2 x 4 BLOCKING AT 16" O.C.
2 x 2
2 x 4 BLOCKING
JOIST

PARTITIONS PERPENDICULAR TO JOISTS
PARTITIONS PARALLEL TO JOISTS
BALLOON AND BRACED

BEARING INTERIOR PARTITIONS

PLYWOOD SUBFLOOR
FINISH
STUD
JOIST
JOIST
JOIST
PARTITIONS BEARING BETWEEN JOISTS
2 x 4 BLOCKING AT 16" O.C.
2 x 6 BLOCKING AT 16" O.C.
2" SOLID BRIDGING
TOP PLATE
FINISH
STUD
FINISH
STUD
1 x 6 NAILER
2 x 2 LEDGER
DOUBLE JOIST SPACE TO ALLOW FOR PIPES
FINISH
DOUBLE JOISTS UNDER PARTITIONS
2 x 4 BLOCKING AT 16" O.C.

NO PARTITION ABOVE
NO PARTITION BELOW
NO PARTITION ABOVE
NO PARTITION BELOW

PARTITIONS PERPENDICULAR TO JOISTS
PARTITIONS PARALLEL TO JOISTS

NONBEARING INTERIOR PARTITIONS

2 x 4 BLOCKING AT 16" O.C.
BLOCKING
WOOD LATH
2 x 4
4 x 6
2 x 2
1 x 6
3-2 x 4's
3-2 x 4's
3-2 x 4's
3-2 x 4's
3-2 x 4's
3-2 x 4's
2-2 x 6's
3-2 x 4's
PLYWOOD SHEATHING
WALL FINISH

PLANS OF OUTSIDE CORNERS
PLANS OF INTERSECTING PARTITIONS

2 x 4 WALL FRAMING

2 x 2
3 x 3
3-2 x 6's
3-2 x 6's

PLAN

2 x 6 CORNER WALL FRAMING

MESH REINFORCING
CERAMIC TILE
CONCRETE CEMENT OR PORTLAND CEMENT GROUT BED
CHAMFER
1 1/4" MIN. PLYWOOD SUBFLOOR
JOIST
CLEATS (LEDGER)

DEPARTMENT OF AGRICULTURE HANDBOOK NO. 73 (1975)

CERAMIC TILE FLOOR

DOUBLE JOIST
JOIST DIRECTION
JOIST HANGER
TAIL JOIST
STRINGER
DOUBLE STRINGER
DOUBLE JOIST
JOIST
JOIST DIRECTION
HEADER
20 d NAIL
TYPES OF CUTS IN BLOCKING. SEE NOTE
HEADER
2'-0"
EXTENSION *
20 d NAIL
2'-0"
EXTENSION *
FOUNDATION WALL
FOUNDATION WALL

NOTE: IF SPACE ABOVE IS TO BE HEATED, INSULATE BETWEEN JOISTS AND PROVIDE CUTS IN BLOCKING AS SHOWN

* ANY EXTENSION GREATER THAN 2'-0" MUST BE ENGINEERED

PERPENDICULAR TO JOISTS
PARALLEL TO JOISTS

FLOOR CANTILEVERS

John Ray Hoke, Jr., AIA; Washington, D.C.

ROUGH CARPENTRY 6

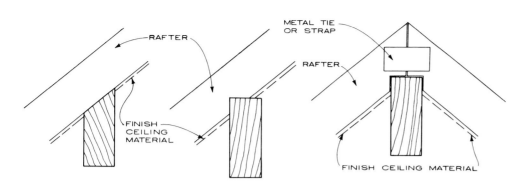

EXPOSED BEAMS AT SLOPING RAFTERS

SLOPED BEAM   BIRD'S MOUTH   RIDGE BEAM

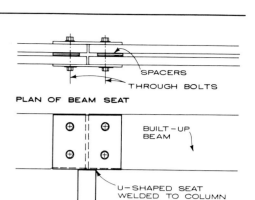

PLAN OF BEAM SEAT

BEAM SEAT

PLAN OF INTERMEDIATE SEAT

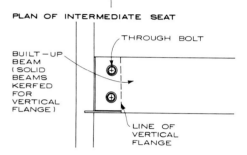

INTERMEDIATE BEAM SEAT

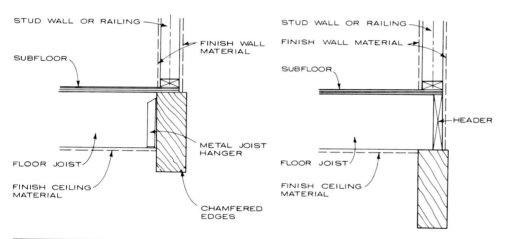

EXPOSED BEAMS AT FLOORS

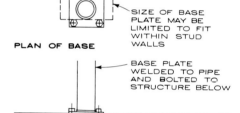

PLAN OF BASE

BASE

STEEL PIPE COLUMNS

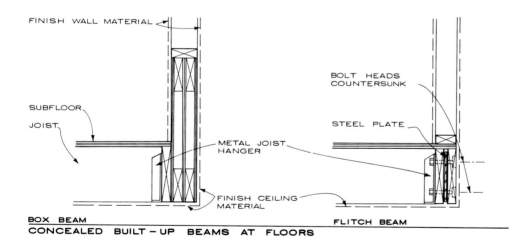

BOX BEAM   FLITCH BEAM

CONCEALED BUILT-UP BEAMS AT FLOORS

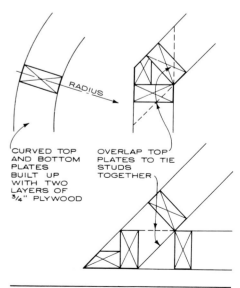

NON-RIGHT ANGLE WALL CORNERS

EXPOSED POSTS AT STUD WALLS

The Bumgardner Partnership/Architects; Seattle, Washington

ROUGH CARPENTRY

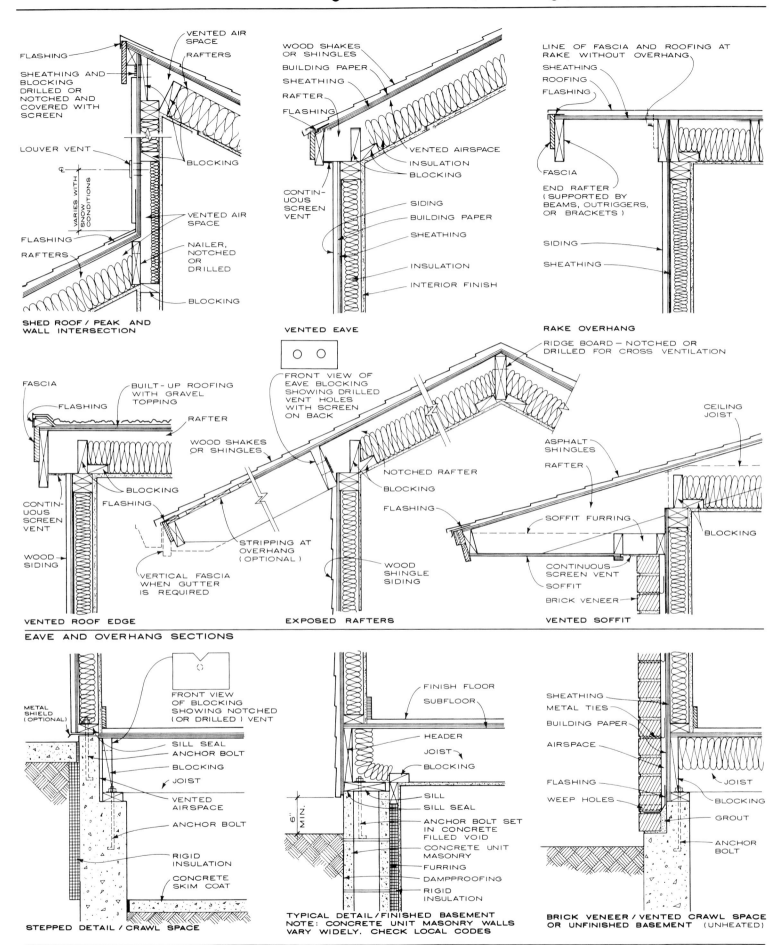

FLASHING

SHEATHING AND BLOCKING DRILLED OR NOTCHED AND COVERED WITH SCREEN

VENTED AIR SPACE

RAFTERS

LOUVER VENT

VARIES WITH SNOW CONDITIONS

BLOCKING

VENTED AIR SPACE

FLASHING

RAFTERS

NAILER, NOTCHED OR DRILLED

BLOCKING

SHED ROOF / PEAK AND WALL INTERSECTION

WOOD SHAKES OR SHINGLES

BUILDING PAPER

SHEATHING

RAFTER

FLASHING

VENTED AIRSPACE

INSULATION

BLOCKING

CONTIN-UOUS SCREEN VENT

SIDING

BUILDING PAPER

SHEATHING

INSULATION

INTERIOR FINISH

VENTED EAVE

FRONT VIEW OF EAVE BLOCKING SHOWING DRILLED VENT HOLES WITH SCREEN ON BACK

LINE OF FASCIA AND ROOFING AT RAKE WITHOUT OVERHANG

SHEATHING

ROOFING

FLASHING

FASCIA

END RAFTER (SUPPORTED BY BEAMS, OUTRIGGERS, OR BRACKETS)

SIDING

SHEATHING

RAKE OVERHANG

FASCIA

FLASHING

BUILT-UP ROOFING WITH GRAVEL TOPPING

RAFTER

BLOCKING

FLASHING

CONTIN-UOUS SCREEN VENT

WOOD SIDING

VERTICAL FASCIA WHEN GUTTER IS REQUIRED

STRIPPING AT OVERHANG (OPTIONAL)

WOOD SHAKES OR SHINGLES

VENTED ROOF EDGE

RIDGE BOARD — NOTCHED OR DRILLED FOR CROSS VENTILATION

NOTCHED RAFTER

BLOCKING

FLASHING

WOOD SHINGLE SIDING

EXPOSED RAFTERS

CEILING JOIST

ASPHALT SHINGLES

RAFTER

SOFFIT FURRING

CONTINUOUS SCREEN VENT

SOFFIT

BRICK VENEER

BLOCKING

VENTED SOFFIT

EAVE AND OVERHANG SECTIONS

FRONT VIEW OF BLOCKING SHOWING NOTCHED (OR DRILLED) VENT

METAL SHIELD (OPTIONAL)

SILL SEAL

ANCHOR BOLT

BLOCKING

JOIST

VENTED AIRSPACE

ANCHOR BOLT

RIGID INSULATION

CONCRETE SKIM COAT

STEPPED DETAIL / CRAWL SPACE

FINISH FLOOR

SUBFLOOR

HEADER

JOIST

BLOCKING

SILL

SILL SEAL

ANCHOR BOLT SET IN CONCRETE FILLED VOID

CONCRETE UNIT MASONRY

FURRING

DAMPPROOFING

RIGID INSULATION

6" MIN.

TYPICAL DETAIL / FINISHED BASEMENT
NOTE: CONCRETE UNIT MASONRY WALLS VARY WIDELY. CHECK LOCAL CODES

SHEATHING

METAL TIES

BUILDING PAPER

AIRSPACE

FLASHING

WEEP HOLES

JOIST

BLOCKING

GROUT

ANCHOR BOLT

BRICK VENEER / VENTED CRAWL SPACE OR UNFINISHED BASEMENT (UNHEATED)

FOUNDATION WALL SECTIONS

The Bumgardner Partnership/Architects; Seattle, Washington

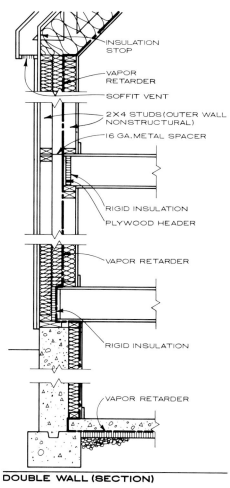

INSULATION STOP

VAPOR RETARDER

SOFFIT VENT

2×4 STUDS (OUTER WALL NONSTRUCTURAL)

16 GA. METAL SPACER

RIGID INSULATION

PLYWOOD HEADER

VAPOR RETARDER

RIGID INSULATION

VAPOR RETARDER

DOUBLE WALL (SECTION)

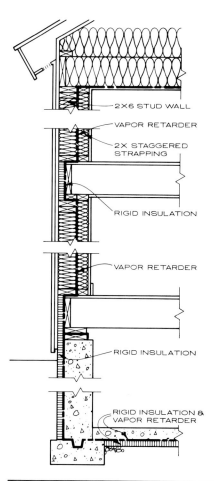

2×6 STUD WALL

VAPOR RETARDER

2× STAGGERED STRAPPING

RIGID INSULATION

VAPOR RETARDER

RIGID INSULATION

RIGID INSULATION & VAPOR RETARDER

STRAPPED WALL (SECTION)

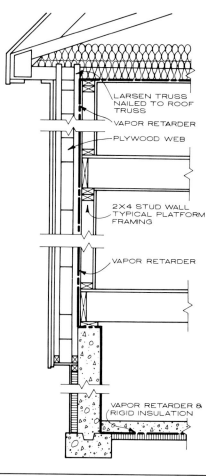

LARSEN TRUSS NAILED TO ROOF TRUSS

VAPOR RETARDER

PLYWOOD WEB

2×4 STUD WALL TYPICAL PLATFORM FRAMING

VAPOR RETARDER

VAPOR RETARDER & RIGID INSULATION

LARSEN TRUSS (SECTION)

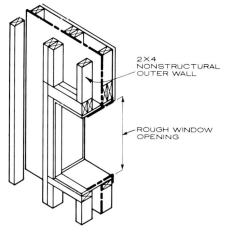

2×4 NONSTRUCTURAL OUTER WALL

ROUGH WINDOW OPENING

WINDOW DETAIL

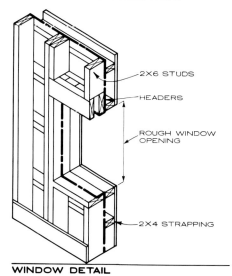

2×6 STUDS

HEADERS

ROUGH WINDOW OPENING

2×4 STRAPPING

WINDOW DETAIL

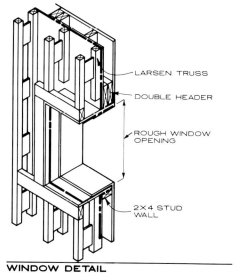

LARSEN TRUSS

DOUBLE HEADER

ROUGH WINDOW OPENING

2×4 STUD WALL

WINDOW DETAIL

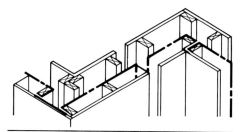

DOUBLE WALL (CORNER DETAILS)

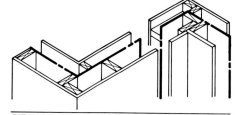

STRAPPED WALL (CORNER DETAILS)

LARSEN TRUSS (CORNER DETAILS)

Timothy B. McDonald; Washington, D.C.

 6   **ROUGH CARPENTRY**

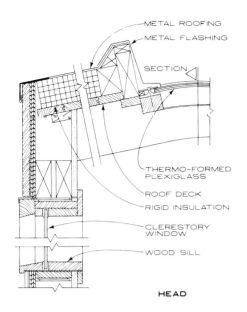

METAL ROOFING
METAL FLASHING
SECTION
THERMO-FORMED PLEXIGLASS
ROOF DECK
RIGID INSULATION
CLERESTORY WINDOW
WOOD SILL

HEAD

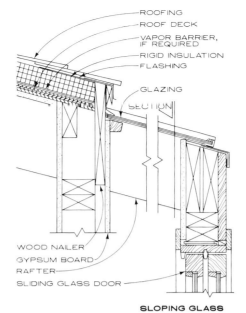

ROOFING
ROOF DECK
VAPOR BARRIER, IF REQUIRED
RIGID INSULATION
FLASHING
GLAZING
SECTION
WOOD NAILER
GYPSUM BOARD
RAFTER
SLIDING GLASS DOOR

SLOPING GLASS

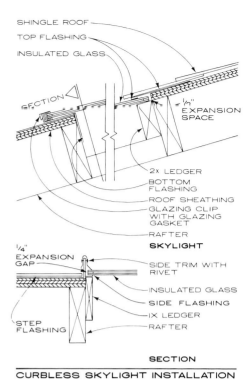

SHINGLE ROOF
TOP FLASHING
INSULATED GLASS
SECTION
1/2" EXPANSION SPACE
2x LEDGER
BOTTOM FLASHING
ROOF SHEATHING
GLAZING CLIP WITH GLAZING GASKET
RAFTER

SKYLIGHT

1/4" EXPANSION GAP
SIDE TRIM WITH RIVET
INSULATED GLASS
SIDE FLASHING
1x LEDGER
RAFTER
STEP FLASHING

SECTION

CURBLESS SKYLIGHT INSTALLATION

SCREW WITH NEOPRENE WASHER
ALUMINUM CLAMPING BAR AND RUBBER GASKET
GASKET
RAFTER
THERMO-FORMED PLEXIGLASS

SECTION

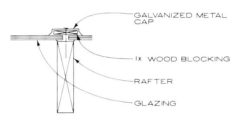

GALVANIZED METAL CAP
1x WOOD BLOCKING
RAFTER
GLAZING

SECTION

FIXED GLASS AT RAFTERS

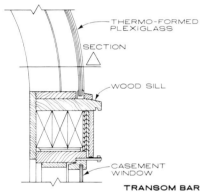

THERMO-FORMED PLEXIGLASS
SECTION
WOOD SILL
CASEMENT WINDOW

TRANSOM BAR

SUNSPACE DETAILS

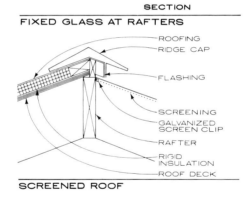

ROOFING
RIDGE CAP
FLASHING
SCREENING
GALVANIZED SCREEN CLIP
RAFTER
RIGID INSULATION
ROOF DECK

SCREENED ROOF

RAFTER
HEADER
1x WOOD TRIM
1 1/2" X 1 1/2" SCREEN STOP
SCREENING
2x SCREEN STOP AND BASEBOARD
WOOD DECK

SCREENED DECK

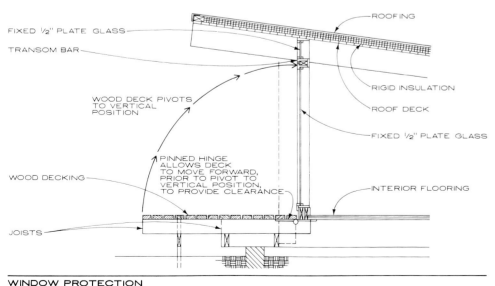

FIXED 1/2" PLATE GLASS
TRANSOM BAR
ROOFING
WOOD DECK PIVOTS TO VERTICAL POSITION
RIGID INSULATION
ROOF DECK
FIXED 1/2" PLATE GLASS
PINNED HINGE ALLOWS DECK TO MOVE FORWARD, PRIOR TO PIVOT TO VERTICAL POSITION, TO PROVIDE CLEARANCE
WOOD DECKING
INTERIOR FLOORING
JOISTS

WINDOW PROTECTION

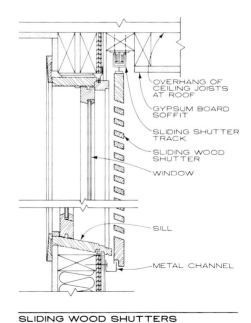

OVERHANG OF CEILING JOISTS AT ROOF
GYPSUM BOARD SOFFIT
SLIDING SHUTTER TRACK
SLIDING WOOD SHUTTER
WINDOW
SILL
METAL CHANNEL

SLIDING WOOD SHUTTERS

Daniel Tinney, AIA; The Russell Partnership, Inc.
Hoffman, see data sources

ROUGH CARPENTRY 6

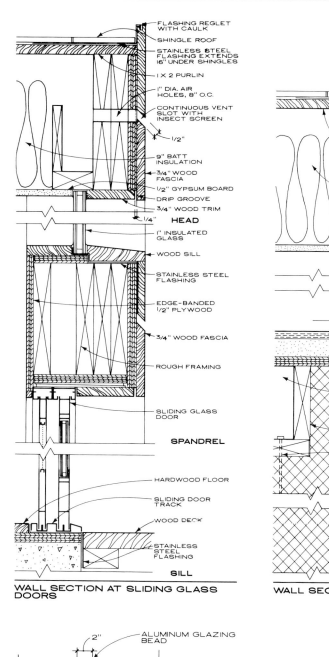

FLASHING REGLET WITH CAULK
SHINGLE ROOF
STAINLESS STEEL FLASHING EXTENDS 16" UNDER SHINGLES
1 X 2 PURLIN
1" DIA. AIR HOLES, 8" O.C.
CONTINUOUS VENT SLOT WITH INSECT SCREEN
1/2"
9" BATT INSULATION
3/4" WOOD FASCIA
1/2" GYPSUM BOARD
DRIP GROOVE
3/4" WOOD TRIM
1/4"
HEAD
1" INSULATED GLASS
WOOD SILL
STAINLESS STEEL FLASHING
EDGE-BANDED 1/2" PLYWOOD
3/4" WOOD FASCIA
ROUGH FRAMING
SLIDING GLASS DOOR
SPANDREL
HARDWOOD FLOOR
SLIDING DOOR TRACK
WOOD DECK
STAINLESS STEEL FLASHING
SILL

WALL SECTION AT SLIDING GLASS DOORS

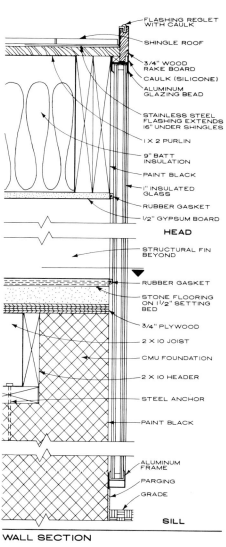

FLASHING REGLET WITH CAULK
SHINGLE ROOF
3/4" WOOD RAKE BOARD
CAULK (SILICONE)
ALUMINUM GLAZING BEAD
STAINLESS STEEL FLASHING EXTENDS 16" UNDER SHINGLES
1 X 2 PURLIN
9" BATT INSULATION
PAINT BLACK
1" INSULATED GLASS
RUBBER GASKET
1/2" GYPSUM BOARD
HEAD
STRUCTURAL FIN BEYOND
RUBBER GASKET
STONE FLOORING ON 1 1/2" SETTING BED
3/4" PLYWOOD
2 X 10 JOIST
CMU FOUNDATION
2 X 10 HEADER
STEEL ANCHOR
PAINT BLACK
ALUMINUM FRAME
PARGING
GRADE
SILL

WALL SECTION

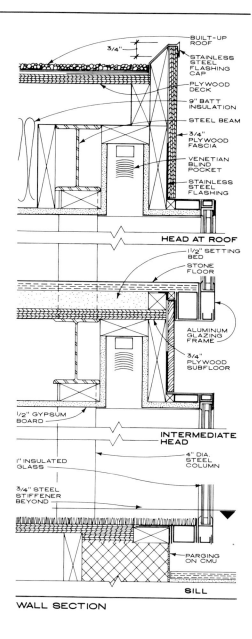

BUILT-UP ROOF
3/4"
STAINLESS STEEL FLASHING CAP
PLYWOOD DECK
9" BATT INSULATION
STEEL BEAM
3/4" PLYWOOD FASCIA
VENETIAN BLIND POCKET
STAINLESS STEEL FLASHING
HEAD AT ROOF
1 1/2" SETTING BED
STONE FLOOR
ALUMINUM GLAZING FRAME
3/4" PLYWOOD SUBFLOOR
1/2" GYPSUM BOARD
INTERMEDIATE HEAD
4" DIA. STEEL COLUMN
1" INSULATED GLASS
3/4" STEEL STIFFENER BEYOND
PARGING ON CMU
SILL

WALL SECTION

2"
ALUMINUM GLAZING BEAD
1" INSULATED GLASS
WOOD TRIM
STRUCTURAL STEEL FRAME
1/2" PLYWOOD
HINGED SHUTTER
2 X 4 STUD

CURTAIN WALL STRUCTURAL FIN

2"
ALUMINUM GLAZING BEAD
1" INSULATED GLASS
WOOD TRIM
STRUCTURAL STEEL FRAME
1/2" PLYWOOD
2X BLOCKING
3/4" WOOD TRIM

CURTAIN WALL STRUCTURAL FIN

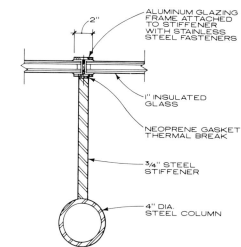

2"
ALUMINUM GLAZING FRAME ATTACHED TO STIFFENER WITH STAINLESS STEEL FASTENERS
1" INSULATED GLASS
NEOPRENE GASKET THERMAL BREAK
3/4" STEEL STIFFENER
4" DIA. STEEL COLUMN

COLUMN WITH STIFFENER AT WINDOW WALL

Hugh Newell Jacobsen, FAIA; Washington, D.C.

 ROUGH CARPENTRY

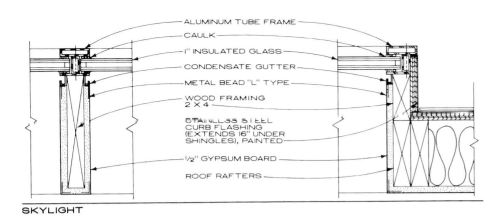

ALUMINUM TUBE FRAME
CAULK
I" INSULATED GLASS
CONDENSATE GUTTER
METAL BEAD "L" TYPE
WOOD FRAMING 2 X 4
STAINLESS STEEL CURB FLASHING (EXTENDS 16" UNDER SHINGLES), PAINTED
1/2" GYPSUM BOARD
ROOF RAFTERS

SKYLIGHT

SHINGLE ROOF
9" FOIL-ENCASED INSULATION
INBOARD STAINLESS STEEL GUTTER
CAULK — VARIES
VARIES
1/2" GYPSUM BOARD
ALIGN TRIM AT FASCIA BOTTOM
SPRING FLASHING
1 X 12 WOOD FASCIA

HEAD AT GUTTER

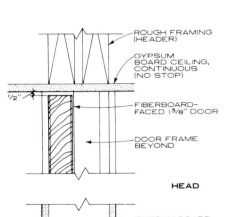

ROUGH FRAMING (HEADER)
GYPSUM BOARD CEILING, CONTINUOUS (NO STOP)
1/2"
FIBERBOARD-FACED 1 3/8" DOOR
DOOR FRAME BEYOND

HEAD

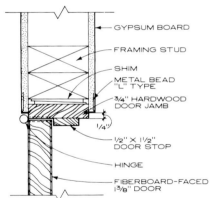

GYPSUM BOARD
FRAMING STUD
SHIM
METAL BEAD "L" TYPE
3/4" HARDWOOD DOOR JAMB
1/4"
1/2" X 1 1/2" DOOR STOP
HINGE
FIBERBOARD-FACED 1 3/8" DOOR

JAMB

TYPICAL INTERIOR DOOR

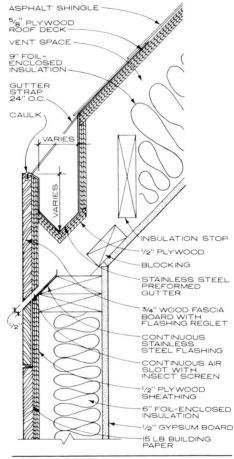

ASPHALT SHINGLE
5/8" PLYWOOD ROOF DECK
VENT SPACE
9" FOIL-ENCLOSED INSULATION
GUTTER STRAP 24" O.C.
CAULK
VARIES
VARIES
1/2'
INSULATION STOP
1/2" PLYWOOD
BLOCKING
STAINLESS STEEL PREFORMED GUTTER
3/4" WOOD FASCIA BOARD WITH FLASHING REGLET
CONTINUOUS STAINLESS STEEL FLASHING
CONTINUOUS AIR SLOT WITH INSECT SCREEN
1/2" PLYWOOD SHEATHING
6" FOIL-ENCLOSED INSULATION
1/2" GYPSUM BOARD
15 LB BUILDING PAPER

WALL SECTION AT CONCEALED GUTTER

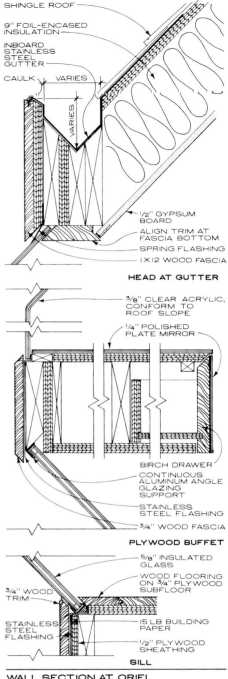

3/8" CLEAR ACRYLIC, CONFORM TO ROOF SLOPE
1/4" POLISHED PLATE MIRROR
BIRCH DRAWER
CONTINUOUS ALUMINUM ANGLE GLAZING SUPPORT
STAINLESS STEEL FLASHING
3/4" WOOD FASCIA

PLYWOOD BUFFET

5/8" INSULATED GLASS
WOOD FLOORING ON 3/4" PLYWOOD SUBFLOOR
3/4" WOOD TRIM
STAINLESS STEEL FLASHING
15 LB BUILDING PAPER
1/2" PLYWOOD SHEATHING

SILL

WALL SECTION AT ORIEL

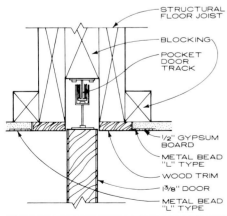

STRUCTURAL FLOOR JOIST
BLOCKING
POCKET DOOR TRACK
1/2" GYPSUM BOARD
METAL BEAD "L" TYPE
WOOD TRIM
1 3/8" DOOR
METAL BEAD "L" TYPE

CONCEALED POCKET DOOR HEAD

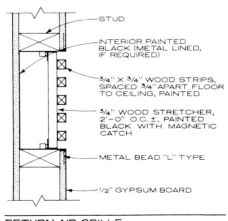

STUD
INTERIOR PAINTED BLACK (METAL LINED, IF REQUIRED)
3/4" X 3/4" WOOD STRIPS, SPACED 3/4" APART FLOOR TO CEILING, PAINTED
3/4" WOOD STRETCHER, 2'-0" O.C. ±, PAINTED BLACK WITH MAGNETIC CATCH
METAL BEAD "L" TYPE
1/2" GYPSUM BOARD

RETURN AIR GRILLE

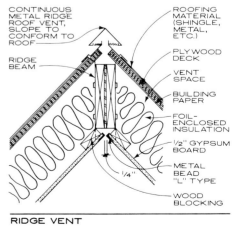

CONTINUOUS METAL RIDGE ROOF VENT, SLOPE TO CONFORM TO ROOF
RIDGE BEAM
ROOFING MATERIAL (SHINGLE, METAL, ETC.)
PLYWOOD DECK
VENT SPACE
BUILDING PAPER
FOIL-ENCLOSED INSULATION
1/2" GYPSUM BOARD
METAL BEAD "L" TYPE
1/4"
WOOD BLOCKING

RIDGE VENT

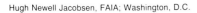

Hugh Newell Jacobsen, FAIA; Washington, D.C.

ROUGH CARPENTRY   6

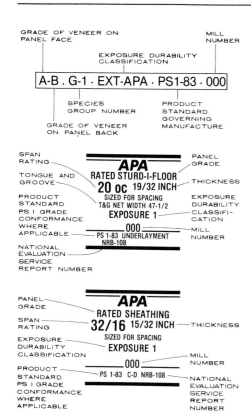

APA TRADEMARKS

GRADE DESIGNATIONS

Construction and industrial panel grades are generally identified in terms of the veneer grade used on the face and back of the panel (e.g., A-B, B-C, etc.), or by a name suggesting the panel's intended end-use (e.g., APA RATED SHEATHING, APA RATED STURD-I-FLOOR, etc.).

Veneer grades define veneer appearance in terms of natural unrepaired growth characteristics and allowable number and size of repairs that may be made during manufacture. The highest quality veneer grades are N and A. The minimum grade of veneer permitted in Exterior plywood is C-grade. D-grade veneer is used only for backs and inner plies of panels intended for interior use or applications protected from exposure to permanent or severe moisture.

VENEER GRADES

N Smooth surface "natural finish" veneer. Select, all heartwood or all sapwood. Free of open defects. Allows not more than 6 repairs, wood only, per 4 x 8 panel, made parallel to grain and well matched for grain and color.

A Smooth, paintable. Not more than 18 neatly made repairs, boat, sled, or router type, and parallel to grain, permitted. May be used for natural finish in less demanding applications.

B Solid surface. Shims, circular repair plugs and tight knots to 1 inch across grain permitted. Some minor splits permitted.

C Plugged Improved C veneer with splits limited to $1/8$ inch width and knotholes and borer holes limited to $1/4$ x $1/2$ inch. Admits some broken grain. Synthetic repairs permitted.

C Tight knots to $1-1/2$ inch. Knotholes to 1 inch across grain and some to $1-1/2$ inch if total width of knots and knotholes is within specified limits. Synthetic or wood repairs. Discoloration and sanding defects that do not impair strength permitted. Limited splits allowed. Stitching permitted.

D Knots and knotholes to $2-1/2$ inch width across grain and $1/2$ inch larger within specified limits. Limited splits allowed. Stitching permitted. Limited to Interior, Exposure 1 and Exposure 2 panels.

John D. Bloodgood, Architects, P.C.; Des Moines, Iowa
American Plywood Association

SPAN RATINGS

APA RATED SHEATHING, APA RATED STURD-I-FLOOR and APA 303 SIDING panels carry numbers in their trademarks called Span Ratings. These denote the maximum recommended center-to-center spacing in inches of supports over which the panels should be placed in construction applications.

The Span Rating in the trademark on APA RATED SHEATHING panels appears as two numbers separated by a slash, such as 32/16, 48/24, etc. The left-hand number denotes the maximum recommended spacing of supports when the panel is used for roof sheathing with the long dimension of the panel across three or more supports. The right-hand number indicates the maximum recommended spacing of supports when the panel is used for subflooring with the long dimension of the panel across three or more supports. A panel marked 32/16, for example, may be used for roof sheathing over supports 32 inches on center or for subflooring over supports 16 inches on center.

The Span Ratings in the trademarks on APA RATED STURD-I-FLOOR and 303 SIDING panels appear as a single number. APA RATED STURD-I-FLOOR panels are designed specifically for residential or other light-frame single-floor (combined subfloor-underlayment) applications and are manufactured with Span Ratings of 16, 20, 24 and 48 inches. These ratings, like those for APA RATED SHEATHING, are based on application of the panel with the long dimension across three or more supports.

APA 303 SIDINGS are manufactured with Span Ratings of 16 and 24 inches and may be used direct to studs or over nonstructural wall sheathing (Sturd-I-Wall construction), or over nailable panel or lumber sheathing (double-wall construction). Panels with a Span Rating of 16 inches may be applied vertically direct to studs spaced 16 inches on center. Panels bearing a Span Rating of 24 inches may be used vertically direct to studs spaced 24 inches on center. All 303 SIDING panels may be applied horizontally direct to studs 16 or 24 inches on center provided horizontal joints are blocked. When used over nailable structural panel or lumber sheathing, the 303 SIDING Span Rating refers to the maximum recommended spacing of vertical rows of nails rather than to stud spacing.

GROUP NUMBER

Plywood can be manufactured from over 70 species of wood. These species are divided on the basis of bending strength and stiffness into five Groups under U.S. Product Standard PS 1. Stiffest species are in Group 1, the next stiffest in Group 2, and so on. The Group number that appears in the trademark on some APA trademarked panels—primarily sanded grades—is based on the species of face and back veneers. Where face and back veneers are not from the same species Group, the higher Group number is used, except for sanded and decorative panels $3/8$ inch thick or less. These are identified by face species because they are chosen primarily for appearance and used in applications where structural integrity is not critical. Sanded panels greater than $3/8$ inch are identified by face species if C or D grade backs are at least $1/8$ in. and are no more than one species group number larger. Some species are used widely in plywood manufacture; others rarely. Check local availability before specifying if a particular species is desired.

EXPOSURE DURABILITY

Plywood manufactured under Product Standard PS1-83 is produced in two basic types: Exterior type with 100 percent waterproof glueline and Interior type with highly moisture resistant glueline. Interior type panels can be manufactured with exterior, intermediate or interior glue, although most Interior type plywood today is manufactured with exterior glue (Exposure 1). Exposure 1 panels are suitable for applications where ability to resist moisture during long construction delays or where exposure to conditions of similar severity is required. However, because the lower grade of veneer permitted for backs and inner plies of Interior type panels may affect glueline performance, only Exterior type plywood should be used for permanent exposure to the weather or moisture.

APA Performance-Rated Panels can be manufactured in three exposure durability classifications—Exterior, Exposure 1 and Exposure 2. Panels marked Exterior are designed for applications subject to continuous exposure to the weather or moisture and are comparable to panels designated under PS 1 as Exterior type. Panels with an Exposure 1 designation are intended for protected construction applications where ability to resist moisture during long construction delays or where exposure to conditions of similar severity is required. Exposure 1 panels are comparable to panels designated under PS 1 as Exposure 1 or Interior type with exterior glue. Panels with an Exposure 2 designation are intended for protected construction applications where moderate delays in providing protection from moisture may be expected or where water leakage or conditions of high humidity may exist. Exposure 2 panels are comparable to panels designated under PS 1 as Interior type with intermediate glue.

SANDED, UNSANDED AND TOUCH-SANDED PANELS

Panels with B-grade or better veneer faces are always sanded smooth in manufacture to fulfill the requirements of their intended end-use—applications such as cabinets, shelving, furniture, built-ins, etc. APA RATED SHEATHING panels are unsanded since a smooth surface is not a requirement of their intended end-use. Still other panels—APA UNDERLAYMENT, APA RATED STURD-I-FLOOR, APA C-D PLUGGED, and APA C-C PLUGGED—require only touch-sanding for "sizing" to make the panel thickness more uniform.

CLASSIFICATION

GROUP 1	GROUP 2		GROUP 3	GROUP 4	GROUP 5
Apitong	Cedar, Port	Maple, Black	Alder, Red	Aspen	Basswood
Beech,	Orford	Mengkulang	Birch, Paper	Bigtooth	Poplar,
American	Cypress	Meranti,	Cedar, Alaska	Quaking	Balsam
Birch	Douglas	Red[b]	Fir,	Cativo	
Sweet	Fir 2[a]	Mersawa	Subalpine	Cedar	
Yellow	Fir	Pine	Hemlock,	Incense	
Douglas	Balsam	Pond	Eastern	Western	
Fir 1[a]	California	Red	Maple	Red	
Kapur	Red	Virginia	Bigleaf	Cottonwood	
Keruing	Grand	Western	Pine	Eastern	
Larch,	Noble	White	Jack	Black	
Western	Pacific	Spruce	Lodgepole	(Western	
Maple, Sugar	Silver	Black	Ponderosa	Poplar)	
Pine	White	Red	Spruce	Pine	
Caribbean	Hemlock,	Sitka	Redwood	Eastern	
Ocote	Western	Sweetgum	Spruce	White	
Pine, South.	Lauan	Tamarack	Engelmann	Sugar	
Loblolly	Almon	Yellow-	White		
Longleaf	Bagtikan	Poplar			
Shortleaf	Mayapis				
Slash	Red				
Tanoak	Tangile				
	White				

NOTES

a. Douglas Fir from trees grown in the states of Washington, Oregon, California, Idaho, Montana, Wyoming, and the Canadian Provinces of Alberta and British Columbia shall be classed as Douglas Fir No. 1. Douglas Fir from trees grown in the states of Nevada, Utah, Colorado, Arizona and New Mexico shall be classed as Douglas Fir No. 2.

b. Red Meranti shall be limited to species having a specific gravity of 0.41 or more based on green volume and oven dry weight.

ROUGH CARPENTRY

Unsanded and touch-sanded panels, and panels with B-grade or better veneer on one side only, usually carry the APA trademark on the panel back. Panels with both sides of B-grade or better veneer, or with special overlaid surfaces (such as Medium Density Overlay), carry the APA trademark on the panel edge.

APA 303 SIDING FACE GRADES

APA 303 plywood siding products are manufactured in four basic classes—Special Series 303, 303-6, 303-18 and 303-30. Each class as shown below, is further divided into grades according to categories of repair and appearance characteristics. The grade designations appear within the APA trademark on panels so graded, thus making it easy to select and specify the siding appropriate for any particular project. Depending on species, type of repair, finishing, etc., premium products can be found in all grades.

303 SIDING FACE GRADES

| CLASS | GRADE[1] | PATCHES | |
		WOOD	SYNTHETIC
Special Series 303	303-OC[2,3]	Not permitted	Not permitted
	303-OL[4]	Not applicable for overlays	
	303-NR[5]	Not permitted	Not permitted
	303-SR[6]	Not permitted	Permitted as natural-defect shape only
303-6	303-6-W	Limit 6	Not permitted
	303-6-S	Not permitted	Limit 6
	303-6-S/W	Limit 6—any combination	
303-18	303-18-W	Limit 18	Not permitted
	303-18-S	Not permitted	Limit 18
	303-18-S/W	Limit 18—any combination	
303-30	303-30-W	Limit 30	Not permitted
	303-30-S	Not permitted	Limit 30
	303-30-S/W	Limit 30—any combination	

NOTES

1. Limitations on grade characteristics are based on 4 ft. x 8 ft. panel size. Limits on other sizes vary in proportion. All panels except 303-NR allow restricted minor repairs such as shims. These and such other face appearance characteristics as knots, knotholes, splits, etc., are limited by both size and number in accordance with panel grades, 303-OC being most restrictive and 303-30 being least. Multiple repairs are permitted only on 303-18 and 303-30 panels. Patch size is restricted on all panel grades. For additional information, including finishing recommendations, see *APA Product Guide: 303 Plywood Siding, E300.*
2. Check local availability.
3. "Clear"
4. "Overlaid" (e.g., Medium Density Overlay siding)
5. "Natural Rustic"
6. "Synthetic Rustic"

APA SANDED & TOUCH-SANDED PANEL[3][4][6]

APA A-A

Use where appearance of both sides is important for interior applications such as built-ins, cabinets, furniture, partitions; and exterior applications such as fences, signs, boats, shipping containers, tanks, ducts, etc. Smooth surfaces suitable for painting. EDC: Interior, Exposure 1, Exterior. COMMON THICKNESSES: ¼, ⅜, ½, ⅝, ¾.[7]

APA A-B

For use where appearance of one side is less important but where two solid surfaces are necessary. EDC: Interior, Exposure 1, Exterior. COMMON THICKNESSES: ¼, ⅜, ½, ⅝, ¾.[7]

APA A-C

For use where appearance of only one side is important in exterior applications, such as soffits, fences, structural uses, boxcar and truck linings, farm buildings, tanks, trays, commercial refrigerators, etc. EDC: Exterior. COMMON THICKNESSES: ¼, ⅜, ½, ⅝, ¾.[7]

APA A-D

For use where appearance of only one side is important in interior applications, such as paneling, built-ins, shelving, partitions, flow racks, etc. EDC: Interior, Exposure 1. COMMON THICKNESSES: ¼, ⅜, ½, ⅝, ¾.[7]

Bloodgood Architects, PC; Des Moines and New York
American Plywood Association

APA B-B

Utility panels with two solid sides. EDC: Interior, Exposure 1, Exterior. COMMON THICKNESSES: ¼, ⅜, ½, ⅝, ¾.[7]

APA B-C

Utility panel for farm service and work buildings, boxcar and truck linings, concrete forms, containers, tanks, agricultural equipment, as a base for exterior coatings and other exterior uses or applications subject to high or continuous moisture. EDC: Exterior. COMMON THICKNESSES: ¼, ⅜, ½, ⅝, ¾.[7]

APA B-D

Utility panel for backing, sides of built-ins, industry shelving, slip sheets, separator boards, bins and other interior or protected applications. EDC: Interior, Exposure 1. COMMON THICKNESSES: ¼, ⅜, ½, ⅝, ¾.[7]

APA UNDERLAYMENT

For application over structural subfloor. Provides smooth surface for application of carpet and pad and possesses high concentrated and impact load resistance. EDC: Interior, Exposure 1. COMMON THICKNESSES: ⅜, ½, ¹⁹⁄₃₂, ⅝, ²³⁄₃₂, ¾, ¹¹⁄₃₂.

APA C-C PLUGGED

For use as an underlayment over structural subfloor, refrigerated or controlled atmosphere storage rooms, pallet fruit bins, tanks, boxcar and truck floors and linings, open soffits, tile backing and other similar applications where continuous or severe moisture may be present. Provides smooth surface for application of carpet and pad and possesses high concentrated and impact load resistance. EDC: Exterior. COMMON THICKNESSES: ⅜, ½, ¹⁹⁄₃₂, ⅝, ²³⁄₃₂, ¾, ¹¹⁄₃₂.

APA C-D PLUGGED

For built-ins, wall and ceiling tile backing, cable reels, walkways, separator boards and other interior or protected applications. Not a substitute for Underlayment or APA Rated Sturd-I-Floor as it lacks their puncture resistance. EDC: Interior, Exposure 1. COMMON THICKNESSES: ⅜, ½, ¹⁹⁄₃₂, ⅝, ²³⁄₃₂, ¾.

APA SPECIALTY PANELS[6]

APA 303 SIDING

Proprietary plywood products for exterior siding, fencing, etc. Special surface treatment such as V-groove, channel groove, striated, brushed, rough-sawn and texture-embossed (MDO). Stud spacing (Span Rating) and face grade classification indicated in trademark. EDC: Exterior. COMMON THICKNESSES: ¹¹⁄₃₂, ⅜, ¹⁵⁄₃₂, ½, ¹⁹⁄₃₂, ⅝.

APA TEXTURE 1-11

Special 303 Siding panel with grooves ¼" deep, ⅜" wide, spaced 4" or 8" o.c. Other spacings may be available on special order. Edges shiplapped. Available unsanded, textured and MDO. EDC: Exterior. THICKNESSES: ¹⁹⁄₃₂ and ⅝ only.

APA DECORATIVE

Rough-sawn, brushed, grooved, or striated faces. For paneling, interior accent walls, built-ins, counter facing, exhibit displays. Can also be made by some manufacturers in Exterior for siding, gable ends, fences, etc. Use recommendations for Exterior panels vary with the particular product. Check with manufacturer. EDC: Interior, Exposure 1, Exterior. COMMON THICKNESSES: ⁵⁄₁₆, ⅜, ½, ⅝.

APA HIGH DENSITY OVERLAY (HDO)[5]

Has a hard semi-opaque resin-fiber overlay both sides. Abrasion resistant. For concrete forms, cabinets, countertops, signs, tanks. Also available with skid-resistant screen-grid surface. EDC: Exterior. COMMON THICKNESSES: ⅜, ½, ⅝, ¾.

APA MEDIUM DENSITY OVERLAY (MDO)[5]

Smooth, opaque, resin-fiber overlay one or both sides. Ideal base for paint, indoors and outdoors. Also available as a 303 Siding. EDC: Exterior. COMMON THICKNESSES: ¹¹⁄₃₂, ⅜, ½, ⅝, ¾, ¹⁵⁄₃₂, ¹⁹⁄₃₂, ²³⁄₃₂.

APA MARINE

Ideal for boat hulls. Made only with Douglas fir or western larch. Special solid jointed core construction. Subject to special limitations on core gaps and face repairs. Also available with HDO or MDO faces. EDC: Exterior. COMMON THICKNESSES: ¼, ⅜, ½, ⅝, ¾.

APA B-B PLYFORM CLASS I AND CLASS II

Concrete form grades with high reuse factor. Sanded both sides and mill-oiled unless otherwise specified. Special restrictions on species. Class I panels are stiffest, strongest and most commonly available. Also available in HDO for very smooth concrete finish. In Structural I (all plies limited to Group 1 species), and with special overlays. EDC: Exterior. COMMON THICKNESSES: ⅝, ¾, ¹⁹⁄₃₂, ²³⁄₃₂.

APA PLYRON

Hardboard face on both sides. Faces tempered, untempered, smooth or screened. For countertops, shelving, cabinet doors, flooring. EDC: Interior, Exposure 1, Exterior. COMMON THICKNESSES: ½, ⅝, ¾.

APA PERFORMANCE-RATED PANELS[1][2][6]

APA RATED SHEATHING

Specially designed for subflooring and wall and roof sheathing. Also good for broad range of other construction and industrial applications. Can be manufactured as conventional veneered plywood, as a composite, or as a nonveneered panel. For special engineered applications, veneered panels conforming to PS 1 may be required. EDC: Exterior, Exposure 1, Exposure 2. COMMON THICKNESSES: ⁵⁄₁₆, ⅜, ⁷⁄₁₆, ½, ⅝, ¾, ¹⁵⁄₃₂, ¹⁹⁄₃₂, ²³⁄₃₂.

APA STRUCTURAL I AND II RATED SHEATHING[3]

Unsanded all-veneer PS 1 plywood grades for use where strength properties are of maximum importance, such as box beams, gusset plates, stressed-skin panels, containers, pallet bins. Structural I more commonly available. EDC: Exterior, Exposure 1. COMMON THICKNESSES: ⁵⁄₁₆, ⅜, ½, ⅝, ¾, ¹⁵⁄₃₂, ¹⁹⁄₃₂, ²³⁄₃₂.

APA RATED STURD-I-FLOOR

Specially designed as combination subfloor-underlayment. Provides smooth surface for application of carpet and pad and possesses high concentrated and impact load resistance. Can be manufactured as conventional veneered plywood, as a composite, or as a nonveneered panel. Available square edge or tongue-and-groove. EDC: Exterior, Exposure 1, Exposure 2. COMMON THICKNESSES: ¹⁹⁄₃₂, ⅝, ²³⁄₃₂, ¾.

APA RATED STURD-I-FLOOR 48 OC (2-4-1)

For combination subfloor-underlayment on 32- and 48-inch spans and for heavy timber roof construction. Manufactured only as conventional veneered plywood. Available square edge or tongue-and-groove. EDC: Exposure 1. THICKNESS: 1⅛.

NOTES

1. Specify Performance-Rated Panels by thickness and Span Rating. Span Ratings are based on panel strength and stiffness. Since these properties are a function of panel composition and configuration as well as thickness, the same Span Rating may appear on panels of different thickness. Conversely, panels of the same thickness may be marked with different Span Ratings.
2. All plies in Structural I panels are special improved grades and limited to Group 1 species. All plies in Structural II panels are special improved grades and limited to Group 1, 2, or 3 species.
3. Exterior sanded panels, C-C Plugged, C-D Plugged and Underlayment grades can also be manufactured in Structural I (all plies limited to Group 1 species) and Structural II (all plies limited to Group 1, 2 or 3 species).
4. Some manufacturers also produce panels with premium N-grade veneer on one or both faces. Available only by special order.
5. Can also be manufactured in Structural I (all plies limited to Group 1 species) and Structural II (all plies limited to Group 1, 2 or 3 species).
6. EDC: Exposure Durability Classifications (typical).
7. Also available in ¹¹⁄₃₂, ¹⁵⁄₃₂, ¹⁹⁄₃₂, ²³⁄₃₂.

EXTERIOR TYPE PANELS

APPEARANCE (1, 3)

GRADE (2)	COMMON USES	F	M	B	1/4	5/16	11/32 3/8	15/32 1/2	19/32 5/8	23/32 3/4
A-A EXT APA (5)	Use where both sides are visible	A	C	A	•		•	•	•	•
A-B EXT APA (5)	Use where view of one side is less important	A	C	B	•		•	•	•	•
A-C EXT APA (5)	Use where only one side is visible	A	C	C	•		•	•	•	•
B-B EXT APA (5)	Utility panel with two solid faces	B	C	B	•		•	•	•	•
B-C EXT APA (5)	Utility panel. Also used as base for exterior coatings on walls and roofs	B	C	C	•		•	•	•	•
HDO EXT-APA (5)	High density overlay plywood has a hard, semi-opaque resin fiber overlay on both faces. Abrasion resistant. Use for concrete forms, cabinets, and countertops	A B	C	A B			•	•	•	•
MDO EXT APA (5)	Medium density overlay with smooth resin fiber overlay on one or two faces. Recommended for siding and other outdoor applications. Ideal base for paint	B	C	B C			•	•	•	•
303 SIDING EXT-APA (7)	Special surface treatment such as V-groove, channel groove, striated, brushed, rough sawn	(6)	C	C			•	•	•	
T1-11 EXT-APA (7)	Special 303 panel having grooves 1/4 in. deep, 3/8 in. wide, spaced 4 in. or 8 in. o.c. Other spacing optional. Edges shiplapped. Available unsanded, textured, and medium density overlay	A B C	C	C					•	
PLYRON EXT-APA	Hardboard faces both sides, tempered, smooth or screened	HB	C	HB				•	•	•
UNDER-LAYMENT C-C PLUGGED EXT-APA (5)	For application over structural subfloor. Provides smooth surface for application of resilient floor coverings where severe moisture conditions may be present. Touch-sanded	C	C	C				•	•	•
C-C PLUGGED EXT-APA (5)	For refrigerated or controlled atmosphere rooms. Touch-sanded	C	C	C			•	•	•	•
B-B PLYFORM CLASS I and CLASS II EXT-APA (4)	Concrete form grades with high reuse factor. Sanded both sides and mill-oiled unless otherwise specified. Special restrictions on species. Also available in HDO for very smooth concrete finish	B	C	B					•	•

PERFORMANCE RATED (3)

GRADE	COMMON USES	F	M	B	1/4	5/16	11/32 3/8	15/32 1/2	19/32 5/8	23/32 3/4
SHEATH-ING EXT-APA	Exterior sheathing panel for subflooring and wall and roof sheathing, siding on service and farm buildings. Manufactured as conventional veneered plywood	C	C	C		•	•	•	•	•
STRUC-TURAL I and II SHEATH-ING EXT-APA	For engineered applications in construction and industry where full exterior type panels are required. Unsanded. See Note 5 for species group requirements	C	C	C		•	•	•	•	•
STURDI-I-FLOOR EXT-APA	For combination subfloor underlayment under carpet and pad where severe moisture conditions exist, as in balcony decks. Touch-sanded and tongue and groove	C	C (11)	C					•	•

INTERIOR TYPE PANELS

APPEARANCE (1, 3)

GRADE (2) (12)	COMMON USES	F	M	B	1/4	5/16	11/32 3/8	15/32 1/2	19/32 5/8	23/32 3/4
N-N, N-A N-B INT-APA	Cabinet quality. For natural finish furniture. Special order items	N	C	NA B						•
N-D INT-APA	For natural finish paneling. Special orders	N	D	D	•					
A-A INT-APA	For applications where both sides are visible. Smooth face; suitable for painting	A	D	A	•		•	•	•	•
A-B INT-APA	Use where view of one side is less important but two solid surfaces are needed	A	D	B	•		•	•	•	•
A-D INT-APA	Use where only one side is visible	A	D	D	•		•	•	•	•
B-B INT-APA	Utility panel with two solid sides	B	D	B	•		•	•	•	•
B-D INT-APA	Utility panel with one solid side	B	D	D	•		•	•	•	•
Decorative panels-INT-APA	Rough sawn, brushed, grooved, or striated faces for walls and built-ins	A B C	D	D		•	•	•		
PLYRON INT-APA	Hardboard face on both sides, tempered smooth or screened for counters and doors	HB	C D	HB				•	•	•
UNDER-LAYMENT INT-APA (5)	For application over structural subfloor. Provides smooth surface for application of resilient floor coverings. Touch-sanded. Also available with exterior glue	C	C D	D				•	•	•
C-D PLUGGED INT-APA (5)	For built-ins, wall and ceiling tile backing, cable reels, walkways, separator boards. Not a substitute for UNDERLAYMENT or STURD-I-FLOOR as it lacks their indentation resistance. Touch-sanded. Also made with exterior glue	C	D	D			•	•	•	•

PERFORMANCE RATED (3, 8)

GRADE	COMMON USES	VENEER (13) F	M	B	1/4	5/16	3/8	15/32 1/2	19/32 5/8	23/32 3/4
SHEATH-ING EXP 1 and 2-APA	Commonly available with exterior glue for sheathing and subflooring. Specify Exposure 1 treated wood foundations	C	D	D		•	•	•	•	•
STRUC-TURAL I and II SHEATH-ING EXP 1-APA	Unsanded structural grades where plywood strength properties are of maximum importance. Made only with exterior glue for beams, gusset plates, and stressed-skin panels	C (10)	D (10)	D (10)		•	•	•	•	•
STURD-I-FLOOR EXP 1 and 2-APA	For combination subfloor and underlayment under carpet and pad. Specify Exposure 1 where moisture is present. Available in tongue and groove	C	C D (11)	D					•	•
STURD-I-FLOOR 48 o.c. (2, 4, 1) EXP 1-APA (9)	Combination subfloor underlayment on 32 and 48 in. spans and for heavy timber roofs. Use in areas subject to moisture; or if construction may be delayed as in site built floors. Unsanded or touch-sanded as specified	C	C D	D						1 1/8

GENERAL NOTES

1. Sanded on both sides except where decorative or other surfaces specified.
2. Available in Group 1, 2, 3, 4, or 5 unless otherwise noted.
3. Standard 4 × 8 panel sizes; other sizes available.
4. Also available in Structural I.
5. Also available in Structural I (all plies limited to Group I species) and Structural II (all plies limited to Group 1, 2, or 3 species).
6. C or better for five plies; C Plugged or better for three-ply panels.
7. Stud spacing is shown on grade stamp.
8. Exposure 1 made with exterior glue, Exposure 2 with intermediate glue.
9. Made only in woods of certain species to conform to APA specifications.
10. Special improved grade for structural panels.
11. Special construction to resist indentation from concentrated loads.
12. Interior type panels with exterior glue are identified as Exposure 1.
13. Also available as nonveneer or composite panels.

Bloodgood Architects, PC; Des Moines and New York
American Plywood Association

 ROUGH CARPENTRY

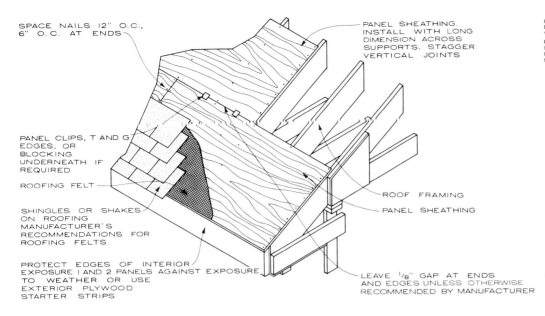

SPACE NAILS 12" O.C., 6" O.C. AT ENDS

PANEL CLIPS, T AND G EDGES, OR BLOCKING UNDERNEATH IF REQUIRED

ROOFING FELT

SHINGLES OR SHAKES ON ROOFING MANUFACTURER'S RECOMMENDATIONS FOR ROOFING FELTS

PROTECT EDGES OF INTERIOR EXPOSURE I AND 2 PANELS AGAINST EXPOSURE TO WEATHER OR USE EXTERIOR PLYWOOD STARTER STRIPS

PANEL SHEATHING. INSTALL WITH LONG DIMENSION ACROSS SUPPORTS. STAGGER VERTICAL JOINTS

ROOF FRAMING

PANEL SHEATHING

LEAVE ⅛" GAP AT ENDS AND EDGES UNLESS OTHERWISE RECOMMENDED BY MANUFACTURER

PANEL SHEATHING INSTALLED WITH LONG DIMENSION ACROSS STUDS, STAGGER VERTICAL JOINTS

LEAVE ⅛" GAP AT EDGES AND ENDS UNLESS OTHERWISE RECOMMENDED BY MANUFACTURER

WALL FRAMING

SIDING MATERIAL

SPACE NAILS 12" O.C., 6" O.C. AT EDGES

PANEL SHEATHING USED AS CORNER BRACING. INSTALL WITH LONG DIMENSION PARALLEL TO STUDS

STRUCTURAL-USE PANEL ROOF SHEATHING

STRUCTURAL-USE PANEL WALL SHEATHING

PLYWOOD ROOF SHEATHING

Plywood grades commonly used for roof (and wall) sheathing are A.P.A. rated sheathing with span ratings: 16/0, 20/0, 24/0, 24/16, 32/16, 40/20, 48/20; exposure durability classifications: Exterior, Exposure 1, Exposure 2. Refer to American Plywood Association recommendations for unsupported edges.

PLYWOOD WALL SHEATHING

Common grade is same as used in roof sheathing. Refer to American Plywood Association recommendations for unsupported edges.

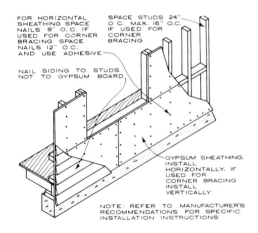

FOR HORIZONTAL SHEATHING SPACE NAILS 8" O.C. IF USED FOR CORNER BRACING SPACE NAILS 12" O.C. AND USE ADHESIVE

SPACE STUDS 24" O.C. MAX. 16" O.C. IF USED FOR CORNER BRACING

NAIL SIDING TO STUDS NOT TO GYPSUM BOARD

GYPSUM SHEATHING. INSTALL HORIZONTALLY. IF USED FOR CORNER BRACING INSTALL VERTICALLY

NOTE: REFER TO MANUFACTURER'S RECOMMENDATIONS FOR SPECIFIC INSTALLATION INSTRUCTIONS

GYPSUM WALL SHEATHING

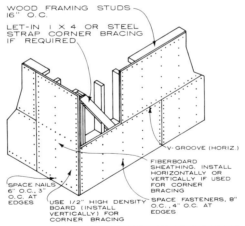

WOOD FRAMING STUDS 16" O.C.

LET-IN I X 4 OR STEEL STRAP CORNER BRACING IF REQUIRED

V-GROOVE (HORIZ.)

FIBERBOARD SHEATHING. INSTALL HORIZONTALLY OR VERTICALLY IF USED FOR CORNER BRACING

SPACE NAILS 6" O.C., 3" O.C. AT EDGES

USE 1/2" HIGH DENSITY BOARD (INSTALL VERTICALLY) FOR CORNER BRACING

SPACE FASTENERS, 8" O.C., 4" O.C. AT EDGES

FIBERBOARD SHEATHING

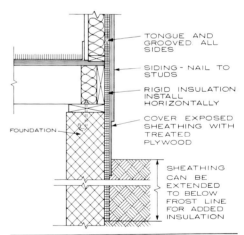

TONGUE AND GROOVED ALL SIDES

SIDING - NAIL TO STUDS

RIGID INSULATION INSTALL HORIZONTALLY

COVER EXPOSED SHEATHING WITH TREATED PLYWOOD

FOUNDATION

SHEATHING CAN BE EXTENDED TO BELOW FROST LINE FOR ADDED INSULATION

PLASTIC SHEATHING

GYPSUM WALL SHEATHING

Fire rated panels are available in ½ and ⅝ in. thicknesses. Gypsum board is not an effective vapor barrier.

FIBERBOARD SHEATHING

Also called insulation board. Can be treated or impregnated with asphalt. Available in regular or ½ in. high density panels.

PLASTIC SHEATHING

Usually made of polyurethane or polystyrene. Can be considered an effective vapor barrier, hence wall must be effectively vented. All edges are usually tongue and groove.

SHEATHING MATERIALS

CHARACTERISTICS	PLYWOOD	GYPSUM	FIBERBOARD	PLASTIC
Nailable base	Yes	No	Only high density	No
Vapor barrier	No	No	If asphalt treated	Yes
Insulation R value (½ in. thickness)	1.2	0.7	2.6	6.25
Corner bracing provided	Yes	Yes (see manufacturer's recommendation)	Only high density	No
Panel sizes (ft.)	4 x 8, 4 x 9, 4 x 10	4 x 8, 4 x 10, 4 x 12, 4 x 14	4 x 8, 4 x 9, 4 x 10, 4 x 12	16 x 96, 24 x 48, 24 x 96
Panel thickness (in.)	5/16, 3/8, 7/16, 15/32, 1/2, 19/32, 5/8, 23/32, 3/4	1/4, 3/8, 1/2, 5/8	1/2, 25/32	3/4 to 6 (for roof)

Timothy B. McDonald; Washington, D.C.
John D. Bloodgood, Architects, P.C.; Des Moines, Iowa
American Plywood Association

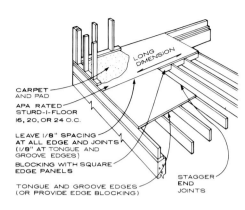

CARPET AND PAD

APA RATED STURD-I-FLOOR 16, 20, OR 24 O.C.

LEAVE 1/8" SPACING AT ALL EDGE AND JOINTS (1/8" AT TONGUE AND GROOVE EDGES)

BLOCKING WITH SQUARE EDGE PANELS

TONGUE AND GROOVE EDGES (OR PROVIDE EDGE BLOCKING)

LONG DIMENSION

STAGGER END JOINTS

APA RATED STURD-I-FLOOR

APA RATED STURD-I-FLOOR (1)

SPAN RATING (MAXIMUM JOIST SPACING) (IN.)	PANEL THICKNESS (2) (IN.)	FASTENING NAIL SIZE AND TYPE	GLUE-NAILED (3) SPACING (IN.) PANEL EDGE		NAILED ONLY SPACING (IN.) INTERMEDIATE
16	19/32, 5/8, 21/32	6d Ring or Screw-Shank (4)	12 / 6	12	10
20	19/32, 5/8, 23/32, 3/4	6d Ring or Screw-Shank (4)	12 / 6	12	10
24	11/16, 23/32, 3/4	6d Ring or Screw-Shank (4)	12 / 6	12	10
	7/8, 1	8d Ring or Screw-Shank (4)	12 / 6	12	10
48 (2-4-1 Panels)	1 1/8	8d Ring or Screw-Shank (5)	6 / 6	(6)	(6)

STURD-I-FLOOR NOTES

1. For conditions not listed, see APA literature.
2. Use only APA Specification AFG-01 adhesives, properly applied. Use only solvent-based glues on non-veneered panels with sealed surfaces and edges.
3. 8d common nails may be substituted if ring- or screw-shank nails are not available.
4. 10d common nails may be substituted with 1 1/8 in. panels if supports are well seasoned.
5. Space nails 6 in. for 48 in. spans and 10 in. for 32 in. spans.

ALLOWABLE CLEAR SPANS FOR APA: GLUED FLOOR SYSTEM (1,4,5)

		APA GLUED FLOOR SPANS			
		JOIST SPACING		19.2'' O.C.	24'' O.C.
		16'' O.C.			
		APA RATED STURD-I-FLOOR			
SPECIES GRADE	JOIST SIZE	16'' OR 20'' O.C.	24'' O.C.	20'' O.C.	24'' O.C.
Douglas fir Larch-No. 2	2 x 6	10'-5''	10'-6''	9'-7''	8'-7''
	2 x 8	13'-7''	13'-10''	12'-7''	11'-3''
	2 x 10	17'-2''	17'-7''	16'-1''	14'-5''
	2 x 12	20'-9''	21'-5''	19'-7''	17'-6''
Douglas fir South-No. 1	2 x 6	9'-10''	10'-8''	9'-11''	9'-1''
	2 x 8	12'-9''	13'-8''	12'-8''	12'-0''
	2 x 10	16'-2''	17'-4''	15'-11''	15'-4''
	2 x 12	19'-7''	20'-5''	19'-1''	18'-4''
Hem-fir No. 1	2 x 6	10'-0''	10'-3''	9'-5''	8'-5''
	2 x 8	13'-1''	13'-7''	12'-5''	11'-1''
	2 x 10	16'-6''	17'-4''	15'-10''	14'-2''
	2 x 12	20'-0''	20'-10''	19'-3''	17'-2''
Mountain hemlock No. 2	2 x 6	9'-2''	9'-6''	8'-8''	7'-9''
	2 x 8	11'-11''	12'-7''	11'-6''	10'-3''
	2 x 10	15'-0''	16'-0''	14'-8''	13'-1''
	2 x 12	18'-2''	19'-2''	17'-9''	15'-11''
Southern pine KD No. 2	2 x 6	10'-2''	10'-8''	9'-9''	8'-8''
	2 x 8	13'-4''	14'-0''	12'-10''	11'-6''
	2 x 10	16'-10''	17'-8''	16'-4''	14'-8''
	2 x 12	20'-5''	21'-2''	19'-10''	17'-9''

John D. Bloodgood, Architects, P.C.; Des Moines, Iowa
American Plywood Association

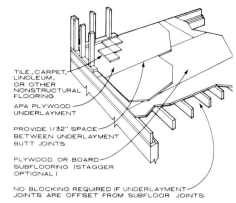

TILE, CARPET, LINOLEUM, OR OTHER NONSTRUCTURAL FLOORING

APA PLYWOOD UNDERLAYMENT

PROVIDE 1/32" SPACE BETWEEN UNDERLAYMENT BUTT JOINTS

PLYWOOD OR BOARD SUBFLOORING (STAGGER OPTIONAL)

NO BLOCKING REQUIRED IF UNDERLAYMENT JOINTS ARE OFFSET FROM SUBFLOOR JOINTS

PLYWOOD UNDERLAYMENT

PLYWOOD UNDERLAYMENT (1)

PLYWOOD GRADES AND SPECIES GROUP	APPLICATION (2)	MINIMUM PLYWOOD THICKNESS (IN.)
Groups 1, 2, 3, 4, 5 UNDERLAYMENT INT-APA (with interior or exterior glue), or UNDERLAYMENT EXT-APA (C-C plugged) EXT	Over smooth subfloor	1/4
	Over lumber subfloor or other uneven surfaces	11/32
Same grades as above, but Group 1 only	Over lumber floor up to 4 in. wide. Face grain must be perpendicular to boards	1/4

UNDERLAYMENT NOTES

1. For tile, carpeting, linoleum, or other nonstructural flooring. (Ceramic tile not recommended.)
2. Where floors may be subject to unusual moisture conditions, use panels with exterior glue (Exposure 1) or UNDERLAYMENT C-C Plugged EXT-APA. C-D Plugged is not an adequate substitute for underlayment grade, since it does not ensure equivalent dent resistance.
3. Recommended grades have a solid surface backed with a special inner ply construction that resists punch-through, dents, and concentrated loads.

UNDERLAYMENT NAILING SCHEDULE

Use 3d ring shank nails for underlayment up to 1/2 in. thickness, 4d for 5/8 in. and thicker. Use 16 gauge staples, except that 18 gauge may be used with 1/4 in. thick underlayment. Crown width should be 3/8 in. for 16 gauge staples, 3/16 in. for 18 gauge. Length should be sufficient to penetrate subflooring at least 5/8 in. or extend completely through. Space fasteners at 3 in. along panel edges and at 6 in. each way in the panel interior, except for 3/8 in. or thicker underlayment applied with ring shank nails. In this case, use 6 in. spacing along edges and 8 in. spacing each way in the panel interior. Unless subfloor and joists are of thoroughly seasoned material and have remained dry during construction, countersink nail heads below surface of the underlayment just prior to laying finish floors to avoid nail popping. If thin resilient flooring is to be applied, fill and thoroughly sand joints.

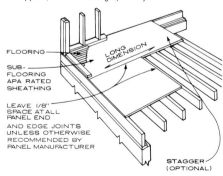

FLOORING

SUB-FLOORING APA RATED SHEATHING

LEAVE 1/8" SPACE AT ALL PANEL END AND EDGE JOINTS UNLESS OTHERWISE RECOMMENDED BY PANEL MANUFACTURER

LONG DIMENSION

STAGGER (OPTIONAL)

APA PANEL SUBFLOOR

APA PANEL SUBFLOORING (1)

PANEL SPAN RATING (OR GROUP NUMBER)	PANEL THICKNESS (IN.)	MAXIMUM SPACING (2, 3, 5) (IN.)
24/16	7/16, 1/2	16
32/16	15/32, 1/2, 5/8	16(4)
40/20	19/32, 5/8, 3/4, 7/8	20(4)
48/24	23/32, 3/4, 7/8	24
1 1/8 in. groups (1, 2)	1 1/8	32 (2x joists) 48 (4x joists)

SUBFLOORING NOTES

1. Applies to APA rated sheathing grades only.
2. The spans assume plywood continuous over two or more spans with long dimension across supports.
3. In some nonresidential buildings special conditions may require construction in excess of minimums given.
4. May be 24 in. if 25/32 in. wood strip flooring is installed at right angles to joists.
5. Spans are limited to the values shown because of the possible effect of concentrated loads.

SUBFLOORING NAILING SCHEDULE

For 7/16 in. panel, 16 in. span, use 6d common nails at 6 in. o.c. at panel edges, 10 in. o.c. at intermediate supports. For 15/32 in. to 7/8 in. panels, 16 in. to 24 in. spans, use 8d common nails at 6 in. o.c. at panel edges, 10 in. o.c. at intermediate supports. For 1 1/8 in. and 1 1/4 in. panels up to 48 in. span, use 10d common nails 6 in. o.c. at panel edges, and 6 in. at intermediate supports.

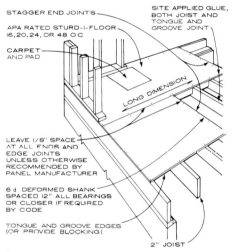

STAGGER END JOINTS

APA RATED STURD-I-FLOOR 16, 20, 24, OR 48 O C

CARPET AND PAD

SITE APPLIED GLUE, BOTH JOIST AND TONGUE AND GROOVE JOINT

LONG DIMENSION

LEAVE 1/8" SPACE AT ALL ENDS AND EDGE JOINTS UNLESS OTHERWISE RECOMMENDED BY PANEL MANUFACTURER

6 d DEFORMED SHANK SPACED 12" ALL BEARINGS OR CLOSER IF REQUIRED BY CODE

TONGUE AND GROOVE EDGES (OR PROVIDE BLOCKING)

2" JOIST

APA GLUED FLOOR SYSTEM

GLUED FLOOR NOTES

1. For complete information on glued floors, including joist span tables (based on building code criteria and lumber sizes), application sequence, and a list of recommended adhesives, contact the American Plywood Association.
2. Place APA STURD-I-FLOOR T&G across the joists with end joints staggered. Leave 1/8 in. space at all end and edge joints.
3. Although T&G is used most often, square edge may be used if 2 x 4 blocking is placed under panel edge joints between joists.
4. Based on live load of 40 psf, total load of 50 psf, deflection limited to 1/360 at 40 psf.
5. Glue tongue and groove joints. If square edge panels are used, block panel edges and glue between panels and between panels and blocking.

GLUED FLOOR NAILING SCHEDULE

Panels should be secured with power driven fasteners or nailed with 6d deformed shank nails, spaced 12 in. at supports. (8d common smooth nails may be substituted.)

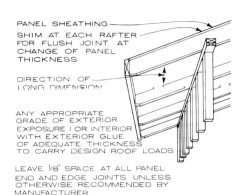

PANEL SHEATHING

SHIM AT EACH RAFTER FOR FLUSH JOINT AT CHANGE OF PANEL THICKNESS

DIRECTION OF LONG DIMENSION

ANY APPROPRIATE GRADE OF EXTERIOR EXPOSURE I OR INTERIOR WITH EXTERIOR GLUE OF ADEQUATE THICKNESS TO CARRY DESIGN ROOF LOADS

LEAVE 1/8" SPACE AT ALL PANEL END AND EDGE JOINTS UNLESS OTHERWISE RECOMMENDED BY MANUFACTURER

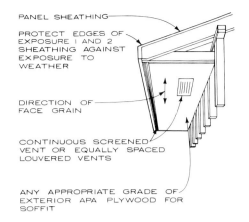

PANEL SHEATHING

PROTECT EDGES OF EXPOSURE I AND 2 SHEATHING AGAINST EXPOSURE TO WEATHER

DIRECTION OF FACE GRAIN

CONTINUOUS SCREENED VENT OR EQUALLY SPACED LOUVERED VENTS

ANY APPROPRIATE GRADE OF EXTERIOR APA PLYWOOD FOR SOFFIT

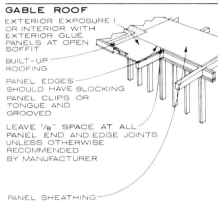

LEAVE 1/8" SPACE AT ALL PANEL END AND EDGE JOINTS UNLESS OTHERWISE RECOMMENDED BY MANUFACTURER

ASPHALT, ASBESTOS, OR WOOD SHINGLES FOLLOW MANUFACTURER'S RECOMMENDATIONS FOR ROOFING FELT

PANEL SHEATHING

PROTECT EDGES OF EXPOSURE I AND 2 PANELS AGAINST EXPOSURE TO WEATHER, OR USE EXTERIOR PLYWOOD STARTER STRIP

EXTERIOR PLYWOOD SOFFIT

PANEL CLIP

GABLE ROOF

EXTERIOR EXPOSURE I OR INTERIOR WITH EXTERIOR GLUE PANELS AT OPEN SOFFIT

BUILT-UP ROOFING

PANEL EDGES SHOULD HAVE BLOCKING PANEL CLIPS OR TONGUE AND GROOVED

LEAVE 1/8" SPACE AT ALL PANEL END AND EDGE JOINTS UNLESS OTHERWISE RECOMMENDED BY MANUFACTURER

PANEL SHEATHING

FLAT-LOW PITCHED ROOF

OPEN SOFFIT
EXTERIOR OPEN SOFFITS/ COMBINED CEILING DECKING (1)

PANEL DESCRIPTIONS, MINIMUM RECOMMENDATIONS	GROUP	MAXIMUM SPAN (IN.)
15/32'' APA 303 siding	1, 2, 3, 4	16
15/32'' APA sanded	1, 2, 3, 4	
15/32'' APA 303 siding	1	24
15/32'' APA sanded	1, 2, 3	
19/32'' APA 303 siding	1, 2, 3, 4	
19/32'' APA sanded	1, 2, 3, 4	
19/32'' APA 303 siding	1	32 (2)
19/32'' APA sanded	1	
23/32'' APA 303 siding	1, 2, 3, 4	
23/32'' APA sanded	1, 2, 3, 4	
1 1/8'' APA textured	1, 2, 3, 4	48 (2)

NOTES
1. Plywood is assumed to be continuous across two or more spans with face grain across supports.
2. For spans of 32 or 48 in. in open soffit construction, provide adequate blocking, tongue-and-groove edges, or other support such as panel clips. Minimum loads are at least 30 psf live load, plus 10 psf dead load.

NAILING SCHEDULE: For open soffits, use 6d common smooth, ring shank, or spiral thread nails for 1/2 in. or smaller thicknesses; use 8d nails for plywood 5/8 to 1 in. thick. Use 8d ring shank or spiral thread or 10d common smooth shank nails for 1 1/8 in. textured panels. Space nails 6 in. at panel edges, 12 in. at intermediate supports, except for 48 in. spans where nails should be spaced 6 in. at all supports.

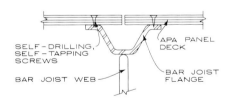

SELF-DRILLING, SELF-TAPPING SCREWS

APA PANEL DECK

BAR JOIST WEB

BAR JOIST FLANGE

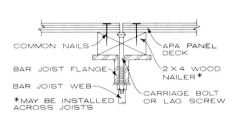

COMMON NAILS

APA PANEL DECK

BAR JOIST FLANGE

2 X 4 WOOD NAILER*

BAR JOIST WEB

CARRIAGE BOLT OR LAG SCREW

*MAY BE INSTALLED ACROSS JOISTS

CONNECTIONS TO OPEN WEB STEEL JOISTS

CLOSED SOFFIT
EXTERIOR CLOSED PLYWOOD SOFFITS

NOMINAL PLYWOOD THICKNESS	GROUP	MAXIMUM SPAN (IN.) ALL EDGES SUPPORTED
11/32'' APA 303 siding or APA sanded		24
15/32'' APA 303 siding or APA sanded	1, 2, 3, 4	32
19/32'' APA 303 siding or APA sanded		48

NOTE: Plywood is assumed to be continuous across two or more spans with face grain across supports.

NAILING SCHEDULE: For closed soffits, use nonstaining box or casing nails, 6d for 11/32 and 15/32 in. panels and 8d for 19/32 in. panels. Space nails 6 in. at panel edges and 12 in. along intermediate supports.

APA PANEL ROOF DECKING (1)

PANEL SPAN RATING	PANEL THICKNESS (IN.)	MAXIMUM SPAN (IN.)		NAIL SIZE AND TYPE	NAIL SPACING (IN.)	
		WITH EDGE SUPPORT	WITHOUT EDGE SUPPORT		PANEL EDGES	INTERMEDIATE
12/0	5/16	12	12	6d common	6	12
16/0	5/16, 3/8	16	16			
20/0	5/16, 3/8	20	20			
24/0	3/8, 7/16, 1/2	24	20			
24/16	7/16, 1/2	24	24			
32/16	15/32, 1/2	32	28			
32/16	5/8	32	28			
40/20	5/8, 19/32, 3/4, 7/8	40	32	8d common		
48/24	23/32, 3/4, 7/8	48	36			

				STAPLING SPACES (IN.)		
				LEG LENGTH	PANEL EDGES	INTERMEDIATE
(see above)	5/16''	(see above)		1 1/4''	4	8
	3/8''			1 3/8''		
	7/16'', 15/32'', 1/2''			1 1/2''		

NAILING SCHEDULE
Use 6d common smooth, ring shank, or spiral thread nails for plywood 1/2 in. thick or thinner and 8d for plywood to 1 in. thick. Use 8d ring shank or spiral thread or 10d common smooth for 2-4-1, and 1 1/8 in. panels. Space nails 6 in. at panel edges and 12 in. at intermediate supports, except for 48 in. or longer spans where nails should be spaced 6 in. at all supports.

NOTES
1. Apply to APA rated panel sheathing.
2. All panels will support at least 30 psf live load plus 10 psf dead load at maximum span. Uniform load deflection limit is 1/180 span under live load plus dead load, or 1/240 under live load only.
3. Special conditions may require construction in excess of the given minimums.
4. Panel is assumed to be continuous across two or more spans with long dimension across supports.

John D. Bloodgood, Architects, P.C.; Des Moines, Iowa
American Plywood Association

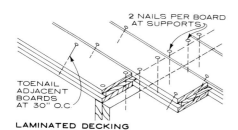

TOENAIL ADJACENT BOARDS AT 30" O.C.
2 NAILS PER BOARD AT SUPPORTS

LAMINATED DECKING

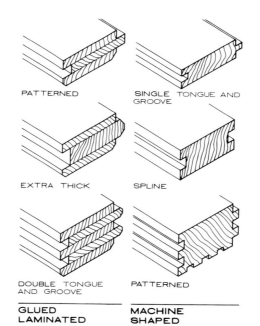

PATTERNED SINGLE TONGUE AND GROOVE

EXTRA THICK SPLINE

DOUBLE TONGUE AND GROOVE PATTERNED

GLUED LAMINATED **MACHINE SHAPED**

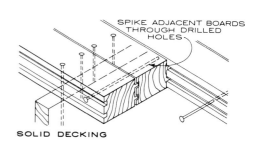

SPIKE ADJACENT BOARDS THROUGH DRILLED HOLES

SOLID DECKING

LAMINATED SIZES (IN.)

THICKNESS		WIDTH	
NOMINAL	ACTUAL	NOMINAL	ACTUAL
3	$2^{3}/_{16}$, $2^{1}/_{4}$	6,8	$5^{1}/_{4}$,7
3 STX	$2^{7}/_{8}$		
5	$3^{21}/_{32}$, $3^{13}/_{16}$		

MACHINE SHAPED SIZES (IN.)

THICKNESS		WIDTH	
NOMINAL	ACTUAL	NOMINAL	ACTUAL
2	$1^{1}/_{2}$	5,6,8,10,12	4, 5, $6^{3}/_{4}$ $8^{3}/_{4}$, $10^{3}/_{4}$
3	$2^{1}/_{2}$	6	$5^{1}/_{4}$
4	$3^{1}/_{2}$	6	$5^{1}/_{4}$

WEIGHT AND INSULATION VALUES

SPECIES	DECKING THICKNESS NOMINAL IN.	DECKING WEIGHTS PSF	DECKING ONLY R
Inland Red Cedar	3	4	4.00
	3 STX	5	5.02
	5	7	6.16
Cedar Face IWP/W Fir Core & Back	3	5	3.70
	3 STX	7	4.58
	5	8	5.59
White Fir Idaho White & Ponderosa Pine	3	5	3.58
	3 STX	7	4.47
	5	9	5.48
Douglas Fir	3	6	3.08
	3 STX	8	3.81
	5	11	4.63
Southern Pine	3	7	3.05
	3 STX	9	3.69
	5	12	4.63

NOTES

1. Insulation value may be increased with added rigid insulation.
2. Use of random lengths reduces waste.

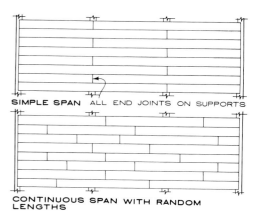

SIMPLE SPAN ALL END JOINTS ON SUPPORTS

CONTINUOUS SPAN WITH RANDOM LENGTHS

LAMINATED DECK—ALLOWABLE UNIFORMLY DISTRIBUTED TOTAL ROOF LOADS GOVERNED BY DEFLECTION (1)

	SPAN IN FEET (2)	SOUTHERN PINE—E1.8 (3) F = 2640				INLAND RED CEDAR—E1.2 (INLAND RED CEDAR FACE AND BACK) F = 1590				PONDEROSA PINE—E1.3 INLAND RED CEDAR—E1.3 (IDAHO WHITE PINE OR WHITE FIR BACK) F = 1590				IDAHO WHITE PINE—E1.5 IDAHO WHITE FIR—E1.5 F = 1850				DOUGLAS FIR/LARCH—E1.8 F = 2640			
		SIMPLE SPAN END-JOINTS OVER SUPPORTS		RANDOM LENGTH CONTINUOUS OVER THREE OR MORE SPANS		SIMPLE SPAN END-JOINTS OVER SUPPORTS		RANDOM LENGTH CONTINUOUS OVER THREE OR MORE SPANS		SIMPLE SPAN END-JOINTS OVER SUPPORTS		RANDOM LENGTH CONTINUOUS OVER THREE OR MORE SPANS		SIMPLE SPAN END-JOINTS OVER SUPPORTS		RANDOM LENGTH CONTINUOUS OVER THREE OR MORE SPANS		SIMPLE SPAN END-JOINTS OVER SUPPORTS		RANDOM LENGTH CONTINUOUS OVER THREE OR MORE SPANS	
		$^1/_{180}$ PSF	$^1/_{240}$ PSF	$^1/_{180}$ PSF	$^1/_{240}$ PSF	$^1/_{180}$ PSF	$^1/_{240}$ PSF	$^1/_{180}$ PSF	$^1/_{240}$ PSF	$^1/_{180}$ PSF	$^1/_{240}$ PSF	$^1/_{180}$ PSF	$^1/_{240}$ PSF	$^1/_{180}$ PSF	$^1/_{240}$ PSF	$^1/_{180}$ PSF	$^1/_{240}$ PSF	$^1/_{180}$ PSF	$^1/_{240}$ PSF	$^1/_{180}$ PSF	$^1/_{240}$ PSF
3 IN. NOMINAL	8	—	—	—	—	71	54	121	91	77	58	127(F)	98	89	67	151	113	107	80	181	136
	9	80	60	136	101	50	38	85	64	54	41	92	69	63	47	106	80	75	56	127	96
	10	59	44	99	74	37	27	62	46	40	30	67	50	46	34	77	58	55	41	93	70
	11	44	32	74	56	27	21	47	35	30	22	50	38	34	26	58	44	41	31	70	52
	12	33	25	57	42	21	16	36	27	23	17	39	29	26	20	45	34	32	24	54	40
	13	26	20	45	33	17	12	28	21	18	14	31	23	21	16	35	26	25	19	42	32
3 IN. STX	10	125	94	212	159	83	63	141	106	90	68	144(F)	115	104	78	168(F)	132	125	94	212	159
	11	94	70	159	119	63	47	106	79	68	51	115	86	78	59	132(F)	99	94	70	159	119
	12	72	54	122	92	48	36	82	61	52	39	88	66	60	45	102	77	72	54	122	92
	13	57	43	96	72	38	28	64	48	41	31	70	52	47	36	80	60	57	43	96	72
	14	46	34	77	58	30	23	51	39	33	25	56	42	38	28	64	48	46	34	77	58
	15	37	28	63	47	25	19	42	31	27	20	45	34	31	23	52	39	37	28	63	47
	16	31	23	52	39	20	15	34	26	22	17	37	28	25	19	43	32	31	23	52	39
	17	25	19	43	32	17	13	29	22	18	14	31	23	21	16	36	27	25	19	43	32
5 IN. NOMINAL	15	89	66	150	113	51	38	86	64	55	41	93	70	63	47	107	80				
	16	73	55	124	93	42	31	71	53	45	34	76	57	52	39	88	66				
	17	61	46	103	77	35	26	59	44	38	28	64	48	43	33	74	55				
	18	51	38	87	65	29	22	50	37	32	24	54	40	37	27	62	46				
	19	44	33	74	55	25	19	42	32	27	20	46	34	31	23	53	40				
	20	37	28	63	47	21	16	36	27	23	17	39	29	27	20	45	34				
	21	32	24	55	41	18	14	31	23	20	15	34	25	23	17	39	29				

SPAN TABLE NOTES

1. Values followed by (f) are governed by stress. Allowable loads for floors when governed by deflection are half of those listed in the 1/180 columns.
2. Span loads shown assume compliance to layup rules. Longer spans may require specific lengths differing from the standard shipment.
3. Custom Grade 3 in. and 5 in. Southern Pine deflection values are 83% of the E1.8 values shown. 3 in. STX Southern Pine values are equal to E1.5 Idaho White Pine values except when bending governs.
4. E = Modulus of elasticity psi.
5. Information derived from data supplied by the Potlatch Corporation.

Timothy B. McDonald; Washington, D.C.

6 **ROUGH CARPENTRY**

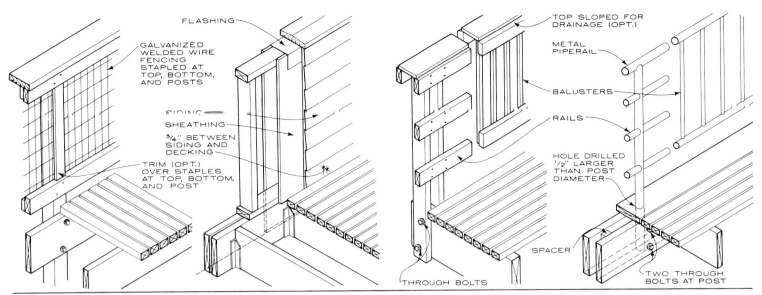

RAILINGS

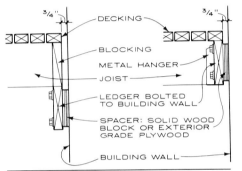

CONNECTIONS AT BUILDING WALL

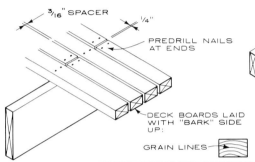

DECKING APPLICATIONS

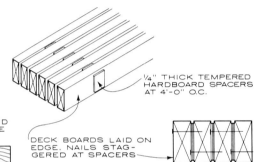

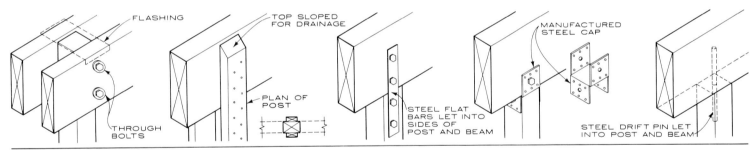

POST AND BEAM CONNECTIONS

RELATIVE COMPARISON OF VARIOUS QUALITIES OF WOOD USED IN DECK CONSTRUCTION

	DOUGLAS FIR—LARCH	SOUTHERN PINE	HEMLOCK FIR*	SOFT PINES†	WESTERN RED CEDAR	REDWOOD	SPRUCE	CYPRESS
Hardness	Fair	Fair	Poor	Poor	Poor	Fair	Poor	Fair
Warp resistance	Fair	Fair	Fair	Good	Good	Good	Fair	Fair
Ease of working	Poor	Fair	Fair	Good	Good	Fair	Fair	Fair
Paint holding	Poor	Poor	Poor	Good	Good	Good	Fair	Good
Stain acceptance†	Fair	Fair	Fair	Fair	Good	Good	Fair	Fair
Nail holding	Good	Good	Poor	Poor	Poor	Fair	Fair	Fair
Heartwood decay resistance	Fair	Fair	Poor	Poor	Good	Good	Poor	Good
Proportion of heartwood	Good	Poor	Poor	Fair	Good	Good	Poor	Good
Bending strength	Good	Good	Fair	Poor	Poor	Fair	Fair	Fair
Stiffness	Good	Good	Good	Poor	Poor	Fair	Fair	Fair
Strength as a post	Good	Good	Fair	Poor	Fair	Good	Fair	Fair
Freedom from pitch	Fair	Poor	Good	Fair	Good	Good	Good	Good

*Includes West Coast and eastern hemlocks.
†Includes western and northeastern pines.
†Categories refer to semitransparent oil base stain.

The Bumgardner Partnership/Architects; Seattle, Washington

MAXIMUM SPAN OF DECK BOARDS

	FLAT		ON EDGE	
	1 x 4	2 x 2 (x3)(x4)	2 x 3	2 x 4
Douglas fir, larch, and southern pine	1'-4''	5'-0''	7'-6''	12'-0''
Hemlock-fir, Douglas-fir, southern	1'-2''	4'-0''	6'-6''	10'-0''
Western pines and cedars, redwoods, spruce	1'-0''	3'-6''	5'-6''	9'-0''

NOTES

Size and spacing of joists, posts, and beams may be selected according to other pages in chapter.

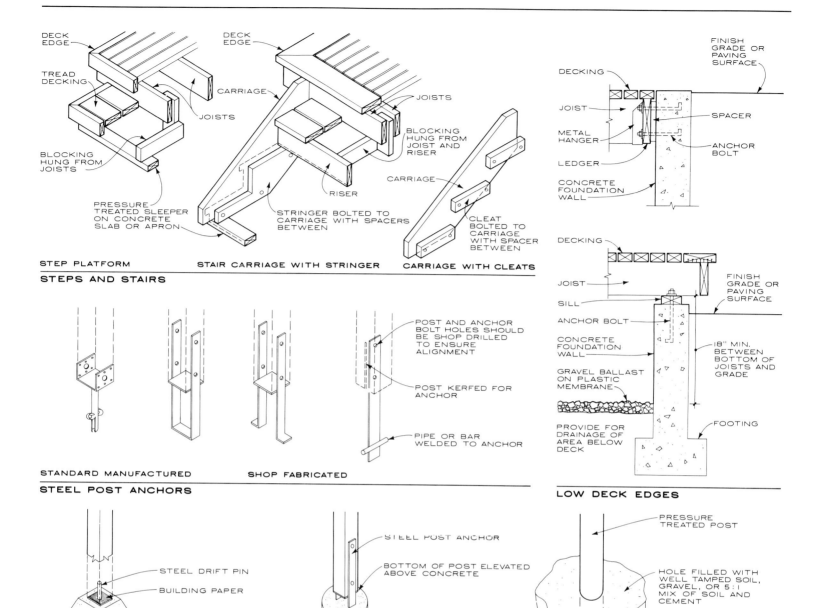

STEPS AND STAIRS

STEP PLATFORM   STAIR CARRIAGE WITH STRINGER   CARRIAGE WITH CLEATS

STANDARD MANUFACTURED   SHOP FABRICATED

STEEL POST ANCHORS

LOW DECK EDGES

PRECAST CONCRETE PLINTH/UNTREATED POST   POURED FOOTING/UNTREATED POST   POURED OR PRECAST FOOTING/TREATED POST

POSTS AND FOOTINGS

FASTENERS

1. Smooth shank nails lose holding strength after repeated wet/dry cycles. Ring or spiral grooved shank nails are preferable.
2. Use galvanized or plated fasteners to avoid corrosion and staining.
3. To reduce board splitting by nailing: blunt nail points; predrill (3/4 of nail diameter); stagger nailing; place nails no closer to edge than one half of board thickness.
4. Avoid end grain nailing and toenailing if possible.
5. Use flat washers under heads of lag screws and bolts, and under nuts.

MOISTURE PROTECTION

1. All wood members should be protected from weather by pressure treatment or field application of preservatives, stains, or paints.
2. All wood in direct contact with soil must be pressure treated.
3. Bottoms of posts on piers should be 6 in. above grade.
4. Sterilize or cover soil with membrane to keep plant growth away from wood members so as to minimize moisture exchange.
5. Treat all ends, cuts, holes, and so on with preservative prior to placement.
6. Decking and flat trim boards, 2 x 6 and wider, should be kerfed on the underside with 3/4 in. deep saw cuts at 1 in. on center to prevent cupping.
7. Avoid horizontal exposure of endgrain or provide adequate protection by flashing or sealing. Avoid or minimize joint situations where moisture may be trapped by using spacers and/or flashing, caulking, sealant, plastic roofing cement.

CONSTRUCTION

1. WOOD SELECTION: Usual requirements are good decay resistance, nonsplintering, fair stiffness, strength, hardness, and warp resistance. Selection varies according to local climate and exposure.
2. BRACING: On large decks, or decks where post heights exceed 5 ft, lateral stability should be achieved with horizontal bracing (metal or wood diagonal ties on top or bottom of joists, or diagonal application of decking) in combination with vertical bracing (rigid bolted or gusseted connections at top of posts, knee bracing, or "X" bracing between posts), and/or connection to a braced building wall. Lateral stability should be checked by a structural engineer.

The Bumgardner Partnership/Architects; Seattle, Washington

ROUGH CARPENTRY

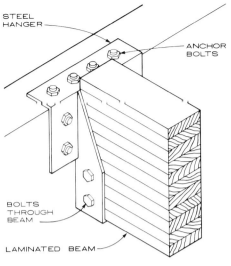

BEAM HANGER

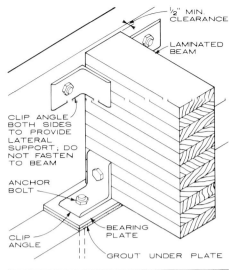

BEAM ANCHOR

BEAM ANCHOR

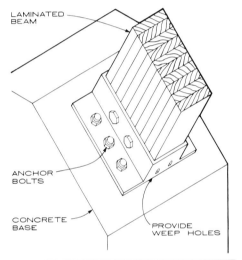

FIXED ARCH ANCHORAGE

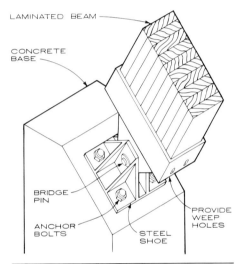

TRUE HINGE ANCHORAGE FOR ARCHES

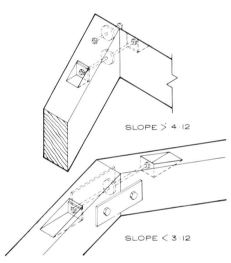

ARCH PEAK CONNECTION

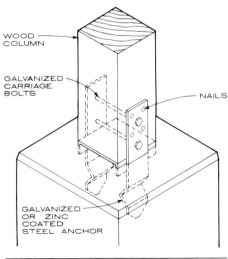

WET POST ANCHORAGE TO CONCRETE BASE

This detail is recommended for heavy duty use where moisture protection is desired. Anchor is set and leveled in wet concrete after screeding.

Timothy B. McDonald; Washington, D.C.

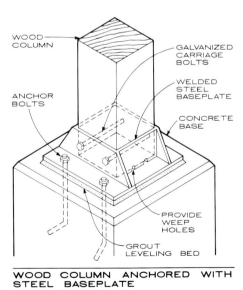

WOOD COLUMN ANCHORED WITH STEEL BASEPLATE

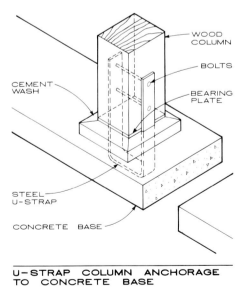

U-STRAP COLUMN ANCHORAGE TO CONCRETE BASE

This detail is recommended for industrial buildings and warehouses to resist both horizontal forces and uplift. Moisture barrier is recommended. It may be used with shear plates.

HEAVY TIMBER CONSTRUCTION 6

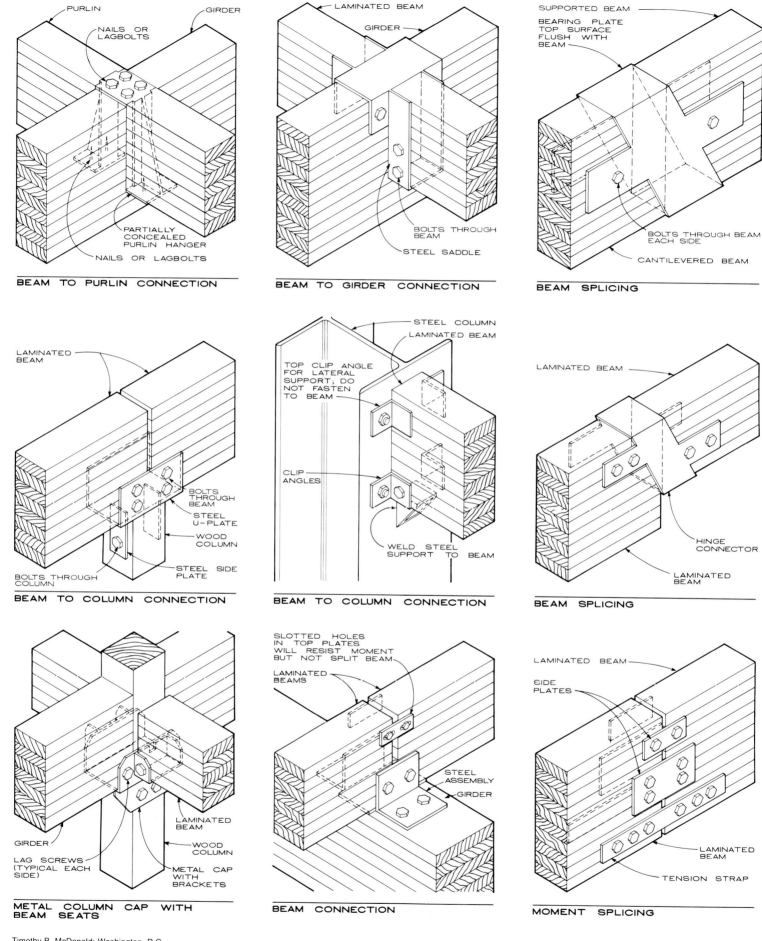

PURLIN

GIRDER

NAILS OR LAGBOLTS

PARTIALLY CONCEALED PURLIN HANGER

NAILS OR LAGBOLTS

BEAM TO PURLIN CONNECTION

LAMINATED BEAM

GIRDER

BOLTS THROUGH BEAM

STEEL SADDLE

BEAM TO GIRDER CONNECTION

SUPPORTED BEAM

BEARING PLATE TOP SURFACE FLUSH WITH BEAM

BOLTS THROUGH BEAM EACH SIDE

CANTILEVERED BEAM

BEAM SPLICING

LAMINATED BEAM

BOLTS THROUGH BEAM

STEEL U-PLATE

WOOD COLUMN

STEEL SIDE PLATE

BOLTS THROUGH COLUMN

BEAM TO COLUMN CONNECTION

STEEL COLUMN

LAMINATED BEAM

TOP CLIP ANGLE FOR LATERAL SUPPORT; DO NOT FASTEN TO BEAM

CLIP ANGLES

WELD STEEL SUPPORT TO BEAM

BEAM TO COLUMN CONNECTION

LAMINATED BEAM

HINGE CONNECTOR

LAMINATED BEAM

BEAM SPLICING

GIRDER

LAMINATED BEAM

WOOD COLUMN

LAG SCREWS (TYPICAL EACH SIDE)

METAL CAP WITH BRACKETS

METAL COLUMN CAP WITH BEAM SEATS

SLOTTED HOLES IN TOP PLATES WILL RESIST MOMENT BUT NOT SPLIT BEAM

LAMINATED BEAMS

STEEL ASSEMBLY

GIRDER

BEAM CONNECTION

LAMINATED BEAM

SIDE PLATES

LAMINATED BEAM

TENSION STRAP

MOMENT SPLICING

Timothy B. McDonald; Washington, D.C.

HEAVY TIMBER CONSTRUCTION

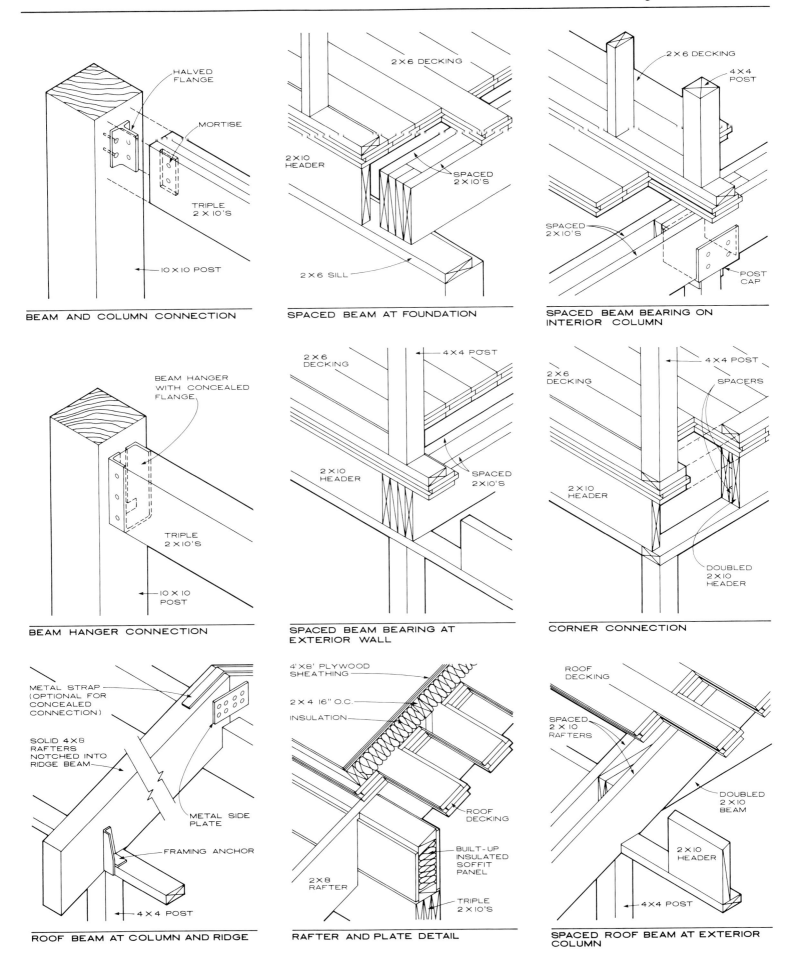

BEAM AND COLUMN CONNECTION

HALVED FLANGE

MORTISE

TRIPLE 2×10'S

10×10 POST

SPACED BEAM AT FOUNDATION

2×6 DECKING

2×10 HEADER

SPACED 2×10'S

2×6 SILL

SPACED BEAM BEARING ON INTERIOR COLUMN

2×6 DECKING

4×4 POST

SPACED 2×10'S

POST CAP

BEAM HANGER CONNECTION

BEAM HANGER WITH CONCEALED FLANGE

TRIPLE 2×10'S

10×10 POST

SPACED BEAM BEARING AT EXTERIOR WALL

2×6 DECKING

4×4 POST

2×10 HEADER

SPACED 2×10'S

CORNER CONNECTION

2×6 DECKING

4×4 POST

SPACERS

2×10 HEADER

DOUBLED 2×10 HEADER

ROOF BEAM AT COLUMN AND RIDGE

METAL STRAP (OPTIONAL FOR CONCEALED CONNECTION)

SOLID 4×8 RAFTERS NOTCHED INTO RIDGE BEAM

METAL SIDE PLATE

FRAMING ANCHOR

4×4 POST

RAFTER AND PLATE DETAIL

4'×8' PLYWOOD SHEATHING

2×4 16" O.C.

INSULATION

ROOF DECKING

2×8 RAFTER

BUILT-UP INSULATED SOFFIT PANEL

TRIPLE 2×10'S

SPACED ROOF BEAM AT EXTERIOR COLUMN

ROOF DECKING

SPACED 2×10 RAFTERS

DOUBLED 2×10 BEAM

2×10 HEADER

4×4 POST

Timothy B. McDonald; Washington, D.C.

HEAVY TIMBER CONSTRUCTION 6

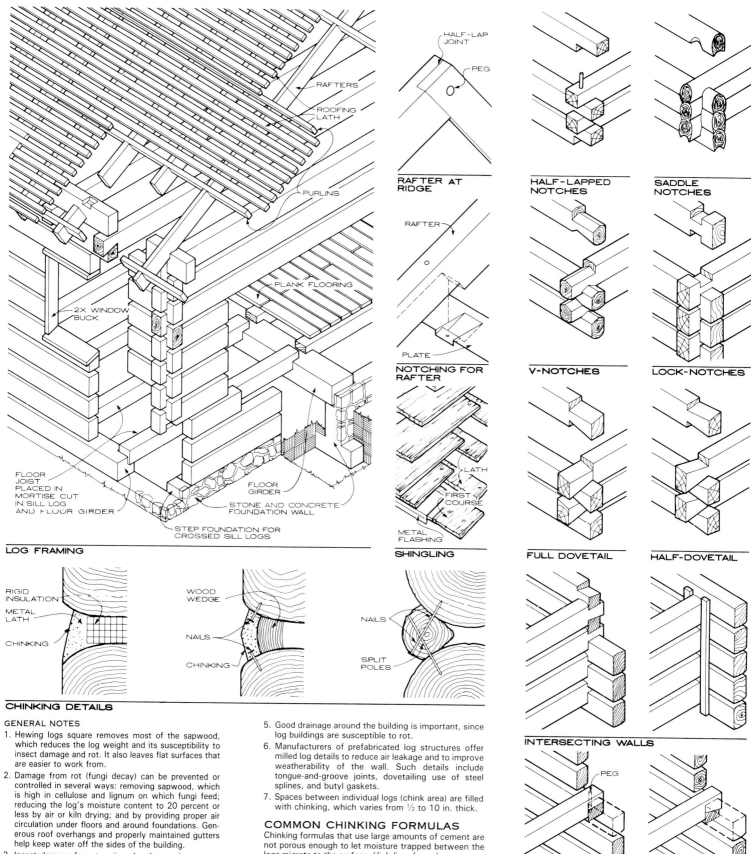

LOG FRAMING

RAFTERS
ROOFING LATH
PURLINS
PLANK FLOORING
2X WINDOW BUCK
FLOOR JOIST PLACED IN MORTISE CUT IN SILL LOG AND FLOOR GIRDER
FLOOR GIRDER
STONE AND CONCRETE FOUNDATION WALL
STEP FOUNDATION FOR CROSSED SILL LOGS

RAFTER AT RIDGE

HALF-LAP JOINT
PEG

NOTCHING FOR RAFTER

RAFTER
PLATE

SHINGLING

LATH
FIRST COURSE
METAL FLASHING

CHINKING DETAILS

RIGID INSULATION
METAL LATH
CHINKING

WOOD WEDGE
NAILS
CHINKING

NAILS
SPLIT POLES

HALF-LAPPED NOTCHES

SADDLE NOTCHES

V-NOTCHES

LOCK-NOTCHES

FULL DOVETAIL

HALF-DOVETAIL

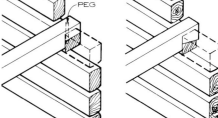

INTERSECTING WALLS

PEG

SECOND FLOOR JOISTS

GENERAL NOTES

1. Hewing logs square removes most of the sapwood, which reduces the log weight and its susceptibility to insect damage and rot. It also leaves flat surfaces that are easier to work from.

2. Damage from rot (fungi decay) can be prevented or controlled in several ways: removing sapwood, which is high in cellulose and lignum on which fungi feed; reducing the log's moisture content to 20 percent or less by air or kiln drying; and by providing proper air circulation under floors and around foundations. Generous roof overhangs and properly maintained gutters help keep water off the sides of the building.

3. Insect damage from termites, beetles, and carpenter ants can be prevented by properly seasoning the wood (kiln or air drying), and by providing continuous vapor barriers under ground floors. Also, good air circulation can help prevent infestations.

4. Exposed interior logs must be coordinated carefully with placement of plumbing, electrical wiring, and mechanical equipment.

5. Good drainage around the building is important, since log buildings are susceptible to rot.

6. Manufacturers of prefabricated log structures offer milled log details to reduce air leakage and to improve weatherability of the wall. Such details include tongue-and-groove joints, dovetailing use of steel splines, and butyl gaskets.

7. Spaces between individual logs (chink area) are filled with chinking, which varies from ½ to 10 in. thick.

COMMON CHINKING FORMULAS

Chinking formulas that use large amounts of cement are not porous enough to let moisture trapped between the logs migrate to the surface. High-lime formulas are more porous, allowing the surface to dry more quickly. They are more elastic.

1. 1 part portland cement, 4–8 parts lime, 7–10 parts sand.

2. ¼ part cement, 11 parts lime, 4 parts sand, ⅛ part dry color, excelsior.

3. 1 part cement, 4 parts lime, 6 parts sand.

Timothy B. McDonald; Washington, D.C.

 HEAVY TIMBER CONSTRUCTION

NOTES

1. Pole embedment depth depends on soil, slope and seismic zone.

2. Cross-bracing between poles may be required to resist lateral loads if shallow embedment. Treat all exposed surfaces with approved pressure treatment.

3. Pole notching for major beams can help align beams and walls that otherwise would be out of plumb due to pole warp. Notching improves bearing of major beams but weakens poles.

4. Roofs, walls and floors should be insulated to suit local climatic conditions. Wall and soffit insulation should meet continuously at the joint. Penetration of insulation should be minimal.

5. Various siding types can be used.

6. Dapping is a U.S. carpentry term for cutting wood to receive timber connectors.

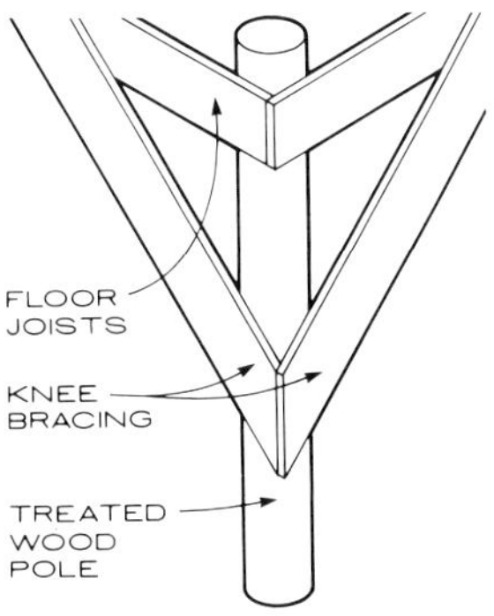

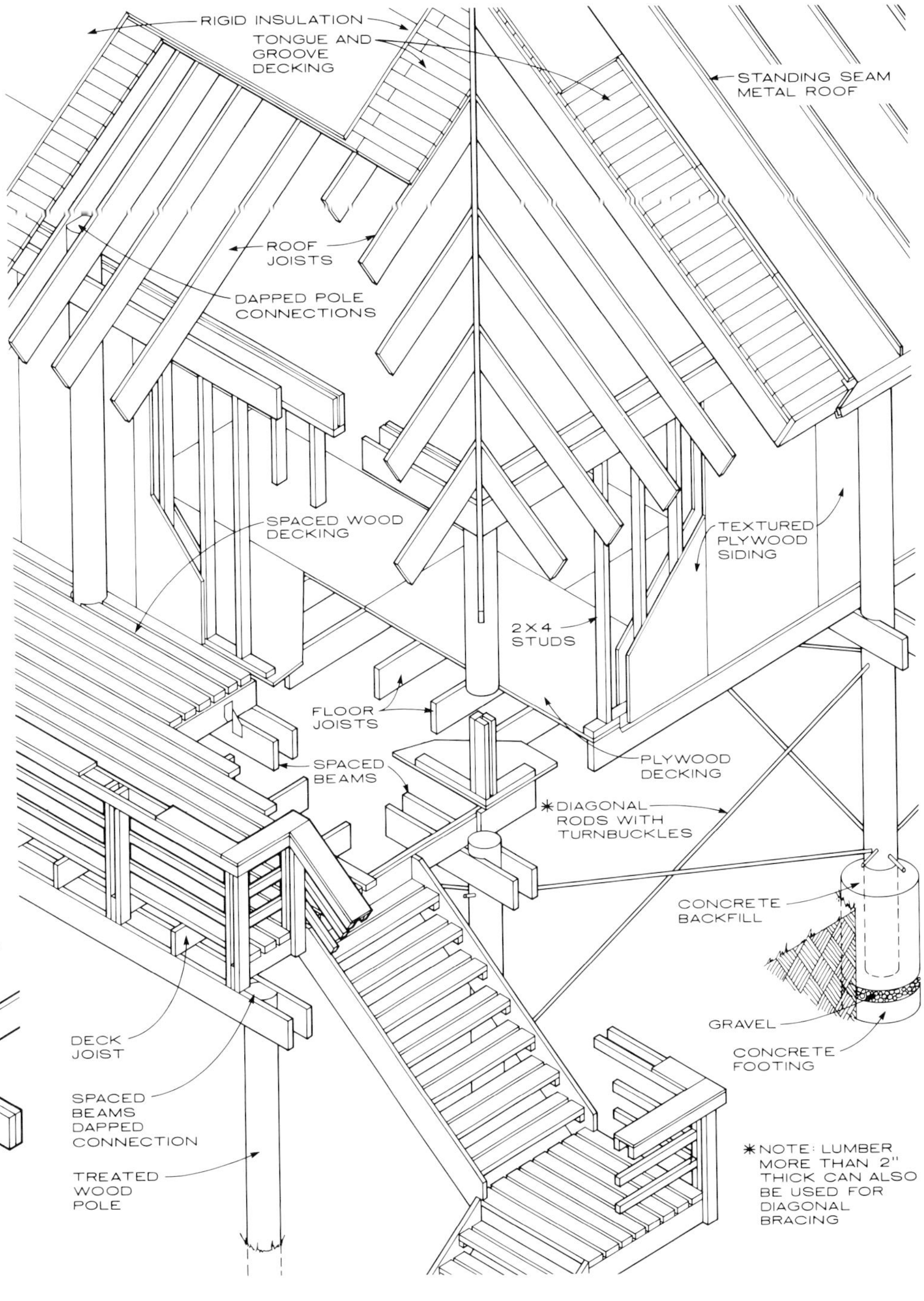

RIGID INSULATION
TONGUE AND GROOVE DECKING
STANDING SEAM METAL ROOF
ROOF JOISTS
DAPPED POLE CONNECTIONS
SPACED WOOD DECKING
TEXTURED PLYWOOD SIDING
2 X 4 STUDS
FLOOR JOISTS
SPACED BEAMS
PLYWOOD DECKING
*DIAGONAL RODS WITH TURNBUCKLES
CONCRETE BACKFILL
GRAVEL
CONCRETE FOOTING

FLOOR JOISTS
KNEE BRACING
TREATED WOOD POLE

KNEE BRACING

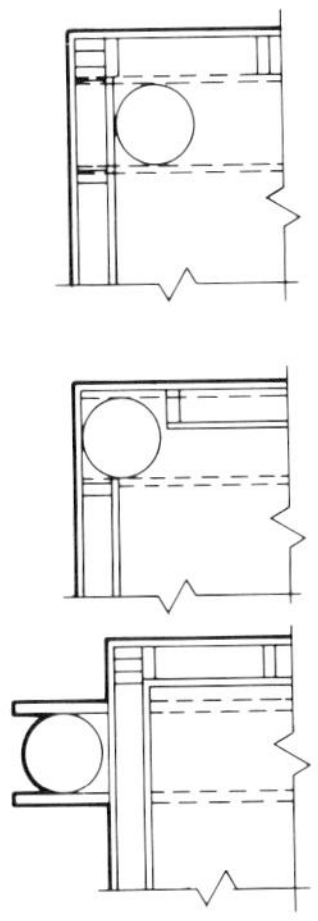

EXTERIOR WALL FRAMING OPTIONS

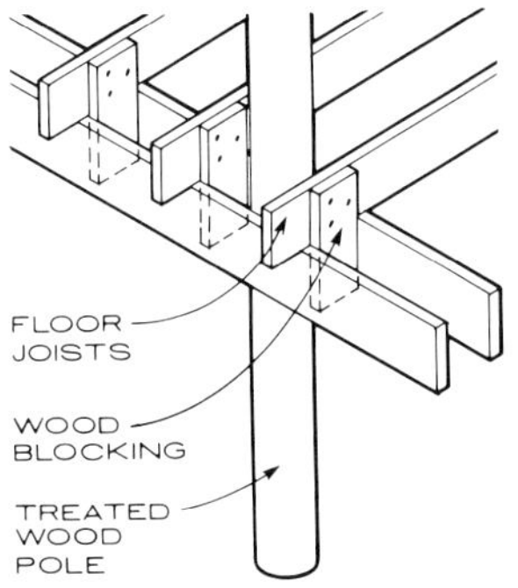

FLOOR JOISTS
WOOD BLOCKING
TREATED WOOD POLE

JOIST ANCHORS

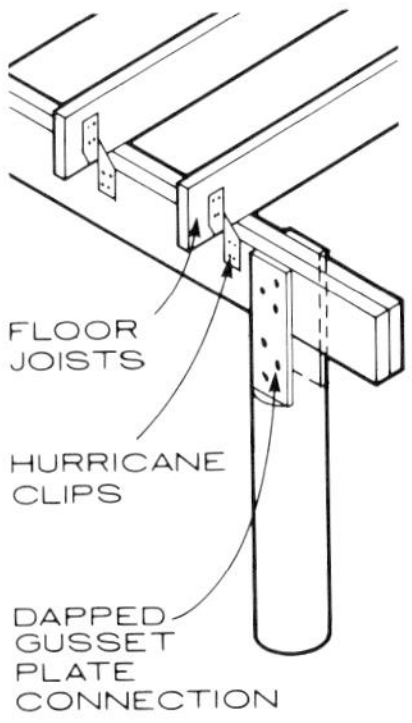

FLOOR JOISTS
HURRICANE CLIPS
DAPPED GUSSET PLATE CONNECTION

JOIST ANCHORS

DECK JOIST
SPACED BEAMS DAPPED CONNECTION
TREATED WOOD POLE

ISOMETRIC OF POLE HOUSE

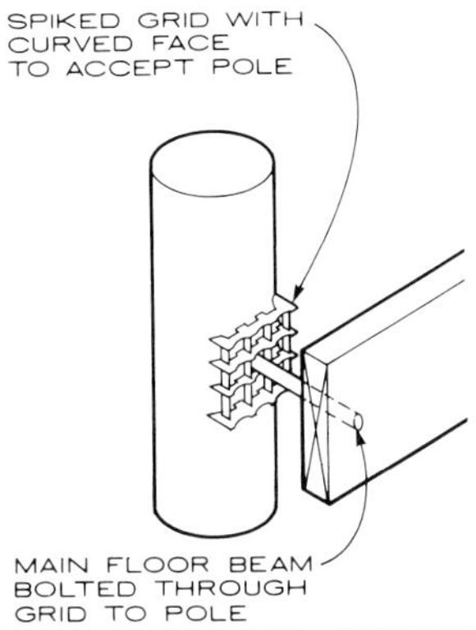

*NOTE: LUMBER MORE THAN 2" THICK CAN ALSO BE USED FOR DIAGONAL BRACING

SPIKED GRID WITH CURVED FACE TO ACCEPT POLE
MAIN FLOOR BEAM BOLTED THROUGH GRID TO POLE

POLE CONSTRUCTION

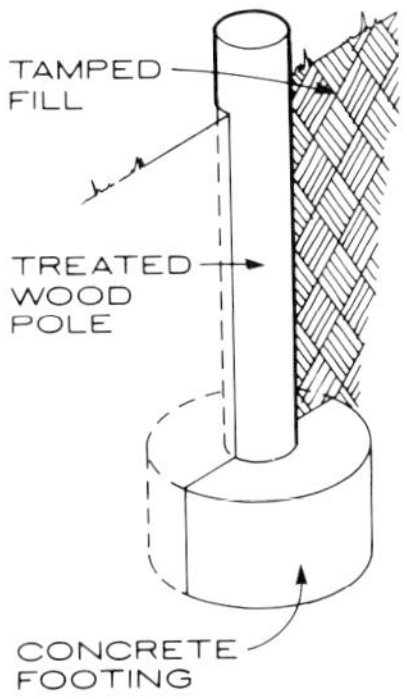

TAMPED FILL
TREATED WOOD POLE
CONCRETE FOOTING

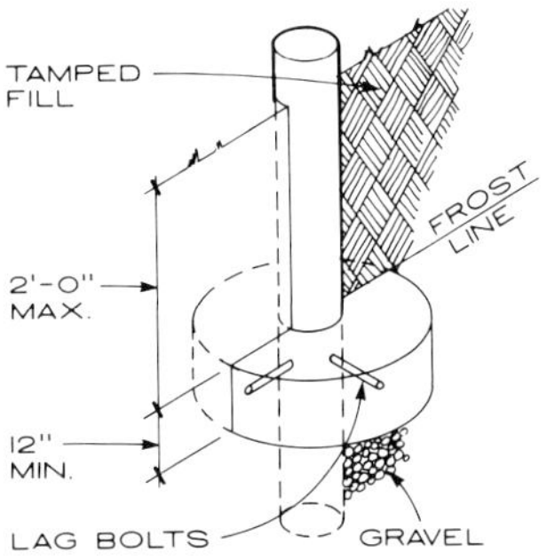

CONCRETE FOOTING

TAMPED FILL
2'-0" MAX.
12" MIN.
FROST LINE
LAG BOLTS
GRAVEL
FOR USE IN TEMPERATE CLIMATES (FROST LINE NO DEEPER THAN 2'-0")

REINFORCED CONCRETE COLLAR

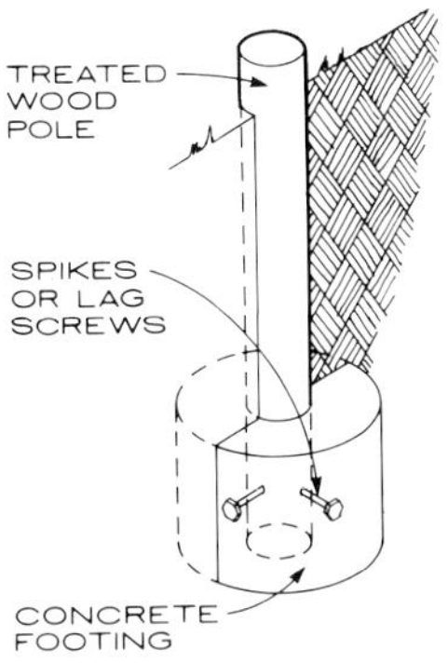

TREATED WOOD POLE
SPIKES OR LAG SCREWS
CONCRETE FOOTING

CONCRETE FOOTING WITH SPIKED ANCHORAGE

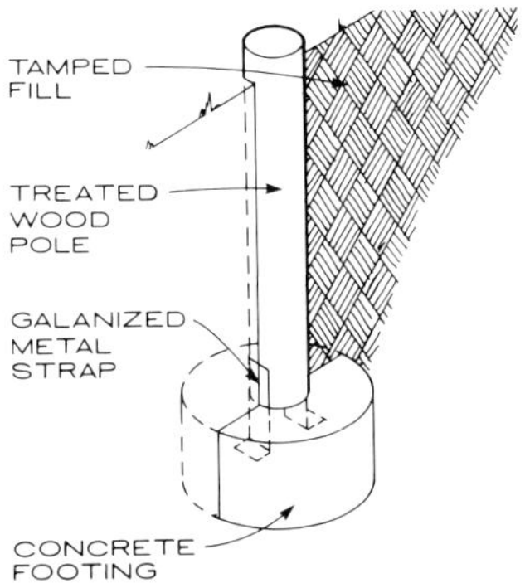

TAMPED FILL
TREATED WOOD POLE
GALANIZED METAL STRAP
CONCRETE FOOTING

CONCRETE FOOTING WITH STRAP ANCHOR

Timothy B. McDonald; Washington, D.C.

HEAVY TIMBER CONSTRUCTION

6

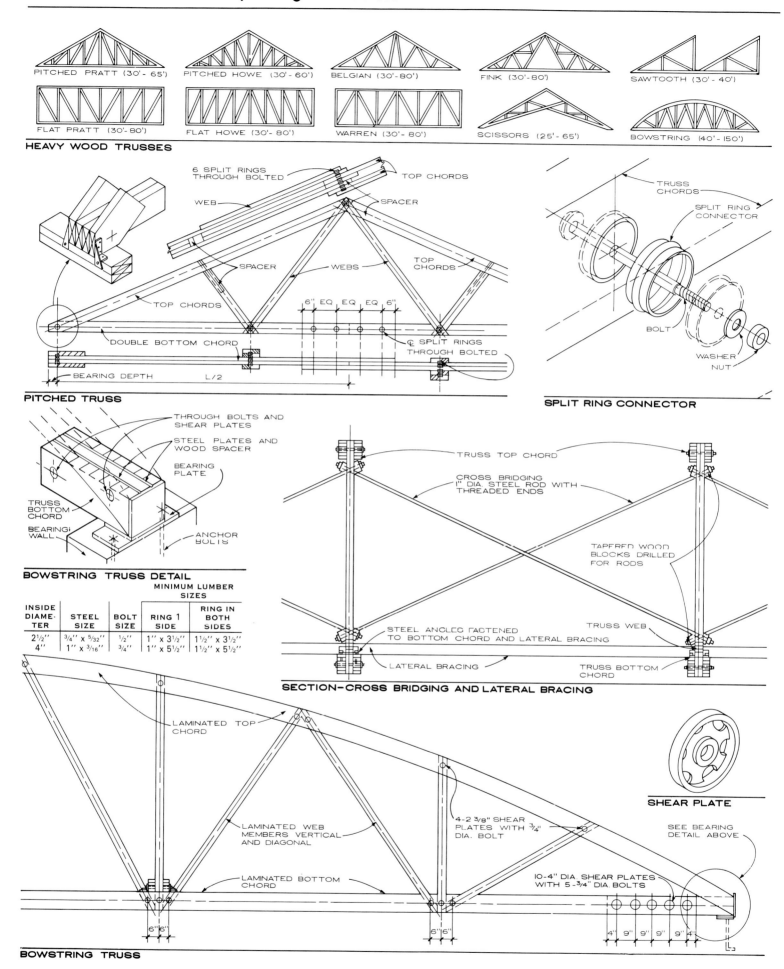

HEAVY WOOD TRUSSES

PITCHED PRATT (30'- 65') PITCHED HOWE (30'- 60') BELGIAN (30'- 80') FINK (30'- 80') SAWTOOTH (30' - 40')

FLAT PRATT (30'- 80') FLAT HOWE (30'- 80') WARREN (30'- 80') SCISSORS (25'- 65') BOWSTRING (40'- 150')

PITCHED TRUSS

6 SPLIT RINGS THROUGH BOLTED — TOP CHORDS
WEB — SPACER
SPACER — WEBS — TOP CHORDS
TOP CHORDS
DOUBLE BOTTOM CHORD
6" EQ EQ EQ 6"
℄ SPLIT RINGS THROUGH BOLTED
BEARING DEPTH   L/2

SPLIT RING CONNECTOR

TRUSS CHORDS
SPLIT RING CONNECTOR
BOLT
WASHER
NUT

BOWSTRING TRUSS DETAIL

THROUGH BOLTS AND SHEAR PLATES
STEEL PLATES AND WOOD SPACER
BEARING PLATE
TRUSS BOTTOM CHORD
BEARING WALL
ANCHOR BOLTS

SECTION–CROSS BRIDGING AND LATERAL BRACING

TRUSS TOP CHORD
CROSS BRIDGING 1" DIA. STEEL ROD WITH THREADED ENDS
TAPERED WOOD BLOCKS DRILLED FOR RODS
STEEL ANGLES FASTENED TO BOTTOM CHORD AND LATERAL BRACING
LATERAL BRACING
TRUSS WEB
TRUSS BOTTOM CHORD

INSIDE DIAMETER	STEEL SIZE	BOLT SIZE	RING 1 SIDE	RING IN BOTH SIDES
MINIMUM LUMBER SIZES				
2½"	¾" x 5/32"	½"	1" x 3½"	1½" x 3½"
4"	1" x 3/16"	¾"	1" x 5½"	1½" x 5½"

SHEAR PLATE

BOWSTRING TRUSS

LAMINATED TOP CHORD
LAMINATED WEB MEMBERS VERTICAL AND DIAGONAL
LAMINATED BOTTOM CHORD
4-2 3/8" SHEAR PLATES WITH ¾" DIA. BOLT
SEE BEARING DETAIL ABOVE
10-4" DIA. SHEAR PLATES WITH 5-¾" DIA. BOLTS
6" 6"
6" 6"
4" 9" 9" 9" 9" 4"

Timothy B. McDonald; Washington, D.C.

PREFABRICATED STRUCTURAL WOOD

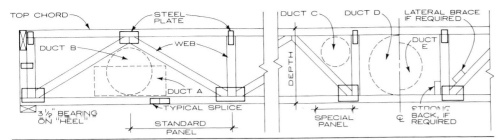

RESIDENTIAL TYPE TRUSSED FLOOR JOIST STEEL PLATE CONNECTED

DUCT SIZES

Ease of running electrical and mechanical services through framing is a major advantage of trussed joists. Most manufacturers provide a large rectangular open panel at midspan; this void will generally accommodate a trunk line.

Sizes given here are approximations. Because web size and angles vary with different brands, the designer is cautioned to verify individual sizes carefully. Note that shape E is the duct that will fit in a flat truss with double chords top and bottom.

DEPTH OF TRUSS AND SIZE OF DUCTWORK

DEPTH	12″	16″	20″	24″
SHAPE				
A	4 x 9	6 x 12	7 x 13	8 x 14
B	7″	10″	12″	14″
C	5″	7″	8″	9″
D	9″	13″	17″	21″
E	6″	10″	14″	18″

GENERAL

Monoplaner trusses are usually made up from 2 x 4 or 2 x 6 lumber. Spacing, normally 24 in. o.c., varies for special uses, especially in agriculture. Camber is designed for dead load only. Bottom chord furring generally is not required for drywall ceiling. Joints in plywood floor or roof should be staggered. Many trusses are approved by model codes, such as BOCA, ICBO, FHA, and SBC.

$$\text{CAMBER (USUAL)} = \frac{L(FT)}{60}$$

BRACING

Adequate bracing of trusses is vital. Sufficient support at right angles to plane of truss must be provided to hold each truss member in its designated position. Consider bracing during design, fabrication, and erection. In addition, provide permanent bracing/anchorage as an integral part of the building. Strongbacks are often used.

WOOD TRUSSED RAFTERS SPANS FOR PRELIMINARY DESIGN

	RESIDENTIAL LIVE LOADS								
	FLOORS 55 PSF (A)			ROOFS 40 PSF (B)		55 PSF (C)		(DOUBLE CHORDS) 55 PSF (C)	
	TRUSSED RAFTERS SPACING (C TO C)								
DEPTH	12″	16″	24″	16″	24″	16″	24″	16″	24″
12″	23-6	21-0	17-1	24-0	21-4	21-11	18-2		
13″	24-11	22-0	17-11						
14″	26-4	22-11	18-8	27-5	23-3	24-5	19-10		
15″	27-7	23-10	19-5						
16″	28-7	24-9	20-1	30-3	25-0	26-4	21-4	31-10	27-10
18″	30-6	26-4	21-5	32-11	26-9	28-1	22-9	35-1	30-7
20″	32-4	27-11	22-8	34-8	28-0	29-7	23-11	38-1	33-1
22″	34-0	26-9	23-11						
24″	35-8	30-10	25-0	38-3	30-11	32-7	26-4	43-10	36-7
28″				41-6	33-6	35-5	28-7	49-2	39-11
32″				44-3	35-7	37-8	30-4	52-9	42-9
36″				47-0	37-10	40-1	32-3	56-3	45-7
48″								60-0	53-3

	COMMERCIAL LIVE LOADS								
	FLOORS 80 PSF (D)			100 PSF (E)			120 PSF (F)		
	TRUSSED RAFTERS SPACING (C TO C)								
DEPTH	12″	16″	24″	12″	16″	24″	12″	16″	24″
12″	19-0	17-3	15-1	17-3	15-8	13-7	16-0	14-7	12-4
14″	21-4	19-4	16-6	19-4	17-7	14-9	18-0	16-4	13-6
16″	23-6	21-5	17-10	21-5	19-5	15-11	19-10	17-11	14-6
18″	25-8	23-4	19-0	23-4	21-0	17-0	21-8	19-2	15-6
20″	27-8	24-10	20-2	25-2	22-3	18-0	23-4	20-3	16-5
24″	31-6	27-5	22-2	28-5	24-6	19-10	25-11	22-4	18-1
16″*	27-7	25-1	21-11	25-1	22-9	19-11	23-2	21-1	18-5
24″*	38-0	34-6	30-1	34-6	31-4	27-4	32-0	29-1	25-1
32″*	47-1	42-9	36-1	42-9	38-10	32-3	39-8	36-1	29-5

Top chord live load	40 psf	20 psf	35 psf	60 psf	80 psf	100 psf
Top chord dead load	10 psf	10 psf	10 psf	10 psf	10 psf	10 psf
Bottom chord dead load	5 psf	10 psf	10 psf	10 psf	10 psf	10 psf
Total load	(A) 55 psf	(B) 40 psf	(C) 55 psf	(D) 80 psf	(E) 100 psf	(F) 120 psf

NOTES

1. Spans are clear, inside to inside, for bottom chord bearing. Values shown would vary very slightly for a truss with top chord loading.
2. Spans should not exceed 24 x depth of truss.
3. Designed deflection limit under total load is ℓ/240 for roofs, ℓ/360 for residential floors, and ℓ/480 for commercial floors.
4. Roof spans include a +15% short term stress.

5. Asterisk (*) indicates that truss has double chords, top and bottom.
6. Spans shown are for only one type of lumber; in this case—#2 Southern pine, with an f_b value of 1550. Charts are available for other grades and species. Lumber and grades may be mixed in the same truss, but chord size must be identical. Repetitive member bending stress is used in this chart.

Michael Bengis, AIA; Hopatcong, New Jersey

SMALL TO MEDIUM 20′-60′

LIGHTWEIGHT $\frac{3}{8}$″ PLYWOOD WEB, 2 X 3 LAMINATED FLANGE

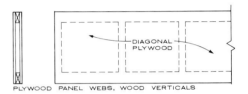

PLYWOOD PANEL WEBS, WOOD VERTICALS

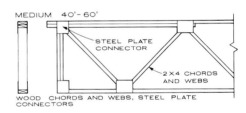

MEDIUM 40′-60′

WOOD CHORDS AND WEBS, STEEL PLATE CONNECTORS

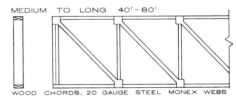

MEDIUM TO LONG 40′-80′

WOOD CHORDS, 20 GAUGE STEEL MONEX WEBS

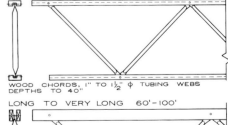

WOOD CHORDS, 1″ TO 1½″ φ TUBING WEBS DEPTHS TO 40″

LONG TO VERY LONG 60′-100′

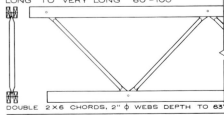

DOUBLE 2×6 CHORDS, 2″ φ WEBS DEPTH TO 63″

TYPES OF FABRICATED TRUSSES

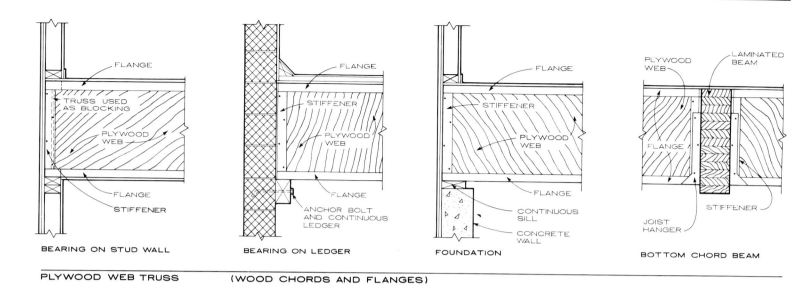

BEARING ON STUD WALL

BEARING ON LEDGER

FOUNDATION

BOTTOM CHORD BEAM

PLYWOOD WEB TRUSS (WOOD CHORDS AND FLANGES)

BOTTOM CHORD BEARING ON STUD WALL

TOP CHORD BEARING— MASONRY WALL

TOP CHORD BEARING ON STUD WALL

TOP CHORD BEARING

OPEN WEB TRUSS (STEEL WEB WOOD CHORD)

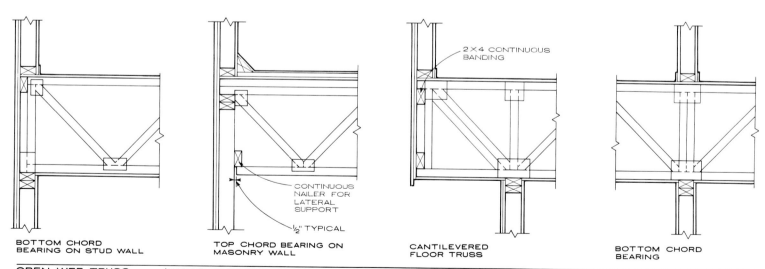

BOTTOM CHORD BEARING ON STUD WALL

TOP CHORD BEARING ON MASONRY WALL

CANTILEVERED FLOOR TRUSS

BOTTOM CHORD BEARING

OPEN WEB TRUSS (WOOD CHORDS AND WEB, METAL PLATE CONNECTORS)

Timothy B. McDonald; Washington, D.C.

 PREFABRICATED STRUCTURAL WOOD

NOTES

1. For light trusses (trussed rafters), average spacing is 2 ft. o.c., but varies up to 4 ft. o.c. The average combined dead and live loads is 45 lbs. per sq.ft. Spans, usually 20 ft. to 32 ft., can be up to 50 ft. in some applications.

2. Early in the design process, consult engineer or truss supplier for preengineered truss designs to establish the most economical and efficient truss proportions. Supplier may provide final truss engineering design.

3. Permanent and temporary erection bracing must be installed as specified to prevent failure of properly designed trusses.

4. Some locales require an engineer's stamp when prefab trusses are used. Check local codes.

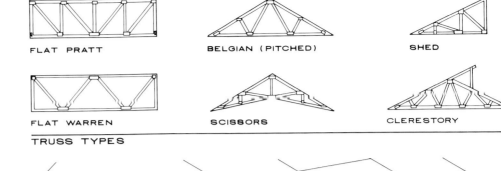

TRUSS TYPES

FLAT PRATT   BELGIAN (PITCHED)   SHED

FLAT WARREN   SCISSORS   CLERESTORY

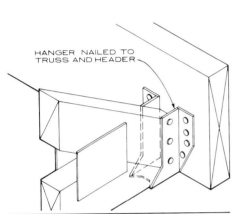

TRUSS HANGER (DETAIL)

HANGER NAILED TO TRUSS AND HEADER

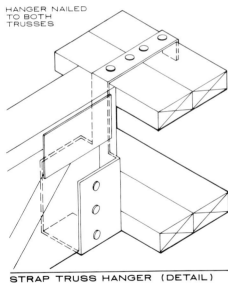

STRAP TRUSS HANGER (DETAIL)

HANGER NAILED TO BOTH TRUSSES

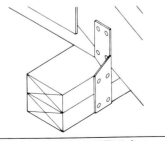

FRAMING ANCHOR (DETAIL)

Timothy B. McDonald; Washington, D.C.

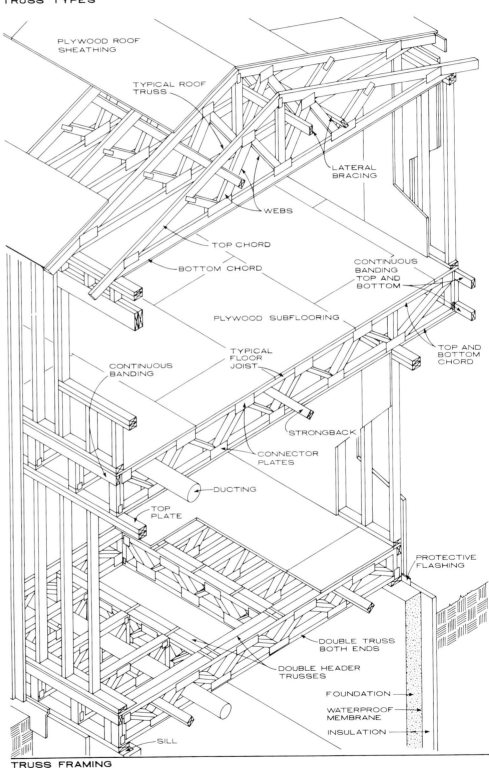

TRUSS FRAMING

PLYWOOD ROOF SHEATHING

TYPICAL ROOF TRUSS

LATERAL BRACING

WEBS

TOP CHORD

BOTTOM CHORD

CONTINUOUS BANDING TOP AND BOTTOM

PLYWOOD SUBFLOORING

TOP AND BOTTOM CHORD

TYPICAL FLOOR JOIST

CONTINUOUS BANDING

STRONGBACK

CONNECTOR PLATES

DUCTING

TOP PLATE

PROTECTIVE FLASHING

DOUBLE TRUSS BOTH ENDS

DOUBLE HEADER TRUSSES

FOUNDATION

WATERPROOF MEMBRANE

INSULATION

SILL

PREFABRICATED STRUCTURAL WOOD 6

COMPARATIVE TABLE FOR SELECTION OF WOOD SPECIES—CONSULT WITH THE ARCHITECTURAL WOODWORK INSTITUTE

SPECIES	HARDNESS	PRINCIPAL USES	APPEARANCE			REMARKS
			COLOR	FIGURE	GRAIN	
Ash, white	Hard	Trim, cabinetry	Creamy white to light brown	High	Open	Excellent strength; bold grain
Basswood	Soft	Decorative moldings and carvings	Creamy white	No figure	Closed	Good for moldings; uniform grain
Beech	Hard	Semiexposed cabinet parts	White to reddish brown	Medium	Closed	Good utility hardwood
Birch, yellow-"natural"	Hard	Trim, paneling and cabinetry	White to dark red	Medium	Closed	Excellent architectural wood, plentiful supply
Birch, yellow-"select red" (heartwood)	Hard	Trim, paneling and cabinetry	Dark red	Medium	Closed	Rich color
Birch, yellow-"select white" (sapwood)	Hard	Trim, paneling and cabinetry	Creamy white	Medium	Closed	Uniform appearance
Butternut	Medium	Trim, paneling and cabinetry	Pale brown	High	Open	Beautiful wood
Cedar, western red	Soft	Trim, paneling exterior and interior	Reddish brown to nearly white sapwood	Medium	Closed	Decay resistant; rough texture
Cherry, American black	Hard	Trim, paneling and cabinetry	Reddish brown	High	Closed	Beautiful wood
Chestnut-wormy	Medium	Paneling and trim	Greyish brown	High	Open with wormholes	Very limited supply
Cypress, yellow	Medium	Trim, frames and special siding	Yellowish brown	High	Closed	Subject to regional availability
Fir, Douglas-flat grain	Medium	Trim, frames and paneling	Reddish tan	High	Closed	Good supply
Fir, Douglas-vertical grain	Medium	Trim, frames and paneling	Reddish tan	Low	Closed	Very limited supply
Mahogany, African-plain sawn	Medium	Trim, frames, paneling, and cabinetry	Reddish brown	Medium	Open	Fine hardwood
Mahogany, African-quarter sawn	Medium	Trim, frames, paneling, and cabinetry	Reddish brown	Low	Open	Limited supply
Mahogany, tropical American-"Honduras"	Medium	Trim, frames, paneling, and cabinetry	Rich golden brown	Medium	Open	One of the world's finest cabinet woods
Maple, hard-natural	Very hard	Trim, paneling and cabinetry	White to reddish brown	Medium	Closed	Plentiful supply; excellent properties
Maple, hard-select white (sapwood)	Very hard	Trim, paneling and cabinetry	White	Medium	Closed	Uniform appearance
Maple, soft-natural	Medium	Trim, semiexposed cabinet parts	White to reddish brown	Low	Closed	Good utility hardwood
Oak, English brown	Hard	Veneered paneling and cabinetry	Leathery brown	High	Open	Distinctive appearance; high cost
Oak, red-plain sawn	Hard	Trim, paneling and cabinetry	Reddish tan to brown	High	Open	Excellent architectural wood; plentiful supply
Oak, red-rift sawn	Hard	Trim, paneling and cabinetry	Reddish tan to brown	Low	Open	Closer grain pattern; limited supply
Oak, red-quarter sawn	Hard	Trim, paneling and cabinetry	Reddish tan to brown	Low	Open	Shows flakes; limited supply
Oak, white-plain sawn	Hard	Trim, paneling and cabinetry	Greyish tan	High	Open	Excellent architectural wood; moderate supply
Oak, white-rift sawn	Hard	Trim, paneling and cabinetry	Greyish tan	Low	Open	Close grain pattern; limited supply
Oak, white-quarter sawn	Hard	Trim, paneling and cabinetry	Greyish tan	Low figure accented with flakes	Open	Shows flakes; limited supply
Pecan	Hard	Trim, paneling and cabinetry	Reddish brown with brown stripes	Medium	Open	Subject to regional availability; attractive
Pine, eastern or northern white	Soft	Trim, frames, paneling, and cabinetry	Creamy white to pink	Medium	Closed	True white pine, wide range of applications for general use
Pine, Idaho, sugar	Soft	Trim, frames, paneling, and cabinetry	Creamy white	Low	Closed	True white pine, wide range of applications for general use
Pine, ponderosa	Soft	Trim, frames, paneling, and cabinetry	White to pale yellow	Medium	Closed	Most widely used pine, wide range of application for general use
Pine, southern yellow-shortleaf	Soft	Trim, frames, paneling, and cabinetry	White to pale yellow	High	Closed	Wide range of applications for general use
Poplar, yellow	Medium	Trim, paneling and cabinetry	White to brown with green cast	Medium	Closed	Good utility hardwood; excellent paintability
Redwood, flat grain (heartwood)	Soft	Trim, frames and paneling	Deep red	High	Closed	Superior exterior wood, high natural decay resistance
Redwood, vertical grain (heartwood)	Soft	Trim, frames and paneling	Deep red	Low	Closed	Superior exterior wood, high natural decay resistance
Rosewood, Brazilian	Very hard	Veneered paneling and cabinetry	Mixed reds, browns, and blacks	High	Open	Exotic figure; high cost
Spruce, Sitka	Soft	Trim, frames	Light yellowish tan	High	Closed	Limited general availability

Architectural Woodwork Institute; Arlington, Virginia

6 FINISH CARPENTRY

COMPARATIVE TABLE FOR SELECTION OF WOOD SPECIES—CONSULT WITH THE ARCHITECTURAL WOODWORK INSTITUTE

SPECIES	HARDNESS	PRINCIPAL USES	APPEARANCE: COLOR	APPEARANCE: FIGURE	APPEARANCE: GRAIN	REMARKS
Teak	Hard	Trim, paneling and cabinetry	Tawny yellow to dark brown	High	Open	Outstanding wood for decorative applications; high cost
Walnut, American black	Hard	Trim, paneling and cabinetry	Chocolate brown	High	Open	Fine domestic hardwood; extremely limited width/length, readily available veneer
Zebrawood, African-quarter sawn	Hard	Trim, paneling and cabinetry	Light gold color/streaked and dark brown to black	High	Closed	Highly decorative

COMPARATIVE TABLE OF WOOD SPECIES FOR DESIGN CRITERIA—CONSULT WITH THE ARCHITECTURAL WOODWORK INSTITUTE

SPECIES	BOTANICAL NAME	FINISHING: PAINT	FINISHING: TRANSPARENT	PRACTICAL SIZE LIMITATIONS: MAX. PRACTICAL THICKNESS WITHOUT LAMINATION	MAX. PRACTICAL WIDTH	MAX. PRACTICAL LENGTH	AVAILABILITY OF MATCHING PLYWOOD (A)	DIMENSIONAL STABILITY (B)
Ash, white	Fraxinus americana	Not normally used	Excellent	1 1/2"	7 1/2"	12'	3	10/64"
Basswood	Tilia, americana	Excellent	Excellent	1 1/2"	7 1/2"	10'	4	10/64"
Beech	Fagus grandifolia	Excellent	Good	1 1/2"	7 1/2"	12'	4	14/64"
Birch, yellow-"natural"	Betula alleghaniensis	Excellent	Good	1 1/2"	7 1/2"	12'	1	12/64"
Birch, yellow-"select red" (heartwood)	Betula alleghaniensis	Not normally used	Excellent	1 1/2"	5 1/2"	11'	2	12/64"
Birch, yellow-"select white" (sapwood)	Betula alleghaniensis	Not normally used	Excellent	1 1/2"	5"	11'	2	12/64"
Butternut	Juglans cinerea	Not normally used	Excellent	1 1/2"	5 1/2"	8'	3	8/64"
Cedar, western red	Thuja plicata	Not normally used	Good	3 1/4"	11"	16'	1 & 3	10/64"
Cherry, American black	Prunus serotina	Not normally used	Excellent	1 1/2"	5 1/2"	7'	2	9/64"
Chestnut-wormy	Castanea dentata	Not normally used	Excellent	3/4"	7 1/2"	10'	4	9/64"
Cypress, yellow	Taxodium distichum	Good	Good	2 1/2"	9 1/2"	16'	4	8/64"
Fir, Douglas-flat grain	Pseudotsuga taxifolia	Fair	Fair	3 1/4"	11"	16'	1	10/64"
Fir, Douglas-vertical grain	Pseudotsuga taxifolia	Good	Good	1 1/2"	11"	16'	4	6/64"
Mahogany, African-plain sawn	Khaya ivorensis	Good	Excellent	2 1/2"	11"	15'	3	7/64"
Mahogany, African-quarter sawn	Khaya ivorensis	Not normally used	Excellent	2 1/2"	7 1/2"	15'	3	5/64"
Mahogany, tropical American-"Honduras"	Sweitenia macrophylla	Not normally used	Excellent	2 1/2"	11"	15'	3	6/64"
Maple, hard-natural	Acer saccharum	Excellent	Good	3 1/2"	9 1/2"	12'	3	12/64"
Maple, hard-select white (sapwood)	Acer saccharum	Not normally used	Excellent	2 1/2"	9 1/2"	12'	3	12/64"
Maple, soft-natural	Acer saccharum	Excellent	Not normally used	3 1/4"	9 1/2"	12'	4	9/64"
Oak, English brown	Quercus robur	Not normally used	Excellent	1 1/2"	5 1/2"	8'	3	
Oak, red-plain sawn	Quercus rubra	Not normally used	Excellent	1 1/2"	7 1/4"	12'	1	11/64"
Oak, red-rift sawn	Quercus rubra	Not normally used	Excellent	1 1/16"	5 1/2"	10'	3	7/64"
Oak, red-quarter sawn	Quercus rubra	Not normally used	Excellent	1 1/6"	5 1/2"	8'	3	7/64"
Oak, white-plain sawn	Quercus alba	Not normally used	Excellent	1 1/2"	5 1/2"	10'	2	11/64"
Oak, white-rift sawn	Quercus alba	Not normally used	Excellent	3/4"	4 1/2"	10'	3	7/64"
Oak, white-quarter sawn	Quercus alba	Not normally used	Excellent	3/4"	4 1/2"	10'	3	7/64"
Pecan	Carya species	Not normally used	Good	1 1/2"	5 1/2"	12'	3	11/64"
Pine, eastern or northern white	Pinus strobus	Good	Good	1 1/2"	9 1/2"	14'	3	8/64"
Pine, Idaho, sugar	Pinus monticola	Good	Good	1 1/2"	9 1/2"	14'	4	8/64"
Pine, ponderosa	Pinus ponderosa	Good	Good	1 1/2"	9 1/2"	16'	3	8/64"
Pine, southern yellow-shortleaf	Pinus echinata	Fair	Good	1 1/2"	7 1/2"	16'	3	10/64"
Poplar, yellow	Liriodendron tulipfera	Excellent	Good	2 1/2"	7 1/2"	12'	3	9/64"
Redwood, flat grain (heartwood)	Sequoia sempervirens	Good	Good	2 1/2"	11"	16'	1 & 3	6/64"
Redwood, vertical grain (heartwood)	Sequoia sempervirens	Excellent	Excellent	2 1/2"	11"	16'	3	3/64"
Rosewood, Brazilian	Dalbergia nigra	Not normally used	Excellent				3	
Spruce, Sitka	Picea sitchensis	Fair	Fair	3 1/4"	9 1/2"	16'	4	10/64"
Teak	Tectona grandis	Not normally used	Excellent	1 1/2"	7 1/2"	10'	2	6/64"
Walnut, American black	Juglans	Not normally used	Excellent	1 1/2"	4 1/2"	6'	1	10/64"
Zebrawood, African-quarter sawn	Brachystegea fleuryana	Not normally used	Excellent	1 1/2"	9"	16'	3	7/64"

(A) Rated from 1 to 4 as follows:

1. Warehouse stock in good quantities and fair assortment of thicknesses and lengths.
2. Warehouse stock in fair quantity but not in thicknesses other than 1/4 and 3/4 in.; or sizes other than 4 x 8 feet.
3. Produced on a special order only.
4. Not generally available.

(B) These figures represent possible width change in a 12 in. board when moisture content is reduced from 10 to 5%. Figures are for plain sawn unless indicated otherwise in species column.

Architectural Woodwork Institute; Arlington, Virginia

GUIDELINES

1. Check current local building code regulations for requirements that may differ from the general recommendations shown or stated on this page.
2. Interior stair width: 3 ft (36 in.) minimum.
3. Minimum headroom should be 6 ft 8 in. as measured vertically from a diagonal line connecting tread nosings to the underside of the finished ceiling or stair landing directly above the stair run. Recommended headroom is 7 ft.
4. Only handrails and stair stringers may project into the required width of a stair.
 Handrail projection: 3½ in. maximum.
 Stringer projection: 1½ in. maximum.
5. The width of a landing or platform should be the same as the actual width of the stair.
6. Maximum vertical rise of stair between landings: 12 ft.
7. Maximum riser height: 7 in.
 Minimum riser height: 4 in.
 Minimum tread width: 11 in.

Tolerances for variation in tread or riser dimension should not exceed ³⁄₁₆ in. for adjacent tread width or riser height. The maximum difference between the largest and smallest tread width or riser height for an entire flight of stairs should be ³⁄₈ in.

8. Height of handrail: 2 ft 6 in. to 2 ft 10 in. (at stair and landings). Handrails should be designed to be easily gripped and to fit the hand. Recommended diameter is 1½ in. for round handrail and similar size for elliptical or rounded edge square section. Handrails should be structurally designed so that both downward (vertical) and lateral (horizontal) thrust loads are considered.
9. Extensions of handrail at top and bottom of stair may affect total length of required run. Verify extensions required by local code before starting stair design.
10. Construction details on this page are for shop-built stairs reflecting Architectural Woodwork Institute Premium Grade Standards.

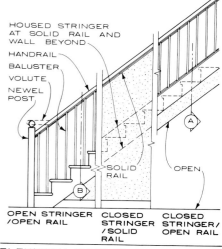

ELEVATION OF FACE STRINGER

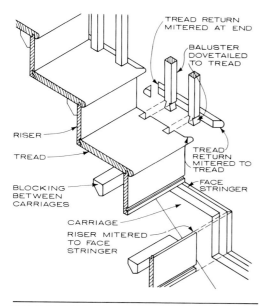

BALUSTERS AND TRIM AT FACE STRINGER

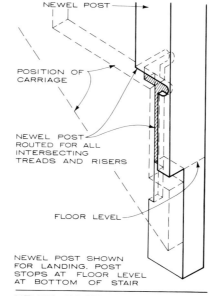

NEWEL POST

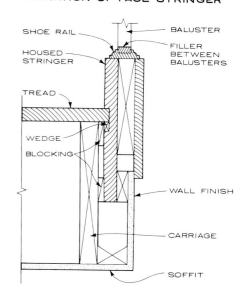

SECTION A

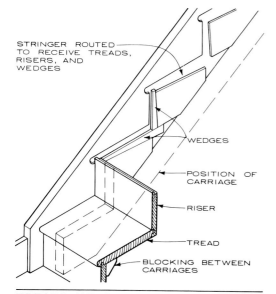

TREADS AND RISERS AT HOUSED STRINGER

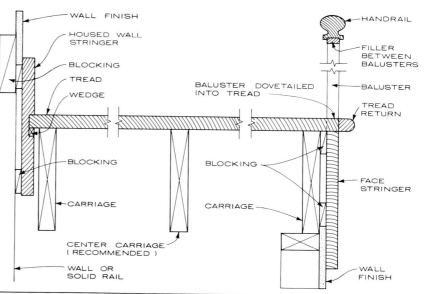

SECTION B

The Bumgardner Partnership/Architects; Seattle, Washington

 FINISH CARPENTRY

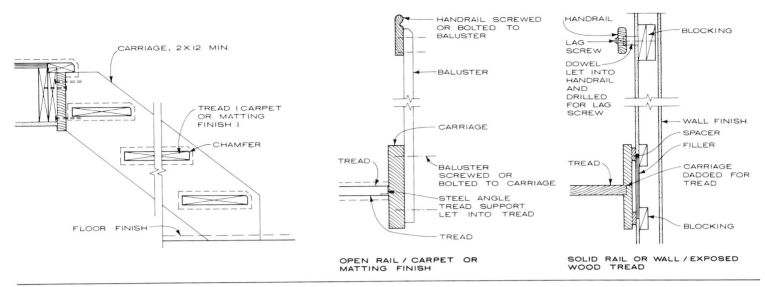

CARRIAGE, 2×12 MIN.

TREAD (CARPET OR MATTING FINISH)

CHAMFER

FLOOR FINISH

HANDRAIL SCREWED OR BOLTED TO BALUSTER

BALUSTER

CARRIAGE

BALUSTER SCREWED OR BOLTED TO CARRIAGE

TREAD

STEEL ANGLE TREAD SUPPORT LET INTO TREAD

TREAD

HANDRAIL

LAG SCREW

DOWEL LET INTO HANDRAIL AND DRILLED FOR LAG SCREW

BLOCKING

WALL FINISH

SPACER

FILLER

CARRIAGE DADOED FOR TREAD

TREAD

BLOCKING

OPEN RAIL / CARPET OR MATTING FINISH

SOLID RAIL OR WALL / EXPOSED WOOD TREAD

OPEN RISER STAIR

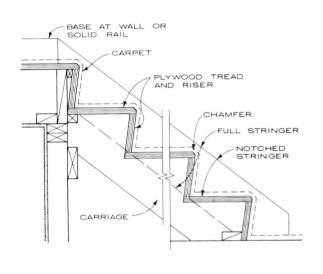

BASE AT WALL OR SOLID RAIL

CARPET

PLYWOOD TREAD AND RISER

CHAMFER

FULL STRINGER

NOTCHED STRINGER

CARRIAGE

CLOSED RISER STAIR/CARPET FINISH

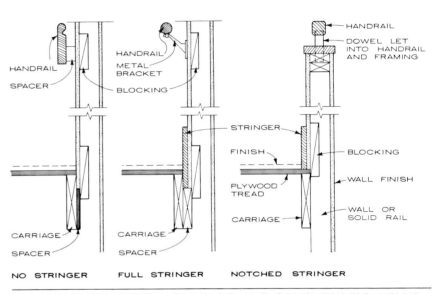

HANDRAIL

SPACER

HANDRAIL

METAL BRACKET

BLOCKING

HANDRAIL

DOWEL LET INTO HANDRAIL AND FRAMING

STRINGER

FINISH

PLYWOOD TREAD

CARRIAGE

BLOCKING

WALL FINISH

WALL OR SOLID RAIL

CARRIAGE

SPACER

CARRIAGE

SPACER

NO STRINGER   FULL STRINGER   NOTCHED STRINGER

CLOSED RISER STAIRS AT WALLS AND SOLID RAILING WALLS

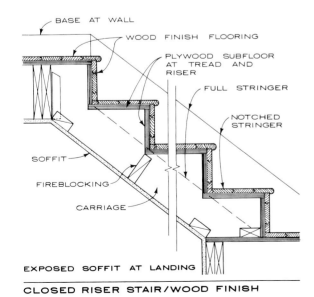

BASE AT WALL

WOOD FINISH FLOORING

PLYWOOD SUBFLOOR AT TREAD AND RISER

FULL STRINGER

NOTCHED STRINGER

SOFFIT

FIREBLOCKING

CARRIAGE

EXPOSED SOFFIT AT LANDING

CLOSED RISER STAIR/WOOD FINISH

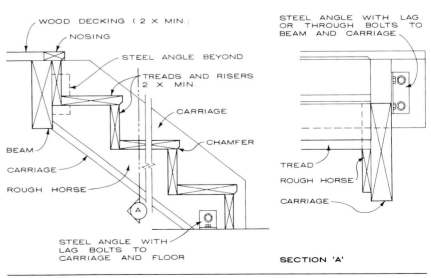

WOOD DECKING (2 X MIN.)

NOSING

STEEL ANGLE BEYOND

TREADS AND RISERS 2 X MIN.

CARRIAGE

CHAMFER

BEAM

CARRIAGE

ROUGH HORSE

STEEL ANGLE WITH LAG BOLTS TO CARRIAGE AND FLOOR

STEEL ANGLE WITH LAG OR THROUGH BOLTS TO BEAM AND CARRIAGE

TREAD

ROUGH HORSE

CARRIAGE

SECTION 'A'

HEAVY TIMBER STAIR

The Bumgardner Partnership/Architects; Seattle, Washington

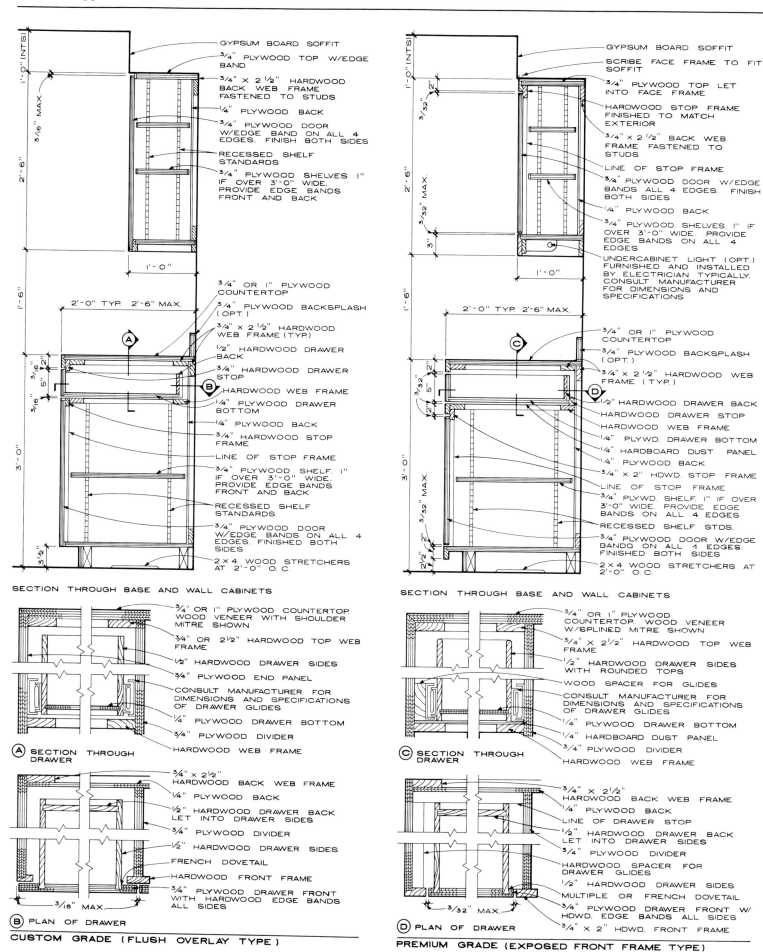

GYPSUM BOARD SOFFIT

3/4" PLYWOOD TOP W/EDGE BAND

3/4" X 2 1/2" HARDWOOD BACK WEB FRAME FASTENED TO STUDS

1/4" PLYWOOD BACK

3/4" PLYWOOD DOOR W/EDGE BAND ON ALL 4 EDGES. FINISH BOTH SIDES

RECESSED SHELF STANDARDS

3/4" PLYWOOD SHELVES 1" IF OVER 3'-0" WIDE. PROVIDE EDGE BANDS FRONT AND BACK

3/4" OR 1" PLYWOOD COUNTERTOP

3/4" PLYWOOD BACKSPLASH (OPT.)

3/4" X 2 1/2" HARDWOOD WEB FRAME (TYP.)

1/2" HARDWOOD DRAWER BACK

3/4" HARDWOOD DRAWER STOP

HARDWOOD WEB FRAME

1/4" PLYWOOD DRAWER BOTTOM

1/4" PLYWOOD BACK

3/4" HARDWOOD STOP FRAME

LINE OF STOP FRAME

3/4" PLYWOOD SHELF. 1" IF OVER 3'-0" WIDE. PROVIDE EDGE BANDS FRONT AND BACK

RECESSED SHELF STANDARDS

3/4" PLYWOOD DOOR W/EDGE BANDS ON ALL 4 SIDES. FINISHED BOTH SIDES

2 X 4 WOOD STRETCHERS AT 2'-0" O.C.

SECTION THROUGH BASE AND WALL CABINETS

3/4" OR 1" PLYWOOD COUNTERTOP WOOD VENEER WITH SHOULDER MITRE SHOWN

3/4" OR 2 1/2" HARDWOOD TOP WEB FRAME

1/2" HARDWOOD DRAWER SIDES

3/4" PLYWOOD END PANEL

CONSULT MANUFACTURER FOR DIMENSIONS AND SPECIFICATIONS OF DRAWER GLIDES

1/4" PLYWOOD DRAWER BOTTOM

3/4" PLYWOOD DIVIDER

HARDWOOD WEB FRAME

Ⓐ **SECTION THROUGH DRAWER**

3/4" X 2 1/2" HARDWOOD BACK WEB FRAME

1/4" PLYWOOD BACK

1/2" HARDWOOD DRAWER BACK LET INTO DRAWER SIDES

3/4" PLYWOOD DIVIDER

1/2" HARDWOOD DRAWER SIDES

FRENCH DOVETAIL

HARDWOOD FRONT FRAME

3/4" PLYWOOD DRAWER FRONT WITH HARDWOOD EDGE BANDS ALL SIDES

Ⓑ **PLAN OF DRAWER**

CUSTOM GRADE (FLUSH OVERLAY TYPE)

GYPSUM BOARD SOFFIT

SCRIBE FACE FRAME TO FIT SOFFIT

3/4" PLYWOOD TOP LET INTO FACE FRAME

HARDWOOD STOP FRAME FINISHED TO MATCH EXTERIOR

3/4" X 2 1/2" BACK WEB FRAME FASTENED TO STUDS

LINE OF STOP FRAME

3/4" PLYWOOD DOOR W/EDGE BANDS ALL 4 EDGES. FINISH BOTH SIDES

1/4" PLYWOOD BACK

3/4" PLYWOOD SHELVES. 1" IF OVER 3'-0" WIDE. PROVIDE EDGE BANDS ON ALL 4 EDGES

UNDERCABINET LIGHT (OPT.) FURNISHED AND INSTALLED BY ELECTRICIAN TYPICALLY. CONSULT MANUFACTURER FOR DIMENSIONS AND SPECIFICATIONS

3/4" OR 1" PLYWOOD COUNTERTOP

3/4" PLYWOOD BACKSPLASH (OPT.)

3/4" X 2 1/2" HARDWOOD WEB FRAME (TYP.)

1/2" HARDWOOD DRAWER BACK

HARDWOOD DRAWER STOP

HARDWOOD WEB FRAME

1/4" PLYWD. DRAWER BOTTOM

1/4" HARDBOARD DUST PANEL

1/4" PLYWOOD BACK

3/4" X 2" HDWD. STOP FRAME

LINE OF STOP FRAME

3/4" PLYWD. SHELF. 1" IF OVER 3'-0" WIDE. PROVIDE EDGE BANDS ON ALL 4 EDGES

RECESSED SHELF STDS.

3/4" PLYWOOD DOOR W/EDGE BANDS ON ALL 4 EDGES. FINISHED BOTH SIDES

2 X 4 WOOD STRETCHERS AT 2'-0" O.C.

SECTION THROUGH BASE AND WALL CABINETS

3/4" OR 1" PLYWOOD COUNTERTOP. WOOD VENEER W/SPLINED MITRE SHOWN

3/4" X 2 1/2" HARDWOOD TOP WEB FRAME

1/2" HARDWOOD DRAWER SIDES WITH ROUNDED TOPS

WOOD SPACER FOR GLIDES

CONSULT MANUFACTURER FOR DIMENSIONS AND SPECIFICATIONS OF DRAWER GLIDES

1/4" PLYWOOD DRAWER BOTTOM

1/4" HARDBOARD DUST PANEL

3/4" PLYWOOD DIVIDER

HARDWOOD WEB FRAME

Ⓒ **SECTION THROUGH DRAWER**

3/4" X 2 1/2" HARDWOOD BACK WEB FRAME

1/4" PLYWOOD BACK

LINE OF DRAWER STOP

1/2" HARDWOOD DRAWER BACK LET INTO DRAWER SIDES

3/4" PLYWOOD DIVIDER

HARDWOOD SPACER FOR DRAWER GLIDES

1/2" HARDWOOD DRAWER SIDES

MULTIPLE OR FRENCH DOVETAIL

3/4" PLYWOOD DRAWER FRONT W/ HDWD. EDGE BANDS ALL SIDES

3/4" X 2" HDWD. FRONT FRAME

Ⓓ **PLAN OF DRAWER**

PREMIUM GRADE (EXPOSED FRONT FRAME TYPE)

John S. Fornaro, AIA; Columbia, Virginia

ARCHITECTURAL WOODWORK

CABINET CLASSIFICATIONS

The Architectural Woodworking Institute classifies cabinets in three groups: economy, the lowest grade; custom, the average grade; and premium, the best grade. These details show the progression to higher quality and generally follow the AWI standards, but do not show all possible variations of cabinet details. Woodworking shops frequently set their own quality standards; thus many higher quality details can be found in lower quality work, and vice versa. Also, an architect's design may require crossover of details between the different quality groups.

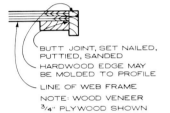

BUTT JOINT, SET NAILED, PUTTIED, SANDED
HARDWOOD EDGE MAY BE MOLDED TO PROFILE
LINE OF WEB FRAME
NOTE: WOOD VENEER
3/4" PLYWOOD SHOWN

ECONOMY GRADE

EDGE DETAIL

SHOULDER MITER SHOWN, TONGUE AND GROOVE MITER AND WOOD SPLINE MITER ALSO USED
LINE OF WEB FRAME
NOTE: WOOD VENEER
3/4" PLYWOOD SHOWN

CUSTOM GRADE

EDGE DETAIL

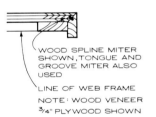

WOOD SPLINE MITER SHOWN, TONGUE AND GROOVE MITER ALSO USED
LINE OF WEB FRAME
NOTE: WOOD VENEER
3/4" PLYWOOD SHOWN

PREMIUM GRADE

EDGE DETAIL

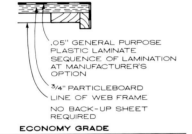

.05" GENERAL PURPOSE PLASTIC LAMINATE SEQUENCE OF LAMINATION AT MANUFACTURER'S OPTION
3/4" PARTICLEBOARD
LINE OF WEB FRAME
NO BACK-UP SHEET REQUIRED

ECONOMY GRADE

EDGE DETAIL

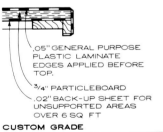

.05" GENERAL PURPOSE PLASTIC LAMINATE EDGES APPLIED BEFORE TOP.
3/4" PARTICLEBOARD
.02" BACK-UP SHEET FOR UNSUPPORTED AREAS OVER 6 SQ FT

CUSTOM GRADE

EDGE DETAIL

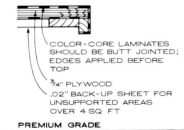

COLOR-CORE LAMINATES SHOULD BE BUTT JOINTED; EDGES APPLIED BEFORE TOP
3/4" PLYWOOD
.02" BACK-UP SHEET FOR UNSUPPORTED AREAS OVER 4 SQ FT

PREMIUM GRADE

EDGE DETAIL

SOAPSTONE, SLATE, OR MARBLE ON THIN-SET BED

2-LAYERS 3/4" PLYWOOD

PREMIUM GRADE

STONE COUNTER

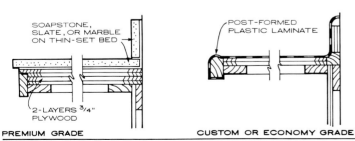

POST-FORMED PLASTIC LAMINATE

CUSTOM OR ECONOMY GRADE

POST-FORMED COUNTER

GYPSUM BOARD SOFFIT (OPTIONAL)
3/4" X 2 1/2" HARDWOOD CLEAT FASTENED TO STUDS
II PLY PLYWOOD LIPPED DOOR WITHOUT EDGE BANDING
3/4" PLYWOOD WITH NAILED AND GLUED EDGE BAND ON FRONT
1/8"-3/16" φ HOLES FOR SHELF SUPPORTS, CONSULT MANUFACTURER FOR DIMENSIONS

3/4" PLYWOOD COUNTERTOP
3/4" PLYWOOD BACKSPLASH (OPTIONAL)
3/4" X 2 1/2" HARDWOOD WEB FRAME
HARDWOOD TILT STRIP
1/2" HARDWOOD DRAWER BACK
1/8" HARDBOARD DRAWER BOTTOM. 1/4" IF OVER 1'-0" WIDE
3/4" THICK HARDWOOD DRAWER SUPPORT
3/4" PLYWOOD SHELF WITH NAILED AND GLUED EDGE BAND ON FRONT
HOLES FOR SHELF SUPPORT; SPACING OPTIONAL 1" TYPICAL
II PLY PLYWOOD LIPPED DOOR WITHOUT EDGE BANDING
2 X 4 WOOD SLEEPER AT 2'-8" O.C.

ECONOMY GRADE

SECTION THROUGH BASE AND WALL CABINETS

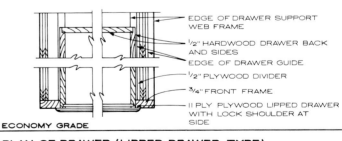

EDGE OF DRAWER SUPPORT WEB FRAME
1/2" HARDWOOD DRAWER BACK AND SIDES
EDGE OF DRAWER GUIDE
1/2" PLYWOOD DIVIDER
3/4" FRONT FRAME
II PLY PLYWOOD LIPPED DRAWER WITH LOCK SHOULDER AT SIDE

ECONOMY GRADE

PLAN OF DRAWER (LIPPED DRAWER TYPE)

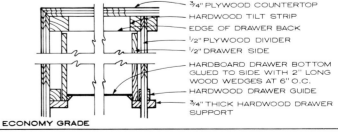

3/4" PLYWOOD COUNTERTOP
HARDWOOD TILT STRIP
EDGE OF DRAWER BACK
1/2" PLYWOOD DIVIDER
1/2" DRAWER SIDE
HARDBOARD DRAWER BOTTOM GLUED TO SIDE WITH 2" LONG WOOD WEDGES AT 6" O.C.
HARDWOOD DRAWER GUIDE
3/4" THICK HARDWOOD DRAWER SUPPORT

ECONOMY GRADE

SECTION THROUGH DRAWER

John S. Fornaro, AIA; Columbia, Virginia

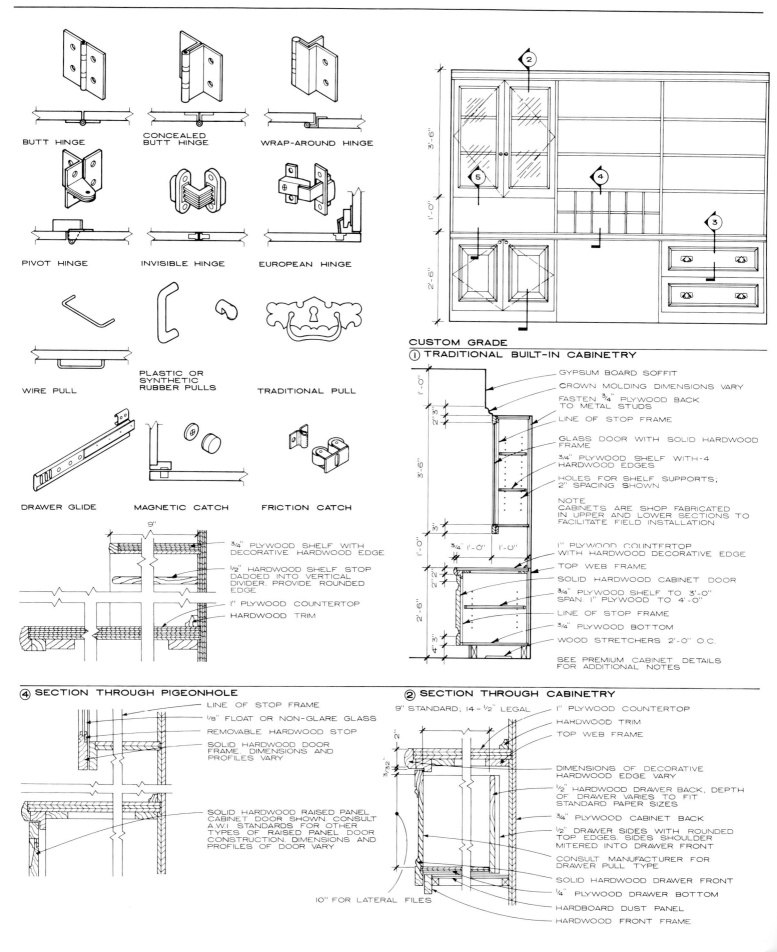

BUTT HINGE

CONCEALED BUTT HINGE

WRAP-AROUND HINGE

PIVOT HINGE

INVISIBLE HINGE

EUROPEAN HINGE

WIRE PULL

PLASTIC OR SYNTHETIC RUBBER PULLS

TRADITIONAL PULL

DRAWER GLIDE

MAGNETIC CATCH

FRICTION CATCH

3/4" PLYWOOD SHELF WITH DECORATIVE HARDWOOD EDGE

1/2" HARDWOOD SHELF STOP DADOED INTO VERTICAL DIVIDER. PROVIDE ROUNDED EDGE

1" PLYWOOD COUNTERTOP

HARDWOOD TRIM

CUSTOM GRADE

① TRADITIONAL BUILT-IN CABINETRY

GYPSUM BOARD SOFFIT

CROWN MOLDING DIMENSIONS VARY

FASTEN 3/4" PLYWOOD BACK TO METAL STUDS

LINE OF STOP FRAME

GLASS DOOR WITH SOLID HARDWOOD FRAME

3/4" PLYWOOD SHELF WITH-4 HARDWOOD EDGES

HOLES FOR SHELF SUPPORTS; 2" SPACING SHOWN

NOTE
CABINETS ARE SHOP FABRICATED IN UPPER AND LOWER SECTIONS TO FACILITATE FIELD INSTALLATION

1" PLYWOOD COUNTERTOP WITH HARDWOOD DECORATIVE EDGE

TOP WEB FRAME

SOLID HARDWOOD CABINET DOOR

3/4" PLYWOOD SHELF TO 3'-0" SPAN. 1" PLYWOOD TO 4'-0"

LINE OF STOP FRAME

3/4" PLYWOOD BOTTOM

WOOD STRETCHERS 2'-0" O.C.

SEE PREMIUM CABINET DETAILS FOR ADDITIONAL NOTES

④ SECTION THROUGH PIGEONHOLE

LINE OF STOP FRAME

1/8" FLOAT OR NON-GLARE GLASS

REMOVABLE HARDWOOD STOP

SOLID HARDWOOD DOOR FRAME. DIMENSIONS AND PROFILES VARY

SOLID HARDWOOD RAISED PANEL CABINET DOOR SHOWN. CONSULT A.W.I STANDARDS FOR OTHER TYPES OF RAISED PANEL DOOR CONSTRUCTION. DIMENSIONS AND PROFILES OF DOOR VARY

② SECTION THROUGH CABINETRY

9" STANDARD; 14 - 1/2" LEGAL

1" PLYWOOD COUNTERTOP

HARDWOOD TRIM

TOP WEB FRAME

DIMENSIONS OF DECORATIVE HARDWOOD EDGE VARY

1/2" HARDWOOD DRAWER BACK, DEPTH OF DRAWER VARIES TO FIT STANDARD PAPER SIZES

3/4" PLYWOOD CABINET BACK

1/2" DRAWER SIDES WITH ROUNDED TOP EDGES. SIDES SHOULDER MITERED INTO DRAWER FRONT

CONSULT MANUFACTURER FOR DRAWER PULL TYPE

SOLID HARDWOOD DRAWER FRONT

1/4" PLYWOOD DRAWER BOTTOM

HARDBOARD DUST PANEL

HARDWOOD FRONT FRAME

10" FOR LATERAL FILES

⑤ SECTION THROUGH GLASS AND WOOD DOOR

③ SECTION THROUGH LATERAL FILE

John S. Fornaro, AIA; Columbia, Virginia

⑥ **ARCHITECTURAL WOODWORK**

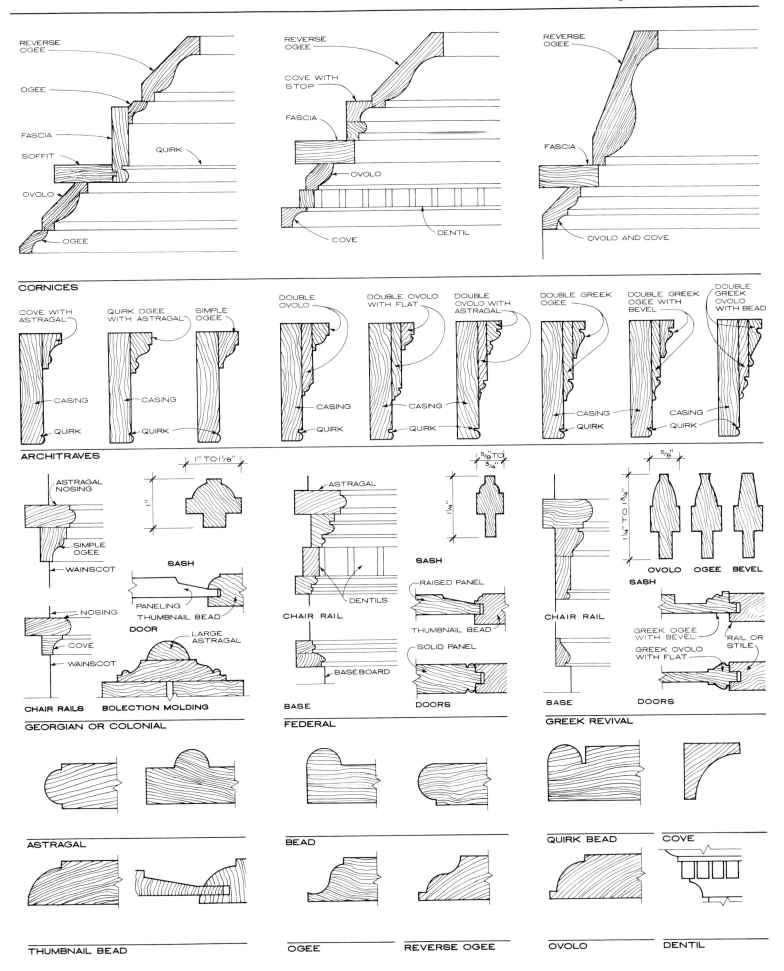

REVERSE OGEE
OGEE
FASCIA
SOFFIT
QUIRK
OVOLO
OGEE

REVERSE OGEE
COVE WITH STOP
FASCIA
OVOLO
COVE
DENTIL

REVERSE OGEE
FASCIA
OVOLO AND COVE

CORNICES

COVE WITH ASTRAGAL
QUIRK OGEE WITH ASTRAGAL
SIMPLE OGEE
CASING
QUIRK

DOUBLE OVOLO
DOUBLE OVOLO WITH FLAT
DOUBLE OVOLO WITH ASTRAGAL
CASING
QUIRK

DOUBLE GREEK OGEE
DOUBLE GREEK OGEE WITH BEVEL
DOUBLE GREEK OVOLO WITH BEAD
CASING
QUIRK

ARCHITRAVES

ASTRAGAL NOSING
SIMPLE OGEE
WAINSCOT
1" TO 1⅛"
1"
SASH
PANELING
THUMBNAIL BEAD
NOSING
COVE
WAINSCOT
DOOR
LARGE ASTRAGAL
CHAIR RAILS
BOLECTION MOLDING

GEORGIAN OR COLONIAL

ASTRAGAL

THUMBNAIL BEAD

ASTRAGAL
DENTILS
CHAIR RAIL
BASEBOARD
BASE
⅝" TO ¾"
1¼"
SASH
RAISED PANEL
THUMBNAIL BEAD
SOLID PANEL
DOORS

FEDERAL

BEAD

OGEE   REVERSE OGEE

CHAIR RAIL
BASE
⅝"
1¼" TO 1¾"
OVOLO   OGEE   BEVEL
SASH
GREEK OGEE WITH BEVEL
GREEK OVOLO WITH FLAT
RAIL OR STILE
DOORS

GREEK REVIVAL

QUIRK BEAD   COVE

OVOLO   DENTIL

Timothy B. McDonald; Washington, D.C.

ARCHITECTURAL WOODWORK   6

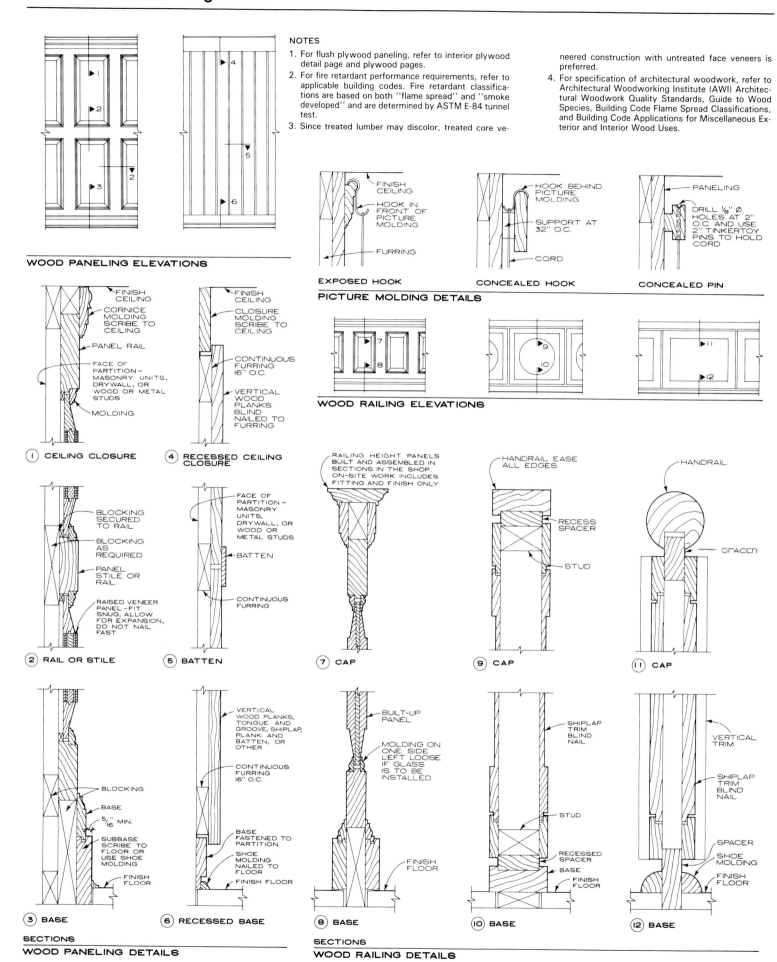

NOTES

1. For flush plywood paneling, refer to interior plywood detail page and plywood pages.
2. For fire retardant performance requirements, refer to applicable building codes. Fire retardant classifications are based on both "flame spread" and "smoke developed" and are determined by ASTM E-84 tunnel test.
3. Since treated lumber may discolor, treated core veneered construction with untreated face veneers is preferred.
4. For specification of architectural woodwork, refer to Architectural Woodworking Institute (AWI) Architectural Woodwork Quality Standards, Guide to Wood Species, Building Code Flame Spread Classifications, and Building Code Applications for Miscellaneous Exterior and Interior Wood Uses.

WOOD PANELING ELEVATIONS

PICTURE MOLDING DETAILS

EXPOSED HOOK   CONCEALED HOOK   CONCEALED PIN

WOOD RAILING ELEVATIONS

① CEILING CLOSURE
④ RECESSED CEILING CLOSURE
② RAIL OR STILE
⑤ BATTEN
⑦ CAP
⑨ CAP
⑪ CAP
③ BASE
⑥ RECESSED BASE
⑧ BASE
⑩ BASE
⑫ BASE

SECTIONS
WOOD PANELING DETAILS

SECTIONS
WOOD RAILING DETAILS

Charles Szoradi, AIA; Washington, D.C.

ARCHITECTURAL WOODWORK

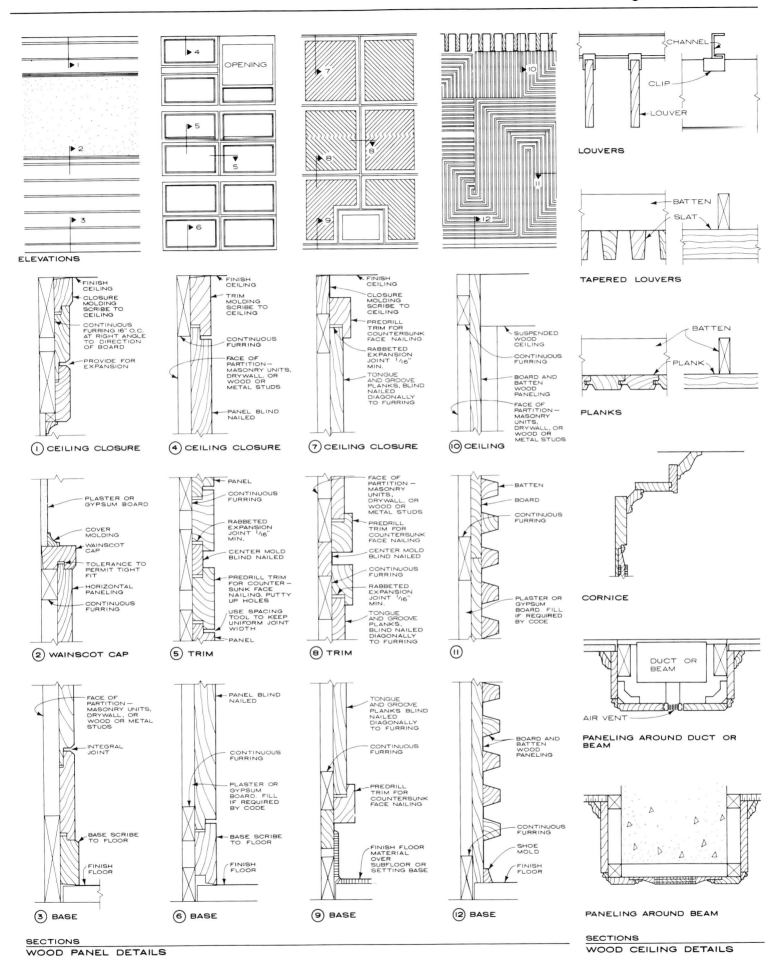

ELEVATIONS

① CEILING CLOSURE
④ CEILING CLOSURE
⑦ CEILING CLOSURE
⑩ CEILING

② WAINSCOT CAP
⑤ TRIM
⑧ TRIM
⑪

③ BASE
⑥ BASE
⑨ BASE
⑫ BASE

SECTIONS
WOOD PANEL DETAILS

LOUVERS

TAPERED LOUVERS

PLANKS

CORNICE

PANELING AROUND DUCT OR BEAM

PANELING AROUND BEAM

SECTIONS
WOOD CEILING DETAILS

Charles Szoradi, AIA; Washington, D.C.

ARCHITECTURAL WOODWORK   6

REFERENCES

GENERAL REFERENCES

Heavy Timber Construction Details, National Forest Products Association (NFPA)

National Design Specification for Wood Construction, National Forest Products Association (NFPA)

Typical Construction Details, American Institute of Timber Construction (AITC)

Timber Construction Manual, American Institute of Timber Construction (AITC)

Timber Design and Construction Sourcebook, 1989, Gotz, Hoor, Mohler, and Netterer, McGraw-Hill

Wood Engineering and Construction Handbook, Keith F. Faherty and Thomas G. Williamson, McGraw-Hill

Western Woods Use Book, Western Wood Products Association (WWPA)

DATA SOURCES: ORGANIZATIONS

American Institute of Timber Construction (AITC), 138

American Insurance Association, 109

American Plywood Association (APA), 124–129

American Society for Testing and Materials (ASTM), 150

Architectural Woodwork Institute (AWI), 144, 145, 150, 151

American Wood Preserver's Institute (AWPI), 109

Automated Building Components, Inc., 139

Dow Chemical Company, 127

Federal Housing Administration (FHA), U.S. Department of Housing and Urban Development (HUD), 139

Forest Products Division, Koppers Company, Inc., 109

Hydro-Air Engineering, Inc., 139

Lumbermate, Inc., 139

Monex Corporation, 139

Simpson Company, 131, 132, 141

Truss Plate Institute, 139

Trus-Joist Company, 139

Underwriters' Laboratories, Inc. (U.L.), 109

Weyerhaeuser Company, 130

Wood Fabricators, Inc., 139

Wood Products Group, Potlatch Corporation, 130

DATA SOURCES: PUBLICATIONS

Basic Building Code, Building Officials and Code Administrators International (BOCA), 139, 109

Bauen mit Holz, c. 1966, Kurt Hoffmann and Helga Griese, Verlag Julius Hoffman, Stuttgart, 121

Curbless Skylights, Rob Thallon, Fine Homebuilding, 121

National Design Specification for Wood Construction, National Forest Products Association (NFPA), 109

Southern Standard Building Code, Southern Building Code Congress (SBCC), 109, 139

Southwest Sunspace, Valerie Walsh, Fine Homebuilding, 120

Uniform Building, 1982 ed., 1985 ed., International Conference of Building Officials (ICBO). Reprinted with permission of the publisher, 109, 139

CHAPTER 7

THERMAL AND MOISTURE PROTECTION

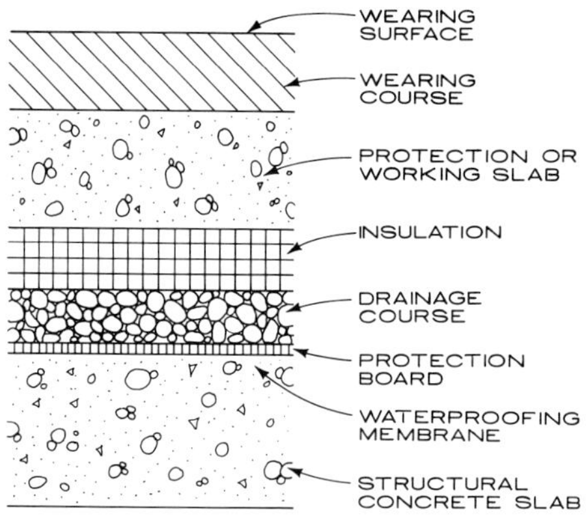
WEARING SURFACE
WEARING COURSE
PROTECTION OR WORKING SLAB
INSULATION
DRAINAGE COURSE
PROTECTION BOARD
WATERPROOFING MEMBRANE
STRUCTURAL CONCRETE SLAB

BASIC COMPONENTS OF WATERPROOFING SYSTEMS

GENERAL

The basic components, subsystems, and features for a building deck waterproofing system are the structural building deck or substrate to be waterproofed, waterproofing membrane, protection of membrane, drainage, insulation, and wearing course. See following pages for generic membrane applications.

SUBSTRATE

The substrate referred to is reinforced cast-in-place structural concrete. Precast concrete slabs pose more technical problems than cast-in-place concrete and the probability of lasting watertightness is greatly diminished and difficult to achieve because of the multitude of joints which have the capability of movement and must be treated accordingly.

The concrete used for the substrate should have a minimum density of 1762 kg/m^3 (110 lb/ft^3) and have a maximum moisture content of 8% when cured.

SLOPE FOR DRAINAGE

A monolithic concrete substrate slope of a minimum 11 mm/m (1/8 in./ft) should be maintained. Slope is best achieved with a monolithic structural slab and not with a separate concrete fill layer.

MEMBRANE

Detection of leakage can be a significant problem when the membrane is not bonded to the structural slab or when additional layers of materials separate it from the structural slab. Therefore, only membranes that can be bonded to the substrate should be used.

The membrane should be applied under dry, frost-free conditions on the surface as well as throughout the depth of the concrete slab.

When the membrane is turned up on a wall, it is preferable to terminate it above the wearing surface to eliminate the possibility of ponded surface water penetrating the wall above the membrane and running down behind it into the building.

Penetrations should be avoided wherever possible. For protection at such critical locations, pipe sleeves should be cast into the structural slab against which the membrane can be terminated.

Treatment at reinforced and nonreinforced joints depends on the membrane used. See following pages.

There are basically two concepts that could be considered in the detailing of expansion joints at the membrane level. These are the positive seal concept directly at the membrane level and the watershed concept with the seal at a higher lever than the membrane. Where additional safeguards are desired, a drainage gutter under the joint could be considered. Flexible support of the membrane is required in each case. Expansion joint details should be considered and used in accordance with their movement capability.

The positive seal concept entails a greater risk than the watershed concept, since it relies fully on positive seal joinery of materials at the membrane level, where the membrane is most vulnerable to water penetration. Since the precision required is not always attainable, this concept is best avoided.

The watershed concept, although requiring a greater height and more costly concrete forming, is superior in safeguarding against leakage, having the advantage of providing a water dam at the membrane level. However, if a head of water rises to the height of the materials joinery, this concept becomes almost as vulnerable as the positive seal concept. Therefore, drainage is recommended at the membrane level.

PROTECTION BOARD

The membrane should be protected from damage prior to and during the remainder of construction. Protection board should be applied after the membrane is installed. The proper timing of application after placement of the membrane is important and could vary with the type of membrane used. The manufacturer's printed instructions should be followed.

DRAINAGE SYSTEM

Drainage should be considered as a total system from the wearing surface down to the membrane, including use of multilevel drains.

Drainage at the wearing surface is generally accomplished in one of two ways:

1. By an open joint and pedestal system permitting most of the rainwater to penetrate rapidly down to the membrane level and subsurface drainage system, and
2. By a closed-joint system designed to remove most of the rainwater rapidly by slope to surface drains and to allow a minor portion to infiltrate to membrane.

A drainage course of washed, round gravel should be provided above the protection board, over the membrane. This permits water to filter to the drain and provides a place where it can collect and freeze without potential damage to the wearing course.

INSULATION

When required, insulation should be located above the membrane, but not in direct contact with it.

PROTECTION OR WORKING SLAB

A concrete slab could be placed soon after the membrane, protection board, drainage course, and insulation, if required, have been installed. It would serve as protection for the permanent waterproofing materials and insulation below, provide a working platform for construction traffic and storage of materials (within weight limits), and provide a substantial substrate for the placement of the finish wearing course materials near the completion of the project.

WEARING COURSE

The major requirements for the wearing course are a stable support of sufficient strength, resistance against lateral thrust, adequate drainage to avoid ponding of water, and proper treatment of joints.

Joints in which movement is anticipated should be treated as expansion joints.

Various proprietary compression seals are available that can be inserted into a formed joint under compression. Most of these, however, are not flush at the top surface and could fill up with sand or dirt.

Wet sealants are the materials most commonly used in moving joints at the wearing surface level. Dimension A is the design width dimension or the dimension at which the joint will be formed. The criterion normally used for determining this dimension with sealants capable of ±25% movement is to multiply the maximum expected movement in one direction by 4. Generally, this is expected to be about three-fourths of the total anticipated joint movement, but if there is any doubt, multiply the total anticipated joint movement by 4. It is better to have the joint too wide than too narrow. Dimension B (sealant depth) is related to dimension A and is best established by the sealant manufacturer. Generally, B is equal to A for widths up to 13 mm (1/2 in.), 15 mm (9/16 in.) for a 16 mm (5/8 in.) width, and 16 mm (5/8 in.) for 19 mm (3/4 in.) and greater widths. This allows some tolerance for self-leveling sealants.

Reference: ASTM C 898 and C 981. Highlights of text and figures are reprinted with permission from ASTM Committee C-24 of the American Society for Testing Materials.

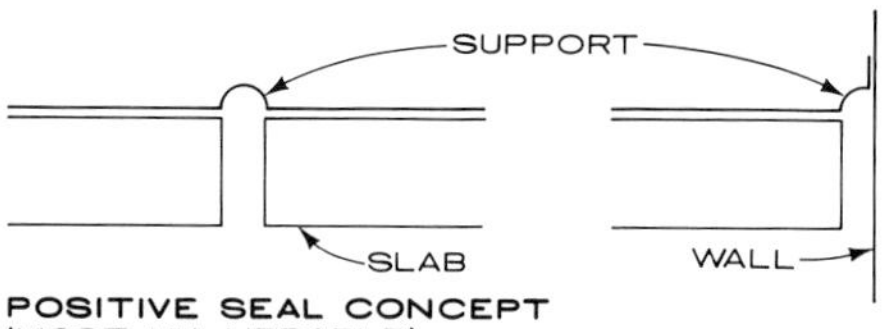
SUPPORT
SLAB
WALL

POSITIVE SEAL CONCEPT (MOST VULNERABLE)

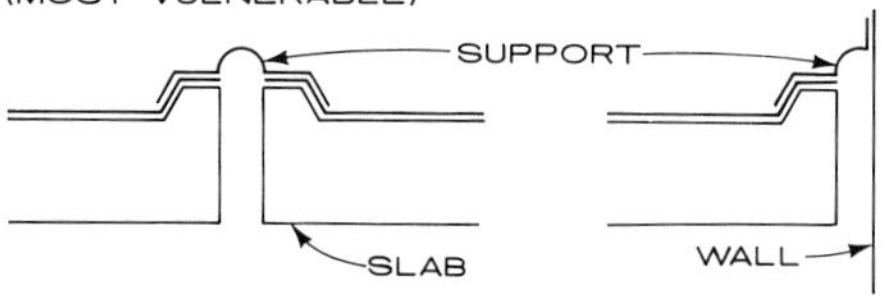
SUPPORT
SLAB
WALL

WATERSHED CONCEPT (PREFERRED)

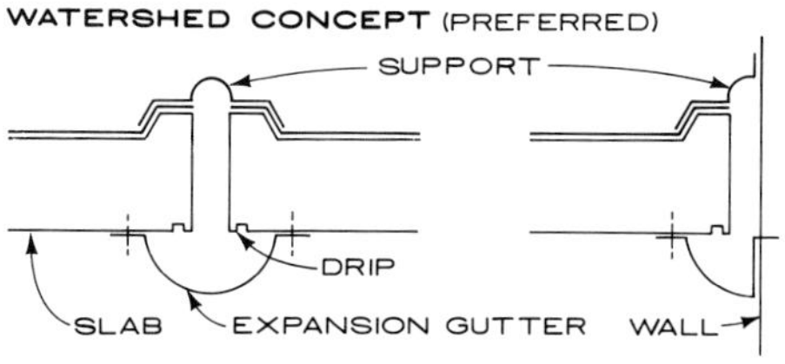
SUPPORT
DRIP
SLAB
EXPANSION GUTTER
WALL

COMBINATION POSITIVE SEAL OR WATERSHED (SHOWN) PLUS EXPANSION GUTTER CONCEPT (PROVIDES ADDITIONAL SAFEGUARD)

EXPANSION JOINT CONCEPTS AT MEMBRANE LEVEL

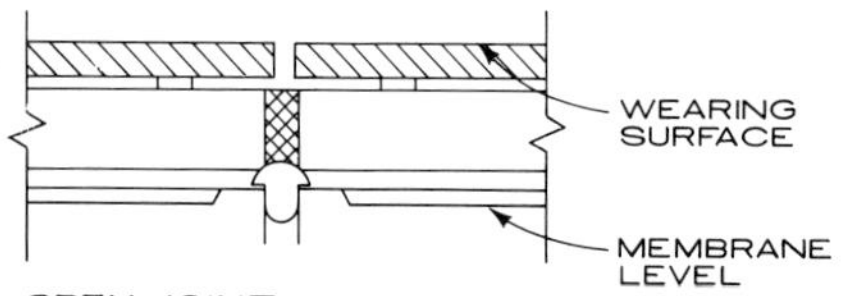
WEARING SURFACE
MEMBRANE LEVEL

OPEN JOINT

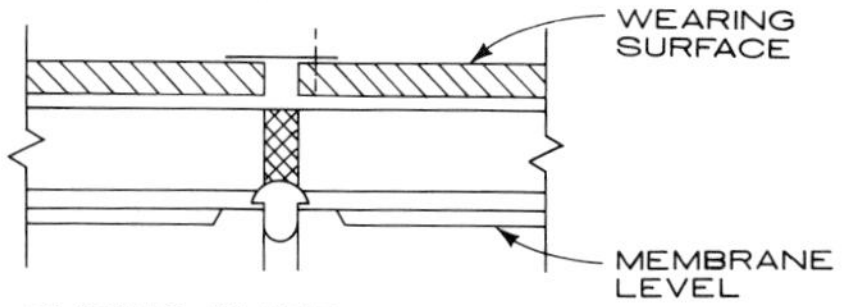
WEARING SURFACE
MEMBRANE LEVEL

SLIDING PLATE

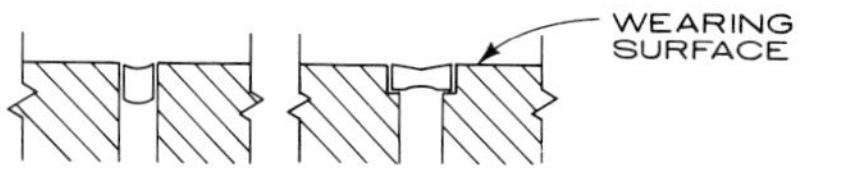
WEARING SURFACE

COMPRESSION SEAL

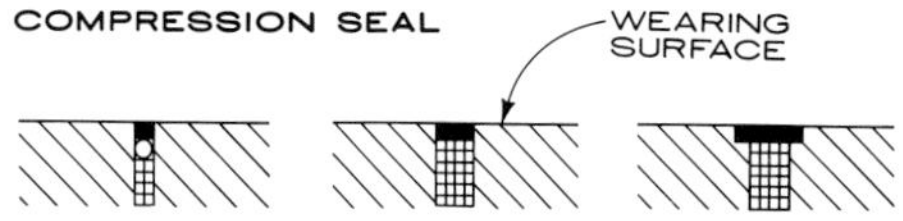
WEARING SURFACE

"WET" SEALANTS

EXPANSION JOINT CONCEPTS AT WEARING SURFACE LEVEL

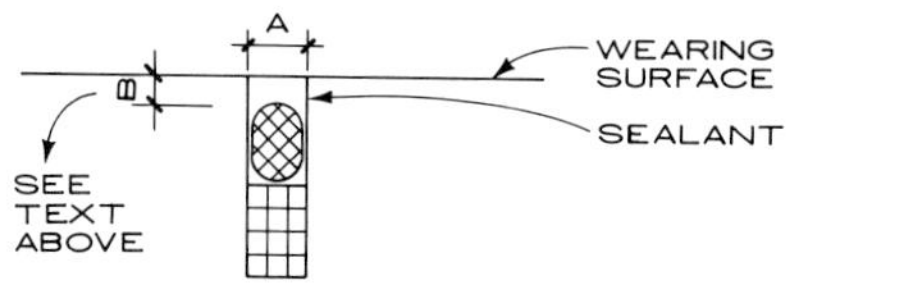
A
B
WEARING SURFACE
SEALANT
SEE TEXT ABOVE

FOR JOINTS UP TO 1/2" WIDE

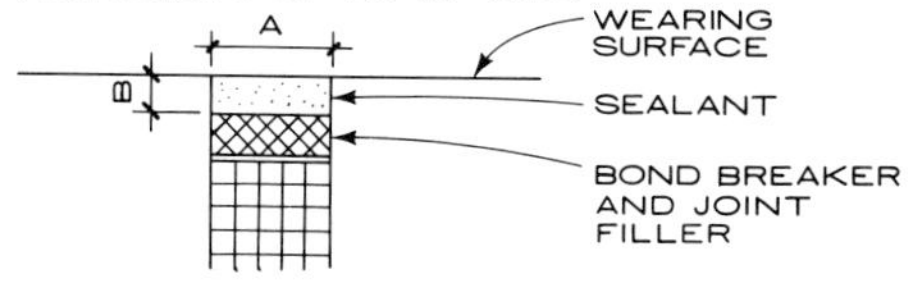
A
B
WEARING SURFACE
SEALANT
BOND BREAKER AND JOINT FILLER

FOR JOINTS UP TO 1 1/2" WIDE

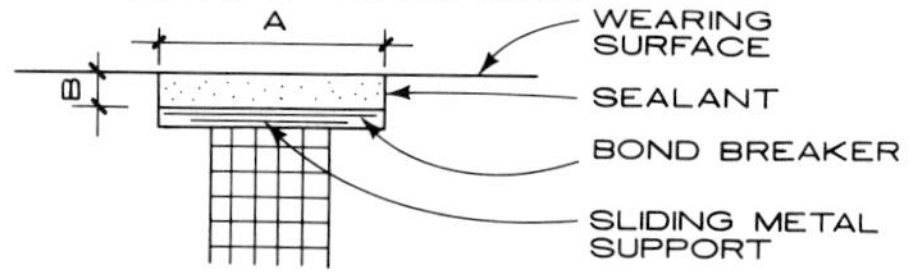
A
B
WEARING SURFACE
SEALANT
BOND BREAKER
SLIDING METAL SUPPORT

FOR JOINTS WIDER THAN 1 1/2"

SEE OTHER PAGES FOR JOINT DESIGN DIMENSIONS

WET SEALANT DETAILS AT WEARING SURFACE

Charles J. Parise, FAIA, FASTM; Smith, Hinchman & Grylls Associates, Inc.; Detroit, Michigan

SUBSTRATE

The building deck or substrate referred to is reinforced cast-in-place structural concrete.

Polymeric, latex, or other organic chemical-based admixtures or modifiers can coat the concrete particles and reduce the ability of the membrane to bond to the substrate. Admixtures should not be used in the concrete unless determined that they are acceptable for use with the membrane.

The underside of the concrete deck should not have an impermeable barrier. A metal liner or coating that forms a vapor barrier on the underside traps moisture in the concrete and destroys or prevents the adhesive bond of the membrane to the upper surface of the concrete.

The surface should be of sufficiently rough texture to provide a mechanical bond for the membrane, but not so rough as to preclude achieving continuity of the membrane of the specified thickness across the surface.

The concrete should be cured a minimum of 7 days and aged a minimum of 28 days, including curing time, before application of the liquid-applied membrane. Curing is accomplished chemically with moisture and should not be construed as drying. Liquid or chemical curing compounds should not be used unless approved by the manufacturer of the liquid-applied membrane as the material may interfere with the bond of the membrane to the structural slab.

MEMBRANE

The membrane should be applied under dry, frost-free conditions on the surface as well as throughout the depth of the concrete slab. Use manufacturer's requirements for the particular membrane.

TERMINATION ON WALLS

A liquid-applied membrane, because of its inherent adhesive properties, may be terminated flush on the wall without the use of a reglet. However, the use of a reglet in a concrete wall has the advantage of providing greater depth protection at the terminal.

TERMINATION AT DRAINS

Drains should be designed with a wide flange or base as an integral part. The drain base should be set flush with the structural slab.

TREATMENT AT REINFORCED JOINTS

One recommended treatment of reinforced concrete joints in the structural slab is to apply a double layer of membrane over the crack. This type of detail is quite limited and implicitly relies on the membrane's crack-bridging ability. An alternative approach is to prevent the membrane from adhering to the substrate for a finite width centered on the joint or crack by means of a properly designed compatible bond-breaker tape.

TREATMENT AT NONREINFORCED JOINTS

Since the joints are not held together with reinforcing steel, some movement, however slight, should be anticipated and provided for, since the liquid-applied membrane has limited ability to take movement.

TREATMENT AT EXPANSION JOINTS

Gaskets and flexible preformed sheets lend themselves better to absorbing large amounts of movement. Since such materials, when used at an expansion joint, must be joined to the liquid-applied membrane, the watershed concept should be used.

PROTECTION BOARD

The liquid-applied membrane should be protected from damage prior to and during the remainder of deck construction. The proper timing of the application of the board is important and the manufacturer's printed instructions should be followed.

Reference: ASTM C 898. Highlights of text and figures are reprinted with permission from ASTM Committee C-24 of the American Society for Testing and Materials.

Charles J. Parise, FAIA, FASTM; Smith, Hinchman & Grylls Associates, Inc.; Detroit, Michigan

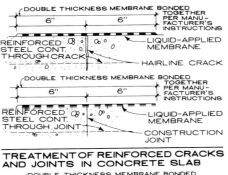

TREATMENT OF REINFORCED CRACKS AND JOINTS IN CONCRETE SLAB

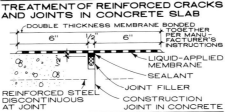

TREATMENT OF NONREINFORCED BUTTED JOINT IN CONCRETE SLAB

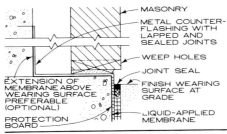

TERMINAL CONDITION WITH MASONRY ABOVE FINISH WEARING SURFACE AT GRADE

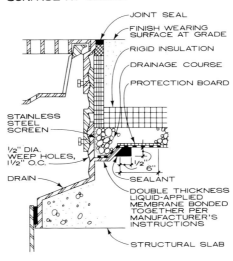

TERMINATION AT DRAIN

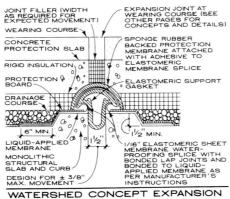

WATERSHED CONCEPT EXPANSION JOINT

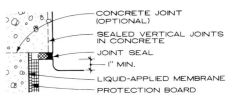

TERMINAL CONDITION ABOVE FINISH GRADE ON CONCRETE WALL

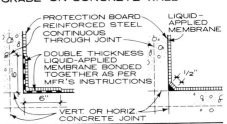

TURNUP DETAILS AT REINFORCED JOINT

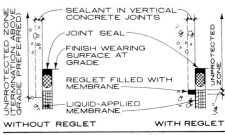

TERMINAL CONDITIONS ON CONCRETE WALL BELOW FINISH WEARING SURFACE AT GRADE

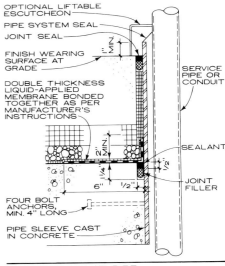

TERMINATION AT PIPE PENETRATIONS

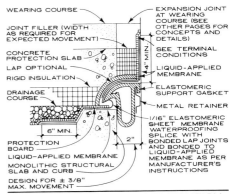

WATERSHED CONCEPT EXPANSION JOINT

WATERPROOFING   7

SUBSTRATE

The building deck or substrate referred to is reinforced cast-in-place structural concrete.

The structural slab should have a finish of sufficiently rough texture to provide a mechanical bond for the membrane, but not so rough to preclude achieving continuity of the membrane across the surface.

The concrete should be cured a minimum of 7 days and aged a minimum of 28 days, including curing time, before application of the bituminous membrane. Curing is accomplished chemically with moisture and should not be construed as drying. Liquid or chemical curing compounds should not be used unless approved by the manufacturer of the built-up bituminous membrane as the material may interfere with the bond of the membrane to the structural slab.

MEMBRANE

A built-up bituminous waterproofing membrane consists of components joined together and bonded to its substrate at the site. The major membrane components include primers, bitumens, reinforcements, and flashing materials.

Surfaces to receive waterproofing must be clean, dry, reasonably smooth, and free of dust, dirt, voids, cracks, laitance, or sharp projections before application of materials.

Concrete surfaces should be uniformly primed to enhance the bond between the membrane and the substrate, so as to inhibit lateral movement of water.

The number of plies of membrane reinforcement required is dependent upon the head of water and strength required by the design function of the wearing surface. Plaza deck membranes should be composed of not less than three plies. The composition of the membrane is normally of a "shingle" or "ply-on-ply" (phased) construction.

For application temperatures, follow the recommendations of the manufacturers of the membrane materials.

Over reinforced structural slab joints, one ply of 6-in.-wide membrane reinforcement should be applied before application of the bituminous membrane.

Nonreinforced joints should receive a bead of compatible sealant in a recessed joint before application of the membrane.

At expansion joints, gaskets and flexible preformed sheets are required inasmuch as bituminous membranes have little or no movement capability. Since such materials must be joined to the bituminous membrane, the watershed concept should be used.

Reinforce all intersections with walls and corners with two layers of woven fabric embedded in hot bitumen.

Flashing membranes should extend above the wearing surface and the highest possible water level and not less than 150 mm (6 in.) onto the deck membrane.

The flashing should extend over the wall dampproofing or membrane waterproofing not less than 100 mm (4 in.).

Drains must be provided with a wide metal flange or base and set slightly below the drainage level. Metal flashing for the drain, if required, and the clamping ring should be set on the membrane in bituminous plastic cement. The metal flashing should be stripped in with a minimum of two plies of membrane reinforcement and three applications of bituminous plastic cement.

Penetrations through the membrane such as conduits and pipes should be avoided whenever possible. Penetrations must be flashed to a height above the anticipated water table that may extend above the wearing surface.

The built-up bituminous membrane should be protected from damage. Protection board should be placed on the waterproofing membrane when the final mopping is being placed. It will then be adhered to the membrane.

Reference: ASTM C 981. Highlights of text and figures are reprinted with permission from ASTM Committee C-24 of the American Society for Testing and Materials.

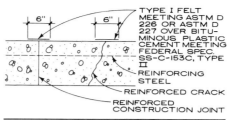
TREATMENT AT REINFORCED JOINTS

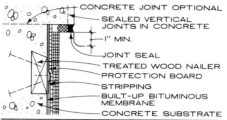
TERMINAL CONDITION ABOVE FINISH GRADE ON CONCRETE WALL

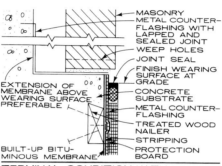
TERMINAL CONDITION WITH MASONRY ABOVE FINISH WEARING SURFACE AT GRADE

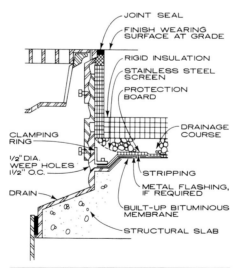
TERMINATION AT DRAIN

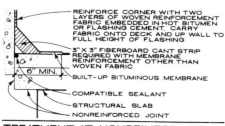
TREATMENT AT NONREINFORCED JOINTS

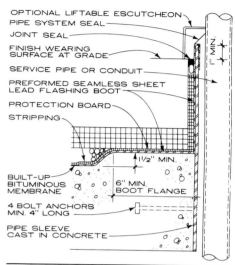
TERMINAL CONDITIONS ON CONCRETE WALL BELOW FINISH WEARING SURFACE AT GRADE

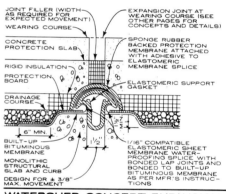
TERMINATION AT PIPE PENETRATIONS

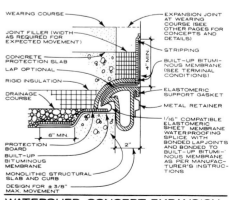
WATERSHED CONCEPT EXPANSION JOINT

WATERSHED CONCEPT EXPANSION JOINT

Charles J. Parise, FAIA, FASTM; Smith, Hinchman & Grylls Associates, Inc.; Detroit, Michigan

NOTES

1. Consult a soils engineer to determine soil types and groundwater levels and their effect on selection of drainage and waterproofing methods.

2. Most membranes require a stable, rigid, and level substrate for their application. Generally a subslab (mudslab) is used when the membrane is below the structural slab. When placed on the structural slab, a protective cover, such as another concrete slab, is required.

3. Bentonite panels may be placed over level, well-compacted fill. Cover them with polyethylene film to prevent premature expansion from wet concrete placed over them. Note: Bentonite forms an impermeable barrier when confined by foundation backfill or by lagging or sheet piling. The material may swell, exerting pressure on adjacent construction. Consult with structural engineer and manufacturer to assure appropriate use and structural adequacy.

4. Protect the water-resistant membrane during construction and backfill operations by covering it with a protection course of parging or solid sheets of protection boards.

5. Some drainage membranes or composites may also serve as the protection course.

6. Footing drains recommended when groundwater level may rise above top of floor slab or when subject to hydrostatic pressure after heavy rain. The drainage composite conveys water to the drain, thus reducing hydrostatic pressure.

7. Water-resistant membrane of interior face of foundation wall only recommended when outside is not accessible.

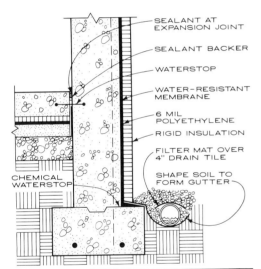

FOOTING WATER RESISTANCE—TYPE 1

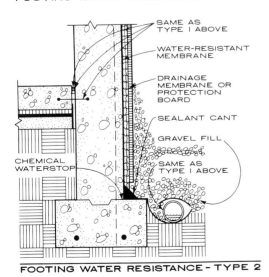

FOOTING WATER RESISTANCE—TYPE 2

FOUNDATION CONDITIONS

WATER RESISTANCE APPLICATIONS

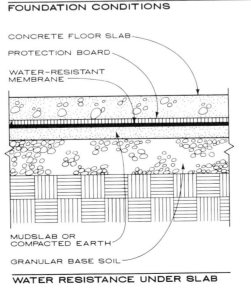

WATER RESISTANCE UNDER SLAB

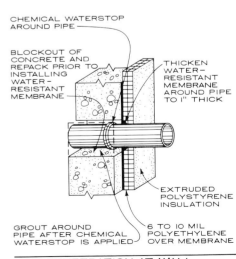

PIPE PENETRATION AT WALL

Krommenhoek/McKeown & Associates; San Diego, California

WATERPROOFING

RED CEDAR HANDSPLIT SHAKES

GRADE	LENGTH AND THICKNESS	DESCRIPTION
No. 1 handsplit and resawn	15" starter-finish 18 x ½" medium 18 x ¾" heavy 24 x ⅜" 24 x ½" medium 24 x ¾" heavy	These shakes have split faces and sawn backs. Cedar logs are first cut into desired lengths. Blanks or boards of proper thickness are split and then run diagonally through a bandsaw to produce two tapered shakes from each blank
No. 1 tapersplit	24 x ½"	Produced largely by hand, using a sharp bladed steel froe and a wooden mallet. The natural shinglelike taper is achieved by reversing the block, end-for-end, with each split
No. 1 straight	18 x ⅜" side wall 18 x ⅜" 24 x ⅜"	Produced in the same manner as tapersplit shakes except that by splitting from the same end of the block, the shakes acquire the same thickness throughout

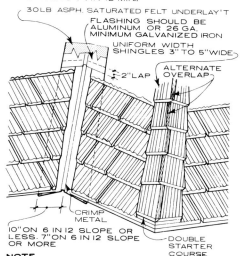

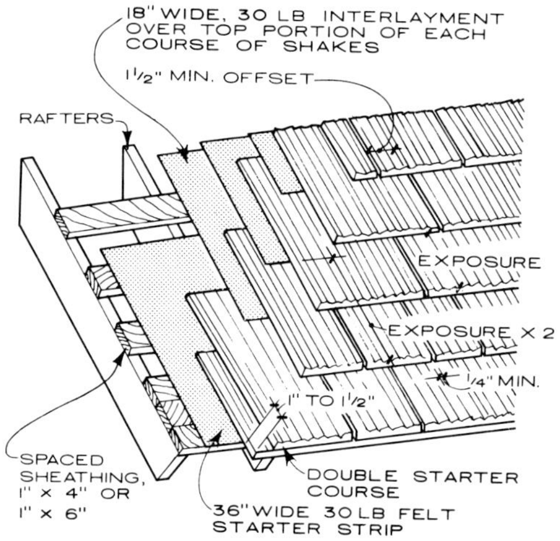

INSTALLATION OF SHAKES OVER SPACED SHEATHING (4 IN 12 MIN.)

RED CEDAR SHINGLES

	NO. 1 BLUE LABEL*			NO. 2 RED LABEL†			NO. 3 BLACK LABEL‡		
	MAXIMUM EXPOSURE RECOMMENDED FOR ROOFS								
ROOF PITCH	16"	18"	24"	16"	18"	24"	16"	18"	24"
3 in 12 to 4 in 12	3¾"	4¼"	5¾"	3½"	4"	5½"	3"	3½"	5"
4 in 12 and steeper	5"	5½"	7½"	4"	4½"	6½"	3½"	4"	5½"

*Premium Grade: 100% heartwood, 100% clear, 100% edge grain, for highest quality.
†Intermediate Grade: not less then 10" clear on 16" shingles, 11" clear on 18" shingles, 16" clear on 24" shingles. Flat grain and limited sapwood permitted.
‡Utility Grade: 6" clear on 16" and 18" shingles, 10" clear on 24" shingles. For economy applications.

UNDERLAYMENT AND SHEATHING

ROOFING TYPE	SHEATHING	UNDERLAYMENT	NORMAL SLOPE		LOW SLOPE	
Wood shakes and shingles	Solid or spaced	No. 30 asphalt saturated felt (interlayment)	4 in 12 and up	Underlayment starter course; interlayment over entire roof	3 in 12 to 4 in 12	Single layer underlayment over entire roof; interlayment over entire roof

NOTES
1. Shakes not recommended on slopes less than 4 in 12.
2. Breathing type building paper—such as deadening felt—may be applied over either type of sheating, although paper is not used in most applications.

NOTE
Copper flashing should not be used with red cedar.

VALLEY HIP AND RIDGE APPLICATION OF SHAKES AND SHINGLES

SHINGLES AND SHAKES USED FOR ROOFING

EXPOSURE FOR SHINGLES AND SHAKES USED FOR SIDING

SHINGLE LENGTH	EXPOSURE OF SHINGLES	
	SGL. COURSE	DBL. COURSE
16"	6" TO 7½"	8" TO 12"
18"	6" TO 8½"	9" TO 14"
24"	8" TO 11½"	12" TO 20"

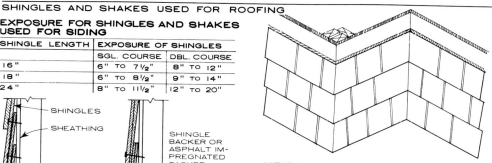

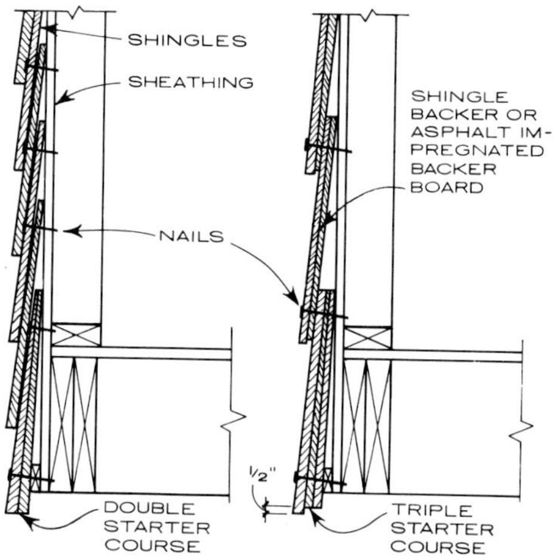

WOOD SHINGLES AND SHAKES FOR SIDING

SINGLE COURSING APPLICATION

DOUBLE COURSING APPLICATION

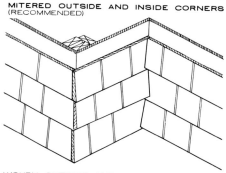

MITERED OUTSIDE AND INSIDE CORNERS (RECOMMENDED)

WOVEN OUTSIDE AND INSIDE CORNERS (MORE ECONOMICAL)

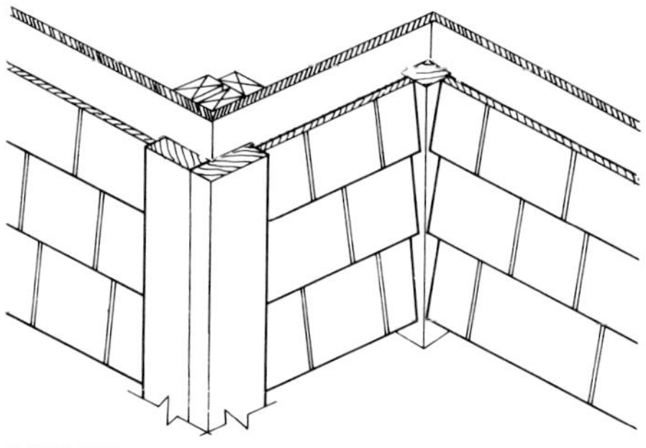

CORNER BOARDS OUTSIDE AND INSIDE CORNERS

NAILING (DEFORMED SHANK NON-FERROUS)
THICKNESS AND NAILS

16" long	5 butts = 2"	3d
18" long	5 butts = 2 ¼"	3d
24" long	4 butts = 2"	4d
25" to 27"	1 butt = ½"	5 or 6d
25" to 27"	1 butt = ⅝" to 1 ¼"	7 or 8d

SHEATHING NOTES

Sheathing may be strip-type, solid 1" x 6" diagonal type, plywood, fiberboard or gypsum. Horizontal wood nailing strips, 1" x 2", should be used over fiberboard and gypsum sheathing. Space strips equal to shingle exposure.

Developed by Holroyd and Gray, Architects; Charlotte, North Carolina; from data furnished by Robert M. Stafford, P.E.; Consulting Engineer; Charlotte, North Carolina

SHINGLES AND ROOFING TILES

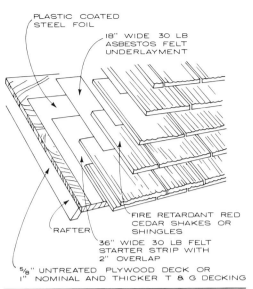

FIRE RATED ROOF CONSTRUCTION

NOTES

In treating shakes, fire retardant chemicals are pressure impregnated into the wood cells, and chemicals are then fixed in the wood to prevent leaching. Treatment does not alter appearance. Fire retardant red cedar shakes are classified as Class C by U.L. With the addition of the deck constructed of $5/8$ in. plywood with exterior glue or 1 in. nominal T&G boards, overlaid with a layer of approved asbestos felt lapped 2 in. on all joints and between each shake is an 18 in. wide strip of approved asbestos felt not exposed to the weather, Class B classification by U.L. is used. Decorative stains may be applied.

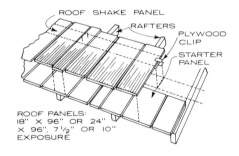

ROOF PANEL

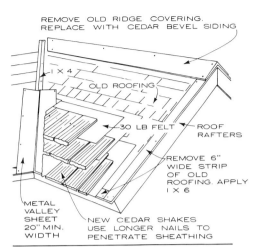

WOOD SHAKES APPLIED TO EXISTING ROOF

NOTES

Shakes can also be applied over any existing wall or roof. Brick or other masonry requires vertical frameboards and horizontal nailing strips.

Over stucco, horizontal nailing strips are attached directly to wall. Nails should penetrate shading or studs. Over wood, apply shakes directly just as if on new sheathing.

NOTES

Shakes and shingles plus sheathing go up in one operation. 8 ft roof panels have 16 individual handsplit shakes bonded to 6 in. wide $1/2$ in. plywood strip, which form a solid deck when the panels are nailed. A 4 to 12 in. or steeper roof pitch is recommended.

After application of starter panels, attach panels directly to rafters. Although designed to center on 16 or 24 in. spacing, they may meet between rafters. Use two 6d nails at each rafter.

NOMENCLATURE

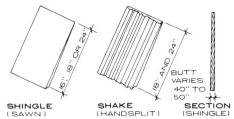

SHINGLE (SAWN)   SHAKE (HANDSPLIT)   SECTION (SHINGLE)

Species: Shingles and shakes are available in red cedar, redwood, and tidewater red cypress.

GENERAL NOTES

1. Wood shingles and shakes are manufactured from wood species that are naturally resistant to water, sunlight, rot, and hail. They are typically installed in the natural state, although stains, primers, and paint may be applied.
2. Nails must be hot dipped in zinc or aluminum. Nail heads should be driven flush with the surface of the shingle or shake, but never into the wood.
3. Underlayment and sheathing should be designed to augment the protection provided by the shingles or shakes, depending on roof pitch and climate. For instance, a low pitched roof in an area subject to wind driven snow should have solid sheathing and an additional underlayment.

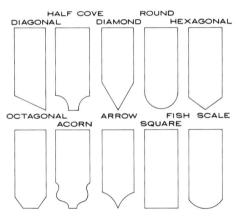

DIAGONAL   HALF COVE   ROUND   DIAMOND   HEXAGONAL

OCTAGONAL   ACORN   ARROW   SQUARE   FISH SCALE

NOTE

Fancy butt shingles are 5 in. wide and $7^1/2$ in. long. Custom produced to individual orders.

FANCY BUTT RED CEDAR SHINGLES

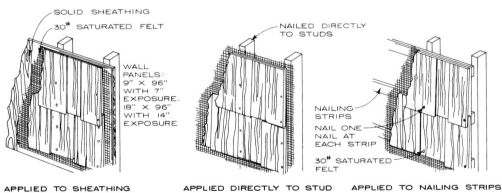

APPLIED TO SHEATHING   **APPLIED DIRECTLY TO STUD**   **APPLIED TO NAILING STRIPS**

NOTES

8 ft sidewall panels are of three-ply construction.

1. Surface layer of individual #1 grade shingles or shakes.
2. Cross binder core of plywood veneer.
3. Undercourse layer of shingle backing panels.

Panels can be applied to nailing strips or directly to studs where Code permits. Use 30 lb saturated fill lapped 3 in. vertically and horizontally. Stagger joints between panels. Matching sidewall or mansard style corners are available.

SIDEWALL PANELS

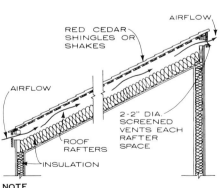

NOTE

A recommended ratio of total free area to adding area should not be less than 1:150 for adequate ventilation.

SECTION

VENTILATION OF ROOF

Robert E. Fehlberg, FAIA; CTA Architects Engineers; Billings, Montana

SCHEDULE OF UNDERLAYMENT

SLOPE	TYPE OF UNDERLAYMENT
Normal slope: 4 in 12 and up	Single layer of 15 lb asphalt saturated felt over entire roof
Low slope: 3 in 12 to 4 in 12	Two layers of 15 lb asphalt saturated felt over entire roof

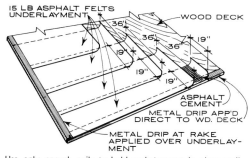

Use only enough nails to hold underlayment in place until shingles are laid.

APPLICATION OF UNDERLAYMENT ON LOW SLOPE ROOFS

NORMAL SLOPE

LOW SLOPE

EAVE FLASHING

EAVE FLASHING

Eave flashing is required wherever the January daily average temperature is 30°F or less or where there is a possibility of ice forming along the eaves.

NORMAL SLOPE—4 IN./FT OR OVER

A course of 90 lb mineral surfaced roll roofing or a course of 50 lb smooth roll roofing is installed to overhang the underlay and metal edge from 1/4 to 3/8 in. Extend up the roof far enough to cover a point at least 24 in. inside the interior wall line of the building. When the overhang requires flashing wider than 36 in., the horizontal lap joint is cemented and located on the roof deck extending beyond the exterior line of the building.

LOW SLOPE—3 TO 4 IN./FT

Cover the deck with two layers of 15# asphalt saturated felt. Begin with a 19 in. starter course laid along the eaves, followed by a 36 in. wide sheet laid even with the eaves and completely overlapping the starter course. The starter course is covered with asphalt cement. Thereafter, 36 in. sheets are laid in asphalt cement, each to overlap the preceding course 19 in., exposing 17 in. of the underlying sheet.

The plies are placed in asphalt cement to a point at least 36 in. inside the interior wall line of the building.

SCHEDULE OF SHINGLE TYPES (1)

DESCRIPTION	DESIGN	MATERIAL	U.L. RATING	WEIGHT	SIZE
Three-tab square butt		Fiberglass Organic felts	A C (4)	205–225 lb/sq 235–300 lb/sq	36″ x 12″
Two-tab square butt		Fiberglass Organic felts	A C (4)	260–325 lb/sq 300 lb/sq	36″ x 12″
Laminated overlay (2)		Fiberglass Organic felts	A C (3)	300 lb/sq 330–380 lb/sq	36″ x 14″
Random edge cut		Fiberglass Organic felts	A C (3)	225–260 lb/sq 250 lb/sq	36″ x 12″

NOTE: Exposure 5″, edge lap 2″.

NOTES

1. Exposure 5 in., edge lap 2 in., for all designs.
2. More than one thickness for varying surface texture.
3. Many rated as wind resistant.
4. All rated as wind resistant.

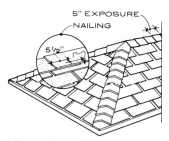

HIP AND RIDGE

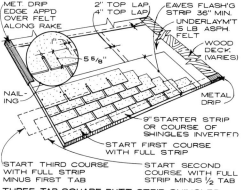

THREE TAB SQUARE BUTT STRIP SHINGLES

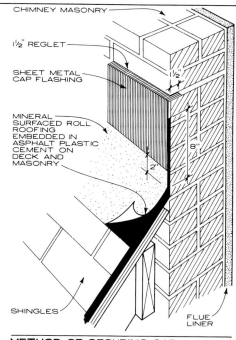

METHOD OF SECURING CAP FLASHING TO CHIMNEY MASONRY

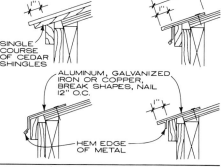

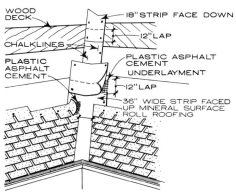

OPEN VALLEY

•Valley width should be 6″ wide at ridge and spread wider at the rate of 1/8″/foot downward to eave. Establish valley width using chalkline from ridge to cove.

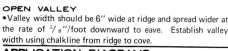

APPLICATION DIAGRAMS

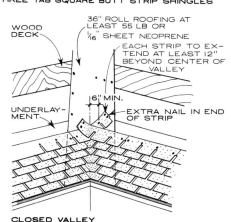

CLOSED VALLEY

NAIL TYPES

SMOOTH

ANNULAR THREADED

SCREW THREADED

DRIP EDGE DETAILS

DECK TYPE	NAIL LENGTH
1″ Wood sheathing	1 1/4″
3/8″ Plywood	7/8″
1/2″ Plywood	1″
Reroofing over asphalt shingles	1 3/4″

NAILING OF SHINGLES RECOMMENDATION

Robert E. Fehlberg, FAIA; CTA Architects Engineers; Billings, Montana

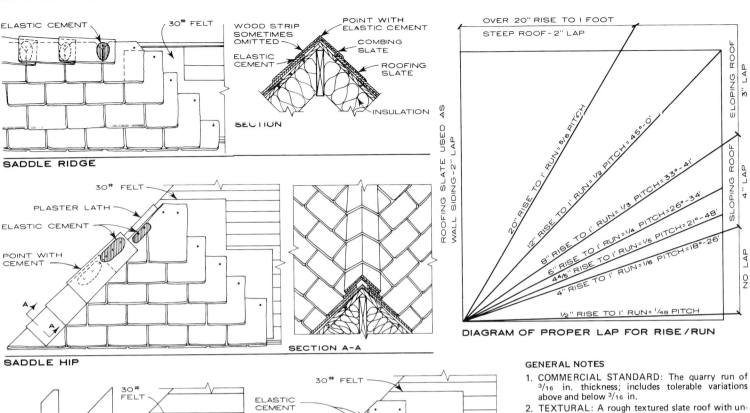

SADDLE RIDGE

ELASTIC CEMENT — 30# FELT — WOOD STRIP SOMETIMES OMITTED — POINT WITH ELASTIC CEMENT — COMBING SLATE — ELASTIC CEMENT — ROOFING SLATE — INSULATION — SECTION

SADDLE HIP

30# FELT — PLASTER LATH — ELASTIC CEMENT — POINT WITH CEMENT — A A

SECTION A-A

ROOFING SLATE USED AS WALL SIDING-2" LAP

OVER 20" RISE TO I FOOT STEEP ROOF - 2" LAP

ELOPING ROOF 3" LAP — SLOPING ROOF 4" LAP — NO LAP

20" RISE TO I' RUN = 5/6 PITCH
12" RISE TO I' RUN = 1/2 PITCH = 45°-0'
8" RISE TO I' RUN = 1/3 PITCH = 33°-4'
6" RISE TO I' RUN = 1/4 PITCH = 26°-34'
4 4/5" RISE TO I' RUN = 1/5 PITCH = 21°-48'
4" RISE TO I' RUN = 1/6 PITCH = 18°-26'
1/2" RISE TO I' RUN = 1/48 PITCH

DIAGRAM OF PROPER LAP FOR RISE / RUN

GENERAL NOTES

1. COMMERCIAL STANDARD: The quarry run of $3/16$ in. thickness; includes tolerable variations above and below $3/16$ in.

2. TEXTURAL: A rough textured slate roof with uneven butts; the slates vary in thickness and size, which is generally not true of slate more than $3/8$ in. thick.

3. GRADUATED: A textural roof of large slates; more variation in thickness, size, and color.

4. A SQUARE OF ROOFING SLATE: A number of slates of any size sufficient to cover 100 ft² with a 3 in. lap. Weight per square: $3/16$ in.—800 lb; $1/4$ in. —900 lb; $3/8$ in.—1100 lb; $1/2$ in.—1700 lb; $3/4$ in.— 2600 lb.

5. STANDARD NOMENCLATURE FOR SLATE COLOR: Black, blue black, mottled gray, purple, green, mottled purple and green, purple variegated, red; to be preceded by the word "Unfading" or "Weathering." Other colors and combinations are available.

6. PROPER JOINTING FOR PITCHED ROOFS: Requires a 3 in. minimum vertical overlap. Overlap varies with pitch; see graph above.

7. FELT: With Commercial Standard Slate use 30# saturated felt. With graduated roofs use 30# for $1/4$ in. slate and 45#, 50#, or 65# prepared roll roofing for heavier slate.

8. NAIL FASTENING: Use large head, slaters' hard copper wire nails, cut copper, cut brass, or cut yellow metal slating nails. Each slate punched with two nail holes. Use nails that are 1 in. longer than thickness of slate. Cover all exposed heads with elastic cement. In dry climates hot dip galvanized nails may be used.

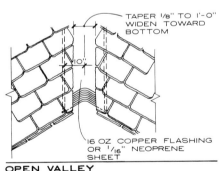

BOSTON HIP

30# FELT — A B — ELASTIC CEMENT — POINT WITH CEMENT — B A B A — B A

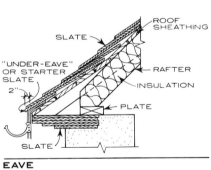

MITERED HIP

30# FELT — ELASTIC CEMENT — POINT WITH CEMENT

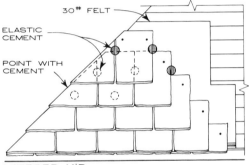

OPEN VALLEY

TAPER 1/8" TO 1'-0" WIDEN TOWARD BOTTOM — 10" — 16 OZ COPPER FLASHING OR 1/16" NEOPRENE SHEET

EAVE

ROOF SHEATHING — SLATE — RAFTER — "UNDER-EAVE" OR STARTER SLATE — 2" — INSULATION — PLATE — SLATE

GABLE RAKE

SLATE — SLATE — 1/2" TO 1"

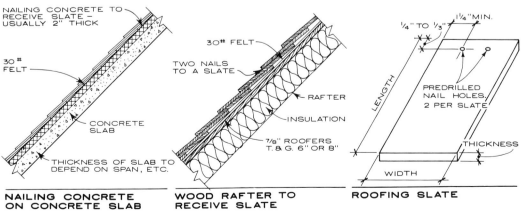

NAILING CONCRETE ON CONCRETE SLAB

NAILING CONCRETE TO RECEIVE SLATE - USUALLY 2" THICK — 30# FELT — CONCRETE SLAB — THICKNESS OF SLAB TO DEPEND ON SPAN, ETC.

WOOD RAFTER TO RECEIVE SLATE

30# FELT — TWO NAILS TO A SLATE — RAFTER — INSULATION — 7/8" ROOFERS T. & G. 6" OR 8"

ROOFING SLATE

1/4" TO 1/3" — 1/4" MIN. — LENGTH — PREDRILLED NAIL HOLES, 2 PER SLATE — THICKNESS — WIDTH

STANDARD SLATE DIMENSIONS*

LENGTH (IN.)	WIDTH (IN.)
10†	6, 7, 8, 9, 10
12†	6, 7, 8, 9, 10, 12
14†	7, 8, 9, 10, 11, 12
16	8, 9, 10, 11, 12, 14
18	9, 10, 11, 12, 13, 14
20	9, 10, 11, 12, 13, 14
22	10, 11, 12, 13, 14
24	11, 12, 13, 14, 16

*The slates are split in these thicknesses: $3/16$, $1/4$, $3/8$, $1/2$, $3/4$, 1, $1 1/4$, and $1 1/2$ in.
†$1/2$ in. and larger slates are not often used in these sizes. Random widths are usually used.

Domenic F. Valente, AIA, Architect & Planner; Medford, Massachusetts

SHINGLES AND ROOFING TILES 7

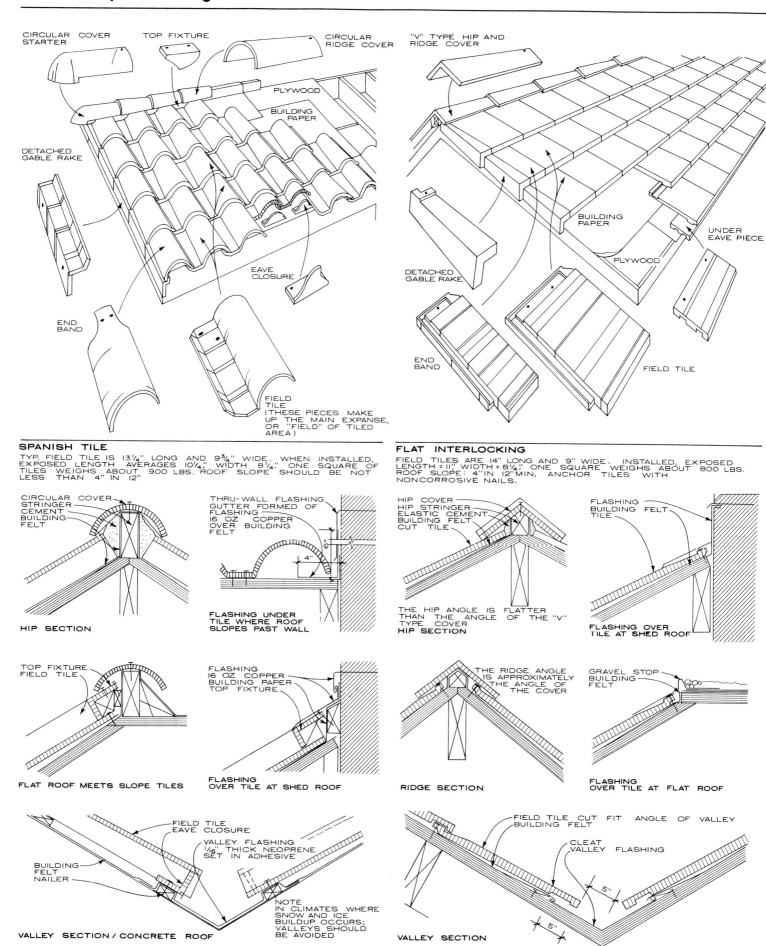

CIRCULAR COVER STARTER

TOP FIXTURE

CIRCULAR RIDGE COVER

"V" TYPE HIP AND RIDGE COVER

PLYWOOD

BUILDING PAPER

DETACHED GABLE RAKE

EAVE CLOSURE

END BAND

FIELD TILE (THESE PIECES MAKE UP THE MAIN EXPANSE, OR "FIELD" OF TILED AREA)

BUILDING PAPER

UNDER EAVE PIECE

PLYWOOD

DETACHED GABLE RAKE

END BAND

FIELD TILE

SPANISH TILE

TYP. FIELD TILE IS 13¼" LONG AND 9¾" WIDE. WHEN INSTALLED, EXPOSED LENGTH AVERAGES 10¼", WIDTH 8¼". ONE SQUARE OF TILES WEIGHS ABOUT 900 LBS. ROOF SLOPE SHOULD BE NOT LESS THAN 4" IN 12"

FLAT INTERLOCKING

FIELD TILES ARE 14" LONG AND 9" WIDE. INSTALLED, EXPOSED LENGTH = 11", WIDTH = 8¼". ONE SQUARE WEIGHS ABOUT 800 LBS. ROOF SLOPE: 4" IN 12" MIN. ANCHOR TILES WITH NONCORROSIVE NAILS.

CIRCULAR COVER STRINGER CEMENT BUILDING FELT

HIP SECTION

THRU-WALL FLASHING GUTTER FORMED OF FLASHING 16 OZ COPPER OVER BUILDING FELT

FLASHING UNDER TILE WHERE ROOF SLOPES PAST WALL

HIP COVER HIP STRINGER ELASTIC CEMENT BUILDING FELT CUT TILE

THE HIP ANGLE IS FLATTER THAN THE ANGLE OF THE "V" TYPE COVER
HIP SECTION

FLASHING BUILDING FELT TILE

FLASHING OVER TILE AT SHED ROOF

TOP FIXTURE FIELD TILE

FLAT ROOF MEETS SLOPE TILES

FLASHING 16 OZ COPPER BUILDING PAPER TOP FIXTURE

FLASHING OVER TILE AT SHED ROOF

THE RIDGE ANGLE IS APPROXIMATELY THE ANGLE OF THE COVER

RIDGE SECTION

GRAVEL STOP BUILDING FELT

FLASHING OVER TILE AT FLAT ROOF

FIELD TILE EAVE CLOSURE

VALLEY FLASHING 1/16" THICK NEOPRENE SET IN ADHESIVE

BUILDING FELT NAILER

NOTE IN CLIMATES WHERE SNOW AND ICE BUILDUP OCCURS; VALLEYS SHOULD BE AVOIDED

VALLEY SECTION / CONCRETE ROOF

FIELD TILE CUT FIT ANGLE OF VALLEY BUILDING FELT

CLEAT VALLEY FLASHING

5"

5"

VALLEY SECTION

Darrel Downing Rippeteau, Architect; Washington, D.C.

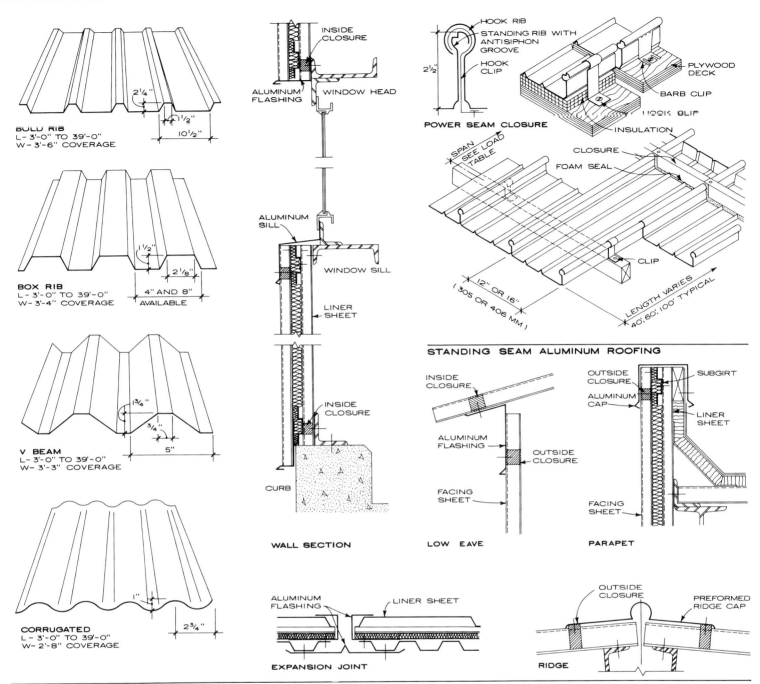

FORMED ALUMINUM ROOFING AND SIDING

NOTES

1. Endlaps for roofing and siding shall be at least 6 in. and fastened at every rib. Two fasteners may be required when designing for a negative (uplift) loading condition.
2. Minimum sidelaps shall be equal to one rib or corrugation and laid away from prevailing wind. Fasteners shall be spaced a maximum of 12 in. on center for all types of roofing and siding.
3. For roofing, fasteners shall pierce only the high corrugation. For siding, fasteners shall pierce either the high or low corrugation. Consult manufacturer for proper sheet metal fasteners and accessories.
4. Minimum slopes for sheet roofing are as follows:
   a. 1 in. depth corrugated—3 in 12.
   b. 1½ in. depth ribbed—2 in 12.
   c. 1¾ in. v-corrugated—2 in 12.
5. See page on Metal Walls for insulation details and fire rated wall assemblies.

John A. Schulte; Hellmuth, Obata & Kassabaum, Inc.; St. Louis, Missouri

MAXIMUM SPAN TABLE FOR FORMED ALUMINUM ROOFING AND SIDING (IN.)

DESIGN LOAD (PSF)	BOLD RIB		4" BOX RIB		V BEAM		CORRUGATED		STANDING SEAM	
	0.032 IN. THICK	0.040 IN. THICK	0.032 IN. THICK	0.040 IN. THICK	0.032 IN. THICK	0.040 IN. THICK	0.032 IN. THICK	0.040 IN. THICK	0.032 IN. THICK	0.040 IN. THICK
20	95	123	100	120	131	151	90	98	103	124
30	77	100	82	98	107	124	73	80	86	104
40	67	87	71	85	92	107	64	69	77	92
50	60	76	63	76	83	96	57	62	70	83

NOTE: Values are based on uniform positive (downward) and walking loads on single span only.

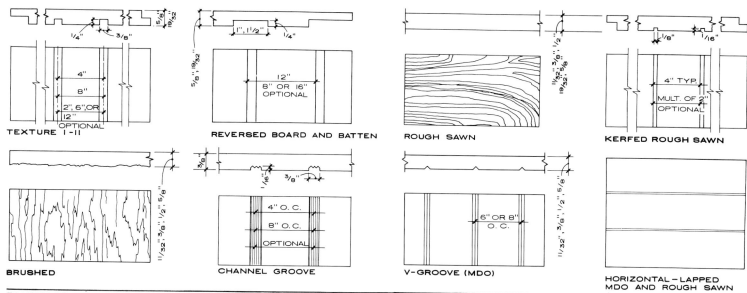

TEXTURE 1-11 — 1/4", 3/8", 5/8", 19/32", 4", 8", 2", 6", OR 12" OPTIONAL

REVERSED BOARD AND BATTEN — 1", 1 1/2", 1/4", 5/8", 19/32", 12", 8" OR 16" OPTIONAL

ROUGH SAWN — 11/32", 3/8", 1/2", 5/8", 19/32", 5/8"

KERFED ROUGH SAWN — 1/8", 1/16", 4" TYP., MULT. OF 2" OPTIONAL

BRUSHED — 11/32", 3/8", 1/2", 5/8"

CHANNEL GROOVE — 3/8", 1/16", 3/8", 4" O.C., 8" O.C. OPTIONAL

V-GROOVE (MDO) — 11/32", 3/8", 1/2", 5/8", 6" OR 8" O.C.

HORIZONTAL – LAPPED MDO AND ROUGH SAWN — 11/32", 3/8", 1/2", 5/8"

PLYWOOD SIDING 303 AND T1-11 (303 SPECIAL)

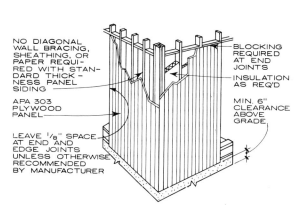

Medium density overlay (MDO) plywood lap siding: standard thickness is 3/8 in. in lengths to 16 ft on order; standard widths are 12 or 16 in.

NO DIAGONAL WALL BRACING, SHEATHING, OR PAPER REQUIRED WITH STANDARD THICKNESS PANEL SIDING

APA 303 PLYWOOD PANEL

LEAVE 1/8" SPACE AT END AND EDGE JOINTS UNLESS OTHERWISE RECOMMENDED BY MANUFACTURER

BLOCKING REQUIRED AT END JOINTS

INSULATION AS REQ'D

MIN. 6" CLEARANCE ABOVE GRADE

PANEL SIDING VERTICAL APPLICATION

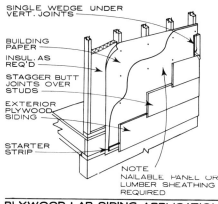

SINGLE WEDGE UNDER VERT. JOINTS

BUILDING PAPER

INSUL. AS REQ'D

STAGGER BUTT JOINTS OVER STUDS

EXTERIOR PLYWOOD SIDING

STARTER STRIP

NOTE NAILABLE PANEL OR LUMBER SHEATHING REQUIRED

PLYWOOD LAP SIDING APPLICATION

1/8" SPACING AT ALL PANEL EDGES

CAULK VERTICAL JOINTS OR BACK WITH BUILDING PAPER

2 X 4 BLOCKING AT HORIZONTAL JOINTS

6" MIN. CLEAR ABOVE GRADE

MAY USE BATTENS TO CONCEAL BUTT JOINTS

PANEL SIDING HORIZONTAL

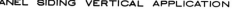

CAULK OR BACK WITH BUILDING PAPER

BUTT AND CAULK — 1/8" WIDE

VERTICAL BATTEN

SHIPLAP

VERTICAL JOINTS

APA STURD-I-WALL CONSTRUCTION RECOMMENDATIONS (SIDING DIRECT TO STUDS AND OVER NONSTRUCTURAL SHEATHING)

PLYWOOD PANEL SIDING DESCRIPTION (ALL SPECIES GROUPS)	NOMINAL THICKNESS (IN.)	MAX. STUD SPACING (IN.)		NAIL SIZE (USE NONSTAINING BOX, SIDING, OR CASING NAILS (1)(2)	NAIL SPACING (IN.)	
		FACE GRAIN VERTICAL	FACE GRAIN HORIZONTAL		PANEL EDGES	INTERMEDIATE
APA MDO EXT	11/32 and 3/8	16	24	6d for panels 1/2" thick or less 8d for thicker panels	6(4)	12
	1/2 and thicker	24	24			
APA 303 siding—16 o.c. EXT (including T1-11)	11/32 and thicker	16	24			
APA 303 siding— 24 o.c. EXT	15/32 and thicker (3)	24	24			

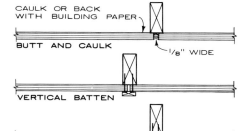

NOTES

1. If siding is applied over sheathing thicker than 1/2 in. use next regular nail size. Use nonstaining box nails for siding installed over foam insulation sheathing.

2. Hot-dipped or hot-tumbled galvanized steel nails are recommended for most siding applications. For best performance, stainless steel nails or aluminum nails should be considered. APA tests also show that electrically or mechanically galvanized steel nails appear satisfactory when plating meets or exceeds thickness requirements of ASTM A641 Class 2 coatings and is further protected by yellow chromate coating.

3. Only panels 15/32 in. and thicker which have certain groove depths and spacings qualify for 24 in. o.c. Span Rating.

4. For braced wall section with 11/32 in. or 3/8 in. siding applied horizontally over studs 24 in. o.c.

MINIMUM BENDING RADII FOR PLYWOOD PANELS PANEL THICKNESS (IN.)	1/4	3/8	1/2	5/8	3/4
Across grain (ft)	2	3	6	8	12
Parallel to grain (ft)	5	8	12	16	20

NOTES

The types of plywood recommended for exterior siding are: A.P.A. grade trademarked medium density overlay (MDO), Type 303 siding or Texture 1-11 (T1-11 special 303 siding). T1-11 plywood siding is manufactured with 3/8 in. wide parallel grooves and ship-lapped edges. MDO is recommended for paint finishes and is available in variety of surfaces. 303 plywood panels are also available in a wide variety of surfaces. The most common A.P.A. plywood siding panel dimensions are 4 x 8 ft but the panels are also available in 9 and 10 ft lengths, lap siding to 16 ft.

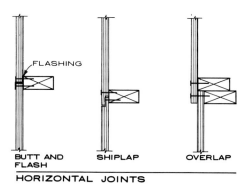

FLASHING

BUTT AND FLASH

SHIPLAP

OVERLAP

HORIZONTAL JOINTS

John D. Bloodgood, Architect, P.C.; Des Moines, Iowa
American Plywood Association

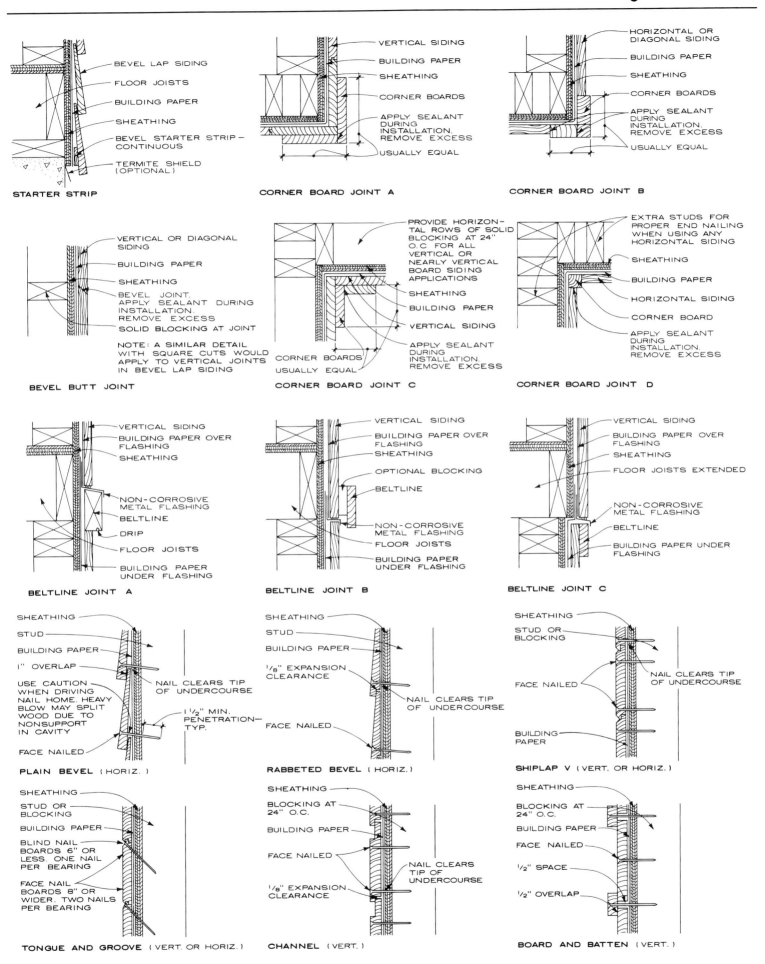

STARTER STRIP
- BEVEL LAP SIDING
- FLOOR JOISTS
- BUILDING PAPER
- SHEATHING
- BEVEL STARTER STRIP—CONTINUOUS
- TERMITE SHIELD (OPTIONAL)

CORNER BOARD JOINT A
- VERTICAL SIDING
- BUILDING PAPER
- SHEATHING
- CORNER BOARDS
- APPLY SEALANT DURING INSTALLATION. REMOVE EXCESS
- USUALLY EQUAL

CORNER BOARD JOINT B
- HORIZONTAL OR DIAGONAL SIDING
- BUILDING PAPER
- SHEATHING
- CORNER BOARDS
- APPLY SEALANT DURING INSTALLATION. REMOVE EXCESS
- USUALLY EQUAL

BEVEL BUTT JOINT
- VERTICAL OR DIAGONAL SIDING
- BUILDING PAPER
- SHEATHING
- BEVEL JOINT. APPLY SEALANT DURING INSTALLATION. REMOVE EXCESS
- SOLID BLOCKING AT JOINT
- NOTE: A SIMILAR DETAIL WITH SQUARE CUTS WOULD APPLY TO VERTICAL JOINTS IN BEVEL LAP SIDING

CORNER BOARD JOINT C
- PROVIDE HORIZONTAL ROWS OF SOLID BLOCKING AT 24" O.C FOR ALL VERTICAL OR NEARLY VERTICAL BOARD SIDING APPLICATIONS
- SHEATHING
- BUILDING PAPER
- VERTICAL SIDING
- APPLY SEALANT DURING INSTALLATION. REMOVE EXCESS
- CORNER BOARDS USUALLY EQUAL

CORNER BOARD JOINT D
- EXTRA STUDS FOR PROPER END NAILING WHEN USING ANY HORIZONTAL SIDING
- SHEATHING
- BUILDING PAPER
- HORIZONTAL SIDING
- CORNER BOARD
- APPLY SEALANT DURING INSTALLATION. REMOVE EXCESS

BELTLINE JOINT A
- VERTICAL SIDING
- BUILDING PAPER OVER FLASHING
- SHEATHING
- NON-CORROSIVE METAL FLASHING
- BELTLINE
- DRIP
- FLOOR JOISTS
- BUILDING PAPER UNDER FLASHING

BELTLINE JOINT B
- VERTICAL SIDING
- BUILDING PAPER OVER FLASHING
- SHEATHING
- OPTIONAL BLOCKING
- BELTLINE
- NON-CORROSIVE METAL FLASHING
- FLOOR JOISTS
- BUILDING PAPER UNDER FLASHING

BELTLINE JOINT C
- VERTICAL SIDING
- BUILDING PAPER OVER FLASHING
- SHEATHING
- FLOOR JOISTS EXTENDED
- NON-CORROSIVE METAL FLASHING
- BELTLINE
- BUILDING PAPER UNDER FLASHING

PLAIN BEVEL (HORIZ.)
- SHEATHING
- STUD
- BUILDING PAPER
- 1" OVERLAP
- USE CAUTION WHEN DRIVING NAIL HOME. HEAVY BLOW MAY SPLIT WOOD DUE TO NONSUPPORT IN CAVITY
- FACE NAILED
- NAIL CLEARS TIP OF UNDERCOURSE
- 1 1/2" MIN. PENETRATION—TYP.

RABBETED BEVEL (HORIZ.)
- SHEATHING
- STUD
- BUILDING PAPER
- 1/8" EXPANSION CLEARANCE
- NAIL CLEARS TIP OF UNDERCOURSE
- FACE NAILED

SHIPLAP V (VERT. OR HORIZ.)
- SHEATHING
- STUD OR BLOCKING
- FACE NAILED
- NAIL CLEARS TIP OF UNDERCOURSE
- BUILDING PAPER

TONGUE AND GROOVE (VERT. OR HORIZ.)
- SHEATHING
- STUD OR BLOCKING
- BUILDING PAPER
- BLIND NAIL BOARDS 6" OR LESS. ONE NAIL PER BEARING
- FACE NAIL BOARDS 8" OR WIDER. TWO NAILS PER BEARING

CHANNEL (VERT.)
- SHEATHING
- BLOCKING AT 24" O.C.
- BUILDING PAPER
- FACE NAILED
- 1/8" EXPANSION CLEARANCE
- NAIL CLEARS TIP OF UNDERCOURSE

BOARD AND BATTEN (VERT.)
- SHEATHING
- BLOCKING AT 24" O.C.
- BUILDING PAPER
- FACE NAILED
- 1/2" SPACE
- 1/2" OVERLAP

Jerry Graham; CTA Architects Engineers; Billings, Montana

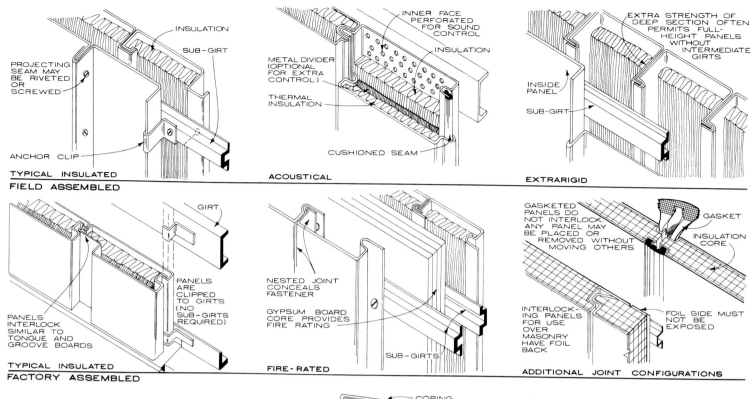

TYPICAL INSULATED FIELD ASSEMBLED

INSULATION
SUB-GIRT
PROJECTING SEAM MAY BE RIVETED OR SCREWED
ANCHOR CLIP

ACOUSTICAL

INNER FACE PERFORATED FOR SOUND CONTROL
INSULATION
METAL DIVIDER (OPTIONAL FOR EXTRA CONTROL)
THERMAL INSULATION
CUSHIONED SEAM

EXTRARIGID

EXTRA STRENGTH OF DEEP SECTION OFTEN PERMITS FULL-HEIGHT PANELS WITHOUT INTERMEDIATE GIRTS
INSIDE PANEL
SUB-GIRT

TYPICAL INSULATED FACTORY ASSEMBLED

GIRT
PANELS ARE CLIPPED TO GIRTS (NO SUB-GIRTS REQUIRED)
PANELS INTERLOCK SIMILAR TO TONGUE AND GROOVE BOARDS

FIRE-RATED

NESTED JOINT CONCEALS FASTENER
GYPSUM BOARD CORE PROVIDES FIRE RATING
SUB-GIRTS

ADDITIONAL JOINT CONFIGURATIONS

GASKETED PANELS DO NOT INTERLOCK; ANY PANEL MAY BE PLACED OR REMOVED WITHOUT MOVING OTHERS
GASKET
INSULATION CORE
INTERLOCKING PANELS FOR USE OVER MASONRY HAVE FOIL BACK
FOIL SIDE MUST NOT BE EXPOSED

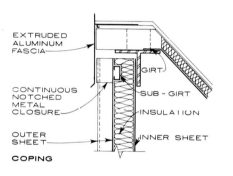

COPING

EXTRUDED ALUMINUM FASCIA
GIRT
CONTINUOUS NOTCHED METAL CLOSURE
SUB-GIRT
INSULATION
OUTER SHEET
INNER SHEET

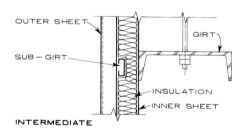

INTERMEDIATE

OUTER SHEET
GIRT
SUB-GIRT
INSULATION
INNER SHEET

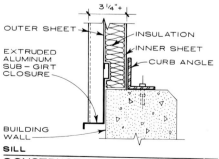

SILL

3 1/4"+
OUTER SHEET
INSULATION
INNER SHEET
EXTRUDED ALUMINUM SUB-GIRT CLOSURE
CURB ANGLE
BUILDING WALL

CONSTRUCTION DETAILS OF FIELD-ASSEMBLED INSULATED METAL WALLS

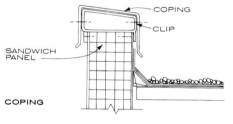

COPING

COPING
CLIP
SANDWICH PANEL

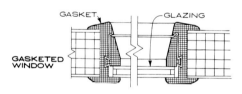

GASKETED WINDOW

GASKET
GLAZING

PREDESIGNED DETAILS – MAY BE HAD IN COMPLETE PACKAGE WITH CERTAIN FACTORY ASSEMBLED SYSTEMS

NOTES

Types of panels shown are representative of plain basic designs with an assortment of connection details. A vast array of folded, ribbed, and grooved sheet configurations is available.

Typical applied finishes available for outer sheets are acrylics, vinyls, alkyds, fluoropolymers, porcelain enamel, and, on aluminum only, various anodized finishes. Typical available length of sheets is 40 ft. Span and wind load must be considered in the selection of panel components and spacing of girts.

Panels typically can span from 9 ft 6 in. to 26 ft clear, more if placed in multispan arrangement. Face panel configuration and wind load value are determining factors.

Consult manufacturers for verification of these data and for thermal and acoustical ratings of panels designed for these purposes.

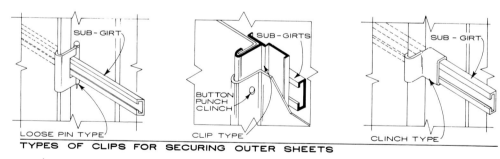

SUB-GIRT
SUB-GIRTS
SUB-GIRT
BUTTON PUNCH CLINCH
LOOSE PIN TYPE
CLIP TYPE
CLINCH TYPE

TYPES OF CLIPS FOR SECURING OUTER SHEETS

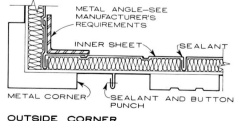

OUTSIDE CORNER

METAL ANGLE—SEE MANUFACTURER'S REQUIREMENTS
INNER SHEET
SEALANT
METAL CORNER
SEALANT AND BUTTON PUNCH

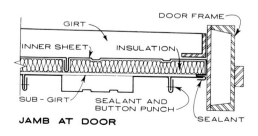

JAMB AT DOOR

GIRT
DOOR FRAME
INNER SHEET
INSULATION
SUB-GIRT
SEALANT AND BUTTON PUNCH
SEALANT

FACING MATERIALS AVAILABLE

1. Aluminum.
2. Aluminized steel.
3. Galvanized steel.

FINISHES AVAILABLE

1. Anodized aluminum.
2. 50% silicone—modified polyester baked enamel paint.
3. Fluorocarbon baked enamel paint.
4. Porcelain enamel on aluminized steel.

INSULATING VALUES	MAX. U FACTOR
2 in. urethane core	0.065
3 in. honeycomb core	0.41
2 in. honeycomb with fill	0.107

NOTE

Some codes restrict the use of the urethane core panel. The honeycomb panels are more acceptable.

Urethane panel = 25 flame spread rating
Honeycomb panel = 15 flame spread rating
See manufacturer for span tables.

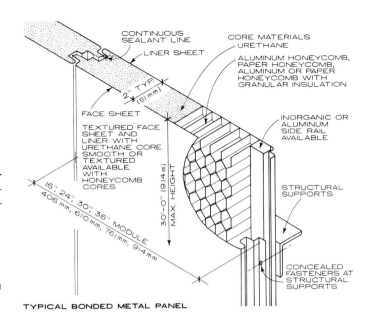

TYPICAL BONDED METAL PANEL

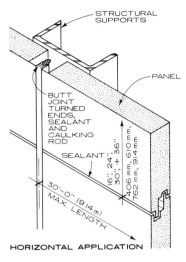

HORIZONTAL APPLICATION

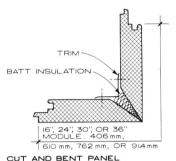

CUT AND BENT PANEL

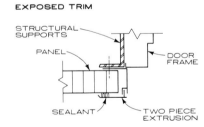

EXPOSED TRIM

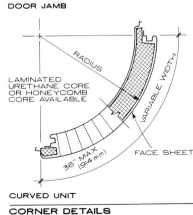

DOOR JAMB

CORNER DETAILS

CURVED UNIT

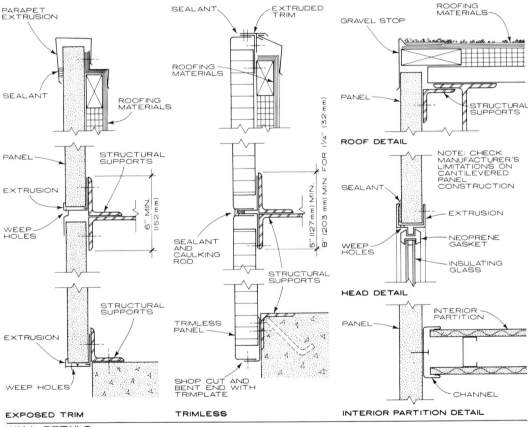

ROOF DETAIL

HEAD DETAIL

INTERIOR PARTITION DETAIL

EXPOSED TRIM — **TRIMLESS**

WALL DETAILS

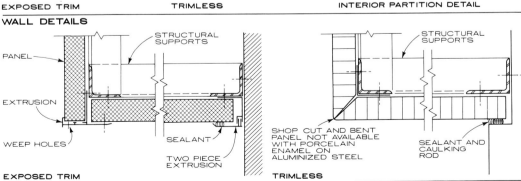

EXPOSED TRIM — **TRIMLESS**

SOFFIT DETAILS

John A. Schulte; Hellmuth, Obata, & Kassabaum, Inc.; St. Louis, Missouri

PREFORMED ROOFING AND CLADDING/SIDING 7

NOTE

Polyvinyl chloride (PVC) is a semirigid material that requires the addition of plasticizers to fabricate a flexible roofing membrane. PVC exhibits excellent weldability for making lap joints or attaching to PVC clad metal flashing.

TYPES OF MEMBRANE

Unreinforced sheet
Sheet reinforced with fiberglass or polyester

METHOD OF MANUFACTURE

Calendering
Spread coating
Extruding

GENERAL

Single ply roofing systems are also referred to as flexible sheet roofing systems. Consult manufacturers for specific requirements regarding materials selection and installation requirements. Compatibility of materials comprising total roofing system is essential.

MATERIAL PROPERTIES

Thickness: Typically 48 and 60 mil; 45 mil minimum

Color: Typically gray; other colors available

Contaminants to avoid: Bitumen, oils, animal fats, and coal tar pitch. See manufacturer's chemical resistance list.

Minimum standards: ASTM has developed standard test methods to evaluate the materials properties of PVC roof membranes. These test results form a useful basis for comparing various PVC membranes. ASTM's standard specification establishes minimum performance criteria for tensile strength, elongation, tear resistance, heat aging, weathering, and water absorption.

INSTALLATION

General guidelines: It is recommended that all roofing materials be installed on roofs with positive slope to drainage. Check with manufacturers regarding their specific requirements.

Lap joining methods: Hot air or solvent weld

Flashing methods: Membrane or PVC coated metal

Types of preformed accessories available: Inside and outside corners; pipe stacks

Weather restrictions during installation: 0°–120°F temperature range. Substrates and welding/bonding surfaces must be dry.

Method of repair: Clean surface; hot air or solvent weld of PVC patch

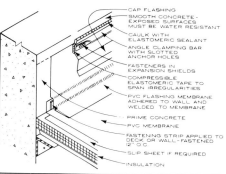

TYPICAL PARAPET FLASHING

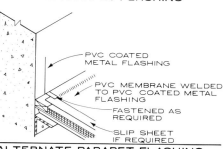

ALTERNATE PARAPET FLASHING

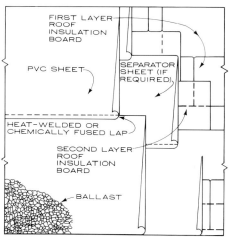

Membrane sheets are laid loose over roof insulation (also laid loose) and secured at the perimeter and around penetrations only. The membrane is then covered with a ballast of river-washed stones (typically 10 lb/sq ft) or appropriate pavers.

This system works efficiently with insulation approved by the membrane manufacturer and on roofs with a slope not exceeding 2 in 12.

LOOSE-LAID BALLASTED SHEETS

Membrane sheets are laid loose over a sloped roof deck and with the insulation on top of it. When the roof deck is dead level, tapered roof insulation is either loose laid or mechanically attached under the membrane to achieve positive slope to drainage. In either instance, a layer of insulation is placed over the membrane and held in place by one of two methods: Either a loose fabric is laid over the insulation, with a minimum of 10 lb/sq ft of ballast laid over the fabric, or insulation with an integrally bonded concrete facing is used in place of the fabric and loose ballast. Membrane manufacturers should be consulted for their approved insulation list. In this roofing system, the membrane is protected from year-round temperature extremes, direct exposure to weather, and damage from other sources. The heat gain or loss is just the same as if the insulation were installed under the membrane. Since the waterproofing membrane is placed on the warm side of the insulation, it functions as a vapor retarder. For high humidity conditions with a dead level roof deck utilizing tapered insulation, a separate vapor barrier should be placed directly beneath the tapered insulation to prevent condensation.

PROTECTED MEMBRANE SHEET

CTA Architects Engineers; Billings, Montana

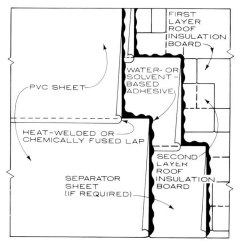

For system with no slope limitations which secures membrane to substrate with bonding adhesive and by mechanically fastening the membrane to perimeter and penetrations. System is appropriate for contoured roofs and roofs that cannot withstand weight of ballasted system.

Membrane can be directly applied to deck surface of concrete, wood surfaces, or be applied to compatible insulation that is mechanically fastened to the deck.

FULLY ADHERED SHEETS

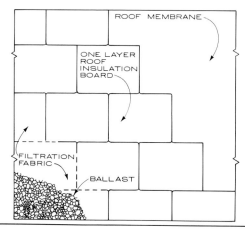

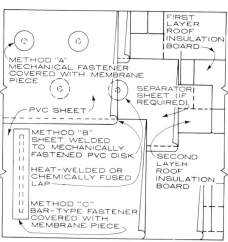

A mechanically anchored roof system is appropriate for roofs that cannot carry the additional load of ballasted roof systems. Systems are available with fasteners that penetrate the membrane or that require no membrane penetration.

The membrane is anchored to the roof using metal bars or individual clips, and it may be installed over concrete, wood, metal, or compatible insulation.

MECHANICALLY ATTACHED SHEETS

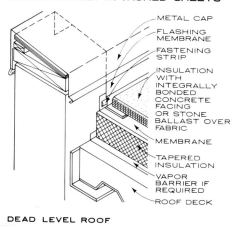

DEAD LEVEL ROOF

NOTES

There are three generic installation methods for EPDM roofing:

1. Fully Adhered: Membrane roofing is rolled onto the substrate and allowed to relax. Underside is then fully coated with bonding adhesive. After both surfaces are tacky, the membrane is pressed onto the substrate with a push broom. Adjoining sheets must overlap at least 3 in., with laps spliced and cemented. Membrane is mechanically secured at perimeter and penetration edges. Flashing protects all edges, openings, and penetrations.

2. Loose Laid: Roofing in this application is laid loose over the substrate, either deck or rigid insulation, and ballasted in place. It is positioned without stretching, allowed to attain its natural shape, and adjacent sheets spliced with adjoining sheets overlapping at least 3 in. Sheets are cemented and rolled together to seal seams. The membrane is mechanically secured at perimeter and penetration edges, and flashing is installed. For ballast, a sufficient amount of river-washed gravel is laid over the membrane to provide 10 lb/sq ft of weight. As an alternate, a precast roof paver system is applied to hold the roofing membrane.

3. Mechanically Fastened: Membrane roof is directly attached to the roof deck with mechanical fasteners. The substrate is anchored to the roof deck, and the fasteners either go through both membrane and insulation or only go through the insulation and deck, with the membrane held down by retainer and cap over the base. Sealant protects against moisture.

Many EPDM membranes are field surfaced to improve resistance to weathering and fire, or to enhance appearance.

GENERAL NOTES

EPDM elastomeric roofing is synthesized from ethylene, propylene, and a small amount of diene monomer. Manufactured sheets range in thickness from 30 to 60 mils.

Advantages: EPDM roofing exhibits a high degree of resistance to ozone, ultraviolet, extreme temperature and other elements, and degradation from abrasion. It is resilient, strong, elastic, and less prone to cracking and tearing when compared to other forms of membrane roofing.

Disadvantages: Application methods, specific formulas and configurations for adhesives, fasteners, and coatings are unique with each system manufactured. Materials, design, and appropriate use vary widely. Close supervision and regular inspection by manufacturer are a requirement. Labor cost and time allotted for installation may vary.

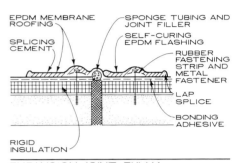

INSULATED ROOF MEMBRANE APPLICATION

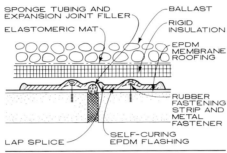

EXPANSION JOINT: INSULATED ROOF MEMBRANE BALLASTED

EXPANSION JOINT: FULLY ADHERED ROOF MEMBRANE

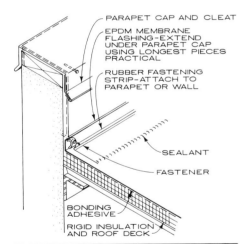

FULLY ADHERED ROOF AT PARAPET OR WALL

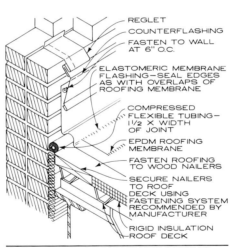

ROOF EDGE AT NONSUPPORTING WALL

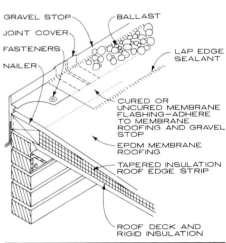

LIGHT METAL ROOF EDGE

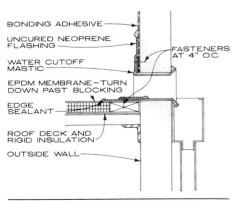

FULLY ADHERED ROOF SCUPPER

Catherine A. Broad; Washington, D.C.

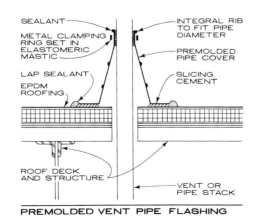

PREMOLDED VENT PIPE FLASHING

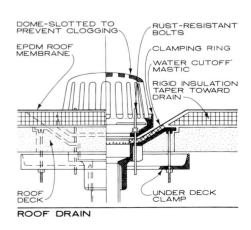

ROOF DRAIN

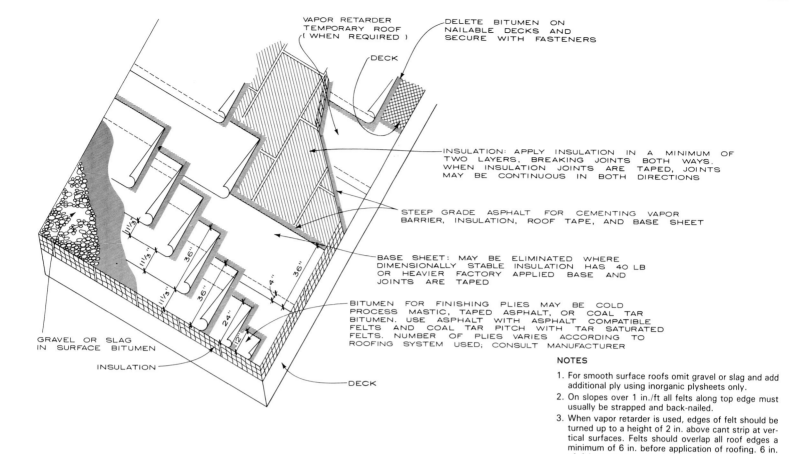

VAPOR RETARDER
TEMPORARY ROOF
(WHEN REQUIRED)

DECK

DELETE BITUMEN ON
NAILABLE DECKS AND
SECURE WITH FASTENERS

INSULATION: APPLY INSULATION IN A MINIMUM OF
TWO LAYERS, BREAKING JOINTS BOTH WAYS.
WHEN INSULATION JOINTS ARE TAPED, JOINTS
MAY BE CONTINUOUS IN BOTH DIRECTIONS

STEEP GRADE ASPHALT FOR CEMENTING VAPOR
BARRIER, INSULATION, ROOF TAPE, AND BASE SHEET

BASE SHEET: MAY BE ELIMINATED WHERE
DIMENSIONALLY STABLE INSULATION HAS 40 LB
OR HEAVIER FACTORY APPLIED BASE AND
JOINTS ARE TAPED

BITUMEN FOR FINISHING PLIES MAY BE COLD
PROCESS MASTIC, TAPED ASPHALT, OR COAL TAR
BITUMEN. USE ASPHALT WITH ASPHALT COMPATIBLE
FELTS AND COAL TAR PITCH WITH TAR SATURATED
FELTS. NUMBER OF PLIES VARIES ACCORDING TO
ROOFING SYSTEM USED; CONSULT MANUFACTURER

GRAVEL OR SLAG
IN SURFACE BITUMEN

INSULATION

DECK

NOTES

1. For smooth surface roofs omit gravel or slag and add additional ply using inorganic plysheets only.
2. On slopes over 1 in./ft all felts along top edge must usually be strapped and back-nailed.
3. When vapor retarder is used, edges of felt should be turned up to a height of 2 in. above cant strip at vertical surfaces. Felts should overlap all roof edges a minimum of 6 in. before application of roofing. 6 in. of felt must be re-turned over the insulation and mopped solidly.

20 YEAR TYPE BUILT-UP ROOF OVER INSULATION

NOTES

1. Over nonnailable deck or insulation omit rosin paper and cement with asphalt. Nailing strips must be provided.
2. Minimum slope for organic felt: ½ in./ft.
3. Minimum slope for fiberglass felt: 0 in./ft.
4. Consult manufacturer for spacing of nails for particular roofing system.

SCHEDULE OF FELT OVERLAP (INCHES)

Organic base sheet	4
Fiberglass or base sheet	2
2-ply felts/plysheets	19
3-ply felts/plysheets	24²/₃
4-ply felts/plysheets	27½
Fiberglass mineral	3 if selvage granulated
Surface cap sheet	2 if selvage granulated

STAGGER NAILS AT 12" O.C.

NAILABLE DECK

MINERAL SURFACE
ROOFING. 2" SIDE LAPS IF
SELVAGE IS UNGRANULATED;
3" SIDE LAPS IF SELVAGE
IS GRANULATED

STEEP GRADE ASPHALT

ROSIN PAPER
(OVER WOOD,
EXCEPT PLYWOOD)

ASPHALT BETWEEN
PLIES OF 15 LB FELT.
ASPHALT TYPE (I, II,
III, OR IV)
DETERMINED BY
ROOF SLOPE

MINERAL SURFACE BUILT-UP ROOF

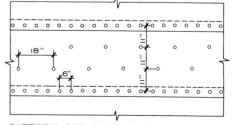

PATTERN FOR NAILING BASE
SHEET OR VAPOR RETARDER OVER
NAILABLE DECK

Kent Wong; Hewlett, Jamison, Atkinson & Luey; Portland, Oregon
Developed by Angelo J. Forlidas, AIA; Charlotte, North Carolina; from data furnished by Robert M. Stafford, P.E., Consulting Engineer; Charlotte, North Carolina

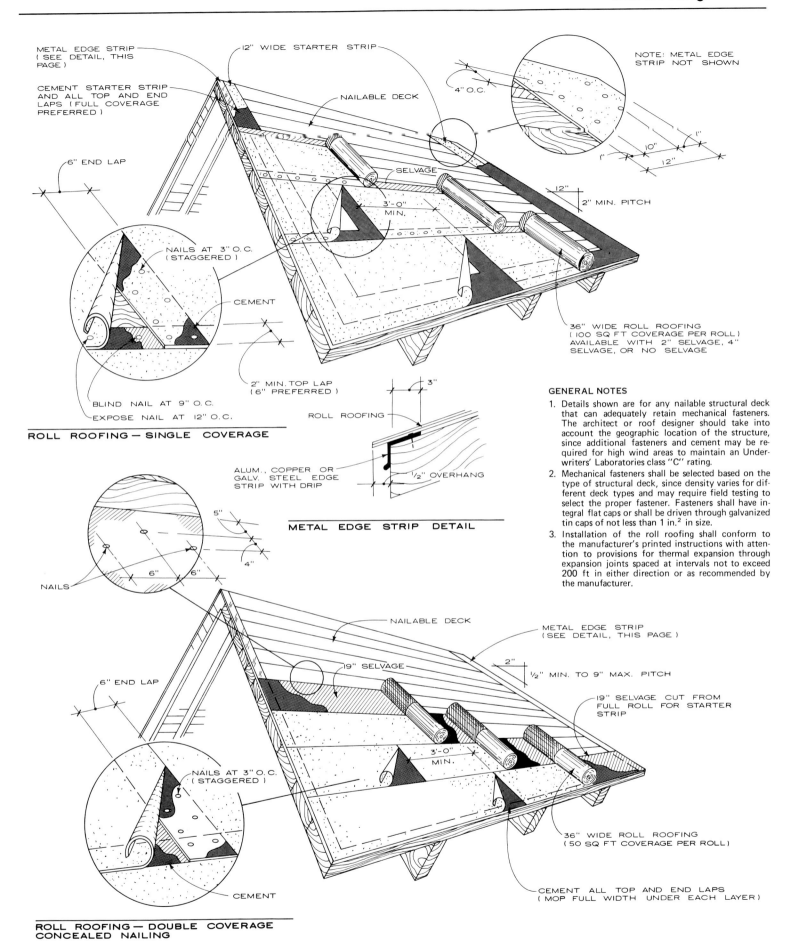

METAL EDGE STRIP
(SEE DETAIL, THIS
PAGE)

CEMENT STARTER STRIP
AND ALL TOP AND END
LAPS (FULL COVERAGE
PREFERRED)

12" WIDE STARTER STRIP

NAILABLE DECK

NOTE: METAL EDGE
STRIP NOT SHOWN

4" O.C.

1"
1"
10"
12"

6" END LAP

SELVAGE

3'-0"
MIN.

12"
2" MIN. PITCH

NAILS AT 3" O.C.
(STAGGERED)

CEMENT

36" WIDE ROLL ROOFING
(100 SQ FT COVERAGE PER ROLL)
AVAILABLE WITH 2" SELVAGE, 4"
SELVAGE, OR NO SELVAGE

BLIND NAIL AT 9" O.C.

EXPOSE NAIL AT 12" O.C.

2" MIN. TOP LAP
(6" PREFERRED)

ROLL ROOFING — SINGLE COVERAGE

3"

ROLL ROOFING

ALUM., COPPER OR
GALV. STEEL EDGE
STRIP WITH DRIP

1/2" OVERHANG

METAL EDGE STRIP DETAIL

GENERAL NOTES

1. Details shown are for any nailable structural deck that can adequately retain mechanical fasteners. The architect or roof designer should take into account the geographic location of the structure, since additional fasteners and cement may be required for high wind areas to maintain an Underwriters' Laboratories class "C" rating.

2. Mechanical fasteners shall be selected based on the type of structural deck, since density varies for different deck types and may require field testing to select the proper fastener. Fasteners shall have integral flat caps or shall be driven through galvanized tin caps of not less than 1 in.[2] in size.

3. Installation of the roll roofing shall conform to the manufacturer's printed instructions with attention to provisions for thermal expansion through expansion joints spaced at intervals not to exceed 200 ft in either direction or as recommended by the manufacturer.

5"

NAILS

6"   6"

4"

6" END LAP

NAILABLE DECK

METAL EDGE STRIP
(SEE DETAIL, THIS PAGE)

19" SELVAGE

2"
1/2" MIN. TO 9" MAX. PITCH

19" SELVAGE CUT FROM
FULL ROLL FOR STARTER
STRIP

NAILS AT 3" O.C.
(STAGGERED)

3'-0"
MIN.

36" WIDE ROLL ROOFING
(50 SQ FT COVERAGE PER ROLL)

CEMENT

CEMENT ALL TOP AND END LAPS
(MOP FULL WIDTH UNDER EACH LAYER)

**ROLL ROOFING — DOUBLE COVERAGE
CONCEALED NAILING**

James E. Phillips; AIA, Liles/Associates/Architects; Greenville, South Carolina

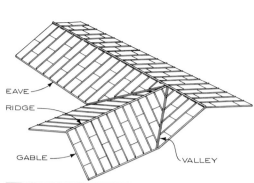

EAVE
RIDGE
GABLE
VALLEY

STANDING SEAM METAL ROOF

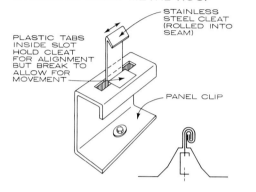

STAINLESS STEEL CLEAT (ROLLED INTO SEAM)

PLASTIC TABS INSIDE SLOT HOLD CLEAT FOR ALIGNMENT BUT BREAK TO ALLOW FOR MOVEMENT

PANEL CLIP

NOTES

To allow for expansion and contraction movement in roof panels, some manufacturers set movable cleats into a stationary panel clip system. The cleat is held in position in the center of a slot in the panel clip by two temporary plastic tabs. This allows for correct alignment of the cleat with the roof panel. Once the cleat has been rolled into the panel seam, it will move with the roof panel by forcing the plastic tabs to break under movement pressure.

MOVABLE CLEAT

NOTES

Roof panels secured at the eave expand up the slope of the roof. Depending on the length of the roof panel, an engineered distance should be left between the end of roof panels on each side of the ridge, thereby allowing for expansion at the ridge. In cases of a very long run of roof panels (usually in excess of 200 ft), expansion joints will be required at other points in addition to the ridge. Any blocking at the ridge should be cut at an angle to provide a space for the panels to bend into when expanding (as in ridge detail A). Ridge coverings can be formed or bowed to move with the expansion of the roof panels (as in ridge details B and C). In addition, the seams can either be flattened or left upright. Upright seams require a closing gasket or panel between seams.

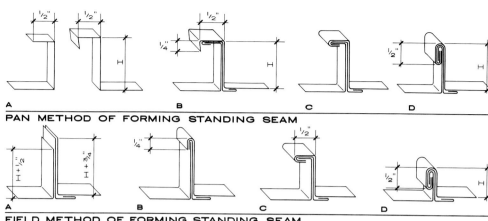

PAN METHOD OF FORMING STANDING SEAM

A   B   C   D

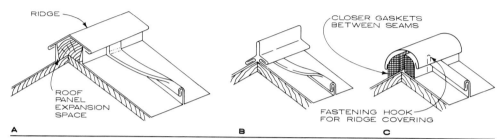

FIELD METHOD OF FORMING STANDING SEAM

A   B   C   D

RIDGE

ROOF PANEL EXPANSION SPACE

CLOSER GASKETS BETWEEN SEAMS

FASTENING HOOK FOR RIDGE COVERING

A   B   C

RIDGE CONSTRUCTION

END SPLICES SHOULD BE STAGGERED FROM ADJACENT SHEETS SPLICES ARE COVERED WITH A CLAMPING PLATE WITH INTEGRAL CHANNELS TO DIVERT WATER AROUND FASTENERS

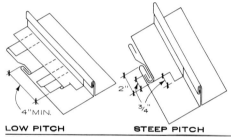

LOW PITCH   STEEP PITCH

4" MIN.   2"   3/4"

SEALANT

TRANSVERSE SEAM AND PANEL SPLICE

STANDARD DOUBLE LOCK SEAM

ALTERNATE SEAMS

A   B   C   D

Standing seam roofing may be installed on slopes as gentle as 1/4 in./ft. Because of the architectural appearance of the roof system, it is more commonly used on steeper roof slopes, allowing the panels to be seen as part of the overall design.

The spacing of seams may vary within reasonable limits to suit the architectural style of a given building. Preformed sheets (as used with preengineered metal buildings) have seam locations set by locations of prepunched holes in the structural framing members.

The two methods of forming a standing seam are the pan method and the roll method. In the pan method, the

top, bottom, and sides of the individual sheets are preformed to allow locking together at each edge. Seams at the top and bottom of each sheet are called transverse seams. In the roll method, a series of long sheets are joined together at their ends with double flat lock seams. These field-formed seams can be executed either manually or with a seaming machine (a wheeled electronic device which runs along the sheet joint forming the seam).

In either method, cleats (spaced as recommended by the manufacturer) are formed into the standing seam. Seam terminations are usually soldered.

STANDING SEAM METHODS AND SHAPES

CONTINUOUS CLEAT

CONTINUOUS CLEAT

GUTTER LINING

PREFORMED SNAP-ON TRANSITION PIECE TO ALLOW SEAM TO CONTINUE TO FASCIA *

6" MIN.

CLEAT

VALLEY

A   B

GABLE DETAILS

A   B   C * LIMITED AVAILABILITY

EAVE DETAILS

VALLEY DETAIL

Raso-Greaves An Architecture Corporation; Waco, Texas
Straub, VanDine, Dziurman/Architects; Troy, Michigan
Emory E. Hinkel, Jr.; A. G. Odell, Jr. and Associates; Charlotte, North Carolina

7

FLASHING AND SHEET METAL

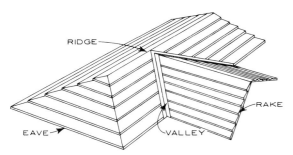

BERMUDA TYPE METAL ROOF

RIDGE — RAKE — VALLEY — EAVE

RECOMMENDED GAUGES OR WEIGHTS FOR PAN WIDTHS

WIDTH OF SHEET (IN.)	WIDTH OF PAN "D" (IN.)	COPPER (OZ)	GALVANIZED STEEL (GAUGE)	STAINLESS STEEL (GAUGE)	PAINTED TERNE 40 LB COATING
20	16½	16	26	28	0.015 IN.
22	18½	16	26	28	0.015 IN.
24	20½	16	26	26	0.015 IN.
26	22½	20	24	26	0.0178 IN.
28	24½	20	24	26	0.0178 IN.

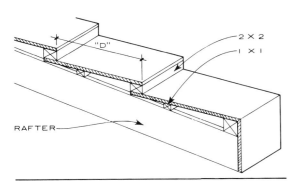

DETAIL 1-WOOD FRAMING

"D" — 2 X 2 — 1 X 1 — RAFTER

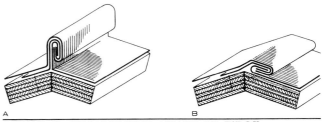

DETAIL 2-SEAM TYPES AT HIP OR RIDGE

A   B

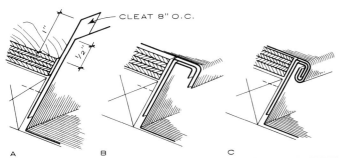

DETAIL 3-CONSTRUCTION AT BATTEN

CLEAT 8" O.C.

A   B   C

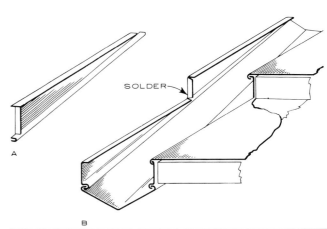

DETAIL 4-CONSTRUCTION AT CLOSURE AND VALLEY

SOLDER

A   B

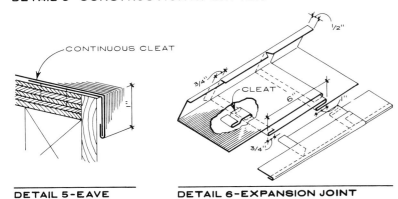

DETAIL 5-EAVE   **DETAIL 6-EXPANSION JOINT**

CONTINUOUS CLEAT — CLEAT — ½" — ¾" — 6" — ¾"

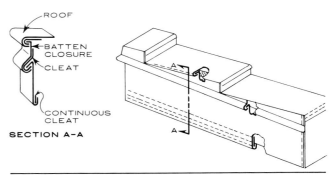

DETAIL 7-CONSTRUCTION AT RAKE

ROOF — BATTEN CLOSURE — CLEAT — CONTINUOUS CLEAT — SECTION A-A

NOTES

1. The Bermuda roof may be used for roofs having a slope greater than 2½ in./ft. Wood framing must be provided as shown in detail 1. Dimension "D" and gauge of metal will depend on the size of sheet used. See chart. Consult general notes on metal roofs for recommended surface preparation.

2. Bermuda roof is applied beginning at the eave. The first pan is hooked over a continuous cleat as shown in detail 5. The upper portion of the first and each succeeding pan is attached as shown in detail 3. Cleats spaced on 8 in. centers are nailed to batten as in A of detail 3. Joint is developed as shown in B of detail 3 and malleted against batten as shown in C of detail 3. All cross seams are single locked and soldered except at expansion joints. Cross seams should be staggered. Expansion joints should be used at least every 25 ft and formed as shown in detail 6. Roofing is joined at hip or ridge by use of a standing seam as shown in A of detail 2. Seam may be malleted down as shown in B of detail 2.

3. Detail 4 shows the method of forming valleys. Valley sections are lapped 8 in. in direction of flow.

Individual closures for sides of valley are formed as shown in A of detail 4 and must be soldered as indicated in B of detail 4. A method of terminating the roof at rake is shown in detail 7. The face plate (optional) is held in place by continuous cleats at both top and bottom. The batten closure is formed as a cleat to hold edge of roof pan as shown in section A-A of detail 7.

See also Metal Roofs for general notes.

Straub, VanDine, Dziurman/Architects; Troy, Michigan
Emory E. Hinkel, Jr.; A. G. Odell, Jr. and Associates; Charlotte, North Carolina

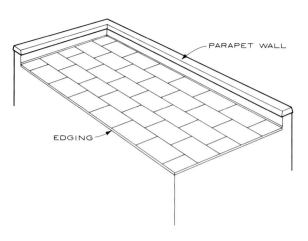

FLAT SEAM ROOF

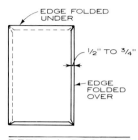

DETAIL 1- ROOFING
SHEET

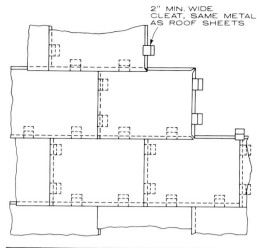

DETAIL 2- FLAT SEAM ROOF

DETAIL 3- EXPANSION BATTEN

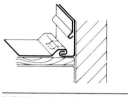

DETAIL 4- JUNCTION AT
PARAPET WALL

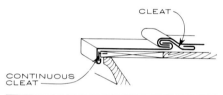

DETAIL 5- ROOF EDGE

NOTES

1. The flat seam method of roofing as illustrated is most commonly used on roofs of slight pitch or for the covering of curved surfaces such as towers or domes.

2. The joints connecting the sheets of roofs having a pitch greater than $1/2$ in./ft may be sealed with caulking compound or white lead. The joints of roofs having a pitch of less than $1/2$ in./ft must be malleted and thoroughly sweated full with solder.

3. Roofs of slight pitch should be divided by expansion batten as shown in detail 3, into sections not exceeding maximum total areas of 30 ft^2.

4. Consult general notes on metal roofs for recommended surface preparation.

5. The metal sheets may be pretinned if required, $1\frac{1}{2}$ in. back from all edges and on both sides of the sheet. Pans are formed by notching and folding the sheets as shown in detail 1.

6. The pans are held in place by cleating as shown. After pans are in place, all seams are malleted and soldered or sealed.

7. Detail 4 shows the junction of a roof and a parapet wall. Metal base flashing is cleated to deck on 2 ft centers and extended up wall; 8 in. pans are locked and soldered to base flashing. Metal counter flashing covers 4 in. of the base flashing. Detail 5 illustrates the installation of flashing at edge of roof. Flashing is formed as shown and attached to the face by a continuous cleat nailed on 1 ft centers and cleated to the roof deck. Pans are locked and soldered or sealed to the flashing. See also general notes below.

GENERAL NOTES

1. Detail drawings for metal roof types are diagrammatic only. The indication of adjoining construction is included merely to establish its relation to the sheet metal work and is not intended as a recommendation of architectural design. Any details that may suggest an architectural period do not limit the application of sheet metal to that or any other architectural style.

2. For weights of metals and roof slopes, see data of the Sheet Metal and Air Conditioning Contractors' National Association and recommendations of manufacturers.

3. Metals used must be of a thickness or gauge heavy enough and in correct proportion to the breadth and scale of the work. Provide expansion joints for freedom of movement.

4. Prevent direct contact of metal roofing with dissimilar metals that cause electrolysis.

5. A wide range of metals, alloys, and finishes are available for metal roofing. The durability as well as the maintenance requirements of each should be taken into consideration when selecting roofing.

6. The surface to receive the metal roofing should be thoroughly dry and covered by a saturated roofing felt in case of leakage due to construction error or wind driven moisture. A rosin paper should be applied over the felt to avoid bonding between felt and metal.

7. Many of the prefabricated batten and standing seam devices are not as watertight as with conventional methods and are therefore more suitable for steeply pitched roofs and mansards.

Straub, VanDine, Dziurman/Architects; Troy, Michigan
Emory E. Hinkel, Jr.; A. G. Odell, Jr. and Associates; Charlotte, North Carolina

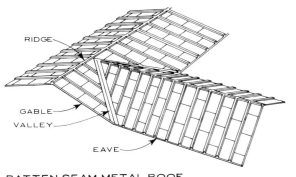

BATTEN SEAM METAL ROOF

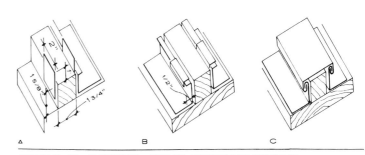

DETAIL 1-BATTEN ALTERNATES FOR METAL ROOFING

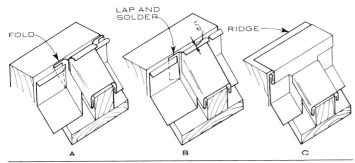

DETAIL 2 - RIDGE CONSTRUCTION

DETAIL 3 - BATTEN JOINT CONSTRUCTION

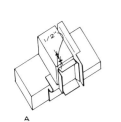 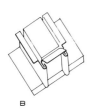 

DETAIL 4 - BATTEN CAP CONSTRUCTION

DETAIL 5 - TRANSVERSE SEAM

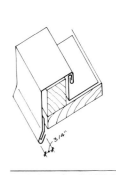

DETAIL 6 - GABLE

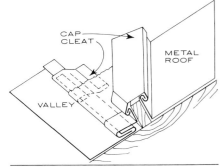

DETAIL 7 - VALLEY

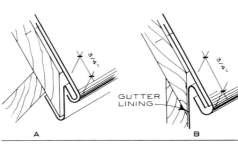

DETAIL 8 - EAVES

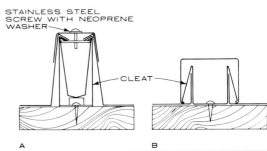

DETAIL 9 - PREFABRICATED BATTENS

NOTES

1. Batten seam roofing may be applied on slopes of 3 in./ft or greater. If the surface to receive the roofing is other than wood, the battens should be bolted into place. All batten fasteners must be countersunk into battens. See general notes on Metal Roofs for recommended surface preparation.

2. The spacing of the wood battens may vary within reasonable limits to suit the architectural style and scale of the building, but the recommended maximum distance is 20 in. between battens. Care should be taken to space the battens in such a manner that waste of metal is held to a minimum. Battens may be shaped as shown in A or B of detail 1.

A is preferred, since it automatically makes allowance for expansion. When battens shown in B are used, care must be taken to provide for expansion by bending the metal where it meets the batten at greater than 90°.

3. Sheets are formed into pans with each side turned up 2 1/8 in. A 1/2 in. flange is turned toward the center of the pan as shown in B of detail 3. At lower end of the pan, the sheet is notched and a hook edge is formed as in A or B of detail 5. For low pitched roofs the upper end of the sheet is formed as in A of detail 5. On steeper roofs the upper end is formed as shown in B of detail 5. Pans

are installed, starting at the eave, and held in place with cleats spaced not over 12 in. on center as shown in A of detail 3. Each pan is hooked to the one below it and cleated into place. After pans are in place, a cap is installed over the batten as shown in B and C of detail 3.

4. A number of manufacturers have developed metal roofing systems using several prefabricated devices. A and B of detail 9 show two common prefabricated battens in use.

5. See also Standing Seam Metal Roofing for details on combination batten and standing or flat seam roofing. See also Metal Roofs for general notes.

Straub, VanDine, Dziurman/Architects; Troy, Michigan
Emory E. Hinkel, Jr.; A. G. Odell, Jr. and Associates; Charlotte, North Carolina

MINIMUM THICKNESS (GAUGES OR WEIGHT) FOR COMMON FLASHING CONDITIONS

MATERIALS	BASE COURSE	WALL OPENINGS HEAD AND SILL	THROUGH WALL AND SPANDREL	CAP AND BASE FLASHING	VERTICAL AND HORIZONTAL SURFACES	ROOF EDGE RIDGES AND HIPS	CRICKETS VALLEY OR GUTTER	CHIMNEY PAN	LEDGE FLASHING	ROOF PENETRATIONS	COPING WIDTH UP TO 12"	COPING WIDTH ABOVE 12"	EDGE STRIPS	CLEATS	NOTE
Copper	10 oz	10 oz	10 oz	16 oz	16 oz	16 oz	16 oz	16 oz	16 oz	16 oz	16 oz	20 oz	20 oz	16 oz	
Aluminum	0.019"	0.019"	0.019"	0.019"	0.019"	0.019"	0.019"	0.019"	0.019"	0.040"	0.032"	0.040"	0.024"	✕	Note 6
Stainless steel	30 GA	30 GA	30 GA	26 GA	30 GA	26 GA	26 GA	30 GA	26 GA	26 GA	26 GA	24 GA	24 GA	✕	Note 5
Galvanized steel	26 GA	26 GA	26 GA	26 GA	26 GA	24 GA	24 GA	26 GA	24 GA	24 GA	24 GA	22 GA	26 GA	22 GA	Note 2
Zinc alloy	0.027"	0.027"	0.027"	0.027"	0.027"	0.027"	0.027"	0.027"	0.027"	0.027"	0.027"	0.032"	0.040"	0.027"	Note 4
Lead	3#	2½#	2½#	2½#	3#	3#	3#	3#	3#	3#	3#	3#	3#	3#	Note 3
Painted terne	40#	40#	40#	20#	40#	20#	40#	20#	40#	40#	✕	✕	20#	40#	Note 8
elastomeric sheet; fabric-coated metal	See Note 7									See Note 7					Note 7

GENERAL NOTES

1. All sizes and weights of material given in chart are minimum. Actual conditions may require greater strength.
2. All galvanized steel must be painted.
3. With lead flashing use 16 oz copper cleats. If any part is exposed, use 3# lead cleats.
4. Coat zinc with asphaltum paint when in contact with redwood or cedar. High acid content (in these woods only) develops stains.
5. Type 302 stainless steel is an all purpose flashing type.
6. Use only aluminum manufactured for the purpose of flashing.
7. See manufacturer's literature for use and types of flashing.
8. In general, cleats will be of the same material as flashing, but heavier weight or thicker gauge.
9. In selecting metal flashing, precaution must be taken not to place flashing in direct contact with dissimilar metals that cause electrolysis.
10. Spaces marked ✕ in the table are uses not recommended for that material.

GALVANIC CORROSION (ELECTROLYSIS) POTENTIAL BETWEEN COMMON FLASHING MATERIALS AND SELECTED CONSTRUCTION MATERIALS

FLASHING MATERIALS	COPPER	ALUMINUM	STAINLESS STEEL	GALVANIZED STEEL	ZINC	LEAD	BRASS	BRONZE	MONEL	UNCURED MORTAR OR CEMENT	WOODS WITH ACID (REDWOOD AND RED CEDAR)	IRON/STEEL
Copper		●	●	◗	●	◗	◗	◗	◗	◗	○	●
Aluminum	○		○	○	○	○	●	●	○	●	●	●
Stainless steel	◗	●		◗	●	●	●	●	●	◗	○	●
Galvanized steel	○	○	○		○	◗	●	◗	◗	◗	●	●
Zinc alloy						○	●	●	●	●	●	●
Lead							●	◗	◗	●	○	○

● Galvanic action will occur, hence direct contact should be avoided.
◗ Galvanic action may occur under certain circumstances and/or over a period of time.
○ Galvanic action is insignificant, metals may come into direct contact under normal circumstances.

GENERAL NOTE: Galvanic corrosion is apt to occur when water runoff from one material comes in contact with a potentially reactive material.

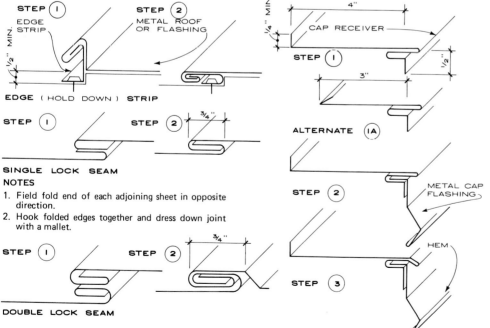

STEP ① EDGE STRIP ½" MIN. STEP ② METAL ROOF OR FLASHING
EDGE (HOLD DOWN) STRIP

STEP ① STEP ② ¾"

SINGLE LOCK SEAM

NOTES
1. Field fold end of each adjoining sheet in opposite direction.
2. Hook folded edges together and dress down joint with a mallet.

STEP ① STEP ② ¾"

DOUBLE LOCK SEAM

NOTES
1. Double fold end of each adjoining sheet in opposite direction with bar folder.
2. Slide edges together and dress down joint with a mallet.

4" CAP RECEIVER ½" ¼" MIN.
STEP ①

3"
ALTERNATE ①A

STEP ② METAL CAP FLASHING

HEM

STEP ③

DEVELOPMENT OF CAP FLASHING
NOTE
Hem in cap flashing recommended for stiffness; but may be omitted if heavier gauge material used.

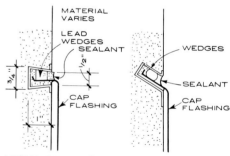

MATERIAL VARIES LEAD WEDGES SEALANT ¾" ½" 1" CAP FLASHING
WEDGES SEALANT CAP FLASHING

METAL REGLETS CAST IN PLACE

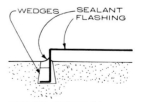

WEDGES SEALANT FLASHING

REGLET SAWED IN MATERIAL

TYPICAL REGLETS

NOTE
Various types of metal reglets are available for cast in place and masonry work; see manufacturer's literature. Where material permits, reglets may be sawn. Flashing is secured in reglets with lead wedges at max. 12" o.c., fill reglet with nonhardening water-resistant compound.

Michael Scott Rudden, The Stephens Associates P.C.—Architects; Albany, New York

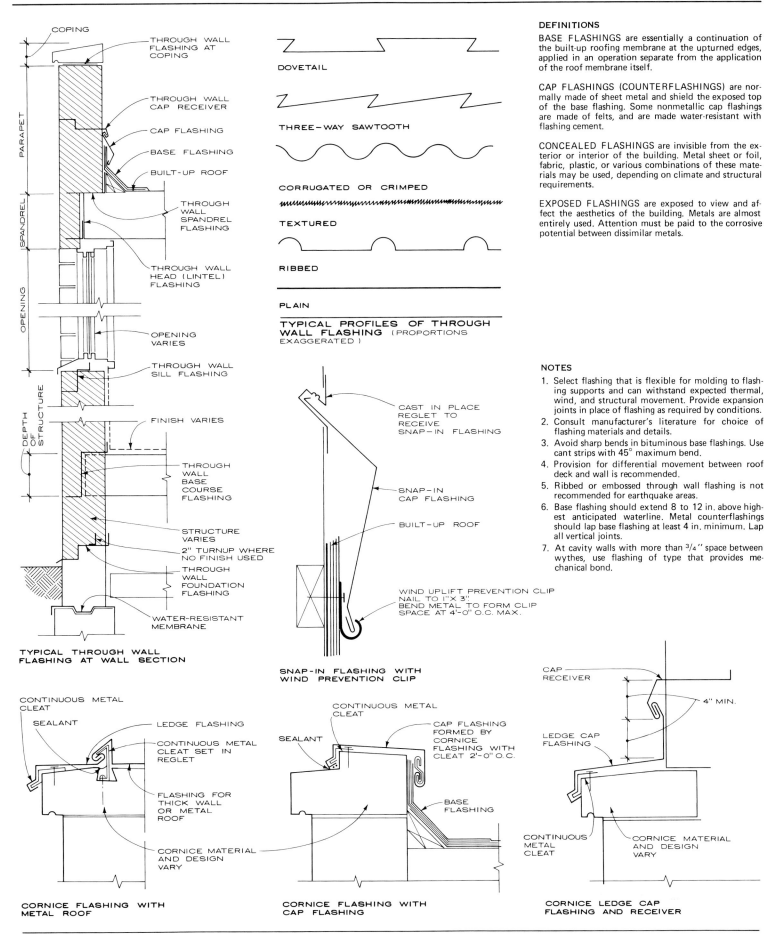

Michael Scott Rudden, The Stephens Associates P.C.—Architects; Albany, New York

DEFINITIONS

BASE FLASHINGS are essentially a continuation of the built-up roofing membrane at the upturned edges, applied in an operation separate from the application of the roof membrane itself.

CAP FLASHINGS (COUNTERFLASHINGS) are normally made of sheet metal and shield the exposed top of the base flashing. Some nonmetallic cap flashings are made of felts, and are made water-resistant with flashing cement.

CONCEALED FLASHINGS are invisible from the exterior or interior of the building. Metal sheet or foil, fabric, plastic, or various combinations of these materials may be used, depending on climate and structural requirements.

EXPOSED FLASHINGS are exposed to view and affect the aesthetics of the building. Metals are almost entirely used. Attention must be paid to the corrosive potential between dissimilar metals.

NOTES

1. Select flashing that is flexible for molding to flashing supports and can withstand expected thermal, wind, and structural movement. Provide expansion joints in place of flashing as required by conditions.
2. Consult manufacturer's literature for choice of flashing materials and details.
3. Avoid sharp bends in bituminous base flashings. Use cant strips with 45° maximum bend.
4. Provision for differential movement between roof deck and wall is recommended.
5. Ribbed or embossed through wall flashing is not recommended for earthquake areas.
6. Base flashing should extend 8 to 12 in. above highest anticipated waterline. Metal counterflashings should lap base flashing at least 4 in. minimum. Lap all vertical joints.
7. At cavity walls with more than 3/4" space between wythes, use flashing of type that provides mechanical bond.

CORNICE FLASHING

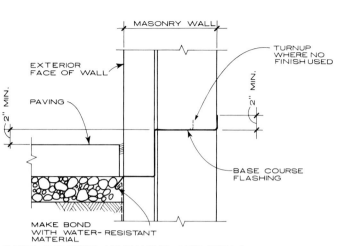

BASE COURSE AT PAVING AND WALL

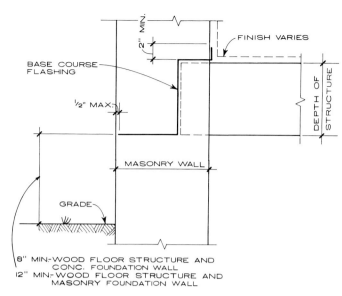

BASE COURSE AT FLOOR CONSTRUCTION

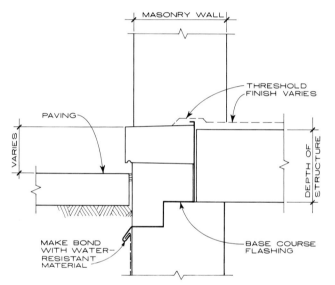

BASE COURSE AT SILL OF MASONRY CONSTRUCTION

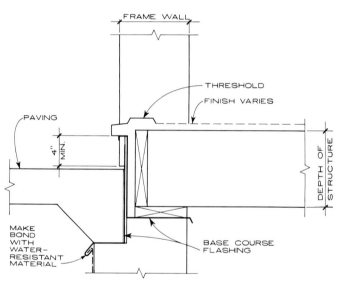

BASE COURSE AT SILL OF FRAME CONSTRUCTION

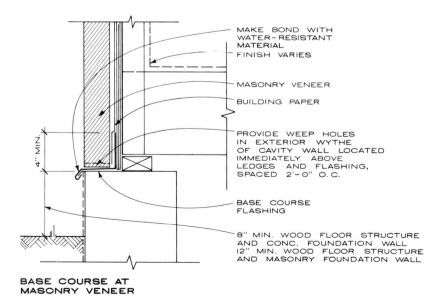

BASE COURSE AT MASONRY VENEER

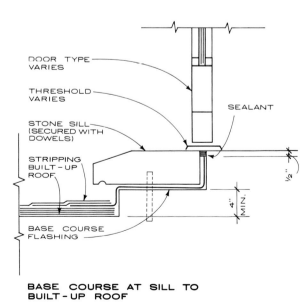

BASE COURSE AT SILL TO BUILT-UP ROOF

Michael Scott Rudden, The Stephens Associates P.C.—Architects; Albany, New York

7   **FLASHING AND SHEET METAL**

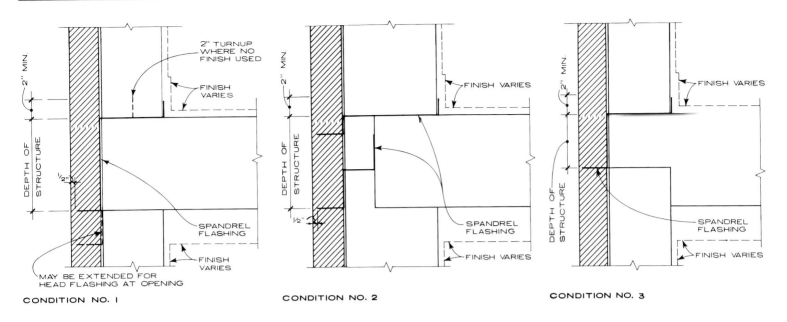

2" TURNUP WHERE NO FINISH USED

FINISH VARIES

2" MIN.

DEPTH OF STRUCTURE

1/2"

SPANDREL FLASHING

FINISH VARIES

MAY BE EXTENDED FOR HEAD FLASHING AT OPENING

CONDITION NO. 1

FINISH VARIES

2" MIN.

DEPTH OF STRUCTURE

1/2"

SPANDREL FLASHING

FINISH VARIES

CONDITION NO. 2

FINISH VARIES

2" MIN.

DEPTH OF STRUCTURE

SPANDREL FLASHING

FINISH VARIES

CONDITION NO. 3

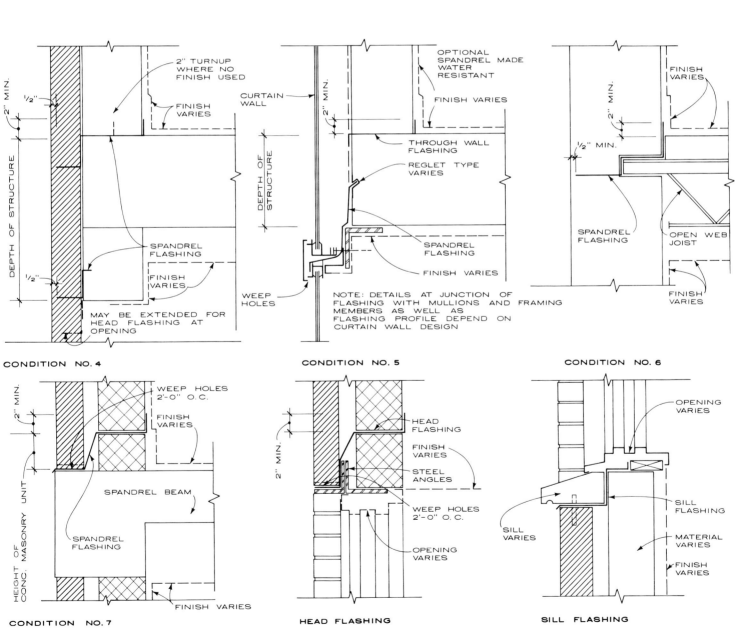

2" TURNUP WHERE NO FINISH USED

FINISH VARIES

2" MIN.

1/2"

DEPTH OF STRUCTURE

1/2"

SPANDREL FLASHING

FINISH VARIES

MAY BE EXTENDED FOR HEAD FLASHING AT OPENING

CONDITION NO. 4

CURTAIN WALL

2" MIN.

DEPTH OF STRUCTURE

OPTIONAL SPANDREL MADE WATER RESISTANT

FINISH VARIES

THROUGH WALL FLASHING

REGLET TYPE VARIES

SPANDREL FLASHING

FINISH VARIES

WEEP HOLES

NOTE: DETAILS AT JUNCTION OF FLASHING WITH MULLIONS AND FRAMING MEMBERS AS WELL AS FLASHING PROFILE DEPEND ON CURTAIN WALL DESIGN

CONDITION NO. 5

FINISH VARIES

2" MIN.

1/2" MIN.

SPANDREL FLASHING

OPEN WEB JOIST

FINISH VARIES

CONDITION NO. 6

WEEP HOLES 2'-0" O.C.

FINISH VARIES

2" MIN.

HEIGHT OF CONC. MASONRY UNIT

SPANDREL BEAM

SPANDREL FLASHING

FINISH VARIES

CONDITION NO. 7

HEAD FLASHING

2" MIN.

FINISH VARIES

STEEL ANGLES

WEEP HOLES 2'-0" O.C.

OPENING VARIES

HEAD FLASHING

OPENING VARIES

SILL FLASHING

SILL VARIES

MATERIAL VARIES

FINISH VARIES

SILL FLASHING

Michael Scott Rudden, The Stephens Associates P.C.—Architects; Albany, New York

FLASHING AND SHEET METAL   7

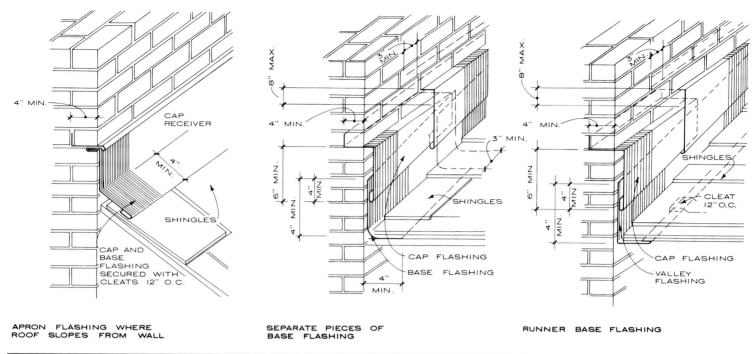

APRON FLASHING WHERE
ROOF SLOPES FROM WALL

SEPARATE PIECES OF
BASE FLASHING

RUNNER BASE FLASHING

PITCHED ROOF WITH WALL FLASHING

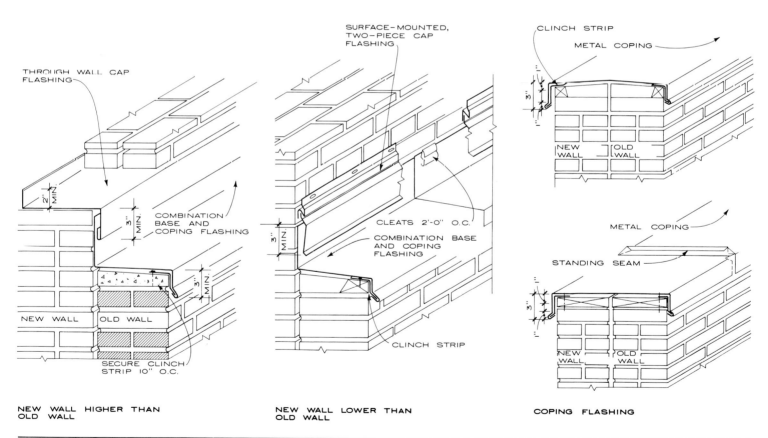

NEW WALL HIGHER THAN
OLD WALL

NEW WALL LOWER THAN
OLD WALL

COPING FLASHING

NEW WALL TO OLD WALL FLASHING

NOTE

Through wall flashing not recommended in earthquake
areas.

Michael Scott Rudden, The Stephens Associates P.C.—Architects; Albany, New York

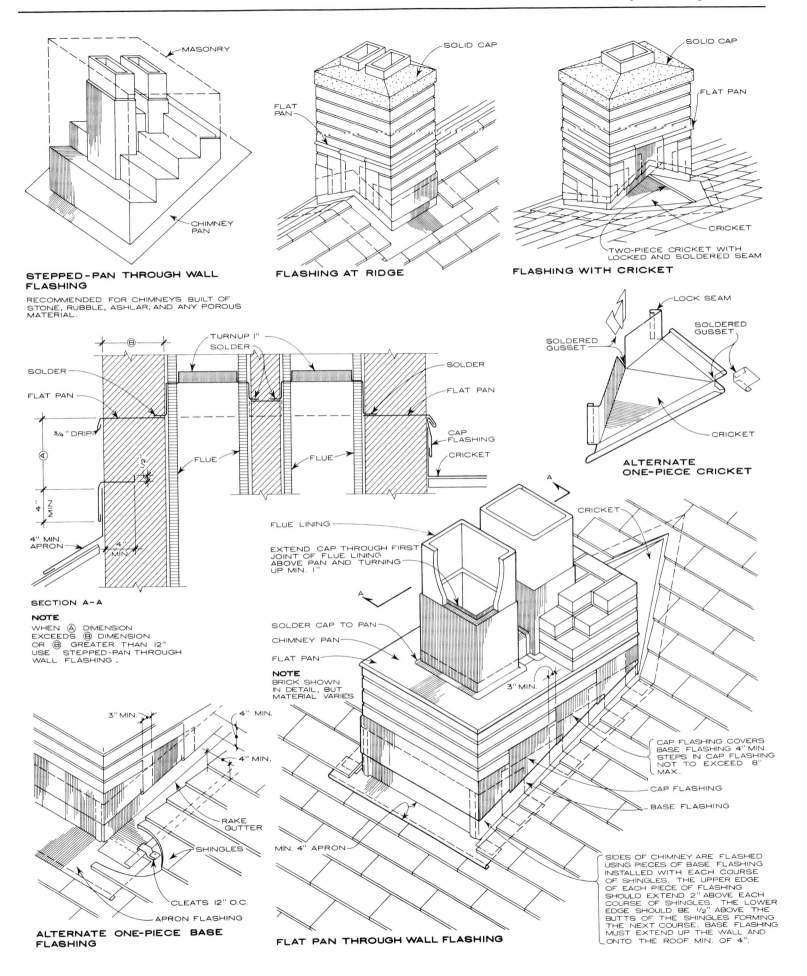

STEPPED-PAN THROUGH WALL FLASHING

RECOMMENDED FOR CHIMNEYS BUILT OF STONE, RUBBLE, ASHLAR, AND ANY POROUS MATERIAL.

MASONRY

CHIMNEY PAN

FLASHING AT RIDGE

SOLID CAP

FLAT PAN

FLASHING WITH CRICKET

SOLID CAP

FLAT PAN

CRICKET

TWO-PIECE CRICKET WITH LOCKED AND SOLDERED SEAM

TURNUP 1"
SOLDER

SOLDER

FLAT PAN

3/4" DRIP

1/2"

4" MIN.

4" MIN. APRON

4" MIN.

FLUE

FLUE

SOLDER

FLAT PAN

CAP FLASHING

CRICKET

SECTION A-A

NOTE

WHEN Ⓐ DIMENSION EXCEEDS Ⓑ DIMENSION OR Ⓑ GREATER THAN 12" USE STEPPED-PAN THROUGH WALL FLASHING.

LOCK SEAM

SOLDERED GUSSET

SOLDERED GUSSET

CRICKET

ALTERNATE ONE-PIECE CRICKET

FLUE LINING

EXTEND CAP THROUGH FIRST JOINT OF FLUE LINING ABOVE PAN AND TURNING UP MIN. 1"

SOLDER CAP TO PAN

CHIMNEY PAN

FLAT PAN

NOTE
BRICK SHOWN IN DETAIL, BUT MATERIAL VARIES

CRICKET

3" MIN.

CAP FLASHING COVERS BASE FLASHING 4" MIN. STEPS IN CAP FLASHING NOT TO EXCEED 8" MAX.

CAP FLASHING

BASE FLASHING

3" MIN.

4" MIN.

4" MIN.

RAKE GUTTER

SHINGLES

CLEATS 12" O.C.

APRON FLASHING

ALTERNATE ONE-PIECE BASE FLASHING

MIN. 4" APRON

FLAT PAN THROUGH WALL FLASHING

SIDES OF CHIMNEY ARE FLASHED USING PIECES OF BASE FLASHING INSTALLED WITH EACH COURSE OF SHINGLES. THE UPPER EDGE OF EACH PIECE OF FLASHING SHOULD EXTEND 2" ABOVE EACH COURSE OF SHINGLES. THE LOWER EDGE SHOULD BE 1/2" ABOVE THE BUTTS OF THE SHINGLES FORMING THE NEXT COURSE. BASE FLASHING MUST EXTEND UP THE WALL AND ONTO THE ROOF MIN. OF 4".

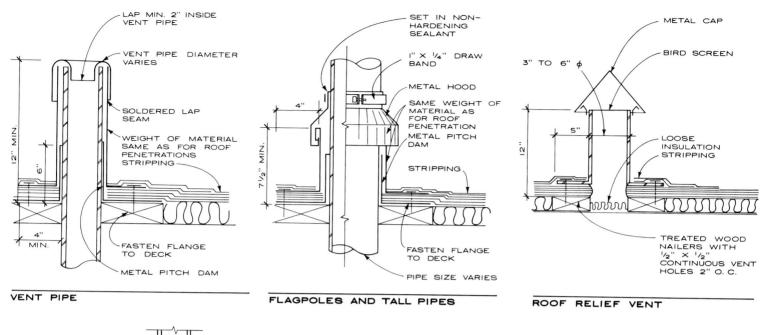

LAP MIN. 2" INSIDE VENT PIPE

VENT PIPE DIAMETER VARIES

SOLDERED LAP SEAM

WEIGHT OF MATERIAL SAME AS FOR ROOF PENETRATIONS STRIPPING

12" MIN.

6"

4" MIN.

FASTEN FLANGE TO DECK

METAL PITCH DAM

VENT PIPE

SET IN NON-HARDENING SEALANT

1" X ¼" DRAW BAND

METAL HOOD

SAME WEIGHT OF MATERIAL AS FOR ROOF PENETRATION METAL PITCH DAM

STRIPPING

4"

7½" MIN.

FASTEN FLANGE TO DECK

PIPE SIZE VARIES

FLAGPOLES AND TALL PIPES

METAL CAP

BIRD SCREEN

3" TO 6" φ

5"

12"

LOOSE INSULATION STRIPPING

TREATED WOOD NAILERS WITH ½" X ½" CONTINUOUS VENT HOLES 2" O. C.

ROOF RELIEF VENT

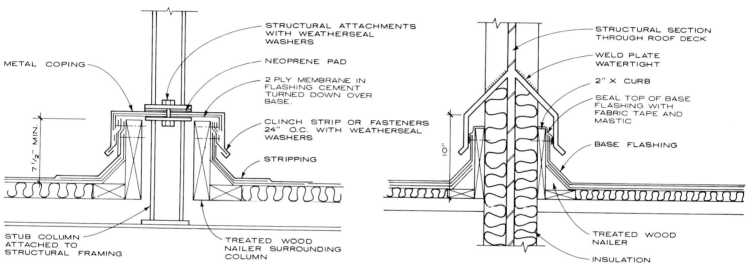

METAL COPING

STRUCTURAL ATTACHMENTS WITH WEATHERSEAL WASHERS

NEOPRENE PAD

2 PLY MEMBRANE IN FLASHING CEMENT TURNED DOWN OVER BASE.

CLINCH STRIP OR FASTENERS 24" O.C. WITH WEATHERSEAL WASHERS

STRIPPING

7½" MIN.

STUB COLUMN ATTACHED TO STRUCTURAL FRAMING

TREATED WOOD NAILER SURROUNDING COLUMN

STRUCTURAL SECTION THROUGH ROOF DECK

WELD PLATE WATERTIGHT

2" X CURB

SEAL TOP OF BASE FLASHING WITH FABRIC TAPE AND MASTIC

BASE FLASHING

10"

TREATED WOOD NAILER

INSULATION

FUTURE COLUMNS, SIGN SUPPORTS, AND STEEL ANGLES

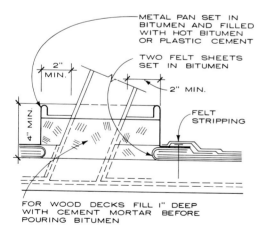

METAL PAN SET IN BITUMEN AND FILLED WITH HOT BITUMEN OR PLASTIC CEMENT

TWO FELT SHEETS SET IN BITUMEN

2" MIN.

2" MIN.

4" MIN.

FELT STRIPPING

FOR WOOD DECKS FILL 1" DEEP WITH CEMENT MORTAR BEFORE POURING BITUMEN

NOTE

Whenever possible avoid the use of pitch pockets in favor of curbs with base and cap flashing around the penetrating member.

PITCH POCKET

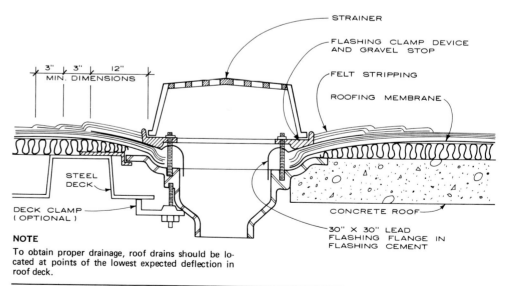

STRAINER

FLASHING CLAMP DEVICE AND GRAVEL STOP

FELT STRIPPING

ROOFING MEMBRANE

3" 3" 12"

MIN. DIMENSIONS

STEEL DECK

DECK CLAMP (OPTIONAL)

CONCRETE ROOF

30" X 30" LEAD FLASHING FLANGE IN FLASHING CEMENT

NOTE

To obtain proper drainage, roof drains should be located at points of the lowest expected deflection in roof deck.

ROOF DRAIN

Michael Scott Rudden, The Stephens Associates P.C.—Architects; Albany, New York

7   **FLASHING AND SHEET METAL**

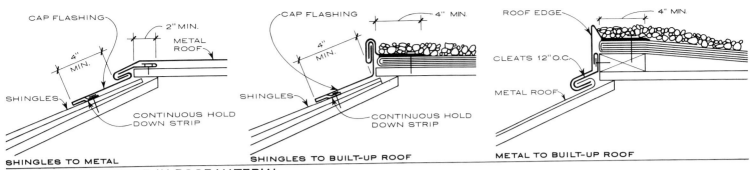

CAP FLASHING — 2" MIN. — METAL ROOF
4" MIN.
SHINGLES
CONTINUOUS HOLD DOWN STRIP

SHINGLES TO METAL

CAP FLASHING — 4" MIN.
4" MIN.
SHINGLES
CONTINUOUS HOLD DOWN STRIP

SHINGLES TO BUILT-UP ROOF

ROOF EDGE — 4" MIN.
CLEATS 12" O.C.
METAL ROOF

METAL TO BUILT-UP ROOF

FLASHING AT CHANGE IN ROOF MATERIAL

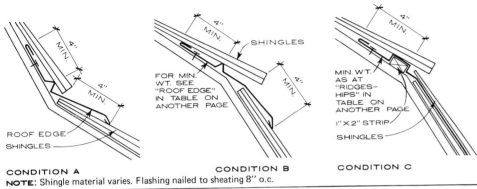

4" MIN.
4" MIN.
ROOF EDGE
SHINGLES

CONDITION A

FOR MIN. WT. SEE "ROOF EDGE" IN TABLE ON ANOTHER PAGE
4" MIN. — SHINGLES
4" MIN.

CONDITION B

4" MIN.
MIN. WT. AS AT "RIDGES-HIPS" IN TABLE ON ANOTHER PAGE
1" X 2" STRIP
SHINGLES

CONDITION C

FLASHING OF BREAK IN SLOPE OF SHINGLE ROOFS
NOTE: Shingle material varies. Flashing nailed to sheating 8" o.c.

SHINGLE MATERIAL VARIES
5" MIN.
CLEATS 2'-0" O.C.
5" MIN.
PROVIDE 1" "V" CRIMP FOR SLOPES LESS THAN 6/12
VALLEY FLASHING

EQUAL SLOPES

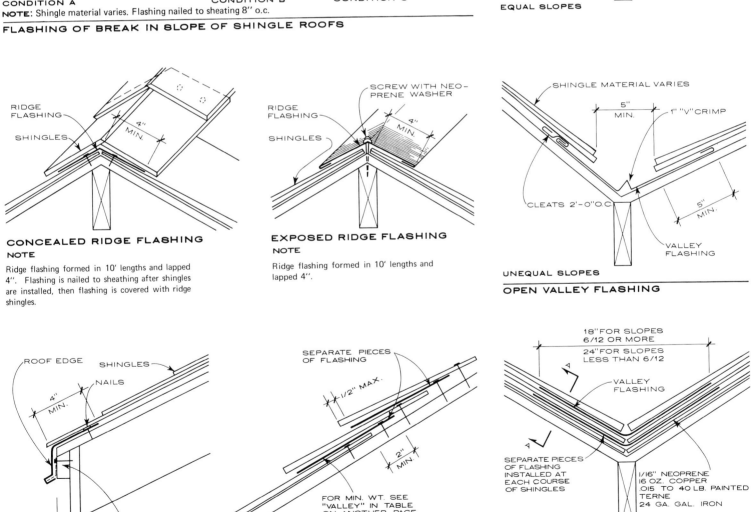

RIDGE FLASHING
SHINGLES
4" MIN.

CONCEALED RIDGE FLASHING
NOTE
Ridge flashing formed in 10' lengths and lapped 4". Flashing is nailed to sheathing after shingles are installed, then flashing is covered with ridge shingles.

SCREW WITH NEO-PRENE WASHER
RIDGE FLASHING
SHINGLES
4" MIN.

EXPOSED RIDGE FLASHING
NOTE
Ridge flashing formed in 10' lengths and lapped 4".

SHINGLE MATERIAL VARIES
5" MIN. — 1" "V" CRIMP
CLEATS 2'-0" O.C.
5" MIN.
VALLEY FLASHING

UNEQUAL SLOPES
OPEN VALLEY FLASHING

ROOF EDGE — SHINGLES
NAILS
4" MIN.
CLINCH STRIP (OPTIONAL)
3/4" MIN.

ROOF EDGE FLASHING

SEPARATE PIECES OF FLASHING
1/2" MAX.
2" MIN.
FOR MIN. WT. SEE "VALLEY" IN TABLE ON ANOTHER PAGE

SECTION A-A
CONCEALED VALLEY FLASHING

18" FOR SLOPES 6/12 OR MORE
24" FOR SLOPES LESS THAN 6/12
VALLEY FLASHING
SEPARATE PIECES OF FLASHING INSTALLED AT EACH COURSE OF SHINGLES
1/16" NEOPRENE 16 OZ. COPPER .015 TO 40 LB. PAINTED TERNE 24 GA. GAL. IRON

CROSS SECTION

Michael Scott Rudden, The Stephens Associates P.C.—Architects; Albany, New York

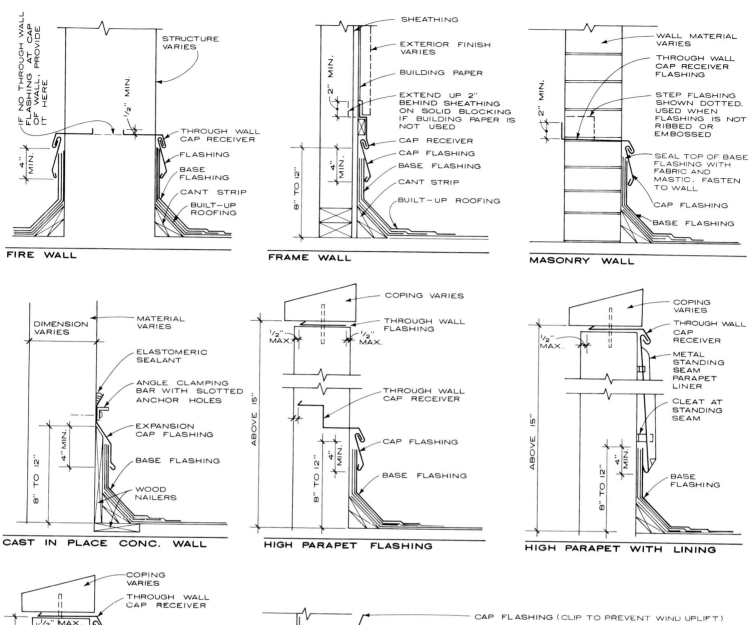

FIRE WALL

- STRUCTURE VARIES
- IF NO THROUGH WALL FLASHING AT CAP OF WALL, PROVIDE IT HERE
- 1/2" MIN.
- THROUGH WALL CAP RECEIVER
- FLASHING
- BASE FLASHING
- CANT STRIP
- BUILT-UP ROOFING
- 4" MIN.

FRAME WALL

- SHEATHING
- EXTERIOR FINISH VARIES
- BUILDING PAPER
- EXTEND UP 2" BEHIND SHEATHING ON SOLID BLOCKING IF BUILDING PAPER IS NOT USED
- CAP RECEIVER
- CAP FLASHING
- BASE FLASHING
- CANT STRIP
- BUILT-UP ROOFING
- 2" MIN.
- 4" MIN.
- 8" TO 12"

MASONRY WALL

- WALL MATERIAL VARIES
- THROUGH WALL CAP RECEIVER FLASHING
- STEP FLASHING SHOWN DOTTED. USED WHEN FLASHING IS NOT RIBBED OR EMBOSSED
- SEAL TOP OF BASE FLASHING WITH FABRIC AND MASTIC. FASTEN TO WALL
- CAP FLASHING
- BASE FLASHING
- 2" MIN.

CAST IN PLACE CONC. WALL

- DIMENSION VARIES
- MATERIAL VARIES
- ELASTOMERIC SEALANT
- ANGLE CLAMPING BAR WITH SLOTTED ANCHOR HOLES
- EXPANSION CAP FLASHING
- BASE FLASHING
- WOOD NAILERS
- 4" MIN.
- 8" TO 12"

HIGH PARAPET FLASHING

- COPING VARIES
- THROUGH WALL FLASHING
- 1/2" MAX.
- 1/2" MAX.
- THROUGH WALL CAP RECEIVER
- CAP FLASHING
- BASE FLASHING
- ABOVE 15"
- 4" MIN.
- 8" TO 12"

HIGH PARAPET WITH LINING

- COPING VARIES
- THROUGH WALL CAP RECEIVER
- METAL STANDING SEAM PARAPET LINER
- CLEAT AT STANDING SEAM
- BASE FLASHING
- 1/2" MAX.
- ABOVE 15"
- 4" MIN.
- 8" TO 12"

LOW PARAPET FLASHING

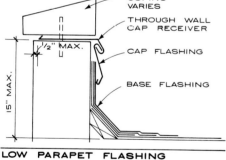

- COPING VARIES
- THROUGH WALL CAP RECEIVER
- CAP FLASHING
- BASE FLASHING
- 1/2" MAX.
- 15" MAX.

GENERAL NOTES

1. Select flashing that is flexible for molding to flashing supports and that can withstand expected thermal, wind, and structural movement. Provide expansion joints in place of flashing as required by conditions.
2. Consult manufacturer's literature for choice of flashing materials and details.
3. Avoid sharp bends in bituminous base flashings. Use cant strips with 45° maximum bend.
4. Provision for differential movement between roof deck and wall is recommended.
5. A ribbed or embossed pattern should be used for all through wall flashing. Through wall flashing is not recommended for earthquake areas.
6. Base flashing should extend 8 to 12 in. above highest anticipated waterline. Metal counterflashing should lap base flashing by at least 4 in. Lap all vertical joints.

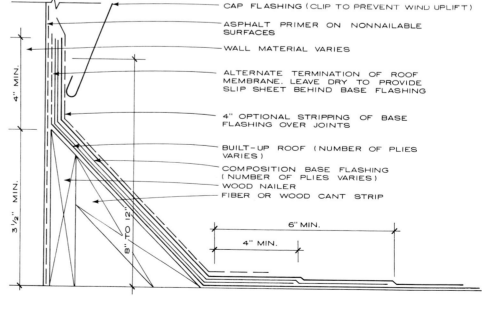

TYPICAL BASE FLASHING

- CAP FLASHING (CLIP TO PREVENT WIND UPLIFT)
- ASPHALT PRIMER ON NONNAILABLE SURFACES
- WALL MATERIAL VARIES
- ALTERNATE TERMINATION OF ROOF MEMBRANE. LEAVE DRY TO PROVIDE SLIP SHEET BEHIND BASE FLASHING
- 4" OPTIONAL STRIPPING OF BASE FLASHING OVER JOINTS
- BUILT-UP ROOF (NUMBER OF PLIES VARIES)
- COMPOSITION BASE FLASHING (NUMBER OF PLIES VARIES)
- WOOD NAILER
- FIBER OR WOOD CANT STRIP
- 4" MIN.
- 3 1/2" MIN.
- 8" TO 12"
- 6" MIN.
- 4" MIN.

Michael Scott Rudden, The Stephens Associates P.C.—Architects; Albany, New York

7 **FLASHING AND SHEET METAL**

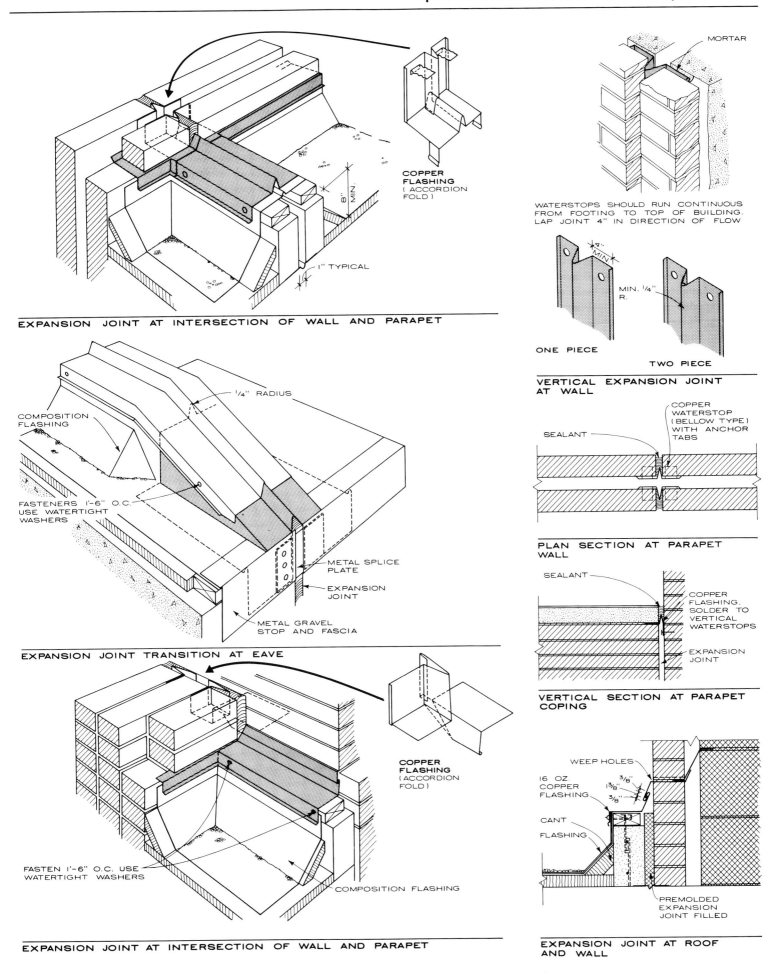

MORTAR

COPPER FLASHING (ACCORDION FOLD)

8" MIN.

1" TYPICAL

EXPANSION JOINT AT INTERSECTION OF WALL AND PARAPET

WATERSTOPS SHOULD RUN CONTINUOUS FROM FOOTING TO TOP OF BUILDING. LAP JOINT 4" IN DIRECTION OF FLOW

4" MIN

MIN. ¼" R.

ONE PIECE

TWO PIECE

VERTICAL EXPANSION JOINT AT WALL

¼" RADIUS

COMPOSITION FLASHING

FASTENERS 1'-6" O.C. USE WATERTIGHT WASHERS

METAL SPLICE PLATE

EXPANSION JOINT

METAL GRAVEL STOP AND FASCIA

EXPANSION JOINT TRANSITION AT EAVE

COPPER WATERSTOP (BELLOW TYPE) WITH ANCHOR TABS

SEALANT

PLAN SECTION AT PARAPET WALL

SEALANT

COPPER FLASHING. SOLDER TO VERTICAL WATERSTOPS

EXPANSION JOINT

VERTICAL SECTION AT PARAPET COPING

COPPER FLASHING (ACCORDION FOLD)

FASTEN 1'-6" O.C. USE WATERTIGHT WASHERS

COMPOSITION FLASHING

EXPANSION JOINT AT INTERSECTION OF WALL AND PARAPET

WEEP HOLES

16 OZ. COPPER FLASHING

⅜"

1⅜"

⅜"

CANT

FLASHING

PREMOLDED EXPANSION JOINT FILLED

EXPANSION JOINT AT ROOF AND WALL

CTA Architects Engineers; Billings, Montana

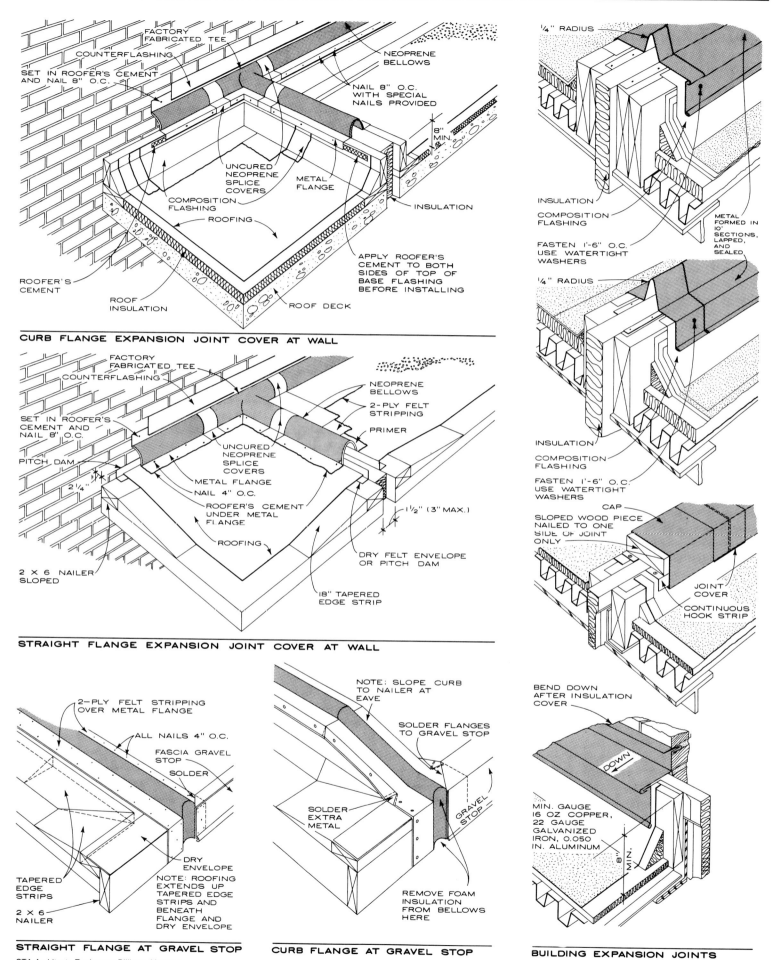

CURB FLANGE EXPANSION JOINT COVER AT WALL

FACTORY FABRICATED TEE
COUNTERFLASHING
SET IN ROOFER'S CEMENT AND NAIL 8" O.C.
NEOPRENE BELLOWS
NAIL 8" O.C. WITH SPECIAL NAILS PROVIDED
UNCURED NEOPRENE SPLICE COVERS
METAL FLANGE
COMPOSITION FLASHING
ROOFING
8" MIN.
INSULATION
ROOFER'S CEMENT
ROOF INSULATION
ROOF DECK
APPLY ROOFER'S CEMENT TO BOTH SIDES OF TOP OF BASE FLASHING BEFORE INSTALLING

STRAIGHT FLANGE EXPANSION JOINT COVER AT WALL

FACTORY FABRICATED TEE
COUNTERFLASHING
SET IN ROOFER'S CEMENT AND NAIL 8" O.C.
PITCH DAM
2¼"
NEOPRENE BELLOWS
2-PLY FELT STRIPPING
PRIMER
UNCURED NEOPRENE SPLICE COVERS
METAL FLANGE
NAIL 4" O.C.
ROOFER'S CEMENT UNDER METAL FLANGE
ROOFING
2 X 6 NAILER SLOPED
1½" (3" MAX.)
DRY FELT ENVELOPE OR PITCH DAM
18" TAPERED EDGE STRIP

STRAIGHT FLANGE AT GRAVEL STOP

2-PLY FELT STRIPPING OVER METAL FLANGE
ALL NAILS 4" O.C.
FASCIA GRAVEL STOP
SOLDER
TAPERED EDGE STRIPS
2 X 6 NAILER
DRY ENVELOPE
NOTE: ROOFING EXTENDS UP TAPERED EDGE STRIPS AND BENEATH FLANGE AND DRY ENVELOPE

CURB FLANGE AT GRAVEL STOP

NOTE: SLOPE CURB TO NAILER AT EAVE
SOLDER FLANGES TO GRAVEL STOP
SOLDER EXTRA METAL
GRAVEL STOP
REMOVE FOAM INSULATION FROM BELLOWS HERE

BUILDING EXPANSION JOINTS

¼" RADIUS
INSULATION
COMPOSITION FLASHING
FASTEN 1'-6" O.C. USE WATERTIGHT WASHERS
METAL FORMED IN 10' SECTIONS, LAPPED, AND SEALED
¼" RADIUS
INSULATION
COMPOSITION FLASHING
FASTEN 1'-6" O.C. USE WATERTIGHT WASHERS
CAP
SLOPED WOOD PIECE NAILED TO ONE SIDE OF JOINT ONLY
JOINT COVER
CONTINUOUS HOOK STRIP
BEND DOWN AFTER INSULATION COVER
DOWN
MIN. GAUGE 16 OZ COPPER, 22 GAUGE GALVANIZED IRON, 0.050 IN. ALUMINUM
8" MIN.

CTA Architects Engineers; Billings, Montana

RECOMMENDED MINIMUM GAUGES GRAVEL STOP–FASCIA

D (MAX.) (IN.)	GALVANIZED STEEL (GAUGE)	COPPER (OZ.)	ALUMINUM (IN.)	ZINC ALLOY (IN.)	STAINLESS STEEL (GAUGE)
4	24	16	0.025	0.020	26
5	24	16	0.032	0.027	26
6	22	20	0.040	0.027	24
7	22	20	0.040	–	22
8	20	20	0.060		20

RECOMMENDED MINIMUM GAUGES FOR COPING

WIDTH OF COPING TOP (IN.)	GALVANIZED STEEL (GAUGE)	STAINLESS STEEL (GAUGE)	ALUMINUM (IN.)	COPPER (OZ.)
Through 12	24	26	0.232	16
13 to 18	22	24	0.040	20

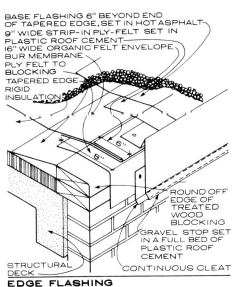

BASE FLASHING 6" BEYOND END OF TAPERED EDGE, SET IN HOT ASPHALT
9" WIDE STRIP-IN PLY-FELT SET IN PLASTIC ROOF CEMENT
16" WIDE ORGANIC FELT ENVELOPE
BUR MEMBRANE
PLY FELT TO BLOCKING
TAPERED EDGE
RIGID INSULATION
STRUCTURAL DECK
ROUND OFF EDGE OF TREATED WOOD BLOCKING
GRAVEL STOP SET IN A FULL BED OF PLASTIC ROOF CEMENT
CONTINUOUS CLEAT

EDGE FLASHING

CONTINUOUS SEALANT
TWO-PIECE METAL COUNTERFLASHING
BASE FLASHING
STRIP-IN PLY-FELT FLASHING
BUR MEMBRANE
FIELD VERIFY
GRAVEL STOP TRANSITION PIECE
SPLICE JOINT
GRAVEL STOP
CONTINUOUS CLEAT

GRAVEL STOP TRANSITION

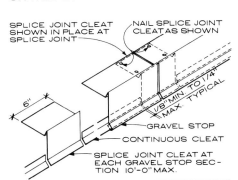

SPLICE JOINT CLEAT SHOWN IN PLACE AT SPLICE JOINT
NAIL SPLICE JOINT CLEAT AS SHOWN
1/8" MIN. TO 1/4" MAX. TYPICAL
6"
GRAVEL STOP
CONTINUOUS CLEAT
SPLICE JOINT CLEAT AT EACH GRAVEL STOP SECTION 10'-0" MAX.

GRAVEL STOP SPLICE JOINT

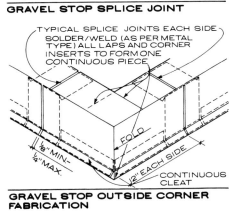

TYPICAL SPLICE JOINTS EACH SIDE
SOLDER/WELD (AS PER METAL TYPE) ALL LAPS AND CORNER INSERTS TO FORM ONE CONTINUOUS PIECE
FOLD
1/8" MIN. 1/4" MAX.
2" EACH SIDE
CONTINUOUS CLEAT

GRAVEL STOP OUTSIDE CORNER FABRICATION

Joseph J. Williams, AIA; A/R/C Associates Inc.; Orlando, Florida

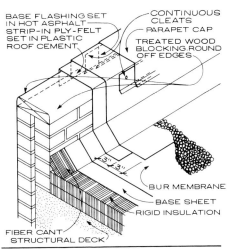

BASE FLASHING SET IN HOT ASPHALT
STRIP-IN PLY-FELT SET IN PLASTIC ROOF CEMENT
CONTINUOUS CLEATS
PARAPET CAP
TREATED WOOD BLOCKING, ROUND OFF EDGES
BUR MEMBRANE
BASE SHEET
RIGID INSULATION
3" 3"
FIBER CANT
STRUCTURAL DECK

PARAPET EDGE DETAIL

1/8" MIN. TO 1/4" MAX. TYPICAL
PARAPET CAP
SPLICE JOINT CLEAT
CONTINUOUS BEAD OF SEALANT AT CENTER AND DOUBLE BOTH SIDES OF SPLICE JOINT
CLEAT. SEALANT TO MATCH COLOR OF METAL
CONTINUOUS CLEAT

SECTION THROUGH SPLICE JOINT

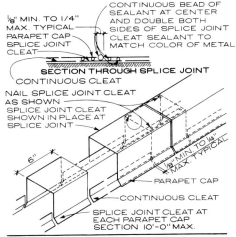

NAIL SPLICE JOINT CLEAT AS SHOWN
SPLICE JOINT CLEAT SHOWN IN PLACE AT SPLICE JOINT
6"
1/8" MIN. TO 1/4" MAX. TYPICAL
PARAPET CAP
CONTINUOUS CLEAT
SPLICE JOINT CLEAT AT EACH PARAPET CAP SECTION 10'-0" MAX.

PARAPET CAP SPLICE JOINT

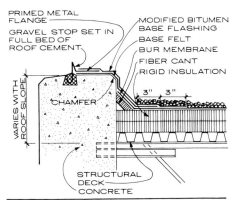

PRIMED METAL FLANGE
GRAVEL STOP SET IN FULL BED OF ROOF CEMENT
VARIES WITH ROOF SLOPE
CHAMFER
MODIFIED BITUMEN BASE FLASHING
BASE FELT
BUR MEMBRANE
FIBER CANT
RIGID INSULATION
3" 3"
STRUCTURAL DECK
CONCRETE

EDGE DETAIL

USER GUIDES TO FLASHING METAL SELECTION

Each commonly used flashing metal has distinctive characteristics, uses, and limitations. Thickness of materials is a function of material size, aesthetic consideration (prevention of oil-canning), and wind uplift due to metal movement during violent storms.

GALVANIZED STEEL

Galvanized steel flashings should be a minimum of 24 gauge with a G-90 galvanized coating. Of commonly used flashing metals, galvanized steel probably is the most common and least expensive. Although galvanized flashing metal may be left exposed, generally it is painted to further protect the steel from corrosion. Before it is painted, galvanized material must be prepared. Plain galvanized material chemically etched in the field is preferred for surfaces to be painted. Factory etching, in which the metal is dipped in an acid bath, etches it on all sides. As a result, exposed edges often rust. Field etching is preferred because only the surfaces to be painted are etched. After etching, the surface should be primed and finish painted, preferably with two coats.

Galvanized steel is easy to solder, low in cost, and easy to work. All flashing metal transitions and terminations should be soldered fully for permanent installation; however, this should not be done at metal flashing joints where movement caused by thermal expansion is expected or at building expansion joints.

STAINLESS STEEL

Stainless steel has many advantages of other steel products, yet generally is corrosion resistant and can be field soldered to accommodate difficult transitions and terminations. If the mill finish appearance is unacceptable, stainless steel may be painted after installation with primer and finish coat.

COPPER

Copper also is a lifetime, relatively maintenance-free material. It can be soldered and molded easily, making it adaptable to complicated transitions and plane changes. Its terminations should be soldered fully. Runoff from the metal can stain adjoining building materials. Generally, copper is softer than other flashing metals and has a moderate expansion coefficient higher than steel, but less than aluminum.

ALUMINUM

Aluminum is a permanent material that corrodes slowly; however, it oxidizes and pits over time, depending on exposure. Since aluminum only can be welded, field connections can be difficult. Although corners can be prefabricated, some plane changes may be difficult. Aluminum has a high expansion and contraction coefficient compared with other flashing metals.

MAJOR COMPONENTS

The major components of a good joint seal are the substrate, primer, joint filler, bond breaker, and sealant.

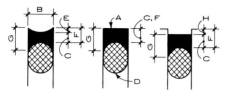

A — sealant
B — sealant width
C — sealant depth
D — joint-filler

E — tooling depth
F — joint-filler depth
G — sealant contact depth
H — sealant recess depth

TYPICAL VERTICAL APPLICATIONS, PROFILES, AND TERMINOLOGY

SUBSTRATE

The more common substrates are masonry concrete, metal, and glass. These are generally classified as porous or nonporous.

Some substrates may not be suitable for achieving a bond unless treated mechanically, chemically, or both.

When the substrate has a coating, the coating must be compatible with the sealant and its bond to the substrate and sealant must be adequate.

Proprietary treatments or protective coatings on metal and waterproofing or water-repellent treatments on concrete may inhibit bonding. Consult both substrate and sealant manufacturers for suitable joint preparation methods and the primers to be used before applying joint materials. Adhesion testing of trial applications in the field is recommended.

Surface laitance and incompatible or bond-inhibiting form release agents on concrete surfaces must be removed.

Substrates must be clean, dry, sound, and free of loose particles, contaminants, foreign matter, water-soluble material, and frost.

Joints in masonry and concrete should be sealed before cleaning exposed surfaces and applying required protective barriers.

PRIMER

The purpose of a primer is to improve the adhesion of a sealant to a substrate. Many sealants require primers on all substrates, some on only certain substrates or on none at all. Most require a primer for maximum adhesion to concrete and masonry surfaces.

JOINT FILLERS

A joint filler is used to control the depth of sealant in the joint and permit full wetting of the intended interface when tooled.

Some joint fillers may be incompatible with the substrate and sealant, causing stains on either one of them or both. Some may be factory coated with a suitable material that provides a barrier to staining. To confirm its suitability, the barrier coating should be acceptable to both the sealant and joint filler manufacturers.

Joint fillers for vertical application may be flexible, compatible, closed cell plastic foam or sponge rubber rod stock and elastomeric tubing of such materials as neoprene, butyl, and EPDM. They should resist permanent deformation before and during sealant application, be nonabsorbent to water or gas, and resist flowing upon mild heating, since this can cause bubbling of the sealant. Open cell sponge type materials such as urethane foam may be satisfactory provided that their water absorption characteristics are recognized. The sealant should be applied immediately after joint filler placement to prevent water absorption from rain. Elastomeric tubing of neoprene, butyl, or EPDM may be applied immediately as a temporary seal until the primary sealant is

put in place, after which they serve to a limited degree as a secondary water barrier. When used as temporary seals, joint fillers should be able to remain resilient at temperatures down to −15°F and have low compression set.

Joint fillers for horizontal application for floors, pavements, sidewalks, patios, and other light-traffic areas may be compatible, extruded, closed cell, high density, flexible foams, corkboard, resin-impregnated fiberboard, or elastomeric tubing or rods. These joint fillers should remain resilient down to −15°F, exhibit good recovery, not cause the sealant to bubble in the joint because of heat, and be capable of supporting the sealant in traffic areas. They should not exude liquids under compression, which could hydraulically cause sealant failure by forcing the sealant from the joint. Combinations of joint filler may be used to form a joint in concrete, and an additional joint filler material may be installed under compression across the width and to the proper depth just before the sealant is applied to provide a clean, dry, compatible backup.

BOND BREAKER

A bond breaker may be necessary to prevent adhesion of the sealant to any surface or material where such adhesion would be detrimental to the performance of the sealant.

The use of a joint filler to which the sealant will not adhere may preclude the need for a bond breaker.

The bond breaker may be a polyethylene tape with pressure-sensitive adhesive on one side or various liquid applied compounds, as recommended by the sealant manufacturer.

SEALANT

Sealants are classified as single component or multicomponent, nonsag or self-leveling, and traffic or nontraffic use, as well as according to movement capability. Characteristics of some generic types are listed in the accompanying table.

CHARACTERISTICS OF COMMON ELASTOMERIC SEALANTS

	ACRYLIC (SOLVENT RELEASES) (ONE PART)	POLYSULFIDE		POLYURETHANE		SILICONE (ONE-PART)
		TWO-PART	ONE-PART	TWO-PART	ONE-PART	
Chief ingredients	Acrylic terpolymer, inert pigments, stabilizer, and selected fillers	Polysulfide polymers, activators, pigments, plasticizers, inert fillers, gelling, and curing agents		Polyurethane prepolymer, inert fillers, pigment, plasticizers, accelerators, activators, and extenders	Polyurethane prepolymer, inert fillers, pigment, and plasticizers	Siloxane polymer, pigment, and selected fillers
Percent solids	85–95	95–100	95–100	95–100	95–100	95–100
Curing process	Solvent release and very slow chemical cure	Chemical reaction with curing agent	Chemical reaction with moisture in the air	Chemical reaction with curing agent	Chemical reaction with moisture in air, also oxygen	Chemical reaction with moisture in air
Curing characteristics	Skins on exposed surface; interior remains soft and tacky	Cures uniformly throughout; rate affected by temperature and humidity	Skins over, cures progressively inward; final cure uniform throughout	Cures uniformly throughout; rate affected by temperature and humidity	Skins over, cures progressively inward; final cure uniform throughout	Cures progressively inward; final cure uniform throughout
Primer	Generally not required	Manufacturer's approved primer required for porous surfaces, sometimes for other surfaces		Manufacturer's approved primer required for most surfaces		Required for most surfaces
Application temperature (°F)	40–120	40–100	60–100	40–120	40–120	0–120
Tackfree time	1–7 days	6–24 hr	6–72 hr	1–24 hr	Slightly tacky until weathered	1 hr or less
Hardness, Shore A Cured 1 to 6 months Aged 5 years	0–25 45–55	15–45 30–60	25–35 40–50	20–40 35–55	25–45 30–50	20–40 35–55
Toxicity	Nontoxic	Curing agent is toxic	Contains toxic ingredients	Toxic; gloves recommended for handling		Nontoxic
Cure time (days)	14	7	14–21	3–5	14	5
Joint movement capability (max.)	±12.5%	±25%	±15%	±25%	±15%	±25% high modulus ±50% low modulus
Ultraviolet resistance (direct)	Very good	Poor to good	Good	Poor to good	Poor to good	Excellent
Dirt resistance cured	Good	Good	Good	Good	Good	Poor
Use characteristics	Excellent adhesion; poor low-temperature flexibility; not usable in traffic areas; unpleasant odor 5–12 days	Wide range of appropriate applications; curing time depends on temperature and humidity	Unpleasant odor; broad range of cured hardnesses available	Sets very fast; broad range of cured hardnesses; excellent for concrete joints and traffic areas	Excellent for concrete joints and traffic areas, but substrate must be absolutely dry; short package stability	Requires contact with air for curing; low abrasion resistance; not tough enough for use in traffic areas

Charles J. Parise, FAIA, FASTM; Smith, Hinchman & Grylls Associates, Inc.; Detroit, Michigan

JOINT DESIGN

The design geometry of a joint seal is related to numerous factors including desired appearance, spacing of joints, anticipated movement in joint, movement capability of sealant to be used, required sealant width to accommodate anticipated movement, and tooling method.

SEALANT WIDTH

The required width of the sealant relative to thermal movement is determined by the application temperature range of the sealant, the temperature extremes anticipated at the site location, the temperature at the time of sealant application, and the movement capability of the sealant to be used. In the absence of specific application temperature knowledge, an ambient application temperature from 4 to 38°C (40 to 100°F) should be assumed in determining the anticipated amount of joint movement in the design of joints. Although affected by ambient temperatures, anticipated joint movement must be determined from anticipated building material temperature extremes rather than ambient temperature extremes.

The accompanying graph provides an average working relationship of recommended joint widths for sealants with various movement capabilities based only on thermal expansion of the more common substrates. These joint widths should be considered as minimal. They do not take into consideration variations in joint dimensions encountered during construction or temperature extremes at the time of sealant application. It is advisable to consider these variables and to also incorporate a safety factor (s.f.) into the joint design by only using a percentage of the stated sealant movement capability, since sealants do not always perform at their stated maximum capabilities.

Many other factors can be involved in building joint movement including, but not limited to, material mass, color, insulation, wind loads, settlement, thermal conductivity, differential thermal stress (bowing), residual growth or shrinkage of materials, building sway, and seismic forces. Of particular importance are material and construction tolerances that can produce joints on the

job site smaller than anticipated. The design joint width should be calculated taking all possible movement and tolerance factors into consideration, as shown with the following examples:

$$J = \text{minimum joint width (inches)}$$
$$= \frac{100}{X} (M_t + M_o) + T$$

X = percentage of stated movement capability of the sealant by ASTM Test Method C719

M_t = joint movement due to thermal expansion of substrates (inches)
$$= (E_c) (\Delta_t) (L)$$

where E_c = coefficient of expansion of substrate from accompanying table (in./in./°F)

Δ_t = temperature change of substrate (°F)

L = substrate length (inches)

M_o = joint movement due to other factors (inches)

T = tolerances for construction (inches)

A sample calculation for joint width between concrete panels of 10 ft lengths, expecting a temperature change in the concrete of 120°F, construction tolerances of 0.25 in., and sealed with a sealant capable of a maximum ±25% (reduced to 20% for s.f.) movement is

$$J = \frac{100}{X} M_t + T$$
$$= \frac{100}{X} (E_c) (\Delta_t) (L) + T$$
$$= \frac{100}{20} (6 \times 10^{-6} \text{ in./in./°F}) (120°F) (120 \text{ in.})$$
$$\quad + 0.25 \text{ in.}$$
$$= 0.68 \text{ in.}$$

A more simplified method (but not as accurate) is to use the accompanying graph as follows:

$$J = (\text{joint width scaled}) + T$$
$$= (0.5 \text{ in./in./°F}) \left(\frac{120°F}{130°F} \right) + 0.25 \text{ in.}$$
$$= 0.71 \text{ in.}$$

SEALANT DEPTH

The sealant depth, when applied, depends on the sealant width. The following guidelines are normally accepted practice.

1. For a recommended minimum width of ¼ in., the depth should by ¼ in.
2. For joints in concrete, masonry, or stone, the depth of the sealant may be equal to the sealant width in joints up to ½ in. For joints ½ to 1 in. wide, the sealant depth should be one-half the width. For joints 1 to 2 in. wide, the sealant depth should not be greater than ½ in. For widths exceeding 2 in., the depth should be determined by the sealant manufacturer.
3. For sealant widths over ¼ in. and up to ½ in. in metal, glass, and other nonporous surface joints, the minimum of ¼ in. in depth applies, and over ½ in. in width the sealant depth shold be one-half the sealant width and should in no case exceed ½ in.

When determining location of the joint filler in the joint, consideration should be given to the reduction in sealant depth with concave and recessed tooled joints, and the joint should be designed accordingly.

COEFFICIENTS OF EXPANSION

MATERIALS	AVERAGE COEFFICIENT OF LINEAR EXPANSION (MULTIPLY BY 10^{-6})	
	CENTIGRADE (MM/MM/°C)	FAHRENHEIT (IN./IN./°F)
Aluminum:		
5005 or 6061 alloy	23.8	13.2
Brass:		
230 alloy	18.7	10.4
Bronze:		
220 alloy	18.4	10.2
385 alloy	20.9	11.6
Clay masonry:		
Clay or shale brick	6.5	3.6
Fire clay brick or tile	4.5	2.5
Concrete masonry:		
Dense aggregate	9.4	5.2
Lightweight aggregate	7.7	4.3
Concrete:		
Calcareous aggregate	9.0	5.0
Siliceous aggregate	10.8	6.0
Quartzite aggregate	12.6	7.0
Copper:		
110 alloy	16.9	9.4
122 alloy	16.9	9.4
Glass	8.8	4.9
Iron:		
Cast, gray	10.6	5.9
Wrought	12.1	6.7
Lead	28.6	15.9
Plastic:		
Acrylic sheet	74.0	41.0
High-impact acrylic sheet	50.0	82.0
Polycarbonate sheet	68.4	38.0
Steel, Carbon	12.1	6.7
Steel, Stainless:		
301 alloy	16.9	9.4
302 alloy	17.3	9.6
304 alloy	17.3	9.6
316 alloy	16.0	8.9
Stone:		
Granite	5.0–11.0	2.8– 6.1
Limestone	4.0–12.0	2.2– 6.7
Marble	6.7–22.1	3.7–12.3
Sandstone	8.0–12.0	4.4– 6.7
Slate	8.0–10.0	4.4– 5.6
Travertine	6.0–10.0	3.3– 5.6
Zinc	32.4	18.0

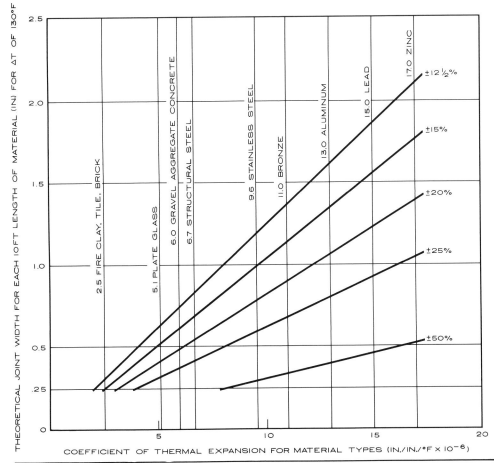

RECOMMENDED JOINT WIDTH FOR SEALANTS WITH VARIOUS MOVEMENT CAPABILITIES

Charles J. Parise, FAIA, FASTM; Smith, Hinchman & Grylls Associates, Inc.; Detroit, Michigan

APPLICATION

To obtain proper adhesion, it is essential that the sealant come in direct contact with the substrate, that the sealant wet the surface of the substrate, and that the substrate be strong enough to provide a firm anchor for the sealant. If any of these conditions is not met, poor adhesion will usually result. The sealant should be installed in such a manner as to completely fill the recess provided in the joint.

Against a porous material, the sealant must enter the pores if good adhesion is to be obtained. Sealants used for this application are thixotropic and will resist flow into the pores unless an external force is applied. Proper filling of the recess accomplishes this, in part, and proper tooling ensures it.

JOINT PREPARATION

Joints to receive sealant should be cleaned out and raked to full width and depth required for installation of joint seal materials. Thoroughly clean all joints, removing all foreign matter such as dust, paint (unless it is a permanent protective coating), oil, grease, waterproofing or water-repellent treatments, water, surface dirt, and frost. Clean porous materials such as concrete, masonry, and unglazed surfaces of ceramic tile by brushing, grinding, blast cleaning, mechanical abrading, acid washing, or a combination of these methods to provide a clean, sound substrate for optimum sealant adhesion. The surface of concrete may be cut back to remove contaminants and expose a clean surface when acceptable to the purchaser.

Remove laitance from concrete by acid washing, grinding, or mechanical abrading and remove form oils from concrete by blast cleaning. Remove loose particles originally present or resulting from grinding, abrading, or blast cleaning by blowing out joints with oil-free compressed air (or vacuuming) prior to application of primer or sealant.

Clean nonporous surfaces, such as metal, glass, porcelain enamel, and glazed surfaces of ceramic tile chemically or by other means that are not harmful to the substrate and are acceptable to the substrate manufacturer.

Remove temporary protective coatings on metallic surfaces by a solvent that leaves no residue. Apply the solvent with clean oil-free cloths or lintless paper towels. Do not dip cleaning cloths into solvent. Always pour the solvent on the cloth to eliminate the possibility of contaminating the solvent. Do not allow the solvent to air-dry without wiping. Wipe dry with a clean dry cloth or lintless paper towels. Permanent coatings that are to remain must not be removed or damaged.

MASKING TAPE

Install masking tape at joint edges when necessary to avoid undesirable sealant smears on exposed visible surfaces. Use a nonstaining, nonabsorbent, compatible type.

PRIMER AND JOINT FILLER

Install primer when and as recommended by the sealant manufacturer for optimum adhesion.

Install compatible joint filler uniformly to proper depth without twisting and braiding.

SEALANT

Install sealant in strict accordance with the manufacturer's recommendations and precautions. Completely fill the recess provided in the joint. Sealants are more safely applied at temperatures above 40°F. Joints must be dry.

TOOLING

Tooling nonsag sealants is essential to force the sealant into the joint and eliminate air pockets and should be done as soon as possible after application and before skinning or curing begins. Tooling also ensures contact of the sealant to the sides of a joint.

Plastic or metal tools may be used. Most applicators use dry tools, but they may be surface-treated to prevent adhesion to the sealant and may be shaped as desired to produce the desired joint profile. Dipping tools in certain liquids decreases adhesion of the sealant to the tool. All liquids should first be tested and accepted for use by the manufacturer. The use of some liquids may result in surface discoloration. In using tooling liquids, care should be taken to ensure that the liquid does not contact joint surfaces prior to the sealant contacting the joint surface. If the sealant overlaps the area contaminated with the liquid, the sealant bond may be adversely affected.

Tool sealant so as to force it into the joint, eliminating air pockets and ensuring contact of the sealant with the sides of the joint. Use appropriate tool to provide a concave, flush, or recessed joint as required.

Immediately after tooling the joint, remove masking tape carefully, if used, without disturbing the sealant.

FIELD TESTING

In cases where the building joints are ready to receive sealant and the question of adhesion of the sealant to novel or untried surfaces arises, it is advisable to install the sealant in a 1.5-m (5 ft) length of joint as a test. It would be good practice to do this as a matter of standard procedure on most projects, even though unusual conditions are not suspected. Following instructions of the sealant manufacturer and using primer as and when recommended, install the sealant in the joint and examine for adhesion after cure to determine whether proper adhesion has been obtained.

Reference: ASTM C-962 "Standard Guide for Use of Elastomeric Joint Sealants." Highlights of text, graph, and figures are reprinted with permission from ASTM Committee C-24 of the American Society for Testing and Materials.

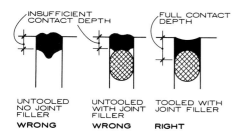

A — sealant
B — removable joint filler
C — premolded joint filler cast in concrete
D — joint filler installed under compression

E — bond breaker (use over sliding metal support in relatively wide joints)
F — concrete shoulder provides vertical support

PURPOSE FOR JOINT FILLER AND TOOLING

USE OF MULTIPLE JOINT FILLERS IN HORIZONTAL APPLICATIONS IN CAST-IN-PLACE CONCRETE

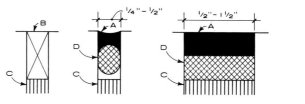

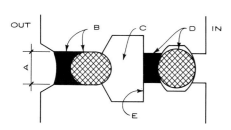

A — 1" minimum for access to interior air seal
B — sealant and joint filler preferred for rain screen; preformed compression seal also used
C — pressure equalization chamber; vent to outside, and chamber baffles at every second floor vertically and same distance horizontally
D — sealant and joint filler installed from outside to facilitate continuity of air seal; building framework hinders application of continuous air seal from interior
E — concrete shoulders required for tooling screed

TWO-STAGE PRESSURE EQUALIZED JOINT SEAL

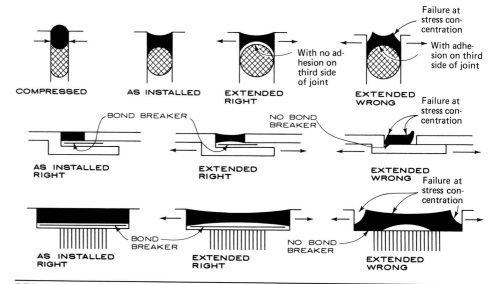

SEALANT CONFIGURATIONS WITH MOVEMENT AND EFFECT OF THREE-SIDED ADHESION

Charles J. Parise, FAIA, FASTM; Smith, Hinchman & Grylls Associates, Inc.; Detroit, Michigan

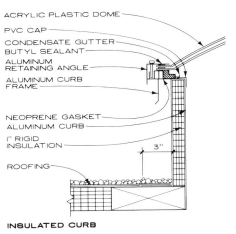

ACRYLIC PLASTIC DOME
PVC CAP
CONDENSATE GUTTER
BUTYL SEALANT
ALUMINUM RETAINING ANGLE
ALUMINUM CURB FRAME
NEOPRENE GASKET
ALUMINUM CURB
1" RIGID INSULATION
ROOFING
3"

INSULATED CURB

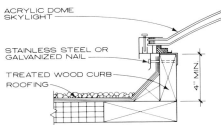

ACRYLIC DOME SKYLIGHT
STAINLESS STEEL OR GALVANIZED NAIL
TREATED WOOD CURB
ROOFING
4" MIN.

WOOD CURB

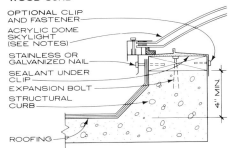

OPTIONAL CLIP AND FASTENER
ACRYLIC DOME SKYLIGHT (SEE NOTES)
STAINLESS OR GALVANIZED NAIL
SEALANT UNDER CLIP
EXPANSION BOLT
STRUCTURAL CURB
ROOFING
4" MIN.

CONCRETE CURB

DETAIL A: CURB TYPES

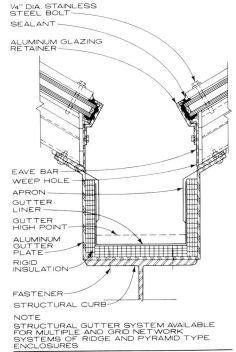

1/4" DIA. STAINLESS STEEL BOLT
SEALANT
ALUMINUM GLAZING RETAINER
EAVE BAR
WEEP HOLE
APRON
GUTTER LINER
GUTTER HIGH POINT
ALUMINUM GUTTER PLATE
RIGID INSULATION
FASTENER
STRUCTURAL CURB
NOTE
STRUCTURAL GUTTER SYSTEM AVAILABLE FOR MULTIPLE AND GRID NETWORK SYSTEMS OF RIDGE AND PYRAMID TYPE ENCLOSURES

DETAIL B: GUTTER

CTA Architects Engineers; Billings, Montana
Wheeler & Guay Architects PC; Alexandria, Virginia

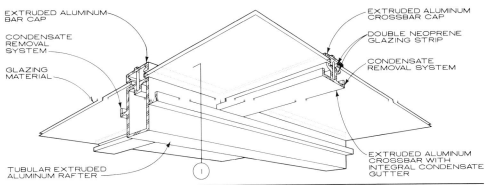

EXTRUDED ALUMINUM BAR CAP
CONDENSATE REMOVAL SYSTEM
GLAZING MATERIAL
TUBULAR EXTRUDED ALUMINUM RAFTER
EXTRUDED ALUMINUM CROSSBAR CAP
DOUBLE NEOPRENE GLAZING STRIP
CONDENSATE REMOVAL SYSTEM
EXTRUDED ALUMINUM CROSSBAR WITH INTEGRAL CONDENSATE GUTTER

DETAIL C: TYPICAL TUBULAR ALUMINUM FRAMING

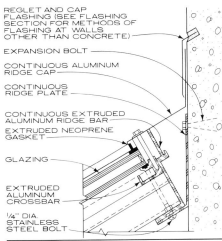

REGLET AND CAP FLASHING (SEE FLASHING SECTION FOR METHODS OF FLASHING AT WALLS OTHER THAN CONCRETE)
EXPANSION BOLT
CONTINUOUS ALUMINUM RIDGE CAP
CONTINUOUS RIDGE PLATE
CONTINUOUS EXTRUDED ALUMINUM RIDGE BAR
EXTRUDED NEOPRENE GASKET
GLAZING
EXTRUDED ALUMINUM CROSSBAR
1/4" DIA. STAINLESS STEEL BOLT

DETAIL D: RIDGE AT SHED

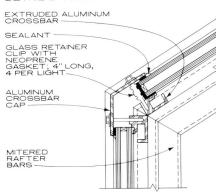

EXTRUDED ALUMINUM CROSSBAR
SEALANT
GLASS RETAINER CLIP WITH NEOPRENE GASKET; 4" LONG, 4 PER LIGHT
ALUMINUM CROSSBAR CAP
MITERED RAFTER BARS

DETAIL E: KNEE EDGE

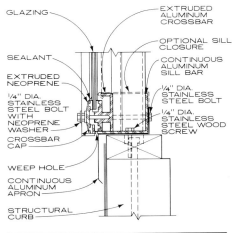

GLAZING
SEALANT
EXTRUDED NEOPRENE
1/4" DIA. STAINLESS STEEL BOLT WITH NEOPRENE WASHER
CROSSBAR CAP
WEEP HOLE
CONTINUOUS ALUMINUM APRON
STRUCTURAL CURB
EXTRUDED ALUMINUM CROSSBAR
OPTIONAL SILL CLOSURE
CONTINUOUS ALUMINUM SILL BAR
1/4" DIA. STAINLESS STEEL BOLT
1/4" DIA. STAINLESS STEEL WOOD SCREW

DETAIL F: VERTICAL SILL

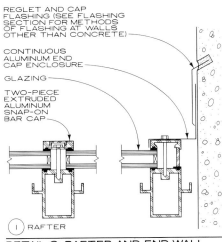

REGLET AND CAP FLASHING (SEE FLASHING SECTION FOR METHODS OF FLASHING AT WALLS OTHER THAN CONCRETE)
CONTINUOUS ALUMINUM END CAP ENCLOSURE
GLAZING
TWO-PIECE EXTRUDED ALUMINUM SNAP-ON BAR CAP
① RAFTER

DETAIL G: RAFTER AND END WALL

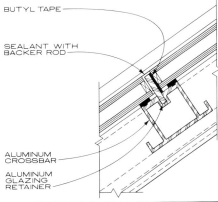

BUTYL TAPE
SEALANT WITH BACKER ROD
ALUMINUM CROSSBAR
ALUMINUM GLAZING RETAINER

DETAIL H: BUTT GLAZING

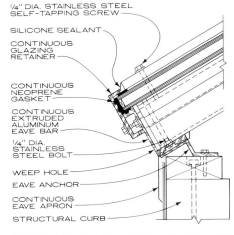

1/4" DIA. STAINLESS STEEL SELF-TAPPING SCREW
SILICONE SEALANT
CONTINUOUS GLAZING RETAINER
CONTINUOUS NEOPRENE GASKET
CONTINUOUS EXTRUDED ALUMINUM EAVE BAR
1/4" DIA. STAINLESS STEEL BOLT
WEEP HOLE
EAVE ANCHOR
CONTINUOUS EAVE APRON
STRUCTURAL CURB

DETAIL J: EAVE OR SILL

SKYLIGHTS 7

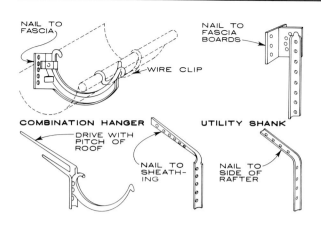

COMBINATION HANGER

DRIVE WITH PITCH OF ROOF

UTILITY SHANK

NAIL TO SHEATH-ING

NAIL TO SIDE OF RAFTER

DRIVE HANGER　　VARIOUS SHANKS

SHANK AND CIRCLE HANGERS

Available in malleable and wrought copper, bronze, stainless steel and aluminum. Only a sampling of the wide variety of shapes available is shown. See mfrs. literature.

GUTTER HANGERS

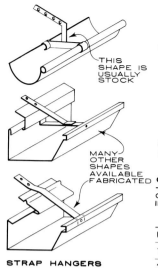

THIS SHAPE IS USUALLY STOCK

MANY OTHER SHAPES AVAILABLE FABRICATED

STRAP HANGERS

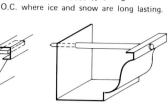

NOTE: Gutter hangers are normally spaced 3'-0" O.C. Reduce to 1'-6" O.C. where ice and snow are long lasting.

BRACKET HANGER
Various shapes are available.

SPIKE AND FERRULE
Not recommended if girth is over 15 in.

GUTTER BRACKET OR STRAP SIZES

GIRTH INCHES	GALV. STEEL INCHES	COPPER INCHES	ALUM. INCHES	STAINLESS INCHES
UP TO 15	1/8 x 1	1/8 x 1	3/16 x 1	1/8 x 1
15 TO 20	3/16 x 1	1/4 x 1	1/4 x 1	1/8 x 1 1/2
20 TO 24	1/4 x 1 1/2	1/4 x 1 1/2	1/4 x 2	1/8 x 2

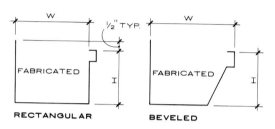

RECTANGULAR　　BEVELED　　OGEE OR STYLE "K"　　SEMICIRCULAR OR HALF-ROUND

OGEE OR STYLE "K"

2 1/2" H x 3" W		
2 3/4" H x 4" W	G A	
3 3/4" H x 5" W	G A	
4 3/4" H x 6" W	G	
5 1/4" H x 7" W		
6" H x 8" W		

SEMICIRCULAR OR HALF-ROUND

4" W	G
5" W	G A
6" W	G A
7" W	G
8" W	G

NOTE: Stock sizes—G = galvanized, A = aluminum.

METAL GUTTER NOTES

Various sizes and other shapes available.

Always keep front 1/2 in. lower than back of gutter.

Do not use width less than 4 in. except for canopies and small porches. Minimum ratio of depth to width should be 3 to 4.

METAL GUTTER SHAPES AND SIZES

NOTES

1. Continuous gutters may be formed at the installation site with cold forming equipment, thus eliminating joints in long runs of gutter.
2. Girth is width of sheet metal from which gutter is fabricated.
3. Sizes listed in table to the left but not marked stock are available on special order.
4. Aluminum and galvanized steel are more commonly used, whereas copper and especially stainless steel are least used.
5. All jointing methods are applicable to most gutter shapes. Lap joints are more commonly used. Seal all joints with mastic or by soldering. Lock, slip, or lap joints do not provide expansion.
6. See SMACNA Architectural Sheet Metal Manual for gutter sizing and details.

EXPANSION JOINTS

Expansion joints should be used on all straight runs over 40 ft. In a 10 ft section of gutter and a 100° temperature change linear expansion will be:

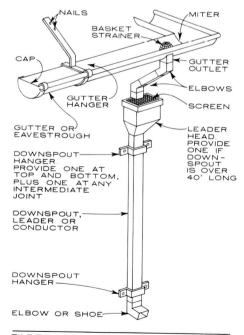

CAP

GUTTER HANGER

GUTTER OR EAVESTROUGH

DOWNSPOUT HANGER PROVIDE ONE AT TOP AND BOTTOM, PLUS ONE AT ANY INTERMEDIATE JOINT

DOWNSPOUT, LEADER OR CONDUCTOR

DOWNSPOUT HANGER

ELBOW OR SHOE

NAILS　MITER

BASKET STRAINER

GUTTER OUTLET

ELBOWS

SCREEN

LEADER HEAD. PROVIDE ONE IF DOWN-SPOUT IS OVER 40' LONG

PARTS OF A GUTTER

NOTE

PVC plastic gutter and downspout parts are similar to metal. See manufacturers' data for shapes and sizes.

Jones/Richards and Associates; Ogden, Utah
Lawrence W. Cobb; Columbia, South Carolina

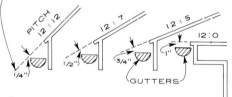

DASH LINE INDICATES ROOF SLOPE

PITCH 12:12　12:7　12:5　12:0

GUTTERS

Gutters should be placed below slope line so that snow and ice can slide clear. Steeper pitch requires less clearance.

PLACING OF GUTTERS

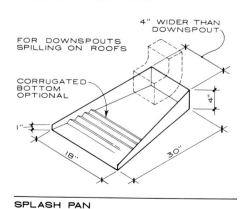

4" WIDER THAN DOWNSPOUT

FOR DOWNSPOUTS SPILLING ON ROOFS

CORRUGATED BOTTOM OPTIONAL

SPLASH PAN

EXPANSION OF METAL GUTTERS IN 40 FT

METAL	COEFFICIENT OF EXPANSION	MOVEMENT
Aluminum	.00128	.15 in.
Copper	.00093	.11 in.
Galvanized steel	.0065	.08 in.

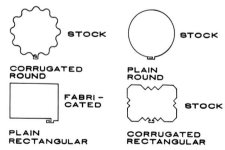

CORRUGATED ROUND　STOCK

PLAIN ROUND　STOCK

PLAIN RECTANGULAR　FABRICATED

CORRUGATED RECTANGULAR　STOCK

NOTES

Space downspouts 20 ft min., 50 ft max., generally. Extreme max. 60 ft.

Do not use size smaller than 7.00 in area except for canopies.

Corrugated shapes resist freezing better than plain shapes.

Elbows available: 45°, 60°, 75°, 90°.

REFERENCES

GENERAL REFERENCES

The NRCA Roofing and Waterproofing Manual, National Roofing Contractors Association (NRCA)

Architectural Sheet Metal Manual, Sheet Metal and Air Conditioning Contractors National Association

Fundamentals of Building Insulation, Insulating Board Institute

Manual of Built-Up Roofing Systems, 2nd ed., 1982, C. W. Griffin, McGraw-Hill

DATA SOURCES: ORGANIZATIONS

Aluminum Company of America (Alcoa), 163, 167
American Plywood Association (APA), 164
Architectural Engineering Products Company, 175
Asphalt Roofing Manufacturers Association (ARMA), 160
Buckingham-Virginia Slate Corporation, 161
Carlisle Corporation, 169
Celotex Corporation, 186
Certain-Teed Corporation, 160
Fisher Skylights, Inc., 191
H. H. Robertson Company, 167
Johns-Manville Sales Corporation, 160, 186
Kaiser Aluminum and Chemical Sales, Inc., 163
Koppers Company, Inc., 158
Long Fir Gutter Company, 192
Ludowici-Celadon Company, 162
MM Systems Corporation, 175
National Roofing Contractors' Association (NRCA), 169, 180, 183, 185, 186
Perma Clad Industries, 175
Red Cedar Shingle and Handsplit Shake Bureau (RCSHSB), 158
Shakertown Corporation, 157, 158
Underwriters' Laboratories, Inc. (U.L.), 171

DATA SOURCES: PUBLICATIONS

Architectural Sheet Metal Manual, Sheet Metal and Air Conditioning Contractors' National Association, Inc. (SMACNA), 173–187, 192

Bob Bates Associates, Various Foundation Waterproofing Methods and Conditions, 157

Underground Waterproofing, Brent Anderson, WEBCO Publishing, Inc., 157

CHAPTER **8**

DOORS AND WINDOWS

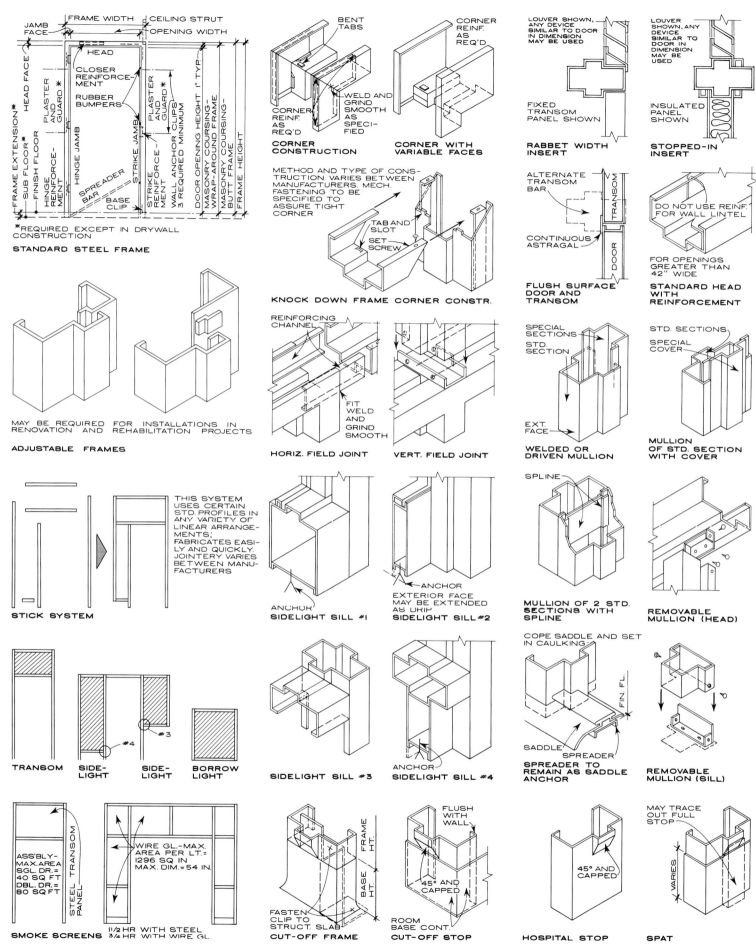

STANDARD STEEL FRAME

*REQUIRED EXCEPT IN DRYWALL CONSTRUCTION

ADJUSTABLE FRAMES

MAY BE REQUIRED FOR INSTALLATIONS IN RENOVATION AND REHABILITATION PROJECTS

STICK SYSTEM

THIS SYSTEM USES CERTAIN STD. PROFILES IN ANY VARIETY OF LINEAR ARRANGEMENTS; FABRICATES EASILY AND QUICKLY. JOINTERY VARIES BETWEEN MANUFACTURERS

TRANSOM **SIDELIGHT** **SIDELIGHT** **BORROW LIGHT**

SMOKE SCREENS

ASS'BLY- MAX.AREA SGL. DR.= 40 SQ FT DBL. DR.= 80 SQ FT

WIRE GL.-MAX. AREA PER LT.= 1296 SQ IN MAX. DIM.= 54 IN.

1½ HR WITH STEEL ¾ HR WITH WIRE GL.

CORNER CONSTRUCTION

CORNER WITH VARIABLE FACES

KNOCK DOWN FRAME CORNER CONSTR.

METHOD AND TYPE OF CONSTRUCTION VARIES BETWEEN MANUFACTURERS. MECH. FASTENING TO BE SPECIFIED TO ASSURE TIGHT CORNER

HORIZ. FIELD JOINT

VERT. FIELD JOINT

SIDELIGHT SILL #1

SIDELIGHT SILL #2

EXTERIOR FACE MAY BE EXTENDED AS DRIP

SIDELIGHT SILL #3

SIDELIGHT SILL #4

CUT-OFF FRAME

CUT-OFF STOP

RABBET WIDTH INSERT

FIXED TRANSOM PANEL SHOWN

LOUVER SHOWN, ANY DEVICE SIMILAR TO DOOR IN DIMENSION MAY BE USED

STOPPED-IN INSERT

INSULATED PANEL SHOWN

LOUVER SHOWN, ANY DEVICE SIMILAR TO DOOR IN DIMENSION MAY BE USED

FLUSH SURFACE DOOR AND TRANSOM

STANDARD HEAD WITH REINFORCEMENT

DO NOT USE REINF. FOR WALL LINTEL

FOR OPENINGS GREATER THAN 42" WIDE

WELDED OR DRIVEN MULLION

MULLION OF STD. SECTION WITH COVER

MULLION OF 2 STD. SECTIONS WITH SPLINE

REMOVABLE MULLION (HEAD)

SPREADER TO REMAIN AS SADDLE ANCHOR

COPE SADDLE AND SET IN CAULKING

REMOVABLE MULLION (SILL)

HOSPITAL STOP

45° AND CAPPED

SPAT

MAY TRACE OUT FULL STOP

VARIES

James W. G. Watson, AIA; Ronald A. Spahn and Associates; Cleveland Heights, Ohio

8   METAL DOORS AND FRAMES

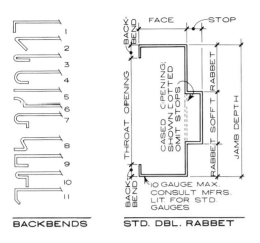

BACKBENDS

STD. DBL. RABBET

Labels on STD. DBL. RABBET drawing: FACE, STOP, BACK-BEND, THROAT OPENING, CASED OPENING; SHOWN SLOTTED, OMIT STOPS, RABBET, SOFFIT, RABBET, JAMB DEPTH, BACK BEND, 10 GAUGE MAX. CONSULT MFRS. LIT. FOR STD. GAUGES

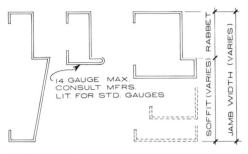

14 GAUGE MAX. CONSULT MFRS. LIT. FOR STD. GAUGES

SOFFIT (VARIES) RABBET, JAMB WIDTH (VARIES)

VARIOUS SINGLE RABBETS

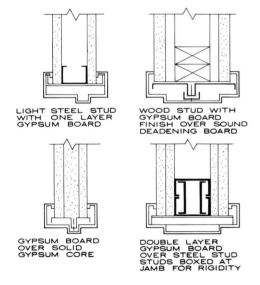

LIGHT STEEL STUD WITH ONE LAYER GYPSUM BOARD

WOOD STUD WITH GYPSUM BOARD FINISH OVER SOUND DEADENING BOARD

GYPSUM BOARD OVER SOLID GYPSUM CORE

DOUBLE LAYER GYPSUM BOARD OVER STEEL STUD STUDS BOXED AT JAMB FOR RIGIDITY

DRYWALL INSTALLATIONS

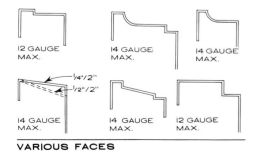

12 GAUGE MAX.   14 GAUGE MAX.   14 GAUGE MAX.

1/4"/2"   1/2"/2"

14 GAUGE MAX.   14 GAUGE MAX.   12 GAUGE MAX.

VARIOUS FACES

VARIOUS STANDARD PROFILES

JAMB DEPTH	2¾	3	3¾	4¾	5½	5¾	6¾	7¾	8¾	12¾
RABBET 3	SINGLE		1 15/16 STD. FOR 1¾" DOOR							
SOFFIT 3	RABBET									
RABBET 3	ONLY		1 9/16 STD. FOR 1⅜" DOOR							
BACKBEND	½	7/16	½	½	¾	½	½	½	½	½
THROAT	1¾	2⅛	2	3¾	4	4¾	5¾	6¾	7¾	11¾

NOTES
1. Many others available. Consult mfrs. list for dimensions and options.
2. Depths vary in 1/8" increments to 12 3/4" max.
3. Omit stops for cased opening frames.
4. Std. stop 5/8", 1/2" min. + std. face 2", 1" min.

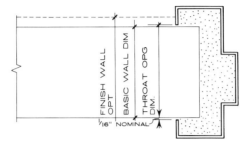

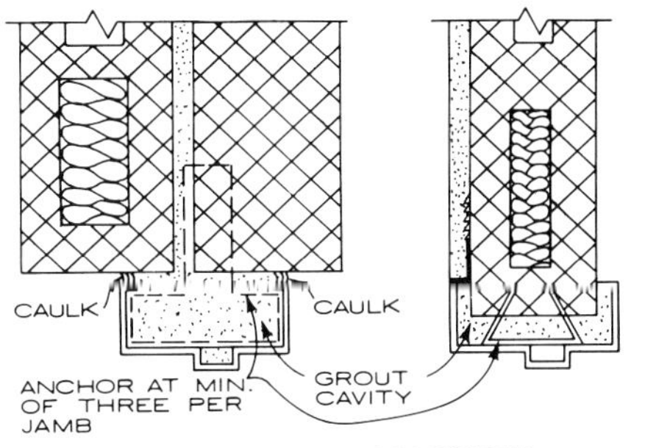

FINISH WALL OPT, BASIC WALL DIM, THROAT OPG. DIM., 1/16" NOMINAL

1. Basic wall dim. < throat opening dim. Fin wall mat'l (dotted may encroach on backbend).
2. Anchors appropriate for wall constr. Req'd. min. 3 per jamb.
3. Fill frame w/mortar or plaster as used in wall.
4. Grout frame, backbend at masonry wall.
5. Backbend may vary as selected.

WRAP-AROUND FRAMES

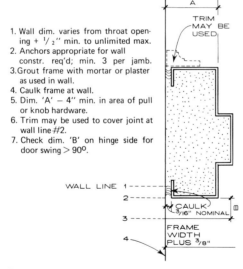

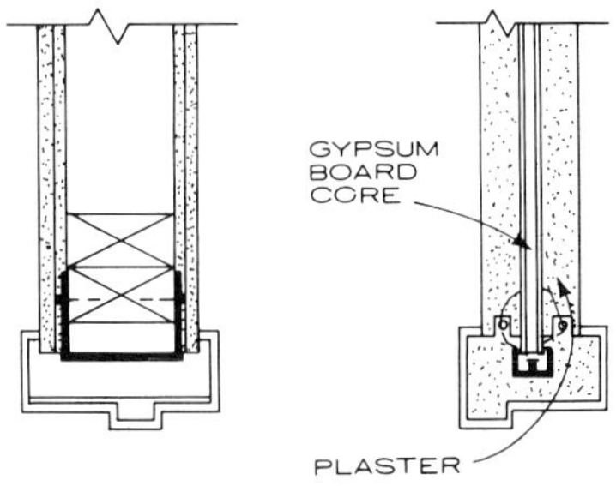

1. Wall dim. varies from throat opening + 1/2" min. to unlimited max.
2. Anchors appropriate for wall constr. req'd; min. 3 per jamb.
3. Grout frame with mortar or plaster as used in wall.
4. Caulk frame at wall.
5. Dim. 'A' — 4" min. in area of pull or knob hardware.
6. Trim may be used to cover joint at wall line #2.
7. Check dim. 'B' on hinge side for door swing > 90º.

A, TRIM MAY BE USED, WALL LINE 1, 2, CAULK 3/16" NOMINAL, 3, 4, FRAME WIDTH PLUS 3/8"

BUTT FRAME

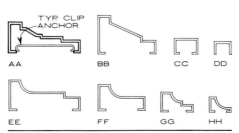

TYP CLIP ANCHOR

AA   BB   CC   DD

EE   FF   GG   HH

VARIOUS TRIM AND SCRIBE MOLDING

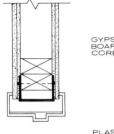

BUTTED TO MASONRY

CAULK, ANCHOR AT MIN. OF THREE PER JAMB

CONCRETE MASONRY UNIT WITH PLASTER FINISH

CAULK, GROUT CAVITY

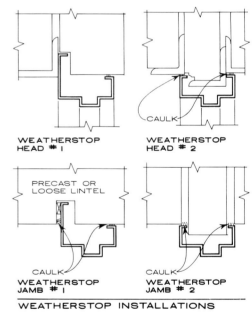

WOOD STUD WITH PLASTER ON PLASTER LATH

SOLID PLASTER

GYPSUM BOARD CORE, PLASTER

VARIOUS INSTALLATIONS

WEATHERSTOP HEAD #1

WEATHERSTOP HEAD #2
CAULK

WEATHERSTOP JAMB #1
PRECAST OR LOOSE LINTEL, CAULK

WEATHERSTOP JAMB #2
CAULK

WEATHERSTOP INSTALLATIONS

NOTES

1. Some details vary between manufacturers.

2. Stock frames stocked in warehouse prior to receipt of order. Certain profiles are warehoused locally.

3. Standard frames manufactured from existing jigs and tooling upon receipt of order. Certain profiles are readily available.

4. Custom frames manufactured in response to specific dimensional requirements of a particular customer. Custom profiles are available with relative delay.

5. Selection should reflect anticipated requirements of construction schedule.

6. Certain detail features will constitute a custom frame, verify with manufacturer.

James W. G. Watson, AIA; Ronald A. Spahn and Associates; Cleveland Heights, Ohio

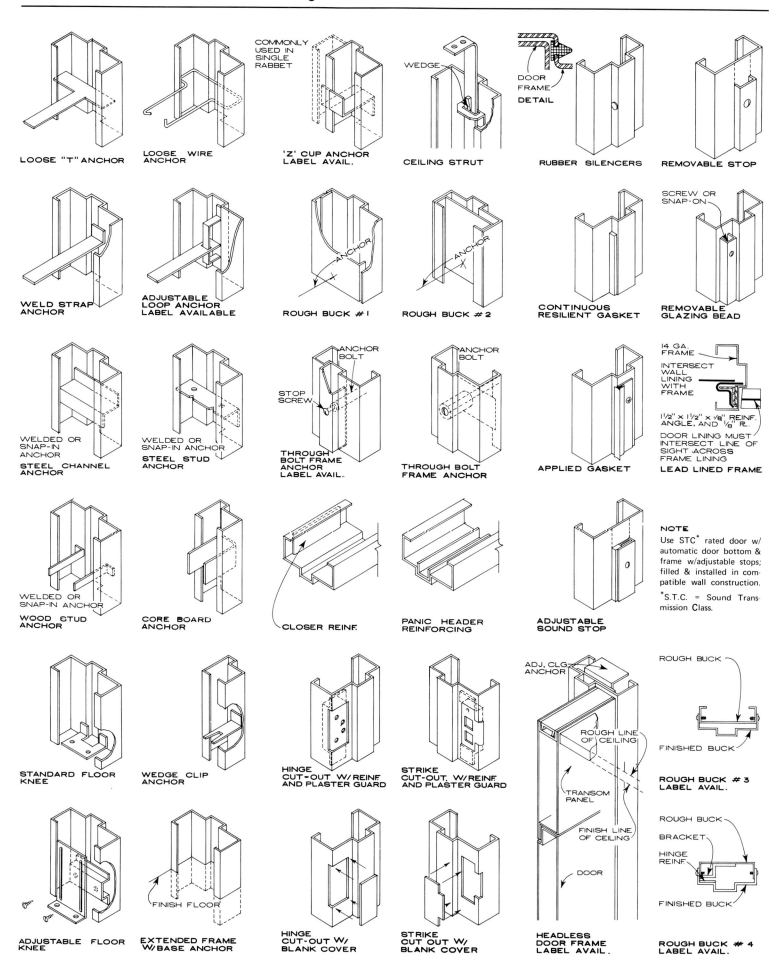

LOOSE "T" ANCHOR

LOOSE WIRE ANCHOR

'Z' CUP ANCHOR LABEL AVAIL.

COMMONLY USED IN SINGLE RABBET

CEILING STRUT

WEDGE

DOOR FRAME DETAIL

RUBBER SILENCERS

REMOVABLE STOP

WELD STRAP ANCHOR

ADJUSTABLE LOOP ANCHOR LABEL AVAILABLE

ROUGH BUCK #1

ANCHOR

ROUGH BUCK #2

ANCHOR

CONTINUOUS RESILIENT GASKET

SCREW OR SNAP-ON

REMOVABLE GLAZING BEAD

WELDED OR SNAP-IN ANCHOR

STEEL CHANNEL ANCHOR

WELDED OR SNAP-IN ANCHOR

STEEL STUD ANCHOR

ANCHOR BOLT

STOP SCREW

THROUGH BOLT FRAME ANCHOR LABEL AVAIL.

ANCHOR BOLT

THROUGH BOLT FRAME ANCHOR

APPLIED GASKET

14 GA. FRAME

INTERSECT WALL LINING WITH FRAME

1 1/2" x 1 1/2" x 1/8" REINF. ANGLE, AND 1/8" PL.

DOOR LINING MUST INTERSECT LINE OF SIGHT ACROSS FRAME LINING

LEAD LINED FRAME

WELDED OR SNAP-IN ANCHOR

WOOD STUD ANCHOR

CORE BOARD ANCHOR

CLOSER REINF.

PANIC HEADER REINFORCING

ADJUSTABLE SOUND STOP

NOTE

Use STC* rated door w/ automatic door bottom & frame w/adjustable stops; filled & installed in compatible wall construction.

*S.T.C. = Sound Transmission Class.

STANDARD FLOOR KNEE

WEDGE CLIP ANCHOR

HINGE CUT-OUT W/REINF. AND PLASTER GUARD

STRIKE CUT-OUT, W/REINF. AND PLASTER GUARD

ADJ. CLG. ANCHOR

ROUGH LINE OF CEILING

ROUGH BUCK

FINISHED BUCK

ADJUSTABLE FLOOR KNEE

FINISH FLOOR

EXTENDED FRAME W/BASE ANCHOR

HINGE CUT-OUT W/ BLANK COVER

STRIKE CUT OUT W/ BLANK COVER

TRANSOM PANEL

FINISH LINE OF CEILING

DOOR

HEADLESS DOOR FRAME LABEL AVAIL.

ROUGH BUCK #3 LABEL AVAIL.

ROUGH BUCK

BRACKET

HINGE REINF.

FINISHED BUCK

ROUGH BUCK #4 LABEL AVAIL.

James W. G. Watson, AIA; Ronald A. Spahn and Associates; Cleveland Heights, Ohio

8

METAL DOORS AND FRAMES

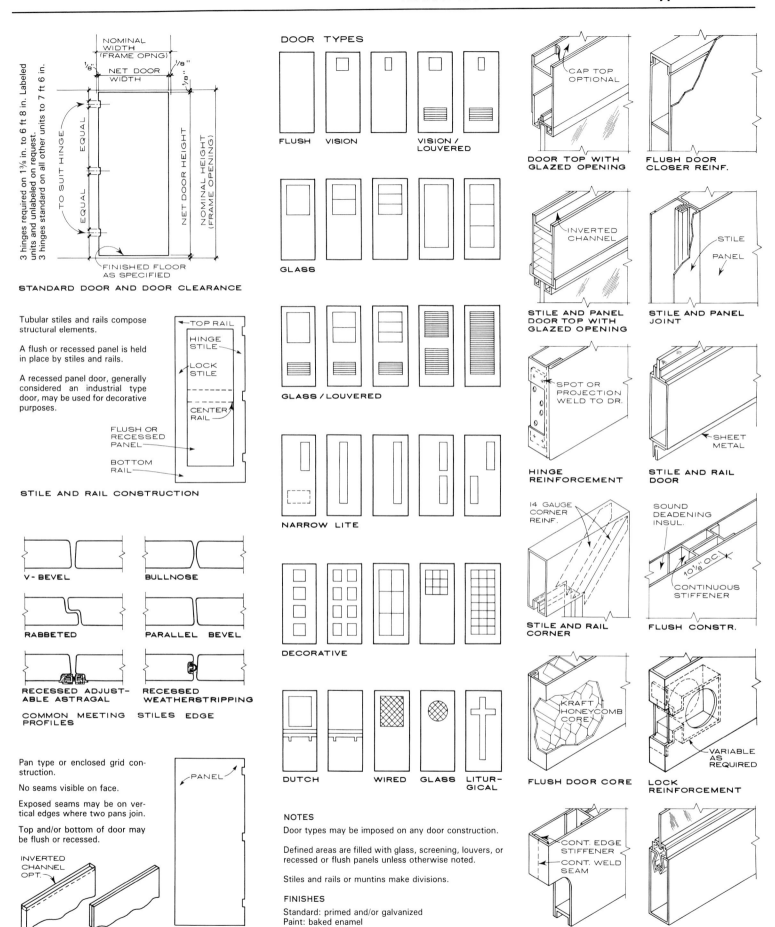

STANDARD DOOR AND DOOR CLEARANCE

NOMINAL WIDTH (FRAME OPNG)

NET DOOR WIDTH

3 hinges required on 1⅜ in. to 6 ft 8 in. Labeled units and unlabeled on request. 3 hinges standard on all other units to 7 ft 6 in.

TO SUIT HINGE

EQUAL / EQUAL / EQUAL

NET DOOR HEIGHT

NOMINAL HEIGHT (FRAME OPENING)

FINISHED FLOOR AS SPECIFIED

Tubular stiles and rails compose structural elements.

A flush or recessed panel is held in place by stiles and rails.

A recessed panel door, generally considered an industrial type door, may be used for decorative purposes.

STILE AND RAIL CONSTRUCTION

TOP RAIL
HINGE STILE
LOCK STILE
CENTER RAIL
FLUSH OR RECESSED PANEL
BOTTOM RAIL

COMMON MEETING STILES EDGE PROFILES

V-BEVEL / BULLNOSE
RABBETED / PARALLEL BEVEL
RECESSED ADJUSTABLE ASTRAGAL / RECESSED WEATHERSTRIPPING

Pan type or enclosed grid construction.

No seams visible on face.

Exposed seams may be on vertical edges where two pans join.

Top and/or bottom of door may be flush or recessed.

FLUSH CONSTRUCTION

INVERTED CHANNEL OPT.
SEAMLESS / FULL FLUSH
PANEL

DOOR TYPES

FLUSH / VISION / VISION / LOUVERED

GLASS

GLASS / LOUVERED

NARROW LITE

DECORATIVE

DUTCH / WIRED / GLASS / LITURGICAL

NOTES

Door types may be imposed on any door construction.

Defined areas are filled with glass, screening, louvers, or recessed or flush panels unless otherwise noted.

Stiles and rails or muntins make divisions.

FINISHES

Standard: primed and/or galvanized
Paint: baked enamel
Applied: vinyl clad
Textured, embossed: stainless steel, aluminum
Polished: stainless steel

CAP TOP OPTIONAL

DOOR TOP WITH GLAZED OPENING

FLUSH DOOR CLOSER REINF.

INVERTED CHANNEL

STILE AND PANEL DOOR TOP WITH GLAZED OPENING

STILE / PANEL

STILE AND PANEL JOINT

SPOT OR PROJECTION WELD TO DR.

HINGE REINFORCEMENT

SHEET METAL

STILE AND RAIL DOOR

14 GAUGE CORNER REINF.

STILE AND RAIL CORNER

SOUND DEADENING INSUL.

10½" O.C.

CONTINUOUS STIFFENER

FLUSH CONSTR.

KRAFT HONEYCOMB CORE

FLUSH DOOR CORE

VARIABLE AS REQUIRED

LOCK REINFORCEMENT

CONT. EDGE STIFFENER
CONT. WELD SEAM

FLUSH DOOR BOTTOM AND EDGE CONST.

STILE AND RAIL DOOR BOTTOM CONST.

James W. G. Watson, AIA; Ronald A. Spahn and Associates; Cleveland Heights, Ohio

METAL DOORS AND FRAMES   8

MINIMUM GAUGES FOR COMMERCIAL STEEL DOORS

ITEM	GAUGE NO.	EQUIVALENT THICKNESS (IN.)
Door frames	16	0.0598
Surface applied hardware reinforcement	16	0.0598
Doors—hollow steel construction		
Panels and stile	18	0.0478
Doors—composite construction		
Perimeter channel	18	0.0478
Surface sheets	22	0.0299
Reinforcement		
Surface applied hardware	16	0.0598
Lock and strike	16	0.0598
Hinge	10	0.1345
Flush bolt	16	0.0598
Glass molding	20	0.0359
Glass muntins	22	0.0299

MINIMUM GAUGES FOR INTERIOR STEEL DOORS

ITEM	GAUGE NO.	EQUIVALENT THICKNESS (IN.)
Door frames, 1³/₈ in. thick	18	0.0478
Door frames, 1³/₄ in. thick	16	0.0598
Stiles and panels	20	0.0359
Reinforcement		
Lock and strike	16	0.0598
Hinge	11	0.1196
Closer	14	0.0747

NOTES

1. The steel door tables represent minimum standards published by the U.S. Department of Commerce for standard stock commercial, 1³/₄ in. thick steel doors and frames, and flush type interior steel doors and frames (doors not more than 3 ft in width).

2. Specifications for custom hollow metal doors and frames are published by the National Association of Architectural Metal Manufacturers. Standards may also vary according to location or the agency—always consult with the local authorities and/or agencies to determine what they require. Doors must be selected according to the project requirements such as frequency of usage, type of traffic, conditions required by the enclosed space, and environmental conditions.

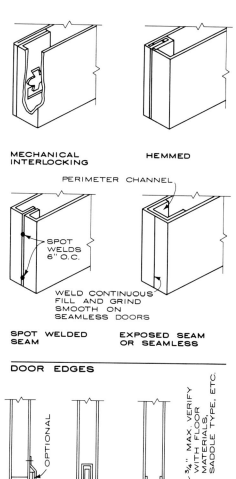

MECHANICAL INTERLOCKING   HEMMED

PERIMETER CHANNEL

SPOT WELDS 6" O.C.

WELD CONTINUOUS FILL AND GRIND SMOOTH ON SEAMLESS DOORS

SPOT WELDED SEAM   EXPOSED SEAM OR SEAMLESS

DOOR EDGES

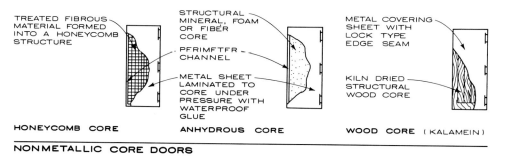

TREATED FIBROUS MATERIAL FORMED INTO A HONEYCOMB STRUCTURE

STRUCTURAL MINERAL, FOAM OR FIBER CORE

PERIMETER CHANNEL

METAL SHEET LAMINATED TO CORE UNDER PRESSURE WITH WATERPROOF GLUE

METAL COVERING SHEET WITH LOCK TYPE EDGE SEAM

KILN DRIED STRUCTURAL WOOD CORE

HONEYCOMB CORE   ANHYDROUS CORE   WOOD CORE (KALAMEIN)

NONMETALLIC CORE DOORS

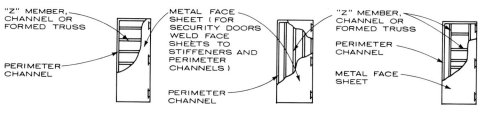

"Z" MEMBER, CHANNEL OR FORMED TRUSS

PERIMETER CHANNEL

METAL FACE SHEET (FOR SECURITY DOORS WELD FACE SHEETS TO STIFFENERS AND PERIMETER CHANNELS)

PERIMETER CHANNEL

"Z" MEMBER, CHANNEL OR FORMED TRUSS

PERIMETER CHANNEL

METAL FACE SHEET

HORIZONTAL STIFFENERS   VERTICAL STIFFENERS   GRID STIFFENERS

STIFFENED CORE DOORS (HEAVY DOORS) **NORMALLY SOUND DEADENED OR INSULATED**

¾" MAX. VERIFY WITH FLOOR MATERIALS, SADDLE TYPE, ETC.

OPTIONAL

AUTOMATIC DOOR BOTTOM

DOOR BOTTOMS

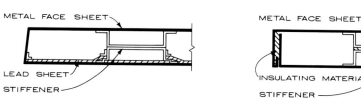

METAL FACE SHEET

LEAD SHEET

STIFFENER

LEAD LINED CORE

METAL FACE SHEET

INSULATING MATERIAL

STIFFENER

THERMAL BREAK CORE

SPECIAL CORE DOORS

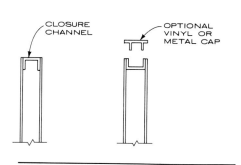

CLOSURE CHANNEL

OPTIONAL VINYL OR METAL CAP

DOOR TOPS

Kelly Sacher & Associates; Architects Engineers Planners; N. Babylon, New York

METAL DOORS AND FRAMES

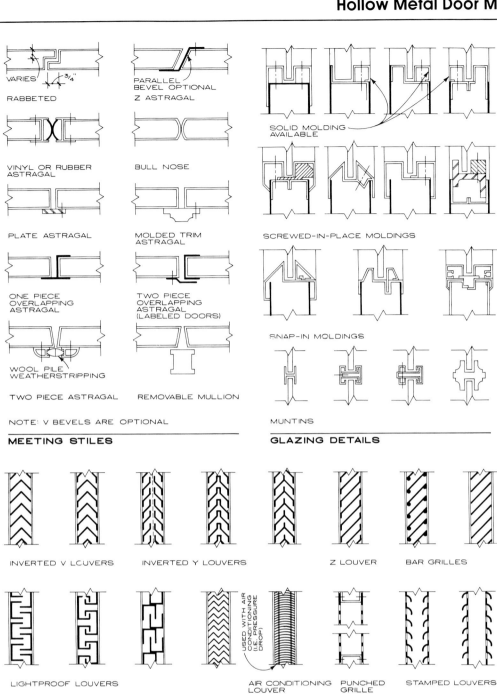

MEETING STILES

VARIES · 3/4"

RABBETED

PARALLEL BEVEL OPTIONAL
Z ASTRAGAL

VINYL OR RUBBER ASTRAGAL

BULL NOSE

PLATE ASTRAGAL

MOLDED TRIM ASTRAGAL

ONE PIECE OVERLAPPING ASTRAGAL

TWO PIECE OVERLAPPING ASTRAGAL (LABELED DOORS)

WOOL PILE WEATHERSTRIPPING

TWO PIECE ASTRAGAL

REMOVABLE MULLION

NOTE: V BEVELS ARE OPTIONAL

GLAZING DETAILS

SOLID MOLDING AVAILABLE

SCREWED-IN-PLACE MOLDINGS

SNAP-IN MOLDINGS

MUNTINS

INVERTED V LOUVERS

INVERTED Y LOUVERS

Z LOUVER

BAR GRILLES

LIGHTPROOF LOUVERS

USED WITH AIR CONDITIONING (I.E. PRESSURE DROP)

AIR CONDITIONING LOUVER

PUNCHED GRILLE

STAMPED LOUVERS

LOUVERS AND VENTS

DOOR LOUVER MOLDINGS

SPOT WELDS OR SCREWS

WEEP HOLES

INSECT OR BIRD SCREEN

INSECT SCREEN

BIRD SCREEN

DOOR LOUVER MOLDINGS

STANDARD FOLDED

EXTRUDED ALUMINUM REWIRABLE

EXTRUDED ALUMINUM REWIRABLE

DOOR SCREENS

Kelly Sacher & Associates; Architects Engineers Planners; N. Babylon, New York

MATERIALS

Hollow metal doors are available in various steel gauges according to where and how they will be used. The following gradings should be used only as guidelines in selecting doors for a particular project. Local codes and governing authorities establish minimum gauges, which should always be consulted.

GRADE	GAUGE
Residential	20 gauge and lighter
Commercial	16 and 18 gauge
Institutional	12 and 14 gauge
High security	Steel plate

Some manufacturers will custom make moldings and muntins to meet a specific design, as long as there is sufficient quantity involved.

For security, the exterior moldings on exterior doors should be welded into the door and all exposed fasteners should be tamperproof.

For fire ratings of hollow metal doors and requirements for fire doors see other pages in this series.

FINISH

Hollow metal doors should receive at least one shop coat of rust inhibitive primer before they are delivered to the job site. In very corrosive atmospheres, such as saltwater beach locations, it is advisable to have the doors and frames hot dipped galvanized for additional protection.

Doors are available from several manufacturers, with factory applied paint finishes in various colors.

GLAZING

The size and type of glass permitted in fire rated doors is determined by local building codes and governing authorities having jurisdiction. The following table should only be used as a guide:

DOOR RATING	GLAZING REQUIREMENTS
*A—3 hr	No glazing permitted
*B—1 1/2 hr	100 sq in. of glazing per door leaf
C—3/4 hr	Max. 1296 sq in. of glazing per light. Max. dim. per light = 54 in. Min. dim. per light = 3 in.
*D—1 1/2 hr	No glazing permitted
E—3/4 hr	Max. 720 sq in. of glazing per light. Max. dim. per light = 54 in.

NOTE: Available on composite doors only. A, B, and D doors are available with Heat Transmission Ratings of 250°F or 650°F, or are not rated.

LOUVERS AND VENTS

Door louvers are available extruded, formed, and stamped in various metals and configurations; operable with or without a fusible link. Punched, stamped, and bar grilles are also available.

The percentage of free area for louvers depends on the louver blade thickness, spacing, and type. For this information consult the manufacturer's catalogs.

Door louvers and grilles are available prefinished, without moldings, and with moldings attached at the factory on one or both sides.

Insert screens are often used in conjunction with louvers or grilles; they may be used by themselves as well, however, in some applications. Screen material is available in various grid and wire sizes and materials.

GENERAL

Fire door assemblies are used for the protection of openings in fire-rated walls. The assembly consists of a fire door, frame, and hardware. Each component is crucial to the overall performance of the assembly as a fire barrier.

NFPA 80 is a national standard to establish the degree of fire protection required at a given opening. Fire doors and frames are classified by the duration of test exposure (hourly rating) and the class of opening the assembly is intended for (letter designation).

Additional information is available in Chapter 7 of the NFPA "Fire Protection Handbook."

TYPES OF OPENINGS

1. CLASS A (3-hour doors): Openings in fire walls and in walls that divide a single building into fire areas.
2. CLASS B (1- or 1½-hour doors): Openings in enclosures of vertical communications through buildings and in 2-hour rated partitions providing horizontal fire separations.
3. CLASS C (¾-hour door): Openings in walls or partitions between rooms and corridors having a fire resistance rating of 1 hour or less.
4. CLASS D (1½-hour door): Openings in exterior walls subject to severe fire exposure from outside of the building.
5. CLASS E (¾-hour door): Openings in exterior walls subject to moderate or light fire exposure from outside of the building.

½- and ⅓-hour doors are used for smoke control in corridor walls.

TYPES OF DOORS

Typical construction for swinging fire doors:

1. COMPOSITE fire doors consist of wood, steel, or plastic sheets bonded to and supported by a solid core material.
2. HOLLOW METAL fire doors are of flush or panel design with not less than 20 gauge steel face.
3. METAL CLAD fire doors are of flush or panel design consisting of metal covered wood cores or stiles and rails and insulated panels covered with steel of 24 gauge or lighter.
4. SHEET METAL fire doors are formed of 22 gauge or lighter steel and are corrugated, flush sheet, or panel design.
5. TINCLAD fire doors consist of a wood core with a terne plate or galvanized steel facing (#30 or #24 gauge).
6. WOOD core-type doors consist of wood, hardboard, or plastic face sheets bonded to a wood block or wood particleboard core material with untreated wood edges.

TYPES OF FRAMES

Fire-rated door frames can be factory or field assembled. All frames must be adequately anchored at the jambs and floor per the manufacturers' specifications.

1. WOOD: Head and jamb members, with or without solid transom panel (20 minute maximum rating).
2. LIGHT GAUGE METAL FRAME: Head and jamb members with or without transom panel made from aluminum (45 minute maximum rating) or light gauge steel (1½ hour maximum rating). Frame is installed over finished wall.
3. PRESSED STEEL (HOLLOW METAL): Head and jamb members, with or without solid or glazed transoms or sidelights made from 18 gauge or heavier steel (3 hour maximum rating). This frame is required for most metal doors.

HARDWARE

Door hardware is either provided by the builder or furnished by the manufacturer. Generally the door and frame must be prepared to receive hardware by the manufacturer to insure that the integrity of the fire-rated assembly is maintained.

Fire doors are hung on steel ball bearing hinges. A fire door must close and latch at the time of a fire. Labeled automatic latches and door closers can be self-operated or controlled by failsafe devices that activate in a fire situation. Pairs of doors require coordinators with astragals to ensure both doors close. Gasketing to seal the head and jambs should be provided where smoke control is required.

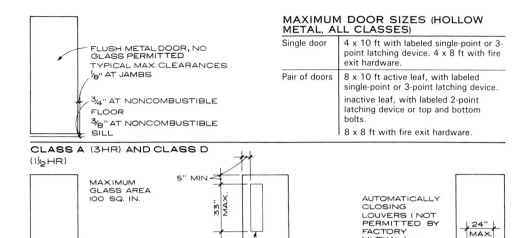

MAXIMUM DOOR SIZES (HOLLOW METAL, ALL CLASSES)

Single door	4 x 10 ft with labeled single-point or 3-point latching device. 4 x 8 ft with fire exit hardware.
Pair of doors	8 x 10 ft active leaf, with labeled single-point or 3-point latching device.
	inactive leaf, with labeled 2-point latching device or top and bottom bolts.
	8 x 8 ft with fire exit hardware.

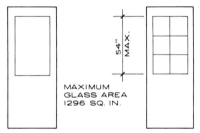

HINGE REQUIREMENTS (ALL CLASSES)

All hinges or pivots must be steel. Two hinges are required on doors up to 5 ft in height and an additional hinge is required for each additional 2 ft 6 in. of door height or fraction thereof. The same requirement holds for pivots.

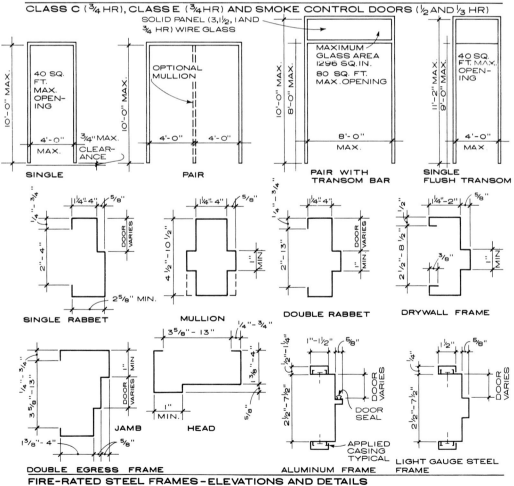

FIRE-RATED STEEL FRAMES—ELEVATIONS AND DETAILS

Thomas Emme, AIA; Albert C. Martin & Associates; Los Angeles, California
William G. Miner, AIA; Architect; Washington, D.C.
NFPA, see data sources

METAL DOORS AND FRAMES

NOTES

CONSTRUCTION

Solid or built-up stiles, rails, and vertical members or mullions, doweled as in NWWDA standard. Stock material includes ponderosa pine or other Western pine, fir, hemlock, or spruce, and hardwood veneers. Hardboard, metal, and plastic facings available in patterns simulating panel doors.

GRADES

Premium (select) grade: for natural, clear, or stained finish. Exposed wood free of defects that affect appearance.

Standard grade: for opaque finishes. Defects, discoloration, mixed species, and finger joints permitted if undetectable after finishing.

BUILT-UP MEMBERS

Core as in solid core of flush doors. Edge and end strips as in flush doors. Face veneer: hardwood at 1/8 in. minimum.

PANELS

Flat: 3-ply hardwood or softwood. Raised—two sides: solid hardwood or softwood built-up of two or more plies. Doors 1 ft 6 in. wide and narrower are one panel wide.

STICKING, GLASS STOPS, AND MUNTINS

Cove, bead, or ovolo; solid, matching face.

GLAZING

Must be safety glazing. Insulated (dual) glazing is available.

THICKNESS

Interior doors: 1 3/8 in.
Exterior doors: 1 3/8 in. or 1 3/4 in.
Storm and screen doors: 1 1/8 in.

See index for other door types and door hardware.

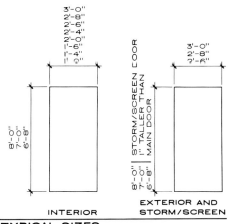

TYPICAL SIZES

INTERIOR

EXTERIOR AND STORM/SCREEN

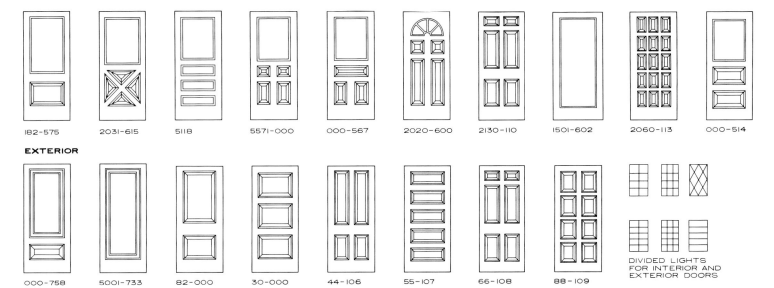

182-575 2031-615 5118 5571-000 000-567 2020-600 2130-110 1501-602 2060-113 000-514

EXTERIOR

000-758 5001-733 82-000 30-000 44-106 55-107 66-108 88-109

DIVIDED LIGHTS FOR INTERIOR AND EXTERIOR DOORS

SCREEN/STORM   **INTERIOR**

SELECTED STANDARD DOOR TYPES (NUMBERS CORRESPOND TO NWWDA STANDARD)

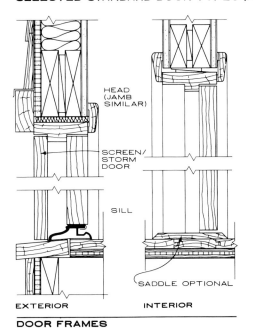

HEAD (JAMB SIMILAR)

SCREEN/ STORM DOOR

SILL

SADDLE OPTIONAL

EXTERIOR   **INTERIOR**

DOOR FRAMES

Jeffrey R. Vandevoort; Talbott Wilson Associates, Inc.; Houston, Texas

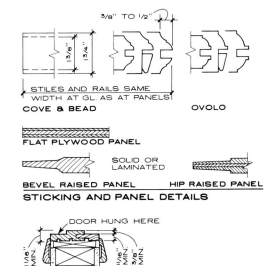

3/8" TO 1/2"

STILES AND RAILS SAME WIDTH AT GL. AS AT PANELS

COVE & BEAD   **OVOLO**

FLAT PLYWOOD PANEL

SOLID OR LAMINATED

BEVEL RAISED PANEL   **HIP RAISED PANEL**

STICKING AND PANEL DETAILS

DOOR HUNG HERE

1/16" MIN 1/16" MIN 3/8" MIN

ADJUSTABLE DOOR FRAME

NOTES

Top operable alone or with bottom using joining hardware.

Can swing in or out.

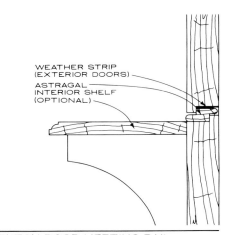

WEATHER STRIP (EXTERIOR DOORS)

ASTRAGAL
INTERIOR SHELF (OPTIONAL)

DUTCH DOOR MEETING RAIL

WOOD AND PLASTIC DOORS

GENERAL NOTES FOR ALL WOOD DOORS

Kiln dried wood, moisture content @ 6-12%.

Type 1 doors: Fully waterproof bond ext. and int.
Type 11 doors: Water resistant bond. Interior only.

Tolerances: Height, width, thickness, squareness and warp per NWMA STANDARDS and vary with solid vs. built-up construction.

Prefit: Doors @ $3/16$" less in width and $1/8$" less in height than nominal size, ± $1/32$" tolerance, with vertical edges eased.

Premachining: Doors mortised for locks and cut out for hinges when so specified.

Premium: For transparent finish. Good/custom: For paint or transparent finish. Sound: For paint, with 2 coats completely covering defects.

FLUSH WOOD DOORS
CORE MATERIAL
SOLID CORES

Wood block, single specie, @ $2^1/2$" max. width, surfaced two sides, without spaces or defects impairing strength or visible thru hdwd. veneer facing.

HOLLOW CORES

Wood, wood derivative, or class A insulation board.

TYPES OF WOOD FACES

Standard thickness face veneers @ $1/16$"-$1/32$", bonded to hardwood, crossband @ $1/10$"-$1/16$". Most economical and widely used, inhibits checking, difficult to refinish or repair face damage, for use on all cores.

$1/8$" Sawn veneers, bonded to crossband, easily refinished and repaired.

For use on staved block and stile and rail solid cores. $1/4$" Sawn veneers: same as $1/8$" but without crossband on stile and rail solid cores with horizontal blocks. Decorative grooves can be cut into faces.

LIGHT & LOUVER OPENINGS

Custom made to specifications. Wood beads and slats to match face veneer. 5" min. between opening and edge of door.

Hollow core: Cut-out area max. $1/2$ height of door. Door not guaranteed with openings greater than 40%. Exterior doors: Weatherproofing required to prevent moisture from leaking into core.

FACTORY FINISHING

Partial: Sealing coats applied, final job finish.
Complete: Requires prefit and premachining.

SPECIAL FACING

High or medium-low density overlay faces of phenolic resins and cellulose fibers fused to inner faces of hardwood in lieu of final veneers as base for final opaque finish only.

$1/16$" min. laminated plastic bonded to $1/16$" min. wood back of two or more piles.

$1/8$" hardboard, smooth one or two sides.

SPECIAL CORES
SOUND INSULATING DOORS

Thicknesses $1^3/4$", $2^1/4$". Transmission loss rating C Stc 36 for $1^3/4$", 42 for $2^1/4$". Barrier faces separated by a void or damping compound to keep faces from vibrating in unison. Special stops, gaskets, and threshold devices required. Mfrs. requirements as to wd. frames and wall specs.

FIRE RATED DOORS

$3/4$ hr "C" label and 1 hr "B" label-maximum size 4'0" x 10'0".
$1^1/2$ hr "B" label-maximum size 4'0" x 9'0". All doors $1^3/4$" minimum thickness.

LEAD LINED DOORS

See U/L requirements. Optional location within door construction of $1/32$" to $1/2$" continuous lead sheet from edge to edge which may be reinforced with lead bolts or glued.

GROUNDED DOORS

Wire mesh located at center of core, grounded with copper wire through hinges to frame.

TYPES OF HOLLOW CORE DOORS

ACOUSTICAL DOOR
Uses gasketed stops and neoprene bottom seals to cut sound transmission.

- ACOUSTICAL DAMPING MATERIAL
- HARDBOARD CROSSBAND
- HARDBOARD FACE

HONEYCOMB FIBER
INSTITU-TIONAL:
With cross rail.
INTERIOR:
Without cross rail. Uniform core of honeycomb fiber to form $1/2$" air cells.

IMPLANTED BLANKS
Spirals or other forms separated or joined, implanted between & supporting outer faces of door.

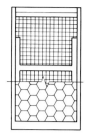

MESH
Interlocked, horizontal & vertical strips, equally spaced, notched into stiles, or expandable cellular or honey-comb core.

TYPES OF SOLID CORES

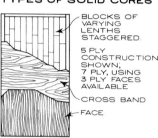

CONTINUOUS BLOCK STAVED CORE
Bonded staggered blocks bonded to face panels. Most widely used & economical solid core.

FRAMED BLOCK STAVED CORE
Non-bonded staggered blocks laid up within stile rail frame, bonded to face panels.

- BLOCKS OF VARYING LENTHS STAGGERED.
- 5 PLY CONSTRUCTION SHOWN; 7 PLY, USING 3 PLY FACES AVAILABLE
- CROSS BAND
- FACE

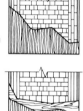

STILE AND RAIL
Horizontal blocks when cross banding is not used. Vertical panel blocks when cross banding is used.

PARTICLE BOARD
Extremely heavy, more soundproof, economical door, available in hardwood face veneer or high pressure laminate face.

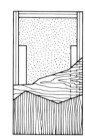

MINERAL COMPOSITION
Lightest weight of all cores. Details, as cut-outs, difficult. Low screw holding strength.

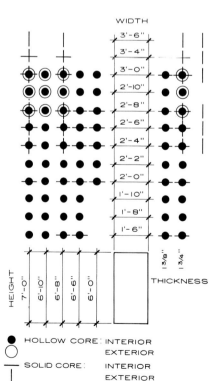

STANDARD SIZES

● HOLLOW CORE: INTERIOR / EXTERIOR
○ SOLID CORE: INTERIOR / EXTERIOR

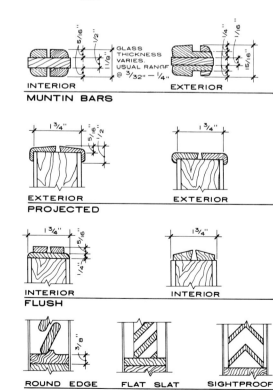

MUNTIN BARS
INTERIOR / EXTERIOR

PROJECTED
EXTERIOR / EXTERIOR

FLUSH
INTERIOR / INTERIOR

LOUVERS · METAL LOUVERS ALSO AVAILABLE
ROUND EDGE / FLAT SLAT / SIGHTPROOF
STOCK OPENING AND LOUVER DETAIL

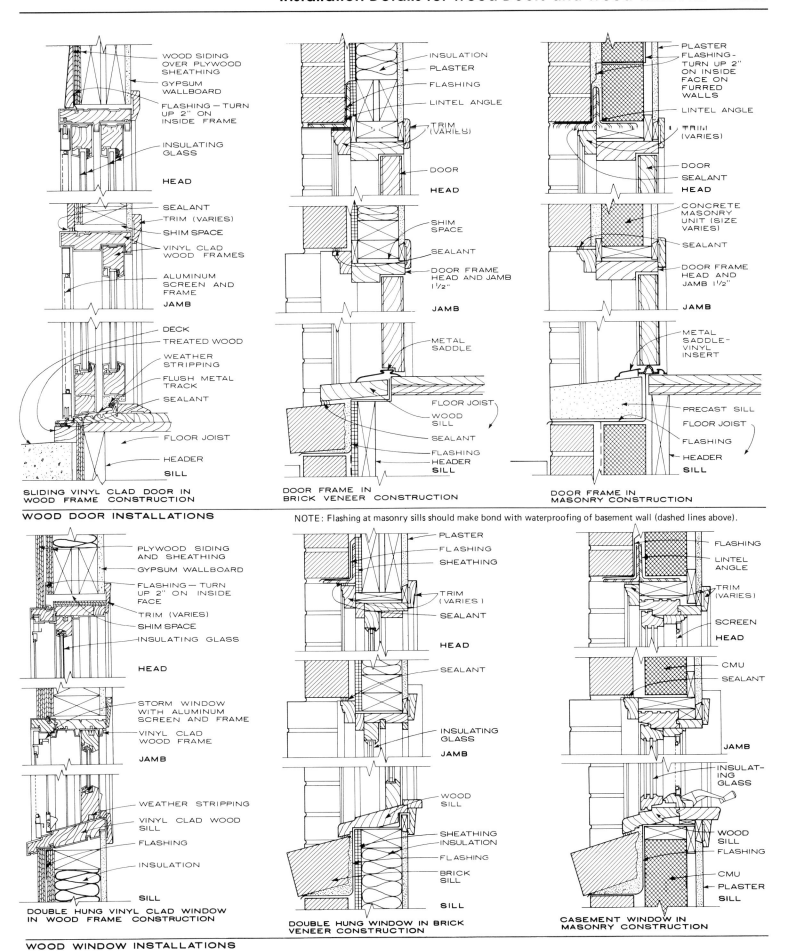

WOOD SIDING OVER PLYWOOD SHEATHING

GYPSUM WALLBOARD

FLASHING — TURN UP 2" ON INSIDE FRAME

INSULATING GLASS

HEAD

SEALANT

TRIM (VARIES)

SHIM SPACE

VINYL CLAD WOOD FRAMES

ALUMINUM SCREEN AND FRAME

JAMB

DECK

TREATED WOOD

WEATHER STRIPPING

FLUSH METAL TRACK

SEALANT

FLOOR JOIST

HEADER

SILL

SLIDING VINYL CLAD DOOR IN WOOD FRAME CONSTRUCTION

INSULATION

PLASTER

FLASHING

LINTEL ANGLE

TRIM (VARIES)

DOOR

HEAD

SHIM SPACE

SEALANT

DOOR FRAME HEAD AND JAMB 1½"

JAMB

METAL SADDLE

FLOOR JOIST

WOOD SILL

SEALANT

FLASHING

HEADER

SILL

DOOR FRAME IN BRICK VENEER CONSTRUCTION

PLASTER

FLASHING - TURN UP 2" ON INSIDE FACE ON FURRED WALLS

LINTEL ANGLE

TRIM (VARIES)

DOOR

SEALANT

HEAD

CONCRETE MASONRY UNIT (SIZE VARIES)

SEALANT

DOOR FRAME HEAD AND JAMB 1½"

JAMB

METAL SADDLE - VINYL INSERT

PRECAST SILL

FLOOR JOIST

FLASHING

HEADER

SILL

DOOR FRAME IN MASONRY CONSTRUCTION

WOOD DOOR INSTALLATIONS

NOTE: Flashing at masonry sills should make bond with waterproofing of basement wall (dashed lines above).

PLYWOOD SIDING AND SHEATHING

GYPSUM WALLBOARD

FLASHING — TURN UP 2" ON INSIDE FACE

TRIM (VARIES)

SHIM SPACE

INSULATING GLASS

HEAD

STORM WINDOW WITH ALUMINUM SCREEN AND FRAME

VINYL CLAD WOOD FRAME

JAMB

WEATHER STRIPPING

VINYL CLAD WOOD SILL

FLASHING

INSULATION

SILL

DOUBLE HUNG VINYL CLAD WINDOW IN WOOD FRAME CONSTRUCTION

PLASTER

FLASHING

SHEATHING

TRIM (VARIES)

SEALANT

HEAD

SEALANT

INSULATING GLASS

JAMB

WOOD SILL

SHEATHING

INSULATION

FLASHING

BRICK SILL

SILL

DOUBLE HUNG WINDOW IN BRICK VENEER CONSTRUCTION

FLASHING

LINTEL ANGLE

TRIM (VARIES)

SCREEN

HEAD

CMU

SEALANT

JAMB

INSULATING GLASS

WOOD SILL

FLASHING

CMU

PLASTER

SILL

CASEMENT WINDOW IN MASONRY CONSTRUCTION

WOOD WINDOW INSTALLATIONS

WOOD AND PLASTIC DOORS AND WINDOWS

8

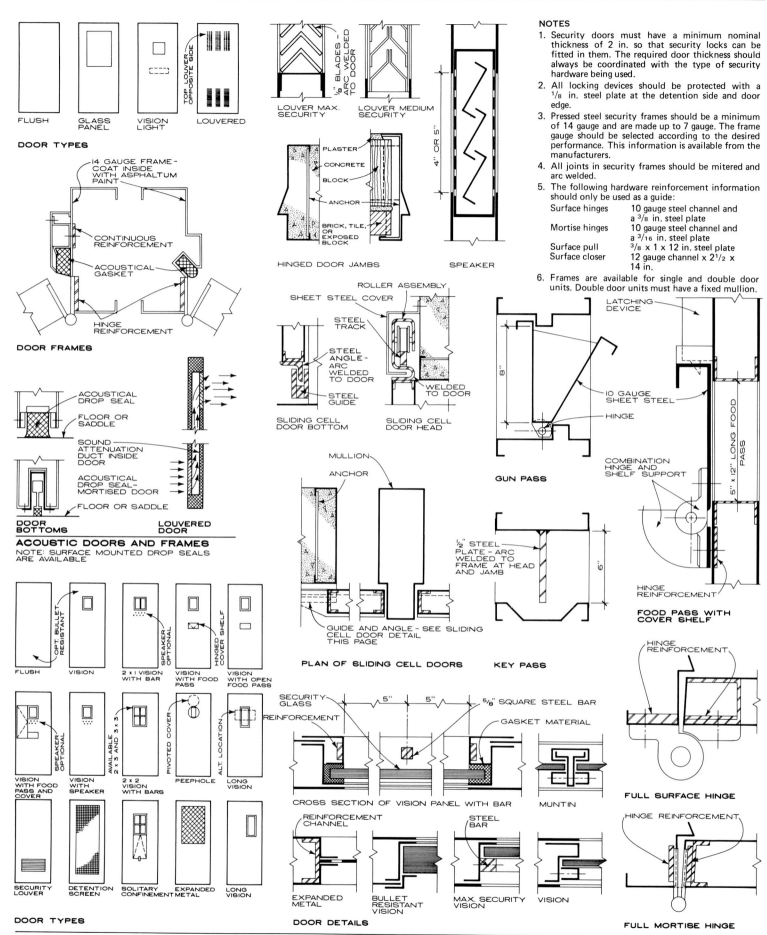

Kelly Sacher & Associates; Architects Engineers Planners; N. Babylon, New York

SPECIAL DOORS

SWINGING DOOR ASSEMBLIES

A door, in addition to providing a portal for entry, should resist unwanted intruders. This resistance can be accommodated by requiring that all exterior doors comply with ANSI/ASTM standard F476-76 Standard Test Methods for Security of Swinging Door Assemblies. The security of a door assembly depends not only on the lock but also on the strike, buck, hinge, door, and even the surrounding wall.

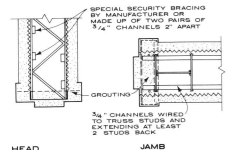

SPECIAL SECURITY BRACING BY MANUFACTURER OR MADE UP OF TWO PAIRS OF ³/₄" CHANNELS 2" APART

GROUTING

³/₄" CHANNELS WIRED TO TRUSS STUDS AND EXTENDING AT LEAST 2 STUDS BACK

HEAD   JAMB

DOOR BUCK DETAIL

GLAZING, LAMINATED OR POLYCARBONATE

GUARDED LOCK CYLINDER

BRACE AT LOCK AND HINGE POINTS

SECURE STRIKE PLATE

GROUT HOLLOW METAL BUCKS (MIN. OF 24") AT LOCK POINT SOLID SHIMMING OF WOOD BUCKS

HINGE WITH NONREMOVABLE PINS

SECURITY DOOR ELEVATION

NOTE: Brace at lock point is essential; brace at hinge points for additional security. If two hinges, braces required at both; if three hinges, brace only at middle hinge. Braces should extend two studs back.

SUGGESTED MATERIALS AND METHODS FOR DOORS

1. GRADE 40: Hollow metal steel doors, 16 gauge.
2. GRADE 30: Hollow metal, 18 gauge; flush wood, lumber core, 1³/₄ in. thick.
3. GRADE 20: Flush wood, particle core, 1³/₄ in. thick, lock block of dense solid wood at least 6 in. wide x 24 in. high. Hinge blocks, 6 in. wide, x 12 in. high.
4. GRADE 10: Flush wood, particle core, 1³/₄ in. thick; wood panel door with minimum thickness of panel at ¹/₂ in. including rebate, stiles minimum dimension 1³/₄ x 6 in.

FRAME

The stiffness of the bucks is critical; wood bucks should be a minimum of 2 in. thick and have solid, secure shims for 24 in. at the locking point and 12 in. at each hinge point; stops should be milled integral with the buck; wood bucks for Grade 20 should be of hard wood premium grade; Grade 20 bucks should be 16 gauge steel; Grade 40 bucks should be 15 gauge steel; all steel bucks should be grouted full.

WALL

Fire stops or braces should be located at the lock point and each hinge point—for one stud space at Grade 10, two stud spaces for Grade 20 and above; if wood studs appear, plywood sheathing should be used on both sides of the studs for two stud spaces to each side of the doorway; if it is a masonry wall, grout all space between frame and wall.

John Stroik, Architect, and Porter Driscoll, AIA, Architect; Center for Building Technology, National Bureau of Standards; Washington, D.C. William G. Miner, AIA; Washington, D.C.

GRADE SELECTION FACTORS

The following items should be considered when designing and selecting components for an entrance door:

1. LOCATION: If the doorway is hidden from public view, or if security lighting is not provided, a higher grade is required than that normally used in the area.
2. ACCESS: If entry is controlled by a guard or protected by a detection device, a lower grade should be adequate.
3. USE: If the doorway provides access to particularly valuable or desirable property, a higher grade is required.
4. TYPE: In a double door, each door should be tested. If the door has solid or glazed panels make sure they meet the test requirements; mail slots are not recommended in the door.

GRADE 10

Minimum security level; adequate for single family residential buildings located in stable, comparatively low crime areas.

GRADE 20

Low to medium security level; provides security for residential buildings located in average crime rate areas or for apartments in both low and average crime rate areas.

GRADE 30

Medium to high security level; provides security for residential buildings located in higher than average crime rate areas or for small commercial buildings in average or low crime rate areas.

GRADE 40

High security level; provides security for commercial buildings located in medium to high crime rate areas.

SLIDING DOOR UNITS

Sliding glass doors are a particular concern in securing a building. Performance requirements specified in the NILECJ-STD-0318, Physical Security of Sliding Glass Door Units should be complied with.

The locking devices should include vertical rod, or lever bolts, at top and bottom; the frame should be solid or reinforced at the locking points; the stile must also be reinforced at the lock points. The operating panels should be designed so that they cannot be lifted out of their tracks when in the locked position.

Glazing and other components should be installed from the inside so that entry cannot be gained by disassembly. As with windows and other doors, a hidden location requires a higher grade.

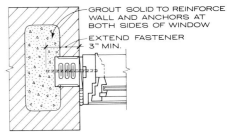

PROVIDE LEVER BOLT AT TOP AND BOTTOM WITH I" MINIMUM THROW

INTERLOCKING MEETING STILE

HEAVY DUTY LOCK WITH HOOK TYPE HARDENED DEAD BOLT

FIXED PANEL SECURED ON THE INSIDE

OPERABLE DOOR SECURED AGAINST LIFTOUT

GROUT FRAME FULL OR BRACE SOLID FROM FLOOR TO 12" ABOVE LOCK

POLYCARBONATE OR LAMINATED GLASS

SLIDING GLASS DOOR

WINDOW FORCED ENTRY DESIGN CRITERIA

EXTERIOR DESIGN ELEMENTS

1. The following items should be considered when designing and selecting windows:
   LOCATION: If accessible (residential: 12 ft vertical, 6 ft horizontal; commercial: 18 ft vertical, 10 ft horizontal) and hidden from public view, a higher grade is required.
   PROTECTED: If windows are protected by a detection device (such as shutters, security screens, or bars), the window grade could be irrelevant. If security screens, bars, or shutters are used, requirements for fire exiting must be met.
2. The existence of windbreaks near a building may provide cover for intruders.
3. The use of shades and window coverings may deter intruders, depending on the ease of removal of these devices or the noise from breakage. The use of lockable shutters or rolldown blinds is very effective.
4. WINDOW UNITS: Window units should at least comply with ANSI/ASTM F 588-79 Standard Test Methods for Resistance of Window Assemblies to Forced Entry for a minimum grade performance and with NILECJ-STD-0316, Physical Security of Window Units, for higher grade performance.
5. As with a door assembly, the security of a window does not rely on the lock alone.

FRAME DESIGN ELEMENTS

1. A rigid frame and sash is important to resist prying and should be removable from the inside only.
2. The quality of the hardware and its placement and anchorage are critical to security. Exposed removable hinges should not be used.
3. Special attention must be given to the use of weather stripping, since this can permit insertion of wires to unlock windows.

GLAZING DESIGN ELEMENTS

1. Multiple glazing systems provide a greater hazard to entry/exit through broken-out windows.
2. Reflective glazing impedes outside daytime surveillance.

MATERIALS AND METHODS FOR WINDOWS

1. Grade 40: Very heavy fixed frames with laminated glass over ¹/₄ in. thick or security screen, bars, or shutters with special locking device.
2. Grade 30: Heavy duty sash with laminated glass over ¹/₄ in. thick or polycarbonate glazing ¹/₄ in. thick. Lock should include at least two heavy duty dead locking bolts.
3. Grade 20: Heavy duty sash with laminated glass or polycarbonate glazing; if wood, sash must be reinforced or heavy; double locks required.
4. Grade 10: Regular glazing in commercial sash with double locks; can be wood frame.

GROUT SOLID TO REINFORCE WALL AND ANCHORS AT BOTH SIDES OF WINDOW

EXTEND FASTENER 3" MIN.

WINDOW JAMB DETAIL

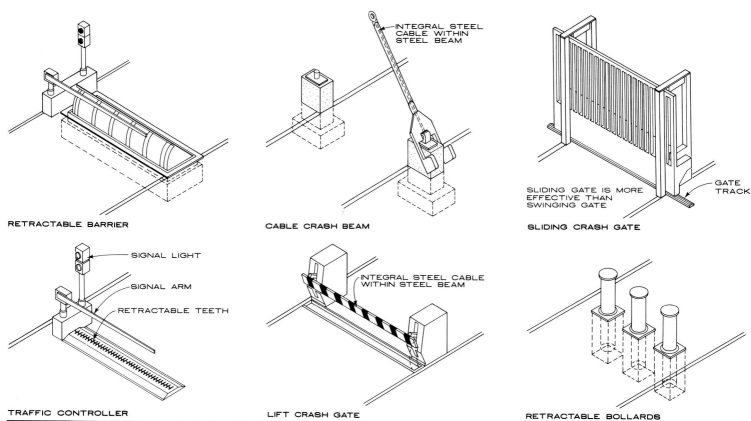

RETRACTABLE BARRIER

INTEGRAL STEEL CABLE WITHIN STEEL BEAM

CABLE CRASH BEAM

SLIDING GATE IS MORE EFFECTIVE THAN SWINGING GATE

GATE TRACK

SLIDING CRASH GATE

SIGNAL LIGHT

SIGNAL ARM

RETRACTABLE TEETH

TRAFFIC CONTROLLER

INTEGRAL STEEL CABLE WITHIN STEEL BEAM

LIFT CRASH GATE

RETRACTABLE BOLLARDS

MECHANICAL BARRIERS

VEHICLE BARRIERS

1. Active barriers at access/egress points in high security areas should be fully engaged until vehicle is cleared for passage. A visible signal light or drop arm should indicate the barrier's status to approaching vehicles. Operating time should not exceed 3–4 sec. The barrier system must maintain its position, preventing access in case of power failure, be capable of manual operation, and should be connected to emergency power. Remote controls should include a status indicator.

2. Passive vehicle barriers (walls, bollards, planters, trench/berms, and ponds) can enhance site design and be inexpensive, low-maintenance vehicle barriers.

3. Concrete bollards and walls require heavy reinforcement tied into massive continuously reinforced concrete footings.

9'-0" HIGH FENCE

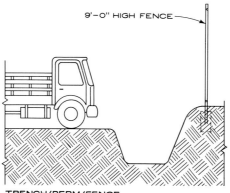

TRENCH/BERM/FENCE

60°

3'-0" O.C.

3'-0"

3'-0"

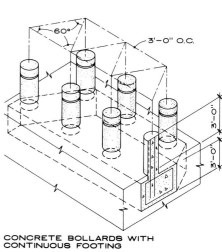

CONCRETE BOLLARDS WITH CONTINUOUS FOOTING

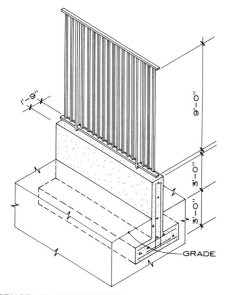

1'-9"

9'-0"

3'-0"

3'-0"

GRADE

FENCE ON BARRIER WALL

SMOOTH FACE TO DETER SCALING

9'-0"

3'-0"

3'-0"

GRADE

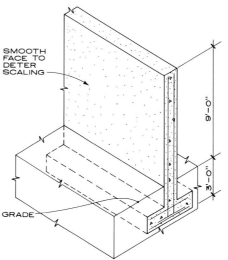

CONCRETE BARRIER WALL

12" INTERMEDIATE CONCRETE WALLS AT 4'-0" O.C.

12"-6" 6"

3'-0"

6'

GRADE

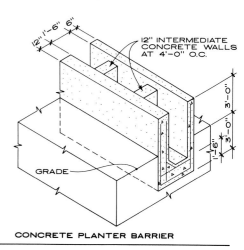

CONCRETE PLANTER BARRIER

FIXED BARRIERS

Edwin Daly, AIA, and Ellen Delaney; Joseph Handwerger, Architects; Washington, D.C.
William G. Miner, AIA; Washington, D.C.

 SPECIAL DOORS

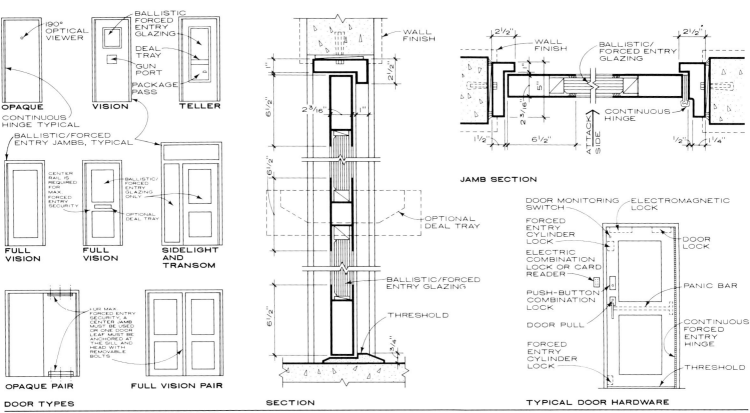

DOOR TYPES

SECTION

TYPICAL DOOR HARDWARE

BALLISTIC/FORCED ENTRY DOORS

NOTES

1. Ballistic/forced entry modular units from manufacturers can be combined to form a wall or room.

2. Fire-rated opaque security doors are available.

3. Ballistic resistant glazing is manufactured in various thicknesses to attain required levels of resistant standards; e.g., 9 mm, high-powered rifle.

4. To maximize forced entry resistance, security doors must swing toward the attack side.

5. Custom doors can be fabricated when designed within manufacturers' parameters.

6. Walls must be constructed to meet the same level of resistance as the windows and doors installed in them.

7. Doors and windows must be anchored in strict accordance with manufacturers' directions to attain resistant standards.

8. Ballistic/forced entry windows for use in exterior building openings are similar to the teller windows detailed on this page.

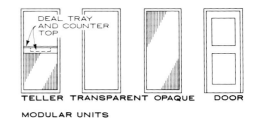

MODULAR UNITS

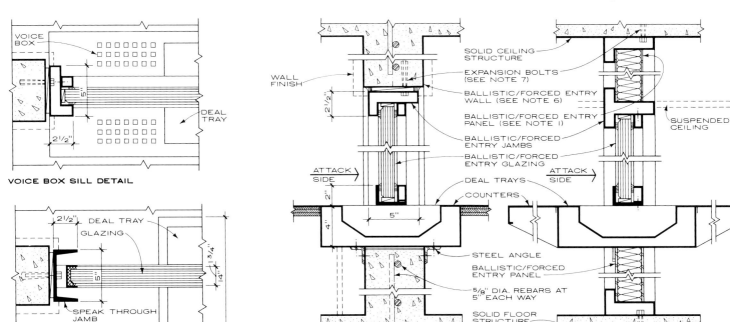

VOICE BOX SILL DETAIL

SPEAK THROUGH JAMB DETAIL

SECTION THROUGH TELLER WINDOW MOUNTED IN BALLISTIC/FORCED ENTRY CONCRETE WALL

SECTION THROUGH TELLER WINDOW MODULAR UNIT

BALLISTIC/FORCED ENTRY TELLER WINDOWS

Edwin Daly, AIA; Joseph Handwerger, Architects; Washington, D.C.
William G. Miner, AIA; Washington, D.C.

SPECIAL DOORS

8

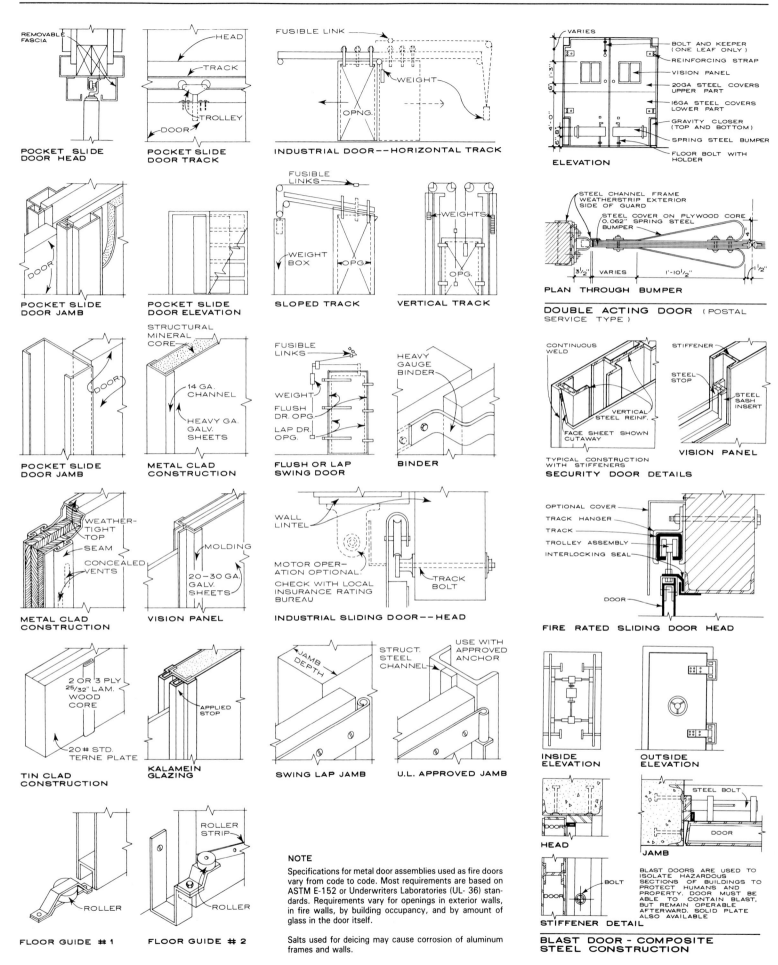

POCKET SLIDE DOOR HEAD

POCKET SLIDE DOOR TRACK

INDUSTRIAL DOOR -- HORIZONTAL TRACK

ELEVATION

POCKET SLIDE DOOR JAMB

POCKET SLIDE DOOR ELEVATION

SLOPED TRACK

VERTICAL TRACK

PLAN THROUGH BUMPER

DOUBLE ACTING DOOR (POSTAL SERVICE TYPE)

POCKET SLIDE DOOR JAMB

METAL CLAD CONSTRUCTION

FLUSH OR LAP SWING DOOR

BINDER

SECURITY DOOR DETAILS

VISION PANEL

METAL CLAD CONSTRUCTION

VISION PANEL

INDUSTRIAL SLIDING DOOR -- HEAD

FIRE RATED SLIDING DOOR HEAD

TIN CLAD CONSTRUCTION

KALAMEIN GLAZING

SWING LAP JAMB

U.L. APPROVED JAMB

INSIDE ELEVATION

OUTSIDE ELEVATION

HEAD

JAMB

FLOOR GUIDE #1

FLOOR GUIDE #2

NOTE

Specifications for metal door assemblies used as fire doors vary from code to code. Most requirements are based on ASTM E-152 or Underwriters Laboratories (UL- 36) standards. Requirements vary for openings in exterior walls, in fire walls, by building occupancy, and by amount of glass in the door itself.

Salts used for deicing may cause corrosion of aluminum frames and walls.

STIFFENER DETAIL

BLAST DOOR - COMPOSITE STEEL CONSTRUCTION

BLAST DOORS ARE USED TO ISOLATE HAZARDOUS SECTIONS OF BUILDINGS TO PROTECT HUMANS AND PROPERTY. DOOR MUST BE ABLE TO CONTAIN BLAST, BUT REMAIN OPERABLE AFTERWARD. SOLID PLATE ALSO AVAILABLE

Darrel Downing Rippeteau, Architect; Washington, D.C.
James W. G. Watson, AIA; Ronald A. Spahn and Associates; Cleveland Heights, Ohio

SPECIAL DOORS

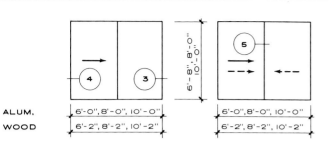
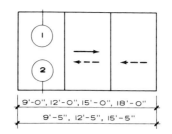
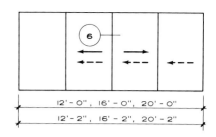

	ALUM.	WOOD
	6'-0", 8'-0", 10'-0"	6'-2", 8'-2", 10'-2"
	6'-0", 8'-0", 10'-0"	6'-2", 8'-2", 10'-2"
	9'-0", 12'-0", 15'-0", 18'-0"	9'-5", 12'-5", 15'-5"
	12'-0", 16'-0", 20'-0"	12'-2", 16'-2", 20'-2"

RESIDENTIAL SLIDING DOOR DIMENSIONS
DIMENSIONS SHOWN ARE NOMINAL STOCK SIZES

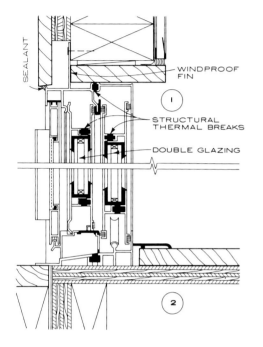

SEALANT

WINDPROOF FIN

STRUCTURAL THERMAL BREAKS

DOUBLE GLAZING

NOTES

1. Residential sliding door dimensions shown are nominal stock sizes. Custom sizes are available in accordance with individual manufacturing limitations and availability of glass sizes.

2. Details shown are for wood frame construction. Interior and exterior finishes and trim are optional. See manufacturer's data for typical installation details.

3. Tempered glass should always be used to reduce the chance of breakage and to avoid dangerous glass shards if breakage occurs.

4. Screens are available for all doors. Details show screens on the exterior for both the metal and wood doors. Consult individual manufacturer's literature to determine if screens are interior only, exterior only, or available either way.

5. Energy conservation is enhanced through the use of structural thermal breaks in aluminum sliding doors along with windproof mounting fins and double glazing. Standard aluminum sliding doors are also available.

6. See manufacturer's data for special sizes, locking devices, finishes, and specific limitations.

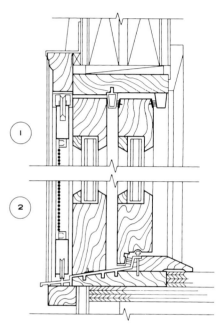

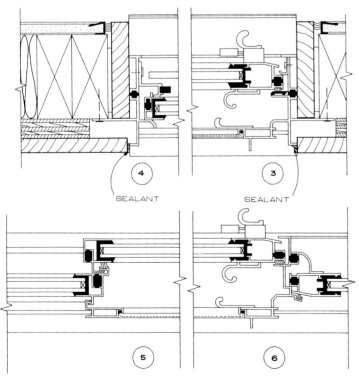

SEALANT   SEALANT

ALUMINUM SLIDING DOOR DETAILS WITH ENERGY CONSERVATION FEATURES

Leo A. Daly; Architecture-Engineering-Planning; Omaha, Nebraska

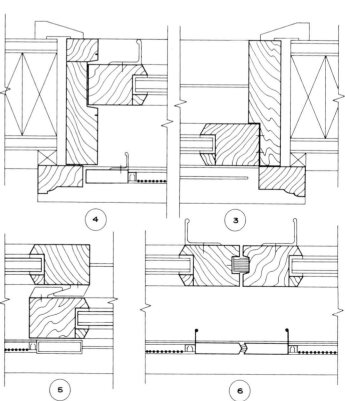

WOOD SLIDING DOOR DETAILS

SPECIAL DOORS 8

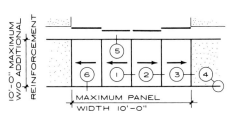

BYPASS DOOR ELEVATION

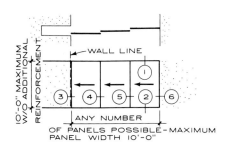

POCKET DOOR ELEVATION

MULTIPLE SLIDING DOOR ELEVATION

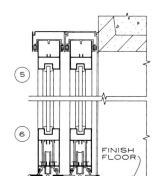

BYPASS DOOR DETAILS

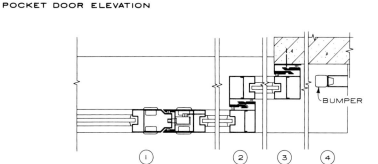

BUMPER

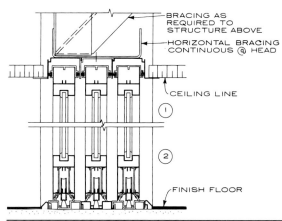

BRACING AS REQUIRED TO STRUCTURE ABOVE

HORIZONTAL BRACING CONTINUOUS @ HEAD

CEILING LINE

FINISH FLOOR

POCKET DOOR DETAILS

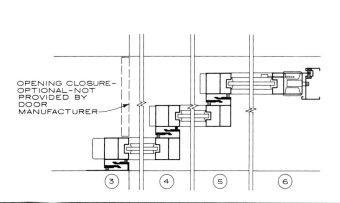

OPENING CLOSURE- OPTIONAL-NOT PROVIDED BY DOOR MANUFACTURER

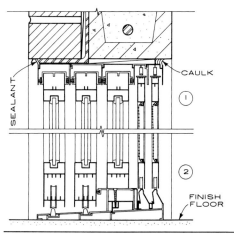

CAULK

SEALANT

FINISH FLOOR

MULTIPLE SLIDING DOOR DETAILS

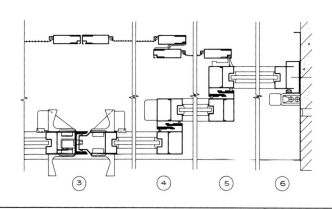

NOTES

1. Details shown are for masonry construction. Interior and exterior finishes are optional. Consult manufacturer's data for typical installation details.
2. Screens are available for all doors if required. Where shown, the details indicate screens on the interior. Consult specific manufacturer's literature to determine if screens are available for interior only, exterior only, or both. Glazing should be of safety glass, tempered, or insulating glass. Maximum manufacturable sizes of individual glass types will be the governing factor in determining maximum panel sizes. Consult industry standards for applicable data.
3. Consult manufacturer's data for available sizes, locking devices, and finishes.

Leo A. Daly; Architecture-Engineering-Planning; Omaha, Nebraska

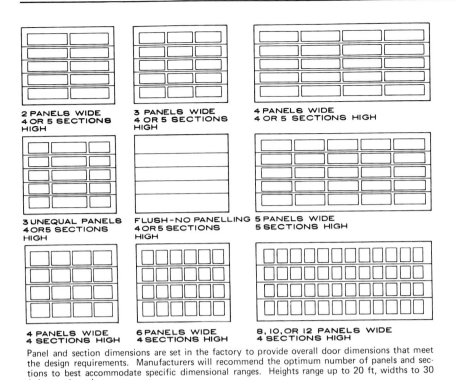

2 PANELS WIDE 4 OR 5 SECTIONS HIGH

3 PANELS WIDE 4 OR 5 SECTIONS HIGH

4 PANELS WIDE 4 OR 5 SECTIONS HIGH

3 UNEQUAL PANELS 4 OR 5 SECTIONS HIGH

FLUSH-NO PANELLING 4 OR 5 SECTIONS HIGH

5 PANELS WIDE 5 SECTIONS HIGH

4 PANELS WIDE 4 SECTIONS HIGH

6 PANELS WIDE 4 SECTIONS HIGH

8, 10, OR 12 PANELS WIDE 4 SECTIONS HIGH

Panel and section dimensions are set in the factory to provide overall door dimensions that meet the design requirements. Manufacturers will recommend the optimum number of panels and sections to best accommodate specific dimensional ranges. Heights range up to 20 ft, widths to 30 ft (approximate).

WOOD DOORS STANDARD STOCK DESIGNS

NOTE

Glazed panels may be located as desired. 3 section doors also available. Other stock designs and sizes available varying with manufacturers.

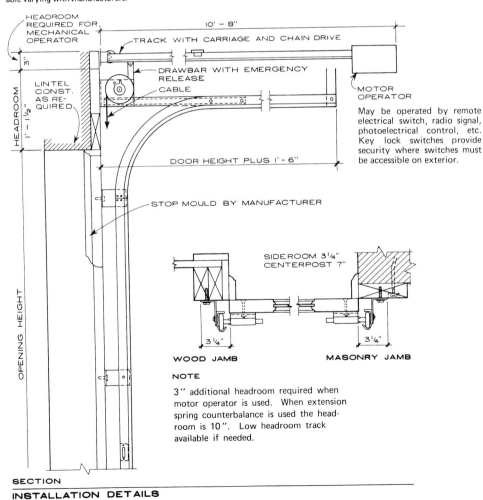

May be operated by remote electrical switch, radio signal, photoelectrical control, etc. Key lock switches provide security where switches must be accessible on exterior.

NOTE

3" additional headroom required when motor operator is used. When extension spring counterbalance is used the headroom is 10". Low headroom track available if needed.

INSTALLATION DETAILS

Eugene Patrick Holden, AIA; Dale E. Selzer, AIA, Architect; Dallas, Texas

TYPICAL DETAILS OF WOOD DOORS

All doors available with torsion or extension spring counterbalance.

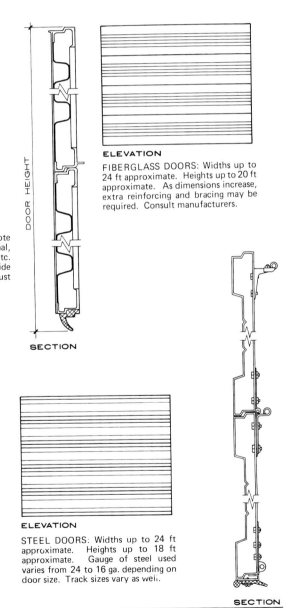

ELEVATION

FIBERGLASS DOORS: Widths up to 24 ft approximate. Heights up to 20 ft approximate. As dimensions increase, extra reinforcing and bracing may be required. Consult manufacturers.

ELEVATION

STEEL DOORS: Widths up to 24 ft approximate. Heights up to 18 ft approximate. Gauge of steel used varies from 24 to 16 ga. depending on door size. Track sizes vary as well.

FIBERGLASS AND STEEL DOORS

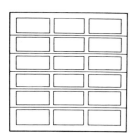

WOOD PANEL DOOR

ELEVATION

SIZE LIMITATIONS

2″ Track—not to exceed 240 sq. ft., 24′-2″ wide or 16′-1″ high.

3″ Track—not to exceed 600 sq. ft., 33′-2″ wide or 25′-1″ high.

Wood doors are easily repaired, but are more susceptible to moisture and heat damage than are metal and fiberglass doors.

NOTE

Number of panels varies from 2 for an 8′-6″ wide door, through 14 for widths from 30′-4″ to 33′-3″; number of vertical sections varies from 4 for doors up to 8′-6″ high through 13 sections for doors from 24′-2″ to 25′-1″ high. Number of panels and sections depends on increments in height and width established by manufacturer.

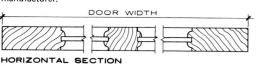

HORIZONTAL SECTION

SECTION

GLASS OR ALUM. PANELS

ELEVATION

PANORAMIC ALUMINUM

SIZE LIMITATIONS

2 in. track is not to exceed 240 sq. ft. or 20 ft. 2 in. wide or 16 ft. 1 in. high. Rails and stiles are of extruded aluminum. Stiles and rails are bolted with 1/4 in. rods for the length of the stile.

This and other doors are available with slats. Check manufacturer's literature.

NOTE

Number of panels varies from 2 for doors up to 8′-11″ wide, through 6 for widths from 18′-0″ to 20′-2″; number of vertical sections varies from 4 for doors up to 8′-6″ high, through 8 sections for doors from 14′-2″ to 16′-1″ high. Number of panels and sections depends on increments in height and width established by manufacturer.

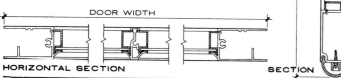

HORIZONTAL SECTION

SECTION

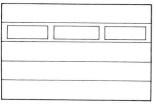

ELEVATION

16 GAUGE STEEL DOOR

SIZE LIMITATIONS

2 in. track is not to exceed 180 sq. ft. or 16 ft. 2 in. wide or 14 ft. 1 in. high. 3 in. track is not to exceed 450 sq. ft. or 33 ft. 2 in. wide or 22 ft. 1 in. high.

This and other doors are available with varying amounts of insulation. Check manufacturer's literature.

NOTE

Number of panels varies from 2 for doors up to 9′-11″ wide through 10 for widths from 31′-11″ to 33′-2″; number of vertical sections varies from 5 for doors up to 8′-0″ high, through 14 sections for doors from 20′-11″ to 22′-1″ high. Number of panels and sections depends on increments in height and width established by particular manufacturers.

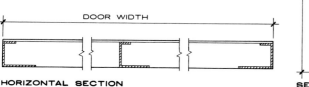

HORIZONTAL SECTION

SECTION

ELEVATION

FLUSH WOOD DOOR

SIZE LIMITATIONS

2″ Track—not to exceed 240 sq. ft., 24′-2″ wide or 16′-1″ high.

3″ Track—not to exceed 600 sq. ft., 33′-2″ wide or 25′-1″ high.

MATERIAL

1/8″ hardboard secured with waterproof adhesive on both sides of 1 1/2″ wood frame. Pressure bonded between the hardboard walls are thick, tough waterproof core strips of styrofoam.

NOTE

Number of vertical sections varies from 4 for doors up to 7′-0″ high through 15 sections for doors from 24′-7″ to 25′-1″ high, depending on increments in height established by particular manufacturers.

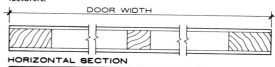

HORIZONTAL SECTION

SECTION

GLASS OR ALUM. PANELS

ELEVATION

HEAVY DUTY ALUMINUM

SIZE LIMITATIONS

2″ Track—not to exceed 336 sq. ft. 24′-2″ wide or 16′-1″ high.

3″ Track—not to exceed 384 sq. ft., 24′-2″ wide or 16′-1″ high.

Stiles and rails of extruded aluminum. Stiles are bolted to rails with 1/4″ rods the length of the stile.

NOTE

Number of panels varies from 2 for doors up to 8′-11″ wide through 8 for widths from 21′-0″ to 23′-11″; number of vertical sections varies from 4 for doors up to 8′-6″ high, through 8 sections for doors from 14′-2″ to 16′-1″ high. Number of panels and sections depends on increments in height and width established by manufactures.

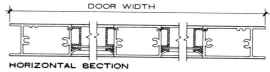

HORIZONTAL SECTION

SECTION

ELEVATION

FIBERGLASS

SIZE LIMITATIONS

2″ Track—not to exceed 340 sq. ft., 26′-2″ wide or 16′-1″ high.

3″ Track—optional.

Stiles and rails made of extruded aluminum.

Doors made of fiberglass fastened to both the rails and stiles.

NOTE

Number of stiles varies from 2 for doors up to 12′-2″ wide, through 7 for widths from 22′-3″ to 26′-2″; number of vertical sections varies from 4 for doors up to 8′-1″ high, through 8 sections for doors from 14′-2″ to 16′-1″ high. Number of stiles and sections depends on increments in height and width established by particular manufacturers.

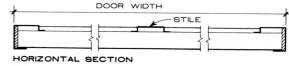

HORIZONTAL SECTION

SECT.

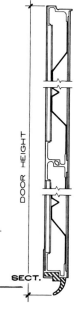

Eugene Patrick Holden, AIA; Dale E. Selzer, AIA, Architect; Dallas, Texas

SPECIAL DOORS

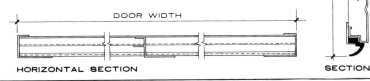

ELEVATION

CENTER STILE		SECTION	
DOOR WIDTH	NO. OF STILES	DOOR HEIGHT	NO. OF SECTIONS
to 8'-2''	2	to 8'-1''	4
8'-3'' to 12'-2''	3	8'-2'' to 10'-1''	5
12'-3'' to 16'-2''	4	10'-2'' to 12'-1''	6
16'-3'' to 19'-2''	5	12'-2'' to 14'-1''	7
19'-3'' to 22'-2''	6	14'-2'' to 16'-1''	8
22'-3'' to 26'-2''	7	16'-2'' to 18'-1''	9
		18'-2'' to 20'-1''	10
		20'-2'' to 22'-1''	11
		22'-2'' to 24'-1''	12

SIZE LIMITATIONS FOR STANDARD SIZES ON STANDARD TRACK:
20 gauge, 3 in. track—not to exceed 600 sq. ft., 33 ft. 2 in. wide or 24 ft. 1 in. high.
24 gauge, 2 in. track—not to exceed 340 sq. ft., 26 ft. 2 in. wide or 16 ft. 1 in. high.

DOOR WIDTH

HORIZONTAL SECTION

DOOR HEIGHT

SECTION

GENERAL INFORMATION

1. Standard commercial doors are designed to 20 lbs. per sq. ft. wind load.
2. All doors are available with sash sections or sash openings in standard section.
3. Doors are available using 20 gauge or 24 gauge steel sections on the top and bottom and intermediate fiberglass sections.
4. Larger openings can be enclosed by using 2 or more doors with removable or swing-up center posts. When the center posts are removed or raised, the entire opening is clear.
5. Larger size doors can be manufactured with special engineering.
6. Consider the range of energy-conscious options now available, such as weatherstripping and anti-infiltration hoods.
7. In some applications doors may require specific fire ratings. Check local building codes.
8. Doors are available with built-in pass-through doors, vision panels, insulation, and many other options. Check manufacturers' literature for availability.

COMBINED DOOR - 20 AND 24 GAUGE STEEL AND FIBERGLASS

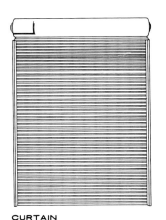

CURTAIN
Available in sizes listed below.

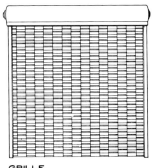

GRILLE
Maximum push-up grille sizes: 95 sq. ft. in steel, 130 sq. ft. in aluminum.

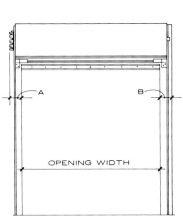

FRAME ELEVATION

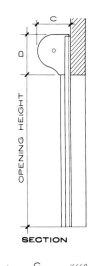

OPENING HEIGHT

SECTION

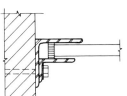

JAMB MOUNTED, STEEL

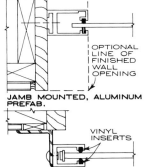

OPTIONAL LINE OF FINISHED WALL OPENING

JAMB MOUNTED, ALUMINUM PREFAB.

VINYL INSERTS

FACE MOUNTED, WEATHER STRIPPED

FACE MOUNTED WITH VINYL INSERTS TO EASE OPERATION

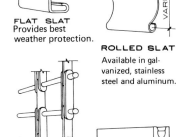

ROLLING GRILLE

FLAT SLAT
Provides best weather protection.

VARIES

ROLLED SLAT
Available in galvanized, stainless steel and aluminum.

EXTRUDED ALUMINUM SLAT
For use with rolling counter doors.

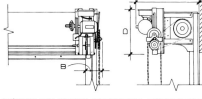

FRONT OF HOOD MOUNTED OPERATOR
Refer to manufacturers' literature for dimensions.

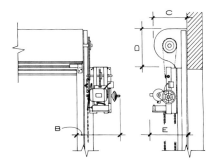

WALL MOUNTED OPERATOR
Refer to manufacturers' literature for dimensions.

GUIDE DETAILS (THESE VARY AMONG MANUFACTURERS)

NOTE

Doors and grilles are manufactured in a wide range of sizes. Many makers provide standard products up to approximately 30 ft high and 33 ft wide. Larger items may require special engineering. Operator dimensions A, B, C, D, and E vary with size and type of rolling door. Small units may be obtained in preassembled form.

ROLLING METAL DOORS & GRILLES

Eugene Patrick Holden, AIA; Dale E. Selzer, AIA, Architect; Dallas, Texas

SPECIAL DOORS 8

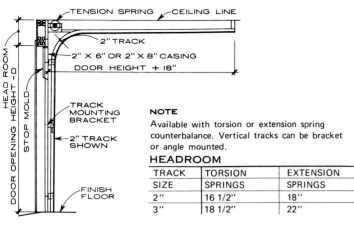

NOTE

Available with torsion or extension spring counterbalance. Vertical tracks can be bracket or angle mounted.

HEADROOM

TRACK SIZE	TORSION SPRINGS	EXTENSION SPRINGS
2"	16 1/2"	18"
3"	18 1/2"	22"

STANDARD HEADROOM TRACK – 2" OR 3"

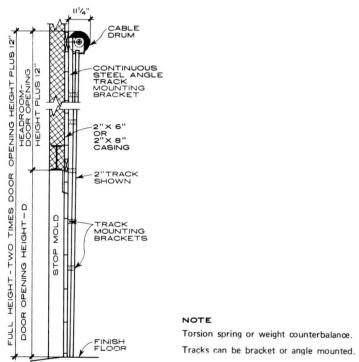

NOTE

Torsion spring or weight counterbalance.

Tracks can be bracket or angle mounted.

FULL VERTICAL TRACK – 2" OR 3"

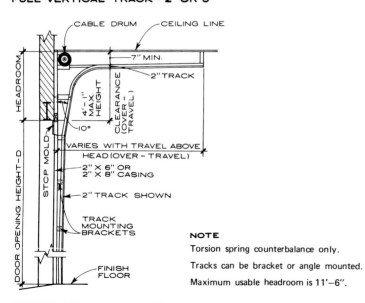

NOTE

Torsion spring counterbalance only.

Tracks can be bracket or angle mounted.

Maximum usable headroom is 11'–6".

LIFT CLEARANCE TRACK – 2" OR 3"

Eugene Patrick Holden, AIA; Dale E. Selzer, AIA, Architect; Dallas, Texas

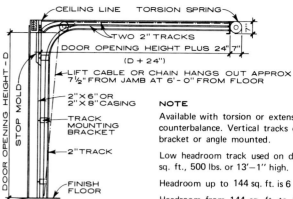

NOTE

Available with torsion or extension spring counterbalance. Vertical tracks can be bracket or angle mounted.

Low headroom track used on doors to 180 sq. ft., 500 lbs. or 13'–1" high.

Headroom up to 144 sq. ft. is 6 1/2".

Headroom from 144 sq. ft. to 180 sq. ft. is 10".

LOW HEADROOM TRACK – 2"

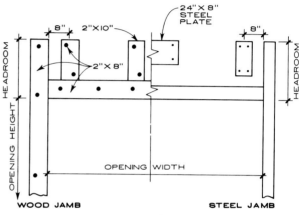

All pads and plates to be flush with wood or steel jambs.

Wide or heavy doors which require more than two springs will require pads additional to those shown in the above detail.

INTERIOR ELEVATION OF DOOR OPENING

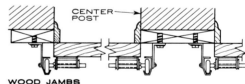

WOOD JAMBS

NOTE

For weight counterbalance doors, additional sideroom is required.

See note for asterisk at Table for Steel Jamb sideroom below.

SIDEROOM

TRACK SIZE	SIDEROOM	FOR DOORS		CENTER POST
2"	3"	to 12'–1" high		6"
2"	3 1/2"	12'–2" to 14'–1"	*	7"
2"	4 1/2"	14'–2" to 16'–1"	*	9"
3"	5"	to 320 sq. ft.	*	10"
3"	5 1/2"	over 320 sq. ft.	*	11"

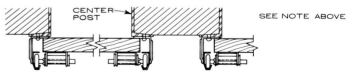

STEEL JAMBS

SEE NOTE ABOVE

SIDEROOM

TRACK SIZE	SIDEROOM	FOR DOORS		CENTER POST
2"	4"	to 12'–1" high		8"
2"	4 1/2"	12'–2" to 14'–1"	*	9"
2"	5 1/2"	14'–2" to 16'–1"	*	11"
3"	6"	to 320 sq. ft.	*	12"
3"	7"	over 320 sq. ft.	*	14"

* 16 ga. steel doors over 168 sq. ft. Use 3" angle mounted track with 7" sideroom, 14" center post.

SPECIAL DOORS

NOTE

If door is not electric operated, a chain hoist is recommended for all doors exceeding 160 sq. ft. or 13'-0" high. For 16 ga. steel use chain hoist on doors exceeding 120 sq. ft. or 12'-0" high.

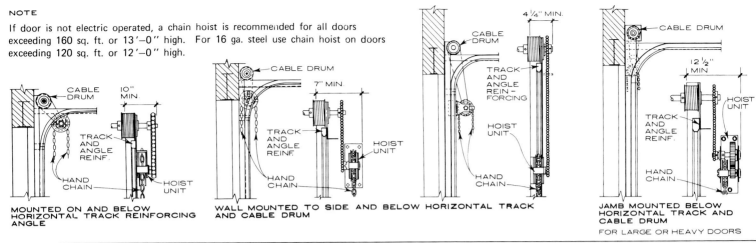

MOUNTED ON AND BELOW HORIZONTAL TRACK REINFORCING ANGLE

WALL MOUNTED TO SIDE AND BELOW HORIZONTAL TRACK AND CABLE DRUM

JAMB MOUNTED BELOW HORIZONTAL TRACK AND CABLE DRUM
FOR LARGE OR HEAVY DOORS

CHAIN HOIST OPERATORS – MINIMUM SIDE ROOM CLEARANCE

NOTE: All chain hoist operators require additional sideroom clearance. Operator may be mounted on left or right side as shown; on the left greater sideroom is required. Dimensions shown are from door jamb to projection of operator.

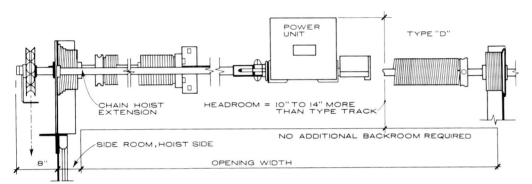

CENTER MOUNTED OPERATOR

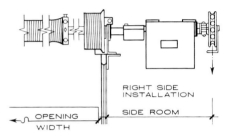

SIDEROOM WIDTHS FOR HEAVY COMMER-CIAL USE – 20" FOR 2" TRACK AND 21" FOR 3" TRACK. FOR INDUSTRIAL USE, WIDTHS ARE 23" FOR 2" TRACK AND 24" FOR 3" TRACK

SIDE MOUNTED OPERATOR

NOTES
CENTER MOUNTED

Same principle as side mounted operator except power unit is located on front wall above door opening. No additional sideroom is needed. Needs from 10" to 18" additional headroom; 3" additional sideroom on chain hoist side.

NOTES
SIDE MOUNTED

Power unit is mounted on inside front wall to the right or left of the door and is connected to the crosshead shaft with a drive chain and sprockets or an adjustable coupling. Power is applied to the shaft to raise the door. The door closes by its own weight with the speed controlled by the operator.

No extra headroom required. Needs 20" to 24" of sideroom on mounting side.
Side mounted operators are available with direct coupled or chain drive, depending on installation condition.

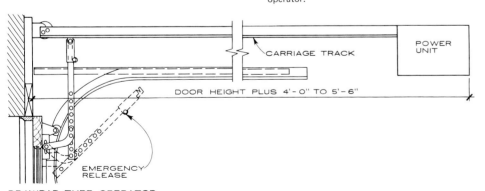

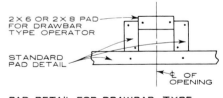

PAD DETAIL FOR DRAWBAR TYPE OPERATORS

DRAWBAR TYPE OPERATOR

NOTE
Power unit is mounted between, above and to the rear of horizontal tracks of door. A chain-driven carriage slides forward and back in its own tracks, which run from power unit to front wall above door. An arm linking the carriage and

the door applies force to open and close the door as the carriage moves backward and forward. Door requires a minimum of 2" additional head room above tracks plus 1" to 3 1/2" more at power unit. No additional sideroom is required.

Drawbar type is not recommended for use on extra large doors nor with lift clearance track installations. Emergency chain hoists are not normally used on drawbar type operators.

ELECTRIC MOTOR OPERATORS

Available in all standard voltages, frequency and phase. Control can be by 2 or 3 button push button station, pull switches, photoelectric, radio control (single or multiple), time delay closing and/or reversing or stop only safety switch. For Operator Selector chart see manufacturers data.

Eugene Patrick Holden, AIA; Dale E. Selzer, AIA, Architect; Dallas, Texas

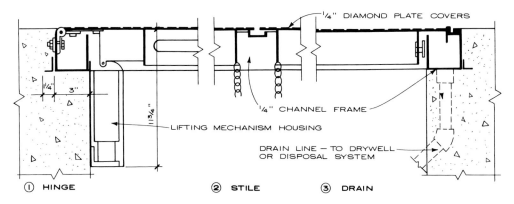

① HINGE   ② STILE   ③ DRAIN

DETAILS

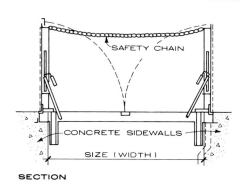

SECTION

SIDEWALK DOORS are available in single and double leaf openings. Single leaf doors range in size from 2 ft to 3 ft 6 in. in 6 in. increments. Double leaf doors range in size from 4 to 6 ft in 1 ft increments. Special sizes are available.

Units are constructed in steel or aluminum. The door leafs are made of 1/4 in. diamond plate and are reinforced to withstand 300 psf of live load. Doors can be reinforced for greater loading conditions. The channel frames are made of 1/4 in. steel or aluminum with an anchor flange around the perimeter. Each door leaf is equipped with forged brass hinges, stainless steel pins, spring operators, and an automatic hold-open arm with release handle and is locked with a concealed snap lock. A drain coupling is provided to drain the internal gutter system. Safety chains are required to protect the opening.

PLAN

SIDEWALK DOOR

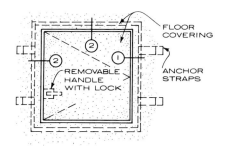

PLAN

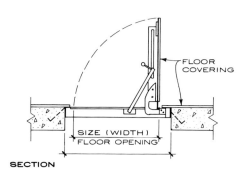

SECTION

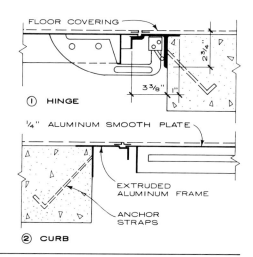

① HINGE

② CURB

FLOOR DOORS are available in single and double leaf openings. Single leaf doors range in size from 2 ft to 3 ft 6 in. in 6 in. increments. Double leaf doors range in size from 4 to 6 ft in 1 ft increments. Special sizes are available. Units are constructed in aluminum.

The door leafs are made of 1/4 in. extruded aluminum. Doors are made to accept 1/8 or 3/16 in. flooring. Each leaf has cast steel hinges and torsion bars. Doors open by a removable handle and are locked with a concealed snap lock.

FLOOR DOOR

CONCEALED HINGES

HOLD-OPEN DEVICE

SLIDE LOCK

OUTLINE OF AREAWAY

ISOMETRIC

DOOR, FRAME AND STRINGER PROVIDED BY MANUFACTURER

DROP GRADE 2" MIN.

CEILING HEIGHT

HEAD ROOM 6'-2" MIN.

AREAWAY DEPTH

SECTION

CELLAR DOOR

CELLAR DOOR DIMENSIONS

TYPE	LENGTH	WIDTH	HEIGHT
S/L	3'-7 1/4''	4'-3''	4'-4''
O	4'-10''	3'-11''	2'-6''
B	5'-4''	4'-3''	1'-10''
C	6'-0''	4'-7''	1'-7 1/2''

AREAWAY DIMENSIONS (INSIDE)

TYPE	LENGTH	WIDTH	HEIGHT
S/L	3'-4''	3'-8''	3'-5 1/4''
O	4'-6''	3'-4''	4'-9 3/4''
B	5'-0''	3'-8''	5'-6''
C*	5'-8''	4'-0''	6'-2 1/4''

*Type C door can have a deeper areaway dimension with the use of stringer extensions.

Ronald C. Olech; SRGF, Inc., Architects; Champaign, Illinois

DOOR TYPES — NOTE: DOORS WITH NARROW STILES SHOULD NOT BE USED IN HEAVILY TRAFFICKED AREAS.

CONTINUOUS TOP AND BOTTOM LOCK	BOTTOM CONTINUOUS	BOTTOM LOCK BOLT SETTING	PLAIN	NARROW STILE/UNEVEN RAILS	NARROW STILE/EVEN RAILS	MEDIUM STILE	WIDE STILE	CUSTOM

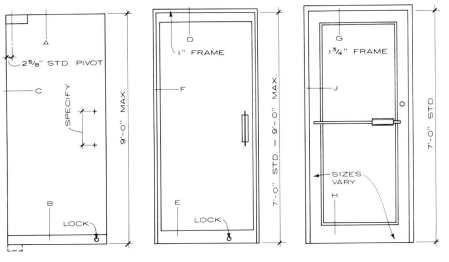

FRAMELESS DOOR   NARROW FRAMED DOOR   STANDARD FRAMED DOOR

ELEVATION — TYPICAL GLASS DOORS

CLOSED POSITION   PARTLY OPEN   COMPLETELY OPEN

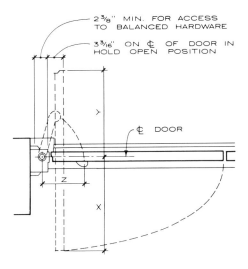

2 3/8" MIN. FOR ACCESS TO BALANCED HARDWARE

3 3/16" ON ℄ OF DOOR IN HOLD OPEN POSITION

℄ DOOR

PLAN
BALANCED DOOR

SPACE REQUIREMENTS—VARIOUS DOOR WIDTHS (IN.)

	34	36	38	40	42	44
X	21 1/4	23 1/4	25 1/4	23 1/4	25 1/4	27 1/4
Y	12 3/4			16 1/4		
Z	7 1/8			8 7/8		

NOTES

1. Consult applicable codes for safety requirements, glass size, thickness, and tempering.
2. Frameless 1/2 in. glass doors are available in clear, grey, or bronze tints in sizes up to 60 in. x 108 in. Frameless 3/4 in. glass doors are available only in clear tint in sizes up to 48 in. x 108 in.
3. Consult manufacturer's data on structural adequacy for required loads and for frames and transom bars reinforcement.
4. Aluminum doors and frames are available in all standard aluminum finishes in sizes up to 6 ft. x 7 ft.
5. Frameless doors may not permit adequate weather-stripping. The use of frameless doors in exterior walls in northern climates should be evaluated for energy efficiency and comfort.

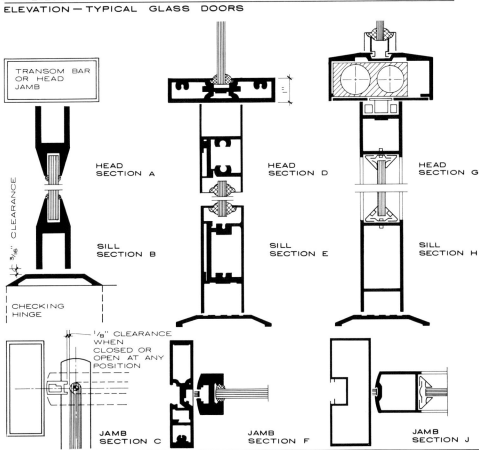

DETAILS — TYPICAL GLASS DOORS

TRANSOM BAR OR HEAD JAMB

HEAD SECTION A   HEAD SECTION D   HEAD SECTION G

3/16" CLEARANCE

SILL SECTION B   SILL SECTION E   SILL SECTION H

CHECKING HINGE

1/8" CLEARANCE WHEN CLOSED OR OPEN AT ANY POSITION

JAMB SECTION C   JAMB SECTION F   JAMB SECTION J

G. Lawson Drinkard, III, AIA; The Vickery Partnership, Architects; Charlottesville, Virginia

ENTRANCES AND STOREFRONTS   8

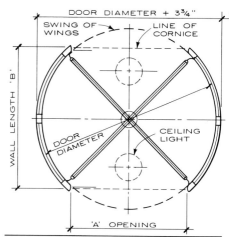

KEY TO TABLE DIMENSIONS

STANDARD DOOR DIMENSIONS

DIAMETER	A (OPENING)	B (WALL LENGTH)
6'-6"	4'-5 1/4"	4'-11 5/8"
6'-8"	4'-6 11/16"	5'-1 1/16"
6'-10"	4'-8 1/8"	5'-2 1/2"
7'-0"	4'-9 1/2"	5'-3 7/8"
7'-2"	4'-10 15/16"	5'-5 5/16"
7'-4"	5'-0 3/8"	5'-6 3/4"
7'-6"	5'-1 3/4"	5'-8 1/8"

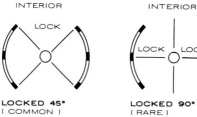

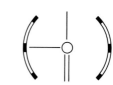

LOCKED 45° (COMMON)   **LOCKED 90°** (RARE)

CENTRAL OPEN   **ONE WING COLLAPSED FOR NIGHT SWING DOOR** (RARE)

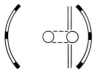

SIDE OPEN (NOTE: REQUIRES OVERHEAD SPEED CONTROL)   **FULL PANIC COLLAPSED POSITION** (ALL DOORS)

Curved sliding night door available for security if code permits. Enclosure walls and wings may be designed to roll aside.

PLANS SHOWING LOCKED AND FOLDED WING POSITIONS

48" PLUS DOOR SWING

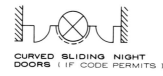

CURVED SLIDING NIGHT DOORS (IF CODE PERMITS)

48" PLUS DOOR SWING

LAYOUT TYPES

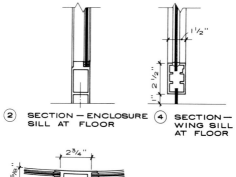

DOOR ELEVATION

NOTES

1. Circular glass enclosure walls may be simply annealed 1/4 in. glass. However, this varies with different government bodies. Some jurisdictions require laminated or wire glass. Tempered glass is not available for this use. Refer to Consumer Products Safety Commission Standards for Glazing.
2. Theoretical capacity each way = 2880 per hour. Practical capacity = 2000 per hour.
3. Doors fabricated from stainless steel, aluminum, or bronze sections are available. Wall enclosure may be all metal, all glass, partial glass, or housed-in construction.
4. Provide heating and cooling source integral with or immediately adjacent to enclosure.
5. Motor drive recommended with constant low speed.
6. For general use, use 6 ft 6 in. diameter. For hotels, department stores, or other large traffic areas, use 7 ft or greater diameter.
7. Codes may allow 50% of legal exiting requirements by means of revolving doors. Some do not credit any and require hinged doors adjacent. Verify with local authorities.

① **SECTION—ENCLOSURE HEAD AT CEILING**   ③ **SECTION—WING HEAD AT CEILING**   ⑤ **DETAIL AT PIVOT HEAD**   ⑥ **CEILING LIGHT DETAIL**

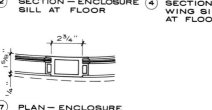

② **SECTION—ENCLOSURE SILL AT FLOOR**   ④ **SECTION—WING SILL AT FLOOR**

⑦ **PLAN—ENCLOSURE AT MULLION**

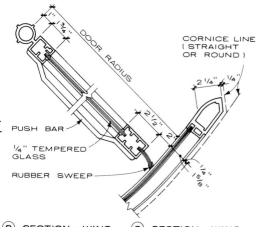

⑧ **SECTION—WING AT CENTER SHAFT**   ⑨ **SECTION—WING AT ENCLOSURE TERMINAL**

TYPICAL DOOR DETAILS

Skidmore, Owings & Merrill

ENTRANCES AND STOREFRONTS

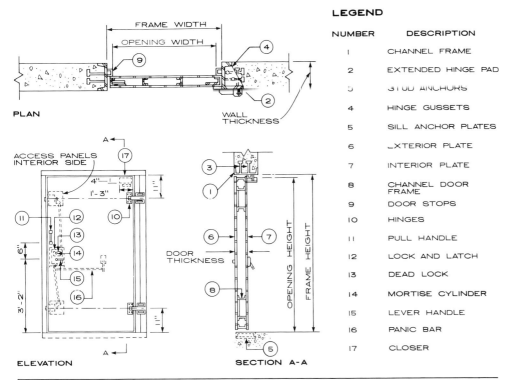

LEGEND

NUMBER	DESCRIPTION
1	CHANNEL FRAME
2	EXTENDED HINGE PAD
3	STUD ANCHORS
4	HINGE GUSSETS
5	SILL ANCHOR PLATES
6	EXTERIOR PLATE
7	INTERIOR PLATE
8	CHANNEL DOOR FRAME
9	DOOR STOPS
10	HINGES
11	PULL HANDLE
12	LOCK AND LATCH
13	DEAD LOCK
14	MORTISE CYLINDER
15	LEVER HANDLE
16	PANIC BAR
17	CLOSER

BLAST-RESISTANT DOOR DETAILS

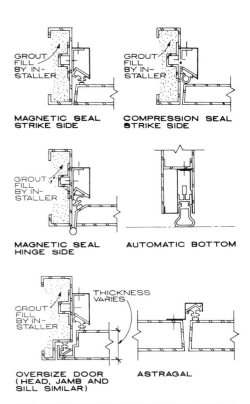

SOUND-RESISTANT DOOR COMPONENTS

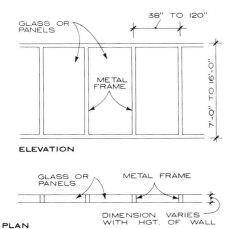

METAL FRAME SYSTEM

NOTES

All glass wall systems are engineered, custom fabricated combinations of clear glass vertical mullion lights with silicone structural sealant at the mullion and vision light interfaces.

Glass mullion systems replace conventional masonry, wood, or metal supports for large glass walls, and they may be used inside or out. No opaque materials are used except for simple metal sections at the head and sill. Engineers usually rely on ¾ in. thick mullions as the principal supporting element. The thickness and width of large vision lights for clear glass (or, under special conditions, tinted glass) are governed by glass and silicone design requirements at the design wind load or other loading requirements. When an all-glass system is proposed, reputable glass manufacturers with expertise in this type of construction should be consulted from the beginning.

Glass thickness varies with width, height, and loading conditions. Consult glass manufacturer for glass sizing recommendations for vision lights and glass mullions.

LARGE GLASS WALLS

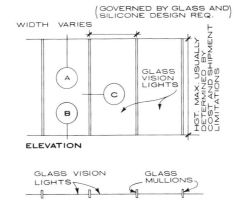

ALL GLASS SYSTEM

Local, state, and federal regulations regarding use and application of safety glazing materials and glass walls must be heeded.

Each component (other than glass) should be designed so that deflections normal to the wall plane at required loading will not exceed 1/200 of the component's clear span; but the deflection of glass-supporting members is limited to 1/300 of the distance over which such glass is supported. Deflections parallel to the wall plane must not exceed 75 percent of the glass edge clearances or other clearances provided between component parts. Calculations for such deflections are based on the combination of maximum direct loading, building deflections, thermal stresses, and fabrication and erection tolerances. Permanent deflections in this type of work are not permitted.

AUTOMATIC DOORS (POWER OPERATED)

Hand- or floor-mat-activated and pneumatic, hydraulic, or electric-powered automatic doors are available from various sources. This type of door is either horizontally sliding (both single and biparting) or pivotal (single or double). Both types usually have break out features from inside that allow them to be used as exit doors. Power-off safety features can be provided to ensure safe public passage, including for the handicapped. Minimum clear opening width for the handicapped is 32 in.

All glass used in doors, sidelights, and vestibule return lights must comply with safety glazing requirements. See "Glass Doors: Entrances."

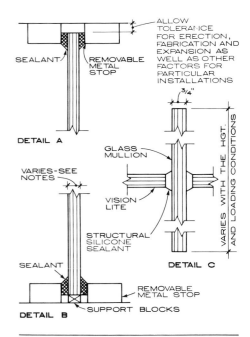

ALL GLASS DETAILS

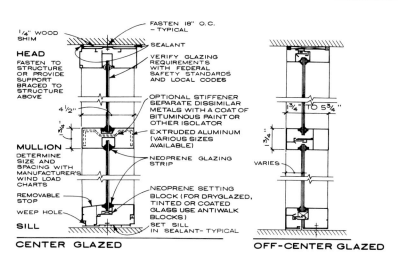

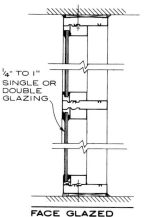

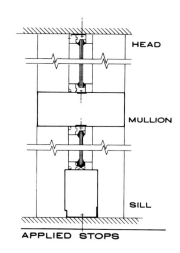

CENTER GLAZED   **OFF-CENTER GLAZED**   **FACE GLAZED**   **APPLIED STOPS**

NOTES

1. Review tinted and coated glass applications and details to eliminate possibility of thermal breakage due to shading devices and shadow patterns.
2. Review setting block spacing, size, and hardness to prevent glass slippage and breakage.
3. Weep holes are required at sill for double glazing.
4. Refer to manufacturer's current recommendations for specific applications.
5. Other materials such as hollow metal or wood can be used for custom work and in saltwater atmospheres where aluminum will corrode.

6. Various aluminum anodized color finishes are available. Class I (0.7 mil) or Class II (0.4 mil) in black, bronze, or clear are standard with most manufacturers.
7. To extend life of aluminum and to reduce tendency of surface pitting, wash aluminum periodically with water and mild detergent.
8. Glass edges mitered at corners are not recommended. Maximum vertical span for butt glazing is 10 ft. x 8 ft. wide.
9. Mullions are clear glass. Tinted or coated glass lights may be considered for small areas. Maximum vertical span is 30 ft.

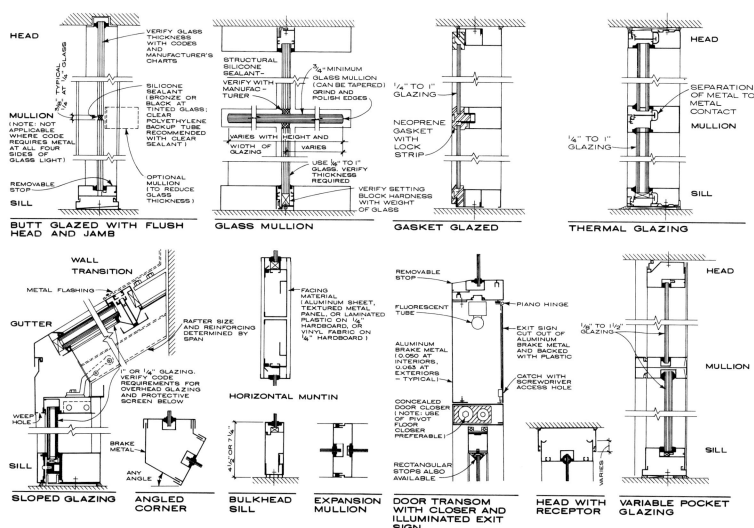

BUTT GLAZED WITH FLUSH HEAD AND JAMB   **GLASS MULLION**   **GASKET GLAZED**   **THERMAL GLAZING**

SLOPED GLAZING   **ANGLED CORNER**   **BULKHEAD SILL**   **EXPANSION MULLION**   **HORIZONTAL MUNTIN**   **DOOR TRANSOM WITH CLOSER AND ILLUMINATED EXIT SIGN**   **HEAD WITH RECEPTOR**   **VARIABLE POCKET GLAZING**

Care should be taken to protect the public from the possibility of overhead glass breakage.

Higher bulkheads can be built up with aluminum tubing and applied stops. Locate expansion mullions 20 ft o.c.

Use receptor for deflection or dimensional tolerance problems.

O'Leary Terasawa Takahashi DeChellis & Chaffin, AIA Architects; Los Angeles, California

ENTRANCES AND STOREFRONTS

TYPICAL OPERATING HARDWARE FOR METAL WINDOWS

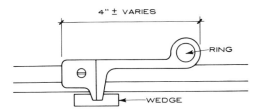

TYPICAL (CAM) LOCKING HANDLE

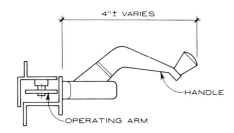

TYPICAL CRANK (ROTO) OPERATOR

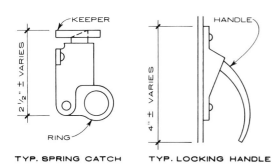

TYP. SPRING CATCH   **TYP. LOCKING HANDLE**

TYPICAL STAY BAR (PUSH BAR)

OTHER TYPES OF HARDWARE

1. Concealed cam hardware.
2. Hardware with removable handles for A.C. buildings. Also key locks.
3. Sliding window hardware.
4. D. H. window hardware (sweeplock).
5. Telescoping adjuster.
6. Chain, pole & cord operated hardware.
7. Hardware for security windows.
8. Heavy duty, electrical powered hardware for group window control.

FINISHES INCLUDE

1. Steel: diecast, lacquered & painted.
2. Aluminum: wide range of finishes and colors. Generally match window finish.
3. Bronze
4. White bronze & nickel bronze

Charles F. D. Egbert, AIA, Architect; Washington, D.C.

EXTRUDED ALUMINUM SILLS

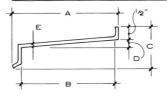

For Lug Sills
Extend into brick joints at window jambs and allow 1/4" space for expansion at ends.

For Continuous Sills
At joints allow 1/4" to 3/8" expansion and flash joints.

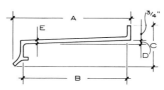

Used for continuous line of windows. Provide 1/4" to 3/8" expansion space at jamb or butt joints of continuous sills.

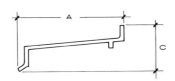

A	B	C	D	E	Std. No.*
3 7/16"	3"	1 9/16"	3/16"	3/32"	37734
3 29/32"		1 1/2"			P-3684
3 15/16"	3 1/2"	1 19/32"	7/32"	3/32"	37735
4 13/32"		1 17/32"			P-3683
4 7/16"	4"	1 5/8"	1/4"	3/32"	37736
4 7/8"		1 9/16"			3686
4 15/16"	4 1/2"	1 21/32"	9/32"	3/32"	37737
5 3/8"		1 9/16"			3687
5 7/16"	5"	1 11/16"	5/16"	3/32"	37738
5 7/8"		1 5/8"			3685
5 15/16"	5 1/2"	1 23/32"	11/32"	3/32"	37739
9 1/16"	8 1/2"	1 31/32"	7/32"	5/32"	37745
3 1/2"	2 3/4"	1 13/16"	3/16"	1/8"	54684
4"	3 1/4"	1 27/32"	7/32"	1/8"	54685
4 1/2"	3 3/4"	1 7/8"	1/4"	1/8"	54686
					9558
5"	4 1/4"	1 29/32"	9/32"	1/8"	54687
					13008
5 1/2"	4 3/4"	1 15/16"	5/16"	1/8"	54688
					13009
6"	5 1/4"	1 31/32"	11/32"	1/8"	54689
6 9/16"	5 3/4"	2"	3/8"	5/32"	54690
7 9/16"	6 3/4	2 1/16"	7/16"	5/32"	54691
8 1/8"	7 1/4"	2 5/32"	15/32"	3/16"	54692
9 1/8"	8 1/4"	2 7/32"	17/32"	3/16"	54693
3 1/2"		1 9/16"			P-3692
4"		1 19/32"			P-3691
4 1/2"		1 5/8"			P-3690
5"		1 21/32"			P-3126
5 1/2"		1 11/16"			P-3127
6"		1 23/32"			P-3128
9 1/16"		1 29/32"			P-3230

Sills may be made to fit posts or mullions, and may be mitered at corners. Sills over eight feet in length should have central anchorage to keep them in proper position.

* Non-warehouse items

Refer to aluminum manufacturers catalogs.

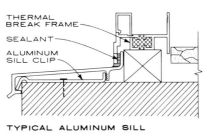

TYPICAL ALUMINUM SILL

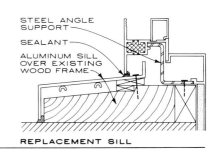

REPLACEMENT SILL

INSTALLATION DETAILS

TYPICAL FORMED METAL SILLS
SHAPES MADE TO ORDER

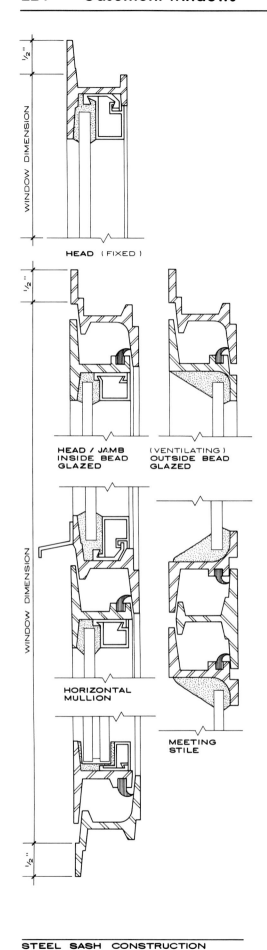

HEAD (FIXED)

HEAD / JAMB INSIDE BEAD GLAZED

(VENTILATING) OUTSIDE BEAD GLAZED

HORIZONTAL MULLION

MEETING STILE

WINDOW DIMENSION

STEEL SASH CONSTRUCTION

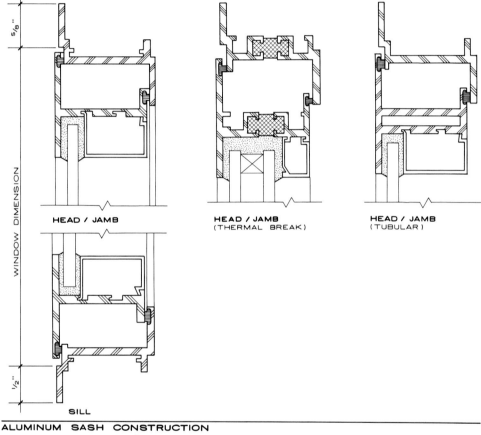

HEAD

MULLION

FIXED GLASS

HORIZONTAL MULLION

MEETING STILE

CASEMENT VENTILATING SASH

JAMB

SILL

EXTERIOR

WINDOW NOMENCLATURE

WINDOW DIMENSION

HEAD / JAMB

SILL

ALUMINUM SASH CONSTRUCTION

HEAD / JAMB (THERMAL BREAK)

HEAD / JAMB (TUBULAR)

NOTES

1. Window sizes and dimensioning methods, as listed, are not uniform for all manufacturers. Some manufacturers have no stock sizes, producing only custom work. Check with those who supply sash for each geographical area.

2. In general, heavier grades of windows offer greater configuration flexibility. Larger operating sash can be produced with heavier members than with lighter members. Thus the fixed lights shown for taller steel sash can be avoided, if desired.

3. Insect screens are necessarily installed on the interior and must be taken into account when selecting hardware.

4. The raindrip indicated on the horizontal mullion may be required at ventilating heads if sash is placed flush with exterior face of wall.

5. Drawings or specification must contain the following information: window size and location, installation details, sills, stools, flashing, sealing, and anchors; sash material and finish; glazing material; glazing method (tape, putty, or bead, inside or outside); weatherstripping, insect screen material, and hardware.

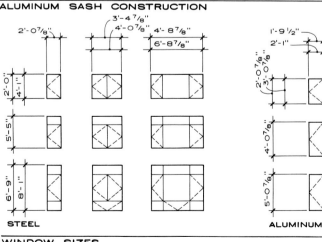

STEEL

ALUMINUM

WINDOW SIZES

William A. Klene, AIA, Architect; Herndon, Virginia

METAL WINDOWS

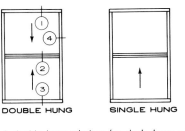

DOUBLE HUNG   **SINGLE HUNG**

A double hung window (or single hung window) is used where maximum light and flush interior and exterior building appearance are important factors.

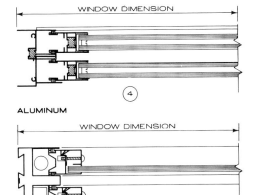

WINDOW DIMENSION

ALUMINUM

WINDOW DIMENSION

STEEL

JAMB SECTIONS

SINGLE AND DOUBLE HUNG WINDOWS

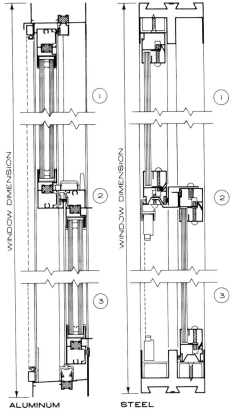

WINDOW DIMENSION

WINDOW DIMENSION

ALUMINUM   **STEEL**

VERTICAL SECTIONS

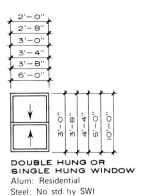

2'-0"
2'-8"
3'-0"
3'-4"
3'-8"
6'-0"

3'-0" 3'-8" 4'-4" 5'-0" 10'-0"

DOUBLE HUNG OR SINGLE HUNG WINDOW
Alum: Residential
Steel: No std. by SWI

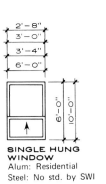

2'-8"
3'-0"
3'-4"
6'-0"

6'-0" 10'-0"

SINGLE HUNG WINDOW
Alum: Residential
Steel: No std. by SWI

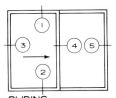

SLIDING

A horizontal sliding glass window (single or double) is used where maximum light, flush interior and exterior building appearance, simple manual operation, and accessibility are important factors.

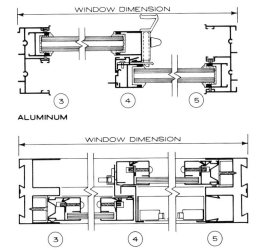

WINDOW DIMENSION

ALUMINUM

WINDOW DIMENSION

STEEL

JAMB SECTIONS

SLIDING WINDOWS

WINDOW DIMENSION

WINDOW DIMENSION

ALUMINUM   **STEEL**

VERTICAL SECTIONS

2'-0"
3'-0"
4'-0"
5'-0"
6'-0"

2'-0"

2'-0"
3'-0"
4'-0"
5'-0"
6'-0"

3'-0"

4'-0"
5'-0"
6'-0"

4'-0" 5'-0" 6'-0"

HORIZONTAL SLIDING WINDOW
Alum: Residential
Steel: No std. sizes by SWI

6'-0"
7'-0"

2'-0" 3'-0" 4'-0" 5'-0"

8'-0"

2'-0" 3'-0" 4'-0" 6'-0"

9'-0"

2'-0" 3'-0" 4'-0" 5'-0"

10'-0"

2'-0" 3'-0" 4'-0" 5'-0"

COMBINATION WINDOW (HOR. SLIDING–FIXED)
Alum: Residential
Steel: No std. sizes by SWI

David W. Johnson; Washington, D.C.

METAL WINDOWS   8

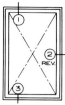

ELEVATION

NOTE

A reversible window is used mostly in multistory, air conditioned buildings where window washing from the interior is desired. It is normally opened for cleaning only; however, it may be combined with a hopper if ventilation is required.

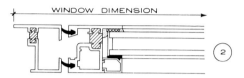

ALUMINUM

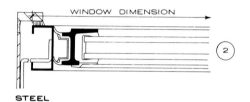

STEEL

JAMB SECTIONS
REVERSIBLE WINDOWS

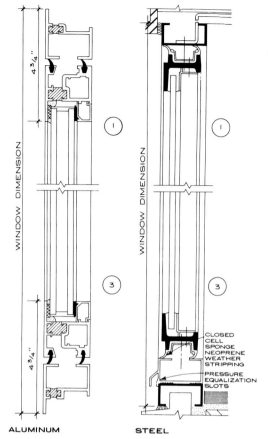

ALUMINUM   **STEEL**

VERTICAL SECTIONS

CLOSED CELL SPONGE NEOPRENE WEATHER STRIPPING

PRESSURE EQUALIZATION SLOTS

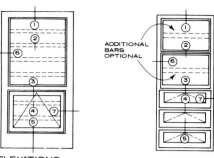

ELEVATIONS

ADDITIONAL BARS OPTIONAL

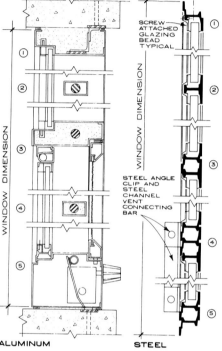

SCREW ATTACHED GLAZING BEAD TYPICAL

STEEL ANGLE CLIP AND STEEL CHANNEL VENT CONNECTING BAR

ALUMINUM   **STEEL**

VERTICAL SECTIONS

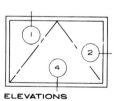

ELEVATIONS
NOTE

A projected (special) window is used mostly in multistory, air conditioned buildings where window washing from the interior is desired. It is normally opened for cleaning only; however, it may be combined with a hopper if ventilation is required. For such use see alternate above.

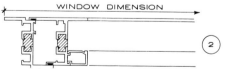

ALUMINUM

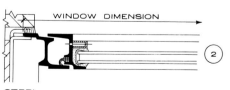

STEEL

JAMB SECTIONS
PROJECTED WINDOWS

David W. Johnson; Washington, D.C.

ALUMINUM   **STEEL**

VERTICAL SECTIONS

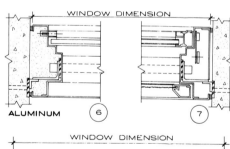

ALUMINUM

6   7

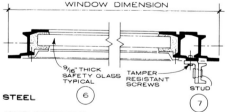

9/16" THICK SAFETY GLASS TYPICAL

TAMPER RESISTANT SCREWS

STUD

STEEL   6   7

JAMB SECTIONS

NOTES

1. Housing sill frame size varies with manufacturer of window operator.
2. Muntin and mullion tubes are 12 gauge maximum and 14 gauge medium security, grouted full, and contain a 7/8 in. diameter tamper resistant bar.
3. Tempered glass is 1/2 in. on exterior side.
4. Horizontal tube/bars to have maximum spacing of 5 in.

SECURITY WINDOWS

METAL WINDOWS

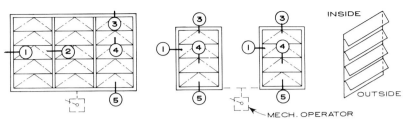

AWNING

AN AWNING WINDOW is one whose movable units consist of a group of hand operated or gear operated outward projecting ventilators, all of which move in unison. It is used where maximum height and ventilation is required in inaccessible areas such as upper parts of gymnasiums or auditoriums. Hand operation is limited to one window only, while a single gear operator may be connected to two or more awning windows, and may be motorized.

MECH. OPERATOR

INSIDE
OUTSIDE

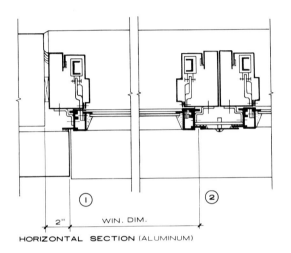

2" WIN. DIM.

HORIZONTAL SECTION (ALUMINUM)

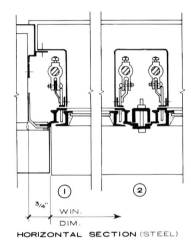

3/4" WIN. DIM.

HORIZONTAL SECTION (STEEL)

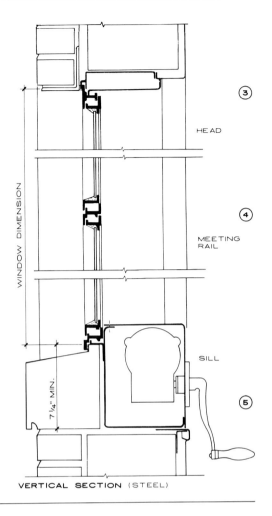

WINDOW DIMENSION

HEAD

MEETING RAIL

7 1/4" MIN.

SILL

VERTICAL SECTION (STEEL)

AWNING WINDOWS

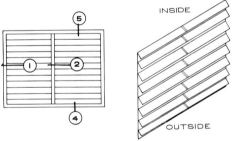

INSIDE
OUTSIDE

JALOUSIE

A JALOUSIE WINDOW (ALUMINUM) consists of a series of operable overlapping glass louvers which pivot in unison. It may be combined in the same frame with a series of operable opaque louvers for climate control. It is used mostly in residential type constructions in southern climates, where maximum ventilation and flush exterior and interior appearance is desired.

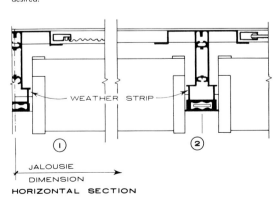

WEATHER STRIP

JALOUSIE DIMENSION

HORIZONTAL SECTION

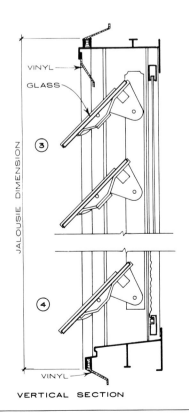

VINYL
GLASS

JALOUSIE DIMENSION

VINYL

VERTICAL SECTION

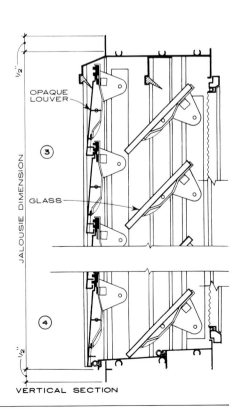

OPAQUE LOUVER

GLASS

JALOUSIE DIMENSION

1/2"

1/2"

VERTICAL SECTION

JALOUSIE WINDOWS

METAL WINDOWS 8

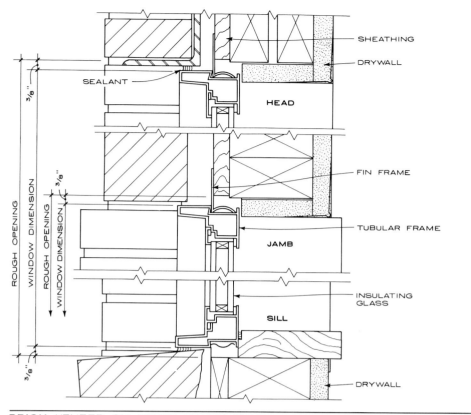

BRICK VENEER ON WOOD FRAME WALL

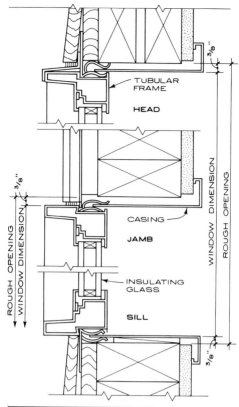

WOOD FRAME WALL

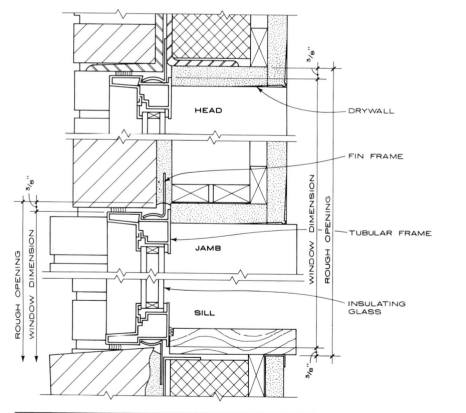

MASONRY WALL

CONCRETE WALL

NOTES

1. Fins and interior casings are available to meet various installation requirements. Interior trims are available in depths of 2 to 10 in., in 1/2 in. increments.

2. Thermal-break type extrusions are available. Consult with manufacturers for sizes and shapes.

Nicanor A. Alano, Architect; Tacoma, Washington

METAL WINDOWS

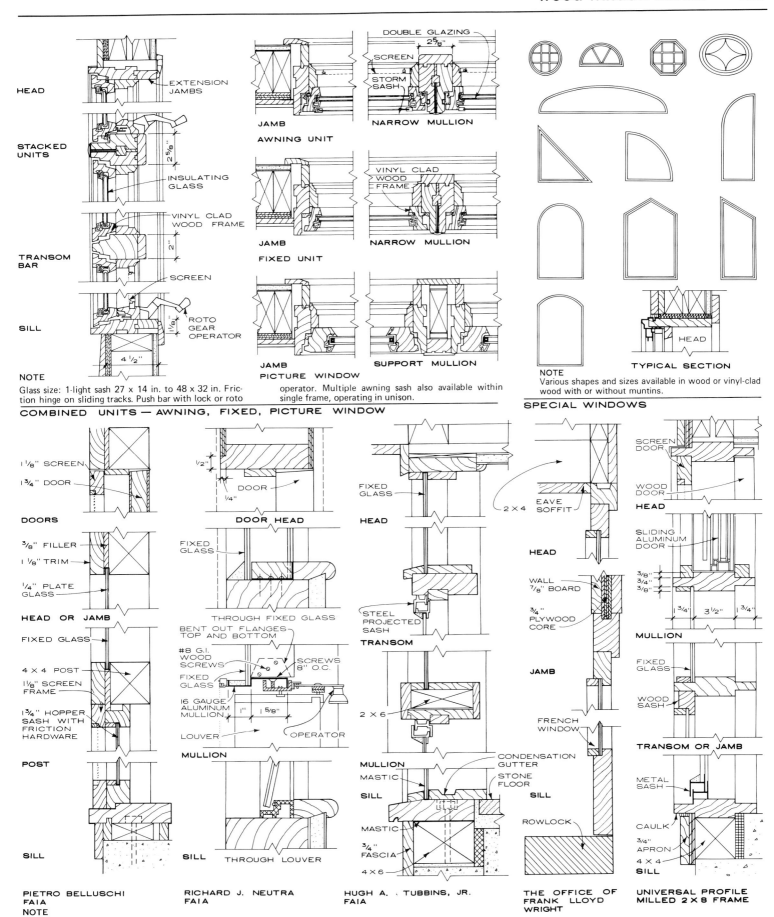

HEAD

EXTENSION JAMBS

STACKED UNITS

2 5/8"

INSULATING GLASS

VINYL CLAD WOOD FRAME

2"

TRANSOM BAR

SCREEN

SILL

1/8"

ROTO GEAR OPERATOR

4 1/2"

NOTE

Glass size: 1-light sash 27 x 14 in. to 48 x 32 in. Friction hinge on sliding tracks. Push bar with lock or roto

COMBINED UNITS — AWNING, FIXED, PICTURE WINDOW

DOUBLE GLAZING 2 5/8"

SCREEN

STORM SASH

JAMB

NARROW MULLION

AWNING UNIT

JAMB

VINYL CLAD WOOD FRAME

NARROW MULLION

FIXED UNIT

JAMB

SUPPORT MULLION

PICTURE WINDOW

operator. Multiple awning sash also available within single frame, operating in unison.

NOTE

Various shapes and sizes available in wood or vinyl-clad wood with or without muntins.

HEAD

TYPICAL SECTION

SPECIAL WINDOWS

1 1/8" SCREEN

1 3/4" DOOR

DOORS

3/8" FILLER

1 1/8" TRIM

1/4" PLATE GLASS

HEAD OR JAMB

FIXED GLASS

4 X 4 POST

1 1/8" SCREEN FRAME

1 3/4" HOPPER SASH WITH FRICTION HARDWARE

POST

SILL

PIETRO BELLUSCHI FAIA

1/2"

DOOR

1/4"

DOOR HEAD

FIXED GLASS

THROUGH FIXED GLASS

BENT OUT FLANGES TOP AND BOTTOM

#8 G.I. WOOD SCREWS

FIXED GLASS

SCREWS 8" O.C.

16 GAUGE ALUMINUM MULLION

1" 1 5/8"

LOUVER

OPERATOR

MULLION

SILL

THROUGH LOUVER

RICHARD J. NEUTRA FAIA

FIXED GLASS

HEAD

STEEL PROJECTED SASH

TRANSOM

2 X 6

MULLION

MASTIC

SILL

MASTIC

3/4" FASCIA

4 X 6

HUGH A. STUBBINS, JR. FAIA

2 X 4

EAVE SOFFIT

HEAD

WALL 7/8" BOARD

3/4" PLYWOOD CORE

JAMB

FRENCH WINDOW

CONDENSATION GUTTER

STONE FLOOR

SILL

ROWLOCK

THE OFFICE OF FRANK LLOYD WRIGHT

SCREEN DOOR

WOOD DOOR

HEAD

SLIDING ALUMINUM DOOR

3/8"
3/4"
3/8"

3/4" 3 1/2" 3/4"

MULLION

FIXED GLASS

WOOD SASH

TRANSOM OR JAMB

METAL SASH

CAULK

3/4" APRON

4 X 4

SILL

UNIVERSAL PROFILE MILLED 2 X 8 FRAME

NOTE

Selected examples indicating joinery to achieve weathertight narrow profiles. Adaptable to insulating glass for energy conservation where dictated by local conditions. See also pages on metal windows.

CUSTOM DETAILS — FIXED GLASS, HOPPER, CASEMENTS, JALOUSIE, AWNING, AND TRANSOM SASH

Carleton Granbery, FAIA; Guilford, Connecticut

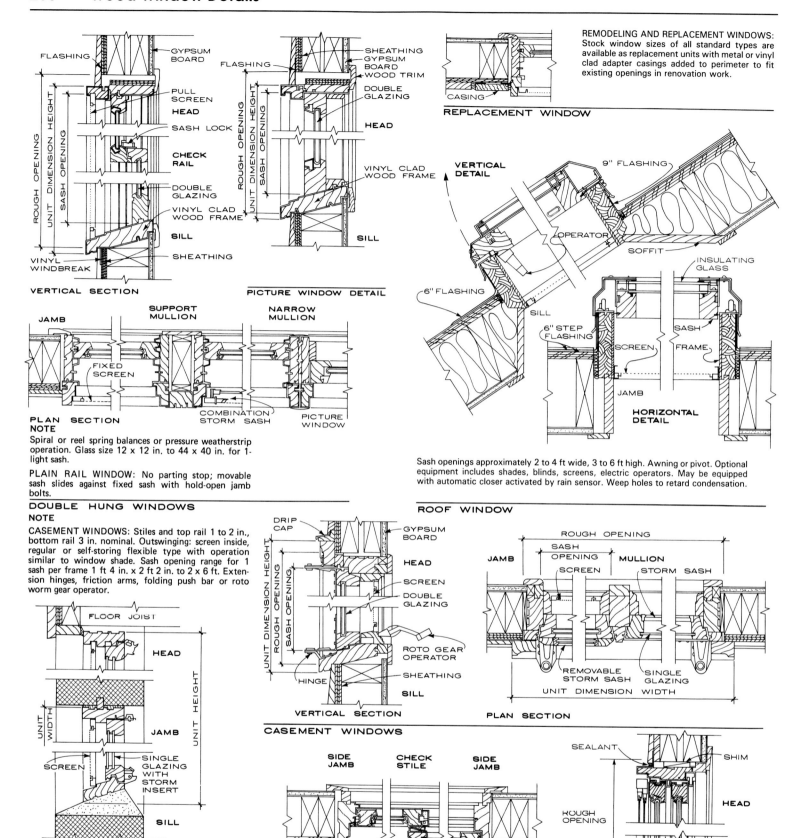

VERTICAL SECTION

FLASHING
GYPSUM BOARD
PULL SCREEN
HEAD
SASH LOCK
CHECK RAIL
DOUBLE GLAZING
VINYL CLAD WOOD FRAME
SILL
SHEATHING
VINYL WINDBREAK

ROUGH OPENING
UNIT DIMENSION HEIGHT
SASH OPENING

PICTURE WINDOW DETAIL

FLASHING
SHEATHING
GYPSUM BOARD
WOOD TRIM
DOUBLE GLAZING
HEAD
VINYL CLAD WOOD FRAME
SILL

ROUGH OPENING
UNIT DIMENSION HEIGHT
SASH OPENING

REPLACEMENT WINDOW

REMODELING AND REPLACEMENT WINDOWS: Stock window sizes of all standard types are available as replacement units with metal or vinyl clad adapter casings added to perimeter to fit existing openings in renovation work.

CASING

PLAN SECTION

JAMB
SUPPORT MULLION
NARROW MULLION
FIXED SCREEN
COMBINATION STORM SASH
PICTURE WINDOW

NOTE

Spiral or reel spring balances or pressure weatherstrip operation. Glass size 12 x 12 in. to 44 x 40 in. for 1-light sash.

PLAIN RAIL WINDOW: No parting stop; movable sash slides against fixed sash with hold-open jamb bolts.

DOUBLE HUNG WINDOWS

NOTE

CASEMENT WINDOWS: Stiles and top rail 1 to 2 in., bottom rail 3 in. nominal. Outswinging: screen inside, regular or self-storing flexible type with operation similar to window shade. Sash opening range for 1 sash per frame 1 ft 4 in. x 2 ft 2 in. to 2 x 6 ft. Extension hinges, friction arms, folding push bar or roto worm gear operator.

FLOOR JOIST
HEAD
JAMB
SINGLE GLAZING WITH STORM INSERT
SCREEN
SILL
UNIT WIDTH
UNIT HEIGHT

MAIN SILL AND UNDERSILL
MAIN SILL AND NOSING

NOTE

Removable sash and dual purpose hinges for opening from top or bottom.

BASEMENT WINDOWS

Carleton Granbery, FAIA; Guilford, Connecticut

VERTICAL DETAIL

9" FLASHING
OPERATOR
SOFFIT
6" FLASHING
SILL
INSULATING GLASS
6" STEP FLASHING
SCREEN
SASH FRAME
JAMB

HORIZONTAL DETAIL

ROOF WINDOW

Sash openings approximately 2 to 4 ft wide, 3 to 6 ft high. Awning or pivot. Optional equipment includes shades, blinds, screens, electric operators. May be equipped with automatic closer activated by rain sensor. Weep holes to retard condensation.

VERTICAL SECTION

DRIP CAP
GYPSUM BOARD
HEAD
SCREEN
DOUBLE GLAZING
ROTO GEAR OPERATOR
HINGE
SHEATHING
SILL
UNIT DIMENSION HEIGHT
ROUGH OPENING
SASH OPENING

PLAN SECTION

ROUGH OPENING
SASH OPENING
MULLION
SCREEN
STORM SASH
JAMB
REMOVABLE STORM SASH
SINGLE GLAZING
UNIT DIMENSION WIDTH

CASEMENT WINDOWS

HORIZONTAL SECTION

SIDE JAMB
CHECK STILE
SIDE JAMB
TRIPLE GLAZING UNIT

Sash opening for 2 sash per frame approximately 3 to 6 ft wide by 3 to 5 ft high. Plastic weatherstrip track top and bottom, center lock with handle.

HORIZONTAL SLIDING WINDOWS

VERTICAL SECTION

SEALANT
SHIM
HEAD
ROUGH OPENING
SILL
SEALANT
TRIM

NOTE

Threshold profiles vary from mfr. to mfr. Consult mfr. catalog for additional sizes. Std. length is 18' to 20' or saddles may be cut to size. Anchors to wood floors are screws; to terrazzo or cement floors, screws in fiber plugs or expansive metal anchors; to concrete, screws tapped to clips set in concrete.

PLAIN TYPE

BRASS		ALUMINUM				BRONZE	
A	B	A	B	A	B	A	B
3"	1/4"	4 5/64"	3/32"	4"		2 1/2 & 3	1/4"
2 1/4"	3/16"	2 1/4"	3/16"	4 5/64"	1/2"	4, 5	
4,5 & 6	1/2"	2 1/2, 3"	1/4"	5 & 6		& 6	1/2"
		2 1/4"	3/16"	4"	7/16"		

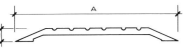

FLUTED TYPES

BRASS		ALUM.		BRONZE		STEEL	
A	B	A	B	A	B	A	B
3, 3 1/2		3, 4		3	5/16"	3 & 4	1/2"
4,5	1/2"	5,6		3	3/8"	5 1/2"	9/16"
& 6		6 1/4"	1/2"	4, 4 1/2		5 1/2	
		7		5, 6	1/2"	& 7	5/8"
		7 1/2		& 7			
		3, 4		6 & 7			
		5 & 6	5/8"	6 & 7	5/8"		

JOINT STRIP

Used for division of floors of different materials

PLAIN AND FLUTED SADDLES AND JOINT STRIPS FOR INTERIORS

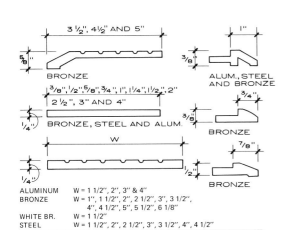

ASSEMBLED SADDLE COMPONENTS

ALUMINUM   W = 1 1/2", 2", 3" & 4"
BRONZE   W = 1", 1 1/2", 2", 2 1/2", 3", 3 1/2", 4", 4 1/2", 5", 5 1/2", 6 1/8"
WHITE BR.   W = 1 1/2"
STEEL   W = 1 1/2", 2", 2 1/2", 3", 3 1/2", 4", 4 1/2"

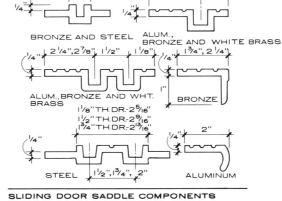

SLIDING DOOR SADDLE COMPONENTS

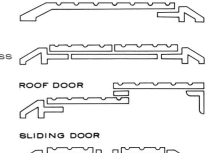

ROOF DOOR

SLIDING DOOR

TYPICAL ASSEMBLED SADDLES

By combining components saddles may be made to any width, joints will not show as fluting pattern is identical.

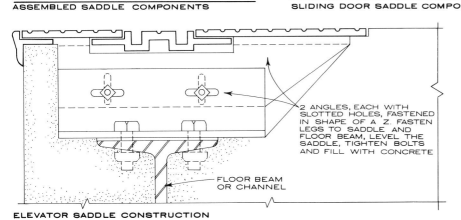

2 ANGLES, EACH WITH SLOTTED HOLES, FASTENED IN SHAPE OF A Z. FASTEN LEGS TO SADDLE AND FLOOR BEAM, LEVEL THE SADDLE, TIGHTEN BOLTS AND FILL WITH CONCRETE

ELEVATOR SADDLE CONSTRUCTION

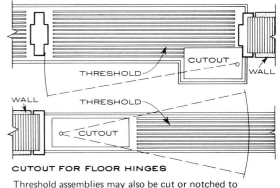

CUTOUT FOR FLOOR HINGES

Threshold assemblies may also be cut or notched to fit mullions or columns.

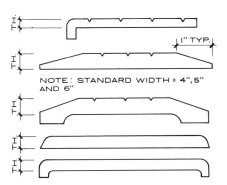

NOTE: STANDARD WIDTH = 4", 5" AND 6"

RECOMMENDED PRACTICE

TH.	IRON	BRONZE	ALUMINUM	NICKEL
1/4		to 6" wide	to 10" wide	to 6" wide
5/16	to 6" wide	to 10" wide	to 18" wide	to 10" wide
3/8	to 12" wide	to 18" wide	to 24" wide	to 14" wide
7/16	to 24" wide	to 24" wide	to 36" wide	to 18" wide
1/2	to 30" wide	to 30" wide	to 42" wide	to 24" wide
5/8	to 42" wide	to 42" wide	to 42" wide	to 30" wide
3/4	to 42" wide	to 42" wide	to 42" wide	to 30" wide

Length, to 9'-6". When width exceeds 32", length should not exceed 7'-6".

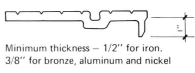

Minimum thickness — 1/2" for iron. 3/8" for bronze, aluminum and nickel

ELEVATOR DOOR SADDLE

Saddles with floor hinge cut-outs, as shown above also available.

CAST METAL ABRASIVE SURFACE SADDLES

Dan Cowling and Associates, Inc.; Little Rock, Arkansas

TOP HINGE 5" FROM JAMB RABBET TO TOP EDGE OF BARREL

THIRD HINGE CENTERED BETWEEN TOP AND BOTTOM HINGES

BOTTOM HINGE 10" FROM BOTTOM EDGE OF BARREL TO FINISHED FLOOR

NOTE: THE ABOVE IS U.S. STANDARD PROCEDURE. CERTAIN WESTERN STATES USE AS STANDARD 7" FROM TOP AND 11" FROM THE BOTTOM

LOCATION OF HINGES ON DOORS

HINGE WIDTH

THICKNESS OF DOOR (IN.)	CLEARANCE REQUIRED* (IN.)	OPEN WIDTH OF HINGES (IN.)
1 3/8	1 1/4	3 1/2
	1 3/4	4
1 3/4	1	4
	1 1/2	4 1/2
	2	5
	3	6
2	1	4 1/2
	1 1/2	5
	2 1/2	6
2 1/4	1	5
	2	6
2 1/2	3/4	5
	1 3/4	6
3	3/4	6
	2 3/4	8
	4 3/4	10

*Note: Clearance is computed for door flush with casing.

FREQUENCY OF DOOR OPERATION

TYPE OF BUILDING AND DOOR	ESTIMATED FREQUENCY		HINGE TYPE
	DAILY	YEARLY	
HIGH FREQUENCY			
Large department store entrance	5,000	1,500,000	
Large office building entrance	4,000	1,200,000	
School entrance	1,250	225,000	Heavy Weight
School toilet door	1,250	225,000	
Store or bank entrance	500	150,000	
Office building toilet door	400	118,000	
AVERAGE FREQUENCY			
School corridor door	80	15,000	Standard Weight
Office building corridor door	75	22,000	Antifriction Bearing
Store toilet door	60	18,000	(except on heavy doors)
Dwelling entrance	40	15,000	
LOW FREQUENCY			
Dwelling toilet door	25	9,000	Plain Bearing Hinges
Dwelling corridor door	10	3,600	may be used
Dwelling closet door	6	2,200	on light doors

HINGE HEIGHT

THICKNESS (IN.)	WIDTH OF DOORS (IN.)	HEIGHT OF HINGES (IN.)
Doors 3/4 to 1 1/8 cabinet	to 24	2 1/2
7/8 and 1 1/8 screen or combination	to 36	3
1 3/8	to 32	3 1/2 − 4
	over 32	4 − 4 1/2
1 3/4	to 36	*4 1/2
	over 36 to 48	*5
	over 48	*6
2, 2 1/4 and 2 1/2	to 42	5 heavy
	over 42	6 weight
Transoms 1 1/4 and 1 3/8	....	3
1 3/4	....	3 1/2
2, 2 1/4 and 2 1/2	....	4

*Note: Heavy weight hinges should be specified for heavy doors and for doors where high frequency service is expected. The heavy weight hinges should be of 4 1/2 in., 5 in. and 6 in. sizes as shown in table.

HINGE SELECTION DESIGN FACTORS

1. Material of door and frame
2. Size, thickness and weight of door with all hardware accessories
3. Clearance required
4. Use—exterior or interior exposure; frequency
5. Exposure to corrosive atmospheric elements (such as sea air, dust, etc.)
6. Quality desired
7. Special application or use (e.g., schools)
8. Door accessories (overhead holders, closers, stops, kick plates, etc.), which affect hinge performance
9. Hinge edge of door—beveled or squared

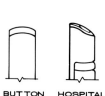

STEEPLE   BALL   BUTTON   HOSPITAL

NOTES
1. HOSPITAL TIPS ARE ROUNDED FOR EASE OF CLEANING.

2. CONSULT MANUFACTURERS FOR A WIDE VARIETY OF ORNAMENTAL TIPS

TYPES OF TIPS

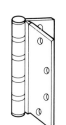

FULL MORTISE   HALF MORTISE   HALF SURFACE   FULL SURFACE

TYPES OF HINGES

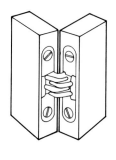

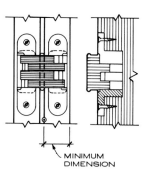

DOOR LEAF — JAMB LEAF

BALL BEARING OR WASHER

℄ OF LEAF USUALLY ON ℄ OF DOOR

HEIGHT VARIES

CLEARANCE

LEAF WIDTH

MINIMUM DIMENSION

WIDTH MAY VARY INDEPENDENT OF HEIGHT

RIGHT HAND HINGE SHOWN

INVISIBLE HINGE

OLIVE KNUCKLE HINGE

Narcisa P. Sanchez; Sanchez & Sanchez; Falls Church, Virginia

HARDWARE

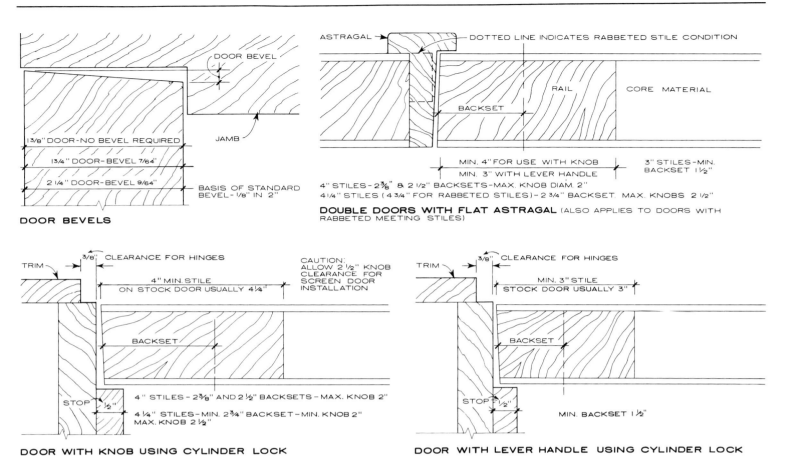

DOOR BEVELS

1 3/8" DOOR-NO BEVEL REQUIRED
1 3/4" DOOR-BEVEL 7/64"
2 1/4" DOOR-BEVEL 9/64"
BASIS OF STANDARD BEVEL- 1/8" IN 2"

DOOR BEVEL
JAMB

ASTRAGAL   DOTTED LINE INDICATES RABBETED STILE CONDITION
RAIL   CORE MATERIAL
BACKSET

MIN. 4" FOR USE WITH KNOB   3" STILES-MIN. BACKSET 1 1/2"
MIN. 3" WITH LEVER HANDLE
4" STILES-2 3/8" & 2 1/2" BACKSETS-MAX. KNOB DIAM. 2"
4 1/4" STILES (4 3/4" FOR RABBETED STILES)-2 3/4" BACKSET. MAX. KNOBS 2 1/2"

DOUBLE DOORS WITH FLAT ASTRAGAL (ALSO APPLIES TO DOORS WITH RABBETED MEETING STILES)

TRIM   3/8" CLEARANCE FOR HINGES
4" MIN. STILE ON STOCK DOOR USUALLY 4 1/4"
CAUTION: ALLOW 2 1/2" KNOB CLEARANCE FOR SCREEN DOOR INSTALLATION
BACKSET
STOP 1/2"
4" STILES - 2 3/8" AND 2 1/2" BACKSETS - MAX. KNOB 2"
4 1/4" STILES-MIN. 2 3/4" BACKSET-MIN. KNOB 2" MAX. KNOB 2 1/2"

DOOR WITH KNOB USING CYLINDER LOCK

TRIM   3/8" CLEARANCE FOR HINGES
MIN. 3" STILE STOCK DOOR USUALLY 3"
BACKSET
STOP 1/2"
MIN. BACKSET 1 1/2"

DOOR WITH LEVER HANDLE USING CYLINDER LOCK

DOOR STILES

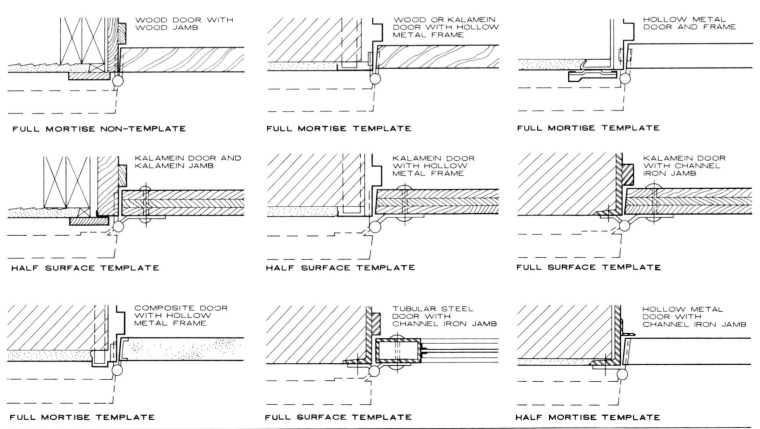

WOOD DOOR WITH WOOD JAMB

FULL MORTISE NON-TEMPLATE

WOOD OR KALAMEIN DOOR WITH HOLLOW METAL FRAME

FULL MORTISE TEMPLATE

HOLLOW METAL DOOR AND FRAME

FULL MORTISE TEMPLATE

KALAMEIN DOOR AND KALAMEIN JAMB

HALF SURFACE TEMPLATE

KALAMEIN DOOR WITH HOLLOW METAL FRAME

HALF SURFACE TEMPLATE

KALAMEIN DOOR WITH CHANNEL IRON JAMB

FULL SURFACE TEMPLATE

COMPOSITE DOOR WITH HOLLOW METAL FRAME

FULL MORTISE TEMPLATE

TUBULAR STEEL DOOR WITH CHANNEL IRON JAMB

FULL SURFACE TEMPLATE

HOLLOW METAL DOOR WITH CHANNEL IRON JAMB

HALF MORTISE TEMPLATE

MORTISE TEMPLATES

F. J. Trost, SMS Architects; New Canaan, Connecticut
Door and Hardware Institute; Arlington, Virginia

HARDWARE   8

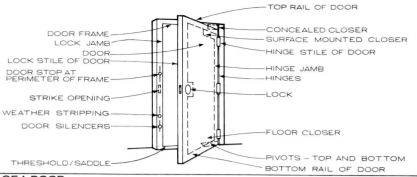

PARTS OF A DOOR

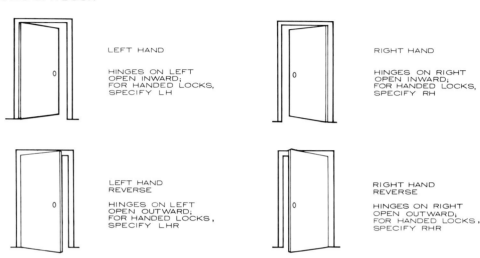

LEFT HAND

HINGES ON LEFT
OPEN INWARD;
FOR HANDED LOCKS,
SPECIFY LH

RIGHT HAND

HINGES ON RIGHT
OPEN INWARD;
FOR HANDED LOCKS,
SPECIFY RH

**LEFT HAND
REVERSE**

HINGES ON LEFT
OPEN OUTWARD;
FOR HANDED LOCKS,
SPECIFY LHR

**RIGHT HAND
REVERSE**

HINGES ON RIGHT
OPEN OUTWARD;
FOR HANDED LOCKS,
SPECIFY RHR

HANDS OF DOORS

DOOR FINISHES

NEAREST U.S. EQUIVALENT	BHMA CODE	FINISH DESCRIPTION	BASE MATERIAL
USP	600	Primed for painting	Steel
US1B	601	Bright japanned	Steel
US2C	602	Cadmium plated	Steel
US2G	603	Zinc plated	Steel
US3	605	Bright brass, clear coated	Brass*
US4	606	Satin brass, clear coated	Brass*
US9	611	Bright bronze, clear coated	Bronze*
US10	612	Satin bronze, clear coated	Bronze*
US10B	613	Oxidized satin bronze, oil rubbed	Bronze*
US14	618	Bright nickel plated, clear coated	Brass, Bronze*
US15	619	Satin nickel plated, clear coated	Brass, Bronze*
US19	622	Flat black coated	Brass, Bronze*
US20A	624	Dark oxidized, statuary bronze, clear coated	Bronze*
US26	625	Bright chromium plated	Brass, Bronze*
US26D	626	Satin chromium plated	Brass, Bronze*
US27	627	Satin aluminum, clear coated	Aluminum
US28	628	Satin aluminum, clear anodized	Aluminum
US32	629	Bright stainless steel	Stainless steel 300 series
US32D	630	Satin, stainless steel	Stainless steel 300 series
—	684	Black chrome, bright	Brass, Bronze*
—	685	Black chrome, satin	Brass, Bronze*

*Also applicable to other base metals under a different BHMA code number.
Note: BHMA—Builders' Hardware Manufacturers Association

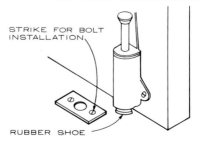

STRIKE FOR BOLT
INSTALLATION

RUBBER SHOE

PLUNGER TYPE HOLDER OR BOLT

A MINIATURE
DEADLOCK, WITH
BOLT PROJECTED
OR RETRACTED BY
A TURN OF THE
SMALL KNOB

MORTISE BOLT

F. J. Trost, SMS Architects; New Canaan, Connecticut
Door and Hardware Institute; Arlington, Virginia

GLOSSARY

Coordinator—A device used on a pair of doors to insure that the inactive leaf is permitted to close before the active leaf.

Cylinder (of a lock)—The cylindrical shaped assembly containing the tumbler mechanism and the keyway, which can be actuated only by the correct keys.

Cylinder Lock—A lock in which the locking mechanism is controlled by a cylinder.

Deadbolt (of a lock)—A lock bolt having no spring action or bevel, and which is operated by a key or a turn piece.

Door Bolt—A manually operated rod or bar attached to a door providing means of locking.

Door Holder—A device to hold a door open at selected positions.

Door Stop—A device to stop the swing or movement of a door at a certain point.

Electric Strike—An electrical device that permits releasing of the door from a remote control.

Exit Device—A door locking device which grants instant exit by pressing on a crossbar to release the locking bolt or latch.

Flush Bolt—A door bolt set flush with the face or edge of the door.

Hand (of a lock, etc.)—A term used to indicate the direction of swing or movement, and locking security side of a door.

Lock Set—A lock, complete with trim, such as knobs, escutcheons, or handles.

Mortise—A cavity made to receive a lock or other hardware; also the act of making such a cavity.

Mortise Lock (or Latch)—A lock designed to be installed in a mortise rather than applied to the door's surface.

Rabbet—The abutting edges of a pair of doors or windows, shaped to provide a tight fit.

Reversible Lock—A lock which, by reversing the latch bolt, may be used by any hand. On certain types of locks, other parts must also be changed.

Rose—A trim plate attached to the door under the knob. It sometimes acts as a knob bearing.

Shank (of a knob)—The projecting stem of knob into which the spindle is fastened.

Spindle (of a knob)—The bar or tube connected with the knob or lever handle that passes through the hub of the lock or otherwise engages the mechanism to transmit the knob action to the bolt(s).

Stop (of a lock)—The button, or other small device, which serves to lock the latch bolt against the outside knob or thumb piece or unlock it if locked. Another type holds the bolt retracted.

Strike—A metal plate or box which is pierced or recessed to receive the bolt or latch when projected. Sometimes called "keeper."

Three-Point Lock—A device sometimes required on three-hour fire doors to lock the active leaf of a pair of doors at three points.

NOTES

1. See also Hollow Metal Frames and Doors: Glossary.
2. Face the outside of the door to determine its hand. The outside of the door is the "key side" or that side which would be secured should a lock be used. This would usually be the exterior of an entrance or the corridor side of an office door.

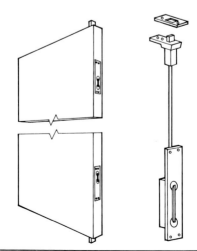

EXTENSION FLUSH BOLT

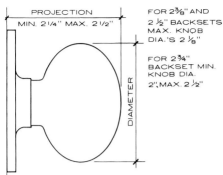

PROJECTION
MIN. 2 1/4" MAX. 2 1/2"

FOR 2 3/8" AND 2 1/2" BACKSETS MAX. KNOB DIA.'S 2 1/8"

FOR 2 3/4" BACKSET MIN. KNOB DIA. 2", MAX. 2 1/2"

DIAMETER

DOOR KNOB

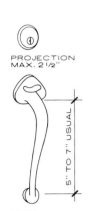

PROJECTION MAX. 2 1/2"

5" TO 7" USUAL

NOTE

Entrance door handle complete lockset includes mortise lock, handle outside, and knob and rose inside.

ENTRANCE HANDLE

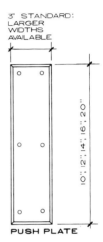

3" STANDARD: LARGER WIDTHS AVAILABLE

10", 12", 14", 16", 20"

PUSH PLATE

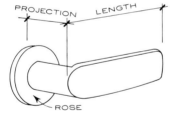

PROJECTION LENGTH

ROSE

NOTES

Projection—1 3/4 in. to 2 1/2 in.
Length—2 in. to 4 in.
Rose—max. diameter 1 1/2 in. for 3 in.
Stile—larger stile takes larger rose.

LEVER HANDLE

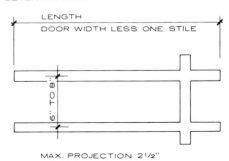

LENGTH
DOOR WIDTH LESS ONE STILE

6" TO 8"

MAX. PROJECTION 2 1/2"

NOTE

Double push-pull bars may be used on the pull side of single acting doors or on either side of double acting doors.

PUSH—PULL BAR

KNOB, HANDLES, PLATE AND BAR

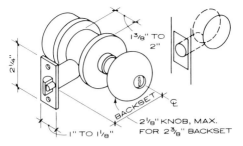

1 3/8" TO 2"

2 1/4"

BACKSET

1" TO 1 1/8"

2 1/8" KNOB, MAX. FOR 2 3/8" BACKSET

NOTES

1. Installation requires 2 1/8 in. hole in door face. Door edge requires 7/8 in. or 15/16 in. hole for standard lock, 1 in. hole for heavy duty lock.
2. Backsets: standard lock—2 3/8 in. (regular), 2 in., 2 3/4 in., 3 3/4 in., 5 in., 7 in., 8 in., 10 in., 18 in. Heavy duty lock 2 3/4 in. (regular), 3 3/4 in., 5 in., 6 in., 7 in., 8 in., 18 in., 19 in. (42 in. special).

CYLINDER

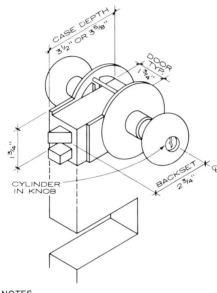

CASE DEPTH
3 1/2" OR 3 5/8"

DOOR TYPE 1 3/4"

1 3/4"

CYLINDER IN KNOB

BACKSET 2 3/4"

NOTES

1. Also available for other door thicknesses.
2. Also available without deadbolt for use as latch.
3. Installation requires notch cut in lock side of door to suit case size. Complete factory assembly eliminates much adjustment on the job.

UNIT

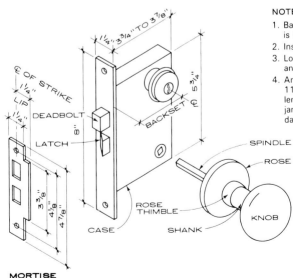

1 1/8", 3 1/4" TO 3 7/8"

C OF STRIKE
1/4"
LIP
1/4"

1 3/4"

DEADBOLT

LATCH

BACKSET 2 3/4"

5 3/4"

3 3/8"
4 1/8"
4 7/8"

CASE

SPINDLE
ROSE
ROSE THIMBLE
SHANK
KNOB

MORTISE

LOCK TYPES

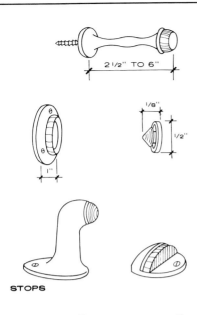

2 1/2" TO 6"

1/8"
1/2"
1"

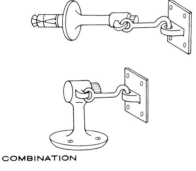

STOPS

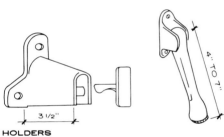

COMBINATION

3 1/2"

4" TO 7"

HOLDERS

STOPS AND HOLDERS

NOTES

1. Backset 2 3/4 in. for 1 3/4 in. door. For 1 3/8 in. door, front is 7/8 in. or 1 in. and backset 2 1/2 in. or 2 3/4 in.
2. Installation requires mortise opening in door.
3. Locks available with rabbeted fronts and many key and latch functions.
4. American Standards Association Lock Strikes A-115V-1959 for metal door frames. To determine lip length measure from centerline of strike to edge of jamb and add 1/4 in. Outside strike dimensions standard for all lock types shown.

F. J. Trost, SMS Architects; New Canaan, Connecticut
Door and Hardware Institute; Arlington, Virginia

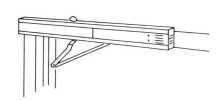

CLOSER, HOLDER, AND DETECTOR
PUSH-SIDE MOUNTED

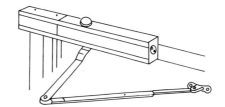

CLOSER AND HOLDER ONLY
PUSH-SIDE MOUNTED

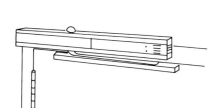

CLOSER, HOLDER, AND DETECTOR
PULL-SIDE MOUNTED

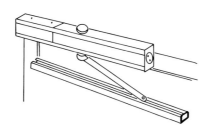

CLOSER AND HOLDER ONLY
PULL-SIDE MOUNTED

A COMBINATION DOOR CLOSER, HOLDER, AND FIRE AND SMOKE DETECTOR is available with ionization, photoelectric, or heat sensing detectors for smoke or any combustion products and for holding the door open.

A COMBINATION CLOSER AND HOLDER (only) will hold door in open position when incorporated with an independent detector or when wired into any type of fire detecting system.

All these units have unlimited hold-open from 0° to approximately 170°, or limited hold-open from 85° to 170° for cross-corridor doors.

FIRE AND SMOKE DETECTION SYSTEMS

1. Heat sensing detectors operate on the basis of fixed temperature or a rate of temperature rise. Door closers are activated upon release of a heat activated device such as a fusible link. Closing mechanisms may consist of gravity operated weights or wound steel springs.

2. Smoke sensing detectors detect both visible and invisible airborne particles. Various operating principles include ionization, photoelectric, resistance, sampling, and cloud chamber detection.

3. Ionization detection closers contain a small quantity of radioactive material within the sensing chamber. The resulting ionized air permits an electric current flow between electrodes. When smoke particles reduce the flow of ionized air between electrodes to a certain level, the detection circuit responds. Closing mechanisms usually consist of a detector, electromechanical holding device, and a door closer.

4. Ionization detectors sense ordinary products of combustion from sources such as kitchens, motors, power tools, and automobile exhausts.

5. Photoelectric detection closers consist of a light source and a photoelectric cell. They activate when smoke becomes dense enough to change the reflectance of light reaching the photoelectric device. Photoelectric detectors may be spot or beam type. Closing mechanisms consist of a detector, electromechanical holding device, and a door closer.

6. Other types of smoke detectors include electrical bridging, sampling, and cloud chambers. Each has operating characteristics similar to ionization and photoelectric detectors.

7. Requirements for closers and detectors vary by code and governing jurisdiction. Refer to local building codes, the National Fire Protection Association's life safety code (NFPA) and other applicable regulations.

SURFACE MOUNTED COMBINATION CLOSERS, HOLDERS, AND DETECTORS

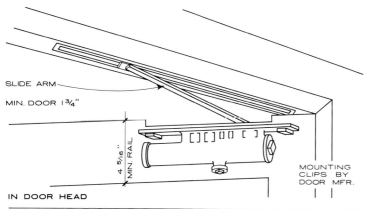

SLIDE ARM
MIN. DOOR 1¾"
4⁵⁄₁₆" MIN. RAIL
MOUNTING CLIPS BY DOOR MFR.
IN DOOR HEAD

CONSULT MANUFACTURERS FOR MIN. SIZES
4½" MAX.
LEVER ARM
SLIDING SHOE IN DOOR HEAD
IN FRAME HEAD

CONCEALED CLOSERS

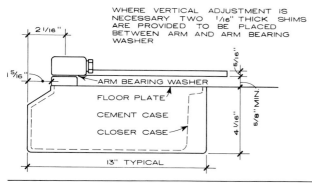

2¹⁄₁₆"
1⁵⁄₁₆"
WHERE VERTICAL ADJUSTMENT IS NECESSARY TWO ¹⁄₁₆" THICK SHIMS ARE PROVIDED TO BE PLACED BETWEEN ARM AND ARM BEARING WASHER
⁵⁄₁₆"
ARM BEARING WASHER
FLOOR PLATE
CEMENT CASE
CLOSER CASE
4¹⁄₁₆"
⁵⁄₈" MIN.
13" TYPICAL

EXTERIOR DOOR CLOSER CONCEALED IN FLOOR

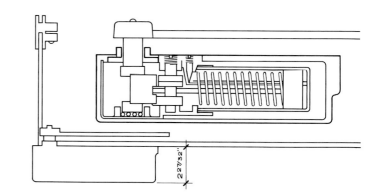

22³²"

CHECKING FLOOR HINGE FOR INTERIOR DOORS

Lee A. Anderson; SRGF, Inc., Architects; Champaign, Illinois
Sam A. Buzbee, AIA; Mott, Mobley, Richter, McGowan & Griffin; Fort Smith, Arkansas

HARDWARE

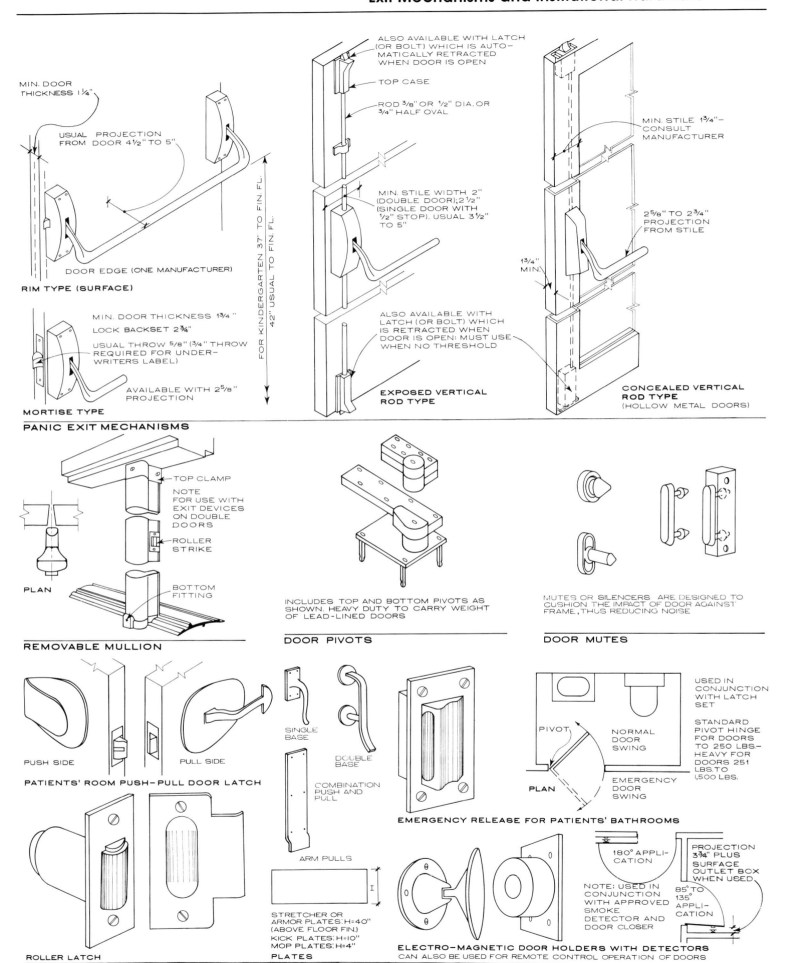

ALSO AVAILABLE WITH LATCH (OR BOLT) WHICH IS AUTO-MATICALLY RETRACTED WHEN DOOR IS OPEN

TOP CASE

ROD 3/8" OR 1/2" DIA. OR 3/4" HALF OVAL

MIN. DOOR THICKNESS 1 1/4"

USUAL PROJECTION FROM DOOR 4 1/2" TO 5"

MIN. STILE 1 3/4"– CONSULT MANUFACTURER

MIN. STILE WIDTH 2" (DOUBLE DOOR); 2 1/2" (SINGLE DOOR WITH 1/2" STOP). USUAL 3 1/2" TO 5"

2 5/8" TO 2 3/4" PROJECTION FROM STILE

FOR KINDERGARTEN 37" TO FIN. FL. 42" USUAL TO FIN. FL.

1 3/4" MIN.

DOOR EDGE (ONE MANUFACTURER)

RIM TYPE (SURFACE)

MIN. DOOR THICKNESS 1 3/4"

LOCK BACKSET 2 3/4"

USUAL THROW 5/8" (3/4" THROW REQUIRED FOR UNDER-WRITERS LABEL)

AVAILABLE WITH 2 5/8" PROJECTION

MORTISE TYPE

ALSO AVAILABLE WITH LATCH (OR BOLT) WHICH IS RETRACTED WHEN DOOR IS OPEN: MUST USE WHEN NO THRESHOLD

EXPOSED VERTICAL ROD TYPE

CONCEALED VERTICAL ROD TYPE (HOLLOW METAL DOORS)

PANIC EXIT MECHANISMS

TOP CLAMP

NOTE FOR USE WITH EXIT DEVICES ON DOUBLE DOORS

ROLLER STRIKE

BOTTOM FITTING

PLAN

REMOVABLE MULLION

INCLUDES TOP AND BOTTOM PIVOTS AS SHOWN. HEAVY DUTY TO CARRY WEIGHT OF LEAD-LINED DOORS

DOOR PIVOTS

MUTES OR SILENCERS ARE DESIGNED TO CUSHION THE IMPACT OF DOOR AGAINST FRAME, THUS REDUCING NOISE

DOOR MUTES

PUSH SIDE   PULL SIDE

PATIENTS' ROOM PUSH–PULL DOOR LATCH

SINGLE BASE

DOUBLE BASE

COMBINATION PUSH AND PULL

ARM PULLS

STRETCHER OR ARMOR PLATES: H=40" (ABOVE FLOOR FIN.) KICK PLATES: H=10" MOP PLATES: H=4"

PLATES

ROLLER LATCH

EMERGENCY RELEASE FOR PATIENTS' BATHROOMS

PIVOT

NORMAL DOOR SWING

PLAN

EMERGENCY DOOR SWING

USED IN CONJUNCTION WITH LATCH SET

STANDARD PIVOT HINGE FOR DOORS TO 250 LBS.– HEAVY FOR DOORS 251 LBS. TO 1,500 LBS.

180° APPLI-CATION

PROJECTION 3 3/4" PLUS SURFACE OUTLET BOX WHEN USED

NOTE: USED IN CONJUNCTION WITH APPROVED SMOKE DETECTOR AND DOOR CLOSER

85° TO 135° APPLI-CATION

ELECTRO-MAGNETIC DOOR HOLDERS WITH DETECTORS CAN ALSO BE USED FOR REMOTE CONTROL OPERATION OF DOORS

HARDWARE FOR HOSPITALS, INSTITUTIONAL BUILDINGS, AND NURSING HOMES

F. J. Trost, SMS Architects; New Canaan, Connecticut
Door and Hardware Institute; Arlington, Virginia

HARDWARE 8

GLASS: DEFINITION

A hard, brittle amorphous substance made by fusing silica (sometimes combined with oxides of boron or phosphorus) with certain basic oxides (notably sodium, potassium, calcium, magnesium, and lead) and cooling rapidly to prevent crystallization or devitrification. Most glasses melt at 800°C to 950°C. Heat-resisting glass usually contains a high proportion of boric oxide. The brittleness of glass is such that minute surface scratches in manufacturing greatly reduce its strength.

INDUSTRY QUALITY STANDARDS

FEDERAL SPECIFICATION DD-G-451: Establishes thickness and dimensional tolerances and quality characteristics of flat glass products.

FEDERAL SPECIFICATION DD-G-1403: Establishes standards for tempered glass, heat strengthened glass, and spandrel glass.

AMERICAN NATIONAL STANDARD 2971: Establishes standards for testing safety glazing material.

INSULATING GLASS CERTIFICATION COUNCIL (IGCC): Conducts periodic inspection and independent laboratory tests of insulating glass products.

ASTM STANDARD E546: Test method for frost point of sealed insulating glass units (horizontal position).

ASTM STANDARD E576: Dew/frost point of sealed insulating glass units in vertical position.

ASTM STANDARD E773: Test method for seal durability of sealed insulating glass units.

ASTM STANDARD E774: Specification for sealed insulating glass units.

NOTE

Consult glass manufacturers for current information because processes, qualities, finishes, colors, sizes, thicknesses, and limitations are revised continuously. The following information represents one or more manufacturers' guidelines.

BASIC TYPES OF GLASS (CLEAR GLASS)

WINDOW AND SHEET GLASS

Manufactured by a horizontally flat or vertical draw process, then annealed slowly to produce natural flat fired, high gloss surfaces. Generally has residential and industrial applications. Inherent surface waves are noticeable in sizes larger than 4 sq. ft. For minimum distortion, larger sizes are installed with the wave running horizontally. The width is listed first when specifying.

FLOAT GLASS

Generally accepted as the successor to polished plate glass, float glass has become the quality standard of the glass industry in architectural, mirror, and specialty applications. It is manufactured by floating on a surface of molten tin, then annealing slowly to produce a transparent flat glass, thus eliminating grinding and polishing.

PLATE GLASS

Transparent flat glass is ground and polished after rolling. Within limits, cylindrical and conic shapes can be bent to desired curvature.

VARIATIONS OF BASIC TYPES OF GLASS

PATTERNED GLASS

Known also as rolled or figured glass, it is made by passing molten glass through rollers that are etched to produce the appropriate design. Most often only one side of the glass is imprinted with a pattern; however, it is possible to imprint both sides.

WIRE GLASS

Available as clear polished glass or in various patterns, most commonly with embedded welded square or diamond wire. Some distortion, wire discoloration, and misalignment are inherent. Some ¼ in. (6 mm) wired glass products are recognized as certified safety glazing materials for use in hazardous locations. For applicable fire and safety codes that govern their use, refer to ANSI Z97.1.

CATHEDRAL GLASS

Known also as art glass, stained glass, or opalescent glass. It is produced in many colors, textures, and patterns, is usually ⅛ in. thick, and is used primarily in decorating leaded glass windows. Specialty firms usually contract this highly exacting art.

OBSCURE GLASS

To obscure a view or create a design, the entire surface on one or both sides of the glass can be sandblasted, acid etched, or both. When a glass surface is altered by any of these methods, the glass is weakened and may be difficult to clean.

HEAT-ABSORBING OR TINTED GLASS

The glass absorbs a portion of the sun's energy because of admixture contents and thickness. It then dissipates the heat to both the exterior and interior. The exterior glass surface reflects a portion of energy depending on the sun's position. Heat-absorbing glass has a higher temperature when exposed to the sun than clear glass does; thus the central area expands more than the cooler shaded edges, causing edge tensile stress buildup.

DESIGN CONSIDERATIONS

1. To avoid shading problems, provide conditions so glass edges warm as rapidly as other lights. An example is framing systems with low heat capacity and minimal glass grip or stops. Structural rubber gaskets can be used.
2. The thicker the glass, the greater the solar energy absorption.
3. Indoor shading devices such as blinds and draperies reflect energy back through the glass, thus increasing the glass temperature. Spaces between indoor shading and the glass, including ceiling pockets, should be vented adequately. Heating elements always should be located on the interior side of shading devices, directing warm air away from the glass.

REFLECTIVE COATED GLASS

Reflective glass coatings may be applied to float plate, heat strengthened, tempered, laminated, insulated, or spandrel glass; the number is vast. Design considerations for heat absorbing glass also apply to reflective coated glass.

Reflective coating glass falls in three basic classifications:

1. Single glazing with a coating on one surface.
2. Laminated glass coated between the glass plies or on the exterior surface.
3. Insulating glass units with coating on the exterior surface or on either of the interior surfaces.

Application of a reflective coating on the exterior surface creates a visually uniform surface on any or all these glass classifications. Extreme care must be taken in handling, glazing, and cleaning this type of glass to avoid scratching the coating. Some reflective coatings are available only with insulating units.

HEAT STRENGTHENED AND TEMPERED GLASS

Produced by reheating and rapidly cooling annealed glass, it has greatly increased mechanical strength and resistance to thermal stresses. Neither type can be altered after fabrication; the manufacturer must furnish the exact size and shape. The inherent warpage may cause glazing problems. Refer to Federal Specifications DD-G-1404 for allowable tolerances.

HEAT STRENGTHENED GLASS

Twice as strong as annealed glass. Unlike tempered glass, it does not pulverize into crystal-like form when broken.

TEMPERED GLASS

Four to five times the strength of annealed glass; it breaks into innumerable small, cubed fragments. It can be much safer than annealed glass. Shallow patterned glass also may be tempered. Tong marks are visible near the edge on the short side when the glass is held vertically during tempering. Some manufacturers temper horizontally to eliminate these marks. Strain patterns are inherent and can be seen under some lighting conditions or through polarized eyeglasses.

SPANDREL GLASS

Heat strengthened by firefusing an opaque ceramic color to the interior surface of sheet, plate, or float glass. May be tempered fully if it conforms with GSA guide specification No. PBS-4-0885.

A variety of colors and special finishes are available. Supplied with a reflective coating, color frit, or opacifier film and with insulation or as part of an insulating glass unit. Pinholes and nonuniformity of color are apparent if used without solid opaque backup. If monolithic spandrel glass is supplied without integral insulation, at least 2 in. air space is required between glass back and insulation material.

SOUND CONTROL GLASS

Laminated, insulating, laminated insulating, and double laminated insulating glass products commonly are used for sound control. STC ratings from 31 to 51 are available depending on glass thicknesses, air space size, polyvinyl butyl film thickness, and number of laminated units used in insulating products.

LAMINATED GLASS

SAFETY GLASS
(See also Wire Glass, Mirrors)

A tough, clear plastic film sheet (interlayer) 0.015 in. (0.636 mm) thick minimum is sandwiched, under heat and pressure, between plies of sheet, plate, float, wired, heat absorbing, tinted, reflective, heat strengthened, full-tempered glass, or combinations of each.

When fractured, particles tend to adhere to the plastic film. Always weep the glazing cavity to the exterior.

SECURITY GLASS

Safety glass with a plastic film of 0.060 in. (1.5 mm) minimum thickness for bullet resistant and burglar resistant glass. Bullet resisting glass consists of three to five plies of glass and, in some cases, high performance plastics, with an overall ¾ in. to 3 in. thickness. Avoid sealants with organic solvents or oil, which can react with the plastic film. (See Plastics in Glazing.)

GENERAL CONSIDERATIONS FOR GLAZING ASSEMBLIES

1. Thermal movement in frame and glass.
2. Deflection, vertical framing members.
3. Deflection, horizontal framing members.
4. Clearances, shims, drainage.

Expansion and contraction of the glazing material and the resulting movement and stresses the glazing system must cope with are determined by:

1. Size of light to be glazed.
2. Maximum exposure temperatures for glazing materials.
3. Sealed insulating units (hotter trapped air.)

Consult manufacturer for load capacities.

Some factors impacting transfer of wind loads to surrounding structure are:

1. Proportion and size of opening, span between supports, and thickness and deflection of glass.
2. Method of support for the glass pane.
3. Movement of the surrounding structure.
4. Setting blocks placed under bottom edge of glass.
5. Spacer shims—to assure proper clearances between face of glazing material and framing channels.
6. Squareness, flatness tolerances surrounding channel.

GLAZING

STRUCTURAL SEALANT CURTAIN WALL SYSTEMS

Structural sealant glazing is a system of retaining glass or other materials to the aluminum members of curtain walls using a structural quality sealant specifically designed, tested, and recommended for structural sealant glazing. In structural glazing applications, wind-induced and other loadings are transferred by the structural sealant from the glass to the aluminum curtain wall system. There are no mechanical fasteners. Presently only certain silicone sealants are suitable for use in these systems, and reference in the balance of the text is to silicone materials.

The design, testing, fabrication, erection, and maintenance of these systems require utmost care and meticulous detailing by the design professional. If the design professional is not fully knowledgeable of structural sealant glazing, then a curtain wall consultant should be retained to be responsible for development and implementation. All parties from the owner to the glazier should be aware of the serious potential liabilities of structural sealant glazing and should be willing to assume their appropriate share of responsibility.

The applicable codes and regulations that apply to the jurisdiction where the structural sealant glazed curtain wall will be erected should be consulted early in the development of the system. Some jurisdictions have regulations that can impact the design as well as the subsequent development and implementation of the system.

Preference should be given to those curtain wall systems, whether 2-side or 4-side structurally glazed, that permit as part of their design the ability to apply the structural silicone sealant in the factory rather than at the construction site. Factory glazing of the structural silicone sealant has fewer variables to control and permits better quality assurance procedures to obtain the high level of sealant workmanship that is necessary for these systems. Construction site glazing is often subject to a multitude of conditions (e.g., rain, dust, storage condition) that can be very detrimental to achieving a quality installation of structural silicone sealant.

The following text includes concerns that need to be resolved when developing structurally glazed curtain walls. It is not all inclusive; additional issues may need resolving for each curtain wall system and its particular performance criteria.

QUALITY ASSURANCE

FABRICATION OF COMPONENTS

A quality assurance program should be implemented that adequately monitors and checks the fabrication of the system components, whether in a factory or at the construction site. This type of quality assurance is best performed by an independent inspection agency that has been properly trained to perform this service.

The objectives of the program are to periodically monitor the materials and workmanship to ensure that no undesirable changes occur which would be detrimental to the performance of the system. For example, the quality of materials would be verified (i.e., cleaning solvents for purity, structural sealants for proper mixing of storage life, adhesion of structural sealants to the intended substrates, and lack of adhesion of sealants to joint fillers and backing) as well as workmanship (i.e., substrate cleaning procedures, sealant application, and that the parts of the system are being installed correctly). This monitoring could also include periodic static load testing of assembled components as a statistical check of the fabrication process.

ERECTION OF COMPONENTS

Quality assurance during this part of the process is equally important, particularly if construction site structural sealant glazing is to be performed. A program should be developed that adequately addresses the training of workmen to the system requirements, monitors the initial installation to fine tune procedures, and then periodically monitors the continuing installation.

The Spector Group; North Hills, New York
Thomas F. O'Connor, AIA, ASTM; Smith, Hinchman & Grylls; Detroit, Michigan

COMPONENTS

Developing a structurally glazed curtain wall system requires careful, conservative design and consideration of all system components and their interaction, including structural silicone sealant, insulating glass, monolithic glass, aluminum finishes, spacer gaskets, and setting blocks.

STRUCTURAL SILICONE SEALANT

The structural silicone sealant should be chosen by the professional designer, sealant manufacturer, and curtain wall contractor and glazier, all working together to establish the necessary strength, adhesive and cohesive properties, curing characteristics, and fabrication concerns for the intended sealant. An appropriate design factor should be established which includes consideration of the above and also indeterminate variables such as application procedures, whether factory or field installed, and secondary stresses induced in the structural sealant by thermal movement, wind-induced building movement, gravity loads, and other factors.

INSULATING GLASS

Insulating glass units should be dual seal units, with a secondary seal of structural quality silicone sealant, certified by the Insulating Glass Certification Council (IGCC) to a CBA quality level. Compatibility of the structural silicone sealant with the secondary insulating glass structural sealant should be verified by the sealant manufacturer and the insulating glass manufacturer. If the structural silicone sealant used with the insulating glass units is acetoxy curing (acetic acid liberating), the sealant details must be approved for compatibility by the sealant and insulating glass manufacturers. Caution should be exercised when choosing the structural silicone sealant if it is being used with insulating glass.

Design considerations for the secondary structural silicone seal of insulating glass units include adequate dimensions to resist wind loading and other secondary stresses previously described. The surfaces of insulating glass units should be tested by the sealant and insulating glass manufacturers for compatibility and adhesion of the intended structural silicone sealant. The insulating glass units should be certified by the manufacturer for use in structural silicone sealant glazing.

MONOLITHIC GLASS

Compatibility and adhesion of the structural silicone sealant to the coated or uncoated glass surface should be tested by the sealant manufacturer. Certain silicone sealants may not develop adequate adhesion to some reflective and low emissivity coated glasses. Monolithic glass used for a spandrel area may require an opacifier applied to the interior glass surface. The opacifier should be cut back for the full contact area on all sides where structural adhesion is required. The sealant manufacturer should test for compatibility of the structural silicone sealant with the opacifier and any other adjacent materials that may come in contact with or be in close proximity to the structural silicone sealant.

ALUMINUM FINISHES

The finish of aluminum framing members and trim pieces where structural adhesion will occur should be tested for compatibility and adhesion with the intended structural silicone sealant. The sealant manufacturer should verify this by laboratory tests performed before the components are fabricated and also periodically on samples of production run components. If factory applied organic coatings are used, then the adhesion and fatigue resistance of the organic coating to the aluminum is as important as the adhesion and fatigue resistance of the structural sealant to the organic coating and should be laboratory tested to verify the coating's suitability for use in structural sealant glazing. Only high-quality coatings with proven durability, applied by licensed applicators, should be considered.

SPACER GASKETS AND SETTING BLOCKS

Compatibility with the structural silicone sealant of spacer gaskets, setting blocks, glazing gaskets, and other accessories should be established before those components are fabricated and also verified periodically on samples of production run components, with laboratory testing by the sealant manufacturer. Preference should be given to the use of silicone rubber for most of these components.

SILICONE WEATHER SEALANTS

Silicone sealants used as a weather seal should be laboratory tested by the sealant manufacturer for adhesion to substrates and for compatibility and stain resistance with adjacent materials before component fabrication and also periodically on samples of production run components.

TESTING OF ASSEMBLED COMPONENTS

Realistic, comprehensive testing criteria for a mock-up of the assembled curtain wall system should be developed by the design professional or curtain wall consultant and the testing laboratory. Performance criteria that should be considered for testing include static air infiltration; static and dynamic water infiltration; wind loading structural adequacy at design loads, at 1.5 times design loads, and perhaps to destruction; deflection characteristics; seismic or racking load resistance; cyclic structural loading; steady state thermal performance; verification of reglazing procedures; verification of fabrication and erection techniques; condensation resistance; and aesthetic evaluation.

Mock-up testing helps to verify the curtain wall system design adequacy; it does not predict long-term durability.

The mock-up must be of sufficient size. It also must be representative of the building conditions and should be constructed using the actual production run materials and components, as well as fabrication and erection methods to be used for the building. The mock-up should be erected by the personnel, both supervisory and production, who will fabricate and erect the system. More than one mock-up may be necessary.

Any changes or modifications resulting from mock-up testing may require additional laboratory testing of components as well as the mock-up. Any changes or modifications after mock-up testing has been completed should be carefully evaluated. Certain aspects of the mock-up testing and perhaps the curtain wall system design could be invalidated by the changes or modifications.

Production and fabrication of the system for erection on the building should not begin until successful mock-up performance is achieved.

MAINTENANCE

The structural sealant curtain wall system design must be capable of being maintained without the need for elaborate or expensive procedures or methods. Glass will break or insulating glass seals will fail, leaks may develop, and the surface will be cleaned periodically. These basic needs should be resolved by the system design. The reglazing of glass is of particular importance, and procedures should be developed in advance of the need. Reglazing may necessitate the use of a different structural sealant from that used for the original work. If this occurs, then this sealant will also have to be tested for compatibility and adhesion during the system design. Factory glazed systems can be designed to greatly ease the field reglazing process.

Consideration should be given to a periodic inspection of the system (particularly a 4-side structurally glazed system) by a qualified professional after installation to verify the continuing performance of the curtain wall system.

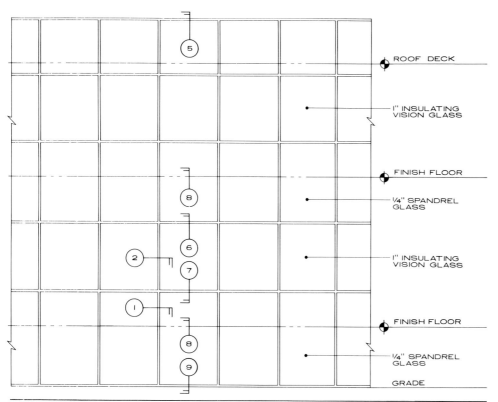

CURTAIN WALL ELEVATION

NOTE

Detail section cut number 8 is for insulation with sheet metal vapor barrier and insulation against glass. If foil vapor barrier is used, then insulation must be of same material and rating as fire-safing material, and if insulation is 2 in. from glass, then a sheet metal vapor barrier with stiffeners is necessary.

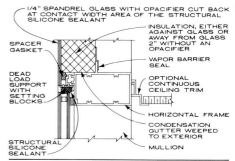

COPING DETAIL 5

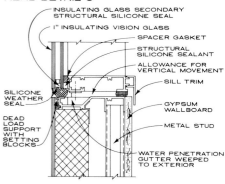

HEAD DETAIL 6

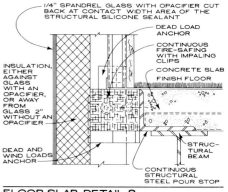

SILL DETAIL 7

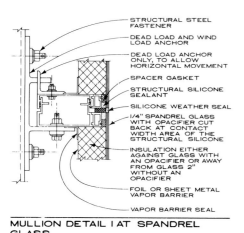

MULLION DETAIL 1 AT SPANDREL GLASS

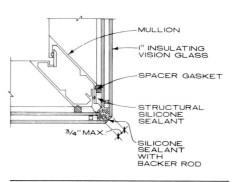

MULLION DETAIL 3 AT OUTSIDE CORNER

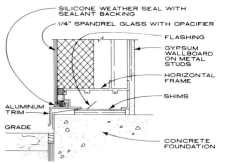

FLOOR SLAB DETAIL 8

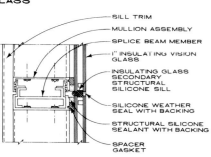

MULLION DETAIL 2 AT VISION GLASS

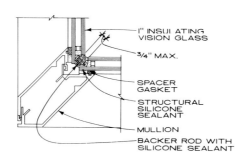

MULLION DETAIL 4 AT INSIDE CORNER

GRADE DETAIL 9

The Spector Group; North Hills, New York
Thomas F. O'Connor, AIA, ASTM; Smith, Hinchman & Grylls; Detroit, Michigan

 GLAZING

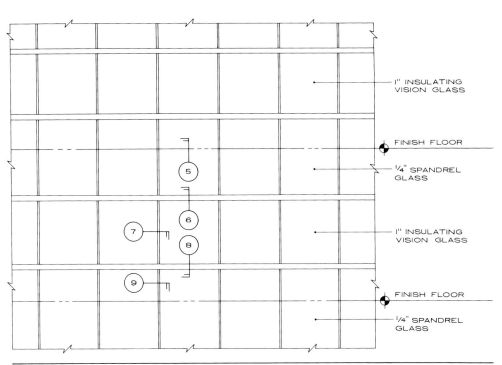

CURTAIN WALL ELEVATION

Labels on elevation:
- 1" INSULATING VISION GLASS
- FINISH FLOOR
- 1/4" SPANDREL GLASS
- 1" INSULATING VISION GLASS
- FINISH FLOOR
- 1/4" SPANDREL GLASS

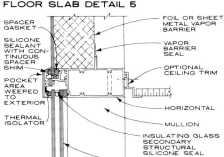

FLOOR SLAB DETAIL 5

Labels:
- 1/4" SPANDREL GLASS WITH OPACIFIER CUT BACK AT CONTACT WIDTH AREA OF THE STRUCTURAL SILICONE SEALANT
- DEAD LOAD ANCHOR
- CONTINUOUS FIRE-SAFING WITH IMPALING CLIPS
- CONCRETE SLAB
- FINISH FLOOR
- INSULATION EITHER AGAINST GLASS WITH AN OPACIFIER OR AWAY FROM GLASS 2" WITHOUT AN OPACIFIER
- DEAD AND WIND LOADS ANCHOR
- STRUCTURAL BEAM

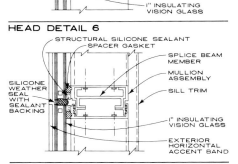

HEAD DETAIL 6

Labels:
- SPACER GASKET
- SILICONE SEALANT WITH CONTINUOUS SPACER SHIM
- POCKET AREA WEEPED TO EXTERIOR
- THERMAL ISOLATOR
- FOIL OR SHEET METAL VAPOR BARRIER
- VAPOR BARRIER SEAL
- OPTIONAL CEILING TRIM
- HORIZONTAL
- MULLION
- INSULATING GLASS SECONDARY STRUCTURAL SILICONE SEAL
- 1" INSULATING VISION GLASS

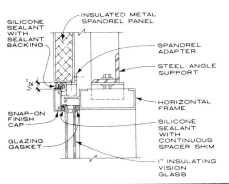

HEAD DETAIL 1 AT METAL SPANDREL

Labels:
- SILICONE SEALANT WITH SEALANT BACKING
- INSULATED METAL SPANDREL PANEL
- SPANDREL ADAPTER
- STEEL ANGLE SUPPORT
- HORIZONTAL FRAME
- SILICONE SEALANT WITH CONTINUOUS SPACER SHIM
- 1" INSULATING VISION GLASS
- SNAP-ON FINISH CAP
- GLAZING GASKET
- 1/2"

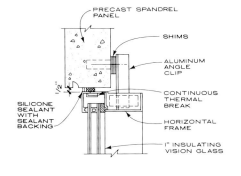

HEAD DETAIL 3 AT PRECAST SPANDREL

Labels:
- PRECAST SPANDREL PANEL
- SHIMS
- ALUMINUM ANGLE CLIP
- CONTINUOUS THERMAL BREAK
- HORIZONTAL FRAME
- 1" INSULATING VISION GLASS
- SILICONE SEALANT WITH SEALANT BACKING
- 1/2"

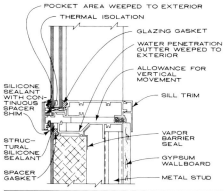

MULLION DETAIL 7 AT VISION GLASS

Labels:
- STRUCTURAL SILICONE SEALANT
- SPACER GASKET
- SPLICE BEAM MEMBER
- MULLION ASSEMBLY
- SILL TRIM
- SILICONE WEATHER SEAL WITH SEALANT BACKING
- 1" INSULATING VISION GLASS
- EXTERIOR HORIZONTAL ACCENT BAND

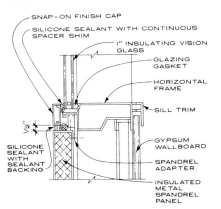

SILL DETAIL 2 AT METAL SPANDREL

Labels:
- SNAP-ON FINISH CAP
- SILICONE SEALANT WITH CONTINUOUS SPACER SHIM
- 1" INSULATING VISION GLASS
- GLAZING GASKET
- HORIZONTAL FRAME
- SILL TRIM
- GYPSUM WALLBOARD
- SPANDREL ADAPTER
- INSULATED METAL SPANDREL PANEL
- SILICONE SEALANT WITH SEALANT BACKING
- 1/2"

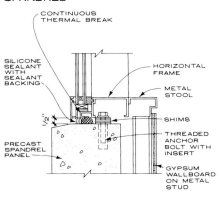

SILL DETAIL 4 AT PRECAST SPANDREL

Labels:
- CONTINUOUS THERMAL BREAK
- SILICONE SEALANT WITH SEALANT BACKING
- HORIZONTAL FRAME
- METAL STOOL
- SHIMS
- THREADED ANCHOR BOLT WITH INSERT
- GYPSUM WALLBOARD ON METAL STUD
- PRECAST SPANDREL PANEL
- 1/2"

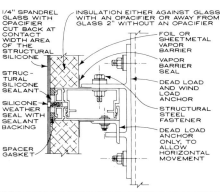

MULLION DETAIL 9 AT SPANDREL GLASS

Labels:
- POCKET AREA WEEPED TO EXTERIOR
- THERMAL ISOLATION
- GLAZING GASKET
- WATER PENETRATION GUTTER WEEPED TO EXTERIOR
- ALLOWANCE FOR VERTICAL MOVEMENT
- SILL TRIM
- SILICONE SEALANT WITH CONTINUOUS SPACER SHIM
- STRUCTURAL SILICONE SEALANT
- SPACER GASKET
- VAPOR BARRIER SEAL
- GYPSUM WALLBOARD
- METAL STUD

SILL DETAIL 8 AT SPANDREL GLASS

Labels:
- 1/4" SPANDREL GLASS WITH OPACIFIER CUT BACK AT CONTACT WIDTH OF THE STRUCTURAL SILICONE
- INSULATION EITHER AGAINST GLASS WITH AN OPACIFIER OR AWAY FROM GLASS 2" WITHOUT AN OPACIFIER
- STRUCTURAL SILICONE SEALANT
- SILICONE WEATHER SEAL WITH SEALANT BACKING
- SPACER GASKET
- FOIL OR SHEETMETAL VAPOR BARRIER
- VAPOR BARRIER SEAL
- DEAD LOAD AND WIND LOAD ANCHOR
- STRUCTURAL STEEL FASTENER
- DEAD LOAD ANCHOR ONLY, TO ALLOW HORIZONTAL MOVEMENT

NOTES

1. Coping detail and base detail similar to details 5 and 9 of four-sided structural curtain wall system.
2. Detail section cut numbers 1–4 are not shown on elevation, but represent its intended use for two-sided structural curtain wall system with precast and metal spandrel panel at the head and sill.
3. Detail section cut number 5 refers to note on four-sided structural sealant glazing system.

The Spector Group; North Hills, New York
Thomas F. O'Connor, AIA, ASTM; Smith, Hinchman & Grylls; Detroit, Michigan

GLAZING

GENERAL NOTES

1. Information on this page is representative of industry recommendations for vertical glazing applications (within 15° of vertical). Consult with the applicable manufacturers and fabricators for specific applications or for applications at greater than 15° from vertical.
2. It is good practice to glaze at temperatures above 40°F (4°C) to preclude condensation and frost contamination of surfaces that will receive sealants. For sealant glazing below 40°F (4°C), consult the glazing sealant manufacturer.
3. Glazing materials should not be installed more than one day in advance of glass placement to avoid potential damage to the glazing materials by other trades or contamination of the materials.

4. Glazing materials used with high-performance reflective coated glass may require the consideration of additional factors for the glazing materials.
5. Glass should always be cushioned in the glazing opening by resilient glazing materials and should also be free to ''float in the opening'' so there is no direct contact of the glass with the perimeter framing system.
6. For glazing of polycarbonate and acrylic plastic sheet, particular attention should be given to thermal movement of the sheet and adhesion and compatibility of the sheet with glazing materials, as well as proper preparation of the glazing opening. Consult the manufacturer or fabricator for glazing recommendations.

7. Insulating, wired, and laminated glass must be installed in glazing pockets that are weeped to the exterior to preclude the detrimental effects of moisture.
8. For large glass lites the deflection characteristics of the glass should be investigated to preclude detrimental deflection which can cause glazing seal failure and glass breakage by contact of an edge or corner with the framing.
9. For setting and edge block requirements for casement, vertically pivoted and horizontally pivoted windows refer to the Flat Glass Marketing Association (FGMA) Glazing Manual.

SETTING BLOCK NOTES

1. Blocks should always be wider than the thickness of glass or panel, no more or less than two per glass or panel, and be of identical material.
2. For glass using the alternate method, verify acceptability of method with glass manufacturer or fabricator.
3. Setting block length per block
   a. Neoprene, EPDM, or silicone block = 0.1 in./sq ft of glass area; never less than 4 in. long.
   b. Lead block = 0.05 in./sq ft of glass area; never less than 4 in. long.
   c. Lock-strip gasket block = 0.5 in./sq ft of glass area; never less than 6 in. long.
4. For neoprene, EPDM, silicone, or lead blocks, the material should be 85 ± 5 shore A durometer.
5. Lead blocks should never be used with laminated, insulating, or wired glass or in lock-strip gaskets, nor should they be used with glass less than ½ in. thick.

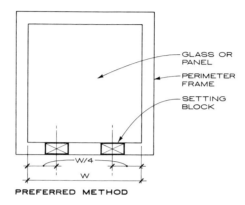

PREFERRED METHOD

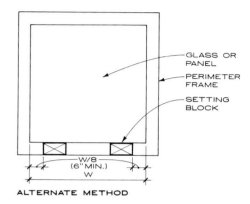

ALTERNATE METHOD

SETTING BLOCK LOCATIONS

EDGE BLOCK NOTES

1. Edge blocking is used to limit lateral movement of the glass or panel caused by horizontal thermal movement, building vibration, and other causes.
2. Method A is preferred.
3. Material should be neoprene, EPDM, or silicone rubber.
4. Hardness should be 65 ± 5 shore A durometer.
5. Blocks should be a minimum of 4 in. long.
6. Blocks should be placed in vertical frame spaces.
7. Blocks should be sized to permit a nominal ⅛ in. of clearance between the edge of the glass or panel and the block.

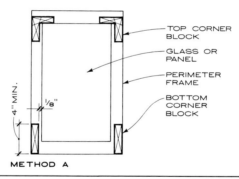

METHOD A

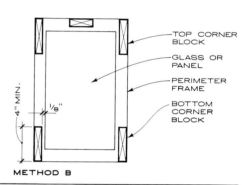

METHOD B

EDGE BLOCK LOCATIONS

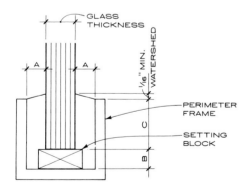

NOTES

1. The typical clearances indicated in the adjacent table may vary by glass manufacturer or fabricator, particularly for special products or applications. Consult the glass manufacturer, fabricator, and sealing material supplier for those conditions.
2. The permissible bow and warp of large lites of heat-strengthened and tempered glass can be substantial, which may require extra face clearance.

FACE AND EDGE CLEARANCE AND BITE

TYPICAL FACE AND EDGE CLEARANCE AND BITE

GLASS THICKNESS		MINIMUM CLEARANCES		
IN.	MM	A = FACE	B = EDGE	C = BITE
MONOLITHIC GLASS				
SS*	2.5	1/16	1/8	1/4
1/8–DS†	3	1/8	1/8	1/4
1/8–DS‡	3	1/8	1/4	3/8
3/16†	5	1/8	3/16	5/16
3/16‡	5	1/8	1/4	3/8
1/4	6	1/8	1/4	3/8
5/16	8	3/16	5/16	7/16
3/8	10	3/16	5/16	7/16
1/2	12	1/4	3/8	7/16
5/8	15	1/4	3/8	1/2
3/4	19	1/4	1/2	5/8
7/8	22	1/4	1/2	3/4
INSULATING GLASS				
1/2	12	1/8	1/8	1/2
5/8	15	1/8	1/8	1/2
3/4	19	3/16	1/4	1/2
1	25	3/16	1/4	1/2
CERAMIC COATED SPANDREL GLASS				
1/4	6	3/16	1/4	1/2

*SS, Single strength; DS, double strength.
†Annealed glass only.
‡Tempered glass only.

Thomas F. O'Connor, AIA, ASTM; Smith, Hinchman & Grylls; Detroit, Michigan

GLAZING

GLAZING SYSTEMS NOTES

1. Only rubber materials formulated to recognized standards and of proven durability such as neoprene, EPDM; and silicone should be used for gaskets and blocking.
2. At least two ¼ to ⅜ in. diameter weep holes for the glazing pocket per glass lite or panel are necessary with access to weep holes not prevented by setting blocks or sealants.
3. Glazing compound or putty should not be used to glaze laminated or insulating glass in openings.
4. Sealants in contact or close proximity to gaskets, rubber blocking, and other sealants must be compatible with those materials to preclude loss of adhesion or lessened durability. Consult with the sealant manufacturer.

5. Sealant must be compatible with the insulating glass edge seal and the butyral laminate of laminated glass to preclude failure of the edge seal or delamination and discoloration of the laminate.
6. The dry glazing method requires careful design and control of tolerances of the frame opening and glazing materials to ensure the development of adequate compression sealing pressure (generally 4–10 lb/lin in. to achieve weathertightness.
7. Closed cell gaskets for dry glazing should have molded or vulcanized corners as the preferred method so as to form a continuous, joint-free glazing material around all sides of the opening.
8. The following table lists sources for specifications and installation practices for glazing materials which should be consulted when designing and specifying.

LOCK-STRIP GASKET NOTES

1. Lock-strip gasket glazing requires careful design and control of framing, gasket, and glazing tolerances to achieve the anticipated weather sealing pressures and structural capacity to resist lateral loads.
2. The best weather sealing performance is achieved with a continuous gasket having factory-formed, injection-molded joints.
3. Concrete gasket lugs require a draft on some surface of the lug to facilitate mold removal. Draft is permissible either on the sides or on top (preferred), not both. Draft on top should slope to the exterior.

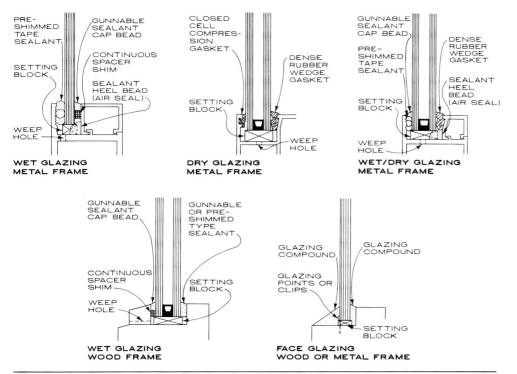

TYPICAL GLAZING SYSTEMS

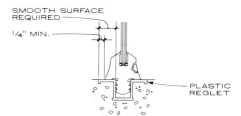
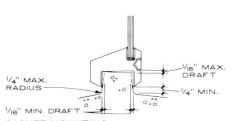
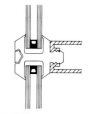
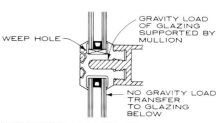

LOCK-STRIP GASKETS

GLAZING SPECIFICATIONS*

PART	MATERIAL	SPECIFICATION	INSTALLATION PRACTICE
Closed cell rubber gasket	Neoprene Silicone EPDM	ASTM C0509	FGMA Glazing Manual
Dense wedge rubber gasket	Neoprene Silicone EPDM	ASTM C0864	FGMA Glazing Manual
Gunnable sealant	Silicone Polyurethane Polysulfide	ASTM C0920	ASTM C0962
Tape sealant	Butyl Polyisobutylene	AAMA 804.1, 806.1, 807.1	FGMA Glazing Manual
Lock-strip gasket	Neoprene EPDM	ASTM C0542	ASTM C0716, C0963, C0964
Setting and edge blocks	Neoprene Silicone EPDM	ASTM C0864	See setting block and edge block location details and FGMA Glazing Manual
Glazing compound	Oil or resin based	ASTM C0570, C0669	ASTM C0797

*AAMA, Architectural Aluminum Manufacturers Association.
ASTM, American Society for Testing and Materials.
FGMA, Flat Glass Marketing Association.

Thomas F. O'Connor, AIA, ASTM; Smith, Hinchman & Grylls; Detroit, Michigan

GLAZING 8

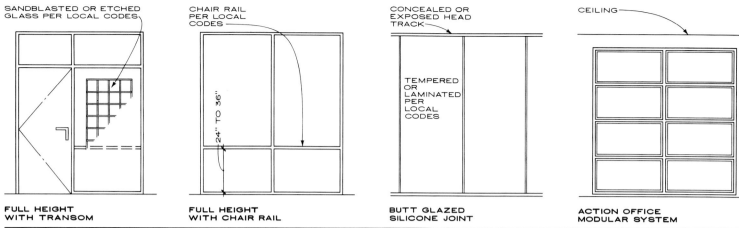

FULL HEIGHT WITH TRANSOM

FULL HEIGHT WITH CHAIR RAIL

BUTT GLAZED SILICONE JOINT

ACTION OFFICE MODULAR SYSTEM

GLASS PARTITION ELEVATIONS

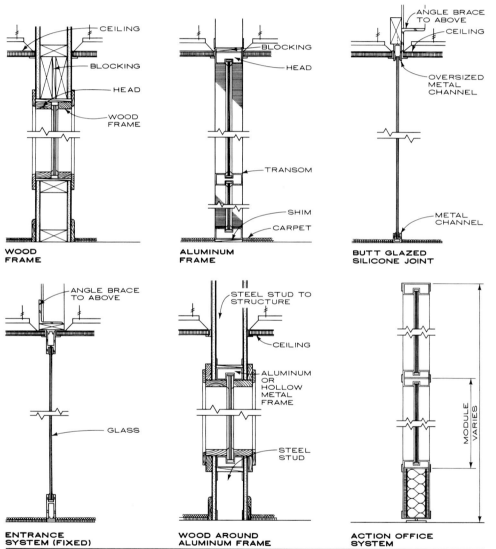

WOOD FRAME

ALUMINUM FRAME

BUTT GLAZED SILICONE JOINT

ENTRANCE SYSTEM (FIXED)

WOOD AROUND ALUMINUM FRAME

ACTION OFFICE SYSTEM

GLASS PARTITION SECTIONS

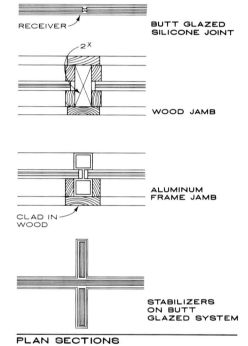

PLAN SECTIONS

GLAZED PARTITION NOTES

1. Interior glazed partitions are available in a variety of standard sizes, materials, and colors. Many manufacturers accommodate special or custom designs.

2. Finishes: Aluminum frames usually come in standard anodized or painted finishes. Many manufacturers now offer rich colors as well. Wood and hollow metal frames can be painted or finished in any tone or color. Action office systems are available in a wide array of colors and finishes, trimmed in wood, metal, or plastic.

3. Silicone glazing (butt glazing) partitions are framed at the top and bottom with either exposed or concealed frames. It is important that the glass thickness be in correct proportion to the unbraced length. If thickness alone cannot handle the span, then glass stabilizers should be used (see diagram).

4. Most manufacturers of action office systems offer a variety of glazed units to be incorporated in their system. Many systems are available with patterned, etched, or tinted glass for safety and privacy.

DRAPERIES

Draperies usually are custom made to specification. Drapery length is unlimited. Fabric width, usually 48 to 118 in. wide, does not limit final drapery width, but affects fabrication only. Considerations in drapery selection include: fabric weight, pleating (fullness), number of seams, track capacity, type of mounting track, type of draw, and control cords location.

SHADES

In addition to the common opaque shade, many shades with excellent shading coefficients that retain a high degree of transparency are available. Single shades usually are limited to 72 in. wide x 198 in. long (manual) or 312 in. long (motorized).

SHUTTERS

Interior shutters are available with fixed or operable vanes in all sizes up to 18 x 78 in. for ¾ in. thick units and 48 x 96 in. for 1¼ in. thick units. Frames usually are painted or stained wood. Some styles use panels of cane, metal, plastic, or solid wood in lieu of vanes.

GLASS COATINGS

A full array of shading films and screens is available for use in new and existing glazing. Films range from totally reflective to slightly tinted. Many also provide excellent shading coefficients.

Sterling Thompson, AIA, and Larry Gawloski, AIA; ARCHIFORMS; Waco, Texas

GLAZING

ACRYLIC PLASTIC AND POLYCARBONATE SHEETS

Both materials are relatively tough, break, shatter, or crack resistant thermoplastics. They are commonly used in the clear transparent form for glazing in schools, factories, skylights, domes, display cases, and protective shields for stained glass assemblies. Certain conditions of varying temperatures and/or humidity on opposing surfaces of a single light may cause it to bow in the direction of the higher temperature and/or humidity. Though this does not affect visibility, it may cause distorted reflections. The surfaces of these materials are susceptible to scratching and abrasions. Progress is being made in developing abrasion resistant coatings. As compared with clear glass of equal size and thickness, they maintain greater resistance to impact and breakage and are lighter in weight. Polycarbonates have softer surfaces and are more impact resistant than acrylics. Acrylics generally weather better than polycarbonates. Because of a somewhat higher coefficient of thermal expansion than in clear glass and other materials with which they are used in construction, acrylics and polycarbonates are subject to a greater degree of dimensional change. In applications that must allow for wide ranges of thermal expansion, avoid inflexible installation methods. Both may be produced with or without light absorbing properties. The allowable continuous service temperature for polycarbonates is slightly higher than that for acrylics. Both may be cold formed to a smooth arc if the resulting radius of curvature is at least 100 times the thickness of the sheet for polycarbonates (180 times for acrylics) and both are supported by curved channel supports following this radius.

Mirrored coatings applied to acrylic sheets are available for interior applications and may be installed with recommended contact cements, double faced tape, clip and channel mounting, and through fastening. Distortion problems indicate that they should not be used for precise image reflectance requirements.

Certain polycarbonate sheets may be used in some bullet resisting and burglar resisting applications.

Consult the manufacturers for current information. Refer to and adhere to all applicable codes and governing authorities on fire and safety.

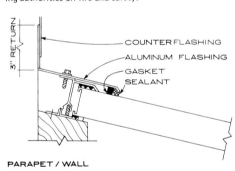

PARAPET / WALL

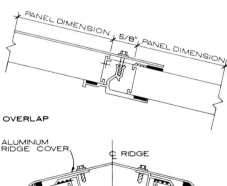

OVERLAP

RIDGE

SKYROOF SYSTEM DETAILS

Skidmore, Owings & Merrill

POLYCARBONATE GLAZING

	POLY-CARBONATE SHEET THICKNESS	SHORT DIMEN-SION	RABBET DEPTH
Small lights	1/8″	24″	1/2″
Intermediate lights	3/16″ 1/4″	36″ 48″	3/4″ 3/4″
Large lights	3/8″ 1/2″	60″ 72″	1″ 1″

NOTES
1. Rabbet width is determined by sheet thickness plus sealant and tape as recommended by sealant tape manufacturers.
2. To select polycarbonate sheet thickness based on wind loads refer to manufacturers' information.

SMALL ACRYLIC LIGHTS

Maximum dimension to 24″
Minimum thickness—0.100″
Minimum rabbet depth 9/32″

INTERMEDIATE ACRYLIC LIGHTS

ACRYLIC THICK-NESS	MAXIMUM SASH OPENING		RABBET DIMENSIONS	
	SQUARE	RECTAN-GULAR	DEPTH	WIDTH
0.125″	40″ x 40″	30″ x 42″	1/2″	3/8″
0.125″	55″ x 55″	36″ x 68″	3/4″	3/8″
0.187″	42″ x 42″	30″ x 45″	1/2″	7/16″
0.187″	63″ x 63″	36″ x 72″	3/4″	7/16″
0.250″	44″ x 44″	30″ x 46″	1/2″	1/2″
0.250″	69″ x 69″	36″ x 72″	3/4″	1/2″

LARGE ACRYLIC LIGHTS

ACRYLIC THICKNESS	LONG DIMENSIONS	RABBET DIMENSIONS*	
		DEPTH	WIDTH
0.187	57″ to 85″	3/4″	7/16″
0.250	78″ to 96″	1″	5/8″
0.250	108″ to 144″	1 1/8″	3/4″
0.375	72″ to 108″	1″	3/4″
0.375	108″ to 144″	1 1/8″	7/8″
0.500	114″ to 144″	1 1/8″	1″

* When darker (less than 60% light transmittance) transparent tints of acrylic plastic are used, rabbet depth shown above should be increased by 1/4″ to allow for greater thermal expansion resulting from solar energy absorption.

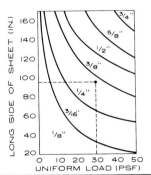

ACRYLIC GLAZING GRAPH
Design load data—large area acrylic glazing

Problem:
Size = 48 x 96 in.
Design load = 30 psf

Solution:
Select 1/4 in.
Sheet thickness

Data apply to square and rectangular lights of acrylic sheets when the length is no more than three times the width. All edges continuously held.

Sheet thickness section is based on total deflection under uniform load limited to 5% of the short side, or 3 in., whichever is smaller.

ACRYLIC SHEET EXPANSION ALLOWANCE

SASH LENGTH OR HEIGHT (IN.)	REDUCE ACRYLIC GLAZING LENGTH OR HEIGHT	
	CLEAR ACRYLIC (IN.)	TINTED ACRYLIC (IN.)
0 to 36	1/16	1/16
36 to 60	1/8	3/16
60 to 96	3/16	5/16
96 to 132	1/4	3/8
132 to 144	5/16	1/2

Note: Both length and height must be reduced according to this table. For polycarbonate glazing expansion allowance, refer to manufacturer's literature.

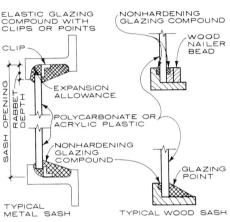

SMALL LIGHTS

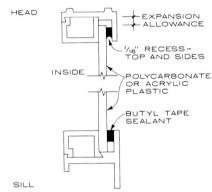

INTERMEDIATE LIGHTS

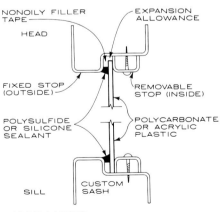

LARGE LIGHTS

PLASTIC GLAZING DETAILS

GLAZING

METAL CURTAIN WALLS

Exterior metal and glass enclosure walls require more careful development and skilled erection than traditional wall construction. Because metal and glass react differently to environmental conditions than do other wall materials, the technology is different from all other enclosure systems.

Errors in judgment can be avoided if behavior of the wall is understood. Some of the important considerations for successful curtain wall development are delineated below. Further in-depth material is available from the Architectural Aluminum Manufacturers Association (AAMA), the Flat Glass Marketing Association (FGMA), and standards developed by American Society for Testing and Materials (ASTM) committees C24 on building seals and sealants and EO6 on performance of building constructions. See index under "Structural Sealant Glazing" for additional information that should be considered when developing a structural sealant curtain wall system.

FUNCTION OF THE WALL

The metal and glass curtain wall functions as an "enclosure system" which, when properly developed, can serve multiple functions: (1) withstand the action of the elements; (2) control the passage inward and outward of heat, light, air, and sound; (3) prevent or control access from outside.

NATURAL FORCES

Curtain wall development is determined in part by the impact of natural forces. Natural forces that cause the most concern and failures are (1) water, (2) wind, (3) sunlight, (4) temperature, (5) gravity, and (6) seismic forces. To understand the impact of these forces on curtain wall development, the effects of each should be separately examined.

WATER

The most frequent cause of problems with all enclosures is leakage from rain, snow, vapor, or condensate. Wind driven moisture can enter very small openings and may move within the wall, appearing far from its point of entry. Water vapor can penetrate microscopic pores and will condense on cool surfaces. Such moisture trapped within a wall can result in lessened durability of the wall which can result in serious damage that is difficult to detect. Leaks are usually limited to joints and openings, which must be designed to provide a weathertight enclosure.

WIND

Structural design development of the wall must take into account both positive and negative pressures caused by wind action, increasing in effect depending on the height and shape of the building. Increases in wind loading will occur in corner areas of the building and must be considered accordingly. Framing members, panels, and glass thicknesses should be determined by maximum wind load anticipated and permissible deflection allowable. Winds contribute to the movement of the wall, affecting joint seals and wall anchorage. The effect of positive or negative wind pressure can cause stress reversal on framing members and glass and will cause water to travel in any direction (including upward) across the face of the wall. The state of the art is to conduct scale model wind studies in a boundary layer wind tunnel to more realistically establish expected prevailing wind patterns and their effects on the building cladding. Wind is a major factor in potential water leakage.

SUNLIGHT

The ultraviolet spectrum of sunlight will cause breakdown of organic materials such as color pigments, various rubber gaskets, plastics, and sealants. Fading and failure of these materials will cause problems with the appearance and weathertightness of the curtain wall. Only quality organic materials should be used, and they should be tested for resistance to ultraviolet radiation and ozone attack.

Sunlight passing through glass can cause excessive brightness and glare and will cause fading of interior furnishings and finishes. Shading devices and the use of glare-reducing or high-performance types of glass should be considered in development of the wall.

TEMPERATURE

Change in temperature causes the expansion and contraction of materials. Control of the passage of heat or cold through the wall is also required. Thermal movement as a result of solar heating is one of the major problems in curtain wall development. Minimum outdoor temperatures vary about 80°F. Throughout the country, the maximum surface temperature of the darker colored surfaces on buildings can range as high as 170°F. This temperature fluctuation, both daily and seasonally, critically affects wall development. Thermal expansion and contraction is much greater in metals than in wood or masonry.

Heat passage through the wall causes heat gain in hot weather and heat loss in cold weather, the relative importance of the two varying with geographic location. Thermal insulation of opaque wall areas becomes an extremely important consideration, especially whenever these areas constitute a large portion of the total wall area. When vision glass areas predominate, the use of high-performance glasses and the minimizing of through metal or "cold bridges" (usually by inserting continuous nonmetallic breaks in the metal assembly) are more effective in lowering the heat transfer (U-value) through the wall.

GRAVITY

Because gravity is constant and static rather than variable and dynamic, gravity is a less critical force affecting the development of a window wall design, but is important in that it should be recognized. It causes deflection in horizontal load-carrying members, particularly under the weight of large sheets of heavy glass. However, because the weight of the wall is transferred at frequent intervals to the building frame, the structural effect of gravity is small in comparison with that imposed by wind action. Far greater gravity forces, in the form of floor and roof loads, are acting on the building frame to which the wall is attached. As these loads may cause deflections and displacements of the frame, connections of the wall to this frame must be designed to provide sufficient relative movement to ensure that the displacements do not impose vertical loads on the wall itself.

SEISMIC

Seismic (earthquake) loadings will produce additional static and dynamic loadings to the window wall system. Seismic loadings will produce both vertical and horizontal deflections of the wall. This will necessitate special energy absorption considerations in the detail of all wall anchorages and adequate consideration of the joints between curtain wall members.

DESIGN DEVELOPMENT CONSIDERATIONS: STRUCTURAL INTEGRITY

Structural integrity of the curtain wall is a prime concern involving the same design procedures used in any other exterior wall. However, deficiencies of weathertightness and temperature movements are more prevalent than deficiencies in strength, which will be elaborated upon further.

The structural integrity of the window wall must be evaluated using two criteria: strength and deflection. Based on numerous window wall tests, it has been found that the ultimate performance of the system is usually dependent on the elastic and inelastic deflections of the system rather than on just the strength of component parts.

Curtain wall fabrication and erection tolerances must be carefully reviewed in conjunction with structural frame tolerances. Many window wall failures have been caused by inadequate anchorage details and inadequate consideration of tolerances.

WEATHERTIGHTNESS

Weathertightness ensures protection against the penetration of water and an excessive amount of air through the wall. This depends on adequate provision for movement and is closely related to proper joint design. A major share of the problems experienced over the years has been due to the lack of weathertightness.

PROVISION FOR MOVEMENT

Development of the wall must accommodate relative movements of the wall components and also differential movements between the wall assembly and the building structure. Relative movements of the wall components will primarily be affected by thermal movements of the wall elements and erection tolerances of the individual wall elements. Erection tolerances may exceed the tolerance for thermal movement. The differential movements between the wall components and the building structure will be a direct function of the dead and live load deflections of the structure and also the creep, shrinkage, thermal, wind, and seismic deformations of the building structure. These differential movements may be of considerable magnitude, and the effects of such differential movements must not be transferred from the structure directly to the window wall system. Usually provisions for such differential movement are provided at the head and jamb anchorage locations between the wall jointery and/or joints between wall and adjacent cladding. Behavior of sealants must be considered. Current recommendations from sealant manufacturers are to limit movement of the joint to a percentage of the sealant's rated movement capacity. This will provide a safety factor to help prevent sealant failure. Temperature of metal parts at time of erection, as well as the anticipated design temperature range, will aid in predicting the extent of movement in a joint. Fabrication and erection tolerances must also be considered when establishing the joint opening width.

MOISTURE CONTROL

Control of condensation is essential because metal and glass are not only impermeable to moisture, but have low heat retention capacity. A vapor barrier should be provided on or near the room side wall face. Impervious surfaces within the wall should be insulated to keep them warmer than the dew point of the air contacting them. Provision should be made for the escape of water vapor to the outside. The wall should be detailed so that any condensation occurring within it will be collected and drained away via weeps to the exterior.

THERMAL INSULATION

High thermal and condensation resistance of the wall is a good long-term investment to minimize heat loss in cold weather or heat gain in hot weather. Such devices as minimizing the exposure of the framing members by using thermal breaks, employing high-performance glass, and insulating opaque surfaces are recommended.

SOUND TRANSMISSION

By careful selection of details and materials, sound transmission characteristics of the metal and glass wall can be made equal to traditional construction.

Use of insulating and laminated glass separately and in combination as well as increasing the mass of the wall will reduce the transmission of sound.

FIRE AND SMOKE STOPS

Prevention of the spread of fire and smoke by continuous firestopping between the curtain wall and the edge of each floor is necessary. Proper detailing and installation of a quality safing material not subject to breakdown by fire will help to avoid what can become an extremely dangerous condition.

CONCLUSION

The following items can be utilized to further refine the techniques of good curtain wall development and construction: It is very beneficial to work with contractors or manufacturers who have specialized for a period of not less than 5 years in the fabrication and installation of curtain walls. Visits to and interviews with owners or managers of buildings will help give an overall view of the performance of curtain wall systems. It is important at the start of design to work with the metal, glass, and sealant manufacturers' technical personnel when developing a metal curtain wall system. Before fabrication and construction starts, wall and component testing should be done under both laboratory and field conditions.

Skidmore, Owings & Merrill
Thomas F. O'Connor, AIA, ASTM; Smith, Hinchman & Grylls; Detroit, Michigan

GLAZED CURTAIN WALLS

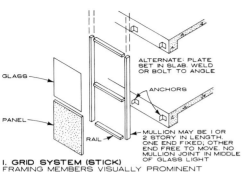

1. GRID SYSTEM (STICK)
FRAMING MEMBERS VISUALLY PROMINENT
COMPONENTS INSTALLED PIECE BY PIECE

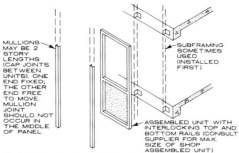

2. GRID SYSTEM (PANEL AND MULLION)
FRAMING MEMBERS VISUALLY PROMINENT
PANEL PREASSEMBLED AND INSTALLED AS SHOWN

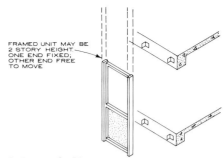

3. PANEL SYSTEM
COMPLETELY PREASSEMBLED UNITS; MAY OR MAY NOT
INCLUDE INTERIOR FINISH

CUSTOM TYPE

Walls designed specifically for one project, using specially designed parts and details. Such walls may be used on buildings of any height, but are more typical of multistoried structures. Included in this category are the highly publicized (and often more expensive) walls that serve as design pacesetters. Methods 1, 2, and 3 above are used for custom-type walls.

COMMERCIAL TYPE

Walls made up principally of parts and details standardized by the manufacturer and assembled either in the manufacturer's stock patterns or in accord with the architect's design. This type is commonly used on one- and two-story buildings and on taller structures. Commercial walls cost less because of quantity production and also offer the advantages of proven performance. Methods 1 and 2 above are used for commercial-type walls.

INDUSTRIAL TYPE

Walls in which ribbed, fluted, or otherwise preformed metal sheets in stock sizes are used along with standard metal sash as the principal components. This type of metal curtain wall has a long history of satisfactory performance and, in its insulated form, is used in buildings other than industrial use-type buildings.

CLASSIFICATION BY CONSTRUCTION AND TYPE

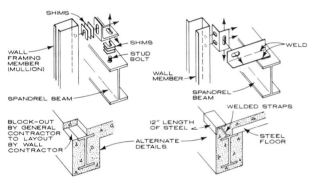

STEEL STRUCTURE

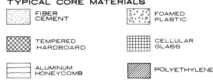

CONCRETE STRUCTURE

NOTES

1. Anchorage devices must permit three-dimensional adjustment. Metal-to-metal connections subject to intentional movement should be designed to eliminate noise caused by movement due to temperature change.
2. Anchors must be designed to withstand wind loads acting outward and inward as well as other required loads.
3. Anchors must be permanently secured in position after final assembly and adjustment of wall components.
4. All anchorage members must be corrosion resistant or protected against corrosive forces.
5. Shim plates may be installed between vertical leg of angle anchor and concrete structure, as required, for proper anchor alignment.

ATTACHMENT AND ANCHORAGE DETAILS

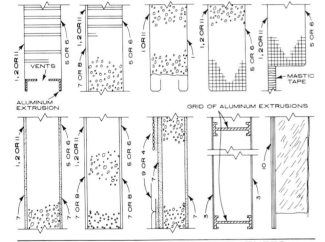

REPRESENTATIVE INSULATING PANEL TYPES
(EXTERIOR FACE ON LEFT)

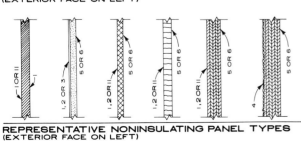

REPRESENTATIVE NONINSULATING PANEL TYPES
(EXTERIOR FACE ON LEFT)

TYPICAL CORE MATERIALS

- FIBER CEMENT
- TEMPERED HARDBOARD
- ALUMINUM HONEYCOMB
- EXTERIOR GRADE PLYWOOD
- PAPER HONEYCOMB
- FOAMED PLASTIC
- CELLULAR GLASS
- POLYETHYLENE
- PERLITE BEADS IN MINERAL BINDER
- FIBERGLASS ◄─ ALUMINUM FOIL

TYPICAL FACING MATERIALS

1. Aluminum or stainless-steel sheet.
2. Porcelain enameled metal.
3. Glass-reinforced plastic sheet.
4. Stone chips in plastic matrix.
5. Galvanized bonderized steel sheet.
6. Aluminum sheet.
7. Fiber cementboard.
8. Tempered hardboard.
9. Ceramic tile in plastic matrix.
10. Opaque tinted glass.
11. Organic color coating on aluminum.

PROPERTIES OF COMMON INSULATING CORE MATERIALS

MATERIAL	DENSITY (LB/CU FT)	APPROXIMATE K VALUE	GENERAL REMARKS
Paper honeycomb	2.5–7.0	0.45–0.55	1. Local codes and ordinances should be consulted for fire resistance requirements of panel construction. This depends, in part, on conditions of use, degree of fire exposure, and core material type.
Paper honeycomb, with foamed plastic fill	4.5–10.0	0.20–0.35	
Paper honeycomb, with vermiculite fill	5–14	0.35–0.40	
Polystyrene foam, extruded	1.7–3.5	0.20–0.26	2. Choice of core material should be made with consideration of potential thermal bowing of panel, flatness of facing materials, oil-canning of facing materials, moisture resistance of panel, and thermal resistance aging characteristics of the core material.
Polyurethane foam	1.5–3.0	0.18	
Polyisocyanurate foam	2.0	0.18	
Phenolic foam	2.5	0.12	
Fiberglass	0.3–2.0	0.23–0.27	
Cellular glass	8.5	0.35	
Perlite beads in mineral binder	11	0.36	

Skidmore, Owings & Merrill
Thomas F. O'Connor, AIA, ASTM; Smith, Hinchman & Grylls; Detroit, Michigan

GLAZED CURTAIN WALLS   8

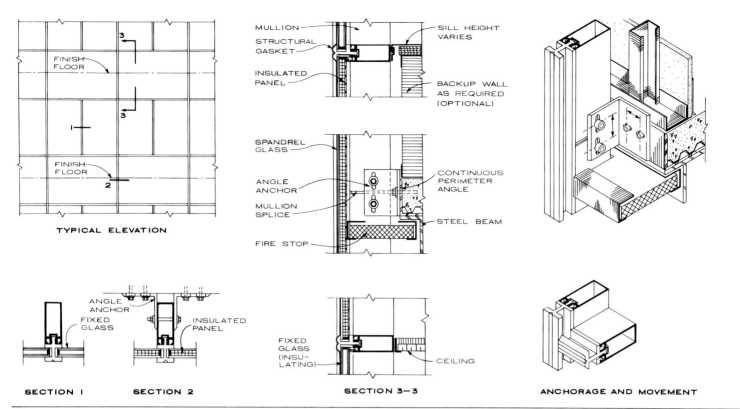

TYPICAL ELEVATION

MULLION
STRUCTURAL GASKET
INSULATED PANEL
SILL HEIGHT VARIES
BACKUP WALL AS REQUIRED (OPTIONAL)

SPANDREL GLASS
ANGLE ANCHOR
MULLION SPLICE
FIRE STOP
CONTINUOUS PERIMETER ANGLE
STEEL BEAM

ANGLE ANCHOR
FIXED GLASS
INSULATED PANEL

SECTION 1   SECTION 2

FIXED GLASS (INSULATING)
CEILING

SECTION 3-3

ANCHORAGE AND MOVEMENT

GRID SYSTEM (STICK OR STUD)—COMMERCIAL TYPE—ALUMINUM—GASKETED
MULTISTORY STICK OR STUD SYSTEM USING STRUCTURAL RUBBER GASKETS

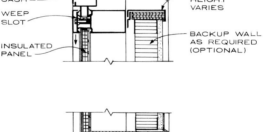
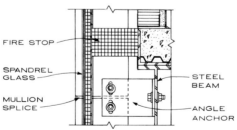
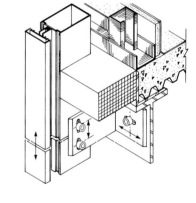
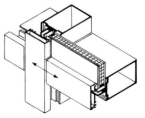
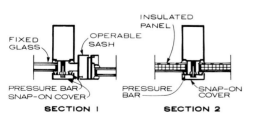
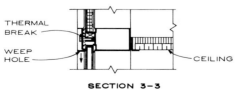

TYPICAL ELEVATION
WINDOW AND PANEL
TYPES OPTIONAL

FINISH FLOOR
FINISH FLOOR

MULLION
OPERABLE SASH
WEEP SLOT
INSULATED PANEL
SILL HEIGHT VARIES
BACKUP WALL AS REQUIRED (OPTIONAL)

FIRE STOP
SPANDREL GLASS
MULLION SPLICE
STEEL BEAM
ANGLE ANCHOR

FIXED GLASS
OPERABLE SASH
INSULATED PANEL
PRESSURE BAR SNAP-ON COVER
PRESSURE BAR
SNAP-ON COVER

SECTION 1   SECTION 2

THERMAL BREAK
WEEP HOLE
CEILING

SECTION 3-3

ANCHORAGE AND MOVEMENT

NOTES

1. Horizontals are weeped for positive performance against water infiltration with slots at glazing pressure plate and holes at cover.
2. See index under "Structural Sealant Glazing" for additional information that should be considered when developing a structural sealant curtainwall system.

GRID SYSTEM (STICK OR STUD)—COMMERCIAL TYPE-ALUMINUM-PRESSURE BAR
TYPICAL MULTISTORY STICK OR STUD SYSTEM USING PRESSURE BARS

Bullock Tice Associates Architects, Inc.; Pensacola, Florida

GLAZED CURTAIN WALLS

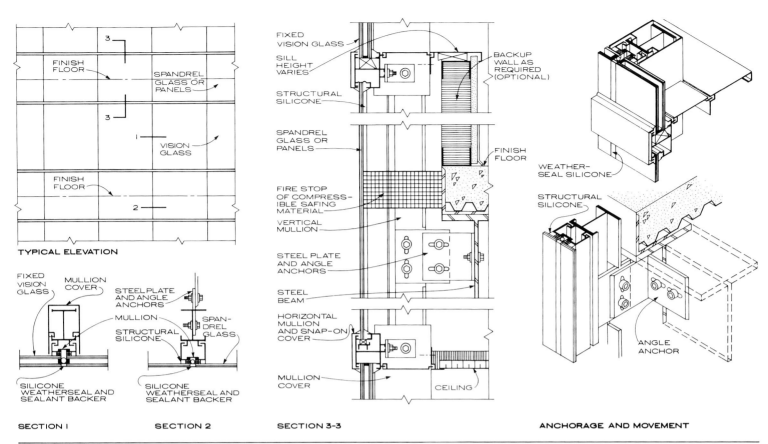

TYPICAL ELEVATION

FINISH FLOOR
SPANDREL GLASS OR PANELS
VISION GLASS
FINISH FLOOR

FIXED VISION GLASS
MULLION COVER
STEEL PLATE AND ANGLE ANCHORS
MULLION
STRUCTURAL SILICONE
SPANDREL GLASS
SILICONE WEATHERSEAL AND SEALANT BACKER
SILICONE WEATHERSEAL AND SEALANT BACKER

SECTION I   SECTION 2

FIXED VISION GLASS
SILL HEIGHT VARIES
STRUCTURAL SILICONE
SPANDREL GLASS OR PANELS
FIRE STOP OF COMPRESS-IBLE SAFING MATERIAL
VERTICAL MULLION
STEEL PLATE AND ANGLE ANCHORS
STEEL BEAM
HORIZONTAL MULLION AND SNAP-ON COVER
MULLION COVER
BACKUP WALL AS REQUIRED (OPTIONAL)
FINISH FLOOR
CEILING

SECTION 3-3

WEATHER-SEAL SILICONE
STRUCTURAL SILICONE
ANGLE ANCHOR

ANCHORAGE AND MOVEMENT

STRUCTURAL GLAZING SYSTEM (STRIP WINDOW)–COMMERCIAL TYPE–ALUMINUM
SYSTEM WITH STRUCTURAL SILICONE SEALANT ATTACHMENT ON TWO SIDES

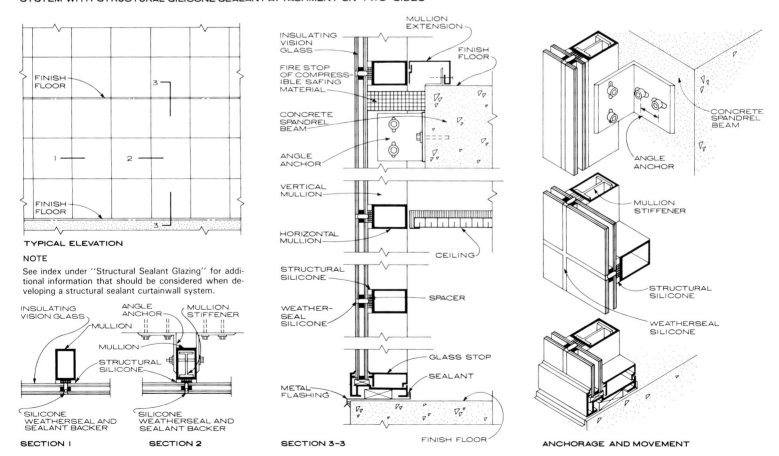

TYPICAL ELEVATION

FINISH FLOOR
FINISH FLOOR

NOTE

See index under "Structural Sealant Glazing" for additional information that should be considered when developing a structural sealant curtainwall system.

INSULATING VISION GLASS
MULLION
MULLION
ANGLE ANCHOR
MULLION STIFFENER
STRUCTURAL SILICONE
SILICONE WEATHERSEAL AND SEALANT BACKER
SILICONE WEATHERSEAL AND SEALANT BACKER

SECTION I   SECTION 2

INSULATING VISION GLASS
FIRE STOP OF COMPRESS-IBLE SAFING MATERIAL
CONCRETE SPANDREL BEAM
ANGLE ANCHOR
VERTICAL MULLION
HORIZONTAL MULLION
STRUCTURAL SILICONE
WEATHER-SEAL SILICONE
METAL FLASHING
MULLION EXTENSION
FINISH FLOOR
CEILING
SPACER
GLASS STOP
SEALANT
FINISH FLOOR

SECTION 3-3

ANGLE ANCHOR
CONCRETE SPANDREL BEAM
MULLION STIFFENER
STRUCTURAL SILICONE
WEATHERSEAL SILICONE

ANCHORAGE AND MOVEMENT

STRUCTURAL GLAZING SYSTEM (STOPLESS)–COMMERCIAL TYPE–ALUMINUM
SYSTEM WITH STRUCTURAL SILICONE SEALANT ATTACHMENT ON FOUR SIDES

Bullock Tice Associates Architects, Inc.; Pensacola, Florida

GLAZED CURTAIN WALLS   8

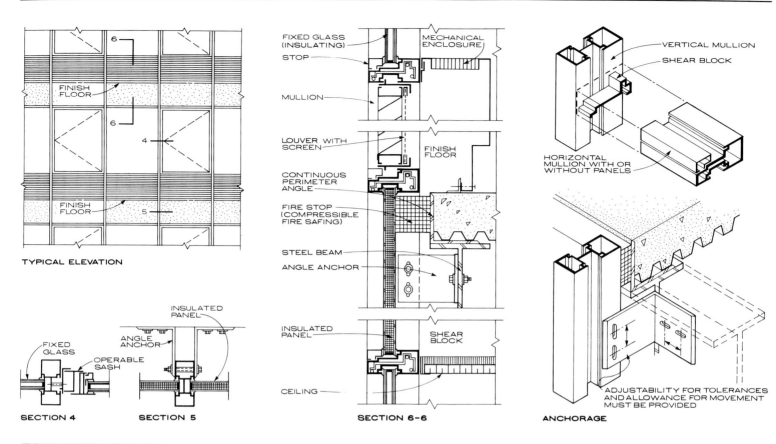

TYPICAL ELEVATION

FIXED GLASS (INSULATING)
STOP
MULLION
MECHANICAL ENCLOSURE

LOUVER WITH SCREEN
FINISH FLOOR
CONTINUOUS PERIMETER ANGLE
FIRE STOP (COMPRESSIBLE FIRE SAFING)
STEEL BEAM
ANGLE ANCHOR

INSULATED PANEL
SHEAR BLOCK
CEILING

SECTION 6-6

VERTICAL MULLION
SHEAR BLOCK
HORIZONTAL MULLION WITH OR WITHOUT PANELS

ADJUSTABILITY FOR TOLERANCES AND ALLOWANCE FOR MOVEMENT MUST BE PROVIDED

ANCHORAGE

INSULATED PANEL
ANGLE ANCHOR
FIXED GLASS
OPERABLE SASH

SECTION 4   SECTION 5

GRID SYSTEM (PANEL AND MULLION) – COMMERCIAL TYPE – ALUMINUM
LOW-RISE APPLICATION USING SHEAR BLOCK FABRICATION

METAL COPING
OPERABLE SASH
FINISH FLOOR
FIXED GLASS
FINISH FLOOR

TYPICAL ELEVATION

INSULATED PANEL
FIXED GLASS (INSULATING)
OPERABLE SASH
SPLIT VERTICAL MULLION WITH FILLER
INSULATED PANEL
METAL FLASHING

CEILING
ADAPTER-SUBFRAME
MECHANICAL ENCLOSURE
FINISH FLOOR

SECTION 6-6

ADJUSTABILITY FOR TOLERANCES AND ALLOWANCE FOR MOVEMENT MUST BE PROVIDED

SPLIT VERTICAL MULLION
SNAP-IN FILLER

NOTE HORIZONTAL MULLIONS SCREW ATTACHED TO SPLIT VERTICAL MULLION AND FILLER FROM BACK SIDE

ANCHORAGE

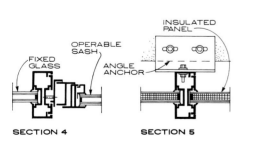

INSULATED PANEL
OPERABLE SASH
ANGLE ANCHOR
FIXED GLASS

SECTION 4   SECTION 5

PANEL SYSTEM – COMMERCIAL TYPE – ALUMINUM
LOW-RISE APPLICATION USING SCREW SPLINE FABRICATION

Bullock Tice Associates Architects, Inc.; Pensacola, Florida

GLAZED CURTAIN WALLS

REFERENCES

DATA SOURCES: ORGANIZATIONS

Acorn Building Components, Inc., 211

Algoma Hardwoods, Inc., 204

American National Standards Institute (ANSI), 207, 238

American Society for Testing and Materials (ASTM), 207

Anderson Corporation, 211, 229, 230

Architectural Aluminum Manufacturers Association (AAMA), 224–227

Bilco Company, 218

Brosco, 229

Ceco Corporation, 198–202, 206

Consumer Products Safety Commission, 220

Darren John Castale Corporation, 240

Door and Hardware Institute, 234, 235, 237

Ellison Bronze Company, 219

Fentron Industries, Inc., 228

Flat Glass Marketing Association, 245

General Services Administration (GSA), 238

Hope's Windows, Inc., 224

House and Home, 229

International Steel Company, 220

Kawneer Architectural Products, 219, 222

Libbey-Owens Ford Company, 219, 222, 238

Malta Manufacturing Company, 230

National Association of Architectural Metal Manufacturers (NAANN), 199, 200, 202

National Wood Window and Door Association (NWWDA), 203

Northrop Architectural Systems, 212, 222, 225

Overhead Door Corporation, 214–216

Overly Manufacturing Company, 210

Peachtree Doors, Inc., 229

Pioneer Industries, 196–202, 206

PPG Industries, Inc., 222, 238

Rolscreen Company, 229

Rusco Industries, Inc., 225

Steel Door Institute (SDI), 199

Steel Window Institute (SWI), 224–227

Trussbilt, Inc., 206

Underwriters' Laboratories, Inc. (U.L.), 210, 247

Velux-America, Inc., 230

Western Integrated Materials, Inc., 202

Weyerhaeuser Company, 204

Woodco Corporation, 230

DATA SOURCES: PUBLICATIONS

Catalog 35, SUN-DOR-CO, 203

General Information Manual, Stanley Hardware, Division of Stanley Works, 235

Hinge Specification Guide, Stanley Hardware, Division of The Stanley Works, 235

Industry Standard for Ponderosa Pine Doors, National Woodwork Manufacturers Association, 203, 204

Metal Curtain Wall Specifications Manual, National Association of Architectural Metal Manufacturers (NAAMM), 246, 247

NFPA 80-1983, National Fire Protection Association, 202

CHAPTER 9

FINISHES

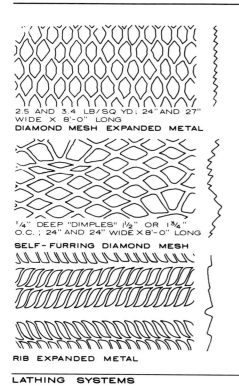

2.5 AND 3.4 LB/SQ YD; 24" AND 27"
WIDE X 8'-0" LONG
DIAMOND MESH EXPANDED METAL

¼" DEEP "DIMPLES" 1½" OR 1¾"
O.C. ; 24" AND 24" WIDE X 8'-0" LONG
SELF-FURRING DIAMOND MESH

RIB EXPANDED METAL

LATHING SYSTEMS

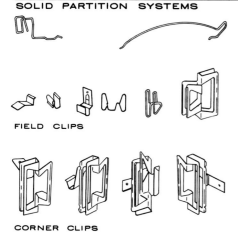

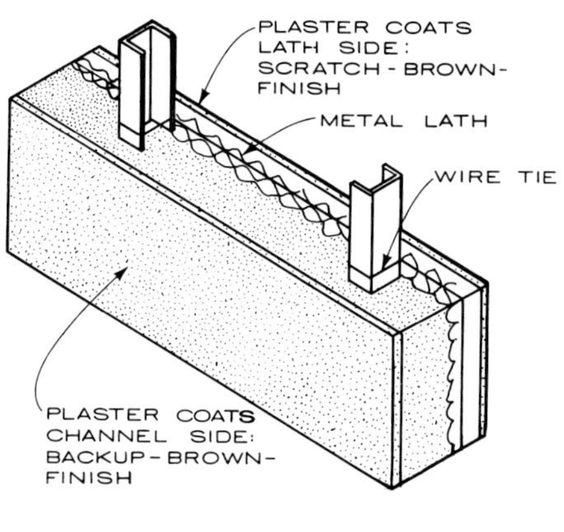

PLASTER COATS
LATH SIDE:
SCRATCH - BROWN-
FINISH

METAL LATH

WIRE TIE

PLASTER COATS
CHANNEL SIDE:
BACKUP - BROWN-
FINISH

SOLID PARTITION SYSTEMS

FIELD CLIPS

CORNER CLIPS

NOTE: OTHER
CLIP TYPES
ARE
AVAILABLE

MISCELLANEOUS

CLIPS FOR GYPSUM LATH SYSTEM

The Marmon Mok Partnership; San Antonio, Texas

NOTES

Self-furring paperbacked reinforcing is available in diamond mesh, welded wire, and hexagonal woven wire. Paperbacks are available to conform to Federal Specifications UU-B-790, Type 1, Grade A, Style 2 for highly water-vapor resistant paper.

Metal lath is also manufactured in large diamond mesh 27 x 96 in., 2.5 or 3.4 lb/sq yd, painted steel or galvanized; ⅛ in. flat rib 27 x 96 in., 2.75 or 3.4 lb/sq yd painted or galvanized; ⅜ in. rib expanded 27 x 96 in., 3.4 lb/sq yd painted or galvanized and ¾ in. rib expanded 24 x 96 in., 5.4 lb/sq yd painted.

Other types of lath are available from some manufacturers.

GYPSUM LATH

Gypsum lath is composed of an air entrained gypsum core sandwiched between two sheets of fibrous absorbent paper and used as a basecoat for gypsum plaster.

1. PLAIN GYPSUM LATH: ⅜ and ½ in. thick, 48 in. long, and 16 in. wide (16⅕ in. in the Western U.S.).
2. PERFORATED GYPSUM LATH: Plain gypsum lath with ¾ in. diameter holes punched 4 in. o.c. in both directions to provide mechanical key to plaster.
3. INSULATING GYPSUM LATH: Plain gypsum lath with aluminum foil laminated to the backside as insulator or vapor barrier.
4. LONG LENGTH GYPSUM LATH: 16 and 24 in. wide, in lengths up to 12 ft, available insulated or plain with square or vee-jointed Tongue and Groove edges or interlocking as ship-lap edge.

SOLID PLASTER PARTITION CONSTRUCTION

PARTITION CONSTRUCTION	THICKNESS	MAXIMUM HEIGHT
¾" cold-rolled channels Diamond mesh lath and plaster	2"	12'-0"
¾" cold-rolled channels Diamond mesh lath and plaster	2½"	16'-0"
1½" cold-rolled channels Diamond mesh lath and plaster	3"	20'-0"
1½" cold-rolled channels Diamond mesh lath and plaster	3½"	22'-0"

NOTE: Maximum partition length is unrestricted if less than 10 ft tall. Twice the height if over 10 ft tall; one and one half the height if over 14 ft tall and equal to the height if over 20 ft tall.

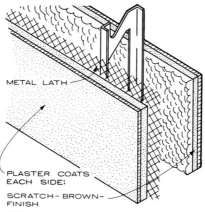

METAL LATH

PLASTER COATS
EACH SIDE:

SCRATCH - BROWN-
FINISH

NOTES

Prefabricated metal studs are used as the supporting elements of lath and plaster hollow partitions. They are available in 1⅝, 2, 2½, 3¼, 4, and 6 in. widths. Lengths are available in various increments up to 24 ft. Prefabricated studs are usually of the nonload bearing type, but load bearing metal studs also are manufactured. Designs vary with the manufacturer, and most manufacturers produce a line of related accessories, such as clips, runners, stud shoes, and similar articles.

HOLLOW PARTITION SYSTEMS

DEFINITIONS

AGGREGATE: Inert material used as a filler with a cementitious material and water to produce plaster or concrete. Usually implies sand, perlite, or vermiculite.

BASECOAT: Any plaster coat applied before the finish coat.

BEAD: Light gauge metal strip with one or more expanded or short perforated flanges and variously shaped noses; used at the perimeter of plastered surfaces.

BROWN COAT: In three-coat plaster, the brown coat is the second coat; in two-coat plaster, the base coat.

CALCINED GYPSUM: Gypsum that has been partially dehydrated by heating.

CLIP: A device made of wire or sheet metal for attaching various types of lath to the substructure and lath sheets to one another.

FIBERED PLASTER: Gypsum plaster containing fibers of hair, glass, nylon, or sisal.

FINISH COAT: The final coat of plaster, which provides the decorative surface.

FURRING: Grillage for the attachment of gypsum or metal lath.

GAUGING: Cementitious material, usually calcined gypsum or portland cement combined with lime putty to control set.

GROUND: A formed metal shape or wood strip that acts as a combined edge and gauge for various thicknesses of plaster to be applied to a plaster base.

GYPSUM: Hydrous calcium sulphate, a natural mineral in crystalline form.

GYPSUM LATH: A base for plaster; a sheet having a gypsum core, faced with paper.

GYPSUM READY MIX PLASTER: Ground gypsum that has been calcined and then mixed with various additives to control its setting and working qualities; used, with the addition of aggregate and water, for basecoat plaster.

HYDRATED LIME: Quicklime mixed with water, on the job, to form a lime putty.

LIME: Obtained by burning various types of limestone, consisting of oxides or hydroxides of calcium and magnesium.

LIME PLASTER: Basecoat plaster of hydrated lime and an aggregate.

NEAT PLASTER: Basecoat plaster, fibered or unfibered, used for job mixing with aggregates.

PERLITE: Siliceous volcanic glass containing silica and alumina expanded by heat for use as a lightweight plaster aggregate.

PLASTER: Cementitious material or combination of cementitious materials and aggregate that, when mixed with water, forms a plastic mass that sets and hardens when applied to a surface.

PORTLAND CEMENT: Manufactured combination of limestone and an argillaceous substance.

SCRATCH COAT: In three-coat plastering, the first coat, which is then scratched to provide a bond for second or brown coat.

SCREED: A device secured to a surface which serves as a guide for subsequent applications of plaster. Thicknesses and widths vary with the thicknesses desired for each operation.

STUCCO PORTLAND CEMENT: Plaster used in exterior application.

VERMICULITE: Micaceous mineral of silica, magnesium, and alumina oxides made up in a series of parallel plates or laminae and expanded by heat for use as a lightweight plaster aggregate.

NOTES

Keene's cement plaster is a specialty finish coat of gypsum plaster primarily used where a smooth, dense, white finish is desired.

Thickness, proportions of mixes of various plastering materials, and finishes vary. Systems and methods of application vary widely depending on local traditions and innovations promoted by the industry.

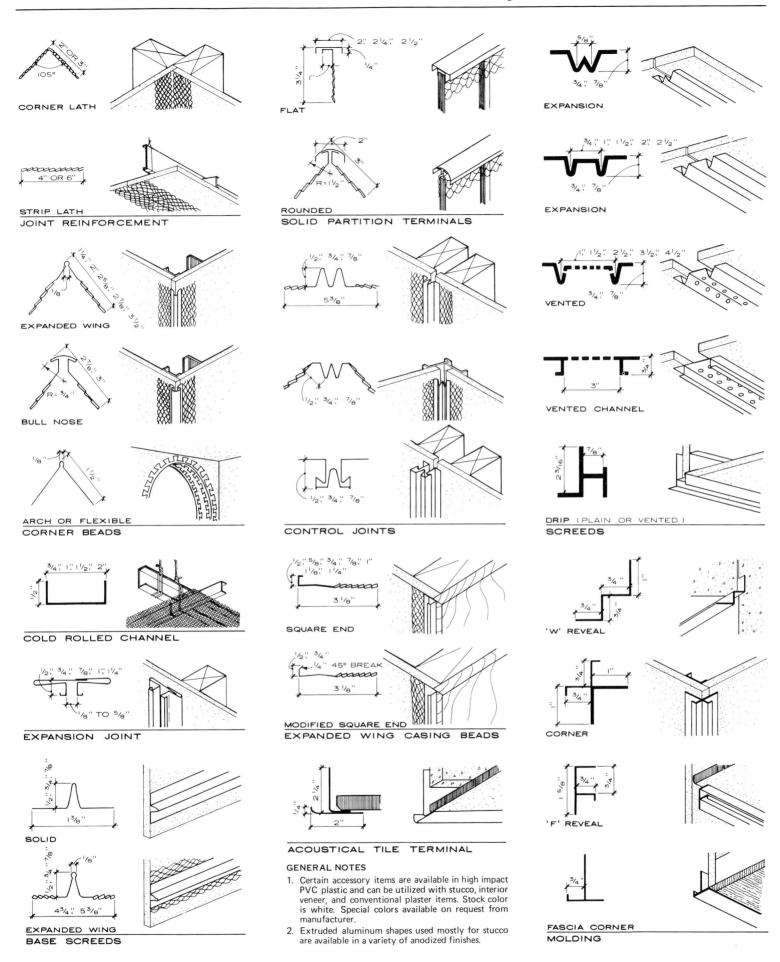

CORNER LATH

STRIP LATH
JOINT REINFORCEMENT

EXPANDED WING

BULL NOSE

ARCH OR FLEXIBLE
CORNER BEADS

COLD ROLLED CHANNEL

EXPANSION JOINT

SOLID

EXPANDED WING
BASE SCREEDS

FLAT

ROUNDED
SOLID PARTITION TERMINALS

CONTROL JOINTS

SQUARE END

MODIFIED SQUARE END
EXPANDED WING CASING BEADS

ACOUSTICAL TILE TERMINAL

GENERAL NOTES
1. Certain accessory items are available in high impact PVC plastic and can be utilized with stucco, interior veneer, and conventional plaster items. Stock color is white. Special colors available on request from manufacturer.
2. Extruded aluminum shapes used mostly for stucco are available in a variety of anodized finishes.

EXPANSION

EXPANSION

VENTED

VENTED CHANNEL

DRIP (PLAIN OR VENTED)
SCREEDS

'W' REVEAL

CORNER

'F' REVEAL

FASCIA CORNER
MOLDING

The Marmon Mok Partnership; San Antonio, Texas

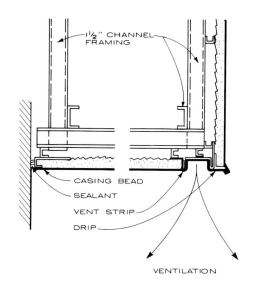

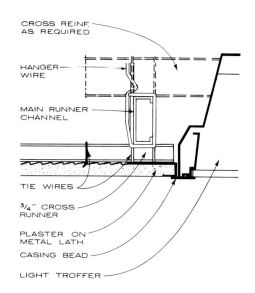

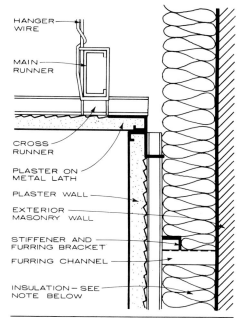

SOFFIT DETAIL

NOTE

Framing details for exterior cement plaster (stucco) are similar to details shown. Wind loads must be considered in designing framing systems for exterior stucco work. Galvanized mesh is available for exterior applications and use in humid areas. Ventilation strips should be used for ventilating all dead airspaces. Where plenum or attic spaces are closed off by ceiling installation, ventilation shall be provided with a minimum of $1/2$ sq. in./sq. ft. of horizontal surface.

SUSPENDED PLASTER CEILING AT RECESSED LIGHT FIXTURE

NOTE

Penetrations of the lath and plaster ceiling—at borrowed light openings, vents, grilles, access panels, and light troffers, for example—require additional reinforcement to distribute concentrated stresses if a control joint is not used. Where a plaster surface is flush with metal, as at metal access panels, grilles, or light troffers, the plaster should be grooved between the two materials.

SUSPENDED PLASTER CEILING AT FURRED MASONRY WALL

NOTE

When interior walls are furred from an exterior masonry wall and insulated, the ceiling should stop short of the furred space. This allows wall insulation to continue above the ceiling line to ceiling or roof insulation, thus forming a complete insulation envelope. In a suspension system that abuts masonry wall, provide 1 in. clearance between ends of main runners or furring channels and wall face.

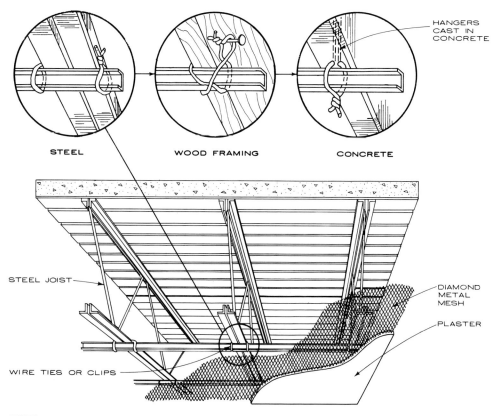

NOTE
RIB METAL LATH MAY BE USED IN LIEU OF DIAMOND MESH LATH AND FURRING CHANNELS IF LATH SPANS DO NOT EXCEED ALLOWABLE MAXIMUM. SEE TABLE 1

FURRED METAL LATH ON STEEL JOIST

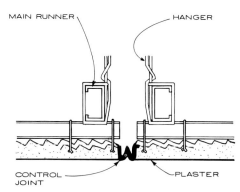

CONTROL JOINT DETAIL

NOTE

Control joints shall be spaced no further than 30 ft on center in each direction for large plastered ceiling areas. Area shall not exceed 900 sq ft without provision for expansion control. Exterior plaster soffits should have control joints spaced no further than 25 ft on center. For portland cement plaster (stucco) areas, interior or exterior, control joints should be placed at 10 ft on center and areas should not exceed 100 sq ft without provisions for expansion/contraction control. Control joints are spaced closer for cement plaster because of its inherent shrinkage during curing.

NOTE

Details shown are for furred (contact) ceilings that are attached directly to the structural members. The architect or ceiling designer should give consideration to the deflection and movement of the structure, since movement and deflection of more than $1/360$ of the span will cause cracking of plaster ceilings. If spacing of structural members exceeds the maximum span of furring members shown in the span charts, the addition of suspended main runners between structural members will be required. Flat rib lath may be attached directly to wood framing members, but is subjected to stresses created by the inherent properties of wood members.

James E. Phillips, AIA; Enwright Associates, Inc.; Greenville, South Carolina

LATH AND PLASTER

DIRECTIONS FOR USING TABLES

1. Select lath and plaster system.
2. Determine spacing of cross furring channels from Table 1—Lath Span.
3. Determine spacing of main runners from Table 2—Maximum Spacing between Runners.
4. Determine hanger support spacing for main runner from Table 3—Maximum Spacing between Hangers.
5. Calculate area of ceiling supported per hanger.
6. Select hanger type from Table 4—Hanger Selection.
7. Select tie wire size from Table 5—Tie Wire Selection.

TABLE 1. LATH SPAN

	LATH TYPE	WEIGHT/SQ.FT.	SPAN (IN.)
Gypsum lath	3/8" plain	1.5#	16
	1/2" plain	2.0#	16
	1/2" veneer	1.8#	16
	5/8" veneer	2.25#	16
	3/8" perforated	1.4#	16
Metal lath	Diamond mesh	0.27#	12
	Diamond mesh	0.38#	16
	1/8" flat rib	0.31#	12
	1/8" flat rib	0.38#	19
	3/8" flat rib	0.38#	24

TABLE 2. MAXIMUM SPACING BETWEEN RUNNERS

CROSS FURRING TYPE	CROSS FURRING SPACING			
	12"	16"	19"	24"
1/4" diam. pencil rod	2'-0"	—	—	—
3/8" diam. pencil rod	2'-6"	—	2'-0"	—
3/4" CRC, HRC (0.3 lb/ft)	—	4'-6"	3'-6"	3'-0"
1" HRC (0.41 lb/ft)	5'-0"	—	4'-6"	4'-0"

CRC = Cold rolled channel
HRC = Hot rolled channel

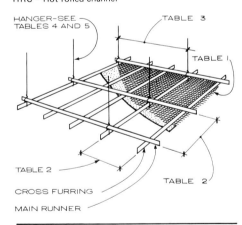

FURRED AND SUSPENSION SYSTEM COMPONENT SELECTION DETAIL

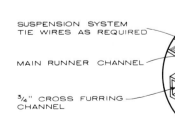

NOTE
Dimensional requirements for support spacing, runner spacing, hanger spacing, hanger type selection, and tie wire selection are given in tables on this page.

James E. Phillips, AIA; Enwright Associates, Inc.; Greenville, South Carolina

TABLE 3. MAXIMUM SPACING BETWEEN HANGERS

MAIN RUNNER TYPE	MAIN RUNNER SPACING				
	3'-0"	3'-6"	4'-0"	4'-6"	5'-0"
3/4" CRC (0.3 lb/ft)	2'-0"	—	—	—	—
1 1/2" CRC (0.3 lb/ft)	3'-0"*	—	—	—	—
1 1/2" CRC (0.875 lb/ft)	4'-0"	3'-6"	3'-0"	—	—
1 1/2" HRC (1.12 lb/ft)	—	—	—	4'-0"	—
2" CRC (0.59 lb/ft)	—	—	5'-0"	—	—
2" HRC (1.26 lb/ft)	—	—	—	—	5'-0"
1/2" x 1/2" x 3/16" ST1	—	5'-0"	—	—	—

*For concrete construction only—a 10-gauge wire may be inserted in the joint before concrete is poured.

TABLE 4. HANGER SELECTION

MAX. CEILING AREA	MIN. HANGER SIZE
12 sq.ft.	9-gauge galvanized wire
16 sq.ft.	8-gauge galvanized wire
18 sq.ft.	3/16" mild steel rod*
25 sq.ft.	1/4" mild steel rod*
25 sq.ft.	3/16" x 1" steel flat*

*Rods galvanized or painted with rust inhibitive paint and galvanized straps are recommended under severe moisture conditions.

TABLE 5. TIE WIRE SELECTION

	SUPPORT	MAX. CEILING AREA	MIN. HANGER SIZE
Cross furring		8 sq.ft.	14-gauge wire
		8 sq.ft.	16-gauge wire (two loops)
Main runners	Single hangers between beams	8 sq.ft.	12-gauge wire
		12 sq.ft.	10-gauge wire
		16 sq.ft.	8-gauge wire
	Double wire loops at supports	8 sq.ft.	14-gauge wire
		12 sq.ft.	12-gauge wire
		16 sq.ft.	11-gauge wire

ERECTION OF METAL LATH SUSPENSIONS

Metal lath suspensions commonly are made below all types of construction for fire rated plaster ceilings. The lath is supported by framing channels and furring channels suspended with wire hangers from the floor or roof structure above. Framing channels normally are spaced up to 4 ft. o.c. perpendicular to joists and should be erected to conform with the contour of the finished ceiling. Framing channels normally are furred with 3/4 in. channels placed at right angles to the framing. Spacing varies by lath types and weights. The lath should be lapped at both sides and ends and secured to the 3/4 in. channels with wire ties every 6 in. Where plaster on metal lath ceilings abuts masonry walls, partitions, or arch soffits, galvanized casing beads should be installed at the periphery.

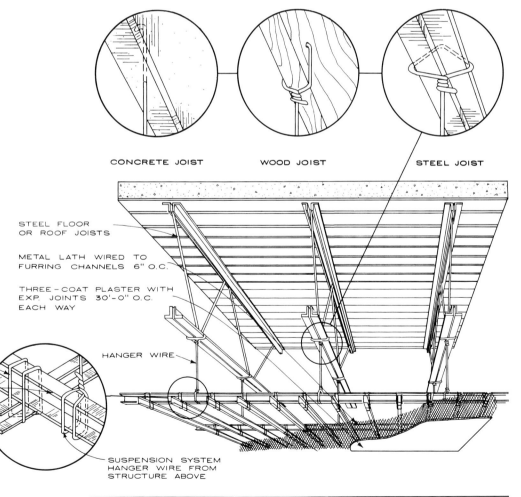

CONCRETE JOIST   WOOD JOIST   STEEL JOIST

STEEL FLOOR OR ROOF JOISTS

METAL LATH WIRED TO FURRING CHANNELS 6" O.C.

THREE-COAT PLASTER WITH EXP. JOINTS 30'-0" O.C. EACH WAY

HANGER WIRE

SUSPENSION SYSTEM HANGER WIRE FROM STRUCTURE ABOVE

METAL LATH SUSPENDED FROM STEEL JOISTS

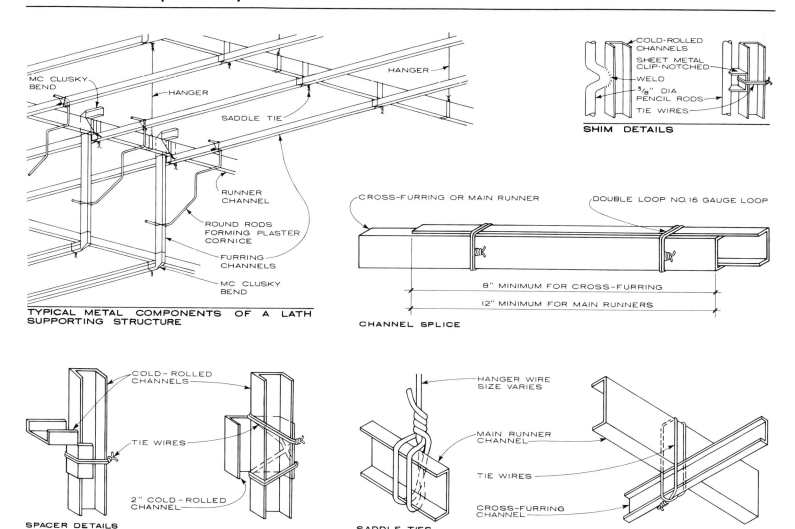

TYPICAL METAL COMPONENTS OF A LATH SUPPORTING STRUCTURE

SHIM DETAILS

CHANNEL SPLICE

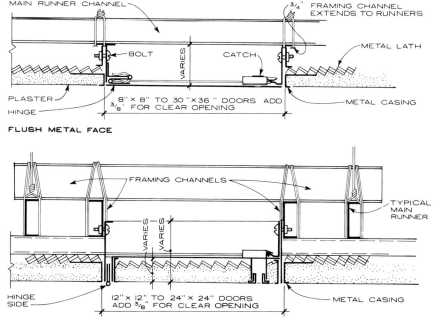

SPACER DETAILS

SADDLE TIES

TYPICAL METAL CHANNEL SUSPENSION AND FURRING DETAILS

FLUSH METAL FACE

FLUSH PLASTER FACE

METAL ACCESS DOORS AND FRAMES

NOTE
GAUGE OF METAL, NO. OF LOCKS, HINGES VARY. FIRE-RATED DOORS AVAILABLE

Douglas S. Stenhouse, AIA; Los Angeles, California

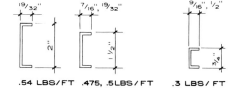

.54 LBS/FT   .475, .5LBS/FT   .3 LBS/FT

RUNNERS   FURRING

TYPICAL COLD-ROLLED CHANNEL SHAPES

Heat-rolled channels (HRC) generally run heavier than cold-rolled channels (CRC). Shapes illustrated are available in 16 gauge, 16 ft. and 20 ft. standard lengths.

Galvanizing of all components is recommended where moisture is a factor. Extra heavy galvanizing is required for swimming pools.

See Suspended Ceiling Systems for instructions for selection of components.

 LATH AND PLASTER

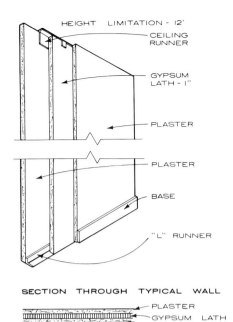

SECTION THROUGH TYPICAL WALL

PLAN

2 IN. SOLID GYPSUM LATH

CHANNEL STUD SPACING

TYPE OF LATH	WEIGHT #/SQ YD	SPACING OF SUPPORTS
Diamond mesh	2.5	16
	3.4	16
Flat rib	2.75	16
	3.4	24*

*Spacing for solid partitions not to exceed 16'-0" in height.

CHANNEL STUD SIZE

PARTITION HEIGHT	PARTITION THICKNESS	CHANNEL
12'	2"	
14'	2¼"	¾ in. 300 lb per 1000 ft
16'	2½"	
18'	2¾"	1½ in. 475 lb per 1000 ft

METAL STUD WITH METAL LATH STUD SPACING AND HEIGHT LIMITATION*

STUD WIDTH	THICKNESS	MAXIMUM HEIGHT		
		16" OC.	19" OC.	24" OC.
2½"	4"	15'	14'	9'
3¼"	4¾"	21'	18'	13'
4"	5½"	22'	20'	16'
6"	7½"	26'	24'	20'

*For length not exceeding 1½ times height; for lengths exceeding this, reduce 20%.

Walter H. Sobel, FAIA & Associates; Chicago, Illinois

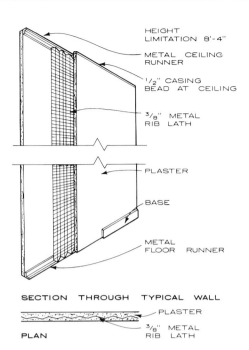

SECTION THROUGH TYPICAL WALL

PLAN

2 IN. SOLID METAL LATH AND PLASTER

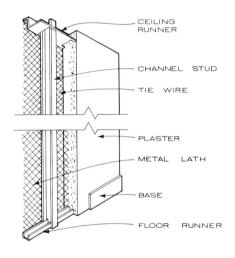

SECTION THROUGH TYPICAL WALL

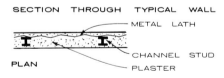

PLAN

METAL LATH–CHANNEL STUD–PLASTER

METAL STUD WITH ⅜" GYPSUM LATH HEIGHT LIMITATIONS

STUD WIDTH	THICKNESS STANDARD SYSTEM	MAX. HEIGHT STUDS 16" OC.
2½"	4¼"	15'
3¼"	5"	21'
4"	5¾"	22'
6"	7¾"	26'

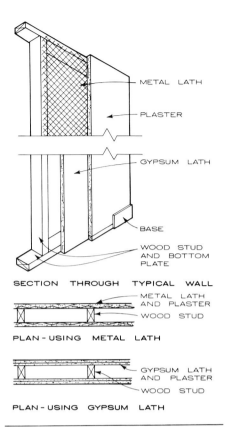

SECTION THROUGH TYPICAL WALL

PLAN – USING METAL LATH

PLAN – USING GYPSUM LATH

WOOD STUD AND LATH

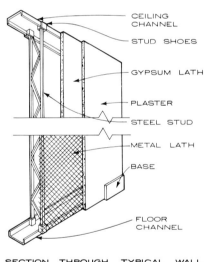

SECTION THROUGH TYPICAL WALL

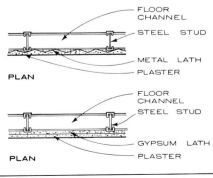

PLAN

PLAN

PREFABRICATED METAL STUD

LATH AND PLASTER

TYPES OF GYPSUM PANEL PRODUCTS

DESCRIPTION	THICKNESS (IN.)	WIDTH/EDGE (FT)	STOCK LENGTH (FT)
Regular gypsum wallboard used as a base layer for improving sound control; repair and remodeling	1/4	4, square or tapered	8-10
Regular gypsum wallboard used in a double wall system over wood framing; repair and remodeling	3/8	4, square or tapered	8-14
Regular gypsum wallboard for use in single layer construction	1/2, 5/8	4, square or tapered	8-16
Rounded taper edge system offers maximum joint strength and minimizes joint deformity problems	3/8 1/2, 5/8	4, rounded taper	8-16
Type X gypsum wallboard with core containing special additives to give increased fire resistance ratings. Consult manufacturer for approved assemblies	1/2, 5/8	4, tapered, rounded taper, or rounded	8-16
Aluminum foil backed board effective as a vapor barrier for exterior walls and ceilings and as a thermal insulator when foil faces 3/4" minimum air space. Not for use as a tile base or in air conditioned buildings in hot, humid climates (Southern Atlantic and Gulf Coasts)	3/8 1/2, 5/8	4, square or tapered	8-16
Water resistant board for use as a base for ceramic and other nonabsorbant wall tiles in bath and shower areas. Type X core is available	1/2, 5/8	4, tapered	8, 10, 12
Prefinished vinyl surface gypsum board in standard and special colors	1/2, 5/8	2, 2 1/2, 4, square and beveled	8, 9, 10
Prefinished board available in many colors and textures. See manufacturers' literature	5/16	4, square	8
Coreboard for use to enclose vent shafts and laminated gypsum partitions	1	2, tongue and groove or square	4-16
Shaft wall liner core board type X with gypsum core used to enclose elevator shafts and other vertical chases	1, 2	2, square or beveled	6-16
Sound underlayment gypsum wallboard attached to plywood subfloor acts as a base for any durable floor covering. When used with resiliently attached gypsum panel ceiling, the assembly meets HUD requirements for sound control in multifamily dwellings	3/4	4, square	6-8
Exterior ceiling/soffit panel for use on surfaces with indirect exposure to the weather	1/2	4, rounded taper	8, 12
Sheathing used as underlayment on exterior walls with type X or regular core	1/2	2, tongue and groove	8
	1/2, 5/8	4, square	8, 9, 10

NOTE: A large range of adhesives, sealants, joint treatments, and texture products are available from the manufacturers of most gypsum board products. Consult available literature for current recommendations and products.

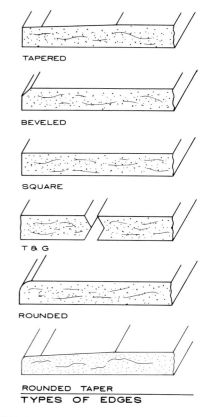

TAPERED

BEVELED

SQUARE

T & G

ROUNDED

ROUNDED TAPER
TYPES OF EDGES

MAX. BENDING FOR DRYWALL

	BENDING RADII	
THICKNESS	LENGTHWISE	WIDTH
1/4"	5'-0"	15'-0"
3/8"	7'-6"	25'-0"
1/2"	20'-0"	—

Shorter radii may be obtained by moistening face and back so that water will soak well into core of board.

MAXIMUM ALLOWABLE PARTITION HEIGHT

STUD SPACING (IN.) (FACING ON EACH SIDE)	STUD DEPTH (IN.)				
	1 5/8 *	2 1/2	3 1/4	3 5/8	4
	MAXIMUM ALLOWABLE HEIGHT				
16 (1/2 one-ply)	11'-0"	14'-8"	17'-10"	19'-5"	20'-8"
24 (1/2 one-ply)	10'-0"	13'-5"	16'-0"	17'-3"	18'-5"
24 (1/2 two-ply)	12'-4"	15'-10"	18'-3"	19'-5"	20'-8"

*1 5/8" stud with single layer of gypsum wallboard recommended for chase walls and closets only.

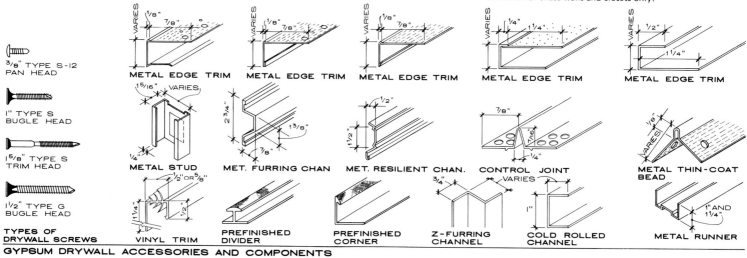

3/8" TYPE S-12 PAN HEAD

1" TYPE S BUGLE HEAD

1 5/8" TYPE S TRIM HEAD

1 1/2" TYPE G BUGLE HEAD

TYPES OF DRYWALL SCREWS

METAL EDGE TRIM

METAL EDGE TRIM

METAL EDGE TRIM

METAL EDGE TRIM

METAL EDGE TRIM

METAL STUD

MET. FURRING CHAN.

MET. RESILIENT CHAN.

CONTROL JOINT

METAL THIN-COAT BEAD

VINYL TRIM

PREFINISHED DIVIDER

PREFINISHED CORNER

Z-FURRING CHANNEL

COLD ROLLED CHANNEL

METAL RUNNER

GYPSUM DRYWALL ACCESSORIES AND COMPONENTS

Ferdinand R. Scheeler, AIA; Skidmore, Owings & Merrill; Chicago, Illinois
James Lloyd; Kennett Square, Pennsylvania

GYPSUM WALLBOARD

FIRE RATING	STC	WALL THICKNESS	CONSTRUCTION DESCRIPTION	WALL SECTIONS
1 HOUR	30 TO 34	4 7/8"	One layer 1/2 in. type X veneer base nailed to each side of 2 x 4 in. wood studs 16 in. o.c. with 5d coated nails 8 in. o.c. Minimum 3/32 in. gypsum veneer plaster. Joints staggered vertically 16 in. and horizontal joints each side at 12 in.	
		4 7/8"	One layer 5/8 in. type X gypsum wallboard or veneer base nailed to each side of 2 x 4 in. wood studs 16 in. o.c. with 6d coated nails 7 in. o.c. Stagger joints 24 in. on each side.	
	35 TO 39	5 1/8"	Two layers 3/8 in. regular gypsum wallboard or veneer base nailed to each side of 2 x 4 in. wood studs 16 in. o.c. First layer attached with 4d coated nails, second layer applied with laminating compound and nailed with 5d coated nails 8 in. o.c. Stagger joints 16 in. o.c. each side.	
	45 TO 49	5 3/8"	Base layer 3/8 in. regular gypsum wallboard or veneer base nailed to each side of 2 x 4 in. wood studs 16 in. o.c. Face layer 1/2 in. (same as base layer). Use 5d coated nails 24 in. o.c. for base layer and 8d coated nails 12 in. o.c. to edge and 24 in. o.c. to intermediate studs. Stagger joints 16 in. o.c. each layer and side.	
		5 7/8"	Base layer 1/2 in. wood fiberboard to each side of 2 x 4 in. wood studs 16 in. o.c. with 5d coated nails 24 in. o.c. on vertical joints and 16 in. o.c. to top and bottom plates. Face layer 5/8 in. type X gypsum wallboard or veneer base applied to each side with laminating compound and nailed with 8d coated nails 24 in. o.c. on vertical joints and 16 in. o.c. to top and bottom plates. Stagger joints 24 in. o.c. each layer and side.	
		5 7/8"	Both sides resilient channels 24 in. o.c. attached with GWB 54 drywall nails to each side of 2 x 4 in. wood studs 16 in. o.c. One layer 5/8 in. type X gypsum wallboard or veneer base attached with 1 in. type S drywall screws 12 in. o.c. to each side and vertical joints back-blocked. GWB filler strips along floor and ceiling both sides. Stagger joints 24 in. o.c. each side.	
	50 TO 54	5 3/8"	Base layer 1/4 in. proprietary gypsum wallboard applied to each side of 2 x 4 in. wood studs 16 in. o.c. with 4d coated nails 12 in. o.c. Face layer 5/8 in. type X gypsum wallboard or veneer base applied with laminating compound and nailed with 6d coated nails 16 in. o.c. to each side. 1 1/2 in. mineral fiber insulation in cavity. Stagger joints 24 in. o.c. each side.	
		5 3/8"	One side resilient channel 24 in. o.c. with 1 1/4 in. type S drywall screws to 2 x 4 in. wood studs 16 in. o.c. Both sides 5/8 in. gypsum wallboard or veneer base attached to resilient channel with 1 in. type S drywall screws 12 in. o.c. and GWB to stud with 1 1/4 in. type W drywall screws. 1 1/2 in. mineral fiber insulation in cavity. Stagger joints 48 in. o.c. each side.	
	60 TO 64	6 7/8"	One side resilient channels 24 in. o.c. attached with 1 in. type S drywall screws to 2 x 4 in. wood studs 16 in. o.c. Two layers of 5/8 in. type X gypsum wallboard or veneer base. First layer attached with 1 in. type S drywall screws, second layer applied with laminating compound. Other side one layer each of 5/8 in. and 1/2 in. gypsum wallboard or veneer base plus top 3/8 in. gypsum wallboard applied with laminating compound. Use 5d coated nails 32 in. o.c. for base, 8d for 1/2 in. center layer. 2 in. glass fiber insulation in cavity. Stagger all joints 16 in. o.c.	
2 HOUR	40 TO 44	6 1/8"	Two layers 5/8 in. type X gypsum wallboard or veneer base applied to each side of 2 x 4 in. wood studs 24 in. o.c. Use 6d coated nails 24 in. o.c. for base layer and 8d coated nails 8 in. o.c. for face layer. Stagger joints 24 in. o.c. each layer and side.	
	50 TO 54	8"	Two layers 5/8 in. type X gypsum wallboard or veneer base applied to each side of 2 x 4 in. wood studs 16 in. o.c. staggered 8 in. o.c. on 2 x 6 in. wood plates. Use 6d coated nails 24 in. o.c. for base layer and 8d coated nails 8 in. o.c. for face layer. Stagger vertical joints 16 in. o.c. each layer and side.	
	55 TO 59	10 3/4"	Two layers 5/8 in. type X gypsum wallboard or veneer base applied to each side of double row of 2 x 4 in. wood studs 16 in. o.c. on separate plates 1 in. apart. Use 6d coated nails 24 in. o.c. for base layer and 8d coated nails 8 in. o.c. for face layer. 3 1/2 in. glass fiber insulation in cavity. Stagger joints 16 in. o.c. each layer and side. GWB fire stop continuous in space between plates.	

CONSULT MANUFACTURER OR GYPSUM ASSOCIATION FOR ADDITIONAL INFORMATION

GYPSUM WALLBOARD

FIRE RATING	STC	WALL THICKNESS	CONSTRUCTION DESCRIPTION	WALL SECTIONS
1 HOUR	35 TO 39	2 7/8"	One layer 5/8 in. type X gypsum wallboard or veneer base applied to each side of 1 5/8 in. metal studs 24 in. o.c. with 1 in. type S drywall screws 8 in. o.c. to edges and 12 in. o.c. to intermediate studs. Stagger joints 24 in. o.c. each side.	
	40 TO 44	3 3/8"	Base layer 3/8 in. regular gypsum wallboard or veneer base applied to each side of 1 5/8 in. metal studs 24 in. o.c. with 1 in. type S drywall screws 27 in. o.c. to edges and 54 in. o.c. to intermediate studs. Face layer 1/2 in. attached on each side to studs with 1 5/8 in. type S drywall screws 12 in. o.c. to perimeter and 24 in. o.c. to intermediate studs. Stagger joints 24 in. o.c. each layer and side.	
		4 7/8"	One layer 5/8 in. type X gypsum wallboard or veneer base applied to each side of 3 5/8 in. metal studs 24 in. o.c. with 1 in. type S drywall screws 8 in. o.c. to vertical edges and 12 in. o.c. to intermediate studs. Stagger joints 24 in. o.c. each side.	
	45 TO 49	3 1/8"	Two layers 1/2 in. regular gypsum wallboard or veneer base applied to each side of 1 5/8 in. metal studs 24 in. o.c. Use 1 in. type S drywall screws 12 in. o.c. for base layer and 1 5/8 in. type S drywall screws 12 in. o.c. for face layer. Stagger joints 24 in. o.c. each layer and side.	
		3 1/8"	Base layer 1/4 in. gypsum wallboard applied to each side of 1 5/8 in. metal studs 24 in. o.c. with 1 in. type S drywall screws 24 in. o.c. to edges and 36 in. o.c. to intermediate studs. Face layer 1/2 in. type X gypsum wallboard or veneer base applied to each side of studs with 1 5/8 in. type S drywall screws 12 in. o.c. Stagger joints 24 in. o.c. each layer and side.	
		5 1/2"	One layer 5/8 in. type X gypsum wallboard or veneer base applied to each side of 3 5/8 in. metal studs 24 in. o.c. with 1 in. type S drywall screws 8 in. o.c. to edge and vertical joints and 12 in. o.c. to intermediate stud. Face layer 5/8 in. (same as other layer) applied on one side to stud with laminating compound and attached with 1 5/8 in. type S drywall screws 8 in. o.c. to edges and sides and 12 in. o.c. to intermediate studs. 3 1/2 in. glass fiber insulation in cavity. Stagger joints 24 in. o.c. each layer and side.	
	50 TO 54	4"	Base layer 1/4 in. regular gypsum wallboard applied to each side of 2 1/2 in. metal studs 24 in. o.c. with 1 in. type S drywall screws 12 in. o.c. Face layer 1/2 in. type X gypsum wallboard or veneer base applied to each side of studs with laminating compound and with 1 5/8 in. type S drywall screws in top and bottom runners 8 in. o.c. 2 in. glass fiber insulation in cavity. Stagger joints 24 in. o.c. each layer and side.	
		4"	Two layers 1/2 in. type X gypsum wallboard or veneer base applied to one side of 2 1/2 in. metal studs 24 in. o.c. Base layer 1 in. and face layer 1 5/8 in. type S drywall screws 8 in. o.c. to edge and adhesive beads to intermediate studs. Opposite side layer 1/2 in. type X gypsum wallboard or veneer base applied with 1 in. type S drywall screws 8 in. o.c. to vertical edges and 12 in. o.c. to intermediate studs. 3 in. glass fiber insulation in cavity. Stagger joints 24 in. o.c. each layer and face.	
	55 TO 59	4 1/4"	Base layer 1/4 in. gypsum wallboard applied to each side of 2 1/2 in. metal studs 24 in. o.c. with 7/8 in. type S drywall screws 12 in. o.c. Face layer 5/8 in. type X gypsum wallboard or veneer base applied on each side of studs with 1 5/16 in. type S drywall screws 12 in. o.c. 1 1/2 in. glass fiber insulation in cavity. Stagger joints 24 in. o.c. each layer and side.	
2 HOUR	40 TO 44	5"	Two layers 5/8 in. type X gypsum wallboard or veneer base applied to each side of 2 1/2 in. metal studs 16 in. o.c. braced laterally. Use 1 in. for base layer and 1 5/8 in. for facelayer type S-12 drywall screws 12 in. o.c. Stagger joints 16 in. o.c. each layer and side.	
	50 TO 54	3 5/8"	Base layer 1/2 in. type X gypsum wallboard or veneer base applied to each side of 1 5/8 in. metal studs 24 in. o.c. Use 1 in. type S drywall screws 12 in. o.c. for base layer and 1 5/8 in. type S drywall screws 12 in. o.c. for face layer. 1 1/2 in. glass fiber insulation in cavity. Stagger joints 24 in. o.c. each layer and side.	
	55 TO 59	6 1/4"	Two layers 5/8 in. type X gypsum wallboard or veneer base applied to each side of 3 5/8 in. metal studs 24 in. o.c. Use 1 in. type S drywall screws 32 in. o.c. for base layer and 1 5/8 in. type S drywall screws 12 in. o.c. to edge and 24 in. o.c. to intermediate studs. One side third layer 1/4 or 3/8 in. gypsum wallboard or veneer base applied with laminating compound. Stagger joints 24 in. o.c. each layer and side.	

CONSULT MANUFACTURER OR GYPSUM ASSOCIATION FOR ADDITIONAL INFORMATION

GYPSUM WALLBOARD

FIRE RATING	STC	WALL THICKNESS	CONSTRUCTION DESCRIPTION	WALL SECTIONS
1 HOUR	35 TO 39	3⅛"	1 in. x 24 in. proprietary type X gypsum panels inserted between 2½ in. floor and ceiling J runners with 2½ in. proprietary vented C-H studs between panels. One layer ⅝ in. proprietary type X gypsum wallboard or veneer base applied parallel to studs on side opposite proprietary gypsum panels with 1 in. type S drywall screws spaced 12 in. o.c. in studs and runners. STC estimate based on 1 in. mineral fiber in cavity. (NLB)	FIRE SIDE 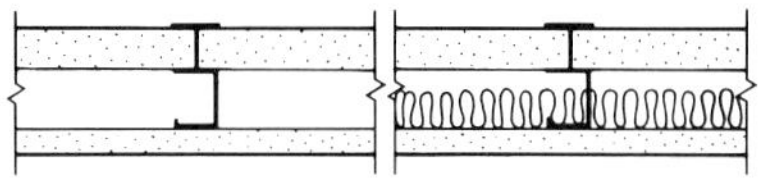 / FIRE SIDE
	40 TO 44	2⅞"	¾ in. x 24 in. proprietary type X gypsum panels inserted between 2¼ in. floor and ceiling track and fitted to proprietary 2¼ in. slotted metal I studs with tab-flange. Face layer ⅝ in. type X gypsum board applied at right angles to studs, with 1 in. type S drywall screws, 12 in. o.c. Sound tested with 1 in. glass fiber friction fit in stud space. (NLB)	FIRE SIDE 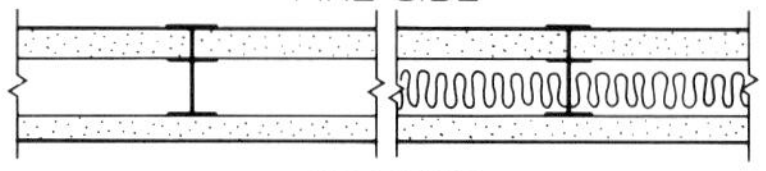 / FIRE SIDE
2 HOURS	30 TO 34	2¼"	One layer ⅝ in. type X gypsum wallboard or veneer base applied vertically to each side of 1 in. gypsum board panels (solid or laminated) with laminating compound combed over entire contact surface. Panel supported by metal runners at top and bottom and horizontal bracing angles of No. 22 gauge galvanized steel ¾ in. x 1¼ in. spaced 5 ft. 0 in. o.c. or less on shaft side. (NLB) *Limiting height shown is based on interior partition exposure conditions. Shaft wall exposure conditions may require reduction of limiting height.	FIRE SIDE 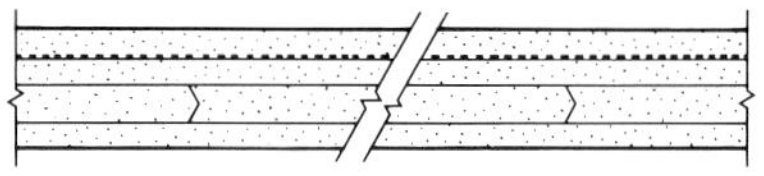
	35 TO 39	4⅛"	Four layers ⅝ in. type X gypsum wallboard or veneer base applied at right angles to one side of 1⅝ in. metal studs 24 in. o.c. Base layer attached to studs with 1 in. type S drywall screws 12 in. o.c. Second layer attached to studs with 1⅝ in. type S drywall screws using only two screws per board. Third layer attached with 2⅝ in. type S drywall screws similar to second layer. Steel strips 1½ in. wide vertically applied over third layer at stud lines and attached 12 in. o.c. to studs with 2⅝ in. type S drywall screws. Third layer also attached to top and bottom track with 2⅝ in. type S drywall screws placed midway between studs. Face layer attached to steel strips with 1 in. type S drywall screws 8 in. o.c. at each stud. Stagger joints of each layer. (NLB)	FIRE SIDE 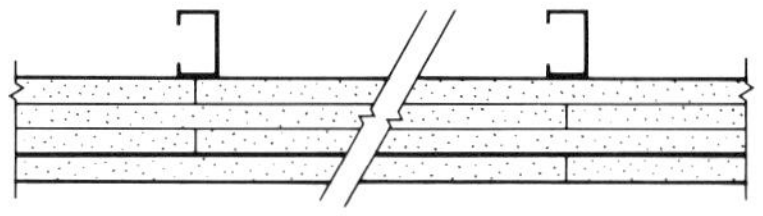 / FIRE SIDE
	40 TO 44	3½"	1 in. x 24 in. proprietary type X gypsum panels inserted between 2½ in. floor and ceiling J track with T section of 2½ in. proprietary C-T metal studs between proprietary gypsum panels. Two layers of ½ in. type X gypsum wallboard applied to face of C-T studs. Base layer applied at right angles to studs with 1 in. type S drywall screws 24 in. o.c. and face layer applied at right angles to studs with 1⅝ in. type S drywall screws 8 in. o.c. Stagger joints 24 in. o.c. each layer. (NLB)	FIRE SIDE 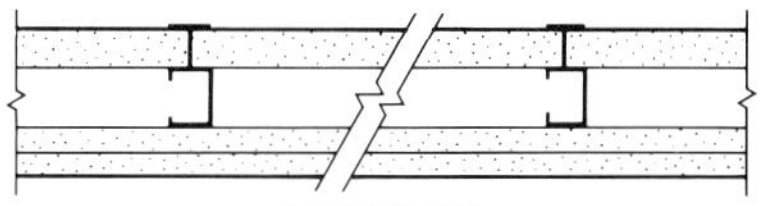 / FIRE SIDE
	45 TO 49	3½"	1 in. x 24 in. proprietary type X gypsum panels inserted between 2½ in. floor and ceiling track with tab-flange section of 2½ in. metal I studs between proprietary gypsum panels. One layer of ½ in. proprietary type X gypsum wallboard or veneer base applied at right angles to each side of metal I studs with 1 in. type S drywall screws 12 in. o.c. Sound tested using 1½ in. glass fiber friction fit in stud space. (NLB)	FIRE SIDE 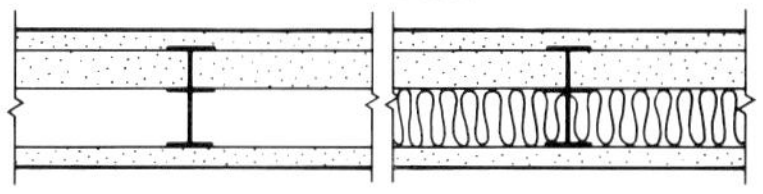 / FIRE SIDE
	50 TO 54	4"	1 in. x 24 in. proprietary type X gypsum panels inserted between 2½ in. floor and ceiling track with tab-flange section of 2½ in. metal I studs between proprietary gypsum panels. One layer of ½ in. proprietary type X gypsum wallboard or veneer base applied at right angles to flanges of I studs adjacent to proprietary gypsum panels with 1 in. type S drywall screws 12 in. o.c. Resilient channels spaced 24 in. o.c. horizontally, screw attached to opposite flanges of I studs with ⅜ in. type S screws, one per channel-stud intersection. ½ in. proprietary type X gypsum wallboard or veneer base applied parallel to resilient furring channels with 1 in. type S drywall screws 12 in. o.c. Sound tested using 1 in. glass fiber friction fit in stud space. (NLB)	FIRE SIDE 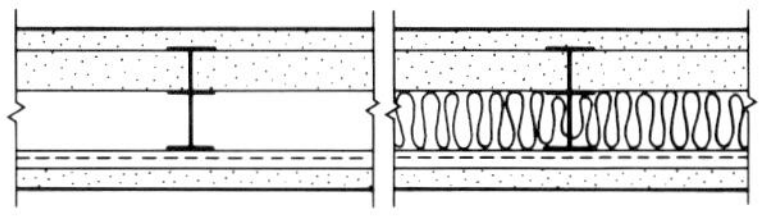 / FIRE SIDE
3 HOURS	40 TO 44	4⅛"	2 in. x 24 in. laminated gypsum board panels installed vertically between floor and ceiling 20 gauge J runners with 25 gauge steel H members between panels. Panels attached at midpoint to 2½ in. leg of J runners with 2⅜ in. type S-12 drywall screws. H studs formed from 20 or 25 gauge 2 in. x 1 in. channels placed back to back and spot welded 24 in. o.c. Base layer ⅝ in. gypsum wallboard or veneer base applied parallel to one side of panels, with 1 in. type S drywall screws 12 in. o.c. to H studs. Rigid furring channels horizontally attached 24 in. o.c. to H studs with 1 in. type S drywall screws. Face layer ⅝ in. gypsum wallboard or veneer base attached at right angles to furring channels with 1 in. type S drywall screws 12 in. o.c. Stagger joints 24 in. o.c. each layer and side. (NLB)	FIRE SIDE 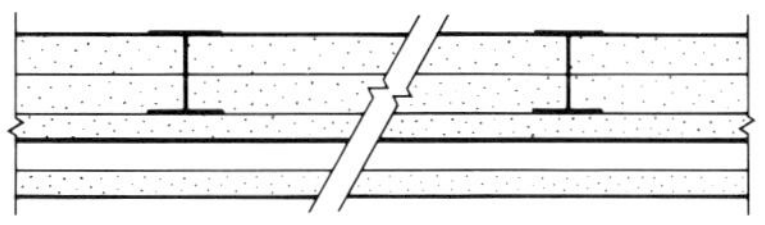
	45 TO 49	5¼"	¾ in. x 24 in. proprietary type X gypsum panels inserted between 2¼ in. floor and ceiling tracks and fitted to 2¼ in. slotted metal I studs with tab-flange. First layer ⅝ in. type X gypsum board applied at right angles to studs with 1 in. type S drywall screws 24 in. o.c. Second layer ⅝ in. type X gypsum board applied parallel to studs with 1⅝ in. type S drywall screws 42 in. o.c. starting 12 in. from bottom. Third layer ⅝ in. type X gypsum board applied parallel to studs with 2¼ in. type S drywall screws 24 in. o.c. Resilient channels applied 24 in. o.c. at right angles to studs with 2¼ in. type S drywall screws. Fourth layer ⅝ in. type X gypsum board applied at right angles to resilient channels with 1 in. type S drywall screws 12 in. o.c. Sound tested with 1 in. glass fiber friction fit in stud space. (NLB)	FIRE SIDE 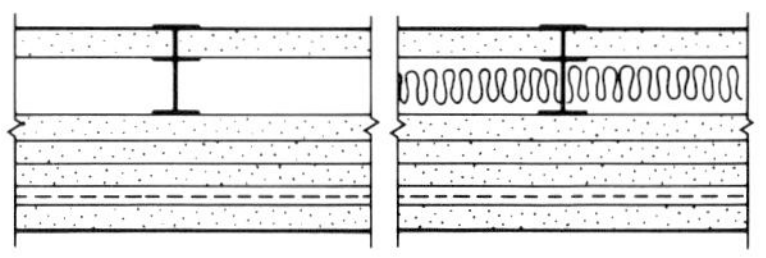 / FIRE SIDE

GYPSUM WALLBOARD   9

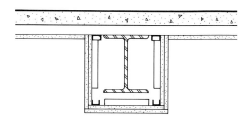

2 HOUR FIRE RATING

Two layers of ⅝ in. type X gypsum wallboard or veneer base around beam. Base layer attached with 1¼ in. type S drywall screws 16 in. o.c., face layer attached with 1¾ in. type S drywall screws 8 in. o.c. to horizontally installed U-shaped steel channels (25 gauge steel 1¹¹⁄₁₆ in. wide and 1 in. legs) located not less than ½ in. from beam flanges. Upper channels secured to steel deck units with ½ in. type S pan head screws spaced 12 in. o.c. U-shaped brackets formed of steel channels spaced 24 in. o.c. suspended from the upper channels with ½ in. type S pan head screws and supported steel channels installed at lower corners of brackets. Outside corners of gypsum board protected by 0.020-in.-thick steel corner beads crimped or nailed. (2 hour restrained or unstrained beam)

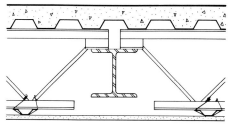

3 HOUR FIRE RATING

One layer ½ in. type X gypsum wallboard or veneer base applied at right angles to rigid furring channels with 1 in. type S drywall screws 12 in. o.c. Wallboard end joints located midway between continuous channels and attached to additional pieces of channel 54 in. long with screws at 12 in. o.c. Furring channels 24 in. o.c. attached with 18 gauge wire ties 48 in. o.c. to open web steel joists 24 in. o.c. supporting ⅜ in. rib metal lath or ⁹⁄₁₆ in. deep, 28 gauge corrugated steel and 2½ in. concrete slab measured from top of flute. Furring channels may be attached to 1½ in. cold-rolled carrying channels 48 in. o.c. suspended from joists by 8 gauge wire hangers not over 48 in. o.c. (3 hour unrestrained beam)

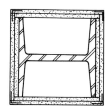

I HOUR FIRE RATING

Base layer ½ in. gypsum wallboard or veneer base tied to column with 18 gauge wire 15 in. o.c. Face layer ½ in. gypsum wallboard or veneer base applied with laminating compound over entire contact surface.

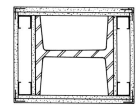

2 HOUR FIRE RATING

Base layer ½ in. type X gypsum wallboard or veneer base against flanges and across web openings fastened to 1⅝ in. metal studs with 1 in. type S drywall screws 24 in. o.c. at corners. Face layers ½ in. type X gypsum wallboard or veneer base screw-attached to studs with 1 in. type S drywall screws 12 in. o.c. to provide a cavity between boards on the flange. Face layers across the web opening laid flat across the base layer and screw attached with 1⅝ in. type S drywall screws 12 in. o.c. Metal corner beads nailed to outer layer with 4d nails 1⅜ in. long, 0.067 in. shank, ¹³⁄₆₄ in. heads, 12 in. o.c.

BEAMS, GIRDERS AND TRUSSES

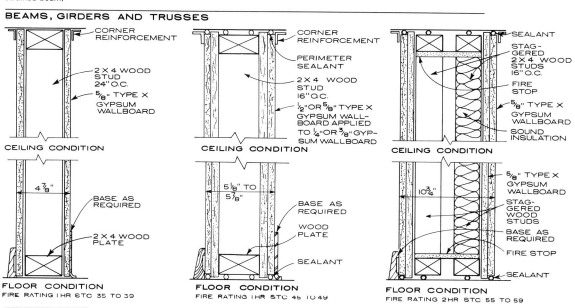

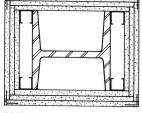

3 HOUR FIRE RATING

Three layers of ⅝ in. type X gypsum wallboard or veneer base screw attached to 1⅝ in. metal studs located at each corner of column. Base layer attached with 1 in. type S drywall screws 24 in. o.c. Second layer with 1⅝ in. type S drywall screws 12 in. o.c. and 18 gauge wire tied 24 in. o.c. Face layer attached with 2¼ in. type S drywall screws 12 in. o.c. and 1¼ in. corner bead at each corner nailed with 6d coated nails, 1⅞ in. long, 0.0915 in. shank, ¼ in. heads, 12 in. o.c.

**COLUMNS
FIRE-RESISTIVE
CONSTRUCTION**

GYPSUM WOOD AND METAL FRAMED TYPE PARTITIONS

Ferdinand R. Scheeler, AIA; Skidmore, Owings & Merrill; Chicago, Illinois
James Lloyd; Kennett Square, Pennsylvania

GYPSUM WALLBOARD

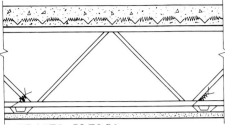

2 HR / STC 50 TO 54

¹/₂ in. type X gypsum wallboard or veneer base applied to drywall furring channels. Furring channels 24 in. o.c. attached with 18 gauge wire ties 48 in. o.c. to open web steel joists 24 in. o.c. supporting ³/₈ in. rib metal lath or ⁹/₁₆ in. deep, 28 gauge corrugated steel and 2¹/₂ in. concrete slab measured from top of flute. Double channel at wallboard end joints.

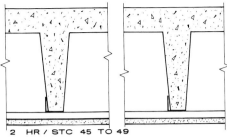

2 HR / STC 45 TO 49

⁵/₈ in. type X gypsum wallboard or veneer base screw attached to drywall furring channels. Furring channels 24 in. o.c. suspended from 2¹/₂ in. precast reinforced concrete joists 35 in. o.c. with 21 gauge galvanized steel hanger straps fastened to sides of joists. Joist leg depth, 10 in. Double channel at wallboard end joints.

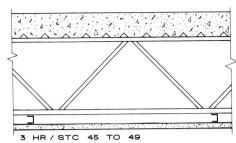

3 HR / STC 45 TO 49

⁵/₈ in. proprietary type X gypsum wallboard or veneer base screw attached to furring channels 24 in. o.c. (double channels at end joints). Furring channel wire tied to open web steel joist 24 in. o.c. supporting 3 in. concrete slab over ³/₈ in. rib metal lath. ⁵/₈ x 2³/₄ in. type X gypsum wallboard strips over butt joints.

FLOOR/CEILING ASSEMBLIES, NONCOMBUSTIBLE

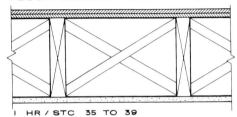

I HR / STC 35 TO 39

⁵/₈ in. type X gypsum wallboard or veneer base applied to wood joists 16 in. o.c. Joists supporting 1 in. nominal wood sub and finish floor, or ⁵/₈ in. plywood finished floor with long edges T & G and ¹/₂ in. interior plywood with exterior glue subfloor perpendicular to joists with joints staggered.

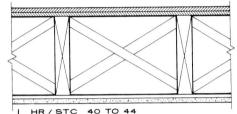

I HR / STC 40 TO 44

¹/₂ in. type X gypsum wallboard or veneer base applied to drywall resilient furring channels 24 in. o.c. and nailed to wood joists 16 in. o.c. Wood joists supporting 1 in. nominal T & G wood sub and finish floor, or ⁵/₈ in. plywood finished floor with long edges T & G and ¹/₂ in. interior plywood with exterior glue subfloor perpendicular to joists with joints staggered.

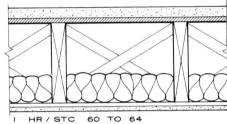

I HR / STC 60 TO 64

¹/₂ in. type X gypsum wallboard or veneer base applied to resilient furring channels. Resilient channels applied 24 in. o.c. to wood joists 16 in. o.c. Wood joists support ¹/₂ in. plywood subfloor and 1¹/₂ in. cellular or lightweight concrete over felt. 3¹/₂ in. glass fiber batts in joist spaces. Sound tested with carpet and pad over ⁵/₈ in. plywood subfloor.

FLOOR/CEILING ASSEMBLIES, WOOD FRAMED

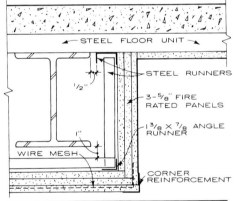

BEAM PROTECTION
3 HR. RESTRAINED   2 HR. UNRESTRAINED

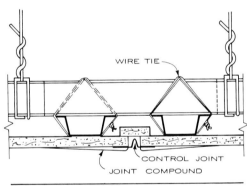

CONTROL JOINT

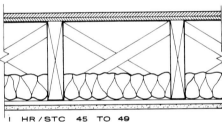

I HR / STC 45 TO 49
ELECTRIC RADIANT HEAT PANEL

⁵/₈ in. proprietary type X gypsum board electrical radiant heating panels attached to resilient furring channels spaced 24 in. o.c. installed to 2 x 10 in. wood joists 16 in. o.c. ³/₁₂ in. glass fiber insulation friction fit in joist space. Wood floor of nominal 1 in. T & G or ¹/₂ in. plywood subfloor and nominal 1 in. T & G or ⁵/₈ in. plywood finish floor.

FLOOR/CEILING ASSEMBLIES, WOOD FRAMED

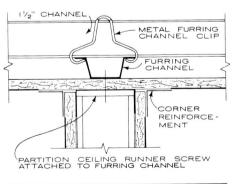

CONTINUOUS CEILING

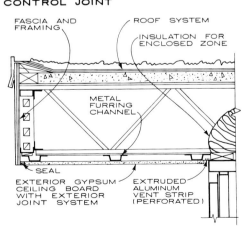

PARTITION ATTACHMENT
(SCREW ATTACHED)

EXTERIOR SOFFIT

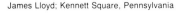

James Lloyd; Kennett Square, Pennsylvania

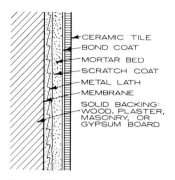

CEMENT MORTAR

Use over solid backing, over wood or metal studs. Preferred method for showers and tub enclosures. Ideal for remodeling.

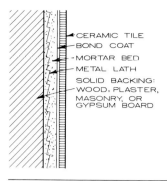

ONE COAT METHOD

Use for remodeling or on surfaces that present bonding problems. Preferred method of applying tile over gypsum plaster or gypsum board in showers and tub enclosures.

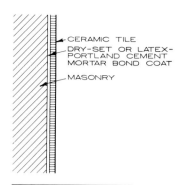

DRY-SET MORTAR

Use over gypsum board, plaster, exterior plywood, or other smooth, dimensionally stable surfaces. Use water-resistant gypsum board in wet areas.

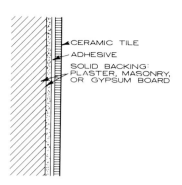

ORGANIC ADHESIVE

Use over gypsum board, plaster, exterior plywood, or other smooth, dimensionally stable surfaces. Use water-resistant gypsum board in wet areas.

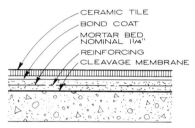

CEMENT MORTAR

Use over structural floors subject to bending and deflection. Reinforcing mesh mandatory; mortar bed nominal 1¼ in. thick and uniform.

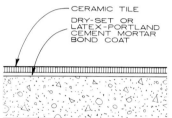

DRY-SET MORTAR

Use on level clean concrete where bending stresses do not exceed 1/360 of span and expansion joints are installed. Scarify existing concrete floors before installing tile.

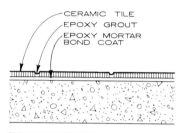

EPOXY MORTAR & GROUT

Use where moderate chemical exposure and severe cleaning methods are used, such as in commercial kitchens, dairies, breweries and food plants.

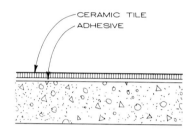

ORGANIC OR EPOXY ADHESIVE

Use over concrete floors in residential construction only. Will not withstand high impact or wheel loads. Not recommended in areas where temperatures exceed 140°F.

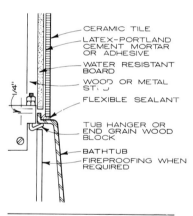

CERAMIC TILE TUB ENCLOSURE

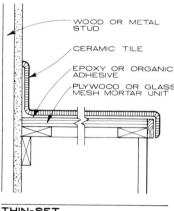

THIN-SET COUNTERTOP

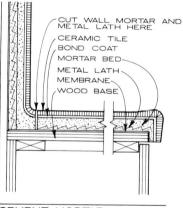

CEMENT MORTAR COUNTERTOP

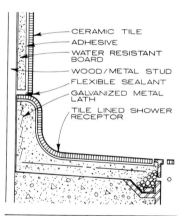

CERAMIC TILE SHOWER RECEPTOR AND WALL

TYPES OF MORTAR

PORTLAND CEMENT MORTAR

A mixture of portland cement and sand (for floor) or sand and lime (for walls) used for thick-bed installation.

DRY-SET MORTAR

A mixture of portland cement with sand and additives, imparting water retention that eliminates the need to soak tiles.

LATEX-PORTLAND CEMENT MORTAR

A mixture similar to dry-set but with latex (an emulsion of rubber or resin particles in water) added to replace all or part of the water in the mortar. It provides better adhesion, density and impact strength than dry-set mortar, and it is more flexible and resistant to frost damage.

MODIFIED EPOXY EMULSION MORTAR

As with epoxy mortars, this mixture contains a resin and hardener along with portland cement and sand. Although

Tile Council of America, Inc.

it is not as chemically resistant as epoxy mortar, it binds well. Compared with straight portland cement, it allows little or no shrinkage.

METHODS OF INSTALLATION

In a thick-bed process, tiles usually are applied over a portland cement mortar bed ¾ in. to 1¼ in. thick. The thick-bed allows for accurate slopes or planes in the finished tile work and is not affected by prolonged contact with water. If the backing surface is damaged, cracked or unstable, a membrane should be used between the surface and the tile.

In a thin-set process, tiles are set or bonded to the surface with a thin coat of material varying from 1/32 in. to 1/8 in. thickness. Bonding materials used include dry-set mortar, latex-portland cement mortar, organic adhesive, and modified epoxy emulsion mortar. Thin-set application requires a continuous, stable and undamaged surface.

THIN-SET MORTAR WITHOUT PORTLAND CEMENT

EPOXY MORTAR

A two- or three-part mixture (resin and hardener with silica filler) used where chemical resistance is important. It has high bond strength and high resistance to impact. This mortar and furan mortar are the only two that can be recommended for use over steel plates.

EPOXY ADHESIVE

Mixture similar to epoxy mortar in bonding capability, but not as chemical or solvent resistant.

ORGANIC ADHESIVE

A one-part mastic mixture that requires no mixing. It remains somewhat flexible (as compared with portland cement mortar), and has good bond strength but should not be used for exterior or wet applications.

TILE

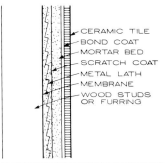

CEMENT MORTAR

Use over dry, well-braced wood studs or furring. Preferred method of installation in showers and tub or enclosures.

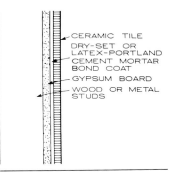

DRY-SET MORTAR

Use in dry interior areas in schools, institutions and commercial buildings. Do not use in areas where temperatures exceed 125° F.

DRY-SET MORTAR WITH GLASS MESH MORTAR UNIT

Use in wet areas over well-braced wood or metal studs. Stud spacing should not exceed 16 in. o.c., and metal studs should be 20 ga. or heavier.

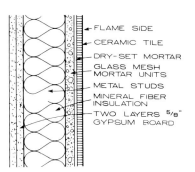

DRY-SET MORTAR (FIRE-RATED WALL)

Use where a fire resistance rating of 2 hours is required with tile face exposed to flame. Stud spacing not to exceed 16 in. o.c. and mortar bed min. thickness 3/32 in.

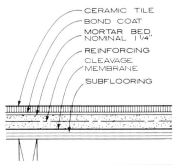

CEMENT MORTAR

Use over wood floors that are structurally sound and where deflection, including live and dead loads, does not exceed 1/360 of span.

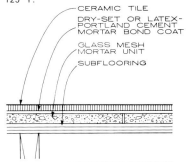

DRY-SET MORTAR

Use in light commercial and residential construction, deflection not to exceed 1/360, including live and dead loads. Waterproof membrane is required in wet areas.

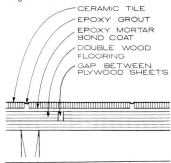

EPOXY MORTAR AND GROUT

Use in residential, normal commercial and light institutional construction. Recommended where resistance to water, chemicals or staining is needed.

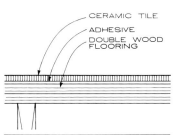

ORGANIC ADHESIVE

Use over wood or concrete floors in residential construction only. Not recommended in wet areas.

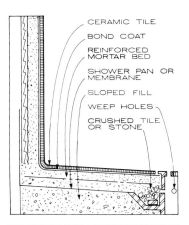

TILE SHOWER RECEPTOR

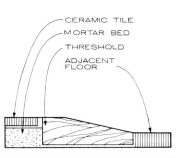

THRESHOLDS, SADDLES

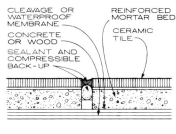

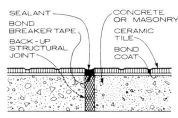

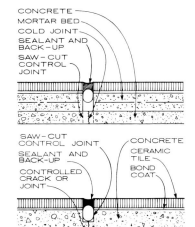

VERTICAL AND HORIZONTAL EXPANSION JOINTS

FURAN MORTAR

A two-part mixture (furan resin and hardener) excellent for chemical resistant uses and its high temperatures (350°F.) tolerance.

GROUT

Grout is used to fill joints between tiles and is selected with a compatible mortar. Types include:

PORTLAND CEMENT BASED GROUTS

Include commercial portland cement grout, sand-portland cement grout, dry-set grout and latex-portland cement grout.

EPOXY GROUT

A two- or three-part mixture (epoxy resin hardener with silica sand filler) highly resistant to chemicals. It has great bond strength. This grout and furan grout are made for different chemical and solvent resistance.

FURAN RESIN GROUT

A two-part furan mixture (similar to furan mortar) that resists high temperatures and solvents.

MASTIC GROUT

A flexible one-part mixture.

SILICONE RUBBER GROUT

An elastomeric mixture based on silicone rubber. It has high bond strength, is resistant to water and staining, and remains flexible under freezing conditions.

Tile Council of America, Inc.

CERAMIC MOSAIC TILE

Ceramic mosaic tile may be either natural clay or por-celain in composition. Special abrasive or slip-resistant surfaces and conductive tile are available only in 1 in. x 1 in. size. Nominal thickness is ¼ in.

GLAZED WALL TILE

Traditional bright and matte glazed wall tile has been supplemented with tile of variegated appearance. Tex-tured, sculptured, embossed, and engraved surface characteristics are coupled with accent designs. Im-ported tile has increased in availability, and it offers a wide range of variation from the native materials used in the manufacturing process as well as the process it-self. Tile from Germany, France, Italy, Mexico, Switzer-land, Austria, Brazil, and Spain currently are represented in manufacturer's literature. Nominal thickness is 5/16 in.

QUARRY AND PAVER TILE

Quarry and paver tile may be natural clay, shale, or por-celain in composition. These tile are characterized by their natural earth-tone coloration, high compressive strength, and slip and stain resistance. They are rec-ommended for interior and exterior applications. Nominal thicknesses are ½ in. and ¾ in. for quarry tile and ⅜ in. and ½ in. for paver tile.

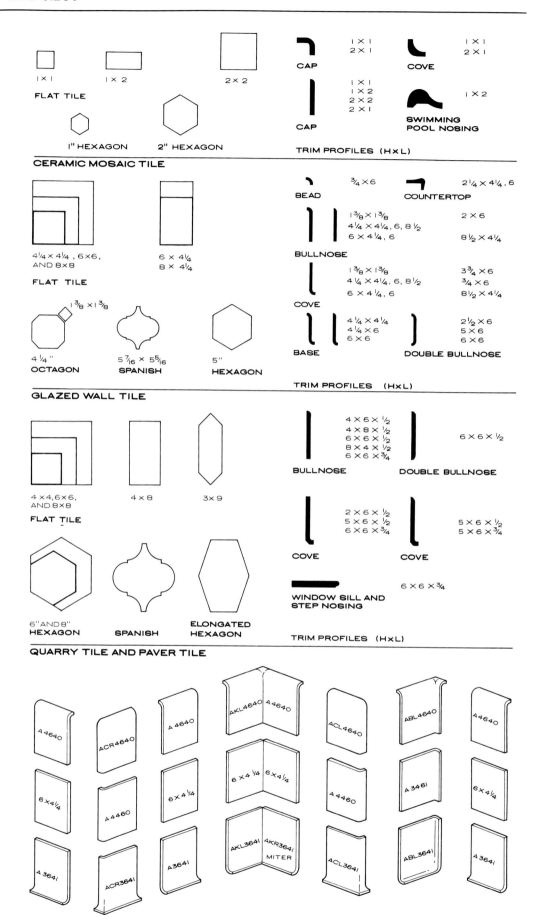

NOTES

1. The trim diagram shows typical shapes available for portland cement mortar installations of glazed wall tile. Similar types are available for thin-set installa-tions and for ceramic mosaic tile, quarry tile, and paver tile. See manufacturer's literature for exact shapes, colors, and glazes available.

2. Mounted tile assemblies (sometimes referred to as ready-set systems) are available for glazed tile and ceramic mosaic applications. These assemblies con-sist of either pregrouted sheets using flexible silicone grout or backmounted sheets that are finished with dry-set grout after installation. Both provide approxi-mately 2 sq ft of coverage per sheet. They are de-signed to simplify installation and improve uniformity.

3. Ceramic bathroom accessories usually are supplied in sets that include bath and lavatory soap holders, roll-paper holder, towel post, and toothbrush tumbler holder. Designs include surface-mounted and fully re-cessed models. They may be used with both conven-tional mortar and thin-set tile installations. Colors and glazes are available to match or harmonize with glazed wall tiles.

Ted B. Richey, AIA; The InterDesign Group; Indianapolis, Indiana

  TILE

Terrazzo is a material composed of stone chips and cement matrix and is usually polished. There are four generally accepted types, classified by appearance:

1. STANDARD TERRAZZO: The most common type; relatively small chip sizes (#1 and #2 size chips).
2. VENETIAN TERRAZZO: Larger chips (size #3 through #8), with smaller chips filling the spaces between.
3. PALLADIANA: Random fractured slabs of marble up to approximately 15 in. greatest dimension, $3/8$ to 1 in. thick, with smaller chips filling spaces between.
4. RUSTIC TERRAZZO: Uniformly textured terrazzo in which matrix is depressed to expose chips, not ground or only slightly ground.

MATRIX DATA

Two basic types exist: portland cement and chemical binders. Color pigments are added to create special effects. Limeproof mineral pigments or synthetic mineral pigments compatible with portland cement are required. Both white and grey portland cement is used depending on final color.

CHEMICAL BINDERS

All five types of chemical binders provide excellent chemical and abrasion resistance, except for latex, which is rated good.

1. EPOXY MATRIX: Two component resinous matrix.
2. POLYESTER MATRIX: Two component resinous matrix.
3. POLYACRYLATE MATRIX: Composite resinous matrix.
4. LATEX MATRIX: Synthetic latex matrix.
5. CONDUCTIVE MATRIX: Special formulated matrix to conduct electricity with regulated resistance, use in surgical areas and where explosive gases are a hazard.

PRECAST TERRAZZO

Several units are routinely available and almost any shape can be produced. Examples include: straight, coved, and splayed bases; window sills; stair treads and risers; shower receptors; floor tiles; and wall facings.

STONE CHIPS

Stone used in terrazzo includes all calcareous serpentine and other rocks capable of taking a good polish. Marble and onyx are the preferred materials. Quartz, granite, quartzite, and silica pebbles are used for rustic terrazzo and textured mosaics not requiring polishing.

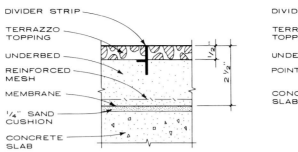

SAND CUSHION TERRAZZO

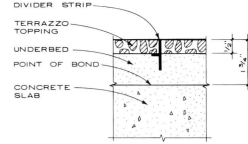

BONDED TERRAZZO

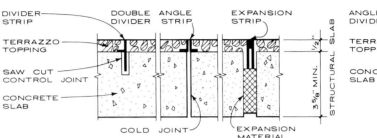

MONOLITHIC TERRAZZO

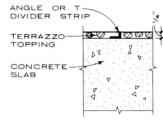

THIN-SET TERRAZZO

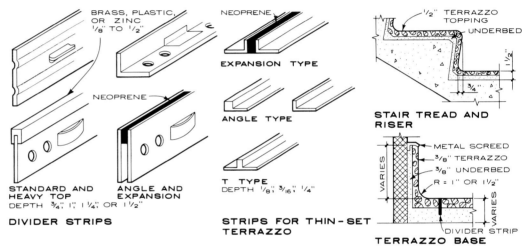

DIVIDER STRIPS

STRIPS FOR THIN-SET TERRAZZO

STAIR TREAD AND RISER

TERRAZZO BASE

TERRAZZO SYSTEMS

TERRAZZO SYSTEM	MINIMUM ALLOWANCE FOR FINISH	MINIMUM WEIGHT/ SQ FT	CONTROL JOINT STRIP LOCATION	SUGGESTED PANEL SIZE AND DIVIDER STRIP LOCATION	COMMENTS
Sand cushion terrazzo	$2^{1}/_{2}$''	27 lb	At all control joints in structure	9 to 36 sq ft	Avoid narrow proportions (length no more than twice the width) and acute angles
Bonded underbed or strip terrazzo	$1^{3}/_{4}$''	18 lb	At all control joints in structure	16 to 36 sq ft	Avoid narrow proportions as in sand cushion
Monolithic terrazzo	$1/_{2}$''	7 lb	At all control joints in structure and at column centers or over grade beams where spans are great	At column centers in sawn or recessed slots maximum 24 x 24 ft	T or L strips usually provide decorative feature only
Thin-set terrazzo (chemical binders)	$1/_{4}$''	3 lb	At all control joints	Only where structural crack can be anticipated	
Modified thin-set terrazzo	$3/_{8}$''	$4^{1}/_{2}$ lb	At all control joints	Only where structural crack can be anticipated	
Terrazzo over permanent metal forms	Varies, 3'' minimum	Varies	Directly over beam	Directly over joist centers and at 3 to 5 ft on center in the opposite direction	
Structural terrazzo	Varies, 4'' minimum	Varies	At all control joints at columns and at perimeter of floor	Deep strip ($1^{1}/_{2}$ in. min.) at all column centers and over grade beams	Use divider strip at any location where structural crack can be anticipated

NOTES

1. Venetian and Palladiana require greater depth due to larger chip size; $2^{3}/_{4}$ in. minimum allowance for finish 28 lb/sq ft.
2. Divider and control joint strips are made of white alloy of zinc, brass, aluminum, or plastic. Aluminum is not satisfactory for portland cement matrix terrazzo; use brass and plastic in chemical binder matrix only with approval of binder manufacturer.
3. In exterior terrazzo, brass will tarnish and white alloy of zinc will deteriorate.

John C. Lunsford, AIA, Varney Sexton Sydnor Architects; Phoenix, Arizona

ACOUSTICAL CEILING SYSTEMS

CEILING TYPE	MAIN, CROSS T	ACCESS T's	Z CHANNEL	H CHANNEL	T SPLINE	FLAT SPLINE	SPACER	MODULAR T	METAL PAN T	SPECIAL	BENT STEEL	BENT STEEL ALUM. CAP	BENT ALUMINUM	EXTRUDED ALUMINUM	GALVANIZED	PAINTED	ANODIZED	EMBOSSED PATTERN	FIRE RATING AVAILABLE	12×12	12×24	24×24	24×48	24×60	20×60	30×60	60×60	48×48	NOTES
GYPSUM WALLBOARD																													
Suspended	•										•				•	•			•										
Exposed grid	•										•	•	•	•	•	•	•	•	•			•	•						
Semiconcealed grid	•					•		•			•				•	•			•			•	•						
Concealed H & T					•	•	•				•				•	•			•	•	•								
Concealed T & G			•								•				•	•			•	•	•								
Concealed Z			•			•					•				•	•			•	•	•								
Concealed access	•	•			•	•	•				•				•	•			•	•		•							
Modular	•					•	•	•			•					•			•					•	•	•	•	•	50 or 60″ sq main grid
Metal pan									•		•		•	•		•	•			•	•								12″ sq pattern
Linear metal									•				•			•													4″ o.c. typical
Perforated metal	•										•		•			•													1 way grid 4′–8′ o.c.
Luminous ceiling									•				•			•													1″ to 4″ sq grid

ACOUSTICAL CEILING MATERIALS

MATERIALS	12×12	12×24	24×24	24×48	24×60	20×60	30×60	60×60	48×48	CUSTOM SIZES	1/2	5/8	3/4	1	1 1/2	3	SQUARE	TEGULAR	T & G	KERFED AND RABBETED	.45–.60	.60–.70	.70–.80	.80–.90	.90–.95	HIGH HUMIDITY	EXTERIOR SOFFIT	HIGH ABUSE/IMPACT	SCRUBBABLE	FIRE RATING AVAILABLE
Mineral fiber:																														
Painted	•	•	•	•	•	•	•			•	•	•	•				•	•	•	•	•	•	•	•						•
Plastic face		•	•										•				•					•							•	•
Aluminum face	•	•	•										•				•					•	•			•			•	•
Ceramic face		•	•										•				•					•				•		•		
Mineral face	•			•									•	•			•	•			•		•					•		•
Glass fiber:																														
Painted		•	•			•					•	•	•				•							•			•			
Film face		•	•				•				•	•	•		•		•						•	•			•			
Glass cloth face		•	•	•	•	•							•	•	•		•							•	•		•	•		
Molded		•	•		•	•	•				Varies						•													
Gypsum		•	•									•					•					•							•	•
Mylar face	•	•	•										•	•			•	•					•			•		•		
Tectum		•	•		•		•	•			1–3						•	•					•					•		

SPECIAL ACOUSTICAL SYSTEMS

SOUND ISOLATION: When it is necessary to isolate a high noise area from a building or a "quiet room" from a high surrounding noise level; floors, walls, and ceilings should be built free of rigid contact with the building structure to reduce sound and vibration transmission.

CUSTOM WALLS: Auditoriums, concert halls, and other special acoustically conditioned space may require both absorptive and reflective surfaces and in some cases surfaces that can be adjusted for varying absorption coefficients to "tune" the space.

LOOSE BATTS

USE: Reduce sound transmission through or over partitions; installed over suspended acoustical tile. Also used between gypsum wall partitions.

MATERIALS: Expanded fiberglass or mineral fiber.

S.T.C.: Based on total designed system, can range from 40 to 60.

Setter, Leach & Lindstrom, Inc.; Minneapolis, Minnesota

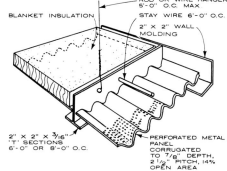

PERFORATED METAL CEILING

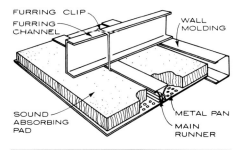

METAL PAN CEILING

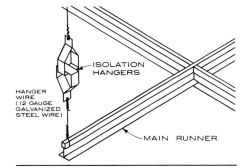

ISOLATION HANGER
CEILING ISOLATION HANGER

Isolates ceilings from noise traveling through the building structure. Hangers also available for isolating ceiling systems to shield spaces from mechanical equipment and/or aircraft noise.

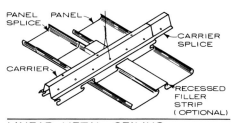

LINEAR METAL CEILING
METAL CEILINGS

USE: Sound absorption depends on batt insulation.

MATERIALS: Bent steel, aluminum, or stainless steel.

N.R.C.: 0.70 to 0.90.

FINISH: Painted, anodized, or stainless steel.

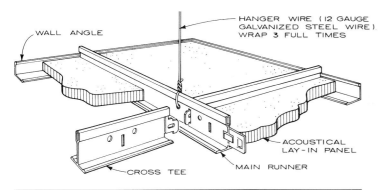

WALL ANGLE

HANGER WIRE (12 GAUGE GALVANIZED STEEL WIRE). WRAP 3 FULL TIMES

ACOUSTICAL LAY-IN PANEL

CROSS TEE

MAIN RUNNER

EXPOSED GRID

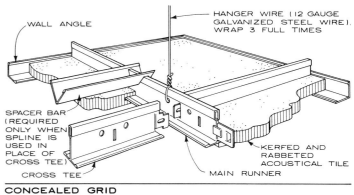

WALL ANGLE

HANGER WIRE (12 GAUGE GALVANIZED STEEL WIRE). WRAP 3 FULL TIMES

SPACER BAR (REQUIRED ONLY WHEN SPLINE IS USED IN PLACE OF CROSS TEE)

KERFED AND RABBETED ACOUSTICAL TILE

CROSS TEE

MAIN RUNNER

CONCEALED GRID

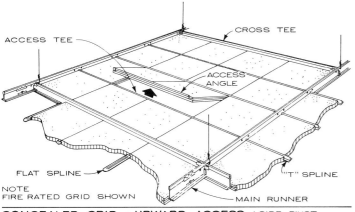

ACCESS TEE

CROSS TEE

ACCESS ANGLE

FLAT SPLINE

"T" SPLINE

NOTE FIRE RATED GRID SHOWN

MAIN RUNNER

CONCEALED GRID – UPWARD ACCESS (SIDE PIVOT SHOWN – END PIVOT AVAILABLE)

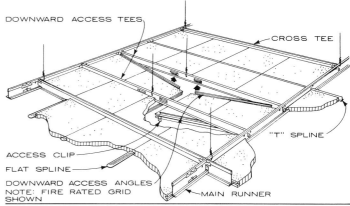

DOWNWARD ACCESS TEES

CROSS TEE

ACCESS CLIP

FLAT SPLINE

DOWNWARD ACCESS ANGLES NOTE: FIRE RATED GRID SHOWN

"T" SPLINE

MAIN RUNNER

CONCEALED GRID – DOWNWARD ACCESS (END PIVOT SHOWN – SIDE PIVOT AVAILABLE)

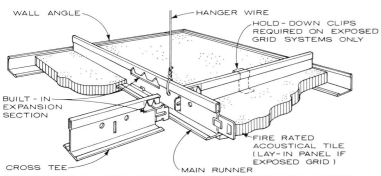

WALL ANGLE

HANGER WIRE

HOLD-DOWN CLIPS REQUIRED ON EXPOSED GRID SYSTEMS ONLY

BUILT-IN EXPANSION SECTION

FIRE RATED ACOUSTICAL TILE (LAY-IN PANEL IF EXPOSED GRID)

CROSS TEE

MAIN RUNNER

FIRE RATED GRID (CONCEALED GRID SHOWN)

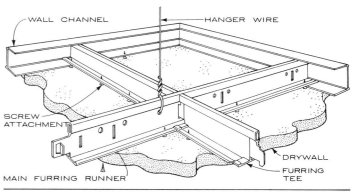

WALL CHANNEL

HANGER WIRE

SCREW ATTACHMENT

MAIN FURRING RUNNER

DRYWALL

FURRING TEE

DRYWALL FURRING SYSTEM

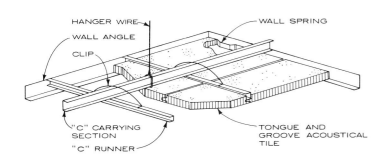

HANGER WIRE

WALL SPRING

WALL ANGLE

CLIP

"C" CARRYING SECTION

"C" RUNNER

TONGUE AND GROOVE ACOUSTICAL TILE

TONGUE AND GROOVE

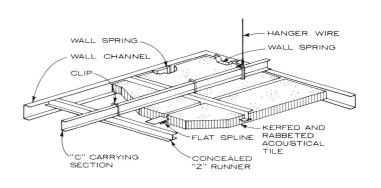

WALL SPRING

HANGER WIRE

WALL CHANNEL

WALL SPRING

CLIP

KERFED AND RABBETED ACOUSTICAL TILE

FLAT SPLINE

"C" CARRYING SECTION

CONCEALED "Z" RUNNER

CONCEALED "Z" SYSTEM

Setter, Leach & Lindstrom, Inc.; Minneapolis, Minnesota

ACOUSTICAL TREATMENT

9

NOTES

1. Flooring can be manufactured from practically every commercially available species of wood. In the United States wood flooring is grouped for marketing purposes roughly according to species and region. There are various grading systems used with various species, and often different specifications for different sized boards in a given species. For instance, nail size and spacing varies among the several board sizes typically available in oak.

2. Information given here should be used for preliminary decision making only. Precise specifications must be obtained from the supplier or from the appropriate industry organization named below.

3. Several considerations in wood flooring selection and installation are applicable industrywide. These are shown graphically at right.

4. The table below includes typical grades and sizes of boards for each species or regional group. Grade classifications vary, but in each case one can assume that the first grade listed is the highest quality, and that the quality decreases with each succeeding grade. The best grade will typically minimize or exclude features such as knots, streaks, spots, checks, and torn grain and will contain the highest percentage of longer boards. Grade standards have been reduced in recent years for practically all commercially produced flooring, hence a thorough review of exact grade specifications is in order when selecting wood flooring.

5. End matching gives a complete tongue and grooved joint all around each board. Board length is reduced as required to obtain the matched ends.

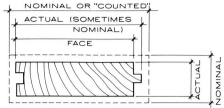

CROSS SECTIONAL DIMENSIONING SYSTEMS VARY AMONG SPECIES, PATTERNS, MANUFACTURERS. TRADE ORGANIZATIONS PROVIDE PERCENTAGE MULTIPLIERS FOR COMPUTING COVERAGE

CROSS SECTIONAL DIMENSIONS

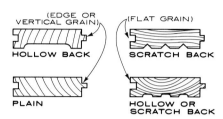

THE UNDERSIDE OF FLOORING BOARDS MAY BE PATTERNED AND OFTEN WILL CONTAIN MORE DEFECTS THAN ARE ALLOWED IN THE TOP FACE. GRAIN IS OFTEN MIXED IN ANY GIVEN RUN OF BOARDS

BOARD CHARACTERISTICS

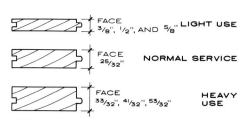

MOST FLOORING MAY BE HAD IN VARYING THICKNESSES TO SUIT WEAR REQUIREMENTS. ACTUAL DIMENSIONS SHOWN ARE AVAILABLE IN MAPLE

VARIOUS THICKNESSES

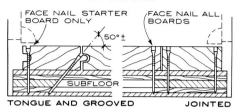

JOINTED FLOORING MUST BE FACE NAILED, USUALLY WITH FULLY BARBED FLOORING BRADS
TONGUE AND GROOVED BOARDS ARE BLIND NAILED WITH SPIRAL FLOOR SCREWS, CEMENT COATED NAILS, CUT NAILS, MACHINE DRIVEN FASTENERS, USE MANUFACTURER'S RECOMMENDATIONS

FASTENING

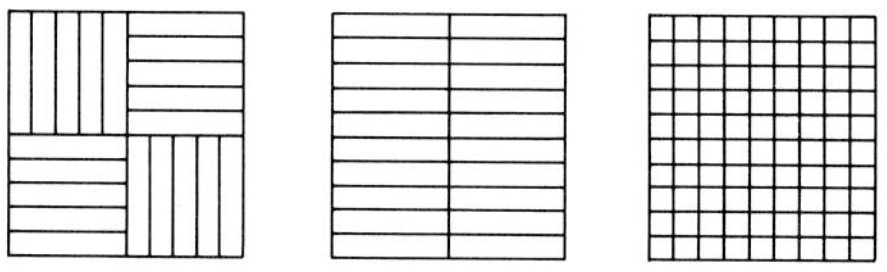

PARQUET FLOORING—SQUARE PANELS

THICKNESS	FACE DIMENSIONS
5/16" (most common) 9/16", 11/16", 3/4"	6" x 6", 6¼" x 6½", 12" x 12", 19" x 19" Other sizes are available from certain manufacturers

PARQUET FLOORING—INDIVIDUAL STRIPS

THICKNESS	FACE DIMENSIONS
5/16"	2" x 12" typical strips can be cut, mitered, etc., to obtain pieces required for special patterns

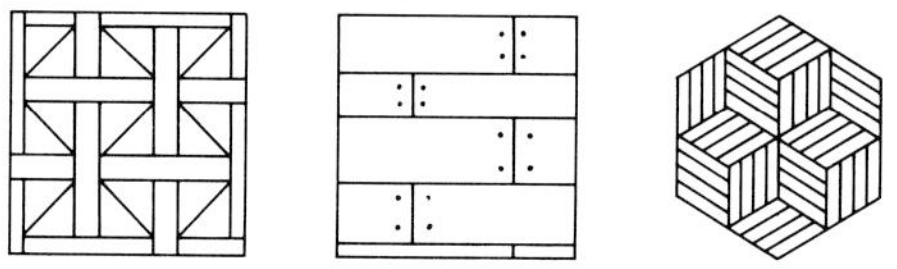

TYPICAL GRADES AND SIZES OF BOARDS BY SPECIES OR REGIONAL GROUP

GROUP	INDUSTRY ORGANIZATION	GRADE	THICKNESS	WIDTH		NOTES
Oak (also beech, birch, pecan, and hard maple)	National Oak Flooring Manufacturers' Assoc.	Quarter Sawn: Clear Select Plain Sawn: Clear Select No. 1 Common No. 2 Common	3/4", 1/2" Standard; also 3/8" 5/16"	Face 1½" 2" 2¼"		This association grades birch, beech, and hard maple. First Grade, Second Grade, Third Grade, and "Special Grades." Pecan is graded: First Grade, First Grade Red, Second Grade, Second Grade Red, Third Grade.
Hard maple (also beech and birch) (acer saccharum—not soft maple)	Maple Flooring Manufacturers' Assoc. Inc.	First Grade Second Grade Third Grade Fourth Grade Combinations	3/8", 12/32" 41/32", 1/2" 33/32", 53/32", 5/8"	Face 1½" 2" 2¼" 3¼"		Association states that beech and birch have physical properties that make them fully suitable as substitutes for hard maple. See manufacturer for available width and thickness combinations.
Southern pine	Southern Pine Inspection Bureau	B & B C C & Btr D No. 2	3/8", 1/2" 5/8", 1" 1¼", 1½"	Nom. 2" 3" 4" 5" 6"	Face 1⅛" 2⅛" 3⅛" 4⅛" 5⅛"	Grain may be specified as edge (rift), near-rift, or flat. If not specified, manufacturer will ship flat or mixed grain boards. See manufacturer for available width and thickness combinations.
Western woods (Douglas fir, hemlock, Englemann spruce, Idaho pine, incense cedar, lodgepole pine, Ponderosa pine, sugar pine, Western larch, Western red cedar)	Western Wood Products Association	Select: 1 & 2 clear- B & Btr C Select D Select Finish: Superior Prime E	2" and thinner	Nominal 3" 4" 6"		Flooring is machined tongue and groove and may be furnished in any grade agreeable to buyer and seller. Grain may be specified as vertical (VG), flat (FG), or mixed (MG). Basic size for flooring is 1" x 4" x 12'; standard lengths 4' and above.
Eastern white pine Norway pine Jack pine Eastern spruce Balsam fir Eastern hemlock Tamarack	Northern Hardwood & Pine Manufacturers' Association	C & Btr Select D Select Stained Select	3/8", 1/2" 5/8", 1", 1¼", 1½"	Nom. 2" 3" 4" 5" 6"	Face 1⅛" 2⅛" 3⅛" 4⅛" 5⅛"	The various species included in this "Lake States Region" group provide different visual features. Consult manufacturer or local supplier to determine precisely what is available in terms of species and appearance.

Darrel Downing Rippeteau, Architect; Washington, D.C.

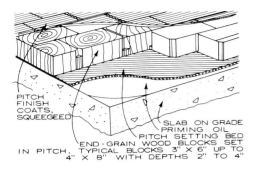

INDUSTRIAL WOOD BLOCK URETHANE FINISH COATS AVAILABLE FOR NONINDUSTRIAL USES

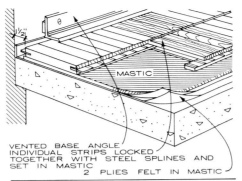

STEEL SPLINED ROWS OF STRIPS CORK UNDERLAYMENT ADDED FOR NON-INDUSTRIAL USE

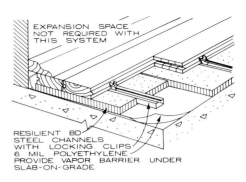

METAL CHANNEL RUNNERS WITH CLIPS

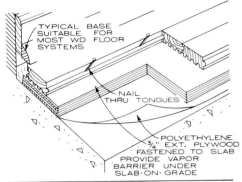

STRIPS OVER PLYWOOD UNDERLAYMENT A NOFMA STANDARD

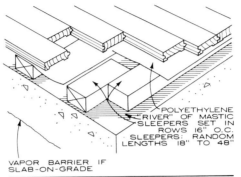

STRIPS OVER STAGGERED 2 X 4 SLEEPERS A NOFMA STANDARD

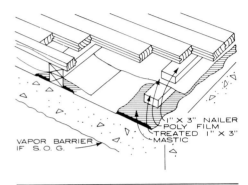

DOUBLE COURSE OF SLEEPER STRIPS A NOFMA STANDARD

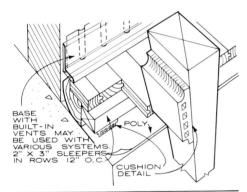

STRIPS OVER CUSHIONED SLEEPERS

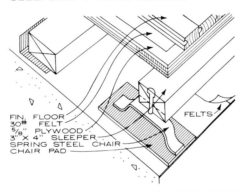

STRIPS OVER SLEEPERS MOUNTED ON SPRING-STEEL CHAIRS

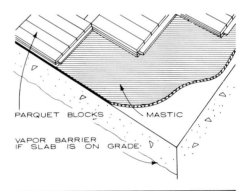

PARQUET BLOCKS SET IN MASTIC

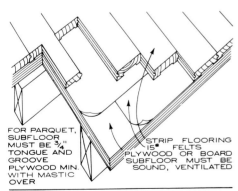

STRIPS OVER SUBFLOOR ON WOOD JOISTS

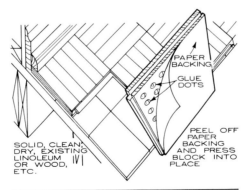

PRESSURE-SENSITIVE "DO-IT-YOURSELF" PANELS (PRE-FINISHED)

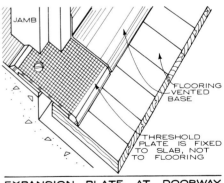

EXPANSION PLATE AT DOORWAY /JOINT WITH DISSIMILAR CONSTRUCTION

Wood flooring is visually attractive and provides an excellent wearing surface. However, wood requires particular care in handling and installation to prevent moisture attack. Minimize moisture attack on wood floors by avoiding proximity to wet areas. Installation should occur after all "wet" jobs are completed. All the permanent lighting and heating plant should be installed to ensure constant temperature and humidity.

Darrel Downing Rippeteau, Architect; Washington, D.C.

Expansion and contraction is a fact of life with most wood flooring. Perimeter base details that allow for movement and ventilation are included in the details above. Moisture control is further enhanced by use of a vapor barrier under a slab on or below grade. This provision should be carefully considered for each installation. Wood structures require adequate ventilation in basement and crawl space.

Wearing properties vary from species to species in wood flooring and should be considered along with appearance. In addition, grain pattern will affect a given species wearability. For instance, industrial wood blocks are typically placed with the end grain exposed because it presents the toughest wearing surface. The thickness of the wood above tongues in T & G flooring may be increased for extra service.

RESILIENT FLOORING CHARACTERISTICS

TYPE OF RESILIENT FLOORING	BASIC COMPONENTS	SUBFLOOR APPLICATION*			RECOMMENDED LOAD LIMIT (PSI)	DURA-BILITY†	RESIS-TANCE TO HEEL DAMAGE	EASE OF MAINTE-NANCE	GREASE RESIS-TANCE	SURFACE ALKALI RESIS-TANCE	RESIS-TANCE TO STAINING	CIGARETTE BURN RESISTANCE	RESIL-IENCE	QUIET-NESS
Vinyl sheet	Vinyl resins with fiber back	B	O	S	75-100	2-3	2-5	1-2	1	1-3	3-4	4	4	4
Homogeneous vinyl tile	Vinyl resins	B	O	S	150-200	1-3	1-4	2-4	1	1-2	1-5	2-5	2-5	2-5
Vinyl composition tile	Vinyl resins and fillers	B	O	S	25-50	2	4-5	2-3	2	4	2	6	6	6
Cork tile with vinyl coating	Raw cork and vinyl resins			S	150	4	3	2	1	1	5	3	3	3
Cork tile	Raw cork and resins			S	75	5	4	4	4	5	4	1	1	1
Rubber tile	Rubber compound	B	O	S	200	2	4	4	3	2	1	2	2	2
Linoleum	Cork, wood, floor, and oleoresins			S	75	3	4-5	4-5	1	4	2	4	4	4

*B: below grade; O: on grade; S: suspended.
†Numerals indicate subjective ratings (relative rank of each floor to others listed above), "1" indicating highest.
  Bruce A. Kenan, AIA, Pederson, Hueber, Hares & Glavin; Syracuse, New York.

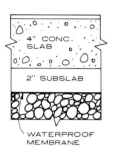 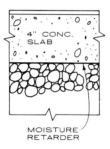 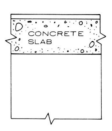 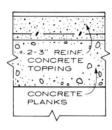 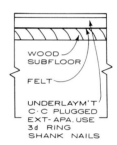 

SLAB BELOW GRADE   SLAB ON GRADE   SLAB ABOVE GRADE   SLAB OVER PRECAST   WOOD SUBFLOOR   WOOD SUBFLOOR

RESILIENT FLOORING

PREPARING OLD WOOD FLOORS

TYPE OF SUBFLOOR		COVER WITH
Single wood floor	Tongue and groove not over 3"	Hardboard or plywood, 1/4" or heavier
	Not tongue and groove	Plywood 1/2" or heavier
Double wood floor	Strips 3" or more	Hardboard or plywood 1" or heavier
	Strips less than 3" tongue and groove	Renail or replace loose boards, remove surface irregularities

PREPARING OLD CONCRETE FLOORS

1. Check for dampness.
2. Remove all existing surface coatings.
3. Wirebrush and sweep dusty, porous surfaces. Apply primer.

PREPARING LIFT SLABS

Remove curing compounds prior to resilient flooring installation.

CONCRETE SLABS BY DENSITY

Density			
	Light	Medium	Heavy
Pounds per cubic foot			
	20/40	60/90	90/120	120/150
Type of concrete			
	Expanded perlite, vermiculite, and others	Expanded slag shale, and clay	Standard concrete of sand, gravel, or stone
Recommendations			
	Top with 1" thickness of standard concrete mix		Approved for use of resilient flooring if troweled smooth and even

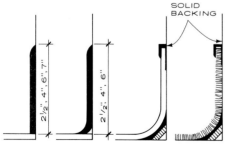  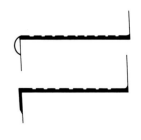

BASES - STRAIGHT OR COVED   COVE STRIP AND CAP STRIP   REDUCERS   STAIR NOSINGS   THRESHOLDS, SADDLES FEATURE STRIP   STAIR TREAD

RESILIENT FLOORING ACCESSORIES, CARPET ACCESSORIES

Broome, Oringdulph, O'Toole, Rudolf & Associates; Portland, Oregon

RESILIENT FLOORING

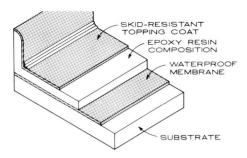

An epoxy resin composition flooring resistant to a large number of corrosive materials, 3/16 in. to 1/4 in. thickness, weight 3 psf. Used in manufacturing areas, food processing, hotel and restaurant kitchens, beverage bottling plants and loading docks.

EPOXY RESIN COMPOSITION FLOORING

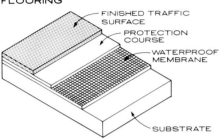

A multicolored installation consisting of a fabric reinforced latex membrane, a neoprene-cement protection course, and a flexible, oil-resistant finish. Thickness 3/16 in., weight 1.5 psf. Used on interior or exterior auto parking facilities.

REINFORCED LATEX MEMBRANE

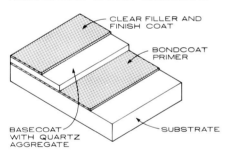

A jointless flooring in which quartz aggregates are embedded either by trowel or broadcast into a wet epoxy binding coat followed by clear filler coat. Used in laboratories, pollution control facilities, locker rooms, light manufacturing.

EPOXY/QUARTZ AGGREGATE

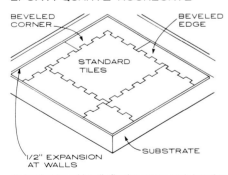

An interlocking rubber tile flooring system made in various thicknesses and types according to user requirements. Can be used in saunas, deck areas, weight, exercise, and locker rooms, on assembly lines, in industrial art rooms.

INTERLOCKING RUBBER FLOORING

Timothy B. McDonald; Washington, D.C.

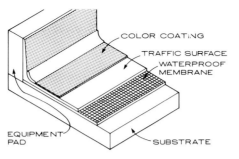

A troweled surface over a fabric reinforced latex-type waterproof membrane. Flooring thickness 3/16 in., weight 2 1/2 psf. Used in mechanical equipment rooms and plenum rooms.

WATERPROOF LATEX MEMBRANE FLOORING

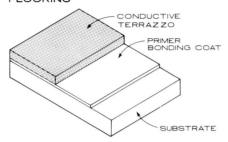

Static-dissipating, nonsparking trowel-applied jointless flooring of elastomeric resin terrazzo, incorporating marble chips. Thickness 1/4 in. to 1/2 in., weighing 3 psf (1/4 in. thick). Used in hospital operating suites.

CONDUCTIVE FLOORING

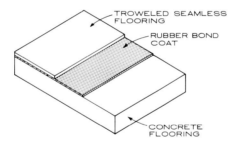

A trowel-applied cupric oxychloride flooring that is nonsparking and solvent resistant, weighing 3.2 psf at 3/8 in. thick. Used in hospitals, arsenals and ammunition plants, light manufacturing areas, warehouses, laboratories.

CUPRIC OXYCHLORIDE FLOORING

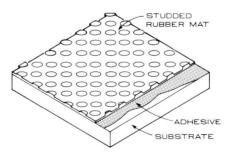

A solid, nonconductive rubber flooring with a raised circular, square, "H" or ribbed pattern. Applied to substrate by use of an adhesive. Used in terminals, malls, recreation facilities, elevators and offices.

STUDDED RUBBER FLOORING

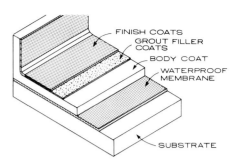

A trowel-applied elastomeric latex resin forming a jointless floor with good chemical resistance, is waterproof in conjunction with membrane. Thickness 1/4 in., weight 3 psf. Used in showers and locker rooms, laboratories, pollution control facilities, TV studios.

ELASTOMERIC LATEX RESIN FLOORING

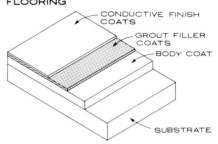

Static-dissipating and nonsparking trowel-applied jointless flooring, 1/4 in. thick, weighing 3 psf. Used in arsenals and ammunition plants, flammable materials storage areas and explosion-hazardous industrial locations.

CONDUCTIVE FLOORING

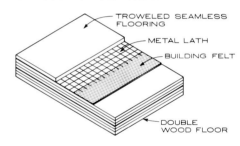

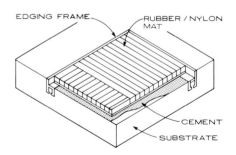

Manufactured from recycled synthetic rubber tires containing nylon fibers for strength and bonded to a glass-cloth backing. Applied to substrate cement adhesive. Used in golf clubs, stores, malls, and air terminals.

RUBBER/NYLON FLOORING

BACKGROUND

The word "carpet" comes from the Latin *carpere*, "to card wool." Carpet production in the U.S. has grown from 100 million square yards in 1910 to over 1 billion square yards per year in the 1980s. Three events account for the major increases:

1. Development of man-made fibers in the 1930s.
2. Replacement of weaving by tufting in the 1950s.
3. Combining of the tufting machine with piece dyeable bulked continuous filament (BCF) nylon in the period beginning 1960. This gave the industry the ability to produce carpet styles with long color lines of up to 50 or more colors without large inventory costs.

CARPET FIBERS

Nature accounted for 100% of face fiber production for floor coverings. The uncertainties of supply of desirable wools from about 20 countries, plus variation in fiber length and increasing costs of scouring and processing encouraged development of man-made fibers. Man-made fibers are easy to clean, mildew resistant, mothproof, and nonallergenic.

Wool: Of 1986 U.S.-produced carpet production, 1% was wool. Its qualities have been copied but never quite duplicated. The natural tendency of animal fibers to stretch and return to their original length makes wool carpet resilient, with excellent recovery from crushing. Problems of supply make it the most expensive fiber and the only one requiring antimoth treatment.

Cotton: Negligible current usage. Early tufted carpet was an offshoot of the "turfed" bedspread cottage industry in the South and had single color, loop, or cut pile fibers made of cotton.

Nylon: Of 1986 carpet production, 80% was nylon—a petrochemical engineered for carpet use, with easy dying characteristics. First successfully introduced into carpet in continuous filament, it was later cut and processed in staple lengths (like wool) to give more natural qualities to the finished product. Recent developments have combined topical treatments with modified extrusions to give antisoil properties to the fibers. Adequate maintenance provisions should accompany specifications for these products, since soil that remains hidden will cause fiber damage unless properly removed by regular vacuuming and cleaning.

Acrylic: Negligible current usage. This hydrocarbon synthetic is considered to be the most wool-like of all man-made fibers.

Polypropylene (olefin): Of 1986 production, 12% and growing. This man-made hydrocarbon normally lacks resilience and the ability to be post dyed. Its simplified extrusion capabilities plus the ability to be solution dyed prior to extrusion have encouraged many carpet makers to install their own polypropylene fiber-making facilities.

Polyester: Of 1986 production, 7%. A high tensile strength synthetic made by the esterification of ethyl glycol, having easy care and water-repellent qualities.

CARPET CONSTRUCTION

Woven carpet represents 2% of the total carpet production in the U.S. today. Whether hand-knotted, loomed, or mechanically produced, there are many similarities in production methods. The side-to-side progression in hand-knotted is accelerated in a loom as the shuttle propels the weft (or woof) yarn back and forth over the 12 or 15 ft width of the finished carpet. This is missing in tufted and later methods. Common to all, however, is a progression of the leading edge of this 12–15 ft finished width in the direction of manufacture. This sets up the direction of lay of the finished face fibers, always in the opposite direction. The exception is in hand-knotted,

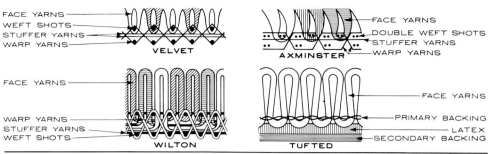

CONSTRUCTION MODES

where the direction of lay of the face fibers falls to one side or the other, depending on the style of knot. In hand-knotted, it will also change after cleaning to follow the direction of brushing.

In all tufted or woven broadloom, it is imperative that the direction of lay be made to run in the same direction on all components of every installation. Otherwise, adjacent widths, although perfectly seamed, will appear to mismatch in perceived color and texture.

Oriental rugs: Defined by the Oriental Rug Retailers of America as "a rug of either wool or silk, knotted entirely by hand by native craftsmen in some parts of Asia, from the shores of the Persian Gulf, North to the Caspian Sea, and Eastward through Iran, the Soviet Union, Afghanistan, Pakistan, India, China, and Japan." An Oriental rug is classed an antique if it is over 75 years old, semiantique if less than 75 years old, and new if made in the past 15 years.

More than 60% of the hand-knotted rugs imported by the U.S. come from China and India. Most machine-made rugs are manufactured in the U.S. or imported from Belgium or Spain. They are available in traditional (floral or curvilinear) and contemporary (geometric) colors and designs.

Dhurrie and Kilim rugs are flat weaves costing less than hand-knotted Orientals. They can be either machine- or hand-made and have primitive as well as modern designs. Other types of rugs are ryas from Scandinavia, American Indian woven rugs, and Greek flotakis. Braided and rag rugs are also finding a niche in the market. Many carpet and rug makers offer custom designs (some computer aided) in a variety of fiber construction.

CONSTRUCTION MODES

Velvet: Simplest of all carpet weaves. Although the simplicity of the loom does not permit patterned designs, beautiful yarn color combinations can be used to produce tweed effects. Pile is formed as the warp yarns are looped over removable "wires" inserted consecutively across the loom (weft-wise). Requires additional space equal to the width of the loom for this rapid operation. Alternate height wires can be used to create high–low loop texture, while wires with a raised knife blade at the trailing end are used to create cut pile upon retraction.

Axminster: Has a smooth cut pile surface, with almost all of the yarn appearing on the surface. Colors and patterns are limited only by the number of tufts in the carpet. Identifying feature is the heavy ribbed backing that only allows the carpet to be rolled lengthwise.

Wilton: Basic velvet loom, improved in the early 1800s by the addition of a Jacquard mechanism to feed yarn through as many as six separate punched hole patterns to vary the texture or colored design. Uses only one color at a time on the surface; the other yarns remain buried; thus the reputation that Wiltons have a hidden quality because of the extra "hand" or feel that this gives to the finished carpet.

Tufted: This technique developed from an early method for making tufted bedspreads. Spacing of as many as 2000 needles on a huge sewing machine (12–15 ft wide) determines the carpet gauge. Face yarn is stitched through the primary backing, where it is bonded to a secondary backing with latex before curing in a drying oven. For energy saving, hot-melt adhesive is substituted for latex by some mills, though this results in a loss of ability to pass flammability tests. Some "single-needle" tufting machines exist having a small stitching head that moves from side to side during carpet construction. They are mainly used for special orders for multiple odd-shaped spaces to eliminate installation waste.

Knitted: Resembles weaving in that knitted carpet is a warp-knitted fabric comprised of warp chains, weft-forming yarns, and face yarns and is knitted in a single operation. Warp-chain stitches run longitudinally and parallel to each other. The backing yarns are laid weft-wise into the warp stitches and pass over 3 or 4 rows of warp stitches overlapping in the back of the carpet for strength and stiffness. As in tufted carpet, latex is applied to the back for stability and tuft lock. An additional backing may also be attached. Knitted carpets usually have solid or tweed colors, with level-loop textures.

Flocked: Made by propelling short strands of pile fiber (usually nylon) electrostatically against an adhesive-coated (usually jute), prefabricated backing sheet. As many as 18,000 pile fibers per inch become vertically embedded in the adhesive before a secondary backing is laminated to the fabric and the adhesive cured. The pile fibers can either be dyed prior to flocking or the finished surface can be printed after fabrication.

Needlepunched: First made of polypropylene fibers in solid colors for outdoor use (patios and swimming pools), they are now made for indoor and automotive use as well, using wool, nylon, acrylic, and/or olefin fibers in variegated colors and designs. They are made by impinging loose layers of random, staple carpet fibers into a solid sheet of polypropylene, from both sides, by means of thousands of barbed needles until the entire mass is compressed to a solid bonded fiber mass of indoor/outdoor carpet.

Fusion bonded: This process produces dense cut pile or level-loop carpet in solid or moresque colors. For cut pile, the face yarn, fed simultaneously from the total width of the supply roll, or "beam," is folded back and forth between two vertically emerging primary backings as they are coated with a viscous vinyl paste that hardens, binding the folded face yarns alternately to the vertical backing sheet on each side. Final operation is a mid-line cutting that separates the vertical "sandwich" into two identical cut pile finished rolls. To make loop pile fusion-bonded carpet, one primary backing and the cutting operation are omitted. Fusion bonding is especially suited to making carpet tiles.

SELECTION CRITERIA

FIBER	DURABILITY	SOIL RESISTANCE	RESILIENCE	ABRASION RESISTANCE	CLEANABILITY
Nylon	Excellent	Good	Good to excellent	Excellent	Very good
Polyester	Very good	Fair	Good	Excellent	Very good
Polypropylene	Excellent	Fair	Poor	Excellent	Very good
Acrylic	Good	Fair	Fair	Good	Very good
Wool	Very good	Good to excellent	Excellent	Good	Very good

Neil Spencer, AIA; North Canton, Ohio

DEFINITIONS

Carpet tiles: Square (from 18 to 36 in.) modules, dense cut pile or loop, heavy backed. Can be made to cover flat, regular wiring; low-voltage lighting systems ("safe-lites"); or underfloor utilities.

Carpet wear: As defined by fiber manufacturers refers to percent of face fiber lost over the life of a guarantee.

Commercial: Includes all contract, institutional, transportation; any use where carpet is specified by other than the end user.

Residential: Includes all carpet specified and purchased for residential use by the owner.

Life-cycle costing: Permits comparison of diverse flooring methods by totaling initial cost, installation, and detailed predictable maintenance expenses over the expected life of the carpet.

Traffic: Usage expressed in terms of foot traffics (person) per unit of time or as light, medium, or heavy, to define need for matching carpet construction, which normally increases in density as traffic increases. See recommendations below.

Pile height: Height of loop or tuft from the surface of the backing to the top of the pile, measured in fractions, or decimals, of an inch.

Pile weight (face weight): total weight of pile yarns in the carpet (measured in oz/sq yd, excluding backing).

Pile density: $D = 36$ times the finished pile weight, in oz/yd, divided by the average pile height.

$$\text{Weight density (WD)} = \frac{(\text{Face weight})^2 \times 36}{\text{Pile height}}$$

Pitch (in woven carpet): The number of yarn ends in a 27 in. finished width of carpet.

Gauge: In tufted carpet, the number of needles per inch across the width of the finished carpet (tufting machine).

Stitches: Number of rows of yarn ends per inch, finished carpet. Tufts per sq in.: Calculation made by multiplying pitch x wires for woven carpet, or gauge x stitches per in. for tufted.

Denier: Weight in grams of 9000 meters (9750 yd) of a single extruded filament of nylon. Based on the standard weight of 450 meters of silk weighing 5 centigrams.

Filament: Continuous strand of extruded synthetic fiber, combined into a "singles" yarn by simply twisting, without the need for spinning.

Ply: Refers to the number of strands of "singles" yarn twisted together for color or texture reasons to create a two-ply or three-ply yarn system.

Point: A single tuft of carpet pile.

BCF: Bulked continuous filament.

Cut pile pattern: Plush or saxony type carpet with woven, tufted, or printed design or pattern.

Level loop: Carpet made from uncut tufts in looped form and having all tufts the same pile height.

Cut pile velvet: Solid color, tweed, or heather blend yarns which give smooth velvety or velour texture.

Cut and loop: Carpet with areas of both cut pile and loop pile, most often with the cut pile being higher than the loop.

Frieze: Cut pile carpet made from highly twisted yarns that are heat set to give a curled random configuration to the pile yarns.

Primary backing: The matrix used in making tufted carpet, consisting of woven or nonwoven fabric, usually jute or polypropylene, into which pile yarn tufts are stitched.

Secondary backing: The woven or nonwoven material adhered to the underside of a carpet during construction to provide additional tuft bind for tufted carpet and dimensional stability and body. Usually jute, or polypropylene, latex foam, or vinyl.

Neil Spencer, AIA; North Canton, Ohio

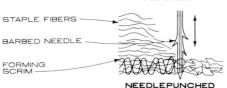

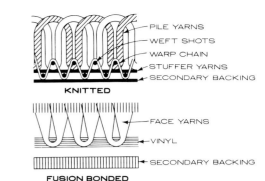

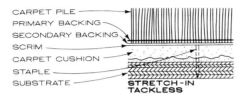

CONSTRUCTION MODES

INSTALLATION (THREE TYPES)

1. Stretch-in (tackless). Over separate cushion. Best condition for maximum carpet wear and most effective cleaning.
2. Direct glue down. For large surface areas which make power-stretching and tackless installations prohibitive. Adhesive must be tailored to match carpet backing and substrate, as recommended by carpet manufacturer.
3. Double glue down. Developed to counter early fiber failure, occurring in direct glue-down carpets in heavy

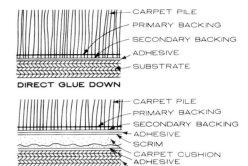

traffic areas, due to lower than normal resilience level of man-made fibers. Provides ease of large area coverage plus benefits of separate pad.

INSTALLATION

CARPET CUSHION OR UNDERLAYMENT

Four reasons for considering separate carpet cushion in wall-to-wall installations are:

1. Adds as much as 50% to the life of the carpet.
2. Absorbs as much as 90% of the traffic noise.
3. Can reduce installation costs by eliminating need for repairs to less than perfect substrate.
4. Improves thermal environment by insulation, which varies depending on material.

Four major categories of carpet cushion are:

1. Felt padding
2. Sponge rubber
3. Urethane foam
4. Foam rubber

TRAFFIC CLASSIFICATION

CARPETED AREAS	TRAFFIC RATING		
	LIGHT	MEDIUM	HEAVY
Educational			
Schools and colleges			
Administration		•	
Classroom			•
Dormitory			•
Corridor			•
Libraries		•	
Museums and art galleries			
Display room			•
Lobby			•
Medical			
Health care			
Executive	•	•	
Patient's room			•
Lounge			•
Nurses' station			•
Corridor			•
Lobby			•
Commercial			
Retail establishments			
Aisle			•
Sales counter			•
Smaller boutiques, etc.			•

TRAFFIC CLASSIFICATION (CONTINUED)

CARPETED AREAS	TRAFFIC RATING		
	LIGHT	MEDIUM	HEAVY
Office buildings			
Executive		•	
Clerical			•
Corridor			•
Cafeteria			•
Supermarkets			•
Food services			•
Recreational			
Recreation areas			•
Club house			•
Locker room			•
Convention centers			
Auditorium			•
Corridor and lobby			•
Religious			
Churches/temples			
Worship	•	•	
Meeting room			•
Lobby			•

NOTE: If rolling traffic is a factor, carpet may be of maximum density for minimum resistance to rollers. Select only level loop or dense low cut pile for safety.

MAINTENANCE PROGRAMMING

The following maintenance-related factors should be considered in the selection of carpet:

Color: Carpets in the mid-value range show less soil than very dark or very light colors. Consider the typical regional soil color. Specify patterned or multicolored carpets for heavy traffic areas in hotels, hospitals, theaters, and restaurants.

Traffic: The heavier the traffic, the heavier the density of carpet construction.

Topical treatment: Note that the soil-hiding qualities of advanced generation fibers do not reduce the need for regular maintenance. They do make soil removal easier, but by disguising the presence of dirt, make it easier for the dirt that remains hidden to contribute to earlier fiber failure unless regularly removed.

Placement: The location of carpeted areas within a building affects the maintenance expense. Walk-off carpet areas can contribute effectively to reducing tracked-in soil near entrances.

TYPICAL COVERINGS AND AVAILABLE SIZES

DESCRIPTION	WIDTH	LENGTH PER SINGLE ROLL	MINIMUM[1] UNIT SOLD	FLAME SPREAD RATING	ADHESIVE USED[2]	GENERAL WEARABILITY
Burlap Vinyl backed Paper backed	30", 36"	4 yards	Single roll	Class A-25	Premixed vinyl adhesive	Durable
Canvas Paper backed	24", 27", 48"	5 yards	Single roll	Class A-25	Premixed vinyl adhesive	Durable
Cork Paper backed Cloth backed	30", 36"	4 yards 5 yards	Single roll	Class A-25 Class B-35	Nonstaining paste Wheat paste Premixed vinyl	Less durable
Fabric (wool, linen, cotton, rayon, jute, etc.) Paper backed Acrylic backed Polyfoam backed	36", 54"	4 yards Continuous rolls	Single roll	Class A-25, 15	Premixed vinyl adhesive	Variable
Felt Paper backed	20½", 24", 30", 36", 54"	5 yards	Single roll	Class A-25	Premixed adhesive	Less durable
Grass cloth Paper backed	30", 36"	4 yards	Single roll	Class A-25	Wheat paste Cellulose paste	Less durable
Paper American	18" 20½" 27"	8 yards 7 yards 5 yards	Single roll	Class A-25 Class B-35	Vinyl adhesive	Less durable
European	18" 20½" 27"	12½ yards 11 yards 8½ yards	Single roll	Class A-25 Class B-35	Vinyl adhesive	Less durable
Flocked	27"	5 yards	Single roll	Class A-25 Class B-35	Vinyl adhesive	Less durable
Foil	27", 30"	5 yards	Single roll	Class A-25	Vinyl adhesive	Less durable
Handprinted sheets	30"	5 yards	Single roll	Class A-25	Vinyl adhesive	Less durable
Murals (variable)	28" Variations	Variable	Single panel	Class A-25	Vinyl adhesive	Less durable
Scenic (variable)	11", 28" Variations	5 yards	Single roll	Class A-25	Vinyl adhesive	Less durable
Silk Paper backed	30", 36"	5 yards	Single roll	Class A-25	Cellulose paste	Less durable
Textures (sand, etc.) Plastic coated Paper backed	3', 4'	5 yards	Single roll	Class A-25	Premixed vinyl nonstaining paste	Durable
Vinyl Cloth backed Paper backed Felt polyester Backed	27", 54"	Variable	Variable	Class A-25, 15 Class B-35	Vinyl adhesive	Durable
Wood veneer	Up to 24" flitch	12' flitch	Single flitch	Class A-25	Premixed adhesive	Durable
Substrate Indian/Bangladesh jute with a stainless jute backing	48"	5 yards	Single roll	Class A-15	Nonstaining and nonbleeding type that causes a crystallization and forms a bond	Very durable

NOTES
1. Large quantities are available in multiple rolls or continuous yardages.
2. Consult manufacturers concerning proper adhesive to be used for specific applications.
3. Consult manufacturers to obtain specific test results for a product's typical flame spread rating.

K. Shahid Rab, AIA; Friesen International; Washington, D.C.

FORMULA FOR COVERAGE

1. Determine number of panels required: total lineal feet of wall divided by width of fabric.
2. Find number of rolls required: number of full (floor to ceiling) panels per roll times number of panels required.
3. Window and door areas may be deducted, but only to the extent that no horizontal seaming occurs.

TYPICAL ROOM COVERAGE

ROOM SIZE (FT)	SINGLE ROLLS REQUIRED USING 30 SQ FT/ROLL			SINGLE ROLLS FOR CEILING
	8-FT CEILING	10-FT CEILING	12-FT CEILING	
9 x 12	11	14	17	4
12 x 14	14	17	21	6
14 x 16	16	20	24	8
16 x 18	18	22	27	10
18 x 20	21	25	30	12

NOTE: Deduct approximately two thirds of the roll for each door and window opening.

CLASSIFICATION OF VINYL WALL COVERINGS

Type I, Light Duty (7 oz/sq yd). For use on surfaces not subjected to abrasion or wear.

Type II, Medium Duty (13 oz/sq yd). For general use in areas of average traffic and scuffing.

TYPE III, Heavy Duty (22 oz/sq yd). For use as wainscot or wall protection for areas exposed to damage, or for decorative effect.

REGULAR FINISH (CLASS I) AND MILDEW RESISTANT FINISH (CLASS II)

Composition may be of three layers, the first being a supporting material of cotton cloth, nonwoven fiberglass, asbestos, or other suitable material. Supporting material for Class II must be mildew resistant. The second layer is a coating compound of specialized vinyl chloride resin which is laminated to the supporting material in a continuous film. This layer is embossed, color printed, or integrally pigmented. A clear coating may be added as a third layer if needed to meet the physical requirements noted in the specification.

AVAILABLE SIZES OF VINYL WALL COVERINGS

TYPE	PIECES PER ROLL	WIDTH PER ROLL	YARDAGE PER ROLL (3 YD LENGTH OR MULTIPLES)
Type I	1 piece	27", 54"	Not less than 72 sq ft plus 1 ft-tolerance
Type II	2 pieces	54"	Not less than 15 yd or more than 45 yd
Type III	4 pieces	54"	15 to 30 yd
	6 pieces		Over 30 yd

Manufacturers should be able to supply all information concerning specification requirements and test data on the covering's breaking strength, tear strength, hydrostatic resistance, abrasion resistance, flame resistance, char length, colorfastness to light, shrinkage, cold crack, blocking, heat aging, and crocking.

SUBSTRATE FABRICS

The material that lies between the wallcovering and the wall itself becomes a substrate which performs a wide variety of functions such as reducing noise, increasing flame retardancy, and allowing a smoother application of a wall covering over surfaces that are imperfect. Manufacturers can supply information on types of substrates they carry and the qualities of each.

THE GYPSUM SUBSTRATE consists of fabric impregnated with uncrystallized gypsum. The gypsum is formulated so that when it is applied to a substrate with an adhesive, it will crystallize and form a secure bond with the substrate. The fabric can be used in many cases as a finished surface over rough walls as well as a surface prepared for an additional covering.

PREFINISHED PANELS

MATERIAL TYPE	USE	THICKNESS									
		1/32	1/16	1/8	3/16	1/4	5/16	3/8	1/2	5/8	3/4
PLYWOOD											
Hardwood veneer	Cabinets, interior paneling, protective surfaces					●		●	●		●
Softwood veneer	Interior paneling					●		●	●	●	●
Printed/embossed	Interior paneling					●		●	●	●	●
Textured	Interior paneling, siding							●	●	●	●
Printed vinyl faced	Decorative interior finish							●	●	●	
HARDBOARD											
Standard	Interior use, cabinet liner			●	●	●	●	●	●		
Tempered	Interior and exterior use, underlayment where strength and wear count			●	●	●	●	●	●		
Plastic finished	Interior paneling, wearing surfaces			●		●		●		●	
Embossed factory finish	Interior decorative paneling				●	●					
FIBERBOARD											
Vinyl covered	Tackboard—interior decorative paneling								●		
Fabric covered	Acoustic, panels, tackboard								●		
LAMINATES											
Plastic laminates	Cabinets, countertops, protective wall finish	●	●	●							
Metal faced	Decorative paneling	●	●	●							
GYPSUM											
Vinyl covered	Interior walls					●		●	●	●	
Fabric covered	Interior walls					●		●	●	●	

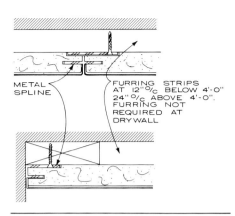

METAL SPLINE

FURRING STRIPS AT 12" O/C BELOW 4'-0" 24" O/C ABOVE 4'-0". FURRING NOT REQUIRED AT DRYWALL

FABRIC COVERED FIBERBOARD

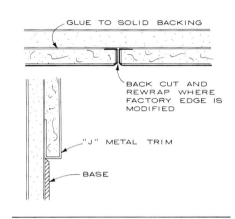

GLUE TO SOLID BACKING

BACK CUT AND REWRAP WHERE FACTORY EDGE IS MODIFIED

"J" METAL TRIM

BASE

VINYL COVERED FIBERBOARD

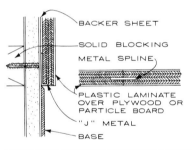

BACKER SHEET

SOLID BLOCKING

METAL SPLINE

PLASTIC LAMINATE OVER PLYWOOD OR PARTICLE BOARD

"J" METAL

BASE

PLASTIC LAMINATE PANELS

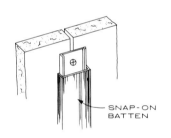

SNAP-ON BATTEN

VINYL COVERED GYPSUM BOARD

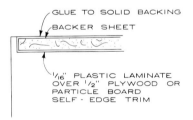

GLUE TO SOLID BACKING

BACKER SHEET

1/16" PLASTIC LAMINATE OVER 1/2" PLYWOOD OR PARTICLE BOARD SELF-EDGE TRIM

PLASTIC LAMINATE PANELS

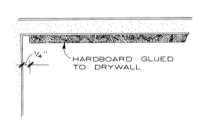

1/4"

HARDBOARD GLUED TO DRYWALL

TEMPERED HARDBOARD

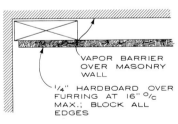

VAPOR BARRIER OVER MASONRY WALL

1/4" HARDBOARD OVER FURRING AT 16" O/C MAX.; BLOCK ALL EDGES

TEMPERED HARDBOARD

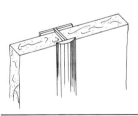

DIVIDER

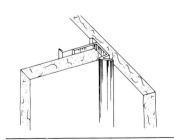

INSIDE CORNER TRIM

OUTSIDE CORNER TRIM

END CAP

Broome, Oringdulph, O'Toole, Rudolf & Associates; Portland, Oregon

WALL COVERING 9

WALL TREATMENT

1. USE: Sound absorption.
2. MATERIALS: Fabric-wrapped glass fiber or mineral wool.
3. N.R.C.: .55–.85
4. NOTES: Wall panels may be used individually or grouped to form an entire wall system. Noise reduction coefficient varies with material thickness and acoustical transparency of fabric facing. Maximum panel sizes vary with manufacturer up to 4 x 12 ft.

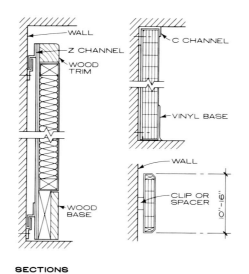

SECTIONS

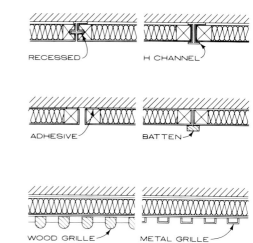

PLAN SECTIONS

WALL TREATMENT

PLENUM BARRIER

1. USE: Reduce sound transmission through plenum above partitions.
2. MATERIALS: 1/64 in. sheet lead, lead-loaded vinyl, perforated aluminum, or foil-wrapped glass fiber.
3. S.T.C.: 18–41 dB improvement.
4. NOTES: All openings through barrier for pipes, ducts, etc., must be sealed airtight for maximum effectiveness.

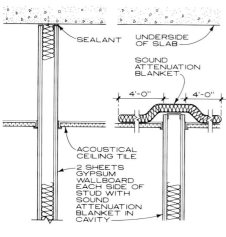

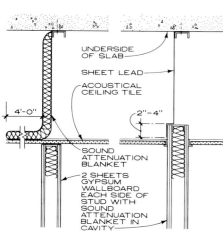

PLENUM BARRIERS

Setter, Leach & Lindstrom, Inc.; Minneapolis, Minnesota
Blythe + Nazdin Architects, Ltd.; Bethesda, Maryland

SUSPENDED PANELS

1. USE: Sound absorption.
2. MATERIALS: Vertical suspension–glass fiber blanket wrapped with perforated aluminum foil or fabric stretched over frame. Horizontal suspension–perforated steel or aluminum with glass fiber blanket, or similar to vertical.
3. N.R.C.: .55–.85
4. NOTES: Panels may be suspended from structure or attached directly to ceiling grid. May be arranged in a variety of patterns including linear, square, zigzag vertical, or regular or random spaced horizontal panels.

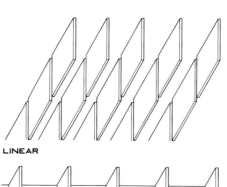

LINEAR

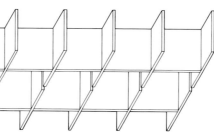

EGGCRATE

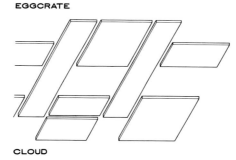

CLOUD

SUSPENDED PANELS

ACOUSTICAL MASONRY UNITS

1. USE: Sound absorption
2. MATERIALS: Concrete masonry unit, 4, 6, or 8 in. thick, with metal baffle and/or fibrous filler in slotted areas.
   Structural glazed facing tile, 4, 6, or 8 in. thick; 8 x 8 in. or 8 x 16 in. (nominal) face dimensions, with fibrous filler in cores.
3. N.R.C.: .45–.65

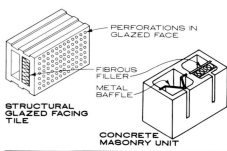

ACOUSTICAL MASONRY UNITS

SPRAY-ON ACOUSTICAL MATERIAL

1. USE: Sound absorption.
2. MATERIALS: Mineral or cellulose fibers spray applied to metal lath or directly to hard surfaces such as concrete, steel, masonry, or gypsum wallboard.
3. N.R.C.: .50–.95.
4. NOTES: Application to metal lath provides slightly better sound absorption and permits irregular shapes. Available with a hard surface for wall applications. Available with fire protection rating.

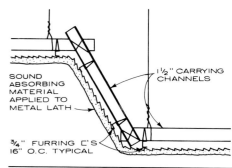

SPRAY-ON ACOUSTICAL MATERIAL

WALL COVERING

REFERENCES

GENERAL REFERENCES

Architectural Acoustics, 1988, M. Egan, McGraw-Hill

Ceiling Systems Handbook, Ceilings and Interior Contractors Association

Handbook for Ceramic Tile Installation, Tile Council of America

Manual of Lathing and Plastering, Gypsum Association

Plaster and Drywall Systems Manual, 3rd ed., 1988, J. P. Gorman, et al., McGraw-Hill

DATA SOURCES: ORGANIZATIONS

Alcan Aluminum Corporation, 270

Chicago Metallic Corporation, 271

Connor Forest Industries, 273

Dow Badische Company, 276

Gypsum Association (GA), 261–265

Keene Association, 254

Manhattan American Terrazzo Strip Company, 269

Maple Flooring Manufacturers' Association, Inc. (MFMA), 272

Metal Lath Institute (MLI), 254, 255

Monsanto Textiles Company, 276

National Gypsum Company, 259, 260, 264, 265

National Oak Flooring Manufacturers Association (NOFMA), 272

National Terrazzo and Mosaic Association, Inc. (NTMA), 269

Northern Hardwood and Pine Manufacturers Association, Inc. (NPHMA), 272

Southern Pine Inspection Bureau (SPIB), 272

Texas Lathing and Plastering Contractors' Association (TLPCA), 254, 255

Tile Council of America, Inc. (TCA), 266, 267

U.S. Gypsum Company, 254, 255, 260, 264, 265

Western Wood Products Association (WWPA), 272

DATA SOURCES: PUBLICATIONS

Carpet and Rugs, The Hoover Company, 276, 277

Specifications for Commercial Interiors, S. C. Reznikoff, Whitney Library of Design, 277

CHAPTER 10

SPECIALTIES

TACKBOARD TYPES AND SIZES

TYPE	VARIATIONS	BACKING	THICKNESS	MAXIMUM SIZE WITHOUT JOINTS
Cork		Unmounted	1/8", 1/4"	4' x 130', 6' x 90'
	Unfaced cork, plain or burlap backed	Particle board	1/2"	4' x 16'
		Hardboard		
		Unmounted	1/4"	4' x 100'
	Vinyl covered cork	Particle board	1/2"	4' x 16'
		Hardboard		4 x 12' fire rated
	Vinyl impregnated cork	Unmounted	1/8", 1/4"	6' x 90'
		Hardboard	1/2"	4' x 12'
Fiber-board	Vinyl covered		1/2"	4' x 12'
	Burlap covered			4' x 8', 4' x 14' spec.

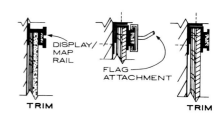

ADDITIONAL VARIETIES OF TRIM AND CHALKTRAYS ARE AVAILABLE

CHALKBOARD TYPES AND SIZES

TYPE	CORE	THICKNESS	MAXIMUM SIZE WITHOUT JOINTS
Porcelain enamel steel (18-28 gauge)*	None	1/32"	4' x 12'
	Plywood	1/4" - 7/16"	4' x 12'
	Hardboard	1/4", 7/16"	5' x 12', 4' x 16'
	Fiberboard	7/16", 1/2"	4' x 12'
	Particle board	3/8" - 1/2"	4' x 16'
	Gypsum board	3/8", 1/2"	4' x 12'
	Honeycomb	3/8", 7/16"	4' x 16'
Painted-on composition	Hardboard	1/4", 1/2"	4' x 16'
	Gypsum board	1/4", 1/2"	4' x 12'
Natural slate		1/4" - 3/8"	4' x 6'

* Available in either chalkboard or liquid marker board.

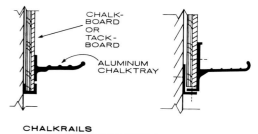

CHALKRAILS

CHALKBOARDS WITH ALUMINUM FRAMING

AVERAGE RECOMMENDED CHALKBOARD MOUNTING HEIGHT
(Chalkrail to Floor)

Nursery	20"
Kindergarten	24"
1st-3rd grade	30"
4th-6th grade	32"
Junior high	36"
Senior high	36"
Adult	36"

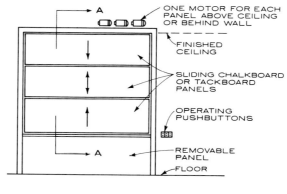

VERTICAL SLIDING PANELS
(MANUAL OR MOTOR OPERATED)

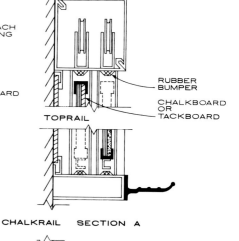

CHALKRAIL   SECTION A

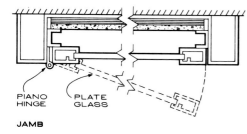

JAMB

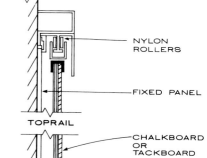

CHALKRAIL   SECTION B

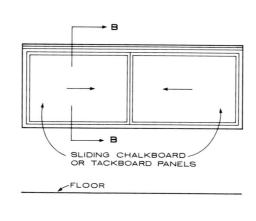

HORIZONTAL SLIDING PANELS

SILL   HEAD

BULLETIN BOARD

SLIDING CHALKBOARDS AND TACKBOARDS

NOTES

1. Compartment types: ceiling hung (marble or metal), overhead braced, wall hung (metal only).
2. Metal finishes: baked-on enamel, porcelain enamel, stainless steel. Phenolic core, plastic laminate, solid polyethylene, tempered glass, and marble panels also are available.
3. A = standard compartment widths: 2 ft. 6 in., 2 ft. 8 in., 2 ft. 10 in., 3 ft. 0 in. (2 ft. 10 in. is used most frequently).
4. B = standard door widths: 1 ft. 8 in., 1 ft. 10 in., 2 ft. 0 in., 2 ft. 2 in., 2 ft. 4 in., 2 ft. 6 in. (2 ft. 0 in. metal doors are standard with marble compartments). Non-standard sizes that sometimes are used: 1 ft. 11 in., 2 ft. 3 in., 2 ft. 5 in.
5. C = standard pilaster widths: 3 in., 4 in., 5 in., 6 in., 8 in., 10 in., 1 ft. 0 in. Nonstandard sizes that sometimes are used: 2 in., 7 in., 1 ft. 2 in.
6. D = standard panel widths: 18 in. to 57 in. in 1 in. increments. All panels are 58 in. high.
7. Wall hung models apply only to metal partitions.
8. Accessories include such items as paper holders, coat hooks, and purse shelves.

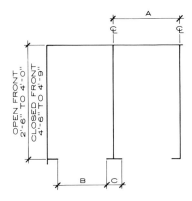

PLAN OF STANDARD W.C. COMPARTMENT (TYPICAL FOR METAL OR PLASTIC LAMINATE)

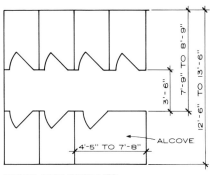

SPACE REQUIREMENTS

GENERAL PLANNING DATA

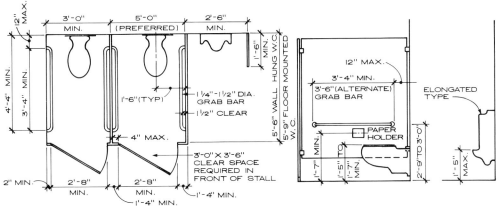

PLAN   SECTION   SECTION AT URINAL   FRONT ELEVATION

HANDICAPPED TOILET LAYOUT

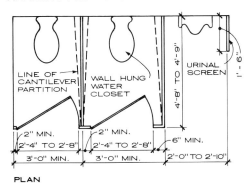

PLAN

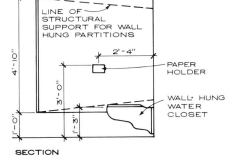

SECTION

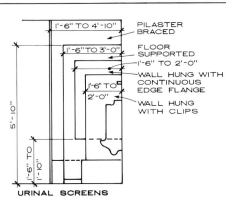

URINAL SCREENS

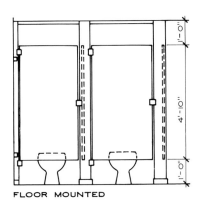

FLOOR MOUNTED

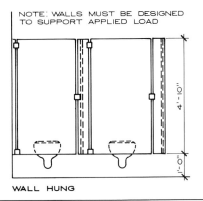

WALL HUNG

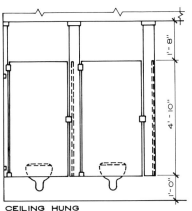

CEILING HUNG

METAL AND PLASTIC LAMINATE TOILET PARTITIONS

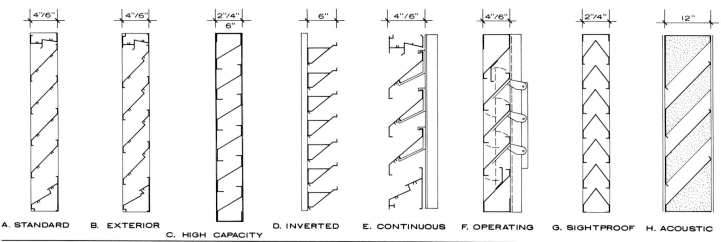

A. STANDARD   B. EXTERIOR
C. HIGH CAPACITY   D. INVERTED   E. CONTINUOUS   F. OPERATING   G. SIGHTPROOF   H. ACOUSTIC

TYPICAL LOUVER AND VENT PROFILES

A. For use in single louver application in small openings or in multiple louver applications where vertical mullion or horizontal joint appearance is desired.

B. Exterior blades provide superior weather protection but reduce free area.
Maximum standard width is 6 ft; minimum width is 1 ft.

C. Used in situations where high velocity and maximum free area are of primary importance.

D. Used primarily as a cooling tower screen where water spray should be contained. They are field assembled and are available in unlimited widths.

E. Used for large openings where continuous horizontal line appearance is desired. Unlimited widths are available; they are field assembled.

F. This permits maximum ventilation capacity when open as well as resistance against weather penetration when closed. Airflow is easily controlled. Recommended maximum blade span is 5 ft; minimum width is 1 ft.

G. This is 100% sightproof from all angles with horizontal blade lines. Maximum recommended width is 7 ft.

H. Used to reduce ambient noise and noise transmission. Blades are backed with mineral fiber. Maximum recommended blade span is 7 ft.

J. "V" BLADE   K. PIVOTED DOOR LOUVER   L. VERTICAL LINE

J. Used for soffit, vertical, continuous horizontal, or sightproof louvers. Blades are field assembled to any desired length or width. They must have horizontal supports at 5 ft maximum.

K. Vertically pivoted intake device provides large volumes of air. It may be individually or gang operated. Units are 24 in. wide and maximum height is 8 ft 5 in.

L. Vertical louver matches standard exterior metal building panel profiles. Maximum recommended blade width is 16 ft; additional length is lapped.

M. Vents for use in foundations, chimney flues, or crawl spaces are made from cast or extruded aluminum and are available with anodic, baked enamel, lacquer, or sandblasted finish. They are made to be compatible with standard, modular, speed, or fuel brick sizes in 4, 6, or 8 in. depths and in lengths to 20 ft.

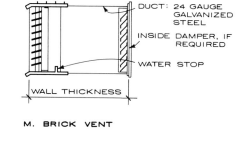

M. BRICK VENT

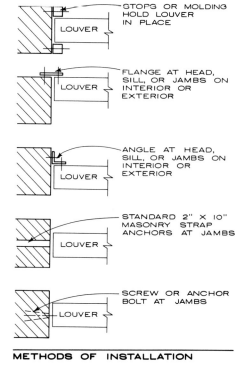

METHODS OF INSTALLATION

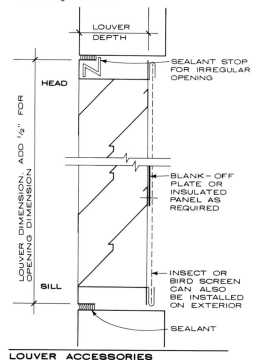

LOUVER ACCESSORIES

GENERAL NOTES

1. The dimensions shown are the most common; others are available.

2. Horizontal louvers can be of unlimited height. Larger louver depths provide more free area per square foot and better weather penetration resistance than smaller depths.

3. Standard materials are 16 gauge galvanized or cold rolled steel and 14 or 12 gauge extruded aluminum alloy. Other metals can be used for special applications. Translucent fiberglass is also a standard blade material where daylighting is desirable.

4. A welded assembly of louvers is preferred to mechanical assembly. This eliminates blade/frame loosening, wear, and vibration noise, as well as providing a better assembly for finishing.

5. Factory finishing is recommended for maximum control of color and durability. The finish for steel louvers is baked enamel in a variety of colors. Aluminum finishes include mill, clear lacquer, baked enamel, and anodic.

6. Screens may be used for protection from insects, birds, or vandalism. Supplied in frames, typical screening for insects is 16 x 18 mesh aluminum or fiberglass; for birds or vandalism 1/2 in. square mesh 14 or 16 gauge aluminum or 1/4 in. square mesh 16 or 18 gauge aluminum.

7. Other options available with louvers include mullions, blank-off plates or insulated panels, frame extensions, sill pieces, sealant stops, and fusible links.

Graham Davidson, Architect; Washington, D.C.

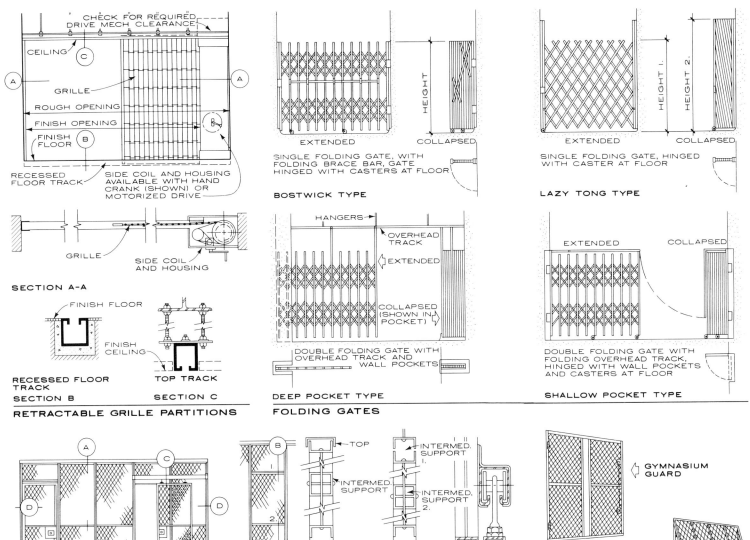

SINGLE FOLDING GATE, WITH FOLDING BRACE BAR, GATE HINGED WITH CASTERS AT FLOOR

BOSTWICK TYPE

SINGLE FOLDING GATE, HINGED WITH CASTER AT FLOOR

LAZY TONG TYPE

SECTION A-A

RECESSED FLOOR TRACK
SECTION B

TOP TRACK
SECTION C

RETRACTABLE GRILLE PARTITIONS

DOUBLE FOLDING GATE WITH OVERHEAD TRACK AND WALL POCKETS

DEEP POCKET TYPE

DOUBLE FOLDING GATE WITH FOLDING OVERHEAD TRACK, HINGED WITH WALL POCKETS AND CASTERS AT FLOOR

SHALLOW POCKET TYPE

FOLDING GATES

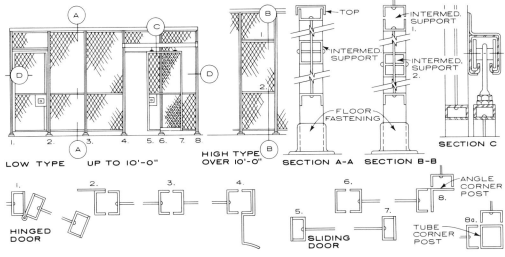

LOW TYPE   UP TO 10'-0"

HIGH TYPE OVER 10'-0"

SECTION A-A   SECTION B-B

SECTION C

HINGED DOOR

SLIDING DOOR

SECTION D-D

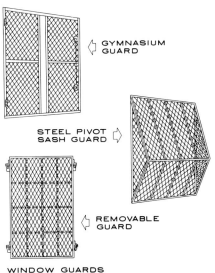

GYMNASIUM GUARD

STEEL PIVOT SASH GUARD

REMOVABLE GUARD

WINDOW GUARDS

RECOMMENDED USES FOR WIRE MESH PARTITIONS

MESH	PATTERN	WIRE SIZE	FRAMES	USES
1 1/4″	◇ ☐	11	1″ [	Animal cages
1 1/2″	◇	10	1″ [	Elevator shafts
1 3/4″	◇	9	1 1/4″ [	Fire escapes
2″	◇	8	1 1/2″ [	Cashier cages
2″	◇	6	1 1/4″ "C"	Runways
			Channel 3/4″ [	Stair enclosures Locker rooms Departmental divisions Stock rooms Tool rooms

OTHER USES FOR WOVEN WIRE MESH

MESH	PATTERN	WIRE SIZE	FRAMES	USES
3/4″	◇ ☐	12	5/16″ ○ 3/4″ [1″ L	Air intake screens Bird screens
1″	◇ ☐	12	3/8″ ○ 1″ [1″ L	Basement window guards Shelves and trays Skylight guards
1 1/2″	◇ ☐		3/8″ ○ 1″ [	Door and window guards
2 1/4″	◇ ☐	7	7/16″ ○	Wire roof signs
2 1/2″	◇	6	1 1/2″ [	Fencing gratings

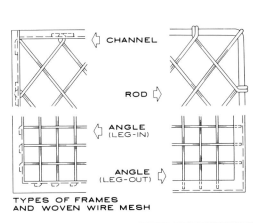

CHANNEL

ROD

ANGLE (LEG-IN)

ANGLE (LEG-OUT)

TYPES OF FRAMES AND WOVEN WIRE MESH

WIRE MESH PARTITIONS

Harnish, Morgan & Causey, Architects; Ontario, California

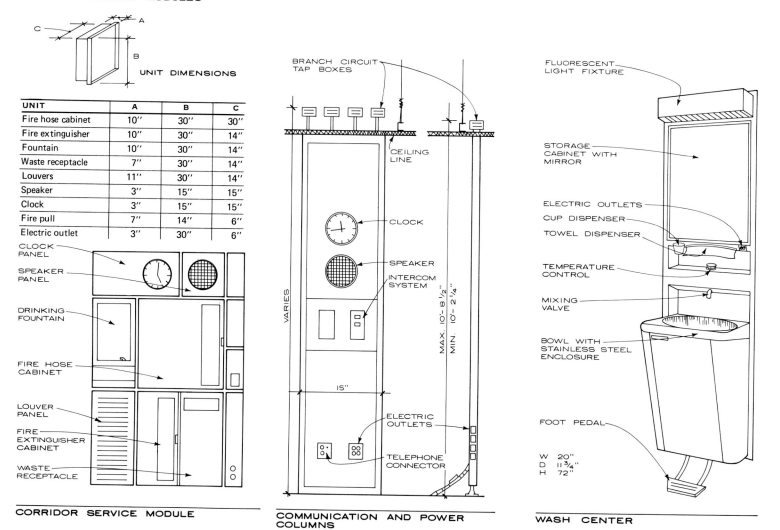

TIME LAPSE CLOCK

GENERAL EXAMINATION OVERHEAD LIGHT

RECESSED MONITOR STORAGE

REMOVABLE PANELS

CABINETS

SPHYGMOMANOMETER

ARM WRAP CLIP

STORAGE

SHELVES

PORTABLE X-RAY 208V OUTLET

BED BUMPER

CONSOLE CONTAINS AIR OUTLETS, OXYGEN OUTLETS, VACUUM OUTLETS, ELECTRIC CURTAIN, CONTROL SWITCH, DUPLEX 110V OUTLETS, NIGHT LIGHT, EXAMINATION DIMMER

RECESSED VACUUM STORAGE UNIT

INTENSIVE CARE UNIT

VARIES

NURSES' CALL SYSTEM

SPEAKER UNITS

RETRACTABLE EXAMINATION LIGHTS

TWO-BED UNIT

HOSPITAL SERVICE MODULES

UNIT DIMENSIONS

UNIT	A	B	C
Fire hose cabinet	10''	30''	30''
Fire extinguisher	10''	30''	14''
Fountain	10''	30''	14''
Waste receptacle	7''	30''	14''
Louvers	11''	30''	14''
Speaker	3''	15''	15''
Clock	3''	15''	15''
Fire pull	7''	14''	6''
Electric outlet	3''	30''	6''

CLOCK PANEL

SPEAKER PANEL

DRINKING FOUNTAIN

FIRE HOSE CABINET

LOUVER PANEL

FIRE EXTINGUISHER CABINET

WASTE RECEPTACLE

CORRIDOR SERVICE MODULE

BRANCH CIRCUIT TAP BOXES

CEILING LINE

CLOCK

SPEAKER

INTERCOM SYSTEM

VARIES

MAX. 10'-8½'' MIN. 10'-2¼''

15''

ELECTRIC OUTLETS

TELEPHONE CONNECTOR

COMMUNICATION AND POWER COLUMNS

FLUORESCENT LIGHT FIXTURE

STORAGE CABINET WITH MIRROR

ELECTRIC OUTLETS

CUP DISPENSER

TOWEL DISPENSER

TEMPERATURE CONTROL

MIXING VALVE

BOWL WITH STAINLESS STEEL ENCLOSURE

FOOT PEDAL

W 20''
D 11¾''
H 72''

WASH CENTER

John Sava; The Architects Collaborative, Inc.; Cambridge, Massachusetts

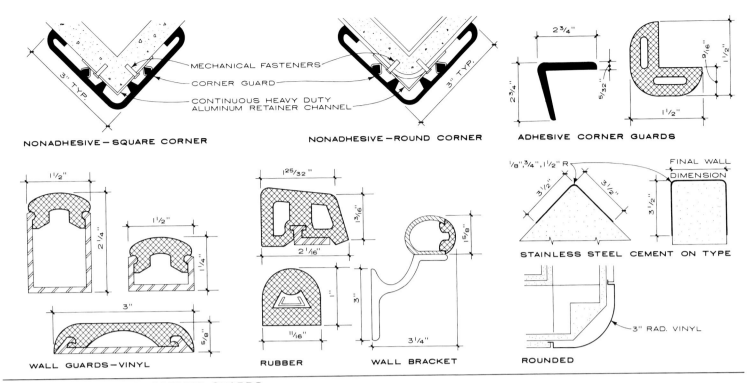

NONADHESIVE—SQUARE CORNER

MECHANICAL FASTENERS
CORNER GUARD
CONTINUOUS HEAVY DUTY
ALUMINUM RETAINER CHANNEL

NONADHESIVE—ROUND CORNER

ADHESIVE CORNER GUARDS

WALL GUARDS—VINYL

RUBBER

WALL BRACKET

STAINLESS STEEL CEMENT ON TYPE

FINAL WALL DIMENSION

ROUNDED

INTERIOR WALL AND CORNER GUARDS

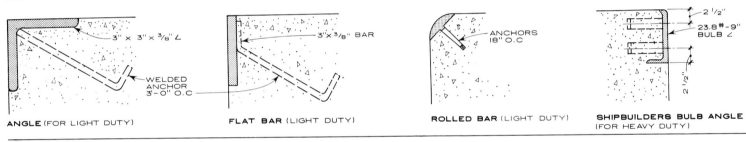

ANGLE (FOR LIGHT DUTY)

FLAT BAR (LIGHT DUTY)

ROLLED BAR (LIGHT DUTY)

SHIPBUILDERS BULB ANGLE (FOR HEAVY DUTY)

CURB GUARDS

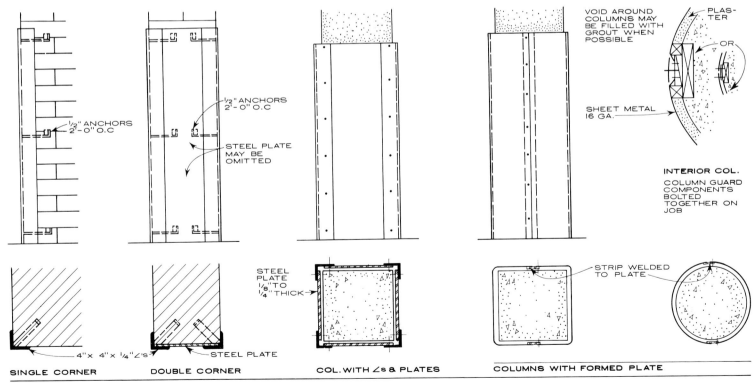

SINGLE CORNER

DOUBLE CORNER

COL. WITH ∠s & PLATES

COLUMNS WITH FORMED PLATE

INTERIOR COL.

COLUMN GUARD COMPONENTS BOLTED TOGETHER ON JOB

CORNER AND COLUMN GUARDS

John Sava; The Architects Collaborative, Inc.; Cambridge, Massachusetts
Vicente Cordero, AIA; Arlington, Virginia

WALL AND CORNER GUARDS

10

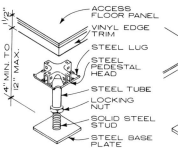

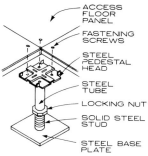

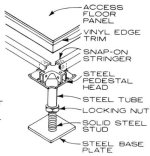

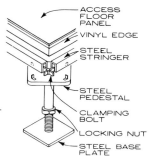

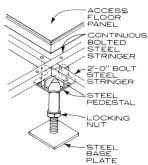

STRINGERLESS

This system is used in general construction or small computer rooms. It provides maximum accessibility, optimum underfloor space, and electrical continuity. Note that it is dependent on panels being restrained by perimeter walls. Maximum load: 150 psf. Concentrated load: 400 lb.

PANEL LOCK

This system is used in general construction and is designed without a stringer connection at the edge. Bolted at the corner, it provides added rigidity over stringerless systems and maximum access and flexibility.

SNAP-ON-GRID

This system is used in computer rooms and in general construction where frequent access is required. It provides improved lateral stability when compared to stringerless systems, electrical continuity, and plenum seal.

CLAMPED STRINGER

This system is used in computer rooms and provides high lateral stability, complete access to the below-floor cavity, electrical continuity for grounding, and static control. The system's contact between panel edge and stringer provides a plenum seal.

RIGID GRID

This system is used in computer rooms and areas of heavy loading. It provides maximum rigidity for seismic or dynamic loading, electrical continuity for grounding or static control, and plenum seal. Maximum load: 400 psf. Concentrated load: 1250 lb.

TYPES OF SUPPORT SYSTEMS – LEAST STABLE TO MOST STABLE

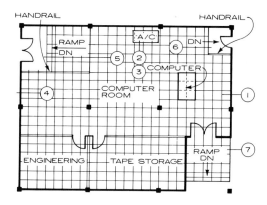

TYPICAL COMPUTER ROOM PLAN

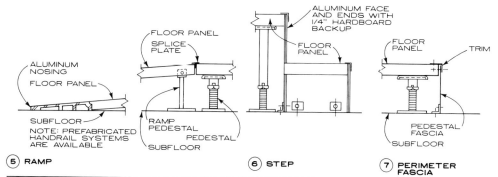

TYPICAL ACCESS FLOOR CONDITIONS

COMPUTER ROOMS

Computers place high demands on electrical, mechanical and floor systems. The floor surface must be conductive and grounded to avoid static electricity and dust accumulation. An automatic fire detection system should be installed in below-floor plenums. Plenums may not exceed 10,000 sq. ft., and they must be divided by noncombustible bulkheads. Computer rooms should be separated from all other occupancies within buildings by fire-resistant walls, floors, and ceilings with a resistance rating of not less than 1 hour. Structural floors beneath access floors should provide for water drainage to reduce damage to computer systems. All access floor openings should be protected from debris. Computer rooms require precision temperature and humidity control. Package air-conditioning units suitable for computer rooms can supply air within a tolerance of ± 1.5° and ± 5% humidity.

Computer room heat gains often are concentrated. For minimum room temperature gradients, supply air distribution should match closely the load distribution. The distribution system should be flexible enough to accommodate location changes and heat gain with minimum change in the basic distribution system. Supply air systems require about 74 litres per second per kilowatt of cooling to satisfy computer room conditions. This provides enough air change rate for even air temperature distribution. Packaged air-conditioning systems using the underfloor air supply plenum should supply the large computer area adequately. The zoning area is controlled by various floor registers and perforated floor panels.

Setter, Leach and Lindstrom, Inc.; Minneapolis, Minnesota

ACCESS FLOORS

Access floor systems are used in business offices, hospitals, laboratories, open area schools, television systems, computer rooms, and telephone-communication centers. They provide mechanical and electrical accessibility and flexibility in placing desks, telephone services, machines, and general office equipment. Equipment can be moved and reconnected quickly. Raised access floors in large areas offer maximum flexibility for future change. They also can be used in a recessed structural floor area.

Reinforced steel panels, aluminum, steel-encased wood core, and cementitious fill are available with finish surfaces of vinyl tile, plastic laminate, and carpet. Basic panel sizes are 24 in. x 24 in. Panel systems rely on gravity-held connections, but they can be held mechanically, increasing rigidity. Wraparound, butt, and protective plastic edge carpet systems are available; some are available with Class A flame-spread ratings. Panels are available in structural grades ranging from general office to light industrial construction.

Using modular wiring increases installation speed and simplifies panel variation. Space beneath floors can be used as an air-conditioning plenum. Special panels provide perforation for air distribution, cable slots, and sound and thermal insulation. Various support systems can be provided in steel. Possible difficulties encountered with access floor systems are restricted minimal floor heights and structural integrity of older buildings. Wet washing techniques cannot be used, and poor placement of exceedingly heavy loads can damage floor systems.

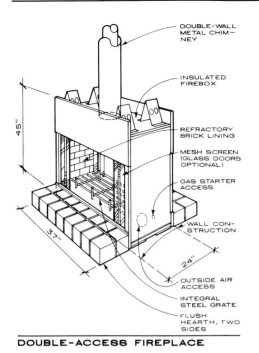

DOUBLE-ACCESS FIREPLACE

Labels: DOUBLE-WALL METAL CHIMNEY; INSULATED FIREBOX; REFRACTORY BRICK LINING; MESH SCREEN (GLASS DOORS OPTIONAL); GAS STARTER ACCESS; WALL CONSTRUCTION; OUTSIDE AIR ACCESS; INTEGRAL STEEL GRATE; FLUSH HEARTH, TWO SIDES; 45"; 37"; 24"

CORNER FIREPLACE

Labels: DOUBLE-WALL METAL CHIMNEY; OUTSIDE AIR ACCESS; GAS STARTER ACCESS; INSULATED FIREBOX; REFRACTORY BRICK LINING; MESH SCREEN (GLASS DOORS OPTIONAL); INTEGRAL STEEL GRATE; FLUSH HEARTH, TWO SIDES; 41½"; 37"; 22"

GENERAL NOTES

1. Verify local/state codes for maximum and minimum chimney height clearances above roof deck.
2. Chimney pipe requires a 2-in. clearance to combustible surfaces. In a multichase installation, chimney pipes should be 20 in. apart, center to center. Chase top must be constructed of noncombustible material.
3. See manufacturer's specifications for chimney joint band and stabilizer locations.
4. Fire-stop spacer must be used whenever a ceiling, floor, or sidewall is penetrated.
5. No special floor support is usually necessary for prefabricated fireplaces; however, local/state codes should be checked to determine exact requirements.
6. Facing material must not obstruct louvered or screened area at sides, top, or bottom of fireplace opening; however, noncombustible finishing material may be used over the black metal on fireplace fronts. See manufacturer's specifications.
7. Inadequate ventilation can occur from air conditioning, heating, or other mechanical systems that generate negative air pressures in the fireplace room. Plan for proper ventilation to ensure smoke-free operation.
8. There is no minimum or maximum horizontal distance for outside air access line.
9. A noncombustible hearth extension must extend at least 8 in. on either side of firebox openings and 16–20 in. in front of firebox.
10. Distances from combustible walls perpendicular to the front of the fireplace—including mantles—vary. Consult manufacturer's specifications.
11. Outlet grilles must be at least 10 in. below ceiling for ducted heat-circulating fireplace.
12. Room furnishings such as drapes, curtains, and chairs must be at least 4 ft 0 in. from firebox opening.

HEAT-CIRCULATING FIREPLACE

Labels: DOUBLE-WALL METAL CHIMNEY; HEATED AIR RETURN; EXTERNAL DAMPER CONTROL; INSULATED FIREBOX; REFRACTORY BRICK LINING; MESH SCREEN (OPTIONAL GLASS DOORS); INTEGRAL TIP-UP GRATE; GAS STARTER ACCESS; OUTSIDE AIR ACCESS; ROOM AIR ENTRY WITH OPTIONAL FANS; HEARTH; 41½"; 48½"; 24"

DUCTED HEAT-CIRCULATING FIREPLACE

Labels: DOUBLE-WALL METAL CHIMNEY; HEATED AIR RETURN—TWIN DUCTS; HEATED AIR RETURN; INSULATED FIREBOX; EXTERNAL DAMPER CONTROL; REFRACTORY BRICK LINING; MESH SCREEN (OPTIONAL GLASS DOORS); GAS STARTER ACCESS; OUTSIDE AIR ACCESS; ROOM AIR ENTRY WITH OPTIONAL FANS; INTEGRAL TIP-UP GRATE; FLUSH HEARTH; 38½"; 46"; 24½"

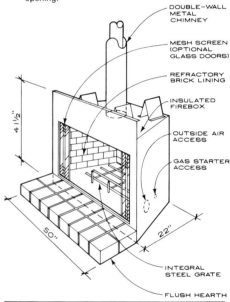

TRADITIONAL FIREPLACE

Labels: DOUBLE-WALL METAL CHIMNEY; MESH SCREEN (OPTIONAL GLASS DOORS); REFRACTORY BRICK LINING; INSULATED FIREBOX; OUTSIDE AIR ACCESS; GAS STARTER ACCESS; INTEGRAL STEEL GRATE; FLUSH HEARTH; 41½"; 50"; 22"

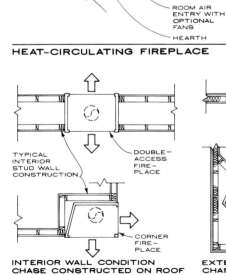

INTERIOR WALL CONDITION CHASE CONSTRUCTED ON ROOF

Labels: TYPICAL INTERIOR STUD WALL CONSTRUCTION; DOUBLE-ACCESS FIREPLACE; CORNER FIREPLACE

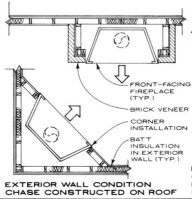

EXTERIOR WALL CONDITION CHASE CONSTRUCTED ON ROOF

Labels: FRONT-FACING FIREPLACE (TYP.); BRICK VENEER; CORNER INSTALLATION; BATT INSULATION IN EXTERIOR WALL (TYP.)

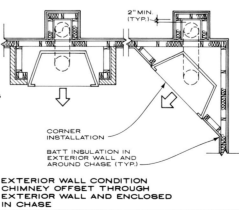

EXTERIOR WALL CONDITION CHIMNEY OFFSET THROUGH EXTERIOR WALL AND ENCLOSED IN CHASE

Labels: 2" MIN. (TYP.); CORNER INSTALLATION; BATT INSULATION IN EXTERIOR WALL AND AROUND CHASE (TYP.)

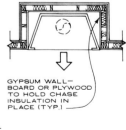

EXTERIOR WALL CONDITION FIREPLACE AND CHIMNEY ENCLOSED IN CHASE

Labels: GYPSUM WALLBOARD OR PLYWOOD TO HOLD CHASE INSULATION IN PLACE (TYP.)

INSTALLATION CONDITIONS FOR PREFABRICATED FIREPLACES

Richard J. Vitullo; Washington Grove, Maryland

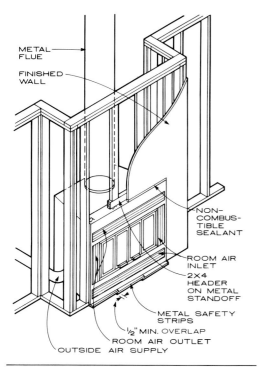

- METAL FLUE
- FINISHED WALL
- NON-COMBUSTIBLE SEALANT
- ROOM AIR INLET
- 2×4 HEADER ON METAL STANDOFF
- METAL SAFETY STRIPS
- 1/2" MIN. OVERLAP
- ROOM AIR OUTLET
- OUTSIDE AIR SUPPLY

HEAT CIRCULATING FIREPLACE

Specially constructed steel fireplaces must be properly enclosed in masonry to obtain a complete wood burning unit. When placed on a firebrick hearth, a steel fireplace includes all essential combustion and smoke handling spaces. A circulator provides a heat transfer chamber with inlets and outlets that draw in cool air, heat it, and expel warm air by natural convection. The air heating cycle can be augmented with electric fans in the intakes (not in the outlets). A steel shell provides a form for the masonry enclosure, but it is not a structural element. Enclosing masonry must be held at least 1/2 in. away from the shell to allow for expansion and contraction in the metal. The 1/2 in. space is taken up with fireproof insulation that covers the entire circulator. The fireplace rear wall should be at least 8 in. thick if exposed to the exterior. Placing the fireplace within the exterior stud wall gives better thermal insulation in exchange for some lost indoor floor space.

Steel circulatory fireplaces are manufactured in various sizes with proportions set for proper burning action and air heating. An incorrect flue size may negate the fireplace design. The flue must be independently supported.

NOTES

Circulator must be entirely wrapped in insulation to control heat and to help space the masonry away from the steel shell.

1. Some manufacturers recommend using a chimney cap with a heat-circulating fireplace.
2. Check local codes for minimum clearance requirements to combustible materials such as walls and mantles.

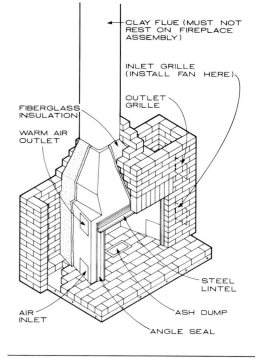

- CLAY FLUE (MUST NOT REST ON FIREPLACE ASSEMBLY)
- INLET GRILLE (INSTALL FAN HERE)
- OUTLET GRILLE
- FIBERGLASS INSULATION
- WARM AIR OUTLET
- STEEL LINTEL
- ASH DUMP
- ANGLE SEAL
- AIR INLET

HEAT CIRCULATING FIREPLACE SET IN STUD WALL

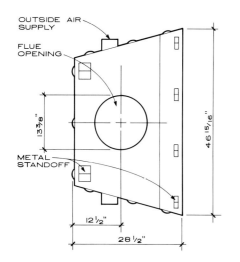

- OUTSIDE AIR SUPPLY
- FLUE OPENING
- METAL STANDOFF
- 13 3/8"
- 46 15/16"
- 12 1/2"
- 28 1/2"

PLAN

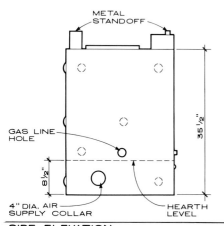

- METAL STANDOFF
- GAS LINE HOLE
- 35 1/2"
- 8 1/2"
- 4" DIA. AIR SUPPLY COLLAR
- HEARTH LEVEL

SIDE ELEVATION

Timothy B. McDonald; Washington, D.C.

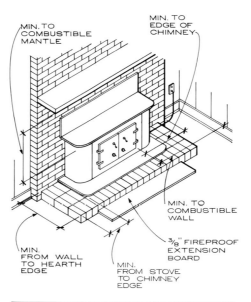

- MIN. TO COMBUSTIBLE MANTLE
- MIN. TO EDGE OF CHIMNEY
- MIN. TO COMBUSTIBLE WALL
- 3/8" FIREPROOF EXTENSION BOARD
- MIN. FROM WALL TO HEARTH EDGE
- MIN. FROM STOVE TO CHIMNEY EDGE

HEAT CIRCULATING FIREPLACE

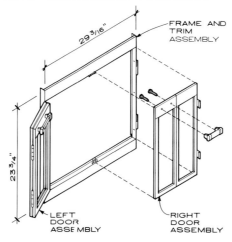

- 29 3/16"
- FRAME AND TRIM ASSEMBLY
- 23 3/4"
- LEFT DOOR ASSEMBLY
- RIGHT DOOR ASSEMBLY

FIREPLACE DOOR ASSEMBLY

HEAT CIRCULATING FIREPLACE SET IN MASONRY

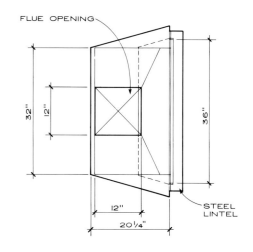

- FLUE OPENING
- 32"
- 12"
- 36"
- 12"
- 20 1/4"
- STEEL LINTEL

PLAN

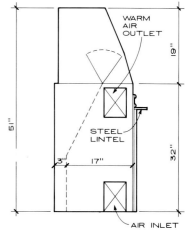

- WARM AIR OUTLET
- 19"
- STEEL LINTEL
- 51"
- 32"
- 3"
- 17"
- AIR INLET

SIDE ELEVATION

10   **FIREPLACES AND STOVES**

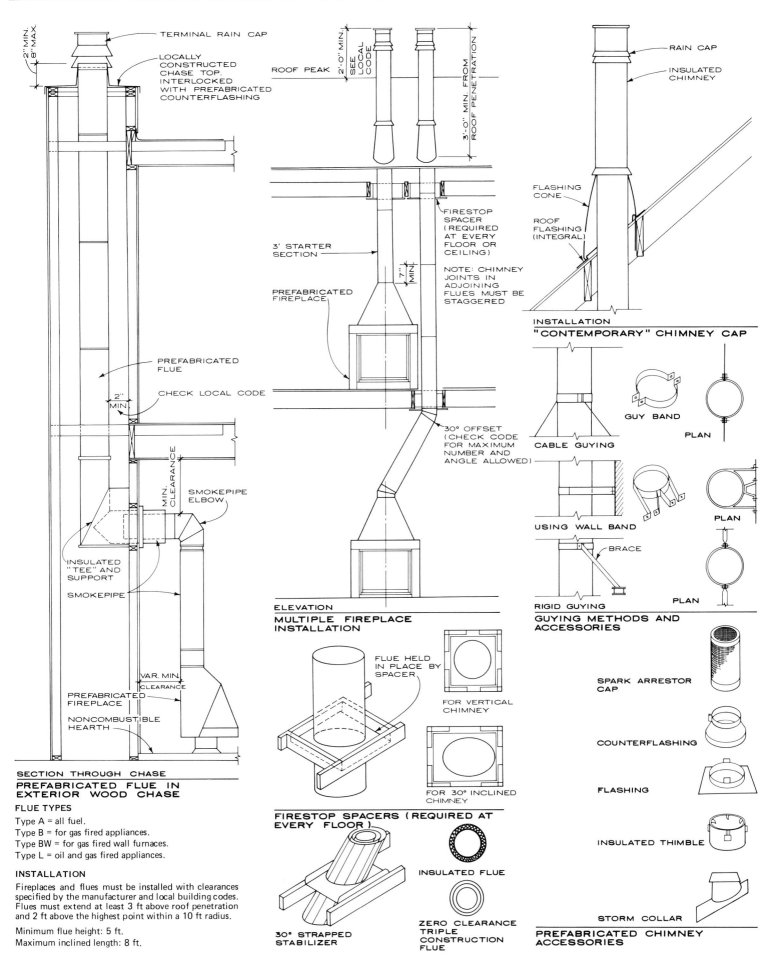

TERMINAL RAIN CAP

2" MIN. 8" MAX.

LOCALLY CONSTRUCTED CHASE TOP. INTERLOCKED WITH PREFABRICATED COUNTERFLASHING

PREFABRICATED FLUE

CHECK LOCAL CODE

2" MIN.

MIN. CLEARANCE

SMOKEPIPE ELBOW

INSULATED "TEE" AND SUPPORT

SMOKEPIPE

VAR. MIN. CLEARANCE

PREFABRICATED FIREPLACE

NONCOMBUSTIBLE HEARTH

SECTION THROUGH CHASE

PREFABRICATED FLUE IN EXTERIOR WOOD CHASE

FLUE TYPES

Type A = all fuel.
Type B = for gas fired appliances.
Type BW = for gas fired wall furnaces.
Type L = oil and gas fired appliances.

INSTALLATION

Fireplaces and flues must be installed with clearances specified by the manufacturer and local building codes. Flues must extend at least 3 ft above roof penetration and 2 ft above the highest point within a 10 ft radius.

Minimum flue height: 5 ft.
Maximum inclined length: 8 ft.

Olga Barmine; Darrel Downing Rippeteau, Architect; Washington, D.C.

ROOF PEAK

2'-0" MIN. SEE LOCAL CODE

3'-0" MIN. FROM ROOF PENETRATION

FIRESTOP SPACER (REQUIRED AT EVERY FLOOR OR CEILING)

NOTE: CHIMNEY JOINTS IN ADJOINING FLUES MUST BE STAGGERED

3' STARTER SECTION

7" MIN.

PREFABRICATED FIREPLACE

30° OFFSET (CHECK CODE FOR MAXIMUM NUMBER AND ANGLE ALLOWED)

ELEVATION

MULTIPLE FIREPLACE INSTALLATION

FLUE HELD IN PLACE BY SPACER

FOR VERTICAL CHIMNEY

FOR 30° INCLINED CHIMNEY

FIRESTOP SPACERS (REQUIRED AT EVERY FLOOR)

30° STRAPPED STABILIZER

INSULATED FLUE

ZERO CLEARANCE TRIPLE CONSTRUCTION FLUE

RAIN CAP

INSULATED CHIMNEY

FLASHING CONE

ROOF FLASHING (INTEGRAL)

INSTALLATION
"CONTEMPORARY" CHIMNEY CAP

CABLE GUYING

GUY BAND

PLAN

USING WALL BAND

PLAN

BRACE

RIGID GUYING

PLAN

GUYING METHODS AND ACCESSORIES

SPARK ARRESTOR CAP

COUNTERFLASHING

FLASHING

INSULATED THIMBLE

STORM COLLAR

PREFABRICATED CHIMNEY ACCESSORIES

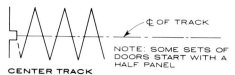

CENTER TRACK

Center track—supported at either the floor or ceiling. Panels are connected to each other and are either manually or power operated.

⊄ OF TRACK

NOTE: SOME SETS OF DOORS START WITH A HALF PANEL

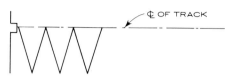

EDGE TRACK

Edge track—supported at either the floor or ceiling. Panels are connected to each other and are either manually or power operated.

⊄ OF TRACK

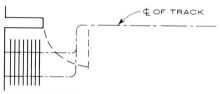

STACKING POCKET

Ceiling suspended, unconnected panels, manually operated only.

⊄ OF TRACK

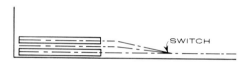

SWITCH

STACKING WITH SWITCHES

LARGE PANEL FOLDING PARTITIONS

SUPPORT

ADJUSTABLE SPACERS SECURED TO SUPPORT

TRACK

DOOR CARRIER

SOUND BAFFLE (OPT)

CEILING

STEEL OR WOOD SOFFIT

TOP SEAL

PANEL

HEAD

RETRACT-ABLE BOTTOM SEAL

FINISHED FLOOR

FIXED SEAL

SILL TYPES

TOP HUNG

BLOCKING AS REQUIRED FOR SUPPORT

CHANNEL TRACK

SOUND SEAL (OPTIONAL)

LINE OF FINISHED CEILING FOR CONCEALED INSTALLATION (CEILING HEIGHT MAY VARY)

HEAD

ADJUSTABLE ROLLERS

GUIDE

STEEL TRACK

STEEL PLATE SECURED FIRMLY

FELT SWEEP STRIPS (OPTIONAL)

FINISHED FLOOR

SILL

FLOOR—SUPPORTED

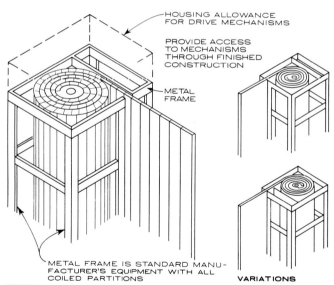

HOUSING ALLOWANCE FOR DRIVE MECHANISMS

PROVIDE ACCESS TO MECHANISMS THROUGH FINISHED CONSTRUCTION

METAL FRAME

METAL FRAME IS STANDARD MANU-FACTURER'S EQUIPMENT WITH ALL COILED PARTITIONS

VARIATIONS

COILED FOLDING PARTITIONS

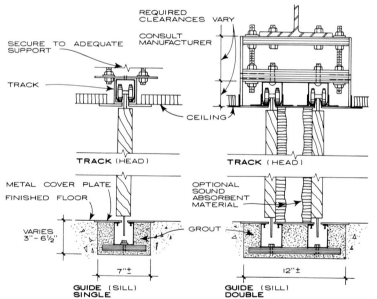

REQUIRED CLEARANCES VARY CONSULT MANUFACTURER

SECURE TO ADEQUATE SUPPORT

TRACK

CEILING

TRACK (HEAD)

TRACK (HEAD)

METAL COVER PLATE

FINISHED FLOOR

VARIES 3"–6½"

OPTIONAL SOUND ABSORBENT MATERIAL

GROUT

7"±

12"±

GUIDE (SILL) SINGLE

GUIDE (SILL) DOUBLE

SECTIONS

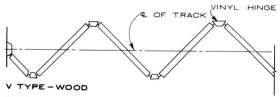

⊄ OF TRACK

VINYL HINGE

V TYPE – WOOD

"V" Type door is available in metal with fabric covering or in solid wood panels.

TYPICAL ACCORDION PARTITIONS

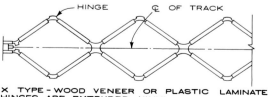

HINGE

⊄ OF TRACK

X TYPE – WOOD VENEER OR PLASTIC LAMINATE HINGES ARE EXTRUDED VINYL

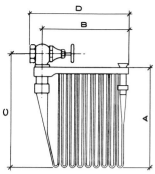

SWING RACK SEMIAUTOMATIC
1½" LINED HOSE

HOSE CAPACITY	25	50	75	100
A	10"	20"	24"	27"
B	15"	16"	19"	20"
C	14"	23"	27"	32"
D	17"	18"	20"	22"
WIDTH	4"	4"	4"	4"

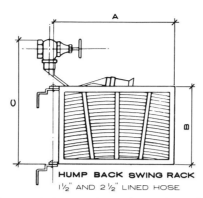

HUMP BACK SWING RACK
1½" AND 2½" LINED HOSE

HOSE CAPACITY	50	100	150	200
A	30"	30"	34"	40"
B	17"	21"	28"	39"
C	30"	33"	40"	50"
WIDTH 1½" HOSE	4"	4"	4"	4"
WIDTH 2½" HOSE	6"	6"	6"	6"

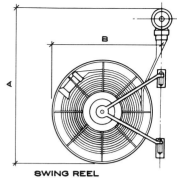

SWING REEL
1½" AND 2½" LINED HOSE

HOSE CAPACITY	50	100	150
A	38"	38"	36"
B	21"	27"	31"
WIDTH 1½" HOSE	4"	4"	4"
WIDTH 2½" HOSE	6"	6"	6"

FIRE HOSE RACK AND REELS

NOTE

Recommended hose size for use with building stand-pipes should not exceed 1½ in. in diameter and 100 ft in length. A larger hose used by amateurs is likely to tangle, cause excessive water damage, and create injuries.

A connection for 2½ in. hose should be available to each station for the use of firemen. Many codes require 2½ in. outlets at all standpipes.

By using a reducing coupling 1½ in. hose can be attached. When a 2½ in. stream is required the coupling may be removed. Industrial installations use 2½ in. hoses and train personnel in the use of the heavier equipment. Valves may be located 5 ft 6 in. above floor (check local code).

Lined synthetic fiber plastic hose is recommended for use on standpipe installations. Cotton rubber lined hose is standard for fire department and heavy equipment hose.

Tables show rack and reels for 1½ and 2½ in. lined hose only. Consult manufacturer's literature for rack and reel dimensions when other types and sizes of hose are used.

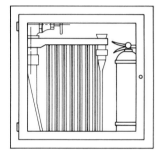

75' 1½" LINED HOSE, RACK, AND ANGLE VALVE; 2½ GAL EXTINGUISHER
2'-9" x 2'-9" x 8½" TO 2'-11" x 2'-11" x 9"

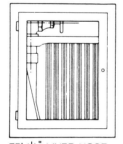

75' 1½" LINED HOSE, RACK, AND ANGLE VALVE
1'-9" x 2'-5" x 8" TO 1'-4" x 2'-7" x 8½"

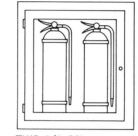

TWO 2½ GAL EXTINGUISHERS
1'-11"X2'-9"X7" TO 2'-2"X2'-11"X8"

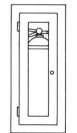

ONE 2½ GAL EXTINGUISHER
1'-0"X2'-6"X8" TO 1'-4"X2'-7"X8½"
NOTE: RESIDENTIAL EXTINGUISHER CABINET 1'-5"X7"X2"

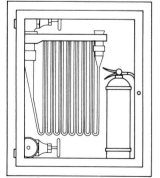

75' 1½" LINED HOSE AND RACK; 1½" AND 2½" ANGLE VALVE; 2½ GAL EXTINGUISHER
2'-9" x 3'-4" x 8½" TO 2'-10" x 3'-7" x 9"

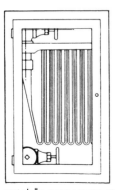

75' 1½" LINED HOSE AND RACK; 1½" AND 2½" ANGLE VALVE
1'-11" x 3'-3" x 8½" TO 2'-4" x 3'-4" x 9"

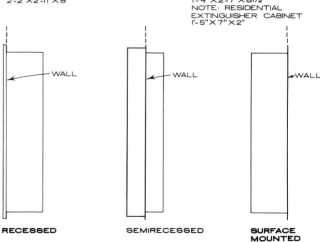

RECESSED   **SEMIRECESSED**   **SURFACE MOUNTED**

FIRE HOSE AND EXTINGUISHER CABINETS

NOTE

Cabinets are #18 gauge steel with glass doors as shown or with doors of metal, wood, mirror, and so on.

Consult manufacturer's literature for cabinets with special features such as revolving door, twin doors, pivoting door with attached extinguisher, and curved door.

Cabinets are obtainable for 25, 50, 75, and 100 ft hose racks. Rough dimensions are shown.

William G. Miner, AIA, Architect; Washington, D.C.

GENERAL NOTES

1. Construction of locker frame and door typically is of 16 gauge steel for sides and back. Top and bottom are typically 20 to 24 gauge steel. Finishes vary. Number plates, a shelf, and coat hooks on back and side walls are generally included. Other construction such as plastic laminate and wood is also used for club facilities.

2. Door types may be solid, perforated (all or part), or louvered (all or part), and ordered in a variety of steel mesh patterns or in special finishes. Doors and locks may be provided with noise-deadening de-vices. Locking mechanisms include built-in adjust-able combination lock, built-in flat or grooved key, and latching locker handle (for padlock use). All lock-ing mechanisms are available for surface or recessed applications.

3. Optional locker equipment includes sloping top for nonrecessed locations with corner miters available, 6 in. legs for open base installation, interior partitions (some models), multiple shelves, coat rods (for models over 18 in. deep), closed base and closed-end base for legs, and attachable bench elements.

4. Ventilation within locker spaces should provide 15 cu ft/min. air movement for locker.

5. Handicapped user access may suggest use of some multiple tier lockers; shelf and coat hooks on single tier lockers are out of reach of most handicapped.

6. Bench arrangements may be attached to locker front or may be freestanding and require a raised installa-tion. Finishes of lockers may be varied as conditions dictate such as stainless steel bottoms or sides when used in areas where long-term chemical contamina-tion may affect finishes.

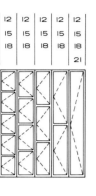
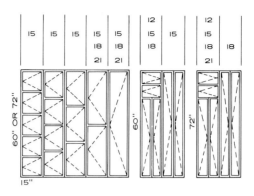
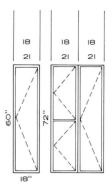
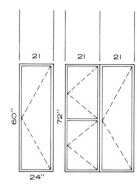

ELEVATIONS

LOCKERS

Checking lockers for heavy duty use are available in enameled steel or stainless steel. Locks are provided with built-in multiple coin selector, which is owner adjustable for coins, tokens, or "free" operation. They may be in-stalled on legs or recessed and may be made movable. Overall height is 6 ft 0 in. on most models, 5 ft 0 in. on some.

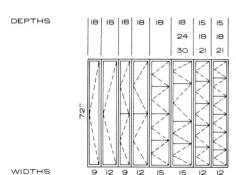

ELEVATION

CHECKING LOCKERS

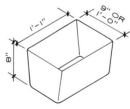

LOCKER SECTION

Basket racks may be arranged in single tier or back to back. Single tier depth is 1 ft 1¼ in. Optional pilfer guards may be installed on sides, top, and bottom, preventing access into adjacent baskets, and should be considered at the back as well. Basket materials include wire mesh (all surfaces), perforated steel ends and mesh sides and bottom, and louvered ends with perforated steel sides and bottom.

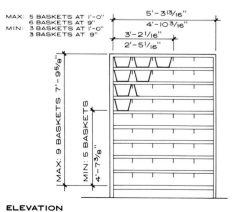

ELEVATION

BASKET RACKS

LOCKER BASKET

FILLER PIECE   **FLUSH WALL JOINT**

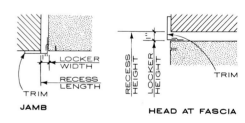

JAMB   **HEAD AT FASCIA**

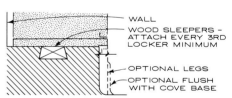

RECESSED/FLUSH BASE AT WALL

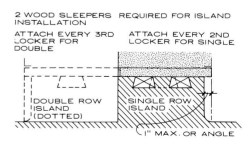

RECESSED/FLUSH BASE AT ISLAND

INSTALLATION DETAILS

Frederick C. Krenson, AIA; Rosser Fabrap International; Atlanta, Georgia

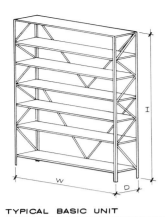

TYPICAL BASIC UNIT

AVAILABLE SIZES

W	D	H
24''	9''	3'-3''
30''	12''	6'-3''
36''	15''	7'-3''
42''	18''	8'-3''
48''	24''	10'-3''
	30''	
	36''	

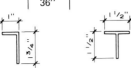

TYPICAL UPRIGHTS

CLASS 1 — STANDARD

CLASS 2 — REINFORCED

CLASS 3 — HEAVY DUTY

LOAD CAPACITY CLASSES

TYPICAL SHELF CAPACITIES

SHELF WIDTH	UNIFORM LOAD (LB)		
	CLASS 1	CLASS 2	CLASS 3
24''	900	1500	2000
30''	800	1300	1800
36''	700	1200	1500
42''	350	800	1200
48''	300	700	1000

NOTES
1. Shelving is available in two types. When bolted, the separate movable units are more permanent. When clipped, the shelving is continuous, but more easily set up and dismantled.
2. Shelves are adjustable at 1 in. increments.
3. Diagonal bracing may be eliminated when solid backs or ends are used.

SOLID SHELVING SYSTEM

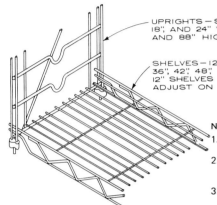

UPRIGHTS — STANDARD OR REINFORCED — 12'', 18'', AND 24'' WIDE AND 53'', 63'', 73'', AND 88'' HIGH

SHELVES — 12'' AND 18'' DEEP AND 24'', 30'', 36'', 42'', 48'', AND 60'' LONG. USE TWO 12'' SHELVES WITH 24'' UPRIGHTS. SHELVES ADJUST ON 5'' CENTERS

NOTES
1. Approved by National Sanitation Foundation for food storage.
2. Available accessories include corner braces, dividers, bottle shelves, back, and side ledges.
3. Finishes may be nickel plated, chrome, stainless steel, and brass.

FLOOR MOUNTED — ERECTA SHELVING

WIRE SHELVING SYSTEM — FOR FOOD AND RESIDENTIAL STORAGE — METROPOLITAN WIRE CORPORATION

VERTICAL MEMBERS ARE AVAILABLE IN 20'', 30'', 39'', AND 84'' HEIGHTS AND HAVE A DEPTH OF 11''

SHELVES AND OTHER COMPONENTS ARE 12'' DEEP AND 31'' WIDE. EACH SHELF CAN CARRY UP TO 200 LB OF DISTRIBUTED WEIGHT

OTHER COMPONENTS AVAILABLE INCLUDE DROP — LEAF CABINETS, MAGAZINE RACKS, AND RECORD STORAGE UNIT

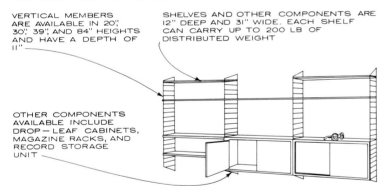

WALL MOUNTED — EUROWALL 73 STORAGE SYSTEM

METAL AND WOOD SHELVING SYSTEM ARCHITECTURAL SUPPLEMENTS INCORPORATED

OTHER CABINET COMPONENTS SUCH AS DROP-LEAF DESKS, BAR CABINETS, AND RECORD STORAGE UNITS CAN ALSO BE OBTAINED. ALL COMPONENTS 31½'' WIDE

BACKBOARD PANELS MATCHING THE WOOD VENEER ON THE COMPONENTS ARE AVAILABLE

NOTE
Standard wall rail lengths (in.) are 19, 39, 59, 69, 79, and 95¾. Standard shelf depths (in.) are 7⅞, 9½, 11¾, 14¾, 15¾, and 22.

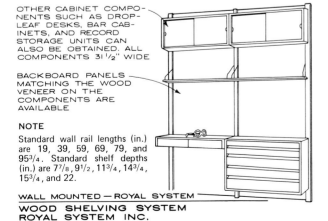

WALL MOUNTED — ROYAL SYSTEM

WOOD SHELVING SYSTEM ROYAL SYSTEM INC.

Charles Szoradi, AIA, and F. Menendez; Washington, D.C.

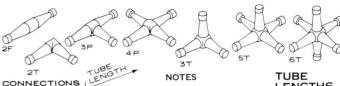

2F   3P   4P   3T   5T   6T

2T

CONNECTIONS

TUBE LENGTH

NOTES
1. Both connectors and tubes are available in chrome and matte black finishes.
2. Tubes are manufactured in heavy gauge stainless steel ½ in. o.d.

TUBE LENGTHS

CM	IN.
65	2.09
130	4.68
275	10.39
395	15.08
460	17.68
530	20.27
595	22.87
805	31.18

FLOOR MOUNTED — ABSTRACTA SHELVING

TUBULAR STEEL SHELVING SYSTEM — FOR DISPLAYS AND EXHIBITS — ABSTRACTA STRUCTURES, INC.

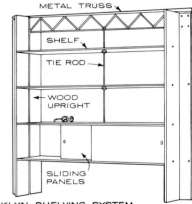

METAL TRUSS

SHELF

TIE ROD

WOOD UPRIGHT

SLIDING PANELS

NOTES
Shelves are hung from a steel truss; thus tension is transferred to metal members, increasing load capacity.

TYPICAL DIMENSIONS:
Height: 81⅞ in.
Depth: 15 in.
Length: 85, 119¼, 121⅝ in.

FLOOR MOUNTED — BROOKLYN SHELVING SYSTEM

METAL AND WOOD SHELVING SYSTEM ACERBIS INTERNATIONAL

NOTES
This storage system can be entirely assembled from the front. Available components include fold-down bar units, desk tops, drawer chests, and hideaway beds. Walk-in closets are also available. All units come in 15¾ and 24 in. depths.

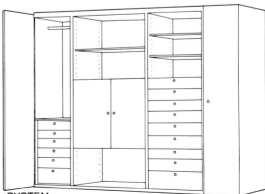

FLOOR MOUNTED — WALL SYSTEM

PANEL AND COMPONENT SHELVING SYSTEM INTERLUBKE - ICF

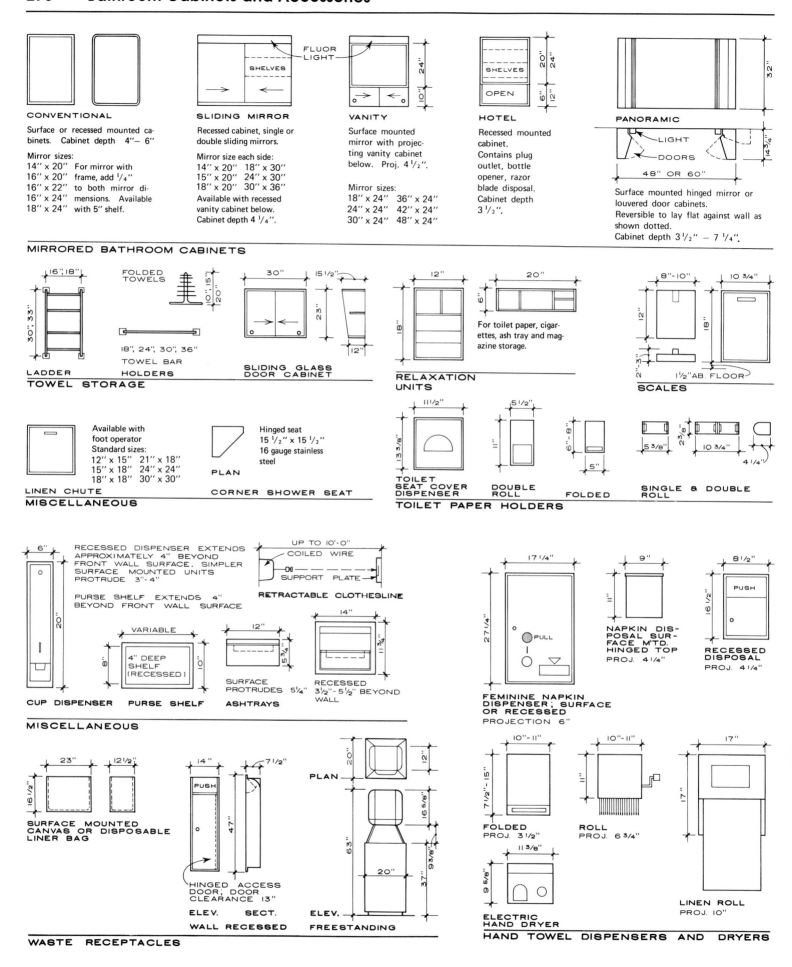

MIRRORED BATHROOM CABINETS

CONVENTIONAL

Surface or recessed mounted cabinets. Cabinet depth 4"– 6"

Mirror sizes:
14" x 20"   For mirror with
16" x 20"   frame, add 1/4"
16" x 22"   to both mirror dimensions. Available
16" x 24"   with 5" shelf.
18" x 24"

SLIDING MIRROR

Recessed cabinet, single or double sliding mirrors.

Mirror size each side:
14" x 20"   18" x 30"
15" x 20"   24" x 30"
18" x 20"   30" x 36"
Available with recessed vanity cabinet below. Cabinet depth 4 1/4".

VANITY

Surface mounted mirror with projecting vanity cabinet below. Proj. 4 1/2".

Mirror sizes:
18" x 24"   36" x 24"
24" x 24"   42" x 24"
30" x 24"   48" x 24"

HOTEL

Recessed mounted cabinet. Contains plug outlet, bottle opener, razor blade disposal. Cabinet depth 3 1/2".

PANORAMIC

Surface mounted hinged mirror or louvered door cabinets. Reversible to lay flat against wall as shown dotted. Cabinet depth 3 1/2" – 7 1/4".

TOWEL STORAGE

LADDER   HOLDERS   SLIDING GLASS DOOR CABINET

RELAXATION UNITS

For toilet paper, cigarettes, ash tray and magazine storage.

SCALES

MISCELLANEOUS

LINEN CHUTE

Available with foot operator
Standard sizes:
12" x 15"   21" x 18"
15" x 18"   24" x 24"
18" x 18"   30" x 30"

CORNER SHOWER SEAT

Hinged seat 15 1/2" x 15 1/2" 16 gauge stainless steel

TOILET PAPER HOLDERS

TOILET SEAT COVER DISPENSER   DOUBLE ROLL   FOLDED   SINGLE & DOUBLE ROLL

MISCELLANEOUS

RECESSED DISPENSER EXTENDS APPROXIMATELY 4" BEYOND FRONT WALL SURFACE. SIMPLER SURFACE MOUNTED UNITS PROTRUDE 3"- 4"

PURSE SHELF EXTENDS 4" BEYOND FRONT WALL SURFACE

RETRACTABLE CLOTHESLINE

CUP DISPENSER   PURSE SHELF   ASHTRAYS

4" DEEP SHELF (RECESSED)

SURFACE PROTRUDES 5 1/4"

RECESSED 3 1/2"- 5 1/2" BEYOND WALL

FEMININE NAPKIN DISPENSER; SURFACE OR RECESSED PROJECTION 6"

NAPKIN DISPOSAL SURFACE MTD. HINGED TOP PROJ. 4 1/4"

RECESSED DISPOSAL PROJ. 4 1/4"

WASTE RECEPTACLES

SURFACE MOUNTED CANVAS OR DISPOSABLE LINER BAG

HINGED ACCESS DOOR; DOOR CLEARANCE 13"

ELEV.   SECT.
WALL RECESSED

PLAN

ELEV.
FREESTANDING

HAND TOWEL DISPENSERS AND DRYERS

FOLDED PROJ. 3 1/2"

ROLL PROJ. 6 3/4"

LINEN ROLL PROJ. 10"

ELECTRIC HAND DRYER

H. E. Hallenbeck, Capuccilli-Bell Architects, AIA; Syracuse, New York

10   TOILET AND BATH ACCESSORIES

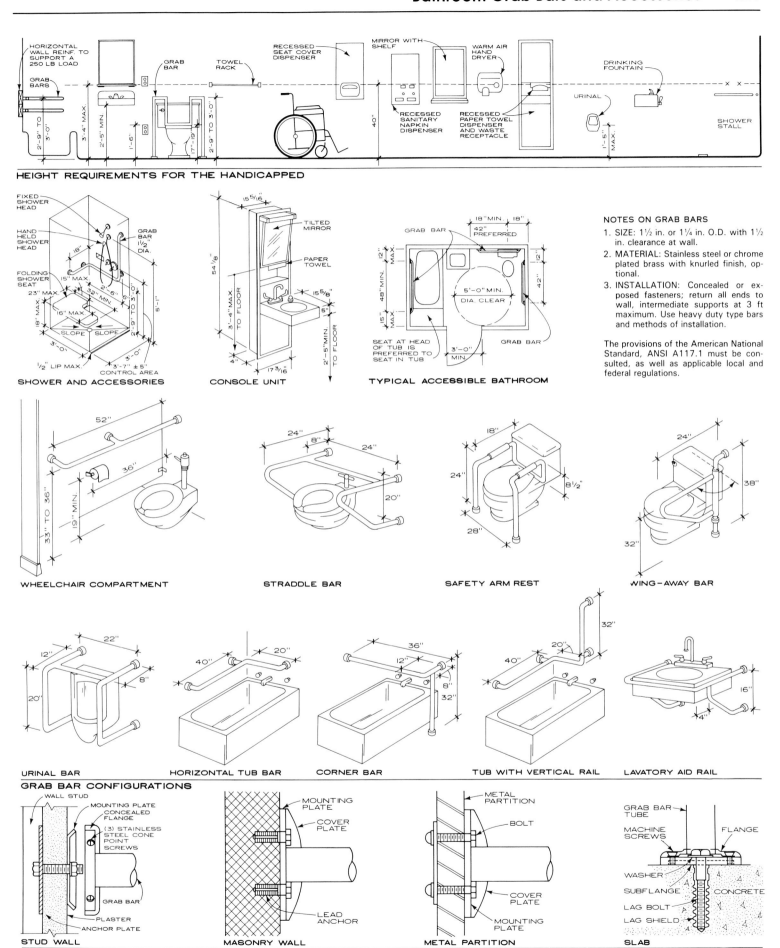

HEIGHT REQUIREMENTS FOR THE HANDICAPPED

SHOWER AND ACCESSORIES

CONSOLE UNIT

TYPICAL ACCESSIBLE BATHROOM

NOTES ON GRAB BARS

1. SIZE: 1½ in. or 1¼ in. O.D. with 1½ in. clearance at wall.
2. MATERIAL: Stainless steel or chrome plated brass with knurled finish, optional.
3. INSTALLATION: Concealed or exposed fasteners; return all ends to wall, intermediate supports at 3 ft maximum. Use heavy duty type bars and methods of installation.

The provisions of the American National Standard, ANSI A117.1 must be consulted, as well as applicable local and federal regulations.

WHEELCHAIR COMPARTMENT

STRADDLE BAR

SAFETY ARM REST

WING-AWAY BAR

URINAL BAR

HORIZONTAL TUB BAR

CORNER BAR

TUB WITH VERTICAL RAIL

LAVATORY AID RAIL

GRAB BAR CONFIGURATIONS

STUD WALL

MASONRY WALL

METAL PARTITION

SLAB

ATTACHMENT DETAILS

Jones/Richards and Associates; Ogden, Utah

REFERENCES

DATA SOURCES: ORGANIZATIONS

Abstract Structures, Inc., 297
Acerbis International, 297
Airolite Company, 286
American Dispenser Company, 298, 299
American National Standards Institute (ANSI). 299

Architectural Power Systems, 288
Architectural Supplements, Inc., 297
Bobrick Washroom Equipment, Inc., 299
Bradley Corporation, 299
Electro/Systems, Inc., 288
General Fire Extinguisher Corporation, 295
Heatilator, 291, 293
Interlubke Mubei Fabrik, 297
Liskey, Inc., 290

Metropolitan Wire Goods Corporation, 297
Nutone Housing Products, 298
Parker Company, 298
Pawling Rubber Company, 289
Robertson Company, 286
Royal Systems, Inc., 297
Tate Architectural Products, Inc., 290
Tubular Specialties Manufacturing, Inc., 299
Van Packer Company, Inc., 293

CHAPTER 11

EQUIPMENT

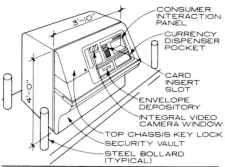

DRIVE-UP AUTOMATIC TELLER MACHINE (ATM)

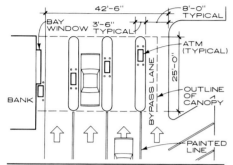

PLAN OF DRIVE-UP TELLERS

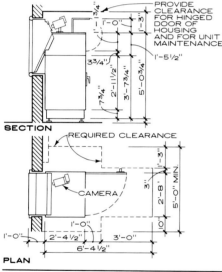

SECTION

PLAN

AUTOMATIC TELLER MACHINE (ATM)

GENERAL NOTES

1. STANDARDS: Comply with the latest edition of "Comptroller's Manual for National Banks, Minimum Security Devices and Procedures" except when higher standards are shown in the construction documents.

2. SURVEILLANCE SYSTEM:
   a. 35 mm hold-up stile cameras.
   b. Device should be capable of enlarging images of persons to produce a 1 in. vertical head size.
   c. Device should be reasonably silent in operation.
   d. Capable of taking at least one picture every 2 sec.
   e. Capable of operating not less than 3 min.
   f. Surveillance devices other than at teller's station or window should be located so as to reproduce identifiable images of persons either leaving the banking office or in a position to transact business at each such station or window, and capable of actuation by initiating devices located at each teller's station or window.
   g. Surveillance devices for teller stations or windows should be located in such a manner as to reproduce

Charles Szoradi, AIA; Washington, D.C.

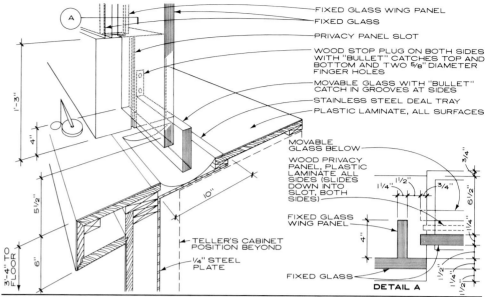

BULLETPROOF GLASS AT TELLER'S STATION

DETAIL A

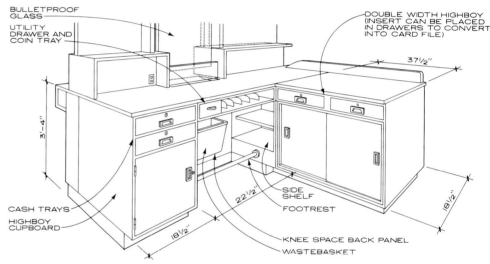

TELLER STATION

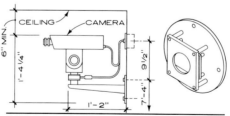

SURVEILLANCE CAMERA AND VOICE PORT (TELLER SIDE)

identifiable images of persons in a position to transact business at each such station or window and areas of such station or window that are vulnerable to robbery or larceny. Such devices should be capable of actuation by one or more initiating devices located within or in close proximity to such station or window. The teller should have access to a device to actuate a surveillance system that covers the area of vulnerability or the exits to the banking office.

3. ROBBERY ALARM SYSTEM:
   a. Four wire interphase control box.
   b. Money clip.
   c. Designated to transmit to the police through an intermediary, a signal indicating that a crime against the banking office has occurred or is in progress.

   d. Capable of actuation by initiating devices located at each teller's station or window.
   e. Safeguarded against accidental transmission.
   f. Equipped with a visual and audible signal capable of indicating improper functioning of or tampering with the system.
   g. Equipped with an independent source of power sufficient to assure continuously reliable operation of the system for at least 24 hr.

4. BURGLARY ALARM SYSTEM:
   a. Capable of detecting promptly an attack on the outer door, walls, floor, or ceiling of each vault and each safe not stored in a vault, each Night Depository (ND) and each Automated Teller Machine (ATM) in which currency, negotiable securities, or similar valuables are stored when the office is closed, and any attempt to move any such safe.
   b. Designed to transmit to the police, through an intermediary, a signal indicating that any such attempt is in progress.
   c. Safeguarded against accidental transmission of an alarm.
   d. Equipped with a visual and audible signal capable of indicating improper functioning of or tampering with the system.
   e. Equipped with an independent source of power (such as a battery) sufficient to assure continuously reliable operation of the system for at least 80 hr in the event of failure of the usual source of power.

5. Equipment information was furnished by Diebold, Inc., Canton, OH.

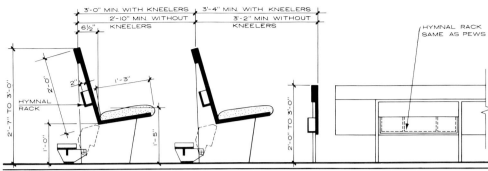

PEW AND FRONTAL

PEW SPACING

BACK-TO-BACK BETWEEN PEWS			PEW LENGTH*		
NO. OF SPACES	2'-10'' SPACING	3'-0'' SPACING	NO. OF PERSONS	1'-8'' PER PERSON	1'-10'' PER PERSON
5	14'-2''	15'-0''	3	5'-0''	5'-6''
10	28'-4''	30'-0''	5	8'-4''	9'-2''
20	56'-8''	60'-0''	7	11'-8''	12'-10''
30	85'-0''	90'-0''	9	15'-0''	16'-6''
			11	18'-4''	20'-0''
			12	20'-0''	

* Minimum space allowed per person is 1 ft 6 in. Based on NFPA 101 Life Safety Code (1985), the maximum number of seats allowed in a row with aisles at both ends of the row is 14; maximum length allowed for a row is 21 ft 0 in.

INTRODUCTION

Ecclesiastical furnishings are as much or more a part of the ambiance, symbolism, and meaning of a worship environment as the structure and architecture itself. Virtually all ecclesiastical furnishings are available from various manufacturers in predesigned, prefabricated form. In many cases, especially with regard to pews and chairs, such stock or semicustom items can be highly satisfactory and economical. Where special scale, material, or symbolism is desired, custom-designed and custom-built furnishings may be more appropriate, as is often true of chancel/sanctuary furnishings including pulpit, table, font, and clergy chairs. The illustrations on these pages provide information concerning the general size and character of such furnishings. The theology and liturgical attitudes of each church should provide primary guidance in the design and execution of ecclesiastical furnishings.

PEWS

Most pew manufacturers offer a diverse selection of styles, materials, and finishes, and many will custom build special designs prepared by the architect. Pew ends contribute most to style and are available in numerous designs from closed to semiopen to fully open. Kneelers are optional and some are available with hydraulic pistons to govern the speed (and noise) with which they are lowered and raised. Other options include book, card, pencil, and communion cup holders.

PULPIT/AMBO

The pulpit (Protestant) or ambo (Roman Catholic) has historically been a fixed chancel/sanctuary furnishing. However, with increasing demands for multiple uses of worship spaces, the need for flexibility often requires that all furnishings be movable.

Among the most important features of a pulpit/ambo is an adjustable top to accommodate the physical variations of speakers. A drop-down step may also be desirable. A pulpit should include a concealed reading lamp (especially where A/V darkening is employed) and a built-in clock. Although extensive use is being made of lavalier or wireless microphones, a concealed microphone cable raceway should be provided and the pulpit top padded to minimize the noise of rustling notes that sensitive microphones may amplify.

LECTERN

The lectern is almost always movable. In small churches or chapels, a lectern may be used as a pulpit. Features similar to those required of the pulpit should be provided.

COMMUNION RAIL

Communion rails should provide for comfortable kneeling. The rail may need to provide for the disposition of individual communion cups (as illustrated below). In worship spaces also used for concerts or drama, communion rails may need to be easily removable.

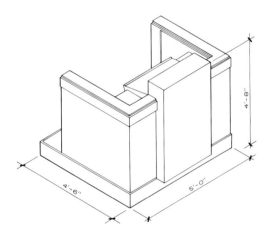

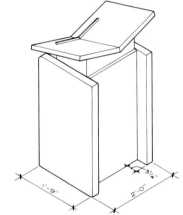

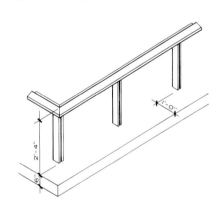

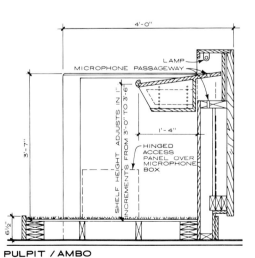

PULPIT / AMBO

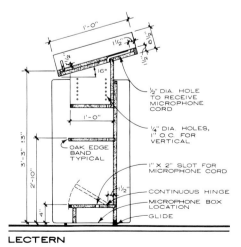

LECTERN

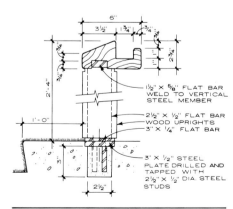

COMMUNION RAIL

Randall S. Lindstrom, AIA; Ware Associates, Inc.; Rockford, Illinois

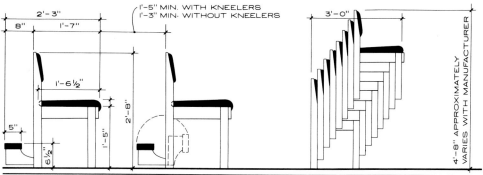

STACKING CHAPEL/CHOIR CHAIRS

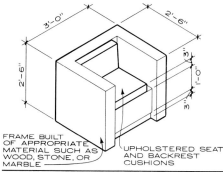

CLERGY/PRESIDER CHAIR

FRAME BUILT OF APPROPRIATE MATERIAL SUCH AS WOOD, STONE, OR MARBLE

UPHOLSTERED SEAT AND BACKREST CUSHIONS

STACK CHAIRS

A variety of stacking or modular chairs are available and well suited to uses such as small churches, chapels, and choir areas where flexibility of arrangement or complete removal is desired. Like pews, these chairs may be upholstered in differing degrees and equipped with kneelers, book holders, and other features. In addition, most manufacturers offer an interlocking device that enables the user to join rows of chairs together for temporarily fixed arrangements. Stacking capability allows efficient storage of chairs. When worship spaces become large enough to require a sloped floor for proper sight and sound lines, chairs are generally not advisable.

ALTAR/COMMUNION TABLE

In most churches, the altar or communion table is the primary focus and therefore the most visually prominent

furnishing. Style and symbolism of the altar/table are deeply rooted in the liturgy of individual churches and usually require the participation and theological direction of both clergy and laity during design. Appropriateness of scale and material are particularly important and widely variable. The altar/table is among the most suitable furnishings for artist collaboration in design and execution.

BAPTISMAL FONT

A font for ceremonial sprinkling of infants and/or adults may be placed in various locations including at the chancel/sanctuary or at the entrance to the church in the narthex. In some cases, the font may be alternately moved between these locations. Usually space for gathering of family and friends is required around the font and, in many churches, the font is required to be in a position that permits general viewing of a baptism by the entire congregation. Churches practicing baptism by im-

mersion or submersion require an altogether different style of baptistry involving a pool or tank that allows full entry by laity and clergy. Prefabricated baptistry tanks are available and custom installations possible.

TABERNACLE

The tabernacle generally associated with Roman Catholic, Orthodox, and Episcopalian ("ambry" rather than tabernacle) churches is a very significant element in the worship environment, acting as the place of repose for the consecrated Host—the body of Christ. It is often a highly artistic and custom furnishing. Careful attention to the liturgical attitudes of the individual church and review of the document "*Environment and Art in Catholic Worship*" (for Roman Catholic churches) should guide the design and placement of the tabernacle.

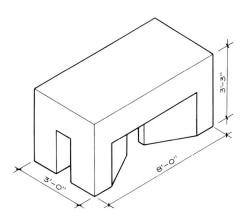

ALTAR

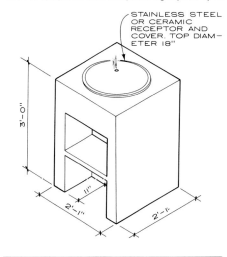

STAINLESS STEEL OR CERAMIC RECEPTOR AND COVER. TOP DIAMETER 18"

BAPTISMAL FONT

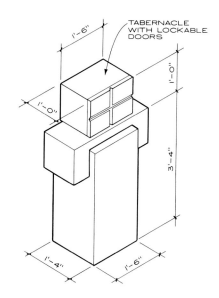

TABERNACLE WITH LOCKABLE DOORS

TABERNACLE

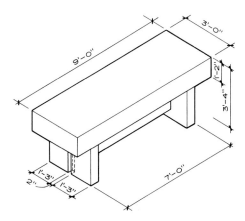

COMMUNION TABLE

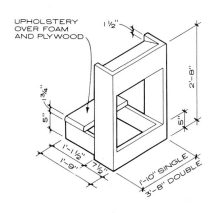

UPHOLSTERY OVER FOAM AND PLYWOOD

INDIVIDUAL KNEELER

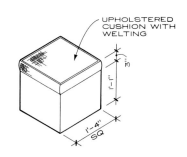

UPHOLSTERED CUSHION WITH WELTING

ACOLYTE STOOL

Ware Associates, Inc.; Rockford, Illinois/Chicago/Los Angeles

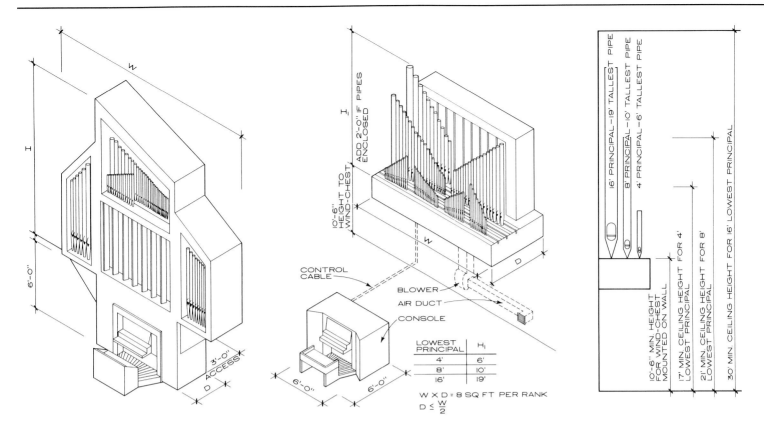

MECHANICAL ACTIONED ORGAN (TRACKER)

ELECTROMECHANICAL OR ELECTROPNEUMATIC ORGAN

PIPE ORGANS

Organ builders recommend that the pipes and casework be located within the space they are to serve, not in an organ chamber. Organ and console, located in proximity to one another, should be placed so that sound can travel freely and directly to the listeners. No furnishings, people, or other barriers should be located in front of the organ pipes. Drafts and sudden temperature changes to the pipes may necessitate more frequent tuning.

While blowers may be built in to the organ casework, quieter operation can be achieved placing the blower in a remote space. However, air for the blower should be drawn from the room in which the organ is located to avoid tuning changes. Sound isolation, power requirements, serviceability, and need for a large duct chase to the organ must be considered when designing the blower room.

The number of stops or ranks required for an organ installation is related to musical flexibility rather than the loudness of an organ. The number of manuals will also vary depending on need for flexibility in the musical program. The table below outlines general guidelines to select the number of ranks for an organ installation.

ELECTROMECHANICAL AND ELECTROPNEUMATIC ORGANS

In these types of instruments, air that passes from the wind-chests into the pipes is controlled by either electromechanical or electropneumatic means. The required size of the organ pipe space will vary depending on the organ builder, but 8 sq ft per rank may be used as a general rule of thumb. If height is available, divisions may be stacked, reducing the floor area required by approximately 25%. All pipes must be accessible for tuning.

Weight of the organ will also vary. A general average is 450 lb per rank. If the organ is enclosed in a case, 50 lb per rank should be added. A stacked arrangement of pipe divisions will increase the floor loading proportionately.

MECHANICAL ACTIONED ORGANS

Commonly know as tracker organs, these instruments introduce air into the pipes through a valve mechanically attached to the keys on the console. The size of tracker organs is measured in terms of stops rather than ranks. Tracker organs are self-contained in wooden cases that house pipes, wind-chests, manuals, and mechanical components. Such wooden cases may be designed to complement the architecture of the surrounding space. Compared to electromechanical and electropneumatic organs, a tracker organ will usually require more height for pipe cases but consequently less floor area. Often used in chapels because of their compactness, tracker organs are not limited to use in small worship spaces. In larger installations the console may be separated from the pipe chests by a limited distance, but must nonetheless be fixed, due to the mechanical connections between manuals and pipes.

Blowers for this type of instrument are built into the organ casework. Electrical power for the blower must be provided.

Mechanical actioned organs have an average weight of 400–500 lb per stop. A 3 ft 0 in. minimum access space behind the instrument is required for servicing and tuning.

Additional information is available through the Associated Pipe Organ Builders of America.

GENERAL SIZE REQUIREMENTS BASED UPON VARIOUS SEATING CAPACITIES

NO. OF SEATS	NO. OF STOPS	NO. OF RANKS	NO. OF DIVISIONS (1)	LOWEST PRINCIPAL (2)
150	4–9	6–12	2–3	4'
200	9–13	12–16	3	8'
250	12–18	16–23	3	8'
300	15–25	18–34	3	8'
400	20–30	26–44	3	16'
500	25–35	34–50	3–4	16'
750	30–45	44–64	4	16'
1000	35–50	50–78	4	16'

MINIMUM DIMENSIONS FOR A TRACKER ORGAN CASE BASED UPON VARIOUS NUMBERS OF STOPS

NO. OF SEATS	NO. OF STOPS	NO. OF RANKS	NO. OF DIVISIONS	LOWEST PRINCIPAL	W WIDTH	D DEPTH	H HEIGHT
150	4–9	6–12	2–3	4	10'	28''	10'
200	9–13	12–16	3	8	12'	28''	12'
250	12–18	16–23	3	8	15'	36''	14'
300	15–25	18–34	3	8	18'	42''	17'
400	20–30	26–44	3	16	20'	48''	23'
500	25–55	34–50	3–4	16	22'	52''	25'
750	30–45	44–64	4	16	22'	56''	25'
1000	35–50	50–78	4	16	22'	60''	25'

Randall S. Lindstrom, AIA; Ware Associates, Inc.; Rockford, Illinois

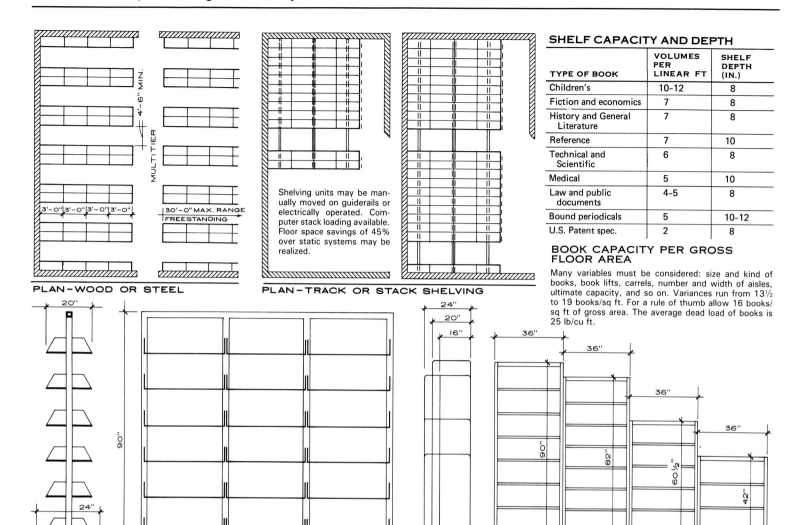

PLAN—WOOD OR STEEL

PLAN—TRACK OR STACK SHELVING

Shelving units may be manually moved on guiderails or electrically operated. Computer stack loading available. Floor space savings of 45% over static systems may be realized.

SHELF CAPACITY AND DEPTH

TYPE OF BOOK	VOLUMES PER LINEAR FT	SHELF DEPTH (IN.)
Children's	10-12	8
Fiction and economics	7	8
History and General Literature	7	8
Reference	7	10
Technical and Scientific	6	8
Medical	5	10
Law and public documents	4-5	8
Bound periodicals	5	10-12
U.S. Patent spec.	2	8

BOOK CAPACITY PER GROSS FLOOR AREA

Many variables must be considered: size and kind of books, book lifts, carrels, number and width of aisles, ultimate capacity, and so on. Variances run from 13½ to 19 books/sq ft. For a rule of thumb allow 16 books/ sq ft of gross area. The average dead load of books is 25 lb/cu ft.

ADJUSTABLE SHELF UNIT, STEEL

ADJUSTABLE SHELF UNIT, WOOD

SIDE DOUBLE FACED

FRONT

SINGLE FACED 8", 10", 12" DEPTH. 90" HEIGHT ONLY 10" DEPTH. DOUBLE FACED 16", 20", 24" DEPTH. 90" HEIGHT ONLY, 20" DEPTH

CARRELS

FRONT

SIDE, SINGLE FACED   SIDE, DOUBLE FACED

FRONT MICROFICHE READER

SIDE

FRONT MICROREADER FOR FICHE OR FILM

SIDE

NOTE

Generally microfilm and microfiche readers and video display terminals (VDT) are positioned on tables.

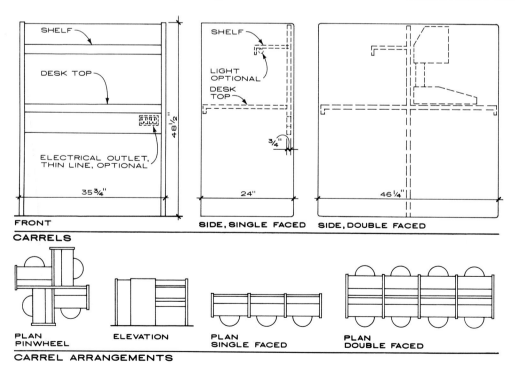

PLAN PINWHEEL   ELEVATION   PLAN SINGLE FACED   PLAN DOUBLE FACED

CARREL ARRANGEMENTS

LIBRARY EQUIPMENT

Walter Hart Associates, AIA; White Plains, New York

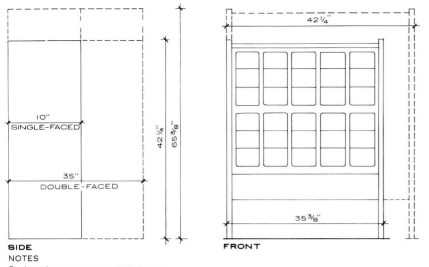

SIDE

FRONT

NOTES

Card catalog cases are available in units:
Single-faced 15–60 trays, 42¼'' H; double-faced 30–120 trays, 42¼'' H; high, single, or double faced with pullout shelves, 72–144 trays, 65⅜'' H. Effective tray card filing depth 14¾'', tray capacity 1250–1300 standard cards of 3'' x 5''.

CARD CATALOG CASES

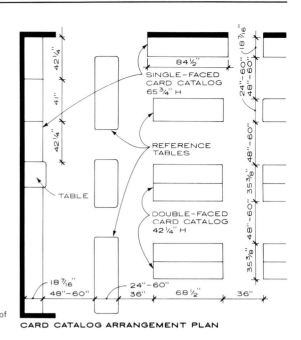

CARD CATALOG ARRANGEMENT PLAN

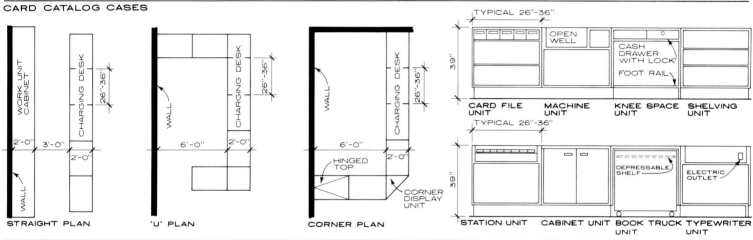

STRAIGHT PLAN   **'U' PLAN**   **CORNER PLAN**

CARD FILE UNIT   **MACHINE UNIT**   **KNEE SPACE UNIT**   **SHELVING UNIT**

STATION UNIT   **CABINET UNIT**   **BOOK TRUCK UNIT**   **TYPEWRITER UNIT**

CHARGING DESKS

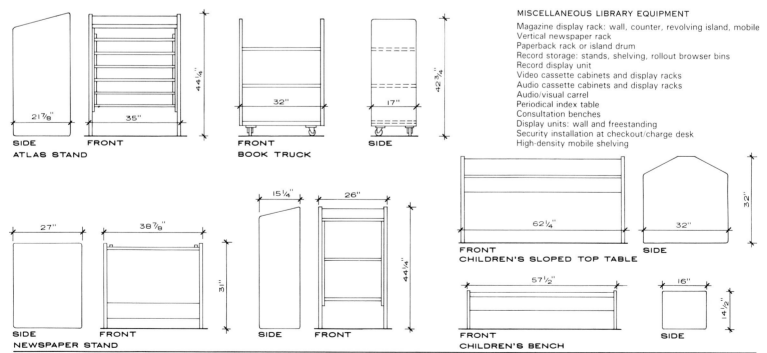

SIDE   **FRONT**
ATLAS STAND

FRONT   **SIDE**
BOOK TRUCK

MISCELLANEOUS LIBRARY EQUIPMENT

Magazine display rack: wall, counter, revolving island, mobile
Vertical newspaper rack
Paperback rack or island drum
Record storage: stands, shelving, rollout browser bins
Record display unit
Video cassette cabinets and display racks
Audio cassette cabinets and display racks
Audio/visual carrel
Periodical index table
Consultation benches
Display units: wall and freestanding
Security installation at checkout/charge desk
High-density mobile shelving

SIDE   **FRONT**
NEWSPAPER STAND

SIDE   **FRONT**

FRONT   **SIDE**
CHILDREN'S SLOPED TOP TABLE

FRONT   **SIDE**
CHILDREN'S BENCH

MISCELLANEOUS LIBRARY EQUIPMENT

Walter Hart Associates, AIA; White Plains, New York

REFERENCES

DATA SOURCES: ORGANIZATIONS

Herman Miller, Inc., 306, 307

Library Bureau, Inc., Catalog LB-76, 306, 307

Library Bureau, Inc., Steel Book Stack Catalog, 306

CHAPTER 12

FURNISHINGS

OFFICE FURNISHINGS   310

OVERFILE STORAGE

TYPE	W	H	D	WEIGHT*
Over 2-drawer letter	30	26 or 37	29	170
Over 2-drawer legal	36		29	308
Over 3-drawer letter	43		29	377
Over 3-drawer legal	54		29	445

VERTICAL FILES

TYPE	W	H	D	WEIGHT*
5-drawer letter	15	60	29	405
5-drawer legal	18	60	29	430
4-drawer letter	15	50	29	324
4-drawer legal	18	50	29	344
3-drawer letter	15	41	29	258
3-drawer legal	18	41	29	162
2-drawer letter	15	30	29	162
2-drawer legal	18	30	29	172

INSIDE DRAWER DIMENSIONS

TYPE	W	H	D
Letter	$12\frac{1}{4}$	$10\frac{1}{2}$	$26\frac{3}{4}$
Legal	$15\frac{1}{4}$	$10\frac{1}{2}$	$26\frac{3}{4}$

*Weights = fully loaded file.

VERTICAL FILE CABINETS

LATERAL FILES

TYPE	W	H	D	WEIGHT*
5-drawer	30, 36, 42	64	18	610–843
4-drawer	30–36–42	52	18	524–720
3-drawer	30, 36, 42	40	18	401–553
2-drawer	30, 36, 42	32	18	285–391

*Weights = fully loaded file.

LATERAL FILE CABINETS

SPECIAL FILES

TYPE	W	H	D
A. Custom stack system	36	52	18
B. Check file	15	52	27
C. Special/double check	22	52	27
D. Card record file	22	52	27
6 drawer (3 × 5, 4 × 6 cards)	22	52	27
5 drawer (3 × 5, 4 × 6, 5 × 8)	22	52	27
E. Pedestal file	15	28	24
Library card file (see index)			

SPECIAL FILING CABINETS

FIRE INSULATED FILES

TYPE	W	H	D	WEIGHT*
4-drawer letter	17	52	30	600
4-drawer legal	20	52	30	660
3-drawer letter	17	51	30	465
3-drawer legal	20	41	30	515
2-drawer letter	17	28	30	330
2-drawer legal	20	28	30	370
3-drawer lateral	39	56	24	1220
2-drawer lateral	39	39	24	875

*Weight = fully loaded.

FIRE INSULATED FILE CABINETS

Associated Space Design, Inc.; Atlanta, Georgia

PLANNING

1. Users' filing needs should be tabulated in inches and in turn converted into number of cabinets. Consult manufacturer for inches available in specific cabinets.
2. For open space planning, the following square footage allowances should be used:

TYPES	SPACE ALLOWANCE (FT²)
Vertical and 36 in. lateral files	10
Lateral file for computer printout	15

NOTE: All dimensions shown are approximate. Consult manufacturer for actual dimensions.

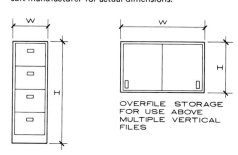

OVERFILE STORAGE FOR USE ABOVE MULTIPLE VERTICAL FILES

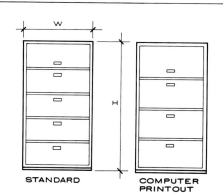

STANDARD   COMPUTER PRINTOUT

FILE CLEARANCES

	VERTICAL FILES	LATERAL FILES
A	106–120	82–94
B	29	18
C	48–62	46–58
D	18–26	16–22
E	30–36	30–36

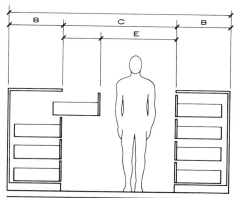

DIMENSIONS FOR PLANNING

NOTES

1. Basic types accommodate multiple configurations of drawers, doors, and shelves.
2. 6 in. drawer accommodates cards and vouchers not exceeding 5 in. in one direction.
3. 12 in. drawer accommodates letter and legal files.
4. 15 in. drawer accommodates computer printouts.
5. Files are available to five-drawer height. Files more than five drawers high are not recommended.
6. Typical overfile storage is 26 or 37 in. high.

    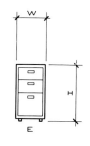

A   B   C   D   E

VERTICAL LETTER   VERTICAL LEGAL   LATERAL

These units are designed to resist forced entry and are fabricated from heavy gauge steel plate. They are available only in legal size vertical format and are essentially the same size as fire insulated cabinets. They are available with or without fire protection.

SECURITY FILES

TYPE	WEIGHT*
5-drawer	1350
5-drawer fire insulated	1650
4-drawer	1050
4-drawer fire insulated	1400
2-drawer	650
2-drawer fire insulated	825

*Weight = fully loaded

SECURITY FILE CABINETS

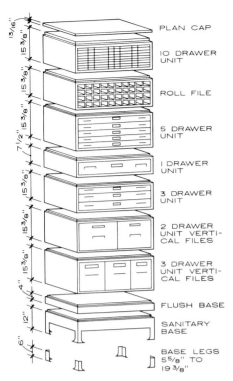

STEEL SHOWN, WOOD SIMILAR; DEPTH
28 1/2"– 50 1/2"; WIDTH 40 3/4"– 79 5/16";
DRAWER EXTENDS 26"– 42"

PLAN FILE SYSTEM

BIFILE SYSTEM

Units at rear are fixed, while units at front slide from side to side on floor-mounted tracks. Files may be operated either manually or electrically. Sizes of individual units vary by manufacturer.

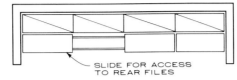

SLIDE FOR ACCESS
TO REAR FILES

BIFILE PLAN

BIFILE
(2 UNITS DEEP, 12' WIDE, FULLY LOADED)

TYPE	WEIGHT (LB)
9 Tier, legal	6200
9 Tier, letter	4850
8 Tier, legal	5550
8 Tier, letter	4350
7 Tier, legal	4900
7 Tier, letter	3850

CONDENSED FILE SYSTEMS

ROTATING FILE SYSTEM

Typically, units at ends of room are single loaded and fixed. Middle units are double loaded and move from side to side on floor-mounted tracks. Files may be operated either manually, mechanically, or electrically. This system permits one aisle to serve many banks of files, resulting in significant square footage savings. This filing system produces concentrated loads and requires close consultation between structural engineer, designer, and manufacturer.

In areas where the designer must consider seismic shock, check with manufacturer for equipping the file units with special seismic anchors.

NOTE

These units rotate on a ball bearing raceway located in the base. Pushing a foot pedal releases the carriage, which rotates 90° to the next locking position, allowing for access to both banks of files or closure of unit. The system is available in 3- to 8-tier arrangements.

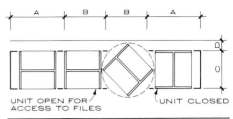

UNIT OPEN FOR
ACCESS TO FILES

UNIT CLOSED

ROTATING FILE PLAN

ROTATING FILES (SINGLE UNIT, FULLY LOADED)

TYPE	WEIGHT (LB)
8 Tier, legal	1450
8 Tier, letter	900
7 Tier, legal	1275
7 Tier, letter	825
5 Tier, legal	950
5 Tier, letter	625

DIMENSIONS FOR PLANNING

	LETTER (IN.)	LEGAL (IN.)
A. End unit	37	45
B. Middle unit	31	38
C. Depth of unit	25	31
D. Clearance from wall	6	7

PAPER WEIGHTS

FILE TYPE	POUNDS PER LINEAL INCH
Letter	1.5
Legal	2.0
Computer printout, hanging	1.75

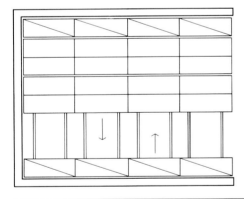

HIGH DENSITY FILE SYSTEM

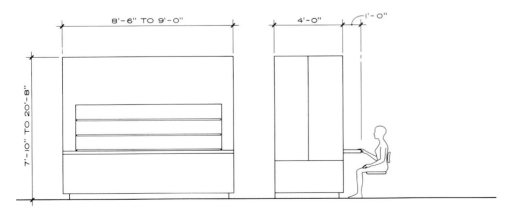

NOTES

An automated system permits the retrieval of records within seconds. Records are stored in the unit on carriers. Each carrier is individually suspended and equally spaced on a conveyor system. The operator sits or stands at a posting board, and at the touch of a button the proper carrier moves into position so that a record may be pulled or filed.

Records that may be stored in these units include file folders, binders, reference books, ledgers, tape reels, microfilm, and cards.

AUTOMATED FILE SYSTEM

Blythe + Nazdin Architects, Ltd.; Bethesda, Maryland
Associated Space Design, Inc.; Atlanta, Tampa, Washington, D.C.
Steven L. Kipples

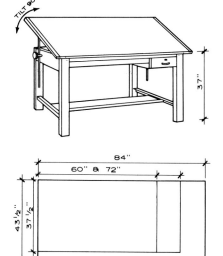

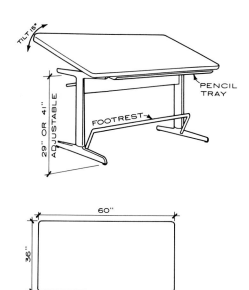

ROTATES 360°

BOARD SIZES:
29.5" X 41.3" (75 X 105 CM)
31.5" X 47.3" (80 X 120 CM)
31.5" X 55" (80 X 140 CM)

ADJUSTABLE TILT TO 90°

ADJUSTABLE HEIGHT

Several manufacturers produce an array of drawing tables with adjustable tops, optional footrests, and pencil drawers.

COUNTERBALANCED AUTOMATIC DRAFTING TABLE

PLAN

Drafting and/or engineering table is available in wood, in steel, or in combination. Various drawer and pedestal arrangements are available.

DRAFTING TABLE WITH ADJUSTABLE TOP

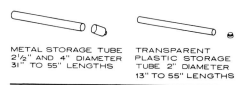

PLAN

ADJUSTABLE WORKING SURFACE

NO. OF TUBES: 27, 48, AND 108
SQ. TUBE SIZES: 4½", 3⅜", AND 2⅛"

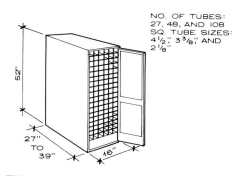

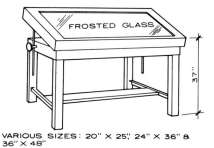

VARIOUS SIZES: 20" X 25", 24" X 36" & 36" X 48"

FLUORESCENT TRACING TABLE

METAL STORAGE TUBE 2½" AND 4" DIAMETER 31" TO 55" LENGTHS

TRANSPARENT PLASTIC STORAGE TUBE 2" DIAMETER 13" TO 55" LENGTHS

STORAGE TUBES

CABINET ROLL FILE

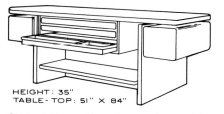

HEIGHT: 35"
TABLE-TOP: 51" X 84"

Service table provides a large worktop and integral storage compartments. Entire offices can be furnished with coordinated units.

SERVICE TABLE

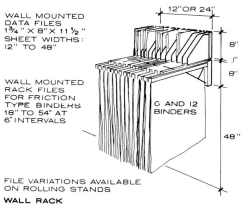

WALL MOUNTED DATA FILES 1¾" X 8" X 11½" SHEET WIDTHS: 12" TO 48"

WALL MOUNTED RACK FILES FOR FRICTION TYPE BINDERS 18" TO 54" AT 6" INTERVALS

12" OR 24"

6 AND 12 BINDERS

FILE VARIATIONS AVAILABLE ON ROLLING STANDS

WALL RACK

PIVOT FILING SYSTEM

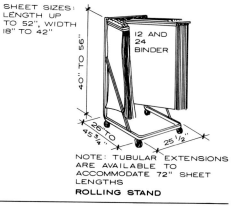

SHEET SIZES: LENGTH UP TO 52", WIDTH 18" TO 42"

12 AND 24 BINDER

NOTE: TUBULAR EXTENSIONS ARE AVAILABLE TO ACCOMMODATE 72" SHEET LENGTHS

ROLLING STAND

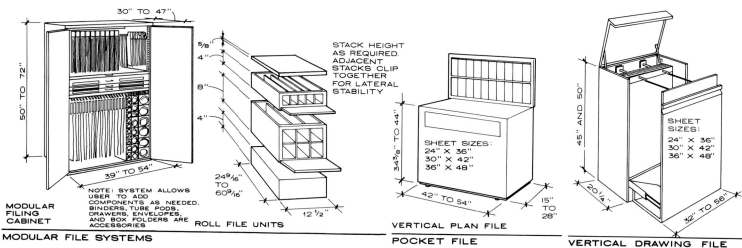

30" TO 47"

50" TO 72"

39" TO 54"

NOTE: SYSTEM ALLOWS USER TO ADD COMPONENTS AS NEEDED. BINDERS, TUBE PODS, DRAWERS, ENVELOPES, AND BOX FOLDERS ARE ACCESSORIES

MODULAR FILING CABINET

MODULAR FILE SYSTEMS

5/8"
4"
8"
4"

STACK HEIGHT AS REQUIRED. ADJACENT STACKS CLIP TOGETHER FOR LATERAL STABILITY

24⁹⁄₁₆" TO 60⁹⁄₁₆"

12½"

ROLL FILE UNITS

34⅜" TO 44"

SHEET SIZES: 24" X 36" 30" X 42" 36" X 48"

42" TO 54"

15" TO 28"

VERTICAL PLAN FILE

POCKET FILE

45" AND 50"

SHEET SIZES: 24" X 36" 30" X 42" 36" X 48"

20¼"

32" TO 56"

VERTICAL DRAWING FILE

DESIGN RATIONALE

Systems furniture is designed primarily for utilization in an open office plan which uses few fixed floor-to-ceiling partitions as compared to conventional office layouts. Open office planning receives its impetus from its ability to respond to requirements for increased flexibility and lower long term expenses. Some of the major areas of response are the following:

1. FLEXIBILITY OF PLANNING: Systems furniture in an open plan maximizes the efficient use of net plannable space. This is the result of the use of more vertical space without fixed floor-to-ceiling partitions, thereby freeing floor area and reducing space planning inefficiencies.

2. FLEXIBILITY OF FUNCTION: Systems furniture allows individual workstation modification so that workstation design can reflect functional requirements of the task performed. In this way, changes in function can be accommodated without total furniture replacement.

3. FLEXIBILITY OF PLAN MODIFICATION: Systems furniture in open office planning allows institutions to respond more easily to organizational changes of size, structure, and function. Open planning allows institutions to respond to change at lower cost by reducing expenses related to partition relocation, HVAC modification, lighting relocation, construction, and moving time.

NOTES

1. Any open office plan as commonly applied will utilize some enclosed spaces having fixed, floor-to-ceiling partitions.
2. Systems furniture requires careful planning and engineering consultation to achieve the maximum functional advantage.
3. Systems furniture components are not compatible from one manufacturer to another regardless of generic type.
4. The generic types listed below are broad classifications for descriptive purposes only.

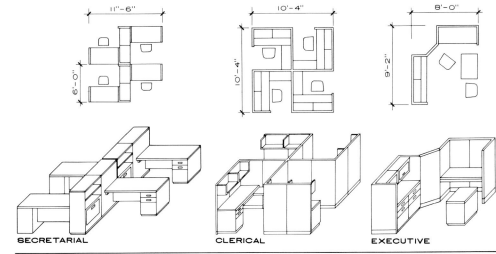

SECRETARIAL   CLERICAL   EXECUTIVE

CONFIGURATIONS

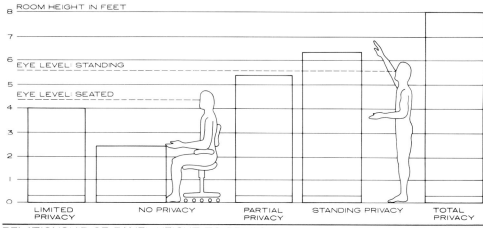

RELATIONSHIP OF PANEL HEIGHT TO PRIVACY

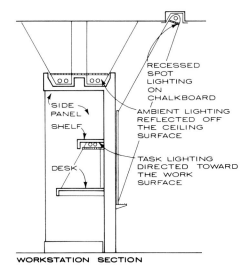

WORKSTATION SECTION

INTEGRATED LIGHTING

Artificial lighting is integrated into most open office furniture systems. The components consist of task oriented downlights located directly over work surfaces, which provide the user with control of intensity and direction of light. Uplights are mounted in the top of workstations to provide indirect light reflected off the ceiling to the ambient surroundings.

Task/ambient lighting provides more flexibility than do standard ceiling mounted fixtures. It can reduce energy consumption by decreasing general light levels and utilizing more efficient light sources. It can also improve acoustics, since fewer fixtures are installed in the acoustical ceiling.

SYSTEMS FURNITURE COMPONENTS

Interspace Incorporated; Washington, D.C.

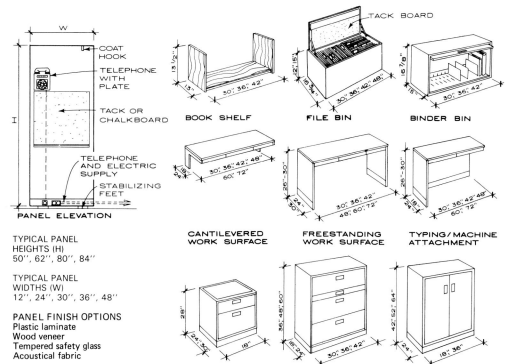

PANEL ELEVATION

TYPICAL PANEL
HEIGHTS (H)
50'', 62'', 80'', 84''

TYPICAL PANEL
WIDTHS (W)
12'', 24'', 30'', 36'', 48''

PANEL FINISH OPTIONS
Plastic laminate
Wood veneer
Tempered safety glass
Acoustical fabric

NOTE: Consult manufacturer for specific sizes and finishes available.

BOOK SHELF   FILE BIN   BINDER BIN

CANTILEVERED WORK SURFACE   FREESTANDING WORK SURFACE   TYPING/MACHINE ATTACHMENT

DRAWER BASE   FILE CASE   WARDROBE

REFERENCES

DATA SOURCES: ORGANIZATIONS

Herman Miller, Inc., 312

Luxo Lamp Corporation, 312

Martin Industries, 312

Mayline Company, 312

Steelcase, Inc., 310, 313

Vemco, 312

DATA SOURCES: PUBLICATIONS

Designing the Automated Office, William Pulgram,
  Whitney Library of Design, 313

CHAPTER 13

SPECIAL CONSTRUCTION

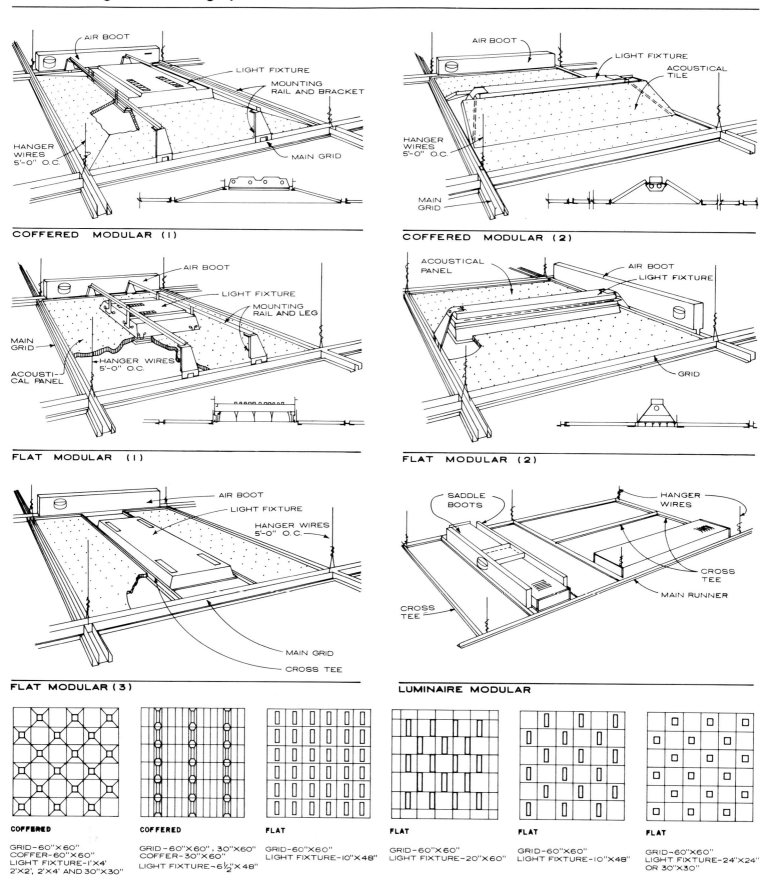

COFFERED MODULAR (1)

AIR BOOT
LIGHT FIXTURE
MOUNTING RAIL AND BRACKET
HANGER WIRES 5'-0" O.C.
MAIN GRID

COFFERED MODULAR (2)

AIR BOOT
LIGHT FIXTURE
ACOUSTICAL TILE
HANGER WIRES 5'-0" O.C.
MAIN GRID

FLAT MODULAR (1)

AIR BOOT
LIGHT FIXTURE
MOUNTING RAIL AND LEG
MAIN GRID
HANGER WIRES 5'-0" O.C.
ACOUSTICAL PANEL

FLAT MODULAR (2)

ACOUSTICAL PANEL
AIR BOOT
LIGHT FIXTURE
GRID

FLAT MODULAR (3)

AIR BOOT
LIGHT FIXTURE
HANGER WIRES 5'-0" O.C.
MAIN GRID
CROSS TEE

LUMINAIRE MODULAR

SADDLE BOOTS
HANGER WIRES
CROSS TEE
MAIN RUNNER
CROSS TEE

COFFERED

GRID-60"X60"
COFFER-60"X60"
LIGHT FIXTURE-1'X4'
2'X2', 2'X4' AND 30"X30"

COFFERED

GRID-60"X60", 30"X60"
COFFER-30"X60"
LIGHT FIXTURE-6½"X48"

FLAT

GRID-60"X60"
LIGHT FIXTURE-10"X48"

FLAT

GRID-60"X60"
LIGHT FIXTURE-20"X60"

FLAT

GRID-60"X60"
LIGHT FIXTURE-10"X48"

FLAT

GRID-60"X60"
LIGHT FIXTURE-24"X24"
OR 30"X30"

REFLECTED CEILING PLANS (INTEGRATED CEILINGS)

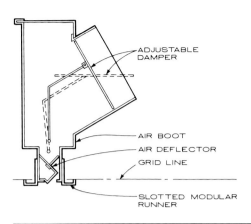

AIR BOOT SECTION AND DETAIL

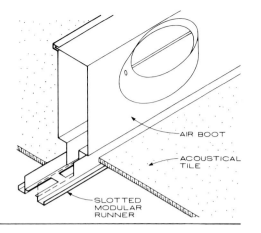

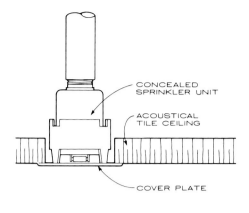

CONCEALED SPRINKLER

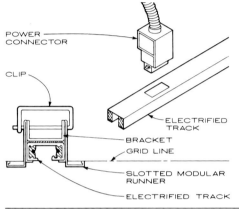

LIGHT TRACK SECTION AND DETAILS

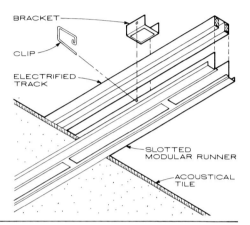

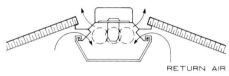

COFFERED FIXTURE

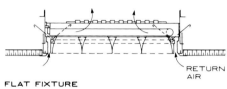

FLAT FIXTURE
LIGHTING FIXTURES

INTEGRATED CEILINGS

Integrated ceilings combine lighting, air diffusion, fire protection, and acoustical control into a single, unified unit. Demountable partitions can be accommodated by the use of an adaptor attached on the modular grid lines. A 60 x 60 in. module is basic to most integrated ceiling systems. Custom sized modules are also available.

LUMINAIRE MODULAR CEILING

The basic configuration is a 60 x 60 in. module divided into four 15 x 60 in. modules.

A recess in the modular defining grid will accommodate demountable partitions, sprinkler heads, and slots for air diffusion.

The basic lighting unit is a $14^1/_2$ x 48 in. recessed troffer. Air return is by return air light fixtures.

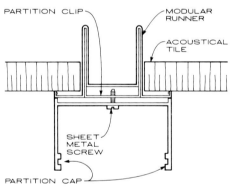

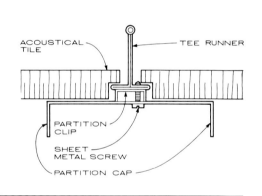

PARTITION ASSEMBLIES

COMPONENTS

CEILING SYSTEMS	HANGER SPACING (o.c.)	WALL MOLDINGS			MAIN RUNNERS			SPACING	CROSS MEMBERS			SPACING (o.c.)	AIR BAR AIR BOOT			ACOUSTIC PANELS			LIGHT FIXTURES		
		L	W	H	L	W	H		L	W	H		L	W	H	L	W	H	L	W	H
Flat modular	2'-6''	10'	$3/_4$''	$3/_4$''	10'	$3/_4$''	$1^1/_2$''	5'	60''	$3/_4$''	$1^1/_2$''	20''	5'	$3^1/_8$''	$9^3/_4$''	5'	20''	$5/_8$''	—	1.	—
Coffered lighting	30''	60''	$1^1/_4$''	$1^1/_4$''	5'	$2^1/_4$''	$1^1/_4$''	5'	60''	$2^1/_4$''	$1^1/_4$''	5'	5'	$7^1/_4$''	8''	5'	15''	$5/_8$''	48''	$14^1/_2$''	5''
Luminair modular	5'	—	—	—	$58^1/_2$''	3''	$1^1/_2$''	5'	57''	$15/_{16}$''	$1^1/_2$''	5'	5'	$7^1/_4$''	8''	5'	15''	$5/_8$''	48''	$14^1/_2$''	5''
Vertical screen	7' Max.	—	—	—	16'	$1^1/_2$''	$1^7/_8$''	7' Max.	16' Max.	$5/_8$''	4''	2'-6''	—	2.	—	—	—	—	—	2.	—
Linear screen	5' Max.	—	—	—	16'	$1^{27}/_{32}$''	$1^1/_4$''	50''	3'-16'	3''	$5/_8$''	2''	—	3.	—	—	4.	—	—	5.	—

NOTES

1. Size can vary.
2. No special type necessary.
3. Utilizes slots between panels for delivery and return.
4. Acoustic blanket.
5. Designed to fit panel width.

Timothy B. McDonald; Washington, D.C.

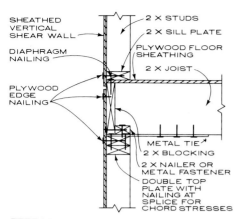

JOIST PERPENDICULAR TO WALL

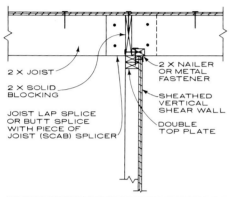

JOIST PERPENDICULAR TO WALL

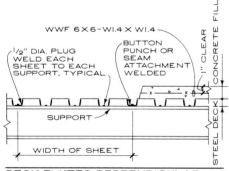

DECK FLUTES PERPENDICULAR TO SUPPORT

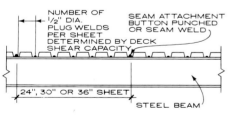

DECK PERPENDICULAR TO SUPPORT

DECK PARALLEL TO SUPPORT
NOTE: PLUG WELD TO BE 1/2" DIA. EFFECTIVE FUSION DIAMETER

1-1/2" STEEL DECK WELDING PATTERN

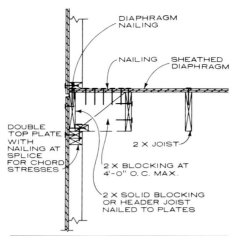

JOIST PARALLEL TO WALL

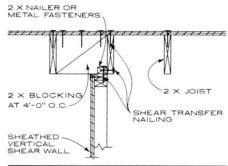

JOIST PARALLEL TO WALL

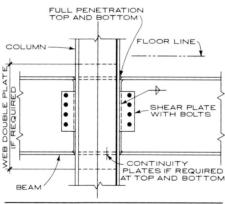

TYPICAL GIRDER AND COLUMN MOMENT CONNECTION

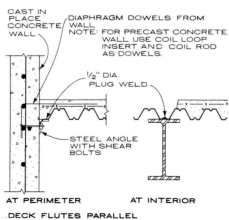

AT PERIMETER   **AT INTERIOR**

DECK FLUTES PARALLEL TO SUPPORT

STEEL DECK WITH CONCRETE FILL

NOTE: SEISMIC DETAILS SHOULD BE ENGINEERED TO MEET SPECIFIC FORCES AND TO CONFORM TO APPLICABLE CODES.

PLYWOOD SHEATHED SHEAR WALL WITH TIE-DOWNS

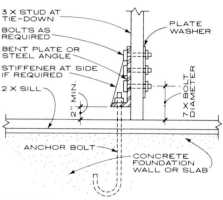

TIE DOWN

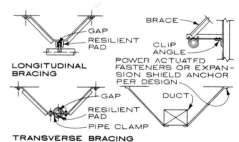

LONGITUDINAL BRACING

TRANSVERSE BRACING

BRACING FOR PIPES AND DUCTS

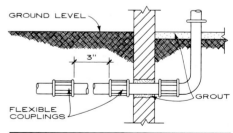

PIPE ENTERING BUILDING

NOTE
Details shown are representative of possible construction detailing. In addition to code defined structural requirements, safety considerations require nonstructural building elements and furnishings to be anchored in areas subjected to seismic movement. These pages show selected details as samples of recommended bracing and anchorage.

Attila L. Mocsary, PE; Hope Architects & Engineers; San Diego, California
Harold P. King, CEC; King, Benioff, Steinmann, King; Sherman Oaks, California

SEISMIC DESIGN

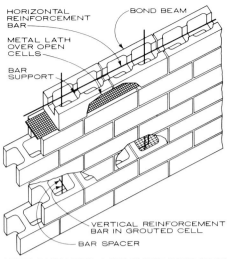

SECURING OF REINFORCEMENT

HORIZONTAL REINFORCEMENT BAR
BOND BEAM
METAL LATH OVER OPEN CELLS
BAR SUPPORT
VERTICAL REINFORCEMENT BAR IN GROUTED CELL
BAR SPACER

NOTE: OMIT METAL LATH UNDER BOND BEAM BLOCK WHERE ALL CELLS ARE SOLID GROUTED.

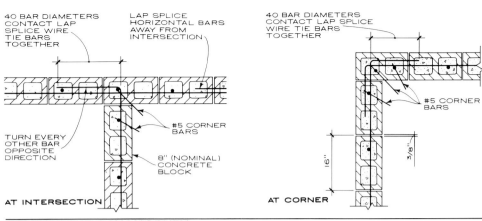

CONCRETE BLOCK MASONRY

40 BAR DIAMETERS CONTACT LAP SPLICE WIRE TIE BARS TOGETHER
LAP SPLICE HORIZONTAL BARS AWAY FROM INTERSECTION
TURN EVERY OTHER BAR OPPOSITE DIRECTION
#5 CORNER BARS
8" (NOMINAL) CONCRETE BLOCK

AT INTERSECTION

40 BAR DIAMETERS CONTACT LAP SPLICE WIRE TIE BARS TOGETHER
#5 CORNER BARS
16"
3/8"

AT CORNER

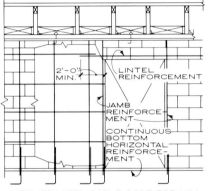

2'-0" MIN.
LINTEL REINFORCEMENT
JAMB REINFORCEMENT
CONTINUOUS BOTTOM HORIZONTAL REINFORCEMENT

NOTE: SEE APPLICABLE CODE FOR MIN. REINFORCEMENT REQUIRED.

MASONRY WALL

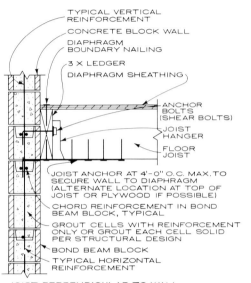

TYPICAL VERTICAL REINFORCEMENT
CONCRETE BLOCK WALL
DIAPHRAGM BOUNDARY NAILING
3 X LEDGER
DIAPHRAGM SHEATHING
ANCHOR BOLTS (SHEAR BOLTS)
JOIST HANGER
FLOOR JOIST
JOIST ANCHOR AT 4'-0" O.C. MAX. TO SECURE WALL TO DIAPHRAGM (ALTERNATE LOCATION AT TOP OF JOIST OR PLYWOOD IF POSSIBLE)
CHORD REINFORCEMENT IN BOND BEAM BLOCK, TYPICAL
GROUT CELLS WITH REINFORCEMENT ONLY OR GROUT EACH CELL SOLID PER STRUCTURAL DESIGN
BOND BEAM BLOCK
TYPICAL HORIZONTAL REINFORCEMENT

JOIST PERPENDICULAR TO WALL

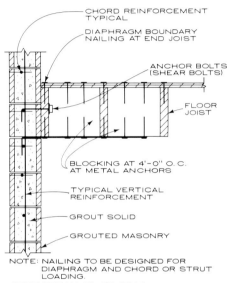

CHORD REINFORCEMENT TYPICAL
DIAPHRAGM BOUNDARY NAILING AT END JOIST
ANCHOR BOLTS (SHEAR BOLTS)
FLOOR JOIST
BLOCKING AT 4'-0" O.C. AT METAL ANCHORS
TYPICAL VERTICAL REINFORCEMENT
GROUT SOLID
GROUTED MASONRY

NOTE: NAILING TO BE DESIGNED FOR DIAPHRAGM AND CHORD OR STRUT LOADING.

JOIST PARALLEL TO WALL

WOOD DIAPHRAGM WITH MASONRY SHEAR WALL CONNECTIONS

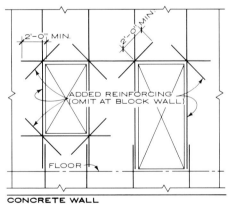

2'-0" MIN.
2'-0" MIN.
ADDED REINFORCING (OMIT AT BLOCK WALL)
FLOOR

CONCRETE WALL

OPENINGS IN MASONRY AND CONCRETE WALLS

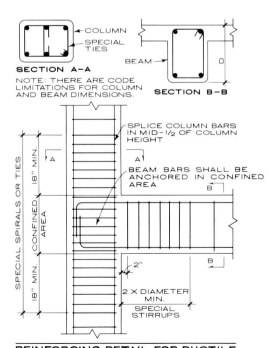

COLUMN
SPECIAL TIES

SECTION A-A

NOTE: THERE ARE CODE LIMITATIONS FOR COLUMN AND BEAM DIMENSIONS.

BEAM
D

SECTION B-B

SPECIAL SPIRALS OR TIES
18" MIN. CONFINED AREA
18" MIN.
SPLICE COLUMN BARS IN MID-1/2 OF COLUMN HEIGHT
BEAM BARS SHALL BE ANCHORED IN CONFINED AREA
2"
2 X DIAMETER MIN.
SPECIAL STIRRUPS

REINFORCING DETAIL FOR DUCTILE MOMENT RESISTING SPACE FRAME CONFINED JOINT

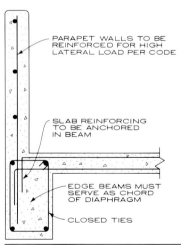

PARAPET WALLS TO BE REINFORCED FOR HIGH LATERAL LOAD PER CODE
SLAB REINFORCING TO BE ANCHORED IN BEAM
EDGE BEAMS MUST SERVE AS CHORD OF DIAPHRAGM
CLOSED TIES

CONCRETE DIAPHRAGM WITH CONCRETE SPANDREL BEAM AND PARAPET

NOTE

Details shown are representative of possible construction detailing. In addition to code-defined structural requirements, safety considerations require nonstructural building elements and furnishings to be anchored in areas subjected to seismic movement. These pages show selected details as samples of recommended bracing and anchorage.

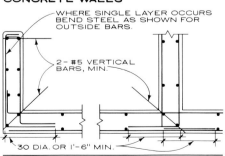

WHERE SINGLE LAYER OCCURS BEND STEEL AS SHOWN FOR OUTSIDE BARS.
2 - #5 VERTICAL BARS, MIN.
30 DIA. OR 1'-6" MIN.

INTERSECTION OF CONCRETE OR REINFORCED MASONRY WALLS

Attila L. Mocsary, PE; Hope Architects & Engineers; San Diego, California
Gary L. McGavin; Wyle Laboratories; El Segundo, California
Alfred M. Kemper, AIA; Kemper & Associates; Los Angeles, California

REFERENCES

GENERAL REFERENCES

Architectural Acoustics, 1988, M. Egan, McGraw-Hill

Architectural Interior Systems: Lighting, Air-Conditioning, Acoustics, 1988, J. Flynn and A. Segil, Van Nostrand Reinhold

Building Configuration and Seismic Design, 1985, C. Arnold and R. Reitherman, Wiley

Noise and Vibration Control in Buildings, 1984, R. Jones, McGraw-Hill

The Seismic Design Handbook, 1989, F. Naiem, Van Nostrand Reinhold

CHAPTER **14**

CONVEYING SYSTEMS

GENERAL NOTES

Lowrise buildings may use either the hydraulic or the electric elevator systems. Elevator selection, arrangement, and design of lobby and cars are similar in both cases. The primary differences between the two systems are in their operational requirements. The hydraulic elevator system is described below; the electric elevator system on the next page.

The major architectural considerations of the hydraulic elevator are the machine room, normally located at the base, and the hoistway serving as a fire protected, ventilated passageway for the elevator car. Adequate structure must be provided at the base of the hoistway to bear the load of the elevator car and its supporting piston or cylinder.

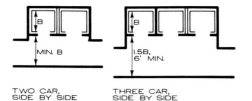

TWO CAR,
SIDE BY SIDE

THREE CAR,
SIDE BY SIDE

B = DEPTH OF CAR

NOTES

Certain guidelines lead to effective placement, grouping, and arrangement of elevators within a building. Elevators should be: (a) centrally located, (b) near the main entrance, and (c) easily accessible on all floors. If a building requires more than one elevator, they should be grouped, with possible exception of service elevators.

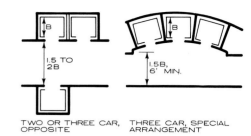

TWO OR THREE CAR,
OPPOSITE

THREE CAR, SPECIAL
ARRANGEMENT

Within each grouping, elevators should be arranged to minimize walking distance between cars. Sufficient lobby space must be provided to accommodate group movement.

ELEVATOR ARRANGEMENT, TWO AND THREE CARS (TYPICAL FOR LOWRISE APPLICATIONS)

HYDRAULIC ELEVATOR DIMENSIONS

RATED LOAD (LB)	DIMENSIONS (FT-IN.)				
	A	B	C	D	E
1500	4-10	5-0	6-8	5-9	2-8
2000	6-0	5-0	7-4	5-9	3-0
2500	7-0	5-0	8-4	5-9	3-6
3000	7-0	5-6	8-4	6-3	3-6
3500	7-0	6-2	8-4	6-11	3-6
4000	5-8	8-9	7-4	9-8	4-0

Rated speeds are 75 to 200 fpm.

NOTES

Elevator car and hoistway dimensions of the preengineered units listed above are for reference purposes only. A broad selection of units is available. Representatives of the elevator industry should be contacted for the dimensions of specific systems.

Hoistway walls normally serve primarily as fireproof enclosures. Check local codes for required fire ratings. Guide rails extend from the pit floor to the underside of the overhead. When excessive floor heights are encountered consult the elevator supplier for special requirements.

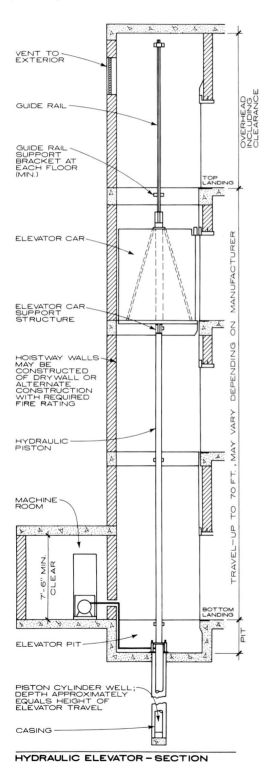

HYDRAULIC ELEVATOR – SECTION

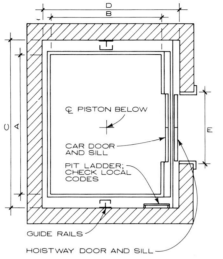

ELEVATOR CAR AND HOISTWAY

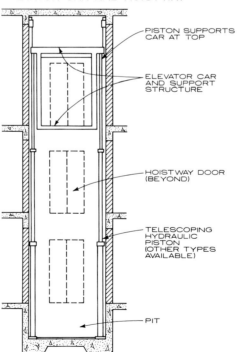

One type of holeless hydraulic elevator uses a telescoping hydraulic piston as the driving machine, eliminating the need for cylinder well excavation. This system is presently limited to a height of three stories or 21 ft 6 in. Other types of holeless hydraulic elevator units are also available using an inverted cylinder attached to the side of the elevator car.

HOLELESS HYDRAULIC ELEVATOR – SECTION

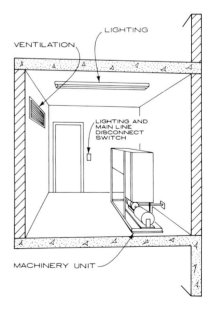

MACHINE ROOM

The MACHINE ROOM of a hydraulic elevator system is usually located next to the hoistway at or near the bottom terminal landing. Consult with elevator manufacturers for required dimensions. Refer to local codes.

Machinery consists of a pump and motor drive unit, hydraulic fluid storage tank, and control panel. Adequate ventilation, lighting, and entrance access (usually 3 ft 6 in. x 7 ft) should be provided.

Alexander Keyes; Darrel Downing Rippeteau, Architect; Washington, D.C.

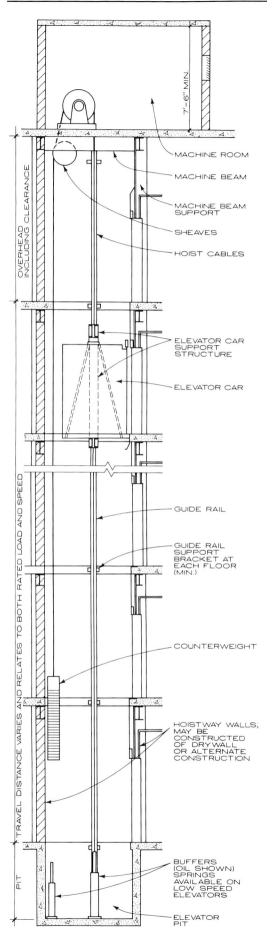

ELECTRIC ELEVATOR — SECTION

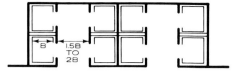

B = DEPTH OF CAR

NOTES

The largest practical grouping of elevators in a building is eight cars. One row of more than four cars is generally unacceptable. With groupings of four or six cars, waiting lobbies may be alcoved (one end closed) or open at both ends. In case of several elevator groupings, one grouping may serve lower floors, while others are express elevators to upper floors.

ELEVATOR ARRANGEMENTS — FOUR, SIX, AND EIGHT CARS (TYPICAL FOR HIGHRISE APPLICATIONS)

CONTROLS

MACHINE BEAM
HOISTING CABLES
HOISTWAY WALL

MACHINE ROOM (GEARLESS ELEVATOR)

COUNTERWEIGHT AND GUIDES

CAR

GUIDES

PIT LADDER; CHECK CODES

STEEL BEAM SUPPORT FOR GUIDE RAIL AT EACH FLOOR (MIN.)

HOISTWAY DOOR AND SILL

ELEVATOR HOISTWAY AND CAR — ELECTRIC ELEVATOR

NOTES

Medium and highrise buildings utilize ELECTRIC GEARED TRACTION and ELECTRIC GEARLESS TRACTION elevator systems. The main difference between the two systems lies in the hoisting machinery. General design considerations involving hoistway, machine room, and elevator planning are similar.

ELECTRIC GEARLESS TRACTION ELEVATOR systems are available in preengineered units with speeds of 200 to 1200 fpm. Systems with greater speeds are also available. Gearless elevators, when used in conjunction with appropriate controls, offer the advantages of a long life and smoothness of ride.

ELECTRIC GEARED TRACTION ELEVATOR systems are designed to operate within the range of 100 to 350 fpm, which restricts their use to medium rise buildings.

Both geared and gearless drive units are governed by CONTROLS, which coordinate car leveling, passenger calls, collective operation of elevators, door operation, car acceleration and deceleration, and safety applications. A broad range of control systems are available to meet individual building requirements.

STRUCTURAL REQUIREMENTS call for the total weight of the elevator system to be supported by the MACHINE BEAMS and transmitted to the building (or hoistway) structure. Consult with elevator and structural engineers.

If the elevator machine is to be supported solely by the machine room floor slab, the floor slab shall be designed in accordance with the requirements of ANSI A17.1.

Check local codes for required fire enclosures.

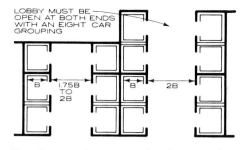

Where 4 or more elevators serve all or the same portion of a building, they shall be located in not less than 2 hoistways, but in no case shall more than 4 elevators be located in any one hoistway.

MACHINE HOISTING BEAM
GEARLESS HOISTING MACHINE
MOTOR – GENERATOR SET

NOTES

The MACHINE ROOM for electric elevators is normally located directly above the hoistway. Space must be provided for the elevator drive, control equipment, and governor with sufficient clearance for equipment installation, repair, or removal. Space requirements vary substantially according to code capacity and speed of the system selected. Adequate lighting and ventilation are required by codes, and sound insulation should be provided.

ELECTRIC ELEVATOR DIMENSIONS

RATED LOAD (LB)	DIMENSIONS (FT-IN.)				
	A	B	C	D	E
2000	6-0	5-0	7-4	6-10	3-0
2500	7-0	5-0	8-4	6-7	3-6
3000	7-0	5-6	8-4	7-1	3-6
3500	7-0	6-2	8-4	7-7	3-6
4000	5-8	8-9	7-8	9-8	4-0

NOTES

Dimensions of preengineered units, listed above, are for reference purposes only. Elevator manufacturers should be consulted for a complete selection.

BASEMENT ELECTRIC ELEVATORS ARE USED IN NEW AND EXISTING BUILDINGS WHERE OVERHEAD CLEARANCE IS LIMITED

COUNTERWEIGHT

ELEVATOR CAR

BASEMENT MACHINE ROOM

BASEMENT ELECTRIC ELEVATOR — SECTION

Alexander Keyes; Darrel Downing Rippeteau, Architect; Washington, D.C.

RESIDENTIAL ELEVATORS

Typical car sizes, A x B: 36 in. x 36 in., 42 in. x 42 in., 36 in. x 48 in.

12 sq ft platform maximum size allowed by National Elevator Code for residential elevators, ANSI A17.1. This platform size does not meet the National Handicapped Access Code, ANSI A117.1, for use by an unassisted wheelchair-bound person.

Load capacity of drum-type machine is 450 lb. Speed is 30 ft per minute.

Load capacity of traction machine is 700 lb. Speed is 36 ft per minute.

Elevators operate on 220/230 volt, single phase power supply. A disconnect switch must be provided within sight of the machine. A 110V, single phase power supply is required for lighting of machine area of hoistway.

Enclosures are recommended for all hoistways. Fire rating of hoistway enclosure and access doors must be consistent with the fire rating of the building construction. See local codes.

NOTES

1. Dimensions may vary among manufacturers and according to system selected. Elevators carrying greater loads or operating at higher speeds require more clearance overhead and in pit areas.
2. Elevator cars may have higher interior clearances if desired, which increases overhead clearance required in the hoistway.
3. Guide rails usually are provided by the manufacturer in 5 ft sections. Some manufacturers supply rails that can span from floor structure to floor structure. If the existing structure cannot support the guide rails, manufacturers can provide a self-supporting tower that transmits the load to its base. Increased horizontal clearance in the hoistway is required. If a third guide rail is required, it is supplied in 3 ft 4 in. sections.
4. Dimensions given are appropriate for most applications. For exact dimensions required in specific circumstances, consult manufacturers.
5. Elevator cars can be provided with openings on two sides; guide rails must be located accordingly. Consult manufacturers.

DUMBWAITERS

Typical car sizes, A x B: 24 in. x 24 in., 30 in. x 30 in., 36 in. x 36 in., 30 in. x 48 in. Smaller sizes are available.

9 sq ft platform maximum size allowed by National Elevator Code for dumbwaiters, ANSI A17.1.

48 in. high car is maximum allowed by National Elevator Code for dumbwaiters, ANSI A17.1.

Load capacity for drum-type machines is 500 lb. Speed is 50 ft per minute.

Drum-type machines are not recommended for installations with total travel of more than 36 ft–40 ft. Maximum total travel 50 ft.

Load capacity of traction machines is 500 lb. Speeds to 500 ft per minute are available.

Dumbwaiters require 3 phase electrical power. For exact voltage consult manufacturer.

NOTES

1. Dimensions may vary among manufacturers and according to system selected. Dumbwaiters carrying greater loads or operating at higher speeds require more clearance overhead and in pit areas.
2. Guide rails usually are provided by the manufacturer in 5 ft sections. Some manufacturers supply rails that can span from floor structure to floor structure. If existing structure cannot support the guide rails, manufacturers can provide a self-supporting tower that transmits the load to its base. Increased horizontal clearance in the hoistway is required.
3. Vertical dimensions given assume the use of vertical bi-parting doors. The entire door may slide up or down; however, required clearances will vary. Swing hoistway doors also are available. Consult manufacturers.

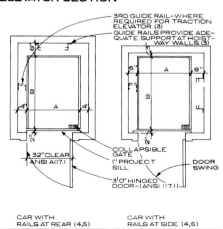

RESIDENTIAL ELEVATOR PLANS

Beth D. Buffington, AIA; Wilkes, Faulkner, Jenkins, and Bass Architects; Washington, D.C.

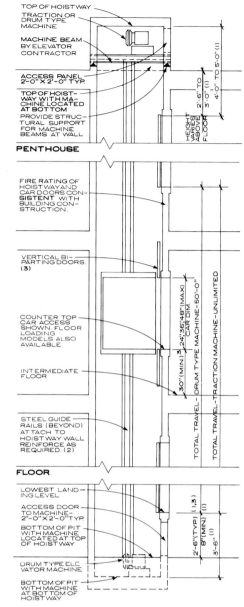

DUMBWAITER SECTION

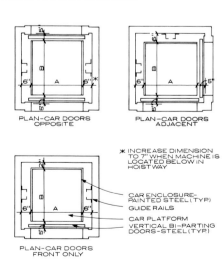

PLANS OF TYPICAL DUMBWAITERS

SERVICE ELEVATORS

Service elevators in industrial, residential, and commercial buildings are often standard passenger elevator packages modified for service use. These modified systems, when compared with custom made freight elevator systems, are generally more economical, are delivered in less time, and have more stringent load ratings related to the platform area. Special provisions include interior cab protection (steel or oak rubbing strips or suitable abuse resistant finish surface) and a door and cab of sufficient size to handle expected loads. Standard horizontal sliding doors can often meet service needs. If the full width of the car platform is needed for loading, vertical biparting doors can be used. If bulky loads are expected only occasionally, a removable car front with swinging hoistway door panels can be provided.

Vertically sliding doors and vertically sliding gates, where permitted by ANSI A17.1, shall conform to the following requirements:

1. At entrances used by passengers they shall be:
   a. Of the balanced counterweighted type which slide in the up direction to open.
   b. Power operated.
2. At entrances used exclusively for freight, they shall be:
   a. Of the balanced counterweighted type or the biparting counterbalanced type.
   b. Manually or power operated.

CAPACITY: Size to largest expected load, with the exception of single one piece loading, which is restricted to 25% of the rated capacity.

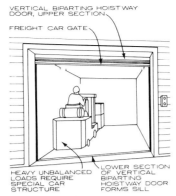

INTERIOR VIEW

FREIGHT ELEVATOR DIMENSIONS

CAPACITY (LB)	PLATFORM		HOISTWAY	
	WIDTH	DEPTH	WIDTH	DEPTH
2,500	5'-4''	7'-0''	7'-4''	8'-2''
6,000	8'-4''	10'-0''	10'-4''	11'-2''
10,000	8'-4''	12'-0''	11'-4''	13'-2''
16,000	10'-4''	14'-0''	14'-0''	15'-2''
20,000	12'-4''	20'-4''	16'-6''	21'-6''

FREIGHT ELEVATOR

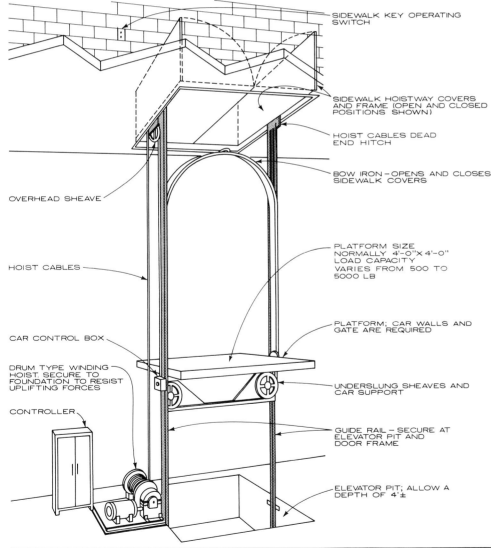

SIDEWALK ELEVATOR

Alexander Keyes; Darrel Downing Rippeteau, Architect; Washington, D.C.

FREIGHT ELEVATORS

Freight elevators are usually classed as general freight loading, motor vehicle loading, industrial truck or concentrated loading elevators. General freight loading elevators, described below, may be electric drum type or traction or hydraulic elevators.

General freight loading elevators satisfy a variety of material handling requirements with capacities of 2000 to 8000 lb. Industrial truck loading freight elevators require special design considerations to handle truck loads of 10,000 to 20,000 lb or more.

General freight or industrial truck elevators may have either hydraulic or electric drive systems, similar to those described on previous pages. The units are usually custom designed with vertical biparting doors and special structural support to carry increased loads and eccentric loading conditions.

Freight elevators usually operate at slower speeds with simple control systems. Capacity must be sized for the largest expected load.

LIGHT DUTY FREIGHT ELEVATORS with capacities of 1000 to 2500 lb may utilize hydraulic or traction drives. Standard systems are illustrated on other pages of this section. Two special types of light freight elevators, with rises limited according to manufacturer, are the SIDEWALK ELEVATOR and the SELF-SUPPORTING ELEVATOR.

The SIDEWALK ELEVATOR, illustrated on this page with an electric winding drum type machine, rises to a top level through hatch doors. Note that local codes often forbid the raising of an elevator in a public sidewalk; elevators may have to be located within building lines.

The SELF-SUPPORTING FREIGHT ELEVATOR is similar to the sidewalk elevator illustrated and operates within a building up to three stories (rise varies with manufacturer). Weight of the car is transferred through the supporting guide rails to the elevator pit.

With the electric winding drum machine, machinery must lift the full weight of car and its load. The drum must be anchored to the floor to resist uplifting forces. Safety codes forbid use of electric winding drum machines for passenger elevators and restrict their use on freight elevators to a speed not exceeding 50 fpm and a travel not exceeding 40 ft; they shall not be provided with counterweights.

SELF-SUPPORTING ELEVATOR DIMENSIONS

CAPACITY (LB)	PLATFORM		HOISTWAY	
	WIDTH	DEPTH	WIDTH	DEPTH
1,500	5'-4''	6'-1''	6'-11''	6'-9''
2,000	6'-4''	7'-0''	7'-11''	7'-8''
2,500	6'-4''	8'-0''	7'-11''	8'-8''

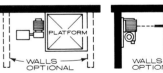 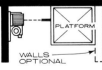

SIDE MOUNTED **WALL MOUNTED**

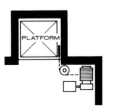 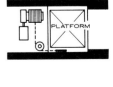

AROUND THE CORNER **MACHINE IN BACK**

MACHINE LAYOUTS – WINDING DRUM TYPE

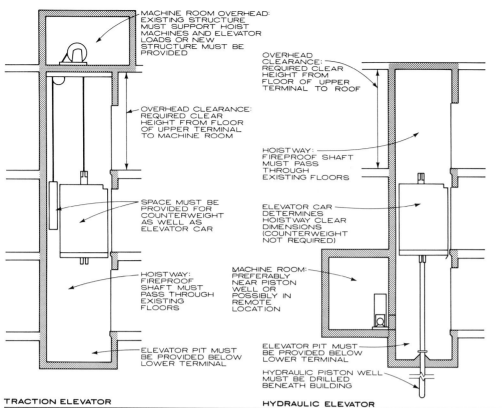

MACHINE ROOM OVERHEAD: EXISTING STRUCTURE MUST SUPPORT HOIST MACHINES AND ELEVATOR LOADS OR NEW STRUCTURE MUST BE PROVIDED

OVERHEAD CLEARANCE: REQUIRED CLEAR HEIGHT FROM FLOOR OF UPPER TERMINAL TO ROOF

OVERHEAD CLEARANCE: REQUIRED CLEAR HEIGHT FROM FLOOR OF UPPER TERMINAL TO MACHINE ROOM

HOISTWAY: FIREPROOF SHAFT MUST PASS THROUGH EXISTING FLOORS

SPACE MUST BE PROVIDED FOR COUNTERWEIGHT AS WELL AS ELEVATOR CAR

ELEVATOR CAR DETERMINES HOISTWAY CLEAR DIMENSIONS (COUNTERWEIGHT NOT REQUIRED)

HOISTWAY: FIREPROOF SHAFT MUST PASS THROUGH EXISTING FLOORS

MACHINE ROOM: PREFERABLY NEAR PISTON WELL OR POSSIBLY IN REMOTE LOCATION

ELEVATOR PIT MUST BE PROVIDED BELOW LOWER TERMINAL

ELEVATOR PIT MUST BE PROVIDED BELOW LOWER TERMINAL

HYDRAULIC PISTON WELL MUST BE DRILLED BENEATH BUILDING

TRACTION ELEVATOR

HYDRAULIC ELEVATOR

ELEVATOR RETROFIT

MACHINE ROOM: HOISTING MACHINES MAY BE OVERHAULED OR MODERNIZED TO PROVIDE GREATER SPEED OR HOISTING CAPACITY. AGE OF MACHINERY AND PRESENT USAGE DEMANDS ARE DETERMINING FACTORS

MODERN CONTROLS ARE OFTEN INSTALLED TO SYNCHRONIZE GROUP ELEVATOR SERVICE AND REDUCE CAR STOPPING AND STARTING TIME

SOUNDPROOFING OR STRUCTURAL REINFORCEMENT MAY BE REQUIRED

ELEVATOR CAR: EXISTING CAR MAY BE RENOVATED OR REPLACED

IF RENOVATED, CONTROLS AND DOORS MAY BE AUTOMATED TO PROVIDE SELF-SERVICE ELEVATORS, AND REDUCE DOOR OPERATING TIME. CENTER OPENING (HORIZONTAL BIPARTING) DOORS WITH ENTRANCE SAFETY DEVICES (SEE "ELEVATOR CAR DESIGN") REPLACE SINGLE SLIDE DOORS FOR INCREASED EFFICIENCY. THE CAR INTERIOR MAY BE RENOVATED OR RESTORED TO RETAIN ORIGINAL APPEARANCES

IF REPLACED, A FULLY AUTOMATED CAR WITH MODERN CONTROLS MAY BE INSERTED INTO AN EXISTING ELEVATOR HOISTWAY

CONSULT REPRESENTATIVES OF THE ELEVATOR INDUSTRY

HOISTWAY: ADDITIONAL FIREPROOFING OF HOISTWAY WALLS MAY BE REQUIRED. CHECK LOCAL CODES

HOISTWAY WALLS AND GUIDE RAILS MAY BE SOUNDPROOFED

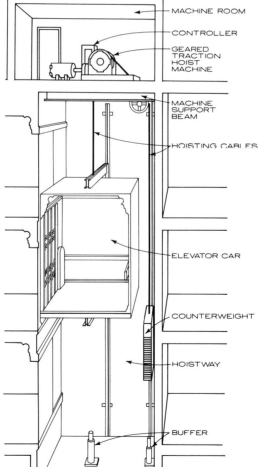

MACHINE ROOM

CONTROLLER

GEARED TRACTION HOIST MACHINE

MACHINE SUPPORT BEAM

HOISTING CABLES

ELEVATOR CAR

COUNTERWEIGHT

HOISTWAY

BUFFER

ELEVATOR PIT

ELEVATOR RENOVATION

ELEVATOR RETROFIT

Existing buildings may be retrofitted with the elevator systems previously illustrated. General selection, location, and arrangement guidelines apply. Additional constraints imposed by existing building conditions must also be considered.

HYDRAULIC ELEVATORS generally require the least initial installation expense in buildings of 2 to 6 stories. The hoistway need only be a fireproof shaft, separating the elevator passageway from the rest of the building. Elevator car guide rails are attached from within the hoistway to the existing structural frame at each floor. A machine room is located near the lower terminal, often in an existing basement. The weight of the system bears upon a concrete pad at the base of the hoistway, beneath which a hole must be drilled to accommodate the hydraulic piston, approximately equal in length to the distance of elevator travel. A HOLELESS HYDRAULIC system eliminates the need for this hole but is limited to a rise of 3 stories.

ELECTRIC ELEVATORS can serve buildings of higher rises at greater speeds and generally lower operating costs. Hoisting machines are located above the hoistway and bear the weight of the elevator system. A structural frame must be designed to support these machines within the existing structural system. Sufficient space for a machine room must be provided, often on an existing roof. The hoistway is designed as a fireproof shaft with elevator guide rails attached to the building structure at each floor. An alternate elevator system permits the hoist machines to be located in the basement (see ELECTRIC ELEVATOR SYSTEMS) in situations where low overhead clearance is available. The weight of the system must still be supported at the top of the hoistway.

In all cases, representatives of the elevator industry must be contacted for proper elevator selection and design specifications.

ELEVATOR RENOVATION AND MODERNIZATION

Elevator systems in older buildings may be renovated and modernized to provide improved service. Certain service components (controls, hoist machines, door operators) may be overhauled or modernized, while visual components (elevator car, lobby) may be renovated or restored to original appearance. The extent of modernization will vary in each case; consult representatives of the elevator industry.

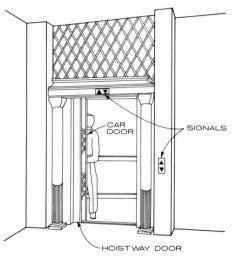

CAR DOOR

SIGNALS

HOISTWAY DOOR

ELEVATOR LOBBY: LOBBY MAY BE RESTORED TO RETAIN ORIGINAL APPEARANCES. NEW SIGNALS AND INDICATORS MAY BE INSERTED INTO AN EXISTING LOBBY WALL (SEE "ELEVATOR LOBBY DESIGN"). HOISTWAY DOORS MAY BE REPLACED FOR INCREASED EFFICIENCY

Olga Barmine; Darrel Downing Rippeteau, Architect; Washington, D.C.

14   ELEVATORS

Escalators are a very efficient form of vertical transportation for very heavy traffic where the number of floors served is limited, normally a maximum of five to six floors. Escalators are not usually accepted as a required exit.

Dimensions shown are general and will vary somewhat with the manufacturer. Consult manufacturers for structural support, electrical supply, and specific dimensional requirements.

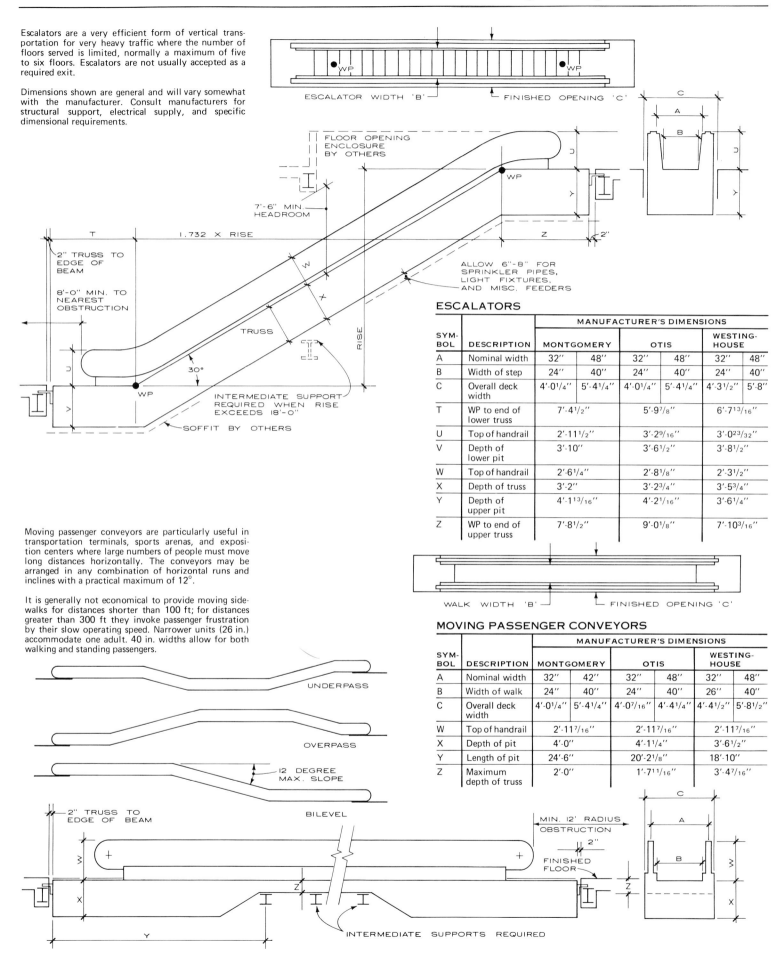

ESCALATORS

SYM-BOL	DESCRIPTION	MANUFACTURER'S DIMENSIONS					
		MONTGOMERY		OTIS		WESTING-HOUSE	
A	Nominal width	32″	48″	32″	48″	32″	48″
B	Width of step	24″	40″	24″	40″	24″	40″
C	Overall deck width	4′-0¼″	5′-4¼″	4′-0¼″	5′-4¼″	4′-3½″	5′-8″
T	WP to end of lower truss	7′-4½″		5′-9⅞″		6′-7¹³⁄₁₆″	
U	Top of handrail	2′-11½″		3′-2⁹⁄₁₆″		3′-0²³⁄₃₂″	
V	Depth of lower pit	3′-10″		3′-6½″		3′-8½″	
W	Top of handrail	2′-6¼″		2′-8⅛″		2′-3½″	
X	Depth of truss	3′-2″		3′-2¾″		3′-5¾″	
Y	Depth of upper pit	4′-1¹³⁄₁₆″		4′-2¹⁄₁₆″		3′-6¼″	
Z	WP to end of upper truss	7′-8½″		9′-0⅛″		7′-10³⁄₁₆″	

Moving passenger conveyors are particularly useful in transportation terminals, sports arenas, and exposition centers where large numbers of people must move long distances horizontally. The conveyors may be arranged in any combination of horizontal runs and inclines with a practical maximum of 12°.

It is generally not economical to provide moving sidewalks for distances shorter than 100 ft; for distances greater than 300 ft they invoke passenger frustration by their slow operating speed. Narrower units (26 in.) accommodate one adult. 40 in. widths allow for both walking and standing passengers.

MOVING PASSENGER CONVEYORS

SYM-BOL	DESCRIPTION	MANUFACTURER'S DIMENSIONS					
		MONTGOMERY		OTIS		WESTING-HOUSE	
A	Nominal width	32″	42″	32″	48″	32″	48″
B	Width of walk	24″	40″	24″	40″	26″	40″
C	Overall deck width	4′-0¼″	5′-4¼″	4′-0⁷⁄₁₆″	4′-4¼″	4′-4½″	5′-8½″
W	Top of handrail	2′-11⁷⁄₁₆″		2′-11⁷⁄₁₆″		2′-11⁷⁄₁₆″	
X	Depth of pit	4′-0″		4′-1¼″		3′-6½″	
Y	Length of pit	24′-6″		20′-2⅛″		18′-10″	
Z	Maximum depth of truss	2′-0″		1′-7¹¹⁄₁₆″		3′-4⁷⁄₁₆″	

Alan H. Rider, AIA; Daniel, Mann, Johnson & Mendenhall; Washington, D.C.

REFERENCES

GENERAL REFERENCES

Electric and Electrohydraulic Elevators, Moving Sidewalks and Ramps, Fred A. Annett, McGraw-Hill

National Electric Code Handbook, National Fire Protection Agency (NFPA)

Standard Elevator Layouts, National Elevator Industry

Vertical Transportation: Elevators and Escalators, George R. Strakosch, Wiley

DATA SOURCES: ORGANIZATIONS

American National Standards Institute (ANSI), 323, 325

Montgomery Elevator Company, 327

National Elevator Industry, Inc., 322, 323, 325, 326

Otis Elevator Company, 327

Westinghouse Electric Corporation, 327

CHAPTER **15**

ENERGY DESIGN

STRATEGIES OF CLIMATE CONTROL

Dry, clear atmospheres lead to high insolation levels, high daytime air temperatures, very high sol-air temperatures, and large thermal radiation losses. These factors produce daily temperature ranges in excess of 30°F. Although daytime air temperatures may be too high for ventilation, nighttime temperatures often fall below comfort limits and are useful for cooling. Arid regions in the U.S. have winter heating requirements, especially at night. Clear skies greatly favor passive solar heating.

High daytime temperatures and solar loads require measures that reduce heat gain. Evaporative roof spray systems dissipate absorbed solar heat, but consume large quantities of water and decrease in value with increases in roof insulation. Evaporative space cooling systems are often effective substitutes for refrigerant air conditioning. Deep ground temperatures are too high and soil thermal conductivity too low in hot, arid regions for the earth to be a useful cooling sink in conventional construction. Low conductivity makes the soil a good buffer against surface conditions, and earth-integrated design can take advantage of seasonal cold storage, so earth coupling does offer opportunities.

MINIMIZE SOLAR GAINS

Plant trees to shade roof and east and west walls. Shape building to minimize solar load on envelope. Cluster buildings to shade one another. Provide shading for outdoor pedestrian and living areas (ramadas and pergolas), and shade all glazing during overheated period. Use carport or garage as buffer on west side. Use light-colored surfacing on walls and roof.

MINIMIZE CONDUCTIVE GAINS

Insulate envelope components in proportion to (sol-air–indoor) temperature difference. Use radiant barrier in attic or cathedral ceiling. Use thermally massive envelope materials. Insulate perimeter of slab-on-grade floors.

PROMOTE VENTILATION LOSSES

Site building to exploit nighttime breezes. Arrange floor plan for internal air movement, especially to cool thermal mass. Consider a whole-house fan for night cooling. Ventilate building envelope (attic or roof, walls).

THERMAL MASS AND INSULATION CONCEPTS

Massive walls of sufficient thickness can average daily outdoor temperatures and maintain nearly constant indoor surface temperatures. This thickness (in feet) for an uninsulated homogeneous wall must be greater than $6.4\ (k/wc)^{1/2}$, where k is thermal conductivity in Btu/ft(hr)F, w is density in lb/cu ft, and c is specific heat in Btu/(lb)F. The minimum thickness is 14 in. for poured concrete, 12 in. for brick, 9 in. for adobe, and 6 in. for pine log. Less thick walls reduce, but do not eliminate, the temperature swing. The ratio of interior to exterior fluctuation is termed the "decrement factor." Values for some composite walls are given in the table.

A completely shaded, uninsulated massive wall can do no better than maintain a temperature near the outdoor daily average at the interior, unless the space is ventilated at night. Uninsulated mass walls have low R values and are not economically suitable for heated and air-conditioned buildings. Insulating outside the mass has the greatest benefit: It reduces heat gain while allowing the wall to store "coolth" from nighttime ventilation. Insulation also allows less mass to be used. The thermally optimal storage thickness (in feet) of mass that is well insulated on the outside is $3.3\ (k/wc)^{1/2}$. Less thickness is still beneficial.

Insulating inside the mass or adding mass outside an insulated frame wall (brick veneer) improves performance over either case alone. Both are inferior to outside insulation and slightly less effective than walls with integral insulation (masonry with core insulation). The optimal insulation and mass combinations vary with climate and conditioning hours of the building.

THERMAL MASS TIME DELAY

Mass delays the transfer of heat to the interior. Its usefulness depends on occupancy and air-conditioning schedules. While a masonry west wall can relieve an office building of peak loads during business hours, for example, it would be inappropriate for a west-facing bedroom. The delay rate in hours per foot for a homogeneous wall is about $1.4(wc/k)^{1/2}$ in thickness.

INTERIOR ZONING AND DAYLIGHTING

Vernacular house design in hot, arid regions uses low mass construction for sleeping areas and high mass for daytime activity areas. The low mass zone is ventilated and cools off quickly at night, while the massive zone has little window area. Evaporative space coolers can provide comfort more than 90% of the time at elevations above 1500 ft and more than 50% at elevations below 1500 ft throughout the Southwest. Ducts should be sized for 1200 fpm (for silence and efficiency) to 1600 fpm.

Clear, sunny skies make daylighting dependable and predictable for design. Small window and skylight areas are effective. Apertures should be shaded at the exterior. Reflected light from the ground and from light shelves is useful, but glare from uncontrolled reflecting surfaces must be kept from view.

REFERENCES

1. K. Clark and P. Paylore, *Desert Housing: Balancing Experience and Technology for Dwelling in Hot Arid Zones*, Office of Arid Land Studies, University of Arizona, Tucson.
2. J. Cook, *Cool Houses for Desert Suburbs*, Arizona Solar Energy Commission, Phoenix, 1984.
3. H. Kessler, *Passive Solar Design for Arizona*, Arizona Solar Energy Commission, Phoenix, 1983.
4. A. Olgyay and V. Olgyay, *Solar Control and Shading Devices*, Princeton University Press, Princeton, 1957.
5. S. Byrne and R. Ritschard, "A Parametric Analysis of Thermal Mass in Residential Buildings," LBL-20288, Lawrence Berkeley Laboratory, Berkeley, CA 94720, 1985.

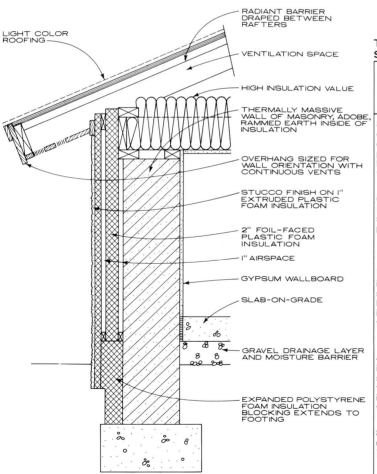

LIGHT COLOR ROOFING

RADIANT BARRIER DRAPED BETWEEN RAFTERS

VENTILATION SPACE

HIGH INSULATION VALUE

THERMALLY MASSIVE WALL OF MASONRY, ADOBE, RAMMED EARTH INSIDE OF INSULATION

OVERHANG SIZED FOR WALL ORIENTATION WITH CONTINUOUS VENTS

STUCCO FINISH ON 1" EXTRUDED PLASTIC FOAM INSULATION

2" FOIL-FACED PLASTIC FOAM INSULATION

1" AIRSPACE

GYPSUM WALLBOARD

SLAB-ON-GRADE

GRAVEL DRAINAGE LAYER AND MOISTURE BARRIER

EXPANDED POLYSTYRENE FOAM INSULATION BLOCKING EXTENDS TO FOOTING

ENERGY-EFFICIENT WALL SECTION INTERIOR MASS WITH OUTSIDE INSULATION

THERMAL PERFORMANCE (TIME LAG) OF VARIOUS WALL SECTIONS

WALL DESCRIPTION	U VALUE (WINTER)	HEAT GAIN BTU/HR/SQ FT (DARK COLOR)		TIME LAG (HR)	AMPLITUDE DECREMENT FACTOR
		AVERAGE ORIENTATION	WEST ORIENTATION		
8" brick and lightweight concrete (100 lb density) block 2" polystyrene insulation board ½" gypsum wallboard	0.073	2.06	1.75	4	0.40
6" precast concrete (140 lb density) sandwich panel 2" polyurethane core	0.065	1.82	1.55	4	0.40
½" plywood siding ½" insulation board sheathing, wood studs. Full batt (R-11) insulation ½" gypsum wallboard	0.076	3.05	4.60	2	0.75
4" brick veneer ½" insulation board sheathing. Wood studs full batt (R-11) insulation ½" gypsum wallboard	0.077	2.18	1.95	4	0.62
8" brick wall (hollow units) 1" x 2" furring. ½" gypsum wallboard	0.316	7.37	5.90	6	0.25

Donald Watson, FAIA; Trumbull, Connecticut
Kenneth Labs; New Haven, Connecticut

15 **ENERGY DESIGN**

STRATEGIES OF CLIMATE CONTROL

Underheated conditions occur in both humid and arid regions and dominate much of the U.S. The strategies are to minimize conduction and infiltration losses and to take advantage of winter solar gain. Humidity affects sky clearness and availability of solar radiation, making optimization of solar glazing area one of the main opportunities of regional design. Moisture movement through the building shell must be controlled. It is driven by air leakage (exfiltration) and by vapor diffusion, which is related to temperature differences.

MINIMIZE CONDUCTION LOSSES

Minimize ratio of envelope to heated floor area. Minimize foundation perimeter length. Insulate envelope components in proportion to indoor–outdoor temperature difference. Minimize areas of windows, doors, and other envelope components of inherently low R value. Detail to avoid thermal bridging. Provide movable insulation for glazed areas.

MINIMIZE INFILTRATION LOSSES

Plant vegetation to create wind-sheltered building sites. Shape building to minimize exposure to winter wind. Orient doors and windows away from winter wind. Specify weatherstripping and infiltration barrier.

CAPTURE SOLAR GAIN

Provide high-transmittance south-facing glazing. Provide thermal mass indoors to store solar gains.

INSULATION

Insulation requirements are proportional to heating loads. The foundation is often underinsulated and can be a major source of heat loss. The desirable insulation level depends on basement temperature and insulation levels in the rest of the building. An approximate thermal optimum is:

$$R_{ins} = \frac{T_{bsmt} - T_0}{T_1 - T_0} R_{ref} - R_{wall}$$

R_{ins} = R value to be added to basement wall above grade

R_{ref} = R value of superstructure wall

R_{wall} = R value of uninsulated basement foundation wall

T_{bsmt} = average seasonal temperature of basement

T_1 = average seasonal temperature of living space

T_0 = average seasonal outdoor temperature

The added foundation insulation above grade is R_{ins}. It should decrease with depth by R − 2 per foot in ordinary soils and R − 1.5 in wet soils. A horizontal skirt can be used to reduce floor perimeter losses. Exterior insulation keeps the wall warm and eliminates condensation and thermal bridges. As seasonal basement temperature decreases, losses to it from the superstructure increase, and basement ceiling R value should increase. As a very rough rule, the basement ceiling R value should be greater than (R_{ref} − R_{ins}).

SOLAR DESIGN AND DAYLIGHTING

The most advantageous south glazing area depends on thermal and climatic factors. Rules of thumb have been prepared (Los Alamos National Laboratory) and more sophisticated methods are available for desktop computers.

The advantage of glazing for daylighting has to be weighed against the penalty of winter heat loss. In predominantly cloudy climates, skylighting can be designed without significant shading, but not without concern for glare. In clear, sunny climates and in warmer regions, daylight glazing may require shading to reduce undesired heat gain. South glazing has the combined advantages of daylighting, winter heat gain, and economical summer shading.

REFERENCES

1. Los Alamos National Laboratory, *Passive Solar Heating Analysis*, ASHRAE, Atlanta, 1984.
2. National Research Council, Canada, Ottawa, Ontario, K1A OR6: *Construction Details for Air Tightness* (nonresidential), NRCC 18291, 1980; *Exterior Walls: Understanding the Problems*, NRCC 21203, 1983; *Humidity, Condensation and Ventilation in Houses*, NRCC 23293, 1984; J. Latta, *The Principles and Dilemmas of Designing Durable House Envelopes for the North*, Building Practice Note 52, 1985.

Donald Watson, FAIA; Trumbull, Connecticut
Kenneth Labs; New Haven, Connecticut

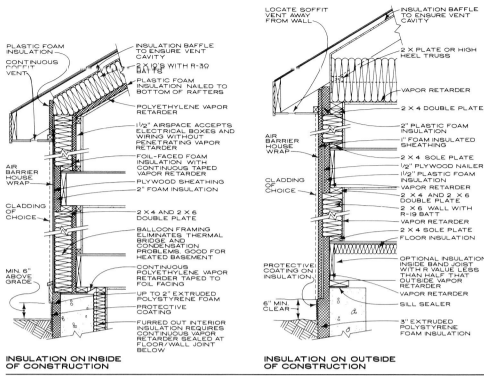

INSULATION ON INSIDE OF CONSTRUCTION

INSULATION ON OUTSIDE OF CONSTRUCTION

ENERGY-EFFICIENT WALL SECTIONS

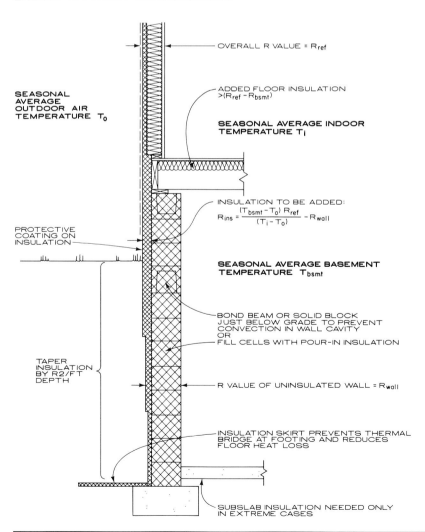

BASEMENT FOUNDATION AND FLOOR INSULATION

STRATEGIES OF CLIMATE CONTROL

Humid overheated conditions are most severe along the Gulf Coast, but occur across the entire southeastern U.S. Atmospheric moisture limits radiation exchange, resulting in daily temperature ranges less than 20°F. High insolation gives first priority to shading. Much of the indoors overheated period is only a few degrees above comfort limits, so air movement can cool the body. Ground temperatures are generally too high for the earth to be useful as a heat sink, although slab-on-grade floor mass is useful. The strategies are to resist solar and conductive heat gains and to take best advantage of ventilation.

MINIMIZE SOLAR GAINS

1. Plant trees to shade roof and east and west walls.
2. Shape building to minimize solar load on envelope.
3. Shade all glazing during overheated period.
4. Shade north elevation in subtropical latitudes.
5. Use light-colored surfacing on walls and roof.

MINIMIZE CONDUCTIVE GAINS

1. Insulate envelope components in proportion to sol-air–indoor temperature difference.
2. Use radiant barrier in attic space.
3. Consider thermally massive envelope materials to reduce peak air-conditioning loads.
4. Use slab-on-grade instead of crawl space and insulate only at perimeter.

PROMOTE VENTILATION LOSSES

1. Orient building to benefit from breezes.
2. Use plantings to funnel breezes into building, but be careful not to obstruct vent openings.
3. Use wing walls and overhangs to direct breezes into building.
4. Locate openings and arrange floor plan to promote cross ventilation.

5. Plan interior for effective use of whole-house fan.
6. Ventilate building envelope (attic or roof, walls).

SPACE VENTILATION

"Air-change ventilation" brings outdoor temperatures indoors by breezes or whole-house exhaust fans. Whole-house fans yield about 60 air changes per hour (ACH) and are useful only as long as outdoor conditions are within comfort limits (72°–82°F). They may offer 30–50% savings in electricity costs over air conditioning. Whole-house fans do not provide high enough airflow rates for body ventilation. Ceiling (paddle) fans are recommended for air movement and can maintain comfort with indoor temperatures up to 85°F ET*. Air conditioning is necessary above 85°F ET*. The issue of when to ventilate and when to air condition is a function of building type, occupancy hours, heat and moisture capacity of the structure, and climatic subregion. Humidity is a factor, as night air may be cool but excessively humid.

ROOFS AND ATTICS

The attic should be designed to ventilate naturally. Most of the heat gain to the attic is by radiation from the underside of the roof. While ventilation is unable to interrupt this transfer, most of it can be stopped by an aluminum foil radiant barrier. Foil facings on rigid insulation and sheathing can be used as radiant barriers when installed facing an airspace.

Roof spray systems can dissipate most of the solar load, leaving the roof temperature near the ambient dry-bulb instead of the sol-air temperature. The theoretical lowest temperature that the roof can be cooled to by evaporation is the wet-bulb, but is not attainable under real daytime conditions. The cost-effectiveness of spray systems depends on the roof section, R value, building type, climatic region, and other factors. Spray systems are most advantageous for poorly insulated flat roofs.

WALLS

Radiant barriers enhance the performance of walls by reducing solar gain. They are most effective on east and west walls and are recommended for predominantly overheated regions [< 2000 heating degree days (HDD), >2500 cooling degree days (CDD)]. They are not recommended on south walls except where CDD exceed 3500. Radiant barriers must face an airspace and can be located on either side of the wall structure. Outside placement allows the cavity to be vented. This enhances summer wall performance, but admitting cold air degrades it during winter. Venting is recommended for regions having more than 3500 CDD. Discharging the cavity into the attic ensures best vent action. Thermal mass in walls reduces peak air-conditioning loads and delays peak heat gain. By damping off some of the peak load, massive walls help keep indoor temperatures in the range where ceiling (paddle) fans and airflow from cross ventilation provide comfort.

DAYLIGHTING

Windows and skylights should be shaded to prevent undesired heat gain. North- and south-facing glazing is shaded most easily for predictable daylighting. Light-colored reflective sunshades and ground surfaces will bounce the light and minimize direct gain. Cloudy or hazy sky conditions are a source of brightness and glare.

REFERENCES

1. S. Chandra et al. *Cooling with Ventilation*, Solar Energy Research Institute, Golden, CO, 1982.
2. P. Fairey, "Radiant Barrier Systems," Design Notes 6 and 7, Florida Solar Energy Center, Cape Canaveral, 1984.
3. P. Fairey, S. Chandra, A. Kerestecioglu, "Ventilative Cooling in Southern Residences: A Parametric Analysis," PF-108-86, Florida Solar Energy Center, Cape Canaveral, 1986.

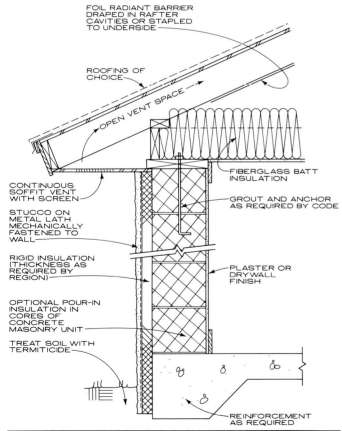

ENERGY-EFFICIENT WALL SECTION: VENTED SKIN MASONRY WALL WITH INSIDE INSULATION

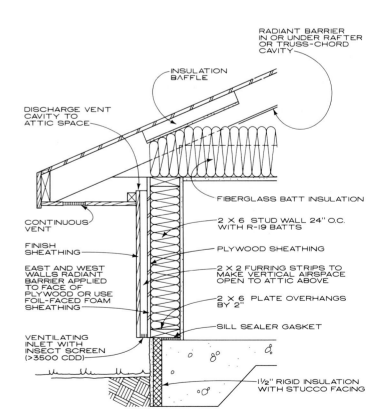

ENERGY-EFFICIENT WALL SECTION: VENTED SKIN WALL WITH RADIANT BARRIER

Donald Watson, FAIA; Trumbull, Connecticut
Kenneth Labs; New Haven, Connecticut

15 ENERGY DESIGN

The design of a solar collector array and its support structure can have an important influence on overall building appearance and be a key determinant of the total cost of the solar heating system. It is also the aspect of the system that the architect can most easily control.

Because there are no industry standards for collector size, piping, or mounting hardware, it is essential that the architect know which collector system will be installed before he or she begins final detailing and design. If the collector array is to be selected as part of a total bid package, for example, sizing and coordination problems may result, and the architect may lose control of the array's structural underpinnings and the building's overall appearance.

ANCHORING THE SUPPORT STRUCTURE

Rooftop collector supports should be anchored directly to structural members, not to wood or metal decking; otherwise, wind-induced uplift forces and point loading may cause roofing—and possibly structural—failure. In steel buildings, vertical supports must be secured directly to joists or beams. In wood buildings, securing the collector supports directly to structural members will normally require the installation of some form of blocking, under the decking and between rafters, to transfer the load.

DESIGNING THE ARRAY

When a collector array is to be placed on a light steel-framed roof, the direction of the joints in the array's support structure becomes a critical design issue. It is often necessary to stagger the array's vertical supports to ensure an even distribution of the load. Some roofs cannot support such a load and thus must be clear-spanned. The array support structure in such cases is likely to be particularly expensive; intricate long-span space-frame structures are invariably costly and cost-ineffective.

AVOIDING ROOFING PROBLEMS

Leaky roofs are a persistent problem in solar installations. Problems can be anticipated and minimized by following these guidelines:

- Minimize roof penetrations. Collector supports constructed of pipe, if used in a large array as shown, require one roof penetration for every 60 sq ft of roof area, approximately; long-span design, by comparison, calls for one roof penetration roughly every 225 sq ft. Roof penetrations can also be avoided by using solar piping supports that rest directly on the roof, as shown; these prevent undue roof stress caused by pipe movement.
- Properly detail the flashing of vertical supports at the roofline. Except on pitched roofs (and often even then), wood-blocking bolted directly through the roof will ultimately generate leaks, regardless of the amount of roofing cement applied. The best approach is to use a neoprene roofing sleeve. The next best is base flashing and canopy detail. Less preferable is a pitch pocket, properly constructed. Other approaches—those using site-fabricated curbs and other techniques—tend to fail. If blocking is to be secured directly to a sloped roof, then roofing cement should be applied between each layer of shingles, between shingles and deck, and between shingles and blocking.

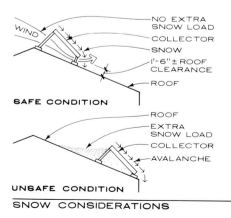

SAFE CONDITION

WIND
NO EXTRA SNOW LOAD
COLLECTOR
SNOW
1'-6" ± ROOF CLEARANCE
ROOF

UNSAFE CONDITION

ROOF
EXTRA SNOW LOAD
COLLECTOR
AVALANCHE

SNOW CONSIDERATIONS

Stephen Weinstein, AIA; The Ehrenkrantz Group; New York, New York

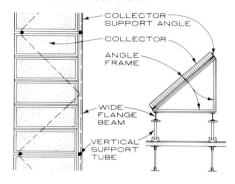

WIND BRACING
VERTICAL SUPPORT TUBE
HORIZONTAL WIND BRACING
COLLECTORS
COLLECTOR SUPPORT ANGLES

PLAN

COLLECTOR SUPPORT

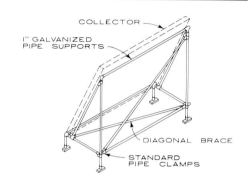

COLLECTOR
COLLECTOR SUPPORT ANGLE
DIAGONAL SUPPORT ANGLE
WIDE FLANGE BEAM
VERTICAL TUBE SUPPORT

SECTION

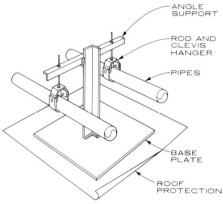

COLLECTOR SUPPORT ANGLE
COLLECTOR
ANGLE FRAME
WIDE FLANGE BEAM
VERTICAL SUPPORT TUBE

PLAN   **SECTION**

COLLECTOR SUPPORT

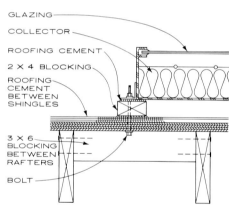

COLLECTOR
1" GALVANIZED PIPE SUPPORTS
DIAGONAL BRACE
STANDARD PIPE CLAMPS

PIPE RACK MOUNTING

ANGLE SUPPORT
ROD AND CLEVIS HANGER
PIPES
BASE PLATE
ROOF PROTECTION

PIPE SUPPORT

GLAZING
COLLECTOR
ROOFING CEMENT
2 X 4 BLOCKING
ROOFING CEMENT BETWEEN SHINGLES
3 X 6 BLOCKING BETWEEN RAFTERS
BOLT

SLOPED ROOF

- Do not create dams. Any form of continuous blocking or curb will—unless installed at a right angle to the slope of a pitched roof—invariably dam a portion of the roof and ultimately cause built-up roofing to fail.
- Specify that all work be performed by the appropriate trade. Support flashing, for instance, is often installed by the steel erector or the plumbing contractor rather than by the roofing contractor.
- Protect the roof. Specify that the roof in general be protected during construction and that permanent walkways be installed to provide access to the system once it is in use.
- Mount collectors on a sloped roof unless the pitch is so flat that the loss of year-round efficiency in performance will be too great. When collectors and

sloped roof are parallel, allow a 1½ in. airspace between them to prevent deterioration of the roofing material and the collector enclosures. Do not mount collectors integrally with the roofing unless the collectors are specifically designed for integral mounting; as a rule, only air collectors are so designed. In cold regions, mount collectors as near the roof peak as possible to minimize damming and snow buildup and to lessen the chance of a dangerous snow slide—a particular threat when an array is located above an entry.

- On a flat roof, mount collectors between 2 ft 6 in. and 3 ft above the roof rather than directly on the roof. This prevents snow buildup, permits adequately sloped pipe runs, and—most important—allows for the installation of proper roof penetrations and for future roof repair and replacement.

PRINCIPLES

Thermal storage wall systems are solar space heating devices that can also be used for space cooling in some climates. They consist generally of south-facing massive walls, an airspace, and are then sealed to the exterior by a glass or plastic glazing system. As solar radiation is transmitted through the glazing material, the wall is heated during sunlit hours; in turn the heated wall then radiates warmth to the interior space during the night. Additional components can be added to enhance cold climate performance, such as selective surface foils, night insulation systems, reflectors, and exterior vents to control overheating in mild climates.

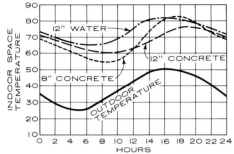

FIGURE 1

WALL PERFORMANCE

Figure 1 illustrates the characteristic performance of three thermal storage walls during one clear January day 24-hr cycle in a well-insulated house with ½ sq ft of wall for each square foot of room area, located in the U.S. Pacific Northwest. The two thicknesses of concrete wall shown in the graph demonstrate that by adding wall depth the resulting fluctuation in interior space temperature is reduced, and wall peak temperature is shifted toward the night hours when heat is most needed. Also it can be seen that by using a water wall with the same volume as the 12 in. concrete wall, the response of the wall to solar heating is enhanced; however, maximum heat transmission to the building interior occurs earlier in the evening when less heat is needed.

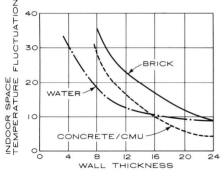

FIGURE 2

TEMPERATURE FLUCTUATION

Figure 2 illustrates space temperature fluctuations that can be expected for a one-day cycle using three different wall materials of varying thicknesses and the same design conditions as depicted in Figure 1. The wall types shown are solid brick, concrete or concrete masonry units grouted solid, and water.

WALL AREA VS. FLOOR AREA

Figure 3 gives rule of thumb guidelines for surface area of storage wall, using a wall thickness of between 8 and 18 in., compared to square feet of floor area to be heated for four latitudes. Example: Find the required wall area for a 250 sq ft room located at 40° north latitude with an average outdoor temperature of 34°F during the coldest winter month. On the "Y" axis find 34°, move right on the graph to the 40° latitude line, and then down the graph to the "X" axis, finding the wall vs. floor ratio of 0.45. Multiply 0.45 times the floor area of 250 sq ft, for a suggested wall area of 112.5 sq ft.

W. Fred Roberts Jr., AIA; Roberts & Kirchner Architects; Lexington, Virginia

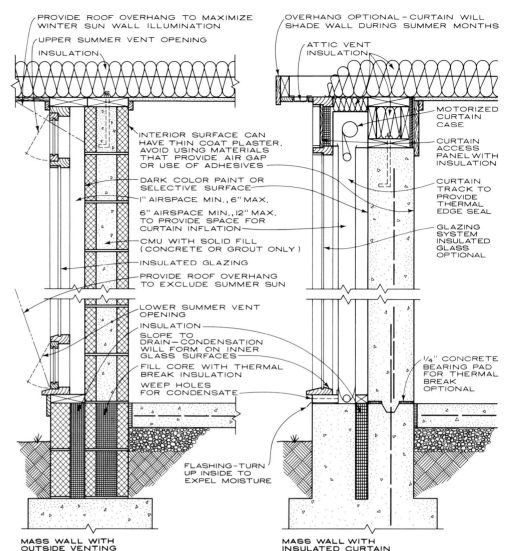

PROVIDE ROOF OVERHANG TO MAXIMIZE WINTER SUN WALL ILLUMINATION

UPPER SUMMER VENT OPENING

INSULATION

INTERIOR SURFACE CAN HAVE THIN COAT PLASTER. AVOID USING MATERIALS THAT PROVIDE AIR GAP OR USE OF ADHESIVES

DARK COLOR PAINT OR SELECTIVE SURFACE

1" AIRSPACE MIN., 6" MAX.

6" AIRSPACE MIN., 12" MAX. TO PROVIDE SPACE FOR CURTAIN INFLATION

CMU WITH SOLID FILL (CONCRETE OR GROUT ONLY)

INSULATED GLAZING

PROVIDE ROOF OVERHANG TO EXCLUDE SUMMER SUN

LOWER SUMMER VENT OPENING

INSULATION

SLOPE TO DRAIN—CONDENSATION WILL FORM ON INNER GLASS SURFACES

FILL CORE WITH THERMAL BREAK INSULATION

WEEP HOLES FOR CONDENSATE

FLASHING—TURN UP INSIDE TO EXPEL MOISTURE

MASS WALL WITH OUTSIDE VENTING

OVERHANG OPTIONAL—CURTAIN WILL SHADE WALL DURING SUMMER MONTHS

ATTIC VENT INSULATION

MOTORIZED CURTAIN CASE

CURTAIN ACCESS PANEL WITH INSULATION

CURTAIN TRACK TO PROVIDE THERMAL EDGE SEAL

GLAZING SYSTEM INSULATED GLASS OPTIONAL

¼" CONCRETE BEARING PAD FOR THERMAL BREAK OPTIONAL

MASS WALL WITH INSULATED CURTAIN

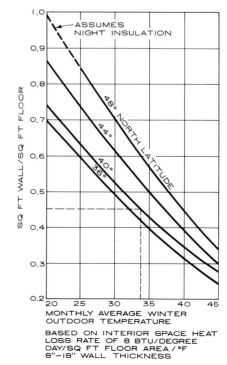

FIGURE 3

ASSUMES NIGHT INSULATION

48° NORTH LATITUDE
44°
40°
36°

BASED ON INTERIOR SPACE HEAT LOSS RATE OF 8 BTU/DEGREE DAY/SQ FT FLOOR AREA/°F 8"–18" WALL THICKNESS

WATER WALLS

Thermal storage walls of the water container type are generally designed as an integral part of the heated space. Fiberglass, plastic, glass, or metal containers can be used; however, if steel is used, a rust inhibitor should be added to the water, and in all cases algicide should be added to prevent algae growth. Water containers are also manufactured that fit within wood-framed walls and appear as translucent windows from the interior or that can be covered with dry wall.

INTERNAL MASS

Mass thermal walls can also be used within rooms that are directly heated by solar radiation entering through windows (direct gain system), but where the wall is not directly illuminated by the sun. In this application the wall acts as a heat sink, absorbing excess spacial heat during sunlit hours and giving back heat during the night, reducing spacial temperature swings. As a rule of thumb, provide internal mass wall area at the rate of six times the direct gain window area.

COOLING

The use of thermal storage walls for cooling involves the isolation of the wall from the exterior and, in particular, solar radiation during the sunlit hours, then exposing the wall surfaces to air jets of cool night air either by forced or natural ventilation to reduce the wall's internal temperature. The wall then functions as a heat sink during the warm hours the following day, to absorb internal spacial heat, thereby maintaining comfortable indoor temperatures.

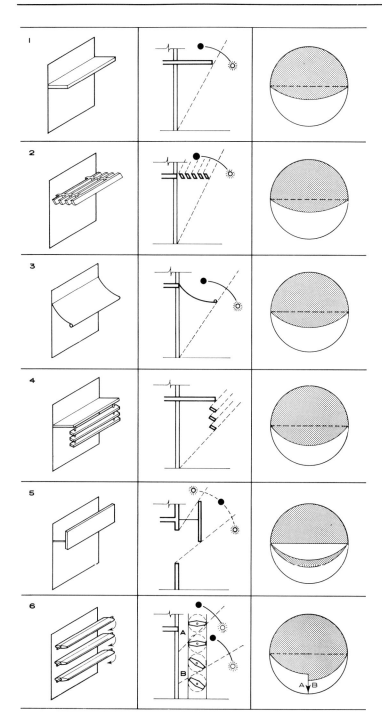

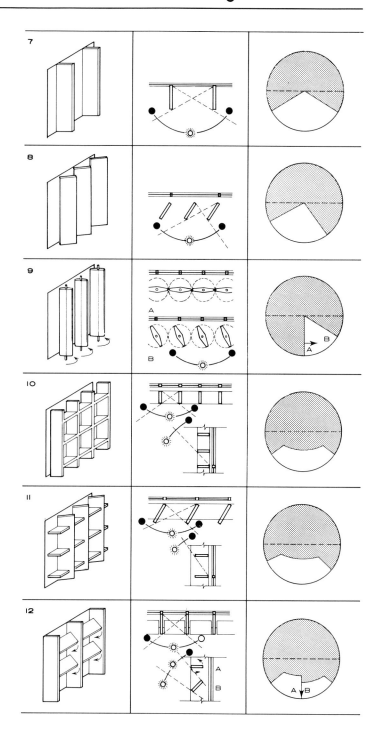

EXAMPLES OF VARIOUS TYPES OF SHADING DEVICES

The illustrations show a number of basic types of devices, classified as horizontal, vertical, and eggcrate types. The dash lines shown in the section diagram in each case indicate the sun angle at the time of 100% shading. The shading mask for each device is also shown, the extent of 100% shading being indicated by the gray area.

General rules can be deduced for the types of shading devices to be used for different orientations. Southerly orientations call for shading devices with segmental mask characteristics, and horizontal devices work in these directions efficiently. For easterly and westerly orientations vertical devices serve well, having radial shading masks. If slanted, they should incline toward the north, to give more protection from the southern positions of the sun. The eggcrate type of shading device works well on walls facing southeast, and is particularly effective for southwest orientations. Because of this type's high shading ratio and low winter head admission; its best use is in hot climate regions. For north walls, fixed vertical devices are recommended; however, their use is needed only for large glass surfaces, or in hot regions. At low latitudes on both south and north exposures eggcrate devices work efficiently.

Whether the shading devices be fixed or movable, the same recommendations apply in respect to the different orientations. The movable types can be most efficiently utilized where the sun's altitude and bearing angles change rapidly: on the east, southeast, and especially, because of the afternoon heat, on the southwest and west.

Victor Olgyay, AIA; Associate Professor; School of Architecture, Princeton University; Princeton, New Jersey

HORIZONTAL TYPES 1. Horizontal overhangs are most efficient toward south, or around southern orientations. Their mask characteristics are segmental. 2. Louvers parallel to wall have the advantage of permitting air circulation near the elevation. Slanted louvers will have the same characteristics as solid overhangs, and can be made retractable. 4. When protection is needed for low sun angles, louvers hung from solid horizontal overhangs are efficient. 5. A solid, or perforated screen strip parallel to wall cuts out the lower rays of the sun. 6. Movable horizontal louvers change their segmental mask characteristics according to their positioning.

VERTICAL TYPES 7. Vertical fins serve well toward the near east and near west orientations. Their mask characteristics are radial. 8. Vertical fins oblique to wall will result in asymmetrical mask. Separation from wall will prevent heat transmission. 9. Movable fins can shade the whole wall, or open up in different directions according to the sun's position.

EGGCRATE TYPES 10. Eggcrate types are combinations of horizontal and vertical types, and their masks are superimposed diagrams of the two masks. 11. Solid eggcrate with slanting vertical fins results in asymmetrical mask. 12. Eggcrate device with movable horizontal elements shows flexible mask characteristics. Because of their high shading ratio, eggcrates are efficient in hot climates.

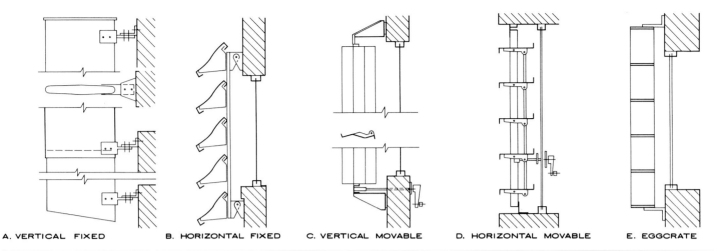

A. VERTICAL FIXED   B. HORIZONTAL FIXED   C. VERTICAL MOVABLE   D. HORIZONTAL MOVABLE   E. EGGCRATE

TYPICAL SUN SHADES AND CONTROLS

A. This device is effective on an east or west wall and can be attached at any degree of angle to facade. If slanted, it should incline to north. Fins are made in floor-to-floor lengths, capped at top and bottom, and telescoped top into bottom at intermediate levels.

B. This device is effective on any side of a building. Blades have a maximum length of 20 ft with supports of 6 ft on center.

C. Used on east or west side of building. This type may interfere with view. Many models are available up to 27 in. wide and 12 ft high.

D. Although this is effective on any side of a building, it is the least restrictive to view when used on the south side. It is usually hinged at the head for emergency exit and window washing. Blades are 9 in. deep; maximum width is 6 ft.

E. This type is very effective on southeast and southwest orientations. It is efficient in hot climates especially if bars can be tilted to more effective angles. All dimensions are variable according to desired function.

EXTERIOR SUN CONTROLS

The incidence of the sun's rays on a building transmits solar energy to the interior of the building. Since the heat gain through glass is particularly high, various forms of solar control for fenestration have been developed to reduce the use of mechanical equipment for cooling.

The most efficient of these is exterior shading, that is, avoiding the penetration of solar heat through the skin of the building. Exterior shading devices vary according to climate, orientation, and building function and are manufactured to suit specific conditions. They are strong design elements.

Sunshades (fixed horizontal or vertical fins, outriggers, and grills) shade glass completely or partially at critical times. Sun controls (movable horizontal or vertical fins) regulate the quantity of solar heat and light admitted through the glass, which is clear. Adjusting mechanisms can be manual or electric and can be automatically operated with time or photoelectric controls.

Aluminum, either sheet or extruded, is the standard material. Anodic and baked enamel coatings are available as finishes.

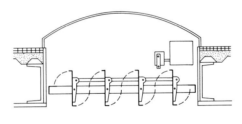

F. OUTRIGGER

F. Overhangs are most effectively used on the south side of a building. Wall brackets are made of cast aluminum. Projections greater than 6 ft require structural support or hangers.

G. SKYLIGHT SHUTTER

G. Perimeter framing should be designed to suit mounting conditions. Electrically operated shutters are available. Maximum width is 10 ft; length is unlimited.

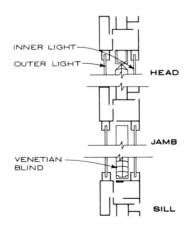

SLAT   STRINGER   45°   22½°   PROJECTED   VERTICAL

H. SHUTTER PANELS

I. INTEGRAL VENETIAN BLINDS
INNER LIGHT   OUTER LIGHT   HEAD   JAMB   VENETIAN BLIND   SILL

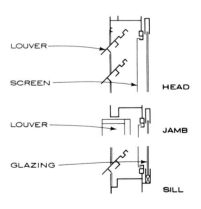

LOUVER   SCREEN   HEAD   LOUVER   JAMB   GLAZING   SILL

J. INTEGRAL HORIZONTAL SHADES

SPECIAL WINDOW TREATMENT

H. These panels are effective solar screens. The aluminum louvers are spaced to preserve the outside view and admit soft, diffused light while eliminating heat and glare. Horizontal slats snap onto stringer supports which can be easily attached to most structures.

I. This window type combines the thermal insulating values of dual glazing with the advantage of semi-external shading. An aluminum blind is provided between two pieces of glass, each in its own frame and each frame pivoted horizontally or vertically to make cleaning possible. The cavity between the two pieces of glass is ventilated to avoid condensation and to equalize air pressure.

The venetian blind can be tilted and, in some

models, raised with controls on the interior window frame.
Window frames are constructed of aluminum, teak or pine.

J. A combination of exterior adjustable horizontal louvers and window frame, this window can be double hung, sliding, jalousie, or fixed. Louvers can be aluminum alloy extrusions, redwood, or glass.

Graham Davidson, Architect; Washington, D.C.

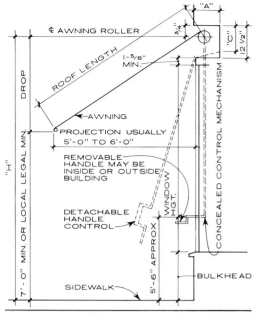

DIAGRAMMATIC SECTION
RECESSED BOX INSTALLATION

AWNING MATERIALS:
1. Canvas
2. Interlocking metal slats
   a. aluminum
   b. bronze
   c. stainless steel
3. Fiberglass

AWNING OPERATORS:
1. Detachable handle control
2. Gear box & shaft (concealed or exposed) with removable handle inside or outside of building
3. Electric control

AWNING BOX CLEARANCES:

Recessed box sizes		"H"	"A"	"B"	"C"
A. lateral arm type		9'-6" to 11'-0"	10"	10 1/2"	10"
		9'-6" to 12'-0"	10 1/2"	12"	10"
		9'-6" to 14'-0"	11"	13 1/2"	10"
B. outrigger arm type	varies		6'-2"	6'-2"	6'-2"

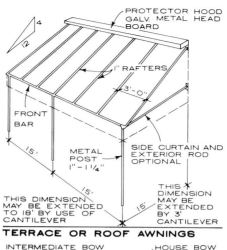

TERRACE OR ROOF AWNINGS

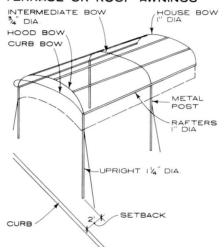

CANOPIES - LOW CURVED BOW SHOWN

TERRACE OR ROOF AWNINGS

To provide complete sun protection and shade, the overall length of the awning bar should extend 3 in. past the glass line on both sides. For proper sunshade protection, awnings should project at least as far forward from the face of the window as the bottom of the window is below the front bar of the awning.

The wall measurement of an awning is the distance down the face of the building from the point where the awning attaches to the face of the building (or from the center of the roller in the case of the roller type awning).

The projection of an awning is the distance from the face of the building to the front bar of the awning in its correct projected position.

Right and left of an awning are your right and left as you are facing the awning looking into the building.

Framework consists of galvanized steel pipe, with non-rattling fittings. Awning is lace-on type canvas with rope reinforced eave. Protector hood is galvanized sheet metal or either bronze, copper, or aluminum.

Sizes of members should be checked by calculation for conditions not similar to those shown on this page.

Consult local building code for limitations on height and setback.

COVERED WALKWAYS

Covered walkways are available with aluminum fascia and soffit panels in a number of profiles. The fascia panels are supported with pipe columns and steel or aluminum structural members if necessary. Panels can cantilever up to 30% of span. Canopy designs can be supported from above.

Another method of providing covered exterior space is with stressed membrane structures. Using highly tensile synthetic fabric and cable in collaboration with compression members, usually metal, dynamic and versatile tentlike coverings can be created. Membrane structures are especially suited to temporary installations.

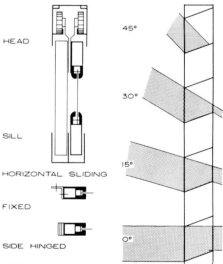

NOTE

These miniature external louvers shade windows from direct sunlight and glare while allowing a high degree of visibility, light, ventilation, insect protection, and daytime privacy. Much like a woven metal fabric, they are not strong architectural elements but present a uniform appearance in the areas covered. The solar screen is installed in aluminum frames and can be adapted to suit most applications.

SOLAR SCREEN SIZES

MATE-RIAL	LOUVERS	TILT	VERTI-CAL SPAC-ING	SIZE (WIDTHS)
Aluminum	17"	17°	1" o.c.	18"-48"
Bronze	17", 23"	20°	1/2" o.c.	Up to 72 1/2"

Aluminum screens are available in black or light green. Bronze screens come in black only.

SOLAR SCREENS

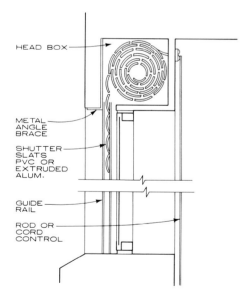

NOTE

Rolling shutters provide sun control not only by shading windows from direct sun rays but also by way of two dead airspaces—one between shutter and window, the other within the shutter extrusions to serve as insulation. The dead airspaces work as well in winter to prevent the escape of heat from the interior. In addition, shutters are useful as privacy and security measures. They can be installed in new or existing construction and are manufactured in standard window sizes.

ROLLING SHUTTERS

Graham Davidson, Architect; Washington, D.C.

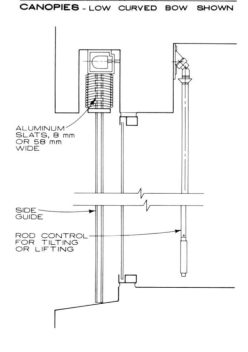

NOTE

External blinds protect the building interior from solar gain and glare, but can be raised partially or fully to the head when not needed. Manual or electric control is from inside the building.

EXTERNAL VENETIAN BLINDS

STRUCTURAL CONSIDERATIONS

Earth sheltered structures are usually deeper and the loads greater than for basements. Hydrostatic and compaction loads add to the triangular soil loading on walls (Figure 1). Floors below water level are subjected to uplift of 62.4 psf per foot depth below water level and may require special design (Figure 2) to resist the load and to provide a uniform support plane for the waterproof membrane. Roof live loads in urban areas may include public assembly at 100 psf, in addition to soil, plants, and furnishings. Saturated soils and gravel are usually taken at 120 pcf. Tree loads are related to species and size. Tree weights can be estimated for preliminary design by the logarithmic relation

$$\log(wt) = x + 2.223 \log(dia.) + 0.339 \log(ht)$$

where (wt) is in pounds, (dia.) is trunk diameter in inches at breast height, and (ht) is in feet. Forest trees range in x from 0.6 for fir to 0.8 for birch, with spruce and maple at about 0.7. The equation has not been tested for lawn trees, so it must be used with caution. Site investigation is important to determine soil bearing and drainage capacity, shearing strength, and water level. Hillside designs produce unbalanced lateral loads that may recommend interior wall buttressing.

LANDSCAPE CONSIDERATIONS

Rooftop plantings require adequate soil depth (Figure 3), underdrainage, and irrigation. Lightweight soil mixes reduce roof loads, but are not suitable under foot. Highly trafficked roofs may require special sandy soil mixes used for golf greens and athletic fields to resist compaction and root damage. Plant materials should be drought-resistant and hardier than normal, since roof soil may be colder than lawn soil.

DRAINAGE AND MOISTURE CONSIDERATIONS

Footing drains draw down the water table and prevent ponding in the backfill. Exterior location is more effective, but is subject to abuse during backfilling and to subsequent settlement. Underslab drains are easier to install correctly and are less likely to fail. Unless both are used, weep holes should be installed through the footing to connect underfloor and perimeter systems. A polyethylene sheet keeps water vapor from entering the slab, and through-joint flashing prevents capillary transfer of soil moisture through the footing to the wall. The waterproofing system must be suited to the structural system and the surface condition of the substrate. Plastic waterstops complicate joint forming and may conceal the source of leaks, disadvantages that usually outweigh whatever benefit they may provide. Chemical (e.g., bentonite base) waterstops do not have these disadvantages.

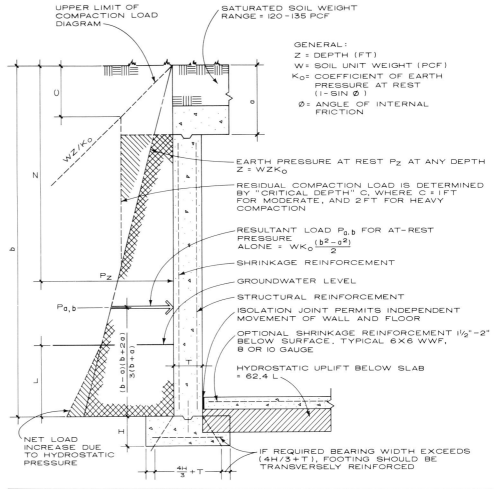

GENERAL:
Z = DEPTH (FT)
W = SOIL UNIT WEIGHT (PCF)
K_o = COEFFICIENT OF EARTH PRESSURE AT REST ($1 - \sin \emptyset$)
$\emptyset$ = ANGLE OF INTERNAL FRICTION

SATURATED SOIL WEIGHT RANGE = 120 – 135 PCF

UPPER LIMIT OF COMPACTION LOAD DIAGRAM

EARTH PRESSURE AT REST P_z AT ANY DEPTH $Z = WZK_o$

RESIDUAL COMPACTION LOAD IS DETERMINED BY "CRITICAL DEPTH" C, WHERE C = 1FT FOR MODERATE, AND 2FT FOR HEAVY COMPACTION

RESULTANT LOAD $P_{a,b}$ FOR AT-REST PRESSURE ALONE = $WK_o \frac{(b^2 - a^2)}{2}$

SHRINKAGE REINFORCEMENT

GROUNDWATER LEVEL

STRUCTURAL REINFORCEMENT

ISOLATION JOINT PERMITS INDEPENDENT MOVEMENT OF WALL AND FLOOR

OPTIONAL SHRINKAGE REINFORCEMENT 1½"–2" BELOW SURFACE, TYPICAL 6×6 WWF, 8 OR 10 GAUGE

HYDROSTATIC UPLIFT BELOW SLAB = 62.4 L

NET LOAD INCREASE DUE TO HYDROSTATIC PRESSURE

IF REQUIRED BEARING WIDTH EXCEEDS (4H/3+T), FOOTING SHOULD BE TRANSVERSELY REINFORCED

FIGURE 1 COMPOSITE LOAD DIAGRAM

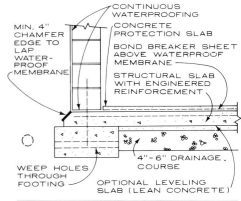

MIN. 4" CHAMFER EDGE TO LAP WATER-PROOF MEMBRANE

CONTINUOUS WATERPROOFING

CONCRETE PROTECTION SLAB

BOND BREAKER SHEET ABOVE WATERPROOF MEMBRANE

STRUCTURAL SLAB WITH ENGINEERED REINFORCEMENT

WEEP HOLES THROUGH FOOTING

4"-6" DRAINAGE COURSE

OPTIONAL LEVELING SLAB (LEAN CONCRETE)

FIGURE 2 REINFORCED SLAB (GERMAN APPROACH)

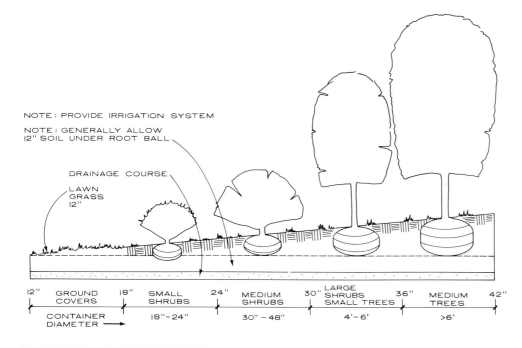

NOTE: PROVIDE IRRIGATION SYSTEM

NOTE: GENERALLY ALLOW 12" SOIL UNDER ROOT BALL

DRAINAGE COURSE

LAWN GRASS 12"

12"	GROUND COVERS	18"	SMALL SHRUBS	24"	MEDIUM SHRUBS	30"	LARGE SHRUBS SMALL TREES	36"	MEDIUM TREES	42"
CONTAINER DIAMETER →			18"–24"		30"–48"		4'-6'		>6'	

FIGURE 3 PLANT SOIL COVER REQUIREMENTS

Kenneth Labs; New Haven, Connecticut

RECOMMENDED REFERENCES

1. B. Anderson, "Waterproofing and the Design Professional," *The Construction Specifier*, March 1986, pp. 84–97.
2. J. Carmody and R. Sterling, *Earth Sheltered Housing Design*, 2nd Ed., Van Nostrand Reinhold, New York, 1985, 350 pp.
3. R. Sterling, W. Farnan, J. Carmody, *Earth Sheltered Residential Design Manual*, Van Nostrand Reinhold, New York, 1982, 252 pp.
4. U.S. Navy, *Earth Sheltered Buildings*, NAVFAC Design Manual 1.4, U.S. Government Printing Office, 1983.
5. Moreland Associates, *Earth Covered Buildings: An Exploratory Analysis for Hazard and Energy Performance*, Federal Emergency Management Agency, 1981.

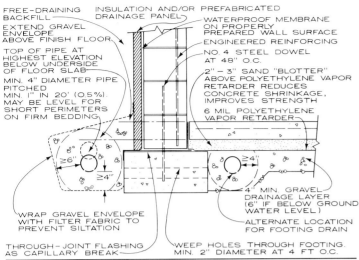

TYPICAL FOOTING CONDITION

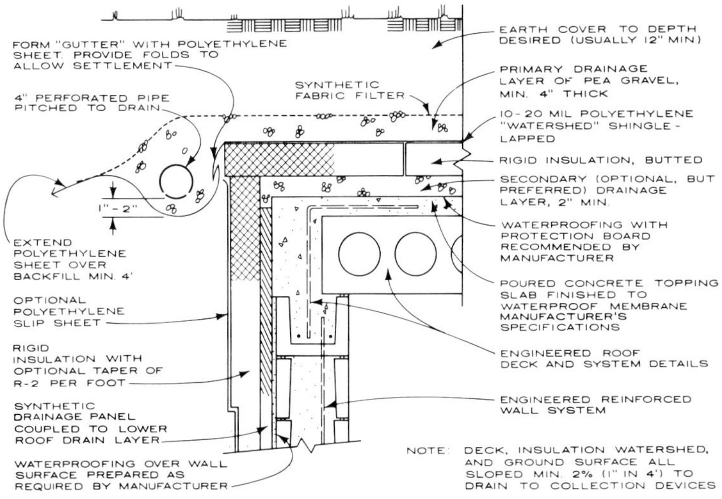

Labels (top-left detail):
- FREE-DRAINING BACKFILL
- EXTEND GRAVEL ENVELOPE ABOVE FINISH FLOOR
- TOP OF PIPE AT HIGHEST ELEVATION BELOW UNDERSIDE OF FLOOR SLAB
- MIN. 4" DIAMETER PIPE PITCHED MIN. 1" IN 20' (0.5%). MAY BE LEVEL FOR SHORT PERIMETERS ON FIRM BEDDING
- INSULATION AND/OR PREFABRICATED DRAINAGE PANEL
- WATERPROOF MEMBRANE ON PROPERLY PREPARED WALL SURFACE
- ENGINEERED REINFORCING
- NO. 4 STEEL DOWEL AT 48" O.C.
- 2" – 3" SAND "BLOTTER" ABOVE POLYETHYLENE VAPOR RETARDER REDUCES CONCRETE SHRINKAGE, IMPROVES STRENGTH
- 6 MIL POLYETHYLENE VAPOR RETARDER
- ≥6"
- ≥4"
- ≥4"
- WRAP GRAVEL ENVELOPE WITH FILTER FABRIC TO PREVENT SILTATION
- THROUGH-JOINT FLASHING AS CAPILLARY BREAK
- WEEP HOLES THROUGH FOOTING. MIN. 2" DIAMETER AT 4 FT O.C.
- 4" MIN. GRAVEL DRAINAGE LAYER (6" IF BELOW GROUND WATER LEVEL)
- ALTERNATE LOCATION FOR FOOTING DRAIN

ROOF EDGE DETAIL

Labels (top-right detail):
- FORM "GUTTER" WITH POLYETHYLENE SHEET. PROVIDE FOLDS TO ALLOW SETTLEMENT
- 4" PERFORATED PIPE PITCHED TO DRAIN
- SYNTHETIC FABRIC FILTER
- EXTEND POLYETHYLENE SHEET OVER BACKFILL MIN. 4'
- OPTIONAL POLYETHYLENE SLIP SHEET
- RIGID INSULATION WITH OPTIONAL TAPER OF R-2 PER FOOT
- SYNTHETIC DRAINAGE PANEL COUPLED TO LOWER ROOF DRAIN LAYER
- WATERPROOFING OVER WALL SURFACE PREPARED AS REQUIRED BY MANUFACTURER
- 1" – 2"
- EARTH COVER TO DEPTH DESIRED (USUALLY 12" MIN)
- PRIMARY DRAINAGE LAYER OF PEA GRAVEL, MIN. 4" THICK
- 10–20 MIL POLYETHYLENE "WATERSHED" SHINGLE-LAPPED
- RIGID INSULATION, BUTTED
- SECONDARY (OPTIONAL, BUT PREFERRED) DRAINAGE LAYER, 2" MIN
- WATERPROOFING WITH PROTECTION BOARD RECOMMENDED BY MANUFACTURER
- POURED CONCRETE TOPPING SLAB FINISHED TO WATERPROOF MEMBRANE MANUFACTURER'S SPECIFICATIONS
- ENGINEERED ROOF DECK AND SYSTEM DETAILS
- ENGINEERED REINFORCED WALL SYSTEM
- NOTE: DECK, INSULATION WATERSHED, AND GROUND SURFACE ALL SLOPED MIN 2% (1" IN 4') TO DRAIN TO COLLECTION DEVICES

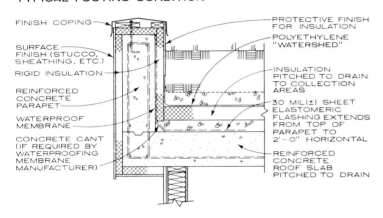

CONCRETE PERIMETER PARAPET

Labels:
- FINISH COPING
- SURFACE FINISH (STUCCO, SHEATHING, ETC.)
- RIGID INSULATION
- REINFORCED CONCRETE PARAPET
- WATERPROOF MEMBRANE
- CONCRETE CANT (IF REQUIRED BY WATERPROOFING MEMBRANE MANUFACTURER)
- PROTECTIVE FINISH FOR INSULATION
- POLYETHYLENE "WATERSHED"
- INSULATION PITCHED TO DRAIN TO COLLECTION AREAS
- 30 MIL(±) SHEET ELASTOMERIC FLASHING EXTENDS FROM TOP OF PARAPET TO 2'-0" HORIZONTAL
- REINFORCED CONCRETE ROOF SLAB PITCHED TO DRAIN

MASONRY INTERIOR PARAPET

Labels:
- INTERIOR SPACE
- ANCHOR BOLT
- INTERIOR FINISH
- REINFORCED GROUTED CONCRETE MASONRY PARAPET WALL
- WATERPROOFING ON PREPARED MASONRY SURFACE
- CONCRETE CANT (IF REQUIRED BY WATERPROOFING MEMBRANE MANUFACTURER)
- CLERESTORY WINDOW
- PROTECTIVE FINISH FOR INSULATION
- POLYETHYLENE "WATERSHED" ON TOP OF INSULATION
- 6" CLEAR (FOR RAINSPLASH)
- INSULATION PITCHED TO DRAIN TO COLLECTION AREAS
- 30 MIL(±) SHEET ELASTOMERIC FLASHING EXTENDS FROM TOP OF PARAPET TO 2'-0" HORIZONTAL
- REINFORCED CONCRETE ROOF SLAB PITCHED TO DRAIN

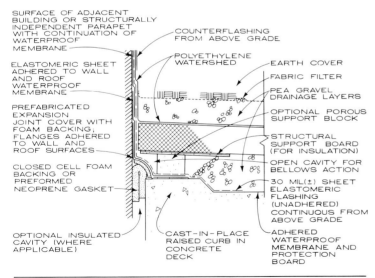

FLEXIBLE JOINT AT ROOF EDGE

Labels:
- SURFACE OF ADJACENT BUILDING OR STRUCTURALLY INDEPENDENT PARAPET WITH CONTINUATION OF WATERPROOF MEMBRANE
- ELASTOMERIC SHEET ADHERED TO WALL AND ROOF WATERPROOF MEMBRANE
- PREFABRICATED EXPANSION JOINT COVER WITH FOAM BACKING; FLANGES ADHERED TO WALL AND ROOF SURFACES
- CLOSED CELL FOAM BACKING OR PREFORMED NEOPRENE GASKET
- OPTIONAL INSULATED CAVITY (WHERE APPLICABLE)
- COUNTERFLASHING FROM ABOVE GRADE
- POLYETHYLENE WATERSHED
- EARTH COVER
- FABRIC FILTER
- PEA GRAVEL DRAINAGE LAYERS
- OPTIONAL POROUS SUPPORT BLOCK
- STRUCTURAL SUPPORT BOARD (FOR INSULATION)
- OPEN CAVITY FOR BELLOWS ACTION
- 30 MIL(±) SHEET ELASTOMERIC FLASHING (UNADHERED) CONTINUOUS FROM ABOVE GRADE
- ADHERED WATERPROOF MEMBRANE AND PROTECTION BOARD
- CAST-IN-PLACE RAISED CURB IN CONCRETE DECK

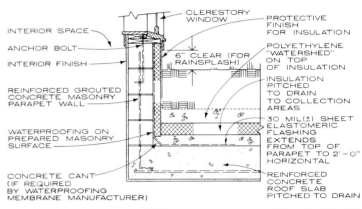

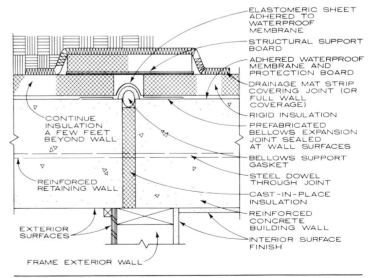

THERMAL BREAK AT RETAINING WING WALL (PLAN)

Labels:
- CONTINUE INSULATION A FEW FEET BEYOND WALL
- REINFORCED RETAINING WALL
- EXTERIOR SURFACES
- FRAME EXTERIOR WALL
- ELASTOMERIC SHEET ADHERED TO WATERPROOF MEMBRANE
- STRUCTURAL SUPPORT BOARD
- ADHERED WATERPROOF MEMBRANE AND PROTECTION BOARD
- DRAINAGE MAT STRIP COVERING JOINT (OR FULL WALL COVERAGE)
- RIGID INSULATION
- PREFABRICATED BELLOWS EXPANSION JOINT SEALED AT WALL SURFACES
- BELLOWS SUPPORT GASKET
- STEEL DOWEL THROUGH JOINT
- CAST-IN-PLACE INSULATION
- REINFORCED CONCRETE BUILDING WALL
- INTERIOR SURFACE FINISH

THERMAL CONSIDERATIONS

Exterior insulation keeps walls and roofs warm and at a stable temperature. This minimizes dimensional change and indoor surface condensation and keeps elastomeric waterproofing pliable. Exterior insulation consumes no indoor space, but it is sometimes attacked by rodents and insects. Extruded polystyrene is usually preferred for its resistance to water absorption. Roof insulation should be placed within the drainage layer so that it does not

sit in water or impede drainage. Gravel is not always needed under the insulation, especially if the insulation is pitched to drain and is covered with polyethylene sheets. All seepage planes should be sloped a minimum of 1 in. in 4 ft.

Soil has little thermal resistance, so roof winter thermal performance depends largely on added insulation. Heat

loss from earth-covered roofs is nearly constant at

$$Q = (T_1 - T_0)/R$$

where Q is heat loss in Btu/ft^2(hr)$^\circ$F, T_1 and T_0 are indoor and outdoor air temperatures ($^\circ$F) averaged over the preceding few days, and R is the thermal resistance of the overall roof assembly. Wet soil has an R value of slightly less than 1.0 per foot thickness.

Kenneth Labs; New Haven, Connecticut

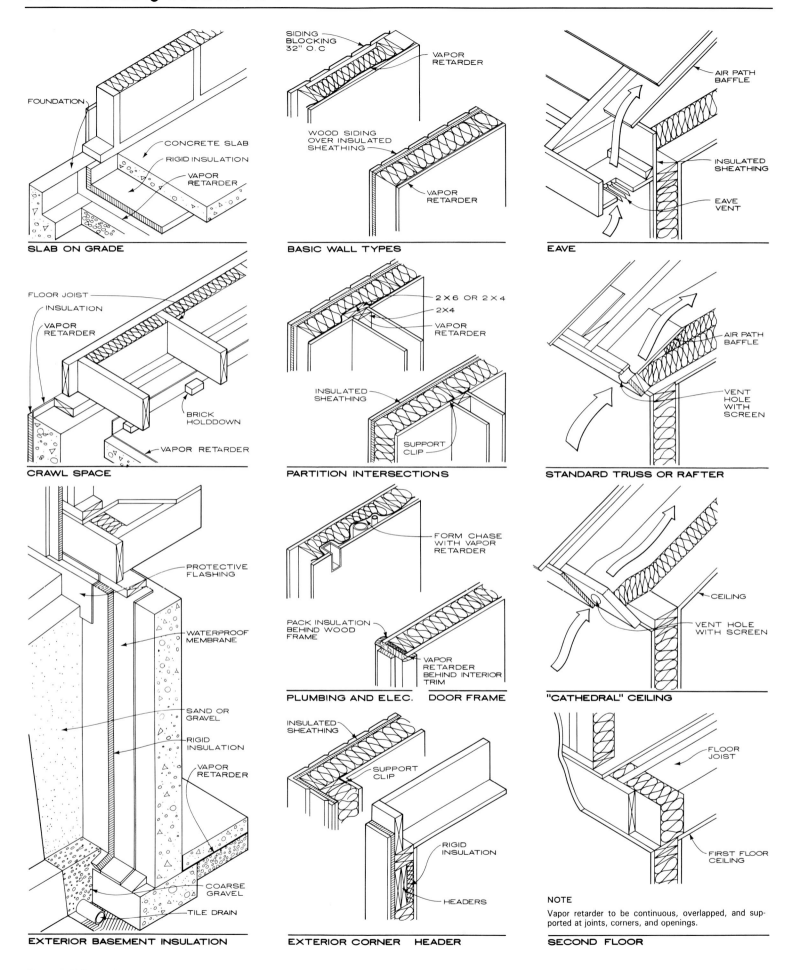

FOUNDATION

CONCRETE SLAB

RIGID INSULATION

VAPOR RETARDER

SLAB ON GRADE

FLOOR JOIST

INSULATION

VAPOR RETARDER

BRICK HOLDDOWN

VAPOR RETARDER

CRAWL SPACE

PROTECTIVE FLASHING

WATERPROOF MEMBRANE

SAND OR GRAVEL

RIGID INSULATION

VAPOR RETARDER

COARSE GRAVEL

TILE DRAIN

EXTERIOR BASEMENT INSULATION

SIDING BLOCKING 32" O.C

VAPOR RETARDER

WOOD SIDING OVER INSULATED SHEATHING

VAPOR RETARDER

BASIC WALL TYPES

2 X 6 OR 2 X 4

2 X 4

VAPOR RETARDER

INSULATED SHEATHING

SUPPORT CLIP

PARTITION INTERSECTIONS

FORM CHASE WITH VAPOR RETARDER

PACK INSULATION BEHIND WOOD FRAME

VAPOR RETARDER BEHIND INTERIOR TRIM

PLUMBING AND ELEC.   **DOOR FRAME**

INSULATED SHEATHING

SUPPORT CLIP

RIGID INSULATION

HEADERS

EXTERIOR CORNER   **HEADER**

AIR PATH BAFFLE

INSULATED SHEATHING

EAVE VENT

EAVE

AIR PATH BAFFLE

VENT HOLE WITH SCREEN

STANDARD TRUSS OR RAFTER

CEILING

VENT HOLE WITH SCREEN

"CATHEDRAL" CEILING

FLOOR JOIST

FIRST FLOOR CEILING

NOTE

Vapor retarder to be continuous, overlapped, and supported at joints, corners, and openings.

SECOND FLOOR

Timothy B. McDonald; Washington, D.C.

15   **BUILDING INSULATION**

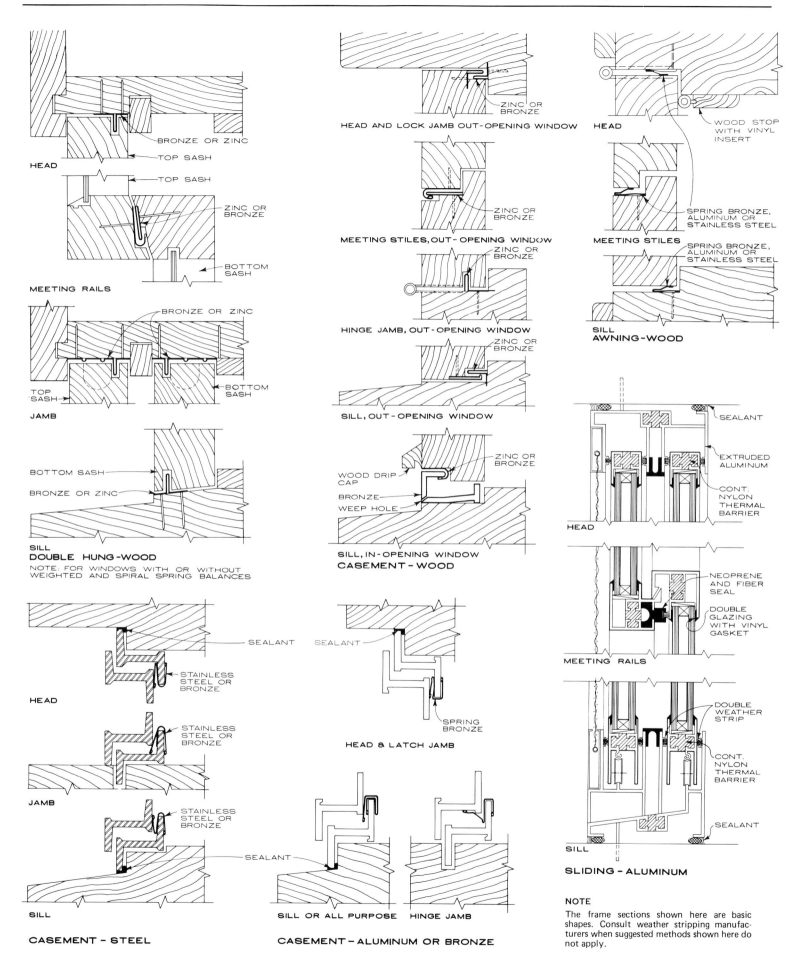

CASEMENT – STEEL

CASEMENT – ALUMINUM OR BRONZE

SLIDING – ALUMINUM

NOTE
The frame sections shown here are basic shapes. Consult weather stripping manufacturers when suggested methods shown here do not apply.

Dan Cowling & Associates, Inc.; Little Rock, Arkansas

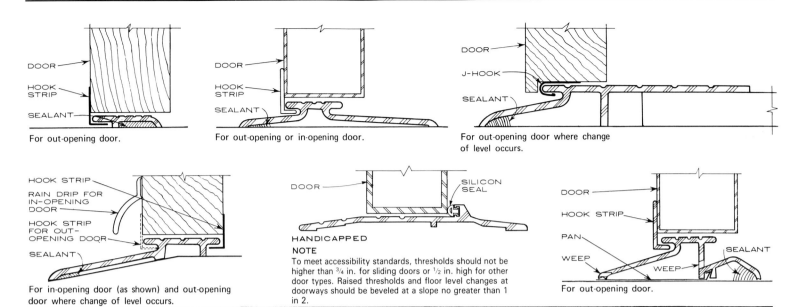

DOOR
HOOK STRIP
SEALANT

For out-opening door.

DOOR
HOOK STRIP
SEALANT

For out-opening or in-opening door.

DOOR
J-HOOK
SEALANT

For out-opening door where change of level occurs.

HOOK STRIP
RAIN DRIP FOR IN-OPENING DOOR
HOOK STRIP FOR OUT-OPENING DOOR
SEALANT

For in-opening door (as shown) and out-opening door where change of level occurs.

DOOR
SILICON SEAL

HANDICAPPED

NOTE
To meet accessibility standards, thresholds should not be higher than 3/4 in. for sliding doors or 1/2 in. high for other door types. Raised thresholds and floor level changes at doorways should be beveled at a slope no greater than 1 in 2.

DOOR
HOOK STRIP
PAN
WEEP
WEEP
SEALANT

For out-opening door.

INTERLOCKING THRESHOLDS

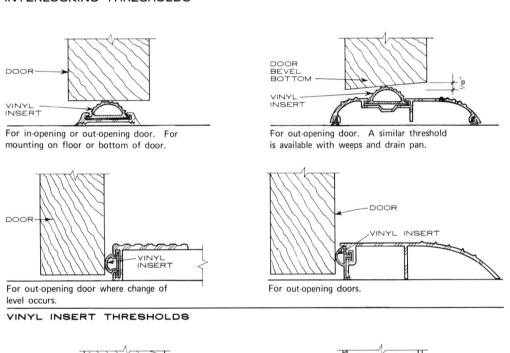

DOOR
VINYL INSERT

For in-opening or out-opening door. For mounting on floor or bottom of door.

DOOR BEVEL BOTTOM
VINYL INSERT

For out-opening door. A similar threshold is available with weeps and drain pan.

DOOR
VINYL INSERT

For out-opening door where change of level occurs.

DOOR
VINYL INSERT

For out-opening doors.

VINYL INSERT THRESHOLDS

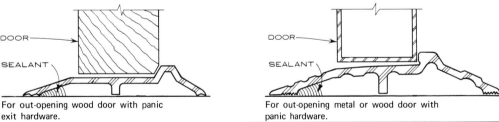

DOOR
SEALANT

For out-opening wood door with panic exit hardware.

DOOR
SEALANT

For out-opening metal or wood door with panic hardware.

LATCH TRACK THRESHOLDS

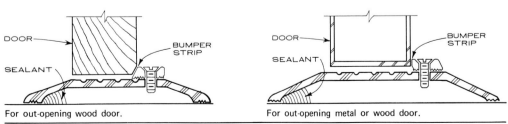

DOOR
SEALANT
BUMPER STRIP

For out-opening wood door.

DOOR
SEALANT
BUMPER STRIP

For out-opening metal or wood door.

FLAT SADDLE THRESHOLDS

Dan Cowling & Associates, Inc.; Little Rock, Arkansas

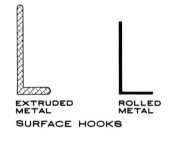

EXTRUDED METAL   ROLLED METAL

SURFACE HOOKS

EXTRUDED METAL

ROLLED METAL

CONCEALED HOOKS

INTERLOCKING HOOK STRIPS

NOTE
Hook strips are available in aluminum, brass, bronze, and zinc, and vary in thickness and dimensions. Consult manufacturers' catalogs.

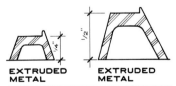

EXTRUDED METAL   EXTRUDED METAL

THRESHOLD ELEVATORS

NOTE
Available in alum. and bronze. Consult manufacturers' catalogs.

GENERAL NOTE
Thresholds are available in bronze and aluminum with a wide selection of shapes and dimensions.

15   **WEATHER STRIPPING**

GENERAL NOTES

Building attics, crawl spaces, and basements must be ventilated to remove moisture and water vapor resulting from human activity within the building. Moisture in basements and crawl spaces can occur, in addition, from water in the surrounding soil. The quantity of water vapor depends on building type (e.g., residence, school, hospital), activity (e.g., kitchen, bathroom, laundry), and air temperature and relative humidity. Proper ventilation and insulation must be combined so that the temperature of the ventilated space does not fall below the dew point; this is especially critical with low outdoor temperatures and high inside humidity. Inadequate ventilation will cause condensation and eventual deterioration of framing, insulation, and interior finishes.

The vent types shown allow natural ventilation of roofs and crawl spaces. Mechanical methods (e.g., power attic ventilators, whole house fans) can combine living space and attic ventilation, but openings for natural roof ventilation must still be provided. Protect all vents against insects and vermin with metal or fiberglass screen cloth. Increase net vent areas as noted in table.

VENTILATION REQUIREMENTS TO PREVENT CONDENSATION

SPACE	ROOF TYPE	TOTAL NET AREA OF VENTILATION	REMARKS
Joist (ceiling on underside of joists)	Flat	$1/300$. Uniformly distributed at eaves	Vent each joist space at both ends. Provide at least $1\frac{1}{2}''$ free space above insulation for ventilation
	Sloped	Ditto	Ditto. On gable roofs, drill 1'' diameter holes through ridge beam in each joist space to provide through-ventilation to both sides of roof
Attic (unheated)	Gable	$1/300$. At least two louvers on opposite sides near ridge	
	Hip	$1/300$. Uniformly distributed at eaves. Provide additional $1/600$ at ridge, with all vents interconnected	Ridge vents create stack effect from eaves; both are recommended over eaves vents alone

Total net vent area = $1/300$ of building area at eaves line. With screens increase net area by: $1/4''$ screen, 1.0; #8 screen, 1.25; #16 screen, 2.00.

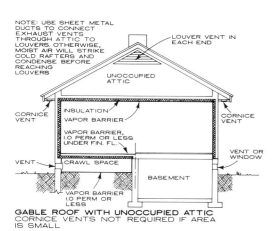

GABLE ROOF WITH UNOCCUPIED ATTIC
CORNICE VENTS NOT REQUIRED IF AREA IS SMALL

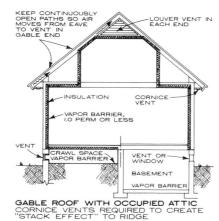

GABLE ROOF WITH OCCUPIED ATTIC
CORNICE VENTS REQUIRED TO CREATE "STACK EFFECT" TO RIDGE

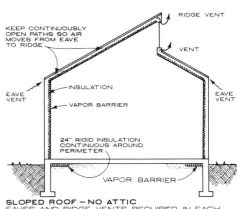

SLOPED ROOF – NO ATTIC
EAVES AND RIDGE VENTS REQUIRED IN EACH JOIST SPACE

TYPICAL ATTIC AND CRAWL SPACE VENTILATION APPLICATIONS

NOTE

Vapor barriers minimize moisture migration to attics and crawl spaces; their use is required for all conditions. Always locate vapor barriers on the warm (room) side of insulation. Provide ventilation on the cold side; this permits cold/hot weather ventilation while minimizing heat gain/loss.

CRAWL SPACES VENTILATION

Crawl spaces under dwellings where earth is damp and uncovered require a high rate of ventilation. Provide at least one opening per side, as high as possible. Calculate total net area by the formula:

$$a = \frac{2L}{100} + \frac{A}{300}$$

where

L = crawl space perimeter (linear ft)
A = crawl space area (sq ft)
a = total net vent area (sq ft)

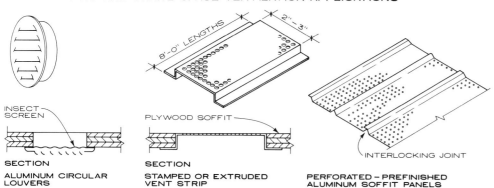

SECTION
ALUMINUM CIRCULAR LOUVERS
1''–3'' DIA.

INSECT SCREEN

SECTION
STAMPED OR EXTRUDED VENT STRIP

PLYWOOD SOFFIT

PERFORATED – PREFINISHED ALUMINUM SOFFIT PANELS
10'' × 10'-0'' LONG. ALSO IN ROLLS

INTERLOCKING JOINT

8'-0'' LENGTHS
2''-3''

EAVES VENTILATING MATERIALS

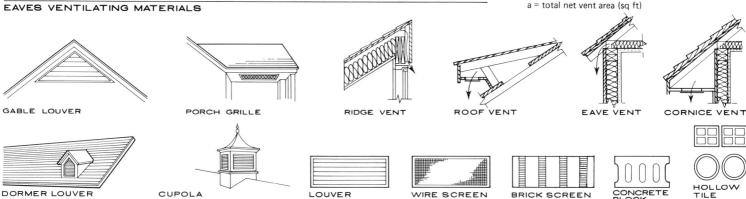

GABLE LOUVER

PORCH GRILLE

RIDGE VENT

ROOF VENT

EAVE VENT

CORNICE VENT

DORMER LOUVER

CUPOLA

LOUVER

WIRE SCREEN

BRICK SCREEN

CONCRETE BLOCK

HOLLOW TILE

TYPICAL ATTIC AND CRAWL SPACE VENT OPENINGS

David Metzger, Architect, CSI; Wilkes and Faulkner Associates; Washington, D.C.

VENTILATION 15

REFERENCES

GENERAL REFERENCES

AIA Architect's Handbook of Energy Practice: Predesign/Climate and Site, American Institute of Architects (AIA)

Energy-Efficient Housing Design, 1986, Jonathan Lane, Van Nostrand Reinhold

Mechanical and Electrical Equipment for Buildings, 7th ed., 1986, Stein, Reynolds, and McGuinness, Wiley

Sun, Wind, and Light: Architectural Design Strategies, 1985, G. Z. Brown, Wiley

Sunlight as a Formgiver for Architecture, 1986, William M. C. Lam, Van Nostrand Reinhold

DATA SOURCES: ORGANIZATIONS

American-German Industries, 337

Brown Manufacturing Company, 336

Clearview Corporation, 336

Disco Aluminum Products Company, 336

Fisher-Insley Corporation, 341

Koolshade Corporation, 337

Remco Weatherstripping, 341, 342

Willard Shutter Corporation, 336

Zero Weatherstripping Company, Inc., 341, 342

CHAPTER 16

HISTORIC PRESERVATION

INTRODUCTION

Architectural metal features—such as cast-iron facades, porches, and steps; sheet metal cornices, siding, roofs, roof cresting, and storefronts; and cast or rolled metal doors, window sash, entablatures, and hardware—are often highly decorative and may be important in defining the overall historic character of the building.

Metals commonly used in historic American building construction include lead, tin, zinc, copper, bronze, brass, iron, steel, and, to a lesser extent, nickel alloys, stainless steel, and aluminum. A high degree of craftsmanship went into fabrication of the metals in older American buildings. Often it was local artisans who designed and built fine staircases, exterior light standards, railings, or metal sculptures.

PRESERVATION APPROACHES

Before beginning any preservation work on metal features, it is critical that the metal be correctly identified; different metals have unique properties and thus require distinct preservation treatments. Inappropriate treatments to metal features can inadvertently result in their damage or loss.

Changes to architectural metal finishes can result in changing the historic character of a building.

Protecting architectural metals from corrosion should be the focus of a cyclical maintenance program. Proper drainage should be provided so that water does not stand on flat, horizontal surfaces or accumulate in curved, decorative features.

Incompatible metals should never be placed together without a reliable separation material or galvanic corrosion of the less noble metal will occur; e.g., copper corrodes cast iron, steel, tin, and aluminum.

Architectural metals should be carefully cleaned with the gentlest method possible to remove corrosion prior to repainting or applying other appropriate protective coatings. Local codes should also be checked to ensure compliance with environmental safety requirements. For some metals, such as bronze or copper, the surface coating or patina may serve as a protective coating and should not be removed. Soft metals such as lead, tin, copper, terneplate, and zinc should be cleaned with appropriate chemical methods because their finishes can be abraded by blasting methods, such as grit blasting.

Harder metals, such as cast iron, wrought iron, and steel, may be hand scraped and wire-brushed to remove paint buildup and corrosion. If these methods prove ineffective, low-pressure dry grit blasting may be appropriate if the surface is not damaged or abraded. Adjacent wood or masonry should be protected from all cleaning efforts.

Applying appropriate paint or other coating systems immediately after cleaning decreases the corrosion rate of metals or alloys. If an architectural metal is being repainted, the colors should be appropriate to the historic building or district.

Architectural metal features can often be repaired by patching, splicing, or otherwise reinforcing the metal following recognized preservation methods. Repairs also involve the limited replacement in kind of those extensively deteriorated or missing parts of features when there are surviving prototypes. Examples are porch railings or roof cresting. An architectural metal feature that is too deteriorated to repair should be replaced in kind. If the historic form and detailing are still evident, they can be used to guide the new work.

If an architectural metal feature is completely missing and there is sufficient historical, pictorial, and physical documentation, the missing features should be accurately restored. In the absence of sufficient documentation, the replacement metal feature may be a new design that is compatible with the size, scale, material, and color of the historic building.

Finally, for both repair and replacement treatments, using the same kind of metal is always preferred. If this is not feasible, a compatible substitute material may be used if it conveys the same visual appearance as the historic material and is chemically and physically compatible.

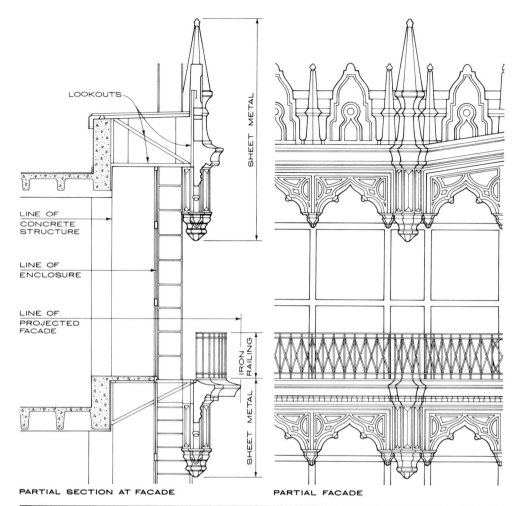

PARTIAL SECTION AT FACADE   PARTIAL FACADE

HALLIDIE BUILDING, SAN FRANCISCO, CA, 1918 (WILLIS POLK—ARCHITECT)

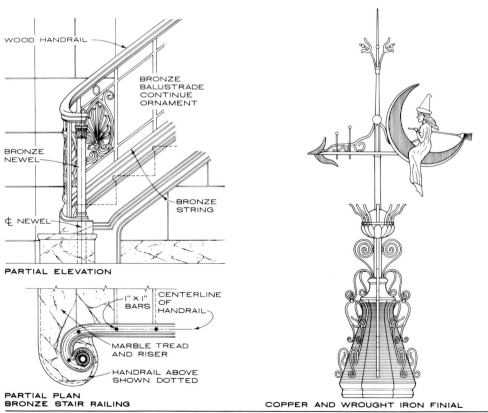

PARTIAL ELEVATION

PARTIAL PLAN
BRONZE STAIR RAILING

METAL ORNAMENT

COPPER AND WROUGHT IRON FINIAL

Lee H. Nelson, FAIA, H. Ward Jandl, Camille Martone, Kay D. Weeks; Preservation Assistance Division, National Park Service; Washington, D.C.
Eric J. Gastier; Darrel Downing Rippeteau Architects, PC; Washington, D.C.

 ARCHITECTURAL METALS

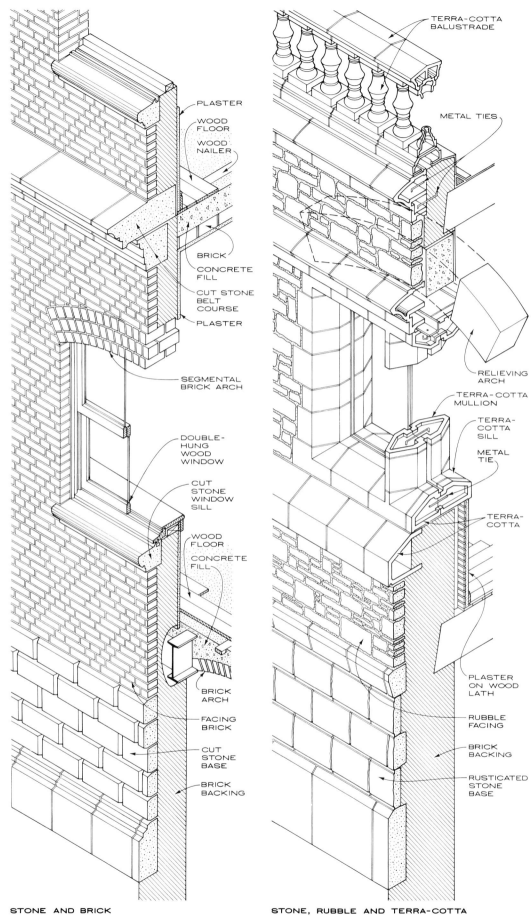

STONE AND BRICK

Labels (left diagram):
- PLASTER
- WOOD FLOOR
- WOOD NAILER
- BRICK
- CONCRETE FILL
- CUT STONE BELT COURSE
- PLASTER
- SEGMENTAL BRICK ARCH
- DOUBLE-HUNG WOOD WINDOW
- CUT STONE WINDOW SILL
- WOOD FLOOR
- CONCRETE FILL
- BRICK ARCH
- FACING BRICK
- CUT STONE BASE
- BRICK BACKING

STONE, RUBBLE AND TERRA-COTTA

Labels (right diagram):
- TERRA-COTTA BALUSTRADE
- METAL TIES
- RELIEVING ARCH
- TERRA-COTTA MULLION
- TERRA-COTTA SILL
- METAL TIE
- TERRA-COTTA
- PLASTER ON WOOD LATH
- RUBBLE FACING
- BRICK BACKING
- RUSTICATED STONE BASE

MASONRY — TYPICAL WALL SECTIONS

Lee H. Nelson, FAIA, H. Ward Jandl, Anne Grimmer, Kay D. Weeks; Preservation Assistance Division, National Park Service; Washington, D.C.
Eric J. Gastier; Darrel Downing Rippeteau Architects, PC; Washington, D.C.

INTRODUCTION

The function of masonry units such as brick or stone is related to the thickness of a wall, the mortar, the bond, and the quality of workmanship. The relationship of all these materials determines the historic building's structural soundness as well as its appearance. While masonry is among the most durable of historic building materials, it is also the most susceptible to damage by improper maintenance or repair techniques and harsh or abrasive cleaning methods.

Stone is one of the more lasting of masonry building materials and has been used throughout the history of American building construction. In the 17th and 18th centuries, stone was primarily used for decorative details and trim work on brick buildings. Where stone was plentiful, even simple buildings had stone foundations and chimneys. Stonework on most buildings was roughly finished, but more elaborate stone structures often featured finely tooled or carved decorative surfaces. The kinds of stone most commonly encountered on historic buildings in the U.S. include various types of sandstone (brownstone), limestone, marble, granite, slate, and fieldstones.

Brick varied considerably in size and quality. Before 1870, brick clays were pressed into molds and were often unevenly fired. The quality of brick depended on the type of clay available and the brick-making techniques; by the 1870s—with the perfection of an extrusion process—bricks became more uniform and durable.

Terra-cotta is also a kiln-dried clay product popular from the late 19th century until the 1930s. Brownstone terra-cotta was the earliest type used throughout the last half of the 19th century. It was hollow cast, glazed or unglazed, and was generally used in conjunction with brick to imitate brownstone. Fireproof terra-cotta was developed for use in high-rise buildings. Inexpensive, lightweight, and fireproof, these rough-finished hollow building blocks were well suited to span I-beams in floor, wall, and ceiling construction. Glazed architectural terra-cotta consists of hollow units hand cast in molds or carved in clay and heavily glazed and fired. The development of the steel-frame office building in the early 20th century and the eclectic taste of the time contributed to its widespread use.

Adobe, which consists of sun-dried earthen bricks, was one of the earliest permanent building materials used in the U.S., primarily in the Southwest where it is still a popular building material.

Mortar is used to bond together masonry units. Historic mortar was generally quite soft and consisted primarily of lime, sand, and other additives such as crushed oyster shells, partially burned lime, animal hair, particles of clay, or pigments to color the mortar to match or contrast with the masonry units. While natural cement was included in some mortars beginning in the early 19th century, most historic mortar did not contain portland cement until after 1880 when it was used in combination with the newly available, harder extruded bricks, which required a more rigid and nonabsorbing mortar.

Traditional stucco, sometimes referred to as plaster, was also heavily lime based and had much the same composition as historic mortar, with regional variations that reflected the availability of certain materials. Like mortar, the composition of stucco increased in hardness with the addition of portland cement toward the end of the 19th century. In the 18th and 19th centuries, stucco was often scored to resemble cut stone and was used as a finish coat directly over stone, brick, or log construction. In the early 20th century, stucco took on significance as a building material in its own right and was applied (often with a decorative textured finish) directly over wood or metal lath attached to the building's structural framework.

Concrete has a long history, being variously made of tabby, volcanic ash, and later of natural hydraulic cements; the latter was first given limited use in the early 19th century in some mortars before the introduction of portland cement in the 1870s. From that time on, concrete has been used in its precast form for structural blocks or "cast stone" to simulate entire stone facades or smaller architectural details. In the 20th century, this has further evolved into precast structural elements.

PRESERVATION APPROACHES

Masonry features that are important in defining the overall historic character of the building include walls, brackets, railings, cornices, window architraves, door pediments, steps, and columns, with tooling and bonding patterns, coatings, color, and joint details.

Making inappropriate visual changes to historic masonry surfaces in the process of rehabilitation, such as applying paint or other coatings to masonry that has been historically unpainted, can easily change the entire character of the building. Similarly, paint should not be removed from historically painted masonry.

The various causes of mortar joint deterioration (such as leaking roofs or gutters, differential settlement of the building, capillary action, or extreme weather exposure) should be identified before selecting an appropriate remedial treatment.

Masonry should only be cleaned in order to halt deterioration or to remove heavy soiling. Cleaning masonry surfaces when they are not heavily soiled in order to create a new appearance can needlessly introduce chemicals or moisture into historic materials. If it is determined that cleaning is necessary, tests should be conducted prior to cleaning and observed over a sufficient period of time so that both the immediate effects and the long-range effects are known.

Brick or stone surfaces should be cleaned with the gentlest method possible, such as water and detergents, using natural bristle brushes. They should never be sandblasted using dry or wet grit or other abrasives. These methods of cleaning permanently erode the surface of the material. Cleaning methods involving water or liquid chemical solutions should not be used when there is any possibility of freezing temperatures, and chemical products should never be used that will damage masonry, such as using acid on limestone or marble.

If repainting of historically painted masonry is necessary, the damaged paint should be removed to the next sound layer using the gentlest method possible prior to repainting. Colors should be used that are historically appropriate to the building and district.

Masonry walls and other masonry features should be repaired whenever there is evidence of deterioration. This may include disintegrating mortar, loose bricks, damp walls, or damaged plasterwork.

In preparation for repointing, deteriorated mortar should be removed by carefully hand-raking the joints to avoid damaging the masonry. Electric saws should never be used.

Old mortar should be duplicated in strength, composition, color, and texture. Repointing with mortar of high portland cement content can create a bond that is stronger than the historic material, damaging historic masonry as a result of the differing coefficient of expansion and the differing porosity of the material and the mortar.

When repointing, the use of traditional materials and methods is strongly recommended rather than synthetic caulking compounds and ''scrub'' coating techniques. Old mortar joints should be duplicated in width and in joint profile.

Stucco should be repaired by removing only the damaged material and patching with new stucco that duplicates the old in strength, composition, color, and texture. Mud plaster should be used as a surface coating over unfired, unstabilized adobe, in order to bond to the adobe. Cement stucco, on the other hand, will not bond properly, enabling moisture to become entrapped between materials. Concrete may be repaired by cutting the deteriorated portion back to a sound surface, then removing the source of deterioration—often corrosion on metal reinforcement bars—by sandblasting or chemical cleaning of the re-bars. The new concrete patch must be applied carefully so it will bond satisfactorily with, and match, the historic concrete.

Masonry features may be repaired by patching, piecing in, or consolidating the masonry using recognized preservation methods. Repair may also include the limited replacement in kind of those extensively deteriorated or missing parts of masonry features such as terra-cotta brackets or stone balusters when there are surviving prototypes.

A masonry feature that is too deteriorated or damaged to repair should be replaced in kind. If the historic form and detailing are still evident, they should be used to restore the feature.

If a masonry feature is completely missing and there is sufficient historical, pictorial, and physical documentation, the missing feature should be accurately restored. In the absence of documentation, the replacement masonry feature may be a new design that is compatible with the size, scale, and color of the historic building.

Finally, for both repair and replacement treatments, using the same kind of material is always preferred; however, if this is not technically or economically feasible, a compatible substitute material with the same visual and physical qualities may be considered.

INCORRECT

MORTAR NOT CLEANED OUT TO A SUFFICIENT UNIFORM DEPTH

EDGES OF BRICKS DAMAGED BY TOOL OR GRINDER, CREATES WIDER JOINT

CORRECT

MORTAR CLEANED OUT TO A UNIFORM DEPTH OF ABOUT 1"

UNDAMAGED EDGES OF BRICK

PREPARATION OF MORTAR JOINTS FOR REPOINTING

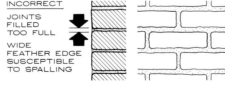

INCORRECT

JOINTS FILLED TOO FULL

WIDE FEATHER EDGE SUSCEPTIBLE TO SPALLING

CORRECT

JOINTS SLIGHTLY RECESSED

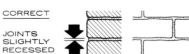

PROPER REPOINTING OF MASONRY JOINTS

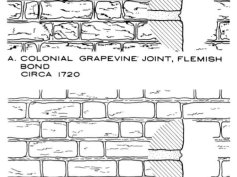

A. COLONIAL GRAPEVINE JOINT, FLEMISH BOND CIRCA 1720

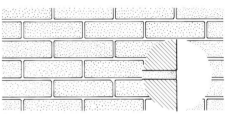

B. BEADED JOINT, FLEMISH BOND CIRCA 1809

C. FLUSH JOINT, COMMON BOND MID-19TH CENTURY

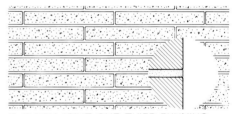

D. RAKED JOINT, ENGLISH BOND EARLY 20TH CENTURY

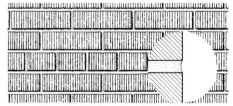

E. FLUSH JOINT, ONE-THIRD RUNNING BOND EARLY 20TH CENTURY

F. CONCAVE JOINT, COMMON BOND EARLY 20TH CENTURY

NOTE THE DIFFERENCE IN UNIFORMITY OF HANDMADE (A AND B) AND MACHINE-MADE (C–F) BRICKS. IN A, B AND F, THE VERTICAL JOINTS WERE STRUCK BEFORE THE HORIZONTALS. IN B AND E, THE VERTICAL JOINTS ARE NARROWER THAN THE HORIZONTALS

JOINT TYPES AND BRICK BONDING PATTERNS

	A. FLEXIBLE MORTAR (LIME)	B. INFLEXIBLE MORTAR (CEMENT)
NORMAL		
HOT (BRICKS EXPAND)	MORTAR COMPRESSES	SPALLING
COLD (BRICKS CONTRACT)	MORTAR FLEXES	CRACKS OPEN UP

FLEXIBLE MORTAR (A) EXPANDS AND CONTRACTS WITH TEMPERATURE CHANGES. BRICKS BONDED BY INFLEXIBLE MORTAR (B) TEND TO SPALL AT THE EDGES (THE AREA OF GREATEST STRESS) IN HOT WEATHER AND SEPARATE FROM THE MORTAR IN COLD WEATHER

EFFECTS OF TEMPERATURE CHANGE ON MASONRY

Lee H. Nelson, FAIA, H. Ward Jandl, Anne Grimmer, Kay D. Weeks; Preservation Assistance Division, National Park Service; Washington, D.C.

Eric J. Gastier; Darrel Downing Rippeteau Architects, PC; Washington, D.C.

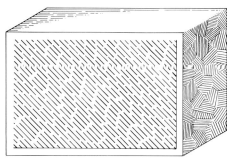

POINTED

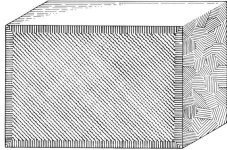

BROACHED

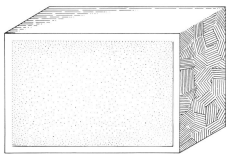

BUSH-HAMMERED

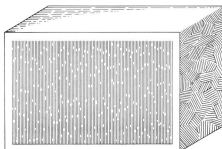

PATENT-HAMMERED

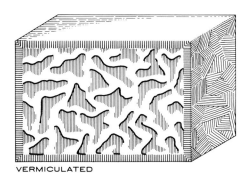

VERMICULATED

STONEWORK FINISHES

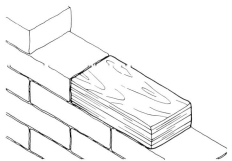

THE CORRECT CONSTRUCTION METHOD IS TO PLACE STONE ON ITS NATURAL BED AS IT ORIGINALLY LAY IN THE QUARRY

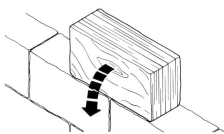

A FACE-BEDDED STONE SCALES IN LAYERS BECAUSE IT WAS PLACED ON END WITH ITS BEDDING PLANES PARALLEL TO THE FACE OF THE WALL. FACE BEDDING ACCOUNTS FOR THE POOR CONDITION OF MANY MID-19TH CENTURY BROWNSTONE BUILDINGS (ARROW INDICATES SCALING)

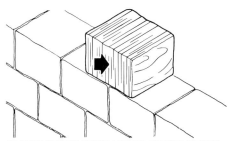

AN EDGE-BEDDED STONE HAS ITS BEDDING PLANES PERPENDICULAR TO THE FACE OF THE WALL. SEAMS ON THE EXPOSED SURFACE (INDICATED BY THE ARROW) WILL WASH OUT IN TIME

STONE BEDDING METHODS

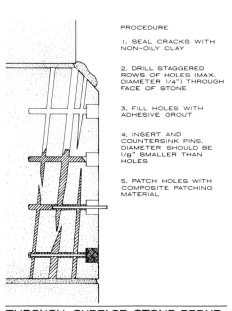

PROCEDURE

1. SEAL CRACKS WITH NON-OILY CLAY

2. DRILL STAGGERED ROWS OF HOLES (MAX. DIAMETER 1/4") THROUGH FACE OF STONE

3. FILL HOLES WITH ADHESIVE GROUT

4. INSERT AND COUNTERSINK PINS. DIAMETER SHOULD BE 1/8" SMALLER THAN HOLES

5. PATCH HOLES WITH COMPOSITE PATCHING MATERIAL

THROUGH-SURFACE STONE REPAIR

PROCEDURE

1. CLEAN SURFACES TO BE JOINED

2. PROTECT ADJACENT SURFACES WITH RUBBER CEMENT

3. DRILL STAGGERED ROWS OF HOLES. DEPTH = 4 X PIN DIAMETER DIAMETER = PIN DIAMETER + 1/8"

4. FILL HOLES WITH RIGID (HIGH MODULUS) EPOXY ADHESIVE

5. SET PINS

6. COAT STONE SURFACES TO BE JOINED WITH FLEXIBLE (LOW MODULUS) EPOXY ADHESIVE

7. SET DETACHED PIECE IN PLACE. GENTLY TAP WITH RUBBER MALLET TO SEAT STONE

8. CLEAN OFF RUBBER CEMENT

CONCEALED REPAIR FOR STONE

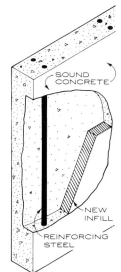

PROCEDURE

1. REMOVE LOOSE DETER-IORATED CONCRETE TO SOUND CONCRETE. CUT SQUARE SHOULDERS AT EDGE OF REPAIR AREA. EXPOSE ALL SIDES OF REINFORCING STEEL

2. SANDBLAST CONCRETE AND REINFORCING STEEL CLEAN

3. IMMEDIATELY APPLY PROTECTIVE COATING SYSTEM TO REINFORCEMENT

4. MOISTEN CONCRETE SURFACE AND ALLOW TO DRY UNTIL DAMP

5. INSTALL MORTAR, EPOXY-MODIFIED BOND COAT AND CONCRETE, OR EPOXY-MODIFIED BOND COAT AND PORTLAND CEMENT CONCRETE, DEPENDING ON REPAIR DEPTH

6. CURE AS NECESSARY

SOUND CONCRETE

NEW INFILL

REINFORCING STEEL

SPALLED CONCRETE REPAIR (EXTERIOR WALLS)

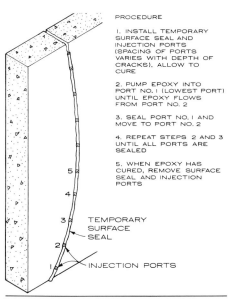

PROCEDURE

1. INSTALL TEMPORARY SURFACE SEAL AND INJECTION PORTS (SPACING OF PORTS VARIES WITH DEPTH OF CRACKS). ALLOW TO CURE

2. PUMP EPOXY INTO PORT NO.1 (LOWEST PORT) UNTIL EPOXY FLOWS FROM PORT NO.2

3. SEAL PORT NO.1 AND MOVE TO PORT NO.2

4. REPEAT STEPS 2 AND 3 UNTIL ALL PORTS ARE SEALED

5. WHEN EPOXY HAS CURED, REMOVE SURFACE SEAL AND INJECTION PORTS

TEMPORARY SURFACE SEAL

INJECTION PORTS

FRACTURED CONCRETE REPAIR (WALLS AND SLABS)

Lee H. Nelson, FAIA, H. Ward Jandl, Anne Grimmer, Kay D. Weeks; Preservation Assistance Division, National Park Service; Washington, D.C.
Eric J. Gastier; Darrel Downing Rippeteau Architects, PC; Washington, D.C.

INTRODUCTION

Because it can be easily shaped by sawing, planing, carving, and gouging, wood is used for architectural features such as clapboards, cornices, brackets, entablatures, shutters, columns, and balustrades. These wooden features, both functional and decorative, may be important in defining the historic character of the building and thus their retention, protection, and repair are important in rehabilitation projects.

Wood has played a central role in American building during every period and in every style. Whether as structural membering, exterior cladding, roofing, interior finishes, or decorative features, wood is frequently an essential component of historic and older buildings.

PRESERVATION APPROACHES

While loss of some exterior wood to weathering is inevitable, taking steps to maximize its retention should be an integral part of any work on a historic building.

Radical changes to the historic appearance of wood surfaces should be avoided, such as changing the type of finish or its color, or stripping historically painted surfaces to bare wood, then applying clear finishes or stains in order to create a ''natural'' look. Special finishes, such as marbling or graining, are evidence of individual craftsmanship and should be retained and preserved.

The causes of wood deterioration should be identified and corrected, such as faulty flashing, leaking gutters, cracks and holes in siding, deteriorated caulking, plants growing too close to wood surfaces, or insect or fungus infestation.

Painted wood surfaces should be inspected to determine whether repainting is necessary or if cleaning is all that is required. Paint should not be removed that is firmly adhering to, and thus, protecting wood surfaces. If surfaces need painting, the damaged or deteriorated paint should only be removed to the next sound layer, using the gentlest method possible (hand scraping and hand sanding).

It is never appropriate to use destructive paint removal methods such as propane or butane torches, sandblasting, or waterblasting. These methods can irreversibly damage woodwork and could penetrate through to damage interior fabric.

Electric hot-air guns may be used effectively on decorative wood features and electric heat plates on flat wood surfaces when paint is so deteriorated that total removal is necessary prior to repainting.

Wood features can be repaired by patching, consolidating, or otherwise reinforcing the wood using recognized preservation methods. More often, however, repair will involve the replacement in kind of extensively deteriorated or missing parts of wood features where there are surviving prototypes. Examples include brackets, moldings, balusters, or sections of siding.

A wood feature too deteriorated to repair should be replaced in kind. If the historic form and detailing are still evident, they should be used to restore the feature. If a wood feature is missing and there is sufficient historical, pictorial, and physical documentation, the missing feature should be restored. Replacing a deteriorated or missing wood feature based on insufficient documentation can create a false historic appearance and can have a more significant negative impact on the historic character than not replacing the feature at all.

For both repair and replacement, using the same kind of material is always preferred. If this is not feasible, a compatible substitute material may be used if it conveys the same historic appearance as wood and is physically and chemically compatible.

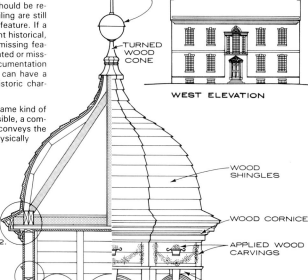

COPPER-COVERED WOOD BALL

TURNED WOOD CONE

WEST ELEVATION

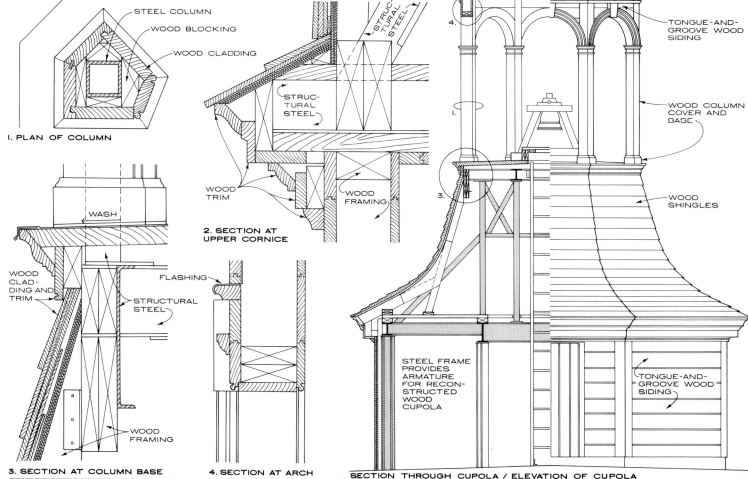

I. PLAN OF COLUMN

STEEL COLUMN
WOOD BLOCKING
WOOD CLADDING

2. SECTION AT UPPER CORNICE

STRUCTURAL STEEL
STRUCTURAL STEEL
WOOD TRIM
WOOD FRAMING

WASH
WOOD CLADDING AND TRIM
STRUCTURAL STEEL
WOOD FRAMING

3. SECTION AT COLUMN BASE

FLASHING

4. SECTION AT ARCH

WOOD SHINGLES
WOOD CORNICE
APPLIED WOOD CARVINGS
TONGUE-AND-GROOVE WOOD SIDING
WOOD COLUMN COVER AND BASE
WOOD SHINGLES

STEEL FRAME PROVIDES ARMATURE FOR RECONSTRUCTED WOOD CUPOLA

TONGUE-AND-GROOVE WOOD SIDING

SECTION THROUGH CUPOLA / ELEVATION OF CUPOLA

OLD STATE HOUSE, DOVER, DE (McCUNE ASSOCIATES, RESTORATION ARCHITECTS, 1977)
Lee H. Nelson, FAIA, H. Ward Jandl, Sharon C. Park, AIA, Michael J. Auer; Preservation Assistance Division, National Park Service; Washington, D.C.
Eric J. Gastier; Darrel Downing Rippeteau Architects, PC; Washington, D.C.

 WOOD

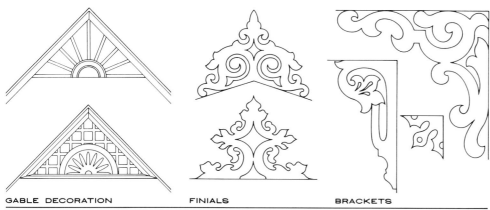

GABLE DECORATION   FINIALS   BRACKETS

DECORATIVE WOOD ELEMENTS

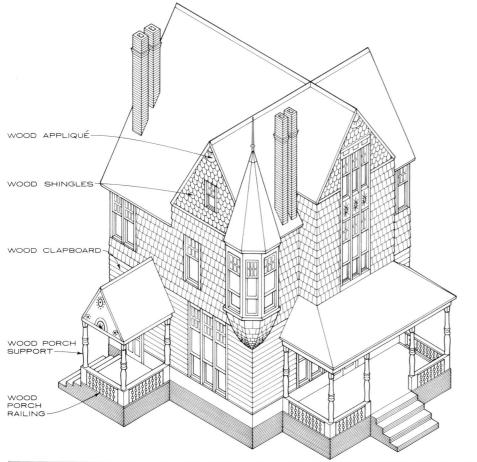

WOOD APPLIQUÉ

WOOD SHINGLES

WOOD CLAPBOARD

WOOD PORCH SUPPORT

WOOD PORCH RAILING

TYPICAL QUEEN ANNE HOUSE, CIRCA 1880 (BASED ON A DESIGN OF LAMB AND WHEELER, ARCHITECTS)

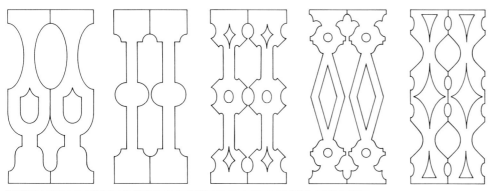

WOOD PORCH RAILING PATTERNS (CUT BY SCROLL SAW FROM THIN WOOD STOCK)

Lee H. Nelson, FAIA, H. Ward Jandl, Sharon C. Park, AIA, Michael J. Auer; Preservation Assistance Division, National Park Service; Washington, D.C.
Eric J. Gastier; Darrel Downing Rippeteau Architects, PC; Washington, D.C.

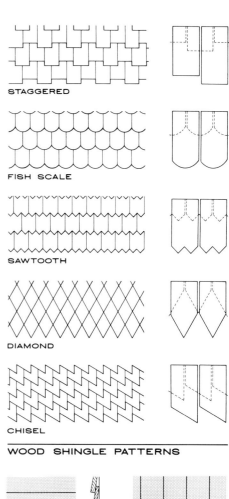

STAGGERED

FISH SCALE

SAWTOOTH

DIAMOND

CHISEL

WOOD SHINGLE PATTERNS

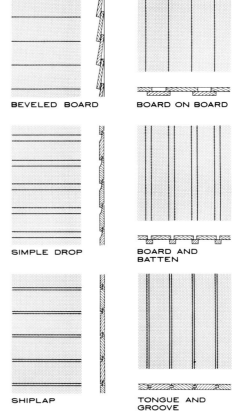

BEVELED BOARD   BOARD ON BOARD

SIMPLE DROP   BOARD AND BATTEN

SHIPLAP   TONGUE AND GROOVE

WOOD SIDING - PROFILES AND PATTERNS

INTRODUCTION

The visible features of historic heating, lighting, ventilating, and plumbing systems may sometimes help define the overall historic character of the building and should thus be retained and repaired whenever possible. Realistically, the systems themselves (the compressors, boilers, generators, and their ductwork, wiring, and pipes) will generally need to be upgraded or entirely replaced in order to accommodate the new use and to meet code requirements. However, the visible portions of a system, the grilles, registers, lighting fixtures, and ornamental switchplates may be important in helping to define the interior historic character of a building. Therefore, the identification of such character-defining features should take place together with an evaluation of their physical condition early in project planning. The significant visual features of a building's mechanical, plumbing, and electrical system should be retained as part of historic preservation.

Mechanical, lighting, and plumbing systems were largely a product of the industrial age. The 19th century interest in hygiene, personal comfort, and the reduction of the spread of disease were met with the development of central heating, piped water, piped gas, and a network of underground cast iron sewers. Vitreous tiles in kitchens, baths, and hospitals could be cleaned easily and regularly. The mass production of cast iron radiators made central heating affordable to many; some radiators were elaborate and included special warming chambers for plates or linens. Ornamental grilles and brass registers created decorative covers for functional heaters in public spaces. By the turn of the 20th century, it was common to have all these modern amenities as an integral part of the building.

The greatest impact of the 20th century was the use of electricity for interior lighting, forced air ventilation, elevators for tall buildings, exterior lighting, and electric heat. The new age of technology brought an increasingly high level of design and decorative art to the functional elements of mechanical, electrical, and plumbing systems.

PRESERVATION APPROACHES

Mechanical, plumbing, and electrical systems and their features should be maintained through cyclical cleaning and other appropriate measures. Adequate ventilation of attics, crawl spaces, and cellars should be provided to prevent accelerated deterioration of mechanical systems due to moisture problems.

New systems should be installed in a manner that does not destroy or damage significant architectural material and that make use of decorative elements of older systems—switchplates, ventilator grilles, lighting fixtures, etc.

Before total replacement of historic mechanical systems is considered, efforts should be made to evaluate the upgrading of the present system. Any ornamental features, such as significant lighting fixtures, should be retained after rewiring.

Often, to accommodate a continuing or new use, the historic mechanical system needs to be totally replaced with a new system. This new system needs to be installed in a manner that minimizes alterations to the building's floor plan and exterior elevations and causes the least damage to the historic building materials.

If a new mechanical system needs to be installed in a historic building, the vertical runs of ducts, pipes, and cables should be placed in closets, service rooms, and wall cavities rather than in architecturally significant spaces. Mechanical equipment should not be concealed in walls or ceilings in a manner that requires the removal of significant historic building materials.

New "dropped" acoustical ceilings that hide mechanical equipment should not be installed when this destroys the proportions of character-defining interior spaces, obscures window openings, or covers over decorative ceilings.

Cutting through features such as masonry walls in order to install heating/air-conditioning units should always be avoided. If new air-conditioning units are installed in window frames, the sash and frames should be protected from moisture condensation. Window installations should be considered only when all other viable heating/cooling systems would result in significant damage to historic materials.

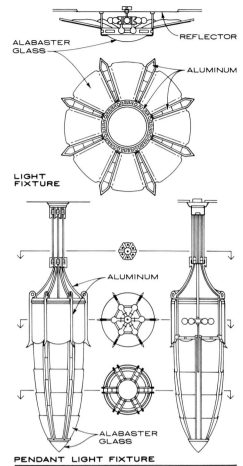

LIGHT FIXTURE

PENDANT LIGHT FIXTURE

DETAILS FROM THE DEPARTMENT OF JUSTICE BUILDING, WASHINGTON, DC, 1933 (ZANTZINGER, BORIE AND MEDARY)

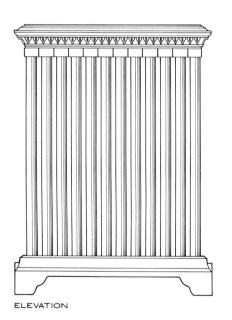

ELEVATION

SECTION

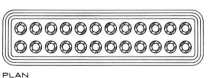

PLAN

STEAM RADIATOR

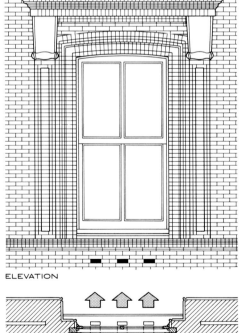

ELEVATION

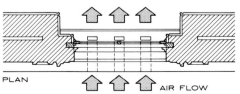

PLAN   AIR FLOW

NATURAL VENTILATION SYSTEM (AT FIRST STORY WINDOW)

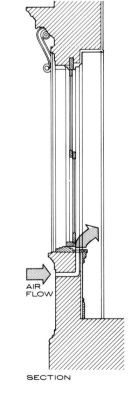

AIR FLOW

SECTION

DETAILS FROM THE PENSION BUILDING, WASHINGTON, DC, 1882 (MONTGOMERY C. MEIGS – ARCHITECT)

Lee H. Nelson, FAIA, H. Ward Jandl, Sharon C. Park, AIA, Kay D. Weeks; Preservation Assistance Division, National Park Service; Washington, D.C.
Eric J. Gastier; Darrel Downing Rippeteau Architects, PC; Washington, D.C.

16 MECHANICAL SYSTEMS

INTRODUCTION

The roof—with its shape; features such as cresting, dormers, cupolas, and chimneys; and the size, color, and patterning of the roofing material—is an important design element of many historic buildings. In addition a weathertight roof is essential to the long-term preservation of the entire structure.

Historic roofing is in large measure a reflection of available materials, levels of construction technology, the weather, and cost. For example, throughout the country in all periods of history, wood shingles have been used—their size, shape, and detailing differing according to regional craft practices. European settlers used clay tile for roofing as early as the mid-17th century. In some cities, such as New York and Boston, clay was popularly used as a precaution against fire. The Spanish influence in the use of clay tiles is found in the southern, southwestern, and western states. In the mid-19th century, tile roofs were often replaced by sheet-metal roofs, which were lighter and easier to install and maintain. Another practice settlers brought to the New World was slate roofing, and evidence of its use dates from the mid-17th century. Slate has been popular for its durability, fireproof qualities, and its decorative applications. The use of metals for roofing and roof features dates from the 18th century and includes the use of sheet iron, corrugated iron, galvanized metal, tinplate, and zinc. Awareness of these and other traditions of roofing materials and their detailing will contribute to more sensitive treatments.

PRESERVATION APPROACHES

The configuration of a historic building can be radically changed by adding new features to the roof, such as dormer windows, vents, skylights, or mechanical and service equipment. Adding an additional floor or floors at the roofline is possibly the most difficult rehabilitation change to accomplish without dramatically changing the historic character of the building. For this reason, the roof's shape, size, color, and patterning should be retained in any preservation project.

Routine maintenance of the building includes cleaning of gutters and downspouts and replacing deteriorated flashing. Roof sheathing should also be checked for proper venting to prevent moisture condensation and water penetration and to ensure that materials are free from insect infestation. When water and debris are permitted to collect, damage may occur to roof fasteners, sheathing, and the underlying structure.

In certain cases, such as storm or fire damage, only portions of a roof or a damaged roofing feature will need repair. The repaired area should match the visual qualities of the historic roof. Some repairs involve less difficulty than others. Normally, individual slates can be replaced without major disruption to the rest of the roof; replacing flashing, on the other hand, can require substantial removal of surrounding materials. If it is the substrate or a support material that has deteriorated, many of the more durable surface materials such as slate or tile can be reused if handled carefully during the repair.

A roof feature that is too deteriorated to repair should be replaced in kind. With some exceptions, most historic roofing materials are available today. Special roofing materials, such as tile or embossed metal shingles, can be produced by manufacturers of related products that are commonly used elsewhere, either on the exterior or interior of a structure. With some creative thinking and research, the historic materials usually can be found. Examples include a large section of roofing, a dormer, decorative roof cresting, or a chimney.

For both repair and replacement of historic roofing, compatible substitute materials may be considered if the same kind of material is technically or economically infeasible; however, the substitute material needs to convey the same visual appearance and be physically and chemically compatible with the surrounding materials.

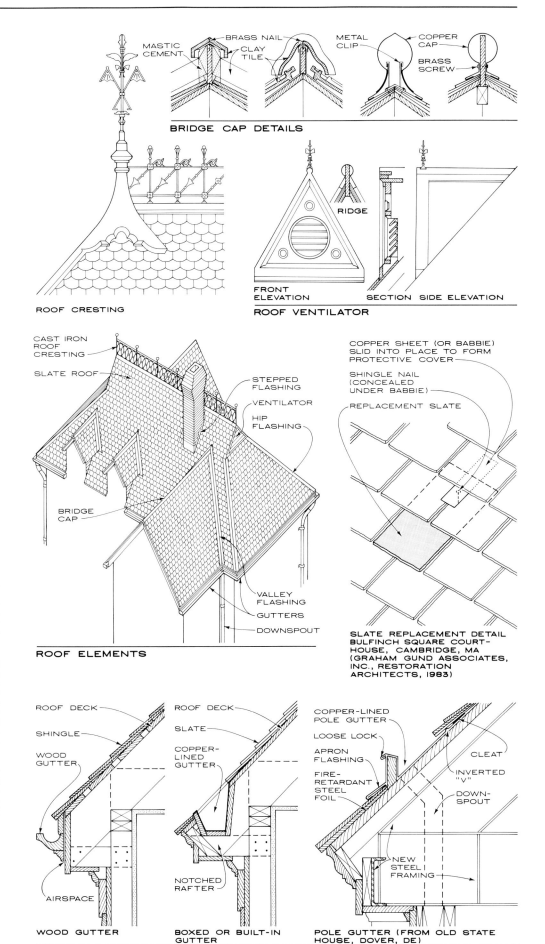

BRIDGE CAP DETAILS

ROOF CRESTING

ROOF VENTILATOR

FRONT ELEVATION — SECTION — SIDE ELEVATION

ROOF ELEMENTS

SLATE REPLACEMENT DETAIL BULFINCH SQUARE COURTHOUSE, CAMBRIDGE, MA (GRAHAM GUND ASSOCIATES, INC., RESTORATION ARCHITECTS, 1983)

WOOD GUTTER

BOXED OR BUILT-IN GUTTER

POLE GUTTER (FROM OLD STATE HOUSE, DOVER, DE)

GUTTER DETAILS

Lee H. Nelson, FAIA, H. Ward Jandl, Sharon C. Park, AIA; Preservation Assistance Division, National Park Service; Washington, D.C.
Eric J. Gastier; Darrel Downing Rippeteau Architects, PC; Washington, D.C.

INTRODUCTION

As one of the few parts of a building serving both as an interior and exterior feature, windows are nearly always an important part of the historic character of a building. In most buildings, windows also comprise a considerable amount of the historic fabric of the wall plane and thus are deserving of special consideration. It is essential that the historic character of the windows be assessed together with their physical condition before specific repair or replacement work is undertaken. Emphasis should be placed on repairing existing windows, where possible, and improving their performance, such as with retrofitting weatherstripping to reduce air infiltration. Replacement windows should closely match the historic ones.

PRESERVATION APPROACHES

Technology and prevailing architectural styles have shaped the history of windows in the United States, starting in the 17th century with wooden casement windows with tiny glass panes seated in lead cames. From the transitional single-hung sash in the early 1700s to the true double-hung sash later in the same century,

VENETIAN WINDOW FROM THE OLD STATE HOUSE
DOVER, DE (McCUNE ASSOCIATES, RESTORATION ARCHITECTS)

these early wooden windows were characterized by small panes, wide muntins, and the way in which decorative trim was used on both the exterior and interior of the window. As the sash thickness increased by the turn of the 19th century, muntins narrowed in width but increased in thickness according to the size of the window and design practices. Regional traditions continued to have an impact on window design, such as with the long-term use of ''French windows'' in the deep South. By the mid-19th century, two-over-two lights were common; the manufacturing of plate glass in the United States by the late 19th century allowed for dramatic use of large sheets of glass in commercial and office buildings. With mass-produced windows, mail order distribution, and changing architectural styles, it was possible to obtain a wide range of window designs and light patterns in sash. Popular versions of Arts and Crafts houses constructed in the early 20th century frequently utilized smaller lights in the upper sash set in groups or pairs and saw the reemergence of casement windows. In the early 20th century, the desire for fireproof building construction in dense urban areas contributed to the growth of a thriving steel window industry along with a market for hollow metal and metal clad wooden windows.

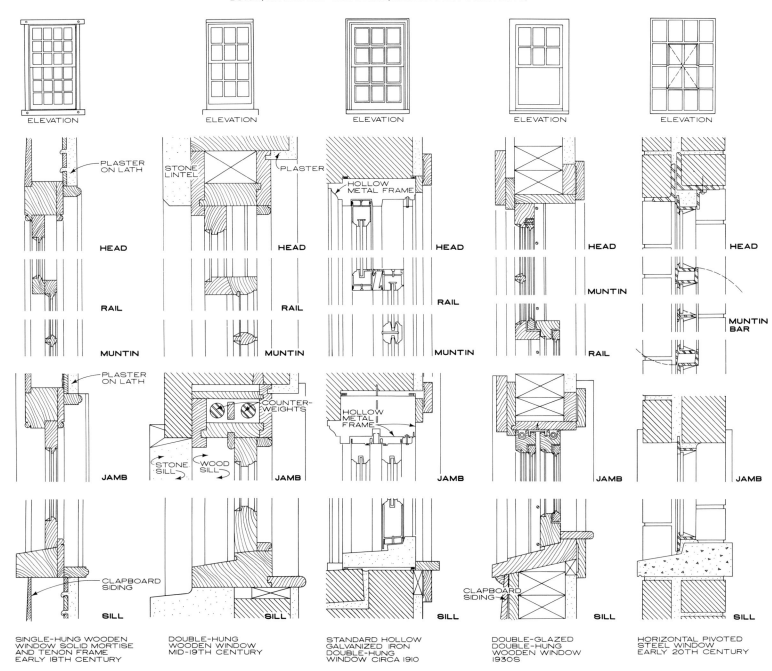

SINGLE-HUNG WOODEN WINDOW SOLID MORTISE AND TENON FRAME EARLY 18TH CENTURY

DOUBLE-HUNG WOODEN WINDOW MID-19TH CENTURY

STANDARD HOLLOW GALVANIZED IRON DOUBLE-HUNG WINDOW CIRCA 1910

DOUBLE-GLAZED DOUBLE-HUNG WOODEN WINDOW 1930S

HORIZONTAL PIVOTED STEEL WINDOW EARLY 20TH CENTURY

Lee H. Nelson, FAIA, H. Ward Jandl, Charles Fisher; Preservation Assistance Division, National Park Service; Washington, D.C.
Eric J. Gastier; Darrel Downing Rippeteau Architects, PC; Washington, D.C.

WINDOWS

PRESERVATION APPROACHES

An in-depth survey of the condition of existing windows should be undertaken early in the planning of a rehabilitation to allow time to fully explore repair and upgrading methods and possible replacement options, if merited. Peeling paint, broken glass, stuck sash, and high air infiltration are no indication that existing windows are beyond repair and that their performance cannot be enhanced.

The wood and architectural metal which comprise the window frame, sash, muntins, and surrounds should be maintained through appropriate surface treatments such as cleaning, rust removal, limited paint removal, reapplication of protective coating systems, and reglazing where necessary.

Windows should be made weathertight by recaulking and replacing or installing weatherstripping. These actions also improve thermal efficiency. Retrofitting or replacing windows should never be a substitute for proper maintenance of the sash, frame, and glazing.

Window frames and sash can be repaired by patching, splicing, consolidating, or otherwise reinforcing historic materials.

Window repair can include replacement of deteriorated components such as sash cords, muntins, and sills.

Serviceable window hardware such as brass lifts and sash locks can be reused in the course of repairs and should not be discarded in favor of new hardware.

Thermal efficiency can be improved with weatherstripping, storm windows, caulking, interior shades, and, if historically appropriate, blinds and awnings. Replacing historic multipaned sash with new thermal sash is inappropriate when the historic sash are in repairable condition.

Interior storm windows should have airtight gaskets, ventilating holes, and/or removable clips or operability features to ensure proper maintenance and to avoid potential condensation damage to historic windows.

Exterior storm windows should be selected that do not damage or obscure the windows and frames. It is not appropriate to install new exterior storm windows that are inappropriate in size and are not painted the same color as the sash trim.

Tinted or reflective glazing should never be used on character-defining or other conspicuous elevations. Lightly tinted glazing could be used on non-character-defining elevations if other energy retrofitting alternatives are not possible and after conclusively establishing a need for such a treatment.

A historic window that is too deteriorated to repair should in most cases be replaced in kind, that is, using the same kind of material (wood for wood; steel for steel) and using the same sash and pane configuration and other design details.

In some cases, the historic windows (frame, sash, and glazing) may be completely missing. The preferred option for replacement is always an accurate restoration using historical, pictorial, and physical documentation.

Where fixed windows are being installed, the glass and frames should be set in the same planes as the historic sash, with all detailing duplicated.

When replacing historic multipaned sash with new sash, true integral muntins should be used, particularly on smaller buildings, windows on large buildings close to the pedestrianway, on ornate windows, where windows are part of a significant interior space, and where a building has high historic merit.

On certain types of large buildings, particularly high-rises, aluminum windows may be a suitable replacement for historic wooden sash provided wooden replacements are not practical and the design detail of the historic windows can be matched. Historic color duplication, custom contour panning, incorporation of ⅝ in. deep trapezoidal exterior muntin grids where applicable, retention of the same glass-to-frame ratio, matching of the historic reveal, and duplication of the frame width, depth, and such existing decorative details as arched tops should all be components in aluminum replacement windows selected for use on historic buildings.

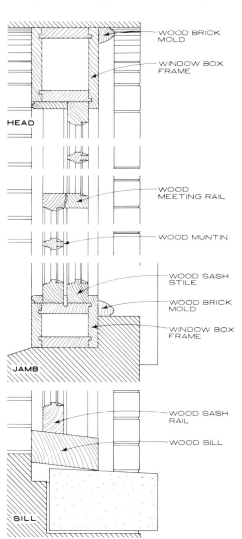

LATE 19TH CENTURY MILL WINDOW

REPAIR WHENEVER POSSIBLE. IN SOME CASES, REPLACEMENT OF SASH AND REUSE OF FRAMES AND HARDWARE MAY BE POSSIBLE

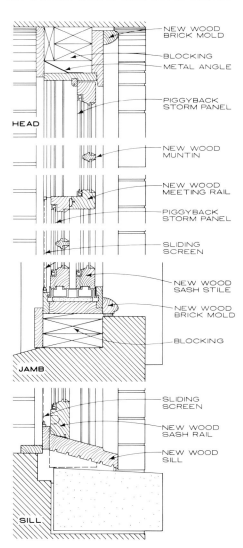

WOOD REPLACEMENT WINDOW

APPROPRIATE WHEN HISTORIC WINDOW IS BEYOND REPAIR. IN MANY CASES, PIGGYBACK INTERIOR STORM PANELS ATTACHED TO NEW SASH AND/OR INTERIOR MOUNTED INSECT SCREENS ARE SUITABLE UPGRADED FEATURES. EXTERIOR APPEARANCE OF HISTORIC WINDOW SHOULD BE RETAINED

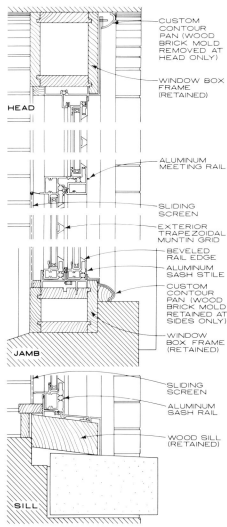

ALUMINUM REPLACEMENT WINDOW (CUSTOM)

APPROPRIATE IN SOME CASES, PARTICULARLY IN EARLY 20TH CENTURY HIGH-RISES. SPECIAL FEATURES TO BE SPECIFIED: BEVELED RAIL AND STILE EDGES, CUSTOM CONTOUR PANNING, CUSTOM COLOR, TRAPEZOIDAL EXTERIOR MUNTIN GRID, AND CLOSELY MATCHED SIGHT LINES

REPAIR/REPLACEMENT STRATEGIES FOR HISTORIC WOOD WINDOWS

Lee H. Nelson, FAIA, H. Ward Jandl, Charles Fisher; Preservation Assistance Division, National Park Service; Washington, D.C.
Eric J. Gastier; Darrel Downing Rippeteau Architects, PC; Washington, D.C.

INTRODUCTION

Entrances and porches are quite often the focus of historic buildings, particularly when they occur on primary elevations. Together with their functional and decorative features such as doors, steps, balustrades, pilasters, and entablatures, they can be extremely important in defining the overall character of a building.

Usually entrances and porches were integral components of a historic building's design; for example, porches on Greek Revival houses, with Doric or Ionic columns and pediments, echoed the architectural elements and features of the larger building. Central one-bay porches or arcaded porches are evident in Italianate style buildings of the 1860s. Doors of Renaissance Revival style buildings frequently supported entablatures or pediments. Porches were particularly prominent features of Eastlake and Stick Style houses; porch posts, railings, and balusters were characterized by a massive and robust quality, with members turned on a lathe. Porches of bungalows of the early 20th century were characterized by tapered porch posts, exposed post and beams, and low-pitched roofs with wide overhangs. Art Deco commercial buildings were entered through stylized glass and stainless steel doors.

PRESERVATION APPROACHES

The materials that comprise entrances and porches—masonry, wood, and architectural metal—should be protected and maintained through appropriate surface treatments such as cleaning, rust removal, limited paint removal, and reapplication of protective coating systems. The overall condition of materials should be evaluated to determine whether more than protection and maintenance are required.

Removing or radically changing primary entrances will in most cases change the overall appearance of the building. Entrances and porches should never be removed because the building has been reoriented to accommodate a new use.

If barrier-free access is required to a historic building, it should be introduced in such a manner that does not destroy significant material or that does not interfere with the historic design.

Entrances and porches can be repaired by reinforcing deteriorated historic materials—patching, splicing, and reinforcing with epoxies are examples. Limited replacement in kind of those extensively deteriorated or missing parts of repeated features may be undertaken where there are surviving prototypes. Examples include balustrades, cornices, entablatures, columns, sidelights, and stairs.

Only when an entire entrance or porch is too deteriorated to repair—or is missing—should total replacement be considered. If the historic form and detailing are still evident, this evidence should be used to restore the entrance or porch.

If the entrance or porch is missing, restoration should be based on historical, pictorial, and physical evidence rather than on conjectural designs or the availability of elements from neighboring buildings.

When insufficient documentation exists for an accurate restoration, the replacement entrance or porch may be a new design that is consistent with the size, scale, material, and color of the historic building. Care must be taken not to create a false historic appearance in the new work.

Compatible substitute material may be considered if replicating with the historic material is technically or economically infeasible; the substitute material needs to convey the same visual appearance and be physically and chemically compatible.

PORCH AND ENTRY

**655 HUGHES STREET,
CAPE MAY, NJ**

PORCH AND ENTRY

**FENDALL HALL, EUFAULA, AL
(NICHOLAS H. HOLMES,
RESTORATION ARCHITECT, 1975)**

PORCH AND ENTRY

**GUNSTON HALL,
FAIRFAX COUNTY, VA**

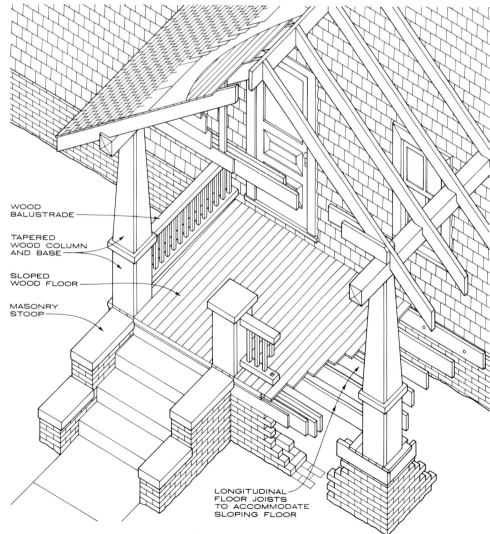

WOOD
BALUSTRADE

TAPERED
WOOD COLUMN
AND BASE

SLOPED
WOOD FLOOR

MASONRY
STOOP

LONGITUDINAL
FLOOR JOISTS
TO ACCOMMODATE
SLOPING FLOOR

TYPICAL BUNGALOW PORCH AND ENTRY, EARLY 20TH CENTURY

Lee H. Nelson, FAIA, H. Ward Jandl, Camille Martone, Kay D. Weeks; Preservation Assistance Division, National Park Service; Washington, D.C.
Eric J. Gastier; Darrel Downing Rippeteau Architects, PC; Washington, D.C.

INTRODUCTION

The storefront is usually the most prominent feature of a historic commercial building, playing a crucial role in a store's advertising and merchandising strategy. Although a storefront normally does not extend beyond the first story, the rest of the building is often related to it visually through a unity of form and detail. Planning should always consider the entire building; window patterns on the upper floors, cornice elements, and other decorative features should be carefully retained, in addition to the storefront itself.

The earliest extant storefronts in the United States, dating from the late 18th and early 19th centuries, had bay or oriel windows and provided limited display space. The 19th century witnessed the progressive enlargement of display windows as plate glass became available in increasingly larger units. The use of cast iron columns and lintels at ground floor level permitted structural members to be reduced in size. Recessed entrances provided shelter for sidewalk patrons and further enlarged display areas. In the 1920s and 1930s, aluminum, colored structural glass, stainless steel, glass block, neon, and other new materials were introduced to create Art Deco

storefronts. The growing appreciation of historic buildings in recent years has prompted many owners to remove inappropriate changes and restore the historic appearance.

PRESERVATION APPROACHES

Functional and decorative features that make up the historic storefront include display windows, lower window panels, transoms, business signs, entrance doors, and entablatures. Materials that make up a storefront—cast iron, bronze, wood, pressed metal, structural glass—should be identified before undertaking any preservation work.

Removal of inappropriate, nonhistoric cladding as well as later alterations such as oversized awnings and signs can enhance a historic storefront.

The historic storefront should be secured by boarding up windows and installing alarm systems prior to and during rehabilitation. Unsecured doors and broken windows permit interior features and finishes to be subjected to damage by weather or vandalism.

Historic features such as cracked display windows, deteriorated wooden lower window panels, and rusted metal structural members should be repaired wherever possible rather than replaced.

Repairs are best made using historic materials; however, substitute materials may be appropriate if they convey the same visual appearance as the surviving components of the storefront.

Only if an entire storefront is missing or is too deteriorated to repair should total replacement be considered. The historic form and detailing should be used to restore the storefront.

Restoration should be based on historical and pictorial evidence rather than on conjectural designs or the availability of elements from neighboring buildings. When insufficient documentation exists for an accurate restoration, the replacement storefront may be a new design that is consistent with the size, scale, material, and color of the historic building.

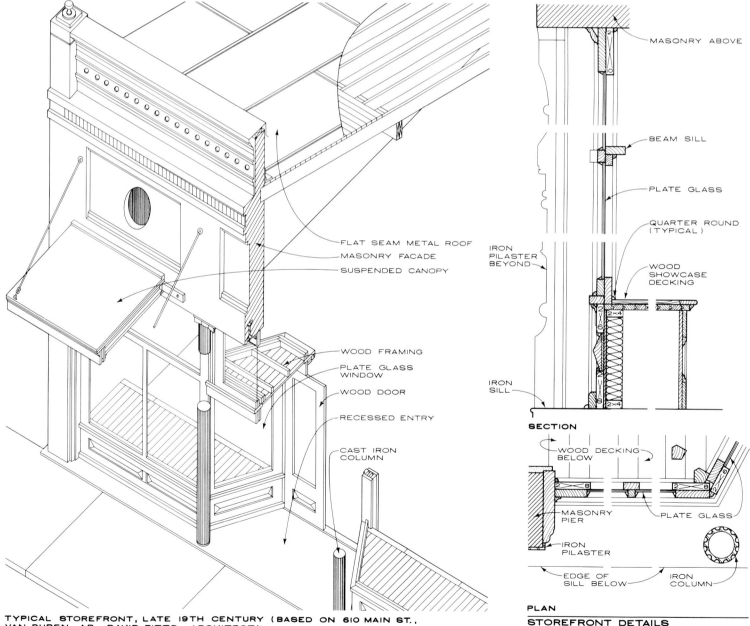

TYPICAL STOREFRONT, LATE 19TH CENTURY (BASED ON 610 MAIN ST., VAN BUREN, AR, DAVID FITTS - ARCHITECT)

STOREFRONT DETAILS

Lee H. Nelson, FAIA, H. Ward Jandl, Michael J. Auer; Preservation Assistance Division, National Park Service; Washington, D.C.

Eric J. Gastier; Darrel Downing Rippeteau Architects, PC; Washington, D.C.

INTRODUCTION

If features of the structural system are exposed, such as load-bearing brick walls, cast iron columns, roof trusses, posts and beams, vigas, or stone foundation walls, they may be important in defining the building's overall historic character.

Structural systems in architecture are composed of structural elements (such as beams, piers, and trusses) and building materials (wood, steel, and masonry) that together form the walls, floors, and roofing of buildings.

The types of structural systems found in America include, but certainly are not limited to, the following: wooden frame construction (17th century), balloon frame construction (19th century), load-bearing masonry construction (18th century), brick cavity wall construction (19th century), heavy timber post and beam industrial construction (19th century), fireproof iron construction (19th century), heavy masonry and steel construction (19th century), skeletal steel construction (19th century), and concrete slab and post construction (20th century).

PRESERVATION APPROACHES

A significant structural system or distinctive structural features should be identified prior to any work. To accommodate new uses within a historic building, structural upgrading should be done in a sensitive manner. Installing equipment or mechanical systems that result in numerous cuts, splices, or alterations to historic structural members should always be avoided.

If excavations or regrading—either adjacent to or within a historic building—are being planned, studies should be

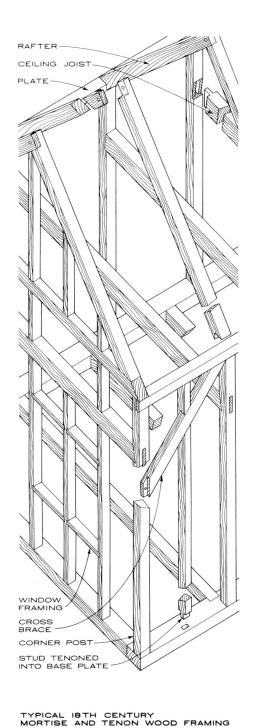

**TYPICAL 18TH CENTURY
MORTISE AND TENON WOOD FRAMING**

RAFTER
CEILING JOIST
PLATE
WINDOW FRAMING
CROSS BRACE
CORNER POST
STUD TENONED INTO BASE PLATE

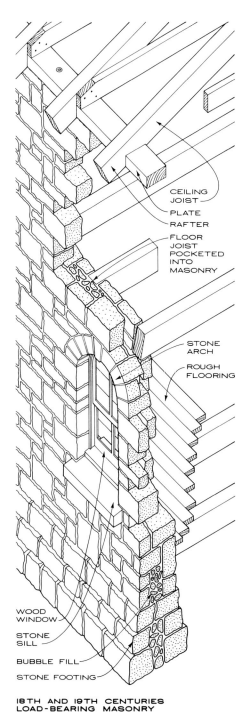

**18TH AND 19TH CENTURIES
LOAD-BEARING MASONRY**

CEILING JOIST
PLATE
RAFTER
FLOOR JOIST POCKETED INTO MASONRY
STONE ARCH
ROUGH FLOORING
WOOD WINDOW
STONE SILL
BUBBLE FILL
STONE FOOTING

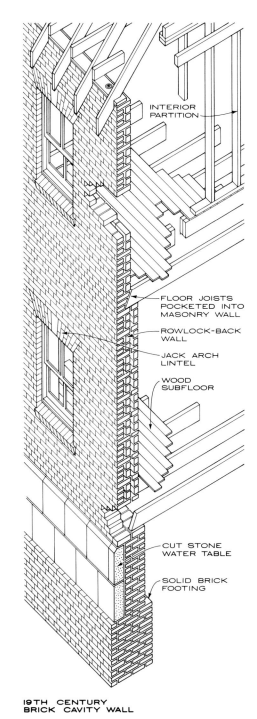

**19TH CENTURY
BRICK CAVITY WALL**

INTERIOR PARTITION
FLOOR JOISTS POCKETED INTO MASONRY WALL
ROWLOCK-BACK WALL
JACK ARCH LINTEL
WOOD SUBFLOOR
CUT STONE WATER TABLE
SOLID BRICK FOOTING

STRUCTURAL SYSTEMS

Lee H. Nelson, FAIA, H. Ward Jandl, Sharon C. Park, AIA, Kay D. Weeks; Preservation Assistance Division, National Park Service; Washington, D.C.

Eric J. Gastier; Darrel Downing Rippeteau Architects, PC; Washington, D.C.

STRUCTURAL SYSTEMS

done first to ascertain potential damage. Inappropriate excavations can cause the historic foundation to settle, shift, or fail.

Structural problems, such as deflection of beams, racking of structural members, or cracking and bowing of walls, should be treated—not cosmetically covered over. A deteriorated load-bearing masonry wall should be reinforced and retained wherever possible, not replaced with a new wall that is veneered using old brick.

Structural systems may be protected by cyclical cleaning of roof gutters and downspouts; replacing roof flashing;

keeping masonry, wood, and architectural metals in a sound condition; and assuring that structural members are free from insect infestation.

The structural system should be repaired by augmenting or upgrading individual parts or features. For example, weakened structural members such as floor framing can be paired with a new member, braced, or otherwise supplemented and reinforced.

Structural upgrading should never be undertaken in a manner that diminishes the historic character of the building, such as installing exterior strapping channels.

In instances where seismic upgrading is necessary, it is best to use grouted bolts as opposed to exposed plates and to locate diaphragms on unornamented surfaces or to consider other options that reduce the visual and physical impact of the code-required change.

If exposed elements of the structural system are beyond repair, the replacements need to convey the same form, design, and overall visual appearance as the historic feature, to equal the load-bearing capabilities of the historic material, and to be physically and chemically compatible.

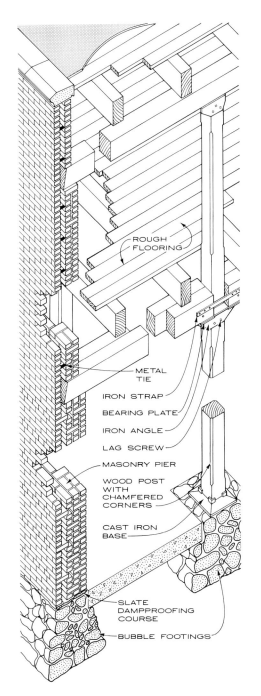

ROUGH FLOORING
METAL TIE
IRON STRAP
BEARING PLATE
IRON ANGLE
LAG SCREW
MASONRY PIER
WOOD POST WITH CHAMFERED CORNERS
CAST IRON BASE
SLATE DAMPPROOFING COURSE
BUBBLE FOOTINGS

19TH AND EARLY 20TH CENTURIES HEAVY TIMBER POST AND BEAM

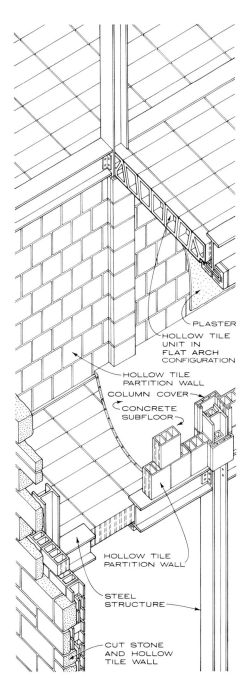

PLASTER
HOLLOW TILE UNIT IN FLAT ARCH CONFIGURATION
HOLLOW TILE PARTITION WALL
COLUMN COVER
CONCRETE SUBFLOOR
HOLLOW TILE PARTITION WALL
STEEL STRUCTURE
CUT STONE AND HOLLOW TILE WALL

LATE 19TH AND EARLY 20TH CENTURIES FIREPROOF CONSTRUCTION

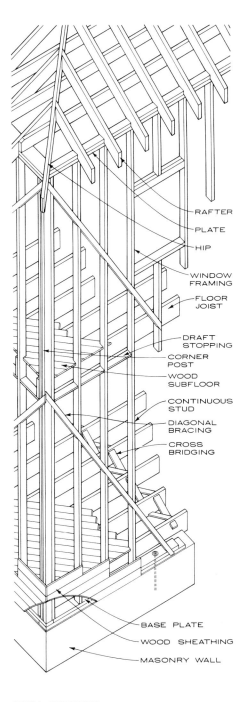

RAFTER
PLATE
HIP
WINDOW FRAMING
FLOOR JOIST
DRAFT STOPPING
CORNER POST
WOOD SUBFLOOR
CONTINUOUS STUD
DIAGONAL BRACING
CROSS BRIDGING
BASE PLATE
WOOD SHEATHING
MASONRY WALL

20TH CENTURY BALLOON FRAMING

STRUCTURAL SYSTEMS

Lee H. Nelson, FAIA, H. Ward Jandl, Sharon C. Park, AIA, Kay D. Weeks; Preservation Assistance Division, National Park Service; Washington, D.C.
Eric J. Gastier; Darrel Downing Rippeteau Architects, PC; Washington, D.C.

INTRODUCTION

An interior floor plan, the arrangement and sequence of spaces, and built-in features and applied finishes are individually and collectively important in defining the historic character of the building. Their identification, retention, protection, and repair should be given prime consideration in every rehabilitation project.

In evaluating historic interiors prior to rehabilitation, it should be kept in mind that interiors are comprised of a series of primary and secondary spaces. This is applicable to all buildings, from courthouses to cathedrals to cottages and office buildings. Primary spaces, including entrance halls, parlors, living rooms, assembly rooms, and lobbies, are defined not only by their features and finishes, but by the size and proportion of the rooms themselves—purposely created to be the visual attraction or functioning "core" of the building. Care should be taken to retain the essential proportions of primary interior spaces and not to damage, obscure, or destroy distinctive features and finishes.

Secondary spaces include areas and rooms that "service" the primary spaces and may include kitchens, bathrooms, mail rooms, utility spaces, secondary hallways, firestairs, and office cubicles in a commercial or office space. Extensive changes can often be made in these less important areas without having a detrimental effect on the overall historic character.

PRESERVATION APPROACHES

Distinctive interior spaces, features, and finishes should be identified, then carefully retained and preserved in any work project. Examples include columns, cornices, baseboards, fireplaces and mantels, paneling, light fixtures, hardware, flooring, and wallpaper, plaster, paint, and finishes such as stenciling, marbling, and graining.

Distinctive interior spaces should not be altered by inserting a floor, cutting through the floor, lowering ceilings, or adding or removing walls.

Historically finished surfaces such as paint, plaster, or other finishes should not be stripped (e.g., removing plaster to expose masonry surfaces such as brick walls or a chimney piece). It is also inappropriate to strip painted wood to a bare wood surface, then apply a clear finish or stain to create a "natural, new look." Distinctive finishes such as marbling or graining on doors or paneling should be repaired, not covered over or removed. Conversely, paint, plaster, or other finishes should not be applied to surfaces that have been historically unfinished to create a new appearance.

Code-required fire suppression systems (such as a sprinkler system for a wood-frame mill building) should be sensitively designed so that character-defining features are not covered.

Interior features should be protected against gouging, scratching, and denting during project work by covering them with heavy canvas or plastic sheets. Destructive methods of paint removal such as propane or butane torches or sandblasting should never be used because they can irreversibly damage the historic materials that comprise interior features.

Interior features and finishes can often be repaired and preserved by reinforcing the historic materials. Repair may involve the limited replacement in kind of those extensively deteriorated or missing parts of repeated features when there are surviving prototypes such as stairs. Examples include balustrades, wood paneling, columns, or decorative wall coverings or ornamental tin or plaster ceilings. If an interior feature or finish is too deteriorated to repair or is missing, its replacement should be based on historical and pictorial evidence rather than on conjectural designs or the availability of elements from neighboring buildings.

In cases where insufficient documentation exists for an accurate restoration of an interior feature or finish, the replacement should be compatible in scale, design, materials, color, and texture with the surviving interior features and finishes. A new design element should be distinguishable from the old and not create a false historic appearance.

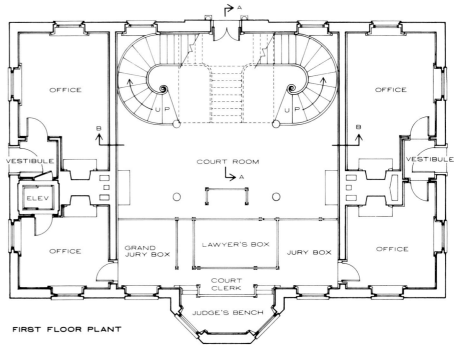

FIRST FLOOR PLAN

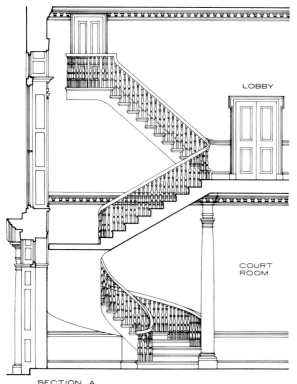

SECTION A

PARTIAL TRANSVERSE SECTION

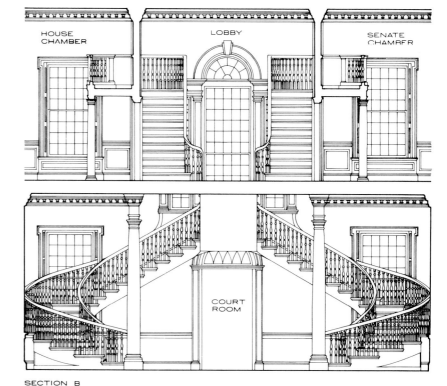

SECTION B

PARTIAL LONGITUDINAL SECTION

OLD STATE HOUSE, DOVER, DE (McCUNE ASSOCIATES, RESTORATION ARCHITECTS, 1977)
Lee H. Nelson, FAIA, H. Ward Jandl, Camille Martone, Kay D. Weeks; Preservation Assistance Division, National Park Service; Washington, D.C.
Eric J. Gastier; Darrel Downing Rippeteau Architects, PC; Washington, D.C.

INTERIORS

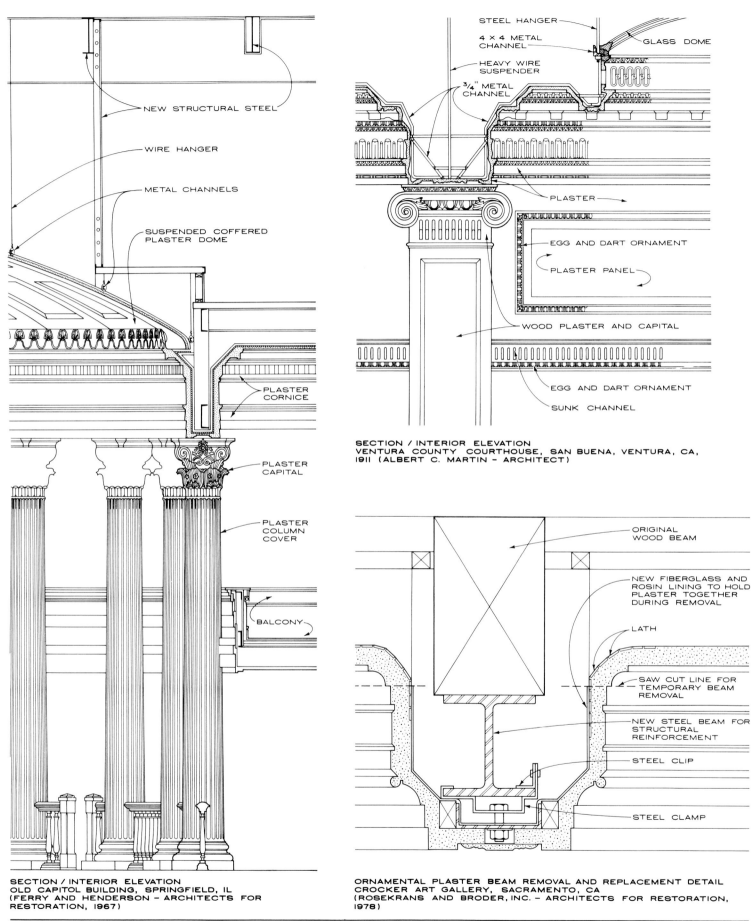

NEW STRUCTURAL STEEL

WIRE HANGER

METAL CHANNELS

SUSPENDED COFFERED PLASTER DOME

PLASTER CORNICE

PLASTER CAPITAL

PLASTER COLUMN COVER

BALCONY

STEEL HANGER

4 X 4 METAL CHANNEL

HEAVY WIRE SUSPENDER

3/4" METAL CHANNEL

GLASS DOME

PLASTER

EGG AND DART ORNAMENT

PLASTER PANEL

WOOD PLASTER AND CAPITAL

EGG AND DART ORNAMENT

SUNK CHANNEL

SECTION / INTERIOR ELEVATION
VENTURA COUNTY COURTHOUSE, SAN BUENA, VENTURA, CA,
1911 (ALBERT C. MARTIN - ARCHITECT)

SECTION / INTERIOR ELEVATION
OLD CAPITOL BUILDING, SPRINGFIELD, IL
(FERRY AND HENDERSON - ARCHITECTS FOR
RESTORATION, 1967)

ORIGINAL WOOD BEAM

NEW FIBERGLASS AND ROSIN LINING TO HOLD PLASTER TOGETHER DURING REMOVAL

LATH

SAW CUT LINE FOR TEMPORARY BEAM REMOVAL

NEW STEEL BEAM FOR STRUCTURAL REINFORCEMENT

STEEL CLIP

STEEL CLAMP

ORNAMENTAL PLASTER BEAM REMOVAL AND REPLACEMENT DETAIL
CROCKER ART GALLERY, SACRAMENTO, CA
(ROSEKRANS AND BRODER, INC. - ARCHITECTS FOR RESTORATION,
1978)

ORNAMENTAL PLASTER

Lee H. Nelson, FAIA, H. Ward Jandl, Camille Martone, Kay D. Weeks; Preservation Assistance Division, National Park Service;
Washington, D.C.
Eric J. Gastier; Darrel Downing Rippeteau Architects, PC; Washington, D.C.

INTERIORS

16

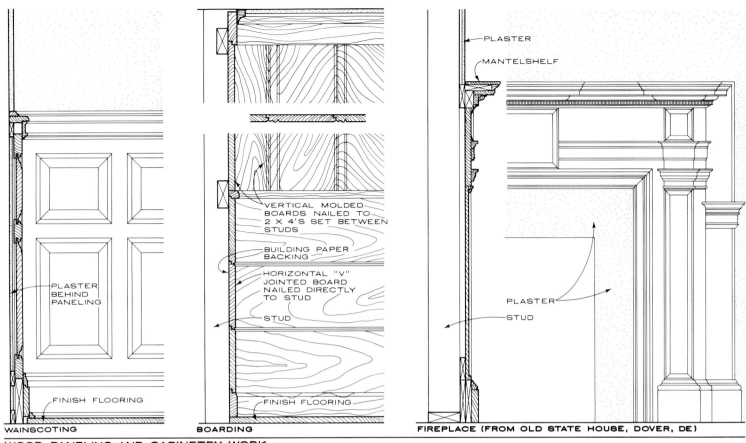

PLASTER
BEHIND
PANELING

FINISH FLOORING

WAINSCOTING

VERTICAL MOLDED
BOARDS NAILED TO
2 X 4'S SET BETWEEN
STUDS

BUILDING PAPER
BACKING

HORIZONTAL "V"
JOINTED BOARD
NAILED DIRECTLY
TO STUD

STUD

FINISH FLOORING

BOARDING

PLASTER

MANTELSHELF

PLASTER

STUD

FIREPLACE (FROM OLD STATE HOUSE, DOVER, DE)

WOOD PANELING AND CABINETRY WORK

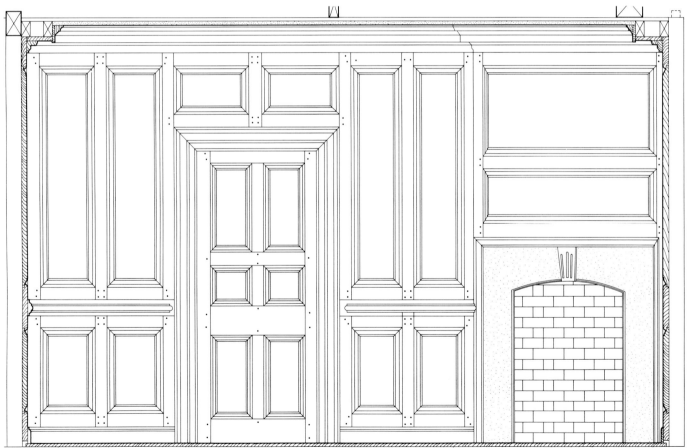

WOOD PANELING FROM THE LIVING ROOM OF THE TAYLOE HOUSE, WILLIAMSBURG, VA (PERRY, SHAW AND HEPBURN, CONSULTING ARCHITECTS FOR RESTORATION, 1949)

Lee H. Nelson, FAIA, H. Ward Jandl, Camille Martone, Kay D. Weeks; Preservation Assistance Division, National Park Service; Washington, D.C.
Eric J. Gastier; Darrel Downing Rippeteau Architects, PC; Washington, D.C.

16   **INTERIORS**

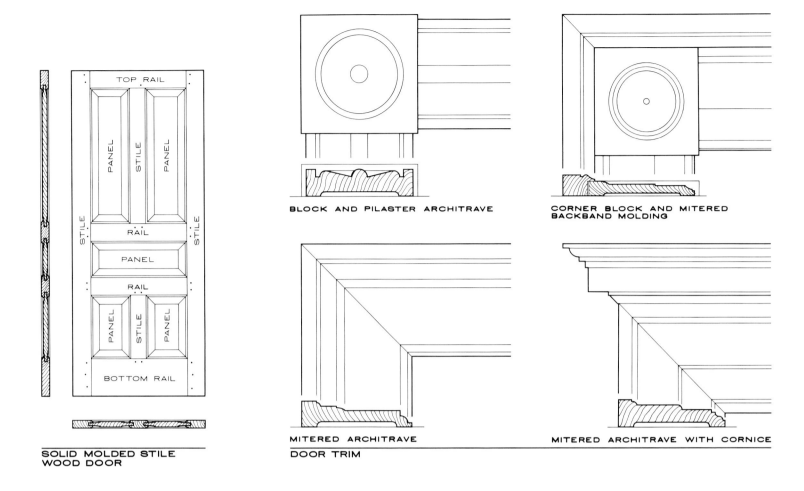

TOP RAIL

STILE

PANEL STILE PANEL

STILE RAIL STILE

PANEL

RAIL

PANEL STILE PANEL

BOTTOM RAIL

**SOLID MOLDED STILE
WOOD DOOR**

BLOCK AND PILASTER ARCHITRAVE

**CORNER BLOCK AND MITERED
BACKBAND MOLDING**

MITERED ARCHITRAVE

MITERED ARCHITRAVE WITH CORNICE

DOOR TRIM

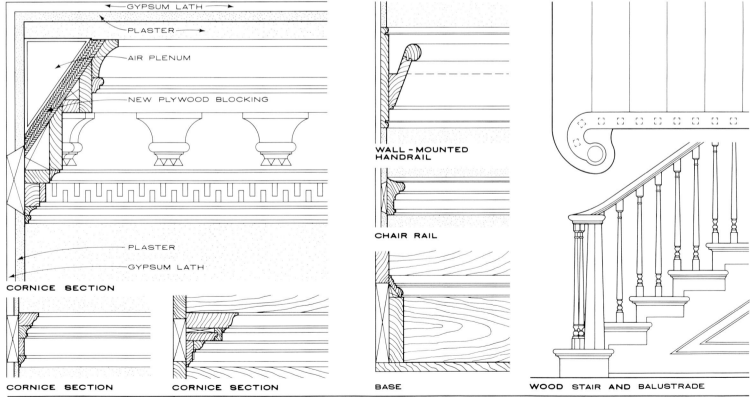

GYPSUM LATH

PLASTER

AIR PLENUM

NEW PLYWOOD BLOCKING

PLASTER

GYPSUM LATH

CORNICE SECTION

CORNICE SECTION

CORNICE SECTION

**WALL-MOUNTED
HANDRAIL**

CHAIR RAIL

BASE

WOOD STAIR AND BALUSTRADE

**INTERIOR WOOD DETAILS FROM THE OLD STATE HOUSE, DOVER, DE (McCUNE ASSOCIATES, RESTORATION
ARCHITECTS, 1977)**

Lee H. Nelson, FAIA, H. Ward Jandl, Camille Martone, Kay D. Weeks; Preservation Assistance Division, National Park Service;
Washington, D.C.
Eric J. Gastier; Darrel Downing Rippeteau Architects, PC; Washington, D.C.

INTERIORS   16

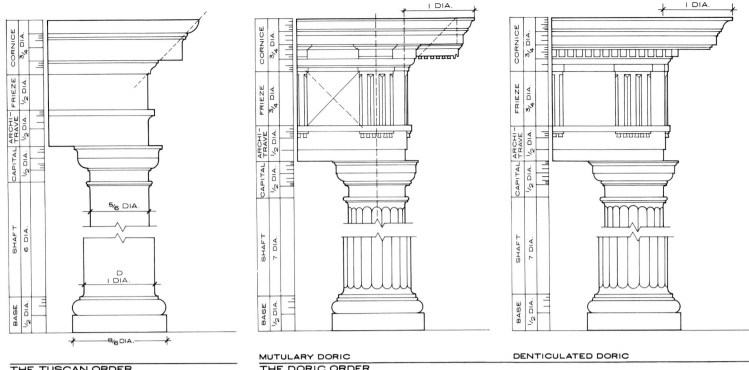

THE TUSCAN ORDER

MUTULARY DORIC
THE DORIC ORDER

DENTICULATED DORIC

A PARALLEL COMPARISON BASED ON VIGNOLA PROPORTIONS IN TERMS OF A CONSTANT
LOWER DIAMETER

TUSCAN   DORIC   IONIC   CORINTHIAN   COMPOSITE

THE FIVE CLASSICAL ORDERS

FILLET – RAISED AND SUNK

CAVETTO

SCOTIA

¾ HOLLOW

OVOLO

TORUS IF LARGE BEAD OR ASTRAGAL IF SMALL

¾ ROUND

CYMA RECTA

CYMA REVERSA

BEAK

THUMB

FASCIA OR FACE

CYMA RECTA WITH ACANTHUS

OVOLO WITH EGG AND DART
ASTRAGAL WITH BEAD AND REEL

CYMA REVERSA WITH WATER LEAF AND TONGUE

CYMA REVERSA WITH ACANTHUS

TORUS WITH BAY LEAF AND GARLAND

CYMA RECTA
CYMA REVERSA
FASCIA
OVOLO
BEAD
DENTILS
CYMA REVERSA
FILLET
FILLET

TYPES OF MOLDING AND ORNAMENTS

David Kulick and Roy W. Lewis, Jr.; Alvin Holm AIA, Architects; Philadelphia, Pennsylvania

16   THE CLASSICAL ORDERS

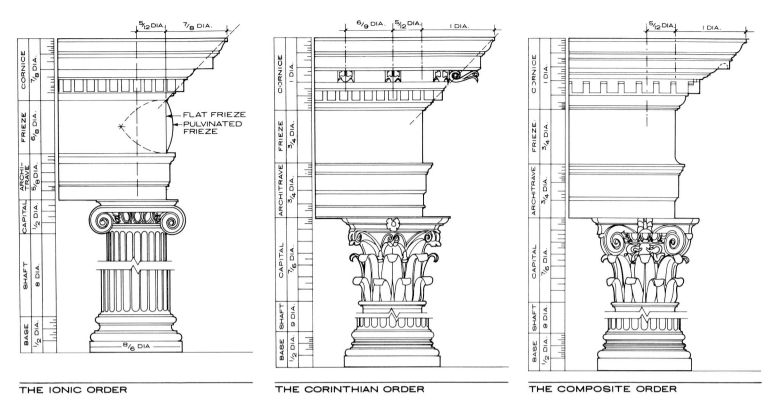

5/12 DIA.	7/8 DIA.	

CORNICE 7/8 DIA.
FRIEZE 6/9 DIA. — FLAT FRIEZE — PULVINATED FRIEZE
ARCHI-TRAVE 5/8 DIA.
CAPITAL 1/2 DIA.
SHAFT 8 DIA.
BASE 1/2 DIA.
8/6 DIA.

THE IONIC ORDER

| 6/9 DIA. | 5/12 DIA. | I DIA. |

CORNICE I DIA.
FRIEZE 3/4 DIA.
ARCHITRAVE 3/4 DIA.
CAPITAL 7/6 DIA.
SHAFT 9 DIA.
BASE 1/2 DIA.

THE CORINTHIAN ORDER

| 5/12 DIA. | I DIA. |

CORNICE I DIA.
FRIEZE 3/4 DIA.
ARCHITRAVE 3/4 DIA.
CAPITAL 7/6 DIA.
SHAFT 9 DIA.
BASE 1/2 DIA.

THE COMPOSITE ORDER

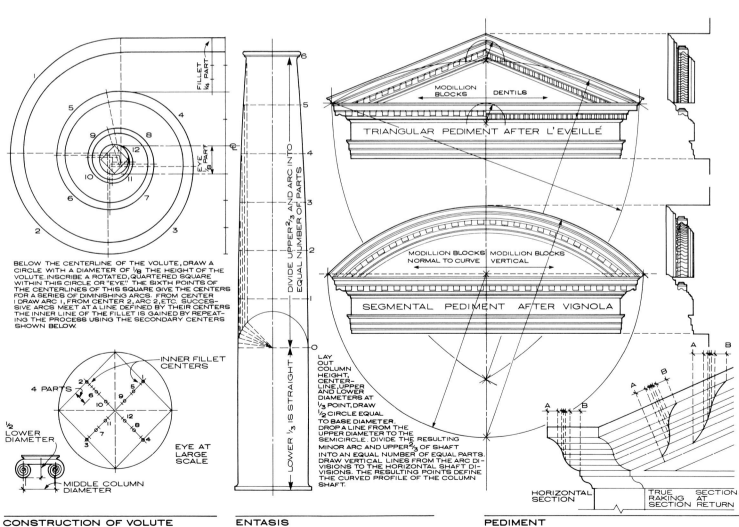

BELOW THE CENTERLINE OF THE VOLUTE, DRAW A
CIRCLE WITH A DIAMETER OF 1/8 THE HEIGHT OF THE
VOLUTE. INSCRIBE A ROTATED, QUARTERED SQUARE
WITHIN THIS CIRCLE OR "EYE." THE SIXTH POINTS OF
THE CENTERLINES OF THIS SQUARE GIVE THE CENTERS
FOR A SERIES OF DIMINISHING ARCS. FROM CENTER
I DRAW ARC I, FROM CENTER 2, ARC 2, ETC. SUCCES-
SIVE ARCS MEET AT A LINE DEFINED BY THEIR CENTERS
THE INNER LINE OF THE FILLET IS GAINED BY REPEAT-
ING THE PROCESS USING THE SECONDARY CENTERS
SHOWN BELOW.

FILLET 1/4 PART
EYE 1/8 PART

INNER FILLET CENTERS
4 PARTS
1/2 LOWER DIAMETER
LOWER DIAMETER
MIDDLE COLUMN DIAMETER
EYE AT LARGE SCALE

CONSTRUCTION OF VOLUTE

DIVIDE UPPER 2/3 AND ARC INTO EQUAL NUMBER OF PARTS

LOWER 1/3 IS STRAIGHT

LAY OUT COLUMN HEIGHT, CENTER-
LINE, UPPER AND LOWER DIAMETERS AT
1/3 POINT, DRAW 1/2 CIRCLE EQUAL
TO BASE DIAMETER. DROP A LINE FROM THE
UPPER DIAMETER TO THE SEMICIRCLE. DIVIDE THE RESULTING
MINOR ARC AND UPPER 2/3 SHAFT
INTO AN EQUAL NUMBER OF EQUAL PARTS.
DRAW VERTICAL LINES FROM THE ARC DI-
VISIONS TO THE HORIZONTAL SHAFT DI-
VISIONS. THE RESULTING POINTS DEFINE
THE CURVED PROFILE OF THE COLUMN
SHAFT.

ENTASIS

MODILLION BLOCKS   DENTILS

TRIANGULAR PEDIMENT AFTER L'EVEILLÉ

MODILLION BLOCKS NORMAL TO CURVE   MODILLION BLOCKS VERTICAL

SEGMENTAL PEDIMENT AFTER VIGNOLA

HORIZONTAL SECTION   TRUE RAKING SECTION   SECTION AT RETURN

PEDIMENT

David Kulick and Roy W. Lewis, Jr.; Alvin Holm AIA, Architects; Philadelphia, Pennsylvania

THE CLASSICAL ORDERS 16

REFERENCES

GENERAL REFERENCES: PUBLICATIONS

Kidder-Parker Architects' and Builders' Handbook, 1931, 18th ed., Harry Parker (Editor-in-Chief), Wiley

New Construction for Older Buildings, 1990, Peter Smeallie and Peter Smith, Wiley

New Life for Old Houses, 1989, George Steven, The Preservation Press (National Trust for Historic Preservation)

Secretary of the Interior's Standards for Rehabilitation and Guidelines for Rehabilitating Historic Buildings, Superintendent of Documents, Government Printing Office, Washington, DC.

Traditional Details for Building Restoration, Renovation, and Rehabilitation, 1991, John Bealle, John Ray Hoke, and Steven Kliment, Wiley

GENERAL REFERENCES: ORGANIZATIONS

The Association for Preservation Technology
P.O. Box 2487, Station D
Ottawa, Ontario
Canada K1P 5W6

Historic Resources Committee
American Institute of Architects
1735 Massachusetts Avenue, NW
Washington, DC 20006

National Conference of State Historic Preservation Officers
Hall of the States
444 N. Capitol Street, NW
Washington, DC 20001

National Park Service
P.O. Box 37127
Washington, DC 20013-7127

National Trust for Historic Preservation
1785 Massachusetts Avenue, NW
Washington, DC 20036

The Old-House Journal
69A Seventh Avenue
Brooklyn, NY 11217

DATA SOURCES: PUBLICATIONS

A Field Guide to American Houses, 1984, Virginia and Lee McAlester, Knopf, 351

American Shelter—An Illustrated Encyclopedia of the American Home, 1981, Lester Walker, Overlook Press, 351

APPENDIX

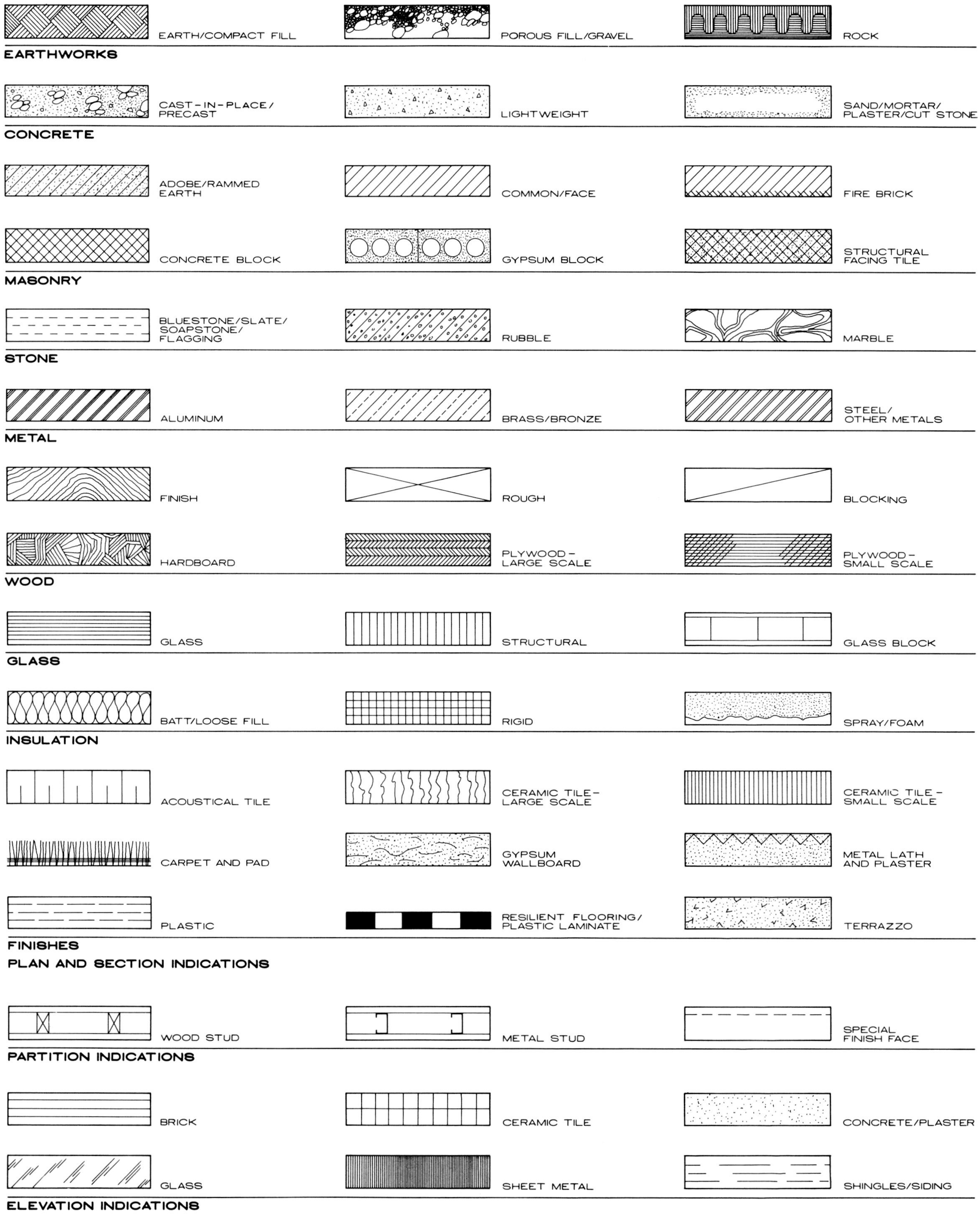

 EARTH/COMPACT FILL  POROUS FILL/GRAVEL  ROCK

EARTHWORKS

 CAST-IN-PLACE/PRECAST  LIGHTWEIGHT  SAND/MORTAR/PLASTER/CUT STONE

CONCRETE

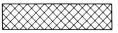 ADOBE/RAMMED EARTH  COMMON/FACE 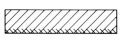 FIRE BRICK

 CONCRETE BLOCK  GYPSUM BLOCK  STRUCTURAL FACING TILE

MASONRY

 BLUESTONE/SLATE/SOAPSTONE/FLAGGING  RUBBLE  MARBLE

STONE

 ALUMINUM  BRASS/BRONZE  STEEL/OTHER METALS

METAL

 FINISH  ROUGH  BLOCKING

 HARDBOARD  PLYWOOD – LARGE SCALE 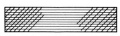 PLYWOOD – SMALL SCALE

WOOD

 GLASS  STRUCTURAL  GLASS BLOCK

GLASS

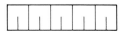 BATT/LOOSE FILL 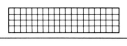 RIGID 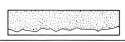 SPRAY/FOAM

INSULATION

 ACOUSTICAL TILE  CERAMIC TILE – LARGE SCALE 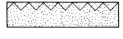 CERAMIC TILE – SMALL SCALE

 CARPET AND PAD  GYPSUM WALLBOARD  METAL LATH AND PLASTER

PLASTIC RESILIENT FLOORING/PLASTIC LAMINATE TERRAZZO

FINISHES

PLAN AND SECTION INDICATIONS

 WOOD STUD 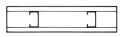 METAL STUD 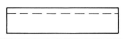 SPECIAL FINISH FACE

PARTITION INDICATIONS

 BRICK 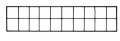 CERAMIC TILE  CONCRETE/PLASTER

 GLASS SHEET METAL  SHINGLES/SIDING

ELEVATION INDICATIONS

John Ray Hoke, Jr., AIA; Washington, D.C.

 GRAPHIC STANDARDS

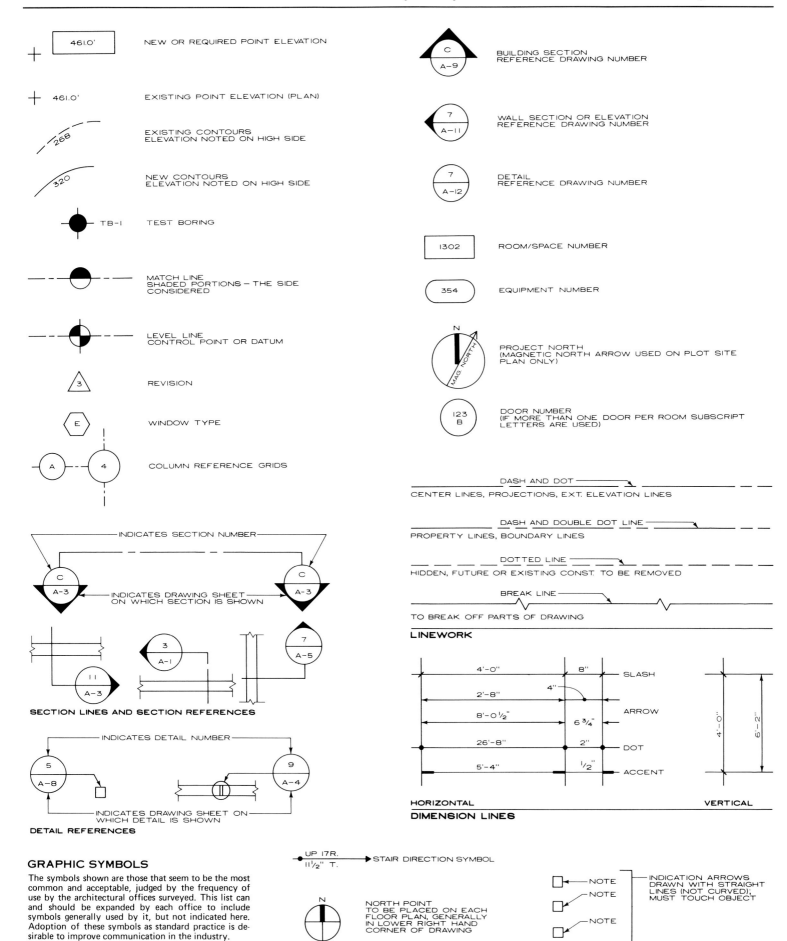

NEW OR REQUIRED POINT ELEVATION

461.0' EXISTING POINT ELEVATION (PLAN)

268 EXISTING CONTOURS
ELEVATION NOTED ON HIGH SIDE

320 NEW CONTOURS
ELEVATION NOTED ON HIGH SIDE

TB-1 TEST BORING

MATCH LINE
SHADED PORTIONS – THE SIDE
CONSIDERED

LEVEL LINE
CONTROL POINT OR DATUM

REVISION

WINDOW TYPE

COLUMN REFERENCE GRIDS

INDICATES SECTION NUMBER

INDICATES DRAWING SHEET
ON WHICH SECTION IS SHOWN

SECTION LINES AND SECTION REFERENCES

INDICATES DETAIL NUMBER

INDICATES DRAWING SHEET ON
WHICH DETAIL IS SHOWN

DETAIL REFERENCES

BUILDING SECTION
REFERENCE DRAWING NUMBER

WALL SECTION OR ELEVATION
REFERENCE DRAWING NUMBER

DETAIL
REFERENCE DRAWING NUMBER

ROOM/SPACE NUMBER

EQUIPMENT NUMBER

PROJECT NORTH
(MAGNETIC NORTH ARROW USED ON PLOT SITE
PLAN ONLY)

DOOR NUMBER
(IF MORE THAN ONE DOOR PER ROOM SUBSCRIPT
LETTERS ARE USED)

DASH AND DOT
CENTER LINES, PROJECTIONS, EXT. ELEVATION LINES

DASH AND DOUBLE DOT LINE
PROPERTY LINES, BOUNDARY LINES

DOTTED LINE
HIDDEN, FUTURE OR EXISTING CONST. TO BE REMOVED

BREAK LINE
TO BREAK OFF PARTS OF DRAWING

LINEWORK

SLASH
ARROW
DOT
ACCENT

HORIZONTAL   **VERTICAL**
DIMENSION LINES

GRAPHIC SYMBOLS

The symbols shown are those that seem to be the most
common and acceptable, judged by the frequency of
use by the architectural offices surveyed. This list can
and should be expanded by each office to include
symbols generally used by it, but not indicated here.
Adoption of these symbols as standard practice is desirable to improve communication in the industry.

John Ray Hoke, Jr., AIA; Washington, D.C.

UP 17R.
11½" T. STAIR DIRECTION SYMBOL

N NORTH POINT
TO BE PLACED ON EACH
FLOOR PLAN, GENERALLY
IN LOWER RIGHT HAND
CORNER OF DRAWING

NOTE
NOTE
NOTE

INDICATION ARROWS
DRAWN WITH STRAIGHT
LINES (NOT CURVED);
MUST TOUCH OBJECT

GRAPHIC STANDARDS

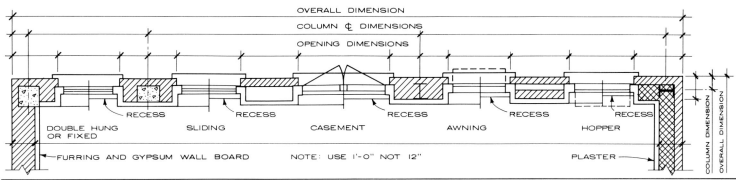

METHOD FOR DIMENSIONING EXTERIOR WINDOW OPENINGS IN MASONRY WALLS (DOORS SIMILAR)

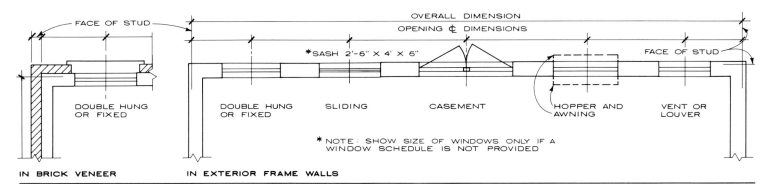

METHOD FOR DIMENSIONING EXTERIOR WINDOW OPENINGS IN FRAME WALLS (DOORS SIMILAR)

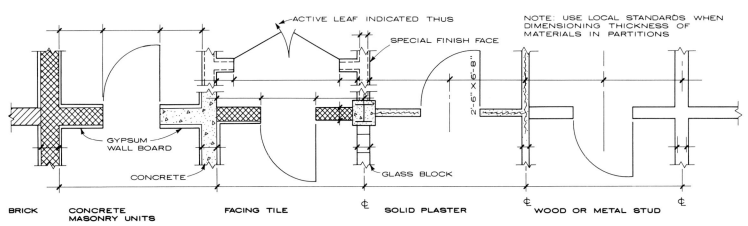

METHOD FOR DIMENSIONING AND INDICATIONS OF INTERIOR PARTITIONS AND DOORS

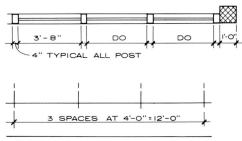

REPETITIVE DIMENSIONING

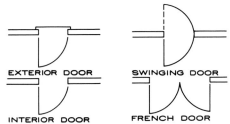

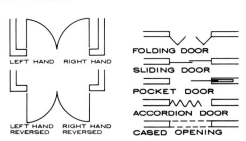

GENERAL NOTES

Dimensioning should start with critical dimensions and should be kept to a minimum. Consideration must be given to the trades using them and the sequencing adjusted to their respective work. It is also necessary to bear in mind that tolerances in actual construction will be varied. This means that as-built dimensions do not always coincide with design dimensions. Dimensioning from established grids or structural elements, such as columns and structural walls, assists the trades that must locate their work prior to that of others.

John Ray Hoke, Jr., AIA; Washington, D.C.

RECOMMENDATIONS

1. Dimensions under 1 ft shall be noted in inches. Dimensions 1 ft and over shall be expressed in feet.
2. Fractions under 1 in. shall NOT be preceded by a zero. Fractions must have a diagonal dividing line between numerator and denominator.
3. Dimension points to be noted with a short blunt 45° line. Dash to be oriented differently for vertical (*) and horizontal (*) runs of dimensions. Modular dimension points may be designated with an arrow or a dot.
4. Dimension all items from an established grid or reference point and do not close the string of

dimensions to the next grid or reference point.
5. Dimension: to face of concrete or masonry work; to centerlines of columns or other grid points; to centerlines of partitions. In nonmodular wood construction dimension to critical face of studs. When a clear dimension is required, dimension to the finish faces and note as such. Do not use the word "clear."
6. Dimension as much as possible from structural elements.
7. Overall readability, conciseness, completeness, and accuracy must be foremost in any dimensional system. It takes experience to determine how to use dimensions to the best advantage.

 GRAPHIC STANDARDS

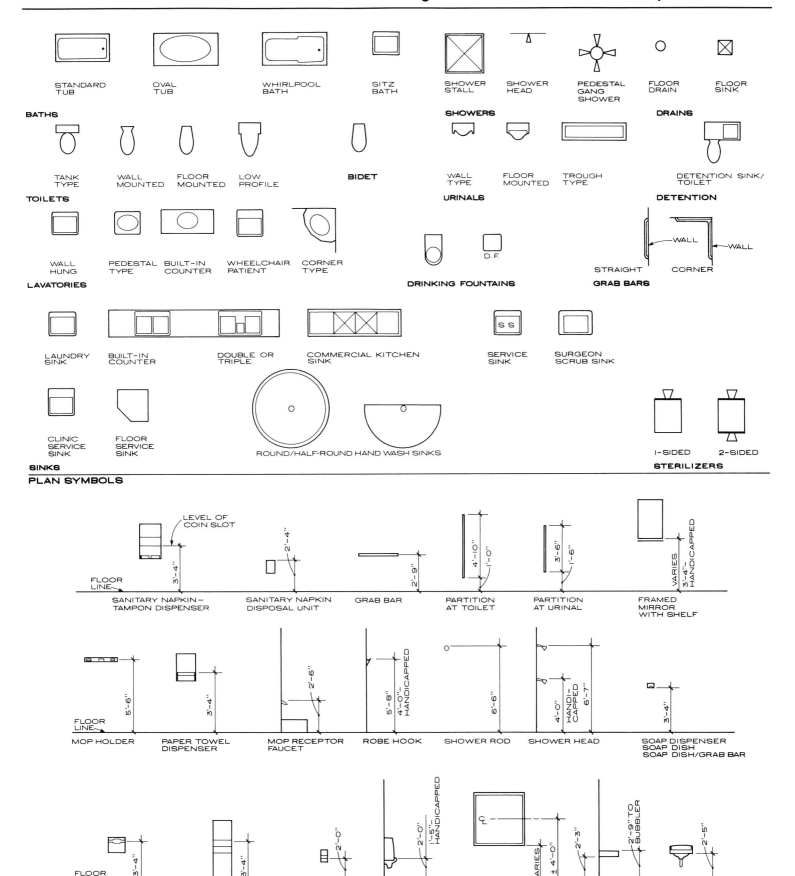

BATHS

STANDARD TUB | OVAL TUB | WHIRLPOOL BATH | SITZ BATH

SHOWERS

SHOWER STALL | SHOWER HEAD | PEDESTAL GANG SHOWER

DRAINS

FLOOR DRAIN | FLOOR SINK

TOILETS

TANK TYPE | WALL MOUNTED | FLOOR MOUNTED | LOW PROFILE | BIDET

URINALS

WALL TYPE | FLOOR MOUNTED | TROUGH TYPE

DETENTION

DETENTION SINK/ TOILET

LAVATORIES

WALL HUNG | PEDESTAL TYPE | BUILT-IN COUNTER | WHEELCHAIR PATIENT | CORNER TYPE

DRINKING FOUNTAINS

D.F.

GRAB BARS

STRAIGHT | CORNER | WALL | WALL

SINKS

LAUNDRY SINK | BUILT-IN COUNTER | DOUBLE OR TRIPLE | COMMERCIAL KITCHEN SINK | SERVICE SINK | SURGEON SCRUB SINK

CLINIC SERVICE SINK | FLOOR SERVICE SINK | ROUND/HALF-ROUND HAND WASH SINKS

STERILIZERS

1-SIDED | 2-SIDED

PLAN SYMBOLS

LEVEL OF COIN SLOT

FLOOR LINE

SANITARY NAPKIN— TAMPON DISPENSER | SANITARY NAPKIN DISPOSAL UNIT | GRAB BAR | PARTITION AT TOILET | PARTITION AT URINAL | FRAMED MIRROR WITH SHELF

MOP HOLDER | PAPER TOWEL DISPENSER | MOP RECEPTOR FAUCET | ROBE HOOK | SHOWER ROD | SHOWER HEAD | SOAP DISPENSER SOAP DISH SOAP DISH/GRAB BAR

TOILET SEAT COVER DISPENSER | TOWEL DISPENSER/ WASTE RECEPTACLE | TOILET PAPER HOLDER | URINAL (ADULT) | CHALKBOARD TACKBOARD | ELECTRIC WATER COOLER | LAVATORY

MOUNTING HEIGHTS

Dale Switzer, AIA; Hope Architects & Engineers; San Diego, California

GRAPHIC STANDARDS   A

GENERAL REFERENCES

References for the individual chapters of this book are given at the end of each chapter. Those lists include both general references for additional information and the sources for information used in developing the chapter contents.

This group of publications consists of references that have additional information that spans over the topics of several chapters of this book.

Architectural Graphic Standards, 8th ed., 1988, Ramsey/Sleeper and the American Institute of Architects, John Ray Hoke Jr., Editor in Chief for the 8th edition, Wiley.
This book (the Construction Details Edition) consists of approximately one half of the 8th edition; as a result, the full copy of the 8th edition should be considered as a resource for additional information on many special topics.

Construction Principles, Materials, and Methods, 5th ed., 1983, Harold B. Olin, John L. Schmidt, and Walter H. Lewis, Van Nostrand Reinhold.
Although somewhat dated, this book represents a rich resource of information for the general topic of light and residential construction.

Time-Saver Standards for Architectural Design Data, 6th ed., 1982, John Hancock Callendar, McGraw-Hill.
A general reference for data and details for building construction and planning.

Building Design and Construction Handbook, 4th ed., 1982, Frederick S. Merritt, McGraw-Hill.
A general technical reference on all aspects of the design of building construction and the various building subsystems.

Mechanical and Electric Equipment for Buildings, 7th ed., 1986, Benjamin Stein, John Reynolds, and William McGuinness, Wiley.
The most comprehensive reference on design of building subsystems for all topics other than structures and general building construction.

Building Structures, 1988, James Ambrose, Wiley.
The most comprehensive single volume on building structures, from basic concepts through systems design.

The following books contain presentations of details of building construction; a topic of endless variety.

House Construction Details, 7th ed., 1986, Nelson Burbank, Arnold Romney, and Charles Phelps, McGraw-Hill.

Building Construction Illustrated, 1975, Francis Ching, Van Nostrand Reinhold.

Means Graphic Construction Standards, 1986, R. S. Means Co.

Wall Systems: Analysis by Detail, 1986, Herman Sands, McGraw-Hill. (Analysis of the curtain wall systems of ten buildings.)

Construction Details for Commercial Buildings, 1988, Glenn E. Wiggins, Whitney.

Architect's Detail Library, 1990, Fred A. Stitt, Van Nostrand Reinhold. (Computer-generated details.)

Professional Handbook of Architectural Detailing, 2nd ed., 1987, Osamu A. Wakita and Richard M. Linde, Wiley.

Architectural Drafting and Construction, 4th ed., 1989, Ernest R. Weidhaas, Allyn and Bacon.

Handbook of Architectural Details for Commercial Buildings, 1980, Joseph De Chiara, McGraw-Hill.

INDEX